Encyclopedia of Data Science and Machine Learning

John Wang
Montclair State University, USA

Volume V

Published in the United States of America by
    IGI Global
    Engineering Science Reference (an imprint of IGI Global)
    701 E. Chocolate Avenue
    Hershey PA, USA 17033
    Tel: 717-533-8845
    Fax: 717-533-8661
    E-mail: cust@igi-global.com
    Web site: http://www.igi-global.com

Library of Congress Cataloging-in-Publication Data

Names: Wang, John, 1955- editor.
Title: Encyclopedia of data science and machine learning / John Wang,
  editor.
Description: Hershey, PA : Engineering Science Reference, an imprint of IGI
  Global, [2023] | Includes bibliographical references and index. |
  Summary: "This book examines current, state-of-the-art research in the
  areas of data science, machine learning, data mining, optimization,
  artificial intelligence, statistics, and the interactions, linkages, and
  applications of knowledge-based business with information systems"--
  Provided by publisher.
Identifiers: LCCN 2021027689 (print) | LCCN 2021027690 (ebook) | ISBN
  9781799892205 (h/c) | ISBN 9781799892212 (ebook)
Subjects: LCSH: Big data. | Data mining. | Machine learning.
Classification: LCC QA76.9.B45 E54 2022 (print) | LCC QA76.9.B45 (ebook)
  | DDC 005.7--dc23
LC record available at https://lccn.loc.gov/2021027689
LC ebook record available at https://lccn.loc.gov/2021027690

British Cataloguing in Publication Data
A Cataloguing in Publication record for this book is available from the British Library.

All work contributed to this book is new, previously-unpublished material. The views expressed in this book are those of the authors, but not necessarily of the publisher.

For electronic access to this publication, please contact: eresources@igi-global.com.

Editorial Advisory Board

List of Contributors

Alphabetical Table of Contents

Volume I: 1-618; Volume II: 619-1246; Volume III: 1247-1870; Volume IV: 1871-2498; Volume V: 2499-3143

Table of Contents by Category

Volume I

Section: Accounting Analytics

Section: Approximation Methods

Section: Autonomous Learning Systems

Section: Big Data Applications

Section: Big Data as a Service

Section: Big Data Systems and Tools

Section: Business Intelligence

Volume II

Section: Causal Analysis

Section: Computational Statistics

Section: Computer Vision

Section: Customer Analytics

Section: Data Processing, Data Pipeline, and Data Engineering

Volume III

Section: Data Visualization and Visual Mining

Section: Decision, Support System

Section: Deep Neural Network (DNN) of Deep Learning

Section: E-Learning Technologies and Tools

Section: Emerging Technologies, Applications, and Related Issues

Section: Feature Engineering

Volume IV

Section: Financial Services Analytics

Section: Fuzzy Logic and Soft Computing

Section: Gradient-Boosting Decision Trees

Section: Graph Learning

Section: High-Throughput Data Analysis

Section: Industry 4.0

Section: Information Extraction

Section: Internet of Things

Section: Malware Analysis

Section: Management Analytics

Section: Marketing Analytics

Section: Object Detection

Section: Performance Metrics

Section: Predictive Analytics

Mustapha Kamal Benramdane, CNAM, France
Samia Bouzefrane, CNAM, France
Soumya Banerjee, MUST, France
Hubert Maupas, MUST, France
Elena Kornyshova, CNAM, France

Section: Reinforcement Learning

Section: Simulation and Modeling

Section: Smart City

Section: Social Media Analytics

Section: Supply Chain Analytics and Management

Section: Symbolic Learning

Section: Time Series Analysis

Section: Transfer Learning

Section: Transport Analytics

Section: Unsupervised and Supervised Learning

Foreword

There has been tremendous progress made in Data Science and Machine Learning over the last $10 - 15$ years, leading to the Data Science becoming the major driving force of the Fourth Industrial Revolution and a significant factor in the current cycle of economic expansion. The need for data scientists is growing exponentially and machine learning has become one of the "hottest" professions in the labor market.

The field of Data Science is expanding both in-depth and in-breadth. In particular, we have witnessed widespread adoption of data science methods across a broad class of industries and functional areas, including health sciences and pharmaceuticals, finance, accounting, marketing, human resource management, operations and supply chains. Data-driven approaches have been deployed in such diverse set of applications as drug discovery, analysis of medical data and decision support tools for physicians, financial applications, including robo-advising, predictive maintenance of equipment and defect detection, Internet of Things (IoT), precision agriculture, physics and chemistry, to name a few. All these industries and applications enjoy adoption of a wide range of machine learning methods, the scope of which grew significantly over the last $10 - 15$ years. In addition to the evolutionary growth and expansion of classical machine learning techniques, the last decade has witnessed revolutionary breakthroughs in such areas as Deep Learning, scalable machine learning methods capable of handling Big Data, the size of which grows exponentially over time in many applications, and the analysis of unstructured data, such as text using NLP-based methods, images and videos using Computer Vision techniques, and voice using Speech Recognition methods.

Given all this progress in Machine Learning and Data Science, it is high time to aggregate all this new knowledge "under one roof," and this Encyclopedia of Data Science and Machine Learning serves this purpose. It covers 188 different topics across the whole spectrum of the field written by leading academic scholars and industry practitioners describing the progress made in the respective areas over the last $10 - 15$ years and reflecting the State-of-the-Art for each topic.

Since data science and machine learning are evolving rapidly, the authors also describe the challenges and present promising future research directions in their respective areas, delineating interesting work that lies ahead for the scholars to address these challenges. Therefore, this Encyclopedia remains what it is – a milestone on a long and exciting road that lies ahead of us in Data Science and Machine Learning.

Alexander Tuzhilin
New York University, USA
May 2022

Preface

Big Data and Machine Learning (BDML) are driving and harnessing the power of the Fourth Industrial Revolution, also referred to as Industry 4.0 or 4IR, which revolutionizes the way companies, organizations, and institutions operate and develop. With the age of Big Data upon us, we risk drowning in a flood of digital data. Big Data has now become a critical part of the business world and daily life, as the synthesis and synergy of Machine Learning (ML) and Big Data (BD) have enormous potential.

BDML not only deals with descriptive and predictive analytics but also focuses on prescriptive analytics through digital technology and interconnectivity. It has continuously explored its "depth" and expanded its "breadth". BDML will remain to maximize the citizens' "wealth" while promoting society's "health".

The *Encyclopedia of Data Science and Machine Learning* examines current, state-of-the-art research in the areas of data science, ML, data mining (DM), optimization, artificial intelligence (AI), statistics, and the interactions, linkages, and applications of knowledge-based business with information systems. It provides an international forum for practitioners, educators, and researchers to advance the knowledge and practice of all facets of BDML, emphasizing emerging theories, principles, models, processes, and applications to inspire and circulate cutting-edge findings into research, business, and communities (Wang, 2022).

How can a manager get out of a data-flooded "mire"? How can a confused decision-maker navigate through a "maze"? How can an over-burdened problem solver clean up a "mess"? How can an exhausted scientist bypass a "myth"? The answer to all of the above is to employ BDML.

As Roy et al. (2022) point out, data has become the center point for almost every organization. For quite a long time, we are familiar with Descriptive Analytics (what happened in the past) and Diagnostic Analytics (why something happened in the past), as well as Predictive Analytics (what is most likely to happen in the future). However, BDML could go much above and beyond them with Prescriptive Analytics (what should be done now), which recommends actions companies, and organizations can take to affect those outcomes. The digital transformation, the horizontal and vertical integration of these production systems, as well as the exploitation via optimization models, can make a gigantic jump with this giant digital leverage.

BDML can turn *Data* into *value;* Transform *information* into *intelligence;* Change *patterns* into *profit;* Convert *relationships* into *resources.* Companies and organizations can make *Faster* (real-time or near real-time), *Frequent,* and *Fact-based* decisions. In an ever-evolving market, 4IR with a set of technologies can stimulate innovations and rapid responses. Knowledge workers can proactively take action before an unfriendly event occurs (Wang, 2008).

Having been penetrated and integrated into almost every aspect of our work and life, as well as our society itself, AI and related cutting-edge technologies will enhance human capacities, improve efficiencies, and optimize people's lives. AI would not replace human intelligence, rather than amplify it. As *AI evolves* and *humans* adapt, AI and humans go forward together in the long run because AI and people both bring different capabilities to society.

According to Klaus Schwab, the World Economic Forum Founder and Executive Chairman, 4IR intellectualizes precipitous change to industrial and societal prototypes and processes in the 21st century due to increasing interconnectivity and smart automation and finally blurs the lines among the physical, digital, and biological worlds. Part of the 4IR is the manner in which all types of machines and devices interact, correspond, and cooperate with each other. Even though there will be obvious job losses due to the replacement of tasks that humans have conducted for years by autonomous machines and/or software. On the contrary, there could be new business opportunities and plenty of new jobs for controlling "the new electricity" (Philbeck & Davis, 2018; Moll, 2022).

There are 207 qualified full chapters among 271 accepted proposals. Finally, the encyclopedia contains a collection of 187 high-quality chapters, which were written by an international team of more than 370 experts representing leading scientists and talented young scholars from more than 45 countries and regions, including Algeria, Argentina, Austria, Bangladesh, Brazil, Canada, Chile, China, Colombia, Cuba, Denmark, Egypt, El Salvador, Finland, France, Germany, Ghana, Greece, Hong Kong, Hungary, Indonesia, Iraq, Japan, Lebanon, Macau, Malaysia, Mexico, Netherland, New Zealand, Poland, Portugal, Saudi Arabia, Serbia, Singapore, South Africa, Sweden, Switzerland, Syria, Taiwan, Tunisia, Turkey, UK, USA, Venezuela, Vietnam, etc.

They have contributed great effort to create a source of solid, practical information, informed by the sound underlying theory that should become a resource for all people involved in this dynamic new field. Let's take a peek at a few of them:

Jaydip Sen has published around 300 articles in reputed international journals and referred conference proceedings (IEEE Xplore, ACM Digital Library, Springer LNCS, etc.), and 18 book chapters in books published by internationally renowned publishing houses. He is a Senior Member of ACM, USA a Member of IEEE, USA. He has been listed among the top 2% scientists in the globe as per studies conducted by Stanford University for the last consecutive three years 2019 - 2021. In his contributed chapter Prof. Sen and his co-author, Dutta have evaluated the performance of two risk-based portfolio design algorithms.

Leung - who has authored more than 300 refereed publications on the topics of data science, ML, BDM and analytics, and visual analytics (including those in ACM TODS, IEEE ICDE, and IEEE ICDM) - presents two encyclopedia articles. One of them presents up-to-date definitions in BDM and analytics in the high-performance computing environment and focuses on mining frequent patterns with the MapReduce programming model. Another one provides the latest comprehensive coverage on key concepts and applications for BD visualization; it focuses on visualizing BD, frequent patterns, and association rules.

Lorenzo Magnani is Editor-in-Chief of the Series Sapere, Springer. Thanks to his logico-epistemological and cognitive studies on the problem of abductive cognition (that regards all kinds of reasoning to hypotheses) explained in this chapter both virtues and limitations of some DL applications, taking advantage of the analysis of the famous AlphaGo/AlphaZero program and the concepts of locked and unlocked strategies. Furthermore, he is the author of many important articles and books on epistemology, logic, cognitive science, and the relationships between ethics, technology, and violence.

The chapter 'AI is transforming insurance with five emerging business models' is the culmination of three years of research into how AI is disrupting insurance. Zarifis has recently won a 'best paper award' at a leading conference and Cheng has recently been published in MIS Quarterly for related work. AI is disrupting many distinct parts of our life, but insurance is particularly interesting as some issues like risk and privacy concerns are more important. After several case studies, this chapter identifies that there are five emerging models in insurance that are optimal for AI.

In "Artificial Intelligence, Consumers, and the Experience Economy," Chang and Mukherjee's excellent synthesis of AI and consumers in the modern economy provides a much-needed knowledge base for stakeholders tasked to deploy AI. In "Using Machine Learning Methods to Extract Behavioral Insights from Consumer Data," they present a comprehensive discussion of new data sources and state-of-the-art techniques for researchers and practitioners in computational social science. The chapters are built on their projects supported by the Ministry of Education, Singapore, under its Academic Research Fund (AcRF) Tier 2 Grant No. MOE2019-T2-1-183 and Grant No. MOE2018-T2-1-181, respectively.

Based on many years of application development by CY Pang and S. Pang's cognitive data analysis of many industrial projects, this chapter proposes a programming paradigm specific to BD processing. Pang was the lead architect of a $1.6 billion enterprise software project and was awarded a special architectural design trophy. He has received awards of $20,000 and $5,000 for outstanding innovation from a company he previously worked for. By the way, CY Pang was awarded a Prestige Scholarship from Peter House, Cambridge to complete his Ph.D. at the University of Cambridge, UK.

Vitor provides an excellent overview of multidimensional search methods for optimization and the potential these methods have to solve optimization problems more quickly. With almost ten years of industry experience, Vitor is an expert in optimization methods and the modeling of complex systems using operations research and data analytics techniques. He is also a recipient of the Nebraska EPSCoR FIRST Award, supported by the National Science Foundation to advance the research of early-career tenure-track faculty.

Lee's chapter on evidence-based data-driven pain management bears multi-facet importance. Nearly 40 million anesthetics are administered each year in the United States. And over 10.7% of Americans use prescription pain medication on a regular basis. The findings highlight the optimal safe dose and delivery mechanism to achieve the best outcome. The study showcases the persistence of overprescription of opioid-type drugs, as it finds that the use of fentanyl has little effect on the outcome and should be avoided.

Auditors must evaluate the volatility and uncertainty of the client company at the initial stage of the audit contract because it directly influences the audit risk. Takada contributes to auditing research and accounting education for 40 years. He has been awarded for his research and contributions to his excellent papers and accounting education by the *Chinese Auditing Association* and by the *Japanese Auditing Association*.

Nguyen and Quinn propose an optimal approach to tackle the well-known issue of the imbalance in bankruptcy prediction. Their approach has been evaluated through a rigorous computation including the most popular current methods in the literature. They have also made other main contributions in the area of imbalanced classification by winning the 2020 Literati Awards for Outstanding Author Contribution.

Rodríguez is the Bioethics of Displacement pioneer, a field that merges futurism, belongingness, and life. He has also published analytic papers and fieldwork on crises and big social changes such as pandemics, Anthropocene, AI takeover, cyborgs, digital securitization and terrorist attacks. As a chair, the author leads the research on the first decolonized corruption index. Torres shares his more than 15 years of wealth of experience in Predictive Maintenance management as a speaker at global summits such as Scalable and PMM Tech Dates. The author leads the first non-taxonomic error mode proponent of AI implementation.

Kurpicz-Briki, Glauser, and Schmid are using unique API technologies to measure the impact of online search behavior using several different online channels. Their method allows the identification of the specific channels, where keywords have been searched, and a restriction of regions, using the domains. Such technologies provide a major benefit for different application domains, including public health. In times such as a pandemic crisis, it is highly relevant for different stakeholders to identify the impact of their communications on the user community as well as the well-being of the population. Using the method proposed by the authors, this can be done while fully respecting the privacy of the users.

Sensors sense the environment and process large sets of data. Monitoring the data to detect malicious content is one of the biggest challenges. The previous work used mean variation to ease the surveillance of information. Ambika's proposal minimizes the effort by classifying the streamed data into three subsets. It uses the k-nearest neighbor procedure to accomplish the same. The work conserves 10.77% of energy and tracks 27.58% of more packets. Map-reduce methodology manages large amounts of data to a certain extent. Ambika's other proposal aims to increase processing speed by 29.6% using a hashing methodology.

In today's world, text-based sentiment analysis brings the attention of all. By looking at the people requirement, Tripathy and Sharaff propose a hybridized Genetic Algorithm (GA)-based feature selection method to achieve a better model performance. In the current study, they have customized the GA by using the SVM to evaluate the fitness value of the solutions. The proposed idea is essential as the technique reduces the computational cost by reducing sufficient features without affecting the performance. The proposed model can be implemented in any field to filter out the sentiment from the user's review.

Alberg and Hadad present the novel Interval Gradient Prediction Tree ML Algorithm that can process incoming mean-variance aggregated multivariate temporal data and make stable interval predictions of a target numerical variable. Empirical evaluations of multi-sensor aircraft datasets have demonstrated that this algorithm provides better readability and similar performance compared to other ML regression tree algorithms.

The environmental, societal, and cultural imperatives press for innovative, prompt, and practical solutions for grave humanitarian problems we face in the 21st century. The climate crisis is felt everywhere; natural disasters are rampant. Can technology provide reasonable means to humanitarian supply chains? What potential uses can AI offer in establishing sustainable humanitarian logistics (SHL)? Ülkü, an award-winning professor and the director of CRSSCA-Centre for Research in Sustainable Supply Chain Analytics, and his research associate Oguntola of Dalhousie University - Canada review the latest research on the applications of AI technology on SHL.

Aguiar-Pérez, the leading author of this chapter, provides the audience an insight into what ML is and its relation with AI or DL. He has an extended experience in the field of ML, DL, BD, and IoT in various sectors (automotive, smart roads, agriculture, livestock, heritage, etc.), including collaboration with companies, EU-funded research projects, publications, and postgraduate teaching experience. The rest of the authors work with him in the Data Engineering Research Unit of the University of Valladolid.

Bagui, a highly accomplished author of several books on databases and Oracle, presents a very timely chapter on the improvements made in Oracle 19c's multitenant container architecture and shows how these improvements aid in the management of Big Data from the perspective of application development. The added functionality that comes with the integration of Big Data platforms, alongside the flexibility and improvement that comes with a container and pluggable databases, has allowed Oracle to be in the forefront in the handling of Big Data.

As an internationally renowned interdisciplinary information and data professional, Koltay's chapter on Research Data Management (RDM) is of interest not only for both professionals of DS and ML but is related to any research activity. He is also a widely published author in these fields. In 2021, his contribution to IGI Global books included an entry on information overload. His book, titled Research Data Management and Data Literacy (Chandos, 2021) contains a more detailed explanation of the subjects, contained in this chapter.

Zhao is a DS professional with experience in industry, teaching, and research. He is a leading BD expert in the IR BD & AI Lab in New Jersey, USA. He provides multiple chapters to the book by covering a broad range of BD applications in vast perspectives of urgent demands in DS research objectives, such as DSS, DL, computer vision, BD architecture designs, and applied BD analytics in Covid-19 research. As such, he did excellent work in those chapters and made significant contributions to the book.

Based on their discovery of action rules and meta-actions from client datasets, Duan and Ras propose a strategy for improving the number of promoters and decreasing the number of detractors among customers. Moreover, the improved/enhanced action rules can be utilized in developing actionable strategies for decision makers to reduce customer churn, which will contribute to the overall customer churn study in the business field. The authors target the domain represented by many clients, each one involved with customers in the same type of business. Clients are heavy equipment repair shops, and customers are owners of such equipment.

The A2E Process Model for Data Analytics is simple without being simplistic and comprehensive without being complicated. It balances technology with humanity and theories with practices. This model reflects Jay Wang's decades-long multi-disciplinary training and experience in STEM, Behavioral Science, and Management Science. While existing process models such as CRISP-DM, SEMMA, and KDD were developed for technical professionals with limitations and low adoption rates, the A2E Model is more approachable to subject matter experts, business analysts, and social scientists. The A2E Model will elevate the analytics profession by fostering interdisciplinary collaborations of all stakeholders and increasing the effectiveness and impacts of analytics efforts.

Turuk explores Audio and video-based Emotion Recognition using the Backpropagation Algorithm, which is the backbone of ML and DL architectures. This chapter analyses everyday human emotions such as Happy, Sad, Neutral, and Angry using audio-visual cues. The audio features such as Energy & MFCC and video features using the Gabor filter are extracted. Mutual information is computed using video features. The readers will benefit and motivated to conduct further research in this domain. The application may be extended to a lie detector using Emotions.

Stojanović and Marković-Petrović focus on continuous cyber security risk assessment in Industrial Internet of Things (IIoT) networks, and particularly on possibilities of DL approaches to achieve the goal. The authors successfully complement their previous work regarding the cyber security of industrial control systems. They concisely review the theoretical background and provide an excellent framework for the continuous risk assessment process in the IIoT environment. DL can be integrated into edge-computing-based systems and used for feature extraction and risk classification from massive raw data. The chapter ends with a list of proposals for further studies.

Climate change is a very important issue and each person on our planet must have a culture of keeping it clean. Pollution increased yearly due to the increased consumption of fossil fuels. Alsultanny has many research papers in climate change and renewable energy. He led a UNDP team for writing reports on energy consumption in Bahrain. Alsultanny did an innovative method in his chapter, by utilizing the pollution gases data, these data currently are BD, because they are registered yearly in every minute, and from many monitoring pollutions stations.

Deliyska and Ivanova conducted timely research and practical work representing an important contribution to data modeling in sustainable science. Applying ontological engineering and a coevolutionary approach, a unique metamodel of sustainable development is created containing structured knowledge and mutual links between environmental, social, and economic dimensions in this interdisciplinary area. Specialists in different fields can use the proposed metamodel as a tool for terminology clarification, knowledge extraction, and interchange and for the structuring of ML models of sustainable development processes.

Hedayati and Schniederjans provide a broad spectrum of issues that come into play when using digital technologies to benefit healthcare. This is even more important where the pandemic has forced healthcare models to rapidly adjust towards compliance with local, regional, and national policy. The dissemination and creation of knowledge become paramount when considering the benefits and drawbacks of the rapid changes in technology applications worldwide. The authors consider several insights from the American Hospital Association Compliance to provide some questions researchers and practitioners may consider when addressing knowledge management via digital technology implementation in healthcare settings.

Pratihar and Kundu apply the theory of fuzzy logic to develop a classification and authentication system for beverages. It emphasizes the versatility of fuzzy logic to deal with the higher dimensional and highly non-linear sensor data obtained from e-tongue for different beverage samples. Commonly used mapping techniques (for dimension reduction of a data set) and clustering techniques (for classification) were also briefly discussed. This study provides a perspective on developing a fuzzy logic-based classifier/authenticator system in the future for beverages, foods, and others and their quality control and monitoring.

Drake discusses the use of IoT technology to improve SCM. As firms look to improve their supply chain resilience in response to the COVID-19 pandemic and other disruptions, IoT data increases visibility, traceability, and can help firms to mitigate risks through added agility and responsiveness. The improved decision-making made possible by IoT data creates a competitive advantage in the market.

Today, high-dimensional data (multi-omics data) are widely used. The high dimensionality of the data creates problems (time, cost, diagnosis, and treatment) in studies. Ipekten et al. introduce the existing solutions to these problems and commonly used methods. Also, the authors present the advantages of the methods over each other and enlighten the researchers that using suitable methods in terms of performance can increase the reliability and accuracy of the studies. Finally, the authors advise on what can be done in the future.

Learning analytics (LA), a promising field of study that started more than a decade ago but has blossomed in recent years, addresses the challenges of LA specifically in education, integrating it as a fundamental element of the Smart Classroom. Ifenthaler and Siemens among others discuss the primary features, the benefits, and some experiences. In addition, the team of authors of the chapter has contributed more than twelve publications on this topic in the last 3 years in leading journals and publishers.

Current advances in AI and ML in particular have raised several concerns regarding the trustworthiness and explainability of deployed AI systems. Knowledge-Based approaches based on symbolic representations and reasoning mechanisms can be used to deploy AI systems that are explainable and compliant with corresponding ethical and legal guidelines, thus complementing purely data-driven approaches.

Batsakis and Matsatsinis, both having vast theoretical backgrounds and experience in this research area, offer an overview of knowledge-based AI methods for the interested AI practitioner.

Noteboom and Zeng provide a comprehensive review of applications of AI and ML and data analytics techniques in clinical decision support systems (CDSSs) and make contributions including, 1) the current status of data-driven CDSSs, 2) identification and quantification of the extent to which theories and frameworks have guided the research, 3) understanding the synergy between AI/ML algorithms and modes of data analytics, 4) directions for advancing data-driven CDSSs to realize their potential in healthcare.

Fisogni investigates the emotional environment which is grounded in any human/machine interaction. Through the lenses of metaphysics and system thinking the author sketches a highly valuable insight, for sure an unprecedented challenge for DSs. In fact, only a philosophical foundation of the big issues of this realm can bring about a change in the quality of understanding an increasingly melted environment humans/machines in the Onlife era.

In "Hedonic Hunger and Obesity", Demirok and Uysal touch upon a remarkable topic and explain ways of identification for people with hedonic nutrition and the conditions that are effective in the states that trigger hunger state in humans. In addition, in this text, the authors ensample hormones that suppress and trigger hunger.

Yen and her coauthors contributed a chapter on how ML creates the virtual singer industry. Virtual singers have great market potential and even advantages over their human counterparts. Despite the bright future of virtual singers, the chapter has discussed difficulties virtual singers face, especially their copyright protection by legislation. Literature on the technical aspects of virtual singers is also reviewed, and a list of additional readings is provided for readers interested in the ML algorithms behind virtual singers.

Rastogi is working on Biofeedback therapy and its effect on Diabetes diseases, a currently very active healthcare domain. He brings back the glory of Indian Ancient Vedic Sciences of Jap, Pranayama, Healing techniques, and the effect of Yajna and Mantra science on Diseases and pollution control. Also, He has developed some interesting mathematical models with algorithms on Swarm Intelligence approaches like PSO, ACO BCO, etc. for better human life via Spiritual Index and higher consciousness.

Isikhan presents a comparison of a new proposal for the modeling of Ceiling and Floor Effect dependent variables and classical methods. It has been noticed that there are very few publications evaluating the regression modeling of ceiling and floor effect observations in recent years. The modeling method with regression-based imputation, which clinicians can use as an alternative to classical models for ceiling and floor effective observations, is explained in detail. The performances of the newly proposed imputation-based regression and other classical methods were validated based on both real clinical data, synthetic data, as well as a 500 replicated cross-validation method.

Drignei has extensive experience with time series modeling and analysis. Prior to this work, he addressed statistical modeling aspects of space-time data, such as temperatures recorded over space and time. His research has been published in leading statistics journals. The current work deals with seasonal times series recorded at a large number of time points. Such data sets will become more common in the future, in areas such as business, industry, and science. Therefore, this chapter is timely and important because it sheds new light on modeling aspects of this type of data sets.

Data visualization plays a key role in the decision-making process. Visualization allows for data to be consumable. If data is not consumable, there is a tendency to ignore the facts and rely more on biases. Researchers have found that cognitive biases do exist within data visualizations and can affect decision-making abilities. Anderson and Hardin provide background on cognitive biases related to data visualizations, with a particular interest in visual analytics in BD environments. A review of recent studies related to mitigating cognitive biases is presented. Recommendations for mitigating biases in visualizations are provided to practitioners.

Puzzanghera explores the impact of AI on administrative law. He combines IT systems with administrative activity and researches the processors that prepare content and the implications that arise. He analyzes the European Commission's proposal in regard to the legislation of AI in Europe and the importance of safeguarding human rights in the introduction of AI in administrative activity.

How ML impacts the catering industry? Liu et al. provide a comprehensive vision to readers with real-life examples and academic research. Researchers at business schools may have their attention drawn to the impact of ML on operations, management, and marketing, while scholars with solid ML backgrounds may become aware of industry issues, identify new research questions, and link their expertise to practical problems through reading the chapter.

Di Wang's research interests include 4D printing technology, robot control, remanufactured industry, and energy schedule in the smart city. Combinatorial optimization is a widely applied field at the forefront of combinatorics and theoretical computer science. With BD challenges, deep reinforcement learning opens new doors to solve complex combinatorial optimization problems with overwhelming advantages over traditional methods.

Firmansyah and Harsanto focus on exploring BD and Islamic finance. The utilization of BD in Islamic financial institutions (IFIs) has been perceived as a source of competitive advantage in today's era. Many IFIs have been more dependent on BD technologies than ever before in order to keep up with the changing customers' demands, lifestyles, and preferences.

With his experience of working in both industry and academic research, Indraneel highlights progress made in integrating AI with industry and helps bridge the reality and challenges faced while summarizing the state of Industry 4.0. The author engages audiences from different sectors without overburdening the reader with incoherent technical details. A practitioner in the fields of DS and cybersecurity, the author brings experience interacting with clients and customers from different fields, including manufacturing, legal, and product developers.

Yang, Wu, & Forrest examine the textual aspects of consumer reviews. As a critical source of information for online shoppers, researchers have spent considerable time examining the potential impact of consumer reviews on purchasing behavior. The authors contribute to the existing body of knowledge by proposing a conceptual framework for capturing the internal relationships between major textual features discovered in prior research.

Kara and Gonce Koçken are researchers studying mathematical programming problems in fuzzy environments. In the study, a novel fuzzy solution approach to multi-objective solid transportation problems is developed by using different membership functions, which can help the studies in transportation systems.

Millham demonstrates the various spheres of the emerging 4IR and how they interrelate with the application, opportunities, expectations, and challenges of a smart city. Because many of these smart city applications are very complex and interact with each other using various technologies, several nature-inspired algorithms are introduced as a way to provide intelligent and coordinated management of these entities.

The development of novel measurement and detection techniques is a rapidly growing area, where the generation of vast amounts of information requires novel methods for analysis. Murrieta-Rico explores a new direction of his research by combing the know-how for generating a big dataset from a digital frequency measurement, with the application of the principal component analysis (PCA). As a result, a powerful methodology for data analysis is presented. In addition, these results can be used for extending the capabilities of ML systems based on sensors.

Coimbra, Chimenti, and Nogueira contribute to the debate related to human-machine interaction in social media. The work helped to understand the mechanisms and motivators of this relationship. In addition, the article presented a historical evolution of the debate on the interaction between machines and men in decision-making, distributing the result of the literature review in three historical cycles. The research was carried out through a survey of YouTube users to understand the interaction mechanism along with its motivators.

As a transformational general-purpose technology, AI is impacting marketing as a function, and marketing managers' activities, capabilities, and performance. Oberoi emphasizes how the job of a marketing manager will be evolving into understanding which kind of AI can and should be applied to which kind of marketing actions for better performance. Marketing managers will have to go through a learning curve and acquire new skills.

Singh and Dev have discussed the concepts of data warehouse and OLAP technology to deal with real-life applications efficiently. The topic is useful in the modern digital era as businesses are dealing with data from heterogeneous sources. The chapter presents the case study of the tourism industry as it deals with multidimensional data like tourist, hospitality, and tourist products. This chapter will be helpful in understanding how to generate multi-dimensional reports that will show the information according to the needs of policymakers.

Ramos has made many contributions to the potential of Business Intelligence tools, combined with DM algorithms methods to produce insights about the tourism business, highlighting an aspect of the investment potential of tourism organizations in this type of system, from those related to accommodation, management of tourist destinations, to tourist transport, restaurants, among other businesses complementary to the tourist activity, with a view to innovation and increasing financial performance, which includes examples ranging from the application of OLAP techniques to the application of ML methods.

Balsam depicts the meaning and role of metamodels in defining the abstract syntax of the language by which developers communicate, design, and implement systems including the selection of the design, implementation methods, and techniques for increasingly complex systems to satisfy customers' needs, particularly if the system has to be delivered in a considerably fleeting time. The author highlights different aspects of meta-models standards, categories, the process of creating the metamodel, and challenges in the research of metamodeling.

Dharmapala contributes a novel method to the field of research in 'Classification of employee categories in allocating a reward, with input features from survey responses.' In the past, researchers conducted qualitative and quantitative analyses on this subject as it is an important topic to any organization that strives to boost the morale of its employees. The author opened a new direction in future research on the subject by using ML algorithms, and the results obtained were promising.

Mudrakola identifies the gap and future scope for Breast cancer applications like the impact of chemical therapy, prognosis analysis among various treatment types and stages, etc. From basic to the latest trends, the author's extensive literature survey will direct the root to aspects needed to analyze work on medical applications specific to Breast cancer.

Rani et al. highlight the venues of user-generated content (UGC) in Industry 4.0. This chapter's contribution is highly interesting for any digital content creator and non-paid professionals. The importance of UGC on consumer behavior in the era of Industry 4.0 will be explained, allowing stakeholders to assess their efficacy in Internet communication and enhancing the digital process required for modern marketing. The chapter aims to link existing ideas and provide a holistic picture of UGC by concentrating on future research.

Ibrahim et al. seek to provide an understanding of the relationship between member support exchange behavior and self-disclosure intention in online health support communities using a data-driven literature review. Seeking or providing support in online communities may be useful but having to disclose personal information publicly online is a critical privacy risk – intention counts.

Rusko introduces the main perspectives of industrial revolutions. He found interesting backgrounding details for the chapter about the disruptions of the industrial revolutions. Kosonen updates the paper with the effects of Covid-19 and contemporary digitizing development.

I would like to highlight a number of authors who have received special stunning honors: Eva K Lee has published over 220 research articles, and fifty government and state reports, and has received patents on innovative medical systems and devices. She is frequently tapped by a variety of health and security policymakers in Washington for her expertise in personalized medicine, chronic diseases, healthcare quality, modeling and decision support, vaccine research and national security, pandemic, and medical preparedness. Lee has received multiple prestigious analytics and practice excellence awards including INFORMS Franz Edelman award, Daniel H Wagner prize, and the Caterpillar and Innovative Applications in Analytics Award for novel cancer therapeutics, bioterrorism emergency response, and mass casualty mitigation, personalized disease management, ML for best practice discovery, transforming clinical workflow and patient care, vaccine immunity prediction, and reducing hospital-acquired infections. She is an INFORMS Fellow. She is also inducted into the American Institute for Medical and Biological Engineering (AIMBE) College of Fellows, the first IE/OR engineer to be nominated and elected for this honor. Her work has been funded by CDC, HHS, NIH, NSF, and DTRA. Lee was an NSF CAREER Young Investigator and Whitaker Foundation Young Investigator recipient.

Petry and Yager are both internationally known for their research in computational intelligence, in the area of fuzzy set theory and applications, and are both IEEE Fellows and have received prestigious awards from the IEEE. They have collaborated here as it represents extensions of their previous research on this topic. Hierarchical concept generalization is one important approach to dealing with the complex issues involving BD. This chapter provides insights on how to extend hierarchical generalization to data with interval and intuitionistic forms of uncertainty.

The globalization of the software development industry continues to experience significant growth. The increasing trend of globalization brings new challenges and increases the scope of the core functions of the software development process. Pal introduces a distributed software development knowledge management architecture. Kamalendu has published research articles in the software development community in the ACM SIGMIS Database, Expert Systems with Applications, DSSs, and conferences. Kamalendu was awarded the best research paper on data analytic work at a recent international conference. He is a member of the British Computer Society, the IET, and the IEEE Computer Society.

Badia's research has been funded by the National Science Foundation (including a prestigious CAREER Award) and has resulted in over 50 publications in scientific journals and conferences. His chapter demonstrates how to use SQL in order to prepare data that resides in database tables for analysis. The reader is guided through steps for Exploratory Data Analysis (EDA), data cleaning (including dealing with missing data, outliers, and duplicates), and other tasks that are an integral part of the Data Scientist day-to-day. The references provide a guide for further study.

Srinivasan explains the three components of graph analytics and provides illustrative examples as well as code for implementation. His chapter is one of the few primers of graph DS/analytics that covers a variety of topics in the discipline. The author does active research in graph analytics methods and applications in healthcare, ML explainability, and DL and regularly publishes in top journals and conferences in information systems, healthcare, and computer science. He received best paper awards in INFORMS Workshop on Data Science (2021) and the 6th International Conference on Digital Health (2016), respectively.

Knowledge explosion pushes BDML, a multidisciplinary subject, to ever-expanding regions. Inclusion, omission, emphasis, evolution, and even revolution are part of our professional life. In spite of our efforts to be careful, should you find any ambiguities of perceived inaccuracies, please contact me at prof.johnwang@gmail.com.

John Wang
Montclair State University, USA

REFERENCES

Moll, I. (2022). The Fourth Industrial Revolution: A new ideology. *tripleC: Communication, Capitalism & Critique, 20*(1), 45–61.

Philbeck, T., & Davis, N. (2018). The Fourth Industrial Revolution: Shaping a new era. *Journal of International Affairs, 72*(1), 17–22.

Roy, D., Srivastava, R., Jat, M., & Karaca, M. S. (2022). A complete overview of analytics techniques: Descriptive, predictive, and prescriptive. *Decision Intelligence Analytics and the Implementation of Strategic Business Management*, 15-30.

Wang, J. (Ed.). (2008). *Data Warehousing and Mining: Concepts, Methodologies, Tools, and Applications* (Vols. 1–6). IGI Global. doi:10.4018/978-1-59904-951-9

Wang, J. (Ed.). (2022). *Encyclopedia of Data Science and Machine Learning*. IGI Global. https://www.igi-global.com/book/encyclopedia-data-science-machine-learning/276507

Acknowledgment

The editor would like to thank all authors for their insights and excellent contributions to this major volume. I also want to thank the many anonymous reviewers who assisted me in the peer-reviewing process and provided comprehensive and indispensable inputs that improved our book significantly. In particular, the Editorial Advisory Board members, including Xueqi Cheng (Chinese Academy of Science), Verena Kantere (University of Ottawa, Canada), Srikanta Patnaik (SOA University, India), Hongming Wang (Harvard University), and Yanchang Zhao (CSIRO, Australia), have all made immense contributions in terms of advice and assistance, enhancing the quality of this volume. My sincere appreciation also goes to Prof. Alexander Tuzhilin (New York University). Despite his busy schedule, he has written three forewords for my consecutive encyclopaedias, over an 18-year span, in this expanding and exploring area.

In addition, the editor wishes to acknowledge the help of all involved in the development process of this book, without whose support the project could not have been satisfactorily completed. I owe my thanks to the staff at IGI Global, whose support and contributions have been invaluable throughout the entire process, from inception to final publication. Special thanks go to Gianna Walker, Angelina Olivas, Katelyn McLoughlin, and Melissa Wagner, who continuously prodded me via email to keep the project on schedule, and to Jan Travers and Lindsay Wertman, whose enthusiasm motivated me to accept their invitation to take on this project.

I would also like to extend my thanks to my brothers Zhengxian, Shubert (an artist, https://portraitartist. com/detail/6467), and sister Joyce Mu, who stood solidly behind me and contributed in their own unique ways. We are thankful for the scholarships which we have been provided, without which it would not have been possible for all of us to come and study in the U.S.

Finally, I want to thank my family: my parents for supporting me spiritually throughout my life and providing endless encouragement; my wife Hongyu for taking care of two active and rebellious teenagers, conducting all family chores, and not complaining to me too much.

This book was special due to the stresses and difficulties posed by the Covid-19 pandemic. We thank and salute the authors who had to overcome numerous challenges to help make this volume a reality. Our authors had to persevere through unprecedented circumstances to enable this masterful encyclopedia. Now, it is time to celebrate and reap the fruits of our demanding work! Cheese and cheers!

Section 40
Network Modeling and Theory

Binary Search Approach for Largest Cascade Capacity of Complex Networks

Natarajan Meghanathan

Jackson State University, USA

INTRODUCTION

Information Cascade in network theory is a behavioral phenomenon by which every node arrives at a decision (adopt or reject a particular thing) under the influence of the decision taken by its neighbor nodes (Easley & Kleinberg, 2010). The decision could be with regards to anything like adopting a new technology, supporting a particular political party or leader, choosing a lawn maintenance company, eating in a restaurant, etc. Given an initial set of nodes (called the initial adopters), the phenomena of information cascade (Easley & Kleinberg, 2010) goes through a series of iterations in each of which at least one node (that has not yet taken a decision) takes the decision under the influence of the decision taken by its neighbor nodes. The iterations stop when all the nodes have taken a decision or when no new node (i.e., no node other than those who had decided in the previous iterations) takes a decision in an iteration.

We refer to the information cascade as a *complete* information cascade (Easley & Kleinberg, 2010) if all the nodes arrive at a *unanimous* decision (for example: all nodes in a social network decide to support a particular political party in an upcoming election). For complete information cascade to happen, nodes (even if they have their own opinion) are expected to get influenced by the decision of their neighbor nodes so that the decision is eventually unanimous when the iterations stop. We assume a node will be in a position to take the *unanimous* decision when at least a *threshold fraction* of its neighbor nodes have taken/adopted the same decision (Easley & Kleinberg, 2010). For a given set of initial adopters, the maximum value for such a threshold fraction of adopted neighbor nodes in every neighborhood that can eventually enforce a unanimous decision for the entire network is called the *cascade capacity* of the network (Easley & Kleinberg, 2010).

The current approach (Easley & Kleinberg, 2010) used to determine the cascade capacity of a network is to first determine the clusters of the network and then determine their densities. The density of a cluster is the minimum of the intra cluster density (fraction of the incident edges to nodes within the same cluster) of the bridge nodes of the cluster (nodes that have one or more edges to nodes in other clusters). Information cascade can penetrate to a cluster and be complete only if the threshold fraction of adopted neighbor nodes (needed for adopting a unanimous decision) is less than or equal to 1 - the cluster density (Easley & Kleinberg, 2010). The cascade capacity of a network is the minimum of such threshold fractions of adopted neighbor nodes needed for a unanimous decision (Easley & Kleinberg, 2010). A primary weakness with the above approach is that it does not consider the nodes chosen as initial adopters to kick start information cascade while determining the cascade capacity of the network (also reported by Chesney, 2017). We claim that the above approach only gives a lower bound for the cascade capacity of the network and the cascade capacity of the network could be indeed larger if the initial adopters are also considered. Moreover, the above approach is time consuming as it first requires

DOI: 10.4018/978-1-7998-9220-5.ch150

to identify the clusters of a network and then identify the bridge nodes per cluster as well as determine their intra cluster density.

Our hypothesis for this research is that the cascade capacity of a network depends on the number and topological positions of the nodes chosen as initial adopters. To validate our hypothesis, we propose a binary search algorithm to determine the largest possible cascade capacity of a network for a given set of initial adopters. The binary search algorithm is briefly explained here: The search space (range of possible values for the threshold fraction of adopted neighbors for a unanimous decision) of the algorithm ranges from 0 (initial left index) to 1 (initial right index). We maintain an invariant that the information cascade will be complete if the left index is used as the threshold fraction of adopted neighbors and that the information cascade will not be complete if the right index is used as the threshold fraction of adopted neighbors. In each iteration, we find the middle index (average of the left and right index) and check if the information cascade can be complete when the middle index is used as the threshold fraction of adopted neighbors: if the information cascade is complete, we move the left index to the right and set the current value of the middle index to be the latest value of the left index; otherwise, we move the right index to the left and set the current value of the middle index to be the latest value of the right index. We proceed as long as the difference between the latest values of the left index and right index stays greater than or equal to a termination threshold (ε). Once the difference between the left index and right index becomes less than the termination threshold, we stop the algorithm and return the latest value of the left index as the largest possible cascade capacity of the network for the given set of initial adopters. The number of iterations needed by the binary search algorithm is $\log_2(1/\varepsilon)$.

Centrality metrics quantify the topological importance of the nodes in a network and are typically neighborhood-based or shortest path-based (Newman, 2010). We consider the neighborhood-based degree (DEG) and eigenvector (EVC) centrality metrics and the shortest path-based betweenness (BWC) and closeness (CLC) centrality metrics for our analysis. The degree centrality (Newman, 2010) of a node is the number of neighbors of the node. The eigenvector centrality (Bonacich, 1987) of a node is a measure of the degree of the node as well as the degrees of the neighbors of the node. The betweenness centrality (Freeman, 1977) of a node is a measure of the fractions of the shortest paths between any two nodes (in the network) that go through the node. The closeness centrality (Freeman, 1979) of a node is a measure of the distance (number of edges on the shortest path) of the node to the rest of the nodes in the network. After running the proposed binary search algorithm on a suite of 60 real-world networks, we observe the DEG centrality metric, followed by the BWC metric, to be relatively more effective for accomplishing larger cascade capacities for the networks when operated with the different percentages of initial adopters.

The rest of the chapter is organized as follows: The Background section reviews related work in the literature and highlights the unique contributions of this work. The section titled "Hypothesis and Motivating Example" presents our hypothesis and a motivating example to illustrate the impact of initial adopters on the cascade capacity of a network. The section titled "Iterative Algorithm and Information Cascade" presents an iterative algorithm used in this chapter to conduct information cascade in a network for a given set of initial adopters and threshold fraction of adopted neighbors. The section titled "Binary Search Algorithm" presents the proposed binary search algorithm to determine the cascade capacity of a network for a given set of initial adopters. The section titled "Analysis of Real-World Networks" presents the results (largest possible cascade capacities for a suite of 60 real-world networks for 2%, 5% and 10% of the nodes as initial adopters with respect to each of the four centrality metrics) and analyzes the increase in the cascade capacities of the networks with increase in the % of the initial adopters vis-a-vis those determined using the intra cluster density approach. The section titled "Future Research Directions" outlines our plans for future work that extend the proposed work in this chapter. The Conclusions section concludes the chapter by highlighting its contributions and presenting a summary of the evaluation results. Throughout the chapter, the terms 'network' and 'graph', 'node' and 'vertex', 'link' and 'edge' are used interchangeably. They mean the same.

BACKGROUND

Yu & Fei (2009) analyzed the propagation of photos through the Flickr social network. If a user A establishes a contact with a user B in Flickr, then all the photos marked as favorites by B will appear to A who can also mark one or more of these photos as his/her favorites. Such favorite photo information will then propagate to all the users who are in contact with A and so on. Photos are displayed in the favorites list in the temporal order; hence, photos that were recently uploaded are more likely to travel a longer distance (i.e., become favorites for several people through their contacts) in the near future compared to photos that were uploaded in the past. In addition, they also analyzed the structural aspects of the social network that expedite or impede photo propagation. We can consider a generic model of information cascade in social networks wherein a user posts/tweets/chooses as favorites some information if at least a fraction 'q' of his/her neighbors have done so. We can apply the proposed binary search algorithm under such a generic model and determine the maximum value for this fraction 'q' needed for the information to reach all the users of the social network with a given set of initial adopters.

Yang & Leskovec (2011) propose a linear influence model that captures the influence potential of a node i by measuring the number of other nodes (and the subsequent iteration #s of the information cascade) that adopted the same decision as node i due to the adoption decision of node i. They applied the model to the Twitter network and found that initiator nodes with more *active* followers (the actual number of followers need not be very high) and followers with larger in-degree are the ones who are the most influential in propagating hashtags; initiator nodes with simply more followers or larger in-degree need not be more influential. In this chapter, we observed for undirected networks, nodes with larger BWC centrality were found to be almost equally effective as nodes with larger DEG centrality for use as initial adopters and operate the network at a larger cascade capacity. We also observed that nodes with larger CLC (though are relatively closer to the rest of the nodes in the network) need not be effective initial adopters to operate the network at a larger cascade capacity. Our observation coincides with the work of Watts and Dodds (2007) who show that for effective dissemination of new ideas, who the initial adopters are connected to is more important than the number of connections of the initial adopters.

The information cascade model based on a threshold fraction of adopted neighbors is sometimes used to model the spread of a complex contagion (Centola & Macy, 2007). Ghasemiesfeh (2013) show that the diffusion speed of a simple contagion (a node adopts a decision when just one neighbor node adopts the decision) might be simply dependent on the network diameter, but the diffusion speed of a complex contagion depends on the distribution of the weak ties. This observation coincides again with our research findings that the CLC metric (suitable for a simple contagion model) is not an effective metric to choose the initial adopters when we require a threshold fraction of adopted neighbors for a node to adopt a decision.

Jalili & Perc (2017) define a measure called the spreading influence of a node, which in our context could be rephrased as the fraction of nodes that adopt a decision based on the decision adopted by the node. They observed a positive correlation between the degree and betweenness centrality of the nodes vs. the spreading influence of the nodes, whereas observed a negative correlation between the eccentricity (related to CLC) and information index vs. the spreading influence of the nodes. Nodes with largest DEG and BWC were thus observed to speed up the adoption process of the rest of the nodes in the network. Our findings in this research also corroborate the role of the DEG and BWC centrality metrics in information cascade and we show that the number and centrality metric values of the initial adopters have a significant impact on the largest possible cascade capacity of a network.

Meghanathan (2021) proposed a binary search algorithm that could be used to determine the minimum fraction of nodes ($f_{IA}^{\min}$) needed as initial adopters to operate the network with a particular threshold fraction (q) of adopted neighbors for a complete information cascade. Meghanathan observed that the q vs. $f_{IA}^{\min}$ distribution for several real-world networks exhibited a step-function pattern wherein there is an abrupt increase in $f_{IA}^{\min}$ value beyond a certain threshold q (referred to as q_{step}). The value $1 - q_{step}$ is referred to as the cascade blocking index (CBI) of a network; the CBI value for a network could be perceived as a measure of the intra-cluster density of the blocking cluster (of the network) that cannot be penetrated without significantly the fraction of nodes needed as initial adopters. In a most recent work, Zhou et al (2022) present a comprehensive review and categorization of the prediction methods for information popularity ranging from feature engineering and stochastic processes, through graph representation, to deep learning-based approaches.

HYPOTHESIS AND MOTIVATING EXAMPLE

Our hypothesis for this research is that the threshold fraction of adopted neighbors for a unanimous decision needed to accomplish complete information cascade depends on the number and topological positions of the nodes chosen as initial adopters. Figures 1 and 2 present an example to illustrate the importance of considering the initial adopters while determining the cascade capacity of a network. Figure 1 presents the calculation of the cascade capacity of a network using the clustering approach (without taking the initial adopters into consideration): Nodes 2, 4, 5 and 6 are the bridge nodes of the two clusters (1, 2, 3, 4) and (5, 6, 7, 8). The intra cluster density (fraction of neighbor nodes that are in the same cluster) for nodes 2 and 4 are 3/5 and 3/4 respectively, and likewise the intra cluster density for nodes 5 and 6 are 3/4 and 3/5 respectively. The density of a cluster is the minimum of the intra cluster density of its bridge nodes. Accordingly, the densities of clusters (1, 2, 3, 4) and (5, 6, 7, 8) are minimum (3/4, 3/5) = 3/5 each. The maximum possible value for the threshold fraction of adopted neighbors for a unanimous decision for each of these two clusters is 1- the intra cluster density = 1- 3/5 = 2/5; the cascade capacity of the network (the minimum of the threshold fraction of adopted neighbors for a unanimous decision for the clusters) is also 2/5. As noticed in this example walk-through, the cluster densities and the cascade capacity are all determined independent of the initial adopters.

Figure 1. Cascade Capacity of a Network Determined using the Clustering Approach

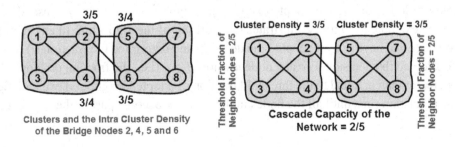

Figure 2 presents an iterative approach (see Algorithm 1 for the pseudo code) to conduct information cascade in the same network of Figure 1 with nodes 2 and 6 (the two nodes with the largest degree centrality in the graph) as the initial adopters. The fraction outside the circle for a node indicates the fraction of adopted neighbor nodes (shaded in green). In the section titled "Binary Search Algorithm," we use the binary search approach to formally determine the largest value for the threshold fraction (q) of adopted neighbor nodes for a unanimous decision (see Table 1 for an example walk-through of the binary search approach). Since the network in Figure 2 is a smaller graph of just 8 nodes and given that nodes 2 and 6 are the initial adopters, it is easy to observe that the cascade cannot proceed if we choose the threshold fraction (q) of adopted neighbor nodes for a unanimous decision to be a value that is greater than the maximum (2/4 = 1/2) of the fractions indicated for the neighbor nodes of the initial adopters. Hence, we proceed with the iterations by using $q = 1/2$ as the threshold fraction of adopted neighbor nodes needed for a node to adopt the unanimous decision.

In Iteration 1, nodes 4 and 5 adopt the decision as their fraction ($f = 1/2$) of adopted neighbor nodes is equal to the threshold fraction ($q = 1/2$) of adopted neighbor nodes. As a result, the fraction (f) of adopted neighbor nodes for nodes 1, 3, 7 and 8 become 2/3 each, which is greater than q (1/2). Hence, in the next iteration (Iteration 2), we say nodes 1, 3, 7 and 8 have also adopted the same decision, leading to a complete information cascade. As mentioned earlier, for the given set of initial adopters {2, 6}, the information cascade cannot proceed (and become complete) if we choose $q > 1/2$. Hence, for {2, 6} as the set of initial adopters, $q = 1/2$ is the largest possible cascade capacity of the network of Figures 1 and 2. We observe our hypothesis to be true with regards to Figures 1 and 2: That is, the cascade capacity of the network determined using the initial adopters 2 and 6 (which are also nodes with relatively larger degree centrality) in Figure 2 is greater than the cascade capacity determined using the clustering approach (that is independent of the initial adopters) in Figure 1.

Figure 2. Cascade Capacity of a Network Determined using the Initial Adopters

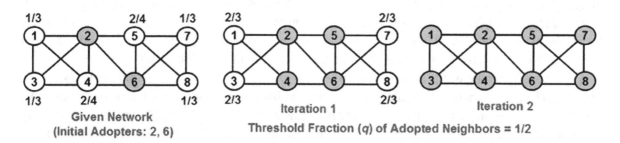

ITERATIVE ALGORITHM AND INFORMATION CASCADE

We use an iterative algorithm to conduct information cascade in a network for a given set of initial adopters (IA) and threshold fraction (q) of adopted neighbors. Algorithm 1 presents the pseudo code of the algorithm and the example in Figure 2 illustrates the working of the algorithm. In any iteration, we go through the vertices that have not yet adopted the decision and determine the fraction (f) of their neighbors that have adopted the decision. For any node u whose $f \geq q$ (i.e., the fraction of adopted neighbors of the node is greater than or equal to the threshold fraction of adopted neighbors), we include node u to the set IA. The algorithm runs until all the nodes in the network become part of the set IA (i.e., adopted

B

the unanimous decision, leading to a complete information cascade) or no new node adopted the decision in the latest iteration (tracked through the boolean variable *CascadeProgress* in the pseudo code of Algorithm 1). In the latter case, the algorithm ends prematurely with the information cascade declared to be *not complete*.

The algorithm would need to run for at most $|V| - |IA|$ iterations (a scenario in which just one vertex per iteration adopts the decision) and in each iteration, we go through at most $|E|$ edges of the graph and determine the fraction of adopted neighbors for each vertex in the set $V - IA$. Thus, the overall time complexity of the iterative algorithm is $O(|V||E|)$, simply written as $O(VE)$. As seen in the example of Figure 2 and the analysis of the real-world networks, the number of iterations needed to accomplish complete information cascade need not be as large as $|V| - |IA|$ iterations. In Figure 2, we accomplish complete information cascade in just 2 iterations (wherein $|V| - |IA| = 6$).

Algorithm 1: Iterative Algorithm to Conduct Information Cascade for a Given Set of Initial Adopters and a Threshold Fraction of Adopted Neighbors

    Input: Graph $G = (V, E)$; Set of Initial Adopters, IA; Threshold Fraction of Adopted Neighbors, q
    Auxiliary Variables: boolean *CascadeProgress*, int *NumAdoptedNeighbors*
    Begin Algorithm *Iterative Information Cascade*
    while $(|IA| < |V|)$ **do**
    CascadeProgress = false
    for vertex $u \in V - IA$ **do**
    N_u = Neighbors of vertex u
    NumAdoptedNeighbors = 0
    for vertex $v \in N_u$ **do**
    if $(v \in IA)$ **then**
    NumAdoptedNeighbors = *NumAdoptedNeighbors* + 1
    end if
    end for
    Fraction f of adopted neighbors = *NumAdoptedNeighbors* $/ |N_u|$
    if $(f \geq q)$ **then**
    $IA = IA \cup \{u\}$
    CascadeProgress = true
    end if
    end for
    if (*CascadeProgress* == false) **then**
    return "Cascade Not complete"
    end if
    end while
    return "Cascade Complete"
    End Algorithm *Iterative Information Cascade*

BINARY SEARCH ALGORITHM

We now present our binary search algorithm (see Algorithm 2 for a pseudo code) to determine the largest possible value for the cascade capacity of a network for a given set of initial adopters. The binary search algorithm runs in a search space ranging from 0 to 1 (as the cascade capacity is always a fraction). If the threshold fraction (q) of adopted neighbors for a unanimous decision is set to 0, then information cascade on a network for any set of initial adopters will be complete. On the other hand, unless the set of initial adopters is large enough such that for at least one un adopted vertex in each iteration of the Iterative Information Cascade algorithm (refer Algorithm 1 for a pseudo code), the fraction of adopted neighbors is 1, the information cascade will not be complete. Hence, as seen in the pseudo code (Algorithm 2) of the algorithm, we first test whether the information cascade can be complete when operated with 1.0 as the threshold fraction (q) of adopted neighbors; if the information cascade can be complete for $q = 1$, we do not need to run the binary search algorithm and simply return 1.0 as the largest possible value for the cascade capacity of the network. There arises a need to run the binary search algorithm on a network for a given set of initial adopters only if the information cascade cannot be complete for $q = 1$.

On the basis of the above discussion, we maintain the following invariant throughout the execution of the binary search algorithm: the value of the left index always corresponds to a threshold fraction (q) of adopted neighbors that can lead to a complete information cascade and the value of the right index always corresponds to a threshold fraction (q) of adopted neighbors that cannot lead to a complete information cascade. The binary search algorithm proceeds in iterations as long as the difference between the right index and left index is greater than or equal to a termination threshold ($\varepsilon = 0.01$ in this chapter). In each iteration, the search space reduces by half, with either the left index moving to the right or the right index moving to the left.

Algorithm 2: Binary Search Algorithm to Determine the Largest Possible Cascade Capacity of a Network for a Given Set of Initial Adopters

> **Input:** Graph $G = (V, E)$; Set of Initial Adopters, *IA*; Termination Threshold, ε
> **Auxiliary Variables:** *Left Index* = 0, *Right Index* = 1
> **Begin** Binary Search Algorithm
> **if** (Iterative Information Cascade(*G, IA, Right Index*) == "Cascade Complete") **then**
> **return** Cascade Capacity = 1
> end if
> **while** (|*Right Index– Left Index*| ≥ ε) **do**
> *Middle Index* = (*Left Index* + *Right Index*)/2
> **if** (Iterative Information Cascade(*G, IA, Middle Index*) == "Cascade Complete") **then**
> *Left Index* = *Middle Index*
> else
> *Right Index* = *Middle Index*
> end if
> end while
> **return** *Cascade Capacity = Left Index*
> **End** Binary Search Algorithm

At the beginning of each iteration, we determine the middle index as the average of the left index and right index. We run the iterative information cascade algorithm (Algorithm 1) on the network with the given set of initial adopters and the middle index value as the threshold fraction (q) of adopted neighbors. If the information cascade is complete, it implies that any value for q ranging from [left index ... middle index] will lead to a complete information cascade: accordingly, we move the left index to the right by setting left index = middle index. If the information cascade is not complete, it implies that any value for q ranging from [middle index ... right index] will not lead to a complete information cascade: accordingly, we move the right index to the left by setting right index = middle index. The algorithm stops when the absolute difference between the right index and left index becomes less than the termination threshold (ε). We then declare the latest value of the left index as the largest possible value for the cascade capacity of the network for a given set of initial adopters.

Table 1. Execution of the Binary Search Algorithm on the Example Graph of Figure 2

Iteration #	Left Index (*LI*)	Right Index (*RI*)	|*RI - LI*|	Middle Index *MI = (LI + RI)/2*	Information Cascade Complete for *MI*?
1	0	1	1	0.5	YES
2	0.5	1	0.5	0.75	NO
3	0.5	0.75	0.25	0.625	NO
4	0.5	0.625	0.125	0.5625	NO
5	0.5	0.5625	0.0625	0.53125	NO
6	0.5	0.53125	0.03125	0.51563	NO
7	0.5	0.51563	0.01563	0.50782	NO
8	0.5	0.50782	|*RI - LI*| = 0.00782 < 0.01, STOP!!! Return *LI* = 0.5 as the largest possible cascade capacity of the network with {2, 6} as the initial adopters		

With the search space (spanning from 0 to 1) reducing by half in each iteration (as is the characteristic of the binary search approach) and a termination threshold of ε, the number of iterations of the algorithm is given by $\log_2$(search space/ε) = $\log_2((1\text{-}0)/\varepsilon)$ = $\log_2(1/\varepsilon)$. In each iteration of the binary search algorithm, we run the information cascade algorithm (Algorithm 1), whose time complexity is O(*VE*). Hence, the overall time complexity of the proposed binary search algorithm is O(*VE**$\log_2(1/\varepsilon)$). Table 1 illustrates the execution of the binary search algorithm on the example graph of Figures 1 and 2: For each iteration, we list the values for the left index, right index and middle index as well as whether the information cascade is complete or not when the middle index value is used for the iteration. As observed in the section titled "Hypothesis and Motivating Example," with {2, 6} as the set of initial adopters, the largest possible cascade capacity of the graph of Figures 1 and 2 is 1/2 (0.5) and in Table 1, we see how the binary search algorithm determines the same.

ANALYSIS OF REAL-WORLD NETWORKS

In this section, we present the results of the analysis conducted for a suite of 60 real-world networks, covering the following domains: Biological Networks (18), Literature Networks (11) and Social Networks (24) and other miscellaneous networks (7). The references for several of these networks are available in (Meghanathan, 2019). The biological networks primarily include 10 genetic interaction networks of various bacteria and virus types as well as the brain networks and metabolic networks of some species, and the food exchange networks of some regions. The literature networks include the interaction networks of characters in a novel/book, citation networks, networks among authors in a particular area, and etc. The social networks include friendship networks and acquaintance networks among politicians, educators focused on a specific mission, employees in organizations, organisms of the same species, people residing in remote locations, etc. Table 2 presents the ranges for the number of nodes and edges as well as their median values for the above three specific network domains. All the 60 real-world network graphs are connected and are considered to be undirected for our analysis.

Table 2. Ranges for the Number of Nodes and Edges and their Median Values for the Network Domains

Network Domain	Min # Nodes	Max # Nodes	Median # Nodes	Min # Edges	Max # Edges	Median # Edges
Biological Networks	35	7,747	375	80	10,375	1,801
Literature Networks	35	1,538	118	118	8,032	425
Social Networks	30	1,133	79	61	10,903	509

For each of the 60 real-world networks, we run the Girvan-Newman clustering algorithm (Girvan & Newman, 2002) based on edge betweenness (Girvan & Newman, 2002) and determine the intra cluster densities of these clusters, using which we determine the cascade capacities of the networks. The Girvan Newman clustering algorithm is a top-down algorithm that iteratively removes the edges (in the decreasing order of their betweenness values) until the network gets partitioned into two or more clusters. The above approach is then applied for each cluster. A hierarchy of clusters can be thus built with the root node being the entire graph and the leaf nodes being the individual nodes; the intermediate nodes are clusters of two or more nodes. We prune the hierarchy at branches whose upstream cluster modularity score (Clauset et al., 2004) is larger than the sum of the modularity scores of the immediate downstream nodes. A cluster whose constituent nodes have more links amongst themselves compared to links with nodes outside the cluster is more likely to incur a larger modularity score.

The cascade capacities of the networks determined using the clustering approach is a lower bound as we observe it to be sufficient enough to cause complete information cascade even with one initial adopter. We then ran the proposed binary search algorithm for three different percentages of nodes chosen as initial adopters: 2%, 5% and 10% with respect to each of the four-centrality metrics (DEG, EVC, BWC and CLC). That is, for each of these four-centrality metrics, we choose the top 2%, 5% and 10% of the nodes with the largest centrality values and consider them as initial adopters. To handle the issue of ties, we run 100 trials of the algorithm for each of the above percentages of initial adopters for each centrality metric and take the average of the results for the largest possible cascade capacities of the networks. For any particular trial, we break the ties arbitrarily.

For each of the 60 real-world networks, we find the difference between the largest possible cascade capacities of the networks for a given percentage of initial adopters and the cascade capacity of the network determined using the clustering approach. We determine the number of real-world networks and thereby the fraction of the 60 real-world networks whose differences in the cascade capacities fall within the following ranges: 0, (0, ..., 0.1], (0.1, ..., 0.2], (0.2, ..., 0.3], (0.4, ..., 0.5] and (0.5, ..., 1]. Figure 3 plots the distribution of these differences for each of the four-centrality metrics and the percentage of initial adopters. We observe the distribution of the differences in the cascade capacities of the networks to follow a Poisson pattern, with the peak fraction of the real-world networks moving to the right as we increase the percentage of initial adopters. For 2%, 5% and 10% of the initial adopters, we observe the peak (maximum fraction of the real-world networks) of the differences in the cascade capacities in the intervals (0, ..., 0.1], (0.1, ..., 0.2] and (0.2, ..., 0.3] respectively. Also, for all the four-centrality metrics, the fraction of real-world networks with differences in the cascade capacities falling in the range (0.5,

B

..., 1] increases with increase in the percentage of initial adopters as well as the fraction of the networks whose differences in the cascade capacities being 0 decreases with increase in the percentage of initial adopters. All of the above observations prove our hypothesis that the largest possible cascade capacity of a network is impacted by the number of initial adopters.

Figure 3. Distribution of the Differences in the Cascade Capacities of the Real-World Networks (with the Clustering Approach): Impact of the Percentage of Initial Adopters and the Centrality Metrics

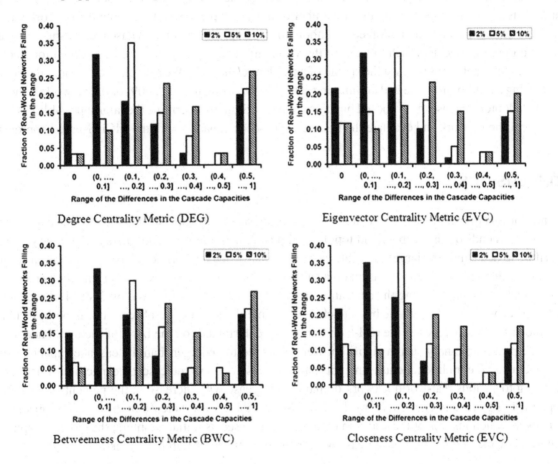

From the point of view of the three network domains (Biological networks, Literature networks and Social networks), for each of DEG and BWC, the median of the differences in the cascade capacities of the Literature networks and Social networks increased with increase in the percentage of initial adopters (as expected). However, for the 18 Biological networks, we had to separately compute the median of the differences in the cascade capacities for the 10 genetic interaction networks and the other 8 networks that are not related to genetic interaction. Irrespective of the network size (# nodes and # edges), the median of the differences in the cascade capacities of the 10 genetic interaction networks remained the same for both the DEG and BWC metrics as well as the same for the different percentages of initial adopters. The median of the differences in the cascade capacities of the other 8 biological networks increased with increase in the percentage of the initial adopters. Overall, the median of the differences in the cascade capacities of the genetic interaction networks were much higher (0.62) than the median of the differences in the cascade capacities of the other biological networks, literature networks and social networks. The median of the differences in the cascade capacities of the social networks was the lowest of all the categories for both DEG and BWC and any value for the percentage of initial adopters.

FUTURE RESEARCH DIRECTIONS

As part of future work, we plan to use a similar strategy and propose a binary search algorithm that could be used to determine the minimum number of initial adopters need to operate the network with a particular threshold fraction of adopted neighbors for a complete information cascade. Further, we plan to extend the proposed approach to identify the vaccination threshold that would be needed for a community in social networks to resist the spread of a pandemic/endemic. We also plan to consider the nodes constituting a minimum connected dominating set (MCDS; Cormen et al., 2009) of the network as the set of initial adopters and use the proposed binary search algorithm to determine the largest possible cascade capacity of the network and evaluate the gain in the cascade capacity with the MCDS-based approach.

CONCLUSIONS

The high-level contributions of this chapter are the proposal of a hypothesis that the cascade capacity of a network depends on the number and topological positions of the initial adopters and a binary search algorithm to determine the largest possible cascade capacity of a network for a given set of initial adopters. We ran the binary search algorithm on a suite of 60 real-world networks by varying the percentage of initial adopters and by using the centrality metrics (Degree: DEG, Eigenvector: EVC, Betweenness: BWC and Closeness: CLC) as the basis to choose the initial adopters. We observe our hypothesis to be true: the cascade capacities of the real-world networks determined (on the basis of the initial adopters) using the proposed binary search algorithm were observed to be larger than the cascade capacities determined using the traditional clustering approach. We also observe the cascade capacities of networks belonging to various real-world network domains to increase with increase in the percentage of initial adopters. The genetic interaction networks demonstrated the largest increase in the cascade capacity of the network when just 2% of the nodes in the network are used as initial adopters; the cascade capacity of these networks did not further increase with increase in the % of initial adopters.

REFERENCES

Bonacich, P. (1987). Power and Centrality: A family of measures. *American Journal of Sociology*, *92*(5), 1170–1182. doi:10.1086/228631

Centola, D., & Macy, M. (2007). Complex contagions and the weakness of long ties. *American Journal of Sociology*, *113*(3), 702–734. doi:10.1086/521848

Chesney, T. (2017). The cascade capacity predicts individuals to seed for diffusion through social networks. *Systems Research and Behavioral Science*, *34*(1), 51–61. doi:10.1002res.2398

Clauset, A., Newman, M. E., & Moore, C. (2004). Finding community structure in very large networks. *Physical Review. E*, *70*(6), 066111. doi:10.1103/PhysRevE.70.066111 PMID:15697438

Cormen, T. H., Leiserson, C. E., Rivest, R. L., & Stein, C. (2009). *Introduction to algorithms* (3rd ed.). MIT Press.

Easley, D., & Kleinberg, J. (2010). *Networks, crowds, and markets: Reasoning about a highly connected world* (1st ed.). Cambridge University Press. doi:10.1017/CBO9780511761942

Freeman, L. (1977). A set of measures of centrality based on betweenness. *Sociometry, 40*(1), 35–41. doi:10.2307/3033543

Freeman, L. (1979). Centrality in social networks: Conceptual classification. *Social Networks, 1*(3), 215–239. doi:10.1016/0378-8733(78)90021-7

Ghasemiesfeh, G., Ebrahimi, R., & Gao, J. (2013). Complex contagion and the weakness of long ties in social networks: Revisited. In *Proceedings of the 14th ACM Conference on Electronic Commerce* (pp. 507-524). ACM.

Girvan, M., & Newman, M. E. J. (2002). Community structure in social and biological networks. *Proceedings of the National Academy of Sciences of the United States of America, 99*(12), 7821–7826. doi:10.1073/pnas.122653799 PMID:12060727

Jalili, M., & Perc, M. (2017). Information cascades in complex networks. *Journal of Complex Networks, 5*(5), 665–693.

Meghanathan, N. (2019). Unit disk graph-based node similarity index for complex network analysis. *Complexity, 2019*(6871874), 1–22. doi:10.1155/2019/6871874

Meghanathan, N. (2021). Exploring the step function distribution of the threshold fraction of adopted neighbors versus minimum fraction of nodes as initial adopters to assess the cascade blocking intra-cluster density of complex real-world networks. *Applied Network Science, 5*(97), 1–33.

Newman, M. E. J. (2010). *Networks: An introduction.* (1st ed.). Oxford University Press. doi:10.1093/acprof:oso/9780199206650.001.0001

Watts, D. J., & Dodds, P. (2007). Influentials, Networks, and Public Opinion Formation. *The Journal of Consumer Research, 34*(4), 441–458. doi:10.1086/518527

Yang, J., & Leskovec, J. (2011). Modeling information diffusion in implicit networks. *Proceedings of the 2010 IEEE International Conference on Data Mining*, 599-608.

Yu, B., & Fei, H. (2009). Modeling social cascade in the Flickr social network. *Proceedings of the 6th International Conference on Fuzzy Systems and Knowledge Discovery*, 7, 566-570. 10.1109/FSKD.2009.719

Zhou, F., Xu, X., Trajcevski, G., & Zhang, K. (2022). A survey of information cascade analysis: Models, predictions and recent advances. *ACM Computing Surveys, 54*(2), 1-36.

ADDITIONAL READING

Alevy, J. E., Haigh, M. S., & List, J. A. (2007). Information cascades: Evidence from a field experiment with financial market professionals. *The Journal of Finance, 62*(1), 151–180. doi:10.1111/j.1540-6261.2007.01204.x

Anderson, L. R., & Holt, C. A. (1997). Information cascades in the laboratory. *The American Economic Review*, *87*(5), 847–862.

Bakshy, E., Rosenn, I., Marlow, C., & Adamic, L. (2012). The role of social networks in information diffusion. *Proceedings of the 21st International Conference on World Wide Web*, 519-528. 10.1145/2187836.2187907

Bhardwaj, N., Yan, K. K., & Gerstein, M. B. (2010). Analysis of diverse regulatory networks in a hierarchical context shows consistent tendencies for collaboration in the middle levels. *Proceedings of the National Academy of Sciences of the United States of America*, *107*(15), 6841–6846. doi:10.1073/pnas.0910867107 PMID:20351254

Blagus, N., Subelj, L., & Bajec, M. (2012). Self-similar scaling of density in complex real-world networks. *Physica A*, *391*(8), 2794–2802. doi:10.1016/j.physa.2011.12.055

de Nooy, W. (1999). A literary playground: Literary criticism and balance theory. *Poetics*, *26*(5-6), 385–404. doi:10.1016/S0304-422X(99)00009-1

Freeman, L. C., Webster, C. M., & Kirke, D. M. (1998). Exploring social structure using dynamic three-dimensional color images. *Social Networks*, *20*(2), 109–118. doi:10.1016/S0378-8733(97)00016-6

Geiser, P., & Danon, L. (2003). Community structure in Jazz. *Advances in Complex Systems*, *6*(4), 563–573.

Gemmetto, V., Barrat, A., & Cattuto, C. (2014). Mitigation of infectious disease at school: Targeted class closure vs. school closure. *BMC Infectious Diseases*, *14*(695), 1–10. doi:10.118612879-014-0695-9 PMID:25595123

Hisakado, M., & Mori, S. (2009). Phase transition and information cascade in a voting model. *Journal of Physics. A, Mathematical and Theoretical*, *43*(31), 1–13.

Hummon, N. P., Doreian, P., & Freeman, L. C. (1990). Analyzing the structure of the centrality-productivity literature created between 1948 and 1979. *Science Communication*, *11*(4), 459–480.

Isella, L., Stehle, J., Barrat, A., Cattuto, C., Pinton, J. F., & Van den Broeck, W. (2011). What's in a crowd? Analysis of face-to-face behavioral networks. *Journal of Theoretical Biology*, *271*(1), 166–180. doi:10.1016/j.jtbi.2010.11.033 PMID:21130777

Jensen, P., Morini, M., Karsai, M., Venturini, T., Vespignani, A., Jacomy, M., Cointet, J. P., Merckle, P., & Fleury, E. (2015). Detecting global bridges in networks. *Journal of Complex Networks*, *4*(3), 319–329. doi:10.1093/comnet/cnv022

Knight, B., & Schiff, N. (2010). Momentum and social learning in presidential primaries. *Journal of Political Economy*, *118*(6), 1110–1150. doi:10.1086/658372

Krackhardt, D. (1999). The ties that torture: Simmelian tie analysis in organizations. *Research in the Sociology of Organizations*, *16*, 183–210.

Lelarge, M. (2012). Diffusion and cascading behavior in random networks. *Games and Economic Behavior*, *75*(2), 752–775. doi:10.1016/j.geb.2012.03.009

Lusseau, D., Schneider, K., Boisseau, O. J., Haase, P., Slooten, E., & Dawson, S. M. (2003). The bottlenose dolphin community of Doubtful sound features a large proportion of long-lasting associations. *Behavioral Ecology and Sociobiology, 54*(3), 396–405. doi:10.100700265-003-0651-y

Meghanathan, N. (2017). Complex network analysis of the contiguous United States graph. *Computer and Information Science, 10*(1), 54–76. doi:10.5539/cis.v10n1p54

Miasnikof, P., Pitsoulis, L., Bonner, A. J., Lawryshyn, Y., & Pardalos, P. M. (2018). Graph clustering via intra-cluster density maximization. *Proceedings of the International Conference on Network Analysis*, 37-48.

Mori, S., Hisakado, M., & Takahashi, T. (2013). Collective adoption of max-min strategy in an information cascade voting experiment. *Journal of the Physical Society of Japan, 82*(8), 1–10. doi:10.7566/JPSJ.82.084004

Newman, M. E. J. (2004). Detecting community structure in networks. *The European Physical Journal B, 38*(2), 321–330. doi:10.1140/epjb/e2004-00124-y PMID:15244693

Prokhorenkova, L., Tikhonov, A., & Litvak, N. (2019). Learning clusters through information diffusion. *Proceedings of the World Wide Web Conference*, 3151-3157. 10.1145/3308558.3313560

Ramezani, M., Khodadadi, A., & Rabiee, H. R. (2018). Community detection using diffusion information. *ACM Transactions on Knowledge Discovery from Data, 12*(2), 1–22. doi:10.1145/3110215

Rodriguez, M. G., Leskovec, J., Balduzzi, D., & Scholkopf, B. (2014). Uncovering the structure and temporal dynamics of information propagation. *Network Science, 2*(1), 26–65. doi:10.1017/nws.2014.3

Subelj, L., & Bajec, M. (2012). Ubiquitousness of link-density and link-pattern communities in real-world networks. *The European Physical Journal B, 85*(1), 1–11. doi:10.1140/epjb/e2011-20448-7

KEY TERMS AND DEFINITIONS

Binary Search: An algorithmic design strategy that proceeds by reducing the search space by half in each iteration until the solution is found or the search space no longer exists.

Bridge Node: A node that has links to one or more nodes in other clusters.

Cascade Capacity: The largest value for the threshold fraction of neighbors that should have made a unanimous decision to result in a complete information cascade.

Centrality Metric: A scalar value that quantifies the topological importance of a node.

Cluster: A grouping of the nodes in a network such that the density of links among nodes within the cluster is larger compared to the density of links to nodes outside the cluster.

Complete Information Cascade: An information cascade in which all the nodes arrive at the same decision irrespective of their personal choice.

Degree: The number of neighbors for a node.

Diffusion: Propagation of information from the initial adopters to the rest of the nodes in a network.

Information Cascade: A behavioral phenomenon by which every node arrives at a decision (adopt or reject a particular thing) under the influence of the decision taken by its neighbor nodes.

Initial Adopters: A set of nodes that trigger information cascade.

Investigating the Character–Network Topology in Marvel Movies

Sameer Kumar
University of Malaya, Malaysia

Tanmay Verma
Independent Researcher, Malaysia

INTRODUCTION

Movies by Marvel Entertainment have seen unprecedented commercial success over the years. The characters such as Spiderman, Hulk or Iron Man, have become household names. Marvel Cinematic Universe's major break came in 2008 after the release of Iron Man and during the last decade, in particular, it has catapulted itself to becoming one of the most successful franchises in the history of film history. Known as the Marvel Cinematic Universe, this media franchise has had its own journey of successes and failures of over 80 years.

In the recent years Social Network Analysis has been applied extensively to understand relationship between entities. A simple relationship could be constructed between any two entity if there is some sort of association between them. This association must be defined, and a connection is then established between them. Several such connections form the network and the network could be then analysed at both the node-level and the network-level.

Martin Goodman started Marvel comics (at that time known as Timely Comics) in 1939. The first comics were a crossover between characters like Namor and the Human Torch. During the time of World War II people wanted to see patriotic heroes, hence characters like Captain America took prominence. In the 1950s, Timely Comics changed its name to Atlas Comics. Stan Lee and Jack Kirby partnered together to make characters like Spiderman, Iron Man, dare devil, fantastic four (team). The characters became more successful commercially than DC (another media franchise) because of team characters like Avengers and X-Men. However, during the 90s they had to suffer bankruptcy as audience were starting to prefer themes where politics and more violence were preferred. During this time they only depended on characters like Punisher, Deadpool, Wolverine and Venom. Marvel Studios had to sell some of the character rights to New World Entertainment. From 2000 onwards they started to make movies like Blade, X-Men, Daredevil and Spiderman. In 2009, after Iron Man and the Incredible Hulk were released, Walt Disney Studios bought Marvel Entertainment. From 2010 onwards they started Marvel Studios and since then on have produced some 22 movies under the franchise.

Our study was driven to find answers to questions like which of the Marvel characters are best connected, holding this famed character-network together; which characters form the bridge and which characters have been a major success both on the yardstick of user ratings and commercial success. To answer these questions, Social Network Analysis is carried out to calculate graph metrics and visualizations. SNA makes it possible to analyse relationships based on the quality (influence, prestige) and quantity (bonding and degree) of connections they form. We also carry out a 2-mode analysis to understand the structure of characters in affiliation to the movies there have starred in.

DOI: 10.4018/978-1-7998-9220-5.ch151

BACKGROUND

Extant literature has looked at several aspects of implementing social network analysis on character interactions. Ding and Yilmaz (2010) used statistical learning to estimate the affinity of characters in movies. Social Network analysis then identified leaders in the communities they formed. Weng, Chu, and Wu (2009) investigated the perspective of social relationships in movies. Using a specially designed method called RoleNet, the authors extract relationships and construct role's social network, thereby leading to identification of corresponding communities. The study was further able to prove the superiority of 'social-based story segmentation approach' over other conventional methods. Using global face name matching Zhang, Xu, Lu, and Huang (2009) identified characters in films and the relationship between characters were mined by applying Social network analysis. A recent study by Lv, Wu, Zhu, and Wang (2018) used a model called as StoryRoleNet to determine relationship among roles. Their study also analysed networks constructed using video and subtitle text.

Audio-visual features are used to analyse movie videos. In addition, constructing networks using co-appearance in movies is often the practice. A study by Ding, Yilmaz, and Ieee (2011) attempts to establish a relationship between visual concepts and social connections between actors. Using a graphical model and experimenting on Youtube videos and theatrical movies, the authors were able to establish relation between actors and also detect communities they form. Park, Oh, and Jo (2012), however, found dialog to be better at constructing social networks, in addition to identifying the quantum of roles (leading, minor, extras), among others. The authors proposed a method called as 'Character-net' to achieve this and also found this to be effective in detecting sequences.

Social network Analysis has been used for movie summarization. Using network analysis, Tran, Hwang, Lee, and Jung (2017) identified protagonists and the other characters and then related them to one another (which the authors call as 'Character Network Analysis') to have a movie summary as close as the original one.

FOCUS OF THE ARTICLE

Most of the studies above, however, have used character roles and relationships within a movie to construct relationships. Rarely have studies looked at character in a movie as a distinct entity which relates to another entity - that may be either a movie, if they have starred in that movie; or another character if they have co-starred in a movie together. Relationships constructed this way could reveal, for example, the best-connected characters or the most 'bridge-forming' characters, at the entity level, and the sparseness of the network or formation of giant component or small world characteristics at the socio-centric level. Our study thus fills this gap in literature by adding the missing dimension.

We have used Marvel Movie production movies as a case study here to investigate network properties of character network. Here we are not interested in understanding association based on what relationship a character has in a particular movie (i.e. father-mother, friend, married couple, love interest, etc.), but rather base it on how we define a common format of relationship. This is done in 2 ways – in the first format of relationship (2-mode) we construct a relationship between a movie and character, if the character has starred a movie (relationship). Hence all the prominent characters (entity) in a movie will tie up with the movie (entity). In the second format (1-mode), a tie or relationship is constructed if the characters have featured in a movie together. A relation is thus seen from purely these two perspectives and topology of the network formed are then investigated.

MATERIAL AND METHODS

List of films was manually recorded by visiting relevant film websites (including IMDB, Mojo,etc). We personally viewed all the films, hence knew the Movie plots of each film, the characters played, etc for each film. Nonetheless, all the films were double checked for the accuracy through the relevant websites. Some film that were not originally produced by Marvel (but later acquired) were excluded. This resulted in a corpus of 67 films. Table 1 depicts the tabulation carried for the movies

Only prominent characters of the movie are taken for analysis. The subjectivity of character selection is apparent here.

Table 1. The cross-section of the list of movies in the data set of 67 films (Refer to Appendix for the complete list)

Movie Title	Year	Characters	Budget $ Approx	Box Office$ Approx	Commercial Success	User Rating (IMDB)
Men In Black (movie)	1997	Agent J| Agent K| Agent Z| Neeble| Jack Jeebs| Dr| Laurel Weaver| Arquillian| Edgar	90,000,000	589,400,000	6.55	7.3
Blade (movie)	1998	Blade| Abraham Whistler| Dr. Karen Jenson| Deacon Frost| Quinn| Vanessa Brooks	45,000,000	131,200,000	2.92	7.1
X-Men (movie)	2000	Wolverine| Professor X| Magneto| Mystique| Rogue| Storm| Iceman| Dr. Jean Grey| Cyclops| Jubilee	75,000,000	296,300,000	3.95	7.4
Blade II (movie)	2002	Blade| Abraham Whistler| Scud| Nyssa| Jared Nomak| Eli Damaskinos| Reinhardt	55,000,000	155,000,000	2.82	6.7
Spider-Man (movie)	2002	Spider-Man| Mary Jane Watson| Flash Thompson| Harry Osborn| Green Goblin| May Parker| Ben Parker| J.J. Jameson	139,000,000	821,700,000	5.91	7.3
Men In Black II (movie)	2002	Agent J| Agent K| Agent Z| Laura Vasquez| Serleena| Jack Jeebs| Scrad| Neeble| Jarra	140,000,000	441,800,000	3.16	6.1
Daredevil (movie)	2003	Daredevil| Elektra| Kingpin| Bullseye| Karen Page| Ben Urich| Foggy Nelson| Jack Murdock	75,000,000	179,200,000	2.39	5.3
X2: X-Men United (movie)	2003	Professor X| Wolverine| Magneto| Mystique| Lady Deathstrike| William Stryker|Rogue| Dr. Jean Grey| Nightcrawler| Storm | Cyclops	110,000,000	407,700,000	3.71	7.5
Hulk (movie)	2003	Hulk| Betty Ross| Thunderbolt Ross| Brian Banner	120,000,000	245,400,000	2.05	5.6
The Punisher (movie)	2004	Punisher| Harry Heck| Howard Saint| Russian| Joan| Livia Saint| Bobby Saint| Quentin Glass	33,000,000	54,700,000	1.66	6.5
Spider-Man 2 (movie)	2004	Spider-Man| Mary Jane Watson| Harry Osborn| May Parker| Dr. Octopus| J.J. Jameson	200,000,000	783,800,000	3.92	7.3
Blade: Trinity (movie)	2004	Blade| Abraham Whistler| Hannibal King| Abigail Whistler| Dracula| Jarko Grimwood| Danica Talos	65,000,000	128,900,000	1.98	5.9

For each film, in addition to the list of main characters, Year of Production, Budget and Box office collections and IMDB User ratings were recorded (see table 1). As the availability of some data was scant, we could not reliably acquire Budget details for four movies (see the data) that were produced during 1998 to 1996.

We used the following method to estimate the relative success of each film:

$$CS = \frac{bc}{mb} \qquad (1)$$

where CS= Commercial Success; bc= Box office Collections and mb= Movie Budget.

The character network formed by combining two characters if they had starred in the same movie together. Hence a movie with 6 mentioned characters, for example, would form a total of 15 connections by being in just one movie (see Figure 1). A degree of a vertex would reveal the number of different characters a character has worked with. However, number of repeat edges (weight) is particularly important here. If any of these characters again work together they would not form a new connection but their edge-weight would increase by 1 (see figure 1). The more movies they work the thicker would be the edge-weight. Edge-weights are crucial to understanding how densely the characters are linked together in the character network

Figure 1. Description of the links formed for a typical movie with 6 characters

Nodes:

Connections formed:

{[a,b];[a,c];[a,d];[a,e];[a,f];

[b,c];[b,d];[b,e];[b,f];

[c,d];[c,e];[c,f];

[d,e];[d,f];

[e,f]}

Figure 2. Example of a network. Larger edge width demonstrates the higher number of times the characters have appeared together

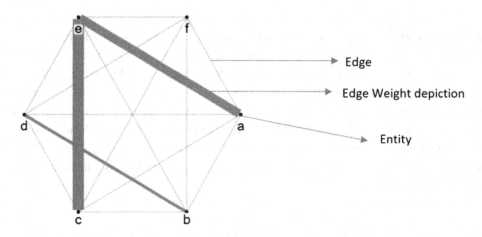

Social network Analysis is a means to quantitatively investigate networks. The networks are typically investigated at three levels – the socio-centric level, relational level and ego-centric level. In the socio-centric level, the overall structure of the graph (other name of network here) is measured to understand if they are small-world (calculated using average geodesic distance), are scale free (calculated using degree distribution), transitivity (calculated through the measurement of clustering coefficient) or what communities they form (number of distinct communities or based on clusters formed within connected communities).

At the relational level, nodes are seen with in the network in relation to other nodes in the network.

Whereas graph metrics such as *degree* calculate the number of immediate direct connections a node has, metrics like *closeness* and *betweenness* centralities are path-based and the profile of entire network is referenced before these calculation results are presented.

Finally, at the egocentric level the investigation is made only on the immediate connections an individual node has. Two metrics are particularly prominent here – Edge Weight or Connectedness (bonding) and Structural holes or absence of connections in the node's immediate neighbourhood. Ego networks with several structural holes may bring more importance to the ego, as the ego (main entity) then becomes a "bridge" for the resources flowing within the personal network. Edge Weight or Strength of connection could be determined by the frequency of interactions, and this is indicated through the thickness of edges between the two nodes. More interactions are also the sign of bondedness. Both bondedness and "weak" connections have their own advantages. While the former is a sign of trust, the other may bring innovation within the community.

Below we mention the specific graph metrics that have been calculated for this study: Density, Degree, betweenness and closeness.

Density of a network is calculated as

$$D = \frac{2*\left(\#L\left(G\right)\right)}{N\left(N-1\right)} \tag{2}$$

Where G represents the network or graph, and N represents the number of nodes. Simply put, a density of a graph is the ratio between the actual edges in the network in ratio to the maximum number of possible edges. The network with a high Density is indicator of high connectedness of the network where resources would flow faster, and vice versa. (Kumar & Markscheffel, 2016; Newman, 2001; Otte & Rousseau, 2002)

A Degree, k_j of vertex i is calculated as

$$k_i = \sum_{j=1}^{n} g_{ij} \qquad (3)$$

where $g_{ij} = 1$, if there is a connection between the vertices i and j. If $g_{ij} = 0$ then it implies that there is no such connection.

Betweenness centrality of a vertex i is the "fraction of geodesic paths which pass through I". Mathematically, betweenness centrality, b of a vertex i is expressed as

$$b(i) = \sum_{j,k} \frac{m_{jik}}{m_{jk}} \qquad (4)$$

where m_{jk} represents geodesic paths from vertex j to vertex $k (j, k \neq i)$ and m_{jik} is the number of geodesic paths from vertex j to vertex k, that is passing through vertex I". (Kumar & Markscheffel, 2016; Newman, 2001; Otte & Rousseau, 2002)

Like betweenness centrality, closeness Centrality too is path-based. Mathematically, closeness centrality c_i of node i is calculated as

$$c_i = \sum_{j} d_{ij} \qquad (5)$$

where d_{ij} represents the number of edges in the geodesic path from vertex i to vertex j. (Kumar & Markscheffel, 2016; Newman, 2001; Otte & Rousseau, 2002). Closeness together with betweenness represent how "central" a node is in the network

FINDINGS AND DISCUSSION

Association Between Commercial Success and User Ratings

Figure 1 depicts the year of release, commercial success and user rating of Marvel Entertainment. The linear trend line shows regular upward progression, meaning that the films, over the years have seen increasing levels of commercial success and higher user ratings. A correlation analysis between commercial Success and user ratings shows a high correlation of 0.62 (Figure 3). This means that high user ratings have also enjoyed relatively high commercial success of these movies and vice versa.

Figure 3. Marvel Movie productions: Year of Release, Commercial Success and User ratings

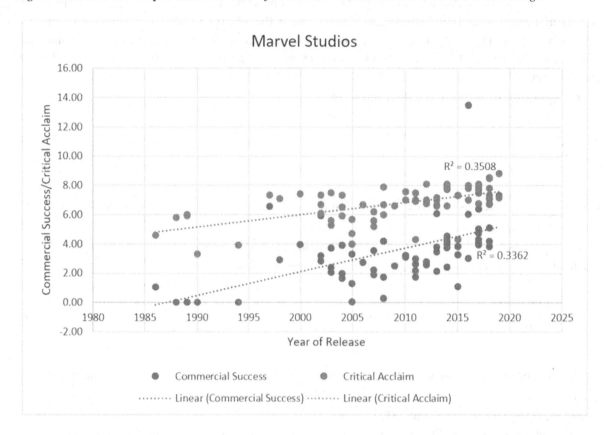

There have been several instances that single hero movies have seen unprecedented success. Examples of this is Spiderman or Ironman series. These movies have certain set of co-actors who also feature in the sequels. In the recent times, there has been a trend to have multi-supermen movies. Naturally these supermen movies have a larger star cast as it also includes the lineage of co-stars of these supermen into a single movie. Example of this trend is most prominently the Avenger Series.

Association Between Larger Star Cast and Movie Success

We next investigated if larger star cast have had movie success, both critically and commercially. A correlation analysis between number of prominent actors in a movie and box office collections and user ratings (for movies between 1997 and 2019, for which we have complete data of box office collections) revealed a correlation result of 0.68 and 0.62, respectively, indicating there may be indeed a relationship. Except for the X-men series, all the movies released till 2009 had a prominent star cast below 10. This has seen a gradual increase since then – X-Men- days of the future past released in 2014 had an even bigger star cast of 18. The Avenger series has led with a massive star cast in the recent years. The results indicate that a larger star cast may be a preferred choice of the audience – especially the ones that bring supermen together. The viewers who have their favourite superman, would like to see him or her matching up with other Superstars and see it compete with them. The recent movie, Avengers- Endgame, a multi hero case movie, broke all records of commercial success.

1-Mode and 2-Mode Network Analyses

The character network (see Figure 4a) formed by connecting 2 actors if they have appeared in a movie together (for the detailed method pl. see Material and Method Section). The network is undirected meaning that the connections are mutual. The network consists of 393 vertices that form 2814 unique edges between them (or 3519 total number of edges). These connections are weighted, meaning that the duplicates edges formed due to repeat connections (if the character works again with the same character in other movies) are merged and counted as 1.

Figure 4. 4(a) – Character Network, force directed layout using Fruchterman-Reingold algorithm 4(b) Movie-Character network force directed layout using Fruchterman-Reingold algorithm. Movie is represented by a diamond whereas the characters are represented by black circles

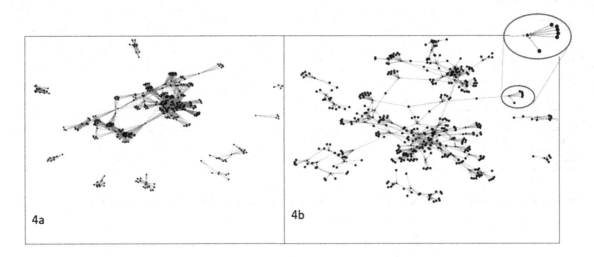

The network is cohesive consisting of a total of 10 components with the largest or giant component capturing over ¾ (76.8%) number of total characters. The GC is the seat of main activity where most of the highly (degree) and densely connected (those having repeat connections) reside. The Average geodesic distance of 3.26 confirms that the network is a "small world". Most self-evolving networks are small world is nature and the same is confirmed by this network too (Amaral, Scala, Barthelemy, & Stanley, 2000; Newman, 2001; Seaton & Hackett, 2004). A graph density of 0.036 nonetheless indicates that the network is not so densely connected.

Complete network visualization at time fails to provide with the granular level of details of some prominent actors that are well connected. Here the weight of the of the edges take prominence. Infact, just the reduction of network on the lines of nodes with higher weight reduces it significantly. The figure 5 shows nodes interaction in the network with the edge weight of 4.

Most of the high weight edges are not the result of two heroes coming together but due to the bond of relationship within the story. Hence these relationships are carried over when they are recast in other movies. Iron Man and Pepper Potts have a weight of 7 meaning the characters have worked together in 7 films. Pepper Potts is a love interest of Tony Stark (Iron Man) in Iron Man Movies. Black Widow has featured with Captain America and Iron Man in 6 movies each. While Black Widow has no specific character relationship with Captain America, it is linked with Iron Man as his secretary. May Parker has appeared with Spider Man as his aunt and they have appeared together in 6 movies. Magneto and Mystique are love interests to each other and they appear in 6 movies together. Similarly, Professor X appears with Mystique in 6 movies as his friend and with Magneto as his Friend-Enemy.

Table 2. Topological Characteristics

Graph	Fig 4a	Fig 4b
Mode	1 mode network: character-character	2-mode network: movie-character
Graph Type	Undirected	Directed
Vertices	393	460
Unique Edges	2814	666
Edges With Duplicates	0	0
Total Edges	2814	666
Self-Loops	0	0
Connected Components	10	10
Maximum Vertices in a Connected Component	302	352
Maximum Edges in a Connected Component	2484	546
Maximum Geodesic Distance (Diameter)	7	14
Average Geodesic Distance	3.263053	6.306843
Graph Density	0.036532	0.003154

Figure 5. Network reduction based on edge weight reveals strong character relationships

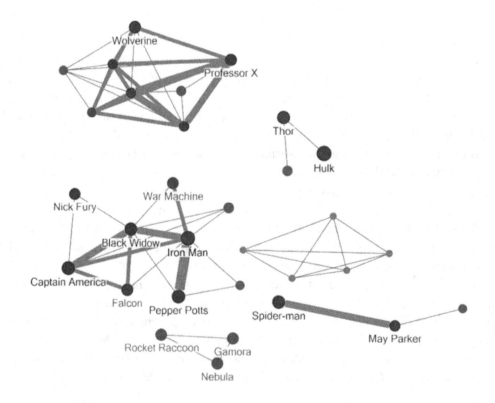

We construct a 2-mode network to understand the characters interactions with the movie they have worked in (see Figure 4b). The network here consists of 460 nodes (movies and characters) forming 666 connections between them. Just like the character network, this network too forms a healthy giant component with the percentage of captured nodes almost the same as the giant component. The diameter and average geodesic distance is almost twice as that of character network. This difference is largely due to the formal introduction of movies as node into the network. In contrast, in a character network, the relationship is formed due to 2 characters working together in a movie. However, in the character network, the movie itself is never represented as a node, but used for defining a relationship. This is also the reason the graph density of this 2-mode network is sparser than the character network (see table 2).

2-mode networks are affiliation-based networks (He, Xie, Luan, Zhang, & Zhang, 2018; Lattanzi & Sivakumar, 2009; Zheleva, Sharara, & Getoor, 2009) where the characters interaction here are formally seen from the perspective of their starring in movies (see Figure2b). On the one hand, all the movie-nodes would have an in-degree of the equivalent of number of characters starring in the movie and the out-degree of 0. Character-nodes, on the other hand, would have the in-degree of 0 and the out-degree representing the total number of different movies they have worked together (Table 2 and Figure 5). Betweenness centrality provides clues on which nodes (movie or characters) have worked as 'bridges' in the network and something interesting emerges.

*Table 3. Topology of movie-character network, By default all Movie would have an out degree of 0 and all Characters would have an in degree of 0. *User rating for the characters is based on the combined movies they have starred in*

Movie Name	In-Degree	Out-Degree	Betweenness Centrality	User Rating*
Avengers: Age Of Ultron (movie)	15	0	46151.89	3.849315
Quicksilver	0	3	39955.34	10.64443
Hulk	0	9	35587.51	24.4193
Avengers: Infinity War (movie)	27	0	30040.49	5.12
X-men: Days Of Future Past (movie)	18	0	26297.71	3.7395
The Trial Of The Incredible Hulk (movie)	8	0	24866.64	0
Avengers: Endgame (movie)	18	0	16698.04	7.303371
Spider-man	0	8	15098.55	34.60231
X-men: Apocalypse (movie)	14	0	14765.38	3.055618
Edgar	0	2	11988	6.548889
Wolverine	0	7	11469.46	26.4565
Iron Man	0	9	11468.43	47.63345
Men In Black (movie)	9	0	11467.67	6.548889
Logan (movie)	15	0	10736.09	6.381444
Captain America	0	8	10641.47	36.07916

Our findings reveal that it is the character of Quicksilver and Hulk that have played an important role in bringing 2 components of a network together, which may have been fragmented components otherwise. Similar action is seen with movies like Avengers series (see Figure 6).

Figure 6. Quicksilver and Hulk emerge as the main "bridging" characters. Movie like Avengers series emerge as central "bridging" movies

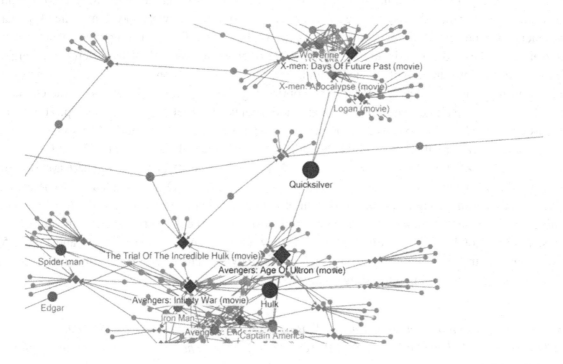

The Clauset-Newman-Moore cluster algorithm detects 18 groups and given the fact that the actual character network already has 10 components, it is apparent that the giant component is fragmented into several sub-clusters. Clusters are other name for communities which are typical socio-centric character-istics of a typical network. The communities demonstrate clumps of nodes. These clumps are relatively more densely connected with one another than the nodes in their neighbourhood. Hence the clumps of nodes may be typically separated with sparse connection of nodes.

SOLUTIONS AND RECOMMENDATIONS

Our cluster analysis shows that there are essentially 2 prominent clusters, the first one capturing most of the prominent star actors of the productions and the second one also managing to capture few. The divisions of clusters within the giant component indicates different communities - meaning those actors who have acted together, but yet may be connected to the overall character network through a character who may have co-acted in two different movies dominated by the different 'universes'. These actors who form a bridge between the clusters tend to have high bridging capacity. The tendency of high bridging behaviour is typically captured by the between-ness centrality.

FUTURE RESEARCH DIRECTIONS

We used Marvel production movies to investigate the network properties in 1-mode and 2-mode manner. The results revealed prominent characters that are best connected and those that form effective bridge at character-character and character-movie levels. Cluster analysis revealed that prominent actors share similar cluster and some actors that serve as potential bridges between communities. More similar research is needed among movies and actors of other universes to establish if indeed such phenomenon is apparent on other networks.

CONCLUSION

The current work is among the first studies that applies social network analysis to understand the movie character connections (1 mode analysis) and how the specific character appearance in movies (2-mode analysis) establish their importance in the series. Whereas the 1 mode analysis presents us with the picture of which characters are best connected and thus typically are holding the network together, the 2 mode isolate those prime characters in relation to their affiliation with movies. Specifically, our study found Quicksilver and Hulk emerging as the main "bridging" characters within the character-movie network. Avengers series emerge as central "bridging" movies.

A high correlation between commercial success of movies and their user ratings confirm that those movies with high user ratings have also enjoyed relatively high commercial success and vice versa. Association between movies with a larger star cast and their success, both critically and commercially indicate that audience prefer a larger star cast– especially the ones that bring supermen together.

Cluster analysis detected clusters within the giant component indicating communities of actors who have acted together but may be connected to the overall character network through a "bridging" character that holds together the two or more communities. This high bridging behaviour is also well captured by the between-ness centrality.

REFERENCES

Amaral, L. A. N., Scala, A., Barthelemy, M., & Stanley, H. E. (2000). Classes of small-world networks. *Proceedings of the National Academy of Sciences of the United States of America, 97*(21), 11149–11152. doi:10.1073/pnas.200327197 PMID:11005838

Ding, L., & Yilmaz, A. (2010). Learning Relations among Movie Characters: A Social Network Perspective. In K. Daniilidis, P. Maragos, & N. Paragios (Eds.), *Computer Vision-Eccv 2010* (Vol. 6314, pp. 410–423). Pt Iv. doi:10.1007/978-3-642-15561-1_30

Ding, L., & Yilmaz, A., & Ieee. (2011). Inferring Social Relations from Visual Concepts. In *2011 IEEE International Conference on Computer Vision* (pp. 699-706). 10.1109/ICCV.2011.6126306

He, J., Xie, Y., Luan, X., Zhang, L., & Zhang, X. (2018). *SRN: The movie character relationship analysis via social network.* Paper presented at the International Conference on Multimedia Modeling. 10.1007/978-3-319-73600-6_25

Kumar, S., & Markscheffel, B. (2016). Bonded-communities in HantaVirus research: A research collaboration network (RCN) analysis. *Scientometrics, 109*(1), 533–550. doi:10.100711192-016-1942-1 PMID:32287514

Lattanzi, S., & Sivakumar, D. (2009). Affiliation networks. *Proceedings of the forty-first annual ACM symposium on Theory of computing.* 10.1145/1536414.1536474

Lv, J. N., Wu, B., Zhu, L. L., & Wang, H. (2018). StoryRoleNet: Social Network Construction of Role Relationship in Video. *IEEE Access: Practical Innovations, Open Solutions, 6,* 25958–25969. doi:10.1109/ACCESS.2018.2832087

Newman, M. E. J. (2001). The structure of scientific collaboration networks. *Proceedings of the National Academy of Sciences of the United States of America, 98*(2), 404–409. doi:10.1073/pnas.98.2.404 PMID:11149952

Otte, E., & Rousseau, R. (2002). Social network analysis: A powerful strategy, also for the information sciences. *Journal of Information Science, 28*(6), 441–453. doi:10.1177/016555150202800601

Park, S. B., Oh, K. J., & Jo, G. S. (2012). Social network analysis in a movie using character-net. *Multimedia Tools and Applications, 59*(2), 601–627. doi:10.100711042-011-0725-1

Seaton, K. A., & Hackett, L. M. (2004). Stations, trains and small-world networks. *Physica A, 339*(3-4), 635–644. doi:10.1016/j.physa.2004.03.019

Tran, Q. D., Hwang, D., Lee, O. J., & Jung, J. E. (2017). Exploiting character networks for movie summarization. *Multimedia Tools and Applications, 76*(8), 10357–10369. doi:10.100711042-016-3633-6

Weng, C. Y., Chu, W. T., & Wu, J. L. (2009). RoleNet: Movie Analysis from the Perspective of Social Networks. *IEEE Transactions on Multimedia, 11*(2), 256–271. doi:10.1109/TMM.2008.2009684

Zhang, Y. F., Xu, C. S., Lu, H. Q., & Huang, Y. M. (2009). Character Identification in Feature-Length Films Using Global Face-Name Matching. *IEEE Transactions on Multimedia, 11*(7), 1276–1288. doi:10.1109/TMM.2009.2030629

Zheleva, E., Sharara, H., & Getoor, L. (2009). Co-evolution of social and affiliation networks. *Proceedings of the 15th ACM SIGKDD international conference on Knowledge discovery and data mining.* 10.1145/1557019.1557128

ADDITIONAL READING

Band, G., & Sao, R. (2018). Bollywood Movies and Social Media Analytics. *Helix, 8*(5), 3843–3845. doi:10.29042/2018-3843-3845

Beyhan, B., & Erkilic, H. (2020). Evolution of Turkish movie cluster: A social network analysis perspective. *Metu Journal of the Faculty of Architecture, 37*(2), 187–216. doi:10.4305/METU.JFA.2020.2.9

He, J., Xie, Y., Luan, X., Zhang, L., & Zhang, X. (2018). *SRN: The movie character relationship analysis via social network.* Paper presented at the International Conference on Multimedia Modeling. 10.1007/978-3-319-73600-6_25

Kumar, S., & Jan, J. M. (2013). On giant components in research collaboration networks: Case of engineering disciplines in Malaysia. *Malaysian Journal of Library & Information Science, 18*(2), 65-78.

Kumar, S., & Jan, J. M. (2014a). Relationship between authors' structural position in the collaboration network and research productivity Case of Indian earth scientists. *Program-Electronic Library and Information Systems, 48*(4), 355–369. doi:10.1108/PROG-01-2013-0002

Kumar, S., & Jan, J. M. (2014b). Research collaboration networks of two OIC nations: Comparative study between Turkey and Malaysia in the field of 'Energy Fuels', 2009-2011. *Scientometrics, 98*(1), 387–414. doi:10.100711192-013-1059-8

Liu, Q. B., Gao, S., Guo, B. F., Liu, H., Feng, Y. Z., & Xia, H. (2019, May 25-26). *Research and Development of Movie Social System.* Paper presented at the 3rd International Conference on Mechatronics and Intelligent Robotics (ICMIR), Kunming, China.

Tran, Q. D., & Jung, J. E. (2015). CoCharNet: Extracting Social Networks using Character Co-occurrence in Movies. *Journal of Universal Computer Science, 21*(6), 796-815.

Viana, W., Santos, P. O., da Silva, A. P. C., & Moro, M. M. (2014, Oct 22-24). *A Network Analysis on Movie Producing Teams and their Success.* Paper presented at the 9th Latin American Web Congress (LA-WEB), Ouro Preto, Brazil. 10.1109/LAWeb.2014.10

Weng, C. Y., Chu, W. T., Wu, J. L., & IEEE. (2007, Jul 02-05). *Movie analysis based on roles' social network.* Paper presented at the IEEE International Conference on Multimedia and Expo (ICME 2007), Beijing, China.

Zhang, X. J., Tang, Y., Xiong, A. O., Wang, W. J., & Zhang, Y. C. (2019). How Network Topologies Impact Project Alliance Performance: Evidence from the Movie Industry. *Entropy (Basel, Switzerland), 21*(9), 859. Advance online publication. doi:10.3390/e21090859

KEY TERMS AND DEFINITIONS

Betweenness Centrality: Betweenness centrality is path-based that determines how much a node forms a 'bridge' between other nodes in a network. Those with high betweenness centrality typically control the flow of resources in a network.

Cinematic Universe: Universe that has significant presence in films and television.

Degree: Degree represents the number of direct connections of a node.

Network Communities: Communities in a network are the clump of densely connected nodes in a network. Communities are detected through cluster algorithms.

Network Density: Density of a network is the ratio between the actual connections in the network in ratio to the maximum number of possible connections. Determines how well connected or sparsely connected a network is.

Social Network: A social network is a connection between any two or more entities joined together through a relationship.

Structural Holes: Structural holes are the absence of connections in the node's immediate neighbourhood.

Social Networks and Analytics

Yuehua Zhao

https://orcid.org/0000-0002-8412-2878

Nanjing University, China

Jin Zhang

https://orcid.org/0000-0002-6665-6606

University of Wisconsin-Milwaukee, USA

INTRODUCTION

Social Network

The notion of social network can be as old as the human species (Knoke & Yang, 2019). In social science, the theory of networks has been adopted to explain social phenomena in a wide variety of disciplines ranging from psychology to economics (Borgatti, Mehra, Brass, & Labianca, 2009). Researchers have realized that the network perspective provides new leverage for answering standard social and behavioral science research questions by defining the political, economic, or social structural environment (Wasserman & Faust, 1994).

With the age of Big Data upon us, power is located in the networks that structure society (Serrat, 2017). Borgatti et al. (2009) regarded social network theory as a gold mine that "provides an answer to a question that has preoccupied social philosophy since the time of Plato, namely, the problem of social order: how autonomous individuals can combine to create enduring, functioning societies" (p. 892).

Social Network Analysis

Of vital significance for the development of methods for the analysis of social network is the fact that the unit of analysis is not the individual, but rather an entity made up of a set of individuals and the linkages among them (Wasserman & Faust, 1994). Special network methods are necessary since the focuses of the analysis are dyads (two actors and their ties), triads (three actors and their ties), or larger systems (subgroups of individuals, or entire networks) (Wasserman & Faust, 1994).

The history of social network analysis can be traced back to the 1930s. By the 1980s, social network analysis had become an established field within the social sciences (Borgatti et al., 2009). About ten years later, social network analysis was applied to a wide range of fields such as physics and biology (Borgatti et al., 2009). To date, social network analysis has been widely employed by a great number of disciplines and has become a multidisciplinary methodology.

To explore the study on social network analysis, we conducted a search using the Web of Science databases on 20 January 2022. The search term "social network analysis" was restricted to the topic field. It resulted in 124,694 publications from 1961 to 2022. The temporal distribution of the retrieved publications is displayed in Figure 1 where the X-axis is the publishing year and the Y-axis is the number of

DOI: 10.4018/978-1-7998-9220-5.ch152

publications related to social network analysis. As we can see from Figure 1, the number of publications regarding social network analysis experienced an apparent surge between 2010 and 2020.

Figure 1. Number of publications in Web of Science Core Collection related to social network analysis

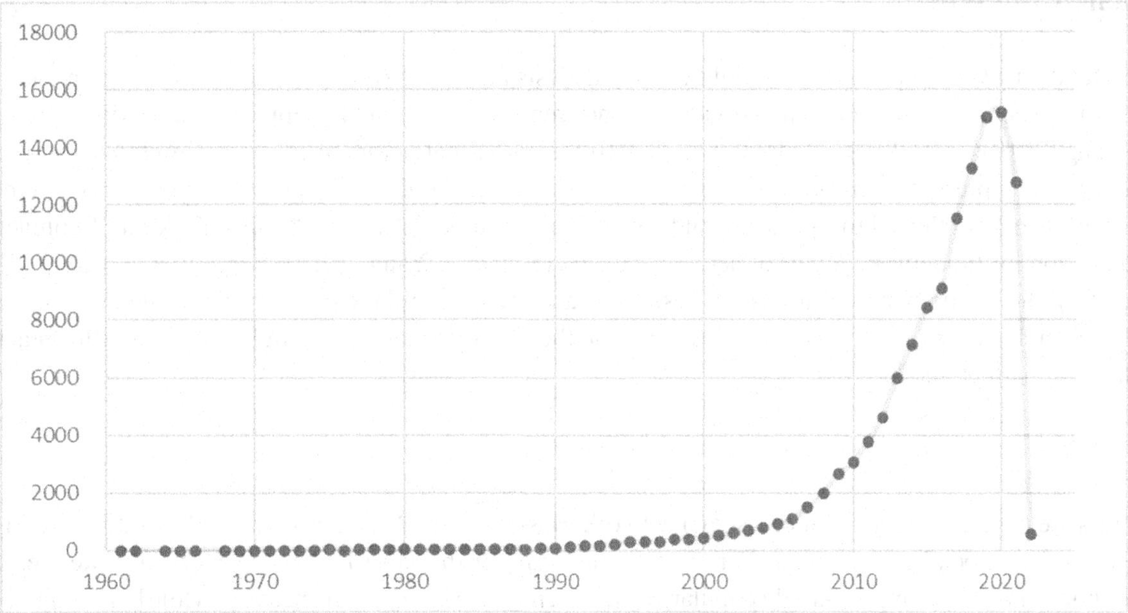

Mission of Social Network Analysis

Social network analysis has been defined as a strategy for investigating social structures through the use of network and graph theories (Otte & Rousseau, 2002). The axiom on which social network analysis rests is that structure matters (Borgatti et al., 2009). Social network analysis provides a framework that measures structural relations between members of a network. While social network analysis has many applications, the ultimate purpose underlying all applications of this method is to reveal useful insights occurring in the behind-the-scenes development and interactions in a network.

Most of the major structural measures derive from insights into empirical phenomena and are motivated by central concepts in social theory (Wasserman & Faust, 1994). One of the main purposes of social network analysis is to identify the core actors in a network. Over the past years, a number of centrality measures have been proposed by sociologists to detect the structural characteristics of entities in a network. The centrality indicators are designed to identify the "core" authors from different perspectives. The degree centrality can be seen as an index of its potential communication activity. Freeman's betweenness centrality is based upon the frequency with which a point falls between pairs of other points on the shortest paths connecting them (Freeman, 1978). Betweenness centrality can be used to assess the potential of an actor for control of communication in the knowledge flow network.

Social network analysis covers a group of methods that reveal the structures of the relational data that are present in different social contexts. It facilitates the delineation of roles within the organizational networks and the evaluation of the relation between organizational structures (Valeri & Baggio, 2021). Disciplines such as sociology, anthropology, and social psychology have concentrated on networks of individuals and the groups that constitute them, while disciplines linked to economics, politics, and management have concentrated on inter-organizational ties (Casanueva et al., 2016). The use of social network analysis in conjunction with epidemiological models aids in the identification of critical transmission features as well as the evaluation of the efficacy of preventative and control efforts (Wang et al., 2022).

Basic Concepts

The fundamental components of social network analysis are actors (nodes/vertices) and relations (ties/edges). An actor may represent an individual or may represent a group of people or organization (Knoke & Yang, 2019). In addition, Hansen et al. (2010) indicated that actors need not be limited to people, but can also represent items such as web pages, keyword tags, or videos. A pair of any two actors in the network is often referred to as a dyad, and so a relation can be defined as "a specific kind of contact, connection, or tie between a pair of actors, or dyad" (Knoke & Yang, 2019). Borgatti et al. (2009) divided dyadic relations into four basic types: "similarities, social relations, interactions, and flows" (p. 894). Social network research focuses primarily on the way that these different kinds of ties affect each other (Borgatti et al., 2009).

Actors

Actors are the main component of a social network. Basically, actors can be construed as entities acting in any sort of social environment. For example, as some of the most famous social media sites (e.g., Facebook, Twitter) being strikingly popular, the platforms can be seen as the network while both ordinary users and high-profile users acting as the actors (Cha et al., 2012). Often the actors represent individual people but some of them could be organizations such as workgroups, teams, institutions, and companies, as well as virtual objects such as brands, TV shows, software, and cartoon roles.

Connections

Connections link actors to one another. The range of connections linking any two actors can be extensive, such as behavioral interaction, physical connection, association or affiliation, etc (Carolan, 2013). When considering a social media application as a social network, connections among users build up the network. All of the social media applications provide certain types of connection capabilities to the users. The basic types of connections occurring in social media sites can be classified into two types: explicit connections or implicit connections (Hansen et al., 2010). Users intentionally and knowingly build explicit connections, whereas implicit connections are inferred from the users' movements in social media (Hansen et al., 2010).

With respect to the analysis of social media, connection data become especially critical since it can help to apply the social network analysis to the social media environment. Both the reciprocated relations (e.g. friending) and the unilateral relations (e.g. following) serve as the links that connect users in networks. Therefore, gathering connections between a certain number of individual users and then building the network among them helps to explain online social behavior and target the influential users.

Networks

Actors and connections together construct networks. The social network perspective concerns the structure of relations and the implication this structure has on individual or group behavior (Carolan, 2013). Taking social networking sites as an example, the activity network refers to the network formed by users who actually interact through the methods provided by the social networking sites (Viswanath et al., 2009). Constructing the activity network enables the discovery of the influential users in the groups, and identification of the interaction patterns among group members. Ye and Pennisi (2022) discovered that out-degree and proximity measurements of online discussion networks are favorably connected with students' academic achievement using social network analysis.

Social Network Measurements

A number of network measurements assist researchers in gaining insights into the structures of the social network. Distances, accesses, or impediments originating from how pathways between players are built up, redundancy in connections, or gaps in links are evaluated by network measures (de Amorim-Ribeiro et al., 2022). Both network-level and actor-level measurements reveal the interaction patterns from different perspectives. Network-level measurements aim to identify the connection patterns among all nodes in a network, while actor-level measurements focus on revealing the characteristics of an individual node. Table 1 summarizes a range of social network measurements that has been widely applied in social science research.

Network-Level Measurements

Network size refers to the number of actors in a network. Network density measures the number of connections in the network expressed as a proportion of the number possible. The network density of a social network implies the speed at which information or resources diffuse among the actors. In the context of an interaction network, reciprocity indicates the extent to which connections in a directed network are mutually linked.

Table 1. A summary of commonly used social network measurements

Level of measurement	Measurement
Network-level	Network size
	Network density
	Reciprocity
	Degree centralization
	Betweenness centralization
	Closeness centralization
Actor-level	In-degree
	Out-degree
	Degree centrality
	Betweenness centrality
	Closeness centrality

Centralization refers to the extent to which a network is dominated by a single node (Borgatti et al., 2013). Freeman's general formula for centralization is measured as summing the difference between each node's centrality and the centrality of the most central node and then dividing the sum by the maximum possible value where the star-shape network would get (Borgatti et al., 2013). Each type of centralization measurements (degree centralization, betweenness centralization, and closeness centralization) can be calculated by using the corresponding centrality measurements (degree centrality, betweenness centrality, and closeness centrality).

Actor-Level Measurements

Actor-level measurements are used to further characterize the actors in a network. The nodal degree is a crucial measure for actors in social networks. It commonly indicates an actor's involvement in network activities (Knoke & Yang, 2019). In a directed network such as the follow relationship network on Twitter, a node possesses two types of degree measures: in-degree (indicating how many followers a user has) and out-degree (indicating how many accounts a user follows). Cha et al. (2012) articulated that the out-degree to in-degree ratio decreases as a user has more followers, which suggested that the less popular a user is, the more actively he/she follows others. In-degree and out-degree measure the frequencies of connections a given actor received and launched. The in-degree of an actor is the number of connections leading to that actor, while the out-degree of an actor is the number of connections leading away from that actor.

Three actor-level centrality measurements (i.e. degree centrality, betweenness centrality, closeness centrality) are most widely adopted to measure the positional importance of group members in the group. Degree centrality refers to the number of connections incident upon a node. The degree centrality implies the potential communication ability of a certain actor. Actors with a higher degree centrality a have higher probability of receiving and transmitting the information flows, and thus can be considered to have influence over other actors in the network (Abraham et al., 2010).

Geodesic distance between two actors refers to the number of edges in the shortest path connecting them. The betweenness centrality of a node j is defined as the share of times that a node i needs the node j in order to reach a node k via the shortest path (Borgatti, 2005). Betweenness centrality evaluates the degree to which an actor controls the flow of information in the network. Actors with higher betweenness centrality act as the "brokers" (Abraham et al., 2010). In the context of online communities, group members with higher betweenness centrality bear more possibility to control the communication among group members.

Closeness centrality basically measures how close a node is located with respect to every other node in the network (Abraham et al., 2010). Closeness centrality can be calculated as the inverse of the sum of the geodesic distances between each actor and every other actor in the network. Actors with higher closeness are able to reach (or be reached by) more other nodes in the network through geodesic or shortest paths. An actor that is close to many others can instantly communicate and interact with others without going through many intermediaries (Makagon et al., 2012). In the contact network, the value of closeness centrality measures the proximity of one case to other cases (Yang et al., 2022).

FUTURE RESEARCH DIRECTIONS

Data challenges today often refer to the growing volume, velocity, or variety of data (Liu et al., 2016). As of January 2021, Facebook ranked as the most popular social networking site worldwide with 2,740 million active users, followed by YouTube and WhatsApp (*Most Used Social Media 2021*, n.d.). Rich sets of implicit, previously unknown, and potentially beneficial information and significant knowledge are embedded in the immense social network data (Leung et al., 2018). With the aid of advanced social network analysis techniques, researchers are able to gain insights from big data on social networking sites about relationships underlying social networks that characterize the social behavior of individuals and groups.

Data gathered from different social media sites has been investigated using social network analysis. Using tweets extracted from Twitter during a series of floods occurring in 2010 and 2011, Cheong and Cheong (2011) applied social network analysis to identify active players in online communities and their effectiveness in disseminating critical information. Gilbert et al. (2008) investigated the behavioral differences between rural and urban social media users based on data collected from MySpace. Through the analysis of those social networks of friends, the authors found that rural users' online friends live much closer than urban users' friends (Gilbert et al., 2008). Concerning the online health forum, Zhong and Liu (2021) and Zhao (2018) both revealed that top contributors to the content in the forum had more interactions than other users in the forum.

Discovering Influential Users

One of the main purposes of applying social network analysis in big data is to identify the core actors in a network. Studying the relative roles of numerous actors/nodes of social media helps us better understand how information is shared on social media sites. By analyzing the structure of the network connection and the distribution of links on Twitter, Cha et al. (2012) classified three types of users in information sharing: 1) mass media sources such as BBC; 2) grassroots users, including most of the ordinary users; and 3) evangelists, consisting of opinion leaders, politicians, celebrities, and local businesses.

The discovery of key players in social networks is commonly done using some of the centrality measures employed in social network analysis (Leung et al., 2018). Within a group of users, each of the group members may serve different roles. Some users occupy central positions, others stay in the periphery, and the remaining members lie somewhere in between (Leung et al., 2018). It was reported that about 1% of group members within an online psychosis support group contributed almost 20% of the overall communication (Chang, 2009). In comparison to other users in social networks, influential users are considered "important" with regard to the potential capacity to impact others.

The ability that a variety of centrality measures have to determine the relative position of an actor within a network has been used to discover influential users in social networks (Leung et al., 2018). Bambina (2007) revealed that a star user played the key function in linking together a highly distributed network in an online discussion forum. Bertoni et al. (2022) used social network analysis (SNA) to identify key players based on the modeling of interactions associated with four abilities of resilient systems.

Detecting Communities

"Community detection" has been an important study component for researchers who attempt to approach the structure of large-scale social networks. Communities are defined in terms of cohesive groups of nodes with more internal connections (between nodes in the same group) than external connections (between nodes in the group and nodes in other groups) (Traud et al., 2012). People who share similar interests or traits tend to gravitate towards each other and become clusters. For example, communities in social networks might correspond to circles of friends or business associates. Researchers investigated the community structures of the Facebook networks, consisting of users as actors and friendship links between those users as edges, from each of the 100 colleges and universities. It turned out that the Facebook friend networks of most of the institutions have community structures that are organized overwhelmingly according to class year, whereas a few institutions are also heavily influenced by dormitory residence (Traud et al., 2012).

An abundant number of community detection methods or algorithms have been proposed to identify the clusters in social networks. These methods can be generally categorized as (1) link-based (topological), (2) content-based (topical), and (3) hybrid (topological and topical) methods (Fani et al., 2020). Various algorithms place individuals into mutually exclusive groups based on distinct heuristics (Smith et al., 2020). Some of the popular community detection algorithms include edge-betweenness, random walktrap, label propagation, infomap, louvain, and spinglass. With the link-based method, Du et al. (2007) proposed the algorithm ComTector which is more efficient for community detection in large-scale social networks. Experimental results show that this algorithm can extract meaningful communities with several real-life networks including the Zachary Karate Club, American College Football, Scientific Collaboration, and Telecommunications Call networks. Selecting specific algorithms should be driven by the research questions in order to leverage each algorithm's different properties to produce a result that best aligns with the question (Smith et al., 2020).

Social Network Visualization

Graph theory has been widely applied in social network analysis as a means of formally representing social relations and quantifying social structural properties since the very beginning of social network analysis. Network visualization has proved to be an important advance for researchers. A sociogram depicts the structure of actors and ties within a group (Nooy et al., 2018). A branch of mathematics employed from graph theory can be used to depict the sociogram (e.g., vertex, line, graph) and most characteristics of networks (e.g., directed graph, undirected graph).

Many software tools perform social network analysis and network visualization (e.g., UCINET, Pajek, Gephi, VOSviewer). The most widely available layout algorithm for social network analysis is the spring embedder variant of Fruchterman and Reingold (1991), which is a force-directed method in which a graph is seen as a physical system of vertices (Brandes et al., 2012).

Visualizing community structures present in social networks and visually identifying key players within a network can reveal interesting information (Gilbert et al., 2011). For instance, studying the social networks of potential terrorists can uncover the organizational structure of terrorist networks and possibly predict terrorist activities (Gilbert et al., 2011). Zhang et al. (2016) investigated the hierarchical and related relationships among categories in the subject directory of a portal. With visual displays of the optimization analysis, the results showed that the recommended connections become stronger than the existing connections after the optimization. Yang et al., (2022) employed social network analysis and visualization approaches to establish a dynamic contact network of the pandemic based on epidemiological studies of 1218 COVID-19 patients in eight districts of China. The findings indicated that a strong association infects more than 65 percent of cases, and over 40 percent of cases had family members afflicted at the same time.

Limitations

Social network analysis has become one of the most popular quantitative methods in the big data era. However, despite the advances of the methods, researchers need to pay attention to the possible issues that may threaten the validity and reliability of the research before applying the methods. Social network researchers proposed that four types of error are of concern: omission errors, commission errors, edge/node attribution errors, and data collection and retrospective errors (Borgatti et al., 2013). Omission errors are associated with missing edges and nodes, while commission errors are cause by the erroneous inclusion of nodes and edges (Borgatti et al., 2013). Edge/node attribution errors result from assigning something to either an edge or node incorrectly (Borgatti et al., 2013). Data collection and retrospective errors are caused by data collection from an individual where the network elicitation question deals with reports of behavior (Borgatti et al., 2013). As for reliability, social network researchers usually adopt test-retest methods to evaluate informant reliability (Knoke & Yang, 2019).

REFERENCES

Abraham, A., Hassanien, A.-E., & Snasel, V. (Eds.). (2010). *Computational Social Network Analysis: Trends, Tools and Research Advances*. Springer-Verlag. doi:10.1007/978-1-84882-229-0

Bertoni, V. B., Saurin, T. A., & Fogliatto, F. S. (2022). How to identify key players that contribute to resilient performance: A social network analysis perspective. *Safety Science*, *148*, 105648. doi:10.1016/j.ssci.2021.105648

Borgatti, S. P., Mehra, A., Brass, D. J., & Labianca, G. (2009). Network Analysis in the Social Sciences. *Science*, *323*(5916), 892–895. doi:10.1126cience.1165821 PMID:19213908

Brandes, U., Indlekofer, N., & Mader, M. (2012). Visualization methods for longitudinal social networks and stochastic actor-oriented modeling. *Social Networks*, *34*(3), 291–308. doi:10.1016/j.socnet.2011.06.002

Carolan, B. V. (2013). *Social Network Analysis and Education: Theory, Methods & Applications*. SAGE Publications.

Casanueva, C., Gallego, Á., & García-Sánchez, M.-R. (2016). Social network analysis in tourism. *Current Issues in Tourism*, *19*(12), 1190–1209. doi:10.1080/13683500.2014.990422

Cha, M., Benevenuto, F., Haddadi, H., & Gummadi, K. (2012). The World of Connections and Information Flow in Twitter. *IEEE Transactions on Systems, Man, and Cybernetics. Part A, Systems and Humans*, *42*(4), 991–998. doi:10.1109/TSMCA.2012.2183359

Cheong, F., & Cheong, C. (2011). *Social Media Data Mining: A Social Network Analysis Of Tweets During The 2010-2011 Australian Floods*. https://works.bepress.com/christopher_cheong/2/

de Amorim-Ribeiro, E. M. B., Carneiro, L. L., Martins, L. F., & Cunha, R. C. (2022). Evaluation Tools of Social Support at Work and Contributions of Social Network Analysis. In M. O. Macambira, H. Mendonça, & M. das G. T. Paz (Eds.), Assessing Organizational Behaviors: A Critical Analysis of Measuring Instruments (pp. 223–241). Springer International Publishing. doi:10.1007/978-3-030-81311-6_10

Du, N., Wu, B., Pei, X., Wang, B., & Xu, L. (2007). Community detection in large-scale social networks. *Proceedings of the 9th WebKDD and 1st SNA-KDD 2007 Workshop on Web Mining and Social Network Analysis*, 16–25. 10.1145/1348549.1348552

Fani, H., Jiang, E., Bagheri, E., Al-Obeidat, F., Du, W., & Kargar, M. (2020). User community detection via embedding of social network structure and temporal content. *Information Processing & Management*, *57*(2), 102056. doi:10.1016/j.ipm.2019.102056

Freeman, L. C. (1978). Centrality in social networks conceptual clarification. *Social Networks*, *1*(3), 215–239. doi:10.1016/0378-8733(78)90021-7

Gilbert, E., Karahalios, K., & Sandvig, C. (2008). The network in the garden: An empirical analysis of social media in rural life. *Proceedings of the SIGCHI Conference on Human Factors in Computing Systems*, 1603–1612. https://dl.acm.org/citation.cfm?id=1357304

Gilbert, F., Simonetto, P., Zaidi, F., Jourdan, F., & Bourqui, R. (2011). Communities and hierarchical structures in dynamic social networks: Analysis and visualization. *Social Network Analysis and Mining*, *1*(2), 83–95. doi:10.100713278-010-0002-8

Hansen, D., Shneiderman, B., & Smith, M. A. (2010). *Analyzing Social Media Networks with NodeXL: Insights from a Connected World* (1st ed.). Morgan Kaufmann.

Knoke, D., & Yang, S. (2019). *Social Network Analysis*. SAGE Publications.

Leung, C. K., Jiang, F., Poon, T. W., & Crevier, P.-É. (2018). Big Data Analytics of Social Network Data: Who Cares Most About You on Facebook? In M. Moshirpour, B. Far, & R. Alhajj (Eds.), *Highlighting the Importance of Big Data Management and Analysis for Various Applications* (pp. 1–15). Springer International Publishing. doi:10.1007/978-3-319-60255-4_1

Liu, O., Man, K. L., Chong, W., & Chan, C. O. (2016). Social network analysis using big data. *Undefined*. https://www.semanticscholar.org/paper/Social-network-analysis-using-big-data-Liu-Man/076bb96cad6 50067c930135e53d47d16d5894aeb

Makagon, M. M., McCowan, B., & Mench, J. A. (2012). How can social network analysis contribute to social behavior research in applied ethology? *Applied Animal Behaviour Science*, *138*(3), 152–161. doi:10.1016/j.applanim.2012.02.003 PMID:24357888

Most used social media 2021. (n.d.). Statista. Retrieved June 25, 2021, from https://www.statista.com/statistics/272014/global-social-networks-ranked-by-number-of-users/

Nooy, W. D., Mrvar, A., & Batagelj, V. (2018). *Exploratory Social Network Analysis with Pajek: Revised and Expanded Edition for Updated Software*. Cambridge University Press.

Otte, E., & Rousseau, R. (2002). Social network analysis: A powerful strategy, also for the information sciences. *Journal of Information Science*, *28*(6), 441–453. doi:10.1177/016555150202800601

Serrat, O. (2017). Social Network Analysis. In O. Serrat (Ed.), *Knowledge Solutions: Tools, Methods, and Approaches to Drive Organizational Performance* (pp. 39–43). Springer. doi:10.1007/978-981-10-0983-9_9

Smith, N. R., Zivich, P. N., Frerichs, L. M., Moody, J., & Aiello, A. E. (2020). A Guide for Choosing Community Detection Algorithms in Social Network Studies: The Question Alignment Approach. *American Journal of Preventive Medicine, 59*(4), 597–605. doi:10.1016/j.amepre.2020.04.015 PMID:32951683

Traud, A. L., Mucha, P. J., & Porter, M. A. (2012). Social structure of Facebook networks. *Physica A, 391*(16), 4165–4180. doi:10.1016/j.physa.2011.12.021

Valeri, M., & Baggio, R. (2021). Italian tourism intermediaries: A social network analysis exploration. *Current Issues in Tourism, 24*(9), 1270–1283. doi:10.1080/13683500.2020.1777950

Viswanath, B., Mislove, A., Cha, M., & Gummadi, K. P. (2009). On the Evolution of User Interaction in Facebook. *Proceedings of the 2Nd ACM Workshop on Online Social Networks*, 37–42. 10.1145/1592665.1592675

Wang, Y., Zhao, Y., & Pan, Q. (2022). Advances, challenges and opportunities of phylogenetic and social network analysis using COVID-19 data. *Briefings in Bioinformatics, 23*(1). doi:10.1093/bib/bbab406

Wasserman, S., & Faust, K. (1994). *Social Network Analysis: Methods and Applications*. Cambridge University Press. doi:10.1017/CBO9780511815478

Yang, Z., Zhang, J., Gao, S., & Wang, H. (2022). Complex Contact Network of Patients at the Beginning of an Epidemic Outbreak: An Analysis Based on 1218 COVID-19 Cases in China. *International Journal of Environmental Research and Public Health, 19*(2), 689. doi:10.3390/ijerph19020689 PMID:35055511

Ye, D., & Pennisi, S. (n.d.). Analysing interactions in online discussions through social network analysis. *Journal of Computer Assisted Learning*. doi:10.1111/jcal.12648

Zhao, Y. (2018). *An Investigation of Autism Support Groups on Facebook*. Academic Press.

Zhong, B., & Liu, Q. (2021). Medical Insights from Posts About Irritable Bowel Syndrome by Adolescent Patients and Their Parents: Topic Modeling and Social Network Analysis. *Journal of Medical Internet Research, 23*(6), e26867. doi:10.2196/26867 PMID:34106078

ADDITIONAL READING

Albert, R., & Barabási, A.-L. (2002). Statistical mechanics of complex networks. *Reviews of Modern Physics, 74*(1), 47–97. doi:10.1103/RevModPhys.74.47

Barabasi, A. L., Jeong, H., Neda, Z., Ravasz, E., Schubert, A., & Vicsek, T. (2002). Evolution of the social network of scientific collaborations. *Physica A, 311*(3–4), 590–614. doi:10.1016/S0378-4371(02)00736-7

Du, N., Wu, B., Pei, X., Wang, B., & Xu, L. (2007). Community detection in large-scale social networks. *Proceedings of the 9th WebKDD and 1st SNA-KDD 2007 Workshop on Web Mining and Social Network Analysis*, 16–25. 10.1145/1348549.1348552

Gilbert, F., Simonetto, P., Zaidi, F., Jourdan, F., & Bourqui, R. (2011). Communities and hierarchical structures in dynamic social networks: Analysis and visualization. *Social Network Analysis and Mining, 1*(2), 83–95. doi:10.100713278-010-0002-8

Smith, M. A., Shneiderman, B., Milic-Frayling, N., Rodrigues, E. M., Barash, V., Dunne, C., Capone, T., Perer, A., & Gleave, E. (2009). Analyzing (Social Media) Networks with NodeXL. *Proceedings of the Fourth International Conference on Communities and Technologies*, 255–264. 10.1145/1556460.1556497

Smith, N. R., Zivich, P. N., Frerichs, L. M., Moody, J., & Aiello, A. E. (2020). A Guide for Choosing Community Detection Algorithms in Social Network Studies: The Question Alignment Approach. *American Journal of Preventive Medicine*, 59(4), 597–605. doi:10.1016/j.amepre.2020.04.015 PMID:32951683

Traud, A. L., Mucha, P. J., & Porter, M. A. (2012). Social structure of Facebook networks. *Physica A*, 391(16), 4165–4180. doi:10.1016/j.physa.2011.12.021

Watts, D. J., & Strogatz, S. H. (1998). Collective dynamics of 'small-world' networks. *Nature*, 393(6684), 440–442. doi:10.1038/30918 PMID:9623998

KEY TERMS AND DEFINITIONS

Actor: Actors refer to any entities acting in any sort of social environment.

Centralization: Centralization refers to the degree to which a network is dominated by a single node.

Connection: Connections refer to the links that connect actors to one another.

Degree Centrality: Degree centrality refers to the number of connections incident upon a node.

In-Degree: An actor's in-degree refers to the number of connections that lead to that actor.

Network: Actors and connections together construct networks.

Network Size: Network size refers to the number of actors in a network.

Section 41
Object Detection

An Image–Based Ship Detector With Deep Learning Algorithms

Peng Zhao

 https://orcid.org/0000-0003-1458-8266
INTELLIGENTRABBIT LLC, USA

Yuan Ren
Shanghai Dianji University, China

Hang Xiao
State Street Corporation, USA

INTRODUCTION

In the era of big data and artificial intelligence, the international logistics system has been developing rapidly towards the next generation of intelligent objects by incorporating the smart sea machine. A smart ship refers to the application of sensors, the Internet of Things (IoT), and other hyper-connected objects to automatically detect and obtain signals and information steams from the ship, the marine environment, logistics, ports, etc. Such a system requires a set of cutting-edge technologies, such as computational science, automatic control theory, big data, machine learning, and computer vision. The intelligent operation of the ship is carried out in aspects of navigation, management, maintenance and cargo transportation; therefore, the logistics system will be safer, more environmentally friendly, cost-efficient and more reliable. A variety of intelligent architectures has been proposed throughout the front-to-end transportation and ship management, including navigation, hull, cabin, energy efficiency control, cargo management, and integration operation. Nowadays, research communities and industrial professionals emphasize the functionality of smart ship projects, which will benefit the construction of smart logistics.

From the technical perspective, a smart ship is designed to empower the sea machines in terms of making decisions without human interactions by incorporating artificial intelligence, which is the core technology of self-driving and vehicle collision warning systems. A smart ship is such a self-driving vehicle that will be competent in sensing its surrounding environment and moving safely in the water, without human operations. A set of state-of-the-art techniques, such as image recognition, object detection, and computer vision, plays a crucial role in the development of smart vehicle objectives, which have attracted attention from the data science community. Most recently, studies on self-driving vehicles have experienced a substantial enhancement due to improvements in deep learning. Deep neural networks have emerged as a powerful tool for image recognition and object detection by incorporating computer vision technologies, which provide the technical advances of smart ships in terms of image classifications.

With the development of deep learning, image classification and object detection techniques have been widely applied in the construction of the smart port and the Unmanned Surface Vehicle (USV) technology, whereas an effective and rapid detection approach is essential for the safe operation of the USV and the port management. With the improvement of the accuracy and real-time requirements of ship detection and classification in the practical application, it is necessary to propose a ship image/

DOI: 10.4018/978-1-7998-9220-5.ch153

video detection and classification method based on an improved regressive deep network. However, such works are still challenging due to the limited data for the model training process, the complexity of model selection, and the difficulty of the ground-truth test. Motivated by the current demand for smart ship operations, this chapter is proposed to focus on the challenges behind the implementation of a smart ship. The objectives of this chapter are listed as follows:

- investigating how deep learning works for constructing the smart ship operation system in terms of the implementation of image recognition and object detection models using satellite images.
- examining how the ship detector is built using a variety of pre-trained object detection models, such as MobileNet, VGGNet, Inception, and ResNet, along with their performances on detecting ships through the model training and testing procedure.
- discussing the capability of the proposed ship detector given a real-world test, which provides a comprehensive understanding of implementations of the ship detector from the industrial application perspectives.

BACKGROUND

In the big data era, data-driven approaches have been becoming the research hotspot in the optimization of ship resource scheduling and the ship collision avoidance. Using Geographic Information System (GIS), Tsou et al. (2010) proposed a genetic algorithm with simulating the biological model, which suggested a plan on economic view for the shortest route of ship collision avoidance. A prediction analysis on ship maneuvering performance has been proposed for estimating the bare hull maneuvering coefficients by using Reynolds-Averaged Navier-Stokes (RANS) based on virtual captive model tests (Sung & Park, 2015). Park et al. (2016) performed a probability flow model for a variety of maritime traffic situations and demonstrated the practical feasibility of the proposed model, which is a semi-analytical approach for estimating the ship collision probability on trajectory uncertainties. A reliability-based structural design framework has been presented in term of ship collision, in which the probabilistic distribution of accidental loads can be predicted according to the occurrence probabilities of different situations of ship loads (Koh et al. 2017). Ramos et al. (2019) explored the human factor on collision avoidance in the operations of maritime surface autonomous ship using Hierarchical Task Analysis for classification.

During the last few years, autonomous driving has been proceeded significantly using computer vision technologies and deep learning algorithms, which have been conducted to detect the pedestrian before the actual accident (Kohli & Chadha 2019). Chen et al. (2019b) proposed a novel network structure based on an end-to-end algorithm, namely Auxiliary Task Network (ATN), which enhances the driving performance with the strength of minimal training data and image semantic segmentations. Inspired by the same ideology of self-driving vehicles, smart ships have been becoming a hot research topic in terms of the decision support system (DSS). Li et al. (2018) designed an integrated information platform for the construction of smart ships based on the cloud computation sub-system and supported by the OPC UA data transmission protocol. Such a platform can implement data interaction and data visualization for the shipbuilding and sailing. A maritime decision support system has been proposed by Sarvari et al. (2019) who suggested the maritime DSS, which comes up with a three-module approach for ferryboat emergency evacuation planning under different emergency conditions. Most recently, a DSS applied to marine navigation has been presented using a discrete planning approach in collision avoidance for smart ships (Lazarowska, 2020). To implement the automatic collision avoidance and navigation, deep learning has been applied by incorporating ship maneuverability, human experience and navigation rules (Guo et al., 2020), of which object detection plays an important role.

Convolutional Neural Network (CNN) has been determined as one of the best algorithms in object detection and image recognition. As one of the most robust deep learning algorithms, CNN has been widely used in many aspects of the binary classification problems, such as image classification (Liu et al., 2016), signal detection (O'Shea et al. 2016), natural language processing and voice recognition (Alu et al., 2017), face recognition (Wu et al., 2018), and motion recognition (Cheng et al., 2020). Particularly, many object detection models, such as region-based CNN (R-CNN), Fast R-CNN, Faster R-CNN, etc., are proposed based on the convolutional networks, which can be applied in implementing the ship detector. Existing studies in ship detection suggest a broad range of deep learning approaches, such as satellite image classification using CNN (Xiao et al., 2019), synthetic aperture radar (SAR) ship detection using CNN-based detection algorithms (Chen et al., 2019a), and video stream processing with embedded ship detection using conventional network structures (Zhao et al., 2019).

FOCUS OF THE ARTICLE

This chapter provides a comprehensive understanding of the image-based ship detector using computer vision technologies with deep learning. Several pre-trained object detection models, such as MobileNet, VGGNet, Inception, and ResNet, have been investigated by illustrating the network architectures. A group of pre-trained models has been proposed and examined by recognizing ships on the sea and in the bay area. The model testing and comparison procedure has also been performed by evaluating the performance matrix and comparing predictive results per model. The optimal model is then chosen with additional tests in terms of capabilities of the ship detection using the satellite image streaming in the real-world application. Such a proposed ship detector can contribute to the development of smart ship operations and may further carve out the possibility for the automated shipping system with smart port management.

SOLUTIONS AND RECOMMENDATIONS

Object Detection with Deep Learning

A ship detector fundamentally belongs to object recognition which discusses a variety of computer vision tasks by classifying objects in digital images. Object recognition, in general, covers three main subjects, including image classification, object localization, and object detection. The category of a certain object can be predicted in an image through image classification, whereas object localization refers to determining the location of single or multiple objects in the image and drawing abounding box around the extent. Those two tasks will be then combined into object detection which localizes and identifies objects. Deep learning is the first choice for image classification as it can achieve better model performance, comparing to the classical machine learning approaches. Modern solutions for image classification can be summarized by three major types, such as the single deep network structure using deep learning models (i.e. the CNN-based architecture), a hybrid method incorporating deep leaning as the feature extractor with machine learning-based classifiers, and the pre-trained models for image classification. The CNN model becomes popular in numerous computer vision tasks (Khan et al., 2018), which is a deep learning algorithm that can be applied in many image classification and recognition tasks. However, it may cause a serious overfitting problem throughout the model training process. Although the hybrid method can avoid the overfitting problem effectively, its model complexity is relatively higher, thereby leading a longer time in model training. Pre-trained models can be applied in terms of the model efficiency that considers the network to be trained faster. Therefore, this chapter employs several pre-trained deep learning models as the image classifiers. Popular pre-trained object detectors, such as MobileNet, VGGNet, ResNet, and Inception, will be investigated and examined as the candidate image classifiers in constructing the ship detection algorithm.

MobileNet

MobileNet, developed by Google, is an open-source object detector based on CNN, which can achieve excellent performance for training the image classifiers efficiently (Howard et al., 2017). MobileNet refers to depth wise separable convolutions, which significantly reduce the model complexity in terms of the lightweight deep neural networks with less parameters. It consists of two main operations, including a Depthwise Convolution (DC) and a Pointwise Convolution (PC). Its original idea is to separate depth and spatial dimension of a filter, of which depthwise separable convolution is a DC followed by a PC in term of the architecture of MobileNet. DC is the channel-wise spatial convolution that maps a single convolution on each input channel separately, whereas PC is the 1 by 1 convolution for changing the dimension. Instead of a single 3 by 3 convolution layer followed by the batch norm and ReLU in a classical CNN, MobileNet splits the convolution into a 3 by 3 depth-wise convolutional layer and a 1 by 1 point-wise convolution.

VGGNet

A typical VGGNet model is VGG-16, which is one of the most powerful pre-trained models for object detection and image classification. Developed by Simonyan & Zisserman (2014), it has been widely adopted by research communities and industrial professionals for most image classification tasks. VGG-16 is a CNN-based architecture, which can achieves more than 92% accuracy in ImageNet. VGG-16 improves AlexNet by modifying the large scale of kernel filters with multiple 3 by 3 convolutional layers. The VGG-16 architecture consists of different layers, such as convolutional layers, pooling layers, and dense layers. The image classification process in VGG-16 starts from inputting a fixed size image (224 by 224 RGB) into the first convolutional layer, where the image can be passed through a stack of the layers. The filters are applied to capture the notion with a smaller receptive field from left to right, through up and down, and at the center. A linear transformation of the input channels is utilized for formatting the 1 by 1 convolution filters in one of the configurations. The convolution stride is fixed per pixel with the spatial padding for the convolutional layer input, in which the spatial resolution is preserved after convolution. Five max-pooling layers are carried out in terms of spatial pooling, along with a 2 by 2 pixel window performed in the second stride. The dense layers consist of three fully-connected layers, which follow a stack of convolutional layers with differences in depth. The final layer is the soft-max layer. The filters are applied at each stage in order to reduce the number of parameters throughout all hidden layers using the ReLU activation function.

Inception

Inception family models can be traced back to 2014 when the paper "Going deeper with convolutions" introduced the first version of Inception architecture (InceptionV1), implemented in the winning ILSVRC 2014 submission GoogLeNet (Szegedy et al., 2015). Inception performs convolutions with multiple filter sizes on the input, with applying max pooling and concatenating the result for the next convolutional operation that recedes the parameters drastically. One of the most significant contribution with respect to CNN is the deeper nets applied for image classification, in which the sparsity can be beneficial to the model performance, along with additional losses tied to the error term of intermediate layers. InceptionV2 has been proposed by the same research group, which extends on the original Inception by implementing a series of smaller convolutions (Szegedy et al., 2016). By following the same ideology on the same network structure, InceptionV3 has been proposed by surpassing the previous versions on the ImageNet benchmark, followed by the latest version, InceptionV4, which is a streamlined version of InceptionV3 with a uniformed architecture and better performance in image recognition (Szegedy et al., 2017). This chapter will apply InceptionV3 as the one of the candidate models for implementing and investigating the optimal ship detector due to its easy and wide availability in Keras and TensorFlow.

ResNet

ResNet-50 is a variant model that belongs to the ResNet family, which has 48 convolution layers with one max pooling layer and one average pool layer. ResNet refers to the residual net, which is the original model of the ResNet family that is another milestone in computer vision (He et al., 2016). The model is motivated by avoiding low accuracy when the network goes more complicated and the model becomes deeper. ResNet-34 is the earliest variant model, which starts off with a single convolution layer and max pooling. Four 3 by 3 convolutional layers are embedded with just varying filter sizes, in which connections are bypassing the layer in between after every two convolutions. Such skipped connections are used as residual blocks, which are so-called "identity shortcut connections". More layers are added in ResNet-50, which follows the same ideology. Such models have been widely used in image recognition tasks, of which ResNet-50 is more popular due to its easy-to-apply property via Keras.

Data Preprocessing and Experimental Design

The demand for global trade is driving huge growth in ship traffic in the worldwide oceans. More ships increase the chances of traffic infractions at sea, including ship accidents, piracy, illegal fishing in protected marine areas, illegal cargo shipping and maritime drug smuggling, which has forced relevant organizations to carry out more effective methods of monitoring ships in the sea. In this chapter, the data is obtained from two sources on Kaggle. One is the data of Ships in Satellite Imagery collected over the San Francisco Bay and San Pedro Bay areas of California. Such data is offered by commercial imagery providers that capture images using constellations of small satellites to help solve the difficulties of detecting large ships' location in satellite images. The second dataset is the Airbus data available from Airbus Ship Detection Challenge. Airbus Defence and Space Company, a global leading provider of optical & radar satellite imagery, offers comprehensive maritime monitoring services by implementing effective solutions with technologies and capabilities. The goal of the challenge held by Airbus is to enhance the accuracy and speed of automatic ship detection and to support the maritime industry on threats anticipation, trigger alerts and efficiency improvement at sea. The difference between these two data sources of satellite imagery is that the first data source contains more bay ship images and the second more maritime ship images. Ship in Satellite Imagery Data consists of 4000 80×80 RGB images with either "ship" or "no-ship" label, in which 1000 images of them are labeled and rest parts are "no-ship" images. The pixel value data for each 80×80 RGB is stored in row-major order with a list of 19,200 integers. The dataset is distributed as a JSON formatted file. The specific data attributes include pixel data, labels, locations and scene IDs. Airbus Data contains totally 192,556 satellite images, in which 65% of them are no ship images and 35% are ship images.

This chapter merges two dataset together for proceeding the model training and testing process. Several data preprocessing is essential as the first stage before the model training procedure. The pixel data can be separated to three parts: the first 6400 red channel values, the second 6400 green channel values and the third 6400 blue channel values. Scene ID is the specific identifier of the PlanetScope visual scene extracted from the image chip. The longitude and latitude coordinate parameters of the image center point are the whole location data of the dataset. The "no-ship" image set covers only ship parts, whereas rest regions of the image are filled by landcover features, involving water, vegetation, bare earth, buildings, etc. On the other side, each ship in the "ship" images is almost centered. Both "ship" and "no-ship" samples are presented in Figure 1 and 2, respectively.

Figure 1. Sample no-ship images

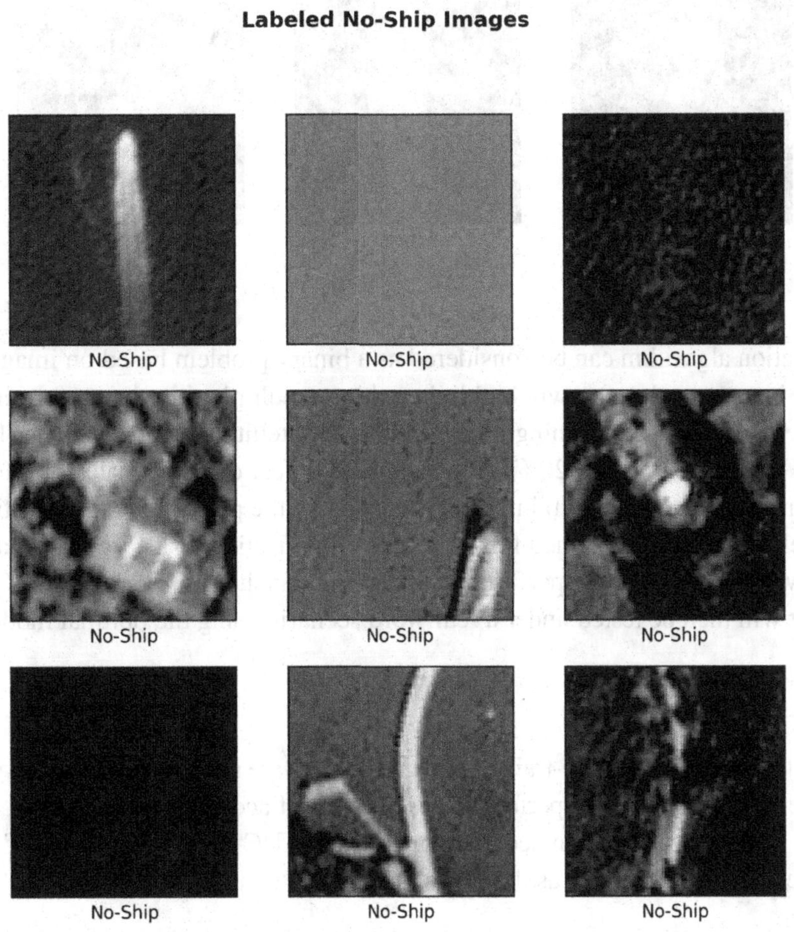

Labeled No-Ship Images

Figure 2. Sample ship images

Labeled Ship Images

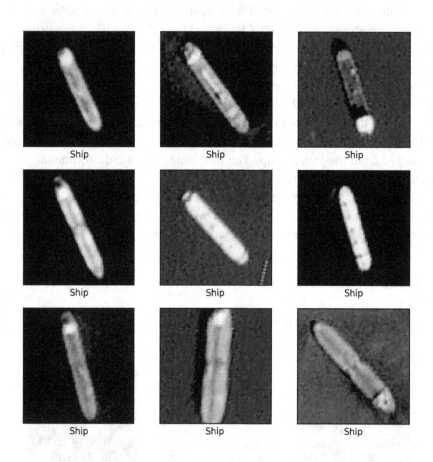

The ship detection algorithm can be considered as a binary problem based on image classification. For each satellite image, the detector will highlight a ship or multiple ships by performing the proposed models. To implement the model training process, Ship in Satellite Imagery Data has been split into a training set (80%) and a testing set (20%). The candidate object detectors, such as MobileNet, VGG, ResNet, InceptionV3, are applied on training set, followed by the prediction on the testing data set. All pre-trained models have been fine-tuned for fitting the classification tasks. The optimal model will be determined by evaluating the model performance measures, including accuracy, AUC, and F1 score. The ship detector will then be tested under a real-word scenario using the optimal model.

Results

The experimental results based on pre-trained object detectors are shown in Table 1. In general, all candidate models can achieve high-level performances in terms of accuracy, AUC, and F1 score. VGG-16 provides the best performance with an accuracy of 98%, an AUC of 0.98, and a F1 of 0.98, therefore, the optimal model can be determined as the object detector.

Table 1. Model performance measures for determining the optimal object detector

	Accuracy	AUC	F1 Score
VGG-16	98.13%	0.98	0.98
VGG-19	96.10%	0.95	0.95
ResNet-18	94.91%	0.94	0.93
ResNet-50	97.01%	0.97	0.96
InceptionV3	95.89%	0.95	0.95
MobileNet	92.26%	0.92	0.91

To understand the predictive result per class, a secondary set of measures has been calculated for both "ship" and "no-ship" categories based on VGG-16. A precision of 0.99 for "no-ship" class indicates that the correctly predictive result will reach 99% when the detector is operated on an image without any ships, while the precision on "ship" class is relatively lower with only 0.95 accuracy for identifying images that have ships. Therefore, the proposed ship detector performances better predictive tasks on images without ships. Similarly, conclusions can be confirmed based on other measurements, such as recall, F1 score, and support, as shown in Table 2.

Table 2. Predictive results evaluation for both "no-ship" and "ship" classes based on VGG-16

	Precison	Recall	F1-score	Support
no-ship	0.99	0.99	0.99	628
ship	0.95	0.96	0.96	172
Avg / total	0.98	0.98	0.98	800

Overall, VGG-16 can be used in constructing the ship detector based on the secondary evaluation measurements. Furthermore, this chapter continuously applied the proposed model to recognize real satellite images in the bay area, as illustrated in Figure 3. Although all the ships are detected correctly in the water, some errors still exist. For instance, a ditch positioned at coordinate (1400, 1800) is incorrectly identified as a ship. Other objects that should not be identified as ships, such as land, shore, and shipyard, are also classified as ships. Such a problem may be caused by the noise in the original datasets. Although similar studies indicate better model performances using different detectors, such as DenseNet (Stofa et al., 2020), HyperLi-Net (Zhang et al., 2020), and RetinaNet (Wang et al., 2019), VGG-16 is still the optimal choice because of the balance between its model efficiency and complexity (Xiao et al., 2019).

FUTURE RESEARCH DIRECTIONS

Despite a high-level model performance achieved by the optimal model, several problems still remain throughout data preparation, model training, and model testing. Firstly, some parts of pixel data are incorrectly labeled in the original datasets. For instance, the satellite image in the up-left corner of Figure 1 should be labeled as ship, while it has been originally annotated as the "no-ship" class. Such mistakes are everywhere in the dataset, thereby may generate a lot of noise in the model training process. Besides, image sizes and scales are different among two datasets, in which images in the Airbus dataset are much smaller, thereby may not be able to recognize ships well. Future studies should focus on how to fix the labeling mistakes and the image pixel issues. Secondly, only four pre-trained object detection models are chosen in this chapter, whereas alternative models may achieve higher model performance measures. Many other similar models, such as MobileNetV2, VGG-19, ResNet-101(152), Xception, etc., can be implemented with the investigation and examination of the ship detector. Besides, some state-of-the-art techniques, such as YOLO family models, SSD, and R-CNN family models, can also be applied. Such alternative models provide lots of research opportunities in the future. Lastly, a wide real-world testing procedure is essential, to the industrial application and deployment perspectives, while such a process is restricted in this chapter due to the limited capacity on data collection. Future research directions should emphasize on data collection and ground-truth testing in the real-world.

Figure 3. Satellite image recognition in the bay area

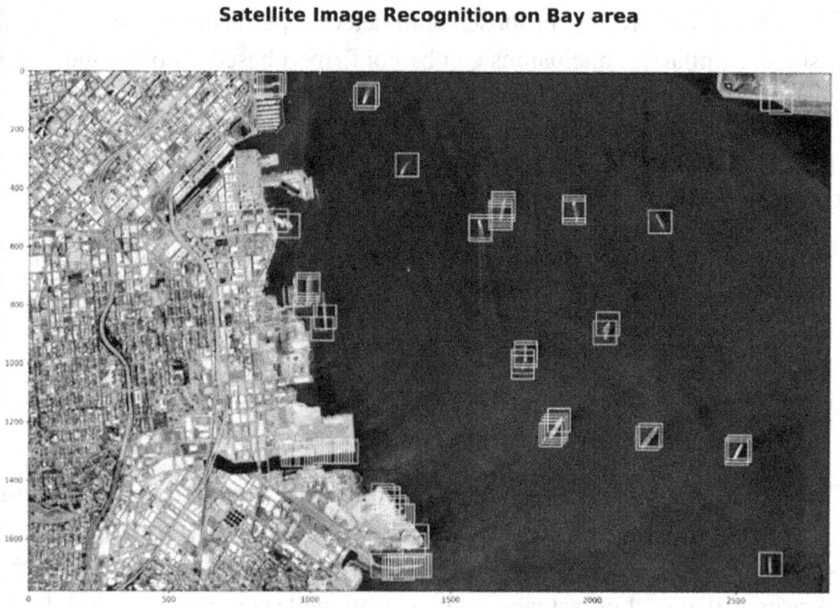

CONCLUSION

In this chapter, a ship detector has been proposed by investigating multiple pre-trained object detection models, including MobileNet, VGG-16, ResNet-50, and InceptionV3. An image classification has been performed through examining the predictive capabilities per model with real-world satellite images. VGG-16 has been determined as the optimal model based on the model performance evaluation and comparison. The optimal model can recognize ships in a satellite image efficiently, with an accuracy of 98.13%. The proposed model has been examined by implementing a real-world testing procedure in the bay area. Although the testing result indicates several problems, such a ship detector can be applied in constructing the recognition system of smart ships based on satellite image classification with deep learning.

REFERENCES

A

Alu, D. A. S. C., Zoltan, E., & Stoica, I. C. (2017). Voice based emotion recognition with convolutional neural networks for companion robots. *Science and Technology*, *20*(3), 222–240.

Chen, C., He, C., Hu, C., Pei, H., & Jiao, L. (2019a). A deep neural network based on an attention mechanism for SAR ship detection in multiscale and complex scenarios. *IEEE Access: Practical Innovations, Open Solutions*, *7*, 104848–104863. doi:10.1109/ACCESS.2019.2930939

Chen, Y., Praveen, P., Priyantha, M., Muelling, K., & Dolan, J. (2019b, January). Learning on-road visual control for self-driving vehicles with Auxiliary tasks. In *2019 IEEE Winter Conference on Applications of Computer Vision (WACV)* (pp. 331-338). IEEE. 10.1109/WACV.2019.00041

Cheng, H. R., Cao, G. Z., Li, C. H., Zhu, A., & Zhang, X. (2020, June). A CNN-LSTM hybrid model for Ankle joint motion recognition method based on sEMG. In *2020 17th International Conference on Ubiquitous Robots (UR)* (pp. 339-344). IEEE. 10.1109/UR49135.2020.9144698

Guo, S., Zhang, X., Zheng, Y., & Du, Y. (2020). An autonomous path planning model for unmanned ships based on deep reinforcement learning. *Sensors (Basel)*, *20*(2), 426. doi:10.339020020426 PMID:31940855

He, K., Zhang, X., Ren, S., & Sun, J. (2016). Deep residual learning for image recognition. In *Proceedings of the IEEE conference on computer vision and pattern recognition* (pp. 770-778). IEEE.

Howard, A. G., Zhu, M., Chen, B., Kalenichenko, D., Wang, W., Weyand, T., . . . Adam, H. (2017). *Mobilenets: Efficient convolutional neural networks for mobile vision applications.* arXiv preprint arXiv:1704.04861.

Khan, S., Rahmani, H., Shah, S. A. A., & Bennamoun, M. (2018). A guide to convolutional neural networks for computer vision. *Synthesis Lectures on Computer Vision*, *8*(1), 1–207. doi:10.1007/978-3-031-01821-3

Koh, H. M., Lim, J. H., Kim, H., Yi, J., Park, W., & Song, J. (2017). Reliability-based structural design framework against accidental loads–ship collision. *Structure and Infrastructure Engineering*, *13*(1), 171–180. doi:10.1080/15732479.2016.1198398

Kohli, P., & Chadha, A. (2019, March). Enabling pedestrian safety using computer vision techniques: A case study of the 2018 Uber inc. self-driving car crash. In *Future of Information and Communication Conference* (pp. 261-279). Springer.

Lazarowska, A. (2020). A discrete planning approach in collision avoidance for smart ships. *Procedia Computer Science*, *176*, 380–389. doi:10.1016/j.procs.2020.08.039

Li, G., Shi, J., Zhu, Q., Lan, J., & Mitrouchev, P. (2018, September). Design of integrated information platform for smart ship. In *International Workshop of Advanced Manufacturing and Automation* (pp. 53-58). Springer.

Liu, C., Cao, Y., Luo, Y., Chen, G., Vokkarane, V., & Ma, Y. (2016, May). Deepfood: Deep learning-based food image recognition for computer-aided dietary assessment. In *International Conference on Smart Homes and Health Telematics* (pp. 37-48). Springer. 10.1007/978-3-319-39601-9_4

O'Shea, T. J., Corgan, J., & Clancy, T. C. (2016, September). Convolutional radio modulation recognition networks. In *International conference on engineering applications of neural networks* (pp. 213-226). Springer. 10.1007/978-3-319-44188-7_16

Park, J., Han, J., Kim, J., & Son, N. S. (2016). Probabilistic quantification of ship collision risk considering trajectory uncertainties. *IFAC-PapersOnLine*, *49*(23), 109–114. doi:10.1016/j.ifacol.2016.10.329

Ramos, M. A., Utne, I. B., & Mosleh, A. (2019). Collision avoidance on maritime autonomous surface ships: Operators' tasks and human failure events. *Safety Science*, *116*, 33–44. doi:10.1016/j.ssci.2019.02.038

Sarvari, P. A., Cevikcan, E., Celik, M., Ustundag, A., & Ervural, B. (2019). A maritime safety on-board decision support system to enhance emergency evacuation on ferryboats. *Maritime Policy & Management*, *46*(4), 410–435. doi:10.1080/03088839.2019.1571644

Simonyan, K., & Zisserman, A. (2014). *Very deep convolutional networks for large-scale image recognition.* arXiv preprint arXiv:1409.1556.

Stofa, M. M., Zulkifley, M. A., & Zaki, S. Z. M. (2020, July). A deep learning approach to ship detection using satellite imagery. *IOP Conference Series. Earth and Environmental Science*, *540*(1), 012049. doi:10.1088/1755-1315/540/1/012049

Sung, Y. J., & Park, S. H. (2015). Prediction of ship manoeuvring performance based on virtual captive model tests. *Journal of the Society of Naval Architects of Korea*, *52*(5), 407–417. doi:10.3744/SNAK.2015.52.5.407

Szegedy, C., Ioffe, S., Vanhoucke, V., & Alemi, A. A. (2017, February). Inception-v4, inception-resnet and the impact of residual connections on learning. *Thirty-first AAAI conference on artificial intelligence.* 10.1609/aaai.v31i1.11231

Szegedy, C., Liu, W., Jia, Y., Sermanet, P., Reed, S., Anguelov, D., ... Rabinovich, A. (2015). Going deeper with convolutions. In *Proceedings of the IEEE conference on computer vision and pattern recognition* (pp. 1-9). IEEE.

Szegedy, C., Vanhoucke, V., Ioffe, S., Shlens, J., & Wojna, Z. (2016). Rethinking the inception architecture for computer vision. In *Proceedings of the IEEE conference on computer vision and pattern recognition* (pp. 2818-2826). 10.1109/CVPR.2016.308

Tsou, M. C., Kao, S. L., & Su, C. M. (2010). Decision support from genetic algorithms for ship collision avoidance route planning and alerts. *Journal of Navigation*, *63*(1), 167–182. doi:10.1017/S037346330999021X

Wu, X., He, R., Sun, Z., & Tan, T. (2018). A light cnn for deep face representation with noisy labels. *IEEE Transactions on Information Forensics and Security*, *13*(11), 2884–2896. doi:10.1109/TIFS.2018.2833032

Wang, Y., Wang, C., Zhang, H., Dong, Y., & Wei, S. (2019). A SAR dataset of ship detection for deep learning under complex backgrounds. *Remote Sensing*, *11*(7), 765.

Xiao, H., Wang, X., & Zhao, P. (2019). Satellite image recognition for smart ships using a convolutional neural networks algorithm. *International Journal of Decision Science*, *10*(2), 85–91.

Zhao, H., Zhang, W., Sun, H., & Xue, B. (2019). Embedded deep learning for ship detection and recognition. *Future Internet, 11*(2), 53.

Zhang, T., Zhang, X., Shi, J., & Wei, S. (2020). HyperLi-Net: A hyper-light deep learning network for high-accurate and high-speed ship detection from synthetic aperture radar imagery. *ISPRS Journal of Photogrammetry and Remote Sensing, 167*, 123–153. doi:10.1016/j.isprsjprs.2020.05.016

ADDITIONAL READING

Brownlee, J. (2019). *Deep learning for computer vision: image classification, object detection, and face recognition in python*. Machine Learning Mastery.

Elgendy, M. (2020). *Deep Learning for Vision Systems*. Simon and Schuster.

Gollapudi, S. (2019). *Learn computer vision using OpenCV: with deep learning CNNs and RNNs*. Apress. doi:10.1007/978-1-4842-4261-2

Goodfellow, I., Bengio, Y., & Courville, A. (2016). *Deep learning*. MIT press.

Gulli, A., & Pal, S. (2017). *Deep learning with Keras*. Packt Publishing Ltd.

More, N., Murugan, G., & Singh, R. P. (2018, August). A survey paper on various inshore ship detection techniques in satellite imagery. In *2018 Fourth International Conference on Computing Communication Control and Automation (ICCUBEA)* (pp. 1-5). IEEE. 10.1109/ICCUBEA.2018.8697866

Princy, D., & Mani, V. R. S. (2021). A survey of ship detection and classification techniques. In *Soft Computing for Intelligent Systems* (pp. 565–602). Springer. doi:10.1007/978-981-16-1048-6_46

KEY TERMS AND DEFINITIONS

Computer Vision: An automation technology that makes computers to gain high-level understanding from images and videos throughout acquiring, processing, analyzing, and recognizing digital data by transforming visual images into numerical or symbolic information.

Convolutional Neural Network: A typical deep learning model that is commonly used to image classification, object detection, natural language procession, and predictive analysis. Such a network structure is a regularized version of fully connected networks, which belong to the class of artificial neural network.

Deep Learning: A broad family of machine learning models based on neural networks. Typical deep learning models are deep neural networks, convolutional neural networks, recurrent neural networks, deep belief networks, and deep reinforcement learning.

Image Recognition: One of the most classical issues in computer vision, image processing, and object detection, which deals with determine whether or not an image contains specific objects, patterns, or features.

Smart Logistics: The large-scale autonomous operation of inland vessels and seagoing machines using information collected by sensors.

Smart Port: An innovative port that applies automation and information technologies by incorporating big data, IoT, artificial intelligence, and blockchain.

Unmanned Surface Vehicle: A water-borne vessel that is able to operate on the surface of the water without any human operators.

Section 42
Performance Metrics

Artificial Intelligence and Machine Learning Innovation in SDGs

Ambar Yoganingrum
National Research and Innovation Agency, Indonesia

Rulina Rachmawati
National Research and Innovation Agency, Indonesia

Cahyo Trianggoro
National Research and Innovation Agency, Indonesia

Arafat Febriandirza
National Research and Innovation Agency, Indonesia

Koharudin Koharudin
National Research and Innovation Agency, Indonesia

Muhammad Yudhi Rezaldi
National Research and Innovation Agency, Indonesia

Abdurrakhman Prasetyadi
National Research and Innovation Agency, Indonesia

INTRODUCTION

In 2015, all United Nations member states adopted the 2030 agenda to jointly achieve the Sustainable Development Goals (SDGs). Several studies using AI-related technologies have been conducted to support this goal. Artificial Intelligence (AI) and machine learning (ML) are believed to accelerate the achievement of the targets of the 17 SDGs. These two terms are often confused. Artificial Intelligence is a broader concept of machines capable of executing commands in "smart" ways. Meanwhile, ML is an AI application that focuses on forecasting by utilizing computational statistics (Gangula et al., 2020).

The rapid progress of AI and ML has significant implications for most of the achievements of the 17 SDGs. Thus, it can be concluded that AI technology may be required to achieve the SDGs targets, although AI-based technologies need to be supported by regulation and oversight to enable sustainable development (Vinuesa et al., 2020).

DOI: 10.4018/978-1-7998-9220-5.ch154

BACKGROUND

AI and ML have become very popular recently and are increasingly becoming a part of our daily life. Figure 1 shows the increasing trend in the number of publications discussing AI and ML across the 17 SDGs. Data were taken from Scopus. The graph illustrates that some goals have long been of interest to AI developers, while others have only been in the last few years.

There have been many studies discussing the role of AI in the achievement of the SDGs. Among them is the role of AI in achieving 137 targets and failing to achieve 59 targets of SDGs (Vinuesa et al., 2020). Then, the role of AI in SDGs as an enabler to address research gaps in academic research, funding institutions, professionals, and industry, with an emphasis on the transportation sector (Gupta et al., 2021). Meanwhile, Sætra (2021) uses the concept of SDGs to provide a new and useful framework for analyzing and categorizing the benefits and harms of AI. To the best of the author's knowledge, the focus of AI research on each of the SDGs has not been identified. This topic is important for analyzing the areas of the SDGs that AI developers are most interested in. In addition to providing information on some issues that AI has not approached. Using a bibliometrics approach, this chapter will provide a brief overview of the areas supported by AI and ML for each SDG. Furthermore, the paper applied narrative review to show the core research of AI and ML in the 17 SDGs and discuss the required future research direction. This study contributes to the academic community, regarding the focus of AI and ML research on the SDGs.

Figure 1. Illustration of the growing number of papers discussing AI and ML for the SDGs

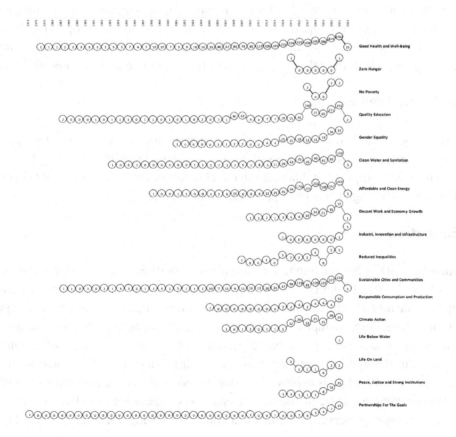

AI AND ML INNOVATION IN THE 17 SDGS

Poverty

No poverty is the first goal of the SDGs. The purpose of this goal is to eradicate poverty in all forms around the world by 2030. Practitioners and policymakers address this goal by using AI and ML techniques to assist in decision-making, estimate the poverty level of vulnerable areas, and monitor progress toward poverty alleviation programs. Several AI and ML that have been developed include a tool that combines spatial interpolation approaches and applied machine learning modeling methods based on the Bayesian geostatistical (BGS) and Artificial neural networks (ANN) to estimate the development over small areas not captured on a national scale, based on socio-economic indicators. Then a tool to evaluate urbanism's effects on the economic dynamism of a neighborhood. The tool could help the government develop poverty prevention programs in mixed neighborhoods. Next, Automated Machine Learning (AutoML) measures poverty risks by evaluating over-indebted household profiles. The technique allowed us to distinguish clusters of over-indebtedness (e.g., low-income, low credit control, and household crisis) and predict families' over-indebtedness risk factors. Hence, it contributes to identifying early-stage poverty.

Hunger

The second goal of the SDGs is zero hunger. This goal aims to stop hunger, achieve food security, improve nutrition, and promote sustainable agriculture. AI and ML-based approaches support these goals in many ways, ultimately preventing crop damage and predicting crop yield. Some researchers propose AI and ML methods to control harmful pests and identify plant diseases in crop damage prevention. Some researchers also report the adoption of AI and ML to predict seasonal crops, contributing to more productive cultivation for farmers and decision-makers adequate agricultural planning and management. Besides predicting crop yield, the ML approach is also reported to be used to forecast food insecurity.

Good Health and Well-Being

The third goal of the SDGs is one that has received much attention from AI developers. ML in good health and well-being is used to develop algorithms to take advantage of the large healthcare administrative databases, measure computational fairness in travel behavior modeling, and build smart Internet of Things (IoT) solutions through decision support mechanisms.

Quality Education

The Development of SDGs has the aim to increase the quality of education. The rapid development of ICT, particularly in Artificial Intelligence and Machine Learning, allows us to exploit massive data to enhance education quality. Digital transformation in the education process, particularly in personalized learning and counseling, helps to improve the academic system. Some researchers showed us that implementing a classroom management system based on improved machine-learning artificial intelligence to analyze student status through intelligent database processing that efficiently embraces students' status could be considered a path and basis to providing personalized feed for college students. Furthermore, in higher education institutions, artificial intelligence enables college students to have a more personalized and interactive learning experience. In the medical education setting, machine learning helps students improve their understanding by utilizing augmented reality simulators and generating many datasets that can be analyzed through machine learning algorithms. However, the adoption of AI and Machine Learning has a challenge regarding accessibility and affordability for Higher Education Institutions in developing countries.

Gender Equality

SDG's goal number five is to achieve gender equality and women's empowerment. Researchers have proposed AI and ML techniques in several areas to support this goal. AI and ML were developed to identify gender gaps in the diagnosis and treatment of COVID-19. Then a system is proposed to measure gender composition and estimate the vulnerable population of women, the elderly, and children in an area. Furthermore, a method using logistic regression (Logistics), SVM with the linear kernel (SVM-Linear) and radial basis function kernel (SVM-RBF), k-nearest neighbor (KNN), and random forest (RF) is proposed to predict the number of births and assist policymakers in developing reproductive health care services or gender-based violence. AI and ML methods were also applied to develop systems to analyze gender-biased programs such as literacy, stunting, and modern contraceptive methods. AI systems were also designed to reveal victims of sexual abuse, especially children, to distinguish child physical abuse from non-abuse and gender, racial, or sexual orientation discrimination, including protection of privacy regarding sensitive information.

Water and Sanitation

Accessibility and water equity as a basic service play an important role in human life. The UN's Sustainable Development Goals are placed at goal number six because there is much water-related homework. The rise of AI and ML has the potential to be a solution to overcome these challenges. In addition, the agricultural sector has a high demand for water management systems that require an Artificial Intelligence approach because manual water distribution to human-operated farms faces several problems and triggers community conflicts. The AI-based systems were developed to include a water management system for adjusting the operation of weir floodgates. AI technologies revealed high performance in Drinking Water Treatment (DWT) processes, such as predicting the coagulant dosage, discrimination of the Disinfection By-Products (DBP) formation potential, advanced control of membrane fouling, membrane preparation and optimization, and water quality prediction.

Clean Energy and Affordable Energy

Clean energy is becoming a significant issue in SDGs due to climate change that occurs during decades and harms our lives, such as the rise of seawater levels, natural disasters caused by high intensity of rainfall, and many more. The adoption of Artificial Intelligence within this field would accelerate the developments of some technologies, and therefore energy generated becomes more affordable and efficient. Artificial Intelligence can be implemented in wind energy sources for demand forecast, optimization of an energy storage operation and wind power, speed prediction, and other purposes. Moreover, in material science, AI can be considered a major driver for the "Operation Warp Speed" of battery research, a framework attached to several worldwide projects. Furthermore, as the cleanest energy source, hydropower also improves storage and effectivity through grey wolf optimization combined with an adaptive neuro-fuzzy inference system (ANFIS) to forecast hydropower generation.

Decent Work and Economic Growth

Industrialization is one of the essential branches of the economy that absorbs labor and provides income. To achieve this SDG, researchers focus on applying AI and ML in various industries. Its application covers the area of production, quality control, security, R&D, supply chain, and any problems that occur in the manufacturing sector. AI and ML also support workforce issues, such as work performance, effects of robots, blockchain and trust, the mediation of hope, leadership, and others. Issues in the financial sector have also become the research focus, such as risk management, stock market, microcredit, price forecasting, financial markets, financial market law, and financial regulations' implications.

Types of ML to support this goal have mainly consisted of supervised learning, such as Gaussian Naïve Bayes algorithm, K-Nearest Neighbor (KNN) Algorithm, Synthetic Minority Oversampling Technique (SMOTE), Multiple Linear Regression (MLR), Classification Trees, Support Vector Machines, Gaussian Mixture Model, Radial Basis Function Neural Network (RBFNN), Multilayer Perceptron Neural Network (MLPNN), and Product-Unit Neural Network (EPUNN) model. Meanwhile, a few papers used deep learning, which includes Gray Level Co-Occurrence Matrix (GLCM), Convolutional Neural Network (CNN), Hierarchical Spatial-Temporal State Machine (HSTSM), Extreme Learning Machine (ELM), Random Forest (RF), Deep Neural Networks, and Extreme Gradient Boosting. In addition, a few papers reported the use of unsupervised learning (e.g., Multivariate Clustering Analysis, K Means algorithm, Principal Component Analysis (PCA), K-mode clustering algorithm, and support vector regression (SVR) method.

Industry, Innovation, and Infrastructure

This term aims to build resilient infrastructure, promote inclusive and sustainable industrialization, and foster innovation. This SDG is an umbrella for other SDGs. Thus, AI and ML research support is categorized into the other SDGs, such as SDG numbers seven and eight.

Reduce and Equalities

Currently, people with disabilities can speak and hear to interact and communicate with the help of AI technology. A sign language recognition system for persons with disabilities has been developed using image recognition technology.

Sustainability Cities and Communities

AI and ML algorithms are increasingly becoming a fundamental segment of some businesses. They are currently developing methods for smart city activities, which aim to build robots and advance city tasks and tasks independently. Several AI-based tools have been developed, such as AI items in homes, sustainable urban systems, and vehicular traffic systems in smart cities.

Responsible Consumption and Production

SDG's goal number ten is to ensure sustainable consumption and production patterns. In this case, AI and ML techniques have been used to optimize resource production, distribution, and consumption (including pollutant reduction) to minimize global climate change. In terms of sustainable consumption of water resources, AI has been used in the remediation of groundwater resources, estimating the amount of water for efficient irrigation, creating global maps of irrigated areas, measuring wind power production, estimating photovoltaic (PV) electricity production of roof buildings and a greenhouse, as well as forecasting heat load in buildings. In terms of industry application, AI and ML methods promote sustainable operations through energy efficiency, reducing labor and operational time, and efficient selection of locations. In addition, AI and ML have also been applied in estimating energy consumption based on call data records, estimating the most efficient locations for plants and depots, creating a decision support system in bioleaching metallurgical processes, determining optimal production schedule, automating vacuum drying process of Algal-based biofuels and wire marking identification, and estimating energy consumption as well as minimizing plastic waste in the plastics processing industry. In the cultivation process, AI and ML have been used for classifying cultivated rapeseed and oil palm.

Climate Action

The application of AI and ML to climate topics mainly focuses on water, gas emissions, and ecology issues. In the field of water, AI and ML are applied primarily for the management and measurement of water quality of rivers, reservoirs, aquifers, pools, and basins for water supply, flood prevention, and survival of aquatic species. In addition, AI and ML support are also applied to research the evapotranspiration process, building rainfall modeling, assessing river-based monsoon flows, estimating frozen soil degradation, and monitoring melt pools.

The application of AI and ML to gas emission subtopics is found in research related to types of building materials that contribute to greenhouse gas emissions, mapping, modeling and carbon measurement, measurement of CO_2 in the atmosphere, prediction of N_2O emissions, temperature-based ozone parameterization, cloud particle characterization, carbon flux, and Solar radiation estimation. Meanwhile, in the term of the ecosystem, AI and ML are widely used to control agriculture/plants, livestock, forest, soil sector, and habitat of various animals

In addition to the main topics mentioned above, AI and ML development are found in weather patterns, energy, temperature, natural disasters, and other specific issues. The weather pattern includes the research related to micrometeorological data prediction and climate data and modeling. AI and ML are also applied to estimate the amount and assess the efficiency of energy consumption in an urban area, identify the factors influencing energy use, and early detection of insulation failure. Research in natural disasters has also utilized AI and ML, especially for disasters of drought, forest fire, heatwave, disease, and flood.

Life Below Water

This goal aims to save marine protected areas, which are essential global resources. The sea is part of the worldwide system and is a source of our food and even oxygen that must be maintained for humankind. AI and Internet of Things (IoT) based on the collaborative business ecosystem (also called an industrial cluster) is an innovative system suggested to the traditional fishery aquaculture. AI and IoT applications are also proposed to monitor the water quality in real-time for small water sources like ponds.

Life on Land

Several types of research report AI and ML adoption to analyze the ecology quality of the land ecosystem. An Artificial intelligence interactive translation (AIIT) and Geographic information system (GIS) software were developed to analyze the spatial distribution of different land ecosystems within different types of ecosystems and comprehensively conduct assessments to improve the ecological quality of the land. AI and ML also were applied to assess the life cycle normalization in Europe.

Peace, Justice, and Strong Institution

SDG's goal number sixteen is to promote peace, build inclusive societies for sustainable development, ensure access to justice for all, and build strong institutions at all levels. AI and ML techniques support this goal by transforming legal/court practices, criminal justice practices (e.g., surveillance and prevention), and policing. A tool was developed to predict the likelihood of re-arrest for patients with serious mental illness. A semi-automatic analysis tool is also proposed to assist mediators between victims and perpetrators during mediation; therefore, the needs of both parties can be accommodated. Moreover, a system is proposed to assess relevant court decisions for plaintiffs and mediators and develop a legal decision-support system.

Partnerships for the Goals

The COVID-19 pandemic has taught the global community that the recurrence of seasonal infections offers completely unexpected possibilities. The challenges facing our world today have grown in complexity and increasingly require great, coordinated efforts: between countries. Given that there are always unthinkable and unprecedented possibilities, it seems wise to proactively address this vulnerability and coordinate efforts: between countries (Mayburd, 2021; Tomašev et al., 2020). Mayburd (2021) outlines a scheme of cost-effective design of multiple anti-viral pharmaceuticals with natural and in-silico-designed libraries. The screening process was conducted with a pool of tested antiviral activity used to train ligand and structure-based methods.

DISCUSSION

This chapter observes that some SDGs are getting more support from AI and ML approaches. Those SDGs are primarily in the areas of health and well-being (Goal 3), followed by education (Goal 4), water (Goal 6), energy (Goal 7), decent work and economic growth (Goal 8), sustainable cities (Goal 11), and climate (Goal 13). The number of papers published yearly supports this finding. However, the number of documents show an increase even though the first paper was detected recently (the goals number 8 and 13).

This paper studied that all goals that receive more support from AI and ML are categorized as having a significant ripple effect, except SDG number 13 (climate). Sætra (2021) analyzed and classified the influence of AI on the SDGs based on the level of impact, direct or indirect effects, and clear and significant ripple effects or not. The goals with much support are categorized as follow: (1) AI in number 3,4 and 11 are categorized as giving direct effect, medium impact, and major ripple effect, and (2) AI in number 8: direct effect, high impact, and major ripple effect, (3) AI in number 6 and 7: indirect effect, minor impact, and major ripple effect, (4) AI in number 13: direct effect, medium impact, and minor ripple effect. The issue of climate change is mitigated with industry, innovation, and infrastructure objectives (Goal number 9). It may have an impact also from applying AI and ML to other SDGs such as energy, water, and goal number 12, namely Responsible consumption and production.

This chapter also learns that much or less support for AI and ML approaches is due to the data availability. ML is a technique that teaches computers to process data. Algorithms use computational methods to "learn" information directly from data. In addition, the importance of data makes one have to be careful in using it because it gives unethical results when using unrepresentative and inaccurate data (Gupta et al., 2021).

Although, in general, AI and ML have a positive impact, several AI developments on the SDGs have a negative impact (Vinuesa et al., 2020). The negative effect is shown on the SDGs with many publications, namely on education. It has been described that several technologies to achieve SDG 4 have been developed but have the potential to create inequality, especially the possibility of the formation of exclusivity and a Western-oriented system (Sætra, 2021). As stated above, the accessibility and affordability of higher education institutions in developing countries remain a challenge. It is important to think about producing AI and ML technologies and how these technologies are evenly distributed. The progress of AI and ML on an SDG can have a negative impact on the other SDG. For example, AI-enhanced farming tools may be inaccessible to smallholders and thus hinder the achievement of the targets of SDG 2 (Vinuesa et al., 2020).

CONCLUSION

This paper shows that the amount of AI and ML research support is not the same for the 17 SDGs. Several SDGs have received high support for a long time (SDGs number 3, 4, 6, 7, and 11), where the five goals provide direct and indirect effects. Meanwhile, SDGs No. 8 and 13 more recently received high support, which had an immediate effect. It is recognized that AI and ML technologies positively impact the achievement of the SDGs in general. However, one must be aware that these technologies can create gaps that will hinder the achievement of other SDGs.

THE FUTURE RESEARCH DIRECTIONS

It is necessary to carry out further research related to the development of AI and ML technology on an SDG, which can be detrimental to the achievement of other SDGs, especially for the SDGs that receive much support from AI and ML research. In addition, it is also necessary to explore and collect the necessary data for the SDGs that are still not supported by AI and ML.

ACKNOWLEDGMENT

Ambar Yoganingrum, Rulina Rachmawati, Cahyo Trianggoro, M. Yudhi Rezaldy, Abdurrakhman Prasetyadi, and Arafat Febriandirza are the main contributors. Koharudin is a member, who helps creating the graphs. All authors have read and approved the final manuscript.

REFERENCES

Gangula, R., Sudha, C., Rekha, S., & Nirmala, M. (2020). A conceptual framework for understanding the role of machine learning in artificial. *International Journal Of Advanced Science And Technology*, *29*(4), 820–825.

Gupta, S., Langhans, S. D., Domisch, S., Fuso-nerini, F., Felländer, A., Battaglini, M., Tegmark, M., & Vinuesa, R. (2021). Assessing whether artificial intelligence is an enabler or an inhibitor of sustainability at indicator level. *Transportation Engineering*, *4*, 100064. doi:10.1016/j.treng.2021.100064

Mayburd, A. (2021). A public-private partnership for the express development of antiviral leads: A perspective view. *Expert Opinion on Drug Discovery*, *16*(1), 23–38. doi:10.1080/17460441.2020.181 1676 PMID:32877233

Sætra, H. S. (2021). AI in context and the sustainable development goals: Factoring in the unsustainability of the sociotechnical system. *Sustainability (Switzerland)*, *13*(1738), 1–19. Academic

Tomašev, N., Cornebise, J., Hutter, F., Mohamed, S., Picciariello, A., Connelly, B., Belgrave, D. C. M., Ezer, D., Haert, F. C., Mugisha, F., Abila, G., Arai, H., Almiraat, H., Proskurnia, J., Snyder, K., Otake-Matsuura, M., Othman, M., Glasmachers, T., Wever, W., ... Clopath, C. (2020). AI for social good: Unlocking the opportunity for positive impact. *Nature Communications*, *11*(1), 2468. Advance online publication. doi:10.103841467-020-15871-z PMID:32424119

Vinuesa, R., Azizpour, H., Leite, I., Balaam, M., Dignum, V., Domisch, S., ... Nerini, F. F. (2020). The role of artificial intelligence in achieving the Sustainable Development Goals. *Nature Communications*, *11*(233), 1–10. doi:10.103841467-019-14108-y PMID:31932590

ADDITIONAL READING

Ak, R., Fink, O., & Zio, E. (2016). Two machine learning approaches for short-term wind speed time-series prediction. *IEEE Transactions on Neural Networks and Learning Systems*, *27*(8), 1734–1747. doi:10.1109/TNNLS.2015.2418739 PMID:25910257

Ancochea, J., Izquierdo, J. L., & Soriano, J. B. (2021). Evidence of gender differences in the diagnosis and management of coronavirus disease 2019 patients: An analysis of electronic health records using natural language processing and machine learning. *Journal of Women's Health*, *30*(3), 393–404. doi:10.1089/jwh.2020.8721 PMID:33416429

Assouline, D., Mohajeri, N., & Scartezzini, J. L. (2017). Quantifying rooftop photovoltaic solar energy potential: A machine learning approach. *Solar Energy*, *141*, 278–296. doi:10.1016/j.solener.2016.11.045

Bogomolov, A., Lepri, B., Larcher, R., Antonelli, F., Pianesi, F., & Pentland, A. (2016). Energy consumption prediction using people dynamics derived from cellular network data. *EPJ Data Science*, *5*(1), 1–15. doi:10.1140/epjds13688-016-0075-3

Bosco, C., Alegana, V., Bird, T., Pezzulo, C., Bengtsson, L., Sorichetta, A., Steele, J., Hornby, G., Ruktanonchai, C., Ruktanonchai, N., Wetter, E., & Tatem, A. J. (2017). Exploring the high-resolution mapping of gender-disaggregated development indicators. *Journal of the Royal Society, Interface*, *14*(20160825), 1–12. doi:10.1098/rsif.2016.0825 PMID:28381641

Boto Ferreira, M., Costa Pinto, D., Maurer Herter, M., Soro, J., Vanneschi, L., Castelli, M., & Peres, F. (2021). Using artificial intelligence to overcome over-indebtedness and fight poverty. *Journal of Business Research*, *131*, 411–425. doi:10.1016/j.jbusres.2020.10.035 PMID:33100428

Bourgeau-chavez, L. L., Lee, Y. M., Battaglia, M., Endres, S. L., Laubach, Z. M., & Scarbrough, K. (2016). Identification of Woodland Vernal Pools with Seasonal Change PALSAR Data for Habitat Conservation. *Remote Sensing*, *8*(6), 1–21. doi:10.3390/rs8060490

Branting, L. K., Pfeifer, C., Brown, B., Ferro, L., Aberdeen, J., Weiss, B., Pfaff, M., & Liao, B. (2021). Scalable and explainable legal prediction. *Artificial Intelligence and Law*, *29*(2), 213–238. doi:10.100710506-020-09273-1

Bu, C. M., Kolditz, O., Fowler, H. J., & Blenkinsop, S. (2007). Future climate scenarios and rainfall e runoff modelling in the Upper Gallego catchment (Spain). *Environmental Pollution*, *148*(3), 842–854. doi:10.1016/j.envpol.2007.02.002 PMID:17428594

Bu, F., & Wang, X. (2019). A smart agriculture IoT system based on deep reinforcement learning. *Future Generation Computer Systems*, *99*, 500–507. doi:10.1016/j.future.2019.04.041

Chahidi, L. O., Fossa, M., Priarone, A., & Mechaqrane, A. (2021). Evaluation of supervised learning models in predicting greenhouse energy demand and production for intelligent and sustainable operations. *Energies*, *14*(6297), 1–15.

Ching, P. M. L., Mayol, A. P., San Juan, J. L. G., Calapatia, A. M., So, R. H. Y., Sy, C. L., Ubando, A. T., & Culaba, A. B. (2021). AI methods for modeling the vacuum drying characteristics of chlorococcum infusionum for algal biofuel production. *Process Integration and Optimization for Sustainability*, *5*(2), 247–256. doi:10.100741660-020-00145-4

Chiogna, G., Marcolini, G., Liu, W., Pérez, T., & Tuo, Y. (2018). Coupling hydrological modeling and support vector regression to model hydropeaking in alpine catchments. *The Science of the Total Environment*, *633*, 220–229. doi:10.1016/j.scitotenv.2018.03.162 PMID:29573688

Cooper, M., Müller, B., Cafiero, C., Bayas, J. C. L., Cuaresma, J. C., & Kharas, H. (2021). Monitoring and projecting global hunger: Are we on track? *Global Food Security*, *30*, 100568. doi:10.1016/j.gfs.2021.100568

D'Amico, B., Myers, R. J., Sykes, J., Voss, E., Cousins-Jenvey, B., Fawcett, W., Richardson, S., Kermani, A., & Pomponi, F. (2018). Machine Learning for Sustainable Structures: A Call for Data B. *Structures*, *19*, 1–4. doi:10.1016/j.istruc.2018.11.013

Dantas, D., De Castro, M., & Santos, N. (2021). Machine learning for carbon stock prediction in a tropical forest in Southeastern Brazil. *Bosque (Valdivia)*, *42*(1), 131–140. doi:10.4067/S0717-92002021000100131

Das, J., & Nanduri, U. V. (2018). Assessment and evaluation of potential climate change impact on monsoon flows using machine learning technique over Wainganga River Basin, India. *Hydrological Sciences Journal*, *63*(7), 1020–1046. doi:10.1080/02626667.2018.1469757

Dehghani, M., Riahi-Madvar, H., Hooshyaripor, F., Mosavi, A., Shamshirband, S., Zavadskas, E. K., & Chau, K. (2019). Prediction of hydropower generation using Grey wolf optimization adaptive neuro-fuzzy inference system. *Energies*, *12*(2), 289. doi:10.3390/en12020289

Demergasso, C., Véliz, R., Galleguillos, P., Marín, S., Acosta, M., Zepeda, V., Zeballos, J., Henríquez, F., Pizarro, R., & Bekios-Calfa, J. (2018). Decision support system for bioleaching processes. *Hydrometallurgy*, *181*, 113–122. doi:10.1016/j.hydromet.2018.08.009

Dikshit, A., & Pradhan, B. (2021). Interpretable and explainable AI (XAI) model for spatial drought prediction. *The Science of the Total Environment*, *801*, 1–12. doi:10.1016/j.scitotenv.2021.149797 PMID:34467917

Dou, X., & Yang, Y. (2018). Comprehensive Evaluation of Machine Learning Techniques for Estimating the Responses of Carbon Fluxes to Climatic Forces in Different Terrestrial Ecosystems. *Atmosphere*, *9*(83), 1–30. doi:10.3390/atmos9030083

El Jelali, S., Fersini, E., & Messina, E. (2015). Legal retrieval as support to eMediation: Matching disputant's case and court decisions. *Artificial Intelligence and Law*, *23*(1), 1–22. doi:10.100710506-015-9162-1

Emami, M., Nazif, S., Mousavi, S., Karami, H., & Daccache, A. (2021). A hybrid constrained coral reefs optimization algorithm with machine learning for optimizing multi-reservoir systems operation. *Journal of Environmental Management*, *286*, 1–10. doi:10.1016/j.jenvman.2021.112250 PMID:33752153

Ezzy, H., Charter, M., Bonfante, A., & Brook, A. (2021). How the small object detection via machine learning and uas-based remote-sensing imagery can support the achievement of sdg2: A case study of vole burrows. *Remote Sensing, 13*(16), 3191, 1-18.

Falconer, E., El-Hay, T., Alevras, D., Docherty, J., Yanover, C., Kalton, A., ... Rosen-Zvi, M. (2014). Integrated multisystem analysis in a mental health and criminal justice ecosystem. *AMIA Annual Symposium Proceedings / AMIA Symposium. AMIA Symposium*, 526–533.

Faria, P., Nogueira, T., Ferreira, A., Carlos, C., & Rosado, L. (2021). AI-powered mobile image acquisition of vineyard insect traps with automatic quality and adequacy assessment. *Agronomy (Basel)*, *11*(4), 1–18. doi:10.3390/agronomy11040731

Fedor, P., Vaňhara, J., Havel, J., Malenovský, I., & Spellerberg, I. (2009). Artificial intelligence in pest insect monitoring. *Systematic Entomology*, *34*(2), 398–400. doi:10.1111/j.1365-3113.2008.00461.x

Franco, D., Oneto, L., Navarin, N., & Anguita, D. (2021). Toward learning trustworthily from data combining face recognition. *Entropy (Basel, Switzerland)*, *23*(1047). PMID:34441187

Gizaw, M. S., & Gan, T. Y. (2016). Regional Flood Frequency Analysis using Support Vector Regression under historical and future climate. *Journal of Hydrology (Amsterdam)*, *538*, 387–398. doi:10.1016/j.jhydrol.2016.04.041

Guo, P., Cheng, W., & Wang, Y. (2017). Hybrid evolutionary algorithm with extreme machine learning fitness function evaluation for two-stage capacitated facility location problems. *Expert Systems with Applications*, *71*, 57–68. doi:10.1016/j.eswa.2016.11.025

Han, H., Im, J., Kim, M., Sim, S., Kim, J., Kim, D & Kang, S. (2016). Retrieval of Melt Ponds on Arctic Multiyear Sea Ice in Summer from TerraSAR-X Dual-Polarization Data Using Machine Learning Approaches : A Case Study in the Chukchi Sea with Mid-Incidence Angle Data. *Remote Sens., 8*(1), 57, 1-23.

Haneef, R., Kab, S., Hrzic, R., Fuentes, S., Fosse-Edorh, S., Cosson, E., & Gallay, A. (2021). Use of artificial intelligence for public health surveillance: A case study to develop a machine Learning-algorithm to estimate the incidence of diabetes mellitus in France. *Archives of Public Health, 79*(1), 1–13. doi:10.118613690-021-00687-0 PMID:34551816

Hipp, J. R., Kane, K., & Kim, J. H. (2017). Recipes for neighborhood development: A machine learning approach toward understanding the impact of mixing in neighborhoods. *Landscape and Urban Planning, 164*, 1–12. doi:10.1016/j.landurbplan.2017.03.006

Huang, X., Hong, S. H., Yu, M., Ding, Y., & Jiang, J. (2019). Demand response management for industrial facilities: A deep reinforcement learning approach. *IEEE Access: Practical Innovations, Open Solutions, 7*, 82194–82205. doi:10.1109/ACCESS.2019.2924030

Huang, Y., Jin, Y., Schwartz, M. W., & Thorne, J. H. (2020). Intensified burn severity in California's northern coastal mountains by drier climatic condition. *Environmental Research Letters, 15*(10), 1–18. doi:10.1088/1748-9326/aba6af

Id, Z. Y., Feng, Q., Yang, L., & Deo, R. C. (2017). Future Projection with an Extreme-Learning Machine and Support Vector Regression of Reference Evapotranspiration in a Mountainous Inland. *Water (Basel), 9*(880), 1–23.

Idowu, S., Saguna, S., Åhlund, C., & Schelén, O. (2016). Applied machine learning: Forecasting heat load in district heating system. *Energy and Building, 133*, 478–488. doi:10.1016/j.enbuild.2016.09.068

Ilić, M. P., Păun, D., Šević, N. P., Hadžić, A., & Jianu, A. (2021). Needs and performance analysis for changes in higher education and implementation of artificial intelligence, machine learning, and extended reality. *Education Sciences, 11*(10), 1–21. doi:10.3390/educsci11100568

Irrgang, C., Saynisch-wagner, J., Dill, R., Boergens, E., & Thomas, M. (2020). Self-validating deep learning for recovering terrestrial water storage from gravity and altimetry measurements. *Geophysical Research Letters, 47*, 1-11.

Jahani, E., Sundsøy, P., Bjelland, J., Bengtsson, L., Pentland, A. S., & de Montjoye, Y. A. (2017). Improving official statistics in emerging markets using machine learning and mobile phone data. *EPJ Data Science, 6*(3), 1–21.

Jang, E., Im, J., Park, G., & Park, Y. (2017). Estimation of Fugacity of Carbon Dioxide in the East Sea Using in Situ Measurements and Geostationary Ocean Color Imager Satellite Data. *Remote Sens., 9*(8), 821, 1-23.

Jiang, Z., Dong, Z., Jiang, W., & Yang, Y. (2021). Recognition of rice leaf diseases and wheat leaf diseases based on multi-task deep transfer learning. *Computers and Electronics in Agriculture, 186*, 106184. doi:10.1016/j.compag.2021.106184

Kaneda, Y., & Mineno, H. (2016). Sliding window-based support vector regression for predicting micrometeorological data. *Expert Systems with Applications, 59*, 217–225. doi:10.1016/j.eswa.2016.04.012

Kang, Y., Lee, S., & Do Chung, B. (2019). Learning-based logistics planning and scheduling for crowd-sourced parcel delivery. *Computers & Industrial Engineering, 132*(April), 271–279. doi:10.1016/j.cie.2019.04.044

Kissos, L., Goldner, L., Butman, M., Eliyahu, N., & Lev-Wiesel, R. (2020). Can artificial intelligence achieve human-level performance? A pilot study of childhood sexual abuse detection in self-figure drawings. *Child Abuse & Neglect, 109*, 104755. doi:10.1016/j.chiabu.2020.104755 PMID:33075702

Kuleto, V., Ilić, M., Dumangiu, M., Ranković, M., Martins, O. M. D., Păun, D., & Mihoreanu, L. (2021). Exploring opportunities and challenges of artificial intelligence and machine learning in higher education institutions. *Sustainability (Switzerland), 13*(18), 1–16. doi:10.3390u131810424

Kurtulmuş, F., & Ünal, H. (2014). Discriminating rapeseed varieties using computer vision and machine learning. *Expert Systems with Applications, 42*(4), 1880–1891. doi:10.1016/j.eswa.2014.10.003

Latif, S. D., & Ahmed, A. N. (2021). Application of Deep Learning Method for Daily Streamflow Time-Series Prediction: A Case Study of the Kowmung River at Cedar Ford, Australia. *International Journal of Sustainable Development and Planning, 16*(3), 497–501. doi:10.18280/ijsdp.160310

Lawson, C. T., Tomchik, P., Muro, A., & Krans, E. (2019). Translation software: An alternative to transit data standards. *Transportation Research Interdisciplinary Perspectives, 2*, 100028. doi:10.1016/j.trip.2019.100028

Li, L., Rong, S., Wang, R., & Yu, S. (2021). Recent advances in artificial intelligence and machine learning for nonlinear relationship analysis and process control in drinking water treatment: A review. *Chemical Engineering Journal, 405*, 126673. doi:10.1016/j.cej.2020.126673

Lou, S., Li, D. H. W., Lam, J. C., & Chan, W. W. H. (2016). Prediction of diffuse solar irradiance using machine learning and multivariable regression. *Applied Energy, 181*, 367–374. doi:10.1016/j.apenergy.2016.08.093

Marchenko, A., Temeljotov-salaj, A., Rizzardi, V., & Oksavik, O. (2020). The Study of Facial Muscle Movements for Non-Invasive Thermal Discomfort Detection via Bio-Sensing Technology. Part I : Development of the Experimental Design and Description of the Collected Data. *Applied Sciences (Basel, Switzerland), 10*(20), 1–29. doi:10.3390/app10207315

Mayburd, A. (2021). A public-private partnership for the express development of antiviral leads: A perspective view. *Expert Opinion on Drug Discovery, 16*(1), 23–38. doi:10.1080/17460441.2020.181 1676 PMID:32877233

Mazzeo, D., Herdem, M. S., Matera, N., Bonini, M., Wen, J. Z., Nathwani, J., & Oliveti, G. (2021). Artificial intelligence application for the performance prediction of a clean energy community. *Energy, 232*, 120999. doi:10.1016/j.energy.2021.120999

Muñoz-mas, R., Lopez-nicolas, A., Martínez-capel, F., & Pulido-velazquez, M. (2016). Shifts in the suitable habitat available for brown trout (Salmo trutta L.) under short-term climate change scenarios. *The Science of the Total Environment, 544*, 686–700. doi:10.1016/j.scitotenv.2015.11.147 PMID:26674698

Nagaraj, D., Proust, E., Todeschini, A., Rulli, M. C., & D'Odorico, P. (2021). A new dataset of global irrigation areas from 2001 to 2015. *Advances in Water Resources, 152*, 1–8. doi:10.1016/j.advwatres.2021.103910

Nasrallah, A., Baghdadi, N., Mhawej, M., Faour, G., Darwish, T., Belhouchette, H., & Darwich, S. (2018). A novel approach for mapping wheat areas using high resolution sentinel-2 images. *Sensors (Switzerland), 18*(7), 1–23. doi:10.339018072089 PMID:29966267

Nemesure, M. D., Heinz, M. V., Huang, R., & Jacobson, N. C. (2021). Predictive modeling of depression and anxiety using electronic health records and a novel machine learning approach with artificial intelligence. *Scientific Reports, 11*(1980), 1-9.

Nik Bakht, M., El-Diraby, T. E., & Hosseini, M. (2018). Game-based crowdsourcing to support collaborative customization of the definition of sustainability. *Advanced Engineering Informatics, 38*, 501–513. doi:10.1016/j.aei.2018.08.019

Nowack, P., Braesicke, P., Haigh, J., Abraham, N. L., Pyle, J., & Voulgarakis, A. (2018). Using machine learning to build temperature-based ozone parameterizations for climate sensitivity simulations Using machine learning to build temperature-based ozone parameterizations for climate sensitivity simulations. *Environmental Research Letters, 13*(10), 1–11. doi:10.1088/1748-9326/aae2be

Okkan, U., & Inan, G. (2014). Statistical downscaling of monthly reservoir inflows for Kemer watershed in Turkey: Use of machine learning methods, multiple GCMs and emission scenarios. *International Journal of Climatology, 35*(11), 3274–3295. doi:10.1002/joc.4206

Park, M., Jung, D., Lee, S., & Park, S. (2020). Heatwave Damage Prediction Using Random Forest Model in Korea. *Applied Sciences (Basel, Switzerland), 10*(8237), 1–12. doi:10.3390/app10228237

Pastick, N. J., Jorgenson, M. T., Wylie, B. K., Nield, S. J., Johnson, K. D., & Finley, A. O. (2015). Remote Sensing of Environment Distribution of near-surface permafrost in Alaska: Estimates of present and future conditions. *Remote Sensing of Environment, 168*, 301–315. doi:10.1016/j.rse.2015.07.019

Peters, D. P. C., McVey, D. S., Elias, E. H., Pelzel-McCluskey, A. M., Derner, J. D., Burruss, N. D., Schrader, T. S., Yao, J., Pauszek, S. J., Lombard, J., & Rodriguez, L. L. (2020). Big data–model integration and AI for vector-borne disease prediction. *Ecosphere, 11*(6), 1–20. doi:10.1002/ecs2.3157

Petrović, A., Nikolić, M., Jovanović, M., Bijanić, M., & Delibašić, B. (2021). Fair classification via Monte Carlo policy gradient method. *Engineering Applications of Artificial Intelligence, 104*, 1–20. doi:10.1016/j.engappai.2021.104398

Philibert, A., Loyce, C., & Makowski, D. (2013). Prediction of N 2 O emission from local information with Random Forest. *Environmental Pollution, 177*, 156–163. doi:10.1016/j.envpol.2013.02.019 PMID:23500053

Ponce-López, V., Escalera, S., Pérez, M., Janés, O., & Baró, X. (2015). Non-verbal communication analysis in Victim-Offender Mediations. *Pattern Recognition Letters, 67*, 19–27. doi:10.1016/j.patrec.2015.07.040

Poursaeid, M., Mastouri, R., Shabanlou, S., & Najarchi, M. (2021). Modelling qualitative and quantitative parameters of groundwater using a new wavelet conjunction heuristic method: Wavelet extreme learning machine versus wavelet neural networks. *Water and Environment Journal: the Journal / the Chartered Institution of Water and Environmental Management, 35*(1), 67–83. doi:10.1111/wej.12595

Rashid, M., Nayan, A.-A., Rahman, M. O., Simi, S. A., Saha, J., & Kibria, M. G. (2021). IoT based Smart Water Quality Prediction for Biofloc Aquaculture. *International Journal of Advanced Computer Science and Applications, 12*(6), 56–62. doi:10.14569/IJACSA.2021.0120608

Reid, A. R., Pérez, C. R. C., & Rodríguez, D. M. (2018). Inference of vehicular traffic in smart cities using machine learning with the internet of things. *International Journal on Interactive Design and Manufacturing*, *12*(2), 459–472. doi:10.100712008-017-0404-1

Rodríguez-González, A., Zanin, M., & Menasalvas-Ruiz, E. (2019). Public Health and Epidemiology Informatics: Can Artificial Intelligence Help Future Global Challenges? An Overview of Antimicrobial Resistance and Impact of Climate Change in Disease Epidemiology. *Yearbook of Medical Informatics*, *28*(1), 224–231. doi:10.1055-0039-1677910 PMID:31419836

Sadeghfam, S., Hassanzadeh, Y., Khatibi, R., Nadiri, A. A., & Moazamnia, M. (2019). Groundwater remediation through pump-treat-inject technology using Optimum Control by Artificial Intelligence (OCAI). *Water Resources Management*, *33*(3), 1123–1145. doi:10.100711269-018-2171-6

Sakaushi, K., & Nishihara, H. (2021). Two-Dimensional π-Conjugated Frameworks as a Model System to Unveil a Multielectron-Transfer-Based Energy Storage Mechanism. *Accounts of Chemical Research*, *54*(15), 3003–3015. doi:10.1021/acs.accounts.1c00172 PMID:33998232

Salawu, E. O., Hesse, E., Stopford, C., Davey, N., & Sun, Y. (2017). Applying machine learning methods for characterization of hexagonal prisms from their 2D scattering patterns – an investigation using modelled scattering data. *Journal of Quantitative Spectroscopy & Radiative Transfer*, *201*, 115–127. doi:10.1016/j.jqsrt.2017.07.001

Saleh, B. M. (2020). D-Talk: Sign Language Recognition System for People with Disability using Machine Learning and Image Processing. *International Journal of Advanced Trends in Computer Science and Engineering*, *9*(4), 4374–4382. doi:10.30534/ijatcse/2020/29942020

Sanober, S., & Dhupia, B. (2020). Performance and Breakdown of Artificial Intelligence and Machine Learning Subsidize to Smart Cities. *International Journal of Advanced Science and Technology*, *29*(4s), 490–495.

Sebbar, A., Heddam, S., & Djemili, L. (2019). Predicting Daily Pan Evaporation (E pan) from Dam Reservoirs in the Mediterranean Regions of Algeria : OPELM vs OSELM. *Environmental Processes*, *6*(1), 309–319. doi:10.100740710-019-00353-2

Şerban, A. C., & Lytras, M. D. (2020). Artificial Intelligence for Smart Renewable Energy Sector in Europe— Smart Energy Infrastructures for Next Generation Smart Cities. *IEEE Access: Practical Innovations, Open Solutions*, *8*, 77364–77377. doi:10.1109/ACCESS.2020.2990123

Shahi, N., Shahi, A. K., Phillips, R., Shirek, G., Lindberg, D. M., & Moulton, S. L. (2021). Using deep learning and natural language processing models to detect child physical abuse. *Journal of Pediatric Surgery*, ●●●, xxxx. PMID:33838900

Slapnik, M., Istenič, D., Pintar, M., & Udovč, A. (2015). Extending life cycle assessment normalization factors and use of machine learning – A Slovenian case study. *Ecological Indicators*, *50*, 161–172. doi:10.1016/j.ecolind.2014.10.028

Suntaranont, B., Aramkul, S., Kaewmoracharoen, M., & Champrasert, P. (2020). Water irrigation decision support system for practicalweir adjustment using artificial intelligence and machine learning techniques. *Sustainability (Switzerland)*, *12*(5), 1–18.

Symonds, P., Taylor, J., Chalabi, Z., Mavrogianni, A., Hamilton, I., Vardoulakis, S., ... Macintyre, H. (2016). Development of an England-wide indoor overheating and air pollution model using artificial neural networks. *Journal of Building Performance Simulation*, *9*(6), 606–619. doi:10.1080/19401493. 2016.1166265

Szajna, A., Kostrzewski, M., Ciebiera, K., Stryjski, R., & Woźniak, W. (2021). Application of the deep cnn-based method in industrial system for wire marking identification. *Energies*, *14*(12), 1–35. doi:10.3390/en14123659

Tian, W., Yang, S., Zuo, J., Li, Z., & Liu, Y. (2014). Relationship between built form and energy performance of office buildings in a severe cold Chinese region. *Building Simulation*, *10*(1), 11–24. doi:10.100712273-016-0314-3

Tien, D., Hoang, N., & Samui, P. (2019). Spatial pattern analysis and prediction of forest fi re using new machine learning approach of Multivariate Adaptive Regression Splines and Differential Flower Pollination optimization: A case study at Lao Cai province (Viet Nam). *Journal of Environmental Management*, *237*, 476–487. doi:10.1016/j.jenvman.2019.01.108 PMID:30825780

Tomašev, N., Cornebise, J., Hutter, F., Mohamed, S., Picciariello, A., Connelly, B., Belgrave, D. C. M., Ezer, D., van der Haert, F. C., Mugisha, F., Abila, G., Arai, H., Almiraat, H., Proskurnia, J., Snyder, K., Otake-Matsuura, M., Othman, M., Glasmachers, T., de Wever, W., ... Clopath, C. (2020). AI for social good: Unlocking the opportunity for positive impact. *Nature Communications*, *11*(1), 2468. doi:10.103841467-020-15871-z PMID:32424119

Traganos, D., & Reinartz, P. (2018). Machine learning-based retrieval of benthic reflectance and Posidonia oceanica seagrass extent using a semi-analytical inversion of Sentinel-2 satellite data. *International Journal of Remote Sensing*, *39*(24), 9428–9452. doi:10.1080/01431161.2018.1519289

Tsimpouris, E., Tsakiridis, N. L., & Theocharis, J. B. (2021). Using autoencoders to compress soil VNIR–SWIR spectra for more robust prediction of soil properties. *Geoderma*, *393*, 114967. doi:10.1016/j. geoderma.2021.114967

Voosen, P. (2018). The earth machine with cash from tech philanthropists, science insurgents plot climate models driven by artificial intelligence. *Science*, *361*(6400), 344–347. doi:10.1126cience.361.6400.344 PMID:30049872

Vulova, S., Meier, F., Duarte, A., Quanz, J., Nouri, H., & Kleinschmit, B. (2021). Modeling urban evapotranspiration using remote sensing, flux footprints, and artificial intelligence. *The Science of the Total Environment*, *786*, 147293. doi:10.1016/j.scitotenv.2021.147293 PMID:33975115

Wang, L. (2021). Urban land ecological evaluation and English translation model optimization based on machine learning. *Arabian Journal of Geosciences*, *14*(22), 2430. doi:10.100712517-021-08905-3

Wang, T., Yang, D., Fang, B., Yang, W., Qin, Y., & Wang, Y. (2019). Science of the Total Environment Data-driven mapping of the spatial distribution and potential changes of frozen ground over the Tibetan Plateau. *The Science of the Total Environment*, *649*, 515–525. doi:10.1016/j.scitotenv.2018.08.369 PMID:30176463

Wang, Y. (2021). An improved machine learning and artificial intelligence algorithm for classroom management of English distance education. *Journal of Intelligent & Fuzzy Systems*, 40(2), 3477–3488. doi:10.3233/JIFS-189385

Willenbacher, M., Scholten, J., & Wohlgemuth, V. (2021). Machine learning for optimization of energy and plastic consumption in the production of thermoplastic parts in SME. *Sustainability (Switzerland)*, 13(12), 1–20. doi:10.3390u13126800

Winkler-Schwartz, A., Bissonnette, V., Mirchi, N., Ponnudurai, N., Yilmaz, R., Ledwos, N., Siyar, S., Azarnoush, H., Karlik, B., & Del Maestro, R. F. (2019). Artificial Intelligence in Medical Education: Best Practices Using Machine Learning to Assess Surgical Expertise in Virtual Reality Simulation. *Journal of Surgical Education*, 76(6), 1681–1690. doi:10.1016/j.jsurg.2019.05.015 PMID:31202633

Woon, W. L., El-hag, A., & Harbaji, M. (2015). Machine learning techniques for robust classification of partial discharges in oil – paper insulation systems. *IET Science, Measurement & Technology*, 10(3), 221–2271. doi:10.1049/iet-smt.2015.0076

Xu, Y., Knudby, A., Shen, Y., & Liu, Y. (2018). Mapping Monthly Air Temperature in the Tibetan Plateau From MODIS Data Based on Machine. *IEEE Journal of Selected Topics in Applied Earth Observations and Remote Sensing*, 11(2), 345–354. doi:10.1109/JSTARS.2017.2787191

Yang, X., Cao, D., Chen, J., Xiao, Z., & Daowd, A. (2020). AI and IoT-based collaborative business ecosystem: A case in Chinese fish farming industry Xiaoping Yang Dongmei Cao * Jing Chen and Zuoping Xiao Ahmad Daowd. *International Journal of Technology Management*, 82(2), 151–171. doi:10.1504/IJTM.2020.107856

Ye, L., Jabbar, S. F., Zahra, M. M. A., & Tan, M. L. (2021). Bayesian Regularized Neural Network Model Development for Predicting Daily Rainfall from Sea Level Pressure Data: Investigation on Solving Complex Hydrology Problem. *Complexity*, 2021, 1–14. doi:10.1155/2021/6631564

Zheng, Y., Wang, S., & Zhao, J. (2021). Equality of opportunity in travel behavior prediction with deep neural networks and discrete choice models. *Transportation Research Part C, Emerging Technologies*, 132, 132. doi:10.1016/j.trc.2021.103410

Zhong, H., Li, X., Lobell, D., Ermon, S., & Brandeau, M. L. (2018). Hierarchical modeling of seed variety yields and decision making for future planting plans. *Environment Systems & Decisions*, 38(4), 458–470. doi:10.100710669-018-9695-4

Zhu, R., Yang, L., Liu, T., Wen, X., Zhang, L., & Chang. (2019). Hydrological Responses to the Future Climate Change in a Data Scarce Region, Northwest China: Application of Machine Learning Models. *Water (Basel)*, 11(8), 1588. doi:10.3390/w11081588

KEY TERMS AND DEFINITIONS

Artificial Intelligence: A computer or robot that requires human intelligence and ingenuity to perform tasks normally performed by humans.

Bibliometrics: An approach to analysis the scientific content of books, articles, and other publications, using statistical methods.

Disinfection By-Products (DBP): Generally formed by the reaction of disinfectants such as chlorine with organic precursors present in water, where these precursors act as precursors of DBP.

Internet of Things: Describes a network of physical objects, where those objects are connected to sensors, software, and other technologies to exchange data over the internet.

Machine Learning: Is a subfield of artificial intelligence where machines are trained to imitate human intelligence, thereby being able to perform complex tasks.

Sustainable Development Goals: Also known as universal calls for all levels of society to act, end poverty, and protect the earth. Therefore by 2030, everyone will enjoy peace and prosperity.

Section 43
Predictive Analytics

A Comparison of SOM and K-Means Algorithms in Predicting Tax Compliance

Felix Bankole
University of South Africa, South Africa

Zama Vara
University of South Africa, South Africa

INTRODUCTION

Revenue administrations oversee the collection and management of domestic revenues such as taxes and customs duties. Tax compliance is a major problem for tax administrations across the world (Jenkins, 2018). Tax noncompliance, is defined as a failure to file on time, capturing incomplete or misleading information on returns, and overdue payment of taxes (Jenkins, 2018). Furthermore, tax noncompliance can be explained as a fraudulent or deliberate misrepresentation of information on income tax returns to decrease the amount of the tax liability (Vanhoeyveld, Martens, & Peeters, 2019). Tax noncompliance is also characterised by false claims for refund, misclassification of goods and services, bogus traders, under-reported sales, and failure to register and failure to pay taxes to the tax administration (Bimo, Prasetyo, & Susilandari, 2019).

The payment of taxes is of significant concern to lawmakers in developed and developing nations. Tax administration in countries worldwide have utilized different methods to quantify the nature of noncompliance, which depends on the social and economic behavior of citizens (Agyeiwa, et al., 2019). In the opinion of Krishnamurthya & Desouza (2014), fiscal revenue deficiencies due to tax noncompliance are very considerable in third world countries of the sub-Saharan Africa, Latin America, Caribbean, and South Asia regions. Sadly, these are the countries which have a greater reliance on tax revenues for their fiscal planning (Krishnamurthya & Desouza, 2014). Compounding the problem is that these countries are the most affected by budget shortages. Moreover, tax administrations are responsible for investing in efficient and effective techniques to select taxpayers for audit. Tax compliance and fraud detection is likely to become even more important with recent developments in Artificial Intelligence (Krishnamurthya & Desouza, 2014).

Auditing tax returns is a slow and costly process that is very prone to errors. Conducting tax audits for example, involves costs to the tax administration, as well as to the taxpayer (Zwick, 2021). Furthermore, the field of anomaly and fraud detection is characterised by unlabelled historical data (Thudumu, Branch, Jin, & Singh, 2020). To this end, here the use of unsupervised machine learning algorithms is suggested. They are well suited to unlabelled datasets. Notwithstanding there is little research on comparing the effectiveness of various unsupervised learning approaches in the income tax realm. In this paper, two clustering techniques are proposed. These are, a K-means algorithm and Self-Organizing Map. Moreover, the efficacy and the predictive accuracy of a Self-Organizing Map (SOM) and K-means algorithms in identifying income tax noncompliance are compared.

DOI: 10.4018/978-1-7998-9220-5.ch155

In this study a SOM and K-means are used to obtain taxpayer cohorts that can easily be labelled as either compliant or otherwise. The objective of this research is to firstly create an Artificial Intelligence based, tax compliance detection framework and secondly, to compare a Self-Organizing Map (SOM) with a K-means algorithm to detect income tax noncompliance. To delineate, this study will utilize taxpayer datasets of the telecommunications industry. Furthermore, to confine the study, unsupervised learning approaches are chosen on income tax noncompliance. Additionally, this study will only use taxpayer datasets of the telecommunications industry.

BACKGROUND

Historical research on tax compliance has been met with a lack of historical data (Battiston & Gamba, 2016). Tax compliance cannot be attributed entirely by the level of enforcement, rather it is also based on behavioural factors affecting the purchaser-seller relations (Lamantia & Pezzino, 2021). Researchers have made attempts to identify and measure the impact of tax morale on tax compliance. Luttmer and Singhal (2014) describe various mechanisms according to which tax morale may affect compliance. One mechanism is based on intrinsic motivation. In every society, there are individuals who believe that paying taxes is a way to contribute to society's welfare and that individuals may obtain private utility from it. There is another important aspect of taxpayers' behaviour related to tax morale and that is the role those social norms and reputation may play (Luttmer & Singhal, 2014).

Tax compliance experiments have been gaining impetus in recent years. The recent phenomenon of an increased number of studies on tax compliance is due to an increase in data availability. These contemporary developments have allowed significant advances in the investigational literature on tax compliance (Mascagni, 2018). As a consequence, tax administrations are investing significant resources in the development of artificial intelligence algorithms to improve tax compliance, according to a new OECD report (OECD, 2021). John McCarthy first coined the term "Artificial Intelligence". He defines it as the science and engineering of making intelligent machines (Rajaraman, 2016). In their study, Faúndez-Ugaldea et al. (2020), consider two applications of artificial intelligence, that is, taxpayers' risk and the automation of tax audit case selection. However, extraordinarily little has been detailed in the literature on how AI, exist side-by-side with taxpayers' rights. Faúndez-Ugaldea et al. (2020) report that in some countries the access to these algorithms is not clearly regulated. Furthermore, they note that general principles derived from the fundamental rights proclaimed by each country make it possible to safeguard taxpayers' right to access this information (Faúndez-Ugaldea et al, 2020).

FOCUS OF THE ARTICLE

Tax Compliance

Tax compliance refers to a taxpayer's decision to comply with tax laws and regulations by paying taxes when expected, filing returns timely and accurately (Youde & S.Lim, 2019). Factors that affecting voluntary tax compliance can be divided into five major groupings, that is, demographic factors like age, gender and education; individual factors like tax knowledge, personal financial constraints and awareness of offense and penalty (Saxunova & Szarkova, 2018); social attributes such as the perception on equity and fairness of tax system; institutional factors such as the simplicity of taxation, role of tax authority, change in government policy and referent group and the probability of being audited; and lastly economic factors corresponding to tax rate, income level, tax audit and perception on government spending (Deyganto, 2018). Honest reporting of taxable income and timely payment of tax dues are foundations of the healthy functioning of societies. However, growth in third-party data has limited the ability to misreport or falsify income (Jensen, 2022). The annual tax gap which derives from noncompliance with taxes is about $381 billion in the US (IRS, 2019) and £35 billion in the UK (HMRC, 2021). The tax administration's understanding of the drivers of tax compliance and the cost effectiveness of further interventions is critical to their ability to reduce noncompliance. To this end the Belgian tax authority conducted a series of experiments that varied their communication with taxpayers. The letters adopted by the Belgian tax administration were shown to be the most effective means of increasing tax compliance (De Neve, Imbert, Spinnewijn, Tsankova, & Luts, 2021). De Neve et al. (2021), ran four experiments for fiscal years 2014 to 2016. In this study, the communication of the tax administration to taxpayers, was changed at four stages of the tax process, namely tax filing, filing reminders, tax payment and payment reminder. In the four experiments the treatment involved simplifying the letter applicable to each process, in such a way that it communicated precisely what the tax administration expected from taxpayers. The study concluded that simplifying communication by the tax administration improved tax compliance (De Neve et al., 2021).

Psychology of Tax Compliance

According to the theory of social psychology, tax compliance behaviours is under the influence of several factors. It originates from certain reasons and emerge in a planned way (Youde & S.Lim, 2019). Tax compliance from a social psychology point of view tries to explain human behaviours towards the tax system, government, and tax authorities (Rantelangi & Majid, 2018). In general tax compliance studies are based on three theoretical models, namely, economic, psychological, and behavioural models (Nguyen, Pham, LE, Truong, & Tran, 2020). According to Nguyen et al. (2020), the probability of audit and severity of sanctions have the strongest impact on tax compliance, particularly the likelihood of being audited. There are many disciplines that have studied the tax compliance phenomenon, economics, law, accounting, and psychology.

Nevertheless, very few researchers have written on the psychology or behaviour of taxpayers towards tax compliance. The findings provided by Saad (2012), reveal that sources of income, attitude, perceived behavioural control, tax knowledge, tax complexity and perceptions of fairness by the tax authority influence tax compliance behaviour (Saad, 2012). Beer et al. (2020) noted that perceptions of fairness is positively correlated to tax compliance rather than tax rates (Beer, Kasper, Kirchler, & Erard, 2020). However, Privitera et al. (2021), found that compliance intentions are significantly correlated with perceptions of a well-functioning tax system (Privitera, Enachescu, Kirchler, & Hartmann, 2021). Additionally, other researchers found that taxpayers' psychological belief, that they could avoid paying taxes without being detected by the tax agency motivated them to continuously not comply with their tax obligations (Kasper & Alm, 2022).

In contrast, Larsen (2018), argues that to understand tax compliance and tax cheating, tax administrators must look beyond law, psychological experiments, and surveys to include tax collectors and taxpayers' practices (Larsen, 2018). Consequently, Larsen (2018), puts forward an anthropological perspective, putting an emphasis on the reciprocal relations that tax, as with any exchange, can be seen to create. Additionally, in his publication Larsen (2018), explore the view of taxpayers as citizens' explicit economic relationship with the state and implicit economic relationship with all other fellow countrymen. Such a view he argues, brings the audience straight to the core of economic anthropology (Larsen, 2018).

Thus, such an economic anthropological view would build and increase tax compliance if taxpayers and tax agencies are to take the creation of reciprocal relations through taxation seriously (Larsen, 2018). Nonetheless, tax compliance is a complex phenomenon which is influenced not just by economic motives but by psychological factors in addition (Kassa, 2021). Thus, psychological factors like tax morale, tax fairness, subjective norms, perceived behavioural control, and moral obligation are major factors impacting on tax compliance (Rantelangi & Majid, 2018).

Artificial Intelligence Aided Tax Compliance Framework

Framework Overview

In this study an Artificial Intelligence Aided Tax Compliance Framework (Figure 1) has been developed. The framework has been inspired by the Big Data Business Model Maturity Index developed by the Data Science Council of America (DASCA) (Schmarzo, 2018). It has already been stated that the AI Aided Tax Compliance framework is both an amalgamation and graphical adaptation of Big Data Business Maturity Model and some aspects have been gleaned from the OECD tax risk identification processes. The framework is designed with the objective of assisting with tax compliance case selection. Furthermore, it has been envisaged that the framework would improve the effectiveness and efficiency of tax administrations in identifying anomalies on Income Tax returns. The framework proposed herein, classify and segregate taxpayers into clusters or categories that have the greatest likelihood of noncompliance. Thus, the framework selects taxpayers for audit on the probability that they will not register on time, file on time, pay on time and declare truthfully.

Figure 1. AI Aided Tax Compliance Framework

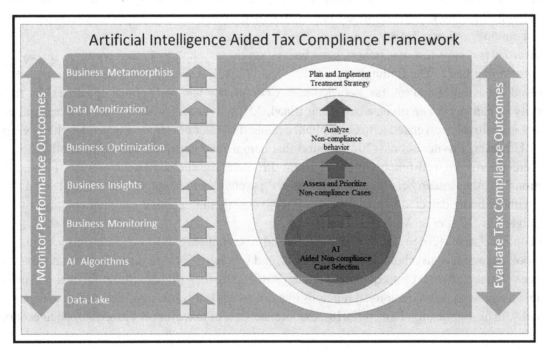

DATA ANALYSIS AND RESULTS

Data Collection

A rich data set, that is the totality of corporate income tax returns (CIT) returns covering 10 years from 2010 to 2019 is used. To delineate the data collection techniques, the chosen focus is on the telecommunications industry. Tax returns have been collected for the complete list of registered firms that were active during the same period. The firms have been anonymised in order that they cannot be connected back to any publicly available data set. Consequently, they are assigned identifying numbers so that the researchers can track a firm over time. The data contains detailed information on the line items in the corporate income tax returns. Importantly, the corporate income tax return form of the South African tax administration is called the ITR14 form. For instance, from the ITR14 dataset it was possible to acquire 26 continuous variables. For ethical and confidentiality reasons, not all these 26 variables will be listed, but only a subset, namely, Turnover, Cost of Sales, Taxable Income, Normal Tax, Table Income and Expenses (Table 1), (Table 2).

Data Preparation

According to Peck et.al (2015) data preparation is the cleansing and organizing of real-world data, which is known to take up more than 80% of the time of a data scientist's work. Real-world data or raw data is dirty, full of missing values, duplicates and in some cases erroneous information (Peck, Olsen, & Devore, 2015). Most machine-learning algorithms cannot deal with missing values. Hence, the data needs to be converted and cleansed. In order to handle missing values, rows were dropped, and then linear interpolation was applied using mean values. Depending on the importance of the variable or feature and amount of the missing values, any one of these solutions could be employed (Peck, Olsen, & Devore, 2015).

It is fortunate that the data set obtained is clean and of a high-quality. Unfortunately, the CIT return dataset was at monthly level, therefore it was necessary to sum up all variables to annual values. The aggregation of all numerical variables of the CIT return span the period 2010 to 2019. Thereafter the rand value amounts were converted into ratios for ease of comparison. It has already been stated that the details of some of the variables that are used in this study could not be reported, due to the confidential nature of the tax audit process. Doing so can increase the potential for reverse engineering of the audit process. This is clearly undesirable and unlawful. However, each CIT return ratio is designed so that a significantly higher or lower ratio value, in relation to the rest of the sample or observations, could arouse suspicion. In the opinion of Castellón et al. (2013) fraud cases are most likely to be found among the extreme values of variables.

Dataset

The telecommunication industry dataset consists of 4838 observations with 26 continuous variables. The observations are of Company Income Tax declarations filed with the South African tax administration. The dataset consists of variables that have been captured by taxpayers on the ITR14 form (Table 1), (Table 2). Due to privacy and data confidentiality concerns, the taxpayer personal information details are not presented in this study. For the same reason, the complete data description or variables cannot be shown in this paper. However, the structure of the dataset showing sample variables can be seen in Table 1 and Table 2.

Table 1. Structure of the Telecommunication Industry Dataset

ID	Turnover	Taxable Income	Normal Tax	Cost of Sales	Expenses	Gross Profit
1	R 440,830,033,374.00	R 133,344,477,590.00	R 37,336,453,725.20	R 185,044,502,778.00	R 144,881,590,649.00	R 255,785,530,596.00
2	R 325,712,763,372.00	R 45,976,984,474.00	R 12,873,555,652.72	R 139,118,478,031.00	R 150,710,119,795.00	R 186,594,285,341.00
3	R 95,855,423,393.00	R 496,854,573.00	R 139,119,280.44	R 21,014,071,385.00	R 78,876,951,826.00	R 74,841,352,008.00
4	R 72,264,085,637.00	R 4,942,946,558.00	R 1,384,025,036.24	R 57,629,068,236.00	R 14,501,578,319.00	R 14,635,017,401.00
5	R 65,130,070,578.00	R 2,311,543,501.00	R 647,232,180.28	R 60,556,471,993.00	R 3,199,077,697.00	R 4,573,598,585.00
6	R 44,545,556,158.00	R 768,268,542.00	R 215,115,191.76	R 41,892,691,162.00	R 2,109,692,354.00	R 2,652,864,996.00
7	R 19,565,447,348.00	R 1,354,031,009.00	R 379,128,682.52	R 16,689,497,901.00	R 3,200,427,668.00	R 2,875,949,447.00
8	R 15,239,654,688.00	R 2,021,074,567.00	R 565,900,878.76	R 529,395,032.00	R 14,305,437,114.00	R 14,710,259,656.00
9	R 11,621,101,618.00	R 102,012,970.00	R 28,563,631.60	R 9,799,841,172.00	R 1,626,742,893.00	R 1,821,260,446.00
10	R 11,486,136,044.00	R 516,024,807.00	R 144,486,945.96	R 10,742,142,559.00	R 435,308,229.00	R 743,993,485.00
.	.	.	.	.	.	.
.	.	.	.	.	.	.
4838						

Table 2. Dataset Variables Descriptions

Variable	Description
Turnover	Turnover is the amount of business or sales that a company makes in a period
Cost of Sales	Is how much a business spending on the products it purchases from suppliers for resale
Gross Profit	The profit a company makes after deducting the costs of making and selling its products
Taxable Income	It is the turnover plus any other income earned by the company or individual after allowable deductions
Normal Tax	Normal Tax is the amount which is paid on taxable income of either an individual or company
Expenses	Expenses incurred in the ordinary course of a business
•	•
•	•
26	26th Variable

Experiments

Data Pre-Processing

Firstly, as part of the data pre-processing, a technique is used called normalization or standardization, to rescale the input and output variables prior to training the SOM and K-means models. The purpose, of scaling the dataset, when training a model, is to normalize the data to obtain a mean close to zero (Imron & Prasetiyo, 2020). The review of the literature reveals that normalization could improve performance of the model (Imron & Prasetiyo, 2020). Normalizing the data speeds up learning and leads to faster convergence. Accordingly, mapping data to around 0 gains much faster training speed than mapping them to the intervals far away from 0 or using un-normalized raw data. This is the way in which Imran & Prasetiyo (2020) point to the importance of data normalization prior to training of a KNN algorithm.

SOM Algorithm

A self-organizing map (SOM) or self-organizing feature map (SOFM) is a type of artificial neural network (ANN). An artificial neural network is an interconnected assembly of simple processing elements, called artificial neurons (Kohonen, 1982), or units or nodes (Figure 2), (Figure 3) and (Figure 4). The SOM is trained using unsupervised learning to produce a low dimensional map. It is a discretized representation of the input space of the training samples, called a map (Figure 4). Self-organizing maps differ from other AI algorithms in that it uses competitive learning instead of error-correction learning (Kohonen, 1982). In a sense, it uses a neighbourhood function to preserve the topological properties of the input space (Bansal & Suman, 2014). During the experimental process with the SOM algorithm, the SOM was coded in R and some parameters are adjusted for an efficient execution of the algorithm.

Training a SOM

The SOM training progress plot is depicted in (Figure 5) and (Figure 6). The SOM training iterations progress is specified in the R programming language with a parameter "rlen= 500". Thus, the distance from each node's weight to the samples represented by that node is reduced. Ideally, this distance should reach a minimum plateau. The graph shows the training progress over time. If the curve is continually decreasing, more iterations are required. In this study a maximum of 500 iterations was set.

Figure 2. Kohonen SOM Neural Network Basic Structure, Source: (Araujo, Silva, & Sampaio, 2008)

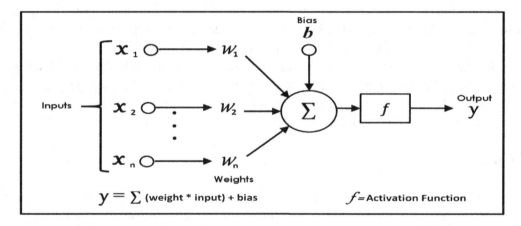

Figure 3. Neural Processing Unit (Neuron) Source: (Araujo, Silva, & Sampaio, 2008)

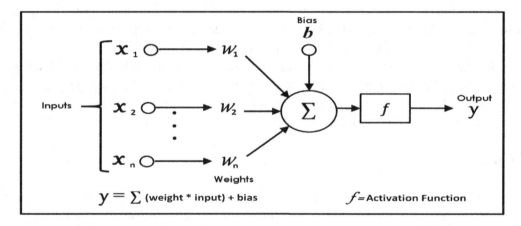

Figure 4. Two Dimensional SOM Neural Network (source: adapted from (Swarnajyoti & & Lorenzo, 2014))

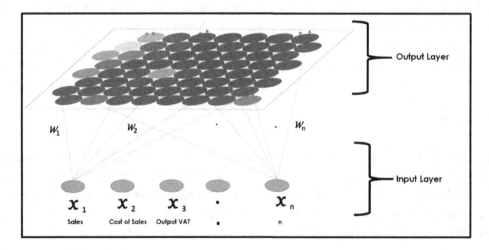

Figure 5. SOM Training Progress (9 Nodes)

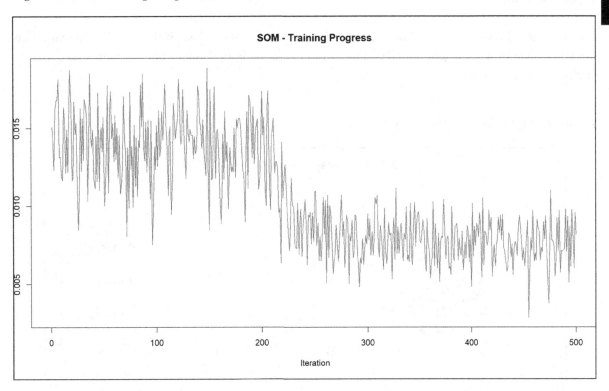

Figure 6. SOM Training Progress (16 Nodes)

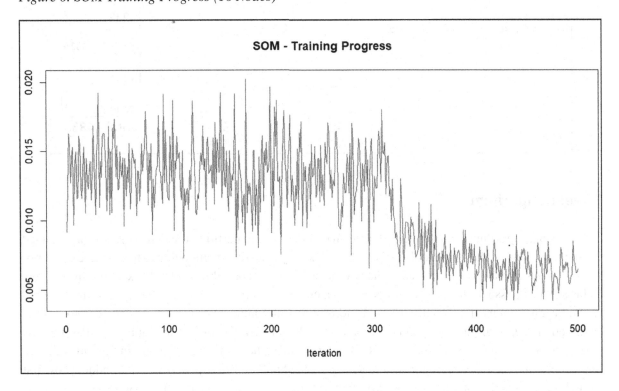

SOM Heat Map

The heat map shows the distribution of all variables across the SOM. Two SOM maps are shown which are comprised of a 3 x 3 grid and 4x4 grid, which give totals of 9 nodes and 16 nodes respectively (Figure 7) and (Figure 8).

Figure 7. SOM Similarity Heat Map (9 Nodes)

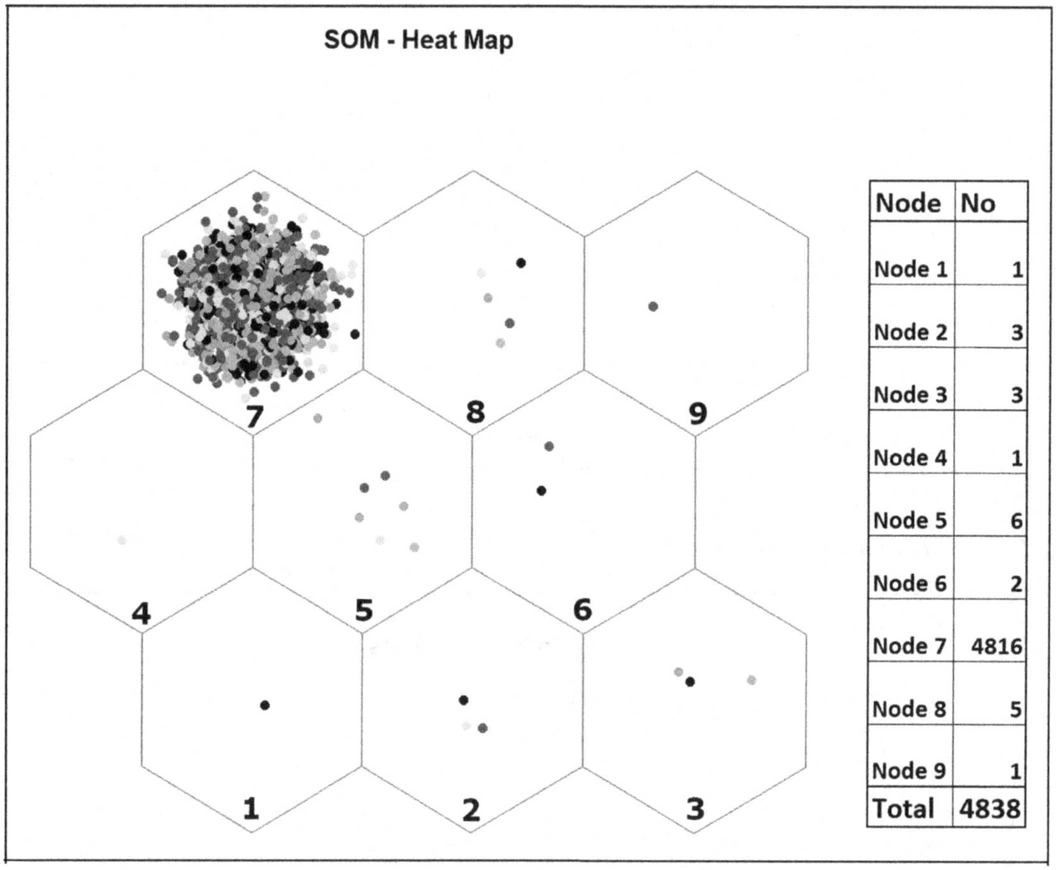

Node	No
Node 1	1
Node 2	3
Node 3	3
Node 4	1
Node 5	6
Node 6	2
Node 7	4816
Node 8	5
Node 9	1
Total	4838

K-Mean Algorithm

The K-means algorithm is an iterative algorithm that attempts to partition the dataset into K pre-defined distinct and non-overlapping number of clusters. Thereby each data point belongs to only one cluster or group. It tries to make the intra-cluster data points as similar as possible while also keeping the clusters as far apart as possible. It assigns data points to a cluster such that the sum of the squared distance between the data points and the cluster's centroid is at the minimum (Dabbura, 2018). The centroid is the arithmetic mean of all the data points that belong to that cluster. According to Dabbura (2018) the less variation there is within K-means clusters, the more similar the data points are within the same cluster. In present study the K-means algorithm was programmed in R and an experiment was conducted by first using 9 clusters and then repeated the experiment using 16 clusters (Figure 9), (Figure 10)

Figure 8. SOM Similarity Heat Map (16 Nodes)

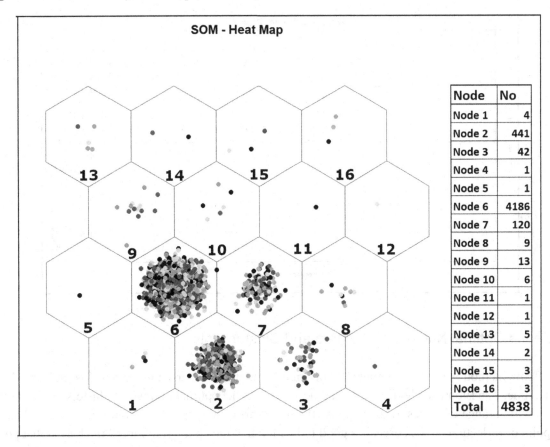

Figure 9. K-means Cluster Plot (9 Clusters)

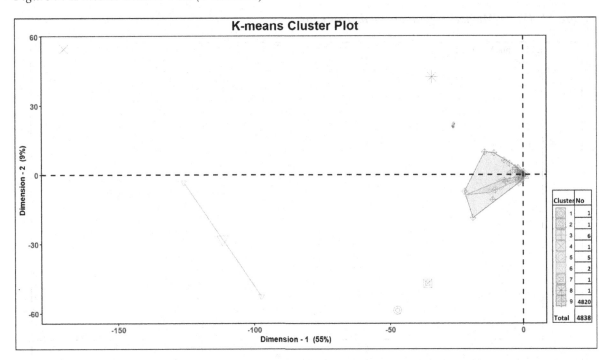

Figure 10. K-means Cluster Plot (16 Clusters)

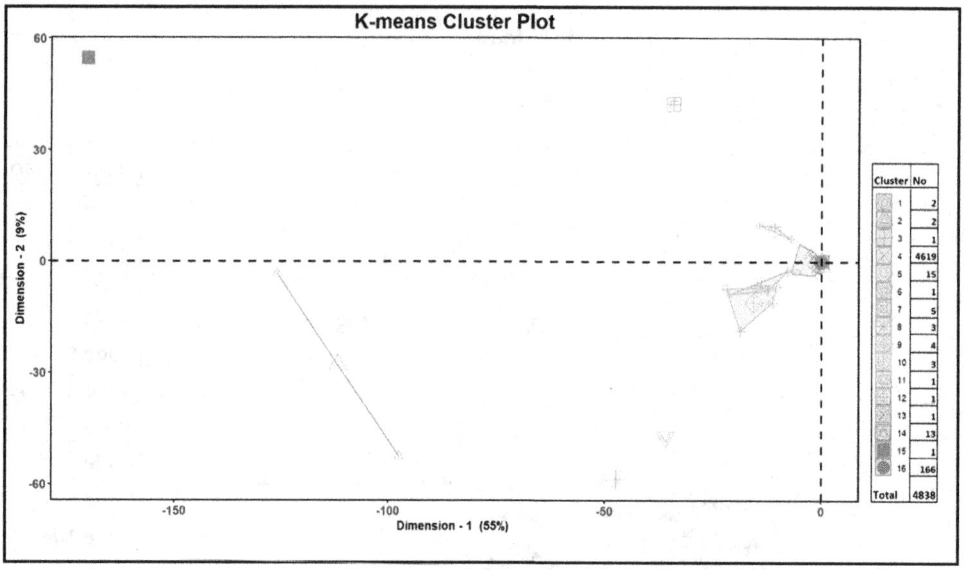

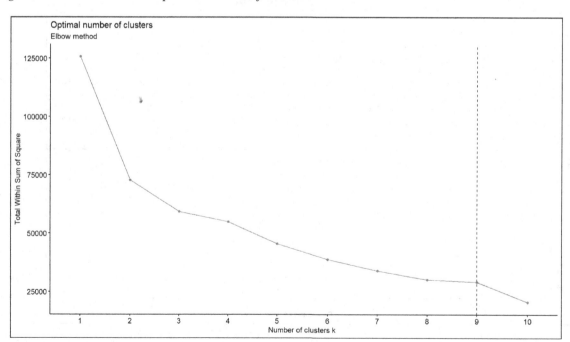

K-Means Optimal Number of Clusters and Cluster Plot

The elbow method is used to compute the optimal number of clusters. The "elbow" is indicated by a dashed line. The Elbow method helps researchers to select the optimal number of clusters by fitting the model with a range of values for **K**. Suppose the line chart resembles an arm, then the elbow, which is the point of inflection on the curve, is a good indication that the underlying model fits best at that point (Figure 11).

Figure 11. Elbow Method - Optimal Number of Clusters

Support Vector Machine (SVM)

SVM belong to a group of supervised learning methods used for classification and regression (Figure 12). They belong to a family of generalized linear classification techniques. SVM simultaneously minimize the empirical classification error and maximize the geometric margin (Durgesh & Lekha, 2010).

Figure 12. Support Vector Machine (Source: (Bahari, Ahmad, & Aboobaider, 2014))

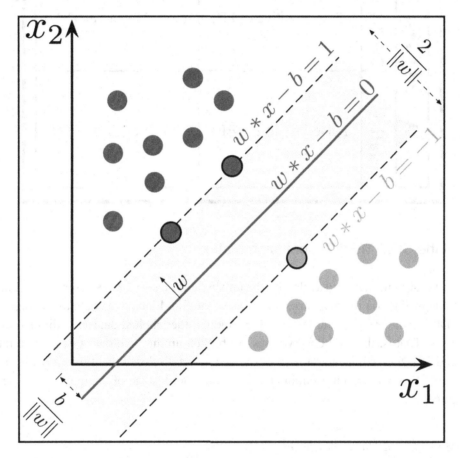

Confusion Matrix

In classification problems, the accuracy degree of a classifier algorithm cannot be considered complete unless it has been evaluated. The accuracy degree shows the congruence between the classes assigned by the sorter and the respective classes of the training dataset that it takes as reference. A typical technique used to evaluate the accuracy of a classification algorithm is called a confusion matrix or error and contingency matrix (Figure 13). This is a **nxn** matrix size, with **n** as the number of classes, with the following tabular form (Expósito, et al., 2021):

Figure 13. Confusion Matrix Basic Idea

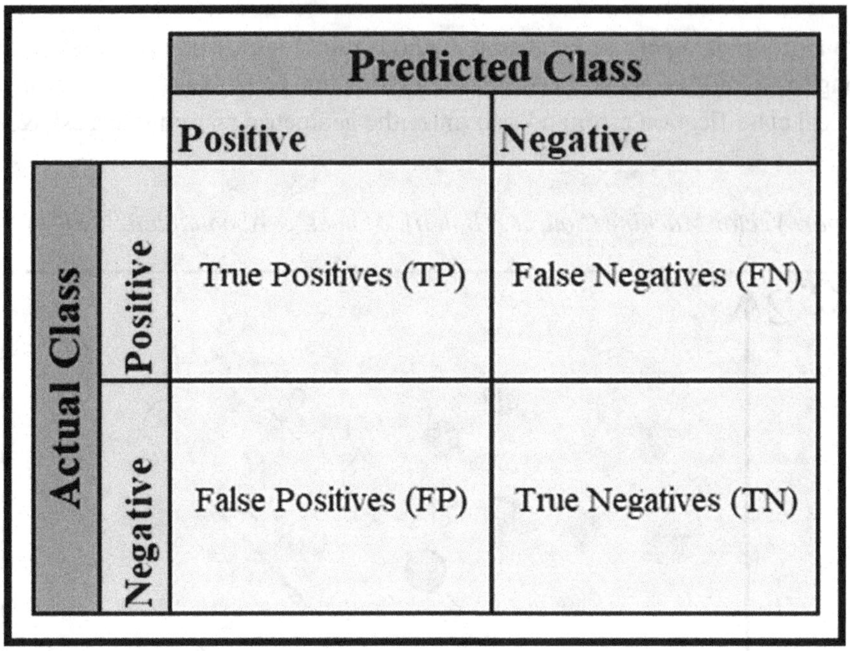

		Predicted Class	
		Positive	**Negative**
Actual Class	**Positive**	True Positives (TP)	False Negatives (FN)
	Negative	False Positives (FP)	True Negatives (TN)

Accuracy of the SOM Model - Confusion Matrix

Initially, the SOM algorithm is used to classify the unlabelled dataset of **4838** observations into **9** clusters or **16** clusters depending on the map size. Afterwards, the SOM labels the data as belonging to any of the clusters. During the training and testing of the model, the labelled dataset is divided into training and test datasets. That is, the total observations are broken up into two datasets, using a ratio of 70% for training and 30% for testing dataset. Earlier on the analyst disclosed that this study uses the Support Vector Machine (SVM) algorithm to train and test the model instead of using either of the compared methods (Figure 12).

Table 3. SOM Confusion Matrix (9 Clusters)

		Actual								
		Node 1	Node 2	Node 3	Node 4	Node 5	Node 6	Node 7	Node 8	Node 9	Total
Predicted	Node 1	0	0	0	0	0	0	0	0	0	0
	Node 2	0	0	0	0	0	0	0	0	0	0
	Node 3	0	0	1	0	0	0	0	0	0	1
	Node 4	0	0	0	0	0	0	0	0	0	0
	Node 5	0	0	0	0	0	0	0	0	0	0
	Node 6	0	0	0	0	0	0	0	0	0	0
	Node 7	0	0	0	0	1	0	1442	0	0	1443
	Node 8	0	0	0	0	0	0	0	2	0	2
	Node 9	0	0	0	0	0	0	0	0	0	0
	Total	0	0	1	0	1	0	1442	2	0	1446

Predicted correctly **1445** from a total of **1446** testing dataset observations - **99.9%** Accuracy

A

The objective of using a different algorithm is to avoid any bias during the training and testing of the compared models. Below two confusion matrices for the SOM map architecture of 9 nodes and 16 nodes are shown. The SOM model performed extremely well during testing, with a prediction accuracy rate of 99.9% using a 9 nodes map and 99.1% in a 16 nodes map. The performance and actual results of the model during testing is shown in the confusion matrix table (Table 3), (Table 4).

Table 4. SOM Confusion Matrix (16 Clusters)

		Actual															
		Node 1	Node 2	Node 3	Node 4	Node 5	Node 6	Node 7	Node 8	Node 9	Node 10	Node 11	Node 12	Node 13	Node 14	Node 15	Node 16	Total
Predicted	Node 1	1	0	0	0	0	0	0	0	0	0	0	0	0	0	0	0	1
	Node 2	0	128	0	0	0	0	3	0	0	0	0	0	0	0	0	0	131
	Node 3	0	0	16	0	0	0	0	2	0	0	0	0	0	0	0	0	18
	Node 4	0	0	0	0	0	0	0	0	0	0	0	0	0	0	0	0	0
	Node 5	0	0	0	0	0	0	0	0	0	0	0	0	0	0	0	0	0
	Node 6	1	4	0	0	0	1246	0	0	0	0	0	0	0	0	0	0	1251
	Node 7	0	0	1	0	0	0	34	0	0	0	0	0	0	0	0	0	35
	Node 8	0	0	0	0	0	0	0	3	0	0	0	0	0	0	0	0	3
	Node 9	0	0	0	0	0	0	0	0	3	0	0	0	0	0	0	0	3
	Node 10	0	0	0	0	0	1	0	0	0	1	1	0	0	0	0	0	3
	Node 11	0	0	0	0	0	0	0	0	0	0	0	0	0	0	0	0	0
	Node 12	0	0	0	0	0	0	0	0	0	0	0	0	0	0	0	0	0
	Node 13	0	0	0	0	0	0	0	0	0	0	0	0	0	0	0	0	0
	Node 14	0	0	0	0	0	0	0	0	0	0	0	0	0	0	0	0	0
	Node 15	0	0	0	0	0	0	0	0	0	0	0	0	0	0	0	0	0
	Node 16	0	0	0	0	0	0	0	0	0	0	0	0	0	0	0	1	1
	Total	2	132	17	0	0	1247	37	5	3	1	1	0	0	0	0	1	1446

Predicted correctly **1433** from a total of **1446** testing dataset observations - **99.1%** Accuracy

Accuracy of the K-means Model - Confusion Matrix

The K-means algorithm is first used to classify the original unlabelled dataset (**4838**) using two K-means experiments of 9 and 16 clusters. Subsequently, K-means labels the data as belonging to any of the identified clusters. During the R experimentation, the labelled dataset is divided into training dataset of **3392** and test dataset **1446** observations using the 70% and 30% split ratio, respectively. In 3.4.9 it was pointed out that the Support Vector Machine (SVM) algorithm is used to train and test the model instead of using either of the compared methods, and that the rationale for using a different algorithm is to avoid any bias during the training and testing of the compared models. The K-means model performed very well during testing, with a prediction accuracy rate of 99.8% using 9 clusters and 99.6% in a 16-cluster configuration. (Table 5) and (Table 6) show the performance results of the model by means of a confusion matrix for a grouping of 9 and 16 clusters.

Interpretation of the Results

SOM

Two SOM experiments were conducted one with 9 nodes and the other with 16 nodes. The spots or specks inside the nodes of the respective heat maps represents individual taxpayers or entities. In the SOM similarity heat maps above, it can be observed that taxpayers or entities, with similar return characteristics, are grouped in the same area or node (Figure 7) (Figure 8). In business, users are more interested in "abnormal clusters" or hot spots. Interest focuses on clusters of income taxpayers who have suspicious rather than those in behaviour rather than those in normal nodes or clusters.

Table 5. K-Means Confusion Matrix – 9 Clusters

		Actual								
		Cluster 1	Cluster 2	Cluster 3	Cluster 4	Cluster 5	Cluster 6	Cluster 7	Cluster 8	Cluster 9	Total
Predicted	Cluster 1	0	0	0	0	0	0	0	0	0	0
	Cluster 2	0	0	0	0	0	0	0	0	0	0
	Cluster 3	0	0	0	0	0	0	0	0	0	0
	Cluster 4	0	0	0	0	0	0	0	0	0	0
	Cluster 5	0	0	0	0	0	0	0	0	0	0
	Cluster 6	0	0	0	1	0	0	0	0	0	1
	Cluster 7	0	0	0	0	0	0	0	0	0	0
	Cluster 8	0	0	0	0	0	0	0	0	0	0
	Cluster 9	0	0	1	0	0	0	0	1	1443	1445
	Total	**0**	**0**	**1**	**1**	**0**	**0**	**0**	**1**	**1443**	**1446**

Predicted correctly **1443** from a total of **1446** testing dataset observations - **99.8%** Accuracy

Table 6. K-Means Confusion Matrix – 16 Clusters

		Actual																
		Cluster 1	Cluster 2	Cluster 3	Cluster 4	Cluster 5	Cluster 6	Cluster 7	Cluster 8	Cluster 9	Cluster 10	Cluster 11	Cluster 12	Cluster 13	Cluster 14	Cluster 15	Cluster 16	Total
Predicted	Cluster 1	0	0	0	0	0	0	0	0	0	0	0	0	0	0	0	0	0
	Cluster 2	0	0	0	0	0	0	0	0	0	0	0	0	0	0	1	0	1
	Cluster 3	0	0	0	0	0	0	0	0	0	0	0	0	0	0	0	0	0
	Cluster 4	0	0	0	1377	0	0	0	0	1	0	0	0	0	0	0	3	1381
	Cluster 5	0	0	0	0	7	0	0	0	0	0	0	0	0	0	0	0	7
	Cluster 6	0	0	0	0	0	0	0	0	0	0	0	0	0	0	0	0	0
	Cluster 7	0	0	0	0	0	0	0	0	0	0	0	0	0	0	0	0	0
	Cluster 8	0	0	0	0	0	0	0	0	0	0	0	0	0	0	0	0	0
	Cluster 9	0	0	0	0	0	0	0	0	0	0	0	0	0	0	0	0	0
	Cluster 10	0	0	0	0	0	0	0	0	0	1	0	1	0	0	0	0	2
	Cluster 11	0	0	0	0	0	0	0	0	0	0	0	0	0	0	0	0	0
	Cluster 12	0	0	0	0	0	0	0	0	0	0	0	0	0	0	0	0	0
	Cluster 13	0	0	0	0	0	0	0	0	0	0	0	0	0	0	0	0	0
	Cluster 14	0	0	0	0	0	0	0	0	0	0	0	0	0	3	0	0	3
	Cluster 15	0	0	0	0	0	0	0	0	0	0	0	0	0	0	0	0	0
	Cluster 16	0	0	0	0	0	0	0	0	0	0	0	0	0	0	0	52	52
	Total	0	0	0	1377	7	0	0	0	1	1	0	1	0	3	1	55	1446

Predicted correctly 1440 from a total of 1446 testing dataset observations - **99.6%** Accuracy

The means that this study uses to identify hot spots is by using the Heat map. Thus, when interpreting the ANN-SOM Heat map the abnormal clusters are those that have a fewer number of entities viz Nodes 1,2,3 (Figure 7). This means that these nodes are composed of taxpayers with doubtful returns. Such firms require detailed human verification by tax audit specialists. Node 7 in Figure 7, and Node 6 in Figure 8, both have the largest number of entities clustered together. The taxpayers clustered in these nodes are relatively homogeneous in nature, and thus depicts entities with normal behaviour. Suspicious taxpayer behaviour can be differentiated by scrutinizing the company financial statements, sales and purchases invoices and comparing with them the tax return attributes such as Turnover, Normal Tax, Cost of Sales and VAT to name just a few variables of interests.

K-Means

Likewise, the K-means algorithm was used to produce one plot with 9 clusters and the other with 16 clusters. The spots inside the clusters of the respective plots represent individual taxpayers. In the K-means plots it can be observed that taxpayers or entities, with similar tax return characteristics, are grouped in the same cluster. Cluster 9 in Figure 9, and Cluster 4 in Figure 10 have the highest concentrations of taxpayers, which can be assumed to constitute normal behaviour filing patterns. In business, key stakeholders are more interested in abnormal clusters or hot spots. That is, clusters of income taxpayers who have suspicious behaviour than normal nodes or clusters. Taxpayers that constitute outliers that require further human scrutiny are found in the clusters that have significantly fewer entities e.g., Clusters 1 to 8 in Figure 9 and Clusters 1,2,3,5, 6, 7 etc in Figure 10.

CONCLUSION AND RECOMMENDATION

In the first experiment the SOM algorithm with a grid made up of 9 nodes, performed almost the same as a K-means algorithm also composed of 9 clusters. The prediction accuracy rate of the SOM was 99.9% and 99.8%. The second experiment was conducted using a larger number of nodes and clusters. It used a SOM map of 16 Nodes and a K-means algorithm of 16 clusters. It was found that the difference in prediction accuracy between the two is negligible, at 99.1% by the SOM and 99.6% from K-means. Moreover, it is perceived that a k-means is the simpler unsupervised learning algorithm compared to a SOM. K-means follows a simple and easy way to classify a given data set through a certain number of clusters and has a low computational cost. The only shortcoming of K-means is that the value of K, which is the number of clusters must be determined ahead of time.

Choosing the number of K clusters can be difficult even if the analyst has a static data set and previous domain knowledge about the data. Similarly, a noted drawback of a SOM is that when datasets are massive and the corresponding maps are large, then training can be a time-consuming process. Put differently, the K-means algorithm is computational efficient and runs faster than a SOM if the number of clusters increases. However, it was found that a K-means is more sensitive to the noise present in the dataset compared to a SOM. In the experiment conducted by Riveros et al. (2019) the model trained with SOM outperformed the model trained with K-means. In their study they found that the SOM improved the identification of patients having vertebral problems (Riveros, Cardenas, & Pico, 2019).

This study has demonstrated the use of ANN-SOM and K-means in exploring clusters and hotspots in a large real-world corporate income tax (CIT) domain. Based on these experiments, the framework combined with the SOM was to be an effective instrument for hot spots and heat map exploration since it employs visualizations techniques that are easy to understand. Auditing returns for tax compliance is a slow and costly process that is very prone to errors. Now, most tax administrations' audit strategy is to randomly select tax returns for audit. In some instance the tax agency selects cases for audit based on inconsistent information on tax returns and the frequency of non-compliance by certain taxpayers. However, the major downside of the random selection technique is that it treats both honest and dishonest taxpayers equally, for the reason that, in a random audit the probability of being selected for audit for both groups is the same.

Nonetheless, it is envisaged that the framework and techniques proposed herein, will significantly reduce the tax administrations' costs relating to the auditing of noncompliant taxpayers. In that, the artificial intelligence aided techniques that have been put forward will increase the detection of noncompliers and drive detection and auditing costs down. This is because the number of cases that are likely to require a detailed human verification and validation of the taxpayer's financial records will be reduced. Since the scope of the human verification required, is limited to the subset of taxpayers that have been flagged as anomalies by the SOM algorithm which is the preferred algorithm in the present work. It is proposed that the effectiveness and efficiency of the methods presented in this report, will enhance the detection of suspicious taxpayers. Consequently, it is anticipated that tax compliance will improve as the fear of detection increases. In future, different profiling or clustering algorithms and sampling techniques can be applied to further improve the performance of the approach proposed herein. Furthermore, the hybrid algorithms may produce higher quality research outcomes

FUTURE RESEARCH

Detection of suspicions noncompliant declarations is a very challenging task as income tax dataset are extremely unbalanced in nature. Furthermore, the tax fraud and noncompliance domain are full of unlabeled data, which in turn makes it difficult to use supervised learning approaches. In this research paper, the efficiency and efficacy of two unsupervised learning approaches were compared. Whatever methods are used it is crucial to have all-encompassing views and strategies on detecting tax noncompliance. Therefore, it is necessary to broaden the understanding and knowledge of the tax noncompliance phenomenon among researchers. Now supervised learning algorithms have proved to be of limited use in the arena of income tax noncompliance detection, since the tax administrations have extremely low to non-existent labelled historic data. This situation in turn cripples the effectiveness of supervised learning approaches.

In as much as this paper's focus was on the comparison of the predictive capability of the SOM and K-means algorithms on corporate income tax (CIT) compliance, the author is confident that the present model together with the algorithms tested herein are applicable to other tax types like Personal Income Tax (PIT), Value Added Tax (VAT) and Customs duties. The outcomes of this research show the potential of artificial intelligence techniques in the realm of corporate income tax noncompliance. Furthermore, this study has proposed a high-level and detailed classification framework on corporate income tax noncompliance, which presents tax auditors with a systemic case selection guide for the identification of suspicious income tax returns.

Furthermore, the author asserts that combining the two algorithms, that is, ANN-SOM and K-means into a single hybrid approach can improve the success of detecting tax noncompliance schemes. Tax administrations may be able to select the most appropriate unsupervised learning technique from this work having considered other alternatives, their operational requirements and business context. This approach could lead to a multitude of available Artificial Intelligence aided tax noncompliance detection algorithms and approaches. Additionally, the techniques proposed in this paper will help tax administrations with precise case selection using an empirical and data-driven approach, which does not depend upon labelled historic tax declarations. Furthermore, it is envisaged that this approach will improve hit rates on suspicious income tax returns, and thus improve tax compliance due to increased likelihood of detection.

REFERENCES

Agyeiwa, H., Amankwaah, E., Abina, S., Kwaku, A., Agyei, N., & Antwi, K. (2019). An empirical assessment of tax knowledge, socio-economic characteristics and their effects on tax compliance behaviour in Sunyani Municipality, Ghana. *Journal of Emerging Trends in Economics and Management Sciences.*

Araujo, E., Silva, C., & Sampaio, D. (2008). Video Target Tracking by using Competitive Neural Networks. *WSEAS Transactions on Signal Processing*, *4*(8), 420–431.

Bahari, N., Ahmad, A., & Aboobaider, B. (2014). Application of Support Vector Machine for classification of multispectral data. *IOP Conferences Series:Earth and Environmental Science*, 1-8.

Bandara, K. G., & Weerasooriya, W. M. (2019). A Conceptual Research Paper on Tax Compliance and Its relationships. *International Journal of Business and Management*, *14*(10).

Bansal, M., & Suman. (2014). Credit Card Fraud Detection Using Self Organised Map. *International Journal of Information & Computation Technology*, *4*(13).

Battiston, P., & Gamba, S. (2016). The impact of social pressure on tax compliance: A field experiment. *International Review of Law and Economics*, *46*, 78–85. doi:10.1016/j.irle.2016.03.001

Beer, S., Kasper, M., Kirchler, E., & Erard, B. (2020). Do audits deter or provoke future tax noncompliance? Evidence on self-employed taxpayers. *CESifo Economic Studies*, *66*(3), 248–264. doi:10.1093/cesifo/ifz018

Bergman, M., & Nevarez, A. (2005, February). Evadir o Pagar Impuestos. Una Aproxi- mación a los Mecanismos Sociales del Cumplimiento. *Política y Gobierno*, *12*(1), 9–40.

Bimo, I., Prasetyo, C., & Susilandari, C. (2019). The effect of internal control on tax avoidance: The case of Indonesia. *Journal of Economic Development*, *21*(2).

Dabbura, I. (2018). *K-means Clustering: Algorithm, Applications, Evaluation Methods, and Drawbacks.* Retrieved July 7, 2020, from https://towardsdatascience.com: https://towardsdatascience.com/k-means-clustering-algorithm-applications-evaluation-methods-and-drawbacks-aa03e644b48a

De Neve, J. D., Imbert, C., Spinnewijn, J., Tsankova, T., & Luts, M. (2021). How to Improve Tax Compliance? Evidence from Population-Wide Experiments in Belgium. *Journal of Political Economy*, *129*(5), 1425–1463. doi:10.1086/713096

Deyganto, K. (2018). Universal Journal of Accounting and Finance. *Universal Journal of Accounting and Finance*, *6*(3), 92–107.

Faúndez-Ugaldea, A., Mellado-Silva, R., & Aldunate-Lizanaa, E. (2020). Use of artificial intelligence by tax administrations: An analysis regarding taxpayers' rights in Latin American countries. *Computer Law & Security Review*, *38*, 38. doi:10.1016/j.clsr.2020.105441

Flach, P. (2012). Machine Learning:The Art and Science of Algorithms that Make Sense of Data. Cambridge University Press. doi:10.1017/CBO9780511973000

HMRC. (2021). *Measuring tax gaps 2021 edition - tax gap estimates for 2019 to 2020.* HMRC.

Imron, M., & Prasetiyo, B. (2020). Improving Algorithm Accuracy K-Nearest Neighbor Using Z-Score Normalization and Particle Swarm Optimization to Predict Customer Churn. *Journal of Soft Computing Exploration*, *1*(1), 56–62.

IRS. (2019). *Understanding the latest Tax Gap estimates and overall taxpayer compliance.* IRS.

Jellis, V., David, M., & Bruno, P. (2020). Value added tax fraud detection with scalable anomaly detection techniques. *Applied Soft Computing*.

Jenkins, M. (2018). *Corruption risks in tax administration, external audits and national statistics.* Transparency International. Retrieved from https://knowledgehub.transparency.org/assets/uploads/helpdesk

Jensen, A. (2022). Employment Structure and the Rise of the Modern Tax System. *The American Economic Review*, *112*(1), 213–234. doi:10.1257/aer.20191528

Kasper, M., & Alm, J. (2022). Audits, audit effectiveness, and post-audit tax compliance. *Journal of Economic Behaviour adn. Organization*, *195*, 87–102.

Kassa, E. (2021). Factors influencing taxpayers to engage in tax evasion: Evidence from Woldia City administration micro, small, and large enterprise taxpayers. *Journal of Innovation and Entrepreneurship*, *10*(8), 8. doi:10.118613731-020-00142-4

Kohonen, T. (1982). Self-organized formation of topologically correct feature maps. *Biological Cybernetics*, *43*(1), 59–69. doi:10.1007/BF00337288

Krishnamurthya, R., & Desouza, K. C. (2014). Big data analytics: The case of the social security administration. *Information Polity*, *19*(1), 165–178. doi:10.3233/IP-140337

Lamantia, F., & Pezzino, M. (2021). Social norms and evolutionary tax compliance. *Manchester School*, *89*(4), 385–405. doi:10.1111/manc.12368

Larsen, L. (2018). *A Fair Share of Tax: A Fiscal Anthropology of Contemporary Sweden.* Springer Nature. doi:10.1007/978-3-319-69772-7

Luttmer, E., & Singhal, M. (2014). Tax Morale. *The Journal of Economic Perspectives*, *28*(4), 143–168. doi:10.1257/jep.28.4.149

Mascagni, G. (2018). From the Lab to the Field: A Review of Tax Experiments. *Journal of Economic Surveys*, *32*(2), 273–301. doi:10.1111/joes.12201

Mayshar, J. (1991). Taxation with Costly Administration. *The Scandinavian Journal of Economics*, *93*(1), 75–88. doi:10.2307/3440422

Netek, R., Pour, T., & Slezakova, R. (2018). Implementation of Heat Maps in Geographical Information System – Exploratory Study on Traflc Accident Data. *Journal of Geosciences (Prague)*, *10*, 367–384.

Nguyen, T., Pham, T., Le, T., Truong, T., & Tran, M. (2020). Determinants Influencing Tax Compliance: The Case of Vietnam. *Journal of Asian Finance, Economics and Business, 7*(2), 65-73.

Nkundabanyanga, S., Mvura, P., Nyamuyonjo, D., Opiso, J., & Nakabuye, Z. (2017). Tax compliance in a developing country: Understanding taxpayers' compliance decision by their perceptions. *Journal of Economic Studies (Glasgow, Scotland)*, *44*(6), 931–957. doi:10.1108/JES-03-2016-0061

OECD. (2014). *Compliance Risk Management: Management and Improving Tax Compliance*. Organisation for Economic Co-operation and Development.

OECD. (2021). *Tax Administration: Comparative Information on OECD and Other Advanced and Emerging Economies*. OECD.

Peck, R., Olsen, C., & Devore, L. (2015). *Introduction to Statistics and Data Analysis* (5th ed.). Brokes Cole.

Privitera, A., Enachescu, J., Kirchler, E., & Hartmann, A. (2021). Emotions in Tax Related Situations Shape Compliance Intentions: A Comparison between Austria and Italy. *Journal of Behavioral and Experimental Economics*, *92*, 101698. Advance online publication. doi:10.1016/j.socec.2021.101698

Rahmayanti, N. P., Sutrisno, T., & Prihatiningtias, T. (2020). Effect of tax penalties, tax audit, and taxpayers awareness on corporate taxpayers' compliance moderated by compliance intentions. *International Journal of Research in Business and Social Science, 9*(2), 118-124.

Rajaraman, V. (2016). The True Father of Artificial Intelligence. *Resonance, 19*(3), 198-207. Retrieved from https://www.bbvaopenmind.com/: https://www.bbvaopenmind.com/en/technology/artificial-intelligence/the-true-father-of-artificial-intelligence/

Rantelangi, C., & Majid, N. (2018). Factors that Influence the Taxpayers Perception on the Tax Evasion. *Advances in Economics, Business and Management Research, 35*.

Riveros, N., Espitia, B., & Pico, L. (2019). Comparison between K-means and Self-Organizing Maps algorithms used for diagnosis spinal column patients. *Informatics in Medicine Unlocked*, *16*, 100206. Advance online publication. doi:10.1016/j.imu.2019.100206

Saad, N. (2012). Tax non-compliance behaviour: Taxpayers view. *Procedia: Social and Behavioral Sciences*, *65*, 344–351. doi:10.1016/j.sbspro.2012.11.132

Saxunova, D., & Szarkova, R. (2018). Global Efforts of Tax Authorities and Tax Evasion Challenge. *Journal of Eastern Europe Research in Business and Economics*, 1-14.

Schmarzo, B. (2018). *The Data Science Handbook*. John Wiley & Sons.

Swarnajyoti, B., & Lorenzo, P. (2014). A novel SOM-SVM based active learning technique for remote sensing image classification. *IEEE Transactions on Geoscience and Remote Sensing*, *52*(11), 6899–6910. doi:10.1109/TGRS.2014.2305516

Thudumu, S., Branch, P., Jin, J., & Singh, J. (2020). A comprehensive survey of anomaly detection techniques for high dimensional big data. *Journal of Big Data*, *7*(42), 42. doi:10.118640537-020-00320-x

Vanhoeyveld, J., Martens, D., & Peeters, B. (2019, October 31). Value-added tax fraud detection with scalable anomaly detection techniques. *Applied Soft Computing*, *86*, 1–20.

Youde, S., & Lim, S. (2019). *Tax Compliance*. Springer.

Zwick, E. (2021). The Costs of Corporate Tax Complexity. *American Economic Journal, 13*(2), 467–500.

Analyzing the Significance of Learner Emotions Using Data Analytics

Shanmugasundaram Hariharan

(iD) https://orcid.org/0000-0001-9686-4329

Vardhaman College of Engineering, India

Magdalene Delighta Angeline D.

(iD) https://orcid.org/0000-0002-0699-9105

Joginpally B. R. Engineering College, India

Ramasubramanian Perumal

Shadan Women's College of Engineering and Technology, India

Samuel PeterJames I.

Independent Researcher, India

INTRODUCTION

Emotional Intelligence is a precondition for developing a good rapport with a group of learners, which subsequently can be the basis for producing learners having more rendezvous, a speediness to work together, a larger eagerness to seize menaces in their learning, a more positive approach, better inspiration, more resourcefulness and more stubbornness. The essential things to be done while using EI in teaching are competent to distinguish and react to own emotions and those of the learners in the learning environment so as to formulate more effectual in each one's individual roles and also to persuade an emotional state in the learners which is favorable to learning as noted in (Peng et al., 2021).

Work described for emotional practice by (Tam et al., 2021) suggests a key task in learning and is an imperative constituent of each school deeds described (Pekrun & Schutz, 2007). Instructor ought to be in control of their emotions and reveal a great covenant of awareness of their learners which can be developed through self-analysis of concert by recognizing potencies and constraints. The instructor has to discover the practices that facilitate both positive and negative emotions throughout teaching and learning environment by (Kaur et al., 2021). Motivation is an inner aspiration to accomplish intentions that are set out during teaching time. High EI of instructor helps them to understand themselves as well as learners. The instructor has to develop circumstances that help out augment group vibrant, initiate activities that endorse effectual rapports among learners and also improving involvement management throughout every subject and offer errands to dissimilar learners.

Academic unease embraces problems such as learning obscurity or disabilities, lack of awareness from instructors, discrimination and underachievement, have an effect on a number of learners all through their academic careers. Academic unease persuades a learner's performance in the learning environment negatively, but they are also expected to have a noteworthy consequence on other areas of life, frequently placing excessive trauma on a learner and inquisitive with work, home and play aspects. A learner who experiences several sorts of academic disquiets possibly will promote from communication to an intel-

DOI: 10.4018/978-1-7998-9220-5.ch156

lectual wellbeing expert. Distress of an academic environment recount to a learner's performance in the learning environment, but they valor too comprise a learner's actions toward instructors or associated learners. A few archetypal academic unease embrace: Learning disabilities, lack of concern in subjects, Lack of appropriate concentration, discrimination at learning environment, bewilderment regarding or misinterpretation of subject, less accomplishment in studies and time managing concerns.

Emotion has a substantial influence on the cognitive processes in humans, including perception, attention, learning, memory, reasoning, and problem solving. Emotion has a particularly strong influence on attention, especially modulating the selectivity of attention as well as motivating action and behavior (Chai et al., 2017). The emotions can be wide-ranging appropriate to the situations faced by the learner inside and outside the learning environment with observations noted in (Samuel et al., 2015). The diverse examinations in the educational viewpoint have exposed that low levels of EI deficiently persuade learner academic attainment as detailed out (Alavinia & Mollahossein, 2012; Costa, 2015).

Recently, several research studies on EI and academic achievement analyzed the results using the techniques like multiple regression. This has emphasized on the emotional construction of positive self-concept learning strategies leading to success in educational environments, social as well as emotional situations. Covid'19 have a greater impact of the learners' learning as the learners' undergoing stressful emotional context. The alternative educational methods facilitated modernism and creativeness in both educators and learners (Yustina, 2020), probably owing to the examination of novel learning methodologies in a diverse educational situation as noted down (Patston, 2020). The pandemic has employed researchers, and facilitators in the growth of digital pedagogy in teaching-learning process. Furthermore, facilitator–learner relationships were personalized, because covid'19 hard-pressed facilitators in the direction of an approach with more stress on learner interests by (Hamilton et al., 2020).

For illustration, an increase in facilitator support and encouragement was recognized throughout the epidemic as mentioned (Daniel, 2020). Consequently, this could further assist learner fine-tuning, interests and academic achievement as described (Lan et al., 2019; Will, 2020). In relation it would be fascinating to scrutinize whether this will last in the post-COVID-19 period is reciprocated by (Chamizo et al., 2021). The COVID-19 pandemic enforced abundant amends to learning. It is imperative to adapt to the newest technologies in the learning process inducing the positive attitude towards the learning overcoming the stressful learning environment. The proposed work implemented in the classroom learning environment helps to identify the learner's emotions even after the stressful situation. The advantage of the proposed work is that it can assist the instructor to know the learners' emotions and direct them towards the positive learning path. The proposed work analyzed the impact of positive and negative emotions in academic achievement utilizing data analytic tools to attain better decisions from the huge volume of data noted down (Ndawo, 2021). The accuracy of the implemented work is measured using Cronbach's Alpha reliability analysis with a reliability coefficient of 0.95 stating that the internal consistency is excellent.

BACKGROUND

Educators and learners were push, nearly suddenly, into an education model with which few had experience narrated down (Doukakis & Alexopoulos, 2020). At the same time as the principal ambition of higher education is academic progression, there is also social and emotional development that takes place during the learning experience and contributes to a learner's success both at learning environment and outside. With over 20 million learners enrolled in higher education, it is imperative to comprehend the developmental method that take place throughout the higher education experience. Modern definitions of emotion have either accentuated the exterior stimuli that activate emotion, or the interior replies engaged in the emotional situation as noted in the work (Levine, 2007). There has been an examination done to find out the pandemic impacted education systems and educational opportunity for students recorded in the work by (Reimers et al., 2022). Digital method of learning stress on the knowledge and abilities required to sustain learners' engagement, learning and well-being in digital environments as briefed in (Greenhow et al., 2020).

According to (Pekrun & Schutz, 2007), the Emotional Intelligence (EI) is concerning on productivity and performance that can be developed and measured. The performance in the academic can be enhanced reducing the emotions of the learners. It is very imperative to have the ability to balance the emotions and high emotions are to be noticed. This engages the pragmatic triangle of thoughts, emotions and actions. Also, the performance in the academic depends on many dissimilar aspects like student's cognitive abilities, emotional intelligence, curriculum, socio-economic status, learning environments, dwelling environments, and instructional materials. A wider range of studies have affirmed that Emotional Intelligence of the students plays a decisive role in their academic performance.

In the modern era, there has been escalating awareness in understanding the association between cognition and emotion in educational and psychological contexts, emphasizing how the interrelation between cognitive and emotional indulgence have an effect on public and academic amendment as illustrated by (Biljana et al., 2017). A lot of investigations connecting teacher self-efficacy and EI are undergoing. Self-efficacy is depicted as referring to the teacher's capability to rely on their individual to deal with crisis, resolve troubles and convey concerning learning amid learners. In the teaching-learning process, emotional aspects play a vital role. EI is defined as the capability to recognize exactly, assess and articulate emotion, the capability to understand emotion and emotional knowledge monitor, perceive, recognize, reason about, and understand emotions, and to use emotions to guide actions, solve problems, enhance thought, and promote growth and the capability to control emotions to endorse emotional and intellectual growth with influence of emotion on learning procedures. Knowledge is an indispensable entity which is required among all (Pekrun, 2021).

Various research has been conducted on the learners' learning. Problem-Based Learning (PBL) and Project-Based Learning (PjBL) let the students to have a few precious classroom activities like carrying out the research, incorporating both theory and practice at the same time, and applying the knowledge and skill in solving the problems that indirectly make the independent students outlined (Temes, 2014). In other research work, the Emotional-Based Approach (EBA) is realized to augment the EI of learners, mostly in realistic areas of study where group capability is normally elapsed. The present study focuses on the relationship between teachers' emotions, their instructional behavior, and students' emotions in class as recorded by (Becker et al., 2014). Concentrating on the individual variations as learners and understanding the learners is a very decisive crisis faced by the instructor. The method of teaching necessitates knowledge, cognition and expertise that develop into an emotional action. Therefore, having a proficiency to understand and cope with emotional knowledge to develop EI is an imperative part of an instructor perpetrate. Besides, the learning environment is modernized for more competent educational succession as it spotlights on the vivacious and relations among the learner, instructor, content and services and technologies.

The success in learning is reliant on cognitive ability, rational skill and the capability to preserve strong associations and legalize emotions creating a basic necessitate for the improvement and realization of courses and practices with the development of equally the cognitive and non-cognitive proficiencies of learners. The learners emotions and with text has been a major study in recent years which is recorded in

(Mingyong et al., 2022). By means of EI measurements and tools, instructors can find out the learners' parts of EI that requires intensification. It is too essential to comprehend the knowledge, both within and exterior of the learning environment that can aid in raising a learner's EI. The preponderance of investigation in the area of EI is learners centered on the rapports amid EI and academic accomplishment. Many investigations have revealed that EI is essential to the growth of learners and educational accomplishment.

By means of EI evaluations and tools, supervisors and instructors can find out the learners' areas of EI which require intensification. It is also vital to recognize the experiences, together within and outside of the learning environment that can aid in increasing a learner's EI. Earlier studies (Van Rooy & Viswesvaran, 2007 & Hasninin et al., 2021) exposed that positive emotions will develop learning by growing motivation and enhancing trouble solving, but others have confirmed the opposite consequence whereby positive emotions are jointly related to learning. A study accomplished by (Samuel et al., 2015) expected that EI was allied with educational performance everywhere group with high EI would carry out higher rationally. Another study recommended the requisite to incorporate EI direction-finding into educational action course of study by extraction and visualization detection approach by (Hasnine et al., 2021). Another author scrutinized the educational obligation of instructors in ascertaining and accomplishing novel exertion forms of teaching (Calkins & Bell, 2010). EI is measured to be the key factor in accomplishing the life objectives which is the basis for inspiration, information and novelty.

Accordingly, EI is useful not only for inspiring learners' learning consequences, but also for improving learners' life objectives (Landy, 2005). EI has been endorsed as an individual disparity changeable that engages in recreations in formative accomplishment in a variety of kinds of individual performance and can be further extended to some point (Van Rooy & Viswesvaran, 2007). The colloborative learning normally finds various affective conditions. In another research, the associations amid EI and instructor efficiency are derived, to a huge amount, from the task of emotions in teaching and in instructors' expert lives and modern attempts to remedy the disregard of emotions in the area of teaching helped recognize this part by (Tiina et al., 2021). The majority of investigation in the area of EI of college learners is centered on the associations among EI and academic attainment.

The learners spent most of the time in the educational institution from where a variety of proficiencies reckoned and appropriate for them to attain achievement in the worldwide. The learning environment is where they will get a perceptive of their position in the world where the learner widens their vision of future, in addition to acquaintance of the dexterities required to attain that ambition. With the intention of obtaining utmost effectiveness in education, much more attention should be given to the learning environment. An eminence learning environment has to be premeditated to sustain all learners in their learning process, and instructors. Appraising the emotional elements in any circumstances, whether it is positive or negative, will help keep the learners betrothed and facilitate the instructor to well again recognize their activities and present state of mind. This research work identifies the relationship between the learners learning and emotion impacted on education.

PROPOSED WORK

The research methodology adopted for this research utilized both qualitative and quantitative data for analyzing learners learning with EI.

Figure 1. Emotion recognition in the learning environment

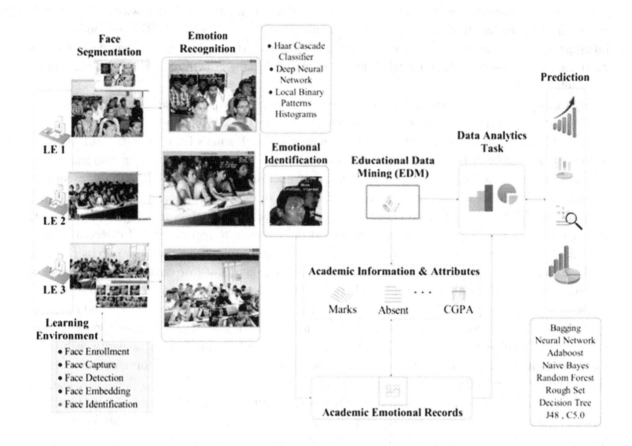

Figure.1 illustrates the process of identifying emotions in the learning environment. Originally, the practice is executed in two stages: training and testing phase. The weight value of each image is spawned during training phase and the testing image is used to make out the emotion of the learner in testing phase. The video input is detained in the learning environment. From the detained video, the face detection is achieved with Haar Cascade Classifier, which a face detector model to perceive face locations.

Subsequently skin segmentation aids in distinguishing the potential regions enclosing the frontal faces and codes every frame relating to 21 emotions: gratitude, contentment, happy, enthusiasm, interest, inspiration, self-control, imaginative, pleasure, hope, anger, detached, irritated, depression, frightened, dependent, antagonistic, anxiety, discouraged, bored and irresponsible. The facial features from the video source is hauled out and mapped with the essential emotions and the yield will be the emotion detection. To recognize the emotion of a face, Naive Bayes algorithm is utilized. From the perceived emotions, the learners with negative emotions are recognized and learning is done equally.

Emotional Based Academic Performance

Next technique exploited webcam to detain the individual learner's face which is then agreed to the anticipated method to scrutinize the emotions of each learner. The populace of the investigation is 10,648 and it is accomplished with 120 learners. The dataset were devised with EBLE and Multi Assessment Method (MAM) where dissimilar learning practices were exploited to haul out the concluding upshots.

The inspected factors like models of Emotional Based- Learning (EBL) and EI are grouped under two kinds: positive and negative. Dissimilar emotions of the learner in the three special learning environments are attained to scrutinize the upshot of a learner. Furthermore, MAM is exploited to assess the performance of the learners. MAM encompasses of assignments, problem scenario, oral examination, written exam, presentations, holistic demonstration, team play, projects, teamwork, discussion, creative empowerment approach and feedback reported (Samuel et al., 2018). The alteration in the emotions of learners is as well viewed that facilitates to endow with learning consequently.

From the recognized face, the emotions of the learners are sorted out by their facial expressions like eyebrow, lip movement and so on. The emotions of the learners are recognized from the input image using Eigen spaces technique. If the input image is alike to a few expressions training set, the renovated image will have less deformation than the image renovated from other eigenvectors of training expressions. The eigenvectors of the covariance matrix ought to be recognized in an attempt to disembark at an elucidation. The paces realized in this technique include the following:

- Appraising of image chosen for input (beside the choosing k Eigen vectors)
- Reforming of input elements.
- Distance calculation of the distance between transformed image and original image.
- The distance between input image and the training images is calculated.
- Diminishing emblematic error in lesser dimensional subspace of input.
- Choose eigenvectors in proportion to m largest Eigen values of total scatter.

The histogram (presented in section 4, analyzed in experimental section) between the skin area and non-skin area worked out in the image by means of skin tone algorithm. After recognizing the emotions of every learner, the learning is afforded to the learners with positive approach. The positive learning environment creates learning openings that support examination and edifice of acquaintance and adroitness. It is noteworthy that the learning environment proffers the finest occasion for learners to be vibrant learners, aggravated to learn more, tackled to take risk, sensitively sustained and feeling usually esteemed.

The benefits of distinguishing emotions are to endow with a positive learning that agrees to the learners to intellect tranquil, confined and engaged. In so doing, the learners will be more open to energetically take part in the activities of the learning environment. Several of the constraints employed in the positive learning environment are spotlighting on each learner, inspiration to be present at learning environment, a probability to learn from and regarding them, keep track of growth of the learner etc,.

Data Analysis

Through good worth of data attained from research review, over and above data from secondary sources composed and obtainable in the current account, descriptive and analytical research was well thought-out most suitable for the investigation. The research problems and the questionnaire were all structured consequently. The implications proffered in the concluding of the current research statement come out from the conjectures strained from the study of the information afforded by sample respondents who are in learning environment. The researcher employed closed-ended questions in the questionnaire to gather main data. The noteworthy tools utilized in the learning process to ascertain the power of EI in learners are

- Listening assist the learners to pay attention with their entire mind, together with their spirits.

- Empathy gives confidences to the learners to permit going of their individual perceptions long adequate to recognize other learners' thoughts and feelings.
- Individual space instructs the learners how to be glad about their individual and other learners' limits.
- Usage of words assists the learners comprehend that the words they prefer make a disparity to the rapports they produce.
- Time bestows the learner's authorization to pick time shrewdly, in means that lend a hand them self-reflect and comprehend others.
- Respecting the learners encourages them into deeper associations.
- Patience facilitates the learners to comprehend that they are sturdy adequate to remain calm which is a precious talent that help out the learners to control their emotions.

Ennobling Education Using Ei

Emotions are instinctive one to human being and it plays a foremost part in the educational sector. Each and every learner arrives out with diverse emotions within the learning environment which is varied consistent with the circumstances faced by the learner in and out of the learning environment. The emotions are grouped under three categories such as positive, negative or neutral. The most intricate emotion is categorized as negative emotion that spotlights on consciousness. Although too many negative emotions can make experience overwhelmed, troubled, exhausted, or tense out. When negative emotions are beyond balance, predicaments may emerge too vast to handle.

The positive emotions augment upcoming growth and success changing brains in ways that increase consciousness, concentration, and reminiscence which support to take in added information, grab plentiful deliberations in mind at one time and comprehend how dissimilar notions are associated to each other. The self-confidence in oneself facilitates to enlarge the positive emotions. The deliberations and deeds are prolonged using positive emotions that throw into upcoming accomplishment. It is extremely indispensable to balance both positive and negative emotions. Therefore, the effect of a learner can be enhanced with the Emotional-Based learning within the learning environment.

Learning Environment

Learning environment refers to the dissimilar substantial locations, perspectives and traditions in which learners learn. As learners learn in an extensive assortment of backgrounds, such as outside locations and open-air environments, the phrase is frequently employed as a more precise or favored option to classroom, which has more inadequate and conventional implications—a space with rows of desks and a chalkboard, for instance. Instructor disputes that learning environments have both a straight and not direct persuade on learners learning, together with their commitment in what is being educated, their inspiration to learn, and their intelligence of comfort, belonging, and individual protection. For case in point, learning environments packed with light and inspiring educational materials would probably be well thought-out more favorable for learning than dreary spaces devoid of panes or adornment.

The intermingle of learners among other learners also be well thought-out facets of a learning environment, and axioms such as "positive learning environment" or "negative learning environment" are generally used in accordance with the public and emotional aspects of a class. The learner be obliged to be energetic and a learning environment be supposed to be intended to be as prevailing as devoted working environments. It has got to be affluent and multifaceted sparkly the indispensable possessions of what has to be learned. The environment must be prearranged. If the affluence of a learning environment is an eminence, its intricacy may diminish learning. It has to afford most favorable learning circumstances as a role of the learner's phase of acquaintance. Learning environments be supposed to be intended as hierarchical acquaintance base producers and ought to present facts as a communication structure.

The learning environment adopted diverse learning approaches to the learners. The instructor explains a topic to the learner with practical implementation as well as the teaching and learning both are in interactive manner. The frustrated learner due to pandemic also participate in learning enthusiastically provide different solutions to the complex topics and problems. The learning is made inducing positive emotion overcoming the negative emotions with thought provoking learning among learners. In the second learning environment, the learners permitted to know about the topic in reality and then the same is discussed in the learning environment. Also, different content related to the specific topic is displayed and discussion in a team is done to know more about the topic and new ideas are shared among the learners. In the next learning environment, the learners themselves work in a team as well as in individual to discover new things related to the subjects. The learners facing negative and unpleasant situation due to pandemic issues are also keenly observed with their emotions and the learning is provided accordingly in the learning environment for each learner.

IMPLEMENTATION, RESULTS AND ANALYSIS

The analysis was performed using the SPSS Modeler statistical package and Data Mining (DM) software analysis and detailed analysis is presented using different methods in different subsections and analyzed.

Cross Tabulation Method

The technique (cross tabulation contingency tables or cross tabs) explores the rapport among multiple variables listed (White, 2003). Cross tabulation groups variables to comprehend the association amid dissimilar variables. Here it confirms on correlations from one variable grouping to the other. It is typically utilized in statistical analysis to discover patterns, trends and probabilities inside raw data. The cross-tabulation procedure suggests trials of autonomy and measures of relationship and accord for nominal and ordinal data. In addition, approximates of the comparative menace of an event is attained known the existence or nonexistence of a meticulous trait. The chi-square test has to be done to ensure this.

Chi-Square Test

This method gauges the inconsistency among the observed cell counts and what probably anticipated if the rows and columns were unconnected as (White, 2003). The degree of influence of the following independent variables relating to the respondents regarding the issues persuading the level of EI is. A chi square (χ^2) statistic is a test that gauges how anticipations evaluate to definite observed data which is then exploited in calculating a chi square statistic be obliged to be indiscriminate, unprocessed, reciprocally elite, and haggard from autonomous variables and drawn from a huge adequate sample. Chi square tests are frequently employed in hypothesis testing. The formula for Chi Square is:

$$X_c^2 = \sum \frac{(O_i - E_i)^2}{E_i} \tag{1}$$

where: c denotes the degrees of freedom, O denotes the Observed value and E denotes the Expected value. The test provides a p-value that notifies that if the test results are important or not. Apart from this, it also gets the p-value, degrees of freedom and alpha level(α).

Reliability Analysis

Reliability decides how constantly a dimension of ability or facts acquiesce related consequences beneath unreliable conditions. If a gauge has elevated reliability, it defers reliable consequences. Case processing summary is presented in Table 1 where N indicates number of instances and percentage indicates valid instances. Table 2 indicates the average inter-correlation among the instances with Cronbach's Alpha value (p = 0.95) that is said to be Excellent as per, commonly accepted rule for describing internal consistency, $0.9 \leq \alpha$ is Excellent.

Table 1. Instance Processing Details

Instance	N	%
Valid Data	10648	100.0
Excluded	0	0
Total	10648	100.0

Table 2. Reliability Statistics

Cronbach's Alpha	N of Items
0.95	6

Cronbach's alpha can be written as a function of the number of test items and the average inter-correlation among the items as shown in equation 2.:

$$\alpha = \frac{N \cdot \overline{c}}{\overline{v} + (N-1) \cdot \overline{c}} \tag{2}$$

Here N denotes the number of items, c represents the average inter-item covariance among the items and v is the average variance. The null hypothesis affirms that the populace means are all equal. From the study, significance level of 0.05 outperforms well.

The scalar estimates for three learning environment with grade are given in figure 2. As the Learning Environment1 increases by 1 standard deviation, the grade decreases by 0.22, 0.27 and 0.30 for LE1, LE2, LE3 respectively. The likelihood of getting critical ratio in absolute value is less than 0.001 for LE1, LE2 and LE3 given in Table 3. Therefore, the estimation of this model is accepted.

Figure 2. Scalar estimates (group number 1 - default model)

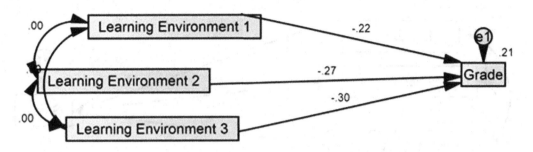

Table 3. Regression Weights: (Group number 1 - Default model)

Group	Estimate	Standard Error	Critical Ratio	Probability
Grade<---LE1	-.054	.002	-26.082	***
Grade<---LE2	-.064	.002	-30.935	***
Grade<---LE3	-.073	.002	-35.411	***
P value which define by *** is less than to .05 that's why estimation of this model is accepted.				

The likelihood of getting critical ratio in absolute value is 1.000 for LE1, LE2 and LE3 given in Table 4. The covariance among LE1 and LE2, LE2 and LE3, LE1 and LE3 is not considerably dissimilar from zero at the 0.05 level.

Table 4. Covariances: (Group number 1 - Default model)

Group	Estimate	Standard Error	Critical Ratio	Probability
LE1<-->LE2	.000	.390	.000	1.000
LE2<-->LE3	.000	.390	.000	1.000
LE1<-->LE3	.000	.390	.000	1.000

The scalar estimates for group number 2 are shown in figure 3.

Table 5 Regression Weights: (Group number 2 - Default model)

Group	Estimate	Standard Error	Critical Ratio	P
Grade<---LEET1	-1.269	.016	-79.093	***
Grade<---LEET2	-1.468	.016	-91.500	***
Grade<---LEET3	-1.697	.016	-105.757	***
P value which define by *** is less than to .05 that's why estimation of this model is accepted.				

Figure 3. Scalar Estimates (Group number 2 - Default model)

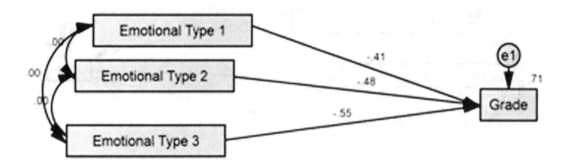

The likelihood of getting a critical ratio as large as 79.093 in absolute value is less than 0.001 is given in table 5. Therefore, the estimation of this model is accepted. The regression weights, covariances, correlations and variances for model 2 are given in table 5 and table 6.

Table 6. Covariances: (Group number 2 - Default model)

Group	Estimate	Standard Error (SE)	Critical Ratio	P
LEET1<-->LEET2	.000	.002	.000	1.000
LEET2<-->LEET3	.000	.002	.000	1.000
LEET1<-->LEET3	.000	.002	.000	1.000

The emotions of learners in three different learning environment was assessed by four different EI dimensions like Self-Emotional Assessment (SEA), Others' Emotional Assessment (OEA), Regulation Of Emotion (ROE), Use of emotion (UOE) given in table 7.

Table 8 confirms the consequences of the "Pearson Chi-Square" row, it is noted that $\chi(1) = 59.950$, p = 0.586 for Learning Environment 1, $\chi(1) = 69.884$, p = 0.257 for Learning Environment 2 and $\chi(1) = 70.000$, p = 0.254 for Learning Environment 3 . This tells that there is no statistically noteworthy association amid LE1 and Emotional Dimensions; that is, both learning environment and Emotional Dimensions equally prefer Emotional Learning Analysis. The null hypothesis is not rejected, as the p-value is greater than the chosen significance level ($\alpha = 0.05$). The finding states that there is an adequate proof to put forward an relationship exists between both learning environment and Emotional Dimensions.

Figure 4, Figure 5 and Figure 6 shows the chart of emotion dimension count in LE1, LE2, LE3. Figure 7, Figure 8 and Figure 9 shows the Chi-Square Contributions in LE1, LE2, LE3 with different emotions.

From table 9, it is depicted that hypothesis H0: "LearningEnvironment1, LearningEnvironment2, LearningEnvironment3" and "EIDimension" are independent. H1: "LearningEnvironment1, LearningEnvironment2, LearningEnvironment3" and "EIDimension" are associated (not independent).

Table 7. EI dimension for Learning Environment

Emotions	EI Dimension for Learning Environment 1				EI Dimension for Learning Environment 2				EI Dimension for Learning Environment 3			
	OEA	ROE	SEA	UOE	OEA	ROE	SEA	UOE	OEA	ROE	SEA	UOE
Anger	117	125	115	127	122	116	131	115	133	115	113	123
Antagonistic	107	120	128	129	129	108	125	122	112	101	118	153
Anxiety	134	120	120	110	130	111	125	118	111	128	128	117
Bored	126	127	111	120	119	111	144	110	115	122	124	123
Contentment	123	125	115	121	141	122	104	117	117	130	123	114
Dependent	117	102	127	138	130	116	117	121	118	119	120	127
Depression	108	126	128	122	122	137	127	98	122	140	112	110
Detached	118	132	117	117	126	117	124	117	115	120	116	133
Discouraged	123	121	133	107	133	121	103	127	131	128	109	116
Enthusiasm	121	123	128	112	115	101	136	132	114	123	128	119
Frightened	136	115	133	100	114	129	116	125	117	115	122	130
Gratitude	109	121	115	139	118	124	127	115	135	121	101	127
Happy	114	121	131	118	137	114	118	115	109	130	123	122
Hope	119	115	111	139	109	120	124	131	120	103	132	129
Imaginative	144	106	102	132	122	127	116	119	125	140	123	96
Inspiration	125	112	125	122	106	116	130	132	112	127	122	123
Interest	110	138	127	109	111	123	110	140	117	119	125	123
Irresponsible	114	129	113	128	107	130	112	135	132	114	133	105
Irritated	132	111	124	117	116	118	125	125	143	109	124	108
Optimism	132	122	116	114	117	116	123	128	112	114	135	123
Pleasure	116	130	117	121	117	138	117	112	136	118	121	109
Self control	117	121	126	120	121	147	108 ·	108	116	126	110	132

Table 8. Chi-Square Tests for Learning Environment

Description	Learning Environment 1			Learning Environment 2			Learning Environment 3		
	Value	Degrees of freedom	Asymp. Sig. (2-sided)	Value	Degrees of freedom	Asymp. Sig. (2-sided)	Value	Degrees of freedom	Asymp. Sig. (2-sided)
Pearson Chi-Square	59.950[a]	63	.586	69.884[a]	63	.257	70.000[a]	63	.254
Likelihood Ratio	59.974	63	.585	69.637	63	.264	69.798	63	.260
N of Valid Cases	10648								
a. 0 cells (0.0%) have expected count less than 5. The minimum expected count is 121.00.									

Figure 4. Emotion Dimension Counts in LE1

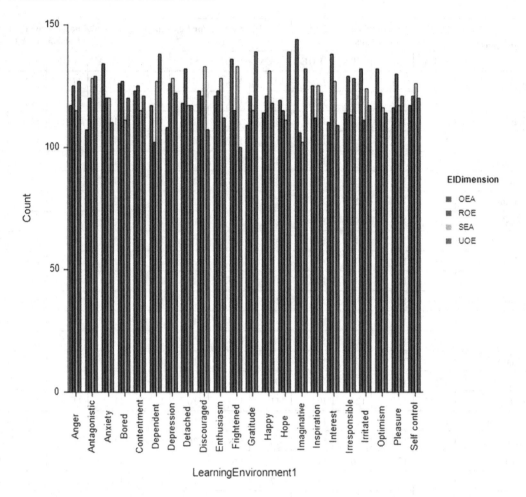

Figure 10 shows the one Sample Chi-Square Test Based on Emotion Dimension. The mean scores of Academic Grade for all the levels of learning environment indicate higher levels of ratings (M=9.0 to 15.1) on Academic performance. However, the pattern of ratings again show that, high Academic performance increases with the designation and highest level of learning environment for the faculty prove that, higher levels of designation containing higher levels of authority and power, esteem and status helps the increase in the Performance of Grade's. Result of One-way ANOVA conducted to compare all the three levels has been significant at 0.000 levels. This shows that, Grade's Academic Performance differs significantly with designation or position in the organization or title holding in the organization. In order to find the significant difference between Leaning Environment and the Self Emotion Appraisal a Chi -square test was employed and the result of the test is shown in the table 9.

Δ Null Hypothesis: There is no significant difference between learning environment and the Self Emotion Appraisal

Δ Alternate Hypothesis: There is a significant difference between learning environment and the Self Emotion Appraisal

Figure 5. Emotion Dimension Counts in LE2

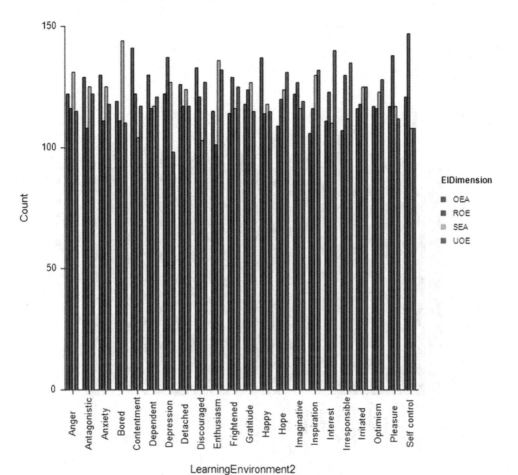

FUTURE RESEARCH DIRECTIONS

The task of the educational sector and institutions is to get ready proficient and self-sufficient learners for verve. To generate proficient, effectual learners is to lend a hand to become skilled at to learn, to make powerful them to map, scrutinize and replicate, support them to recognize more concerning their emotions and their learning, direct them to expand targets, and assist with others, accomplish this huge ambition, a usual cognitively intellectual learner be supposed to be emotionally and deliberately intellectual, as well. The EI is obliged to be implicit and measured fundamental to education. The learners learn more capably if they benefit from learning, instructors can exploit many methods that lend a hand to the learners to develop their EI in a learning environment.

In future, the research ought to be focused on precise facets and tools of online learning environments. Also, the various emotional behaviors and its impact in an online learning environment are to be assessed under different situations and analyze them in more detail. With anticipation the future investigation in this area can prolong to develop acquaintance of the intricate interaction among emotion and non-native language learning. Future research possibly will discover whether the support of positive emotional practices, and acknowledgement and management of the lack thereof, develop dissimilar forms of positive work experiences and decrease yield and absenteeism.

Figure 6. Emotion Dimension Counts in LE3

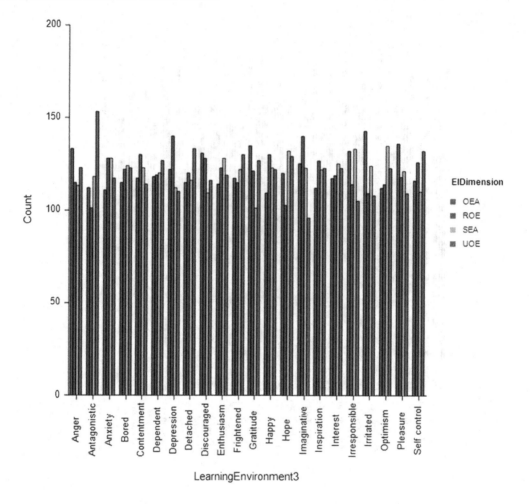

CONCLUSION

The results of the research portray the association amid the learners' positive attitude inside the learning environment. The outcomes designate a rapport amid instructors' level of EI and the way they are evaluated by their learners. The positive association amid the instructors' level of EI and the way they are assessed by their learners designates that learners' success. The results of the study confirm that the learning environment along with the teaching methodologies and emotional happenings in and around decides the performance of the learner. The questionnaire accomplished by the learners exposes interpersonal rapports with the instructor and their responsive and friendly attitude. They also value an improved contact with instructors, motivation, and support inside and outside the learning environment, respect, encouragement, and capability to articulate their feelings and emotional states, free and open discussion throughout the session, sympathy, and equality. Enhancing EI consequently can allow learners to direct their thoughts and actions, and can eventually augment the quality of their rapports with other learners. The questionnaire comprising of the aspects requisite to compute the EI proportion of the learners, is deliberate and then the analysis task is made.

Figure 7. Chi-Square Contributions in LE2

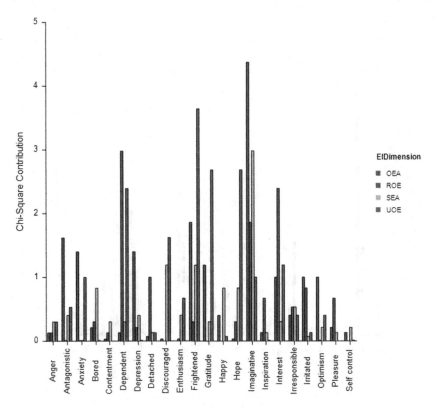

Figure 8. Chi-Square Contributions in LE2

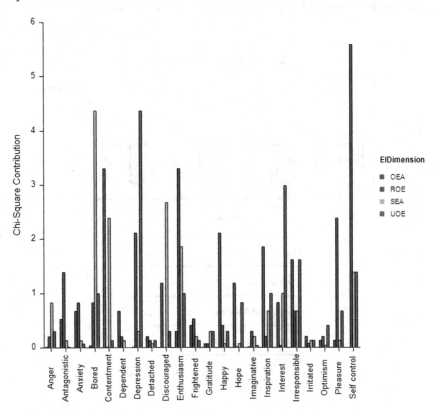

Figure 9. Chi-Square Contributions in LE3

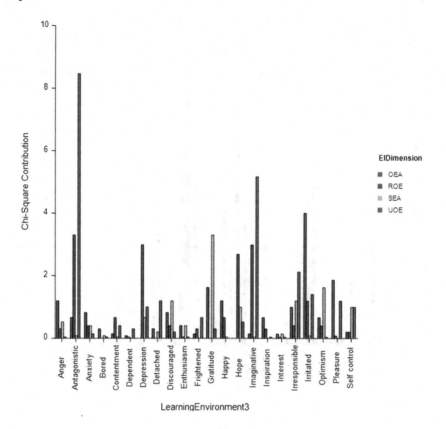

Figure 10. One Sample Chi-Square Test Based on Emotion Dimension

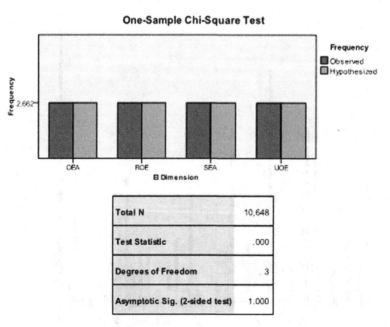

A

Table 9. Hypothesis Analysis for LE

Test	Type	LE1				LE2				LE3		
		Chi-Square Value	Degrees of freedom	Probability Level	Reject H0 at α = 0.05?	Chi-Square Value	Degrees of freedom	Probability Level	Reject H0 at α = 0.05?	Chi-Square Value	Degrees of freedom	Probability Level	Reject H0 at α = 0.05?
Pearson's Chi-Square Yates' Cont. Correction*	2-Sided	59.9504	63	0.58571	No	69.8843	63	0.25746	No	70.0000	63	0.25437	No
Likelihood Ratio Fisher's Exact*	2-Sided	59.9738	63	0.58487	No	69.6368	63	0.26415	No	69.7977	63	0.25979	No

For analyzing the hypothesis, relationship between the LE and EI dimensions is independent. In contrast means among groups, independent-sample t-test was exploited while there were only two groups and ANOVA was used when there were more than two groups. EI to facilitate gain important knowledge of how to hold and control emotions, make use of emotions to attain preferred outcomes, uphold satisfying associations, in addition to articulate sympathy and perceptive towards the learners. Based on the psychoanalysis and understanding made and conversed in this chapter, findings of the study and further implications raised through the findings are to interpret. The scrutiny of data for the purposes of the study was made by means of the following tools: Structural Equation Modeling, Cross tabulation, Correlation, Frequency table, ANOVA, Chi-Square Test and T-test. This work helps the instructor to attain good academic output even after this covid'19 stressful situation. In future, the same work can be extended to analyze the emotional behavior in the online learning environment and its impacts.

REFERENCES

Alavinia, P., & Mollahossein, H. (2012). On the correlation between iranian efl learners' use of meta cognitive listening strategies and their emotional intelligence. *International Education Studies*, *5*(6), 189–203. doi:10.5539/ies.v5n6p189

Biljana, N. C., & Dragana, S. (2017). Educational needs of teacher for introduction and application of innovative models in educational work to improve teaching. *Journal of Cognitive Research in Science. Engineering and Education*, *5*(1), 49–56.

Calkins, S. D., & Bell, M. A. (2010). *Child development at the intersection of emotion and cognition*. American Psychological Association. doi:10.1037/12059-000

Chamizo, N., Arrivillaga, M. T., Rey, C., & Extremera, L. N. (2021). The Role of Emotional Intelligence, the Teacher-Student Relationship, and Flourishing on Academic Performance in Adolescents: A Moderated Mediation Study. *Frontiers in Psychology*, *12*, 695067. doi:10.3389/fpsyg.2021.695067 PMID:34335411

Costa, A., & Faria, L. (2015). The impact of emotional intelligence on academic achievement: A longitudinal study in Portuguese secondary school. *Learning and Individual Differences*, *37*, 38–47. doi:10.1016/j.lindif.2014.11.011

Daniel, S. J. (2020). Education and the COVID-19 Pandemic. *Prospects*, *49*(1-2), 91–96. doi:10.100711125-020-09464-3 PMID:32313309

Doukakis, S., & Alexopoulos, E. C. (2020). Distance learning for secondary education students. The role of educational neuroscience. In *BFAL 2020, LNAI, 12462. Springer Nature Switzerland AG*. doi:10.1007/978-3-030-60735-7_17

Extremera, N., & Berrocal, P. F. (2002). Emotional intelligence as an essential skill at school. *Revista Iberoamericana de Educacion*, *29*(1), 1–6.

Greenhow, C., Lewin, C., & Willet, K. B. S. (2020). The educational response to Covid-19 across two countries: A critical examination of initial digital pedagogy adoption. *Technology, Pedagogy and Education*, *1866654*. Advance online publication. doi:10.1080/1475939X

Gugu, N. (2021). Facilitation of emotional intelligence for the purpose of decision-making and problem-solving among nursing students in an authentic learning environment: A qualitative study. *Journal of Africa Nursing Sciences*, *15*, 100375. doi:10.1016/j.ijans.2021.100375

Hamilton, L. S., Grant, D., Kaufman, J. H., Diliberti, M. K., Schwartz, H. L., Hunter, G. P., Setodji, C. M., & Young, C. J. (2020). COVID-19 and the State of K–12 Schools: Results and Technical Documentation from the Spring 2020 American Educator Panels COVID-19 Surveys. RAND Corporation.

Hau, L. T., Sylvia, Y. C. L., Anna, K., Hui, N. N., Doris, K. Y., & Cin, C. (2021). The significance of emotional intelligence to students' learning motivation and academic achievement: A study in Hong Kong with a Confucian heritage. *Children and Youth Services Review*, *121*, 105847. doi:10.1016/j.childyouth.2020.105847

Jimenez, M. I., & Zafra, E. L. (2008). Autoconcepto Emocional Como Factor De Riesgo Emocional En Estudiantes Universitarios [Emotional Self-concept as an Emotional Risk factor in university students. Differences of Gender and Age]. *Boletín de Psicología*, *93*, 21–39.

Landy, F. J. (2005). Some historical and scientific issues related to research on Emotional Intelligence. *Journal of Organizational Behavior*, *26*(4), 411–424. doi:10.1002/job.317

Levine, D. S. (2007). Neural network modeling of emotion. *Physics of Life Reviews*, *4*(1), 37–63. doi:10.1016/j.plrev.2006.10.001

Li, M., Ge, M., Zhao, H., & An, Z. (2022). Modeling and Analysis of Learners' Emotions and Behaviors Based on Online Forum Texts. *Computational Intelligence and Neuroscience*, *2022*, 9696422. Advance online publication. doi:10.1155/2022/9696422 PMID:35096051

Lyubomirsky, S., Sheldon, K. M., & Schkade, D. (2005). Pursuing happiness: The architecture of sustainable change. *Review of General Psychology*, *9*(2), 111–131. doi:10.1037/1089-2680.9.2.111

Mohammad, N. H., Huyen, T. T., Bui, T. T. T. T., Ho, T. N., & Gökhan, A. (2021). Students' emotion extraction and visualization for engagement detection in online learning. *Procedia Computer Science*, *192*, 3423–3431. doi:10.1016/j.procs.2021.09.115

Neale, S., Arnell, S. L., & Wilson, L. (2009). *Emotional Intelligence Coaching: Improving Performance for Leaders, Coaches and the Individual*. EAN.

Parneet, K. (2021). Affective state and learning environment based analysis of students' performance in online assessment. *Journal of Cognitive Computing in Engineering*, *2*, 12–20. doi:10.1016/j.ijcce.2020.12.003

Patston, T. J., Kennedy, J., Jaeschke, W., Kapoor, H., Leonard, S. N., Cropley, D. H., & Kaufman, J. C. (2021). Secondary Education in COVID Lockdown: More Anxious and Less Creative—Maybe Not? *Frontiers in Psychology*, *12*, 391. doi:10.3389/fpsyg.2021.613055 PMID:33692721

Pekrun, R., & Schutz, P. A. (2007). Where do we go from here? Implications and future directions for inquiry on emotions in education. In P. A. Schutz & R. Pekrun (Eds.), *Emotion in education* (pp. 313–331). Elsevier. doi:10.1016/B978-012372545-5/50019-8

Reimers, F. M. (Ed.). (2022). Learning from a Pandemic. The Impact of COVID-19 on Education Around the World. In Primary and Secondary Education During Covid-19. Springer. doi:10.1007/978-3-030-81500-4_1

Reinhard, P. (2021). Teachers need more than knowledge: Why motivation, emotion, and self-regulation are indispensable. *Educational Psychologist, 56*(4), 312–322. doi:10.1080/00461520.2021.1991356

Rode, J., Mooney, C., Arthaud, M. D., Near, T., Baldwin, R., Rubin, R., & Bommer, W. (2007). Emotional intelligence and individual performance: Evidence of direct and moderated effects. *Journal of Organizational Behavior, 28*(4), 399–421. doi:10.1002/job.429

Rooy, D. L. V., & Viswesvaran, C. (2007). Assessing emotional intelligence in adults: A Review of existing instruments and their application to increase human performance. In R. Bar-On, J. G. Maree, & M. J. Elias (Eds.), *Educating People to be Emotionally Intelligent: Scientific Guidelines for Enhancing Human Performance*. Heinemann Publishers.

Samuel, P. J., Ramasubramanian, P., & Magdalene, D. D. A. (2015). A survey on affective learning context discovery using emotional intelligence. *Journal of Emerging Technologies in Computational and Applied Sciences, 1*(14), 43–44.

Samuel, P. J., Ramasubramanian, P., & Magdalene, D. D. A. (2018). Student learning context analysis by emotional intelligence with data mining tools. *Journal of Intelligent Engineering and Systems, 11*(2), 173–183. doi:10.22266/ijies2018.0430.19

Sancheng, P., Lihong, C., Yongmei, Z., Zhouhao, O., Aimin, Y., Xinguang, L., Weijia, J., & Shui, Y. (2021). A survey on deep learning for textual emotion analysis in social networks. *Digital Communications and Networks*. doi:10.1016/j.dcan.2021.10.003

Svetlana, H. (2007). *Emotional intelligence and academic achievement in higher Education*. Pepperdine University.

Temel, S. (2014). The effects of problem-based learning on pre-service teachers' critical thinking dispositions and perceptions of problem-solving ability. *South African Journal of Education, 34*(1), 1–20. doi:10.15700/201412120936

Tiina, T., & Hanna, J., & Kristiina, M. (2021). All for one and one for all – How are students' affective states and group-level emotion regulation interconnected in collaborative learning? *The Journal of Educational Research, 109*, 101861.

Tyng, C. M., Amin, H. U., Saad, M. N. M., & Malik, A. S. (2017). The Influences of Emotion on Learning and Memory. *Frontiers in Psychology, 1454*(8), 1454. doi:10.3389/fpsyg.2017.01454 PMID:28883804

Van, V. K., & Lasky, S. (2005). Emotions as a lens to explore teacher identity and change: Different theoretical approaches. *Teaching and Teacher Education, 21*(8), 895–898. doi:10.1016/j.tate.2005.06.002

Will, M. (2020). Teachers without internet work in parking lots, empty school buildings during COVID-19. *Education Week*.

Yustina, Y., Syafii, W., & Vebrianto, R. (2020). The Effects of Blended Learning and Project-Based Learning on Pre-Service Biology Teachers' Creative Thinking through Online Learning in the Covid-19 Pandemic. *Journal of Pendidik, 9*(3), 408–420. doi:10.15294/jpii.v9i3.24706

ADDITIONAL READING

Driessen, E., Beatty, A., Stokes, A., Wood, S., & Ballen, C. (2020). Learning principles of evolution during a crisis: An exploratory analysis of student barriers one week and one month into the COVID-19 pandemic. *Ecology and Evolution, 10*(22), 12431–12436. doi:10.1002/ece3.6741 PMID:33250982

Errico, D., Paciello, F., & Cerniglia, L. (2016). When emotions enhance students' engagement in e-learning processes. *Journal of e-Learning and Knowledge Society, 12,* 9–23. . doi:10.20368/1971-8829/1144

Gelles, L., Lord, A., Hoople, S. M., Chen, G. D., & Mejia, J. A. (2020). Compassionate flexibility and self-discipline: Student adaptation to emergency remote teaching in an integrated engineering energy course during COVID-19. *Education Sciences, 10*(11), 304. doi:10.3390/educsci10110304

Heffner, J., Vives, M. L., & Feldman, H. O. (2021). Emotional responses to prosocial messages increase willingness to self-isolate during the COVID-19 pandemic. *Personality and Individual Differences, 170,* 110420. doi:10.1016/j.paid.2020.110420 PMID:33082614

Luan, L., Hong, J. C., Cao, M., Dong, Y., & Hou, X. (2020). Exploring the role of online EFL learners' perceived social support in their learning engagement: A structural equation model. *Interactive Learning Environments,* 1–12. doi:10.1080/10494820.2020.1855211

Magdalene, D.D.A., Ramasubramanian, P., & Samuel, P.J. (2020). The Discriminant Analysis Approach for Evaluating Effectiveness of Learning in an Instructor-Led Virtual Classroom. *Journal on Smart Sensing and Intelligent Systems,* 1-15. doi:10.21307/ijssis-2020-035

Nassr, R., Aborujilah, M., Aldossary, A., & Aldossary, A. (2020). Understanding Education Difficulty During COVID-19 Lockdown: Reports on Malaysian University Students' Experience. *IEEE Access: Practical Innovations, Open Solutions, 8,* 186939–186950. doi:10.1109/ACCESS.2020.3029967 PMID:35127298

Radu, M. C., Schnakovszky, C., Herghelegiu, E., Ciubotariu, V. A., & Cristea, I. (2020). The impact of the COVID-19 pandemic on the quality of educational process: A student survey. *Journal of Environmental Research and Public Health, 17*(21), 7770. doi:10.3390/ijerph17217770 PMID:33114192

Saeed, T., Hongying, M., Rafiq, M., Matus, S., & Pleva, J. (2018). Facial Expression Emotion Detection for Real-Time Embedded Systems Technologies. *Technologies, 6*(1), 1–18.

KEY TERMS AND DEFINITIONS

Chi-Square: Chi square is a measure used to determine how closely the observed data fit the expected data.

Cronbach's Alpha: Cronbach's alpha is a measure of reliability of set of items.

Cross Tabulation: Cross tabulation is a statistical tool that groups variables to understand the correlation between different variables.

Facial Feature: Facial Feature is a distinguishing element of a face, such as an eye, nose, or lips

Haar Cascade Classifier: Haar Cascade Classifier is an Object Detection Algorithm used to identify faces in an image or a real time video.

Learning Environment: Learning Environment refers to the collective combination of active learning, healthy environment, communicative class work, and different locations for learning.

Multi Assessment Method: Multi Assessment Method is an assessment of performance of the learner after undergoing the learning in different learning environment.

Naïve Bayes: A naive Bayes is an algorithm that uses Bayes' theorem to classify objects.

Reliability Analysis: Reliability Analysis is a measurement technique that allows researchers to assess the stability of measures.

Segmentation: Segmentation is partitioning an image into different parts according to their features and properties.

Breast Cancer Disease Exploitation to Recure a Healthy Lifestyle

B

Mudrakola Swapna

https://orcid.org/0000-0003-2816-6857

Vardhaman College of Engineering, India

Nagaratna P. Hegde

Vasavi College of Engineering, India

INTRODUCTION

While cancer has been plaguing the world for decades, people joined together for globally famous cancer advocacy organizations only at the beginning of the 1900s (Slamon, et.al, 1987; Slamon, et.al, 2001). There are several forms of cancer that humans attack. The most regular cancer types that occur are Bladder, Rectal, Colon, Kidney, Endometrial, Leukemia, Pancreatic, Lung, Melanoma, Liver, Prostate, Non-Hodgkin Lymphoma, Thyroid, and Breast are some cancers. Breast Cancer is the next to the first largest in women after skin cancer disease. Early, probably before the spread of breast cancer, mammograms may screen breast cancer. Prevention, screening, treatment, statistics, study, and clinical testing are listed here (Slamon, 1989; Al-Hajj, 2003).

BACKGROUND

Positional cloning methods have identified a powerful applicant for the BRCA1 17q-related gene that affects breast and cervical cancer sensitivity. In five out of eight siblings allegedly segregating BRCA1 susceptibility alloys, possible predisposing mutations founded. Mutations entail 11-base deletion, 1-base pair addition, stopping the codon, halting the missense, and expected procedural mutation. The gene BRCA1, which encodes the 1863 amino acid protein predicted to organs, breasts, and ovaries is demonstrated. In amino-terminal region and protein contains a size of finger region of Zinc which has no interaction otherwise to the previously mentioned protein. Identification of BRCA1 (Schrijver, 2022) may aid early diagnosis and breast cancer molecular awareness and ovarian cancer in individuals. It is represented in Figure 1 (Van't, 2006; Miki, Y., Swensen, 1994)

The collection of adjuvant clinical treatment for patients would be strengthened by an exact method of prediction in breast cancer (Cory, 2022). We listed 295 successive individuals with breast carcinomas with chromosome-expression signatures that can be either a bad prognosis or a good prognosis. Analyzing micro-arrays to assess our potential development 70-gene diagnosis and treatment profile. Patients were all under the age of 53 years and had phase-1 or the phase-2 BC disease. From 295 subjects, 151 had the lymph Node Negative (LN-), 144 were lymph Node-Positive (LN+). Through uni-variable and multi-variant statistical analysis. We try to estimate the predictive strength of the extrapolative outline. For 295 cases, 180 had bad prediction and 115 had positive prediction signatures. The mean average survival rate (+/-SE) for the 10 years was 54.6+/-4.4 percentage and 94.5+/-2.6 percentage. At ten

DOI: 10.4018/978-1-7998-9220-5.ch157

years, in the category with a bad signature and 85 percentage, +4.3 percentage in the class with a strong signature forecast likelihood of lasting free of remote metastases remained50.6+/-4.5 percentage. Inside the party of a bad pregnancy, the calculated risk rating was 5.1 (95 percentage assurance interlude, 2.9 percentage to 9.0; P<0.001) when comparing the group through a strong forecast initial. When groups were analyzed based on the lymph status, this relationship remained important. Multi-Cox regression research has shown that the prognosis profile for the prediction of disease outcome is an independent factor (Zhou, 2020; Van De Vijver, 2002).

FOCUS OF THE ARTICLE

The literature Survey on breast cancer, insight few important notes and conclusions. The statistical analysis has clearly stated the frequency of the BC in women's special very common in white women. The BC is slowly leading the higher sector in the pie-chart compared to other cancer diseases. The detection of BC in the early state will recure the patients with a higher prognosis. The later Stage of disease detection will reduce the life span of the patients. Analysis of the patient's increased pattern has altered and motivated me to study BC. The inference and knowledge extracted from the above literature survey are Different methods used to detect BC. Imaging is a remarkable approach in detection and comparison from the previous spread status of the disease. Different therapies are practiced in the BC treatment, and results are projected in the literature survey. The responsiveness of the treatment varies from gender, Stage of cancer, age of the subject, family history, physical and psychological strength of the subject. The prognosis of the subject after treatment is analyzed.

In several trials, morphological tests of the degree of differentiation provided valuable prognostic relevant information on breast cancer. There are no histology degree values are recognized as a standard technique until recently and largely due to potential reproductively and accuracy issues. The most widely used form by Bloom & Richardson has updated objective criteria. Which are improving in Nottingham / Tenovus principal breast cancer study. In the revamped methodology, three morphological characteristics–the proportion of tubular development, the point of atomic pleomorphism, and the exact mitotic computation on a given area of the field have were assessed semi quantitatively. A numbering system using the synopsis of the actual rating of three factors removes the combined classification. Since 1973, a multiple indicator analysis has experimented among 2,200 subjects with preliminary operable BC. The histological classification had tested in the year 1831 cases, shows a clear link to prognosis cases with classification. I tumors had a substantial increase in survival relative to individuals with tumor positions II and III (P < 0.0001). Such findings suggest that the histological ranking system offers valuable forecast information and reproductive outcomes. The evaluation protocol followed faithfully to streamline treatment for optimal care then the histology assessment is used in the Nottingham Prognostic Scale of the multi-factor (Tur, 2022; Elston, 1991).

Scanning of 10q23 human genome homozygous deletions resulted in autonomy, in a large amount, of human cancer, of the candidate tumor suppressor gene, PTEN. PTEN mutations in the 31 percentage (13/42) of the glioblastoma and xenograft cell lines, 100 percent (4/4) of the lines of the prostate cancer cells, six percent (4/65) of the breast and xenografts cell lines, and 17 percentage (3/18) of the main glioblastomas have been identified in provisional screenings. The PTEN substance predicted has a phosphatase domain of protein tyrosine and extensive tensin homology, a protein that acts together utilizing filaments on concentrating attachments (Veeramani, 2005). The counterparts indicate that PTEN can inhibit the growth of tumor cells as a result of provoking protein tyrosine kinases and can control the invasion and metastases of tumors in oriented adhesions (Li, J,1997).

The metastatic origin of local lymph nodes, bone marrow, lungs, and hepatitis is characterized by breast cancer. The tumor and metastasis migration has some similarities in comparison to leukocyte movement. it was closely observed by chemo kinesis and its antibodies. The receptors of CCR7 and CXCR4 chemokines exist in human breast and metastatic cells (Raza, 2022). The organs serving the primary targets of breast cancelation the corresponding ligands, CXCL12/ SDF-1alpha and CCL21/6Ckine demonstrated tip level in the expression. Activation in BC cells of CXCR4 or CCR7 moderates the development and subsequently causes chemical and invasive reactions of actin polymerization and pseudopodia. In vivo, neutralization of the interactions of CXCL12/CXCR4 damages the metastases of central lymph nodes and the breast cancer system's pulmonary network. Apart from CXCR3 and CCR7, CCR10 levels have been increased by malignant melanoma, which has metastatic characteristics similar to breasted cancer but has elevated rates of skin metastases (Lange, 2022). When assessing the metastatic targets of tumor cells, our results confine concern receptors and chemokines has very importance in BC(Müller,2012).

The likelihood of localized diagnosis in a lymph node or estrogen-receptor-positive BC is wrongly established in clinical and histopathological studies (Obi, 2022). We investigated the probability of a remote scale in National Adjuvant Breast and Bowel Clinical Study B-14 in spatial empty, therapy with tamoxifen, in the results of RT-PCR in paraffin-embedded tumor tissue 21 quantitatively selected genes. Expression rates were used to calculate the recurrence value and assess the risk category (low, middle, or high) for individual patients using a forward-looking algorithm for sixteen cancer and five reference gene. In 668 of 675 tumor fragments, correct RT-PCR profiles have collected. The RT-PCR test classified 51% of medium risk, 22% of moderate risk, and 27% of the patients' high-risk patients. The risk categories are less, moderate, and most-risk have Kaplan-Meier estimated the remote recurrence rates at 10 years of age to be 6.8 percent (95 percent, 4.0 to 9.6) 14.3 percent (95 percent, 8.3 to 20.3), and 2.5 percent (95 percent, 23.6 to 37.4). The frequency rate was slightly lower for the minimal-risk group considering the high-risk group (P-value is less than 0.001). The recurrence score of a multivariate Cox model provided important age-and tumor-related predictive capacity (P<0.001). The average survival rate (P-value is less than 0.001) was also reliable and may perhaps be used as a continuous method to detect a reserved repetition in particular patients (Paik, 2004)

Several randomized experiments have been carried out for adjuvant tamoxifen in females for first breast cancer, with revised findings (Chan, 2022). In 1995, the randomized trial activated in advance 1990 with adjuvant tamoxifen vs. no tamoxifen until reappearance required details about each patient. Details on each of 37000 women in 55 such trials were gathered and analyzed centrally, representing about 87 percent of global data. This doubles the amount of tamoxifen proof for the cases obtained above 5 years next to the optimization of the precedent assessment by bringing all tests together.

Nearly 8000 of the females had their primary tumor at or zero levels calculated by the estrogen-receptor protein (ER) (Krutilina, 2022). The net effect of tamoxifens was low, with the following studies of repetition and absolute mortality of the remaining people limited (18000 ER-positive tumors, plus approximately 12000 more ER-positive tumors, estimated at 8000). The relative recurrence declines of these 30,000 women over around ten years of track and about 21 percent (Standard Deviation 3.0), 29 percent (Standard Deviation 2.0), and 47 percent (Standard Deviation 3.0), with a strong tendency in the direction of a greater effect of extended care (chi2 (1) =52.0, 2p<0.00001) in trials for One, Two and Five years adjuvant tamoxifen. The corresponding relative mortality declines were 12 percentage (Standard Deviation 3), 17 percentage (Standard Deviation 3), and 26 percentage (Standard Deviation 4), whereas the pattern check (chi2(1]=8.8;2p=0.003) was again important. In the first five years, the actual increase in relapse was higher, and if the improvement in survival within the first ten years was gradually increasing. For people with both node-positive and node-negative diseases, relative declines in mortality have been comparable, but actual reductions in node-positive patients have decreased.

The function of histone modifications in cancer growth has been determined by family cancer syndromes. In childhood and adult tumors, the mainly genetic Li-Fraumeni (LFS) condition is especially important because of its complex existence (Omran, 2022). The formal association study was not feasible due to the prevalence and death rate of LFS. The choice of the most likely candidate gene was the alternate solution. The p53 tumor suppressor gene is researched due to earlier reports that the sporadic genes are synthesized (non-family) variants of most LFS related cancers. For all five LFS families tested, Germ line p53 mutations are observed. These mutations are not responsible for aggregates of transmuted p53 protein that are predicted to induce a trans-dominant functional lack of action on wild protein type p53. The occurrence of germ line p53 mutations is currently being studied in the communities of LFS and other healthcare professionals with clinical symptoms that may be correlated with this alteration (Malkin, 1990).

Trastuzumab is a transcription factor with recombinant HER2 (Ling, 2022), which promoted breast cancer clinically and has over-expressed HER2. We also studied its effectiveness and protection following the removal of suspected breast cancer as well as the implementation of chemotherapy. This global, multi-center, comprehensive trial associated 1 to 2 years of Trastuzumab per triple week with findings of patients who had loco regional treatments and four cycles of neoadjuvant to auxiliary chemotherapy for either HER2+ve and node-ve or nodes+ve BC. The randomization of 1,694 females, to 2-year trastuzumab, 1,694 females to 1-year trastuzumab and 1,693 women to be monitored was provided with details. They mention here just one year or assessment of the outcomes of therapy with trastuzumab. In the first expected intermediate study (median follow-up for 1 year of a year) 347 cases are asses: 127 incidents of trastuzumab group, 220 are in the Assessment community. Compared with the experimental community, the unadjusted hazard risk of an occurrence in the trastuzumab population was 0.54 percentages reflecting an absolute advantage of 8.4 points for disease-free survival for two years. In both groups, overall survival did not vary significantly (29 trastuzumab vs. 37 observational deaths). In 0.5 percent of women receiving trastuzumab, serious cardio toxicity was established (Piccart-Gebhart, 2005).

Early breast cancer can also affect the mortality ratio of long-term BC with differences with the local therapies, which greatly influence the likelihood of loco regional recurrence. To investigate this relationship, joint meta-analyses of the related randomized studies completed by 1995 were carried out based on individual patient results. 42,000 women in 78 random therapy compare (**Radiation** vs no of **Radiation therapy**, 23,500 **greater** vs. **fewer** procedure, 9300 **Excuses surgery** vs **Radiation therapy**(Daniel,2022), (9300) were given details. There have been 24 different forms of individual associations of diagnosis. To further the effects on (i.e., local) chronic diseases, these were classified into a breast mortality risk that reached 10 percent of the local recurrence risk over 5 years (<10 percentage, 17,000 women; >10 percentage, 25,000 women).

Within the first five years, nearly 3-Quarters of the possible local reoccurrence risk happened (Hohenschurz,2022). There was no variation in the 15-year survival rate of breast cancer in contrast with minor (< 10 percentage) disparities with a five-year local incidence risk. In 25,000 women who compared major (> 10 percentage) disparities, there were, however, 7 percentage active reoccurrence (> 26 percentage reduction) and 44,6 percentage (total reduction) versus 49,5 percentage (total reduction 5,0 percentage), respectively, active (total reduction 19 percentage) mortality chances for 15 years of breast cancer. Those 25,000 patients included 7300 patients with breast preservation operations of Five-year local recurrence (usually in the retained breast, mostly with axillary and node-ve diseases) 7 percent vs. 26 percentage (reduced to 19 percentage), while the risk for breast cancer is 30.5 percentage vs. 35.9 percentage (red) of 15-years. In comparison, 8,500 with axillaries clearance, node diseases, and mastectomy (usually to the chest and the lymphatic nodes of the region) showed significant actual radiation therapy gains; 5-year local residual threats 6 percent vs. 23 percent and 15-year mortality risk 54.7 percent vs. 60.1 percent. In all patients, regardless of either their age group or characteristics of the tumor and major radiotherapy trials the radiation treatment achieved a comparable relative reduction. There were also significant, total reductions even where the control risks were high. To evaluate the life-threatening radiation therapy side effects, radiation therapy and further surgery experiments were not paired with radiation therapy. There was a substantial excess occurrence of contra lateral BC (rate 1.18, SE=0.06, 2p=0.002) and a considerable amount of NBC (Non-breast Cancer) deaths in irradiated females (rate 1.12, SE 0.04, 2p=0,001) under at least some of these older systems. There was a substantial amount of these shows. For the first five years, they all were small but persisted after the 15th year. The surplus death was primarily due to heart failure (1.27, SE 0.07 and 2p=0.0001 ratios) and lung cancer (1.78 ratio, SE 0.22, 2p=0.0004 ratio) (Trialists',2005)

Unraveling the human genome sequence allowed genetic variations to be detected in unparalleled detail in cancers. The protein code of a gene is determined in tumor types to initiate a systematic investigation of these changes (Küçüksayan,2022). Testing of 13,023 genes in 11 breasts and 11 colorectal cancers showed that, on average, nearly 90 mutant genes are produced by single tumors, but only a fraction of those belong to the neoplasm. We observed a high rate of recurrence of 189 genes (average 11 per tumor) mutating with strict criteria. The mostly the gene are not genetically modified and are potentially vulnerable to a wide broad range of cell behavior, like invasion, transcription, and adhesion. This evidence describes the genomic environment of two cancer forms in humans, offers new diagnosis and therapeutic goals, and offers promising avenues for fundamental tumor biological study (Sjoblom, 2006)

MicroRNAs (miRNAs) are small non-groups that control cell proliferation by addressing the translation or suppression of RNAs (Hironaka-Mitsuhashi, 2022). These may involve aberrant speech, like cancer, in human diseases. In the course of human lymphocytic leukemia miRNA, the aberrant expression has previously been identified where miRNA signatures are linked to particular biological clinical characteristics. We show here that miRNAs are abnormally expressed in human BC rather than normal breast tissue.

The overall miRNA phenomenon can distinguish normal from cancer tissues, with me-125b, mir-145, and mir-21 being the most significantly deregulated miRNAs. Microarray and Northern blot studies have verified findings. Mirrors whose activity was associated with particular histopathology features, such as the activity of estrogen and progesterone hormone, tumor process, index of proliferation, or vascular invasion may be defined (Iorio.2005).

To build a guide for the accuracy of receptor 2(HER 2) growth in human epidermal research and its use as a diagnostic marker for invasive BC (Prat, 2022). A team of experts was assembled by the American Society of Clinical Oncology (ASCO) and the college of American pathologists(AP), who thoroughly reviewed the literature and provided suggestions for optimum test success of HER2. The recommendations were reviewed and accepted by selected experts by the Directors ' Council.Current HER2 results could be flawed around 20 percent. If extensively checked experiments are performed, the results available remain uncertain as to the gain factor of anti-HER2 treatment, the effectiveness either of Immune Histochemistry (IHC) or of In-Situ Hybridization (ISH). The group advises that HER2 for all aggressive breast cancer should be determined. A research algorithm, including newer forms of brightfield ISH, is provided based on detailed and reproducible test results. Elements are given to efficiently minimize variability testing (for example the treatment of materials, omission from testing, and reporting criteria). A +ve HER2 outcome is an IHC staining of 3+ (a consistent, strong membrane staining 3 percent intrusive tumor cell), fluorescence in situ hybridization (FISH) is the product of more than six FISH ratio (HER2-gene signal to chromosome) or HER2 gene copies per nucleus. A +ve HER2 response is suggested. Further action is needed for the final decision to produce equivocal outcomes. To conduct HER2 studies, laboratories are advised to be 95 percent in line with another acknowledged test for optimistic and undesirable test values. The board highly advises the evaluation of training or improvements in labs, the implementation of standardized working protocols, and the introduction of rigorous laboratory accreditation requirements, performance testing, and skill assessment to ensure conformity with current research criteria. The panel suggests that HER2 studies be accomplished in a test center approved by CAP or a laboratory which complies with the criteria set out in this document on accreditation and competence testing (Wolff, 2007).

In women with HER2-Negative expression metastatic BC (Tarantino, 2022), 1-Agent trastuzumab assesses the care and effectiveness of that first-line drug. A first-line 4 mg/kg processing dose followed by 2 mg/kg a week or a higher 8 mg-kg loading dose and 4 mg/kg a week was periodically treated successfully for 114 women with HER2-overexpressing BC. The average response percentage is 26 (95 percentile CI, 18.2 percentile to 34.4 percentile), with 7 full responses and 23 partial responses. Response levels are 35 percentile (95 percentile of CI, 24.4 percentile to 44.7 percentile) and no (95 percentile of CI, 0 percentile to 15.5 percent), respectively, in 111 useful patients with 3 + or 2 + HER 2 over-expression by immunohistochemistry (IHC). Among the assessable HER2-over-expressed cases, the therapeutic benefit levels were 48 percentages and 7 percentages. Response levels were 34 percent (95 percentile CI, 23.9 percentile to 45.7 percentile) and 7 percentile (95 percentile CI, 0.8 percentile to22.8 percentile), in 108 useful patients with and without HER2-gene amplification through in situ-hybridization (FISH) study. Out of 30 patients with quantitative effects, 17 (57 percentage) were not followed up at 12 months or older, and 22 (51 percentage) of 43 patients with therapeutic advantages. Chills (25 percentage of patients), asthenia (23 percentage), fever (22 percentage), pain (18 percentage), and nausea (14 percentage) were the most frequent treatment-related adverse effects. Two patients (2 percent) had heart dysfunctions; all had a history of heart failure and did not need further therapy until trastuzumab was withdrawn. A dose-response association for reaction, longevity, or adverse effects was not explicitly seen (Vogel, 2002).

In a comprehensive multicenter analysis (Fitzal, 2022)177 women with observable metastatic breast cancer were checked both before the beginning of another phase of therapy and at the first follow-up examination for circulating tumor cell rates. Through regular MRI studies at the participating hospitals, the severity of the condition or the response to treatment has been determined. Until patients began a new therapy for metastatic cancer they analyzed the outcomes conferring to reference point rates of socializing tumor cells. The mean overall survivability (2.7 Mon. versus 7.0 Mon. P less than 0.001), and undersized existence (10.1 Mon. versus > 18 Mon., P><0.001) was found in patients in the training set of tumor proliferation levels of equal or greater than five in 7.5 ml of whole blood compared to that of less than five mingling lumps in 7.5 ml. These differences continued at the earliest visit following the start of therapy and the decline of the percentage of patients (from 49 to 30percentage), among the population with an adverse prognosis, suggesting that the procedure benefitted (2.1 months vs. 7.0 Months, progression-free survival, P less than 0.001;) cumulative survival of 8.2 months versus > 18months; P-value is less than 0.001). The multivariate analysis of Cox proportional hazards revealed the most important predictors of increasingly free and total survival of all variables in the predictive model, the circulating tuber cells at baseline, and during the initial follow-up visit (Cristofanilli.2004).

B

The HER2 protein is communicated in 25 to 30 percent of human breast cancer and contributes to an especially assertive disease type. In females through metastatic brain cancer that advanced after chemotherapy for metastatic diseases, recombinant demystified monoclonal anti-HER2 was tested for effectiveness and defense in a single-piece shape. Two hundred and twenty-two females were diagnosed with metastatic HER2-over-breast cancer developing with one or two chemotherapy schedules. Patients acknowledged an intravenous loading dosage of 4 mg/kg followed by a period of 2 mg/kg of treatment. Patients in the study required comprehensive previous treatment and progressive metastatic illness. Eight full response responses and 26 partial response responses were reported by a blinded, neutral response assessment committee and the objective response rate was 15 percent of the targeted care participants (95 percent confidence interval, 11 percentages to 21 percentages). The average response time was 9.1 months; the average survival time was 13 months. Infusion-related fever and / or chills were among the most frequent side effects in around 40 percent of patients, usually after the first infusion only, and were moderate to mild. Acetaminophen and/or diphenhydramine have been used extensively for these effects. Cardiac dysfunction (INGUL 2022) in 4.7 percent of cases was the most clinically significant adverse condition. Despite treatment-related adverse effects, only 1 percent of patients have halted the study (Cobleigh, 1999).

The effectiveness and safety of paclitaxel are similar to that of Paclitaxel plus bevacizumab (Takahashi, 2022) as initial therapy for metastatic BC in an open-label randomized phase-3 trial. On days 1,8 and 15 every 4 four weeks, we allocate patients randomly to take 90 mg paclitaxel per square meter of the body surface, either alone or at 10 mg per kg of body weight on days 1 and 15. The primary endpoint was progression less survival, and the secondary endpoint total survival. A total of 722 patients are enrolled between December 2001 and May 2004. In contrast to paclitaxel alone, Paclitaxel + bevacizumab substantially extended progression-free survival (median, 11.8 vs. 5.9 months; progression threat ratio of 0.60; $P<0.001$), raising the objective rate of reaction (36.9 percentage vs. 21.2 percentage), $P<0.001$. For all classes though, the average survival rate was comparable (median: 26.7 to 25.2 months; danger ratio: 0.88; $P=0.16$). The most frequent of patients undergoing paclitaxel and bevacizumab have been Grade three or four hypertension (14.8 percentage vs. 0.0 percent, $P<0.001$), proteinuria, (3.6 percentage c. 0.0 percentage, $P<0.001$), pain (2.2 percentage vs. 0.08), and stroke (1.9 percent c. 0.0 percentage, $P=0.02$). Paclitaxel plus bevacizumab were more common in cases (9.3 percentage vs 2.9 percentage $P<0.001$), however, febrile neutropenic remained unusual (< 1 percentage overall) (Miller, 2007).

The aggregation of tumor suppressor genes and mutations in on cogenesis (Fierti, 2022) responsible for human cancer. We also removed DNA from eleven breasts and evolved colorectal tumors to classify the genetic variations that exist in the tumor genesis and determined the gene sequences in these samples in the reference sequence database. They suggest that colorectal cancer and genomic environments of breast consist of a few of the frequently mutated pattern grade "mountains" and more in a count of gene "hills" are mutated at below levels, based on a study of exons containing 20,857 transcripts from 18,191 genes. We define statistical and bio informatics instruments to assist in detecting tumor genesis mutations. These findings will help to explain how human cancers are and how heterogeneous they are, and to use clinical genomics for tumor diagnosis and therapy (Jiao, 2019).

The incidence of BC has been raised by the ongoing purpose of hormone replacement therapy (HRT) (Tang,2022). Million Woman Research was conducted to examine the impact on accident and fatal cancer of different forms of HRT. In 1996-2001, 1084110 United Kingdom females aged 50-64 years are recruited Million Women Survey, given reports about the purpose of HRT, among rest of the personal data. Half of the women used HRT; after 2.6 and 4.1 years of cumulative followed for continuous observations, there have been 9364 invasive breast cancer and 637 BC deaths. At hiring, existing HRT customers have been more likely than ever to develop and die of Breast Cancer (adjusted 1.66 [95 percent IC 1.58-1.75], p<0.0001]) (1.22 [1.00-1.48], p=0.05). The probability of an accident or fatal illness was however not improved by the previous applications of HRT (1.01 [0.94-1.09] and 1.05 [0.82-1.34]). The frequency of the oestrogen-progestagen (2.00 [2.88–2.12], and the tibolone (1.45 [1.25–1.68], p<0.0001) for existing patients actually improved slightly (p<0.0001). The resulting danger was greatly higher for the estrogen-progestagen than for the other HRT forms (p<0.0001). This was attributed to a strong rise in the occurrence of estrogens-progestagen. Data are not that far from or from similar estrogen and progestagens or their dosage. For nasal, transversal, and injected estrogen formulations the relative risks were greatly raised separately (1.32 [1.21-1.45]; 1.24 [1.11-1.39]; and 1.65 [1.26-2.16], respectively; all p<0.0001). The risk of BC has increased with an increased cumulative period of usage by current users of the HRT form. It was estimated 10 years ' use of HRT in 5 additional Breast Cancer (95 percent CI 3-7) for 1 000 estrogen-only users and 19 (15-23) for 1000 estrogen-progestagen users for potential carcinogen combinations. The use of hormone replacement therapy (HRT) in British women between the age of 50 to 64 years have contributed to an estimated 20000 new breast cancers over the last decade and 15000 linked with estrogenprogestagen(Million,2003).

SOLUTIONS AND RECOMMENDATIONS

We also carried out a 20-year follow-up on the success of progressive (Halsted) mastectomy relative to that of breast survival. From 1973 to 1980, spontaneous mastectomy (349 patients) and breast-conserving treatment [75] (quadrantectomy), followed by radiation therapy on the ipsilateral mammalian tissue (352 patients), were given to 701 women with breast cancer estimated no more than 2 cm diameter. Since 1976, the adjuvant chemotherapy of cyclophosphamide, methotrexate, and fluorouracil was still used in all classes of active auxiliary nodes.30 participants in the BCT community liable for tumor reappearance on the same breast, while 8 of them had local repeats in the extreme mastectomy community (P<0.001). The average actual frequency of these incidents over 20 years was 8.8 percentages and 2.3 percentages. In comparison, the levels of contra lateral breast carcinomas, remote metastases, or secondary primary cancer did not vary substantially among the two groups. With a mean observation of 20 years, the mortality rate from all sources in the breast-conserving and extreme mastectomy community was 41.7 percent (P=1.0 percentage). (P=1.0) Breast cancer mortality rates were 26.1 percentage and 24.3 percentage respectively (P=0.8) (Veronesi, 2002).

The **Carolina Breast Cancer trial** (Prakash, 2022) (found out in May-1993 to Dec-1996), a workforce-based case-control trial that over-sampled premenopausal and African American participants, has applied immune histochemical replacements for each subtype to 496 occurrence instances of invasive BC. Subtype definitions were as follows: **luminal A** (ER-Positive and/or progesterone receptor-positive [PR+], HER2-), **luminal B** (ER-Positive and/or PR+, HER2+), basal-like (ER-, PR-, HER2-, cytokeratin 5/6 positive, and/or HER1+), HER2+/ER- (ER-, PR-, and HER2+), and unclassified (negative for all 5 markers). We analyzed the prevalence of genetically and menopausal-modified subtypes of breast cancer and determined their correlations with tumor frequency, axillaries nodal status, mitotic indices, nuclear pleomorphism, p53 mutation status, and survival in the BC. The subtype basal BC was more frequent in African American female premenopausal (39 percentage) compared to African American (14 percentage) and non-African American (16 percentage) female premenopausal women (P<0.001), with less prevalence of A (36 percentage vs. 59 percentage and 54 percentage respectively). The HER2+/ER-subtype was not isolated from race or menopause (6 percentage 9 percentages). The TP 53 mutations were of the basal tumors relative to luminal A (44 percentage vs 15 percentage, P <0.001), the mitotic index higher (odds ratio, 11.0; 95 percentage confidence [OR], 5.6-21.7), the nuclear pleomorphism greater than that of the luminary (OR, 9.7; 95 percent CI, 5.3-18.0). (OR, 8.3; 95 percent CI, 4.4-15.6) is greater. Similar breast cancer survivors varied according to the subtype (P<0.001) between HER2+/ ER-and basal-like subtypes with the shortest survival (Carey, 2006).

Gene expression tests may distinguish variations in gene activation sub classifying tumors which could be a better method to determine specific risks in patients with lymph node-negative BC than is currently accessible (Prat,2022). With Affymetrix Human U133a GeneChips, we studied the expression, for 286 non-adjuvant systemic therapy, of 22000 transcripts of total RNA of frozen tumors. We identified a 76-gene fingerprint for 115 tumors, consisting of 60 genes for estrogen receptor (ER) patients and 16 genes for ER-negative patients. In a later experimental study sample of 171 lymph node-negative patients, this signature was 93 percent sensitivity and 48 percentage precision. In detecting patients with remote metastases over 5 years (hazard ratio 5.67 [95 percentage CI 2.59-12.4]), even when adjusted for standard statistical variables for multivariate analysis, the genetic profile was highly insightful (5.55[2.46-12.5]). In subgroups, 84 premenopausal (9.60 [2.18-40.5]), 87 postmenopausal patients (4.04 [1.57-10.4]) and 79 tumor patients (14.1 [3.34-59.2]), a group for which the estimation of prognoses is especially difficult, were all highly pronounced by a 76-gene profile. The estimation is extremely difficult for such patients. A good tool for recognizing patients at high risk of remote recurrence is the trademark that has been identified. The ability to classify patients with a positive forecast may encourage physicians to skip systematic adjuvant therapy or to select less extreme therapeutic options following independent confirmation (Wang, 2005).

In women with BC, the authors note the efficacy and accuracy of intra operative lymphatic mapping with sentinel lymphadenectomy. Breast Cancer dissecting of the auxiliary lymph node (ALND)(Tang, 2022) is widely known for its treatment and prognosis, but dissecting is contentious. A sampling of the blind lymph node or stage I dissection does not involve such nodal metastases, but lymph edema may be due to ALND. Melanoma is an efficient and minimally invasive alternative to ALND for intra-operational lymph node imaging with sentinel lymphadenectomy to locate nodes with metastasis. A hundred and seventy-four methods were used to trace the main site of breast cancer with essential dye. The first ("sentinel") node, excised before ALND, was identified and accompanied by axillaries lymphatic drugs. In 114 of 174 (65.5 percentage) operations, sentinel nodes and axillary nodal were correctly predicted in 109 of 114 (95.6 percentage) cases. In the first section of the analysis, there was a clear learning curve, and all the fake-negative sentinel nodes were identified; sentinel nodes were identified to be 100 percent accurate in the past 87 procedures. The sentinel knot was the only tumor-involved lymph knot found in 16 of the 42 (38.0 percentage) clinically negative / pathologically stable axillae. In 54 more recent operations, the anatomical status of the sentinel node was investigated ten specimens included either nodal level II metastases that may have been absent from the study or weak (stage I) axillaries dissection. This research indicates that the sentinel node— the auxiliary lymph node, which most commonly includes breast cancer metastases— can be correctly identified by intraoperative lymphatic maps in certain cases. The methodology could increase the accuracy of inspection and could change ALND's position with more refinement and practice (Silva, 2021).

In women with MBC who have been developed following therapy based on trastuzumab lapatinib, an inhibitor of the epidermal human development receptor type2 (HER2, also said to be HER2 (Yamamoto,2022) and Neu) as well as the EGFR, is active in conjunction with capecitabine. In this analysis lapatinib plus capecitabine is compared to capecitabine alone. Since diagnosis therapies have trastuzumab, anthracycline, and taxane women have HER2 active, locally advanced or metastatic breast cancers have been randomly allocated both for combined therapy (lapatinib at 1250 mg dose once in a day regularly and capecitabine at 2000 Mg square meter dose in day 1-14 of the body surface area. The key result was improvement time, based on a random evaluation by independent feedback. The intermediate assessment of time to change fulfilled some requirements for early coverage in the combination-therapy community, based on dominance. The hazard ratio for the objectively measured transition period was 0.49 for 49 combination therapy incidents and 72 in the immunotherapy community, with a 95 percent confidence interval (CI), a 0.34-0.71; a P less than 0.001 intervals. In the combined treatment groups the meantime to improvement was 8.4 months compared with immunotherapy groups 4.4 months. Such progress has been accomplished without increased inflammation or symptomatic heart problems (Geyer, 2006).

Breast cancer is typically caused by digenetic changes in breast somatic (diploid) cells; however, susceptibility to the condition is often hereditary. The detection of early lesions that are important to the development of Breast Cancer by the public could also be possible with the genes inherited from breast cancer. Chromosome 17q21 tends in families with the early beginning disease of site and gene for the hereditary susceptibility to Breast Cancer. The genetic study shows in an early stage of the breast cancer risk binding to D17S74 (logarithm of the chance ratio for linkage) of 5.98 and in families of late starting circumstances in the unfavorable weak scores. The likelihood of heterogeneity of relations between families ranged from 2000:1 to over 10(6):1, based on a multi-point study of four different locations in the area (Hall, 1990).

BRCA1 and BRCA2 Germ line mutations [82] are particularly dangerous to Breast, ovarian Cancer and although the general size of these threats is unknown and will differ based on the setting. Multi-cases identified populations be enriched for high-risk mutations and/or other family-related causes, although research focused on unselected case samples has not produced specific risk estimates. We collected pedigree results from 22 trials affecting 8,139 indexes case-with breast cancer (2 percent) of the males (86 percentages) or females (12 percent). Total 500 cases with a germ line mutation in BCRA1 and BRCA2 are founded. To have had unselected case-with the family background. Because of a modified classification study, the rates of prevalence of ovarian and breast cancer in mutation Carriers are calculated base on the frequency of a few cancers in families in cases of the transmission index.

The combined average risk for breast cancer in BRCA1 transporters(Küçüksayan,2022) up to 70 years of age was 65 percentage (95 percentage sure 44 percentage -78 percentage) and 39 percentage (18 percentage -54 percentage) of ovarian cancer. The BRCA2 figures were 45 percentage (31 percentage -56 percentage) and 11 percentage (2.4 percentage -19 percentage), respectively. For the carrier of mutationBRCA1 (P trend 0.0012) associated chances of breast cancer decreased dramatically, however, of age. Carrier changes were greater if they were detected at less than the age of 35 years depending on the index of BC cases. We also have seen evidence that women from prior birth cohorts are at risk reduction and variability in incidence through mutation in both genes. The cancer risk trends were close in many cases, but their actual magnitudes, in particular BRCA2, were smaller. The frequency difference by age at the test case examination is consistent with other genes that change the carriers ' risk of cancer (Antoniou, 2003).

FUTURE RESEARCH DIRECTIONS

The Future Research on breast cancer detection using technology to reduce the risk factors for cancer patients. The breast cancer patient's digital health records can be maintained to monitor the patient's reminder notification for checkup's, medication and lab records. The drug history in prognosis can be used with machine learning concepts to predict the efficiency of the drug. The advance image processing methods can implement on the mammogram images for clear study and automated treatment plan.

B

CONCLUSION

The major contribution required for BC treatment is early detection methods, awareness of breast cancer, Primary examination, regular examinations. The imaging methods can predict and detect tumors at the very early Stage of the disease. The CAD application is built with more accuracy and precision in detecting tumors. The Deep Learning and Machine Learning concepts need to build with a higher detection rate and Stage of the11 cancer.

1. Calculate accuracy by using Deep Learning Technique for Breast Cancer identification.
2. Suggesting medicine for cancer reduction by using prescriptive analytics.

FUNDING INFORMATION

This research received no specific grant from any funding agency in the public, commercial, or not-for-profit sectors.

REFERENCES

Al-Hajj, M., Wicha, M. S., Benito-Hernandez, A., Morrison, S. J., & Clarke, M. F. (2003). Prospective identification of tumorigenic breast cancer cells. *Proceedings of the National Academy of Sciences of the United States of America*, 100(7), 3983–3988. doi:10.1073/pnas.0530291100 PMID:12629218

Antoniou, A., Pharoah, P. D., Narod, S., Risch, H. A., Eyfjord, J. E., Hopper, J. L., Loman, N., Olsson, H., Johannsson, O., Borg, Å., Pasini, B., Radice, P., Manoukian, S., Eccles, D. M., Tang, N., Olah, E., Anton-Culver, H., Warner, E., Lubinski, J., ... Easton, D. (2003). Average risks of breast and ovarian cancer associated with BRCA1 or BRCA2 mutations detected in case series unselected for family history: A combined analysis of 22 studies. *American Journal of Human Genetics*, 72(5), 1117–1130. doi:10.1086/375033 PMID:12677558

Carey, L. A., Perou, C. M., Livasy, C. A., Dressler, L. G., Cowan, D., Conway, K., Karaca, G., Troester, M. A., Tse, C. K., Edmiston, S., Deming, S. L., Geradts, J., Cheang, M. C. U., Nielsen, T. O., Moorman, P. G., Earp, H. S., & Millikan, R. C. (2006). Race, breast cancer subtypes, and survival in the Carolina Breast Cancer Study. *Journal of the American Medical Association*, 295(21), 2492–2502. doi:10.1001/jama.295.21.2492 PMID:16757721

Chan, C. W. H., Li, C., Xiao, E. J., Li, M., Phiri, P. G. M., Yan, T., & Chan, J. Y. W. (2022). Association between genetic polymorphisms in cytochrome P450 enzymes and survivals in women with breast cancer receiving adjuvant endocrine therapy: A systematic review and meta-analysis. *Expert Reviews in Molecular Medicine*, 24, 24. doi:10.1017/erm.2021.28 PMID:34991754

Cheng, Y. Y., Tuzo, E. T., Dalley, J. W., & Tsai, T. H. (2022). Dose-dependent effects of Hedyotis diffusa extract on the pharmacokinetics of tamoxifen, 4-hydroxytamoxifen, and N-desmethyltamoxifen. *Biomedicine and Pharmacotherapy*, *145*, 112466. doi:10.1016/j.biopha.2021.112466 PMID:34839255

Cobleigh, M. A., Vogel, C. L., Tripathy, D., Robert, N. J., Scholl, S., Fehrenbacher, L., Wolter, J. M., Paton, V., Shak, S., Lieberman, G., & Slamon, D. J. (1999). Multinational study of the efficacy and safety of humanized anti-HER2 monoclonal antibody in women who have HER2-overexpressing metastatic breast cancer that has progressed after chemotherapy for metastatic disease. *Journal of Clinical Oncology*, *17*(9), 2639–2639. doi:10.1200/JCO.1999.17.9.2639 PMID:10561337

Collaborative Group on Hormonal Factors in Breast Cancer. (1997). Breast cancer and hormone replacement therapy: Collaborative reanalysis of data from 51 epidemiological studies of 52 705 women with breast cancer and 108 411 women without breast cancer. *Lancet*, *350*(9084), 1047–1059. doi:10.1016/S0140-6736(97)08233-0 PMID:10213546

Cory, L., Brensinger, C., Burger, R. A., Giuntoli, R. L. II, Morgan, M. A., Latif, N., Lin, L. L., & Ko, E. M. (2022). Patterns of adjuvant treatment and survival outcomes in stage I uterine carcinosarcoma. *Gynecologic Oncology Reports*, *39*, 100930. doi:10.1016/j.gore.2022.100930 PMID:35111895

Cristofanilli, M., Budd, G. T., Ellis, M. J., Stopeck, A., Matera, J., Miller, M. C., Reuben, J. M., Doyle, G. V., Allard, W. J., Terstappen, L. W., & Hayes, D. F. (2004). Circulating tumor cells, disease progression, and survival in metastatic breast cancer. *The New England Journal of Medicine*, *351*(8), 781–791. doi:10.1056/NEJMoa040766 PMID:15317891

Daniel, S., Venkateswaran, C., Singh, C., Hutchinson, A., & Johnson, M. J. (2022). "So, when a woman becomes ill, the total structure of the family is affected, they can't do anything…" Voices from the community on women with breast cancer in India: A qualitative focus group study. *Supportive Care in Cancer*, *30*(1), 951–963. doi:10.100700520-021-06475-4 PMID:34420101

Dredze, L. M., Friger, M., Ariad, S., Koretz, M., Delgato, B., Shaco-Levy, R., ... Geffen, D. B. (2022). *Neoadjuvant Therapy with Doxorubicin-Cyclophosphamide Followed by Weekly Paclitaxel in Early Breast Cancer: A Retrospective Analysis of 200 Consecutive Patients Treated in A Single Center with A Median Follow-Up of 9.5 Years*. Academic Press.

Early Breast Cancer Trialists' Collaborative Group. (1998). Polychemotherapy for early breast cancer: An overview of the randomised trials. *Lancet*, *352*(9132), 930–942. doi:10.1016/S0140-6736(98)03301-7 PMID:9752815

Early Breast Cancer Trialists' Collaborative Group. (2005). Effects of radiotherapy and of differences in the extent of surgery for early breast cancer on local recurrence and 15-year survival: An overview of the randomised trials. *Lancet*, *366*(9503), 2087–2106. doi:10.1016/S0140-6736(05)67887-7 PMID:16360786

Elston, C. W., & Ellis, I. O. (1991). Pathological prognostic factors in breast cancer. I. The value of histological grade in breast cancer: Experience from a large study with long-term follow-up. *Histopathology*, *19*(5), 403–410. doi:10.1111/j.1365-2559.1991.tb00229.x PMID:1757079

Fierti, A. O., Yakass, M. B., Okertchiri, E. A., Adadey, S. M., & Quaye, O. (2022). The Role of Epstein-Barr Virus in Modulating Key Tumor Suppressor Genes in Associated Malignancies: Epigenetics, Transcriptional, and Post-Translational Modifications. *Biomolecules*, *12*(1), 127. doi:10.3390/biom12010127 PMID:35053275

Fisher, B., Anderson, S., Bryant, J., Margolese, R. G., Deutsch, M., Fisher, E. R., Jeong, J.-H., & Wolmark, N. (2002). Twenty-year follow-up of a randomized trial comparing total mastectomy, lumpectomy, and lumpectomy plus irradiation for the treatment of invasive breast cancer. *The New England Journal of Medicine, 347*(16), 1233–1241. doi:10.1056/NEJMoa022152 PMID:12393820

Fisher, B., Costantino, J. P., Wickerham, D. L., Redmond, C. K., Kavanah, M., Cronin, W. M., Vogel, V., Robidoux, A., Dimitrov, N., Atkins, J., Daly, M., Wieand, S., Tan-Chiu, E., Ford, L., & Wolmark, N. (1998). Tamoxifen for prevention of breast cancer: Report of the National Surgical Adjuvant Breast and Bowel Project P-1 Study. *Journal of the National Cancer Institute, 90*(18), 1371–1388. doi:10.1093/jnci/90.18.1371 PMID:9747868

Fitzal, F., Bolliger, M., Dunkler, D., Geroldinger, A., Gambone, L., Heil, J., Riedel, F., de Boniface, J., Andre, C., Matrai, Z., Pukancsik, D., Paulinelli, R. R., Ostapenko, V., Burneckis, A., Ostapenko, A., Ostapenko, E., Meani, F., Harder, Y., Bonollo, M., ... Weber, W. P. (2022). Retrospective, multicenter analysis comparing conventional with oncoplastic breast conserving surgery: Oncological and surgical outcomes in women with high-risk breast cancer from the OPBC-01/iTOP2 study. *Annals of Surgical Oncology, 29*(2), 1061–1070. doi:10.124510434-021-10809-1 PMID:34647202

Ford, D., Easton, D. F., Stratton, M., Narod, S., Goldgar, D., Devilee, P., Bishop, D. T., Weber, B., Lenoir, G., Chang-Claude, J., Sobol, H., Teare, M. D., Struewing, J., Arason, A., Scherneck, S., Peto, J., Rebbeck, T. R., Tonin, P., Neuhausen, S., ... Zelada-Hedman, M.Breast Cancer Linkage Consortium. (1998). Genetic heterogeneity and penetrance analysis of the BRCA1 and BRCA2 genes in breast cancer families. *American Journal of Human Genetics, 62*(3), 676–689. doi:10.1086/301749 PMID:9497246

Gail, M. H., Brinton, L. A., Byar, D. P., Corle, D. K., Green, S. B., Schairer, C., & Mulvihill, J. J. (1989). Projecting individualized probabilities of developing breast cancer for white females who are being examined annually. *Journal of the National Cancer Institute, 81*(24), 1879–1886. doi:10.1093/jnci/81.24.1879 PMID:2593165

Geyer, C. E., Forster, J., Lindquist, D., Chan, S., Romieu, C. G., Pienkowski, T., Jagiello-Gruszfeld, A., Crown, J., Chan, A., Kaufman, B., Skarlos, D., Campone, M., Davidson, N., Berger, M., Oliva, C., Rubin, S. D., Stein, S., & Cameron, D. (2006). Lapatinib plus capecitabine for HER2-positive advanced breast cancer. *The New England Journal of Medicine, 355*(26), 2733–2743. doi:10.1056/NEJMoa064320 PMID:17192538

Goldhirsch, A., Gelber, R. D., & Coates, A. S. (2005). What are the long-term effects of chemotherapy and hormonal therapy for early breast cancer? *Nature Clinical Practice. Oncology, 2*(9), 440–441. doi:10.1038/ncponc0296 PMID:16265010

Hall, J. M., Lee, M. K., Newman, B., Morrow, J. E., Anderson, L. A., Huey, B., & King, M. C. (1990). Linkage of early-onset familial breast cancer to chromosome 17q21. *Science, 250*(4988), 1684–1689. doi:10.1126cience.2270482 PMID:2270482

Hironaka-Mitsuhashi, A., Takayama, S., Jimbo, K., Suto, A., Shimomura, A., & Ochiya, T. (2022). Clinical Application of MicroRNAs in Breast Cancer Treatment. *Archives of Breast Cancer*, 20-31.

Hohenschurz-Schmidt, D., Kleykamp, B. A., Draper-Rodi, J., Vollert, J., Chan, J., Ferguson, M., McNicol, E., Phalip, J., Evans, S. R., Turk, D. C., Dworkin, R. H., & Rice, A. S. (2022). Pragmatic trials of pain therapies: A systematic review of methods. *Pain, 163*(1), 21–46. doi:10.1097/j.pain.0000000000002317 PMID:34490854

Hohenschurz-Schmidt, D., Kleykamp, B. A., Draper-Rodi, J., Vollert, J., Chan, J., Ferguson, M., McNicol, E., Phalip, J., Evans, S. R., Turk, D. C., Dworkin, R. H., & Rice, A. S. (2022). Pragmatic trials of pain therapies: A systematic review of methods. *Pain*, *163*(1), 21–46. doi:10.1097/j.pain.0000000000002317 PMID:34490854

Iorio, M. V., Ferracin, M., Liu, C. G., Veronese, A., Spizzo, R., Sabbioni, S., Magri, E., Pedriali, M., Fabbri, M., Campiglio, M., Ménard, S., Palazzo, J. P., Rosenberg, A., Musiani, P., Volinia, S., Nenci, I., Calin, G. A., Querzoli, P., Negrini, M., & Croce, C. M. (2005). MicroRNA gene expression deregulation in human breast cancer. *Cancer Research*, *65*(16), 7065–7070. doi:10.1158/0008-5472.CAN-05-1783 PMID:16103053

Ivanov, O., Ličina, J., Petrović, B., Trivković, J., & Marjanović, M. (2022). Implementation of accelerated partial breast irradiation at the Oncology Institute of Vojvodina. *Srpski Arhiv za Celokupno Lekarstvo*, *150*(00), 10–10. doi:10.2298/SARH200422010I

Jiao, X., Hooper, S. D., Djureinovic, T., Larsson, C., Wärnberg, F., Tellgren-Roth, C., Botling, J., & Sjöblom, T. (2013). Gene rearrangements in hormone receptor negative breast cancers revealed by mate pair sequencing. *BMC Genomics*, *14*(1), 1–11. doi:10.1186/1471-2164-14-165 PMID:23496902

Kayahan, M. (2022). Can Skin Sparing Mastectomy and Immediate Submuscular Implant-Based Reconstruction Be a Better Choice in Treatment of Early-Stage Breast Cancer? *European Journal of Breast Health*, *18*(1), 55–62. doi:10.4274/ejbh.galenos.2021.2021-6-4 PMID:35059592

Kharel, S., Shrestha, S., Yadav, S., Shakya, P., Baidya, S., & Hirachan, S. (2022). BRCA1/BRCA2 mutation spectrum analysis in South Asia: A systematic review. *The Journal of International Medical Research*, *50*(1). doi:10.1177/03000605211070757 PMID:35000471

Krutilina, R. I., Playa, H., Brooks, D. L., Schwab, L. P., Parke, D. N., Oluwalana, D., Layman, D. R., Fan, M., Johnson, D. L., Yue, J., Smallwood, H., & Seagroves, T. N. (2022). HIF-dependent CKB expression promotes breast cancer metastasis, whereas cyclocreatine therapy impairs cellular invasion and improves chemotherapy efficacy. *Cancers (Basel)*, *14*(1), 27. doi:10.3390/cancers14010027 PMID:35008190

Küçüksayan, E., Sansone, A., Chatgilialoglu, C., Ozben, T., Tekeli, D., Talibova, G., & Ferreri, C. (2022). Sapienic Acid Metabolism Influences Membrane Plasticity and Protein Signaling in Breast Cancer Cell Lines. *Cells*, *11*(2), 225. doi:10.3390/cells11020225 PMID:35053341

Lange, T., Luebber, F., Grasshoff, H., & Besedovsky, L. (2022, January). The contribution of sleep to the neuroendocrine regulation of rhythms in human leukocyte traffic. In *Seminars in immunopathology* (pp. 1–16). Springer Berlin Heidelberg. doi:10.100700281-021-00904-6

Li, J., Yen, C., Liaw, D., Podsypanina, K., Bose, S., Wang, S. I., ... Parsons, R. (1997). PTEN, a putative protein tyrosine phosphatase gene mutated in human brain, breast, and prostate cancer. *Science*, *275*(5308), 1943-1947.

Ling, Y., Liang, G., Lin, Q., Fang, X., Luo, Q., Cen, Y., Mehrpour, M., Hamai, A., Liu, Z., Shi, Y., Li, J., Lin, W., Jia, S., Yang, W., Liu, Q., Song, E., Li, J., & Gong, C. (2022). circCDYL2 promotes trastuzumab resistance via sustaining HER2 downstream signaling in breast cancer. *Molecular Cancer*, *21*(1), 1–16. doi:10.118612943-021-01476-7 PMID:34980129

Maheswari, V. U., Prasad, G. V., & Raju, S. V. (2021). Facial expression analysis using local directional stigma mean patterns and convolutional neural networks. *International Journal of Knowledge-based and Intelligent Engineering Systems*, 25(1), 119–128. doi:10.3233/KES-210057

Maheswari, V. U., Raju, S. V., & Reddy, K. S. (2019, November). Local directional weighted threshold patterns (LDWTP) for facial expression recognition. In *2019 Fifth International Conference on Image Information Processing (ICIIP)* (pp. 167-170). IEEE. 10.1109/ICIIP47207.2019.8985829

Malkin, D., Li, F. P., Strong, L. C., Fraumeni, J. F. Jr, Nelson, C. E., Kim, D. H., Kassel, J., Gryka, M. A., Bischoff, F. Z., Tainsky, M. A., & Friend, S. H. (1990). Germ line p53 mutations in a familial syndrome of breast cancer, sarcomas, and other neoplasms. *Science*, 250(4985), 1233–1238. doi:10.1126cience.1978757 PMID:1978757

Meyer. (2018). Vers la modelisation des traitements de radiotherapie. Academic Press.

Miki, Y., Swensen, J., Shattuck-Eidens, D., Futreal, P. A., Harshman, K., Tavtigian, S., Liu, Q., Cochran, C., Bennett, L. M., Ding, W., Bell, R., Rosenthal, J., Hussey, C., Tran, T., McClure, M., Frye, C., Hattier, T., Phelps, R., Haugen-Strano, A., ... Skolnick, M. H. (1994). A strong candidate for the breast and ovarian cancer susceptibility gene BRCA1. *Science*, 266(5182), 66–71. doi:10.1126cience.7545954 PMID:7545954

Miller, K., Wang, M., Gralow, J., Dickler, M., Cobleigh, M., Perez, E. A., Shenkier, T., Cella, D., & Davidson, N. E. (2007). Paclitaxel plus bevacizumab versus paclitaxel alone for metastatic breast cancer. *The New England Journal of Medicine*, 357(26), 2666–2676. doi:10.1056/NEJMoa072113 PMID:18160686

Million Women Study Collaborators. (2003). Breast cancer and hormone-replacement therapy in the Million Women Study. *Lancet*, 362(9382), 419–427. doi:10.1016/S0140-6736(03)14065-2 PMID:12927427

Müller, A., Homey, B., Soto, H., Ge, N., Catron, D., Buchanan, M. E., ... Zlotnik, A. (2001). Involvement of chemokine receptors in breast cancer metastasis. *Nature*, 410(6824), 50-56.

Nathwani, R., Kockerling, D., Mullish, B. H., Cole, A., Lemoine, M., Antoniades, C. G., Thursz, M. R., & Dhar, A. (2022). Non-selective beta-blocker use in cirrhosis: The additional benefit in preventing secondary infections. *Frontline Gastroenterology*, 13(1), 86–88. doi:10.1136/flgastro-2021-101818 PMID:34970431

Obi, N., Werner, S., Thelen, F., Becher, H., & Pantel, K. (2022). Metastatic Breast Cancer Recurrence after Bone Fractures. *Cancers (Basel)*, 14(3), 601. doi:10.3390/cancers14030601 PMID:35158869

Omran, M., Tham, E., Brandberg, Y., Ahlström, H., Lundgren, C., Paulsson-Karlsson, Y., Kuchinskaya, E., Silander, G., Rosén, A., Persson, F., Leonhardt, H., Stenmark-Askmalm, M., Berg, J., van Westen, D., Bajalica-Lagercrantz, S., & Blomqvist, L. (2022). Whole-Body MRI Surveillance—Baseline Findings in the Swedish Multicentre Hereditary TP53-Related Cancer Syndrome Study (SWEP53). *Cancers (Basel)*, 14(2), 380. doi:10.3390/cancers14020380 PMID:35053544

Overgaard, M., Hansen, P. S., Overgaard, J., Rose, C., Andersson, M., Bach, F., Kjaer, M., Gadeberg, C. C., Mouridsen, H. T., Jensen, M.-B., & Zedeler, K. (1997). Postoperative radiotherapy in high-risk premenopausal women with breast cancer who receive adjuvant chemotherapy. *The New England Journal of Medicine*, 337(14), 949–955. doi:10.1056/NEJM199710023371401 PMID:9395428

Paik, S., Shak, S., Tang, G., Kim, C., Baker, J., Cronin, M., Baehner, F. L., Walker, M. G., Watson, D., Park, T., Hiller, W., Fisher, E. R., Wickerham, D. L., Bryant, J., & Wolmark, N. (2004). A multigene assay to predict recurrence of tamoxifen-treated, node-negative breast cancer. *The New England Journal of Medicine, 351*(27), 2817–2826. doi:10.1056/NEJMoa041588 PMID:15591335

Piccart-Gebhart, M. J., Procter, M., Leyland-Jones, B., Goldhirsch, A., Untch, M., Smith, I., Gianni, L., Baselga, J., Bell, R., Jackisch, C., Cameron, D., Dowsett, M., Barrios, C. H., Steger, G., Huang, C.-S., Andersson, M., Inbar, M., Lichinitser, M., Láng, I., ... Gelber, R. D. (2005). Trastuzumab after adjuvant chemotherapy in HER2-positive breast cancer. *The New England Journal of Medicine, 353*(16), 1659–1672. doi:10.1056/NEJMoa052306 PMID:16236737

Prakash, I., Neely, N. B., Thomas, S. M., Sammons, S., Blitzblau, R. C., DiLalla, G. A., Hyslop, T., Menendez, C. S., Plichta, J. K., Rosenberger, L. H., Fayanju, O. M., Hwang, E. S., & Greenup, R. A. (2022). Utilization of neoadjuvant chemotherapy in high-risk, node-negative early breast cancer. *Cancer Medicine, 11*(4), 1099–1108. doi:10.1002/cam4.4517 PMID:34989142

Prat, A., Guarneri, V., Pascual, T., Brasó-Maristany, F., Sanfeliu, E., Paré, L., Schettini, F., Martínez, D., Jares, P., Griguolo, G., Dieci, M. V., Cortés, J., Llombart-Cussac, A., Conte, B., Marín-Aguilera, M., Chic, N., Puig-Butillé, J. A., Martínez, A., Galván, P., ... Perou, C. M. (2022). Development and validation of the new HER2DX assay for predicting pathological response and survival outcome in early-stage HER2-positive breast cancer. *EBioMedicine, 75*, 103801. doi:10.1016/j.ebiom.2021.103801 PMID:34990895

Raza, S., Rajak, S., Tewari, A., Gupta, P., Chattopadhyay, N., Sinha, R. A., & Chakravarti, B. (2022, January). Multifaceted role of chemokines in solid tumors: from biology to therapy. In *Seminars in cancer biology*. Academic Press. doi:10.1016/j.semcancer.2021.12.011

Romond, E. H., Perez, E. A., Bryant, J., Suman, V. J., Geyer, C. E. Jr, Davidson, N. E., Tan-Chiu, E., Martino, S., Paik, S., Kaufman, P. A., Swain, S. M., Pisansky, T. M., Fehrenbacher, L., Kutteh, L. A., Vogel, V. G., Visscher, D. W., Yothers, G., Jenkins, R. B., Brown, A. M., ... Wolmark, N. (2005). Trastuzumab plus adjuvant chemotherapy for operable HER2-positive breast cancer. *The New England Journal of Medicine, 353*(16), 1673–1684. doi:10.1056/NEJMoa052122 PMID:16236738

Schrijver, L. H., Mooij, T. M., Pijpe, A., Sonke, G. S., Mourits, M. J., Andrieu, N., ... Rookus, M. A. (2022). Oral Contraceptive Use in BRCA1 and BRCA2 Mutation Carriers: Absolute Cancer Risks and Benefits. *Journal of the National Cancer Institute.*

Silva, P., Maronezi, M. C., Gasser, B., Pavan, L., Aires, L., Uscategui, R. R. A., ... Feliciano, M. A. R. (2021). Updates in The Evaluation of Locoregional Lymph Nodes in Bitches With Mammary Tumors. *Revista De Ciência Veterinária E Saúde Pública, 8*(1), 59-72.

Sjoblom, T., Jones, S., Wood, L. D., Parsons, D. W., Lin, J., Barber, T. D., ... Velculescu, V. E. (2006). The consensus coding sequences of human breast and colorectal cancers. *Science, 314*(5797), 268-274.

Slamon, D. J., Clark, G. M., Wong, S. G., Levin, W. J., Ullrich, A., & McGuire, W. L. (1987). Human breast cancer: correlation of relapse and survival with amplification of the HER-2/neu oncogene. *Science, 235*(4785), 177-182.

Slamon, D. J., Godolphin, W., Jones, L. A., Holt, J. A., Wong, S. G., Keith, D. E., Levin, W. J., Stuart, S. G., Udove, J., Ullrich, A., & Press, M. F. (1989). Studies of the HER-2/neu proto-oncogene in human breast and ovarian cancer. *Science, 244*(4905), 707–712. doi:10.1126cience.2470152 PMID:2470152

Slamon, D. J., Leyland-Jones, B., Shak, S., Fuchs, H., Paton, V., Bajamonde, A., Fleming, T., Eiermann, W., Wolter, J., Pegram, M., Baselga, J., & Norton, L. (2001). Use of chemotherapy plus a monoclonal antibody against HER2 for metastatic breast cancer that overexpresses HER2. *The New England Journal of Medicine, 344*(11), 783–792. doi:10.1056/NEJM200103153441101 PMID:11248153

Takahashi, S., Takei, Y., Tamura, K., Taneichi, A., Takahashi, Y., Yoshiba, T., ... Fujiwara, H. (2022). Response to and toxicity of weekly paclitaxel and carboplatin in patients with stage IIIC-IV ovarian cancer and poor general condition. *Molecular and Clinical Oncology, 16*(1), 1–7. PMID:34881034

Tang, H. C., Cheng, Y. Y., & Guo, H. R. (2022). Association between hormone replacement therapy and carpal tunnel syndrome: A nationwide population-based study. *BMJ Open, 12*(1), e055139. doi:10.1136/bmjopen-2021-055139 PMID:34983770

Tarantino, P., Gandini, S., Nicolò, E., Trillo, P., Giugliano, F., Zagami, P., Vivanet, G., Bellerba, F., Trapani, D., Marra, A., Esposito, A., Criscitiello, C., Viale, G., & Curigliano, G. (2022). Evolution of low HER2 expression between early and advanced-stage breast cancer. *European Journal of Cancer, 163*, 35–43. doi:10.1016/j.ejca.2021.12.022 PMID:35032815

Tur, C., Grussu, F., De Angelis, F., Prados, F., Kanber, B., Calvi, A., ... Wheeler-Kingshott, C. A. G. (2022). Spatial patterns of brain lesions assessed through covariance estimations of lesional voxels in multiple Sclerosis: The SPACE-MS technique. *NeuroImage. Clinical, 33*, 102904. doi:10.1016/j.nicl.2021.102904 PMID:34875458

Utomo, R. Y., Wulandari, F., Novitasari, D., Susidarti, R. A., Kirihata, M., Hermawan, A., & Meiyanto, E. (2022). Synthesis and cytotoxicity of the boron carrier pentagamaboronon-0-ol for boron neutron capture therapy against breast cancer. *Journal of Advanced Pharmaceutical Technology & Research, 13*(1), 70. PMID:35223445

Van De Vijver, M. J., He, Y. D., Van't Veer, L. J., Dai, H., Hart, A. A., Voskuil, D. W., Schreiber, G. J., Peterse, J. L., Roberts, C., Marton, M. J., Parrish, M., Atsma, D., Witteveen, A., Glas, A., Delahaye, L., van der Velde, T., Bartelink, H., Rodenhuis, S., Rutgers, E. T., ... Bernards, R. (2002). A gene-expression signature as a predictor of survival in breast cancer. *The New England Journal of Medicine, 347*(25), 1999–2009. doi:10.1056/NEJMoa021967 PMID:12490681

Van't Veer, L. J., Dai, H., Van De Vijver, M. J., He, Y. D., Hart, A. A., Mao, M., ... Friend, S. H. (2002). Gene expression profiling predicts clinical outcome of breast cancer. *Nature, 415*(6871), 530-536.

Veeramani, S., Yuan, T. C., Chen, S. J., Lin, F. F., Petersen, J. E., Shaheduzzaman, S., Srivastava, S., MacDonald, R. G., & Lin, M. F. (2005). Cellular prostatic acid phosphatase: A protein tyrosine phosphatase involved in androgen-independent proliferation of prostate cancer. *Endocrine-Related Cancer, 12*(4), 805–822. doi:10.1677/erc.1.00950 PMID:16322323

Veronesi, U., Cascinelli, N., Mariani, L., Greco, M., Saccozzi, R., Luini, A., Aguilar, M., & Marubini, E. (2002). Twenty-year follow-up of a randomized study comparing breast-conserving surgery with radical mastectomy for early breast cancer. *The New England Journal of Medicine, 347*(16), 1227–1232. doi:10.1056/NEJMoa020989 PMID:12393819

Vogel, C. L., Cobleigh, M. A., Tripathy, D., Gutheil, J. C., Harris, L. N., Fehrenbacher, L., Slamon, D. J., Murphy, M., Novotny, W. F., Burchmore, M., Shak, S., Stewart, S. J., & Press, M. (2002). Efficacy and safety of trastuzumab as a single agent in first-line treatment of HER2-overexpressing metastatic breast cancer. *Journal of Clinical Oncology, 20*(3), 719–726. doi:10.1200/JCO.2002.20.3.719 PMID:11821453

Wang, Y., Klijn, J. G., Zhang, Y., Sieuwerts, A. M., Look, M. P., Yang, F., Talantov, D., Timmermans, M., Meijer-van Gelder, M. E., Yu, J., Jatkoe, T., Berns, E. M. J. J., Atkins, D., & Foekens, J. A. (2005). Gene-expression profiles to predict distant metastasis of lymph-node-negative primary breast cancer. *Lancet, 365*(9460), 671–679. doi:10.1016/S0140-6736(05)17947-1 PMID:15721472

Wolff, A. C., Hammond, M. E. H., Schwartz, J. N., Hagerty, K. L., Allred, D. C., Cote, R. J., Dowsett, M., Fitzgibbons, P. L., Hanna, W. M., Langer, A., McShane, L. M., Paik, S., Pegram, M. D., Perez, E. A., Press, M. F., Rhodes, A., Sturgeon, C., Taube, S. E., Tubbs, R., ... Hayes, D. F. (2007). American Society of Clinical Oncology/College of American Pathologists guideline recommendations for human epidermal growth factor receptor 2 testing in breast cancer. *Archives of Pathology & Laboratory Medicine, 131*(1), 18–43. doi:10.5858/2007-131-18-ASOCCO PMID:19548375

Wooster, R., Bignell, G., Lancaster, J., Swift, S., Seal, S., Mangion, J., Collins, N., Gregory, S., Gumbs, C., Micklem, G., Barfoot, R., Hamoudi, R., Patel, S., Rices, C., Biggs, P., Hashim, Y., Smith, A., Connor, F., Arason, A., ... Stratton, M. R. (1995). Identification of the breast cancer susceptibility gene BRCA2. *Nature, 378*(6559), 789–792. doi:10.1038/378789a0 PMID:8524414

Yamamoto, H., & Hirasawa, A. (2022). Homologous Recombination Deficiencies and Hereditary Tumors. *International Journal of Molecular Sciences, 23*(1), 348. doi:10.3390/ijms23010348 PMID:35008774

Zhong, Y. M., Tong, F., & Shen, J. (2022). Lympho-vascular invasion impacts the prognosis in breast-conserving surgery: A systematic review and meta-analysis. *BMC Cancer, 22*(1), 1–9. doi:10.118612885-022-09193-0 PMID:35073848

Zhou, Q., Zhou, L. Q., Li, S. H., Yuan, Y. W., Liu, L., Wang, J. L., Wu, D.-Z., Wu, Y., & Xin, L. (2020). Identification of subtype-specific genes signature by WGCNA for prognostic prediction in diffuse type gastric cancer. *Aging (Albany NY), 12*(17), 17418–17435. doi:10.18632/aging.103743 PMID:32915770

ADDITIONAL READING

Bandyopadhyay, S. K. (2010). Pre-processing of mammogram images. *International Journal of Engineering Science and Technology, 2*(11), 6753-6758.

Gonzalez, R. C. (2009). *Digital image processing.* Pearson Education India.

Han, Y., Kim, D. W., & Kwon, H. J. (2012). Application of digital image cross-correlation and smoothing function to the diagnosis of breast cancer. *Journal of the Mechanical Behavior of Biomedical Materials, 14*, 7-18.

Patel, J. J., & Hadia, S. K. (2021). An enhancement of mammogram images for breast cancer classification using artificial neural networks. *IAES International Journal of Artificial Intelligence, 10*(2), 332. doi:10.11591/ijai.v10.i2.pp332-345

Robertson, S., Azizpour, H., Smith, K., & Hartman, J. (2018). Digital image analysis in breast pathology—From image processing techniques to artificial intelligence. *Translational Research; the Journal of Laboratory and Clinical Medicine, 194*, 19–35. doi:10.1016/j.trsl.2017.10.010 PMID:29175265

Sung, H., Ferlay, J., Siegel, R. L., Laversanne, M., Soerjomataram, I., Jemal, A., & Bray, F. (2021). Global cancer statistics 2020: GLOBOCAN estimates of incidence and mortality worldwide for 36 cancers in 185 countries. *CA: a Cancer Journal for Clinicians, 71*(3), 209–249. doi:10.3322/caac.21660 PMID:33538338

Swapna, M., & Hegde, N. (2021). A Multifarious Diagnosis of Breast Cancer Using Mammogram Images–Systematic Review. *IOP Conference Series. Materials Science and Engineering, 1042*(1), 012012. doi:10.1088/1757-899X/1042/1/012012

Swapna, M., Viswanadhula, U. M., Aluvalu, R., Vardharajan, V., & Kotecha, K. (2022). Bio-Signals in Medical Applications and Challenges Using Artificial Intelligence. *Journal of Sensor and Actuator Networks, 11*(1), 17. doi:10.3390/jsan11010017

KEY TERMS AND DEFINITIONS

BRCA1: Human tumor suppressor gene and is responsible for repairing DNA.

Breast Cancer Symptoms: Cancer cells, lumps, blood discharge, and deformation of shape are symptoms for breast cancer.

Chemotherapy: The drug-based treatment for cancer cells.

HER2: The positive breast cancer is a breast cancer that tests positive for a protein called human epidermal growth factor receptor 2 (HER2).

Radiation Therapy: The cancer cell organs are exposed to ionizing radiation. It kills the cancer cells and also stops growing further.

Convex Nonparametric Least Squares for Predictive Maintenance

William Chung
City University of Hong Kong, Hong Kong

Iris M. H. Yeung
City University of Hong Kong, Hong Kong

INTRODUCTION

With the industrial Internet of Things (IoT) sensors, predictive maintenance (PdM) becomes viable to identify maintenance issues in real-time by predicting the next error of the system. To develop the prediction model for PdM, a certain number of researchers employed machine learning (ML) methods. From the literature, Random Forests (RF), Support Vector Machine (SVM), Artificial Neural Network (ANN), and k-means are the popular ML methods. On the other hand, regression-based methods are considered inappropriate due to their pre-defined function forms and the non-linear nature of the PdM models. However, the convex nonparametric least squares (CNLS) method can overcome the above shortcomings of the regression-based methods. This chapter discusses the use of CNLS for PdM, which can be an alternative method for PdM.

In the Background section, brief descriptions of predictive maintenance, IoT, and machine learning are given. Then, in the Solutions and Recommendations section, after introducing the CNLS method in detail with two simple examples, the application of energy consumption of production systems or equipment is provided with consideration of using IoT devices. Then, how to use the CNLS to develop the predictive model with the energy consumption is discussed for having PdM of production systems. No method is perfect. In the Future Research Directions section, future developments of the CNLS method are given based on its limitations.

BACKGROUND

Predictive Maintenance and IoT

Conventional preventive maintenance (PvM) is schedule-based maintenance with the same time interval for reducing the likelihood of equipment failure. The PvM assumes the likelihood of failure increases with the usage and age of the equipment. Hence, Malik (1979) proposed the "Proportional Age Reduction" model that, for a piece of equipment with age t, its post-maintenance age can be reduced from t to t/β, where $\beta=(1,\infty)$. Age may not be a good indicator, and the PvM approach may result in the unnecessary replacement of some equipment components after a predetermined period. On the other hand, if the equipment runs with abnormal energy consumption, speed, or temperature before replacement, PvM cannot provide the replacement decision.

DOI: 10.4018/978-1-7998-9220-5.ch158

To address the above shortcomings of PvM, Predictive maintenance (PdM) enabled by the industrial Internet of Things (IoT) sensors is proposed by which we can identify maintenance issues in real-time. The PdM approach is prediction-based maintenance. The equipment is continuously monitored by various sensors (IoT sensors), which generate data in real-time to predict the next error. PdM can then be conducted before the failure occurs. In particular, PdM is invaluable if the equipment and the corresponding processes are too expensive to have any critical damages.

Predictive Maintenance and ML

Since PdM comes with high potential in reducing maintenance costs, it has recently attracted a certain number of researchers applying machine learning methods to PdM, such as Samatas et al. (2021), Ayvaz and Alpay (2021), Florian et al. (2021), Chen et al. (2020), Çınar et al. (2020), Sahal et al. (2020), Ruiz-Sarmiento et al. (2020), Wan et al. (2017), Susto et al. (2014), and Susto et al. (2012).

According to the review paper of Carvalho et al. (2019), the popular machine learning methods for PdM are Random Forests (RF), Support Vector Machine (SVM), Artificial Neural Network (ANN), and k-means. They also concluded that "there is no preference for an equipment to perform PdM strategies, and vibration signals are the most common data used to design PdM models, there is a preference for real data to build PdM models."

Ayvaz and Alpay (2021) developed a predictive maintenance model for personal care goods production lines, such as baby care, feminine hygiene, and home care products, in Turkey. They evaluated six algorithms, four ensembles (Random Forest, XGBoost, Gradient Boosting, and AdaBoost), and two constituent machine learning algorithms (Neural Network and Support Vector Regression), developing a model consisting of one dependent output and 47 independent inputs. They also explored the performance of Multiple Regression, Lasso Regression, and Ridge Regression. Due to the non-linear nature of the problem, these three regression-based methods could not capture any variance in the data.

FOCUS OF THE ARTICLE

In this chapter, we would like to introduce a non-parametric regression method, Convex Nonparametric Least Square (CNLS), as an ML approach. A case application is used to discusses how CNLS is used in energy consumption (or efficiency) and PdM.

SOLUTIONS AND RECOMMENDATIONS

Introduction of CNLS

CNLS is a nonparametric regression method shown below.

$$y = f(x) + \varepsilon^{CNLS},$$

where $f(x)$ is a function with shape restrictions, y is the dependent output variable, x is a vector of input variables, and εC^{NLS} is a random variable satisfying $E(\varepsilon CN^{LS|x})=0$. See (Afriat, 1972; Hildreth, 1954) for more details. That is, CNLS is to estimate a f(x) by minimizing ε^{CNLS}. It does not require the functional form's prior specification and a smoothing parameter like the kernel regression.

Kuosmanen (2008) derived the following quadratic programming formulation to estimate any f(x).

[CNLS]

$$min_{a,b,\varepsilon} \sum_{i=1}^{n} \left(\varepsilon_i^{CNLS}\right)^2$$

$$\text{s.t. } y_i = a_i + \sum_{j=1}^{m} b_{ij} x_{ij} + \varepsilon_i^{CNLS} \text{ for } i=1,\ldots,n \tag{1}$$

$$a_i + \sum_{j=1}^{m} b_{ij} x_{ij} \leq a_h + \sum_{j=1}^{m} b_{hj} x_{ij} \text{ for } i,h=1,\ldots,n \text{ and } i \neq h \tag{2}$$

$$b_{ij} \geq 0 \text{ for } i=1,\ldots,n; j=1,\ldots,m. \tag{3}$$

where y_i is the output, x_{ij} is the crisp input j, and ε_i^{CNLS} is the disturbance term representing the deviation of observation i from the estimated function. Due to the concavity constraints (one of the shape constraints), CNLS has attracted considerable interest in the literature productivity efficiency analysis.

If there are n observations, CNLS estimates n equality constraints (different hyperplanes, equation (1)) to approximate the unknown f(x), where a_j and b_{ij} are specific to each observation i. The shape constraints are Afriat concavity inequalities, (2). The monotonicity constraints are represented by the sign-constraints of the slops of hyperplanes (3).

Then, the prediction process can be conducted by using the resulting hyperplanes if they are unique. However, the CNLS may the [CNLS] may not generate a unique optimal solution, but the fitted values are unique, i.e., $\hat{y}_i = \hat{a}_i + \sum_{j=1}^{m} \hat{b}_{ij} x_{ij}$. Thus, we can calculate a low concave envelope for the estimated function. By Kuosmanen & Kortelainen's (2012) results, we can use the Afriat concavity inequalities to estimate the low concave envelope (unique).

[CNLS-LCE$_i$]

$$min_{a_i,b_{ij}} \left\{ a_i + \sum_{j=1}^{m} b_{ij} x_{ij} \mid a_i + \sum_{j=1}^{m} b_{ij} x_{ij} \geq \hat{y}_i \quad \forall i \right\},$$

where a_i and b_{ij} is the unique optimal solution to [CNLS], which may be distinct from the results $\left(\hat{a}_i, \hat{b}_{ij}\right)$ estimated in [CNLS]. The number of unique hyperplanes, k, normally is smaller than that of observations.

Remark 1 CNLS and OLS

C

The [CNLS] can be reduced to the signed ordinary least squares [OLS-sign] regression by adding two constraints: $a_j=a_h$ and $b_{ij}=b_{hj}$ for $i,h=1,\dots,n$. Let $a=a_j$ and $b_j=b_{ij}$, then we have

[OLS-sign]

$$min_{a,b,\varepsilon} \sum_{i=1}^{n} \left(\varepsilon_i^{OLS} \right)^2$$

s.t. $y_i = a + \sum_{j=1}^{m} b_j x_{ij} + \varepsilon_i^{OLS}$ for $i=1,\dots,n$

$b_j \geq 0$

For all observations, there is one hyperplane in the [OLS-sign], $a + \sum_{j=1}^{m} b_j x_{ij}$. If $b_j \geq 0$ is needed due to professional judgment, and we swap the sign of the corresponding j^{th} vector of x_{ij}. Then, it is no harm to introduce $b_j \geq 0$ $\forall j$ to the [OLS-sign].

Efficient Algorithms for [CNLS]

Solving [CNLS] may require efficient algorithms since the CNLS problem size grows quadratically as a function of the number of observations due to the constraint (2). If there are n observations, [CNLS] consists of n(n-1) constraint (2). That is, when $n=100$, the number of constraints (2) is 9900. Lee et al. (2013) proposed an efficient algorithm for solving [CNLS]. They first defined the following relaxed CNLS problem.

[Relaxed-CNLS]

$$min_{a,b,\varepsilon} \sum_{i=1}^{n} \left(\varepsilon_i^{CNLS} \right)^2$$

s.t. $y_i = a_i + \sum_{j=1}^{m} b_{ij} x_{ij} + \varepsilon_i^{CNLS}$ for $i=1,\dots,n$ (1)

$a_i + \sum_{j=1}^{m} b_{ij} x_{ij} \leq a_h + \sum_{j=1}^{m} b_{hj} x_{ij}$ $\forall i,h \in V$ (2V)

$b_{ij} \geq 0$ for $i=1,\dots,n; j=1,\dots,m$.   (3)

where V is a subset of all the observation pairs; hence the concavity constraints (2V) are a subset of all the concavity constraints (2).

With [Relaxed-CNLS], they proposed the following algorithm.

Step 1: Let $r=0$ and let V be a subset of the observation pairs.

Step 2: Solve [Relaxed-CNLS] to find an initial solution, $\left(a_i^{(0)}, b_{ij}^{(0)} \right)$.

Step 3: Do until $\left(a_i^{(r)}, b_{ij}^{(r)} \right)$ satisfies all concavity constraints (2) of [CNLS]:

    3.1 Select a subset of the concavity constraints that $\left(a_i^{(r)}, b_{ij}^{(r)} \right)$ violates and let $V^{(r)}$ be the corresponding observation paris.

    3.2 Set $V = V \cup V^{(r)}$.

    3.3 Solve [RCNLS] to obtain solution $\left(a_i^{(r+1)}, b_{ij}^{(r+1)} \right)$.

    3.4 Set $r=r+1$.

To find the initial solution $\left(a_i^{(0)}, b_{ij}^{(0)} \right)$ in Step 2, Lee et al. (2013) proposed two approaches: elementary Afriat approach and sweet spot approach. Since the sweet spot approach outperformed the Afriat approach, we provide the sweet spot approach here. First, the Euclidean norm between two observations is measured in the $m+1$ dimensional space of inputs and output. Then, For each observation i, the concavity constraints corresponding to the observations, whose distance to observation i is less than a pre-specified value δ_i are added. Empirically, they found that an effective value for δ_i is the 3rd percentile of the distances from all observations to observation i.

To select a subset of the concavity constraints (the set of violated concavity constraints) in Step 3.1, Lee et al. (2013) proposed three approaches:

$$(1) \quad max_{i,h} \left\{ a_i^{(r)} + \sum_{j=1}^{m} b_{ij}^{(r)} x_{ij} - \left(a_h^{(r)} + \sum_{j=1}^{m} b_{hj}^{(r)} x_{ij} \right) \right\} > 0,$$

$$(2) \quad max_h \left\{ a_i^{(r)} + \sum_{j=1}^{m} b_{ij}^{(r)} x_{ij} - \left(a_h^{(r)} + \sum_{j=1}^{m} b_{hj}^{(r)} x_{ij} \right) \right\} > 0 \quad \forall i, \text{ and}$$

$$(3) \quad a_i^{(r)} + \sum_{j=1}^{m} b_{ij}^{(r)} x_{ij} - \left(a_h^{(r)} + \sum_{j=1}^{m} b_{hj}^{(r)} x_{ij} \right) > 0 \quad \forall i, h$$

Empirical results showed that approach (2) outperforms others.

Remark 2 Shape Constraints

There may be different shape constraints (like convexity), as mentioned in Kuosmanen (2008) and Lee et al. (2013). Hence, the application of CNLS is not limited to production efficiency analysis. For convexity, the "$\leq$" is changed to "$\geq$" in constraint (2) of [CNLS]. For monotone decreasing, constraint

(3) is changed to $b_j \leq 0$. Although there is no method to help modellers to select shape constraints and monotone constraints. Modellers are required to select one of the four combinations with the largest adjusted R-squared. In the following example, two types of shape constraints are illustrated. Hence,

Examples with Different Shape Constraints

Two examples are given in this section. The first example is used for the concave pattern of the estimated function. The second example is for the convex one. The first two columns of Table 1 and Table 2 are the first and second examples, respectively. The last two columns of both tables show the resulting hyperplanes accordingly. Figure 1 and Figure 2 are the results of both examples. All [CNLS] models and [CNLS-LCE$_i$] were coded with GAMS and solved by the Pathnlp solver in a PC.

Table 1. Data and the resulting CNLS Hyperplanes of the Example

	Data		Hyperplanes	
i	*x*	*y*	*a*	*b*
1	5	14	**2.775**	**2.245**
2	8	21	7.624	1.635
3	11	25	**7.678**	**1.628**
4	14	31	15.325	1.082
5	17	33	**16.016**	**1.033**
6	19	36	17.054	0.978
7	22	37	**26.762**	**0.467**
8	24	38	16.762	0.467

Table 2. Data and the resulting CNLS Hyperplanes of Example 2

	Data		Hyperplanes	
i	*x*	*y*	*a*	*b*
1	5	29	**27.537**	**0.293**
2	8	30	**25.982**	**0.502**
3	11	31	19.912	1.057
4	14	36	**19.187**	**1.123**
5	17	37	16.386	1.288
6	19	44	**0.169**	**2.242**
7	22	49	**-3.324**	**2.401**
8	24	58	**-44.082**	**4.253**

Performance of CNLS

Obviously, the accuracy of CNLS must be better than that of OLS. The R-squared of CNLS and OLS in Example 1 is 0.998 and 0.944, respectively. In Example 2, we have 0.993 and 0.881, respectively.

Energy Consumption and PdM

From the literature, it is found that predicting abnormal consumption (or energy efficiency) of the production system or equipment is used to activate the maintenance process, for instance, Yan and Hua (2010, December), Fisera and Stluka (2012), Shrouf and Miragliotta (2015), Palasciano et al. (2016), Cupek et al. (2018), Wan et al. (2017), Kulkarni et al. (2018, June), Hollingsworth et al. (2018, December), Paolanti et al. (2018), Bhandari et al. (2020), Fernandes et al. (2020), and Morariu et al. (2020). The energy consumption of equipment increases dramatically as reliability decreases, which indicates a performance degradation. Hence, one of the possible applications of CNLS is to predict abnormal energy consumption (or energy efficiency) of the production system or equipment.

Figure 1. Hyperplanes of Example 1 with concave observations

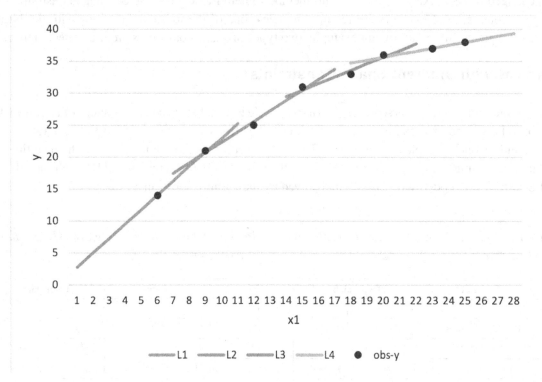

Figure 2. Hyperplanes of Example 2 with convex observations

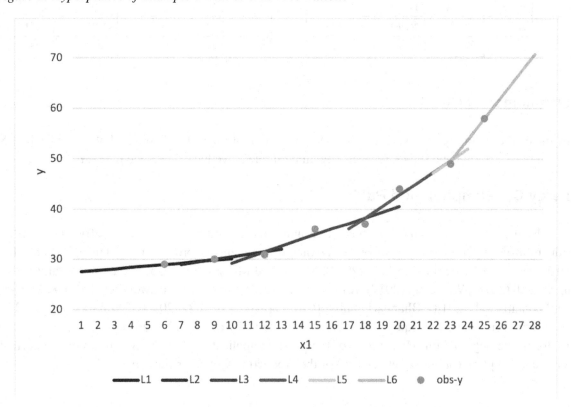

Moreover, introducing an internet-of-things (IoT) enables software applications for real-time energy efficiency monitoring on manufacturing shop floors. While enabling real-time monitoring of energy efficiency, we can apply the CNLS method to develop an energy performance function, $f(x)$, in IoT sensors' real-time data or production performance under normal production processes. The resulting CNLS model can predict if there are abnormal energy consumption patterns on the shop floor. A case application found in Tan et al. (2017) is used to illustrate such an application.

Tan et al. (2017) introduced an IoT-enabled software application for real-time energy efficiency monitoring on manufacturing shop floors. Their application consists of two parts, a monitoring module and benchmarking process. The monitoring module (real-time energy performance monitoring) is used to collect data and to detect if the machine is operating, idling, or not operating. If the machine is operating, energy consumption per production volume (energy efficiency) is calculated. The benchmarking process applies the data envelopment analysis (DEA) technique to find the historical best energy consumption practices. Then, by comparing each practice with these best practices, the relative efficiency is calculated and clustered into quantile classification. Considering hourly energy performance to be benchmarked in DEA with the best practices, the relative efficiency can be calculated every hour. Low relative efficiency indicates abnormal energy consumption patterns, and the PdM may follow. According to Tan et al. (2017), DEA is solved for every benchmarking process.

Tan et al. (2017) illustrated how to benchmark the real-time monitoring of energy efficiency to detect abnormal energy consumption and PdM. Similarly, the CNLS method can be used as a benchmarking development tool.

Predicting Process of CNLS for Energy Consumption and PdM

A simple example is used to illustrate the use of CNLS for PdM. It is interesting to develope a PdM of a machine based on the corresponding energy consumption performance in terms of potential explainable variables such as production volume, product type, operating hours, etc. We first collect the energy consumption and the variables through IoT devices, where y_i is the energy consumption in the observed time slot i, and x_{ij} are the variables. Second, after collecting n observations, we use these observations to find all CNLS residuals ($\varepsilon_1^{CNLS}, \ldots, \varepsilon_n^{CNLS}$) by solving the problem [CNLS]. The ($\varepsilon_1^{CNLS}, \ldots, \varepsilon_n^{CNLS}$) can be used to form a benchmarking table with Q1, Q2, Q3, and Q4. Third, we solve the problem [CNLS-LCE$_i$] in order to find a set of hyperplanes by which we can calculate the approximated energy consumption of the new observation. Fourth, after each predetermined time slot, we have a new observation, $\left(y_t^o, x_{tj}\right)$, and the corresponding residuals, $\hat{\varepsilon}_{it}^{CNLS}$, to be discussed next. Assuming that if $\hat{\varepsilon}_{it}^{CNLS} < Q1$, there is something wrong with the machine, and the PdM is needed. Else, no PdM is needed, and waiting for the new observation of the predetermined time slot.

The calculation of the residual of the new observation, $\hat{\varepsilon}_{it}^{CNLS}$, is given below. It should be noted that this residual is used in predicting if PdM is needed.

It is assumed that CNLS residuals ($\varepsilon_1^{CNLS}, \ldots, \varepsilon_n^{CNLS}$) is composed the half-normal inefficiency term and a normally distributed noise term, $u_i \sim \left|N\left(0, \sigma_u^2\right)\right|$ and $v_i \sim N\left(0, \sigma_v^2\right)$ respectively. Both u_i and v_i are independent and identically distributed. Kuosmannen and Kortleainen (2012) used the method of moments to estimate the variance parameters σ_u^2 and σ_v^2. They first calculate

$$\hat{M}_2 = \sum_{i=1}^{n} \left(\varepsilon_i^{CNLS} - \hat{E}\left(\varepsilon_i^{CNLS} \right) \right)^2 / n \text{ and } \hat{M}_3 = \sum_{i=1}^{n} \left(\varepsilon_i^{CNLS} - \hat{E}\left(\varepsilon_i^{CNLS} \right) \right)^3 / n,$$

and then

$$\hat{\sigma}_u = \sqrt[3]{\sqrt{\frac{\hat{M}_3}{\left(\sqrt{\frac{2}{\pi}} \right)\left[1 - \frac{4}{\pi} \right]}}} \text{ and } \hat{\sigma}_v = \sqrt{\left(\hat{M}_2 - \left[\frac{\pi - 2}{\pi} \right] \hat{\sigma}_u \right)}.$$

With the estimated $\hat{\sigma}_u$ and $\hat{\sigma}_v$ parameters, the conditional expected value of inefficiency can be computed as

$$\hat{E}\left(u_i \mid \hat{\epsilon}_i \right) = -\frac{\hat{\epsilon}_i \hat{\sigma}_u^2}{\hat{\sigma}_u^2 + \hat{\sigma}_v^2} + \frac{\hat{\sigma}_u^2 \hat{\sigma}_v^2}{\hat{\sigma}_u^2 + \hat{\sigma}_v^2} \left[\frac{\varnothing \left(\frac{\hat{\epsilon}_i}{\hat{\sigma}_v^2} \right)}{1 - \Phi \left(\frac{\hat{\epsilon}_i}{\hat{\sigma}_v^2} \right)} \right]$$

where $\hat{\epsilon}_i = \varepsilon_i^{CNLS} - \hat{\sigma}_u \sqrt{2/\pi}$ is the estimator of the composite error term, $\varnothing$ is the standard normal density function, and Φ is the standard normal cumulative distribution function $\hat{E}\left(u_i \mid \hat{\epsilon}_i \right)$ is an unbiased but inconsistent estimator of u_i. Since $\hat{E}\left(u_i \mid \hat{\epsilon}_i \right)$ can be considered a set of efficiency scores, it can be used to form a benchmark table in which $\hat{E}\left(u_i \mid \hat{\epsilon}_i \right)$ is in ascending order for the further benchmark. Note that $\hat{M}_3$ should be negative. If not, it brings all $\hat{E}\left(u_i | \hat{\epsilon}_i \right) = 0$. In some applications, $\hat{M}_3$ may be positive. Hence, we cannot use this approach to build the benchmark table. In Chung and Yeung (2017), they had positive $\hat{M}_3$. They proposed to use ε_i^{CNLS} to form the benchmarking table. Note that $\left\{ \varepsilon_{(1)}^{CNLS}, \ldots, \varepsilon_{(n)}^{CNLS} \right\}$ can be considered to provide an empirical cumulative distribution function of the normalized efficiency scores. The bootstrapping re-sampling technique can be used to provide an efficient percentile estimation for small samples.

Then, the resulting model (a set of unique hyperplanes) of [CNLS-LCE$_i$] can be used for the prediction process. The prediction process for a given new observation is described in (Chung & Yeung, 2020). In short, let x_{ij} be the observed inputs for a given observation t. We first found the fitted values, $\hat{y}_i = \hat{a}_i + \sum_{j=1}^{m} \hat{b}_{ij} x_{ij}$, using the corresponding hyperplane i. Then, the forecasted

$$\hat{y}_t = \min \left\{ \hat{y}_{ti} | \hat{y}_{ti} = \hat{a}_i + \sum_{j=1}^{m} \hat{b}_{ij} x_{tj} \quad \forall i \right\}.$$

Like Tan et al. (2017), after having the benchmarking table, we can start the prediction process to detect abnormal energy consumption. For predicting the abnormal energy consumption (or efficiency) of a new observation t with the benchmarking table, we need to calculate the corresponding $\overset{\wedge CNLS}{\varepsilon}$ by the resulting model (a set of unique hyperplanes) of [CNLS-LCE$_i$]. However, we have $k(<n)$ hyperplanes by solving [CNLS-LCE$_i$]. The problem is how to find the corresponding hyperplane i to calculate the corresponding $\overset{\wedge CNLS}{\varepsilon_t}$. Chung and Yeung (2017) discussed and described the following method to calculate the $\overset{\wedge CNLS}{\varepsilon_t}$.

Chung and Yeung (2017) discussed that any energy efficiency i must satisfy the second set of concavity constraints, Eq (2) of [CNLS]:

$$a_i + \sum_{j=1}^{m} b_{ij} x_{ij} \le a_h + \sum_{j=1}^{m} b_{hj} x_{ij} \text{ for } i,h=1,\ldots,n.$$

The concavity constraints require that for observation i with x_{ij}, the estimated functional value using the parameters associated with hyperplane i will be less than or equal to x_{ij} evaluated using any other hyperplane h. Hence, all hyperplanes which do not associate with i, must be above i's hyperplane. Using this property of the concavity constraints, for any new observation t, we can find the corresponding hyperplane i with the maximum residual εi_t. That is, by hyperplane i and h from Eq (4), we have

$$y_t^o - \varepsilon_{it} = \hat{a}_i + \sum_{j=1}^{m} \hat{b}_{ij} x_{tj} \text{ and } y_t^o - \varepsilon_{ht} = \hat{a}_h + \sum_{j=1}^{m} \hat{b}_{hj} x_{tj} \text{ respectively.}$$

Since the new observation t also satisfies Eq (2),

$$\hat{a}_i + \sum_{j=1}^{m} \hat{b}_{ij} x_{tj} \le \hat{a}_h + \sum_{j=1}^{m} \hat{b}_{hj} x_{tj},$$

we get $\left(y_t^o - \varepsilon_{it}\right) \le \left(y_t^o - \varepsilon_{ht}\right)$ $\forall i,h$ implying that $\varepsilon_{it} \ge \varepsilon_{ht}$ $\forall i,h$.

Hence, we can use the following equation to find the corresponding hyperplane i and the benchmarking performance $\overset{\wedge CNLS}{\varepsilon_{it}}$ for the new observation *t*.

$$\overset{\wedge CNLS}{\varepsilon_{it}} = \max\{\varepsilon_{it} \mid \varepsilon_{it} = y_t^o - \left(\hat{a}_i + \sum_{j=1}^{m} \hat{b}_{ij} x_{tj}\right) \text{ for } i = 1,\ldots,k\}. \tag{4}$$

The computed $\overset{\wedge CNLS}{\varepsilon_{it}}$ is then compared with the values in the benchmark percentile table to find the corresponding efficiency scores. The CNLS residuals ($\varepsilon_1^{CNLS},\ldots,\varepsilon_n^{CNLS}$) are clustered into three efficiency levels using quantile classification. Top 25% of ε_i^{CNLS} ($>Q3$) represents the "normal" energy performance. The lowest 25% of ε_i^{CNLS} ($<Q1$) represents the "abnormal" energy performance. The

middle 50% of ε_i^{CNLS} (Q1> ε_i^{CNLS} >Q3) represents the energy performance with warning status. If $\hat{\varepsilon}_{it}^{CNLS} < Q1$, the equipment performs in "abnormal" status and PdM is needed.

In short, we have the following steps to construct a PdM model based on CNLS estimation.

(1) Collect energy consumption and the related activities and production volume, (y_i, x_{ij}), $i=1,\dots,n$.

(2) Use [CNLS] to find CNLS residuals ($\varepsilon_1^{CNLS},\dots,\varepsilon_n^{CNLS}$) to form a benchmarking quantile table with Q1, Q2, Q3, and Q4. Note that there are different shape and monotone constraints. As mentioned in Remark 2 above, modellers are required to select one of the combinations with the largest adjusted R-squared.

(3) Use [CNLS-LCE$_i$] with the result of [CNLS] to find a set of hyperplanes that representing the energy consumption function $f(x)$

(4) After each predetermined time slot, *t*, a new observation $\left(y_t^o, x_{tj}\right)$ is used to calculate $\hat{\varepsilon}_{it}^{CNLS}$ by Eq. (4). Repeat this step until $\hat{\varepsilon}_{it}^{CNLS} < Q1$, the PdM is needed.

Obviously, such kind of benchmarking table is easy to be implemented and used in daily operations. However, it is necessary to solve a DEA to obtain benchmarking efficiency every time.

FUTURE RESEARCH DIRECTIONS

One of the further research topics is variable selection in CNLS by least absolute shrinkage and selection operator (lasso). According to Tibshirani (1996), the lasso estimate $\left(\hat{\alpha}, \hat{\beta}\right)$ is defined by

$$\left(\hat{\alpha}, \hat{\beta}\right) = \arg\,min\left\{\sum_{i=1}^{n}\left(y_i - \alpha - \sum_{j=1}^{m}\beta_j x_{ij}\right)^2 + s\sum_{j=1}^{m}\left|\beta_j\right|\right\} \tag{5}$$

where $s(\geq 0)$ is a tuning parameter for the additional lasso penalty term $s\sum_{j=1}^{m}\left|\beta_j\right|$. An equivalent definition of the lasso problem can be defined by removing the lasso penalty term ($\sum_{j=1}^{m}\left|\beta_j\right|$) and adding a constraint of the form $\sum_{j=1}^{m}\left|\beta_j\right| \leq t$. That is,

$$\left(\hat{\alpha}, \hat{\beta}\right) = \arg\,min\left\{\sum_{i=1}^{n}\left(y_i - \alpha - \sum_{j=1}^{m}\beta_j x_{ij}\right)^2 \mid \sum_{j=1}^{m}\left|\beta_j\right| \leq t\right\}$$

where $t(\geq 0)$ is a tuning parameter for the additional lasso constraint.

Lee and Cai (2020) studied the lasso variable selection method in the sign-constrained CNLS (sCNLS), which is equal to the [CNLS] with an additional sign constraint, $\varepsilon_i^{CNLS} \leq 0$. According to Kuosmanen and Johnson (2010), the sCNLS can be used to estimate the additive form of the output-oriented VRS-DEA frontier. Lee and Cai (2020 used sCNLS to develop lasso selection in DEA.

[LASSO-sCNLS]

$$min_{a,b,\varepsilon} \sum_{i=1}^{n} \left(\varepsilon_i^{CNLS}\right)^2 + s \sum_{i=1}^{n} \left(\sum_{j=1}^{m} b_{ij}\right)$$

s.t. $y_i = a_i + \sum_{j=1}^{m} b_{ij} x_{ij} + \varepsilon_i^{CNLS}$ for $i=1,\ldots,n$ $\qquad(1)$

$a_i + \sum_{j=1}^{m} b_{ij} x_{ij} \leq a_h + \sum_{j=1}^{m} b_{hj} x_{ij}$ for $i,h=1,\ldots,n$ and $i \neq h$ $\qquad(2)$

$b_{ij} \geq 0$ for $i=1,\ldots,n; j=1,\ldots,m.$ $\qquad(3)$

$\varepsilon_i^{CNLS} \leq 0 \ \forall i.$ $\qquad(6)$

Note that the lasso penalty term is $s \sum_{i=1}^{n} \left(\sum_{j=1}^{m} b_{ij}\right)$. When s increases, any input j with $b_{ij}=0$ for all observation i can be removed from the selected variables.

Obviously, **[LASSO-CNLS]** can be easily derived and is equal to **[LASSO-sCNLS]** without $\varepsilon_i^{CNLS} \leq 0$. That is

[LASSO-CNLS]

$$min_{a,b,\varepsilon} \sum_{i=1}^{n} \left(\varepsilon_i^{CNLS}\right)^2 + s \sum_{i=1}^{n} \left(\sum_{j=1}^{m} b_{ij}\right)$$

s.t. $y_i = a_i + \sum_{j=1}^{m} b_{ij} x_{ij} + \varepsilon_i^{CNLS}$ for $i=1,\ldots,n$ $\qquad(1)$

$a_i + \sum_{j=1}^{m} b_{ij} x_{ij} \leq a_h + \sum_{j=1}^{m} b_{hj} x_{ij}$ for $i,h=1,\ldots,n$ and $i \neq h$ $\qquad(2)$

$b_{ij} \geq 0$ for $i=1,\ldots,n; j=1,\ldots,m.$ $\qquad(3)$

Since Lee and Cai (2020)'s results were supported by small datasets and focused on the curse of dimensionality problem of DEA, it is worthwhile to investigate the performance of [LASSO-CNLS] in some actual applications with large scale datasets.

On the other hand, there are variants of the lasso from the literature, summarized in Tibshirani (2011). Further research is needed to extend the variants of the lasso in CNLS. For example, Tibshirani et al. (2005) introduced an additional lasso penalty term $s_1 \sum_{j=2}^{m} |\beta_j - \beta_{j-1}|$ to (5) for a drawback of the lasso method which encourages sparse solutions (with many coefficients equal to 0). It may be interested in introducing the similar additional lasso penalty term to [LASSO-CNLS] by adding a new constraint (7) shown in [LASSO-ssCNLS]. Further research investigates how to apply the computational approach of Tibshirani et al. (2005) to the [LASSO-ssCNLS].

[LASSO-ssCNLS]

$$min_{a,b,\varepsilon} \sum_{i=1}^{n} \left(\varepsilon_i^{CNLS} \right)^2 + s \sum_{j=1}^{m} b_j + s_1 \sum_{j=2}^{m} |b_j - b_{j-1}|$$

$$\text{s.t. } y_i = a_i + \sum_{j=1}^{m} b_{ij} x_{ij} + \varepsilon_i^{CNLS} \text{ for } i=1,\dots,n \tag{1}$$

$$a_i + \sum_{j=1}^{m} b_{ij} x_{ij} \le a_h + \sum_{j=1}^{m} b_{hj} x_{ij} \text{ for } i,h=1,\dots,n \text{ and } i \ne h \tag{2}$$

$$b_{ij} \ge 0 \text{ for } i=1,\dots,n; j=1,\dots,m \tag{3}$$

$$b_j = \sum_{i=1}^{n} b_{ij} \tag{7}$$

CONCLUSION

In this chapter, we discuss the convex nonparametric least squares (CNLS) method as a machine learning method for predictive maintenance (PdM) to predict the next error of the system. One of the attractive properties of the CNLS method is its regression-based analysis without pre-defined non-linear function forms. In addition, the CNLS method does not need to find the appropriate Kernel function like the Support Vector Machine. Note that no method is perfect. The limitation of the CNLS method comes from the shape constraints. It is because the shape constraints generate a large number of constraints that incur computational burdens. Besides the abovementioned Lee et al. (2013), we can find that Mazumder et al. (2019) proposed another efficient algorithm. Mazumder et al. (2019) used a prototypical version of the alternating direction method of multipliers (ADMM) to develop the multiple-block splitting ADMM algorithm for CNLS. Further research works focus on the parameter selection methods in the

CNLS method and different applications of the PdM problem. Obviously, the use of the CNLS model for PdM with IoT can be easily extended to other applications, such as freezers in supermarkets, vending machines, and the like in the retail service sector.

REFERENCES

Ayvaz, S., & Alpay, K. (2021). Predictive maintenance system for production lines in manufacturing: A machine learning approach using IoT data in real-time. *Expert Systems with Applications*, *173*, 114598. doi:10.1016/j.eswa.2021.114598

Bhandari, G., Joglekar, A., Kulkarni, A., Kulkarni, D., Mahadeva, C., Mohanty, S. B., ... Sundaresan, R. (2020, January). An Implementation of an Industrial Internet of Things on an SMT Assembly Line. In *2020 International Conference on COMmunication Systems & NETworkS (COMSNETS)* (pp. 688-690). IEEE. 10.1109/COMSNETS48256.2020.9027475

Carvalho, T. P., Soares, F. A., Vita, R., Francisco, R. D. P., Basto, J. P., & Alcalá, S. G. (2019). A systematic literature review of machine learning methods applied to predictive maintenance. *Computers & Industrial Engineering*, *137*, 106024. doi:10.1016/j.cie.2019.106024

Chen, C., Liu, Y., Wang, S., Sun, X., Di Cairano-Gilfedder, C., Titmus, S., & Syntetos, A. A. (2020). Predictive maintenance using cox proportional hazard deep learning. *Advanced Engineering Informatics*, *44*, 101054. doi:10.1016/j.aei.2020.101054

Chung, W., & Yeung, I. M. (2017). Benchmarking by convex nonparametric least squares with application on the energy performance of office buildings. *Applied Energy*, *203*, 454–462. doi:10.1016/j.apenergy.2017.06.023

Chung, W., & Yeung, I. M. (2020). A study of energy consumption of secondary school buildings in Hong Kong. *Energy and Building*, *226*, 110388. doi:10.1016/j.enbuild.2020.110388

Çınar, Z. M., Abdussalam Nuhu, A., Zeeshan, Q., Korhan, O., Asmael, M., & Safaei, B. (2020). Machine learning in predictive maintenance towards sustainable smart manufacturing in industry 4.0. *Sustainability*, *12*(19), 8211. doi:10.3390u12198211

Cupek, R., Ziebinski, A., Zonenberg, D., & Drewniak, M. (2018). Determination of the machine energy consumption profiles in the mass-customised manufacturing. *International Journal of Computer Integrated Manufacturing*, *31*(6), 537–561. doi:10.1080/0951192X.2017.1339914

Fernandes, S., Antunes, M., Santiago, A. R., Barraca, J. P., Gomes, D., & Aguiar, R. L. (2020). Forecasting appliances failures: A machine-learning approach to predictive maintenance. *Information (Basel)*, *11*(4), 208. doi:10.3390/info11040208

Fisera, R., & Stluka, P. (2012). Performance monitoring of the refrigeration system with minimum set of sensors. *Iranian Journal of Electrical and Computer Engineering*, *6*(7), 637–642.

Florian, E., Sgarbossa, F., & Zennaro, I. (2021). Machine learning-based predictive maintenance: A cost-oriented model for implementation. *International Journal of Production Economics*, *236*, 108114. doi:10.1016/j.ijpe.2021.108114

Hollingsworth, K., Rouse, K., Cho, J., Harris, A., Sartipi, M., Sozer, S., & Enevoldson, B. (2018, December). Energy anomaly detection with forecasting and deep learning. In 2018 IEEE international conference on big data (Big Data) (pp. 4921-4925). IEEE. doi:10.1109/BigData.2018.8621948

Kulkarni, K., Devi, U., Sirighee, A., Hazra, J., & Rao, P. (2018, June). Predictive maintenance for supermarket refrigeration systems using only case temperature data. In *2018 Annual American Control Conference (ACC)* (pp. 4640-4645). IEEE. 10.23919/ACC.2018.8431901

Kuosmanen, T. (2008). Representation theorem for convex nonparametric least squares. *The Econometrics Journal*, *11*(2), 308–325. doi:10.1111/j.1368-423X.2008.00239.x

Kuosmanen, T., & Johnson, A. L. (2010). Data envelopment analysis as nonparametric least-squares regression. *Operations Research*, *58*(1), 149–160. doi:10.1287/opre.1090.0722

Kuosmanen, T., & Kortelainen, M. (2012). Stochastic non-smooth envelopment of data: Semi-parametric frontier estimation subject to shape constraints. *Journal of Productivity Analysis*, *38*(1), 11–28. doi:10.100711123-010-0201-3

Lee, C. Y., & Cai, J. Y. (2020). LASSO variable selection in data envelopment analysis with small datasets. *Omega*, *91*, 102019. doi:10.1016/j.omega.2018.12.008

Lee, C. Y., Johnson, A. L., Moreno-Centeno, E., & Kuosmanen, T. (2013). A more efficient algorithm for convex nonparametric least squares. *European Journal of Operational Research*, *227*(2), 391–400. doi:10.1016/j.ejor.2012.11.054

Malik, M. A. K. (1979). Reliable preventive maintenance scheduling. *AIIE Transactions*, *11*(3), 221–228. doi:10.1080/05695557908974463

Mazumder, R., Choudhury, A., Iyengar, G., & Sen, B. (2019). A computational framework for multivariate convex regression and its variants. *Journal of the American Statistical Association*, *114*(525), 318–331. doi:10.1080/01621459.2017.1407771

Morariu, C., Morariu, O., Răileanu, S., & Borangiu, T. (2020). Machine learning for predictive scheduling and resource allocation in large scale manufacturing systems. *Computers in Industry*, *120*, 103244. doi:10.1016/j.compind.2020.103244

Palasciano, C., Bustillo, A., Fantini, P., & Taisch, M. (2016). A new approach for machine's management: From machine's signal acquisition to energy indexes. *Journal of Cleaner Production*, *137*, 1503–1515. doi:10.1016/j.jclepro.2016.07.030

Paolanti, M., Romeo, L., Felicetti, A., Mancini, A., Frontoni, E., & Loncarski, J. (2018, July). Machine learning approach for predictive maintenance in industry 4.0. In *2018 14th IEEE/ASME International Conference on Mechatronic and Embedded Systems and Applications (MESA)* (pp. 1-6). IEEE.

Ruiz-Sarmiento, J. R., Monroy, J., Moreno, F. A., Galindo, C., Bonelo, J. M., & Gonzalez-Jimenez, J. (2020). A predictive model for the maintenance of industrial machinery in the context of industry 4.0. *Engineering Applications of Artificial Intelligence*, *87*, 103289. doi:10.1016/j.engappai.2019.103289

Sahal, R., Breslin, J. G., & Ali, M. I. (2020). Big data and stream processing platforms for Industry 4.0 requirements mapping for a predictive maintenance use case. *Journal of Manufacturing Systems*, *54*, 138–151. doi:10.1016/j.jmsy.2019.11.004

Samatas, G. G., Moumgiakmas, S. S., & Papakostas, G. A. (2021, May). Predictive Maintenance-Bridging Artificial Intelligence and IoT. In *2021 IEEE World AI IoT Congress (AIIoT)* (pp. 0413-0419). IEEE. 10.1109/AIIoT52608.2021.9454173

Shrouf, F., & Miragliotta, G. (2015). Energy management based on Internet of Things: Practices and framework for adoption in production management. *Journal of Cleaner Production*, *100*, 235–246. doi:10.1016/j.jclepro.2015.03.055

Susto, G. A., Beghi, A., & De Luca, C. (2012). A predictive maintenance system for epitaxy processes based on filtering and prediction techniques. *IEEE Transactions on Semiconductor Manufacturing*, *25*(4), 638–649. doi:10.1109/TSM.2012.2209131

Susto, G. A., Schirru, A., Pampuri, S., McLoone, S., & Beghi, A. (2014). Machine learning for predictive maintenance: A multiple classifier approach. *IEEE Transactions on Industrial Informatics*, *11*(3), 812–820. doi:10.1109/TII.2014.2349359

Tan, Y. S., Ng, Y. T., & Low, J. S. C. (2017). Internet-of-things enabled real-time monitoring of energy efficiency on manufacturing shop floors. *Procedia CIRP*, *61*, 376–381. doi:10.1016/j.procir.2016.11.242

Tibshirani, R. (1996). Regression shrinkage and selection via the lasso. *Journal of the Royal Statistical Society. Series B. Methodological*, *58*(1), 267–288. doi:10.1111/j.2517-6161.1996.tb02080.x

Tibshirani, R. (2011). Regression shrinkage and selection via the lasso: A retrospective. *Journal of the Royal Statistical Society. Series B, Statistical Methodology*, *73*(3), 273–282. doi:10.1111/j.1467-9868.2011.00771.x

Tibshirani, R., Saunders, M., Rosset, S., Zhu, J., & Knight, K. (2005). Sparsity and smoothness via the fused lasso. *Journal of the Royal Statistical Society. Series B, Statistical Methodology*, *67*(1), 91–108. doi:10.1111/j.1467-9868.2005.00490.x

Wan, J., Tang, S., Li, D., Wang, S., Liu, C., Abbas, H., & Vasilakos, A. V. (2017). A manufacturing big data solution for active preventive maintenance. *IEEE Transactions on Industrial Informatics*, *13*(4), 2039–2047. doi:10.1109/TII.2017.2670505

Yan, J., & Hua, D. (2010, December). Energy consumption modeling for machine tools after preventive maintenance. In *2010 IEEE International Conference on Industrial Engineering and Engineering Management* (pp. 2201-2205). IEEE. 10.1109/IEEM.2010.5674578

ADDITIONAL READING

Chung, W., & Yeung, I. M. (2017). Benchmarking by convex nonparametric least squares with application on the energy performance of office buildings. *Applied Energy*, *203*, 454–462. doi:10.1016/j.apenergy.2017.06.023

Kuosmanen, T., & Johnson, A. L. (2010). Data envelopment analysis as nonparametric least-squares regression. *Operations Research*, *58*(1), 149–160. doi:10.1287/opre.1090.0722

Lee, C. Y., & Cai, J. Y. (2020). LASSO variable selection in data envelopment analysis with small datasets. *Omega*, *91*, 102019. doi:10.1016/j.omega.2018.12.008

Lee, C. Y., Johnson, A. L., Moreno-Centeno, E., & Kuosmanen, T. (2013). A more efficient algorithm for convex nonparametric least squares. *European Journal of Operational Research, 227*(2), 391–400. doi:10.1016/j.ejor.2012.11.054

Mazumder, R., Choudhury, A., Iyengar, G., & Sen, B. (2019). A computational framework for multivariate convex regression and its variants. *Journal of the American Statistical Association, 114*(525), 318–331. doi:10.1080/01621459.2017.1407771

Schwendemann, S., Amjad, Z., & Sikora, A. (2021). A survey of machine-learning techniques for condition monitoring and predictive maintenance of bearings in grinding machines. *Computers in Industry, 125*, 103380. doi:10.1016/j.compind.2020.103380

Tan, Y. S., Ng, Y. T., & Low, J. S. C. (2017). Internet-of-things enabled real-time monitoring of energy efficiency on manufacturing shop floors. *Procedia CIRP, 61*, 376–381. doi:10.1016/j.procir.2016.11.242

Zonta, T., da Costa, C. A., da Rosa Righi, R., de Lima, M. J., da Trindade, E. S., & Li, G. P. (2020). Predictive maintenance in the Industry 4.0: A systematic literature review. *Computers & Industrial Engineering, 150*, 106889. doi:10.1016/j.cie.2020.106889

KEY TERMS AND DEFINITIONS

Abnormal Energy Consumption Patterns: An energy consumption pattern of a system or a device that is not normal compared to the stable operating condition. It can be used to indicate that the system is going to fail.

Conventional Preventive Maintenance (PvM): It is schedule-based maintenance with the same time interval for reducing the likelihood of equipment failure. The PvM assumes the likelihood of failure increases with the usage and age of the equipment.

Convex Nonparametric Least Square (CNLS): A nonparametric regression method that does not require the functional form's prior specification.

Internet of Things (IoT): A network of physical objects (things) embedded with sensors by which the objects can be connected to the Internet.

Predictive Maintenance (PdM): It enabled by the industrial Internet of Things (IoT) sensors is proposed by which we can identify maintenance issues in real-time. The PdM approach is prediction-based maintenance.

Shape Constraints: The constraints of quadratic programming, representing Convex Nonparametric Least Square, are used to provide the estimated regression function's concavity or convexity.

Machine Learning and Sensor Data Fusion for Emotion Recognition

M

Eman M. G. Younis

🆔 https://orcid.org/0000-0003-2778-4231

Minia University, Egypt

Someya Mohsen Zaki

Al-Obour High Institute for Management, Computers, and Information Systems, Obour, Egypt

Essam Halim Houssein

Minia University, Egypt

INTRODUCTION

Emotions have massive influences on our lives. Negative emotions have become determinants of human health. Long-term unpleasant reactions are associated with health issues, including migraines, asthma, ulcers, and heart disease (Kim, J., & André, E., 2008). Growing usage of sensors and wireless networks have led to development of low-cost, efficient wearable devices collecting and transferring data in real-time for long periods (Kanjo, E., Younis, E. M., & Ang, C. S., 2019). These data sources provide a chance to create innovative algorithms for identifying human emotions. This can aid in treatment of chronic diseases, including diabetes, asthma, and heart disease (Pollreisz, D., & TaheriNejad, N., 2017, July).

Researchers made several attempts to integrate ML techniques with sensor datasets for automatic emotion identification (Busso, C., & Deng et al., 2004; Jerritta et al., 2011; Kanjo, E., Kuss, D. J., & Ang, C. S., 2017; Katsis et al., 2008). Many studies on automatic emotion identification have focused on visual, auditory, and movement data (e.g., facial expressions, body postures, speeches) (Busso, C., & Deng et al., 2004; Jerritta et al., 2011; Katsis et al., 2008; Basiri, M., Schill, F., U. Lima, P., & Floreano, D., 2018; Kanjo, E., Al-Husain, L., & Chamberlain, A., 2015). With growing availability of low-cost wearable sensors (e.g., Fitbit, Microsoft wristbands), research interest in using human physiological data for emotion identification has grown. Due to possibility and diversity of human emotional manifestations, automated human emotion categorization remains difficult despite the capacity to sense a wide range of information (from human physiology to surroundings) (Plasqui, G., & Westerterp, K. R., 2007). In addition, they extracted specific emotions based on controlled samples in lab settings using audio-visual stimuli (e.g., showing participants photos or videos or asking participants to complete designed tasks to induce emotional states (Agrafioti, F., Hatzinakos, D., & Anderson, A. K., 2011). That sort of controlled study is limited to strictly controlled environments despite effectiveness.

Authors used several standard ML techniques to capture variability of multi- modal data at sensor and feature levels for mood categorization "in the wild" using smartphones and wristbands, based on integrating many sensors of various modalities (physiological [EDA, HR, Body-Temperature, Motion] and environmental [Air-Pressure, Env-Noise, UV]).

DOI: 10.4018/978-1-7998-9220-5.ch159

The purpose of this chapter is to compare several supervised ML techniques (SVM, KNN, RF, DT) to classify five distinct emotional states. Authors collected data from participants wandering about Minia - university campus using physiological and mobile sensors in real-world settings to develop prediction models. Using sensor data, authors applied ML approach for emotion classification in this work, which incorporates a set of ML algorithms to achieve the following goals: - 1) Using on-body and environmental factors to predict emotional reactions. 2) Constructing a user-dependent model based on various modalities associated with several sensors using various ML techniques.

Authors organize the rest of this chapter as follows. Section 2 presents some background knowledge about affective computing, data fusion and machine learning. Section 3 surveys related research. Section 4 presents system description including data collection and tools used in the experiments. Section 5 presents implementation framework and design of the proposed procedure, data preprocessing, and statistics. Results are presented and discussed in Section 6. Finally, authors present conclusions and future work in Section 7

BACKGROUND

Affective Computing

Affective computing is a cross-disciplinary research area to enable intelligent computers to recognize, predict, and interpret human emotions. It includes computer science, artificial intelligence, cognitive science, neuroscience, neuropsychology, and social science.

Affective computing is a collection of approaches for identifying affect from data in various modalities and granularities. Sentiment analysis and emotion recognition are two of the most common subjects in affective computing research.

Multi-Sensor Data Fusion

Sensor data fusion is the process of fusing sensory input with data from other sources to provide knowledge with less uncertainty than using sources separately. Collecting data from many sources, like video cameras and Wi-Fi localization signals.

The data sources for a fusion process aren't required to come from the same sensor. There are three types of fusion: direct fusion, indirect fusion, and fusion of the outputs of the former two.

Direct fusion is used to combine sensor data from a set of heterogeneous or homogeneous sensors, soft sensors, and sensor data history values. Indirect fusion uses information sources like priori knowledge about the environment and human input. Sensor fusion is a subset of information fusion and also known as (multi-sensor) data fusion.

Authors can apply sensor fusion in various ways, including combining raw data from many sources, extrapolated characteristics, and even single-node decisions.

Sensor fusion is divided into various levels, including (data-level), (feature-level), and (decision-level). These levels are discussed in more detail in the section 3.

Machine Learning

Machine learning (ML) technology enables machines to learn from current inputs to assess specific situations. Scientists classified ML algorithms into three main categories: (supervised, unsupervised, and reinforcement learning). Types of supervised algorithms include Support Vector Machines SVM, neural networks NN, decision trees DT, K-nearest neighbors KNN, Random Forest RF, naive Bayes NB, and others, but unsupervised algorithms involve K-means, Gaussian mixtures, hierarchical clustering, and others.

In this chapter, authors used supervised ML techniques to classify emotional states, ranging from very negative to very positive.

RELATED WORK

Nowadays, smartphones and many wearable devices, including smart-watches and wrist- bands with various sensors, are available to monitor human physiological signals (e.g., heart rate, movements, EDA, and body-temporary).

In addition to data from the surrounding environment (e.g., noise, brightness, etc.). Many large databases have emerged in several study fields, including healthcare and smart cities. This avalanche of on-body and environmental data provides an opportunity for healthcare research, so it necessitates design of new tools and techniques for dealing with massive multidimensional datasets (Kanjo et al., 2019, 2018).

Based on sensor data collected from participants walking around Nottingham city center with a smartphone and wristband 2. This study (Kanjo, E., Younis, E. M., & Sherkat, N., 2018) developed a user-dependent prediction emotion model that depends on integrating physiological (HR, EDA, b-temp, Motion) and environmental (UV, EnvNoise, air pressure) factors. Furthermore, researchers investigated the detrimental effects of noise on human wellbeing thoroughly in the literature, including medical issues like sleep disorders, heart problems, vision problems, and others (Stern, N., & Stern, N. H., 2007). Liisi Koots investigated the Influence of weather on Affective Experience (the relationship between negative and positive emotions and environmental variations in weather like temperature, relative humidity, barometric pressure, and brightness) (Kovats, R. S., & Haines, A., 2005).

Similarly, several research projects have looked at emotions, and their links to wellbeing and physiological changes. However, only one of these (Kanjo et al., 2018) has examined combining physiological and wellbeing sensors with ecological sensors to forecast and model emotion see (Noroozi et al., 2017; Knapp, R. B., Kim, J., & André, E., 2011; Kreibig, S. D., 2010; Balters, S., & Steinert, M., 2017; Guendil et al., 2016; Basiri et al., 2018; Hildén, F., 2019; Gravina et al., 2017). Many sensors were used to monitor physiological data Examine the table 1, which contains a list of health sensors using in emotion identification.

Data Fusion (includes combining numerous data sources to create more consistent and accurate information consists of three levels: a) **data-level fusion** (low-level) attempts to gather diverse data components from multiple sensors to complement one another. During data collection, it is possible to incorporate other data sources, like user self-reported emotions (Agrafioti et al., 2011; Wen et al., 2014). b) During data analysis, the **feature level** (intermediate-level data fusion) is used to select the best set of features for categorization. The best combination of features, like EMC, Respiration, Skin Conductance, and ECC, has been retrieved using feature-level fusion (Gravina et al., 2017). c) At the **decision-making level** (high-level data fusion), the goal is to improve decision-making by integrating results of several techniques.

Table 1. List of some on-body sensors that have been used for emotion detection

Sensor	Signals and features
Body Temperature	Despite its simplicity, we can use body temperature to gauge a Person's emotions and mood shifts (Guendil et al., 2016; Hildén, F., 2019). Wan-Young Chung demonstrated that variations in skin temperature, known as Temperature Variability (TV), may be used to identify Nervous system activity.
Heart Rate	The RR interval refers to the period between 2 successive pulse peaks, and the signal produced by this sensor consists of heart-Beats. According to many emotion recognition studies, They use HR to measure happiness and emotions (Busso et al., 2004; Briggs, D., 2003).
EDA	Sometimes called Galvanic Skin Resistance, is associated with Emotional and stress sensitivity (GSR) (Kim, J., & André, E., 2008; Sultana, M., Al-Jefri, M., & Lee, J., 2020).
Motion	Because modern accelerometers incorporate tri-axial micro-electro-mechanical systems (MEMS) to record three-dimensional acceleration, the motion equation is:- $$\sqrt{X^2 + Y^2 + Z^2}$$ where this equation is the root mean square of all three Components. In recent years, They utilized the accelerometer to identify Emotions (Hildén, F., 2019). In recent years, they used the accelerometer to identify emotions (Hildén, F., 2019).

Raffaele Gravina published research on a study of alternative data fusion techniques and applications on body sensor networks (Ley et al., 2019).

Using a real-world study (Kanjo et al., 2018) using smartphones and wearable devices, they used a deep learning approach for emotion classification through an iterative process of adding and eliminating a large number of sensor signals from diverse modalities. It merged the local interactions of three sensor modalities: on-body, environmental, and location, into a global model that reflects signal dynamics plus temporal linkages between each modality. On the raw sensor data, this method used different learning algorithms, including a hybrid approach that combined Convolutional Neural Network and Long Short-term Memory Recurrent Neural Network (CNN-LSTM).

When using massive number of sensors, the results showed that deep-learning approaches were effective in human emotion classification (average accuracy 95% and F-Measure= 95%), and hybrid models outperformed traditional fully connected deep neural networks (average accuracy 73% and F-Measure=73%). The hybrid models also beat previously developed Ensemble methods that use feature engineering to train the model (average accuracy 83% and F-Measure=82%) (Kanjo et al., 2017).

Table 2. Previous Research on Recognizing Emotion from Physiological Signals

Emotions	Measurement Methods	Data Analysis Methods	Accuracy	ref
Sadness, anger, stress, surprise	ECG, SKT, GSR	SVM	For recognizing three and four categories, the correct classification rates were 78.4%, and 61.8%, respectively.	(Kim, J., & André, E., 2008).
Sadness, anger, fear, surprise, frustration, and amusement	GSR, HRV, SKT	KNN, DFA, MBP	KNN, DFA, and MBP could classify emotions with 72.3%, 75.0%, and 84.1%, respectively.	(Lisetti, C. L., & Nasoz, F., 2004)
Three levels of driver stress	ECG, EOG, GSR and respiration	Fisher projection matrix and a linear discriminant	Three levels of driver stress with an accuracy of over 97%	(Healey, J. A., & Picard, R. W. (2005)).
Fear, neutral, joy	ECG, SKT, GSR, respiration	Canonical correlation analysis	The rate of correct categorization is 85.3%. Fear, neutral, and happy categorization percentages were 76%, 94%, and 84%, respectively.	(Wioleta, S. 2013, June)
The emotional classes identified are high stress, low stress , disappointment, and euphoria	Facial EOG, ECG, GSR, respiration	SVM and adaptive neuro-fuzzy inference system (ANFIS)	The total classification rates for the SVM and the ANFIS using tenfold cross-validation are 79.3% and 76.7%, respectively.	(Busso et al., 2004)
Fatigue caused by driving for extended hours	HRV	Neural Network	The accuracy of the neural network is 90%	(Katsis et al., 2008)
Boredom, pain, surprise	GSR, ECG, HRV, SKT	Machine learning algorithms such as linear discriminate analysis (LDA), classification and regression tree (CART), self-organizing map (SOM), and SVM	SVM produced an average accuracy rate of 100.0%	(Jang et al., 2012)
The arousal classes were calm, medium, aroused, and activated and the valence classes were un-pleasant, neutral, and pleasant	ECG, pupillary response, gaze distance	Support Vector Machine	The optimal classification accuracies of 68.5% for three labels of valence and 76.4% for three labels of arousal.	(Song et al., 2019)
Sadness, fear, pleasure	ECG, GSR, blood volume pulse, pulse	Support vector regression	Recognition rates up to 89.2%	(Knapp et al., 2011)
Terrible, love, hate, sentimental, lovely, happy, fun, shock, cheerful, depressing, exciting, melancholy, mellow	EEG, GSR, blood volume pressure, respiration pattern, SKT, EMG, EOG	Support vector machine, Multilayer perceptron (MLP), K-Nearest Neighbor (KNN), and Meta-multiclass (MMC)	The average accuracies are 81.45%, 74.37%, 57.74% and 75.94% for SVM, MLP, KNN and MMC classifiers respectively. The best accuracy is for 'Depressing' with 85.46% using SVM. Accuracy of 85% with 13 emotions.	(Gravina et al., 2017)

Previously, scientific studies concentrated on recognizing and evaluating emotions by analyzing facial expressions, body posture, and gestures. Table 2 depicts an overview of the most widely utilized sensor analysis and feature extraction methods.

David et.al described an emotion detection system with a compact footprint that is appropriate for wearable devices with low resources in (Pollreisz, D., & TaheriNejad, N., 2017). In addition to distinguishing emotions, the suggested approach offered a confidence level for each recognition (with a success rate of 65%). (An average of 57%). They introduced a new technique for analyzing physiological signals like SKT, EDA, and HR using wearable devices like smart watches by looking for peaks in EDA signal and a simplified method for detecting emotions using EDA signal.

This study utilized the bio-signals obtained during data collection operation like: - the Empatica E4 smart watch to collect EDA, SKT, and HR values of persons with ages ranging from 20 to 25 years old). ML approaches were employed as: SVM (Banzhaf et al., 2014) 66.95%, RSVM (Banzhaf et al., 2014) 75.9%, SVM + GA (Yu, S. N., & Chen, S. F., 2015) 90%, NN (Lee et al., 2006) 80.2%, DFA (Jang et al., 2012) 84.7% of the cases.

The study in (Briggs, D., 2003) classified emotions based on multi-channel EEC signals and multi-modal physiological signals. They reviewed different feature extraction (e.g., wavelet transform and non-linear dynamics), feature reduction (e.g., PCA, LDA), and ML classifier design methods (e.g., KNN, naive Bayesian (NB), SVM and RF). This study achieved an average classification accuracy of over 80%, which seems acceptable for practical applications.

In this chapter, authors propose an empirical user dependent approach for combining environmental and physiological variables using sensor data obtained from thirty members wandering about Minia university campus. Simultaneously, authors obtained environmental and physiological data to create emotion detection models.

SYSTEM DESCRIPTION

Data Collection

To exclude additional variables (i.e., confounders) related to gender, authors collected data from 30 subjects (all females, undergraduate or graduate students) selected for this study. They were between the ages of 18 and 22, with an average age of 20 years. All of the participants were in good health, had no psychiatric problems, and had not consumed any alcohol or taken any medications that could have delayed their emotional response in the previous 72 hours. Before the experiment, each participant signed a written consent form. The Minya University Presidency gave their approval to the study.

Authors used a mobile App, which is as smartphone software wirelessly related to the Microsoft wristband 2 to collect data, which consists of 30 data files collected from 30 participants walking around Minia-university campus on a specific route. The dataset consists of on-body data like HR, galvanic skin response (GSR) or EDA, B-Temp, Motion data (accelerometer and gyro), environmental data like noise levels, UV, air pressure, and GPS locations associated with time stamp and self-report emotion levels (5-step Self-Assessment-Manikin (SAM) Scale for valence) logged by the EnvBodySens mobile application on Android phones, connected wirelessly to Microsoft wrist Band (Kanjo et al., 2019).

Authors used a wearable sensor known as the "Microsoft wristband 2". It's the second-generation smart band featuring smart watch capabilities was the wristband 2, which includes multiple sensors:

- Monitor your heart rate using an optical heart rate monitor.
- Accelerometer data with three axes.
- GPS Sensors.
- Galvanic skin response sensors (EDA).
- UV sensor (light).
- Skin temperature sensor.

Data collected are shown in table 3.

Table 3. Data recorded in mobile app

Data recorded in EnvBodySens

Microsoft wrist-band 2	Android phone 7
Heart Rate (HR)	Self-Report of Emotion (1-5)
Body-Temperature (Body-Temp)	Environmental Noise (Env-Noise)
Electro Dermal Activities (EDA)	GPS Location
Hand Acceleration (Motion as three-axis accelerometer)	
Air Pressure	
Light (UV)	

During data collection, when the user launches the software, the mobile interface displays five unique facial emotions ranging from extremely pessimistic to highly excited. To restructure the persistent labeling procedure, authors used the 5-step SAM Scale for Valence derived from (Balters, S., & Steinert, M., 2017).

The idea of valence fits well into this research setting since it portrays positive or negative emotion evoked by a scenario, an item, or an event.

Posters on walls or word of mouth, for example, urged students at the college of Computers and Information to participate in the study.

Finally, the data-collection setup, which includes a smartphone application and a wristband 2, is shown in figure 1.

Figure 1. Data collection process using wristband

Data collection process

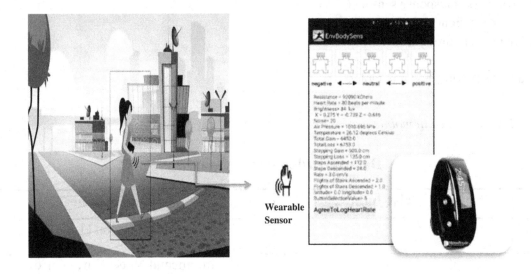

SYSTEM ARCHITECTURE

As shown in Figure 2, the system consists of several components using the three fusion levels (information fusion). Each user's dataset was collected using on-body sensors from the "Microsoft wrist band 2" and user data from the smartphone (e.g., location, ambient noise, and self-reported emotional states) and then merged via data-level fusion.

In the second step, authors cleaned or preprocessed the data and described in detail in the next subsection, 4.2.1 the cleaned data is analyzed using statistical analysis, to discover links between features in the third step. Fourth, authors used decision-level fusion to extract features from preprocessed data sensors or samples to solve the problem of emotion classification.

Then, authors spilt the dataset into two parts: training and testing. So, most of samples of the dataset were trained using specific candidate ML algorithms to produce the final trained model, and the rest are used for testing. After that, the model is then evaluated using new data or test data via performance metrics like (Accuracy, F1-score in classification report) resulting from that predicting emotional response (Labels) based on test data.

Data Pre-Processing

Because of the complicated and subjective nature of raw physiological signals, and the sensitivity to noises from measurement devices, electromagnetic interferences, and movement artifacts, it is vital to preprocess noise effects at the early stage of emotion recognition (Shu et al., 2018).

Because authors deal with much raw data, ML approaches require organizing and cleaning the data before constructing models. Authors cleaned the data and transformed it into a proper format before using ML techniques.

Finding missing, erroneous, or irrelevant data and updating, modifying, or removing it, and eliminating dataset flaws that could damage the prediction model, are all part of data cleaning.

Figure 2. System architecture of the proposed emotion model using information fusion

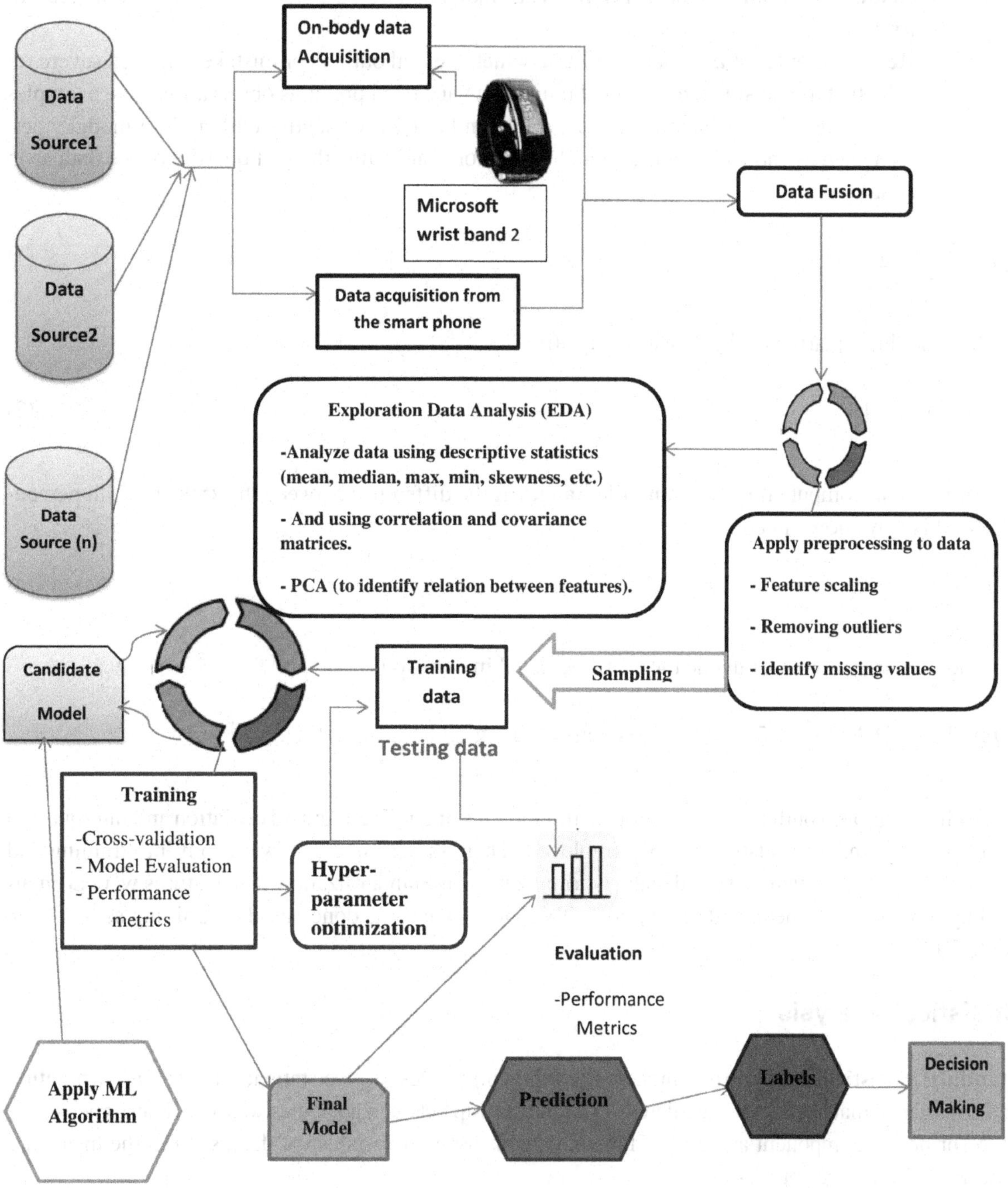

The two most common data preparation operations are **formatting** and **cleaning**.

- *Formatting*: The data may not be in a format you'll work with. The data should be in an excel or CSV file, and it could be stored in a relational database or a text file.

- *Cleaning*
  - **Remove Unwanted Observations**: That includes any observations that are duplicated or irrelevant.
  - **Removing irregular data or outliers**, which are real outliers or mistakes, or even severe results that are outside the predicted range and vary from previous observations, are examples of data cleaning. A boxplot or histogram can be used to identify outliers in a model's performance as shown in Figures 3 and 4. Authors can define the first quartile of the data as in equation:

$$Q1 = X[n / 4]$$ (1)

And the third quartile of the data as in equation:

$$Q3 = X[3n / 4]$$ (2)

Authors can compute IQR (Interquartile Range) as the difference between the 75th and 25th percentiles in this way shown in equation:

$$Q3 - Q1$$ (3)

And outliers are points outside the range depicted in equation:

$$[Q1 - 1.5 * IQR, Q3 + 1.5 * IQR]$$ (Rousseeuw, P. J., & Hubert, M., 2011).

Authors removed outliers using several methodologies, including standard deviation and Interquartile Range (IQR), which are also frequently employed. Then, the cleaned data were split into training and testing sets, with the features scaled using Normalization or Standardization. The features were normalized by removing the mean and scaling to unit variance. That was done based on training set (Sultana et al., 2020).

Statistical Analysis

Standard statistical procedures: include the following: - Descriptive statistics, as well as correlation and covariance matrices, were calculated. The relationship between attributes was also determined using PCA (principal component analysis). The crucial and essential variables of data, such as the mean, are described using descriptive statistics.

Table 4a shows the standard deviation (std), median (Med), minimum (min), 1st Quartile, or Q_1 (25%), 2nd Centile, or Q_2 (50%), 3rd Centile, or Q_3 (75%), maximum (100%), and skewness and kurtosis (kur) of the various body and environmental sensor signals for all participants. On the other hand, a Covariance Matrix is a two-dimensional array that displays the covariance of each pair of variables in a random vector. Positive covariance suggests that the two variables' frequency is increasing. A negative correlation, on the other hand, proposes that the two variables are frequently dropping.

Figure 3. Boxplot of HR and bTemp before and after cleaning

Box-plot representation of (HR, BTemp) before pre-processing

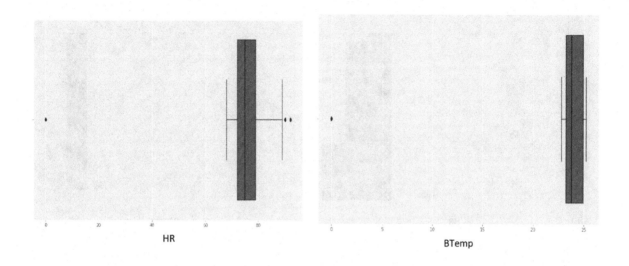

Box-plot representation of (HR, BTemp) after pre-processing

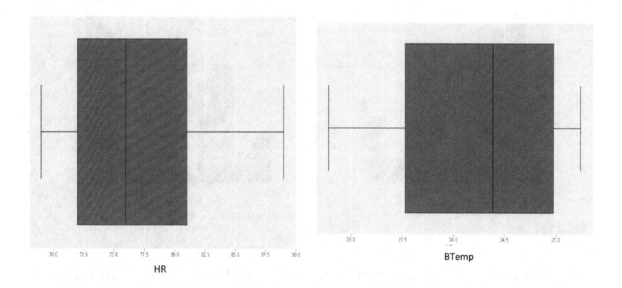

Finally, as demonstrated in Table 4b, if the covariance is 0, there is no association between the two variables. Figure 5c show that (EDA) has a negative association with (HR, UV, b-Temp) and a positive relationship with (Motion, Env-Noise, Air-Pressure). HR is negatively related to (EDA, Env-Noise) and positively related to (UV, Motion, Air-Pressure-Temp). Also, the UV feature has a positive connection with (HR, Motion, Air-Pressure, bTemp) and a negative relationship with (EDA, Env-Noise). Motion is positive with (EDA, HR, UV, Env-Noise, Air-Pressure) and is negative with (bTemp). Env-Noise is negatively related to (HR, UV, b-Temp) and positively related to (EDA, Motion, Air- pressure).

Figure 4. Histogram plot of HR. and bTemp before and after cleaning

Histogram plot representation of (HR, BTemp) before pre-processing

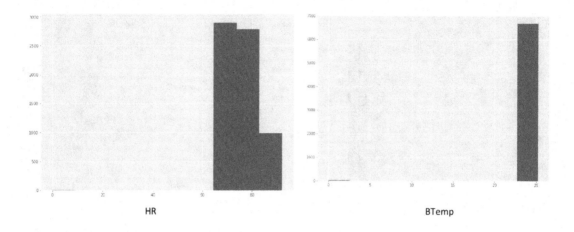

Histogram plot representation of (HR, BTemp) after pre-processing

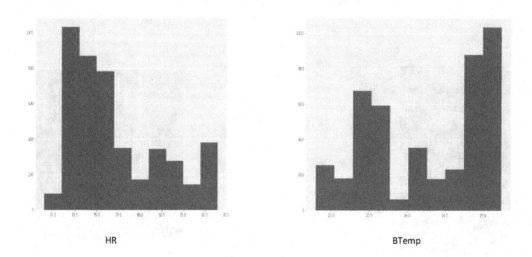

The air-Pressure feature is positive with all (EDA, HR, UV, Motion, Env-Noise, bTemp) features. And bTemp variable has positively related to (HR, UV, Air-Pressure) and negatively related to (EDA, Motion, Env-Noise).

EDA, Motion, and (Env-Noise, Air-Pressure) are positively related to each other because they are on the top-right side of the plot. Also, (HR, Motion, b-Temp) are positive with (UV, Air-Pressure) because (HR, Motion, b-Temp) are on the right side of the plot with (UV, Air-Pressure) although feature (UV) is on the bottom-right side of the figure whereas the rest are on the top-right of the graph. Features (UV, HR) are positive with each other because they are on the right side of the graph. And so on for the remaining independent variables.

Figure 5. Represents Standard statistics of on-body and environmental. (a) (b) represents correlation matrix of on-body and environmental features to label. (c) Represents PCA Plot of features. (d) 3D Scatterplot of each pair of features. (e) Poincare plot during and after noise of HRV. (f) PSD plot of collected dataset

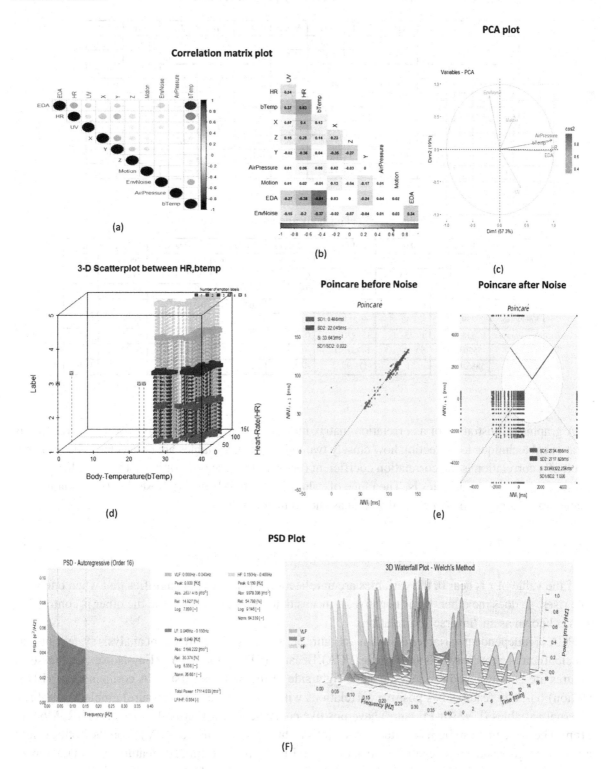

Table 4. Descriptive statistics and Covariance Matrix for all collected on-body and environmental factors corresponding to Label

Descriptive statistics of independent variables

(a)

	Min	Q1	Med	Q2	Mean	Q3	Max	skw	kur	std
EDA	666.0	666.0	666.0	666.0	667.2	669.0	669.0	0.4	-1.9	1.5
HR	77.0	77.0	77.0	77.0	77.5	78.0	79.0	1.1	-0.5	0.8
UV	2209.0	3051.0	3051.0	3051.0	3204.3	3381.5	4295.0	0.3	-0.7	620.6
X	-1.4	-0.7	-0.5	-0.5	-0.5	-0.3	0.3	-0.2	0.6	0.4
Y	-0.3	0.2	0.4	0.4	0.4	0.6	1.3	0.3	-0.5	0.4
Z	-1.3	-0.9	-0.7	-0.7	0.6	-0.4	0.3	0.6	-0.7	0.4
Motion	0.3	0.8	1.2	1.2	1.4	1.9	2.9	0.6	-0.8	0.7
Env Noise	48.0	51.0	53.0	53.0	52.3	54.0	57.0	0.0	-0.5	2.2
Air Pressure	1011.0	1011.0	1011.0	1011.0	1011.0	1011.0	1011.1	0.0	-0.9	0.0
bTemp	32.2	32.3	32.3	32.3	32.3	32.3	32.3	-0.7	-0.2	0.0

Covariance Matrix of on-body and environmental

(b)

	EDA	HR	UV	Motion	EnvNoise	AirPressure	bTemp	Label
EDA	21549661382	-1135089.3	-337117195	1828.78	263392.91	87518.6	-552080.9	5885.4
HR	-1135089.3	411.33	41801.2	0.22	-21.5	19.75	59.30	-0.51
UV	-337117195	41801.2	73553532.01	35.10	-6921.46	1899.9	14763.30	-179
Motion	1828.78	0.22	35.10	0.26	0.072	0.048	-0.028	-0.006
EnvNoise	263392.91	-21.46	-6921.46	0.072	28.62	0.77	-9.19	0.075
Air-Pressure	87518.6	19.75	1899.9	0.048	0.77	260.78	6.30	0.06
bTemp	-552080.9	59.30	14763.30	-0.028	-9.19	6.30	21.4	-0.11
Label	5885.4	-0.51	-178.98	-0.006	0.075	0.06	-0.11	1.49

A graphical illustration of a correlation matrix may be seen in Figure 5b. As a result, correlation is a statistical technique for detecting how closely two independent variables are connected. The principal result of a correlation is the correlation coefficient (or "r"). It's a measure of how strong the linear relationship between two variables is. The range of values is -1.0 to +1 .0. The closer the two variables are related, the closer r is to +1 or -1 calculated as shown in equation:

$$r = \mathrm{cov}(\mathrm{x,y}) \,/\, \sigma\mathrm{x}\sigma\mathrm{y} \tag{5}$$

If the value of r is near 0, the variables are unrelated. If r is positive, it signifies that when one variable rises, so does the other. If r is negative, it means that one is growing while the other is contracting (this is known as an "inverse" correlation).

PCA of independent variables is shown in Figure 5c. A regression component analysis system such as principal component analysis is an example (PCA). Because (EDA, Motion) and (Env-Noise, Air-Pressure) features are both oriented towards the same right side of the plot, the first PCA component of (EDA, Motion) on-body features has positive correlations with (Env-Noise, Air-Pressure) ambient variables. External variables (UV, Air-Pressure) have positive coefficients with on-body variables (HR, Motion, bTemp) because they are both oriented to the plot's right-top side, whereas (UV) is on the bottom-right side of the figure and has a negative association with Env-Noise, b-Temp, HR features are on the top X-axis and are negatively related to (EDA, Env-Noise), whereas (EDA, Env-Noise) features have positive coefficients with (Motion, Air pressure). Thus, authors must take into account the relationship between environmental and on-body elements, as well as their impact on human emotions.

As illustrated in Figure 5d, Authors can generate scatterplots between b-Temp, HR to highlight the relationship between them and the label responses. Both b-Temp and HR have a stronger positive relationship with Emotion Labels.

SYSTEM IMPLEMENTATION

In the emotion recognition model, feature extraction is quite significant. Authors started by combining all sensor data, location data, and self-reported contextual information from various users. Sensor readings were taken every 30 minutes to 60 minutes for each user on different days ranging from 1 to 2 days. The number of samples changes from one user to another; for example, the first user's data range from 1000 to 6688, the second user's data range from 1000 to 11586, and the sixth user's samples range from 1000 to 23086, and so on. The data differ because each person's data collection period differs.

Authors used PCA as shown in Figure 5c to identify the relationship between environmental and physiological factors after analyzing data and investigating the impact of each ambient variable on each body sensor and vice versa, as well as their impact on label responses, using covariance and correlation metrics as shown in Table 4, Figure 5b.

To extract physiological and environmental parameters, authors employed descriptive statistics as shown in Table 4. For:-

- Authors extracted the following features (Mean, Median, Max, Min, STD and Quartiles, Skewness, Kurtosis) from (HR, EDA, bTemp, Motion, UV, Env-Noise, Air-Pressure) variables (Lisetti, C. L., & Nasoz, F., 2004).

For Motion: - Authors combined the X, Y, and Z characteristics into a single component called Motion As shown in equation:

$$Motion = \sqrt{X^2 + Y^2 + Z^2} \tag{6}$$

Authors used a Poincare plot to derive HRV feature distributions and to assess normality defined in time series and frequency domains for HR (Guendil et al., 2016). This plot is a graph with NN (i) on the x-axis and NN (i + 1) (the next NN interval) on the y-axis, with NN intervals in between (the distance between each heartbeat), as illustrated in Figure 5e.

Several metrics were calculated and plotted in the graph, including the SD_1 (standard deviation along the minor axis), which is as follows in equation:

$$SD1 = \sqrt{\left(\frac{1}{2} SDSD^2 \right)} \tag{7}$$

And the SD2 parameter (the standard deviation on the major axis) can be calculated as follows in Equation:

$$SD2 = \sqrt{\left(2SDNN2 - \tfrac{1}{2}SDSD2\right)} \tag{8}$$

Where SDSD is the standard deviation of consecutive differences (Time Domain parameter) SDNN is the standard deviation of the NNI series (), where (SD_1 / SD_2) determines whether a higher or lower heart rate of HRV occurs (Nguyen et al., 2019).

Authors also derive frequency domain that indicates the power spectrum of order 16 by integration of low frequency (LF) heartbeats (0.04 to 0. 5 Hz) and high frequency (HF) (0. 15 Hz to 0.4 Hz), (Nguyen et al., 2019) as shown in Figure 5.

Feature Engineering

The data distribution of most features might be skewed and non-normal. To eliminate this, authors used the 'Box-cox Transformation' power transform method to make the data more Gaussian-like. That is helpful when modeling heteroscedasticity (non-constant variance) or other circumstances when normality is required. A 'Box Cox transformation' converts non-normal dependent variables into a normal shape. For Box-Cox, the input data must be strictly positive. Box-cox is used to find the maximum likelihood estimates of the Box-Cox transform parameters, the coefficients on the independent variables, and the standard deviation of normally distributed errors. While fitting a linear regression model, the purpose of this strategy is to discover the optimum transformation for Y. As a result, the power transformations are taken into consideration, which is defined as follows in Equation:

$$Y` = \left(Y + \lambda 2\right)\lambda 1 \tag{9}$$

After shifting the data, a specific amount λ_2, the data is raised to a power λ_1, where λ is an ideal transformation parameter in series $\lambda \in \left[-1, 1\right]$ (Kanjo et al., 2018). To do this, a Box-Cox transformation gives a shifting parameter. Before executing box cox, such a shift parameter is equal to adding a positive constant to x. This method is part of SCiPy's stats package, and it performs a box-cox power transformation on non-normal data, returning fitted data and the lambda value used to adapt the non-normal distribution to a normal distribution.

For example, authors want to convert the HR feature from a non-normal to a normal feature using the box-cox function as shown in Figure 6.

Feature Fusion

The techniques of feature fusion can be divided into three categories: early, intermediate, and late fusion. The characteristics selected from the sensors are consolidated in a single set before sending to the classifier in early fusion (feature level fusion). The intermediate fusion can reliably deal with incomplete data. The outcome is voted on by the outputs of many classifiers in late fusion, also known as decision level fusion. In signal integration, early fusion and late fusion are the most often employed methods (Shu et al., 2018). For each person, authors concatenated feature sets from many modalities to generate two spaces that reflect them (the environmental and on-Body modalities). As seen in the data preprocessing part, and the previous section, authors extracted **21** features for each user from our dataset. However, not all of these features are required for emotional responses, and some of them are linked. As a result, authors can delete some of them, reducing the number of features in the model. Finally, the model can include the most significant variables to characterize an emotional response.

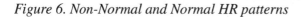

Figure 6. Non-Normal and Normal HR patterns

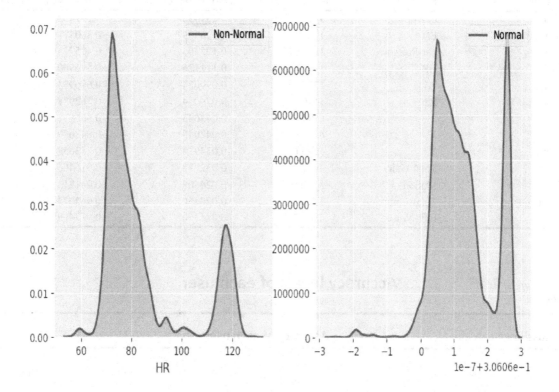

Feature Selection

Authors create a user-dependent prediction model to investigate if authors can accurately forecast a user's affect state based on contextual and physiological data. To make the emotion recognition model more effective, authors intended to reduce the dimension of characteristics by selecting the most efficient features from 21 features. Authors chose the SelectKBest feature selection method, which returned the top k features when the 'mutual-info-classif' evaluation argument was set to true or changing the 'score-func' parameter (classification problem). SelectKBest is a Python library function from the sklearn machine learning package. In this study, the corresponding version was 0.21.1. Sklearn was updated to the newest version using pip or CONDA commands (Shu et al., 2020).

For emotional transition and state identification, and personalized models, this feature selection technique was used independently. As a result, each model (Sultana et al., 2020) has a unique number of features. Authors also decided to develop a user-dependent predictive model with **12 or 13** features that have a strong link with the labels depending on the results of the 'SelectKBest' feature selection. Authors can depict the most relevant features retrieved from the SelectKBest feature-selection technique in Figure 7 depicts the significance of selected features, such that cumulative significance increasing until n =12. (Where n is no. of Features).

Table 5. (a) Feature importance score for each feature and (b) accuracy levels of each user over each classifier

Importance of Features

(a)

Index	Feature	Importance	Normalized Importance	Cumulative Importance
0	bTemp	34711.3	0.231432	0.231432
1	EDA	19338.9	0.128939	0.360371
2	Air-Pressure	18808.5	0.125403	0.485773
3	HR	16667.3	0.111126	0.596900
4	UV	13503.8	0.090034	0.686934
5	Rate	11406.9	0.076054	0.762988
6	Z	6545.8	0.043643	0.806631
7	X	6306.6	0.042048	0.848679
8	Y	5245.6	0.034974	0.883653
9	Total-Gain	4912.4	0.032753	0.916406
10	Motion	3720.8	0.024808	0.941213
11	Total-Loss	3128.6	0.020850	0.962073
12	Env-Noise	2309.2	0.015396	0.977469

Accuracy levels of each user

(b)

Classifier	Accuracy of each user				
	User1	User2	User3	User4	User5
KNN	95%	96%	98%	95.2%	97.7%
SVM	97%	98%	97%	94%	91%
RF	96%	95%	96%	97%	97.2%
DT	98%	97%	96%	94%	96.6%

Using this technique, authors could investigate the impact of significant features on emotion labels and the reactions of the affect labels. As seen in Figure 7, Table 5a illustrates the importance of each feature, as well as its normalized and cumulative importance. Note that the higher the cumulative importance, the lower the significance of each feature, as shown in this Table. As a result, the Env-Noise Feature is less important than the other features. As a result, the irrelevant features were removed.

Machine Learning Models

The main challenge in emotion recognition is to allocate the input signals to one of the available class groups. Other various categorization methods can be used to recognize emotions (Shu et al., 2018). So, to distinguish between the five emotional states (happy, sad, neutral, very happy, very sad) (Shu et al., 2020) and develop personalized models for each person to explore the impact of interpersonal variability on the performance of emotional transition and state detection (Sultana et al., 2020), four classifiers were evaluated: KNN (k-Nearest Neighbor), (Song et al., 2019), RF (Random Forests) (Li et al., 2016; Wen et al., 2014), DT (Decision Tree) (Zhang et al., 2016; Noroozi et al., 2017), SVM (Support Vector Machine). Authors used the sklearn library to create these classification models, which integrated common machine learning approaches (Shu et al., 2020). Emotional state detection is a multiclass classification problem in which authors wanted to categorize the current emotional state of a person into one of five categories: 1, 2, 3, 4, and 5 (Sultana et al., 2020).

Figure 7. [A] Feature Importance. [B] Cumulative importance of selected features

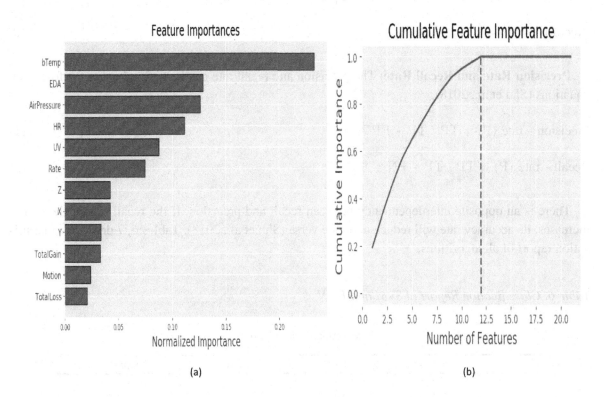

After applying feature-extraction to extract features for each independent variable in our dataset, feature fusion to explain three fusion levels applied on the dataset, feature engineering to depict used technique for transforming specific features from non-normalized to normalized features to make data more Gaussian-like and feature selection to select the most important features with which authors could get higher accuracy levels for each user. But, in particular, times when applying classifiers in our study on the preprocessed dataset with those significant features produced over-fitting at default parameters of classifier so, authors decided to use CridSeacrchCV optimization on each classifier in ML algorithms for each user individually by which authors could reach the optimal hyper-parameters for each person for each classifier, and N-fold cross-validation over the data of each person was performed and then the results over each person are averaged. In subject-dependent training, this processing was done by K-fold cross-validation to evaluate the performance of each person's data.

Now, authors can represent training and testing accuracy levels for each user over each classifier. The next figures depict a comparison between training and testing levels for each person after choosing the optimal parameters. This study (Kanjo et al., 2018) presents accuracy of (86%) based on combining multi-modal classifiers (SVM, RF, and KNN). Table 5b depicts Accuracy levels for each person over each classifier. Tables 6, 7 represent the classification performance of different algorithms.

Performance Measures

Accuracy: the terms accuracy rate and error rate are often used in categorization. The accurate rate refers to the percentage of samples that are correctly categorized out of all the data. The mistake rate is computed by dividing the total number of data (Shu et al., 2018) by the number of misclassified samples. The accuracy rate calculated as follows in Equation (Shu et al., 2020).

$$Accuracy = Ncorrect / Ntotal \tag{10}$$

Precision Rate and Recall Rate: The precision and recall rate can be defined using the following equations (Shu et al., 2018).

$$Precision - rate\ (P) = TP / TP + FP \tag{11}$$

$$Recall - rate\ (P) = TP / TP + FN \tag{12}$$

There is an opposite interdependency between recall and precision. If the recall rate of the output increases, its accuracy rate will reduce and vice versa (Shu et al., 2018). Tables 6, 7 depict the classification report of all algorithms.

Table 6. Classification Report of SVM and KNN

Classification Report of SVM

(a)

	Precision	Recall	F1-Score	Support
1	0.89	1.00	0.94	275
2	1.00	0.79	0.88	717
3	0.94	0.99	0.96	485
4	0.91	0.99	0.95	518
5	0.93	0.99	0.96	496
Accuracy			0.94	2491
Macro avg	0.93	0.95	0.94	2491
Weighted avg	0.94	0.94	0.93	2491

Classification Report of KNN

(b)

	Precision	Recall	F1-Score	Support
1	0.94	0.94	0.94	309
2	0.95	0.93	0.94	585
3	0.95	0.96	0.95	509
4	0.96	0.96	0.96	568
5	0.95	0.97	0.96	520
Accuracy			0.95	2491
Macro avg	0.95	0.95	0.95	2491
Weighted avg	0.95	0.95	0.95	2491

Table 7. Classification Report of DT and RF

Classification Report of DT

(c)

	Precision	Recall	F1-Score	Support
1	0.94	0.96	0.95	302
2	0.98	0.94	0.96	600
3	0.87	0.96	0.92	467
4	0.97	0.93	0.95	594
5	0.93	0.93	0.93	528
Accuracy			0.94	2491
Macro avg	0.94	0.94	0.94	2491
Weighted avg	0.94	0.94	0.94	2491

Classification Report of RF

(d)

	Precision	Recall	F1-Score	Support
1	0.98	0.97	0.97	310
2	0.99	0.95	0.97	596
3	0.96	0.96	0.96	513
4	0.98	0.99	0.98	560
5	0.95	0.98	0.99	512
Accuracy			0.97	2491
Macro avg	0.97	0.97	0.97	2491
Weighted avg	0.97	0.97	0.97	2491

F1-score is defined as the harmonic mean of the precision rate and the recall rate (Shu et al., 2018). F1 can be defined as in Equation:

$$F1 = 2 * P * R / P + R \tag{13}$$

Authors used cross-validation for estimating a model's performance. In k-fold cross-validation, the number of folds is k. Cross-validation is used to train the model ten times (CV= 10). As a result, the k value would be 10. The classifier's accuracy is calculated by scoring='accuracy'. It's used in a grid search in this fashion. Instead of minimizing the actual error, they took the accuracy to maximize and optimize accuracy. These figures depict a comparison between training and testing levels for each person based on the optimal parameters as shown in Figures 8, 9, 10, 11.

Based on variations in the accuracy levels shown in Figures 8,9,10,11,12 and table 5b, authors can depict the variations in the accuracy levels between combined models and single modalities as in Fig 13.

FUTURE RESEARCH DIRECTIONS

In this paper, an emotion detection model was presented for on-body and ecological sensing based on an information fusion approach, which opens up new possibilities for data-intensive methods. The study is noteworthy for detecting emotions using multi-modal sensor inputs (physiological and environmental data) using machine learning algorithms.

Figure 8. Depict training and testing accuracy levels for five users of KNN algorithm

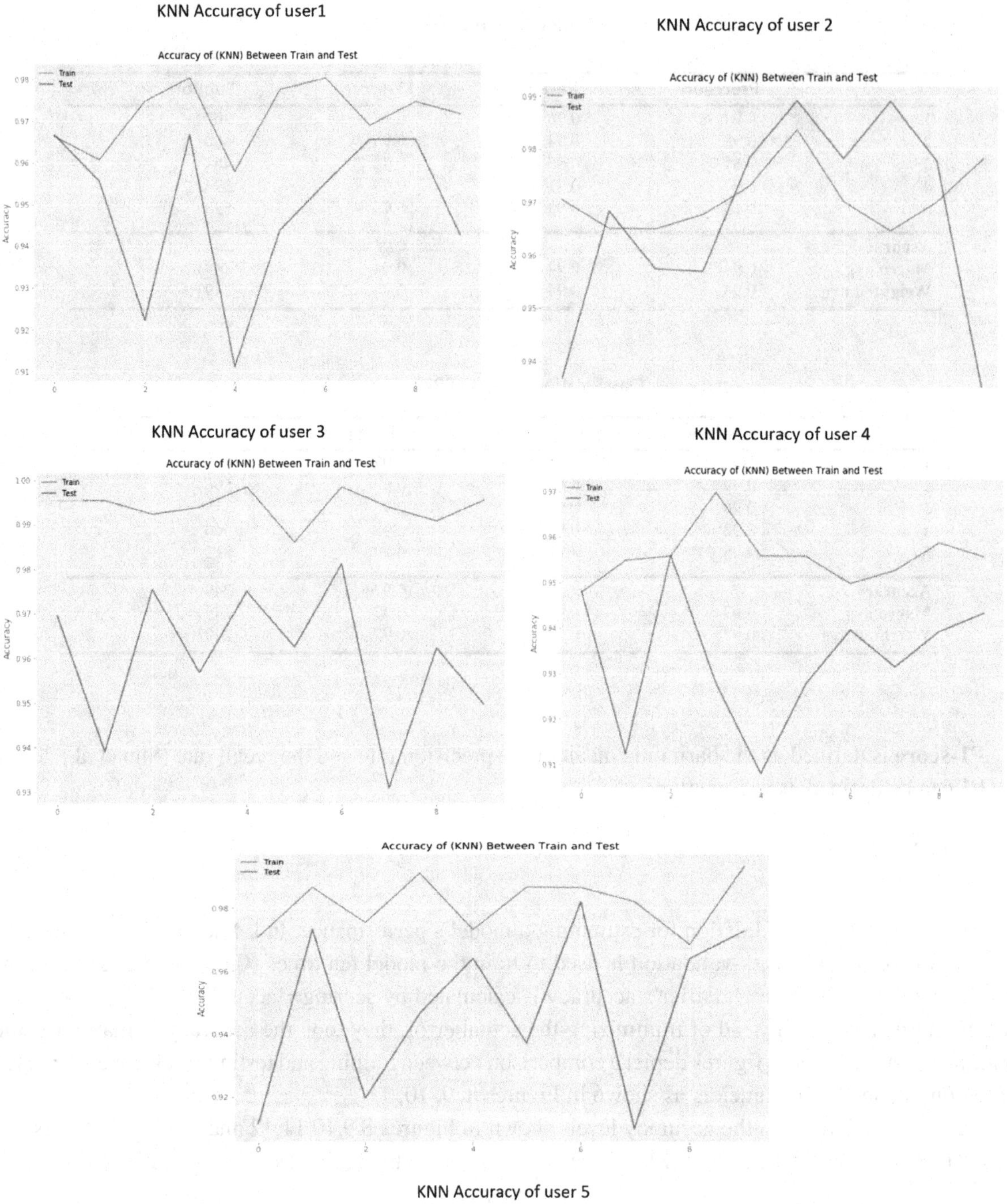

KNN Accuracy of user1

KNN Accuracy of user 2

KNN Accuracy of user 3

KNN Accuracy of user 4

KNN Accuracy of user 5

Authors will try adding more sensors to improve understanding of the underlying links between the environment and health in the future. Moreover, they will look at using a mobile application to model these aspects associated with actual locations in different parts of the city. In addition to using more advanced machine learning methods such as deep learning.

Figure 9. Depict accuracy levels for five users of DT algorithm

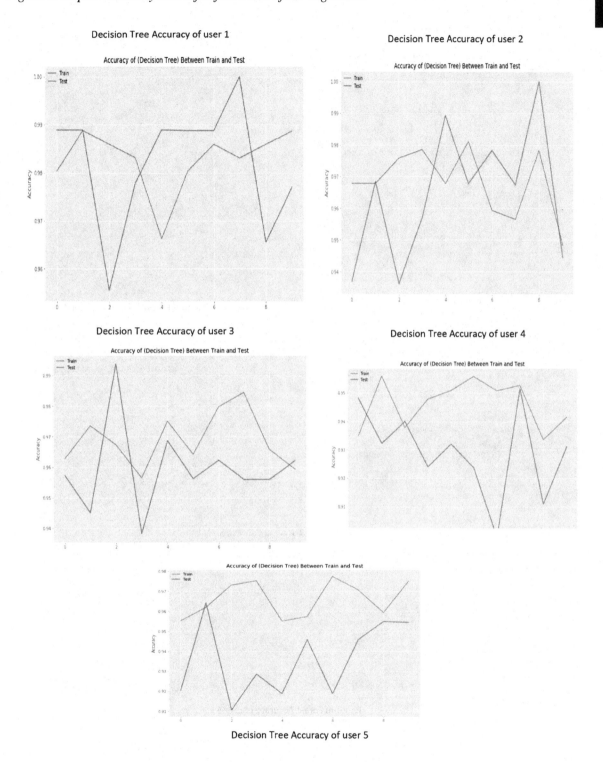

Figure 10. Displays accuracy Levels for five users of RF algorithm

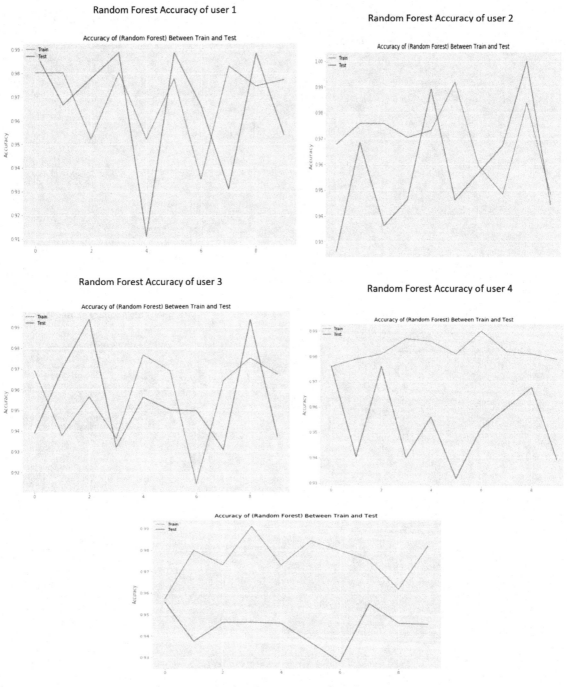

Random Forest Accuracy of user 5

Figure 11. Shows accuracy levels for five users of SVM algorithm

Support Vector Machine Accuracy of user 1

Support Vector Machine Accuracy of user 2

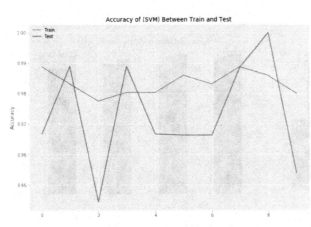

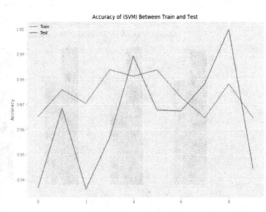

Support Vector Machine Accuracy of user 3

Support Vector Machine Accuracy of user 4

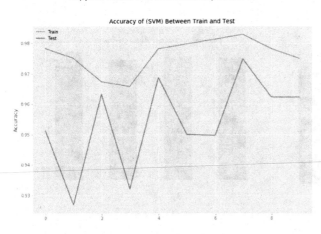

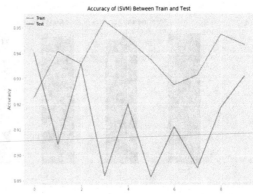

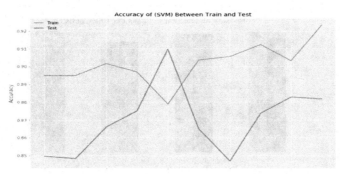

Support Vector Machine Accuracy of user 5

Figure 12. [A] A comparison of accuracy levels of all algorithms for us1. [B] A comparison of accuracy levels of all algorithms for us2. [C] A comparison of accuracy levels of all algorithms for us3. [D] A comparison of accuracy levels of all algorithms for us4. [E] A comparison of accuracy levels of all algorithms for us5

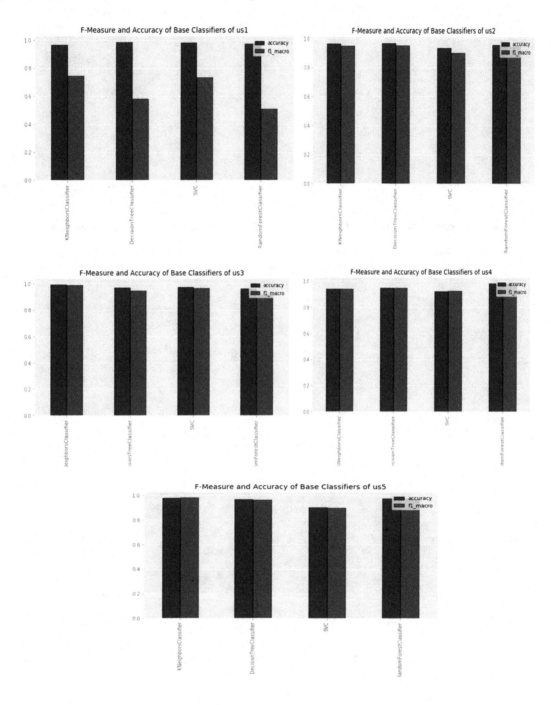

Figure 13. [a], [b] depicts variations of the accuracy levels of ten users between fused and single modalities

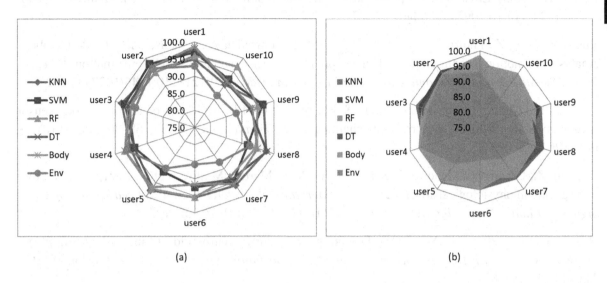

(a)   (b)

CONCLUSION

The accuracy levels achieved are also compared between single modalities (on-body, environmental modality) and combined modalities across all four models. When RF, DT, for example, were trained only on-Body data subset, it achieved an average accuracy of 97%. Whereas SVM and KNN achieved an average accuracy of 94% when training on physiological data only.

While RF, SVM, KNN performed worse on Environment data with an average accuracy lower than 90%. DT achieved an average accuracy of 92%.

SVM achieved an average accuracy of 96% when performed on fused modalities data which is significantly higher than every single modality (p <0.01). Also, KNN achieved an average accuracy of 96.8% and RF achieved an average accuracy of 97% and DT achieved an average accuracy of 97.4%. Moreover, the results depicted that DT, RF outperforms SVM, KNN significantly by 1% or 2% (p <0.01) with an average accuracy 0.97%.

REFERENCES

Agrafioti, F., Hatzinakos, D., & Anderson, A. K. (2011). ECG pattern analysis for emotion detection. *IEEE Transactions on Affective Computing*, *3*(1), 102–115. doi:10.1109/T-AFFC.2011.28

Balters, S., & Steinert, M. (2017). Capturing emotion reactivity through physiology measurement as a foundation for affective engineering in engineering design science and engineering practices. *Journal of Intelligent Manufacturing*, *28*(7), 1585–1607. doi:10.100710845-015-1145-2

Banzhaf, E., de la Barrera, F., Kindler, A., Reyes-Paecke, S., Schlink, U., Welz, J., & Kabisch, S. (2014). A conceptual framework for integrated analysis of environmental quality and quality of life. *Ecological Indicators*, *45*, 664–668. doi:10.1016/j.ecolind.2014.06.002

Basiri, M., Schill, F. U., Lima, P., & Floreano, D. (2018). Localization of emergency acoustic sources by micro aerial vehicles. *Journal of Field Robotics*, *35*(2), 187–201. doi:10.1002/rob.21733

Briggs, D. (2003). Environmental pollution and the global burden of disease. *British Medical Bulletin, 68*(1), 1–24. doi:10.1093/bmb/ldg019 PMID:14757707

Busso, C., Deng, Z., Yildirim, S., Bulut, M., Lee, C. M., Kazemzadeh, A., ... Narayanan, S. (2004, October). Analysis of emotion recognition using facial expressions, speech and multimodal information. *Proceedings of the 6th international conference on Multimodal interfaces*, 205-211. 10.1145/1027933.1027968

Gravina, R., Alinia, P., Ghasemzadeh, H., & Fortino, G. (2017). Multi-sensor fusion in body sensor networks: State-of-the-art and research challenges. *Information Fusion, 35*, 68–80. doi:10.1016/j.inffus.2016.09.005

Guendil, Z., Lachiri, Z., Maaoui, C., & Pruski, A. (2016, March). Multiresolution framework for emotion sensing in physiological signals. *2016 2nd International Conference on Advanced Technologies for Signal and Image Processing (ATSIP)*, 793-797. 10.1109/ATSIP.2016.7523190

Healey, J. A., & Picard, R. W. (2005). Detecting stress during real-world driving tasks using physiological sensors. *IEEE Transactions on Intelligent Transportation Systems, 6*(2), 156–166. doi:10.1109/TITS.2005.848368

Hildén, F. (2019). *Time series clustering by extracted features*. Academic Press.

Jang, E. H., Park, B. J., Kim, S. H., Chung, M. A., & Sohn, J. H. (2012). Classification of three emotions by machine learning algorithms using psychophysiological signals. *International Journal of Psychophysiology, 3*(85), 402–403. doi:10.1016/j.ijpsycho.2012.07.106

Jerritta, S., Murugappan, M., Nagarajan, R., & Wan, K. (2011, March). Physiological signals based human emotion recognition: a review. *2011 IEEE 7th international colloquium on signal processing and its applications,* 410-415. 10.1109/CSPA.2011.5759912

Kanjo, E., Al-Husain, L., & Chamberlain, A. (2015). Emotions in context: Examining pervasive affective sensing systems, applications, and analyses. *Personal and Ubiquitous Computing, 19*(7), 1197–1212. doi:10.100700779-015-0842-3

Kanjo, E., Kuss, D. J., & Ang, C. S. (2017). NotiMind: Utilizing responses to smart phone notifications as affective sensors. *IEEE Access: Practical Innovations, Open Solutions, 5*, 22023–22035. doi:10.1109/ACCESS.2017.2755661

Kanjo, E., Younis, E. M., & Ang, C. S. (2019). Deep learning analysis of mobile physiological, environmental and location sensor data for emotion detection. *Information Fusion, 49*, 46–56. doi:10.1016/j.inffus.2018.09.001

Kanjo, E., Younis, E. M., & Sherkat, N. (2018). Towards unravelling the relationship between on-body, environmental and emotion data using sensor information fusion approach. *Information Fusion, 40*, 18–31. doi:10.1016/j.inffus.2017.05.005

Katsis, C. D., Katertsidis, N., Ganiatsas, G., & Fotiadis, D. I. (2008). Toward emotion recognition in car-racing drivers: A biosignal processing approach. *IEEE Transactions on Systems, Man, and Cybernetics. Part A, Systems and Humans, 38*(3), 502–512. doi:10.1109/TSMCA.2008.918624

Kim, J., & André, E. (2008). Emotion recognition based on physiological changes in music listening. *IEEE Transactions on Pattern Analysis and Machine Intelligence, 30*(12), 2067–2083. doi:10.1109/TPAMI.2008.26 PMID:18988943

Knapp, R. B., Kim, J., & André, E. (2011). Physiological signals and their use in augmenting emotion recognition for human–machine interaction. In *Emotion-oriented systems* (pp. 133–159). Springer. doi:10.1007/978-3-642-15184-2_9

Kovats, R. S., & Haines, A. (2005). Global climate change and health: Recent findings and future steps. *Canadian Medical Association Journal, 172*(4), 501–502. doi:10.1503/cmaj.050020 PMID:15710942

Kreibig, S. D. (2010). Autonomic nervous system activity in emotion: A review. *Biological Psychology, 84*(3), 394–421. doi:10.1016/j.biopsycho.2010.03.010 PMID:20371374

Lee, C., Yoo, S. K., Park, Y., Kim, N., Jeong, K., & Lee, B. (2006, January). Using neural network to recognize human emotions from heart rate variability and skin resistance. In *2005 IEEE Engineering in Medicine and Biology 27th Annual Conference* (pp. 5523-5525). IEEE.

Ley, M., Egger, M., & Hanke, S. (2019, November). Evaluating Methods for Emotion Recognition based on Facial and Vocal Features. In *AmI* (pp. 84–93). Workshops/Posters.

Li, S., Cui, L., Zhu, C., Li, B., Zhao, N., & Zhu, T. (2016). Emotion recognition using Kinect motion capture data of human gaits. *PeerJ, 4*, e2364. doi:10.7717/peerj.2364 PMID:27672492

Lisetti, C. L., & Nasoz, F. (2004). Using noninvasive wearable computers to recognize human emotions from physiological signals. *EURASIP Journal on Advances in Signal Processing, 2004*(11), 1–16. doi:10.1155/S1110865704406192

Nguyen Phuc Thu, T., Hernández, A. I., Costet, N., Patural, H., Pichot, V., Carrault, G., & Beuchée, A. (2019). Improving methodology in heart rate variability analysis for the premature infants: Impact of the time length. *PLoS One, 14*(8), e0220692. doi:10.1371/journal.pone.0220692 PMID:31398196

Noroozi, F., Sapiński, T., Kamińska, D., & Anbarjafari, G. (2017). Vocal-based emotion recognition using random forests and decision tree. *International Journal of Speech Technology, 20*(2), 239–246. doi:10.100710772-017-9396-2

Plasqui, G., & Westerterp, K. R. (2007). Physical activity assessment with accelerometers: An evaluation against doubly labeled water. *Obesity (Silver Spring, Md.), 15*(10), 2371–2379. doi:10.1038/oby.2007.281 PMID:17925461

Pollreisz, D., & TaheriNejad, N. (2017, July). A simple algorithm for emotion recognition, using physiological signals of a smart watch. *2017 39th annual international conference of the ieee engineering in medicine and biology society (EMBC)*, 2353-2356.

Rousseeuw, P. J., & Hubert, M. (2011). Robust statistics for outlier detection. *Wiley Interdisciplinary Reviews. Data Mining and Knowledge Discovery, 1*(1), 73–79. doi:10.1002/widm.2

Shu, L., Xie, J., Yang, M., Li, Z., Li, Z., Liao, D., Xu, X., & Yang, X. (2018). A review of emotion recognition using physiological signals. *Sensors (Basel), 18*(7), 2074. doi:10.339018072074 PMID:29958457

Shu, L., Yu, Y., Chen, W., Hua, H., Li, Q., Jin, J., & Xu, X. (2020). Wearable emotion recognition using heart rate data from a smart bracelet. *Sensors (Basel), 20*(3), 718. doi:10.339020030718 PMID:32012920

Song, T., Zheng, W., Lu, C., Zong, Y., Zhang, X., & Cui, Z. (2019). MPED: A multi-modal physiological emotion database for discrete emotion recognition. *IEEE Access: Practical Innovations, Open Solutions*, *7*, 12177–12191. doi:10.1109/ACCESS.2019.2891579

Stern, N., & Stern, N. H. (2007). *The economics of climate change: the Stern review*. Cambridge University Press. doi:10.1017/CBO9780511817434

Yu, S. N., & Chen, S. F. (2015, August). Emotion state identification based on heart rate variability and genetic algorithm. *2015 37th annual international conference of the IEEE engineering in medicine and biology society (EMBC)*, 538-541. 10.1109/EMBC.2015.7318418

Zhang, Z., Song, Y., Cui, L., Liu, X., & Zhu, T. (2016). Emotion recognition based on customized smart bracelet with built-in accelerometer. *PeerJ*, *4*, e2258. doi:10.7717/peerj.2258 PMID:27547564

ADDITIONAL READING

Sultana, M., Al-Jefri, M., & Lee, J. (2020). Using machine learning and smartphone and smartwatch data to detect emotional states and transitions: Exploratory study. *JMIR mHealth and uHealth*, *8*(9), e17818. doi:10.2196/17818 PMID:32990638

Wen, W., Liu, G., Cheng, N., Wei, J., Shangguan, P., & Huang, W. (2014). Emotion recognition based on multi-variant correlation of physiological signals. *IEEE Transactions on Affective Computing*, *5*(2), 126–140. doi:10.1109/TAFFC.2014.2327617

Wioleta, S. (2013, June). Using physiological signals for emotion recognition. *2013 6th International Conference on Human System Interactions (HSI)*, 556-561. 10.1109/HSI.2013.6577880

KEY TERMS AND DEFINITIONS

Data-Level Fusion: Low-level attempts to gather diverse data components from multiple sensors to complement one another. During data collection, it is possible to incorporate other data sources, like user self-reported emotions.

Decision-Level Fusion: High-level data fusion, the goal is to improve decision-making by integrating results of several algorithms.

Emotion Recognition: Is the process of automatically identifying human emotions.

Feature Engineering: It is the process of identifying the most relevant and important features for machine learning algorithms for creating predictive models for machine learning.

Feature Selection: Is selecting a subset of the variables of the dataset to generate predictive models using machine learning algorithms.

Feature-Level Fusion: Intermediate-level data fusion is used to select the best set of features for categorization. The best combination of features, like EMC, Respiration, Skin Conductance, and ECC, has been retrieved using feature-level fusion.

Machine Learning: Is a kind of Artificial intelligence to enable machines to think using data and algorithms.

Predicting Estimated Arrival Times in Logistics Using Machine Learning

Peter Poschmann
Technische Universität Berlin, Germany

Manuel Weinke
Technische Universität Berlin, Germany

Frank Straube
Technische Universität Berlin, Germany

INTRODUCTION

ML techniques offer great potentials to support decision-making processes in companies by allowing the prediction of unknown information. The ability to extract and approximate system relationships from training data without explicit a priori knowledge makes them highly suitable for modeling highly complex and dynamic real-world systems. Due to the learning capability of ML-based systems, problems can be solved more flexibly, with less effort and with higher accuracy, and there is the potential to automate decisions (Wahlster, 2017). Against this background, ML-based applications are of particular importance, especially in the field of logistics. However, while the majority of logistics companies already use technologies for real-time visibility like Track & Trace, ML-based decision support systems have so far rarely been applied in logistics (Straube, 2019). The goal of the chapter is to demonstrate the application of ML methods on a significant use case in logistics practice: the prediction of ETA in intermodal transport networks as a basis for the detection of process disruptions.

The maritime transport chain serves as the practical use case considered in the chapter. International container transports by ship are handled via complex transport networks involving a large number of logistics actors. The implementation requires the interaction of numerous, closely timed and interdependent sub-processes. At the same time, the execution of the processes is influenced by a variety of impact factors such as resource availability, weather and the human factor. In addition, there is often no complete transparency between the actors, as information on process planning, status and disruptions has so far only been exchanged insufficiently and often manually between the involved logistics companies. Many of the decisions are therefore made under high uncertainty and rather reactively. As a result, according to Poschmann et al. (2019) decisions are often not optimal in regard to the entire chain and lead to high economic and ecological disadvantages in the form of unpunctual deliveries, resources not optimally utilized, cost-intensive special processes and unnecessary risk buffers.

Against this background, early prediction of arrival times and possible delays is highly important. Thus, ETA information enables logistics actors to identify and deal with possible process disruptions at an early stage by initiating appropriate measures. Furthermore, information on arrival times is an important basis to ensure a demand-oriented capacity planning with regard to material stocks, personnel and infrastructure (Walter, 2015). ML-based ETA predictions can thus make an important contribution to

DOI: 10.4018/978-1-7998-9220-5.ch160

improving today's logistics networks, which are affected by increasing customer requirements in terms of reliability, transparency and sustainability and cost efficiency (Handfield et al., 2013).

The chapter aims to demonstrate the application of ML for ETA prediction in logistics. A detailed insight is given into the results of a research project whose objective was to develop an ETA prediction for combined road-rail traffic in the port hinterland. The chapter is organized as follows: In the first step, a general methodology is presented, which contains all essential subphases of the development, starting from the requirements analysis and data collection up to the IT integration. Subsequently, the conception of an approach for the above-mentioned use case is presented and ML approaches for three selected sub-processes are prototypically implemented and evaluated.

BACKGROUND

The following is a brief description of the fundamentals relevant to this chapter. First, a definition of ML is given, followed by an overview of the state of the art in ETA prediction research.

Machine Learning

ML is a sub-domain of Artificial Intelligence (AI) and comprises various methods that enable computer systems to independently extract patterns from extensive data (Murphy, 2012). ML thus enables computer systems to learn inductively. (Nilsson, 2010) This means that inference takes place on the basis of hypothetical correlations that a learning algorithm has acquired in the course of a training process by adapting to observations and generalizing patterns contained therein. (Awad & Khanna, 2015) This automatic extraction of patterns from data enables the recognition of complex relationships that are not recognizable to humans, or only with great effort, and an industrial use, for example, for segmenting and predicting information, deriving rules and solving optimization problems. (Alpaydın, 2010; Döbel, et al., 2018). Approaches to ML can be roughly divided into the three main types supervised, unsupervised and reinforcement learning. (Russell & Norvig, 2010). For ETA prediction, supervised and unsupervised learning are of particular importance, as learning is mainly based on historical transport data.

Prediction of Estimated Times of Arrival

With regard to the existing approaches to ETA prediction in the literature, a basic distinction can be made between model-based approaches, which are based on simulations or analytical models, and data-based approaches, according to Wen et al. (2017). The application of ML for ETA prediction can be regarded as a sub-group of the data-based approaches. Model-based approaches have been widely used in the literature for delay prediction in rail networks. They can be found in Berger et al. (2011) as well as Büker and Seybold (2012), for example. However, their disadvantage lies in the complex modeling and the low adaptability to changing operational conditions. Despite the great potential of ML for ETA prediction, its application has been explored only selectively and with a strong focus on passenger transport. Existing approaches to logistics are usually only related to isolated sub-processes and specific modes of transport.

Initial approaches already exist for maritime transport, which represents the main leg in international maritime transport chains. Parolas et al. (2016) predict the arrival time of ocean vessels at the port of Rotterdam started about 120 hours before arrival using Artificial Neural Networks (ANN) and Support Vector Machines (SVM). Bodunov et al. (2018) and Lechtenberg et al. (2019) developed models for the prediction of ship arrival times at a specific port or in a specific destination region, as well as for the prediction of the destination port and port turnaround time. ANN, SVM as well as ensemble methods such as Extreme Gradient Boosting (XGB) were tested.

Existing approaches to rail transport are almost related to passenger transport. Appropriate concepts are developed, for example, in Oneto et al. (2018), Huang et al. (2020) and Marković et al. (2015), predominantly using ANNs. However, those approaches are only applicable to rail freight transport to a limited extent as passenger transport differs from freight transport by rail in respect of the operational processes and influencing factors. An approach for freight trains, but solely with statistical methods (linear regression), can only be found in Gorman (2009).

For road transport, existing approaches also focus primarily on passenger transport. For example, Fan and Gurmu (2015) use ANN to predict travel times in public bus transport. Due to the different conditions (e.g. stronger timetable dependency, shorter transport distances), these are not suitable for road freight transport. Only Li and Bai (2016) deal with the development of an approach for road freight transport using XGB, where only temporal characteristics are considered.

Except for the port turnaround time prediction by Lechtenberg et al. (2019), no ML-based approaches for the prediction of processes in logistical nodes such as inland terminals and marshalling yards could be found. Similarly rare are approaches for the prediction of more complex transport chains, which are, however, of fundamental importance for the implementation of ETA predictions for logistics. The only application of ML for the prediction of intermodal transport chains was found in Servos et al. (2020), who developed an ETA prediction for container transports within the maritime transport chain. This was done using ensemble methods such as Adaptive Boosting and SVM. The approach only incorporates GPS data, but no other data, so operational factors that influence arrival time are not taken into account.

In summary, there are currently only a few approaches to ETA prediction for both individual logistics processes and complex transport chains. Furthermore, there is especially a lack of a well-proven methodology on how to proceed methodically in the development of corresponding approaches. To close this research gap, in the following section, a general methodology is presented on how to develop ETA predictions for such application cases by using the example of combined road-rail transport based on a practical use case.

METHODOLOGY

The methodology for the development of the ETA prediction was based on the industry-wide standard CRISP-DM for conducting data-based projects (Wirth & Hipp, 2000). CRISP-DM is known to be a generic process model without reference to a specific use case. However, the development of a cross-actor ETA prediction requires certain sub-phases which do not emerge sufficiently concretely from this model. For example, different stakeholders need to be involved in the development process and multiple sub-models need to be developed to predict complex transportation chains. To take these aspects into account, the CRISP-DM was extended and refined for the problem of ETA prediction. The derived methodology is briefly presented below (see Figure 1). Subsequently, the results of these methodical steps are presented in particular sections. In the case of model development, some steps are summarized for the individual sub-problems. The activities of the integration will not be discussed according to the focus of the paper. The presented procedure can serve as a reference for similar problems in this application area.

Figure 1. Methodology for development of ETA prediction

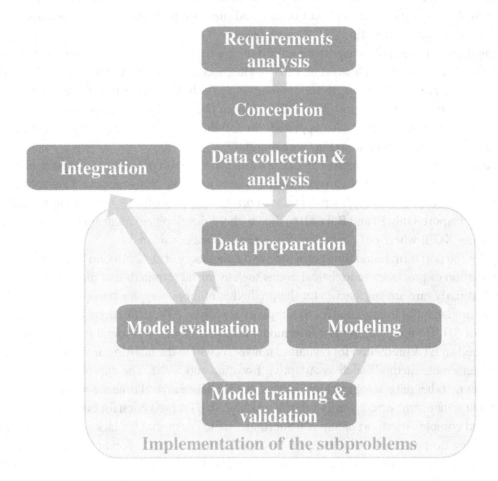

Requirements analysis: To create a practice-oriented solution, the first step was to collect and assess crucial requirements on the solution, similar to the 'Business Understanding' in CRISP-DM. The phase included a process analysis, disruption analysis, and the identification of use cases and requirements for the ETA prediction in practice. As part of the process analysis, the logistics actors to be involved and the relevant logistics processes of the transport chain were first investigated. The goal of the subsequent disruption analysis was to identify all disruption reasons and other influencing factors that affect the process duration and must be considered as features in the models. Due to the high complexity of today's transport networks, it is probably not possible to incorporate all process configurations. Another step was therefore to prioritize use cases for the ETA and to define required prediction horizons, prediction qualities reference objects and events to which an ETA must relate. The requirements analysis was carried out in the form of expert interviews, comprising also a Failure Mode and Effect Analysis (FMEA).

Conception: Due to the complexity of transportation chains, a single model is usually not sufficient for ETA prediction. Rather, the problem must be decomposed into several problems according to the sub-processes and the requirements. Each sub-process is then represented by one or more specific regression or classification models with individual features. Rule-based systems (or simulation methods) can be used later to link the sub-models according to predefined rules and to incorporate prior knowledge. The definition of these sub-problems and the overall logic of the system were done in the conception phase.

Data collection & analysis: An essential precondition for the desired ML approach was the availability of historical data. To ensure a sufficient data basis, various measures were taken to obtain suitable data sources (similar to the phase 'Data Understanding' in CRISP-DM). The data obtained was processed and analyzed. This included both the analysis of process characteristics and the identification of possible factors influencing process times. Data visualization and methods from the field of unsupervised learning like cluster analysis and sequence mining were used for this purpose.

Data preparation: Similar to CRISP-DM, the next step was to properly prepare the data for each sub-problem. Feature engineering is a central task in this process. Here, suitable input variables (features) were designed that represent the identified influencing factors and disruptions as well as possible. This involves using existing variables as well as creating new variables, for example by combining and transforming the existing variables. This phase also included standard ML tasks such as outlier handling, missing value handling and feature encoding.

Modeling: For each sub-problem, a suitable forecasting approach is designed. Supervised learning methods for regression or classification were used, depending on the sub-problem. Aspects such as the type of labels and features, data quantity and data quality were taken into account to choose a proper approach.

Model training & validation: The selected ML methods were finally trained with historical training data for each sub-problem, using Grid Search and Cross-Validation (CV) for hyperparameter tuning. The statistical programming language R and further open source packages were used for implementation and evaluation.

Model evaluation: To determine the achievable prediction quality of the respective trained models, they were applied to independent test data. Various quality measures such as Mean Absolute Error (MAE) were used for regression problems and accuracy, Cohens kappa and no-information rate for classification problems. In addition, other problem-specific metrics were calculated for better external understanding.

Integration: Once sufficient prediction quality had been achieved for each sub-problem, the model was integrated into an overall system (similar to the 'Deployment' phase in CRISP-DM). This enables the models to be linked in the sense of a "door-to-port" prediction. In addition, a rule-based decision support system was developed based on the ETA to detect disruptions in the chain and recommend appropriate measures. The developed prototype is available online at the link www.smecs-eta.de.

REQUIREMENTS ANALYSIS & CONCEPTION

Transport of sea freight containers in combined road-rail transport in the port hinterland (export) was chosen as the use case under investigation. The transport chain consists of five major sub-processes, which are shown in Figure 2. The first sub-process consists of road transport of the container between a shipper and the hinterland terminal. At the hinterland terminal, the container is transferred to rail and then carried by a hinterland train to a marshalling yard. There, the train is broken up and the wagons are distributed to newly formed feeder trains, which finally are moving to the seaport.

Several potential users and use cases could be identified for an ETA prognosis for the described process chain. This resulted in different reference points of the ETA (e.g. arrival of container at hinterland terminal, arrival of train at marshalling yard), reference objects (e.g. container, train, truck) and prediction times. In the disruption analysis, a large number of influencing factors were identified for each of the aforementioned sub-processes, which form the basis for feature engineering. The detailed results of the requirements analysis can be found in Poschmann et al. (2019).

On the basis of the process analysis and real-world requirements, six sub-problems were finally defined, which, together, enable a door-to-port prognosis (see Figure 2). The overall prediction is achieved by a logical connection of all individual sub-models in the sense of a process chain prediction. The output of a model serves as one input information for the subsequent prediction models. The development of the highlighted sub-problems will be discussed in detail in this chapter. In addition, representative transport relations (so-called pilot relations) were defined for the development of prototypes. The pilot relations represent container shipments from a variety of shippers (origin) via three hinterland terminals (transshipment road to rail) and a marshalling yard (transfer from hinterland to feeder train) to a seaport (destination).

Figure 2. Process chain and defined sub-problems for Door-to-port ETA prediction

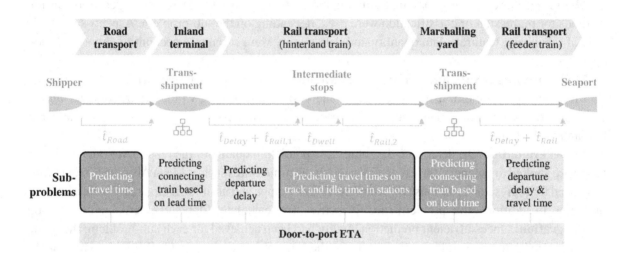

DATA COLLECTION & ANALYSIS

To carry out the development, four years of historical data were obtained from various logistics and transport companies such as a rail transport company, a rail infrastructure operator and a CT operator from the project consortium. The data was obtained from a total of 16 IT systems, in particular booking, scheduling and enterprise resource planning (ERP) systems. In addition, further external data sources were obtained, comprising information about external influencing factors like weather conditions and vacations. Not all data sources were available for the entire time period. Figure 3 provides an overview of the available data for each of the three sub-problems. The data can be roughly divided into two types of information: Information on the physical processes (time stamps and geopositions) and information on the conditions and influencing factors, serving as the basis for feature engineering.

For road transport, a total of about 47,000 truck trips (after data cleansing) were available. The process data includes information about the actual time of departure and arrival as well as information about the locations (manually entered address information). For the construction of possible features, additional data on the load (dangerous goods status, container weight and length), weather conditions (air temperature, precipitation, wind speed and direction, snow) as well as vacation periods and public holidays were available. No information was available on planned times, sub-processes and the route.

The highest data coverage was provided for rail transports. For this sub-process, data on about 2,100 hinterland train journeys (after data cleansing) were available. Unlike for road transport, the process data included detailed route information in the form of waypoints as well as additional planned times from the timetable. In addition, information on planned sub-processes (e.g. locomotive crew changes) was available for each train journey. As a basis for feature construction, data sources on train and locomotive characteristics (e. g. train weight and type of traction unit), construction works (location and period of road works on route and consequences), weather conditions as well as vacation periods and public holidays were available.

For the marshalling yard, wagon-based transport plans for about 16,000 wagon movements (after data cleansing) were available. The dataset used contained information about the planned and actual inbound and outbound trains of each wagon as well as the corresponding arrival and departure times. In addition, information about the timetables of all outbound feeder trains, construction works, weather conditions and vacation periods and public holidays could be considered. Data about the sub-processes within the marshalling yard was not available, so this had to be treated as a black box.

Figure 3. Overview of the used information in the raw data set

	Road transport	Rail transport	Marshalling yard
Process data	• Origin and destination • Actual time of departure and arrival	• Planned route over several waypoints (incl. geopositions) • Actual and planned times of departure and arrival and further timestamps for each waypoint • Planned sub-processes	• Planned and actual times of arrival and departure for inbound and outbound trains • Planned and actual inbound / outbound trains of each wagon • Schedules of alternative trains
Data on the conditions	• Container weight and length • Dangerous goods status • Weather conditions • Vacations and public holidays	• Construction works on track • Train characteristics • Locomotive characteristics • Weather conditions • Vacations and public holidays	• Construction works inside the marshalling yard • Weather conditions • Vacations and public holidays

IMPLEMENTATION OF THE SUB-PROBLEMS

In the following section, the stages from data preparation to model evaluation are described in detail for each of the three selected sub-problems Road Transportation, Rail Transportation and Marshalling Yard.

ROAD TRANSPORT

The first sub-problem relates to the road transport of containers between shippers and the three hinterland terminals on the pilot relations. The considered journeys mainly take place in the near region of the hinterland terminals and therefore have short travel times of only a few hours. The aim of the ML models to be developed is to predict the expected arrival time of a container at the hinterland terminal. In addition to the driving time, the process duration can also include times for rest periods and intermediate parking of the container, which are not known beforehand. Among other things, the process duration is strongly influenced by the traffic situation (congestion) and weather conditions.

During the data cleansing process, journeys were removed that had no plausible or missing time and location information (e.g. journeys with journey times of less than 15 minutes or more than 10 hours). Some of the journeys related to the collection of the empty container were also removed. After data cleaning, 47,278 valid trips remained for the model development.

In the next step, the actual journey times were determined for all journeys from the departure and arrival times. In addition, source-destination relations were defined from the trips and each trip was assigned to a relation. The formation of the relations was based on the postal code area and the respective inland terminal, i.e. all trips from the same postal code area to the same inland terminal belong to the same relation. This resulted in a total of 1,020 possible source-destination relations.

In order to determine the most influencing factors, correlations between travel times and various variables were investigated. Figure 4 shows the correlations between the hour of departure and the dangerous goods status and the travel time. Significant correlations can be seen for time of day, which can be caused by traffic congestion or breaks in the journey. There is also a slight correlation between travel time and the dangerous goods status of the container.

Figure 4. Correlations between travel time and hour of day / dangerous goods status

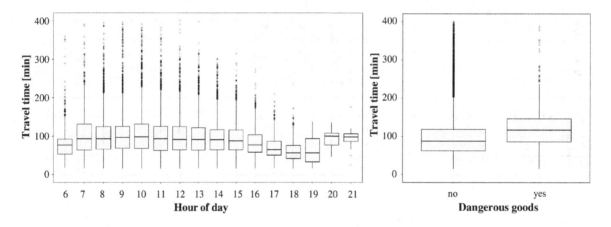

In the next step, an approach for predicting the arrival times of trucks and containers at the hinterland terminals was developed using supervised learning methods. The task is treated as a regression problem with the travel time as target variable. The arrival time (ETA) is determined from the planned or actual departure time and the predicted travel time. Since many trips occur on the same source-destination relations, two types of features can be distinguished. Journey-specific features represent conditions that only refer to a specific journey (e.g. the container weight). Relation-specific features, on the other hand, contain information that is valid equally for all trips of a relation (e.g., the aerial distance). In order to enable the best possible learning of both journey- and relation-specific features, a hybrid approach with several sub-models was chosen (Figure 5). For frequently travelled relations with more than or equal 100 available historical journeys, a relation-specific model was trained in each case. For relations with less than 100 past journeys, a non-relation-specific model was trained on the whole training set, as the amount of training data for relation-specific models is too small. Only relation-specific characteristics are included in the relation-specific sub-models, whereas relation-related characteristics are also taken into account in the non-relation-specific model.

Figure 5. Technical approach for prediction of road travel times

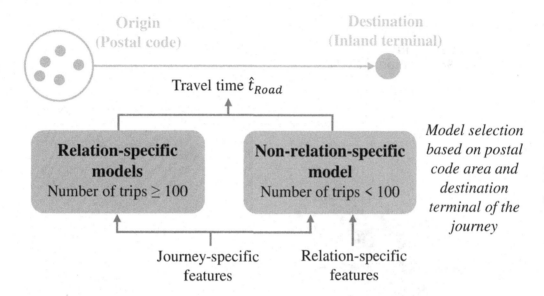

From the available data, eleven journey- and relation-specific features were selected. Trip-specific features include time-related features (hour of departure, weekday, month, holiday density), shipment-related features (weight and length of the container, dangerous goods status) and weather-related features (temperature, precipitation). As relation-specific features, based on the training data, the median travel time on each relation as well as the linear air distance between the starting point (center of the postal code area) and the destination (geo-coordinates of the inland terminal) were calculated. Categorical characteristics (e.g. weekday) were transformed into binary variables by one-hot encoding.

Different ML methods were tested. For the implementation of the relation-specific models, the highest prediction quality was achieved with XGB, whereas a Linear Regression Tree described in Zeileis et al. (2008) was identified as the optimal method for the non-relation-specific model, as it allows for an optimal consideration of the continuous, relation-specific features.

For the purpose of evaluation, the data was split in a ratio of 80% / 20% into a training / validation dataset and a test dataset. For the model selection, hyperparameter tuning was performed using grid search. Finally, a final evaluation of the trained models was carried out using the test set. The MAE is 20.2 minutes. 32.6% of the predicted journeys are within a maximum deviation interval of +/- 10% of the travel time observed. The evaluation results are presented in Figure 6.

It can be seen that the majority of journeys can be predicted with a relatively high accuracy. Nevertheless, there are also cases with larger prediction errors, which can be caused, for example, by additional travel interruptions (e.g. rest periods), waiting times at hinterland terminals and various previously unforeseeable disruptions (e.g. construction sites, traffic jams, technical failures). Also, documentation errors due to the manual data entry of departure and arrival times by the driver can be the cause of existing variations. By improving the data quality and considering further data sources, a further increase in the quality of the prognosis can be expected. Possible additional data sources include, in particular, more detailed information on the planned routes, processes (rest periods, intermediate stops), the traffic situation on the route, planned construction sites and waiting times at the inland terminal.

Figure 6. Evaluation results for prediction of road travel times

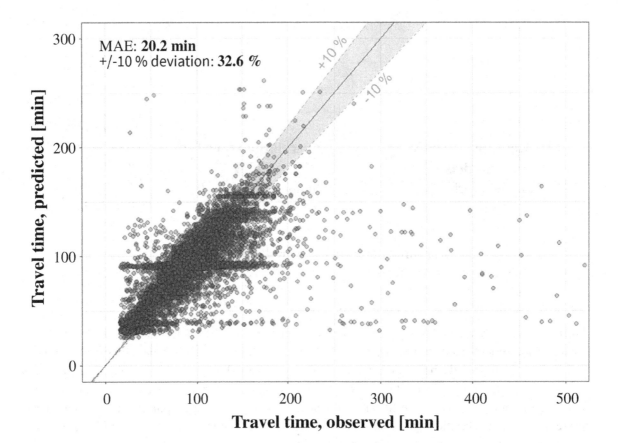

RAIL TRANSPORT

As a further sub-problem, the prediction of container transport by rail should be discussed. The focus is on hinterland trains between hinterland terminals and marshalling yards. Train runs on three source-destination relations are considered (starting from three different hinterland terminals to a marshalling yard). For each relation, however, there are a variety of possible routes through the rail network that connect the respective hinterland terminal with the marshalling yard. Compared to road transport, rail transport is subject to a timetable that clearly defines the spatial and temporal course of a journey via discrete waypoints in the rail network. In addition to traction, rail transport includes intermediate stops, where, among other things, locomotive crew changes and locomotive changes are carried out. Rail transport is characterized by numerous different disruptive and influencing factors that can lead to timetable deviations and must therefore be integrated into the model as input variables. These include, for example, train path conflicts, delays in personnel changes, weather influences, construction sites and

P

technical disruptions. By developing suitable features, it has been attempted to take these influencing factors into account as far as possible.

In the initial processing, non-representative journeys (outliers) were removed. This also included journeys that predominantly ran on rarely used route sections. Due to the relatively small number of train journeys, missing values were replaced as far as possible instead of removing the cases. A total of 2,107 journeys remained in the data set (Relation A: 870 journeys, Relation B: 470 journeys, Relation C: 767 journeys). For relation C, some data sources were not available so that certain features could not be generated.

Subsequently, a comprehensive data analysis was carried out to identify factors influencing the journey time. Figure 7 shows an example of the correlations between influencing factors of different cause groups and the journey times of the trains on the basis of scatterplots and boxplots. The visualization shows that the train weight has a positive influence on the travel time. Furthermore, correlations between the traction unit type and travel time can be observed. The factors shown are therefore to be included in the model as features along with others.

Figure 7. Correlations between travel time and train weight / traction unit type

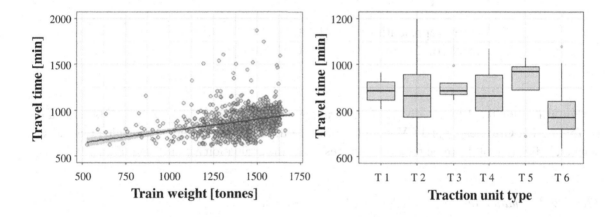

As described at the beginning, each train journey is made up of a sequence of partial sections and intermediate stops, each with fixed planned times. In order to consider the different route configurations in the prediction, an approach was chosen in which several sub-models are trained (see Figure 8). Each sub-model represents a specific route section or a station. In each sub-model, local influencing factors were considered (e.g. local construction works and weather conditions). The target variable (labels) of each sub-model is the travel time on the specific route section or the dwell time at a station. The prediction of the ETA at the destination results from the actual or predicted departure time and the sum of the sub-process times over all planned route sections or stations. A model was estimated for a section or station if at least 30 historical journeys were available for training, otherwise the planned times from the timetable were used for this section, as the amount of data was not sufficient for training a model.

To implement the approach, the data set was transformed and aggregated accordingly, so that each train journey is mapped as a sequence of the planned sub-sections. Subsequently, a total of 21 features were generated and selected. These include information from the timetable, train and locomotive characteristics, staff availability, construction sites, weather conditions and temporal factors. Due to the large number of sub-models, the final features considered in each sub-model were selected as part of the automatic feature selection of the training procedure. Different ML methods were tested for the sub-models described. The highest prediction quality was achieved with the Random Forest method for travel time prediction and XGB for dwell time prediction.

Figure 8. Technical approach for prediction of rail process times

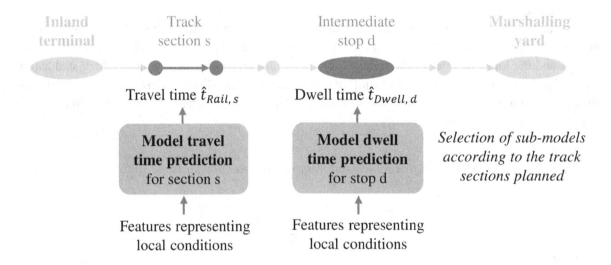

For evaluation the data was divided into a training / validation data set and a test data set in a ratio of 75% / 25%. Grid Search and CV were used to tune the hyperparameters. The evaluation was done separately for each of the three relations. The results of the evaluation are shown in Figure 9.

Figure 9. Evaluation results for prediction of rail travel times

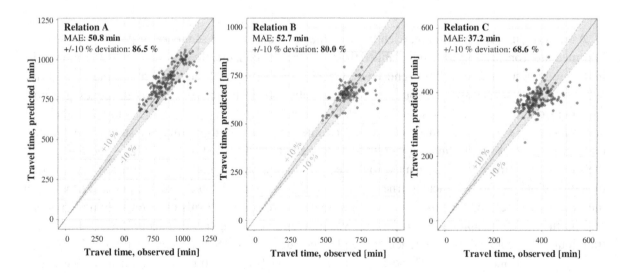

The highest prediction quality was achieved for Relation A. The MAE on this route was 50.8 minutes with a mean total travel time of approx. 900 minutes. 86% of the predictions were within a deviation interval of max. +/-10% compared to the actual travel time. The lowest prediction quality (+/-10%) was achieved on route C with 68%, which can be explained in particular by the poorer data basis. On route B, a high prediction quality was also achieved with a quality of 80%. Overall, it can be concluded that the selected approach allows to predict rail process time with a high precision. However, some influencing factors, in particular technical disruptions, traffic-related influences could not yet be sufficiently considered and require the integration of further data sources.

MARSHALLING YARD

To illustrate the prediction of logistical nodes, the marshalling yard is considered as a third sub-problem. The hinterland trains are broken up in this and the wagons are allocated to multiple feeder trains which serve the seaport terminals. The trains between the marshalling yard and the seaport move several times a day according to a timetable. The process consists of several sub-processes such as train splitting, marshalling and train formation. The allocation of wagons to trains is carried out according to the "first-in-first-out" principle. The transit time depends on various influencing factors to be considered as features in the model, e.g. the timetable of outgoing trains, the degree of utilization of infrastructure and trains, road works, but also planned buffer times.

In the data preparation phase, all complete cases were first determined on the pilot relations. Each case represents the passage of a wagon through the marshalling yard, starting with the arrival of the hinterland train and ending with the departure of the feeder train. The original data set contained many identical cases in which wagons have the same inbound and outbound train. As these duplicates do not provide any gain of information, the data set was first cleansed so that only one case with an identical inbound and outbound train is available. The cleaned data included 15,765 cases. In the following data analysis, factors influencing the turnaround time were investigated. Figure 10 shows an example of the correlations between the weekday and month and the transit time of a wagon. The weekday has a high influence on the throughput time, whereas only minor differences can be observed for the month.

Figure 10. Correlations between transit time and weekday / month in marshalling yard

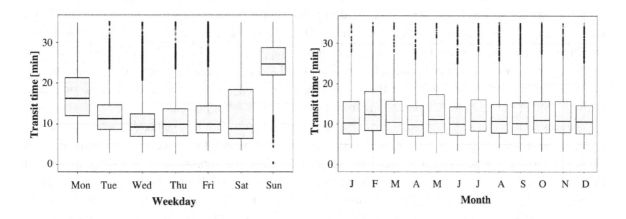

Since the objective is to predict the connecting train of a wagon, the process was treated as a classification problem. The approach used is illustrated in Figure 11. The basis was the connecting train planned for a particular wagon according to the transport plan. With the help of timetable data, further alternative connecting trains to the planned destination were subsequently determined before and after the planned train. These were then mapped to a discrete variable with a total of nine possible states (<-3, -3, -2, -1, 0, 1, 2, 3, >3). Category "0" corresponds to the planned initial train, while "-1", for example, corresponds to the next earlier train moving to the same destination. Categories "> 3" and "< 3" correspond to a connecting train departing at least four trains before or after the scheduled train. The restriction was introduced because a classification implies a restriction on the number of classes. In order to be able to apply supervised learning, the actual connecting trains were also determined for all cases and assigned to the categories.

Figure 11. Technical approach for prediction of connecting trains in marshalling yard

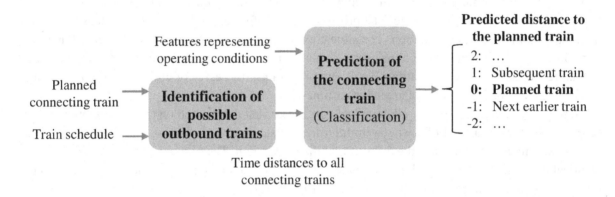

As part of the feature engineering 18 features were designed. These include the available lead times to all possible connecting trains of a wagon as well as temporal features and features on train characteristics, capacity utilization and construction work. Due to the ordinal character of the target variable (labels), the Ordinal Forest model based on Hornung (2020) was used as ML method.

Finally, the developed model was evaluated with a ratio of 90% / 10% for training / validation set and test set. For the test set an accuracy of 0.70 and a kappa coefficient of 0.59 could be achieved. The no-information rate was 0.43. Therefore, the developed model has a clear added value compared to a naive estimator whose output is always the main class of training data (in this case the planned connecting train). In order to better assess the dispersion of the prediction, Figure 12 shows the observable prediction error as the distance between the predicted and actual connecting train. It can be seen that in 84.3% of the cases the model forecasts the connecting train exactly or only has an error of +/- one train. Only in 16% of the cases higher deviations from the actual train were present.

Various factors can be the cause of the existing prediction error. On the one hand, connection scheduling in the marshalling yard is a complex decision-making situation that is carried out manually and often at short-term depending on current operating conditions. An improvement of the prediction can therefore be achieved by integrating further information into the model, e.g. on planned sub-processes within the yard as well as on the infrastructure and train utilization. Furthermore, it seems useful to take into account the closing times of a container's ocean-going vessel, which may also influence transit time in the marshalling yard. Another option for improvement may be the choice of alternative class definitions, which, for example, are based on the time of arrival of the wagon and not on the planned outbound train.

Figure 12. Evaluation results for prediction of connecting trains in marshalling yard

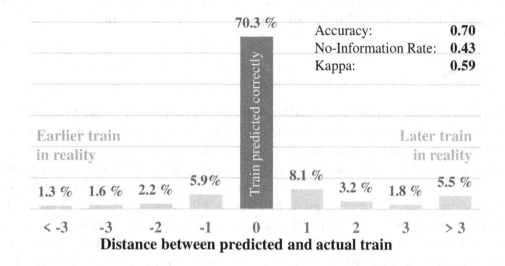

FUTURE RESEARCH DIRECTIONS

In the previous sections, approaches were presented on how ML can be used to predict complex transport chains in logistics. The development and evaluation of these approaches were only carried out under laboratory conditions with historical data and for selected sub-processes, so that no final statements can be made about the feasibility in practice. In addition, only a very limited number of ML methods, data sources, and modeling opportunities could be tested. This results in various directions for future research.

On the first hand, it is important to develop approaches for other logistics processes. These include, for example, other modes of transport such as inland waterways and air transport, but also further approaches for logistical nodes such as the seaport. In addition, testing with more comprehensive training data sets and further characteristics is useful. For example, numerous influencing factors have not yet been sufficiently considered within the tested models. These include, in particular, serious and rare events (e.g., heavy weather, accidents), whose prediction poses a particular challenge due to the limited availability of data. To take into account as many effects on arrival time as possible, a large number of characteristics are often needed. Against this background, the testing of novel feature encoding techniques can also be of great importance, e.g. to reduce the number of features.

In addition to alternative forms of modeling, it appears promising to test other ML methods. For example, deep learning approaches and recurrent neural networks offer high potential for ETA prediction and should be tested. A high potential also arises in the combination with other ML and AI fields. Especially unsupervised learning clustering methods could be used for data aggregation and feature extraction. Symbolic AI approaches (e.g. rule-based systems and fuzzy logic) can be useful to incorporate expert knowledge into the forecast or to implement recommendations for actions based on the ETA in the sense of prescriptive analytics. Another direction for future research concerns approaches for linking the individual sub models in order to be able to predict even complex transport chains with varying process configurations. In the presented use case, this was only done in a simplified way with logical operators. Here, the combination of ML and simulation methods could offer a high potential. For a high user acceptance in real-time operation, the comprehensibility of the predictions will be of great importance. Against this backdrop, approaches of Explainable AI can be highly valuable. Finally, the testing of ETA predictions under real conditions represents another important step in future research. In this phase, further technical and organizational challenges arise, such as the handling of missing data, the re-training of the models and also the user acceptance of ML-based information.

CONCLUSION

In this chapter, a methodology and ML-based approach for implementing ETA predictions for complex transport chains in logistics was presented. The evaluation results based on a real use case show that supervised ML techniques offer a high potential to accurately predict the duration of logistic processes and possible disruptions. However, this quality is fundamentally influenced by the availability and scope of training data fundamentally. Particularly in transport, where numerous companies are often involved, the cross-actor data integration poses a great challenge for ML projects. The optimal ML method and the suitable features are not known in advance and have to be determined in numerous development and evaluation runs. This leads to a highly iterative process, whereas the involvement of domain experts was recognized as an important criterion for success. The provided results and the shown challenges of using ML in the operational environment could be used for further activated in this application field. In general, it can be concluded that the use of ML for logistics represents a high potential for improving process flows through intelligent decision support systems. This applies not only to the presented use case of ETA prediction, which makes an important contribution to increasing the efficiency, reliability and flexibility of logistics networks by higher transparency about process times of transport orders. It also concerns other areas of application of high uncertainty and complexity, most of which have not yet been researched. Interdisciplinary research between ML and logistics will therefore play an important role in the future.

ACKNOWLEDGMENT

The authors thank all participants for their cooperation in the project as well as their confidence in providing comprehensive data and further company-related information. Special thanks apply to the employees of DB Cargo AG and the representatives of the other involved subsidiaries of Deutsche Bahn AG.

The results of this paper are based on the research project SMECS (Smart Event Forecast for Seaports) funded by the German Federal Ministry of Transport and Digital Infrastructure (IHATEC, 2017).

REFERENCES

Alpaydin, E. (2010). *Introduction to machine learning*. The MIT Press.

Awad, M., & Khanna, R. (2015). *Efficient learning machines: Theories, concepts, and applications for engineers and system designers*. Apress Open. doi:10.1007/978-1-4302-5990-9

Berger, A., Gebhardt, A., Müller-Hannemann, M., & Ostrowski, M. (2011). Stochastic delay prediction in large train networks. In Caprara, A., & Kontogiannis, S. (Eds.), *11th Workshop on Algorithmic Approaches for Transportation Modeling, Optimization, and Systems* (pp. 100–111). OASICS. 10.4230/OASIcs.ATMOS.2011.100

Bodunov, O., Schmidt, F., Martin, A., Brito, A., & Fetzer, C. (2018). Real-time destination and ETA prediction for maritime traffic. In *DEBS '18: Proceedings of the 12th ACM International Conference on Distributed and Event-based Systems* (pp. 198–201). New York: ACM. 10.1145/3210284.3220502

Büker, T., & Seybold, B. (2012). Stochastic modelling of delay propagation in large networks. *Journal of Rail Transport Planning & Management*, 2(1-2), 34–50. doi:10.1016/j.jrtpm.2012.10.001

Döbel, I., Leis, M., Molina Vogelsang, M., Welz, J., Neustroev, D., Petzka, H., Riemer, A., Rüping, S., Voss, A., & Wegele, M. (2018). *Maschinelles Lernen: Eine Analyse zu Kompetenzen, Forschung und Anwendung*. Fraunhofer-Gesellschaft.

Fan, W., & Gurmu, Z. (2015). Dynamic travel time prediction models for buses using only GPS data. *International Journal of Transportation Science and Technology*, 4(4), 353–366. doi:10.1016/S2046-0430(16)30168-X

Gorman, M. F. (2009). Statistical estimation of railroad congestion delay. *Transportation Research Part E, Logistics and Transportation Review*, 45(3), 446–456. doi:10.1016/j.tre.2008.08.004

Handfield, R., Straube, F., Pfohl, H.-C., & Wieland, A. (2013). *Trends and strategies in logistics and supply chain management: Embracing global logistics complexity to drive market advantage*. DVV Media Group.

Hornung, R. (2020). Ordinal Forests. *Journal of Classification*, 37(1), 4–17. doi:10.100700357-018-9302-x

Huang, P., Wen, C., Fu, L., Peng, Q., & Tang, Y. (2020). A deep learning approach for multi-attribute data: A study of train delay prediction in railway systems. *Information Sciences*, 516, 234–253. doi:10.1016/j.ins.2019.12.053

IHATEC. (2017). *SMECS - Smart Event Forecast for Seaports*. https://www.innovativehafentechnologien.de/wpcontent/uploads/2017/09/IHATEC_Projektsteckbrief_SMECS_formatiert.pdf

Lechtenberg, S., Siqueira Braga, D., & Hellingrath, B. (2019). Automatic Identification System (AIS) data-based ship-supply forecasting. In *Proceedings of the Hamburg International Conference of Logistics 2019* (pp. 2–24). Berlin: Epubli. 10.15480/882.2487

Li, X., & Bai, R. (2016). Freight vehicle travel time prediction using gradient boosting regression tree. In *15th IEEE International Conference on Machine Learning and Applications (ICMLA)* (pp. 1010–1015). New York: IEEE. 10.1109/ICMLA.2016.0182

Marković, N., Milinković, S., Tikhonov, K. S., & Schonfeld, P. (2015). Analyzing passenger train arrival delays with support vector regression. *Transportation Research Part C, Emerging Technologies*, 56(1), 251–262. doi:10.1016/j.trc.2015.04.004

Murphy, K. P. (2012). *Machine Learning: A probabilistic perspective*. The MIT Press.

Nilsson, N. J. (2010). *The quest for artificial intelligence: A history of ideas and achievements*. Cambridge University Press.

Oneto, L., Fumeo, E., Clerico, G., Canepa, R., Papa, F., Dambra, C., Mazzino, N., & Anguita, D. (2018). Train delay prediction systems: A big data analytics perspective. *Big Data Research*, *11*(3), 54–64. doi:10.1016/j.bdr.2017.05.002

Parolas, I., Tavasszy, L., Kourounioti, I., & van Duin, R. (2016). Prediction of vessel's Estimated Time of Arrival (ETA) using machine learning: A port of Rotterdam case study. In *Transportation Research Board 96th Annual Meeting Compendium of Papers*. Washington, DC: Transportation Research Board.

Poschmann, P., Weinke, M., Balster, A., Straube, F., Friedrich, H., & Ludwig, A. (2019). Realization of ETA predictions for intermodal logistics networks using artificial intelligence. In Clausen U., Langkau S., & Kreuz F. (Eds), *Advances in production, logistics and traffic: Proceedings of the 4th interdisciplinary conference on production logistics and traffic 2019* (pp. 155–176). Cham: Springer. 10.1007/978-3-030-13535-5_12

Russell, S. J., & Norvig, P. (2010). *Artificial intelligence: A modern approach* (3rd ed.). Prentice-Hall.

Servos, N., Liu, X., Teucke, M., & Freitag, M. (2020). Travel time prediction in a multimodal freight transport relation using machine learning algorithms. *Logistics*, *4*(1), 1. Advance online publication. doi:10.3390/logistics4010001

Straube, F. (Ed.). (2019). *Trends and Strategies in Logistics: Pathway of Digital Transformation in Logistics Best Practice Concepts and Future Developments*. Universitätsverlag der TU Berlin.

Wahlster, W. (2017). Künstliche Intelligenz als Grundlage autonomer Systeme. *Informatik-Spektrum*, *40*(5), 409–418. doi:10.100700287-017-1049-y

Walter, F. (2015). *Informationsaustausch in der maritimen Transportkette*. Springer. doi:10.1007/978-3-658-09661-8

Wen, C., Lessan, J., Fu, L., Huang, P., & Jiang, C. (2017). Data-driven models for predicting delay recovery in high-speed rail. In *4th International Conference on Transportation Information and Safety (ICTIS)* (pp. 144–151). Piscataway, NJ: IEEE. 10.1109/ICTIS.2017.8047758

Wirth, R., & Hipp, J. (2000). CRISP-DM: Towards a standard process model for data mining. In *Proceedings of the Fourth International Conference on the Practical Application of Knowledge Discovery and Data Mining* (pp. 29–39). Academic Press.

Zeileis, A., Hothorn, T., & Hornik, K. (2008). Model-Based Recursive Partitioning. *Journal of Computational and Graphical Statistics*, *17*(2), 492–514. doi:10.1198/106186008X319331

ADDITIONAL READING

Alessandrini, A., Mazzarella, F., & Vespe, M. (2019). Estimated Time of Arrival Using Historical Vessel Tracking Data. *IEEE Transactions on Intelligent Transportation Systems*, *20*(1), 7–15. doi:10.1109/TITS.2017.2789279

Cerreto, F., Nielsen, B. F., Nielsen, O. A., & Harrod, S. S. (2018). Application of Data Clustering to Railway Delay Pattern Recognition. *Journal of Advanced Transportation*, *2018*, 1–18. Advance online publication. doi:10.1155/2018/6164534

Oneto, L., Buselli, I., Lulli, A., Canepa, R., Petralli, S., & Anguita, D. (2020). A dynamic, interpretable, and robust hybrid data analytics system for train movements in large-scale railway networks. *International Journal of Data Science and Analytics, 9*(1), 95–111. doi:10.100741060-018-00171-z

Poschmann, P., Weinke, M., Straube, F., Kliewer, J., & Gerhardt, F. (2022). Künstliche Intelligenz in der Binnenschifffahrt: Steigerung der Zuverlässigkeit von Binnenschifftransporten durch datenbasierte Ankunftszeitprognosen. *Internationales Verkehrswesen, 74*(2).

Straube, F., Poschmann, P., Weinke, M., Friedrich, H., Ludwig, A., & Balster, A. (2020). *Smart Event Forecast for Seaports (SMECS) – Schlussbericht*. Technische Universität Berlin, Fachgebiet Logistik.

Strottmann Kern, C., de Medeiros, I. P., & Yoneyama, T. (2015). Data-driven aircraft estimated time of arrival prediction. In *2015 Annual IEEE Systems Conference (SysCon) Proceedings* (pp. 727–733). 10.1109/SYSCON.2015.7116837

Wang, R., & Work, D. B. (2015). Data driven approaches for passenger train delay estimation. In *2015 IEEE 18th International Conference on Intelligent Transportation Systems* (pp. 535–540). 10.1109/ITSC.2015.94

Weinke, M., Poschmann, P., & Straube, F. (2021). Decision-making in Multimodal Supply Chains using Machine Learning. In Adapting to the future: how digitalization shapes sustainable logistics and resilient supply chain management (pp. 301–326). Berlin: Epubli. doi:10.15480/882.3991

KEY TERMS AND DEFINITIONS

Accuracy: Error measure for assessing the quality of a prediction (classification) which corresponds to the proportion of correctly predicted test cases to all test cases.

Estimated Time of Arrival: Expected arrival time of a vehicle, container or shipment at a defined location considering the current conditions.

Feature: Input variable of an ML model, containing formalized and known information about the problem to be learned.

Intermodal Transport: Transport chain which comprises multiple modes of transport (e.g. rail, road).

Label: Target variable of a supervised ML model that is usually known in the training process and is to be predicted when the model is applied.

Machine Learning: Sub-field of Artificial Intelligence which comprises various methods that enable computer systems to extract patterns from data.

Marshalling Yard: Railroad yard used for separating and sorting railroad cars and forming freight trains.

Mean Squared Error: Error measure for assessing the quality of a prediction (regression) which is determined as the mean value of the squared deviations between the predicted and actual values.

Transport Chain: Sequence of several transport and transshipment processes for the shipment of goods from an origin to a destination.

Relative Relations in Biomedical Data Classification

Marcin Czajkowski

Bialystok University of Technology, Poland

INTRODUCTION

Advances in data science continue to improve the precision of biomedical research, and machine learning solutions are increasingly enabling the integration and exploration of molecular data (Huang, Chaudhary & Garmire, 2017). To enable a better understanding of cancer and enhance advances in personalized medicine such data need to be converted to knowledge. An interdisciplinary subfield of computer science called data mining (Han, Kamber & Pei, 2012) aims to reveal important and insightful information hidden in data. It requires appropriate tools and algorithms to effectively identify correlations and patterns within the data. However, the overwhelming majority of systems focus almost exclusively on the prediction accuracy of core data mining tasks like classification or regression. Far less effort has gone into the crucial task of extracting meaningful patterns or molecular signatures of biological processes.

Recently, there is a strong need for "white box", comprehensive machine learning models which may actually reveal and evaluate patterns that have diagnostic or prognostic value in biomedical data (McDermott & Wang, 2013). In this chapter, we focus on algorithms for biomedical analysis in the field of eXplainable Artificial Intelligence (XAI) (Angelov, Soares, et. al., 2021). In particular, we present computational methods that address the concept of Relative Expression Analysis (RXA) (Eddy, Sung, et. al., 2010). The algorithms that are based on this idea access the interactions among genes/molecules to study their relative expression, i.e., the ordering among the expression values, rather than their absolute expression values. One then searches for characteristic perturbations in this ordering from one phenotype to another. The simplest form of such an interaction is the ordering of expression among two genes, in which case one seeks to identify typical reversals' pairs of genes (ordering is usually present in one phenotype and rarely present in the other). Such pairs of genes can be viewed as ''biological switches'' which can be directly related to regulatory "motifs" or other properties of transcriptional networks. The classification algorithms based on RXA are often data-driven and due to the comparison between feature relative expression levels within the same sample, the predictor is robust to inter- and intra-platforms variabilities as well as complex analytical and data processing methods like normalization and standardization procedures.

The purpose of this chapter is to illustrate the concept of RXA and the innovations that the use of relative relationship-based algorithms brings. We will also cover the issues and challenges of biomedical data analysis.

DOI: 10.4018/978-1-7998-9220-5.ch161

BACKGROUND

Data mining is an umbrella term covering a broad range of tools and techniques for extracting hidden knowledge from large quantities of data. Biomedical data can be very challenging due to the enormous dimensionality, biological and experimental noise as well as other perturbations. In the literature, we will find that nearly all standard, off-the-shelf techniques were initially designed for other purposes than omics data (Bacardit, Widera, et. al. 2014), such as neural networks, random forests, SVMs, and linear discriminant analysis. When applied for omics data, the prediction models usually involve nonlinear functions of hundreds or thousands of features, many parameters, and are therefore constrain the process of uncovering new biological understanding that, after all, is the ultimate goal of data-driven biology. Deep learning approaches have also been getting attention (Min, Lee & Yoon, 2016) as they can better recognize complex features through representation learning with multiple layers and can facilitate the integrative analysis by effectively addressing the challenges discussed above. However, we know very little about how such results are derived internally. Such lack of knowledge discovery itself in those 'black box' systems impedes biological understanding and are obstacles to mature applications.

In contrast to data mining systems, statistical methods for analyzing high-dimensional biomolecular data generated with high-throughput technologies permeate the literature in computational biology. Those analyses have uncovered a great deal of information about biological processes (Zhao, Shi, et. al., 2015) such as important mutations and lists of "marker genes" associated with common diseases and key interactions in transcriptional regulation. Statistical methods can enhance our understanding by detecting the presence of disease (e.g., "tumor" vs "normal"), discriminating among cancer subtypes (e.g., "GIST" vs "LMS" or "BRCA1 mutation" vs "no BRCA1 mutation") and predicting clinical outcomes (e.g., "poor prognosis" vs "good prognosis"). The statistical analysis is often based on a relatively small number of features thus a small set of informative variables needs to be identified out of a large number (or dimension) of candidates. Therefore, using popular variable selection methods like LASSO and/or dimension reduction methods like PCA is crucial but still, it may limit the prediction model performance.

High-throughput measurements in cell biology (e.g., transcriptomics, proteomics, metabolomics) generate an enormous amount of information, but only implicitly, in the form of raw e.g., expression values. Extracting such knowledge from this single or multi-omics data is a key to future success in the biomarker field (Huang, Chaudhary & Garmire, 2017). However, there stand several challenges that computational approaches need to face. First of all, the dimensions of the dataset can grow into hundreds or thousands of variables, while the number of observations or biological samples remains limited. This disparity is called the curse of dimensionality or the p >> n problem, where p is the number of variables and n is the number of samples. Moreover, missing values and the class imbalance in the data can also lead to results that are biased or less accurate. A class imbalance problem arises when rare events are analyzed and compared against events that happen much more frequently, a common occurrence in omics datasets. Furthermore, standard data mining solutions may not be suitable e.g. large-scale multi-omics analysis due to computational limitations. Finally, studied data often inherent biological and experimental errors and/or rely on capturing a snapshot of complex and dynamic biological systems. Consequently, an incorrect experimental design, erroneous integrational analysis, or randomness may lead to high noise and the risk of wrong scientific conclusions due to false-positive results.

RELATIVE EXPRESSION ANALYSIS

This paper reviews an idea called Relative Expression Analysis (RXA) that was originally designed for gene expression data. It was proposed in the pioneering research (Geman, d'Avignon, Naiman, & Winslow 2004) to test relative expression among a small number of transcripts. To validate the concept of RXA a Top Scoring Pair (TSP) classifier was developed which is a straightforward prediction rule utilizing building blocks of rank-altered gene pairs in case and control comparison. Discrimination between two classes depends on finding one pair of genes that achieves the highest-ranking value called "score", which is calculated as follows. The general schema of the TSP algorithm is illustrated in Figure 1.

Figure 1. A general schema of Top Scoring Pair (TSP) classifier

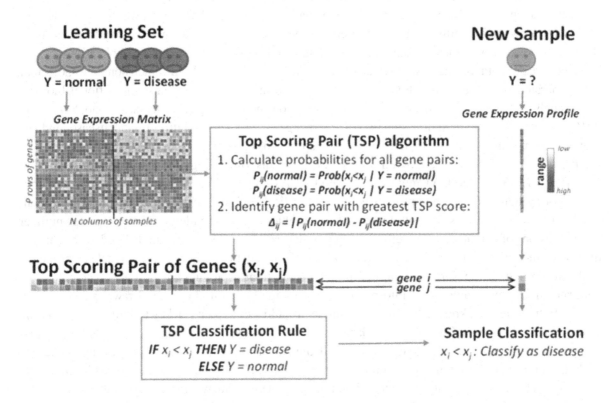

Consider a gene expression dataset consisting of P genes and M samples. Let the data be represented as a $P{\times}M$ matrix in which an expression value of i-th gene from j-th sample is denoted as x_{ij}. Each row represents an observation of a particular gene over M training samples, and each column represents a gene expression instance composed from P genes. Let's for the simplicity of presentation assume that there are only two classes: C_1 and C_2, and instances with indexes from 1 to M_1 ($M_1{<}M$) belong to the first class (C_1) and instances from range $\langle M_1 + 1, M \rangle$ to the second class (C_2). The discriminating power of each pair of genes (i,j) ($i,j \in \{1,...,P\}$, $i^1 j$) is measured by the absolute difference between the probabilities p_{ij} of the event that gene i is expressed more than gene j in the two classes ($x_{im}{<}x_{jm}$ where $m=1,2,...,M$). For each pair of genes (i,j) two probabilities are calculated $p_{ij}(C_1)$ and $p_{ij}(C_2)$:

$$p_{ij}(C_1) = \frac{1}{|C_1|}\sum_{m=1}^{M_1} I(x_{im} < x_{jm}), p_{ij}(C_2) = \frac{1}{|C_2|}\sum_{m=M_1+1}^{M} I(x_{im} < x_{jm}),$$

R

where $|C_1|$ denotes the number of instances from class C_1 and $I(x_{im} < x_{jm})$ is the indicator function defined as:

$$I(x_{im} < x_{jm}) = \begin{cases} 1, if\ x_{im} < x_{jm} \\ 0, if\ x_{im} \geq x_{jm} \end{cases}.$$

TSP is a rank-based method, therefore, for each pair of genes (i,j) the "score" denoted Δ_{ij} is calculated as: $\Delta_{ij}=|p_{ij}(C_1) - p_{ij}(C_2)|$. In the next step, the algorithm chooses a pair with the highest score. The titled top-scoring pair becomes a pair of genes with the highest score estimated from the training data. In case of a tie, a secondary ranking (Tan, Naiman, Xu, Winslow, & Geman, 2005) is used, based on the raw gene expression differences in each class. Finally, for a new test sample, the relation between expression values of the top pair of genes is checked. If the relation holds, then the TSP predictor votes for the class that has the higher probability p_{ij} in the training set, otherwise it votes for the class with a smaller probability.

In the literature, this basic implementation of RXA is extended in several directions, each having its pros and cons. Figure 2 illustrates the relative expression algorithms taxonomy that includes the main development paths that will be now briefly described.

Figure 2. The general taxonomy of the family of relative expression algorithms (RXA)

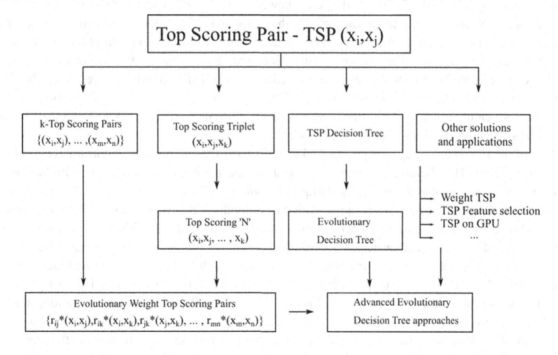

In one of the first extensions called k-TSP (Tan, Naiman, Xu, Winslow, & Geman, 2005) the number of top-scoring pairs included in the final prediction was increased. The classifier uses no more than k top-scoring disjoint gene pairs that have the highest score. The parameter k is determined by internal cross-validation and the simple majority vote is used to make the final decision. The classification decision is made by comparing the expression values for each pair of genes with a new test sample. The k-TSP classifier employs a majority voting to obtain the final prediction, however each vote has the same wage.

This method was later combined with a top-down induced decision tree (Kotsiantis, 2013) in an algorithm called TSPDT (Czajkowski, Kretowski, 2011). In this hybrid solution, each non-terminal node of the tree divides instances according to a splitting rule that is based on TSP or k-TSP algorithm. The authors used decision trees (often referred as classification trees) which have a long history in predictive modeling. DTs have a knowledge representation structure consisting of nodes and branches, where: each internal node is associated with a test on one or more attributes; each branch represents a test result; and each leaf (terminal node) is designed by a class label. Typically, a tree induction algorithm partitions the feature space using axis-parallel hyperplanes according to the given goodness of split. We call such trees univariate because the tests in the internal nodes consist of a single feature. Trees with multivariate tests (usually called oblique) are based mainly on linear combinations of multiple dependent attributes and divide the feature space by a non-orthogonal hyperplane. The success of the tree-based approach can be explained by its ease of use, speed of classification and effectiveness. In addition, the hierarchical structure of the tree, where appropriate tests are applied successively from one node to the next, closely resembles the human way of making decisions. However, when using DT a few new problems rises like under and over-fitting to the data as well as computational issues (Czajkowski, Kretowski, 2019).

Other approaches for the TSP extensions focus on the relationships between more than two genes. Algorithms like Top Scoring Triplet (TST) and Top Scoring N (TSN) (Magis & Price, 2012) analyze all possible ordering relationships between the genes, however, the general concept of TSP is retained. With the three-gene version authors successfully predict the germline BRCA1 mutations in breast cancer. The TSN algorithm uses generic permutations and dynamically adjusts the size to control both the permutation and combination space available for classification. Variable N denotes the size of the classifier; therefore, in case $N=2$ the TSN algorithm simply reduces to the TSP method and when $N=3$, the TSN can be seen as TST. The classifier's size can be defined by the user or by internal cross-validation that checks classification accuracy for different values of N (on training data, in a range specified by the user) and selects the classifier with the highest score.

One of the first heuristic approaches applied to RXA were the evolutionary algorithms (EAs) (Michalewicz, 1996). They belong to a family of metaheuristic methods that are inspired by biological mechanisms of evolution and represent techniques for solving a wide variety of difficult optimization problems. The typical EA operates on a population of individuals that represents possible solutions to the target problem. In each evolutionary iteration, individuals are modified with genetic operators such as mutation and crossover, and evaluated according to the fitness function. Next, individuals are reproduced to a new population of offspring whereas individuals with higher fitness are reproduced more often. The evolutionary loop is stopped when the convergence criteria are satisfied. The first proposed algorithm using EA with RXA was the TIGER (Top Inter-GEne Relations) solution that used weight k-TSP (Czajkowski, Czajkowska, Kretowski, 2016). The authors use a typical framework of evolutionary algorithms (EA) with an unstructured population and a generational selection to perform the search for k-TSP and TSN-like rules. The Evolutionary Heterogeneous Decision Tree (EvoHDTree) is the most recent application of EA to RXA (Czajkowski, Jurczuk, Kretowski, 2021). It uses both classical univariate and bivariate tests in the splitting nodes of DT which focus on the relative ordering and weight relationships between the genes. The search for the decision tree structure, node representation, and splits is performed globally by the evolutionary algorithm.

The RXA analysis and the TSP solution are also applied as a feature selection in machine learning (Kavitha, Neeradha, Athira, Vyshna & Sajith, 2020) like in Bayesian Top Scoring Pair algorithm (Arslan & Braga-Neto 2017) or as an component for more powerful classifiers like SVM (Shi, Ray, Zhu & Kon, 2011). Authors conclude that the TSP ranking algorithm can be used as a computationally efficient, multivariate filter method for feature selection in machine learning. Their simulation studies suggested that this algorithm is better tuned to correlated signal genes, the implication of which should be further explored in real datasets, where differentially expressed genes act in concert due to pathway dependencies. Moreover, many pathways include both up- and down-regulated components. The TSP as a ranking algorithm showed that it is very effective in capturing up-regulated and down-regulated genes simultaneously and, therefore, can be used as an alternative method to generate the rank list in gene set enrichment analysis, which may reveal a unique profile of enriched sets of genes. What's more, the strength and simplicity of RXA have been recognized outside genomics data and the RXA-like solutions are successfully used in other omics analysis.

SOLUTIONS AND RECOMMENDATIONS

The process of biomarker discovery and characterization provides opportunities for more sophisticated solutions that integrate statistical, data mining, and expert knowledge-based approaches. The basic RXA algorithms have the following advantages for gene expression data analysis: (i) the method is non-parametric since the method is constructed based on the relative ranking of gene pairs. Since different transcriptomic studies are usually conducted in different labs and on different platforms, the applicability of non-parametric nature facilitates cross-study validation; (ii) the method is based on one or a few genes pairs. The biological interpretation of the model and the translational application is more straightforward. It is more likely to succeed by designing a reproducible assay for wider clinical applications; (iii) researchers have repeatedly found that the family of TSP algorithms provides good prediction performance in many transcriptomic data (Afsari, Braga-Neto & Geman, 2014).

The main drawback of TSP-family algorithms is that they are focused only on gene expression data and can only be used locally and on a small scale. There are three reasons why: (i) focusing on simple "biological switches" may not work when more advanced relations occur; (ii) exhaustive search performed by TSP-solutions has enormous computational complexity which strongly limits the number of features and inter-relations that can be analyzed (Magis & Price, 2012); (iii) finding accurate values of some parameters like 'k' in k-TSP or N in TSN algorithm.

The first problem can be partially mitigated by using top-down induced decision trees (DT) with TSP splits (Czajkowski, Kretowski, 2011). There are also many other ways to rank the gene pairs of different systems that inherit the RXA methodology (Afsari, Braga-Neto & Geman, 2014). Among them, we can distinguish trend-based approach, AUCTSP classifier that uses the ROC curve (Kim, Lin & Tseng, 2016), vertical and horizontal genes relations and more advanced relations that involve more than simple ordering relations like in (Czajkowski, Jurczuk, Kretowski, 2020).

The complexity of standard RXA algorithms mentioned in the second issue, is $O(k * PN)$, where k is the number of top-scoring groups, P is the number of features, and N is the size of the group of genes with which ordering relationships are compared. This strongly limits the use of algorithms if the sample size or the number of features is large. In the literature, there are some attempts of improving TSP performance by parallelization of the algorithm using a graphic processing unit (GPU) for calculations (Magis & Price, 2012). The popularity of GPUs results from their general availability, relatively low cost, and high computational power. Parallel evaluation of instances is considered much more scalable with respect to the size of the dataset than a population approach. It focuses on gradually distributing the entire dataset among the local memories of all processors. The possible speedup is noticeable as it can shorten the calculation time for the RXA problem even two orders of magnitude.

The third problem considers the most popular TSP extensions like k-TSP, TSN, and their DT hybrids. The parameters k and N need to be defined ad hoc or by internal cross-validation. The first way is strongly dependent on an analyzed dataset and the second one is extremely time-consuming and decreases the size of the training dataset which is usually small in the case of gene-expression data. In addition, it is not clear which extension should be preferred: k-TSP or TSN. It should be noted that the k-TSP algorithm cannot be replaced by the TST as k-TSP has restrictions to use only disjoint gene pairs. On the other side, the k-TST or k-TSN was not even analyzed in the literature, probably due to its computational complexity. This drawback can be limited through evolutionary approach (Czajkowski, Jurczuk, Kretowski, 2020). Using heuristic solutions allow exploring much larger solution space and searches for much complex interaction between genes. Fortunately, EAs are naturally prone to parallelism and in the literature we can find application of EA with RXA solutions that uses various approaches (Czajkowski, Jurczuk, Kretowski, 2021). In the aforementioned paper, authors proposed a hybrid approach with shared address space (OpenMP) paradigm and graphics processing units (GPU)-based parallelization. The individuals from the population are spread over the CPU cores using OpenMP threads. Each OpenMP thread is responsible for subsequent algorithm blocks (genetic operator, evaluation, etc.) for the assigned pool of individuals. This way, the individual are processed in parallel on the CPU. The GPU parallelization is applied in a different way. It is used locally in each non-terminal tree node of the RXA DT in order to speed up the search for the tests in the splitting nodes.

FUTURE RESEARCH DIRECTIONS

There are two promising directions for future research and real-life applications of Relative Expression Analysis. The first one is the integrative analysis and exploration of multi-omics data which is a key to new biomedical discoveries and advancements in precision medicine. This will require additional research that relates to the data integration (both vertical and horizontal), inter- and intra-platforms variabilities as well as understanding the specifics of each omics separately (Zhu, Zhao, Zhao & Ma, 2016). For example, in metabolomics specific issues like a drift of retention time, data deconvolution, peak detection and alignment should be considered. By focusing on multi-omics approach instead of a single-omic analysis RXA will gain some profound advantages. For example, a single change in gene expression may be weakly associated with the pathophysiology of multifactorial disease. However, when this finding is further supported with alterations in mRNA expression and in protein concentration, the possibility that this gene or protein is an important factor in the pathogenesis of the disease increases.

The second direction will focus on knowledge discovery itself to extract meaningful molecular signatures of biological processes. The upcoming algorithms should include even low-ranked features and allow searching for complex but still comprehensible predictions constituted with hierarchical and horizontal dependencies in multi-class data. To achieve that novel hybrid solutions are required that may involve all the aforementioned algorithms. It could be a GPU parallelized evolutionary DT combined with various extensions of RXA and applied to multi-omics datasets.

CONCLUSION

Achieving high classification accuracy for gene expression datasets is still a major problem. When searching for white-box solutions researchers and biologists often use classification algorithms based on RXA because of their simplicity and relatively high prediction power. However, it is not always enough. Such methods are capable of finding interesting patterns but often are limited to various aspects.

In this chapter, we reviewed the relative relations in biomedical data classification. The most important methods from the family of TSP-based algorithms are presented. Every approach has drawbacks and limitations; however, in this particular case, these drawbacks are well known and easily understood. We have discussed how some limitations can be mitigated and included our recommendations. The most important is; however, the fact, that the use of RXA should be taken into consideration for biomedical analysis.

ACKNOWLEDGMENT

The article is funded by National Science Centre in Poland on the basis of decision 2019/33/B/ST6/02386.

REFERENCES

Afsari, B., Braga-Neto, U. M., & Geman, D. (2014). Rank discriminants for predicting phenotypes from RNA expression. *The Annals of Applied Statistics*, 8(3), 1469–1491. doi:10.1214/14-AOAS738

Angelov, P., Soares, E. A., Jiang, R., Arnold, N. I., & Atkinson, P. M. (2021). Explainable artificial intelligence: An analytical review. *Wiley Interdisciplinary Reviews. Data Mining and Knowledge Discovery*, 11(5), 5. doi:10.1002/widm.1424

Arslan, E., & Braga-Neto, U. M. (2017). Bayesian top scoring pairs for feature selection. *51st Asilomar Conference on Signals, Systems, and Computers*, 387-391. 10.1109/ACSSC.2017.8335365

Bacardit, J., Widera, P., Lazzarini, N., & Krasnogor, N. (2014). Hard data analytics problems make for better data analysis algorithms: Bioinformatics as an example. *Big Data*, 2(3), 164–176. doi:10.1089/big.2014.0023 PMID:25276500

Czajkowski, M., Czajkowska, A., & Kretowski, M. (2016). TIGER: An evolutionary search for Top Inter-GEne Relations. *International Journal of Data Mining and Bioinformatics*, 16(2), 2. doi:10.1504/IJDMB.2016.080042

Czajkowski, M., Jurczuk, K., & Kretowski, M. (2020). Generic Relative Relations in Hierarchical Gene Expression Data Classification. LNCS, 12270, 372-384.

Czajkowski, M., Jurczuk, K., & Kretowski, M. (2021). Accelerated Evolutionary Induction of Heterogeneous Decision Trees for Gene Expression-Based Classification. *GECCO'21, Lille, France. GECCO 2021 Proceedings*, 946-954.

Czajkowski, M., & Kretowski, M. (2011). Top scoring pair decision tree for gene expression data analysis. *Software Tools and Algorithms for Biological Systems. Advances in Experimental Medicine and Biology*, 696, 27–35. doi:10.1007/978-1-4419-7046-6_3 PMID:21431543

Czajkowski, M., & Kretowski, M. (2019). Decision Tree Underfitting in Mining of Gene Expression Data. An Evolutionary Multi-Test Tree Approach. *Expert Systems with Applications*, *137*, 392–404. doi:10.1016/j.eswa.2019.07.019

Eddy, J. A., Sung, J., Geman, D., & Price, N. D. (2010). Relative expression analysis for molecular cancer diagnosis and prognosis. *Technology in Cancer Research & Treatment*, *9*(2), 149–159. doi:10.1177/153303461000900204 PMID:20218737

Geman, D., d'Avignon, C., Naiman, D. Q., & Winslow, R. L. (2004). Classifying gene expression profiles from pairwise mRNA comparisons. *Statistical Applications in Genetics and Molecular Biology*, *3*(1), 19. doi:10.2202/1544-6115.1071 PMID:16646797

Han, J., Kamber, M., & Pei, J. (2012). *Data mining: Concepts and techniques* (3rd ed.). Morgan Kaufmann Publishers.

Huang, S., Chaudhary, K., & Garmire, L. X. (2017). More Is Better: Recent Progress in Multi-Omics Data Integration Methods. *Frontiers in Genetics*, *8*, 84. doi:10.3389/fgene.2017.00084 PMID:28670325

Kavitha, K. R., Neeradha, K., Athira, Vyshna, K., & Sajith, S. (2020). Laplacian Score and Top Scoring Pair Feature Selection Algorithms. *2020 Fourth International Conference on Computing Methodologies and Communication (ICCMC)*, 214-219.

Kim, S., Lin, C.-W., & Tseng, G. C. (2016). MetaKTSP: A meta-analytic top scoring pair method for robust cross-study validation of omics prediction analysis. *Bioinformatics (Oxford, England)*, *32*(13), 1966–1973. doi:10.1093/bioinformatics/btw115 PMID:27153719

Loh, W. (2014). Fifty years of classification and regression trees. *International Statistical Review*, *83*(3), 329–348. doi:10.1111/insr.12016

Magis, A. T., & Price, N. D. (2012). The top-scoring 'N' algorithm: A generalized relative expression classification method from small numbers of biomolecules. *BMC Bioinformatics*, *13*(1), 227. doi:10.1186/1471-2105-13-227 PMID:22966958

McDermott, J. E., Wang, J., Mitchell, H., Webb-Robertson, B.-J., Hafen, R., Ramey, J., & Rodland, K. D. (2013). Challenges in Biomarker Discovery: Combining Expert Insights with Statistical Analysis of Complex Omics Data. *Expert Opinion on Medical Diagnostics*, *7*(1), 37–51. doi:10.1517/17530059.2012.718329 PMID:23335946

Michalewicz, Z. (1996). *Genetic algorithms + data structures = evolution programs*. Springer. doi:10.1007/978-3-662-03315-9

Min, S., Lee, B., & Yoon, S. (2016). Deep learning in bioinformatics. *Briefings in Bioinformatics*, *18*(5), 851–869. PMID:27473064

Shi, P., Ray, S., Zhu, Q., & Kon, M. A. (2011). Top scoring pairs for feature selection in machine learning and applications to cancer outcome prediction. *BMC Bioinformatics*, *12*(1), 375. doi:10.1186/1471-2105-12-375 PMID:21939564

Tan, A. C., Naiman, D. Q., Xu, L., Winslow, R. L., & Geman, D. (2005). Simple decision rules for classifying human cancers from gene expression profiles. *Bioinformatics (Oxford, England)*, *21*(20), 3896–3904. doi:10.1093/bioinformatics/bti631 PMID:16105897

Zhao, Q., Shi, X., Xie, Y., Huang, J., Shia, B., & Ma, S. (2015). Combining multidimensional genomic measurements for predicting cancer prognosis: Observations from TCGA. *Briefings in Bioinformatics, 16*(2), 291–303. doi:10.1093/bib/bbu003 PMID:24632304

Zhu, R., Zhao, Q., Zhao, H., & Ma, S. (2016). Integrating multidimensional omics data for cancer outcome. *Biostatistics (Oxford, England), 17*(4), 605–618. doi:10.1093/biostatistics/kxw010 PMID:26980320

ADDITIONAL READING

Earls, J. C., Eddy, J. A., Funk, C. C., Ko, Y., Magis, A. T., & Price, N. D. (2013). AUREA: An open-source software system for accurate and user-friendly identification of relative expression molecular signatures. *BMC Bioinformatics, 14*(1), 78. doi:10.1186/1471-2105-14-78 PMID:23496976

Grzadkowski, M. R., Sendorek, D. H., P'ng, C., Huang, V., & Boutros, P. C. (2018). A comparative study of survival models for breast cancer prognostication revisited: The benefits of multi-gene models. *BMC Bioinformatics, 19*(1), 400. doi:10.118612859-018-2430-9 PMID:30390622

Huang, X., Lin, X., Zhou, L., & Su, B. (2018). Analyzing omics data by pair-wise feature evaluation with horizontal and vertical comparisons. *Journal of Pharmaceutical and Biomedical Analysis, 157*, 20–26. doi:10.1016/j.jpba.2018.04.052 PMID:29754039

Kagaris, D., Khamesipour, A., & Yiannoutsos, C. T. (2018). AUCTSP: An improved biomarker gene pair class predictor. *BMC Bioinformatics, 19*(1), 244. doi:10.118612859-018-2231-1 PMID:29940833

Lin, X., Afsari, B., Marchionni, L., Cope, L., Parmigiani, G., Naiman, D., & Geman, D. (2009). The ordering of expression among a few genes can provide simple cancer biomarkers and signal BRCA1 mutations. *BMC Bioinformatics, 10*(1), 256. doi:10.1186/1471-2105-10-256 PMID:19695104

Mirza, B., Wang, W., Wang, J., Choi, H., Chung, N. C., & Ping, P. (2019). Machine Learning and Integrative Analysis of Biomedical Big Data. *Genes, 10*(2), 87. doi:10.3390/genes10020087 PMID:30696086

Sahu, B., Dehuri, S., & Jagadev, A. K. (2018). A Study on the Relevance of Feature Selection Methods in Microarray Data. *The Open Bioinformatics Journal, 11*(1), 117–139. doi:10.2174/1875036201811010117

Wang, J., Liu, Y., & Chen, T. (2017). Identification of key genes and pathways in Parkinson's disease through integrated analysis. *Molecular Medicine Reports, 16*(4), 3769–3776. doi:10.3892/mmr.2017.7112 PMID:28765971

Wu, C., Zhou, F., Ren, J., Li, X., Jiang, Y., & Ma, S. (2019). A Selective Review of Multi-Level Omics Data Integration Using Variable Selection. *High-Throughput, 8*(1), 4. doi:10.3390/ht8010004 PMID:30669303

Xing, P., Chen, Y., Gao, J., Bai, L., & Yuan, Z. (2017). A fast approach to detect gene–gene synergy. *Scientific Reports, 7*(1), 16437. doi:10.103841598-017-16748-w PMID:29180805

KEY TERMS AND DEFINITIONS

Classification Tree: A decision tree applied to the classification problem, where each leaf node is labeled with one class label. Classification tree is used to predict membership of cases or instances in the classes of a categorical dependent variable from their measurements on one or more predictor variables.

Decision Tree: A decision tree is a graph that uses a branching method to illustrate every possible outcome of a decision. Each branch of the decision tree represents a possible decision or occurrence. The tree structure shows how one choice leads to the next, and the use of branches indicates that each option is mutually exclusive.

Global Induction: A method of decision tree generation, where both the tree structure and all tests are searched at the same time; usually based on evolutionary approach in contrast to top-down induction.

Multi-Omics Data: Data of different omic groups combined together during analysis. The different omic strategies employed during multi-omics are genome, proteome, transcriptome, epigenome, and microbiome.

Ordering Relation: The most typical relation in RXA that involve simple ordering relation between two (or more) genes that constitute rule e.g. $x_i < x_j$ where ($i, j \in \{1, ..., P\}$, $i \neq j$).

Top-Down Induction: A recursive method of decision tree generation. It starts with the entire input dataset in the root node where a locally optimal test for data splitting is searched and branches corresponding to the test outcomes are created. The test searches and data splitting are repeated in the created nodes unless the stopping condition is met.

Weight Relation: A more advanced relation in RXA that involve weight ordering relation between two (or more) genes that constitute rule e.g. $x_i < \alpha * x_j$ where ($i, j \in \{1, ..., P\}$, $i \neq j$).

Use of "Odds" in Bayesian Classifiers

Bhushan Kapoor
California State University, Fullerton, USA

Sinjini Mitra
California State University, Fullerton, USA

INTRODUCTION

The availability of massive amounts of data and the explosive growth of the field of analytics and data science has led to widespread use of machine learning in many different types of problems. Machine learning is a field of study that focuses on algorithms and techniques that learn from data or examples. Performance of machine learning algorithms and techniques improve as these are exposed to more data. According to Arthur Samuel (1959) who first coined the term machine learning, "Machine learning algorithms enable the computers to learn from data, and even improve themselves, without being explicitly programmed".

There are several categories of machine learning techniques, such as Classification, Regression, Clustering, and Association, for different types of problems. The goal of Classification techniques is to predict the output category (or label) given the input data (or predictors). As an example, loan application algorithm predicts if a loan application will be approved, or not by the financial institution. The input data or predictors in this case would be the applicant's credit history, FICO score, annual income, education, and so on. The output category (or label) that the algorithm predicts would be the different output categories, like loan is approved or loan is not approved.

Classification models belong to the category of supervised learning where the models at their development stages are provided with data/ examples on both input (predictor variables) and output category (label). After the model is built and tested, it is put in production to predict the output category (or label) given the input data (or predictors). The bayes classifiers compute prior probabilities and likelihood of input data at the development stage. At the production stage, the classifiers predict posterior probabilities for each output category (or label). In this paper we will introduce the concepts of odds, log odds, and odds ratio and reformulate Bayes' Theorem and multinomial Naïve Bayes' Classifiers in terms of odds. The reformulated bayes classifiers will compute prior odds and likelihood of input data at the development stage. At the production stage, the classifiers will predict posterior odds for each output category (or label).

This paper is divided into five main sections, (1) Introduction, (2) Concept of 'Odds' and its properties, (3) Bayes' Theorem, (4) Naïve Bayes' Classifier, and (5) Conclusion. In Section (2), concept of odds is defined in terms of probabilities. Some of its basic properties are also stated in this section. In Section (3), the authors will discuss Bayes' Theorem and reformulated Bayes' theorem using odds and probabilities. They will then present an example on loan application approval and calculate posterior probabilities and posterior odds using both forms of the Bayes' theorem. Section (4) will be devoted to Multinomial Naïve Bayes' Classifier and its reformulation using odds and probabilities. We will compare the two forms with the help of the example on loan application approval. Finally, the chapter will conclude with a summary and discussion in Section (5).

DOI: 10.4018/978-1-7998-9220-5.ch162

BACKGROUND

Like probability, 'odds' is a measure of the likelihood of an event. But these are defined differently in statistics and have different properties (Lawrence, Francis, Nathaniel & Muzaffer, 2012; Martin, 2021; Ranganathan, Aggarwal & Pramesh, 2015). The probability of an event, E (written here as P(E)) is defined as a real number that always lies between 0 and 1, and it is estimated as the number of times the event occurs over the total number of random trials or examples. When there are only two outcomes, we can use odds instead of the probability of an event. We represent the odds of an event as O(E). And it is defined as follows:

$$O(E) = \frac{P(E)}{P(-E)} = \frac{P(E)}{1 - P(E)} \tag{1}$$

where -E is the complement event of E.

O(E) can assume any real number between 0 and infinity. O(E) = 1 means that the chances of event E happening or not happening are equal. When O(E) is greater than 1, it means that the chance of occurrence of event E is higher than its non-occurrence. And, when O(E) is less than 1, it means that the chance of occurrence event E is lower than its non-occurrence.

Odds of an event, E, is generally expressed in a ratio form as m:n, where m and n are positive integers (whole numbers), and O(E) = m/n. Similarly, odds of the event -E, is generally expressed in a ratio form as n:m, and O(-E) = n/m.

From the above equation (1), we have

$$P(E) = \frac{O(E)}{1 + O(E)} \tag{2}$$

Given P(E) we can find O(E) by using equation (1), and similarly given O(E) we can find P(E) from equation (2). From these equations, it is obvious that

O(E)*O(-E) = 1, O(E) = 1/O(-E), and O(-E) = 1/O(E)

Some people may grasp the concept of "odds" better than probability in certain applications (Grant, 2020; Moran, 2020). For example, they get better understanding when a financial institution informs them of the odds of their loan approval rather than the probability of the loan approval.

BAYES'S THEOREM

Bayes's Theorem, named after 18th century British mathematician Rev. Thomas Bayes, is a mathematical formula that relies on incorporating prior probability distribution to generate posterior probabilities. The Bayes's Theorem is the foundation of the vast field of Bayesian Statistics, and several Machine Learning models are based on Bayesian Statistics (Tyler, Liliana & Jeong, 2018; Bolstad & Curran, 2016; Kruschke, 2014; Lee, 2012; Christensen, Johnson, Branscum & Hanson, 2011). We will explain below both the original Bayes' Theorem and its reformulation using 'odds' and 'odds ratio, and with the help of an example on loan application.

Suppose a local bank received 17,570 personal loan applications during the last 2 years, and they approved 12,550 of them and rejected the remaining 5,020 applications. Let Y denote a discrete random variable that takes two possible values:

$Y = 1$, if the loan application is approved, and
$Y = 2$, if the loan application is not approved.

Let us define a new event, A. Let A denote the event $Y=1$, that is, the bank approved the loan. The -A (complement of event A) denotes the event $Y=2$, that is, the bank did not approve the loan.

$P(A) = 12,550/17,570 = 0.714$, and $P(-A) = 1 - P(A) = 1-0.714 = 0.286$

Using equation (1), $O(A) = 0.714/0.286 = 2.5$

Now, $O(A) = 2.5 = 25/10 = 5/2$, and therefore $O(A)$ will be expressed in ratio form as 5:2. This means that we expect that for every five loan applications approved by the bank, there will be 2 loan applications that will not be approved by the bank.

The bank may consider one or more factors (such as, applicant's credit or FICO score, applicant's income, applicant's savings, home ownership, education level, marital status, profession, etc.) for making the decision on a loan application. We will discuss here three cases: [1]. Bank considers only applicant's FICO score (X_1), [2]. Bank considers only applicant's income (X_2), [3]. Bank considers multiple factors, such as applicant's FICO score (X_1) and income (X_2), for making the decision on the applicant's loan application.

Case 1: Bank Considers Loan Applicant's FICO Score (X_1)

In this case, we assume that the bank grouped the credit scores for all loan applicants into 2 classes, applications with a high FICO score of 750 or more and applications with a low FICO score of less than 750. Let the variable X_1 assumes the value 1 when the application has a FICO score 750 or more, and $X_1 = 2$ otherwise.

Let us define events E_1 and E_2 as follows: E_1: ($X_1 = 1$) and E_2: ($X_1 = 2$).

As stated earlier, the bank approved 12,550 applications and rejected the rest 5,020 applications. Further analysis revealed that the bank approved 8,430 applications with high FICO scores and also approved 4,120 applications with low FICO scores. Of the rejected applications, 2,110 applications had high FICO scores and 2,910 had low FICO scores. Therefore[1],

$P(E_1 | A) = P(\text{high FICO score}| \text{loan is approved}) = 8,430/12,550 = 0.672$

$P(E_1 | -A) = P(\text{high FICO score}| \text{loan is not approved}) = 2,110/5,020 = 0.420$

We already know from above that the overall probability of loan approval is:

$P(A) = 0.714$

Suppose the bank receives a new application. If the FICO score of this new applicant is high (that is event E_1 has occurred), then based on this additional data or information, the probability that the loan will be approved is denoted by $P(A \mid E_1)$. $P(A)$ is called the *prior probability* of A and $P(A \mid E_1)$ is called *posterior probability* of A which can be considered an updated version of the prior probability based on the additional information available about the applicant's FICO score. $P(E_1 \mid A)$ is called the *likelihood* of the data for event A, and $P(E_1 \mid -A)$ is called the *likelihood* of the data for event -A. One way to calculate the posterior probabilities in terms of prior probability and likelihood of data is to use the traditional Bayes' Theorem.

Traditional Bayes Theorem (Posterior Probability)

According to the multiplicative law of probability:

$$P(A \text{ and } E_1) = P(E_1) * P(A \mid E_1) \tag{3}$$

and

$$P(A \text{ and } E_1) = P(A) * P(E_1 \mid A) \tag{4}$$

From these equations (3) and (4),

$$P(A \mid E_1) = \frac{P\left(A \text{ and } E_1\right)}{P\left(E_1\right)}$$

$$= \frac{P\left(A\right) \cdot P(E_1 \mid A)}{P\left(E_1\right)} \tag{5}$$

That is, posterior probability = (prior probability * likelihood of data)/ $P(E_1)$.

The following equation (6) can be used to calculate $P(E_1)$ in terms of the prior probabilities and the likelihood of data. In the next section the Bayes' Theorem will be reformulated to estimate posterior odds of an event. In this reformulation, $P(E_1)$ will not be needed to find posterior odds as will be seen below.

Now, $E_1 = (E_1 \text{ and } A)$ or $(E_1 \text{ and } -A)$

Thus, $P(E_1) = P(E_1 \text{ and } A) + P(E_1 \text{ and } -A)$

$$= P(A)*P(E_1 \mid A) + P(-A) * P(E_1 \mid -A) \tag{6}$$

Substituting this equation in equation (5), we get the final equation of the Bayes' Theorem to calculate the posterior probability of event A in terms of the prior probability and the likelihood of data:

$$P(A \mid E_1) = \frac{P\left(A\right) \cdot P(E_1 \mid A)}{P\left(A\right) \cdot P(E_1 \mid A) + P\left(-A\right) \cdot P(E_1 \mid -A)}$$

Thus,

Posterior probability= Prior probability * Likelihood of data/ P(E₁), where

$$P(E_l) = P(A) \cdot P(E_1|A) + P(-A) \cdot P(E_1|-A) \qquad (7)$$

The following table, Table 1, breaks down the above equation into easy steps to find posterior probabilities of events A and -A for high FICO score applications.

Table 1. Posterior probabilities when considering FICO score (X_l) for loan applications

Event	Prior Prob.	Likelihood of Data	Bayes Numerator	Bayes Denominator	Posterior Prob.
A: Loan Approved	P(A) = 0.714	P(E₁ I A) = 0.672	P(A) * P(E₁ I A) = 0.480	0.6	P(A I E₁) = 0.8
-A: Loan Not approved	P(-A) = 0.286	P(E₁ I -A) = 0.42	P(-A)* P(E₁ I -A) = 0.12	0.6	P(-A I E₁) = 0.2
Total	1				1

Thus, we see from the above table that if a loan applicant's FICO score is high (that is, event E_1 has occurred), then the probability that the loan will be approved is 0.80.

A similar table can be prepared when the FICO score of a new applicant is low (that is event E_2 occurs). The reader may verify that if FICO score is low for a certain loan application, (that is event E_2 occurs), then the probability that the loan will be approved is 0.39.

Next, we will reformulate Bayes' Theorem to calculate posterior odds. The reformulated Bayes' Theorem to calculate the posterior odds is particularly useful when we are assessing the chances of the occurrence of an event with a binary outcome –like that of a loan application, which is either approved or not approved.

Reformulated Bayes' Theorem (Posterior Odds)

We know that overall odds of loan approval is:

O(A) = 2.5 (5:2)

Now, if a loan applicant's FICO score is high (that is event E_1 has occurred), then in the light of this additional data or information, the odds that their loan will be approved can be written as $O(A \mid E_1)$. O(A) is called the *prior odds* of A and $O(A \mid E_1)$ is called the *posterior odds* of A. $P(E_1 \mid A)$ is the likelihood of data for event A, and $P(E_1 \mid -A)$ is the likelihood of data for the event -A. The ratio of these two likelihood terms is called the *Likelihood Ratio* (LR). That is, the likelihood ratio for event A is given by $P(E_1 \mid A)/ P(E_1 \mid -A)$.

$$\text{Prior odds} = O(A) = \frac{P(A)}{P(-A)}$$

$$\text{Posterior odds} = O(A \mid E_1) = \frac{P(A \mid E_1)}{P(-A \mid E_1)}$$

$$= \frac{P(A) \cdot P(E_1 \mid A)}{P(-A) \cdot P(E_1 \mid -A)}$$

$$= O(A) * \text{Likelihood Ratio}$$

$$\text{Posterior odds} = \text{Prior odds} * \text{Likelihood Ratio} \tag{8}$$

As can be seen from the above equation, finding the posterior odds is simpler, more elegant and lot more insightful than the equation to find the posterior probability (Berry & Lindgren, 1996; Grant, 2020). If the likelihood ratio equals one, then the additional data or information has no impact on the odds. But if the likelihood ratio is greater than one, the odds increases, and the odds decrease if the ratio is less than one. The following table, Table 2, breaks down the above equation into easy steps to compute the posterior odds of events A and -A for high income class applications.

Table 2. Posterior odds when considering FICO score (X_1) for loan applications

Event	Prior Odds	Likelihood of Data	Likelihood Ratio	Posterior Odds
A: Loan Approved	$O(A) = 2.5$ (5:2)	$P(E_1 \mid A) = 0.672$	1.6	$O(A \mid E_1) = 4.0$ (4:1)
-A: Loan Not approved	$O(-A) = 0.4$ (2:5)	$P(E_1 \mid -A) = 0.42$	0.625	$O(-A \mid E_1) = 0.25$ (1:4)

In this case, the likelihood ratio (1.6) is greater than 1, implying that the additional data increases the chances of loan approval. The odds of loan approval has also increased from 2.5 to 4.0. And, for every 4 approved loan applications the bank rejects just 1 application if the applicant's FICO score is high.

A similar table can be prepared when the loan applicant's FICO score is low (that is event E_2 occurs). The reader may verify that if the applicant's FICO score is low (that is event E_2 occurs), then the odds of loan approval decreases from 2.5 to 1.42.

Despite the above results, one must be careful when interpreting the magnitude of increase or decrease in the odds. It is known that $O(A)$ can assume any real number between 0 and infinity. $O(A) = 1$ means that the chances of event A happening or not happening are equal. When the likelihood of event A happening is greater than that of it not happening, $O(A)$ spreads out between 1 and infinity. On the other hand, when the likelihood of event A happening is lower than that of it not happening, $O(A)$ is restricted between 0 and 1. In other words, the absolute distances from 1 to $O(A)$ and $O(-A)$ are not same. One way to solve this issue is to use log(odds) instead of odds. The logarithmic base used does not have any effect.

Log (odds) assumes a real number between -infinity (μ) and +infinity (-μ). Log (0) = -infinity, Log (1) = 0, and the logarithm of any other number greater than one range between 0 and infinity. Log $O(A)$ = 0 means that the chances of event A happening or not happening are equal. When the likelihood of event A happening is greater than that of it not happening, Log $O(A)$ lies between 0 and infinity. On the other hand, when the likelihood of event A happening is lower than that of it not happening, Log $O(A)$ lies between 0 and -infinity. That is, the absolute distances from 0 to Log $O(A)$ and Log $O(-A)$ are same.

Log (odds) is also called the *logit function* and is used in several machine learning algorithms, including logistic regression. To avoid lengthier computations, odds will be considered rather than log odds throughout the rest of the chapter.

Case 2: Bank Considers Loan Applicant's Income (X_2)

In this case, we assume that the bank grouped applicant annual incomes into 3 classes, applications with high income ($100,000 or more), moderate income (between $80,000 and $99,999), and low income (less than $80,000). Let variable X_2 assumes 1 when an applicant has high income, $X_2 = 2$ when the applicant has medium income, and $X_2 = 3$ when the applicant has low income.

Let us define events, F_1: ($X_2 = 1$), F_2: ($X_2 = 2$), and F_3: ($X_2 = 3$).

As stated earlier, the bank approved 12,550 applications and rejected the rest 5,020 applications. Analysis of applicant incomes showed that the bank approved 5,050 applications with high incomes, approved 4,080 with moderate incomes and approved 3,420 applications with low incomes. Of the rejected applications, 880 had high incomes, 2,220 had medium incomes and 1,920 applicants had low incomes.

Therefore,

$P(F_1 \mid A) = 5,050/12,550 = 0.402$

$P(F_1 \mid -A) = 880/5,020 = 0.175$

We know that the overall probability and odds of loan approval are:

$P(A) = 0.714$

$O(A) = 2.5 \ (5:2)$

Now, if a loan applicant is in high income class (that is, event F_1 occurs), then in the light of this additional data or information, the odds that their loan will be approved is given by $O(A \mid F_1)$. $O(A)$ is the prior odds of A which is equal to 2.5, and $O(A \mid F_1)$ represents the posterior odds of A. $P(F_1 \mid A)$ is the likelihood of data for event A, and $P(F_1 \mid -A)$ is the likelihood of data for event -A. The ratio of these two likelihood terms is the Likelihood Ratio, just as defined in the earlier case. That is, the likelihood ratio for event A can be calculated as $P(F_1 \mid A)/ P(F_1 \mid -A) = 0.402/0.175 = 2.3$. Now, as we know,

Posterior odds = Prior odds * Likelihood Ratio

The following table, Table 3, has the steps to find posterior odds of events A and -A for high income class applications.

Table 3. Posterior odds when considering income class (X_2) for loan applications

Event	Prior Odds	Likelihood of Data	Likelihood Ratio	Posterior Odds
A: Loan Approved	$O(A) = 2.5 \ (5:2)$	$P(F_1 \mid A) = 0.402$	2.3	$O(A \mid F_1) = 5.75 \ (23:4)$
-A: Loan Not approved	$O(-A) = 0.4 \ (2:5)$	$P(F_1 \mid -A) = 0.175$	0.435	$O(-A \mid F_1) = 0.174 \ (4:23)$

In this case, the likelihood ratio (2.3) is greater than 1, implying that the additional data increases the chances of loan approval. The odds of loan approval have also increased from 2.5 to 5.75. And, for every 23 approved loan applications the bank rejects or does not approve just 4 applications if the applicant's income is high (greater than $100,000).

Similar tables can be prepared for the moderate-income class (that is, when event F_2 occurs) and for the low-income class applicants (that is, when event F_3 occurs). The reader may verify that if a loan applicant belongs to the moderate-income class, then the odds that the loan will be approved decreases from 2.5 to 1.84, and if the applicant belongs to the low-income class, then odds that the loan will be approved decreases from 2.5 to 1.79.

Case 3: Bank Considers Multiple Factors (Both Credit Score and Income)

Realistically, a bank would consider several factors or predictors to decide on loan applications. Let us consider a simple case where the bank considers two factors, the applicant's credit or FICO score (X_1) and the applicant's annual income (X_2) to make a decision on loan applications. X_1 assumes two different values (1 when the applicant has FICO score 750 or more, and 2 when the FICO score is less than 750). X_2 assumes three different values (1 when the applicant has high income, 2 when the applicant has medium income and 3 when the applicant has low income). The joint distribution of X_1 and X_2 will have six different values, and hence we need to find the posterior odds (probabilities) for each possible value of the joint distribution.

Now, suppose that the bank receives a new application, and the applicant's FICO score and income are both known. Further, suppose that the applicant's FICO score is high, and income also belongs to the high-income class. What are odds that the applicant will be offered the loan given this information?

Let M denote the event that $\{X_1 = 1 \text{ and } X_2 = 1\}$, so that the posterior odds given M needs to be calculated, that is, to find O(A | M).

We know from the Reformulated Bayes' Theorem that,

Posterior odds = Prior odds * Likelihood Ratio

Prior odds = O(A) = 2.5 (from before)

Likelihood Ratio (LR) for event A = P(M | A) / P(M | -A)

However, P(M | A) or P(M | -A) may not be known or it may not be possible to find them. This is often the case when the number of predictors is large and there are not enough observations in each possible outcome category.

In general, if the bank considers k factors (X_1, X_2, ..., X_k) and they assume (n_1, n_2, ..., n_k) values, then the joint distribution of X_1, X_2, ..., X_k will assume $n = n_1 * n_2 * ... * n_k$ values. Even for a moderate value of k, n_k will be very large, and without imposing some additional assumptions, finding the posterior odds (or probabilities) in real time will be a formidable task. We will discuss this problem in more details in the next section.

NAIVE BAYES' CLASSIFIER

Naïve Bayes' Classifier is a supervised learning method (used for classification) in machine learning that is based on the Bayes' Theorem. It makes the following assumptions regarding the predictor variables (X_i's):

X_i's are conditionally independent of one another. That is, the conditional joint probability of X_i's is a product of their individual conditional probabilities. In other words,

$$P(X_1, X_2, ..., X_k \mid A) = P(X_1 \mid A) * P(X_2 \mid A) * ... * P(X_k \mid A), \tag{9}$$

$$P(X_1, X_2, ..., X_k \mid -A) = P(X_1 \mid -A) * P(X_2 \mid -A) * ... * P(X_k \mid -A) \tag{10}$$

This classifier is called "Naïve" because of the strong assumption underlying the predictors. It is possible that this assumption is not valid in many real-life applications, yet the algorithm gives better results than some other classifiers in many cases. It usually generalizes well because it has no hyper-parameters to tune. Naïve Bayes' Classifiers haves been used for wide variety of classification problems such as, financial loan approval, Employee churn, Spam email detection, Optical Character Recognition (OCR), Text classification, Medical diagnosis, Fraud detection, Sentiment analysis, Recommender system, and so on.

There are two types of Naïve Bayes' Classifiers, namely Multinomial Naïve Bayes' and Gaussian Naïve Bayes' classifiers. Multinomial Naïve Bayes' classifier deals with discrete or categorical factors or predictors while Gaussian Naïve Bayes' classifier deals with continuous factors. This paper focuses on Multinomial Naïve Bayes' classifier.

Multinomial or Traditional Naïve Bayes' Classifier (Posterior Probability)

The traditional Bayes' Theorem presented in equation (7) can be extended to multiple predictors, as follows:

Posterior probability = (Prior probability * Likelihood of ($\mathbf{X}$)) / P(X),

where $P(\mathbf{X}) = P(A)*P(\mathbf{X} \mid A) + P(-A) * P(\mathbf{X} \mid -A))$ and $\mathbf{X} = (X_1, X_2, ..., X_k)$ is the vector representing the k predictors

Likelihood of ($\mathbf{X}$) = $P(X_1, X_2, ..., X_k \mid A)$

Using the naïve assumption given in equations (9) and (10) above, we can write the likelihood of $\mathbf{X}$, as follows:

Likelihood of ($\mathbf{X}$) = $P(X_1 \mid A) * P(X_2 \mid A) * ... * P(X_k \mid A)$

= Likelihood of (X_1) * Likelihood of (X_2) * ... * Likelihood of (X_k)

The Naïve Bayes' Classifier considers the following hypothesis:

Posterior probability = (Prior probability * Likelihood of (X_1) * Likelihood of (X_2) ... * Likelihood of (X_k)) / P(X), *where*

P(X) = P(A)*P(X | A) + P(-A) * P(X | -A), and

$X = (X_1, X_2, ..., X_k)$ (11)

Reformulated Naive Bayes' Classifier (Posterior Odds)

The reformulated Bayes' Theorem presented in equation (8) can be extended to multiple predictors, as follows:

Posterior Odds = Prior Odds * likelihood ratio of $(X_1$ and X_2 and ... and $X_k)$

Likelihood ratio of $(X_1, X_2, ..., X_k)$ = $\dfrac{P(X_1, X_2,..., X_k \mid A)}{P(X_1, X_2,..., X_k \mid -A)}$

Using equations (9) and (10), the above equation takes the following form

Likelihood ratio of $(X_1, X_2, ..., X_k)$ = $\dfrac{P(X_1 \mid A) \cdot P(X_2 \mid A) \cdot ... P(X_k \mid A)}{P(X_1 \mid -A) \cdot P(X_2 \mid -A) \cdot ... P(X_k \mid -A)}$

$= \dfrac{P(X_1 \mid A)}{P(X_1 \mid -A)} \cdot \dfrac{P(X_2 \mid A)}{P(X_2 \mid -A)} \cdot .... \dfrac{P(X_k \mid A)}{P(X_k \mid -A)}$

= Likelihood ratio of (X_1) * Likelihood ratio of (X_2) * ... * Likelihood ratio of (X_k)

Substituting this in the reformulated Bayes' theorem, we get a very simplified hypothesis for the Naïve Bayes' classifier (posterior odds):

Posterior odds = Prior odds * Likelihood ratio (X_1) * Likelihood ratio (X_2) * .... * Likelihood ratio (X_k) (12)

Next, we will apply the reformulated Naïve Bayes' equation to Case 3 of the loan application example introduced in the previous section. In this case, the bank considers two factors, applicant's FICO score (X_1) and applicant's annual income (X_2) to make decisions on loan applications. X_1 assumes two different values (1 when the application has a FICO score of 750 or more, and 2 when the FICO score is less than 750). X_2 assumes three different values (1 when the applicant has high income, 2 when the applicant has medium income and 3 when the applicant has low income). The joint distribution of X_1 and X_2 will have six different values, and posterior odds (probabilities) will now need to be calculated for each possible value of the joint distribution.

Now, suppose the bank receives a new application, and the applicant's FICO score and income are both known. Suppose the applicant's FICO score and income are both high. What are the odds that the applicant will be offered the loan given this information?

Let M denote the event that $\{X_1 = 1$ and $X_2 = 1\}$, and we need to compute the posterior odds given M. That is, we need to find O(A | M).

We know from the reformulated Naïve Bayes' Theorem that,

Posterior odds = Prior odds * likelihood ratio of (X1) * likelihood ratio of (X2)

Prior odds for loan approval = 2.5

Likelihood ratio of (X_1) = 1.6 (see Table 2)

Likelihood ratio of (X_2) = 2.3 (See Table 3)

Posterior odds = 2.5 * 1.6 * 2.3 = 9.2

Table 4. Posterior odds based on FICO score (X1) and Income (X2)

Event	Prior Odds	Likelihood Ratio (E_1 - High FICO Score)	Likelihood Ratio (F_1 - High Income)	Posterior Odds
A: Loan Approved	O(A) = 2.5 (5:2)	1.6	2.3	O(A | M) = 9.2 (9:1)
-A: Loan not approved	O(-A) = 0.4 (2:5)	0.625	0.435	O(-A| M) = 0.109 (1:9)

If FICO score is high and income is high (that is event M has occurred), then the odds that the loan will be approved jumps from 2.5 to 9.2. And, for every 9 approved loan applications, the bank rejects just 1 loan application if the applicant's FICO score and income are both high.

FUTURE RESEARCH DIRECTION

In this paper we have discussed the use of odds, odds ratio and log odds in Bayes' Theorem and multinomial Naïve Bayes' Classifiers. The reformulated Naïve Bayes' Classifiers has made the algorithm simpler, easier to interpret, and computationally more efficient. Future research may be conducted to investigate how odds, odds ratio and log odds can be used in other machine learning classification and regression models as well.

CONCLUSION

The availability of massive amounts of data today and the explosive growth of the field of Analytics and Data Science today has led to widespread use of predictive models today, and Naïve Bayes' classifier is one of them. It is a probabilistic machine learning technique that is based on a well-known theorem in Statistics, namely Bayes' Theorem. This method is mostly applied to large datasets for both binary and multi-class problems. It is especially known to be robust in case a dataset involves categorical variables compared to other classification techniques such as k-NN, Decision Trees, etc. The underlying simplistic assumption of independence among predictors is often criticized since in the real-world scenario, there is hardly ever a situation where all the predictors are independent. Yet, Naïve Bayes' classifier has found extensive use in applications such as financial loan approvals, detection of spam emails, intrusion detection for computer networks, and sentiment analysis in marketing. It has also been used to build recommender systems (like the ones that Amazon, Netflix use to predict what books or movies a customer may like based on interest and past choices) in an ensemble set up along with other machine learning techniques such as collaborative filtering.

In this paper we discussed how odds, odds ratio and log odds can be used in Bayes' Theorem and multinomial Naïve Bayes' Classifiers. We reformulated Bayes' Theorem and Multinomial Naïve Bayes' classifiers in terms of odds and odds ratio. The reformulated bayes classifiers compute prior odds and likelihood of input data at the development stage. At the production stage, the classifiers predict posterior odds for each output category (or label). The reformulations made the classifiers more efficient, and simpler and easier to understand.

Among other applications, Bayes' theorem and the concept of odds have also been used in the domain of Decision Analysis (Camm et al., 2020). The well-known technique of "expected value" approach used in decision-making can be augmented with additional sample information when available. One way to obtain such information is through experiments and market research studies, which can then be used to "update" or "revise" odds and probabilities used for making decisions.

REFERENCES

Berry, D. A., & Lindgren, B. W. (1996). *Statistics: Theory and Methods* (2nd ed.). Duxbury Press.

Bolstad, W. M., & Curran, J. M. (2016). *Introduction to Bayesian Statistics* (3rd ed.). Wiley Publication.

Camm, J. D., Cochran, J. F., Fry, M. J., & Ohlmann, J. W. (2020). *Business Analytics* (4th ed.). Cengage.

Christensen, R., Johnson, W., Bransecum, A., & Hanson, T. E. (2011). *Bayesian Ideas and Data Analysis*. CRC Press.

Fulton, L. V., Mendez, F. A., Bastian, N. D., & Muzaffer Musal, R. (2012). Confusion between odds and probability, a Pandemic? *Journal of Statistics Education: An International Journal on the Teaching and Learning of Statistics*, 20(3). Advance online publication. doi:10.1080/10691898.2012.11889647

Grant, S. (2020). *The medical test paradox, and redesigning Bayes' rule*. Accessed 18 September 2021. https://www.youtube.com/watch?v=lG4VkPoG3ko

Hicks, T., Rodriguez-campos, L., & Choi, J. H. (2018). Bayesian posterior odds ratio: Statistical tools for collaborative evaluations. *American Journal of Education*, 39(2), 278–289.

Kruschke, J. (2014). *Doing Bayesian Data Analysis: A Tutorial with R, JAGS, and Stan* (2nd ed.). Academic Press.

Lee, P. M. (2012). *Bayesian Statistics: An Introduction* (4th ed.). Wiley Publication.

Martin, K. G. (2018). *Logistic Regression Analysis: Understanding Odds and Probability*. Accessed 18 September 2021. Available from https://www.theanalysisfactor.com/understanding-odds-and-probability/

Moran, K. (2020). *Odds of Dying from COVID-19 vs Other Coronavirus*. Accessed 18 September 2021. Available from https://www.youtube.com/watch?v=1YhzkZvz2lc

Ranganathan, P., Aggarwal, R., & Pramesh, C. S. (2015). Common pitfalls in statistical analysis: Odds versus risk. *Perspectives in Clinical Research*, 6(4), 222–224. doi:10.4103/2229-3485.167092 PMID:26623395

Samuel, A. (1959). Some studies in machine learning using the game of checkers. *IBM Journal of Research and Development*, 3(3), 535–554. doi:10.1147/rd.33.0210

ADDITIONAL READING

Dasgupta, A. (2011). *Probability for Statistics and Machine Learning: Fundamentals and Advanced Topics*. Springer. doi:10.1007/978-1-4419-9634-3

Golden, R. (2020). *Statistical Machine Learning: A Unified Framework* (1st ed.). CRC Press. doi:10.1201/9781351051507

Goodfellow, I., Bengio, Y., & Courville, A. (2016). *Deep Learning, Illustrated edition*. The MIT Press.

Hastie, H., Tibshirani, R., & Friedman, J. (2008). *The Elements of Statistical Learning: Data Mining, Inference, and Prediction* (2nd ed.). Springer Series.

Kroese, D. P., Botev, Z., Taimre, T., & Vaisman, R. (2020). *Data Science and Machine Learning: Mathematical and Statistical Methods* (1st ed.). CRC Press.

Lesmeister, C., & Chinnamgari. (2019). *Advanced Machine Learning with R: Tackle data analytics and machine learning challenges and build complex applications with R 3.5*. Packt Publishing Ltd.

Murphy, K. P. (2022). *Probabilistic Machine Learning: An Introduction*. The MIT Press.

KEY TERMS AND DEFINITIONS

Conditional Probability: Conditional probability is probability of an event (say A) given that another event (say B) has already occurred and is written as P(A|B).

Odds: Odds is a measure of the likelihood of an event. It assumes any value between 1 and infinity.

Posterior Odds: Posterior odds of an event is the odds we estimate for this event after we collect data/ examples and make use of the relevant information contained in the data.

Posterior Probability: Posterior probability of an event is the probability we estimate for this event after we collect data/ examples and make use of the relevant information contained in the data.

Prior Odds: Prior odds of an event is the odds we estimate for this event before data/ examples are collected.

Prior Probability: Prior probability of an event is the probability we estimate for this event before data/ examples are collected.

Supervised Learning: In supervised learning models (at their development stages) are provided with data/ examples on both input (predicator variables) and output (category) labels.

ENDNOTE

[1]   P(A|B) is a commonly used notation in the Statistics literature to denote the probability of occurrence of event A "given" that event B has already occurred.

Section 44
Pricing Analytics

Machine Learning for Housing Price Prediction

Rahimberdi Annamoradnejad
University of Mazandaran, Iran

Issa Annamoradnejad
Sharif University of Technology, Iran

INTRODUCTION

The housing market is one of the earliest and most influential industries with interests among general populations. It has been described as the least transparent industry in our ecosystem, as it keeps changing day in and day out (Varma et al., 2018). In recent years and with the advent of computer approaches, many studies used the latest machine learning models to analyze the housing market and identify its most important influential variables in order to suggest a proper price or to predict price fluctuations. These automated models help homeowners, builders, and business people to perform an objective assessment and reach more profit by knowing about the future market, successful neighborhoods, or demanded building structures. In addition, they assist city administrators and urban planners to organize environmental and locational amenities in a way that would bring success and profit to a wider population of a city.

Earlier works were able to apply statistical and mathematical approaches, such as regression and hedonic price models (Harrison Jr. & Rubinfeld, 1978), on relatively small datasets collected from local real estate agencies. Throughout the years, precision was significantly improved by collecting larger datasets and variables, and with the use of the latest machine learning models, e.g. neural networks, deep learning, and gradient boosting. Most previous studies consider property price prediction as a static task, without any regard for price fluctuations over time. However, in a real-world setting, it is also essential to include time in making a final prediction. Stock market prediction is a similar but more volatile example, where researchers focus on predicting price changes based on daily data.

This chapter follows the general phases of the CRISP-DM process model for data mining, to elaborate on the problem statements, data collection and preparation, modeling, and evaluation. It will take into account the intricacies of the problem in all steps of the process, from the problem definition, data collection, feature engineering, model selection, and evaluation. The discussion contains a classification of tasks, popular machine learning competitions, variable groups, and feature engineering methods. Data sources and methods of data collection will be reviewed in detail and variables are grouped into three categories. Proper ways to design steady and accurate models are proposed in relation to previous methods and approaches for predicting housing prices. While the purpose of this chapter is not to propose a new model or dataset for housing prices, the overall workflow and proposed ideas can empower future studies to design a machine learning approach for predicting housing prices.

DOI: 10.4018/978-1-7998-9220-5.ch163

M

BACKGROUND

Early works studied housing prices using mathematical and statistical approaches. The hedonic pricing is a very popular method in early works of determining influential variables of housing prices, which detects the impact of given variables on the total price of a property and is used for valuation of market goods for their utility-bearing characteristics (Harrison Jr. & Rubinfeld, 1978; Selim, 2011). This conventional method has been widely applied for housing prices (Tse, 2002; Hansen, 2009; Selim, 2011; Liao and Wang, 2012).

In recent decades and with the advent of computer models, many studies applied state of the art models to analyze the housing market, identify its most influential variables, and suggest a proper price. Many machine learning algorithms and approaches have been applied to assess their success in making accurate predictions. Earlier works focused on training general-purpose statistical and machine learning models, such as Fuzzy logic (Kusan et al., 2010), Neural Networks (Nghiep, 2001; Khalafallah, 2008), Linear Regression (Sangani et al, 2017), Random Forest (Antipov and Pokryshevskaya, 2012), Support Vector Machines (Kontrimas and Verikas, 2011), Genetic algorithms (Giudice et al., 2017) and their blended results (Kontrimas and Verikas, 2011; Plakandaras et al., 2015). Antipov and Pokryshevskaya (2012) addressed the missing values problem in most housing variables datasets and showed that the random forest approach is suitable to deal with them. In recent years and with the possibility of creating large datasets, works utilized more complex neural networks (Pai and Wang, 2020), deep learning, and gradient boosting (Sangani et al., 2017; Singh and Sharma, 2020) to tackle the problem. Truong et al. (2020) adopted Stacked Generalization approach, among other ensemble techniques, to optimize the predicted values.

Most previous studies and machine learning competitions consider housing price prediction as a static task, without any consideration for price fluctuations over time. While that is a valuable goal to understand the essential variables on the final pricing, it is also important to predict the overall price changes and consider market fluctuations to reduce external bias from the training. Stock market prediction is a similar but more volatile example, in which many researchers have tried to predict price changes in day to day markets. To this aim, some works applied time series methods, autoregressive and dynamic models to forecast house price growth rates and volatility (Segnon et al., 2020; Bork and Møller, 2015). Plakandaras et al. (2015) designed a model to detect early warning signs for predicting sudden house price drops. Previous studies are mostly fine-tuned on a single dataset of a particular city, as with the several machine learning competitions that target predicting housing prices.

PREDICTING PRICE VALUES

This section discusses the necessary steps in developing a new machine learning model for housing prices, according to CRISP-DM methodology (Wirth & Hipp, 2000) and in line with the general steps of supervised learning algorithms (as described by Kotsiantis et al., 2007). The CRISP-DM process model is shown at Figure 1. The discussion contains exploration of problem definitions, dataset creation methodologies, variable groups, proper feature engineering methods, modeling, and evaluation. We omit the last phase of CRISM-DM, i.e. deployment, in this chapter.

Figure 1. Phases of CRISP-DM process model for Data Mining (Wirth & Hipp, 2000)

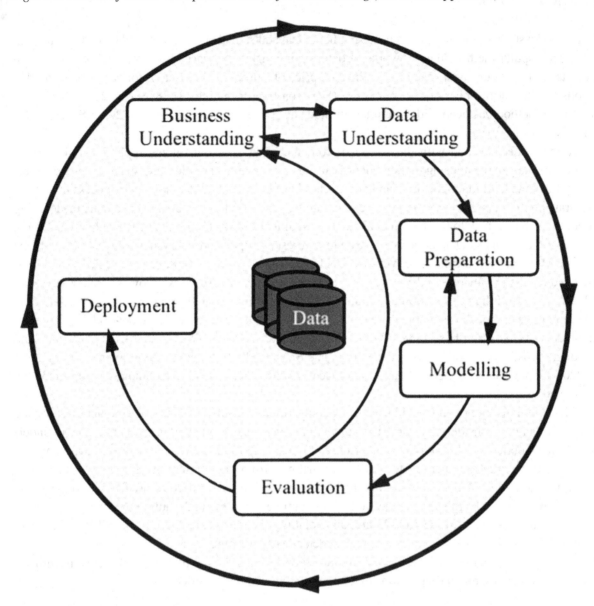

Business Understanding

The housing price prediction falls under the supervised learning tasks, as a model is trained using labeled data. The most common form of pricing prediction task is the regression task to predict prices based on the given structural features, such as base area, age, floor level, number of bedrooms, and floor texture. Based on the nature of the predictors and the goal of research, there exist a number of variants:

- **Static regression task of predicting property price**: This is the most common form of the task, where the focus is on the precision of the predicted values. The task do not include temporal data (such as year), thus, inflation, local and governmental policies, or any other external factor are not considered as determinants. The authors advise to include data only from a single year to prevent the adverse impact of timely factors in the prediction accuracy.

- **Dynamic regression task of predicting property price**: A variant of the previous task, where the objective is to predict the price by knowing the year for each entry. The data should consist of a long period of time for proper comprehension of the underlying relationships. Additional information on the external events may help to explain the causes for price fluctuations. Studies concentrated on the temporal analysis of prices exist in other markets, such as Bitcoin market and Stock market.

- **Determining influential variables of housing prices**: While the objective of a machine learning tasks are generally to predict a target value, it is also essential to understand the influential variables of housing prices and their degree of influence. Earlier works that used Hedonic Pricing Method and Linear Regression, mostly focused on this particular task, as it would give market enthusiasts (such as homeowners or builders) an insight into their future investment.

In addition to independent research works that focus on finding answers to the mentioned questions, some companies from the public and private sectors organize machine learning competitions to find accurate prediction models, especially for the first task. These competitions use online platforms, such as Kaggle, to introduce the competition, share data, evaluate models against the private test set, and announce the winners. Hundreds of teams will compete over a period of 3-4 months, where the top teams are awarded money prizes sometimes up to $500k. Here are a few examples:

- **Zillow Prize 2018 competition**: Zillow, a US real estate market place, organized the competition on Kaggle platform to encourage researchers to come up with accurate house price forecasting algorithms. Zillow website estimates price of houses based on given information for millions of buyers and sellers. The competition attracted 3770 teams and awarded $1.2M in total to the top teams. The competition used MAE (mean-absolute-error) as the evaluation metric, based on which, several teams scored as low as 0.074 (Kaggle n.d.).

- **House Prices - Advanced Regression Techniques:** This is a Kaggle competition organized by the Kaggle platform to entice new users for participation in competitions. While it contains ranking and automated evaluation, it does not awards money to participants and the test set is publicly available for everyone. The dataset contains more than 70 variables, such as lot area, type of alley access, style of dwelling, height of the basement, roof style, electrical system, number of fireplaces, fence quality, and size of garage in car capacity (Kaggle, n.d.).

Data Understanding

The general focus of previous machine learning studies and competitions is to understand the impact of intrinsic variables of a property, such as age, base area, flood level, and the number of bedrooms. However, there are additional influential factors that are not related to the structure of a property. These variables are broadly called extrinsic variables, such as environmental issues, governmental orders, transport amenities, distance to CBD, etc. While the latter group are influential in the overall price of houses, they impact all cases or a large portion of entries together. As a result, it becomes harder to detect their impact in small datasets, especially if all cases are collected from a single city.

Studies that examine the determinants of property prices from both aspects (intrinsic and extrinsic) cluster variables into two or three groups based on the focus of their research (b and c can be merged as extrinsic variables) (Annamorad et al., 2019):

1. **Structural attributes of a unit**, such as base area, floor level, age of the building, number of bedrooms, number of bathrooms, materials, number of windows, number of floors, etc.
2. **Locational variables of the neighborhood**, including distance from CBD, distance to educational centers, population density, and average land price.
3. **Environmental variables**, such as air quality, and green space per capita.

As for datasets and data collection, there are countless datasets available for price prediction from all around the world. Some researchers are using well-known housing datasets, e.g., Boston (Harrison Jr. & Rubinfeld, 1978) and King county (Wang et al., 2014) datasets. China cities are particularly of interest for researchers as government policies, population density and environmental issues are playing great roles alongside structural variables in determining the prices.

Earlier datasets are collected manually with the help of officials or real estate agents. More recent datasets focus on using Web Mining techniques to collect large amounts of entries from brokerage websites (Annamorad et al., 2019). They usually contain more entries in a structured way in less time and can contain data from several cities.

In general, the authors identified three methods of data collection for tasks related to housing prices:

- **Request from officials**: A simple and accurate way to create a dataset regarding housing prices is to use data from local or national officials (government). Generally, every property transaction has to be submitted officially, which will be stored as paper or online records. While access to such data can provide accurate data, such as the exact price or address of the property, they are considered sensitive information; thus cannot be shared publicly with researchers. However, related agencies may publish some insightful high-level information (such as the average price per neighborhood for each year) without compromising any individual data.
- **Request from real-estate agents**: Another traditional method of data collection is to request data from private real-estate companies/agents. They usually store the listings with several variables in a structured way, and they include unsuccessful offers as well as successful ones. One main drawback of this method is that researchers have to contact several independent people to collect a medium-sized dataset encompassing all regions of a city. In addition, stored variables from different companies may be slightly different from each other; thus requiring a merging step.
- **Use of web mining**: In this computer-mediated method, a web crawler program is designed to collect data from web-pages containing listings of brokerage websites. From a technical point, a web crawler program retrieves data from the specified HTML elements of a web page and crawls into linked pages thereafter. This is a very quick and easy way to collect large amounts of public data from the Internet, which may contain listings from multiple cities. While this method solves several problems of the traditional ways of data collection, the generated dataset will be based on unconfirmed user-reported entries.

The advantages, disadvantages, some public dataset examples, and a medium required effort level are presented in Table 1.

Table 1. Various data sources for tasks related to housing prices

Data Source	Effort Level	Advantages	Disadvantages	Dataset Examples
Local officials/agencies	Medium	- Accurate data - Large quantities - Ability to collect from multiple cities	- Hard/No access - Unable to share publicly - May require data entry	- Ames dataset (De Cock, 2011) - Boston Housing dataset (Harrison Jr. & Rubinfeld, 1978) - Average New House Price (Data.gov, n.d.)
Private real-estate agents/agencies	High	- Collecting data on unsuccessful items - Collecting unofficial variables	- Very hard to collect, agent by agent - Low quantities - May require data entry	- Agarwal et al. (2019) - Barwick and Pathak (2015)
Brokerage websites	Low	- Very fast to collect - Large quantities - Ability to collect from multiple cities - No requirement for data entry	- Mostly the listings, not the success result - May contain incorrect submissions	- Annamorad et al. (2019) - Data from 2018 Zillow competition

It should be noted that these methods are to collect structural values related to each property, meaning that they will not include locational attributes. For this reason, it is required to collect the selected extrinsic properties using a separate method. For example, it may be required to locate the place of each entry on a geographical map and calculate its distance to CBD. Similar to the first part, this process too can be performed manually or with the help of computer tools.

Some locational variables, such as air quality, will not differ greatly inside a small city. While one way to resolve the problem is by targeting multiple cities, this method will result in additional city-related variables (such as geographical location, structure, culture, and city regulations) which would defeat the original purpose. In addition, the solution will require multiple data sources, from a few similar cities. A better way to resolve such a problem is to target a mega city, separated by regions.

Finally, if the selected task (previous subsection) is a static one, the authors advise researchers to collect data only from a short timeframe (e.g. a single year). This is to prevent the adverse impact of bias, such as inflation or new regulations, on model training.

Data Preparation

In this step, the data is analyzed, grouped, and transformed to be ready to enter a training process as inputs. This step contains feature engineering, as a step that plays a preliminary, but vital role in reaching an accurate model. It can be performed to increase the number of features, fix missing values, sanitize the data, normalize values, or completely discard unnecessary variables. This is highly dependent on the dataset and selected variables.

Removing outlier/incorrect values is an important step to prevent adverse results. For example, a property with 15 bedrooms or a negative number of bathrooms should be discarded as a possible mistake in the data entry process. However, an apartment on floor -1 can be a real underground place representing valuable information. Another step is to convert textual features to categorical variables. These include neighborhood names, used materials, etc. Normalizing numerical values may have a positive impact on the training process of some models (such as KNN). The target variable should be properly adjusted to fit the prediction task. For example, the average price can be calculated per timeframe per neighborhood; so, the increase or decrease of prices can be detected over time.

Modeling

This step is composed of algorithm selection, training, and parameter tuning with the purpose of reaching a good model that is generalized enough to extract the underlying rules of pricing. In terms of algorithm selection, previous works tried a number of approaches, including Fuzzy logic (Kusan et al., 2010), Neural Networks (Nghiep, 2001; Khalafallah, 2008; Pai and Wang, 2020), Linear Regression (Sangani et al, 2017), Random Forest (Antipov and Pokryshevskaya, 2012), Support Vector Machines (Kontrimas and Verikas, 2011), Genetic algorithms (Giudice et al., 2017) and their blended results (Kontrimas and Verikas, 2011; Plakandaras et al., 2015). and gradient boosting (Sangani et al., 2017; Singh and Sharma, 2020). In general, training and predicting via machine learning models take a longer time compared to traditional numerical methods, such as the hedonic pricing model. Choosing the right algorithm should be made by considering the number of items (dataset size), variable types, and existence of relationships between variables.

By reviewing the approaches taken by the top teams in machine learning competitions (See step 1), it is evident that ensemble learning, especially bagging algorithm, plays an important role in achieving high evaluation scores. In bagging, multiple models are designed and trained separately and their output are merged together using a weighted sum. While the approach is simple, it brings good qualities of multiple models and reduces the impact of outlier predictions.

Evaluation

For evaluation purposes, the test part of the dataset should be split randomly, before any kind of analysis, training, or preprocessing steps. It would be better to allocate at least 20% of the entries for testing/evaluation purposes, as it would contain a variety of combinations. If the dataset is an original work, the authors advise separating and publishing of the train and test sets, separately, so other researchers will be able to reproduce results or evaluate their own models in the same criteria. As for the evaluation metrics, MSE (mean-squared-error) and MAE (mean-absolute-error) are common choices for regression tasks according to previous studies and competitions mentioned in the background section.

It should be remembered that validation on the test part of the dataset should not be performed in the middle of the training process, meaning that the training, fine-tuning, or parameter setting should be performed prior to the final evaluation on the test set. To achieve accurate estimates of the final evaluation scores during the training process, cross-validation is a practical approach that is widely used by researchers and the top teams in machine learning competitions.

SOLUTIONS AND RECOMMENDATIONS

Based on the general guidelines and best practices of machine learning in relation to the intricacies of housing market, the authors propose a few solutions to reach steady robust results and deal with the problems of previous studies.

The biggest concern about previous works and approaches is the lack of robust steady results via generalized models. The authors highly recommend using complex models only on large datasets. It is useless to apply recent deep neural networks or other complex models on conventional datasets of housing prices. These datasets generally include too many variables for a small number of cases (less than 50k), which forces complex models to fit very quickly to the variance of the training dataset; thus, creating a highly over-fit model that is unusable on any other dataset. A good way to combat this problem is to collect a large amount of data from various places to help a complex model in learning underlying rules of pricing. Large websites with verified cases or official sources can be a good resource to reach this goal.

Another major reason for not being able to reach steady robust results is the existence of undetected biases in the training of a machine learning model. Bias exists in models that try to predict prices just based on structural variables of the property by disregarding the importance of locational factors, such as distance to CBD, crime rate, etc. Similarly, if the dataset is collected over a larger period of time, external economic factors, such as inflation or new regulations, will affect the prices of housing and inject bias into training. The bias can also impact training if the data are collected from a small portion of the city. These biases can be detected and neutralized by adding more related variables to the dataset, whether from government reports, external datasets, or even sentiment analysis of social media.

FUTURE RESEARCH DIRECTIONS

Previous research mostly target predicting housing prices by using latest general machine learning models and based on a few selected variables. While this trend can continue in the future to improve the overall precision of prediction systems, great advances can be achieved by further investigation into the following subjects:

- **Dynamic prediction of housing prices**: This is a variant of the problem, in which the objective is to predict the price by knowing the year for each entry. It can contain the analysis of external temporal events, such as local regulations and inflation, on the house market. The results can also be utilized to nullify their impact on large datasets. The data should consist of a long period of time for proper comprehension of the underlying relationships. Additional information on the external events may help to explain the causes for price fluctuations. Studies concentrated on the temporal analysis of prices exist in other markets, such as Bitcoin market and Stock market.
- **Targeting mega cities**: Some variables, such as air quality, will not differ greatly inside a small city. While, one way to resolve such problem is by targeting multiple cities, additional city-related variables (such as geographical location, structure, culture, and city regulations) will enter the calculations and impact the final results. In addition, the solution will require multiple data sources, from a few similar cities. A better way to resolve such problem is to target a mega city, separated by regions.
- **Impact of agents:** It would be a good idea to use human agents (and websites) as a categorical variable to determine their impact on the success of a listing. This can be further investigated by including characteristics of agents (such as age, gender, and experience) to help homeowners in finding suitable agents.

CONCLUSION

Although statistical analysis plays a significant role in the financial industry, supervised learning is making big inroads into the financial world of housing prices. In this chapter, the authors reviewed previous attempts at predicting housing prices by using machine learning models and shed a light on the most important questions in designing a new prediction model. The main discussion elaborates on the intricacies of the problem statement, data collection and preparation, modeling, and evaluation.

As it was evident in the discussion, most previous studies consider housing price prediction as a static task, with less regard for price fluctuations over the years. The main focus of previous attempts is on understanding the impact of intrinsic variables of a property, such as a floor level and the number of bedrooms. Furthermore, they suffer from reaching steady results on multiple datasets. This can be largely traced to the existence of bias in training, as it is essential to predict prices by considering external economic variables. Removing bias and reaching higher accuracies require collecting larger datasets, both in the number of items and variables. This can be achieved with the help of recent automated techniques in collecting, merging, and cleaning data. The proposed ideas and the overall workflow of the current chapter can be used as guidelines to fix the existing issues of previous works or to accelerate future studies.

REFERENCES

Agarwal, S., He, J., Sing, T. F., & Song, C. (2019). Do real estate agents have information advantages in housing markets? *Journal of Financial Economics*, *134*(3), 715–735. doi:10.1016/j.jfineco.2019.05.008

Annamorad, R., Annamorad, I., Safarrad, T., & Habibi, J. (2019, April). Using Web Mining in the Analysis of Housing Prices: A Case study of Tehran. *5th International Conference on Web Research (ICWR)*, 55-60.

Antipov, E. A., & Pokryshevskaya, E. B. (2012). Mass appraisal of residential apartments: An application of Random forest for valuation and a CART-based approach for model diagnostics. *Expert Systems with Applications*, *39*(2), 1772–1778. doi:10.1016/j.eswa.2011.08.077

Average new house price. Data.Gov.IE. (n.d.). Retrieved September 14, 2022, from https://data.gov.ie/dataset/average-new-house-price

Barwick, P. J., & Pathak, P. A. (2015). The costs of free entry: An empirical study of real estate agents in Greater Boston. *The RAND Journal of Economics*, *46*(1), 103–145. doi:10.1111/1756-2171.12082

Bork, L., & Møller, S. V. (2015). Forecasting house prices in the 50 states using Dynamic Model Averaging and Dynamic Model Selection. *International Journal of Forecasting*, *31*(1), 63–78. doi:10.1016/j.ijforecast.2014.05.005

De Cock, D. (2011). Ames, Iowa: Alternative to the Boston housing data as an end of semester regression project. *Journal of Statistics Education: An International Journal on the Teaching and Learning of Statistics*, *19*(3).

Del Giudice, V., De Paola, P., & Forte, F. (2017). Using genetic algorithms for real estate appraisals. *Buildings*, *7*(2), 31–41. doi:10.3390/buildings7020031

Hansen, J. (2009). Australian house prices: A comparison of hedonic and repeat-sales measures. *The Economic Record, 85*(269), 132–145. doi:10.1111/j.1475-4932.2009.00544.x

M

Harrison, D. Jr, & Rubinfeld, D. L. (1978). Hedonic housing prices and the demand for clean air. *Journal of Environmental Economics and Management, 5*(1), 81–102. doi:10.1016/0095-0696(78)90006-2

House prices - advanced regression techniques. (n.d.). Kaggle. Retrieved September 14, 2022, from https://www.kaggle.com/c/house-prices-advanced-regression-techniques/

Khalafallah, A. (2008). Neural network based model for predicting housing market performance. *Tsinghua Science and Technology, 13*(S1), 325–328. doi:10.1016/S1007-0214(08)70169-X

Kontrimas, V., & Verikas, A. (2011). The mass appraisal of the real estate by computational intelligence. *Applied Soft Computing, 11*(1), 443–448. doi:10.1016/j.asoc.2009.12.003

Kotsiantis, S. B., Zaharakis, I., & Pintelas, P. (2007). Supervised machine learning: A review of classification techniques. *Emerging Artificial Intelligence Applications in Computer Engineering, 160*(1), 3-24.

Kuşan, H., Aytekin, O., & Özdemir, İ. (2010). The use of fuzzy logic in predicting house selling price. *Expert Systems with Applications, 37*(3), 1808–1813. doi:10.1016/j.eswa.2009.07.031

Liao, W. C., & Wang, X. (2012). Hedonic house prices and spatial quantile regression. *Journal of Housing Economics, 21*(1), 16–27. doi:10.1016/j.jhe.2011.11.001

Nghiep, N., & Al, C. (2001). Predicting housing value: A comparison of multiple regression analysis and artificial neural networks. *Journal of Real Estate Research, 22*(3), 313–336. doi:10.1080/10835547.2001.12091068

Pai, P. F., & Wang, W. C. (2020). Using machine learning models and actual transaction data for predicting real estate prices. *Applied Sciences (Basel, Switzerland), 10*(17), 5832. doi:10.3390/app10175832

Sangani, D., Erickson, K., & Al Hasan, M. (2017, October). Predicting zillow estimation error using linear regression and gradient boosting. *IEEE 14th International Conference on Mobile Ad Hoc and Sensor Systems (MASS)*, 530-534. 10.1109/MASS.2017.88

Segnon, M., Gupta, R., Lesame, K., & Wohar, M. E. (2021). High-frequency volatility forecasting of US housing markets. *The Journal of Real Estate Finance and Economics, 62*(2), 283–317. doi:10.100711146-020-09745-w

Selim, H. (2009). Determinants of house prices in Turkey: Hedonic regression versus artificial neural network. *Expert Systems with Applications, 36*(2), 2843–2852. doi:10.1016/j.eswa.2008.01.044

Singh, A., Sharma, A., & Dubey, G. (2020). Big data analytics predicting real estate prices. *International Journal of System Assurance Engineering and Management*, 1-12.

Tse, R. Y. (2002). Estimating neighbourhood effects in house prices: Towards a new hedonic model approach. *Urban Studies (Edinburgh, Scotland), 39*(7), 1165–1180. doi:10.1080/00420980220135545

Varma, A., Sarma, A., Doshi, S., & Nair, R. (2018). House Price Prediction Using Machine Learning and Neural Networks. *2018 Second International Conference on Inventive Communication and Computational Technologies (ICICCT)*. 10.1109/ICICCT.2018.8473231

Wang, X., Wen, J., Zhang, Y., & Wang, Y. (2014). Real estate price forecasting based on SVM optimized by PSO. *Optik (Stuttgart)*, *125*(3), 1439–1443. doi:10.1016/j.ijleo.2013.09.017

Wirth, R., & Hipp, J. (2000, April). CRISP-DM: Towards a standard process model for data mining. In *Proceedings of the 4th international conference on the practical applications of knowledge discovery and data mining*. London, UK: Springer-Verlag.

Zillow Prize. Zillow's home value prediction (zestimate). (n.d.). Kaggle. Retrieved September 14, 2022, from https://www.kaggle.com/c/zillow-prize-1

ADDITIONAL READING

Hu, L., He, S., Han, Z., Xiao, H., Su, S., Weng, M., & Cai, Z. (2019). Monitoring housing rental prices based on social media: An integrated approach of machine-learning algorithms and hedonic modeling to inform equitable housing policies. *Land Use Policy*, *82*, 657–673. doi:10.1016/j.landusepol.2018.12.030

Karasu, S., Altan, A., Saraç, Z., & Hacioğlu, R. (2018, May). Prediction of Bitcoin prices with machine learning methods using time series data. In *2018 26th signal processing and communications applications conference (SIU)*. IEEE. 10.1109/SIU.2018.8404760

Kok, N., Koponen, E. L., & Martínez-Barbosa, C. A. (2017). Big data in real estate? From manual appraisal to automated valuation. *Journal of Portfolio Management*, *43*(6), 202–211. doi:10.3905/jpm.2017.43.6.202

Limsombunchai, V. (2004, June). House price prediction: hedonic price model vs. artificial neural network. New Zealand agricultural and resource economics society conference, 25-26. doi:10.3844/ajassp.2004.193.201

Oladunni, T., & Sharma, S. (2016, December). Hedonic housing theory—a machine learning investigation. *15th IEEE International Conference on Machine Learning and Applications (ICMLA)*, 522-527.

Park, B., & Bae, J. K. (2015). Using machine learning algorithms for housing price prediction: The case of Fairfax County, Virginia housing data. *Expert Systems with Applications*, *42*(6), 2928–2934. doi:10.1016/j.eswa.2014.11.040

Pérez-Rave, J. I., Correa-Morales, J. C., & González-Echavarría, F. (2019). A machine learning approach to big data regression analysis of real estate prices for inferential and predictive purposes. *Journal of Property Research*, *36*(1), 59–96. doi:10.1080/09599916.2019.1587489

Rico-Juan, J. R., & de La Paz, P. T. (2021). Machine learning with explainability or spatial hedonics tools? An analysis of the asking prices in the housing market in Alicante, Spain. *Expert Systems with Applications*, *171*, 114590. doi:10.1016/j.eswa.2021.114590

Rosen, S. (1974). Hedonic prices and implicit markets: Product differentiation in pure competition. *Journal of Political Economy*, *82*(1), 34–55. doi:10.1086/260169

KEY TERMS AND DEFINITIONS

M

Central Business District (CBD): The commercial and business center of a city that contains commercial space and offices. Housing prices are usually much higher than suburbs.

Ensemble Learning: A process by which multiple models, such as classifiers or experts, are strategically generated and combined to solve a particular computational intelligence problem.

Hedonic Pricing Method: A model that identifies price factors according to the premise that price is determined both by internal characteristics of the good being sold and external factors affecting it.

House Price Index (HPI): A normalized average (typically a weighted average) of price relatives in a given region, during a given interval of time.

Real Estate Appraisal: A process to develop an opinion of value for real property based on upgrades or improvements. It is an essential step in initiating mortgage loans, settling estates and divorces, taxation, and so on.

Sales Comparison Approach: An approach that relies on the assumption that a matrix of attributes or significant features of a property drive its value.

Spatial Modeling: An analytical process in which an area is divided into a number (often a large number) of similar units conducted in conjunction with a geographical information system (GIS).

Section 45
Qualitative Research

Quantitative Data in Ethnography With Asian Reflections

Parimal Roy

https://orcid.org/0000-0002-0461-2587

University of Malaya, Malaysia

Jahid Siraz Chowdhury

https://orcid.org/0000-0002-1016-0441

University of Malaya, Malaysia

Haris Wahab

https://orcid.org/0000-0001-9834-3797

University of Malaya, Malaysia

Mohd Rashid Mohd Saad

University of Malaya, Malaysia

Sanjay Krishno Biswas

Shahjalal University of Science and Technology, Bangladesh

INTRODUCTION

Statistics have been a powerful tool since colonial times (Tylor, 1889; Gluckman, 1961; Senft, 2007; Morgan, 1928; Herskovits, 1939; Kluckhohn, 1939), even in the Asian context (Hutchinson, 1909; Rizvi, Ed., 1970). At least, that is what we think when we look at the social sciences' birth, growth, and developmental stages. Furthermore, in the case of the Anthropology that surrounds it, statistics and its proper application are reasonably straightforward (Walter, Kukutai, Carroll, & Rodriguez-Lone bear, 2020; Walter and Andersen, 1992). In this matter, there should be no endeavor to disagree with anyone except the Anthropologist of the colonial mentality. Our experiences in the attached introduction lesson in this chapter are not happy. The added role of the overweight person is also something we do not want to read these days for a variety of reasons. Therefore, we did not hire any hair-raising intellectual because he was not given a definite role. Instead, in this chapter, we are talking about this short introduction, what it is, why it needs to be written, who will read it, etc. We understand that the name of the chapter is entirely unexpected.

Rather fluently, we have tried to highlight the beauty of quantitative ethnography, which may be relevant to Data science if we take numbers as an important factor in social research. In the title of the chapter, when we look carefully, there is an implication of the two words not easily pronounced in one breath — a little clumsy. This chapter is about how social scientists can use ethnographic techniques to analyze data statistically. At the same time, it explores anthropology and how to use statistical techniques to expand capabilities and other qualitative approaches to research. It is between qualitative and quantitative research methods, science, and humanity in the digital age. In terms of numbers and understanding,

DOI: 10.4018/978-1-7998-9220-5.ch164

the questions we can ask sometimes limit us. Nevertheless, quantitative ethnography is a 'complement' to a research approach that will help us understand how to position ourselves in a growing data-rich world.

Changes in Western norms in the 1960s and 1970s impacted census data collection. Because demographic statistics significantly influence governance and social services, these numbers have become a critical lens through which indigenous peoples learn about their country and how the Government utilizes them. Statistics describe our demographics, geographic distribution, employment situation, health, and educational attainment. Nations use statistics to show indigenous life's "who, what, where, and how (Chowdhury et al., 2021; Roy et al.,2022)." This data represents a fundamental, deliberate representation of reality. As a result, they create and execute indigenous social programs. Because indigenous peoples are over-represented in the homeless population, it impacts government policies and efforts—other Indigenous organizations back Canada's Indigenous Employment and Training Program (IET). Postsecondary education increasingly utilizes Indigenous student enumeration data. American data are vital in evaluating Native American housing and social service needs. The numbers frame aboriginal understandings. We know who we are as we participate in their categories. We will not go. Let us look at the Bangladeshi context statistically; we can say the Indigenous people are decreasing Table 1.

Table 1. The Indigenous and Bengali settlers' Ratio since 1872 and the Ethnic Liquidation of Banglades

Census Time	Natives	Settlers	Population
1872	61,957 (98.27%)	1,097 (1.73%)	63,054
1901	1,13,074 (92.81%)	8,762 (7.19%)	1,21,836
1959	2,60,517 (90.39%)	27,171 (9.61%)	2,87,688
1981	4,41,796 (59.17%)	3,04,873 (40.83%)	7,46,669
1991	5,00,190 (51.34%)	4,74,255 (48.66%)	9,74,445
2001	736,682 (54.86%)	606,058 (45.14%)	1342,740
2011	845,541 (52.90%) *	752,690 (47.10%)	1598,231

Source: Chowdhury, 2014

Bengalis are rising. The statistics show long-standing deficits in our self-sufficiency. Stats, therefore, generate reality, not simply reflect it. Anthropologists only add. It works. They influence acceptable interpretations of recorded occurrences.

BACKGROUND

As indicated, statistics has been a tool for composing ethnography, so it is not entirely new. Instead, it is inextricably linked with the journey of anthropology. The adjective of the latter for the former can be a laughingstock to many anthropologists! Nevertheless, we have taken bold steps to bridge the gap between "quantity/quality" and keep these two golfers in a match. Here is our simple statement; why can't a combination of ethnographic work be made with numbers? As we have seen, wise people are more interested in a Malinowski mask or Geertz's introspective interpretation than in doing something like yourself. More and more, those who are constantly struggling to acquire 'deeper' knowledge are busy with blows and delays. No, there is nothing wrong with that. At least We are on one side! Discussing this chapter with the research method you have read may embarrass you; we know that. However, this chapter is hopeful in a conversational tone and in a humorous way. This beauty of academia has helped us write this chapter. We have a passion for academic discourse, decision-making, analysis, statistics, and textual judgment numbers.

However, we now have a way of analyzing a large amount of data on socially enriching topics, but in a way that reflects the stringency that has developed over the years, especially in qualitative research, anthropological research, 'step-motherly behavior' and respect for 'school discipline.' Unbeknownst to us, we have become one-of-a-kind 'disciplines of discipline.' However, full knowledge of the Western discipline and its creators has 'disciplined' us. Moreover, we academically became the learning analytics community as 'captives,' 'mimics,' or Malinowski's masks. We can remember Talal Asad's memory of Malinowski.

[w] here I able to embark once more on fieldwork, I would certainly take much more excellent care to measure, weigh and count everything that can be legitimately measured, weighed and counted" We adopted from Asad, (see" Malinowski, 2001; Asad, 1994, p 56)

And very importantly, Talal Asad said,

"The political success of statistics in the modernizing world is a fact of considerable anthropological significance. From this latter standpoint, it is to be analyzed and explained as a cultural feature of modern social life. If I suggest that such an analysis be conducted, it does not follow that I think ethnographic fieldwork has no merit. Nor- I repeat- do I say there is any essential superiority of statistical over ethnographic methods. The only general opinion I offer about ethnography is that the rich historical tradition of anthropology is unduly narrowed if it is defined simply in terms of fieldwork. (Asad's original note, 8, p. 79.)."

Let us see some foundational Works in Table 2 about Quantity.

Table 2. History of statistics with anthropology. Source: Readers' Readings, and all are given in Endnotes

Anthropologists	Works	Year
Dr. Schaaffhauseu, Prof. Virchow	Colour of the eyes, hair, and skin of 2,000,000 school children in Germany (p.645)	1875
Thomas Wilson	Anthropology at the Paris Exposition in 1889	1890
J.E Partington	Ethnographic Album of the Pacific Islands. The Journal of the Anthropological Institute of Great Britain and Ireland.	1891
AF Chamberlain	Anthropology in universities and colleges.	1894
Forrest Clements, E, Sara M. Schenck, and T. K. Brow	A new objective method for showing unique relationships	1926
Franz Boas	Anthropology and statistics	1927
Wilson D Wallis	Probability and the diffusion of culture traits.	1928
E.M Morgan	Morgan, E. M. (1928). The Social Sciences and their Interrelations. Heinonline.org	1928
Forest Clements	The quantitative method in ethnography	1928
Harols Driver & Alfred Kroeber	Quantitative expression of cultural relationships	1932

continues on following page

Table 1. Continued

Anthropologists	Works	Year
Melville Herskovits	Anthropology and economics	1937
Clyde Kluckhohn	On specific recent applications of association coefficients to ethnological data.	1939
Harold Driver	Statistics in anthropology	1953
Anthony Boyce	The value of some methods of numerical taxonomy concerning hominoid classification	1964
Hans Hoffmann	Mathematical anthropology. Biennial review of anthropology, 6, 41-79.	1969
Paul Kay (Eds.)	Explorations in mathematical anthropology.	1971
M.L Burton[1]	Mathematical anthropology	1973
Michael Chibnik	The use of statistics in sociocultural anthropology	1985
Paul Jamison	Anthropology and statistics?	1991
Paul Ballonoff	Mathematical foundations of social anthropology	2011
Sieghard et a.	The cultural challenge in mathematical cognition	2018
B. Silverstein	*The Social Lives of Numbers: Statistics, Reform and the Remaking of Rural Life in Turkey.*	2020
D M Kotliar	Data orientalism: on the algorithmic construction of the non-Western other	2020
Dwight W Read	Mathematical Anthropology	2019
Maggie Walter and her co-authors	2010; 2005; 2016; 2018 Walter & Andersen, 2013; Kukutai & Walter, 2017; Walter & Suina, 2019	
T. Kukutai & Taylor	*Indigenous data sovereignty: Toward an agenda*	2016
Duarte, Vigil-Hayes, Littletree, & Belarde-Lewis	Of Course, Data Can Never	2020
Carroll, S. R., Rodriguez-Lonebear, & Martinez	Indigenous Data Governance: Strategies from United States Native Nations	2019
J. Wilks, Kennedy, Drew & Wilson	Indigenous data sovereignty in higher education: Towards a decolonized data quality framework	2018

If we summarize Table 2, we will say that statistics in anthropology are not minor but not so huge. Instead, the tendency to avoid it was more remarkable. Social and cultural anthropologists have never used statistics like their peers in other social sciences. Franz Boas emphasized the importance of statistics in the 1920s, noting the increasing use of statistics in sociology, political science, and economics. The successful ethnographic phenomenon of the attempt to apply statistics was "more than doubtful (Wilks, Kennedy, Drew, & Wilson, 2018, see Driver & Kroeber, 1932, note 1)."Kluckhohn (1939, p.350) writes that professional folklore includes priority resistance to any use of statistics almost a decade later. Anthropologists have avoided math and statistics "like a mother-in-law (Driver, 1932, p. 54).

NUMBER SPEAKS

Also, at the same time, the use of mathematics in cultural anthropology increased dramatically, and statistical analyzes of field data became commonplace. While the new theoretical and methodological aspects of anthropology influenced this increased emphasis on moderation, the changing nature of the work was also important. Emphasis on intensive examination of specific subjects in 1950s research tended to be problem-based. Since problem-based studies often involve the systematic collection of quantitative data, the need for a statistical approach to description and inference became apparent, as we saw much earlier, good use of statistics in this area. Instead of increasingly multiple methods by psychologists, it tended to be a general bifurcated experiment rather than an effective system. In present-day Bangladesh, Jilawari ' District Gazetteer' came out concomitantly. However, the Assam Gazetteer came out much earlier, in 1905. Baptist Mission Press published the giant volume pair with William Carey. In 1818, the mission established Srirampur College to train the church and Indian administrators. In 1820, Carrie became interested in botany. He supported him and established the Agri Horticultural Society of India at Ali pore, Calcutta. When William Roxburgh went on vacation, Carrie was tasked with maintaining the Calcutta Botanical Garden. The career genus was named after him. Let's look at some phrases: (Botany + James Cook + Colony + Science + Power + Joseph Banks + Sugar + Tea Tree)—can anyone distinguish these names/discourses!).

In this context, we, the researchers, put our imprint on the studied culture — not only are individuals skewed in obvious or conscious ways, but why do we see study informants as "insignificant people" from a social, cultural, economic, and political standpoint? Population statistics, in particular, is a wise foundation that is an essential consideration in the modern state. Which reflects and creates unique perspectives (see James Scott). Statistics are, in a word, very concise statistics of the social world. Statistics alone do not give social shape and are shaped by these. Population statistics also play a substantial role in defining a nation's ideas, such as 15,000 Santals in 1901 and 39,000 in 1911. These illustrate national social and economic trends: education level, age, and gender distribution; Patterns of birth, illness, and death; Labor market statistics; Income dynamics; and many other incidents. Through this mapping process, they provide their portraits of the nation-state and its various populations. The social, cultural, and economic events chosen for inclusion and those not excluded reflect the nation-state's changing social, cultural, and economic priorities and norms. Example: The poverty rate of the Santals is 59.9% as compared to 39.9% of the rural population of Bangladesh (Sarker, Khan, & Musarrat, 2017). An earlier example is the 1900 Census in colonial Bangladesh. These were done to see who opposed the colony and who was in favour. Statistics is the primary tool of countries to determine and present the 'who,' 'what,' 'where,' and 'how' of tribal life will be official. Often located as a sub-set of overall national social trends, this information is a simple, purposeful snapshot of the underlying reality.

The state considers formulating and implementing social policies for indigenous peoples as the yardstick. Numbers are crucial to making the best policy decisions about where and how indigenous people live and how the Government provides social services. See "Eviction: From Chimbuk to Laldia Char." In a real sense, it seems that the figures frame growing tribal understanding. We will not go away. We look at the census of Bangladesh. We can say that the tribals are decreasing and decreasing. Appropriate statistics are being obscured. On the contrary, Bengalis are growing. In any country with indigenous figures, political leaders have used their qualities of life to document long-term gaps.

Raja Debashish Roy, Sanjeev Drong, and Prashanta Tripura talk about segregated data. Statistics, therefore, do not merely describe reality— but make a reality. At least it gives the state a tool to do 'biopolitics.' We anthropologists just help a little bit. They influence how the described events are understood, but they shape their acceptable interpretations.

CULTURAL STRUCTURE OF INDIGENOUS STATISTICS

James Scott's 'Seeing like State' is a must-read here. His main argument is that a combination of four elements is needed to create a social policy catastrophe of genuinely epic proportions.

The first element is establishing a system of administrative orders for the states of the modern state to organize a society. An example is a national census whose purpose is not just to count but to describe a population considered necessary for understanding the population, such as age, gender, and employment.

The second element Scott called a high-modernist ideal. The term translates into confidence about scientific and technological progress associated with a supposedly rational design for social discipline. Similarly, the high-modernist ideology is due to the relatively illegal embrace of big data technologies and the privilege of open data policies required for these technologies to clean up the western countries.

The third element identified by Scott is an authoritarian state, Willing, able to use the total weight of its compulsive power to create these ultra-modernist designs. This combination of state power makes the indigenous people's bureaucratic reasoning (indigenous information) a discipline in social policy. Excessive information on deficient Indigenous peoples informs the procedure to make Indigenous peoples understand the need for reconstruction appropriately compellingly as ideological, good Indigenous citizens (Moreton-Robinson, 2009).

The fourth element of Scott is a society that cannot resist the imposition of state strategies and policies. Again, the dramatic power imbalance is characteristic of the past and present relationship between the Indigenous people and the Indigenous majority (see Smith, Shawn Wilson, Martin Nakata, Gregory Cajete). Scott himself noted that colonial governments test social policies, especially on indigenous peoples.

We are not proposing any real difference by emphasizing the inherent similarity of qualitative and quantitative academic knowledge. In the social sciences, qualitative methods are involved in the groundbreaking work of feminist scholars who have tried to prove how contemporary male-dominated statistical studies tended to cut women's voices from the statistical "truths" they created.

DISCIPLE OF DISCIPLINE

Our Understanding is that Asian scholars, even the west too, mostly and simply follow their supervisors and mentors, which makes, re-creates, and, in effect, reproduces the old 'wine' in new names. Malinowski trained Raymond Firth to MN Srinivas, and this is the lineage, scholars to scholars, west to East. Academic in Bangladesh means social research is a significant activity. It started in 1921 at Dhaka University. In a century of academia, what have we done with the actual work that has brought about qualitative and quantitative change in indigenous peoples? The methodology may be an answer. If we assume that methodology is a factor, why didn't we do something ourselves? Its simplicity means that we have not been able to understand the methodology problem so far. Professor of Social Sciences has been around since Nazmul Karim (1958)!

We know that the academic world is out of context, let alone anything else. However, let us look at that context. We see the context of 2020 through the work of Erving Goffman of the 1960s (Professor Hasan Shafie, Department of Anthropology, Dhaka University), and the Rakhain Society of 2010 with the 'Need Theory' of 1918 (Professor Abdul Awal Biswas, Department of Anthropology, SUST, Bangladesh). Also, in the form of table (Table 3), we have some work on the Santal race, try to see.

Should we conclude in Table 2 that our academy is a situational time and exemplary work? We do this because we are taking everything for granted. We avoided statistics, and if we look at Table 3, most of the cited works are here in (Table 2)

Table 3. Ethnographic works in Bangladesh. Source: Roy et al. (2021, 2022; Chowdhury et al., 2021,2022)

Q

Ethnographic methods and anthropological works	Hossain (2000); O'Malley (1916); Ali (1998); Debnath (2010, 2020); Karim (2012); Shamsuddoha& Jahan (2016); Somers, 1985); Toppo, A., Rahman, M. R., Ali, M. Y., &Javed, A. (2016); Bodding (1887;1925); Troisi (1978); Culshaw (1949); Hembram, R., Ghosh, A., Nair, S., &Murmu, D. (2016); Somers (1985); Mahapatra (1986); Shafie & Kilby (2003); Sur (1977); Anny, N. Z. (2019); Day, A. (2015); Sarker (2015)
Sociological perspective	Uddin (2011, 2009); Shariff (2013); Troisi, J. (1978); Schulte-Droesch, L. (2018); Toru (2007); Murmu, (2004); Tripura, (2016); Ahmed, (2017). Elahee, (2013); Nasrin (2019); Anny (2019); Henry (1976); Barkat, (2016); Mohsin (2001); Rahman (2002); Guhathakurta (2004).
Among them, alive did not even bother to know how the Santals survived this pandemic2020	

We have another purpose in giving the table above. We are doing 'recommended' work at the time of this epidemic. Because, whatever the time, we cannot get out of our legacy. The impact of Anglo-colonialism extends to government policy and administratively strategic measures across the country and academia. Table 4 shows that we can present a partial community without statistics instead of a fuller view of Bangladesh.

In sum, the legibility of a society provides the capacity for large-scale *social engineering, high-modernist* ideology provides the desire, the authoritarian state provides the determination to act on that desire, and an incapacitated civil society provides the leveled social terrain on which to build.

So, in sociology, don't the examples of Bangladesh seem inadequate without accurate statistics? How will it be in man's best interest to prove this truth by mere explanation or qualitative methodology? In contrast, quantitative research tends toward numbers (see Table 4). Probably, the most crucial element of this method becomes abstract. That is, these methods allow researchers to draw information from a local context, validate it, and remove it from the context, providing it with a central point of calculation.

The quantitative methodology will create a place of inspiration for all quantitative practitioners — indigenous and non-indigenous. Not our 'feeling,' but the journey of perception is not without challenges. As you read this chapter, you are entering the place of indigenous statistics, and as a new researcher or long-term ally, we have such thoughts.

We tell you to be careful when using some suffixes. For example, 'Worldview' is considered by many to be equivalent to a paradigm. However, 'Worldview' carries a direct colonial legacy. We would use Life World instead of worldview. 'Life world,' although not entirely compatible with the Indigenous approach, is still accepted by many elders.

So, we have merged with Life world, not with Western-produced worldviews. What are the challenges to domestic data sovereignty?

'COME TOGETHER BY NAMES'

This section will try to understand that the only specific types of data used to collect indigenous peoples are systematically configured to be created. In Canada, Malaysia, and Bangladesh, the quantitative guiding method limits size and data and their utility rather than the quantitative method. The result is that indigenous figures become increasingly political instead of presenting numerical images of reality, as is usually portrayed. Systematically, they are sub-colonial-permanent artifacts and exceptional settlers between the states of Bangladesh who serve their masters and preserve their subjects. They do so in a way that has become the norm, requiring little thought or awareness of their limitations.

Table 4. The Factuality, Ethnography may adopt a Case of Bangladesh. Source: Authors' understanding from different write-ups.

First Census	Aiming to make classifications of obeyed and resistant	*1860-1900*
Forest Act-1865	Taken for modern plantation	covered 26% CHT Land
	A Shift -Statecrafts and Biopower activities Anthropologist Levi-Strauss came in 1952 to CHT, a provoker in the west.	
Paper Mill	Softwood Plantation provides raw materials Only 15-16 People get the job of 10000	1953
Military Janta Ayub Khan	Submitted the special excluded and status of CHT	1964
EPFIDC**	Development policy mainly exploited the natural resources, per se, Plyboard mills, the Lighter industry, and clothing knitting factories.	1953-1960
Kaptai Hydraulic Project, A mega development project,	- displacing 1 m people, migrated to India - one-quarter of the total population, more than 50 thousand acres of the cultivated area went to the dam	1963
EPIC	A. Mechanical logging imposed	Softwood supply
The intention was to grab natural resources and raw materials for industries.	B. Forestal	
Independent Bangladesh since 1971	C. Indigenous Leaders met the President for indigenous inclusion in a nation, but he rejected and called *Bangalees*.	1972
1972	Article 28 says, *as Bengalis as a nation.* D. Article 23A says, *"[t]he state shall take steps to protect and develop the unique local culture and tradition of the tribes [upajati], minor races [khudrojatishaotta], ethnic sects and communities [nrigoshthi o shomprodai]"*	National Constitution 1972
Counter Hegemonic Activities	Bengali Nationality VS Jhumma Nationality All 13 Indigenous people of CHT united under a counter-hegemonic nationalist ideology, bear and born from the land, *Jono Songhoty* for Jhuma nationality.	1972 1973
Forest ordinance for Modernization	By the name of forest conservation, the Government acquired about 30% of the total land of CHT	1976
Settlement Plans for Development	24% "Reserved Forest has mainly used or given to landless plain land Bangle people	
Power and Militarization	About three hundred Military quarters, above two hundred para-militia set-ups, are for ensuring 'peace' as of 1997 *156,552 acres of land occupied by the military under 'development projects*	1997
Expanded bio-power	Between 1990-1998, 217,790 and 82 Mouzas (Villages) were covered in CHT	1990-1998
Ethnicization	State facilitated the resettlement of over 4 million settlers, Settler colonialism.	
Number factors	Consequently, the Bengali population in the CHT increased sharply (Table 3), about 50-50 ratio.	1991

DEFINING AND IDENTIFYING INDIGENOUS PEOPLE

A sample change needs to be noticed. 'Tribal' people have been replaced by 'ethnic' or 'ethnic group.' As seen in our study, the rise of nation-states in the 1960s and the colonial sunset, when nation-states surrounded a geographically specific area or boundary — the colonial administration again defined this boundary. After the 1960s, it was mentioned that 'tribes' were shifted to ethnic or ethnic groups. The truth of Western philosophy is that the constitution of a nation-state cannot give equal place to all peoples, groups, and communities. Thus, the constitution transferred all the pre-determined 'tribes' or 'tribes' to 'ethnic groups. In light of Western philosophy, the hills and plains were also considered ethnic groups in these newly formed states. Yes, this language of Tribal, mostly scholars adopt.

Table 4 is, in fact, nothing but a historical construction of tribal architectural nomenclature, which is 50 of Bangladesh is referred to as ethnic groups; In India, 481 different ethnic groups are called tribals, and in Malaysia, 18 other ethnic groups are called orang Asli. Different countries have different names, but somewhere it is like a thread.

Table 5. Identification of Indigenous people in Asian Nations. Source: Authors' compilations

Country	Number of Indigenous Communities	Addressing Terminology
India	461	Tribal/Ethnics
Bangladesh	51 (54)	Small Ethnic Groups
Malaysia	18	Orang Asli/Aboriginal
China	55	Menu

INDIGENOUS LIQUIDATION: 'INHERITANCE METAPHYSICS' (DERRIDA) AND 'HISTORICAL ONTOLOGY' (FOUCAULT) AS ARGUMENTS FOR EXCLUSION

Every year, people flee to India in the two villages where we (first and second writers) work or live. Sometimes they are forced to sell their land. Sometimes the Government continues to occupy it under the "reserve forest scheme." Before 1975, for example, there were 1,200 Rakhain houses in the village, where now only 300 people with 600 families live; the rest are Bengalis (field's sound)

If you look at the history, you will know that 18 or all the ethnographers were coming because the census was conducted in 1900, laws were made for the tribals, and the protagonists were our Academic Ancestors and anthropologists. Let us give the example of the bay, Bangladesh; the settlers are still at the center of colonialism, flowing much like the *Falgu River*. So, 'critical approach is important.'

SOME MORE INNOCENT STATISTICS

If we look at the early ethnographic figures and recent ethnographic works, one has to be surprised (though not surprisingly); however, we are shocked to see that scholars blindly follow their academic ancestors in creating and constructing neo-liberal states. Let us relate this assumption to table 5.

Is Table 6 what we are seeing? Are these just a number? No matter what — today, the past, or the future? Whatever we say, sitting in an air-conditioned room or on television talk shows, these three tables (4, 5, 6) point fingers at our anthropologists—the reality of work related to indigenous people. The tables contain today's numbers or statistics and the time long ago. In other words, our research brings the 'genealogy of the work to the fore. Would anthropologists still say that ethnographic work does not require statistics? Let us look at the indigenous peoples' living standards within our country's geographical borders; let us put this in table 7.

Table 6. Influence of religion in hilly areas. Source: Tripura, S. B. (2008). Blaming Jhum, denying Jhumia: Challenges of indigenous peoples land rights in the Chittagong Hill Tracts (CHT) of Bangladesh: a case study on Chakma and Tripura (Master's thesis, University Tromsø), p. 90.

Religious group	Year of the census									
	1951		1961		1974		1981		1991	
	N	%	N	%	N	%	N	%	N	%
Buddhist	215,000	74.84	275681	71.59	337586	66.47	394321	52.46	425311	43.65
Hindu	40,984	14.47	47644	12.37	53373	10.51	70583	9.39	87806	9.01
Muslim	18070	6.29	43322	11.77	95633	18.83	25956	34.58	42995	44.12
Christiann	3745	1.30	10160	2.64	13272	2.61	18973	2.52	22206	2.28
Others	9475	3.30	6272	1.63	8050	1.58	8247	1.10	9168	0.94

Table 7. Some more innocent numbers. Source: Authors' Compilations

Elements	Hill People	Bangali Majority of Plainland
Santal	Poverty 59.9%	Rural Bangladesh 39.9%
Child Mortality	75 (in 000)	
	KhagraChari, 117, Bandarban, 35, Rangamati, 61	23.62
Primary Education	Hill people 79.5% (2006) 46.7 (2013)	89.2 (2006)58.6 (2013)

Let us clarify with one more; see figure 1, which gives a more comprehensive picture of the necessity of numbers in Ethnography.

Perhaps, the vital question is that what is the creed of research: Justice, Welfare, and peace. If so, a methodology is a science. Science contains philosophy. Philosophy is a study that seeks to discover all the basic principles related to science, art, and cosmology. Ethnography is if we treat a Science. Compared to technology, which is valuable, useless, or dangerous, it depends on the goals it serves; whether the technology is good or bad is not the matter; rather, its utility of it is important. To Aristotle, Al-Farabi, and Patanjali, science will be for the people; in converse, often said, by the 17th Century New Science, pure science is entirely value-free. Because it only discusses the faculty of our thinking about the world and how to improve it, knowledge itself defines it as 'good.' That being said, science is good, its purpose is positive, and welfare uses knowledge (see *Nichomachean Ethics*, books V and VI). A vital question is from the figure discussion above, where the Gap pertains? The gap is on Gnoseology—we go back to Aristotelian Gnoseology, which covers Episteme, Aesthesis, and Methods, and indeed more than Epistemology. Moreover, this has a good link with Medieval Arab and Ancient India. Therefore, we are thinking of Gnoseology instead of Epistemology, which we placed in figure 2.

Figure 1. A comparative picture of Hill Indigenous people and plain land.

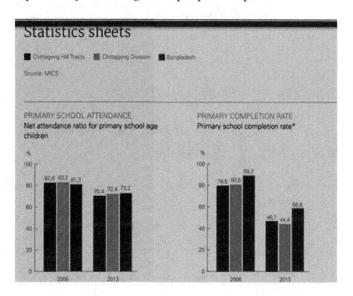

Suppose we adopt this in seeing the Reciprocal world conceivably. In that case, we will be justified Al-Biruni's Anthropological contribution, which is important for academic practice. By no means anthropology or Philosophy is commenced by Kant and Descartes. St. Augustine could be a political thinker, but he is more than that; the best term is 'The Philosopher of western philosophers' David Shills, however, said, "[a] useful case in point is the political theory of the early Christian writer St. Augustine, who, it is sometimes alleged, was not a political theorist at all. The grounds for this allegation, however, usually rest on a different notion of what is plausible; sometimes, it is said that Augustine appealed to revelation rather than reason, that he was unsystematic, or that his arguments were neither confirmable nor refutable by logic or fact." And hence, the Eastern and Arabic Gnoseology is absent. Suppose the Methodology is a part of HSP. In that case, a project broadly known as philosophical anthropology is not a German or Kantian (Clammer & Giri, 2013, p.1). Our Methodological scope is far arching than the New Science Era (figure 2). Let us end our introduction with another icon context. We all know what Charles Darwin's contribution is. Outside of biology, the impact on anthropology, particularly James Frazer, is fatal in botany. This man is called the Victorian Think Tank. Let us share astonishing information. Survival of the fittest and mutations have been around for almost 900 years. In science, the problem-value relationship is built around two aspects. The first is to answer a possible logical restructuring of science, which is biased values accessible. Second, suppose actual science or philosophy is a love of knowledge. In that case, scientific consciousness must proceed with some element of the moral degree. Scientists must have the right to moral control to prevent them from doing evil.

Figure 2. Equation of Gnoseology and Epistemology

$E \triangleq G$ (by Definition: theory of Knowledge),

so, one can say, $E \sim G$

But, in practice, $E = \{TK \text{ and } WP, C, CC\}$

Whereas, $G (E, T, P, TK, RP)$

So, $G \subseteq E$ is not a correct methodological position

But, $\underline{E \subseteq G}$,   (Epistemology is a part of Gnoselogy [Aristotlian Logic, Alfarabian Philosophy, and Saadian theory of Knowledge]

Notes: WP=Western Philosophy, E= Epistemology, RP=Reciprocity, TK= Tacit Knowledge (Karl Polany), T= Techne, C= Colonialism, CC=Christian Commonwealth, P= Phronesis (Wise use of knowledge, Aristotle in Eikerland, 2007, p. 348), G= Gnoseology

FUTURE RESEARCH DIRECTIONS

We are going to say: What are we going to look at the Indigenous and marginalized people, only numbers or beyond? We know by now that Ethnomathematics.[2] Data is the one element we found in the Rakhain communities of Bangladesh; however, globally[3] as a good number of texts already appeared, and regionally[4] And the other one is *Ethnogeometry*, a number of scholars[5] have appeared with valuable texts since 1999; however, we here define and adopt it as a separate tool of research. Because it is more than Ethnmathematcis. For instance, we see when the "Farmers carrying geometrical shape in lay-outing the field to get the maximum sunlight exposure,"[6] Moreover, our field visit with the Buddhist people, who adopt various medicinal pants with their Bodily geometry, directly benefits the community. Since ancient Egyptians, everywhere spatial geometry has been in the practice of daily life. "Most cultures display considerable geometric understanding through their manufactured products, whether these are craftwork, buildings, weapons, utensils, or decorations.[7] Furthermore, in concurrent, we adopt the root of Geometry.[8] We thus define Ethnogeometry, almost following the master of Ethnomathematics, Ubiratan D'Ambrosio (2007), is

Ethno=People+ (Geometry = spatial sensing) + Sanskrit roots as Jyamiti and Para = Peoples' spatial sensing.

Figure 3. An Ethnogeometry and Healing of Buddhist cosmos

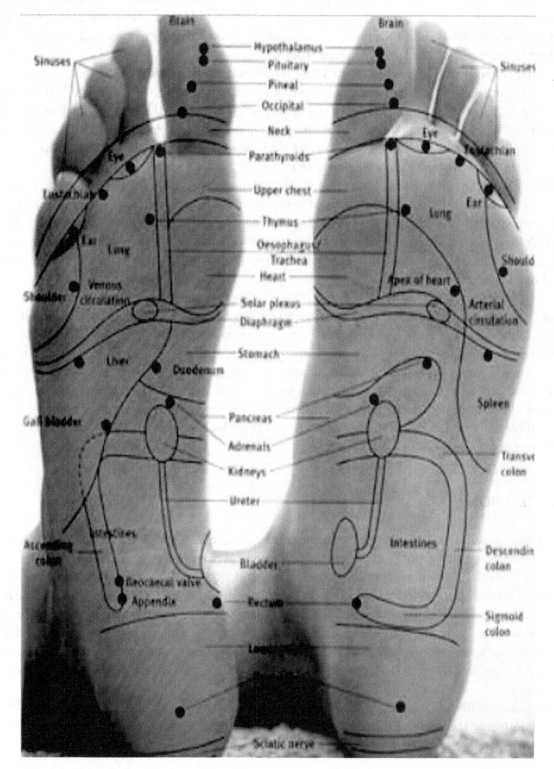

If so, then it is pertinent for us to realize that Ethnogeometry is a concomitant perspective to practice knowledge which, as we said, should be on the tenor of welfare and justice. Let us show an example of Ethnogeometry of the Buddhist Rakhain people, which they use for healing purposes and a combination of Plant-based medical knowledge and Ethnogeometry,

We recommend that we need to follow Indigenous Gnoseology will bring the Ethnomathematical aspect of communities for establishing peace and justice (D'Ambrosio, 2007), a bridge between East and West.[9]. The government and the donor community write down something interesting that has been happening for almost a century, everyone has been saying. It is going on in the academic world. Are these people getting any benefit from all these scholarly words? Or will we keep that question with the 'incest taboo'? We see our faces in the mirror of IG.

Linda Smith, Shawn Wilson, and Gregory Cajete, all concerned with de-democratic practices of interface, knowledge, language, and culture, are raising voices for the people. This process will challenge Western ontology, Western axiology in general, ethical guidance, and presentation. It is not a complete methodology, and the whole methodology is omnipresent. Quantitative and quantitative, two types of data, are the work of Indigenous methodology to understand and hold them separately. We humbly suggest Ethnomathematics is important for understanding culture and Ethnogeometry.

Along with the self-realization of ideas, as if we are improving the masses, such ethnographic work is our purpose. We emphasize that this steering of research perspectives and methodologies, which were central to the quantitative methods of establishing Western colonies, should be axiological aware. The standpoint is central to the indigenous quantitative approach. However, it is exclusively necessary and applicable to address the Ethnomathematical and Ethnogeometrical aspects of the community in all studies. Indigenous methodologists and non-indigenous researchers are very much aware of this social position. We also consider being aware. Because we all know, read, and read, these are basically 'Epistemic Violence' (see Gayatri Spivak, Syed Hussein Alatas, Walter Mignolo, Farid Alatas, and Linda Smith's philosophical position).

CONCLUSION

With sophisticated thinking, we have seen that the article, as mentioned earlier, is not relative but indicates bias, elsewhere we stated more that we need to be Reciprocal (Chowdhury et al., 2022a), regardless of digital or physical (Chowdhury et al., 2022b, 2022c; Roy & Hamidi, 2022); they legitimize and reproduce one-sided relationships, no matter how strongly they claim to be 'indigenous or decolonial. These are, in a word, as silent as the classical 'ethnic' or ethnic work. It is also argued that the Indigenous standpoint theory is a "native perspective" similar to the classical ethnographic position. They reinforced that current research, such as Shan Wilson's work, has "over-simplified" indigenous sciences, stating that research cannot be a program. The term rejects scientific values, detrimental to ethnographic research philosophy and scientific knowledge.

According to our discussion, the position of this methodology that we are talking about may find ways to influence the values of the colonized researchers, the successive levels of knowledge, and the quantitative research in a better and better way for indigenous issues, communities, and people.

REFERENCES

Allen, B. C. (1905). *Assam district gazetteers: Sylhet* (Vol. 2). Printed at the Baptist Mission Press.

Ambagudia, J., & Xaxa, V. (Eds.). (2020). *Handbook of Tribal Politics in India*. Sage Publications Pvt. Limited.

Aristotle. (1966). *Metaphysics*. Indiana University Press.

Asad. (1994). Ethnographic representation, statistics, and modern power. *Social Research*, 55-88.

Ballonoff, P. A. (2011). *Mathematical foundations of social anthropology*. Walter de Gruyter.

Bangladesh Bureau of Statistics. (2011). *Population and housing census 2011*. Government of the Peoples Republic of Bangladesh.

Beller, S., Bender, A., Chrisomalis, S., Jordan, F. M., Overmann, K. A., Saxe, G. B., & Schlimm, D. (2018). *The cultural challenge in mathematical cognition*. HTTP/ psycharchives.org/bit-stream/20.500.12034/1299/1/jnc.v4i2.137.pdf

Boas, F. (1927). Anthropology and statistics. The Social Sciences and Their Interrelations, 1.

Boyce, A. J. (1964). *The value of some methods of numerical taxonomy regarding hominoid classification. In Phenetic and phylogenetic classification*. Systematics Association.

Burton, M. L. (1973). Mathematical anthropology. *Annual Review of Anthropology*, *2*(1), 189–199. doi:10.1146/annurev.an.02.100173.001201

Carroll, S. R., Rodriguez-Lonebear, D., & Martinez, A. (2019). *Indigenous Data Governance: Strategies from United States Native Nations*. Academic Press.

Chamberlain, A. F. (1894). Anthropology in universities and colleges. *The Pedagogical Seminary*, *3*(1), 48–60. doi:10.1080/08919402.1894.10534796

Chibnik, M. (1985). The use of statistics in sociocultural anthropology. *Annual Review of Anthropology*, *14*(1), 135–157. doi:10.1146/annurev.an.14.100185.001031

Chowdhury, J.S., Roy, P., Wahab, H,. & Saad, R. (2021). Quantitative Ethnography in Indigenous Research Methodology. Aditya Anik Prakashani.

Chowdhury, J. S., & Jakaria. (2006). Contested Ethnic Identity, Muslim Manipuries in Bangladesh. In *Anthropology on the Move: Contextualizing Culture Studies in Bangladesh*. Department of Anthropology, The University of Dhaka.

Chowdhury, J. S., Abd Wahab, H., Saad, M. R. M., & Rakhine, M. A. L. (2022b). How Digital Ethnography Can Be a Tool to Indigenous Gnoseology: Seeing With the Rakhain Community of Bangladesh. In *Practices, Challenges, and Prospects of Digital Ethnography as a Multidisciplinary Method* (pp. 94–108). IGI Global. doi:10.4018/978-1-6684-4190-9.ch007

Chowdhury, J. S., Abd Wahab, H., Saad, M. R. M., & Rakhine, M. A. L. (2022c). Are We More Social or Individual by the Digital Ethnographic Tool? A Reflection With the Rakhain Community of Bangladesh. In Practices, Challenges, and Prospects of Digital Ethnography as a Multidisciplinary Method (pp. 78-93). IGI Global.

Chowdhury, J. S., Abd Wahab, H., Saad, M. R. M., Reza, H., & Ahmed, M. M. (2022a). *Reciprocity and Its Practice in Social Research*. IGI Global. doi:10.4018/978-1-7998-9602-9

Chowdhury, M. S. (Ed.). (2014). *Survival Under Threat: Human Rights Situation of Indigenous Peoples in Bangladesh*. Asia Indigenous People Pact.

Clammer, J., & Giri, A. K. (2013). *Philosophy and Anthropology in Dialogues and Conversations. In Philosophy and Anthropology. Border Crossing and Transformations*. Anthem Press.

Clements, F. E., Schenck, S. M., & Brown, T. K. (1926). A new objective method for showing unique relationships. *American Anthropologist*, *28*(4), 585–604. doi:10.1525/aa.1926.28.4.02a00010

Crisp, R. (Ed.). (2014). *Aristotle: Nicomachean Ethics*. Cambridge University Press.

Culross, J. (1882). *William Carey*. AC Armstrong and Son.

Driver, H. E., & Kroeber, A. L. (1932). Quantitative expression of cultural relationships (Vol. 31, No. 4). University of California Press.

Duarte, M. E., Vigil-Hayes, M., Littletree, S., & Belarde-Lewis, M. (2020). Of Course, Data Can Never Fully Represent Reality. *Human Biology*, *91*(3), 163–178. doi:10.13110/humanbiology.91.3.03 PMID:32549034

Endicott, K. (Ed.). (2015). *Malaysia's original people: The Orang Asli's past, present, and future*. NUS Press.

Gluckman, M. (1961). Ethnographic data in British social anthropology. *The Sociological Review*, *9*(1), 5–17. doi:10.1111/j.1467-954X.1961.tb01082.x

Herskovits, M. J. (1939). Anthropology and economics. *Journal of Social Philosophy*, *5*, 127.

Hoffmann, H. (1969). Mathematical anthropology. *Biennial Review of Anthropology*, *6*, 41-79.

Hutchinson, R. H. S. (1909). *Eastern Bengal and Assam District Gazetteer*. Chittagong Hill Tracts.

Jamison, P. L. (1991). Anthropology and statistics? *Revista de Antropologia*, *17*(1-4), 191–199.

Kay, P. (Ed.). (1971). *Explorations in mathematical anthropology*. MIT Press.

Kluckhohn, C. (1939). On specific recent applications of association coefficients to ethnological data. *American Anthropologist*, *41*(3), 345–377. doi:10.1525/aa.1939.41.3.02a00010

Kotliar, D. M. (2020). Data orientalism: On the algorithmic construction of the non-Western other. *Theory and Society*, *49*(5), 919–939. doi:10.100711186-020-09404-2

Kukutai, T., & Taylor, J. (2016). *Indigenous data sovereignty: Toward an agenda*. Anu Press. doi:10.22459/CAEPR38.11.2016

Kukutai, T., & Walter, M. (2017). Indigenous Statistics. Handbook of Research Methods in Health Social Sciences, 1-16.

Lawrence, B. B. (2021). Al-Biruni: Against the Grain 2014. In The Bruce B. Lawrence Reader (pp. 99-112). Duke University Press.

Loriaux, M. (1992). The realists and Saint Augustine: Skepticism, psychology, and moral action in international relations thought. *International Studies Quarterly, 36*(4), 401–420. doi:10.2307/2600732

Macer, D. R. (1998). *Bioethics is a love of life*. Eubios Ethics Institute.

Malinowski, B. (2001). *Coral Gardens and Their Magic: A Study of the Methods of Tilling the Soil and Agricultural Rites in the Trobriand Islands. In The language of magic and gardening. II* (Vol. 8). Psychology Press.

Moreton-Robinson, A. (2009). Imagining the good indigenous citizen: Race war and the pathology of patriarchal white sovereignty. *Cultural Studies Review, 15*(2), 61–79.

Morgan, E. M. (1928). *The Social Sciences and Their Interrelations*. Heinonline.org

Partington, J. E. (1891). Ethnographic Album of the Pacific Islands. *The Journal of the Anthropological Institute of Great Britain and Ireland, 20*, 292-294.

Pines, S., & Gelblum, T. (1966). Al-Biruni's Arabic Version of Bulletin of the School of Oriental and African Studies. *University of London, 29*(2), 302–325.

Raitapuro, M., & Bal, E. (2016). 'Talking about mobility': Garos aspiring migration and mobility in an 'insecure' Bangladesh. *Competitive Preferences and Ethnicity: Experimental Evidence from Bangladesh.*

Read, D. W. (2019). *Mathematical Anthropology*. Oxford University Press. doi:10.1093/obo/9780199766567-0215

Rizvi, S. N. H. (Ed.). (1970). *East Pakistan District Gazetteers: Sylhet* (Vol. 3). East Pakistan Government Press.

Rogers, D. (2015). *A critical analysis of the history of Southern Baptist approaches to interdenominational cooperation in international missions*. Southeastern Baptist Theological Seminary.

Roy, P., Chowdhury, J. S., Abd Wahab, H., & Saad, R. B. M. (2022). Ethnic Tension of the Bangladeshi Santal: A CDA of the Constitutional Provision. In Handbook of Research on Ethnic, Racial, and Religious Conflicts and Their Impact on State and Social Security (pp. 208-226). IGI Global. doi:10.4018/978-1-7998-8911-3.ch013

Roy, P. K., & Hamidi, M. (2022). Digital Ethnography: What We Have Done and What We Need to Do in the New Normal. In Practices, Challenges, and Prospects of Digital Ethnography as a Multidisciplinary Method (pp. 278-287). IGI Global.

Roy, P. K., Hamidi, M., & Roy, S. (2022). Internet as a Field: An Analysis of the Santal Online Communities. In *Practices, Challenges, and Prospects of Digital Ethnography as a Multidisciplinary Method* (pp. 124–137). IGI Global. doi:10.4018/978-1-6684-4190-9.ch009

Sarker, M. A. R., Khan, N. A., & Musarrat, K. M. (2017). Livelihood and vulnerability of the Santals community in Bangladesh. *The Malaysian Journal of Social Administration, 12*(1), 38–55. doi:10.22452/mjsa.vol12no1.2

Sen, A. K., Bridge, T. W., Craven, J. A., Depree, G. C., Hakim, K. S. S. A., Hallett, M. G., . . . Reid, J. (2018). Tribes as Indigenous People of India. In Indigeneity, Landscape and History: Adivasi Self-fashioning in India (Vol. 2, No. 16, pp. ix-x). Allahabad: University of London.

Senft, G. (2007). Bronislaw Malinowski and linguistic pragmatics. *Lodz Papers in Pragmatics, 3*(1), 79–96.

Silverstein, B. (2020). *The Social Lives of Numbers: Statistics, Reform and the Remaking of Rural Life in Turkey.* Springer Nature. doi:10.1007/978-981-15-9196-9

Tylor, E. B. (1889). On a method of investigating the development of institutions; applied to laws of marriage and descent. *Journal of the Anthropological Institute of Great Britain and Ireland, 18*, 245–272. doi:10.2307/2842423

Walter, M. (2005). Using the power of the data within Indigenous research practice. *Australian Aboriginal Studies*, (2), 27.

Walter, M. (2016). Data politics and Indigenous representation in Australian statistics. *Indigenous data sovereignty: Toward an agenda*, 79-98.

Walter, M. (2018). The voice of Indigenous data: Beyond the markers of disadvantage. *Griffith Review, 60*, 256–263.

Walter, M., & Andersen, C. (2013). *Indigenous Statistics: A quantitative research methodology.* Left Coast Press.

Walter, M., Kukutai, T., & Carroll, S. R. (2020). *Rodriguez-Lone bear, D.* Indigenous Data Sovereignty and Policy.

Walter, M., & Suina, M. (2019). Indigenous data, indigenous methodologies, and indigenous data sovereignty. *International Journal of Social Research Methodology, 22*(3), 233–243. doi:10.1080/136455 79.2018.1531228

Walter, M. M. (2010). The politics of the data: How the Australian statistical Indigene is constructed. *International Journal of Critical Indigenous Studies, 3*(2), 45–56. doi:10.5204/ijcis.v3i2.51

Wilks, J., Kennedy, G., Drew, N., & Wilson, K. (2018). Indigenous data sovereignty in higher education: Towards a decolonized data quality framework. *Australian Universities' Review, 60*(2), 4-14.

Wilson, T. (1890). Anthropology at the Paris Exposition in 1889. Report of the United States National Museum for the year ending June 30, 1890, p.642.

Wolfe, A. (1989). *Whose keeper? Social science and moral obligation.* Univ of California Press.

ADDITIONAL READING

Chilisa, B. (2019). *Indigenous research methodologies.* Sage Publications.

Chowdhury, J. S., Abd Wahab, H., Saad, M. R. M., Roy, P., Hamidi, M., & Ahmad, M. M. (2021). Ubuntu Philosophy: 'I Am Because We Are'–A Road to 'Individualism' to Global Solidarity. In Handbook of Research on the Impact of COVID-19 on Marginalized Populations and Support for the Future (pp. 361-381). IGI Global.

Chowdhury. (2022a). *Reciprocity and Its Practice in Social Science.* IGI Global.

Chowdhury. (2022b). A Textbook on Quantitative Ethnography in Decolonial and Indigenous Research. In *Methodology: An Asian Reflection.* Cambridge Scholars Press.

Wilson, S. (2001). What is an indigenous research methodology? *Canadian Journal of Native Education, 25*(2), 175–179.

KEY TERMS AND DEFINITIONS

Disciple of Discipline: Disciple of Discipline, why do we throw our obfuscated knowledge to a local classroom or a global reader? Why am I going to trample on your academic freedom through epistemic violence in the name of academic responsibility? Before adopting and delivering a concept in class or engaging in a conversation with someone, I should, at the very least, understand its origins and journey. I can see my path for myself and my audience with complete comprehension. According to our experience (Jahid, Sanjay, and Primal), teachers can present themselves as experts in front of students. We are aware that reading this book may embarrass you with the research methodology you have read, but we also know that it will provide some food for thought. We will go over this in detail in chapters two and four. On the other hand, being a *Disciple of Discipline* is a rooted concern in anti-colonial research, especially when we sit in Indigenous mountains. As previously stated, we believe in philosophical diffusions, and we do not want Malinowski's ideology to be used to serve colonial administration or linear development.

Indigenous Gnoseology: Indigenous Gnoseology is a philosophical amalgamation of west-east, ancient-modern, conceptuality, and practicality. As previously stated, we require a stand for and by the people. IG is a new theory that covers the Quali-Quanti dynamics in a descent nascent manner. We believe that after providing a brief overview of IG, we will examine the four philosophical foundations of this concept. Gnoseology, according to the Cambridge Dictionary, is " a system of ways of doing, teaching, or studying something" (Cambridge Dictionary). According to the Oxford Dictionary, a methodology is "a set of methods and principles used to carry out a specific task" (Wehmeir, 2007, 963). In practice, Indigenous Gnoseology (hereafter IG). IG, which we generate in accordance with the original spirit of knowledge and philosophy of Aristotle's Nicomachean Ethics (Marcelo, 2020; Zuppolini, 2021), Saadia Gaon's theory of knowledge (Efros 1942), and Buddhist Moral Ethics (Lamirin et al., 2021; Payne, 2020; Sinnett, 1884) that resembles the Rakhain Indigenous Standpoint (Marcelo, 2020; Zuppolini, 20? (Nakata, Foley, Wilson, Smith). As previously stated, our motivation for developing IG stemmed from four philosophical roots.

Indigenous/Ethnic Liquidation: Every year, people flee to India in the two villages where we (first and second writers) work or live. Sometimes they are forced to sell their land. Sometimes the Government continues to occupy it under the "reserve forest scheme." Before 1975, for example, there were most of the Rakhain in the village, where now they were minority people; the rest are Bengalis. Where once upon the Indigenous people were the majority in number, now they are in the minority and deprived of all types of state privileges due to ethnic/ Indigenous liquidation, which is a process of becoming less important by numbering. Let us give the example of the bay, Bangladesh; the settlers are still at the center of colonialism, flowing much like the Falgu River. So, 'critical approach is the important.'

Ubuntu: Although the widely accepted definition of Ubuntu is *I am because we are*, a variety of meanings are visible (Gade, 2012; Ewuoso & Hall, 2019; Ewuoso, 2020; Tagwirei, 2020; Sibanda, 2019) in the western text. Therefore, Desmond Tutu said that Ubuntu is very difficult to render into a Western language (Tutu, 1998). Since 1928, Albert Vitor Murray, Nelson Mandela, and Desmond

Tutu have prolifically adopted this term, as we indicated, in every possible sphere of African Land, in state policy, foreign diplomacy, and even in school. Let us take some definitions of Ubuntu; Richard Bolden (Bolden, 2014, p. 4) says, *The concept of Ubuntu is an alternative to individualistic and utilitarian philosophies that tend to dominate in the West. It is a Zulu/Xhosa word, with parallels in many other African languages. It is most directly translated into English as 'humanness'. Its sense, however, is perhaps best conveyed by the Nguni expression 'umuntungumuntungabantu,' which means a person is a person through other people.* Arch Bishop Desmond Tutu in *No Future without Forgiveness* said, Ubuntu is *our humanity is caught up in that of all others; we are human because we belong, we are made for community, togetherness, family, to exist in a delicate network of interdependence....no one can be human alone" (Tutu 1999,p.145).*

ENDNOTES

[1]   Burton, M. L. (1973). Mathematical anthropology. *Annual Review of Anthropology*, *2*, 189-199.

[2]   "Mathematics is adapted and given a place as "scholarly practical" mathematics, which we will call, from now on, "academic mathematics," i.e., the mathematics which is taught and learned in the schools. In contrast, we will call ethnomathematics— the mathematics practiced among identifiable cultural groups, such as national-tribal societies, labor groups, children of a certain age bracket, professional classes, and so on. Its identity depends largely on the focus of interest, motivation, and certain codes and jargon that do not belong to the realm of academic mathematics. (see d'Ambrosio, 1985,p.45, d'Ambrosio, U. (1985). Ethnomathematics and its place in the history and pedagogy of mathematics. *For learning mathematics*, *5*(1), 44-48.

[3]   D'Ambrosio, U. (2001). *Mathematics across cultures: The history of non-Western mathematics* (Vol. 2). Springer Science & Business Media. And Helaine Selin, (2001, Vol. 1, Mathematics Across Cultures: The History of Non-Western Mathematics,); D'Ambrosio, U. (2007). Peace, social justice, and ethnomathematics. *The Montana Mathematics Enthusiast, Monograph*, *1*(2007), 25-34.

[4]   From Indonesian context, Nursyahidah, F. A., Ulil, I., & Saputro, B. A. (2020, March). Local Wisdom: Mathematics Among Angler's Activities. In *2nd International Conference on Education and Social Science Research (ICESRE 2019), Indonesia.* For Nigeria, see James, A. T., & Tertsea, J. (2021). The Effect of Ethno-mathematics on Junior Secondary School Students' Achievement and Retention in Geometry in Benue State, Nigeria: A Corona Virus Pandemic Case Study. *International Journal of Research and Innovation in Applied Science (IJRIAS)*, *6*(4), 95-100. ; for Zimbabwe, see Chiwa, F. (2013). *Views of Ordinary Level Mathematics teachers on the inclusion of Ehno Mathematics in teaching form 4 Geometrical Transformation; a case of Mufakose Mhuriimwe School* (Doctoral dissertation, BUSE). Spagnolo, F. (2002). History and Ethno-Mathematics in the Interpretation of the process of learning/teaching. *University of Hong Kong*, *13*, 20-25; Prahmana, R. C. I., Yunianto, W., Rosa, M., & Orey, D. C. (2021). Ethnomathematics:" Pranatamangsa" System and the Birth-Death Ceremonial in Yogyakarta. *Journal on Mathematics Education*, *12*(1), 93-112; Herawaty, D., Khrisnawati, D., Widada, W., Mundana, P., & Anggoro, A. F. D. (2020, February). The cognitive process of students in understanding the parallels axiom through ethnomathematics learning. In *Journal of Physics: Conference Series* (Vol. 1470, No. 1, p. 012077). IOP Publishing; Lubis, A. N. M. T., Widada, W., Herawaty, D., Nugroho, K. U. Z., & Anggoro, A. F. D. (2021). The ability to solve mathematical problems through realistic mathematics learning based on ethnomathematics. In *Journal of Physics: Conference Series* (Vol. 1731, No. 1, p. 012050). IOP Publishing.

5   Gerdes, P. (1999). *Geometry from Africa: Mathematical and educational explorations* (Vol. 10). Cambridge University Press.

6   Nursyahidah, F. A., Ulil, I., & Saputro, B. A. (2020, March). Local Wisdom: Mathematics Among Angler's Activities. In *2nd International Conference on Education and Social Science Research (ICESRE 2019), Indonesia*.

7   Sizer, W. S. (2000). Traditional mathematics in Pacific cultures. In *Mathematics Across Cultures* (pp. 253-287). Springer, Dordrecht, p.260.

8   The root meaning of the word self is to measure, and geometry in ancient India came to be known by the name sulba or sulva. Sulbasutras mean the geometric principles of geometry (see Puttaswamy, T. K. (2000). The Mathematical Accomplishments of Ancient Indian Mathematicians. In *Mathematics Across Cultures* (pp. 409-422). Springer, Dordrecht, p. 410.

9   This is also true for Asia's artistic and cultural borrowings prior to 1500. They, too, were often unconscious, and even when they were not, they were regarded as embellishments or decorations rather than in any way a challenge to traditional themes. For example, the incorporation into the Christian calendar and the corpus of edifying literature stories about Saints Baarlam and Josephat, derived as they were from stories of the life of Buddha, resulted not in a Buddhist challenge to the Christian faith but simply in the addition of two new saints to the growing Christian pantheon, Selin, (2000, p.26).

Section 46
Recommender Systems

Content and Context–Aware Recommender Systems for Business

Prageet Aeron

(iD) https://orcid.org/0000-0003-3957-5912

Management Development Institute, Gurgaon, India

INTRODUCTION

Author has already emphasized upon the importance of recommender systems for today's firms irrespective of domain such as grocery, apparel, electronic goods, entertainment services etc in the first part of this series of two articles. Today most retailing companies have proprietary recommender systems that are often highly customized and already into the next generation in terms of bringing together many different algorithms together. Today's recommender systems are no longer standalone proof of concept systems trying to gain credibility but rather are considered to be a major source of revenue booster for the organizations. Popular literature estimate suggests that almost 70% of content consumed online by Netflix viewers is through personal recommendations and according to Gomez-Uribe & Hunt (2016) they could save almost USD 1.2 billion by avoiding cancellations. Similarly, popular literature reports almost 30-35% revenues of Amazon originating through its recommender systems. It is now well established that these systems help in better customer engagement, upselling, customer retention and in boosting revenues.

Author started his discussion with basic collaborative systems and its variants in the earlier chapter and also emphasized on the growing need and logic (Aggarwal, 2015) for combining various methods. This second chapter of the series takes the on from exactly the point where we left off. Author shall start his discussion from content based systems and its variants, then move on to knowledge based systems and ensembles, subsequently author discusses context aware systems and evaluation methods for recommender systems. Finally, the author concludes the chapter with a brief discussion and emphasizing on the need for more work on recent topics in the field.

BACKGROUND

Content Based Recommender Systems

As the name rightly suggests the content-based recommender systems focus on data from users' own ratings as well as attributes or features of the product to make recommendations. As a result, these systems are inherently incapable of identifying novel recommendations and are likely to be recommended products/services more in line with past usage only. By extension of the same argument, content based systems are more appropriate for systems with detailed attribute information irrespective of the knowledge representation available for describing the attributes. Since structured data representation can be considered as subsets of unstructured data representation therefore the analysis of unstructured data can

DOI: 10.4018/978-1-7998-9220-5.ch165

be considered as more generic. Therefore, we look at the analysis of unstructured data only. Natural language processing/text processing and regression models usually form the primary workhorse of content based systems. Like any other recommender systems three parts of content based system comprise, pre-processing of raw data, learning model implementation and prediction utility.

Pre-processing

This involves transforming either text or any other data into vector-based attributes. Usually this is a domain and context centric activity which may differ as per the requirements. Transforming of text based structure into a term-document matrix or identifying most appropriate vector attributes based on a combination of term frequency and inverse document frequency (TF_IDF) is now well understood and this is just one of the ways to deal with basic data at hand. Use of stop-word removal is akin to feature selection and use of TF_IDF is an example of feature weighing in the above setting. However, based on the context methods are likely to change (Gini index or entropy based methods). Further, in addition to vector space representation there may be a need for multi-dimensional attributes from structured data which may include price, and other formal characteristics.

Learning

Learning models will require a training data dsr and testing data dse. These may represent attributes together with user rating as class or weight as per the availability. The training and testing data may even be pure documents or music albums depending upon the context. The model trained on dsr are then tested on dse which can be considered unlabeled and therefore the problem translates into a simple regression or classification kind of problem. Using any similarity metric such as cosine or Jaccard etc. k-similar documents from dse corresponding to each dsr can be identified and average rating assigned to each. As is evident for each example or each user in dsr the process operates at an individual level making it rather complex and computationally intensive. As an improvement to the above process a k-means clustering approach can be used to lower the computational effort. As a part of this approach each independent rating from training set dsr the entire dsr is clustered into a group of x. Therefore, for y independent ratings in dsr this leads to x*y groups to work with which is much lesser as compared to total number in dsr. This leads to reformulation of the vector-space for documents by aggregation across the x documents as the new vector-space representation. Subsequently, any target row of training data-set or document from dsr could be taken up and any k<x closest items could be identified (Aggarwal, 2015; Zhai & Aggarwal, 2012). In addition to above Naive Bayes methods may be applied to learning very effectively with appropriate smoothing methods (Laplace or others) taking care of rare elements or events with zero probability. Also rule-based classifiers have also been successfully utilized in certain cases. Next author focuses on a regression based method for learning in the context of content based recommender systems.

Regression Method

Depending upon the target variable in the data at hand ordinary regression, logistic regression, probit or multinomial probit or ordered probit or any other variant may be successfully used for learning. Here we discuss only the ordinary regression method together with regularization. Consider dsr as the d x t matrix, with documents or datarows and t terms or words as per the context. Assume $\overline{y}, \overline{W}$ to be the column vector for each datarow corresponding to dsr and weight row vector for each of the "t" terms in the matrix. Therefore, the equations for the above can be written as,

$$\overline{y} = dsr * \overline{W} \tag{1}$$

$$Minimize\ J = \left(dsr * \overline{W}^T - \lambda\left(\overline{W}\right)^2\right)\left(dsr^T dsr + \lambda I\right)\overline{W}^T \tag{2}$$

$$= dsr^T \overline{y}\overline{W}^T = \left(dsr^T dsr + \lambda I\right)^{-1} dsr^T \overline{y} \tag{3}$$

Above expression gives the weight vector for the terms associated with the dsr matrix. Using the above weight vector, any unlabeled example from dse may be processed. Content based methods discussed above are often useful for interpretation of the final model so obtained and can be more useful in the scenario of new items being added to the mix as compared to collaboration based models, however, on the flip side they are not suitable if a new user is added to the data set.

KNOWLEDGE BASED RECOMMENDER SYSTEMS

Some objects/items are different in nature so as to be difficult to capture in terms of hard ratings or people are very specific about their requirements or have time varying aspects such as mobile phones, laptop machines or cars etc. Such items may not be bought regularly like vehicles, machines etc so have low dependence on past purchase for an individual. Two kinds of knowledge based recommender systems have been identified and curiously they do share their basic characteristics with expert systems and decision support systems of the 1990s. The two kinds of such systems are constraint based systems and case based systems. A very prominent part of such systems is the interaction or front-end which enables them to converse with the client. This interaction may be either search-based system or navigational or critique based system or generic conversational system. Author briefly overviews the two kinds of knowledge based recommender systems below.

Constraint Based Systems

Constraint based recommender systems allow the users to specify hard constraints which are directly linked to the attributes of the product. However, in addition to the constraints the systems are equipped with a knowledge engine i.e. a set of rules connecting the attributes to the requirements of the customer as not all customers may be equally knowledgeable about the domain or may search based on non-standard attributes. A typical example of a constraint in an investment scenario could be the age of the customer connected to the risk profile or in other words, higher age => lower risk portfolio should be the norm. So even if the customer is not aware an internal domain specific constraint ensures certain product specifications to be shown to the customer based on non-product attributes or demographic attributes or any other inputs from the prospective customer. Another example could be compatibility constraints from the vehicle especially car or two wheeler industry. So a consumer by default has to search in more mileage or more style or more power groups and the system informs the customer that higher mileage with higher power may be incompatible. Such rules are built overtime by either domain specific or subject matter experts or through the mining of historical data from the industry or sector. Some of these constraints and corresponding choice of attributes may have a direct bearing on the price of the product. Therefore, inputs to a system may include user characteristics that may impact product, specific and explicit user requirements, knowledge engine to resolve compatibility issues, knowledge engine to filter user-specific requirements and connect them to appropriate products and lastly a comprehensive user catalog with detailed attributes in relational knowledge representation. Ultimately the inputs from the user are collected, transformed into a query that is executed on the database to throw out the most relevant matches from the system. The information retrieval may be further augmented by ranking the various constraint satisficing options for better utilization at the consumer end. The interaction between the consumer and the system is iterative, usually on a web based platform seeking standard inputs from the customer. The customer may choose to input each variable or certain specific ones. Based on choice when a variable is not chosen, the system identifies a default value which again is based on historic data or subject matter expert view point. These default values are subject to change based on change of mapping between attributes and products and therefore are evolving and can be identified as key elements that impact the quality of the overall solution at times. Nevertheless, if the user so decides, the system can usually guide the user in choosing an appropriate value for the attribute of interest.

Presentation of the results based on explainable ranking is a gold standard and involves building a weighted utility function. Assuming n items P(p1,p2,p3...pn) be the vector of attributes of the matched product, with a dimension of n, w_i be the weight associated with each attribute of the utility vector, and the contribution of each attribute may be captured as fi(pi), then utilizing the superposition principle, the utility may be given by,

$$U\left(\bar{P}\right) = \sum_{i=1}^{n} w_i f_i \left(p_j\right) \tag{4}$$

The actual estimates of weights, function fi(pi) etc are all determined by subject matter experts or through trial and error or utilizing regression models on sample units or through conjoint analysis. At times the results may either be too large or empty. In either case existing constraints need to be modified, needless to say in case of no results constraints need relaxation and usually in case of large result sets additional relevant constraints need to be introduced into the system by the user. Both relaxation and addition of constraints is an important topic of further research with many sophisticated methods suggested by scholars, refer (Felfernig, Friedrich, Jannach & Stumpner, 2004; Jannach, 2006a; Jannach, 2006b; Mahmood & Ricci, 2009; McSherry, 2004).

Case-Based Recommender System

Unlike constraint based recommender systems case based recommender systems cannot incorporate hard constraints but are designed to retrieve data based on similarity metrics. The case based recommender system depends on critiquing the present solution for resolution of the ultimate answer to the query and this search or rather interactive exploration of the item space has been called critiquing. Therefore, similarity metric and critiquing system are the two most important design parameters of such a system. Consider a product which is given by d attributes. We further consider two products Y and T, with both specified over "s" of the overall "d" (s<d) attributes. Then the form of similarity function as well as the similarity function between Y and target T may be defined as,

$$f\left(T,Y\right) = \frac{\sum_{i \in s}\left(w_i\, Similarity\left(t_i, y_i\right)\right)}{\sum_{i \in s} w_i} \tag{5a}$$

C

$$Similarity\left(t_i, y_i\right) = 1 - \frac{\left|t_i - y_i\right|}{max_i - min_i} \tag{5b}$$

In addition to the above similarity metric may add a factor for symmetric or asymmetric attributes. For example, certain products such as microprocessors may specify cycle speed as 2.4 GHz and values above 2.4 GHz are likely to be acceptable on the higher side whereas not acceptable on the lower side. On the contrary, price as an attribute is likely to be preferred on the negative side. Therefore, one could augment the similarity function with reward factor to take care of asymmetric products.

$$Similarity\left(t_i, y_i\right) = 1 - \frac{\left|t_i - y_i\right|}{max_i - min_i} + \alpha_i I\left(y_i > t_i\right)\frac{\left|t_i - y_i\right|}{max_i - min_i} \tag{6}$$

$$Similarity\left(t_i, y_i\right) = 1 - \frac{\left|t_i - y_i\right|}{max_i - min_i} + \alpha_i I\left(y_i < t_i\right)\frac{\left|t_i - y_i\right|}{max_i - min_i} \tag{7}$$

In the above expression only one of the equations is required depending upon the case of positive variance or negative variance and since I is an indicator function, the reward function shall be zero otherwise. The value of alpha parameter lies between (0,1) and so one needs to be careful in interpreting the similarity metric. As can be seen the similarity increases with distance in case of positive values of alpha. However, this case does not consider categorical variables in the vector attributes which is likely to further complicate the analysis and there may be a need to redefine a suitable notion of similarity as compared to use above.

Critiquing methods are based on the idea that at times it is simpler for users to identify what they seek after they have seen the early results of query and their views can be captured through semantics such as roomier, better, airier more power etc. depending upon the context of data being searched. Based on this three different critiquing way have been studied and they are single direction or simple critiques, compound critiques and dynamic critiques. Simple critique deals with the case of a single attribute being modified in a specific direction (increase or decrease) while keeping the other attributes relatively unchanged. Simple in intent this may lead to many iterative loops before converging and even then may pose compatibility constraints as different attributes may not always operate simultaneously in the same region. This problem is removed by the use of compound critiques which involve modifying multiple attributes. However, only subject matter experts can fully define the impact that the compound critique may have on the knowledge engine or the set of rules. For example, a "trendier" bike may stand higher style quotient, higher power, better looks etc. The flip side of compound critique is that it does not work on existing data already brought out by the previous query. In order to overcome this dynamic critique comes into picture which recognizes that modification to existing results is a subset of the existing query. Lastly some work has also been done on trying to explain and interpret the meaning of the critique which is an important aspect for the value it brings to the user or consumer (Burke, Hammond, & Young, 1997; Reilly, McCarthy, McGinty, & Smyth, 2005).

ENSEMBLE BASED RECOMMENDER SYSTEMS

Author has discussed collaborative and content based methods and readers have seen both work with different kinds of data. However, it is unlikely that bringing multiple methods together should not have been thought of and this is exactly the subject matter of ensemble and hybrid recommender systems. The basic architecture of an ensemble or a hybrid could be a set of recommender algorithms working independently and presenting a weighted output or a set of sequential operations leading to improvements in the output. At this point it is important to clarify that ensembles involve combinations of off-the shelf algorithms being utilized directly whereas hybrids are considered a more customized specific combination of algorithms (Aggarwal, 2016). According to Burke (Burke, 2002), hybrid recommender systems can be classified into the following categories: weighted, switching, cascade, feature augmentation, feature combination, meta-level and mixed. We briefly touch upon the primary aspects of each of the above mentioned types in the section below. However, it needs to be pointed out that ensemble methods for classification could form the basis for the ensemble recommender systems and recognize that these systems would require adapting the existing algorithms such as the bagging and boosting algorithms that are known to reduce variance and bias respectively.

Weighted Hybrids

Let R be the original ratings matrix with dimension m x n. This method requires using q different algorithms to completely predict unknown ratings in the original matrix R, to give R'1, R'2, R'q, q different matrices each of the same dimension as the original matrix. Then a set of weights w1, to wq, may be used to predict the final rating matrix which is given by,

$$\hat{R} = \sum_{i=1}^{q} w_i \widehat{R_i} \quad (a)$$
$$\widehat{r_{uj}} = \sum_{i=1}^{q} w_i \widehat{r_{uj}} \quad (b)$$

$$(8)$$

Here $\widehat{r_{uj}}$ refers to the individual rating for user u and item j which is predicted by the model. In order to get to optimal weights a particularly useful method is classification based hold-out method where 30% of all original ratings are kept aside (set H) and model are trained on the other 70% data (across all q algorithms to generate different individual prediction matrices which are combined for the ensemble). Based on above mentioned models, error over the hold out sample or H is calculated and this error in the form of Mean Squared error or Mean Absolute error forms the dependent variable for the linear regression model with weights being set as the coefficients and the "q" different predictions as the independent variables. Minimization of this error gives a good set of estimates for the proposed set of weight wi. Although MSE is the preferred error type to work with, MAE offers better results and is considered robust to outliers and noise. Gradient descent method can be used together with MAE to give an estimate of (w1..wq) and the algorithm may be initialized by setting weights as 1/q. Regularization and other relevant constraints may also be used to augment the minimization problem. In its simplest form it may be given as,

$$MAE\left(\overline{w}\right) = \frac{\sum_{(u,j)\in H}\left|r_{uj} - \widehat{r_{uj}}\right|}{|H|} \tag{9}$$

$$\frac{\partial MAE\left(\overline{w}\right)}{\partial w_i} = \frac{\sum_{(u,j)\in H}\left(sign\,r_{uj} - \widehat{r_{uj}}\right)\widehat{r_{uj,i}}}{|H|} \tag{10}$$

Adapting bagging for collaborative filtering involves use of a base collaborative filtering algorithm that can handle entries with weights. Apart from this, standard bootstrapping may be used for creating q different matrices with replacement or any other sampling/retention technique may be adopted. Subsequently, a collaborative algorithm may be applied to each of the q datasets and predictions are made for the missing item ratings. For each dataset, an item rating can be predicted for a user only if that user is represented at least once in the matrix. The predicted rating from that ensemble component is the average rating of that item over every repeat occurrence of that user. The predicted rating is then averaged over all the ensemble components in which that user is present (Bar, Rokach, Shani, Shapira, & Schclar, 2013). A different approach to bagging could be the random injection of randomness into the matrix factor model or the neighborhood model similar (both have been discussed in a prior chapter) to the concept of random forest as used in simple classification.

Switching Hybrids

Switching mechanisms are used to handle the cold-start problem, in which one recommender performs better with less data, whereas the other recommender performs better with more data. As more data or ratings are available the system would move to the next or more appropriate method. A cross-validation based approach to identify the lowest error model or in general the lowest MSE or MAE approach may also be used.

Cascade Hybrids

The class of recommender systems that sequentially improve upon the previous output are often referred to as cascade hybrids. One of the most successful methods of successive refinement is the Boosting method from classification (Freund & Schapire, 1996). AdaBoost algorithm in classification works in a series of steps putting higher weight on wrongly classified items in each run, finally till the items are all correctly classified in the training set. Like before Boosting needs to be modified to be used with collaborative filtering methods. One such adaptation is the dissociation between weights associated with training examples as rows, instead we have here a set S of the observed ratings in the ratings matrix which form the primary training basis. In each iteration the weight of these S, set of observed ratings are modified based on performance of the iteration. This also presumes the ability of the base collaborative algorithm to work with weights. The algorithm may be applied say T times on the given data. The algorithm usually starts with equal weight assigned to each of the S sets of ratings. After kth iteration, the weight corresponding to $(u,j)^{th}$ entry is given by $W_k(u,j)$. If the (u,j) belongs to set S, and the prediction is not within the required value it is considered an error. The rate of error out of the set S is then calculated and set as ε_K which is multiplied by the weight of all the other entries that are correctly identified. This reduces the weight of the correctly identified items and keeps the weight of wrongly predicted items the same, after normalization this leads to higher weight percentage for the incorrectly identified values. The baseline model is applied again to the re-weighted data. After T iterations, T different predictions are obtained for individual unknown entries, and in the final prediction each of the T predictions are weighted by $\log(1/\varepsilon_K)$ (Bar et al., 2013). Next we look at adapting algorithms to work with weighted values. Let w_{uj} be the weight associated with an entry in the rating matrix at $(u,j)^{th}$ position. In order to modify the neighborhood based algorithm it is required to make changes to the similarity indices like Pearson's coefficient or the cosine similarity. For example, one possible modification could be as shown below.

$$Pearson's\ Coefficient\left(u,v\right) = \frac{\sum_{j \in u \cap v} w_{uj} w_{vj}\left(r_{uj} - \mu_u\right) * \left(r_{vj} - \mu_v\right)}{\sqrt{\sum_{j \in u \cap v}\left(w_{uj}\right)^2\left(r_{uj} - \mu_u\right)^2}\sqrt{\sum_{j \in u \cap v}\left(w_{uj}\right)^2\left(r_{vj} - \mu_v\right)^2}} \tag{11}$$

Similarly, the optimization component of Latent factor models could be modified as,

$$Minimize\ J = \left(1/2\right)\sum_{(i,j) \in s} w_{ij} e_{ij}^2 + \left(\lambda/2\right)\sum_{i=1}^m \sum_{s=1}^k u_{is}^2 + \left(\lambda/2\right)\sum_{j=1}^n \sum_{s=1}^k l_{js}^2 \tag{12}$$

whereas, the gradient descent based updates may be changed as follows,

$$u_{ig} = u_{ig} + \alpha\sum_{i,j \in S}\left(w_{ij} e_{ij} l_{jg} - \lambda u_{ig}\right) \tag{13a}$$

$$l_{jg} = l_{jg} + \alpha\sum_{i,j \in S}\left(w_{ij} e_{ij} u_{ig} - \lambda l_{jg}\right) \tag{13b}$$

Many other algorithms may be suitably modified to work with weighted values as shown above.

Feature Augmentation Hybrids

In the feature augmentation hybrid, the first set of algorithms work to enhance a set of features which act as the subsequent input to the next level algorithms. For example, a content based system may be used to work on text to predict a set of missing ratings and ultimately, the non-sparse matrix can then again be subjected to collaboration filtering for improved prediction. The final prediction may again involve weighing the predictions in each step and the weights themselves may be given by some heuristic (Mellville, Mooney, & Nagarajan, 2002).

Meta-Level Hybrids

Meta-level hybrids work similar to the feature augmentation hybrids in that one set of algorithms are used to identify features of interest which then form the input for the next phase of algorithms. However, operationalization is rather different. A content-based model (Burke, 2002; Barragáns-Martínez, Costa-Montenegro, Burguillo, Rey-López, Mikic-Fonte, & Pel, 2010) is used to construct a set of discriminative features, and then each user is represented as a vector of discriminative words. This reduced vector representation can be used to assess the similarity between the users and subsequently the ratings can be calculated by taking an average over the peers. These hybrids require a lot of customized effort especially for the first phase which is closely connected to the domain.

Feature Combination Hybrids

Before subjecting the input data to predictions the existing data may either be combined with additional data from different sources, creating comprehensive representation or certain features may be created for the purpose of enhanced analysis (Basu, Hirsh, & Cohen, 1998). The common method is using a content based collaboration prediction algorithm enriched by collaborative data. The combination of data could be achieved in very many ways thereby giving an element of innovation and creativity to the process of identifying the same. A parallel approach is creation of an augmented matrix of dimension m x (n+r), where r could be the vector of words from a content based system describing the item. Subsequently either neighborhood or matrix factorization method could be used with weights of vector of words being determined by aggregation of descriptions or user ratings. This requires a combination of two different objective functions optimized over θ as a parameter.

$$J(\theta) = \text{CollaborativeObjective}(\theta) + \text{ContentObjective}(\theta) + \text{RegularizationTerms} \text{ ---} \tag{14}$$

Using elastic net regression and matrix factorization, we can show the above mentioned idea. Assuming R to be (m x n) and content be given by C (n x r). Let W be a (n x n) item-item coefficient matrix utilized for prediction of ratings Rpred = RW or CW. Therefore, our optimization function can be set up as follows assuming appropriate non-negativity constraints;

$$Minimize\ J = \left(R - \widehat{(R)}W\right)^2 + \left(R - \widehat{(C)}W\right)^2 + \lambda\left(W\right)^2 + \mu|W|$$
$$\text{s.t.}, W \geq 0 \tag{15}$$

For prediction though only the former relationship (RW) is utilized, others are more for improving the results. The same approach could be generalized much further (Ning & Karypis, 2012). Next the author discusses the meta-feature approach (Sill et al., 2009) which assumes d meta-features are extracted and their values are $z_1^{ut}, \dots z_d^{ut}$, for user-item combination (u,t). Considering g different algorithms one could compute a weighted average of the g results to establish the predicted value of unknown rating with weights being assessed by linear regression method described in a section above. However, a small change is required as each of the weights is considered an independent linear function of the meta-features, this implies that each predicted rating is equivalent to a completely independent linear regression model in itself. This brings in much needed refinement but increases the number of learning variables as m x n x g which is rather large. But incorporating weights as linear combination and using an additional variable vij in order to express weights as linear combination of meta-features. This brings down the variables to learn considerably and can be further improved by adding regularization terms etc.

$$\left(\left(r^{\char`\^}\right)_{ut}\right) = \sum\nolimits_{i=1}^{g} w_i^{ut}\left(\left(r^{\char`\^}\right)_{ut}^{i}\right) \tag{16a}$$

$$w_i^{ut} = \sum_{j=1}^{d} v_{ij}\left(\left(z^{\hat{}}\right)_j^{ut}\right) \tag{16b}$$

$$\left(\left(r^{\hat{}}\right)_{ut}\right) = \sum_{i=1}^{g}\sum_{j=1}^{d} v_{ij}\left(\left(z^{\hat{}}\right)_j^{ut}\right)\left(\left(r^{\hat{}}\right)_{ut}^{i}\right) \tag{16c}$$

Mixed Hybrids

These recommender systems do not output composite scores but present the outputs as a detailed catalogue. For example, different activities may need a different recommender system and so different outputs from the various such systems could be presented to the users as a bundle of options. However, since the bundle may have inconsistencies or incompatibility issues, an appropriate knowledge engine or a set of rules may be used to transform the original bundle into more acceptable choices (Zanker, Aschinger, & Jessenitschnig, 2007; Zanker, Aschinger, & Jessenitschnig, 2010).

CONTEXT AWARE RECOMMENDER SYSTEMS

Context aware recommender systems add an additional dimension/s of context to the existing recommendations. For example, a particular set of recommendation systems may add specific advice based on either location or time as context. For example, a family movie may be suggested by a recommender system during festival season in India or a Christmas movie may be suggested during the winter holidays. While a traditional setting of recommender system may be understood as a mapping from user and item to ratings matrix which is 2-dimensional. The same idea may be generalized to multiple dimensions by invoking a setup similar to OLAP systems where a function g; maps various dimensions into ratings.

gr: D1 x D2 x D3........Dw --> Ratings (R) (17)

Where ratings data R contain w different dimensions that are mapped to ratings, which results in a w-dimensional cube rather than a 2-dimensional matrix. At a more general level, borrowing from the OLAP world, this can be looked upon as querying for top-ranked combinations of values with the use of two disjoint subsets from D1 . . . Dw, where subsets of dimensions are either "what" dimensions, or they are "for whom" dimensions. Ultimately, the final objective is to determine the top-k possibilities in the "what" dimensions for a set of values in the "for whom" dimensions. Another important aspect of multidimensional recommendations is the existence of hierarchies. The hierarchies are defined on various dimensions, such as sales may be across the cities, states, regions etc, or time may be defined as weeks, months, quarters, years etc. The concept of drill-down or roll-up as used in OLAP models can be used here as well. Therefore, the real problem of a multidimensional, hierarchical, rating estimation problem is described as given an initial set of user-assigned ratings specified as the multi-dimensional cube of ratings, estimation of all other ratings in the cube at all the levels of the OLAP hierarchies. Three methods are used for this estimation, namely, the contextual pre-filtering, contextual post-filtering and contextual modeling.

Contextual Pre-Filtering Approach

As the name suggests w-dimensional data is transformed to 2-dimensional ratings by specifying the values for each of the other w-2 dimensions. For example, if a particular dimension is time then we specify time as say 7PM in the evening. This is akin to running a projection after the selection of appropriate values from the attributes in database operations. Once readers have the relevant 2-dimensional contextual matrix of ratings they can subsequently utilize collaborative algorithms on this data segment for prediction. While the main advantage of this approach is collaborative filtering only on the most relevant segment of data, the flip side is sparsity of data. To some extent averaging of data over larger segments helps overcome sparsity at the cost of refinement. Another approach is averaging over all possible combinations of context relevant data thereby defining new data. For example, the data from say 7PM to 9PM may be combined with the average value for 7-8PM and 8-9PM. Another variation is use of ensemble or hybrid methods within the above by invoking cross-validation over various data segments (say all combinations of contextual data segments) and ultimately identifying the best model and using the test segment data for prediction with the chosen model.

Contextual Post-Filtering Approach

In the post-filtering approach as against the pre-filtering, 2- dimensional ratings matrix is created by aggregating the ratings over all the possible contextual values and then the ratings are filtered by bringing in the context dimension. Like in the previous case w-dimensional ratings are converted into 2 dimensions by averaging over w-2 dimensions (for explicit ratings) and summing across the dimensions for implicit ratings. If for a context no rating is available, then it is rated as zero. Once this matrix is ready it is subjected to regular collaborative methods and the results obtained are then filtered based on the appropriate context values. In a more mathematical approach, machine learning based predictive models can be built using attributes that are considered relevant to estimate context based probability $P(u,i,D)$, where u is the user, I is the item and D is the context. This $P(u,i,D)$ is determined using pre-filtering methods and can be used as weights with predicted rating value r_{ui} to give a ranking for all the predicted values, filtering out lower values of this product and retaining the higher values as relevant contextual predictions.

Contextual Modeling

In either of the above two approaches, we see transforming the w-dimensional data into 2 dimensional versions for analysis which reduces the richness of the user-item relationships which ought to be used in the analysis. Contextual modeling helps incorporate this through the modification of both neighborhood and latent factor model enabling the use of w-dimensions. For adapting neighborhood methods, notion of distance could be utilized with distance between say two points on a 3-dimensional cube may be expressed as,

$$D(A,B) = w1*D(u,u') + w2*D(i,i') + w3*D(h,h') \tag{18}$$

where u and u' stand for users, I and i' for items and h and h' for the context which may be either time or location or any such dimension. This distance may then be utilized for calculating r-nearest ratings which may then be filtered further for recommendations. Determining the distance would require innovation as utilizing either Pearson's coefficient or Cosine similarity could work depending upon the data type available. This will also require determining the Item x, context matrix for say user u and u'. As the users are specified the 2d data slice can be extracted and D(u,u') can be calculated, the same process could be used for D(i,i') and D(h,h'). Next author looks at the adaptation of latent factor models for context aware recommender systems.

Adapting Latent Factor Models

The generalized framework for matrix factorization is presented by Tensor factorization (Karatzoglou, Amatrian, Baltrunas, & Oliver, 2010), however, it is rather computationally intensive and therefore other simpler ways of working with latent factor models have been proposed (Rendle, Gantner, Freudenthaler, & Schmidt-Thieme, 2011). One such method is the Pairwise Interaction Tensor Factorization (PITF) which is a special case of factorization machine. Let R = r [ijc] be a 3-dimensional ratings cube of size m × n × d with m users, n items, and d different values of the contextual dimension. Let U = [u_{is}]; (user-factor matrix), V = [v_{js}]; (item-factor matrix), and W = [w_{cs}]; (context-factor matrix), be m × k, n × k, and d × k, matrices, where k is the rank of the latent factor model, and s is the set of all the observed entries. Using optimization errors over all unobserved samples shall be minimized as,

$$
Minimize\ J = \frac{1}{2}\sum_{i,j,c \in s}\left(r_{ijc} - \sum_{s=1}^{k}\left[u_{is}v_{js} + v_{js}w_{cs} + u_{is}w_{cs}\right]\right)^2
$$
$$
+ \frac{\lambda}{2}\sum_{s=1}^{k}\left(\sum_{i=1}^{m}u_{is}^2 + \sum_{j=1}^{n}v_{js}^2 + \sum_{c=1}^{d}w_{cs}^2\right)
\tag{19}
$$

As per SGD,

$$
u_{iq} = u_{iq} - \alpha\left[\frac{\partial J}{\partial u_{iq}}\right]\forall q \in (1...k)
\tag{20a}
$$

$$
v_{jq} = v_{jq} - \alpha\left[\frac{\partial J}{\partial v_{jq}}\right]\forall q \in (1...k)
\tag{20b}
$$

$$
w_{cq} = w_{cq} - \alpha\left[\frac{\partial J}{\partial w_{cq}}\right]\forall q \in (1...k)
\tag{20c}
$$

The updates to the above system based on stochastic gradient descent can be calculated for each error with ni user, nj item, nc context, are the normalization parameters (number of observed values in the data cube) for regularization term. Updates are as follows:

$$
u_{iq} = u_{iq} + \alpha\left(\left(r_{ijc} - \widehat{r_{ijc}}\right)\left(v_{jq} + w_{cq}\right) - \left(\frac{\lambda u_{iq}}{n_i^{user}}\right)\right)\forall q \in (1...k)
\tag{21a}
$$

$$v_{jq} = v_{jq} + \alpha \left(\left[r_{ijc} - \widehat{\left(r_{ijc} \right)} \right] \left(u_{iq} + w_{cq} \right) - \left(\frac{\lambda v_{jq}}{n_j^{item}} \right) \right) \forall q \epsilon \left(1...k \right) \tag{21b}$$

$$w_{cq} = w_{cq} + \alpha \left(\left[r_{ijc} - \widehat{\left(r_{ijc} \right)} \right] \left(u_{iq} + v_{jq} \right) - \left(\frac{\lambda w_{cq}}{n_c^{context}} \right) \right) \forall q \epsilon \left(1...k \right) \tag{21c}$$

The above 3-dimensional results can be generalized to a w-dimensional setting using the optimization method mentioned above.

Next author briefly looks at the concept of factorization machines which is the generalization of all w-dimensional latent factor models. Consider a 3-dimensional cube containing m users, n items, and d values of the contextual dimension, and each rating is practically a tuple. Such a cube can be transformed into (m + n + d)-dimensional rows with as many rows as the number of observed ratings. Assuming each of the ratings is binary, depending on the specific user-item-context tuple, only observed values are 1s and others 0s. A k-dimensional latent factor vector vi is related to the p (m+n+d) variables with individual bias term bi as well as global bias term g added to refine the model. The model may be presented as,

$$\hat{y}\left(\overline{x} \right) = g + \sum_{i=1}^{p} b_i x_i + \sum_{i=1}^{p} \sum_{j=i}^{p} \left(\overline{\left(v_i \right)} \cdot \overline{\left(v_j \right)} \right) \left(x_i x_j \right) \tag{22}$$

The solution approach is beyond the scope of this work and the reader is advised to refer to (Aggarwal, 2016; Rendle, 2010). Although the author has limited the discussion to the second order factorization model, it could be of higher order as well. A more general approach is known as the contextual content based models.

Contextual Content Based Models

A generalization of content based models (Adomavicius & Tuzhilin, 2011) could be understood based on a 3-dimensional example with user, item and context as the dimensions. The predicted rating r_{ijk} may be given by,

$$r_{ijk}\hat{} = W_1^- y_i^- + W_2^- z_j^- + W_3^- d_k^- + W_4^- \left(y_i^- \otimes z_j^- \right)$$
$$+ W_5^- \left(z_j^- \otimes d_k^- \right) + W_6^- \left(y_i^- \otimes d_k^- \right) + W_7^- \left(y_i^- \otimes z_j^- \otimes w_k^- \right) \tag{23}$$

In the expression above, W1, W2, and W3 stands for feature vector weights for user, feature vector weights for item and feature vector weights for context, and other weight variables represent Kronecker cross product for various interactions of the features of the vectors. Subsequently, any machine learning method can be used to fit a model on the observed data and use the model so obtained for prediction of unobserved values. Author does not dwell deeper into these models and next discusses evaluation methods for recommender systems.

EVALUATION OF RECOMMENDER SYSTEMS

A good design of the evaluation system is pertinent for understanding the performance of the recommender system as well as ensuring that the usage and resources being spent are in line with the business strategy and IT strategy. Two primary techniques are used for evaluation, offline and online evaluation. Online methods require user participation for them to be useful and are often conducted as A/B testing. However, for benchmarking and testing over diverse datasets a better option is offline systems and they form the core of most evaluation systems. Three important aspects of any evaluation methodology for recommender systems are evaluation goals, evaluation design and evaluation metrics. For evaluation design one could look at the acronym "CCARDSS" (similar to cards) to remember generic goals of the recommender system. Author looks at each of the Confidence, Coverage, Accuracy, Robustness, Diversity, Serendipity, and Scalability attributes briefly.

1. Confidence: Confidence or rather confidence and trust, refer to two measures. Confidence measures a system's faith in recommendations made from the supply side whereas trust measures the supply side or customer faith in the recommendations made (Das, Datar, Garg, & Rajaram, 2007).
2. Coverage: Coverage refers to the ability of the system to recommend for every user and recommend every item. It could be broken down into user-coverage and item-coverage. User-coverage is an issue due to sparsity of data and therefore having models with baseline assumptions or defaults is a solution along with assuring appropriate numbers for top-k values (k should be representative for the size of data). Similarly, item-coverage may be measured as catalog coverage CC is defined as the fraction of items that are recommended to at least one user (Aggarwal, 2016).
3. Accuracy: Accuracy is one of the most important goals and measures the error. One could use many different measures of error such as Mean Squared Error, Mean Absolute Error or Root Mean Squared Error etc depending upon context and algorithm utilized. This also requires that separation of training and testing data to be appropriately done as well as right sampling as well for training and testing datasets. One could also bring in utility based measures (expected profit from recommending), or rank-correlation measures (McNee, Riedl, & Konstan, 2006).
4. Robustness: A stable recommender system is immune to the presence of attacks such as fake ratings or false patterns in the data (Mobasher, Burke, Bhaumik, & Williams, 2007; Lam & Riedl, 2004).
5. Diversity: Diversity is measured as average similarity between the various pairs of recommendations made in a list of say top-k values. The idea is to ensure that lower values of average similarity be brought in for richer results and this is in direct contrast to accuracy metrics (Smyth & McClave, 2001).
6. Serendipity: Serendipity is a measure of non-obvious but useful recommendations made by the recommender system, made over and above the obvious values through baseline or primitive recommender systems. Such recommendations may either be online or offline (Ge, Delgado-Battenfeld, & Jannach, 2010).
7. Scalability: In today's context when size of data in terms of users, items could easily reach petabytes in terms of scale. So the design of recommender systems should be such so as to perform effectively and efficiently in terms of memory requirements, training time, and prediction time (Sarwar, Karypis, Konstan, & Riedl, 2002; Takacs, Pilaszy, Nemeth, & Tikk, 2009).

Above attributes or metrics capture the performance of any recommender system in a way that organizations can objectively decide the results obtained by such systems. Next section concludes the article with a brief discussion.

CONCLUSION AND FUTURE RESEARCH DIRECTION

Present chapter has brought out advanced concepts and techniques that are being utilized by the practitioners of recommender systems in the industry today. Article began by explaining the complete cycle of content based models and identifying their suitability for new items especially over other methods. Knowledge based recommender systems are prescribed for less often bought items and among constraint based systems the front-end is a defining characteristic to enable search and among case based systems understanding similarity is the key to better results. Author details the various ensemble based systems and hybrids and the likely many choices that they offer to the users with possibilities of improved results. As mentioned at the beginning of the article, ensembles and hybrids are pretty much the future of the systems in industry. Article also discusses value addition that is enabled by context aware systems and their dependence on factorization methods. Lastly, the article discusses the various metrics for understanding the performance of the recommender systems.

Together with an earlier chapter, which included neighborhood methods, modeling based methods, and this article is aimed at analyzing and bringing forth as many aspects of recommender systems as possible so as to enable the readers to develop a bird's eye view around the various developments over the last two decades. The chapter is highly utilitarian as it serves as an interesting starting point for not just the research oriented readers but also the newbie who wants to get a quick and reasonably in-depth picture of the state of theory about recommender systems. However, the article is in no way a comprehensive literature review of recommender systems. It should be stated that it is still early days and a lot more contemporary work on structural recommendations, social context based recommendations, robust attack-resistant recommendations and many recent additions to literature have not been covered in this brief effort. Author intends to analyze more advanced topics of this domain in the near future in order to bring such topics before a larger interested audience.

REFERENCES

Adomavicius, G., & Tuzhilin, A. (2011). Context-Aware Recommender Systems. In B. Shapira, P. B. Kantor, F. Ricci, & L. Rokach (Eds.), *Recommender Systems Handbook* (pp. 217–253). Springer. doi:10.1007/978-0-387-85820-3_7

Aggarwal, C. C. (2015). *Data Mining: The Textbook*. Springer International Publishing.

Aggarwal, C. C. (2016). *Recommender Systems: The Textbook*. Springer International Publishing. doi:10.1007/978-3-319-29659-3

Bar, A., Rokach, L., Shani, G., Shapira, B., & Schclar, A. (2013). Boosting simple collaborative filtering models using ensemble method. *Multiple Classifier Systems*, 1-12.

Barragáns-Martínez, A. B., Costa-Montenegro, E., Burguillo, J. C., Rey-López, M., Mikic-Fonte, F. A., & Pel, A. (2010). A hybrid content-based and item-based collaborative filtering approach to recommend TV programs enhanced with singular value decomposition. *Information Sciences*, *80*(22), 4290–4311. doi:10.1016/j.ins.2010.07.024

Basu, C., Hirsh, H., & Cohen, W. (1998). Recommendation as classification: using social and content-based information in recommendation. AAAI, 714-720.

Burke, R. (2002). Hybrid recommender systems: Survey and experiments. *User Modeling and User-Adapted Interaction*, *12*(4), 331–370. doi:10.1023/A:1021240730564

Burke, R., Hammond, K., & Young, B. (1997). The FindMe approach to assisted browsing. *IEEE Expert*, *12*(4), 32–40. doi:10.1109/64.608186

Das, A., Datar, M., Garg, A., & Rajaram, S. (2007). Google news personalization: scalable online collaborative filtering. *World Wide Web Conference*, 271-280. 10.1145/1242572.1242610

Felfernig, A., Friedrich, G., Jannach, D., & Stumptner, M. (2004). Consistency-based diagnosis of configuration knowledge bases. *Artificial Intelligence*, *152*(2), 213–234. doi:10.1016/S0004-3702(03)00117-6

Freund, Y., & Schapire, R. (1996). Experiments with a new boosting algorithm. *ICML Conference*, 148-156.

Ge, M., Delgado-Battenfeld, C., & Jannach, D. (2010). Beyond accuracy: evaluating recommender systems by coverage and serendipity. *Proceedings of the fourth ACM conference on Recommender systems (RecSys '10)*, 257-260. 10.1145/1864708.1864761

Gomez-Uribe, C. A., & Hunt, N. (2016). The Netflix Recommender System: Algorithms, Business Value, and Innovation. *ACM Transactions on Management Information Systems*, *6*(4), 1–19. doi:10.1145/2843948

Jannach, D. (2006). Finding preferred query relaxations in content-based recommenders. *Intelligent Techniques and Tools for Novel System Architectures*, 81-97.

Jannach, D. (2006). Techniques for fast query relaxation in content-based recommender systems. *Advances in Artificial Intelligence*, 49–63.

Karatzoglou, A., Amatrian, X., Baltrunas, L., & Oliver, N. (2010). Multiverse recommendation: N-dimensional tensor factorization for context aware collaborative filtering. *ACM Conference on Recommender Systems*, 79-86. 10.1145/1864708.1864727

Lam, S., & Riedl, J. (2004). Shilling recommender systems for fun and profit. *World Wide Web Conference*, 393-402. 10.1145/988672.988726

Mahmood, T., & Ricci, F. (2009). Improving recommender systems with adaptive conversational strategies. *ACM Conference on Hypertext and Hypermedia*, 73-82. 10.1145/1557914.1557930

McNee, S., Riedl, J., & Konstan, J. (2006). Being accurate is not enough: how accuracy metrics have hurt recommender systems. *SIGCHI Conference*, 1097-1101. 10.1145/1125451.1125659

McSherry, D. (2004). Incremental relaxation of unsuccessful queries. In *Proceedings of the European Conference on Case-based Reasoning* (pp. 331-345). Springer. 10.1007/978-3-540-28631-8_25

Mellville, P., Mooney, R., & Nagarajan, R. (2002). Content-boosted collaborative filtering for improved recommendations. *AAAI/IAAI*, 187-192.

Mobasher, B., Burke, R., Bhaumik, R., & Williams, C. (2007). Toward trustworthy recommender systems: An analysis of attack models and algorithm robustness. *ACM Transactions on Internet Technology*, 7(4), 23. doi:10.1145/1278366.1278372

Ning, X., & Karypis, G. (2012). Sparse linear methods with side information for top-n recommendations. *ACM Conference on Recommender Systems*, 155-162. 10.1145/2365952.2365983

Reilly, J., McCarthy, K., McGinty, L., & Smyth, B. (2005). Explaining compound critiques. *Artificial Intelligence Review*, 24(2), 199–220. doi:10.100710462-005-4614-8

Rendle, S. (2010). Factorization machines. *IEEE International Conference on Data Mining*, 995-1000.

Rendle, S., Gantner, Z., Freudenthaler, C., & Schmidt-Thieme, L. (2011). Fast context-aware recommendations with factorization machines. *ACM SIGIR Conference*, 635-644.

Sarwar, B., Karypis, G., Konstan, J., & Riedl, J. (2002). Incremental singular value decomposition algorithms for highly scalable recommender systems. *International Conference on Computer and Information Science*, 27-28.

Sill, J., Takacs, G., Mackey, L., & Lin, D. (2009). *Feature-Weighted Linear Stacking*. Retrieved January 24, 2022, from https://arxiv.org/abs/0911.0460

Smyth, B., & McClave, P. (2001). Similarity vs. diversity. *Proceedings of the 4th International Conference on Case-Based Reasoning: Case-Based Reasoning Research and Development (ICCBR '01)*, 347-361.

Takacs, G., Pilaszy, I., Nemeth, B., & Tikk, D. (2009). Scalable collaborative filtering approaches for large recommender systems. *Journal of Machine Learning Research*, 10(22), 623–656.

Zanker, M., Aschinger, M., & Jessenitschnig, M. (2007). Development of a collaborative and constraint-based web configuration system for personalized bundling of products and services. In *Proceedings of the 8th international conference on Web information systems engineering (WISE'07)* (pp. 273–284). Springer-Verlag. doi:10.1007/978-3-540-76993-4_23

Zanker, M., Aschinger, M., & Jessenitschnig, M. (2010). Constraint-based personalised configuring of product and service bundles. *International Journal of Mass Customisation*, 3(4), 407–425. doi:10.1504/IJMASSC.2010.037653

Zhai, C., & Aggarwal, C. C. (Eds.). (2012). *Mining Text Data*. Springer New York.

ADDITIONAL READING

Ali, W., Kumar, R., Deng, Z., Wang, Y., & Shao, J. (2021). A federated learning approach for privacy protection in context-aware recommender systems. *The Computer Journal*, 64(7), 1016–1027. doi:10.1093/comjnl/bxab025

Chen, L., & Xia, M. (2021). A context-aware recommendation approach based on feature selection. *Applied Intelligence*, 51(2), 865–875. doi:10.100710489-020-01835-9

Guo, J., Zhou, Y., Zhang, P., Song, B., & Chen, C. (2021). Trust-aware recommendation based on heterogeneous multi-relational graphs fusion. *Information Fusion*, 74, 87–95. doi:10.1016/j.inffus.2021.04.001

Javed, U., Shaukat, K., Hameed, I. A., Iqbal, F., Alam, T. M., & Luo, S. (2021). A review of content-based and context-based recommendation systems. *International Journal of Emerging Technologies in Learning*, 16(3), 274–306. doi:10.3991/ijet.v16i03.18851

Li, D., Liu, H., Zhang, Z., Lin, K., Fang, S., Li, Z., & Xiong, N. N. (2021). CARM: Confidence-aware recommender model via review representation learning and historical rating behavior in the online platforms. *Neurocomputing*, 455, 283–296. doi:10.1016/j.neucom.2021.03.122

Lozano Murciego, Á., Jiménez-Bravo, D. M., Valera Román, A., De Paz Santana, J. F., & Moreno-García, M. N. (2021). Context-aware recommender systems in the music domain: A systematic literature review. *Electronics (Basel)*, 10(13), 1555. doi:10.3390/electronics10131555

Polignano, M., Narducci, F., de Gemmis, M., & Semeraro, G. (2021). Towards emotion-aware recommender systems: An affective coherence model based on emotion-driven behaviors. *Expert Systems with Applications*, 170, 114382. doi:10.1016/j.eswa.2020.114382

Suhaim, A. B., & Berri, J. (2021). Context-Aware Recommender Systems for Social Networks: Review, Challenges and Opportunities. *IEEE Access: Practical Innovations, Open Solutions*, 9, 57440–57463. doi:10.1109/ACCESS.2021.3072165

KEY TERMS AND DEFINITIONS

Content-Based Recommender Systems: Content based systems work on data from users' own ratings as well as attributes or features of the product to make recommendations by using unstructured data elements and applying NLP and other methods on the same.

Ensemble and Hybrid-Based Methods: Both ensemble and hybrids involve bringing together more than one algorithm for recommendation, however, ensembles involve off-the shelf algorithms whereas hybrids involve custom algorithms for the context.

Knowledge-Based Recommender Systems: For products not related to past purchase or having uncommon characteristics ordinary ratings may not be useful and such systems are subject to either constraint based systems or case based systems in order to make appropriate recommendations.

ERP and Time Management:
A Recommender System

Anthony Bronner
ADRIA, France

Pascale Zaraté
 https://orcid.org/0000-0002-5188-1616
ADRIA, France

INTRODUCTION

As the performance of business computer hardware evolves, software offers more services to users. The software tool most used in business, management software, also evolves over time. Thus companies, as part of their digital transition, require their employees to use an Enterprise Resource Planning (ERP) in order to centralize management and data. The modern ERP implementation methodology encourages and supports a phased approach to business management (Lutovac and al., 2012). In all sectors, the manager is faced with the difficulty of planning the tasks of the team as well as possible. Management software frequently helps the manager to follow the activity of the company but this does not guarantee that each member of the team takes care of the most suitable task according to the criteria imposed by the management.

Standard management software may be ideal for a company that only needs basic functionalities such as sales management, inventory management or customer management (Bronner and al., 2020). On the other hand, when a company wishes to manage and monitor all the information and operational services that make up its activity, it uses an ERP. The objectives of this tool, which is part of the digital transition of companies, are multiple:

- Ensure centralization, security and rapid access to information
- Automate repetitive and time-consuming tasks (low value-added hunting)
- Improve organization between employees and communication between departments
- Plan tasks and coordinate stakeholders
- Analyze performance and profitability in real time
- Have all the useful information on its staff, customers, products, suppliers and subcontractors

In addition, ERPs are also used for time and activity management (TAM). Thus, department heads, whose mission is to organize the activity and guarantee the productivity of their department through the operational planning of their teams, are assisted by the software which allows them to discharge a certain number of control and input operations to focus on more strategic tasks. TAM creates a climate of trust and transparency by making the monitoring of staff working time more reliable, both in terms of consultation and organization. Indeed, the precision of the input information guarantees infallible output processing.

DOI: 10.4018/978-1-7998-9220-5.ch166

The major challenge of setting up a TAM is optimal operational management, i.e. scheduling the right person, at the right time, for the right activity, while controlling the associated costs.

Thus, in the commercial sector, it is difficult to know if a user is making the right choice when making a quote for customer A while customer B is also waiting, or vice versa. The time spent for each client is an important factor, as it can be seen as the profitability of the project or it could improve customer satisfaction, but neither the employees nor the manager can control all these parameters. The volume of data stored by an ERP is so large that a user can in no way take into account its entirety. The reality is such that even software struggles to be able to process them effectively, hence the birth of the term big data.

Business Intelligence (BI) tools and techniques used to come on top of the ERP systems in order to help decision makers making quality decisions (Elragal, 2014). Indeed, BI can go deeper to find hidden patterns and unknown facts when using data mining techniques. It is therefore obvious that a system allowing the user of an ERP to suggest an action by matching user's preferences and the analysis of the company's activity is essential.

A recommender system, in which criteria would thus be defined, could ensure the choice of the most appropriate alternative under the constraint of these criteria. One alternative is a task to be done in priority. This recommender system could guide the staff in the next to be done.

Some companies have invested millions in business software that is not used by their employees because they spend more time than expected using the software, or because they have been excluded from the software design process. For this reason we included the staff members in the design of the ERP and we aim to test it in real situation.

In this chapter, we discuss the asymmetry between the staff members and the manager for the next task to be done choice. We present the prototype of the recommendation system which will restore a balance in this asymmetry, with its interface and its database. In this article, we discuss the asymmetry between staff members and manager in choosing the next task to do. We present the prototype of the recommendation system which will restore a balance in this asymmetry, with its interface and its database. Regarding the interface, the main configuration forms are produced, and their operation is revealed. We then detail the structure of the database as well as examples of the content of the main tables. In order to clarify the problem of time management, we explain how the use of an ERP can facilitate the operation of the company's activity but generate difficulties in its use, which can be avoided thanks to recommendations. The source code of some forms are exposed, and the development environment as well.

BACKGROUND

The digital transition of companies is the heart of the strategic decisions taken by managers, both for large groups and small companies. This digitization most often materialized by setting up an ERP system, its implementation is generally a great challenge, and typically requires between one to five years (Mabert and al., 2003). The basis of ERP systems is to generate mandatory, relevant, reliable and timely information (Lecic and al., 2013). This implies that upstream, the information is transformed into a convenient form to be used. This objective is achieved on one hand when the user consults this information via the ERP and considers that he has saved time, on the other hand when the organization is able to better execute all its business processes and when the integrated information system can support the development performance of the enterprise (Boota-Genoulaz and al., 2005). Thus, in addition to the computational aspect, there is also the concern for the information presentation. Indeed, each user has a value system and perceives information in a very personal way. The perceived transparency of ERP system information has significant direct effects on perceived usefulness, ease of use, and indirect effects on attitude and adoption (Al-Jabri and al., 2015). In addition, perceived utility fully mediates the relationship between transparency of information and attitude towards ERP system use. There is therefore a cultural dimension in the implementation of ERP knowledge sharing (Jones and al., 2006). In addition, the transmission mode of information plays an important role in the frequency of use. Thus, the web aspect of the system offers significant advantages, as the system is distributed through interoperable, cross-platform and highly pluggable web service components (Tarantilis and al., 2008). In contrast, a local client-server system offers more security, better data control, and more robust offline operation (Ruivo and al., 2015).

The objective of setting up an ERP is to increase commercial and financial performance. However, one study found that operational performance is positively associated with financial performance (Acar and al., 2017). ERP therefore influences all areas of the company and affects its overall functioning. A better understanding of the contribution of ERP systems to operational performance can be obtained if researchers and managers assess changes in operational performance at the modular and system levels. Furthermore, machine learning and predictive analytics can assist ERP in improving processes and predictions, enhancing planning for company operations via learning from experience, and adapting business rules (Jenab and al., 2019).

The nature and modalities of organizational change generated by the implementation of ERP are consistent, as presented and synthesized by Reix (Reix, 2002) for the general framework of relations between information technologies and organizational change, by Rowe (Rowe, 1999) for the understanding of the nature of ERP and their organizational impact and by Azan or Pourtier (Meyssonnier and al., 2004), for the analysis of the concrete systems put in place to allow the success of ERP implementations in companies. We know that the introduction of ERP can involve two approaches: the Big Bang, as is the case in almost 30% of cases (Cannone and al., 2002), or gradually by increasing the number of modules (increasing depth) and entities (increasingly wide spatial field). To analyze the nature of the change in ERP, it is therefore necessary to take into account, as proposed by Tomas (Tomas, 2000), the fundamental dimensions of ERP such as the degree of integration (DI) and operational coverage (CO).

Moreover, for Burns and Scapens (Scapens and al., 2003) in an institutionalist approach, changes in the field of management control can also appear in two forms. This can be a sudden break calling into question a stable overall equilibrium with its formal rules and concrete practices (phenomenon of revolution). In the end, this can appear as a dialectical process of modifying practices and adjusting rules, requiring a certain duration and resulting in a new configuration (phenomenon of evolution). In the latter case, the perception of changes is strongly determined by the moment when the observation takes place (because too early it does not detect any major change).

A large number of studies on the subject show that the complexity of ERP integration raises many organizational issues. Thus, the proliferation of specific or peripheral applications complicates and scleroses the use of data. Consolidation of previous procedures permanently hinders the possibility of restructuring operating methods at different levels. The disaffection of staff and the compartmentalization between several groups of users can slow down the flow of information, reporting procedures and updating of strategic data. Thus, if ERP constitutes an innovative and conceptually remarkable technical framework that can promote a significant improvement in communication between the different services, in the accessibility and security of information, the reality remains nuanced, since the system is imposed on the client staff who rarely participate in the process.

It is essential that the user is strongly involved in the ERP development process with which he will subsequently work. Development project management approaches, such as Agile or Scrum, make it possible precisely to consider the client's involvement during the creation phases, and to take into account the client's analysis and feelings about the content presented to the client at each step, in order to refine the development.

As we mentioned previously, ERPs offer users a wide choice of possible actions. In order to allow the user not to find himself alone in the selection of the tasks that he must accomplish during the working time, it could be interesting to offer the user a suggestion of action. It is precisely for this purpose that we have thought of a recommendation system based on a multi-criteria decision support MCDA which is a sub-domain of decision support, of which the different alternatives or actions, are evaluated through several criteria.

Indeed, the use of a single criterion does not make it possible to effectively separate the different alternatives while taking into account all the preferences of the decision-maker, in this case the user.

There are a very large number of multi-criteria decision support methods. Two "schools" stand out in the MCDA field and follow quite different basic principles (Rakotoarivelo, 2018). The first is the "American School" which most often uses an additive utility function that combines utility values into an overall rating for the stock. The second, the "European school" generally favors the use of methods based on notions of outclassing among potential actions. The notion of upgrading corresponds to saying that one element is preferred over another in relation to one or more points of view. We have chosen the AHP method, from the American school, to create the recommendation system that will be presented later in this article. AHP is a simple, fast, flexible, and easily adaptable decision support approach. The method of binary comparison matrices (Kast, 2002), makes it possible to arrive in a simple and efficient way at weight vectors. Beforehand, we followed the classic method of decomposing the problem and transforming judgments into numerical values with the Saaty scale (Saaty, 2003).

A decision support tool can complicate the evaluation since it indirectly reduces the user's freedom, suggesting an alternative that might not have been the client's choice if he had been given the opportunity to decide by himself (Madapusi and al., 2012). Indeed, the alternative comes from a list programmed in advance and does not always include all the possibilities that the user would have thought of.

SOLUTIONS AND RECOMMENDATIONS

Time Management and ERP

In general, ERP is broken down into modules that stack up according to the needs of the company that uses it. A small business requires commercial management, while a large business will likely have to manage other industries and prioritize the level of privileges of its users according to the department to which they belong. However, and apart from taking into account the size of the company, what guarantee is there that the ERP is used correctly? How do you know if the time that the user spends on the ERP is dedicated to the most suitable, most urgent, or even the most profitable tasks for the company? There is no simple answer to these questions. Because it depends on the criteria used to evaluate the user's choice. It is possible to respond partially by carrying out investigations, then extracting statistics aimed at highlighting the time spent by the user on the ERP and the enhancement of his productivity. To fully answer it, we would have to evaluate all the possibilities. This would imply considering all possible scenarios, and isolating the most effective. It is totally unthinkable that a user, before each action in the ERP, evaluates all the scenarios in order to choose the best one. He would spend the whole day choosing the right action, so he wouldn't do anything, this would be too much time consuming. He would rather do nothing than make a bad decision. Our objective is to introduce a recommender system that would assist the user to decide and choose the next task to be done.

In this recommender system, we have considered three criteria, namely turnover (therefore the total sales made by the company), customer satisfaction (measurable thanks to the frequency of purchase of the same customer), and the margin (calculated by making the difference between the sale price and the purchase price of the same product) (Janssen, 2004). These criteria may involve several business sectors of the company. Thus, the margin can increase if there is an increase in selling prices (commercial sector), but also if there is a decrease in purchase prices.

We have chosen to focus on the commercial sector in order to reduce the volume of data to consider.

Time Management

From the User's Point of View

As an employee of a company, each user has a certain autonomy. However, this employee must complete a pre-established working time, taking into account a job description. Thus, it must be able to make trade-offs among the various tasks awaiting processing. These trade-offs are subjective, and depend on several categories of criteria. The first depends on the preferences of the user himself. Indeed, the preferences of each employee vary in a dynamic and natural way according to three criteria which are the mood, the motivation or the psychological state when he is at work. The involvement of personal factors external to the company is to be expected and influences its choices. The second relates to what is imposed by its managers in a direct way, or the management in a more indirect way. The employee is aware that he must take this into account. These two categories are therefore hierarchically unbalanced. It can therefore easily be understood that the assignment of the weight of one criterion to another by the employee is a difficult task to perform before each decision-making, and could be subject to calculation errors which could compromise the validity of the final decision.

From the Manager's Point of View

The management of a company generally takes two types of measures to adjust its strategy: cyclical measures and structural measures. The structural measures are part of long-term deadlines. They define the internal policy of the company. They embody the vision of the leader. On the other hand, cyclical measures respond to short-term issues. They are the ones who define the assignment of tasks to the employees and the distribution of their working time. It is on the basis of these measures that management adjusts the weight of the criteria in their decisions.

Data Volume and Real Time

As we discussed earlier in this article, the amount of data to consider when making a decision may be too large to be left to the mental arithmetic of any decision maker.

The activity of an employee is concomitant with that of others, which means that in each decision-making, the employee should be informed in real time of the activities of other employees, and take them into account. Even if we admit that the user of the ERP has statistics updated in real time on the current activity of the company, the simple fact of consulting them and integrating them into a calculation would make them obsolete even before the end of the operation.

Another possibility would be calculating the most suitable task to be done integrating several criteria of evaluations defined by the staff members and by the manger. The weight of each criterion is defined by the staff members and the manager. However, the variation in the weight of a criterion following the modification of the vote of a manager is important to take into account in the recommendation process.

The simplest solution therefore remains an algorithm which would take into account all of these parameters and which could draw information from the company's database in real time, in other words a recommender system.

Need of Decision Support

Due to the fact that the user's choice depends on hierarchical factors within the company, personal factors, and the value system of the employee concerned, the number of elements to be taken into consideration in decision-making is an intrinsic source of conflict. By going through a criteria weighting algorithm which would perform the calculations and which would assign a score to each alternative, the decision-maker, and therefore the user, would have the possibility of obtaining a recommendation that he could follow. If the proposed task would not suit to the end-user, other recommendations classified by decreasing score level would be offered to the staff members.

The Combination of ERP and Decision Support

In order to develop such a recommender system, we selected an existing ERP. This ERP, namely "Cortex-Gestion" was developed by a French company, located in Toulouse, from 2012. Since that date, it is still under development and benefits from annual updates. It is currently used by several companies in France, particularly in the building or industrial sector, to manage their activities. Its marketing is likely to be extended to other countries since it includes several languages, including Spanish and English. Its graphical interface was designed in the Microsoft Visual Studio environment, in VB.Net language.

A Recommender System

Tunning

General Presentation

GTiA software is a recommender system designed to improve the time management of ERP users. The ERP is already used in a company and the main objective of this work is to associate GtiA with the existing ERP. To make recommendations, GTiA is therefore linked to the ERP which contains data on which it can perform calculations, according to predefined criteria and user preferences. In this article, we have coupled GTiA to the database of the existing ERP, including modules such as sales, purchasing, logistics, human resources, customers and suppliers, projects, communication, marketing, and others.

Its main interface is designed in the form of a dashboard divided into 4 categories. The first category is devoted to managing the rights and privileges of the logged user, to be defined after their prior authentication. The second is intended to configure the recommendation system, define the criteria, the alternatives, and the influence of the criteria on the alternatives. It is also used to link the database containing the information from which recommendations are to be made. Finally, the last two components are used to view statistics, and finally to enter user preferences (Voter) and get recommendations (Visualiser). Details of the events associated with these GUI buttons will be presented later.

Figure 1. Software Home Interface

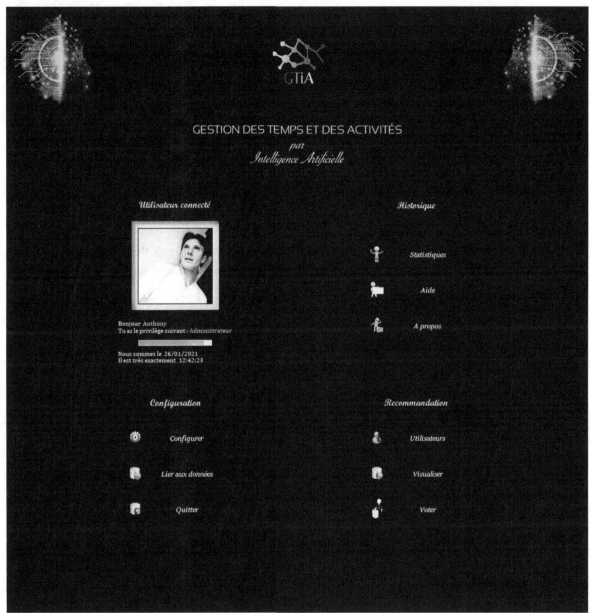

General Configuration Overview

- Configuration form

The configuration form allows the end user to add, modify or delete criteria and alternatives. Datagridviews (Visual Basic forms) display a summary of the information entered in order to obtain an overview and be able to interact. For each criterion, or for each alternative, the latest modification information is kept (date and user).

- Criterion form

This form is intended to create or modify a criterion. The first 3 cells are pre-filled when opening in order to guarantee that the information is not erroneous (identifier, user, date). The wording will then make it possible to select the criterion and associate it (or not) with an alternative.

It is possible to select the unit of the criterion (quantitative, qualitative or monetary) then to adjust the corresponding scale. The meaning is also precise (max or min) in order to define how it must be interpreted in the final algorithm. Finally, the influence (direct or indirect) of the criterion makes it possible to associate a reduction coefficient which attenuates its weight in the final score of the recommendation.

Further down, in the datagridview, each user can assign a weight to the criterion, whose the value will be used to calculate the final score used in the evaluation of the alternatives.

- Alternative form

Regarding the alternatives, the form is designed on the same principle as that of the criterion. The information concerning the date, the user and the identifier are pre-filled, and only the caption remains to be entered.

For each alternative, it is necessary to fill in the list of criteria associated with it. It is thus possible to exclude a criterion if it is considered that it is not applicable to a particular alternative without compromising the whole of the subsequent recommendation.

Evaluation Form

- Alternative Evaluation form

This form allows each user to evaluate each alternative according to all the criteria in order to generate a judgment matrix that the algorithm will then process to extract the priorities. The details of this procedure will be specified in the part of the recommendation algorithm presented at the end of this paper. The author explains the different steps of solving the matrix, namely, the filling of the columns, the calculation of the sum of the columns, the division of the elements by the sum of each column, as well as the calculation of the average of the elements of each row, in order to obtain the first rankings (Saaty, 2003).

- Preferences form's source code

Here is the complete GTiA project in the Visual Studio 2019 development environment, with part of the source code of a form, in VB.Net language.

The recommendation processing part of the algorithm is mainly coded in a module which will be detailed in the last section.

Database

Relational Database Schema

The database was created under Microsoft Access. It is made up of four main tables, namely "Alternatives", "Criteres", "Users" and "Vote", as well as mandatory tables to establish a relationship with the configurations and the made choices from the main tables, namely "Crit_Altern", "Crit_Vote". We can see that some tables are not linked, in particular "Devis_Client", "Commande_Client" and "Facture_Client" that we can translate by quotes, orders and invoices. This means that these tables are independent of the general operation of the software, since they come from an export from the main database of an existing ERP. Time management is only possible if the existing ERP collects this information and records it. In our example, each database tables has a field intended to record the time spent by a user on a task. Thus, statistics are possible to carry out an assessment of the allocated time to each action, and the recommendation takes this parameter into account.

Figure 2.

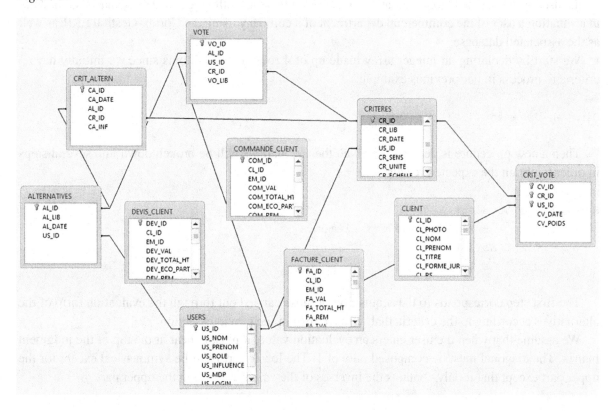

Association Table of Alternatives and Criteria

The records in this table show that certain criteria are associated with alternatives and that the influence is specified each time. This means for example that alternative 5 is concerned by 3 criteria (1 with direct influence, 2 with direct influence, 4 with indirect influence).

Table for Assigning a Weight to the Criteria

Each user assigns a weight to each criterion. In the following example, criterion 2 received the evaluation of 4 users (4 with a weight of 6, 2 with a weight of 5, 1 with a weight of 2 and 3 with a weight of 3).

Table of Alternative's Score According to Users and Criteria

This table contains the foreign keys of the alternative, criterion and user tables, as well as a score. It is the result of the evaluation by the user of each alternative according to each criterion. The score depends on the initial weight of each criterion as the user entered it in the criterion table, as well as on the influence selected in the alternative table.

Algorithm Description

Here is the first part of the recommendation system algorithm. The author presents here the source code model used to obtain the recommendation presented at the end of the section. The scenario studied put in a situation a user of the commercial department of a company using the Cortex-Gestion ERP, as well as the associated database.

We start by declaring an integer array made up of 4 rows and 4 columns since we initially have 3 criteria to process in our previous example.

```
Dim Tab_Jugement(3, 3) As Integer
```

Then a new procedure is declared in which the calculations will be broken down into several steps in order to obtain the expected results.

```
Sub Matrice_Jugement()
        'Step 1 - Remplissage des éléments
        Dim i As Integer = 0
        Dim j As Integer = 0
```

The first step corresponds to the acquisition of those carried out through the evaluation form of the alternatives according to the criteria that we have seen in the previous section.

We assume that when the user enters an evaluation value, it must appear at the top of the judgment matrix. The diagonal must be composed only of 1. The lower part must be symmetrical except for the upper part except that it only contains the inverses of the values entered in the upper part.

```
        For i = 0 To 2 Step 1
            For j = 0 To 2 Step 1
                If i = j Then
                    Tab_Jugement(i, j) = 1
                ElseIf i < j Then
                    Tab_Jugement(i, j) = Form_Vote.dgv_critère.CurrentRow.
Cells(1).Value.ToString
                ElseIf j < i Then
                    Tab_Jugement(i, j) = 1 / Tab_Jugement(j, i)
                End If
            Next
        Next
```

Once the 3x3 matrix is completed, we can calculate the sum of the columns and store it in the fourth row.

```
'Step 2 - Calcul de la somme des colonnes
i = 0
j = 0
For j = 0 To 2
    For i = 0 To 2
        Tab_Jugement(3, j) = Tab_Jugement(3, j) + Tab_Jugement(i, j)
    Next
Next
```

Next, we must divide each element of the matrix, which is included in part (2,2) of our array, by the total of each column, previously calculated, then replace each coordinate of our array by this new value.

```
'Step 3 - Division des éléments par la somme de chaque colonne
i = 0
j = 0
For i = 0 To 2 Step 1
    For j = 0 To 2 Step 1
        Tab_Jugement(i, j) = Tab_Jugement(i, j) / Tab_Jugement(3, j)
    Next
Next
```

Finally, we calculate the average of the elements of each row of the matrix by summing the elements of each row, then dividing them by the number of elements, which is 3 in our example.

```
'Step 4 - Calcul de la moyenne des éléments de chaque ligne
i = 0
j = 0
For i = 0 To 2 Step 1
    For j = 0 To 2 Step 1
        Tab_Jugement(i, 3) = (Tab_Jugement(i, 3) + Tab_Jugement(i, j))
/ 3
    Next
Next
End Sub
```

Extraction of the source code for calculating the normalization of the matrix as well as the consistency.

```
Sub Remplissage_DGV_Norm()
    dgv_norm.Rows.Clear()
    dgv_norm.Columns.Clear()
    dgv_norm.CellBorderStyle = DataGridViewCellBorderStyle.Single
    Obj_Command = New OleDbCommand()
```

```
        Obj_Command.Connection = laConnexionPrincipale
        Obj_Command.CommandText = "SELECT AL_LIB FROM ALTERNATIVES"
        Obj_Reader = Obj_Command.ExecuteReader()
        Dim i As Integer = 0
        dgv_norm.Columns.Add(i, "ALTERNATIVE")
        dgv_norm.Columns(i).Width = 130
        dgv_norm.Columns(i).DefaultCellStyle.Alignment= DataGridViewConten-
tAlignment.MiddleLeft
        While Obj_Reader.Read()
            i = i+1
            dgv_norm.Columns.Add(i, Replace(Obj_Reader.GetValue(0).ToString(),
"/", "'"))
            dgv_norm.Columns(i).Width = 130
            dgv_norm.Columns(i).DefaultCellStyle.Alignment= DataGridViewCon-
tentAlignment.MiddleCenter
            dgv_norm.Rows.Add(Replace(Obj_Reader.GetValue(0).ToString(), "/",
"'"))
            dgv_norm.Rows(i-1).Height = 25
        End While
        Obj_Reader.Close()
        Dim j As Integer = 0
        'Normalisation de la matrice
        For j = 0 To Nbr_Alt - 1
            For i = 0 To Nbr_Alt - 1
                dgv_norm.Rows(j).Cells(i+1).Value= FormatNumber(CDbl(dgv_alt.
Rows(j).Cells(i+1).Value.ToString)/ CDbl(dgv_alt.Rows(3).Cells(i+1).Value.To-
String), 5)
            Next
        Next
        'Calcul du poids des vecteurs propres
        dgv_norm.Columns.Add(i+1, "VECT. PROPRE")
        dgv_norm.Columns(i+1).Width = 130
        dgv_norm.Columns(i+1).DefaultCellStyle.Alignment= DataGridViewConten-
tAlignment.MiddleCenter
        j = 0
        i = 0
        Dim Valeur_Inter As Double
        For j = 0 To Nbr_Alt - 1
            dgv_norm.Rows(j).Cells(Nbr_Alt + 1).Value = 0
            Valeur_Inter = 0
            For i = 0 To Nbr_Alt - 1
                Valeur_Inter = Valeur_Inter + FormatNumber(CDbl(dgv_norm.
Rows(j).Cells(i + 1).Value.ToString), 5)
            Next
            dgv_norm.Rows(j).Cells(Nbr_Alt + 1).Value = FormatNumber(Valeur_
```

```
Inter, 5)
        Next
        'Calcul du poids des vecteurs propres normalisés
        dgv_norm.Columns.Add(i+1, "VECT. PRO. NORM.")
        dgv_norm.Columns(i+1).Width = 130
        dgv_norm.Columns(i+1).DefaultCellStyle.Alignment= DataGridViewConten-
tAlignment.MiddleCenter
        j = 0
        i = 0
    For j = 0 To Nbr_Alt - 1
            dgv_norm.Rows(j).Cells(Nbr_Alt+2).Value= FormatNumber(CDbl(dgv_
norm.Rows(j).Cells(Nbr_Alt + 1).Value) / Nbr_Alt, 5)
        Next
    End Sub
    Sub Remplissage_DGV_Consist()
        dgv_consist.Rows.Clear()
        dgv_consist.Columns.Clear()
        dgv_consist.CellBorderStyle = DataGridViewCellBorderStyle.Single
        Obj_Command = New OleDbCommand()
        Obj_Command.Connection = laConnexionPrincipale
        Obj_Command.CommandText = "SELECT AL_LIB FROM ALTERNATIVES"
        Obj_Reader = Obj_Command.ExecuteReader()
        Dim i As Integer = 0
        dgv_consist.Columns.Add(i, "ALTERNATIVE")
        dgv_consist.Columns(i).Width = 140
        dgv_consist.Columns(i).DefaultCellStyle.Alignment= DataGridViewConten-
tAlignment.MiddleLeft
        While Obj_Reader.Read()
            i = i + 1
            dgv_consist.Columns.Add(i, Replace(Obj_Reader.GetValue(0).To-
String(), "/", "\"))
            dgv_consist.Columns(i).Width = 140
            dgv_consist.Columns(i).DefaultCellStyle.Alignment= DataGridView-
ContentAlignment.MiddleCenter
            dgv_consist.Rows.Add(Replace(Obj_Reader.GetValue(0).ToString(),
"/", "\"))
            dgv_consist.Rows(i - 1).Height = 25
        End While
        Obj_Reader.Close()
        Dim j As Integer = 0
        'Normalisation de la matrice
        For j = 0 To Nbr_Alt - 1
            For i = 0 To Nbr_Alt - 1
                dgv_consist.Rows(j).Cells(i+1).Value= FormatNumber(CDbl(dgv_
alt.Rows(j).Cells(i+1).Value.ToString)* CDbl(dgv_norm.Rows(i).Cells(5).Value.
```

```
ToString), 5)
            Next
        Next
        'Calcul du poids des critères
        dgv_consist.Columns.Add(i + 1, "SOMME POND.")
        dgv_consist.Columns(i + 1).Width = 140
        dgv_consist.Columns(i+1).DefaultCellStyle.Alignment= DataGridViewCon-
tentAlignment.MiddleCenter
        dgv_consist.Columns.Add(i + 2, "VECT. PROPRE NORM.")
        dgv_consist.Columns(i + 2).Width = 140
        dgv_consist.Columns(i+2).DefaultCellStyle.Alignment= DataGridViewCon-
tentAlignment.MiddleCenter
        dgv_consist.Columns.Add(i + 3, "CONSISTANCE")
        dgv_consist.Columns(i + 3).Width = 140
        dgv_consist.Columns(i+3).DefaultCellStyle.Alignment= DataGridViewCon-
tentAlignment.MiddleCenter
        j = 0
        i = 0
        Dim Valeur_Inter As Double
        'Somme pondérée des valeurs par vecteur propre normalisé
        For j = 0 To Nbr_Alt - 1
            Valeur_Inter = 0
            For i = 0 To Nbr_Alt - 1
                Valeur_Inter = Valeur_Inter + FormatNumber(CDbl(dgv_consist.
Rows(j).Cells(i + 1).Value.ToString), 5)
            Next
            dgv_consist.Rows(j).Cells(4).Value = FormatNumber(Valeur_Inter, 5)
        Next
        'Vecteur propre normalisé
        For j = 0 To Nbr_Alt - 1
            dgv_consist.Rows(j).Cells(Nbr_Alt + 2).Value = 0
            Valeur_Inter = 0
            For i = 0 To Nbr_Alt - 1
                Valeur_Inter = Valeur_Inter + FormatNumber(CDbl(dgv_norm.
Rows(j).Cells(i + 1).Value.ToString), 5)
            Next
            dgv_consist.Rows(j).Cells(Nbr_Alt + 2).Value = FormatNumber(Valeur_
Inter / Nbr_Alt, 5)
        Next
        'Consistance
        For j = 0 To Nbr_Alt - 1
            dgv_consist.Rows(j).Cells(Nbr_Alt+3).Value= FormatNumber(dgv_con-
sist.Rows(j).Cells(Nbr_Alt+1).Value/ dgv_consist.Rows(j).Cells(Nbr_Alt +
2).Value, 5)
        Next
```

```
    lbl_lambda.Text = FormatNumber((CDbl(dgv_consist.Rows(0).Cells(Nbr_Alt
+ 3).Value.ToString) + CDbl(dgv_consist.Rows(1).Cells(Nbr_Alt + 3).Value.To-
String) + CDbl(dgv_consist.Rows(2).Cells(Nbr_Alt + 3).Value.ToString)) / 3, 5)
    lbl_CI.Text = FormatNumber((CDbl(lbl_lambda.Text.ToString) - 3) / 2,
5)
    lbl_RI.Text = FormatNumber(CDbl(lbl_CI.Text.ToString) / 0.58, 5)
    If lbl_RI.Text < 0.1 Then
        lbl_RI.ForeColor = Color.LightSkyBlue
    Else
        lbl_RI.ForeColor = Color.PeachPuff
    End If
End Sub
```

Figure 3.

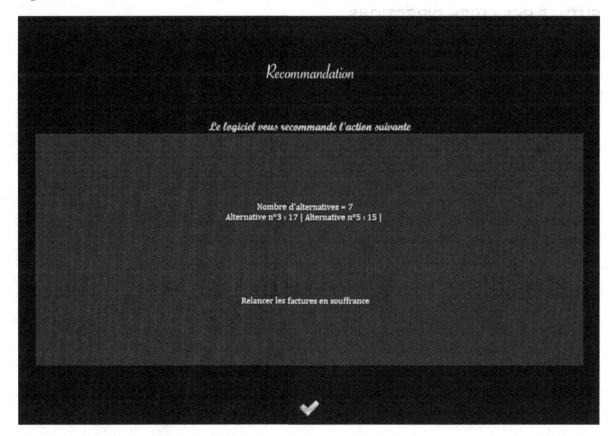

Example of a recommendation proposed by the GTiA software, among a selection of 7 alternatives in the case of a decrease in turnover observed by comparison with the commercial data of the previous year. The recommendation system suggests the user to dunning overdue invoices in order to generate cash.

CONCLUSION

The majority of companies are now equipped with internal management software, such as ERP, which offers a large number of functions in relation to user needs.

In this article, we have introduced the graphical user interface, forms, database and source code snippets of our recommendation system, which is intended to make it easier to manage the activities of employees of a company using an ERP.

As the historical part shows, setting up an ERP is a tight process, which must take into account a large number of constraints, both technical and operational since the risk is that the software will not be used, while the investment for its implementation represents a significant burden for the company.

Our goal is to come up with a recommendation that considers users' choices while giving them the ability to work on the task that best meets the wishes of management as well as the preferences of the end user, through granularity of the customizable recommendation.

FUTURE RESEARCH DIRECTIONS

User preferences are currently considered statically, but we are considering a second version that will handle them dynamically, with Machine Learning. The learning phase requires collecting data to allow our model to rely on a sufficient density of observations to learn. As the ability of a system to recognize and apply knowledge and skills on new tasks is based on the analysis of previous tasks, we must continue to use our static model in real conditions.

Actually, our system can be adapted to any type of ERP insofar as the data is made available in the format expected by the processing algorithm.

Time is a precious commodity which deserves to be used efficiently, without this being perceived by the user as a lack of confidence in the autonomy of decision-making. Our system is an opening towards a recommendation better accepted by the user and taking into account the well-being of the employee on the one hand and the management on the other.

REFERENCES

Acar, M. F., Tarim, M., Zaim, H., Zaim, S., & Delen, D. (2017). Knowledge management and ERP: Complementary or contradictory? *International Journal of Information Management, 37*(6), 703–712. doi:10.1016/j.ijinfomgt.2017.05.007

Al-Jabri, I. M., & Roztock, N. (2015). Adoption of ERP systems: Does information transparency matter? *Telematics and Informatics, 32*(2), 300–310. doi:10.1016/j.tele.2014.09.005

Boota-Genoulaz, V., Millet, P.-A., & Grabot, B. (2005). *A survey on the recent research literature on ERP systems*. Elsevier. doi:10.1016/j.compind.2005.02.004

Bronner A., & Zaraté P. (2020). A Decision Support System for working time management through an ERP. *ICDSST 2020 on Cognitive Decision Support Systems & Technologies,* 201-206.

Cannone, R., & Damret, J.-L. (2002). Résultats d'une enquête sur l'implantation et l'utilisation des ERP en France [Results of a survey on the implementation and use of ERP in France]. *Revue Française de Gestion Industrielle, 21*(4), 29–36.

Elragal, A. (2014). CENTERIS 2014 – ERP and Big Data: The Inept Couple. *Conference on ENTERprise Information Systems / ProjMAN 2014 - International Conference on Project MANagement / HCIST 2014 - International Conference on Health and Social Care Information Systems and Technologies,* 242-249.

Janssen, F. (2004). *L'interchangeabilité des critères de conceptualisation de la croissance: étude empirique* [The Interchangeability of Growth Conceptualization Criteria: Empirical Study]. IAG - LSM Working Papers - 04/118 Louvain School of Management - Strategy and Organisation.

Jenab, K., Staub, S., Moslehpour, S., & Wu, C. (2019). Company Performance Improvement by Quality Based Intelligent-ERP. *Decision Science Letters, 8,* 151–162. doi:10.5267/j.dsl.2018.7.003

Jones, M. C., Cline, M., & Ryan, S. (2006). Exploring Knowledge sharing in ERP implementation: An organizational culture framework. *Decision Support Systems, 41*(2), 411–434. doi:10.1016/j.dss.2004.06.017

Kast, R. (2002). *La théorie de la décision [Decision theory].* La Découverte.

Lecic D., & Kupusinac A. (2013). The Impact of ERP Systems on Business Decision-Making. *TEM Journal,* 323-326.

Lutovac, M., & Manojlov, D. (2012). The Successful Methodology for ERP Implementation. *Journal of Modern Accounting and Auditing, 8*(12), 1838-1847.

Mabert, V. A., Soni, A., & Venkataramanan, M. A. (2003). Enterprise resource planning: Managing the implementation process. *European Journal of Operational Research, 146*(2), 302–314. doi:10.1016/S0377-2217(02)00551-9

Madapusi, A., & D'Souza, D. (2012). The influence of ERP system implementation on the operational performance of an organization. *International Journal of Information Management, 32*(1), 24–34. doi:10.1016/j.ijinfomgt.2011.06.004

Meyssonnier, F., & Pourtier, F. (2004). *Le rôle essentiel du centre de compétences pour la réussite des projets ERP [The essential role of the competence center for the success of ERP projects].* Cahiers de Recherche du CEREMO.

Meyssonnier, F., & Pourtier, F. (2004). ERP, changement organisationnel et contrôle de gestion [ERP, organizational change and management control]. Congrès de l'AFC (Orléans).

Prasada Babu, M. S., & Hanumanth Sastry, S. (2014). Big data and predictive analytics in ERP systems for automating decision making process. *IEEE International Conference on Software Engineering and Service Sciences (ICSESS).*

Rakotoarivelo J. B. (2018). Décision Multicritère: Un système de recommandation pour le choix de l'opérateur d'agrégation [Multi-criteria decision: A recommendation system for the choice of the aggregation operator]. *IRIT.*

Reix, R. (2002). Changements organisationnels et technologies de l'information [Organizational changes and information technologies]. Cahiers du GREGO (Montpellier 2), 12.

Rowe F. (1999). Cohérence, intégration informationnelle et changement: esquisse d'un programme de recherche à partir des progiciels intégrés de gestion. *Systèmes d'information et management, 4*(12), 3-20.

Ruivo, P., Rodrigues, J., & Oliveira, T. (2015). The ERP surge of hybrid models - an exploratory research into five and ten years forecast. *Procedia Computer Science, 64*, 594–600. doi:10.1016/j.procs.2015.08.572

Saaty, T. L. (2003). Decision-making with the AHP: Why is the principal Eigenvector necessary. *European Journal of Operational Research, 145*(1), 85–91. doi:10.1016/S0377-2217(02)00227-8

Scapens, R., & Jazayeri, M. (2003). ERP Systems and Management Accounting Change: Opportunities or Impacts? A Research Note. *European Accounting Review, 12*(1), 201–233. doi:10.1080/0963818031000087907

Tarantilis, C. D., Kiranoudis, C. T., & Theodorakopoulos, N. D. (2008). A Web-based ERP system for business services and supply chain management: Application to real-world process scheduling. *European Journal of Operational Research, 187*(3), 1310–1326. doi:10.1016/j.ejor.2006.09.015

Tomas, J.-L. (2000). ERP et logiciels intégrés [ERP and integrated software] (2nd ed.). Dunod.

Foundational Recommender Systems for Business

Prageet Aeron

https://orcid.org/0000-0003-3957-5912

Management Development Institute, Gurgaon, India

INTRODUCTION

The role of the Internet in commerce has steadily risen with a large number of consumers and firms now completely transacting online. As a result, the need for better exploration and search for appropriate products or rather the most suitable products is an important activity. Starting out as simple catalogues and moving to advanced search, today's recommender systems are advanced prediction systems helping users identify the right products and helping firms improve their revenues and profitability. Recommender systems are also touted as efficient as they help in faster search and lesser transaction times for everyone involved. Since the recommender systems are such a primary component of today's online organizations, it is no surprise that it has been the subject of constant scrutiny and research with state of the art technologies and strategies being developed by the firms to get an edge over their competitors through better and better recommender systems. Right from Amazon to Netflix to Alibaba, no e-commerce website can hope to make it big without recommender systems. Therefore, students of business, executives involved in business and practitioners of technology all have stakes in learning and helping develop better recommender systems.

The present work briefly discusses the basic concepts and explores the state of art techniques in this important techno-commercial space. Author starts with neighborhood based collaborative filtering, subsequently the author discusses model based collaborative filtering, and then discussion proceeds to dimension reduction and latent factor models. Finally, the author touches upon the need and basic concepts of integrating various models and concludes the article with a brief discussion.

BACKGROUND

Any recommender system is likely to either identify top-k users or items or identify missing user-item ratings and both the formulations and all have their own advantages and disadvantages depending upon the business context (Aggarwal, 2016; Zanker, Feidrich & Jannach, 2011). Before delving deeper, it is important to understand the user-rating matrix which is the most important construct in the study of recommender systems. The users could be denoted by the rows and items by the columns with items being marked as per the obtained rating from a user. Therefore, for, m "user" and n "item" scenarios, we have a m x n matrix as the user-rating matrix. In other words, r(i,j) belongs to the m x n matrix, it represents the rating given to jth item by the ith user. A word on rating types is also necessary for the readers to fully comprehend the richness and at times appreciate the complexity of the problem being handled. Ratings in practical systems could be binary (Yes/No or Positive/Negative), interval-based

DOI: 10.4018/978-1-7998-9220-5.ch167

(Likert scale) or continuous ratings. Next we start with discussing neighbourhood based collaborative methods in detail.

NEIGHBOURHOOD BASED COLLABORATIVE FILTERING

Neighbourhood based collaborative filtering algorithms are amongst the earliest algorithms for the purpose of developing recommendations. The foundational idea of these algorithms is that similar consumers are likely to rate on similar lines and at the same time similar items have a higher probability of achieving similar ratings. As has been discussed before, the process of computing similarity is a primary activity among these algorithms. Let us discuss the steps involved in the execution of the neighborhood-based collaborative filtering algorithm and simultaneously develop an understanding about these algorithms. For assessing similarity between users we can utilize various similarity indices such as raw cosine similarity, adjusted cosine similarity or the Pearson's coefficient. Pearson's coefficient is considered better for the algorithm as it has a bias-adjustment effect as compared to other cosine indices. Another variation to similarity index is achieved by using a discount factor in cases when the common ratings are below a threshold value.

User-Based Model

Assuming we utilize the Pearson's coefficient; the first step is calculating the mean rating for each user given the ratings of items excluding the items for which rating is absent. Next we identify users in the user-rating matrix who have rated the same items and Pearson's coefficient is calculated taking into account the mean ratings. The Pearson coefficient is computed between the target user and all the other users and the k highest Pearson coefficient with respect to the target user are identified, and weighted average of the ratings of the missing item for target user are then calculated. Pearson coefficient for assessing similarity, however, can be calculated only across the intersection of the set of item ratings between the two users or in other words only if an item has been rated by both the users. Mathematically speaking, for the ith user,

$$\mu_i = \frac{\sum_j r_{ij}}{\left(number\,of\,items\,with\,ratings\right)} \forall i \left\{1...m\right\} \tag{1}$$

where j is an index representing items. Assuming intersection of set of items rated by user "u" and "v" by $u \cap v$,

$$Pearson's\,Coefficient\left(u,v\right) = \frac{\sum_{j \in u \cap v}\left(r_{uj} - \mu_u\right)*\left(r_{vj} - \mu_v\right)}{\sqrt{\sum_{j \in u \cap v}\left(r_{uj} - \mu_u\right)^2}\sqrt{\sum_{j \in u \cap v}\left(r_{vj} - \mu_v\right)^2}} \tag{2}$$

To further improve the results one may employ the mean centered rating of items for each user and subsequently compute the weighted mean rating for missing user-item rating. Many authors have also suggested usage of normalized or standardized rating as predicted output rather than mean centered ones with mixed response on benefit so obtained. However, in either of these cases appropriate inverse transformation will need to be applied to the rating function.

Item-based Model

Item-based models follow almost the same process as the user-based method with the difference that similarity index now shifts to the columns of the user-rating matrix or similarity between items is the consideration. The first step necessarily involves mean centering about zero for all user ratings and subsequently mean centering for each of the items. After identifying the set of users who have rated an item "i" and another set of users who have rated say item "j", Adjusted cosine similarity is then calculated between the items "i" and "j" respectively. In the expression below s_{ui} represents mean centered rating and Ui represents set of users who have specified ratings for item "i",

$$Adjusted\,Cosine\,Similarity\left(i,j\right) = \frac{\sum_{u \in U_i \cap U_j} s_{ui} * s_{uj}}{\sqrt{\sum_{u \in U_i \cap U_j} s_{ui}^2} \sqrt{\sum_{u \in U_i \cap U_j} s_{uj}^2}} \tag{3}$$

This way similarity between all possible items could also be calculated. Now the problem may be formulated as getting the predicted rating of item "x" for user "U". After identifying top-k similar items to "x" for which user 'U" has marked ratings in the past, weighted average ratings of these items could be used as a prediction for the rating of item "x" for user "U". The weights here are the adjusted cosine similarity between item "j" and "x". So, for predicting rating r_{Ux}, we have,

$$r_{Ux} = \frac{\sum_{j \in top\,k, U} Adjusted\,Cosine\left(j, x\right) * r_{Uj}}{\sum_{j \in top\,k, U} Adjusted\,Cosine\left(j, x\right)} \tag{4}$$

In terms of the implementation of above algorithms, a portion of the calculation can be maintained as static data (infrequently calculated) that could be used in making recommendations when required. Computational complexity of both the user-based and item-based algorithms is similar with upper bound of O(m^2*n) and O(n^2*m) with m users and n items (actual order will be dependent on ratio of item ratings present or sparsity of the matrix) respectively. Since the item-based neighborhood algorithms incorporate user's own ratings they are likely better in performance as compared to user-based models. On the other hand, user-based methods could be utilized for more undiscovered options as compared to conventional options generated by item-based methods. Another advantage in favor of item-based models is that number of items is relatively stable as compared to number of users in a business context and so item based methods are much more likely to be stable overtime. Neighborhood models overall are known for their simple approach and effective outcomes though sparsity of the user-rating matrix is a major computational and storage concern.

Relationship Between Neighborhood Based Algorithms and Clustering

As established in the para above, the offline phase of neighborhood-based algorithms could be computationally intensive especially with a large number of customers and items alike. Clustering methods could help in reducing the computational effort substantially. Any basic clustering algorithm helps create clusters of similar users based on distance over "n" items. This can help in computing weighted average on unknown rating for a given user-item target, with only users from the given cluster forming the basis of weighted average. This process therefore represents a trade-off between intensity of offline computation in the original algorithm versus accuracy of the original algorithm as clustering is more efficient in general. However, the process of clustering has to undergo adaptation in this context due to missing ratings. Authors have suggested using distance measure devoid of missing ratings or normalizing distance measure with number of available ratings as well as shifting to Manhattan distance measure instead of Euclidean norm. Various clustering based variants have been proposed by authors involving not just user-based and item-based methods but also co-clustering based methods (Sarwar, Karypis, Konstan, & Reidl, 2002; Xu, Bu, Chen & Cai, 2012; Xue, in, Yang, Xi, Zeng, Yu, & Chen, 2005; Chee, Hang, & Wang, 2001; Yildirim & Krishnamoorthy, 2008).

RELATIONSHIP BETWEEN NEIGHBORHOOD BASED ALGORITHMS AND REGRESSION BASED METHODS

A careful examination of the above algorithms tells us that the unknown user ratings are weighted linear combinations of the existing user-ratings for similar users or similar items as the case may be. But this could be construed as a special case of the regression model that involves a set of k-similar users or items rather than regression based prediction of unknown user-rating that may include as dependent variables all possible user ratings of item "j" or all ratings by user "u". The choice of weights in a linear regression model are driven by optimization rather than the heuristic driven method which involves choosing k-similar users and their similarity index as weights. Next author examines the user-based nearest neighbor regression method for prediction of user-ratings.

User-Based Nearest Neighbor Regression

In neighborhood based models, the set of similar users $S_u(j)$ was the set of k closest users to target user u, who have specified ratings for item j. In the case of regression methods, the set $S_u(j)$ is defined by first calculating the k closest peers for each user on an absolute basis, and then retaining only those for whom ratings are present. However, parameter k is much larger in the context of regression based models. The idea here is to utilize the k-nearest user ratings to predict the known ratings of a user "u" for each known item rating of the user. This acts like training data and enables the learning of the model with error function as the squared error between actual rating and predicted rating. Standard linear regression algorithm can easily determine the coefficients for the various users and then can be used for predicting the ratings of unrated items.

$$\widehat{r_{uj}} = \mu_u + \sum_{v \in S_u(j)} w_{uv} * \left(r_{vj} - \mu_v \right) \tag{5}$$

$$Minimize \, \phi_u = \sum_{u \in S_u(j)} \left(r_{uj} - \widehat{r_{uj}} \right)^2 \tag{6}$$

The above problem could be formulated as the sum of multiple optimization problems for all users or individual optimization problems for each user as is formulated above. Although it is much more effective if individual problems can be solved using a linear regression process. Any further augmentation to the objective function such as introduction of regularization term etc. have also been proposed and offer further value add in the form of preventing overfitting and reducing model complexity. We do not dwell on these variants in this section.

Item-Based Nearest Neighbor Regression

The process followed is very similar to the one discussed above with the only difference that predictors are the nearest neighbors of the target item and the weights used are adjusted cosine similarity indices. The optimization problems are set up just as explained in the user-based case. The rating prediction for target item "t" is given by expression below where $S_t(u)$ represents the subset of the k nearest neighbors of the target item,

$$\widehat{r_{ut}} = \sum_{j \in S_t(u)} w_{jt} * r_{uj} \qquad (7)$$

Other modeling aspects remain the same.

MODEL BASED COLLABORATIVE FILTERING

While neighborhood-based filtering methods are akin to instance based learning methods which involve pre-processing to predict for a specific instance, model based methods are formal supervised or unsupervised learning methods where a model has been established for prediction of test case. However, collaborative filtering methods bring to fore a slightly different problem as compared to data classification models. Firstly, rows and columns work in an interchangeable way (user vs item) in collaborative filtering problems, secondly, clear separation exists both between training, validation and testing data as well as predicted variables and attributes. In fact, collaborative filtering methods are more data completion problems but given the generic nature of these problems almost all theoretical results from the field of machine learning can be applied with some changes and it has led to more efficient algorithms for collaborative filtering. As an example, the author presents the decision tree method which is an established machine learning method and further explores rule based method and Naive Bayesian methods from the data mining family.

Decision Tree Method

As is well understood, the decision tree method is based on separation of data based on entropy measured by any suitable index such as the Gini Index. At each node beginning the root node, the lowest Gini index is used to identify the most appropriate attribute to partition the data. The process is followed consecutively till sufficient separation or leaf nodes are attained. The process may also be utilized with appropriate variation to continuous dependent variables. Pruning helps in avoiding overfitting. Moving further from conventional decision trees would require tackling problems posed before such as sparsity and missing data etc. For each attribute as a dependent variable a different tree would need to be constructed. While predicting the rating of a particular item (user) for a user (item), the decision tree corresponding to the relevant item (user) is used for prediction. Another parallel approach looks at the process of dimension reduction to transform the m x n-1 ratings matrix (excluding say jth attribute) into m x d matrix, where d << n-1, and every attribute is specified. For projecting the ratings of users one of the methods discussed in the latent factors section is used and the new reduced representation is used for constructing the decision tree for the jth item by treating the problem as a classification or regression method. This approach like the earlier case is used for all attributes from 1 to n, and leads to creation of n decision trees. In other words, to get the rating of item j for a user i, the ith row of the m × d matrix is used and the jth decision tree is used as the model to predict the required rating.

Rule Based Methods

The rule-based collaborative filtering starts by discovering all the association rules at a pre-specified level of minimum support and confidence. Only those rules are kept for analysis where one item is present as a consequent. An association rule is said to be relevant if the itemset in the antecedent of the rule is a subset of the items preferred by that target. All rules are then sorted in order of reducing confidence and the top k items discovered in the consequents are recommended (Sarwar Karypis, Konstan, & Reidl, 2001). This is comparatively a simpler method with a greater dependence on data mining related techniques.

Naive Bayes Method

Similar to the existing theme of discussion where we discuss machine learning methods and their modification to suit the collaboration requirements, we now take up the Naive Bayes method. Naive Bayes assumes categorical values, say, "l" different categories given by {v1,v2,v3...vl}. Similar to the standard formulations discussed before we assume a ratings matrix of m x n with m users and n items. We consider a user "i" who has notified ratings for a set of items which we refer to as Si. For Bayes classifier to be able to predict the user "i" ratings for item "j" which is not a part of set Si, we will invoke the conditional probability rule of Bayes for events A and B,

$$P(A|B) = P(A)*P(B|A)/ P(B) -- \tag{8}$$

So we need to develop an estimate for P(rij = vd | Observed ratings in Si). So for each value of d ∈ {1....l}, we have,

$$P(rij = vd | Observed\ ratings\ in\ Si) = \frac{P\left(rij = vd\right)* P\left(Observed\ ratings \in Si\ /\ rij = vd\right)}{P\left(Observed\ ratings \in Si\right)} \tag{9}$$

The denominator is independent of "d", therefore can be ignored and based on naive assumption conditional independence can be utilized for the estimation purpose, giving us the following expression,

$$P\left(rij = vd\ /\ Observedratings \in Si\right) \propto P\left(rij = vd\right)* \prod_{k\epsilon Si} P\left(rik = vd\ /\ rij = vd\right) \tag{10}$$

This estimate can then be utilized for estimating rij either by employing a process similar to maximum likelihood where in the maximum value of the above expression is understood as the estimate of the rij,

$$\widehat{rij} = argmax_{vd} P\left(rij = vd\right) * \prod\nolimits_{k \in Si} P\left(rik = vd \,/\, rij = vd\right) \tag{11}$$

Another approach is estimating by weighted average of all ratings with probability used as weights,

$$\widehat{rij} = \frac{\sum_{d=1}^{l} vd * P\left(rij = vd\right) * \prod_{k \in Si} P\left(rik \,/\, rij = vd\right)}{\sum_{d=1}^{l} P\left(rij = vd\right) * \prod_{k \in Si} P\left(rik \,/\, rij = vd\right)} \tag{12}$$

Sparsity of real world data often creates a computational problem in the above mentioned methods. Therefore, arises a need for possible reduction in data dimensionality for better efficiency. A reduced representation of the data can be either row-based or column-based latent factors. Depending on the dimension that has been transformed into latent factors, the system may be used for either user-based neighborhood algorithms or item-based neighborhood algorithms. Author next examines latent factor models.

REDUCTION OF DIMENSIONS AND LATENT FACTOR MODELS

In the latent factor method, the m × n user-rating matrix is transformed into a lower-dimensional space by using either principal component analysis (PCA) or singular value decomposition (SVD). The resulting matrix is of size m × d, where d<<n and new user ratings are specified as a d-dimensional vector which is fully specified. After this d-dimensional representation of each user is determined, the similarity is computed from the target user to each user using the transformed data. The similarity computations in the reduced space are not only more robust but also more efficient from a computational point of view. The first step in this method involves filling up the missing values in the user-rating matrix by mean values from either the row or the column. The next step involves the similarity calculation between items or between users. The n x n matrix or the m x m matrix obtained after determining similarity between items or users is then subjected to the SVD process. This reduced dimension system is then used for predicting the user rating for unrated items based on neighborhood algorithms discussed in sections above after identifying the k-similar group from the representation. The process of SVD may be replaced by PCA as well with the difference that instead of similarity matrix covariance matrix comes into picture for analysis purposes. The ratings are often mean centered for reducing bias. Bias can also be reduced by either bringing in an EM algorithm to generate the data, using maximum likelihood estimate for co-variance matrix construction or utilizing truncated SVD factorization method for assessing the similarity between users or items as required.

Direct method for matrix completion is another of latent factor models where the basic idea is that various portions of the rows and columns of data matrices are highly correlated. Therefore, the data has natural redundancy and so the original matrix is approximated well by a low-rank matrix and offers a robust estimation of the missing entries. In order to understand the dimensionality reduction better we need to bring in a perspective from factorization of matrices. The key idea is that any m × n matrix R of rank k <<min {m, n} can always be expressed as a product of rank-k factors, that is, R = UL^T . U

is an m × k matrix, and L is an n × k matrix. The error of this approximation is equal to $\|R - UL^T\|^2$ and the resulting residual matrix is $(R - UL^T)$. The ability to factorize any rank-k and above matrix is a characteristic property and many such factorizations are possible. SVD is one such example wherein the factors are orthogonal to each other. The real strength of the approach is based on no dependency with regard to the matrix R being fully specified, but one can still successfully calculate all the entries of the latent factors U and L. Since latent factor models are the state of the art with respect to recommender systems, next the author discusses the variants of the factorization methods.

Unconstrained Matrix Factorization

In a fully specified ratings matrix, unconstrained matrix factorization can be easily formulated as an unconstrained optimization problem as follows.

$$\text{Minimize } J = 1/2*(R-UL^T)(R-UL^T)^T \tag{13}$$

However, it is unlikely that the ratings matrix will be fully specified and in case of missing entries the above function would need to be modified. Let the set of all user-item pairs (i, j), which are observed in R, be denoted by S. Here, $i \in \{1 \ldots m\}$ is the index of a user, and $j \in \{1 \ldots n\}$ is the index of an item. Therefore, the set S of observed user-item pairs is defined as follows:

$S = \{(i, j): r_{ij} \text{ is observed}\}$

Based on observed values, factorization can be achieved and the predicted values approximating a fully specified matrix can be obtained. The (i, j)th entry of matrix R can be predicted as follows:

$$\widehat{r_{ij}} = \sum_{s=1}^{k} u_{is} * l_{js} \tag{14}$$

The difference between the predicted value and the observed value of a specified entry (i, j) is the error and is given by $e_{ij} = (r_{ij} - \hat{r}_{ij})$. This error term forms the basis of the modified optimization problem (summed over only the observed values) given by,

$$Minimize\ J = \left(1/2\right)\sum_{(i,j)\varepsilon s} e_{ij}^2 = \left(1/2\right)\sum_{(i,j)\varepsilon s}\left(r_{ij} - \sum_{s=1}^{k} u_{is} * l_{js}\right)^2 \tag{15}$$

This minimization problem can be solved by using the conventional gradient descent method and invoking the partial differentiation of the cost function with respect to u_{ig} and l_{jg},

$$\frac{\partial J}{u_{ig}} = \sum_{i,j\varepsilon S}\left(r_{ij} - \sum_{s=1}^{k}\left(u_{is} * l_{is}\right)\right)\left(-l_{jg}\right) = \sum_{i,j\varepsilon S} e_{ij} * \left(-l_{jg}\right), \tag{16}$$

where $\forall i\varepsilon(1,2,3,\ldots,m)$, $\forall g\varepsilon(1,2,3,\ldots,k)$

$$\frac{\partial J}{l_{jg}} = \sum_{i,j\varepsilon S}\left(r_{ij} - \sum_{s=1}^{k}\left(u_{is} * l_{is}\right)\right)\left(-u_{ig}\right) = \sum_{i,j\varepsilon S}e_{ij} * \left(-u_{ig}\right), \tag{17}$$

where $\forall j\varepsilon(1,2,3,\ldots,n)$, $\forall g\varepsilon(1,2,3,\ldots,k)$

The vector of partial derivatives provides the gradient with respect to the vector of (m + n)*k decision variables in the matrices U and L and are updated using small step size α.

$$u_{ig} = u_{ig} + \alpha * \sum_{i,j\varepsilon S}e_{ij} * \left(-l_{jg}\right) \tag{18}$$

$$l_{jg} = l_{jg} + \alpha * \sum_{i,j\varepsilon S}e_{ij} * \left(-u_{ig}\right) \tag{19}$$

This method represents the batch update variant of the gradient descent method. Another more famous variant that is used is the stochastic gradient descent method. In the stochastic method instead of change of weight for the components after one complete epoch, change of weights is affected at each step for the observed rating r_{ij}. Stochastic methods are known to reach convergence much faster as compared to batch methods and are the go to method for larger data sets. The utilization of few values to predict the other values at times may also lead to a prominent machine learning problem of overfitting which can be overcome by bringing in the regularization theory. In regularization, the idea is to discourage very large values of the coefficients in U and L in order to encourage stability. Therefore, a regularization term, (λ /2) ($\|U\|^2 + \|L\|^2$), is added to the objective function, where $\lambda > 0$ is the regularization parameter with the aim to bring down the values of coefficients that do not impact the objective function in a major way. Here we briefly express the objective function and the partial differentials of the decision variables for a quick comparison between non-regularized and regularized problem formulation.

$$Minimize\ J = \left(1/2\right)\sum_{(i,j)\varepsilon s}e_{ij}^{2}$$
$$= \left(1/2\right)\sum_{(i,j)\varepsilon s}\left(r_{ij} - \sum_{s=1}^{k}u_{is} * l_{js}\right)^{2} + \left(\lambda/2\right)\sum_{i=1}^{m}\sum_{s=1}^{k}u_{is}^{2} + \left(\lambda/2\right)\sum_{j=1}^{n}\sum_{s=1}^{k}l_{js}^{2} \tag{20}$$

$$\frac{\partial J}{u_{ig}} = \sum_{i,j\varepsilon S}e_{ij} * \left(-l_{jg}\right) + \lambda * u_{ig}, where\ \forall i\varepsilon\left(1,2,3..m\right), \forall g\varepsilon\left(1,2,3,...k\right) \tag{21}$$

$$\frac{\partial J}{l_{jg}} = \sum_{i,j\varepsilon S}e_{ij} * \left(-u_{ig}\right) + \lambda * l_{jg}, where\ \forall j\varepsilon\left(1,2,3..n\right), \forall g\varepsilon\left(1,2,3,...k\right) \tag{22}$$

Subsequently, the update rule would depend on the variant of the gradient descent algorithm being used for the solution. We present the stochastic version below for the reader below,

$$u_{ig} = u_{ig} + \alpha\sum_{i,j\varepsilon S}\left(e_{ij}l_{jg} - \lambda u_{ig}\right) \tag{23}$$

$$l_{jg} = l_{jg} + \alpha \sum_{i,j \in S} \left(e_{ij} u_{ig} - \lambda l_{jg} \right) \tag{24}$$

We also present the more efficient (computationally) vectorized form over the k-dimensional factor vectors of user i and item j as follows,

$$\vec{u_i} = \vec{u_i} + \alpha \left(e_{ij} \vec{l_j} - \lambda \vec{u_i} \right) \tag{25}$$

$$\vec{l_j} = \vec{l_j} + \alpha \left(e_{ij} \vec{u_i} - \lambda \vec{l_j} \right) \tag{26}$$

Finally, various methods of parameter tuning such as cross validation may be employed to identify the most appropriate value for λ.

Role of User Bias and Item Bias

A variant of the unconstrained method incorporating user or item bias (Sarwar et al., 2001) involves a mean centering of the rating matrix with respect to overall ratings mean. Let the bias of user i be bi and for item j be dj. Now in the predicted rating matrix a part of the (i,j)th rating is explained by bi + dj and the remaining by the product of UL^T. The predicted rating is given by,

$$\widehat{r_{ij}} = b_i + d_j + \sum_{s=1}^{k} u_{is} * l_{js} \tag{27}$$

$$e_{ij} = r_{ij} - \widehat{r_{ij}} = r_{ij} - b_i - d_j - \sum_{s=1}^{k} u_{is} * l_{js} \tag{28}$$

The change from the unconstrained factor model is that now we seek larger factor matrices of size m × (k + 2) and n × (k + 2), respectively and these are the bias columns. The original formulation now incorporates the two constraints, that is, the last column of the user-factor matrix and the second last column of the item-factor matrix is set to all 1s. Just like the original case one can use either the gradient descent or the stochastic gradient descent for the solution of the optimization problem with the same update rules. Only the two columns that have been set as 1s need to stay static and so after each update they need to be reset to 1s. All the previous discussion about initialization, learning rate and regularization all hold true. Below we present the optimization formulation.

$$Minimize \ J = \left(1/2 \right) \sum_{(i,j) \in s} \left(r_{ij} - \sum_{s=1}^{k+2} u_{is} * l_{js} \right)^2 + \left(\lambda / 2 \right) \sum_{i=1}^{m} \sum_{s=1}^{k+2} u_{is}^2 + \left(\lambda / 2 \right) \sum_{j=1}^{n} \sum_{s=1}^{k+2} l_{js}^2 \tag{29}$$

where, (k + 2)th column of U and (k+1) th column of L contains only 1s.

Clearly, baseline ratings can be developed by using item popularity or user generosity and these could help in improving the recommendation models.

Models Incorporating Implicit Feedback

Often buying of products can be considered as implicit acceptance of the product. For such cases two methods have been reported as effective, namely asymmetric factor model and SVD++. The basic idea behind these methods is that the user rating factor can be expressed as the linear combination of the latent factors of item ratings. Author discusses both the approaches below and in addition also presents a brief overview of SVD for completeness.

1. **Asymmetric factor model:** The first step is to derive the implicit feedback matrix from explicit matrix R (mxn) and for this any observed value is replaced by 1 and non-observed value is replaced by a zero. Subsequently, the matrix is normalized with L-2 norm to give the matrix F, so for a user i, every nonzero entry in the ith row is 1/|Ci|(1/2). Another matrix Y which is n x k matrix of implicit item factor ratings together with matrix F above gives the U equivalent matrix of the factorization discussed as above. In other words, replace U by FY and other aspects of the method remain the same. The most important aspect of this method is explain ability of the model based on item ratings and item factors.

2. **SVD++:** In this approach user-factor matrix FY is used to modify the explicit user-factor matrix U by adding FY matrix to it. The new ratings matrix R, m x n is given by $(U + FY)L^T$, where the second term of the expression is the implicit feedback matrix. In case a complete problem formulation including user and item bias is to be incorporated, the following expression is easy to reach after appropriate global mean centering of the given ratings matrix.

$$\widehat{r}_{ij} = \sum_{s=1}^{k+2}\left(u_{is} + \left[FY\right]_{is}\right)l_{js} = \sum_{s=1}^{k+2}\left(u_{is} + \sum_{h\epsilon C_i}\frac{y_{hs}}{\sqrt{|C_i|}}\right)l_{js} \tag{30}$$

$$Minimize\ J = \left(1/2\right)\sum_{(i,j)\epsilon s}\left(r_{ij} - \sum_{s=1}^{k+2}\left(u_{is} + \sum_{h\epsilon C_i}\frac{y_{hs}}{\sqrt{|C_i|}}\right)l_{js}\right)^2$$
$$+\left(\lambda/2\right)\sum_{i=1}^{m}\sum_{s=1}^{k+2}u_{is}^2 + \left(\lambda/2\right)\sum_{j=1}^{n}\sum_{s=1}^{k+2}l_{js}^2 + \left(\lambda/2\right)\sum_{j=1}^{m}\sum_{s=1}^{k+2}y_{js}^2 \tag{31}$$

This is subject to the constraints that the (k + 2)th column of U contains only 1s, (k + 1)th column of L contains only 1s and the last two columns of Y contain only 0s. The last condition is necessitated by the matrix addition requirement of U and FY. The update rules as per the stochastic gradient descent are given by,

$$u_{ig} = u_{ig} + \alpha\left(e_{ij}l_{jg} - \lambda u_{ig}\right)\forall g\epsilon\left\{1,2,3..k+2\right\} \tag{32}$$

$$l_{jg} = l_{jg} + \alpha\left(e_{ij}\left(u_{ig} + \sum_{h\epsilon C_i}\frac{y_{hg}}{\sqrt{|C_i|}}\right) - \lambda l_{jg}\right)\forall g\epsilon\left\{1,2,3..k+2\right\} \tag{33}$$

$$y_{hg} = y_{hg} + \alpha \left(\frac{e_{ij} l_{jg}}{\sqrt{|C_i|}} - \lambda y_{hg} \right) \forall g\epsilon \left\{1,2,3..k+2\right\} \forall h\epsilon\, C_i \tag{34}$$

but the constrained columns do not need to be updated.

3. **Singular Value Decomposition (SVD):** SVD involves factorization of a matrix into two matrices like before but with an additional constraint that requires U and L to be orthogonal. A fully specified matrix ratings matrix R may be factorized as, $R = Q_k \Delta_k P_k^T$, where rank k << min{m,n} and Qk, Δk, and Pk are matrices of size m × k, k × k, and n × k, respectively. The matrix QkΔk (U) contains the transformed and reduced m × k representation of the original ratings matrix in the basis corresponding to Pk (L). As usual the optimization problem can be set up and solved. However, for unspecified ratings matrices a different approach is required. We need to first pre-process and convert existing rating matrix to row-wise mean centered matrix Rc and the missing entries of the matrix Rc are set up as zeros. SVD is then performed and the user and item factor are so obtained. Then, the rating r̂ ij of user i for item j is estimated as the following adjusted dot product of u_i and l_j:

$$\widehat{r_{ij}} = \mu_i + \vec{u_i} \cdot \vec{l_j} \tag{35}$$

where μ_i stands for row mean for ith user. However, this method brings in considerable bias in the solution so either maximum likelihood estimation method may be used or one may resort to iterative SVD. In the iterative SVD, after initialization of the unknown values by the mean of the row of ith user, SVD factorization is conducted, and then the values which substituted earlier in the step are changed based on factorization results till convergence is achieved. Iterative approach may as well be replaced by optimization approach further bolstered by incorporating bias model as well as regularization parameters. However, the author does not present the detailed expressions here and the interested reader is advised to refer to standard work in the domain (Shen & Huang, 2008; Bertsekas, 1995).

INTEGRATING VARIOUS NEIGHBORHOOD MODELS AND LATENT FACTOR MODELS

Author has presented many prominent models and algorithms for the recommendation methods and here the author presents an integrated model formulation for the benefit of the readers. The model presented here draws on many of the concepts and formulation ideas that have been discussed before. The first step in the integrated model is the baseline estimator using a bias-centric model assuming a mean centered ratings matrix. Let b_i^{user}, b_j^{item} be the bias of the user and the item, one can predict the rating by,

$$\widehat{r_{ij}} = b_i^{user} + b_j^{item} \tag{36}$$

and assume S as before be the pairs of indices corresponding to the observed entries in the ratings matrix.

S = {(i, j): r ij is observed}

The objective function is given by:

$$Minimize\ J = \left(1/2\right)\sum_{i,j\in S}\left(r_{ij} - \widehat{r}_{ij}\right)^2 + \left(\frac{\lambda}{2}\right)\left(\sum_{i=1}^{m}\left(b_i^{user}\right)^2 + \sum_{j=1}^{n}\left(b_j^{item}\right)^2\right) \tag{37}$$

The above optimization problem can be solved by invoking the SGD algorithm with the following update rules,

$$b_i^{user} = b_i^{user} + \alpha\left(e_{ij} - \lambda b_i^{user}\right) \tag{38}$$

$$b_j^{item} = b_j^{item} + \alpha\left(e_{ij} - \lambda b_j^{item}\right) \tag{39}$$

After solving for b_i^{user}, b_j^{item} the rating can be predicted and identified as B$_{ij}$ for the subsequent integration process. Next we look at the neighborhood part of the model. It has seen before that incorporating bias into neighborhood model leads to the following predicted ratings,

$$\widehat{r}_{ij} = b_i^{user} + b_j^{item} + \frac{\sum_{l\in Q_j(i)} w_{lj}^{item}\left(r_{il} - b_i^{user} - b_l^{item}\right)}{\sqrt{\left|Q_j(i)\right|}} \tag{40}$$

The variable w^{item}_{lj} represents the item-item regression coefficient between item l and item j. The set $Q_j(i)$ represents the subset of the K nearest items to j that have been rated by the ith user. Within the expression the values of b_i^{user}, b_l^{item} are replaced by B$_{lj}$, which is a constant. The model is further enhanced by bringing in the item-item implicit feedback which author refers to as clj, the overall expression is presented below,

$$\widehat{r}_{ij} = b_i^{user} + b_j^{item} + \frac{\sum_{l\in Q_j(i)} w_{lj}^{item}\left(r_{il} - B_{il}\right)}{\sqrt{\left|Q_j(i)\right|}} + \frac{\sum_{l\in Q_j(i)} c_{lj}}{\sqrt{\left|Q_j(i)\right|}} \tag{41}$$

The optimization expression will be similar to the mentioned above, and the corresponding updates based on above expression are exactly the same for the two bias variables and for the weight variable and item-item implicit feedback is as follows,

$$w_{lj}^{item} = w_{lj}^{item} + \alpha_2\left(\frac{e_{ij} w_{lj}^{item}\left(r_{il} - B_{il}\right)}{\sqrt{\left|Q_j(i)\right|}} - \lambda_2 w_{lj}^{item}\right) \tag{42}$$

$$c_{lj} = c_{lj} + \alpha_2 \left(\frac{e_{ij}}{\sqrt{|Q_j(i)|}} - \lambda_2 c_{lj} \right) \tag{43}$$

Now author bring in the latent factor model part whereby rating is predicted as follows,

$$\widehat{r_{ij}} = \sum_{s=1}^{k+2} \left(u_{is} + \sum_{h \in I_i} \frac{y_{hs}}{\sqrt{|I_i|}} \right) l_{js} \tag{44}$$

with additional constraints that $(k+2)^{th}$ column of U is set to 1s, $(k+1)^{th}$ column of L is set to 1s and the last two columns of Y are set to zeros. This brings reader to the integrated model where all the above mentioned components are brought together as follows,

$$\widehat{r_{ij}} = \frac{\sum_{l \in Q_j(i)} w_{lj}^{item} (r_{il} - B_{il})}{\sqrt{|Q_j(i)|}} + \frac{\sum_{l \in Q_j(i)} c_{lj}}{\sqrt{|Q_j(i)|}} + \sum_{s=1}^{k+2} \left(u_{is} + \sum_{h \in I_i} \frac{y_{hs}}{\sqrt{|I_i|}} \right) l_{js} \tag{45}$$

The optimization formulation for the integrated model is given by the expression below,

$$Minimize\ J = (1/2) \sum_{(i,j) \in s} \left(r_{ij} - \widehat{r_{ij}} \right)^2 + (\lambda_1 / 2) \sum_{i=1}^{m} \sum_{s=1}^{k+2} u_{is}^2 + (\lambda_1 / 2) \sum_{j=1}^{n} \sum_{s=1}^{k+2} l_{js}^2$$
$$+ (\lambda_1 / 2) \sum_{j=1}^{m} \sum_{s=1}^{k+2} y_{js}^2 + (\lambda_2 / 2) \sum_{j=1}^{n} \sum_{l \in Q_j(i)} \left(\left(w_{lj}^{item} \right)^2 + c_{lj}^2 \right) \tag{46}$$

subject to:

(k + 2)th column of U contains only 1s;

(k + 1)th column of L contains only 1s;

and the last two columns of Y contain only zeros.

The solution to the above optimization problem can be obtained by invoking the standard SGD algorithm and the updates are as follows,

$$u_{ig} = u_{ig} + \alpha \left(e_{ij} l_{jg} - \lambda u_{ig} \right) \forall g \in \{1, 2, 3..k+2\} \tag{47}$$

$$l_{jg} = l_{jg} + \alpha \left(e_{ij} \left(u_{ig} + \sum_{h \in I_i} \frac{y_{hg}}{\sqrt{|I_i|}} \right) - \lambda l_{jg} \right) \forall g \in \{1, 2, 3..k+2\} \tag{48}$$

$$y_{hg} = y_{hg} + \alpha \left(\frac{e_{ij} l_{jg}}{\sqrt{|I_i|}} - \lambda y_{hg} \right) \forall g \epsilon \{1,2,3..k+2\} \forall h \epsilon\, I_i \tag{49}$$

$$w_{lj}^{item} = w_{lj}^{item} + \alpha_2 \left(\frac{e_{ij} w_{lj}^{item} \left(r_{il} - B_{il} \right)}{\sqrt{|Q_j(i)|}} - \lambda_2 w_{lj}^{item} \right) \forall l \epsilon\, Q_j(i) \tag{50}$$

$$c_{lj} = c_{lj} + \alpha_2 \left(\frac{e_{ij}}{\sqrt{|Q_j(i)|}} - \lambda_2 c_{lj} \right) \forall l \epsilon\, Q_j(i) \tag{51}$$

Further, the fixed columns of U, L and Y are maintained as such. The accuracy of the above process has been identified as higher than both pure latent factor approach and pure neighborhood approach methods (Koren, 2010). This also forms the genesis of combining various methods together to form the hybrid recommender systems.

CONCLUSION AND FUTURE RESEARCH DIRECTION

Article starts the discussion with basic neighborhood collaborative methods with discussion bringing out the pros and cons of user based as well as item based models as well as the utility of mixed models. The article also explores the close relationship of neighborhood models with both clustering and regression techniques with regard to predicting unknown ratings. Subsequently the article explores the model based methods of recommender systems wherein the author discusses the close relationship between machine learning models and data mining methods such as Naive Bayesian in the larger scheme of recommendations. The sparsity of data and computational complexity involved brings the need for dimensionality reduction and a clear need for latent factor models. Latent factor models have been presented for the benefit of readers in a way to enable them to cross-compare and understand the incremental steps between SVD, SVD++ and asymmetric models as well as a brief description of models incorporating user bias. Lastly, the author presents a typical example of bringing together the various concepts and techniques together in the integrated model which has been known to produce better results than standalone models thereby motivating the need for hybrid models to be explored in the next series of articles.

Clearly, this work reviews and discusses the theoretical basis of neighborhood methods, modeling based methods and dimension reduction methods as well as their interactions in the evolving subject of recommender systems. However, the paucity of space and need for justice toward other equally important topics have prevented the author from discussing related work in the present article. Author intends to analyze topics such as content aware recommender systems, knowledge based systems and context aware recommender systems in the follow up article.

REFERENCES

Adomavicius, G., & Tuzhilin, A. (2011). Context-Aware Recommender Systems. In B. Shapira, P. B. Kantor, F. Ricci, & L. Rokach (Eds.), *Recommender Systems Handbook* (pp. 217–253). Springer. doi:10.1007/978-0-387-85820-3_7

Aggarwal, C. C. (2015). *Data Mining: The Textbook*. Springer International Publishing.

Aggarwal, C. C. (2016). *Recommender Systems: The Textbook*. Springer International Publishing. doi:10.1007/978-3-319-29659-3

Bar, A., Rokach, L., Shani, G., Shapira, B., & Schclar, A. (2013). Boosting simple collaborative filtering models using ensemble method. *Multiple Classifier Systems*, 1-12.

Barragáns-Martínez, A. B., Costa-Montenegro, E., Burguillo, J. C., Rey-López, M., Mikic-Fonte, F. A., & Pel, A. (2010). A hybrid content-based and item-based collaborative filtering approach to recommend TV programs enhanced with singular value decomposition. *Information Sciences*, 80(22), 4290–4311. doi:10.1016/j.ins.2010.07.024

Basu, C., Hirsh, H., & Cohen, W. (1998). Recommendation as classification: using social and content-based information in recommendation. AAAI, 714-720.

Bertsekas, D. P. (1995). *Nonlinear programming*. Athena Scientific.

Burke, R. (2002). Hybrid recommender systems: Survey and experiments. *User Modeling and User-Adapted Interaction*, 12(4), 331–370. doi:10.1023/A:1021240730564

Burke, R., Hammond, K., & Young, B. (1997). The FindMe approach to assisted browsing. *IEEE Expert*, 12(4), 32–40. doi:10.1109/64.608186

Chee, S., Han, J., & Wang, K. (2001). Rectree: An efficient collaborative filtering method. *Data Warehousing and Knowledge Discovery*, 141-151.

Koren, Y. (2010). Factor in the neighbors: Scalable and accurate collaborative filtering. *ACM Transactions on Knowledge Discovery from Data*, 4(1), 1–24. doi:10.1145/1644873.1644874

Sarwar, B., Karypis, G., Konstan, J., & Riedl, J. (2001). Item-based collaborative filtering recommendation algorithms. *World Wide Web Conference*, 285-295.

Sarwar, B., Karypis, G., Konstan, J., & Riedl, J. (2002). Recommender systems for large-scale e-commerce: Scalable neighborhood formation using clustering. *International Conference on Computer and Information Technology*, 50.

Shen, H., & Huang, J. Z. (2008). Sparse principal component analysis via regularized low rank matrix approximation. *Journal of Multivariate Analysis*, 99(6), 1015–1034. doi:10.1016/j.jmva.2007.06.007

F

Xu, B., Bu, J., Chen, C., & Cai, D. (2012). An exploration of improving collaborative recommender systems via user-item subgroups. *World Wide Web Conference*, 21-30. 10.1145/2187836.2187840

Xue, G., Lin, C., Yang, Q., Xi, W., Zeng, H., Yu, Y., & Chen, Z. (2005). Scalable collaborative filtering using cluster-based smoothing. *ACM SIGIR Conference*, 114-121.

Yildirim, H., & Krishnamoorthy, M. (2008). A random walk method for alleviating the sparsity problem in collaborative filtering. *ACM Conference on Recommender Systems*, 131-138. 10.1145/1454008.1454031

Zanker, M., Felfernig, A., Friedrich, G., & Jannach, D. (2011). *Recommender Systems: An Introduction.* Cambridge University Press.

Zhai, C., & Aggarwal, C. C. (Eds.). (2012). *Mining Text Data*. Springer New York.

ADDITIONAL READING

Abdul Hussien, F. T., Rahma, A. M. S., & Abdulwahab, H. B. (2021). An E-Commerce Recommendation System Based on Dynamic Analysis of Customer Behavior. *Sustainability*, *13*(19), 10786. doi:10.3390u131910786

Anitha, J., & Kalaiarasu, M. (2021). Optimized machine learning based collaborative filtering (OMLCF) recommendation system in e-commerce. *Journal of Ambient Intelligence and Humanized Computing*, *12*(6), 6387–6398. doi:10.100712652-020-02234-1

Coussement, K., De Bock, K. W., & Geuens, S. (2021). A decision-analytic framework for interpretable recommendation systems with multiple input data sources: A case study for a European e-tailer. *Annals of Operations Research*, 1–24.

Karthik, R. V., & Ganapathy, S. (2021). A fuzzy recommendation system for predicting the customers interests using sentiment analysis and ontology in e-commerce. *Applied Soft Computing*, *108*, 107396. doi:10.1016/j.asoc.2021.107396

Kersbergen, B., & Schelter, S. (2021, April). Learnings from a Retail Recommendation System on Billions of Interactions at bol. com. In *IEEE 37th International Conference on Data Engineering (ICDE)* (pp. 2447-2452). IEEE.

Wang, Z., Maalla, A., & Liang, M. (2021, December). Research on e-commerce personalized recommendation system based on big data technology. In *IEEE 2nd International Conference on Information Technology, Big Data and Artificial Intelligence (ICIBA)* (Vol. 2, pp. 909-913). IEEE. 10.1109/ICIBA52610.2021.9687955

Xia, H., Wei, X., An, W., Zhang, Z. J., & Sun, Z. (2021). Design of electronic-commerce recommendation systems based on outlier mining. *Electronic Markets*, *31*(2), 295–311. doi:10.100712525-020-00435-2

KEY TERMS AND DEFINITIONS

Latent Factor Methods: In the latent factor method, the user-rating matrix is transformed into a lower-dimensional space by using either principal component analysis (PCA) or singular value decomposition (SVD).

Model-Based Methods: As against neighborhood based methods, model based methods are formal supervised or unsupervised learning methods where a model has been established for prediction of test case.

Neighbourhood Based Methods: These algorithms are based on the idea that similar consumers are likely to rate on similar lines and at the same time similar items have a higher probability of achieving similar ratings.

Singular Value Decomposition: SVD involves factorization of a matrix into two matrices U and L, such that requires U and L to be orthogonal.

Hybrid Machine Learning for Matchmaking in Digital Business Ecosystems

Mustapha Kamal Benramdane
CNAM, France

Samia Bouzefrane
iD https://orcid.org/0000-0002-0979-1289
CNAM, France

Soumya Banerjee
MUST, France

Hubert Maupas
MUST, France

Elena Kornyshova
CNAM, France

INTRODUCTION

Digital Business Ecosystems (DBE) is an up-to-date topic which encompasses traditional Business-to-business (B2B) and Business-to-Customer (B2C) relationships. This concept describes the situation of business transactions or exchange of products between different actors in order to exchange their products, services, or information within a market. The term ecosystem was inspired from nature as the ecosystem term comes from "ecological system" and includes "all the plants and living creatures in a particular area considered in relation to their physical environment" (OxfordLearnersDictionaries.Com, n.d.).

Like for a B2B network representing graph structure in which different nodes presented by companies are linked to each other by specific threads presented by relationships between them (H\aakansson & Ford, 2002; Janke & Prídavok, 2012), DBE is composed in the same manner but can also include final customers. This kind of organization helps businesses communicate and collaborate more easily. Compared to the traditional B2B vision, DBE, developed later, enhances the communication and collaboration within a network by introducing collective learning and knowledge flow between different business actors (Janke & Prídavok, 2012; van Egeraat & Curran, 2010).

DBE can have several aspects such as: a) Transaction-based: In the case of a single company that establishes a transactional method common to all these major customers and suppliers for doing business with them. b) Process-Based: When two companies establish a common business process that enables them to conduct business effectively and efficiently with each other. c) Strategic relationships-based: Two or more companies establishing a strategic partnership relationship based on all major interactions between organizations. This includes transactions, processes and any other collaboration between the two organizations (Kumar & Raheja, 2012).

DOI: 10.4018/978-1-7998-9220-5.ch168

An essential part of any digital DBE and the corresponding platform is the matchmaking process (Alpar, 2010). Matchmaking is the process of matching entities according to different criteria; it "allows one agent with some objective to learn the name of another agent that could take on that objective" (Decker et al., 1996). It is also "the process of searching the space of possible matches between demand and supplies" (Noia et al., 2004). Matchmaking is then essential for suppliers' proposals and customers' requirements to be connected (Alpar, 2010).

The matchmaking process attempts to assess the interest profiles of market players, with the aim of matching agents in the supply chain who have the least conflicting interests, thus supposed to have better profits from the arbitrage phases and subsequent execution (Medjahed et al., 2003). In a DBE environment, the use of an intermediary player who collects data and information on different market players, assists potential customers and suppliers in finding business partners and improves the efficiency of the matchmaking process (Ouksel et al., 2004) as in the financial and commodity digitized trading systems. In the same DBE environment, the authors have an opportunity to use the knowledge of the arbitration policy of the negotiation phase during the matchmaking phase, which strengthens the capacity of the matchmaker (Ouksel et al., 2004).

In this manner, the context of the DBE paradigm is not simple. It must indeed have multiple facets, such as the development of more and more entrepreneurship strategies to bring about the emergence of businesses and the extension of capacity building services for businesses in order to support them in their growth. However, seldom the growth of DBE has been primarily challenged due to non-availability of appropriate data towards precise matchmaking process.

In addition, matchmaking is complicated by incomplete data mainly because companies don't want to share private data. Missing data affects data analysis in a wide range of domains including matchmaking within DBEs. It has been observed that there are a few hybrid models proposed in DBE-related paradigms to address the missing data frames (Jerez et al., 2010). However, most of the business information system model incorporates that the missing values are imputed using association rules by comparing the known attribute values of missing observations and the antecedent part of association rules (Jerez et al., 2010; Lakshminarayan et al., 1999). In the case, when there is no rule present or fired (i.e. no attributes relationship exists in the training data) against the missing value.

This rule-based system seldom becomes ineffective, especially where the business rules for the youngest firms may not be available in database either or due to confidentiality of business data. Hence, the static data and association rule could not be an acceptable solution for the purpose of DBE matchmaking. Thus, the decision support engine for matchmaking often demonstrates vague results while disappointing end-users. The authors investigate that recently deep latent variable models like DLVMs (Kingma & Welling, 2013; Rezende et al., 2014) have been applied to missing data problems in business and statistical domains with an unsupervised setting (Ipsen et al., 2020; Ivanov et al., 2018; Ma, Gong, et al., 2018; Ma, Tschiatschek, et al., 2018; Mattei & Frellsen, 2018, 2019; Nazabal et al., 2020; Rezende et al., 2014; Yoon et al., 2018), while the supervised setting has not seen the same recent attention (Ipsen et al., 2020; Yoon et al., 2018).

The progress of unsupervised learning centers on inference and imputation. This provides more precision in the results than when learning with missing values of a criminalizing model. However, this approach does not necessarily minimize the prediction error (Cole, 2008).

Considering the random and ever-changing DBE context, it is worthy to apply certain bi-focal algorithms which could resolve the missing data features to some extent latently. Following that, the authors use a semi-supervised algorithm to deal with business matchmaking to recommend and infer about most likelihood business match. Our proposal also includes an algorithm to complete the missing data to provide a more precise recommendation of business partners inside DBEs.

Thus, this chapter proposes a novel bifocal algorithm including the following stages:

- Stage 1: Introduce a missing data imputation algorithm in order to fill the missing data features.
- Stage 2: Regenerate the data frame with denoising of synthesized data.
- Stage 3: Apply a semi-supervised model with the new data frame to train the model.
- Stage 4: To label the decision on matchmaking.

For validating and testing the proposed approach, the authors follow three stages of approaches:

1. Stage 1: The complete 3-tier algorithm will be positioned on MUST-VE engine as a live case study
2. Stage 2: The algorithm will be followed by a mathematical estimate of the composite runtime to demonstrate the efficiency.

The remaining paper has been organized as follows: In section II., we describe a state of the related works. In section III., we elaborate the details of the proposed algorithms, the mathematical components, and simulations executed under the MUST case platform. Section IV. presents the components of MUST -VE matchmaking case study together with the obtained results. Finally, section V sums up the paper and discusses the immediate future work. In the appendix, we present the screenshots of the results for live case study (under MUST-VE platform) and the remaining code analysis of both missing data algorithms and machine learning algorithms.

RELATED WORKS

In section II.1., the chapter also solicits the relevance of introducing hybrid machine learning models for these types of B2B matching applications. Section II.2 will introduce the missing data problem for business and statistics, followed by the existing solutions using statistical machine learning.

Usage of Hybrid Machine Learning for Missing Data Imputation

In recent years, the complexity of data mining and recommendation applications demanded more advanced algorithms. For example, to pick and choose a specific inference out of substantially much larger instances, conventional machine learning classification might not be adequate. Moreover, it will be evident that the supervised training model demonstrates unexpected noise in the data itself. The use-cases and applications concerning decision support systems are significantly affected. Seldom, the performance of matching and contextual decision-making may appear precise. However, with respect to the real business market it exhibits erroneous outputs. The authors first come across the normal matrimonial matching prior to focus on the business matchmaking paradigm. Hence, the collaborative approach of algorithms was initiated. At present, another technical argument exists across the machine learning community. This is regarding the acceptance of any missing data imputation as pre-machine learning association. Considering the volume of data and data mining strategies, recent researchers suggest certain insights. Khan et al. (Khan & Hoque, 2020) and Jadhav et al. (Jadhav et al., 2019) investigated two prime considerations respectively. In the first work, the authors emphasized that any data analytics and machine learning may follow statistical imputation as primary components. In the second work, the authors emphasized the numerical presence of data instances to be important for decision or recommendations. This indication is prominent to devise additional pre-matching machine learning components before any type of classification or clustering procedure.

The subsequent challenge is to detect the nature of precision of missing data algorithms in data mining. "Missing at random" (MAR) and "missing not at random" (MNAR) are two very common occurrences visible in many applications (Royston, 2004; Rubin, 2004). Even in those applications, detection of precession becomes important specially for label-free proteomics (Jin et al., 2021). Although, certain research reveals that missing data cannot be the exact replacement over supervised machine learning algorithms. This is primarily because they usually distort the joint and marginal distributions of the data and thus induce the influential bias in estimators (Josse & Reiter, 2018; Little & Rubin, 2019; Mayer et al., 2019). The distribution of post-synthesis data of missing value imputation may still appear to be a skewed distribution. The authors observe two typical facets of the analysis (specially for the MCAR category of missing data, which is predominant for the case study): full likelihood and partial likelihood of observed data. Popularly known as *out of sample*. The robust technique for inserting more precession in the missing data is to leverage the imputation model as training layers of supervised learning procedure. Therefore, multiple imputation or specifying any parametric model and computing the probability distribution of the post-response across the observed values can be a close measure to be consistent with the missing imputation algorithm with reference to machine learning (Jin et al., 2021).

However, in supervised-learning settings, the objective is rather to build a prediction function that minimizes the expected risk by trial and error. Standard empirical risk minimization can be adopted too (Klochkov & Zhivotovskiy, 2021) in the form of stability analysis of learning algorithms under the purview of a generic framework. For investigating better visibility, the related missing data and entropy model towards joint distribution has been detailed in section 3. Keeping this two-tier architecture of the model (i.e. missing data of statistical imputation and traditional classification of machine learning), navigation of the proposed model is supported.

As it is described, hybrid methods combine two or more ML and/or soft computing methods for higher performance and optimum results. In fact, hybrid methods benefit from the advantage of two or more methods to achieve better performance. Sometimes, hybrid methods contain one unit for prediction and one unit for the optimization of the prediction unit to reach an accurate output. Therefore, it can be claimed that hybrid methods contain different single methods and form a method with greater flexibility with a high capability compared with single methods.

Hybrid methods have become more popular due to their high potential and capability. Hybrid methods are the same as a company with different employees with different expertise to achieve a single goal. Ensemble methods may use a series of ML classification trees instead of a single one. Through this technique, the accuracy of the model is substantially improved. Ensemble methods are considered as supervised learning algorithms, and benefit from different and flexible training algorithms to increase the training accuracy for reaching a higher testing accuracy.

Missing Data Problem for Business and Statistics

This section will introduce the missing data problem for business & statistics, followed by the existing solutions using statistical machine learning in section 3.1. Missing data is a typical yet a very common phenomenon for generic business, social data science, and different statistical data mining-based uses-cases.

There are plenty of default reasons for missing and incomplete data to happen. Some of them are quite familiar like non-availability of data features or confidentiality of data itself. In a typical business ecosystem there are possibilities, where the statistical absence across the attributes of data features is prominent.

Consequently, available data may not be so adequate due to the reduced and compressed storage size, but also, could be highly influenced on-account of the diversified sources of data and level of trust during the collection of data. Hence, pure statistical inference or decision-making mechanism may become invalid.

It is worthy to mention that the missing part in the business domain and its associated treatment seldom require different statistical and unsupervised machine learning algorithms. A few mentionable are: Data Augmentation (DA), semi/fully conditional specification and expectation, minimization with several customized boot-strapped techniques. Therefore, there are certain conventional modalities of missing data with imputation models. In this section, we will investigate these notorious w.r.t customization methods adopted for the implementation.

The authors assume g is a data grid, s is the sample size and v is the number of variables g(sxv). Therefore, the distribution of g is with two major components, i.e. mean vector µ and a variance - co-variance matrix M:

g~ V (µ, M), where the variables are continuous.

However, to measure the missing data log in the data grid, we may refer to certain classical mechanisms (Carpenter & Kenward, 2012; King & Zeithaml, 2001; Rubin, 2004) followed by the customization process involved in the work. Hence the mechanisms are: *Missing completely at random (MCAR), Missing at Random (MAR) and Not Missing at Random (NMAR)*. The modalities of these three modes are coordinated with observations of data and variables associated with them. At the imputation stage, the concept of dependent and independent variables is not being considered. This is because imputation is not a causal model, rather it is a predictive model. The important point here is to identify the average information contained in the random variable (Shannon entropy). Significantly, the entropy of missing data will help us to formulate the distribution points where actually observed data and synthesis of new data will fit in.

In this work, the authors investigate a conceptual entropy of missing data, corresponding to the probability of observations and variables.

Let r be a probability vector defined in the continuous trend of data source on a given sample of data $S = \{S_1, ..., S_n\}$, the authors define:

$$g\left(\sigma\right) = \sum\nolimits_{i=1}^{n} \sigma_i \cot^{-1}\left(\frac{1}{r_i^3}\right) - \Pi \qquad (1)$$

Therefore, based on this entropy the authors take a random variable Y for any missing value. So, the authors define:

$$g\left(Y\right) = \sum\nolimits_{y \in Y} \sigma\left(y\right) \cot^{-1}\left(\frac{1}{\sigma\left(y\right)}\right) - \Pi \qquad (2)$$

This is a simple one variable (missing entropy) dependent model. Now, the authors define the joint variable entropy for Y, D as:

$$g(Y, D) = \sum_{d \in D} \sum_{y \in Y} \sigma(d, y) \cot^{-1} \left(\frac{1}{\sigma(d, y)} \right) - \Pi \tag{3}$$

The proportion of these customizations can be viewed as one proposed lemma:

- The $f(y) = \cot^{-1} \left(\frac{1}{y} \right)$ function is convergent on (0, π)

It means that in the proposed use case, the B2B ecosystem could be non-negative. Hence, to apply any of the imputation values the authors could provide this generic entropy for missing data as a random value.

The native entropy of Y and D can be defined by the present model:

$$R(Y \| D) = \int y . \cot^{-1} \left(\frac{y}{d} \right) d\mu - \Pi \tag{4}$$

Where is the relative entropy of the proposed treatment, and μ is a measure on y.

Considering the entropy alignment with respect to the conventional expectation minimization problem to treat missing data leads to a statistical machine learning paradigm. The authors also consider joint distribution of probabilities for occurring the missing data. Based on the relative entropy, as proposed in eq (4), the authors also empirically treat a defined expression of an immediately available data entity further to redefine an embedded data item (it could be existing or hidden according to the design of the database). Hence, if the authors consider any inequality e.g. Johnson inequality, then:

$$\log(\theta)[Ri] \Rightarrow \log Ri(\theta, av_\alpha) = \log \sum^{R_i} i(\theta, av_\alpha, h_\alpha)$$
$$= \log \sum Ri(h_\alpha) \left[\frac{Ri(av_\alpha, \theta, h_\alpha)}{Ri(h_\alpha)} \right] \geq \log \sum Ri(h_\alpha) \log \left(\frac{Ri(av_\alpha, \theta, h_\alpha)}{Ri(h_\alpha)} \right) \tag{5}$$

Where R_i is relative entropy, from eq(4); $a_{v\alpha}$ is available data, θ the phase of data iteration, is embedded or hidden data, $R_i(h_\alpha)$ is a joint distribution of missing data entropy w.r.t hidden data.

Hence, prior to implement EM-algorithm, the entropy model of missing data with a (cot-1) function is proposed and justified if and only if the missing data comprises not only missing data, but also hidden and embedded data. This component of entropy identification will be adequate for completely unsupervised set-up. However, with respect to the present context of the work it will be also supportive for ginger and precise performance of the MICE algorithm. The cot family of functions will help to identify any negative inputs as it is the inverse of tan function.

DETAILS OF PROPOSAL DESCRIPTION

Our proposal includes two main parts: missing data imputation algorithm (Section II.1) and matchmaking algorithm (Section III.1).

Missing Data Algorithm

As the dataset may contain unavailable values for several variables, then it becomes necessary to look for a way to restore or reconstruct them. This non-availability of values may be due to several factors; it is possible that these values are not filled in, are not yet known or are not acquired for their confidential nature, and this depends on the organization that holds them.

Multiple Imputation by Chained Equation (MICE) algorithm allows you to impute missing data in a dataset by following several strategies. It uses via a prediction model a series of imputations which are repeated in several iterations until convergence is obtained (Royston & White, 2011).

Figure 1. MICE algorithm steps

	production_capability	no_of_companies_supplied	expertise_level
supplier 1	1	0	8
supplier2	NaN	NaN	2
supplier 3	4	1	5
supplier 4	3	NaN	5
supplier 5	NaN	2	2

	no_of_companies_sup	expertise_level		production_capability
supplier 1	0	8		1
supplier2	1.5	2	NaN	
supplier 3	1	5		4
supplier 4	1.5	5		3
supplier 5	2	2	NaN	

	no_of_companies_sup	expertise_level		production_capability
supplier 1	0	8		1
supplier2	1.5	2		2.67
supplier 3	1	5		4
supplier 4	1.5	5		3
supplier 5	2	2		3.9

Here, the authors describe the MICE algorithm for a given sample of data $X = \{x1, ...xk\}$ represented by {no_of_companies_sup, expertise_level, production_capability} in Figure 1. Some of these variables have missing values, such as product_capability for supplier 2. Initially, all the missing values that were mandatory marked N/A are imputed with the feature mean like "no_of_companies_sup" feature in the illustrated example. The initial imputation strategy for the MICE algorithm can be the mean feature, median or any other fixed values. Next, the authors take the first variable that has missing values, for example "production_capability", and it is then estimated by applying regression on the rest of the variables i.e. $\{x2, ..., xk\}$. This estimate is limited to the observation of x1. Subsequently, the missing values on x1 are replaced by values known as proper imputation. The next variable that has missing values will undergo the same process. For example, if x3 has missing values, it will be then imputed by applying regression on the other variables i.e. $\{x1, x2, x4, ..., xk\}$.

This same process is repeated in several cycles for all the features that have missing values. For every continuous streaming data from different external APIs, the missing data is handled and the data becomes model-ready. According to Van Buuren (Van Buuren et al., 1999), the authors could use 10 to 20 cycles to stabilize the results. In the proposed study, the authors used up to 20 cycles to impute missing data using the MICE algorithm.

Matchmaking Algorithm

In the authors' study, the MICE algorithm is combined with the Linear Regression algorithm to impute missing data. Since each feature uses its own prediction model, different variable types can be handled by MICE algorithms such as continuous, binary or categorical data types. Here the authors introduce the algorithms used in the authors' study to perform matchmaking with semi-supervised machine learning. In algorithm 1) on one hand, a Logistic Regression model is trained on the database to predict relations between organizations. These relations may be for instance customer/supplier or partnership relations. Algorithm 2) on the other hand describes the steps to be followed to perform smart recommendation for matchmaking.

Algorithm 1 describes all the steps followed to build a recommendation model based on the content of the database. The data is first pre-processed and cleaned. Categorical and numerical data are separated and each treated separately. It is the numerical data that is then imputed via the missing data algorithm. A model based on the MICE algorithm combined with Linear Regression is then trained on the data in order to impute the missing data in each variable of the data set, and this with a mean feature initial strategy.

After imputation of the missing data, the dataset is then trained on a recommendation model based on Logistic Regression (LR). This model then learns from these data whether the customer / supplier relation, for example, exists or not for any pair of organizations contained in the database. This also applies to other types of relationships that may exist between two organizations.

In the end, the authors obtain a smart recommendation model based on the Logistic Regression trained on imputed data. This brings more precise results in the sense that without imputation, the recommendation model would have skipped certain variables due to non-availability of values.

Algorithm 2 describes the steps followed in order to obtain an optimized recommendation list using Smart Recommendation. First, the authors perform static matchmaking. This type of algorithm uses static rules applied to the database to obtain a recommendation list for an input organization. This list of recommendations may contain, depending on the use case, customers, suppliers, partners or distributors.

Secondly, the data of the input organization are linked with those of the organizations contained in the established list. For a pair (A, B), A as the input organization, and B as each organization in the list, the LR model returns a match probability which is taken as a score for each B organization appearing from the previous list. The list is then reorganized according to the new score in descending order.

It is still useful to mention in this case that the imputation model can also be used to restore missing data to the input organization.

Algorithm 1. MICE and model generation

```
Input:CSV files
Output:modelclf: Logistic-Regression model
```

```
1 Procedure main(CSV file)
2 Upload CSV file into raw_data;
3 lr = LinearRegression();
4 imputer_model = Mice(estimator= lr, verbose= 2, max_iter = 20, tol =1e-10,
imputation_order = "roman", initial_strategy = "mean");
5 X_data= prepareData(raw_data);
6 Split X_data into X_train and y_train, X_test and y_test with test_size= 0.1;
7 model_clf= LogisticRegression(X_train, y_train,random_state= 42,max_iter=
400);
8 testResults= testLRModel(X_test,y_test);
9 print(testResults);
10 return model_clf,imputer_model;
11 Procedure prepareData(raw_data)
12 Divide raw data into raw_data_categorical and raw_data_numerical;
13 for each row in raw_data_categorical do
14     for each col in raw do
15         if col is not available then
16             col= "unknown" ;
        end
    end
end
17 raw_data_numerical = imputermodel.transform(raw_data_numerical) ;
18 Scale raw_data_numerical to zero mean and unit variance ;
19 Encode raw_data_categorical with one-hot-encoder method ;
20 Concatenate raw_data_numerical and raw_data_categorical into X_data;
21 Remove redundant rows in X_data;
22 return X_data,imputer_model;
```

Algorithm 2. Perform Smart Recommendation

```
Procedure performSmartRecommendation(input_company_data)
1 companies_list = performStaticMatchmaking(input_company_data);
2 Xdata = prepareData(companies_list * input_company_data);
3 modelclf = loadModel();
4 scores = model_clf.predict_proba(X_data);
5 companies_list=companies_list.sort(scores);
6 return companies_list;
```

CASE STUDY COMPONENTS

In this section, the authors describe the case study components of the proposed matchmaking system and its data components. Figure 2. depicts the ER diagram of the used database. It contains a significant number of "organizations" which may be businesses, companies, investors or non-profit organizations. The "organization" can belong to at least one "category" and operate in at least one "market segment". Each organization can offer various "products" and services to its environment. The products and services may be similar to others in the same "market segment".

"Market segment" defines a group of organizations that share one or more common characteristics. Each market segment is different and unique. "Category" defines a subgroup of a market segment formed according to more precise information about the activity, services and products provided by an organization.

Based on this database, the proposed recommendation system has two types of matchmaking algorithms as shown in Figure 3: A) Algorithms that use static rules, browsing the database to generate a list of customers / suppliers to a given organization as input. The authors call this "Static matchmaking". B) Algorithms based on machine learning, more precisely Logistic Regression, which optimize the results of "Static matchmaking". The authors call it "Smart Recommendation"(Benramdane et al., 2021).

Conventionally, in any data mining applications, the most intensive operation is treated as pre-processing. The pre-processing comprises the generation of missing data values, consistent data trend (noiseless) and defined terminal values. In this application development, the prime consideration is bifocal: firstly, the authors adopt missing data and attributes and secondly the association and relationship of data features in the database.

Therefore, the design follows a couple of specialized notions: To bypass the corresponding data row, where the authors omit the class label in object-oriented design. However, the constraints here are the presence of *Missing Completely at Random (MCAR)* (Royston, 2004; Rubin, 2004). In this case, data mining and association face uncertainty, when the missing observations are dependent on the observed and unobserved measurements.

In the case of selecting the fill up for the target database, the authors consider global constants instead of putting "N/A" in the database entry. Also in this case, in the preprocessing, the authors are faced with the challenges of the second category of missing data, i.e., *"Missing at Random" (MAR)* (Royston, 2004). It signifies that the observed data is statistically related to the missing variables. Although, it is feasible here to estimate the missing values from the observed data. Therefore, instead of concentrating on the missing part, the strategy will be to fill it with global constants in every place of the database.

Figure 2. ER diagram of the database

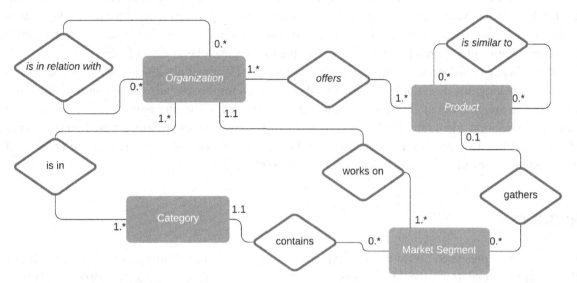

Figure 3. Matchmaking system overview

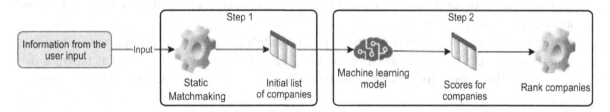

Figure 4. MICE and Decision Tree confusion matrix

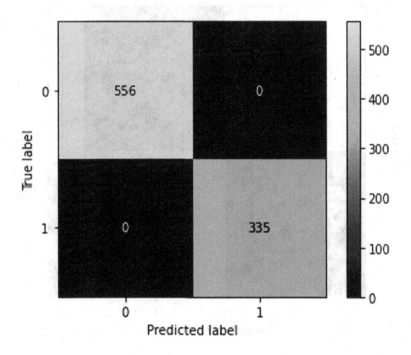

In the third case of exception, the database design is to investigate the control mechanism, where neither MCAR nor MAR actually occurs. This scenario is usually more difficult for the design, the authors initiate a classification approach for all the attributes in the database. This will follow the method of accepting attribute mean for all samples belonging to the same class of data features.

"Data sketch" is important in this kind of preprocessing (Wang et al., 2021). Here, for the application matchmaking, the designing of a distributed data sketch for the scenario occurs with multiple data streams. The larger distributed dataset often initiates a weighted cardinality approach. The authors consider an association and a relation that is associated with a fixed weight or grade based on the domain of matchmaking. However, in the generalized problem, the goal is to estimate the total sum of weights for all unique elements present in a data stream (Cohen et al., 2015).

RESULTS

The algorithms presented above are self-explanatory. However, the authors also investigate different characteristics concerning the MICE imputation matrix. The authors emphasized two models to be hybridized in nature: firstly, the imputation algorithm itself and secondly either Decision Tree (DT) and Logistics Regression (LR). The plots here demonstrate the efficiency of the authors' comparative approaches to cite different characteristics under simple imputation and the MICE techniques. The confusion matrix is evaluated as below.

Figure 4 shows the confusion matrix plots after using the MICE imputation technique and decision tree algorithm. Here, we can see the true positive and false negative sum up to the total, and no false positive or true negative. Thus, the algorithm performs best when used with the MICE imputation technique.

Figure 5. General imputation and Decision Tree confusion matrix

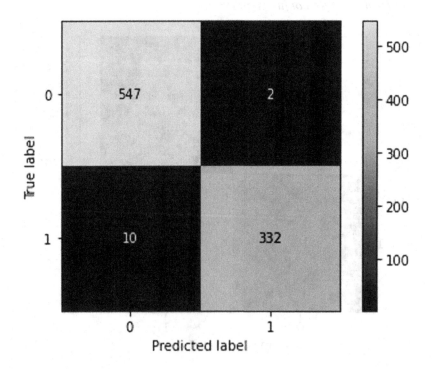

Figure 6. MICE and LR confusion matrix

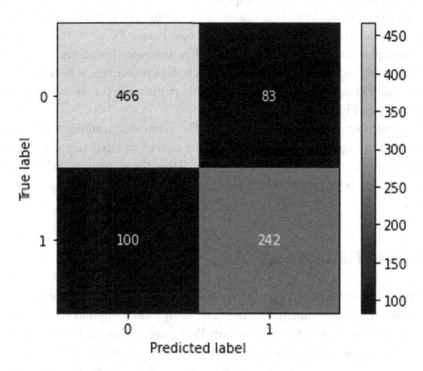

Figure 7. MICE and LR confusion matrix

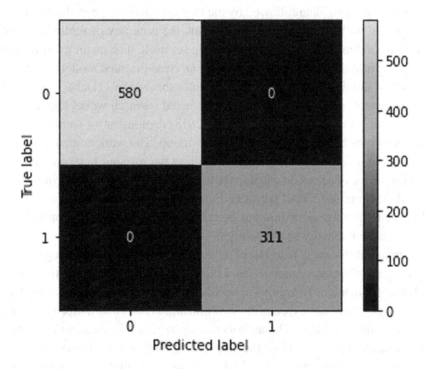

Confusion matrix plot after using general imputation technique and decision tree algorithm is shown in Figure 5. As we can see, there are 10 true negatives and 2 false positives, so it is certainly performing poorly as compared to the MICE imputation technique (see Figure 4).

Confusion matrix plot after using general imputation technique (imputing using column mean in places of NaN values) and logistic regression algorithm is depicted in Figure 6. As we can see, there are 100 true negatives and 83 false positives, so it is certainly performing poorly as compared to the MICE imputation technique (see Figure 4).

The plot of the confusion matrix after using the MICE imputation technique and logistic regression algorithm is presented in Figure 7. Here, we can see the sum of true positive and false negative up to the total, and no false positive or true negative is present. Thus, the algorithm again performs best when used with MICE imputation technique. The code snippet of python associated libraries is included in Appendices B & C.

CONCLUSION AND FUTURE ASPECTS

The chapter elaborates a rudimentary yet novel approach to missing data imputation and recommendations in the digital business environment. The use case, navigation snaps and efficiency were described in a real prototyping environment of the said platform. Performance plots and close precision with hybrid machine learning algorithms were demonstrated suitably with multiple imputations and combining two categories of prediction algorithms, e.g., logistic regression (LR) and decision tree (DT). Both are well performed with respect to accuracy while yielding recommendations to the end users.

The authors faced substantial challenges during the hybridization of two distinct forms of data processing algorithms (like missing data followed by the decision-making procedures). The authors found that for any given model with completely observed data, the accuracy of multiple imputations highly depends on the missing values supported on the training set itself. The mean imputation model used to be more reliable for business data features. However, for any tree-oriented models, more emphasis can be given to the insertion of missing values with data attributes them-selves (Debavelaere & Allassonnière, 2021). During implementations, we refer to two phenomenal research works (Jiang et al., 2020; Yoon et al., 2018). These models in Yoon et al. (Yoon et al., 2018) demonstrate a *Generative Adversarial Imputation Nets (GAIN)* which has been set in a pervasive set-up. The work coined missing data with two components e.g., generator set (which contributes to filling the missing part) and discriminator which can compare with the vector of actual data feature with regard to what has been synthesized. The feature of the paper guided the proposed model partially. Finally, following the theme of Jiang et al. (Jiang et al., 2020), the logistic regression algorithm has been tested. The combination of these two algorithms may impress on the final complexity of the solution.

Therefore, to compensate for the constraints of the supervised model and missing (MICE) in general, it will be advisable to extend the present model with a bifocal vertical: firstly adopt the model by deploying the unsupervised model of machine learning. Especially those models suitable for embedded missing data investigation procedures. There are expectation-maximization (EM) and majority minimization (MM) (Debavelaere & Allassonnière, 2021). The authors anticipate that this algorithm will be fit to generate smooth and precise-matched predictions for the data features of dynamic ecosystems which will closely follow Gaussian multivariate distribution. In addition to this augmentation, we also consider that future works will concentrate on the approaches for high- dimensional data for those business ecosystems following other machine learning models like random forest (Wright & Ziegler, 2015). Finally, the faster convergence of bio-inspired algorithms and graph matching will open another appropriate direction towards the future research perspectives (Zaslavskiy et al., 2008).

H

REFERENCES

Alpar, F. Z. (2010). Matchmaking Framework for B2B E-Marketplaces. *Informações Econômicas, 14*(4), 164–170.

Benramdane, M. K., Maupas, H., Kornyshova, E., & Banerjee, S. (2021). Business Recommender System through Matchmaking with Supervised Machine Learning in Distributed Digital Platforms: Energy Complexity Analysis. *2021 8th International Conference on Future Internet of Things and Cloud (FiCloud)*, 372–376. 10.1109/FiCloud49777.2021.00060

Carpenter, J., & Kenward, M. (2012). *Multiple imputation and its application.* John Wiley & Sons.

Cohen, R., Katzir, L., & Yehezkel, A. (2015). A unified scheme for generalizing cardinality estimators to sum aggregation. *Information Processing Letters, 115*(2), 336–342. doi:10.1016/j.ipl.2014.10.009

Cole, J. C. (2008). How to deal with missing data. *Best Practices in Quantitative Methods*, 214–238.

Debavelaere, V., & Allassonnière, S. (2021). *On the curved exponential family in the Stochatic Approximation Expectation Maximization Algorithm.* Academic Press.

Decker, K., Williamson, M., & Sycara, K. (1996). Matchmaking and brokering. *Proceedings of the Second International Conference on Multi-Agent Systems (ICMAS-96), 432.*

ecosystem noun—Definition, pictures, pronunciation and usage notes. (n.d.). Oxford Advanced Learner's Dictionary at OxfordLearnersDictionaries.com. Retrieved January 30, 2022, from https://www.oxfordlearnersdictionaries.com/definition/english/ecosystem?q=ecosystem,%20Accessed%20January%202022

Haakansson, H., & Ford, D. (2002). How should companies interact in business networks? *Journal of Business Research, 55*(2), 133–139.

Ipsen, N. B., Mattei, P.-A., & Frellsen, J. (2020). *not-MIWAE: Deep generative modelling with missing not at random data.* ArXiv Preprint ArXiv:2006.12871.

Ivanov, O., Figurnov, M., & Vetrov, D. (2018). *Variational autoencoder with arbitrary conditioning.* ArXiv Preprint ArXiv:1806.02382.

Jadhav, A., Pramod, D., & Ramanathan, K. (2019). Comparison of performance of data imputation methods for numeric dataset. *Applied Artificial Intelligence, 33*(10), 913–933.

Janke, F., & Prídavok, M. (2012). B2B Network Performance: Practical Aspects of Network Supply Adequacy Indicator. *IDIMT*, 337–346.

Jerez, J. M., Molina, I., García-Laencina, P. J., Alba, E., Ribelles, N., Martín, M., & Franco, L. (2010). Missing data imputation using statistical and machine learning methods in a real breast cancer problem. *Artificial Intelligence in Medicine, 50*(2), 105–115.

Jiang, W., Josse, J., Lavielle, M., & Group, T. (2020). Logistic regression with missing covariates—Parameter estimation, model selection and prediction within a joint-modeling framework. *Computational Statistics & Data Analysis*, *145*, 106907.

Jin, L., Bi, Y., Hu, C., Qu, J., Shen, S., Wang, X., & Tian, Y. (2021). A comparative study of evaluating missing value imputation methods in label-free proteomics. *Scientific Reports*, *11*(1), 1–11.

Josse, J., & Reiter, J. P. (2018). Introduction to the special section on missing data. *Statistical Science*, *33*(2), 139–141.

Khan, S. I., & Hoque, A. S. M. L. (2020). SICE: An improved missing data imputation technique. *Journal of Big Data*, *7*(1), 1–21.

King, A. W., & Zeithaml, C. P. (2001). Competencies and firm performance: Examining the causal ambiguity paradox. *Strategic Management Journal*, *22*(1), 75–99.

Kingma, D. P., & Welling, M. (2013). *Auto-encoding variational bayes*. ArXiv Preprint ArXiv:1312.6114.

Klochkov, Y., & Zhivotovskiy, N. (2021). *Stability and Deviation Optimal Risk Bounds with Convergence Rate $O(1/n)$*. ArXiv Preprint ArXiv:2103.12024.

Kumar, V., & Raheja, E. G. (2012). Business to business (b2b) and business to consumer (b2c) management. *International Journal of Computers and Technology*, *3*(3b), 447–451.

Lakshminarayan, K., Harp, S. A., & Samad, T. (1999). Imputation of missing data in industrial databases. *Applied Intelligence*, *11*(3), 259–275.

Little, R. J., & Rubin, D. B. (2019). *Statistical analysis with missing data* (Vol. 793). John Wiley & Sons.

Ma, C., Gong, W., Hernández-Lobato, J. M., Koenigstein, N., Nowozin, S., & Zhang, C. (2018). Partial VAE for hybrid recommender system. *NIPS Workshop on Bayesian Deep Learning*.

Ma, C., Tschiatschek, S., Palla, K., Hernández-Lobato, J. M., Nowozin, S., & Zhang, C. (2018). *Eddi: Efficient dynamic discovery of high-value information with partial vae*. ArXiv Preprint ArXiv:1809.11142.

Mattei, P.-A., & Frellsen, J. (2018). *Leveraging the exact likelihood of deep latent variable models*. ArXiv Preprint ArXiv:1802.04826.

Mattei, P.-A., & Frellsen, J. (2019). MIWAE: Deep generative modelling and imputation of incomplete data sets. *International Conference on Machine Learning*, 4413–4423.

Mayer, I., Sportisse, A., Josse, J., Tierney, N., & Vialaneix, N. (2019). *R-miss-tastic: A unified platform for missing values methods and workflows*. ArXiv Preprint ArXiv:1908.04822.

Medjahed, B., Benatallah, B., Bouguettaya, A., Ngu, A. H., & Elmagarmid, A. K. (2003). Business-to-business interactions: Issues and enabling technologies. *The VLDB Journal*, *12*(1), 59–85.

Nazabal, A., Olmos, P. M., Ghahramani, Z., & Valera, I. (2020). Handling incomplete heterogeneous data using vaes. *Pattern Recognition*, *107*, 107501.

Noia, T. D., Sciascio, E. D., Donini, F. M., & Mongiello, M. (2004). A system for principled matchmaking in an electronic marketplace. *International Journal of Electronic Commerce*, *8*(4), 9–37.

Ouksel, A. M., Babad, Y. M., & Tesch, T. (2004). Matchmaking software agents in b2b markets. *37th Annual Hawaii International Conference on System Sciences, 2004. Proceedings.*

Rezende, D. J., Mohamed, S., & Wierstra, D. (2014). Stochastic backpropagation and approximate inference in deep generative models. *International Conference on Machine Learning*, 1278–1286.

Royston, P. (2004). Multiple imputation of missing values. *The Stata Journal*, *4*(3), 227–241.

Royston, P., & White, I. R. (2011). Multiple imputation by chained equations (MICE): Implementation in Stata. *Journal of Statistical Software*, *45*(4), 1–20.

Rubin, D. B. (2004). *Multiple imputation for nonresponse in surveys* (Vol. 81). John Wiley & Sons.

Van Buuren, S., Boshuizen, H. C., & Knook, D. L. (1999). Multiple imputation of missing blood pressure covariates in survival analysis. *Statistics in Medicine*, *18*(6), 681–694.

van Egeraat, C., & Curran, D. (2010). Social Network Analysis of the Irish biotech industry: Implications for digital ecosystems. *International Conference on Open Philosophies for Associative Autopoietic Digital Ecosystem*, 31–43.

Wang, H., Ma, C., Odegbile, O. O., Chen, S., & Peir, J.-K. (2021). Randomized error removal for online spread estimation in data streaming. *Proceedings of the VLDB Endowment International Conference on Very Large Data Bases*, *14*(6), 1040–1052.

Wright, M. N., & Ziegler, A. (2015). *ranger: A fast implementation of random forests for high dimensional data in C++ and R*. ArXiv Preprint ArXiv:1508.04409.

Yoon, J., Jordon, J., & Schaar, M. (2018). Gain: Missing data imputation using generative adversarial nets. *International Conference on Machine Learning*, 5689–5698.

Zaslavskiy, M., Bach, F., & Vert, J.-P. (2008). A path following algorithm for the graph matching problem. *IEEE Transactions on Pattern Analysis and Machine Intelligence*, *31*(12), 2227–2242.

KEY TERMS AND DEFINITIONS

Business Ecosystem: A business ecosystem is an economic community made up of interacting organizations and individuals. This network includes customers, major producers, competitors and other stakeholders. These organizations activate in providing a specific product or service through competition and cooperation. The evolution of such a community can be influenced by leadership societies, which are called "the keystone species".

Digital Business Ecosystem: The digital business ecosystem is an extension of the business ecosystem in a digital environment populated by digital entities such as software applications, hardware and processes. Unlike the classic business ecosystem which has generic organizational interdependence, DBE places more emphasis on the central role of digital technology in the organizational interdependence of companies.

Digital Matchmaking: It is the extension of the concept of matchmaking and its implementation in a digital environment. In this case, the presence of several business actors in a digital platform can then form a digital business network. Consequently, it becomes possible to carry out matchmaking operations using different algorithms which make it possible to optimize the existing relations between these economic actors or to create new ones according to different professional criteria.

Machine Learning: Machine learning is a branch of artificial intelligence (AI) and computing that focuses on experience, the use of data, and algorithms to automate the building of analytical models. Machine learning algorithms build a model based on sample data, called "training data", in order to make predictions or decisions without being explicitly programmed to do so and to mimic the way humans learn, gradually improving its accuracy.

Matchmaking: Matchmaking is the process of matching several entities according to different criteria. In the case of business ecosystems, it is then a question of putting companies in contact based on professional criteria concerning them, and this in order to create relationships between these two economic entities. It then allows an organization with an objective to find another organization that can take on that objective.

Missing Data Imputation: Missing data imputation is the statistical and computerized process which makes it possible to restore or reconstruct missing data values. These data may be unavailable for various reasons: they do not yet exist, they have not been communicated, or they are confidential.

Supervised Machine Learning: Supervised machine learning, is a subcategory of machine learning. This type of algorithm uses labeled sets of data, known as training data, to train models or produce an inferred function, allowing new samples of data to be classified or results to be accurately predicted. Therefore, the more data that is fed into the model, the more optimally it adjusts its weights until the model has been fitted appropriately, which occurs as part of the cross-validation process.

APPENDIX A: SOURCE CODE

Dataset used:

Titanic Dataset (https://www.kaggle.com/c/titanic)

Source Code:

```
import pandas as pd
df = pd.read_csv("./data/train.csv")
# Data Preprocessing
df.columns = ['PassengerId','Survived','Pclass','Name','Sex','Age','SibSp','Pa
rch','Ticket','Fare','Cabin','Embarked']
labels = list(df['Survived'])
df.drop(['PassengerId','Name','Ticket', 'Survived'],axis=1,inplace=True)
df["labels"] = labels
#================================================================
# MICE missing value imputation
#================================================================
# Label encoding for categorical values
df_mice = df.copy()
from sklearn import preprocessing
for i in df_mice:
if df_mice[i].dtype == 'object':
le = preprocessing.LabelEncoder()
df_mice[i]=le.fit_transform(df_mice[i])
# Handling missing values
# By MICE method
import numpy as np
from sklearn.experimental import enable_iterative_imputer
from sklearn.impute import IterativeImputer
imp = IterativeImputer(max_iter=10, random_state=0)
df_mice_transformed = pd.DataFrame(imp.fit_transform(df_mice))
df_mice_transformed.columns = df_mice.columns
# Fitting Decision Tree
from sklearn.tree import DecisionTreeClassifier
clf = DecisionTreeClassifier(random_state=0)
clf.fit(df_mice_transformed.drop(['labels'],axis=1),labels)
y_train = clf.predict(df_mice_transformed.drop(['labels'],axis=1))
# Checking Confusion matrix plot for prediction accuracy
from sklearn.metrics import plot_confusion_matrix
import matplotlib.pyplot as plt
plot_confusion_matrix(clf, df_mice_transformed.drop(['labels'],axis=1),y_train)
plt.show()
# Implementing Logistic Regression along with MICE
from sklearn.linear_model import LogisticRegression
clf= LogisticRegression(random_state=0, max_iter= 500).fit(df_mice_trans-
```

```
formed.drop(['labels'], axis= 1), labels)
y_train = clf.predict(df_mice_transformed.drop(['labels'],axis=1))
plot_confusion_matrix(clf, df_mice_transformed.drop(['labels'],axis=1),y_train)
plt.show()
#=================================================================
# Normal missing value imputation
#=================================================================
# Label encoding for categorical values
df_norm = df.copy()
from sklearn import preprocessing
for i in df_norm:
if df_norm[i].dtype == 'object':
le = preprocessing.LabelEncoder()
df_norm[i]=le.fit_transform(df_norm[i])
# Missing value imputation
for i in df_norm:
df_norm[i].fillna(value=df_norm[i].mean(),inplace=True)
# Training the model
from sklearn.tree import DecisionTreeClassifier
clf = DecisionTreeClassifier(random_state=0)
clf.fit(df_norm.drop(['labels'],axis=1),labels)
y_train = clf.predict(df_norm.drop(['labels'],axis=1))
# Plotting accuracy plot for predictions
from sklearn.metrics import plot_confusion_matrix
import matplotlib.pyplot as plt
plot_confusion_matrix(clf, df_norm.drop(['labels'],axis=1),labels)
plt.show()
# Implementing Logistic Regression along with normal impute
from sklearn.linear_model import LogisticRegression
dft = df_norm.drop(['labels'],axis=1)
clf = LogisticRegression(random_state=0, max_iter = 500).fit(dft,labels)
y_train = clf.predict(df_norm.drop(['labels'],axis=1))
plot_confusion_matrix(clf, df_norm.drop(['labels'],axis=1),labels)
plt.show()
```

APPENDIX B: LIVE RESULTS

The recommendation system set up on the MUST-VE platform makes it possible to generate a list of customers, suppliers or distributors according to the demand of the matchmaking algorithms. The results are presented according to Figure 8.

Figure 8. MUST-VE matchmaking output

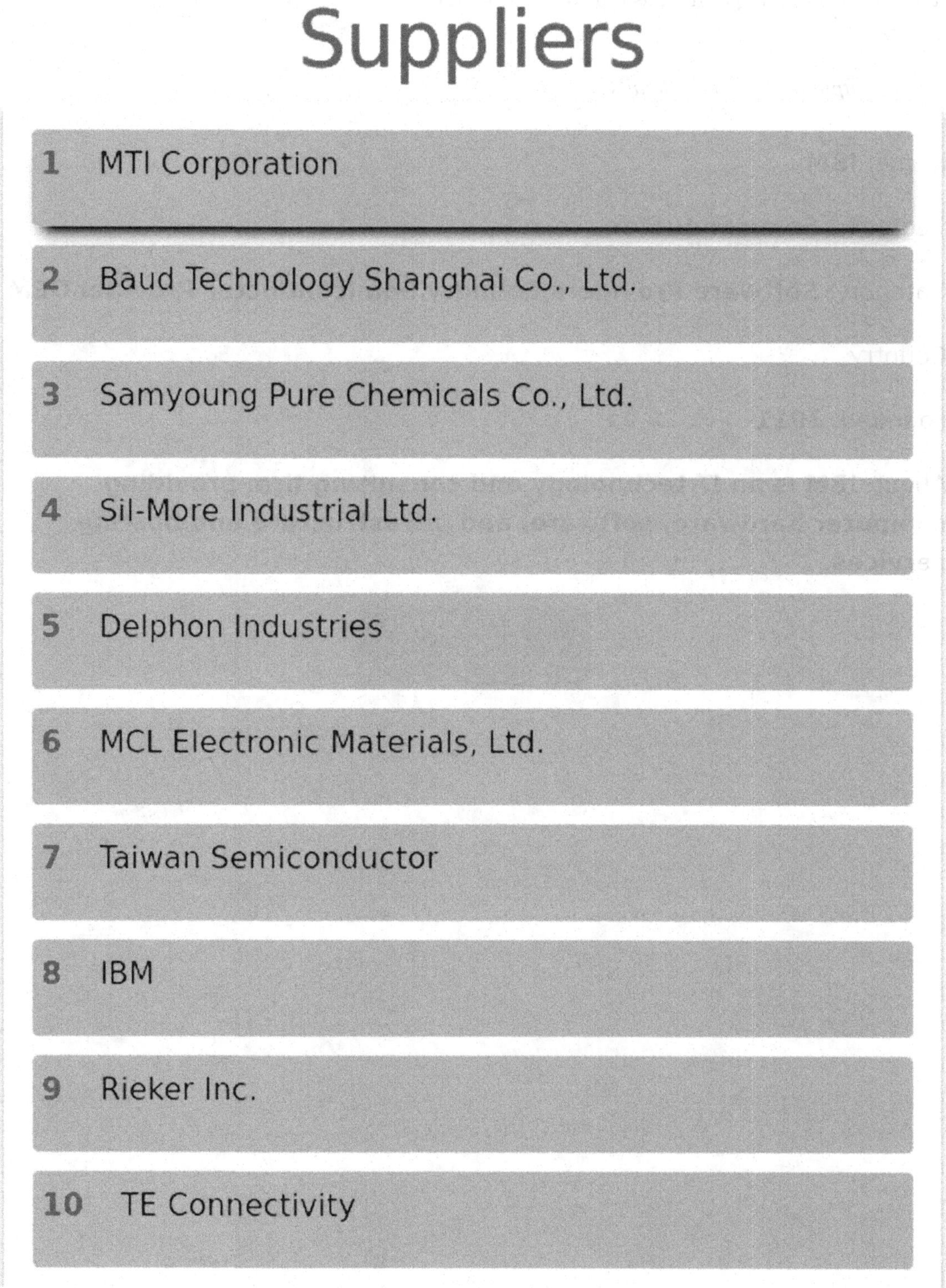

Suppliers

1   MTI Corporation

2   Baud Technology Shanghai Co., Ltd.

3   Samyoung Pure Chemicals Co., Ltd.

4   Sil-More Industrial Ltd.

5   Delphon Industries

6   MCL Electronic Materials, Ltd.

7   Taiwan Semiconductor

8   IBM

9   Rieker Inc.

10   TE Connectivity

When the user clicks on one of the elements of the previous list, the interface offers more detail concerning the organization in question, as represented by Figure 9.

Figure 9. Output organization details

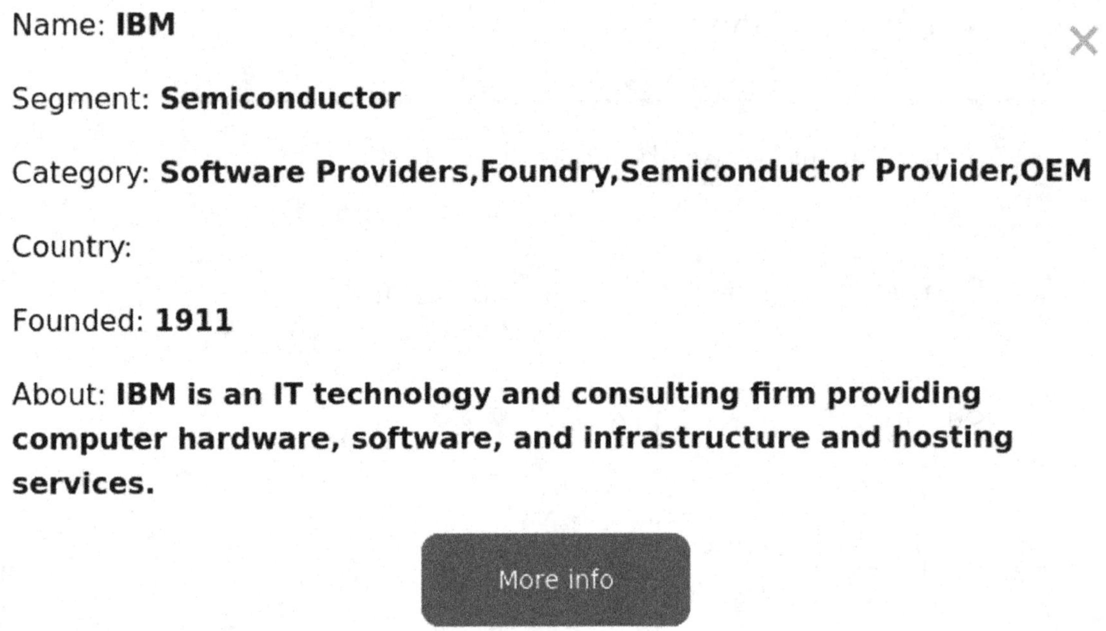

Name: **IBM**

Segment: **Semiconductor**

Category: **Software Providers,Foundry,Semiconductor Provider,OEM**

Country:

Founded: **1911**

About: **IBM is an IT technology and consulting firm providing computer hardware, software, and infrastructure and hosting services.**

More info

Recommendation Systems

R

Houda El Bouhissi

https://orcid.org/0000-0003-3239-8255

LIMED Laboratory, Faculty of Exact Sciences, University of Bejaia, Algeria

INTRODUCTION

As e-commerce expands and Big Data becomes more widespread, a massive quantity of data becomes available, and the number of Internet users increases. On the other hand, users are finding it difficult to acquire the products they desire. In a great knowledge area, the challenge is to help users in discovering and selecting resources. Recommendation systems have recently been a popular topic for researchers. Several big companies, such as Amazon and Netflix (Paul et al., 2017) have adopted these systems. Recommender Systems explore users' preferences in order to supply them with items that best meet their needs.

According to Klašnja-Milićević et al. (2015), Recommender systems are software tools and algorithms that provide suggestions for items that a user could find useful. These systems leverage the dependence principle between user-based and item-based tasks to select the most relevant item (Aggarwal, 2016).

Recommender systems remain to be a significant business tool for both Internet users and service providers; on the one hand, they improve company's sales, profits, and revenues, while also reducing the price of discovery and adoption in an online shopping.

However, Recommender systems are not limited to marketing products but emerged to support the healthcare community for decision-making and predict healthiness. In order to make user recommendations, the Recommender systems collect efficiently simple and standard data from different data sources, such as user evaluations and suggestions. Data belongs to different types and are mainly related to the elements proposed and the users receive the appropriate recommendations. Moreover, Data can be more informational, for example, users or items descriptions or constraints, social relationships, and user's activities (Portugal et al., 2018).

In addition, with the explosion of the Web Services on the internet, such as YouTube, Amazon, eBay, and many others, Recommender systems are becoming increasingly important in our life. Recommender systems are now inevitable in our daily online trips, from e-commerce (suggest articles to buyers that may be of interest) to online advertising (suggest the proper contents to consumers based on their preferences).

Overall, recommender systems are becoming increasingly important in a variety of fields, most particularly healthcare. Here some examples:

- Movies: Netflix and Movielens
- E-commerce: Amazon.com
- Music: lastFM
- Tourism: Tripadvisor.com
- Youtube.com: video

DOI: 10.4018/978-1-7998-9220-5.ch169

Recently, in order to provide users with better recommendations, these systems have introduced Machine-Learning algorithms. However, given the large number of methods presented in the literature and the effectiveness of each approach, selecting an appropriate Machine-Learning algorithm for a Recommender system is challenging (Portugal et al., 2018).

Recommender systems are usually used to manage massive amounts of data and knowledge. Ontologies play a crucial role in knowledge representation, exchange, and reuse in these systems. Ontology-based recommenders are knowledge-based systems that employ ontologies to describe information about items and users in the recommendation process. Indeed, including ontological information in the recommendation process enriches the data with semantics and can overcome the limitations of conventional recommender systems.

According to recent studies (Chicaiza and Valdiviezo-Diaz, 2021), combining ontology domain information about users and items increases the accuracy and quality of suggestions while reducing the downsides of traditional recommender approaches like cold start and score dispersion. The ontology is useful for constructing user profiles with several dimensions, such as user comments, reviews, and ratings. Furthermore, the ontological model makes it easier to comprehend user preferences by representing them from several viewpoints.

Thus, the main contributions of this work are:

- First, we discuss the paradigms of the most popular recommender systems. We detail how they work, their conceptual model, and their strengths and shortcomings.
- Secondly, we present a state-of-art of the main proposals based on Machine-Learning algorithms and ontologies. In addition, we highlight the need to combine Machine-Learning algorithms and ontologies to provide accurate and efficient recommendations.
- Finally, we discuss and give an insight into the future research trends in this area of recommender systems and present a general solution including Machine-Learning algorithms and ontologies.

The remainder of this chapter is organized as follows. Section 2 gives a background about Recommender systems and their techniques. In Section 3, we discuss the challenges faced. In section 4 and 5, we review the basic concepts related to Ontologies and Machine-Learning. The literature review is described in Section 6. In section 7, we discuss how to evaluate a Recommender system. Finally, Section 8 gives a conclusion and points out future directions.

BACKGROUND

Before going into the details of this survey, let us examine some basic terms and ideas related to recommendation systems, machine learning and ontologies. We also discuss the reasons and motivations for introducing Ontologies and Machine-Learning algorithms to Recommender systems.

Overall, recommendation lists are generated based on various collected data, such as user preferences, item features, previous user-item interactions, and some other information. User profiles, item databases, a recommendation engine, and a ranking mechanism are all high-level components of every recommender system. Figure 1 depicts these components and their interrelationship.

Usually, a Recommender system includes two databases: "a database of user profiles and a database of items". The two databases are interlinked in order to express the relationship between a user and an item. This relationship can be one of interest expressed (e.g., a "like") or one of engagement (Chounta,

2018). In the database, a suggestion is made for a certain user. A recommendation algorithm evaluates whether additional things in the database could be of interest to the selected user based on one user profile and the associated items in the database. To generate a suggested list, these algorithms might employ a variety of methodologies.

Figure 1. Recommender System general architecture

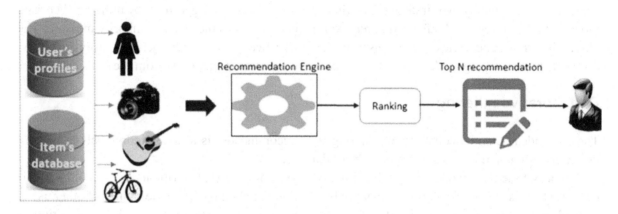

In practice, a Recommender system has mainly four (4) parts:

- A database where the input data is available.
- An interface for communication and exchange like computer, smartphone …etc.
- An algorithm for data processing
- Recommendation component as an output

Recommender systems are categorized in the literature according to the method used to estimate missing scores into different approaches that are extensively utilized in a range of fields (Mckensy-Sambola et al., 2022):

- Collaborative filtering (CF): the most common approach, which involves gathering preferences from a large number of users, filtering using collaborative strategies, and making automatic predictions;
- Content-based filtering (CB), which uses features defined in items liked by users to find and suggest similar items;
- Hybrid approaches, which combine the above techniques.

Content-Based Filtering

CB approaches suggest items that are similar to those that a user previously selected.
The following concepts underlying CB Recommender systems:

- Attempt to analyze a user's description of the goods he or she like to identify the main characteristics (preferences) that may be utilized to distinguish these items. A user profile is used to store these choices.
- Only items that are substantially close to the user's profile will be recommended when the characteristics of each element are compared to the user's profile.

To create recommendations based on the information utilized and the produced systems, CB recommender systems employ two strategies. The first approach generates suggestions by utilizing "heuristic models" and "conventional information retrieval methods" such as the cosine similarity measure. The alternative strategy generates suggestions by utilizing statistical learning and machine learning methods, primarily by developing models capable of understanding users' preferences from previous data.

Collaborative Filtering

The basic idea behind a collaborative filtering (CF) recommender is to assist individuals in making decisions based on the views of others with similar interests.

Memory-based and model-based CF are the two types of CF (AL-Ghuribi and Noah,2021). Memory-based CF is a heuristic algorithm that predicts an item's rating based on the ratings of other users. It involves two types: user-based and item-based. The former uses ratings to identify a collection of neighbors (i.e., like-minded users) for a target user and then recommends a set of goods that interest his neighbors. The latter, on the other hand, suggests things to a target user that share comparable (i.e., shared characteristics) interests in items that the user has previously purchased, seen, or loved. The item-to-item technique, on the other hand, calculates similarities between things depending on whether consumers like them.

Hybrid Recommendation

It is ideal to combine the Recommender systems methodologies in order to increase the performance of Recommender systems and prevent cold start difficulties, data scarcity, and scalability. Many systems use a combination of the CF and CB approaches, which are referred to as hybrid systems.

The above-mentioned strategies are combined in the hybrid recommendation methodology. This method has been proposed as a way to overcome the limitations of existing recommendation approaches and produce better results. Hybrid systems manage content-oriented user profiles, and the comparison between these profiles increases the creation of user communities, allowing collaborative filtering.

In general, hybridization is performed in two stages: (i) developing candidate suggestions using CF and other filtering approaches individually, and (ii) combining these sets of early recommendations using particular methodologies to provide final recommendations for users.

RECOMMENDER SYSTEMS' CHALLENGES

Recommender systems produce good outcomes in many systems, but there are a few issues that must be addressed. Researchers in the field of recommender systems confront a number of obstacles, the most important of which are listed below (Khan et al., 2017) (Khusro et al., 2016):

R

- Data sparsity: when the number of recorded scores is smaller than the number of predicted scores by a given user, the problem is known as "data sparsity." Recommender system concentrates on a single domain while ignoring user interests in other domains, resulting in sparsity and cold start issues. The user-item matrix will be quite sparse in this situation, and Recommender system will be unable to offer the proper opinions to the customer. We distinguish two data sparsity characteristics:
  - Reduced coverage: This refers to the percentage of items for which the systems can provide recommendations. When the number of ratings is relatively small in contrast to the number of things in the system, the suggestions fail.
  - Neighbor transitivity: Due to the limited databases, it is difficult to link users who are favorably associated.
- Cold start: When new users join the system, there is typically insufficient information to generate suggestions for them, and there isn't enough past rating for an item. In such situations, it is impossible for the Recommender system to suggest specific things to new users.
- Semantic: This difficulty occurs when many things have similar qualities but distinct names. When the Recommender system is unable to manage a scenario like this, it may create a suggestion list with comparable items, resulting in a lower recommendation quality. For example, a Recommender system will not distinguish between "book" (reservation) and "book" (manuscript), and both terms have different meanings depending on the context.
- Security and credibility: Recommendation systems are unable to avoid fraud. This makes it simple to create a new identity and commit acts of vandalism, such as giving the system false information. We detect that in distributed systems without a central authority, controlling user identification and punishing harmful activity is more challenging.
- Collection of preferences: Collecting user preferences is one of the most crucial and hardest phases in recommender systems. Gathering feedback from users on a resource that they loved, disliked, or did not like at all is a challenging task. Users are apprehensive about giving their personal information to recommender systems. As a result, a Recommender system should build trust among its users by incorporating randomized perturbation techniques that allow users to publish private data without revealing their identities, as well as utilizing Semantic Web technologies, particularly ontologies, in conjunction with NLP techniques to mitigate undesirable information contact.
- Grey sheep and black sheep: Grey sheep occurs when the opinion of a user does not match with any group, and therefore, is unable to get benefit from any recommendations. Black sheep" are those users who have no or very few people with whom they correlate. Recommendations are very difficult to make in this category.

Ontologies

According to communities, several meanings of the term "ontology" have been suggested. The term ontology, which refers to the topic of existence, has a long history in philosophy. From the standpoint of knowledge engineering, we have opted to define the term "ontology".

Gruber and his Stanford colleagues introduced ontology in 1993. His definition is the most frequently cited in academic articles and research studies. An ontology, according to Gruber (1993), is "*a formal and explicit statement of a common conceptualization*":

- Formal: the fact that an ontology has to be machine-readable, i.e., that a computer could be able to interpret the semantics of the information provided.
- Explicit: indicates that the type of concepts utilized, as well as the restrictions on their usage, must be explicitly specified.
- Conceptualization: refers to an abstract model of certain phenomena in the world that identifies appropriate concepts for this phenomenon.
- Shared: indicates that the ontology supports consensual knowledge, and is not restricted to some individuals.

The three fundamental components of ontology are class, individual, and property. Disease is an example of a class, whereas corona is an example of an individual. Furthermore, the people are described by the property component.

According to their use, four categories of ontologies are classically distinguished (Heijst et al., 1997):

- Generic ontologies are also called top-level ontologies or high-level models. They describe general concepts regardless of a particular domain or problem. Concepts can be time, space, or events.
- Domain ontologies specify general concepts in a particular domain. The vocabulary is generally related to a domain of knowledge like healthcare or law. The different concepts of domain ontologies are often considered a specialization of generic ontologies.
- Task ontologies describe the vocabulary of terms needed to perform generic tasks or activities (e.g., diagnosis) by specializing the concepts provided by the top-level ontology.
- Application ontologies describe the structure of knowledge necessary for the realization of a particular task.

Machine Learning

Machine-Learning is a branch of artificial intelligence whose purpose is to automate processes that previously required human intellect, such as decision-making, pattern identification, and many others. As summarized by Ramzan et al. (2019), Machine-Learning approaches may be classified into three types: Supervised learning, unsupervised learning and semi supervised learning.

In supervised learning, data is provided with the objective of developing a general rule that links inputs to outputs. In other situations, inputs are only partially available, while some desired outputs are either missing or only provided as feedback to actions in a dynamic context (reinforcement learning). In this case, the trained model is used to expect the test data's missing outputs (labels) supervised learning includes KNN (K-Nearest Neighbor), linear regression, Naïve bayes and other techniques.

Unsupervised learning is an approach in which the user does not learn the model. Instead, it allows the model to work alone to identify patterns and information. It is mostly concerned with unlabeled data. Unsupervised learning enables users to perform more tasks. Unsupervised learning includes, for example, clustering, anomaly detection, neural networks, and other algorithms.

Supervised learning requires labeled datasets. When handling large amounts of data, this method is highly expensive. Unsupervised learning also has the issue of having a limited range of applications. To address these issues, the semi-supervised learning algorithms were established. This approach employs both labeled and unlabeled data, allowing it to function with any type of data. Mostly, semi-supervised learning includes a small amount of labeled data and a huge amount of unlabeled data.

LITERATURE REVIEW

Different studies were conducted to review and survey the classical Recommender systems in different domains such as health, e-commerce, and tourism.

In this section, we present the most important works related to Recommender systems. We give a classification of these contributions into two categories: Machine-Learning-based approaches and Ontology-based approaches.

Machine-Learning-Based Approaches

In (Kim et al., 2009), the authors suggest a diet Recommender system for coronary heart disease management in healthcare services. This study presents a customized food recommendation service for consumers who seek coronary heart disease prevention and management. Since a diet suggestion service is only focused on personal illness information, clients who are concerned about their condition receive a personalized diet based on their basic information, vital signs, family history of diseases, food preferences according to seasons, and intakes.

Automatic home medical product suggestion was utilized as a real example in (Luo et al., 2012) to highlight the benefits of incorporating intelligence into Personal Health Records (PHRs). Their technique builds a topic-selection input interface for proposing home medical items by combining treatment and nursing expertise and extending the language modeling method.

Another approach introduced by Verma et al. (2015). The authors propose a recommender system based on hybrid filtering. The study is about numerical data in the form of ranks or ratings for different products and services. These data first filter/transform as per requirement. They analyzed different size files and came with the conclusion that their model was working perfectly and that size was not influencing the execution time. However, the model proposed does not handle text data.

Another method was introduced by Verma et al. (2015). The authors propose a hybrid filtering-based recommender system. The research focuses on numerical data in the form of rankings or ratings for various products and services. This data is first filtered and transformed as needed. They examined various file sizes and concluded that their model was accurate and that file size had no effect on execution time. However, the suggested model does not handle text data.

Dwivedi and Roshni (2017) introduced a recommendation system for education that handles large amounts of data. The research employs collaborative filtering-based recommendation algorithms to propose elective courses to students. The proposal is based on Mahout, a Machine-Learning library of Hadoop, and can be used by schools, colleges, and universities.

The authors, Mayahi et al. (2018), studied the benefits of adopting big data analytics in healthcare. The research is based on current literature studies and secondary data and reveals that using analytics in healthcare is critical. The authors perform an experiment to examine the possible benefits using a real dataset, and the results were quite encouraging.

A novel approach was proposed by (Ratnaparkhi, 2018) for building a Recommender system for new clients. The proposal aims to provide clients with a set of dishes that have been classified into categories (good, average, and bad) based on previous reviews. The author followed the KDD methodology, which is a set of steps that simplify the implementation of any project that aims at generating knowledge from a given dataset. The result was that the prediction model gave good accuracy and could be trained on much larger datasets. This research provides a good implementation for Recommender system in another domain. However, it has the ability to work only with one type of dish, so composed dishes are not taken into account.

In the proposal of Hosseini et al. (2019), the authors introduced a diabetes prediction and recommendation system. Healthcare recommender systems are significant because persons use social media to keep track of their health. To deliver personalized healthcare recommendations, they adopted a hybrid filtering strategy. Data from a variety of sources, used by learning algorithms, which produce significant results. The illness risk diagnosis for future instances is displayed by the prediction engine, which is based on active patients. On the other hand, the trust and security of social health data must be taken into account.

The paper (Serrano, 2019) explores the product rank relevance provided by various commercial big data recommender systems and proposes an intelligent Recommender system based on a random neural network that serves as an interface between the client and the various recommender systems that adapt to the perceived user relevance. The Intelligent Recommender System handles a client's request and collects goods from the recommender system's data set. Serrano shows that employing neural networks in recommender systems is a revolutionary strategy.

Ontology-Based Approaches

Many ontology-based recommendation techniques have been presented in recent years. Rahayu et al. (2022) conduct a comprehensive analysis of the role of ontologies in e-Learning recommender systems. Previous research on ontology-based recommendation systems focused on domain ontologies, restricted vocabulary, and taxonomies. Nowadays, Linked Open Data has opened up new opportunities for improved application recommendation.

In Vicente et al. (2014), the authors developed a novel semantic reasoning-based technique for improving neighborhood generation in order to address the aforementioned fake neighborhood problem. The aim of the method was to make the search for semantic similarities between various items more flexible, without requiring users to score the same products in order to compare them.

Bagherifard et al. (2017) present a new hybrid recommendation approach utilizing a real-world dataset. The goal is to increase efficiency and accuracy by developing a heuristic hybrid recommendation technique that incorporates memory-based and model-based approaches. The authors employ domain ontologies in the CF mechanism and enhance the ontology structure. This innovative technique has the potential to improve the accuracy of CF and CB.

In the proposal of Nilashi et al. (2018), the authors build a new hybrid recommendation method based on CF approaches to solve two main drawbacks of recommender systems, sparsity and scalability, using dimensionality reduction and ontology techniques. Then, the authors use ontology to improve the accuracy of recommendations in CF part.

Table 1 outlines the main elements of the proposed techniques. The table is divided into five columns, and each column includes a comparison criterion, as follows:

- The column "*Approach category*" designates the category to which the approach belongs.
- The column "*Approach*" designates the underlying approach.
- The column "*Domain*" indicates the recommendation domain.
- The column "*Used technique*" specifies the used techniques, what methods are used for recommendation.
- The column "*Advantages*" introduces the main advantages of the approach.

Table 1. Summary of literature review.

Approach Category	Approach	Domain	Used Technique	Advantages
Machine-learning approaches	(Kim et al., 2009)	Data recorder that stores XML Data of user's health	-Content-based filtering	Better recommendation
	(Luo et al., 2012)	Medical exam cases	Knowledge-Based filtering	-Non existence of cold-start -Providing personalized healthcare
	(Verma et al., 2015)	MovieLens	-Hybrid filtering -Machine learning	-Tested with different size file.
	(Liu et al., 2016)	Healthcare big data	-Collaborative filtering -Machine learning	-Handles different formats of data
	(Dwivedi and Roshni, 2017)	Education big data	Collaborative filtering -Machine learning	-Useful for training -Improve the education system quality -Improve the student and teacher performance
	(Mayahi et al., 2018)	UC Irvine machine learning repository	-Machine learning	-Efficient healthcare services -Cost effective -Better performance
	(Ratnaparkhi, 2018)	Yelp (restaurant category)	-NLP -Machine learning	-Larger dataset can be used with this model
	(Hosseini et al., 2019)	Diabetes data collected from hospital	-Hybrid filtering -Machine learning	-Minimize costs -Warn patient of health risks
	(Serrano, 2019)	MovieLens Trip Advisor Amazon	Random Neural Network -Machine learning	Direct connection between customers and products in a reduced time -Rearrange the products until the satisfaction of the customers
Ontology-based approaches	(Vicente et al., 2014)	e-commerce websites	Collaborating filtering. Ontologies	Reduce fake neighborhoods' problem
	(Bagherifard et al., 2017)	e-commerce websites	Hybrid RS Ontologies	User has been clustered in ontology to reduce computing time
	(Nilashi et al., 2018)	Movieslens Yahoo	Hybrid RS Ontologies	Clustering item and user to reduce over generalization

RECOMMENDER SYSTEM EVALUATION

In the domain of Recommender systems, different evaluation approaches are used, categorized into on-line and off-line techniques. The on-line evaluation concerns human judgment and satisfaction and involves real users (students, researchers, and professionals) with computer skills. The off-line techniques are based on well-defined metrics.

For a Recommender system based on a machine-learning algorithm, we need to analyze its performance in order to decide which algorithm best matches the goal condition.

The Precision tries tso address the question, "What percentage of positive identifications were genuinely correct?" It elucidates (Equation 1) how a model may accurately predict class membership. As a result, it assesses the accuracy of the categorization outputs.

$$Precision = \frac{A}{\left(A + C\right)} \tag{1}$$

When there is a high cost associated with number of relevant not recommended items, we use the Recall metric, also known as sensitivity, to select our best model. It (Equation 2) shows how accurate the model is at predicting class membership and thus addresses the quantitative aspect of classification success. It is determined by the percentage of all relevant items that are suggested.

$$Recall = \frac{A}{A + B} \tag{2}$$

Where:

- A: number of relevant recommended items.
- B: number of relevant not recommended items.
- C: number of irrelevant recommended items.

Precision is a good measure to determine, when the costs of False Positive is high. For example, in food recommendation, a false positive means that a particular food that is not specific for a patient (actual negative) has been identified as a recommended food (predicted food). Precision, therefore, calculates the accuracy for the minority class.

When the precision is high the recall is low, in this case, the used classifier is extremely accurate. Nevertheless, the dataset misses a significant number of instances that are difficult to classify, then, this is not very useful.

Another interesting metric, called *accuracy* (Equation 3) which represents the number of correctly classified data instances over the total number of data instances.

$$Accuracy = \frac{D + A}{D + C + A + B} \tag{3}$$

Where:

- D: number of not relevant recommended items (True negative).

In general, accuracy may not be a good measure if the dataset is not balanced (both negative and positive classes have different number of data instances).

When we employ machine-learning methods, we need both precision and recall to be one, which also implies FP and FN should be zero in a good classifier. As a result, we require a metric that considers both accuracy and recall.

One of the most common approaches for measuring cluster accuracy is to utilize the F-measure metric. F-measure is a metric, which takes both accuracy and recall into account. It is based on precision and recall (Equation 4):

$$F\text{-}measure = 2 * \frac{Precision * Recall}{Precision + Recall} \tag{4}$$

When we want to strike a balance between precision and recall, we need the F-measure. The outcome is a number between 0.0 and 1.0, with 0.0 being the worst F-measure and 1.0 representing the best F-measure.

Overall, the F-measure works best when the built-in Recommender system attacks a compromise between Precision and Recall. The F-measure, on the other hand, is not as high if one measure improves at the value of the other.

FUTURE RESEARCH DIRECTIONS

For the recommendation, the systems discussed above employ various types of data sources. The most popular domain is movies. The easy accessibility of data in the cinematic domain is one such reason for this outcome.

The CB method proposes items that are similar in content to those previously experienced by the user. This technique works if the item is described as a set of attributes. Moreover, CB suffers from the ability to change the user's preferences.

The most widespread technique is the CF approach. It matches people with similar preferences by using ratings for items in a certain domain. Compared to CB, CF has several advantages:

- Provides unpredicted recommendations.
- Deals with items whose content is not easily inspected.

The hybrid recommendation approach is promising because it integrates two or more recommendation techniques to limit the weaknesses of CB and CF. It can provide many synergies compared to the CB and CF recommendation algorithms. However, the use of recommendation systems has exposed many challenges: data sparsity, cold start problems, fraud and privacy when it comes to healthcare, and we need techniques that are more efficient.

Recommender systems mostly rely on ratings, which do not always meet the goals of various recommender systems, such as health recommender systems. Users' preferences may differ from their needs (for example, a user may express a taste for ice cream, but he is diabetic, so this is not a product to offer him).

Filtering methods in the health recommender system must be improved. Furthermore, privacy concerns are a key problem that must be addressed. Using data from several sources may raise concerns about the usage of personal information. As a result, it might be a significant issue, particularly in the area of health information, where privacy is a sensitive concern. We also intended to highlight the lack of academic resources in health Recommender systems, as most research is presented at conferences rather than in peer-reviewed publications. The key conclusion is that health recommender systems are an exciting new expansion in healthcare.

Ontologies can be employed to model the semantics of the medical domain, resulting in explicit terminology. An ontology aids in the organization of data by connecting the entities inside the database. Currently, a wide collection of ontologies have been created, ranging from modeling human disease domains to defining medical terminology, allowing medical information systems to be interoperable, and facilitating knowledge interchange across various disciplines. Furthermore, by using the ontology structure, semantic similarity will be calculated between each entity (user and item) for the rating prediction in CF and CB.

Recent studies showed that through the ontology as a semantic model, we increase the Recommender system accuracy and decrease the cold start issues.

Ontologies seem to be promising if they are combined with machine-learning algorithms. Many researches has been conducted on how to improve Recommender systems using ontologies and Machine-Learning algorithms to achieve accuracy. In addition, using ontologies provides Recommender system with a semantic layer to overcome limitations related to traditional Recommender systems. For example, in educational content recommendation, ontologies are used to model learners and learning resources.

The authors (Bahramian and Abbaspour, 2015) proposed a travel CB Recommender system that uses ontology information to compute the degree of similarity between a user's preferences and facts of interest to provide personalized recommendations. The system uses Machine-learning techniques to generalize user preferences. The proposed system overcomes the data sparsity problem of the traditional CB recommender using Spreading Activation.

In the paper of Obeid et al. (2018), the authors propose a new ontology-based Recommender system that use Machine-Learning algorithms. The proposal is dedicated to education domain and provides a personalized recommendation for students. The authors aim to identify the requirements, interests, preferences and capabilities to recommend the appropriate major and university for each one.

ELali (2021) provides a method for making suggestions using intention mining, which is based on a mix of intentional process models, domain ontologies, and contextual data. The suggested approach is divided into two stages. In the first step, the author uses an ontological method to construct the intentional model by merging the contextual information of the activity's traces. The user is guided to complete the next task in the second phase, depending on the generated model.

Joy et al. (2021) suggest a new e-learning recommender system to improve the learning experience. To solve the pure cold-start problem in content recommenders, the proposal recommends a semantic framework based on ontology. The ontology contains both domain information about learners and learning objects.

The approach of El Bouhissi et al. (2021) is a novel knowledge-based food recommendation system in healthcare that includes Machine-Learning techniques and could be used to help people select appropriate meals based on their health situation. The proposal is based on IoT sensors and attempts to combine machine-learning techniques and ontologies to provide recommendations that are more efficient .

According to the presented study, we highlight a general inspired approach combining ontologies and Machine-Learning algorithms. Figure 2, depicts the use of ontologies as a semantic model, understanding and interoperability asset as well as Machine-Learning models for reasoning and recommendation.

The proposed system involves four modules, namely (1) the users' profiles, (2) items, which produce two different ontologies: the user's profile ontology and the item's ontology, (3) the matching module, which matches the two ontologies, and (4) the Recommender engine, based on hybrid filtering, and responsible for providing users with the items that best match their needs.

Figure 2. General Recommender system based on Ontologies and Machine-Learning algorithms

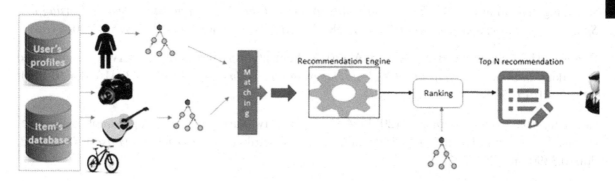

The matching module uses matrix factorization and clustering to search for the user information in a recorded profile. The aim is to increase the recommendation speed. The Recommendation engine uses deep learning to find the top N recommendations.

Finally, to choose the best recommendation from the top N, we use the A-star algorithm. The A-star algorithm (He et al., 2022), based on the Dijkstra algorithm, is a graph-based path-finding algorithm. The A-star algorithm selects the best path by calculating the cost from the start point to reach the target point.

CONCLUSION

As we mentioned in the introduction of this chapter, Recommender systems are becoming essential in many industries and, hence, have received more attention in recent years. In this chapter, we have introduced the basic notions required for a better understanding of the questions related to these systems.

Recommender systems are playing a major role in our everyday lives, and in the last few years, research topics in this field have been increasing. Recently, Big Data Analytics and machine-learning algorithms have come to solve some of the challenges such as data sparsity, scalability, and cold start.

In this chapter, we describe Recommender systems in general and underline the need to combine Machine-Learning algorithms and ontologies to provide better recommendations.

In the future, we plan to extend our proposal the proposal of (El Bouhissi et al., 2021) and propose a new hybrid approach using ontologies to model user preferences and items and deep learning algorithms to build an efficient food recommendation system for diabetics.

REFERENCES

Aggarwal, C. C. (2016). *Recommender systems*. Springer International Publishing. doi:10.1007/978-3-319-29659-3

AL-Ghuribi. S. M., & Noah, S. A. M. (2021). *A Comprehensive Overview of Recommender System and Sentiment Analysis*. arXiv preprint arXiv:2109.08794.

Bagherifard, K., Rahmani, M., Nilashi, M., & Rafe, V. (2017). Performance improvement for recommender systems using ontology. *Telematics and Informatics*, *34*(8), 1772–1792. doi:10.1016/j.tele.2017.08.008

Bahramian, Z., & Abbaspour, R. A. (2015). An ontology-based tourism recommender system based on spreading activation model. *The International Archives of the Photogrammetry, Remote Sensing and Spatial Information Sciences*, *XL-1*(W5), 83–90. doi:10.5194/isprsarchives-XL-1-W5-83-2015

Bouhissi, H. E., Salem, A. B. M., & Tari, A. (2019). Semantic enrichment of web services using linked open data. *International Journal of Web Engineering and Technology*, *14*(4), 383–416. doi:10.1504/IJWET.2019.105594

Chicaiza, J., & Valdiviezo-Diaz, P. (2021). A Comprehensive Survey of Knowledge Graph-Based Recommender Systems: Technologies, Development, and Contributions. *Information (Basel)*, *12*(6), 232. doi:10.3390/info12060232

Chounta, I. A. (2018). *A review of the state-of-art of the use of Machine-Learning and Artificial Intelligence by educational portals and OER repositories* (White Paper). University of Tartu.

Dwivedi, S., & Roshni, V. S. (2017). Recommender system for big data in education. *2017 5th National Conference on E-Learning & E-Learning Technologies (ELELTECH)*, 1-4.

Elali, R. (2021). *An Intention Mining Approach using Ontology for Contextual Recommendations*. Academic Press.

El Bouhissi, H., Adel, M., Ketam, A., & Salem, A. B. M. (2021). Towards an Efficient Knowledge-based Recommendation System. IntelITSIS, 38-49.

Gruber, T. R. (1993). A translation approach to portable ontology specifications. *Knowledge Acquisition*, *5*(2), 199–220. doi:10.1006/knac.1993.1008

He, Z., Liu, C., Chu, X., Negenborn, R. R., & Wu, Q. (2022). Dynamic anti-collision A-star algorithm for multi-ship encounter situations. *Applied Ocean Research*, *118*, 102995. doi:10.1016/j.apor.2021.102995

Heijst Van, G., Schreiber, A. T., & Wielinga, B. J. (1997). Using explicit ontologies in KBS development. *International Journal of Human-Computer Studies*, *46*(2-3), 183–292. doi:10.1006/ijhc.1996.0090

Hosseini, S. M. A., & Pons Valladares, O. (2019). Sustainable building technologies for post-disaster temporary housing: Integrated sustainability assessment and life cycle assessment. *World Academy of Science, Engineering and Technology*, *13*(4), 244–250.

Joy, J., & Raj, N. S., & VG, R. (2021). Ontology-based E-learning Content Recommender System for Addressing the Pure Cold-start Problem. *ACM Journal of Data and Information Quality*, *13*(3), 1–27. doi:10.1145/3429251

Khan, M. M., Ibrahim, R., & Ghani, I. (2017). Cross-domain recommender systems: A systematic literature review. *ACM Computing Surveys*, *50*(3), 1–34. doi:10.1145/3073565

Khusro, S., Ali, Z., & Ullah, I. (2016). Recommender systems: issues, challenges, and research opportunities. In *Information Science and Applications (ICISA)*. Springer. doi:10.1007/978-981-10-0557-2_112

Kim, J. H., Lee, J. H., Park, J. S., Lee, Y. H., & Rim, K. W. (2009). Design of diet recommendation system for healthcare service based on user information. *2009 Fourth International Conference on Computer Sciences and Convergence Information Technology*, 516-518. 10.1109/ICCIT.2009.293

Klašnja-Milićević, A., Ivanović, M., & Nanopoulos, A. (2015). Recommender systems in e-learning environments: A survey of the state-of-the-art and possible extensions. *Artificial Intelligence Review*, *44*(4), 571–604. doi:10.100710462-015-9440-z

Luo, G., Thomas, S. B., & Tang, C. (2012). Automatic home medical product recommendation. *Journal of Medical Systems*, *36*(2), 383–398. doi:10.100710916-010-9483-2 PMID:20703712

Lu, J., Wu, D., Mao, M., Wang, W., & Zhang, G. (2015). Recommender system application developments: A survey. *Decision Support Systems*, *74*, 12–32. doi:10.1016/j.dss.2015.03.008

Al Mayahi, S., Al-Badi, A., & Tarhini, A. (2018). Exploring the potential benefits of big data analytics in providing smart healthcare. In *International Conference for Emerging Technologies in Computing*. Springer. 10.1007/978-3-319-95450-9_21

Mckensy-Sambola, D., Rodríguez-García, M. Á., García-Sánchez, F., & Valencia-García, R. (2022). Ontology-Based Nutritional Recommender System. *Applied Sciences (Basel, Switzerland)*, *12*(1), 143. doi:10.3390/app12010143

Nilashi, M., Ibrahim, O., & Bagherifard, K. (2018). A recommender system based on collaborative filtering using ontology and dimensionality reduction techniques. *Expert Systems with Applications*, *92*, 507–520. doi:10.1016/j.eswa.2017.09.058

Obeid, C., Lahoud, I., El Khoury, H., & Champin, P. A. (2018). Ontology-based recommender system in higher education. *Companion Proceedings of the Web Conference*, 1031-1034.

Paul, P. V., Monica, K., & Trishanka, M. (2017). A survey on big data analytics using social media data. *2017 Innovations in Power and Advanced Computing Technologies (i-PACT)*, 1-4.

Portugal, I., Alencar, P., & Cowan, D. (2018). The use of machine learning algorithms in recommender systems: A systematic review. *Expert Systems with Applications*, *97*, 205–227. doi:10.1016/j.eswa.2017.12.020

Rahayu, N. W., Ferdiana, R., & Kusumawardani, S. S. (2022). A systematic review of ontology use in E-Learning recommender system. *Computers and Education: Artificial Intelligence, 100047*.

Raghuwanshi, S. K., & Pateriya, R. K. Recommendation Systems (2019). Techniques, Challenges, Application, and Evaluation. Advances in Intelligent Systems and Computing, 817, 151–164.

Ramzan, B., Bajwa, I. S., Jamil, N., Amin, R. U., Ramzan, S., Mirza, F., & Sarwar, N. (2019). An intelligent data analysis for recommendation systems using machine learning. *Scientific Programming*, *2019*, 1–20. doi:10.1155/2019/5941096

Ratnaparkhi, K. (2018). *Recommender system for food in a restaurant based on Natural Language Processing and Machine Learning* (Doctoral dissertation). National College of Ireland.

Serrano, W. (2019). Intelligent recommender system for big data applications based on the random neural network. *Big Data and Cognitive Computing*, *3*(1), 15. doi:10.3390/bdcc3010015

Verma, J. P., Patel, B., & Patel, A. (2015, February). Big data analysis: recommendation system with Hadoop framework. *2015 IEEE International Conference on Computational Intelligence & Communication Technology*, 92-97. 10.1109/CICT.2015.86

Martín-Vicente, M. I., Gil-Solla, A., Ramos-Cabrer, M., Pazos-Arias, J. J., Blanco-Fernández, Y., & López-Nores, M. (2014). A semantic approach to improve neighborhood formation in collaborative recommender systems. *Expert Systems with Applications*, *41*(17), 7776–7788. doi:10.1016/j.eswa.2014.06.038

ADDITIONAL READING

George, G., & Lal, A. M. (2019). Review of ontology-based recommender systems in e-learning. *Computers & Education*, *142*, 103642. doi:10.1016/j.compedu.2019.103642

Isinkaye, F. O., Folajimi, Y. O., & Ojokoh, B. A. (2015). Recommendation systems: Principles, methods and evaluation. *Egyptian Informatics Journal, 16*(3), 261-273.

Mckensy-Sambola, D., Rodríguez-García, M. Á., García-Sánchez, F., & Valencia-García, R. (2022). Ontology-Based Nutritional Recommender System. *Applied Sciences (Basel, Switzerland)*, *12*(1), 143. doi:10.3390/app12010143

Mishra, D., Buyya, R., Mohapatra, P., & Patnaik, S. (2019). Intelligent and Cloud Computing. *Proceedings of ICICC*, 1.

Mohanty, S. N., Chatterjee, J. M., Jain, S., Elngar, A. A., & Gupta, P. (Eds.). (2020). *Recommender System with Machine Learning and Artificial Intelligence: Practical Tools and Applications in Medical, Agricultural and Other Industries*. John Wiley & Sons. doi:10.1002/9781119711582

Sahu, R., Dash, M., & Kumar, A. (Eds.). (2017). *Applying Predictive Analytics within the Service Sector*. IGI Global. doi:10.4018/978-1-5225-2148-8

Schwartz, D., & Te'eni, D. (Eds.). (2011). *Encyclopedia of Knowledge Management* (2nd ed.). IGI Global. doi:10.4018/978-1-59904-931-1

Yearwood, J., & Stranieri, A. (2012). *Approaches for Community Decision Making and Collective Reasoning: Knowledge Technology Support*. IGI Global. doi:10.4018/978-1-4666-1818-3

KEY TERMS AND DEFINITIONS

Big Data: Big data also known as mega-data refers to all the digital data produced by the use of new technologies for personal or professional purposes.

Cold Start: An issue that a recommendation system encounters when there is very little data available about the user or the item.

Collaborative Filtering: Recommends items to a specific user based on the interests of many other users.

Dataset: Datasets are commonly used in machine learning. They regroup a set of linked data that can be in various formats (texts, numbers, images, videos, etc.).

Items: Entities that a recommendation system recommends. For example, books are the items that a bookstore recommends.

Machine Learning: Machine learning is an artificial intelligence technology that allows computers to learn without being explicitly programmed for this purpose.

Ontology: The word ontology is of a Greek origin. In computer science, an ontology is a structured set of concepts that makes sense of information.

Recommender System: Software tool that suggests recommendation, which users might apply to achieve their goals.

R

Section 47
Reinforcement Learning

Reinforcement Learning for Combinatorial Optimization

R

Di Wang

https://orcid.org/0000-0002-7992-7743

University of Illinois Chicago, USA

INTRODUCTION

Reinforcement learning (RL) is a subfield of machine learning (ML) that tells what actions the intelligent agent should take to maximize the received cumulative rewards (Arulkumaran, 2017) from environments. Building on Markov Decision Process (MDP), a discrete-time stochastic control process, reinforcement learning is suitable for temporal decision-making problems with long-term and short-term reward trade-offs. Researchers introduce deep learning into reinforcement learning to fully utilize the advanced GPU computation ability and potent representation property of neural networks. Moreover, exploiting deep neural networks (DNN) as function approximators instead of using limited-capacity value memory tables make it possible for DRL to solve large-scale problems. The effectiveness of DRL has been proved with applications across multiple industries, including robot control (Yuan, 2022), computer games (Peng, 2022), natural language processing (Du, 2022), healthcare (Oh, 2022), finance (Asgari, 2022) and others.

As shown in Figure 1, many terminologies and concepts are included in deep reinforcement learning. DRL's four essential constituent parts are states, actions, rewards, and stationary transition functions. Specifically, the state represents the observable environment, which refers to the agent's surroundings or the target optimization problem. Action denotes the behaviors of the agent or decision variables of optimization problems, while policy refers to actions at the sequence of time steps. The stationary transaction function records probabilities of transitioning from one state to another. The reward is the evaluation of the action providing DRL the directions of the training process, because of which, DRL belongs to semi-supervised learning algorithms. Unlike supervised learning algorithms, the ground truth is not provided. Theoretically, DRL updates parameters of neural networks greedily towards the gradient of maximizing the expectation of rewards. In detail, the policy evaluation step and the policy estimation step are the essential steps in the training process. Figure 2 illustrates an example of the cooperation between these two steps. The policy evaluation step iteratively estimates state function v_π, where π denotes the adopted policy. An accurate evaluation can provide accurate instruction to the policy improvement step. The policy improvement step greedily generates better policies, providing more data for training the policy evaluation step.

Furthermore, the discounted accumulative rewards can be approximated by two main function approximators, the state value function or state-action value function (also known as Q value). The main goal of DRL is to maximize the expectation of the cumulative rewards (also known as return). Based on the initial actions' availability, the return's expectation can be modeled as state value function or state-action value function (Q value). Q value measures the quality of an action at a given state followed by a particular policy. State value measures the expectation of future discounted rewards starting from the given state and followed by a specific policy.

DOI: 10.4018/978-1-7998-9220-5.ch170

Figure 1. Main concepts and terminologies in deep reinforcement learning. The deep reinforcement learning algorithm contains the state, actions, reward, and stationary transition function. State value function and state-action value function are two approximations of the discounted accumulative reward. Besides, DQN, A2C, A3C, and PPO are state-of-art DRL algorithms, while CNN, RNN, GAT, and GCN are state-of-art neural network architectures.

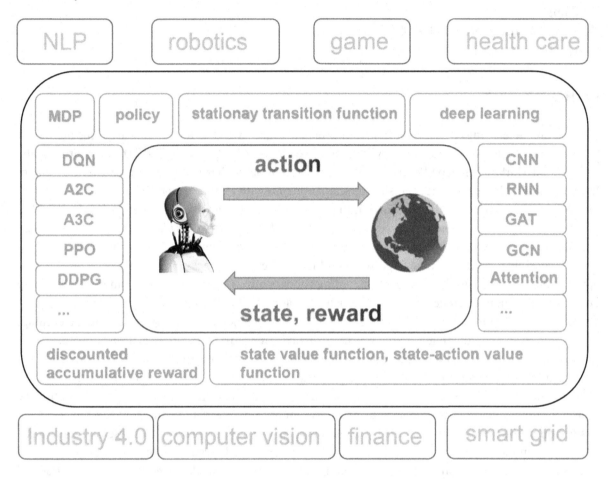

Value-based and policy-based methods are the two main categories of the model-free DRL methods. DQN (Osband, 2016), as the value-based method, is suitable for discrete-action space problems. Actor-critic (Konda, 2000), as the policy-based method, is suitable for both discrete-action and continuous-action space problems. Policy-based methods directly model the agent's policy as a parametric function. Value-based methods first compute the value-action function, then the agent's policy corresponds to picking an action that maximizes the Q value. For complex CO problems, the action space involves discrete actions and continuous actions. For instance, in the energy aware VRP, the remaining task points are discrete actions, while the charged energy is continuous actions. Thus, this chapter focuses on policy-based actor-critic DRL methods.

For developing proper neural networks, researchers adopt different state-of-art neural network architectures like convolutional neural network (CNN), recurrent neural network (RNN), graphical convolutional neural network (GCN) and others. However, different architectures have different characteristics. For instance, RNN is able to extract sequential features from the inputting sequence, while CNN is famous for tackling pictures data. GCN can keep the translation invariance and extract nodes/edges features from graphical networks. This chapter focuses on using deep reinforcement learning (DRL) to solve combinatorial optimization (CO) problems. This chapter aims to illustrate the related concepts in DRL and CO problems, demonstrate recent works, and present the process of solving CO problems with DRL.

Figure 2. Policy improvement and policy estimation steps in deep reinforcement learning. The cooperation among these two steps constitutes the training process of deep reinforcement learning. The green line denotes the policy estimation step, which evaluates the policy at each time step. The red line denotes the policy improvement step, which greedily selects the policy with the highest state value calculated by the state value function. π* denotes the optimal policy while v* refers to the real expectation of the return with the optimal policy.

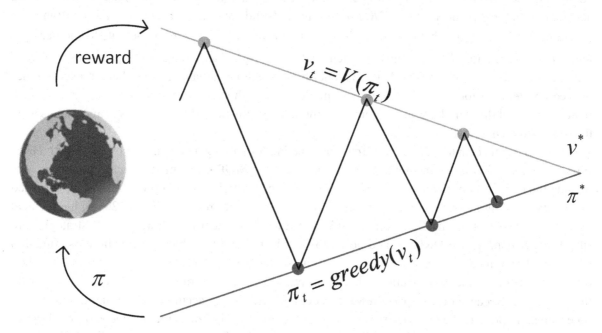

The combinatorial optimization problem aims to find an optimal value of the cost function f: V®R and the corresponding optimal elements in the finite set of elements V (Mazyavkina, 2021). With the power of deep reinforcement learning, CO problems have recently attracted rising attention in social networks, industrial manufacture, transportation, telecommunications and scheduling. Typical CO problems include the traveling salesman (TSP), the vehicle routing problem (VRP) and the bin packing problem (BPP). This chapter will discuss these three CO problems to demonstrate the pipeline of solving a CO problem with DRL, present its advantages over traditional works, and show recent works in this field.

As NP-hard problems, traditional solvers to CO problems include exact algorithms and heuristic algorithms. Based on enumeration and brand-and-bound algorithms, exact algorithms are expensive in computational time and intractable for large-scale problems. On the other hand, heuristic algorithms require domain knowledge and delicately hand-crafted heuristics, which are hard to obtain in many real cases. DRL provides a new avenue to solve complex CO problems with extremely short computational time and guaranteed near-optimal solutions. Besides, once DRL parameters are trained, a new problem case can be solved within an extremely short time. Unlike supervised learning methods, labels are not required in DRL, which is very important since labels are hard to obtain in CO problems.

The agent in RL refers to something interacting with the environment repeatedly through executing actions, making observations and receiving rewards. In most CO problems, the agent is our solver. The environment in RL includes all things except the agent. In CO problems, the environment is our given problem, providing the solver with the solution space, decision variables and cost functions. In order to apply RL to CO, researchers firstly model our problem into Markov Decision Process (MDP), which consists of a tuple $M=(S,A,R,T)$. S denotes state space while $s_t \hat{I} S$ represents the agents' observations received from the environment. For robot control problems, states include the robot's various positions, angles, velocities of mechanical parts. Tile coding is the suggested state representation method (Sutton, 2018). Besides, different state representations are taken in different CO problems. A denotes action space while $a_t \hat{I} A$ is the things that the agent can do in the environment. For CO problems, actions represent an addition to the partial or changing complete solution. R reward function is a mapping from states and actions into the real number $R: S \times A \circledR R$. For CO, rewards indicate the cost function. T is the transition function $T = (s_{t+1} \mid s_t, a_t)$ that represents the probability of transmitting from one state to another state with a particular action. T is problem dependent and model embedded. In many CO problems, like TSP, T is deterministic. DRL can be divided into model-based methods (Huang, 2019) where transition function can be learned for decision making and model-free methods (Henderson, 2018) where the best policy is learned through the trials and errors without the sophisticated model. This chapter focuses on the model-free DRL methods.

The goal of this chapter is to demonstrate the pipeline for solving a general CO problem with DRL. Firstly, the given CO problem should be reformulated as an MDP problem. The main challenges here include the definition of the states, actions, rewards. The constraints in CO problems can be modeled as penalties adding to rewards. For sparse reward issues, curiosity rewards (Burda, 2018), hierarchical deep reinforcement learning (Al-Emran, 2015) and reward engineering (Dewey, 2014) strategies are suggested. Secondly, one DRL method needs to be selected and the objective function/loss function should be determined. For example, researchers can select the A2C method to solve the TSP and add the regularization to the loss function. The actor network's objective function of A2C is to maximize the likelihood. Because of the sparse reward issue, researchers can accumulate the likelihood at each time step and optimize the parameters at the end of the episode. Thirdly, suitable encoder and decoder networks need to be selected, such as RNN (Wang, 2016), CNN (Bharati, 2020), GCN (Wu, 2020), GAT (Guo, 2020). The encoder encodes the information of the states and output features vectors. The decoder encodes the generated feature vectors and numerical output, such as probabilities distributions, state value and Q value. Fourthly, beam search (Zhao, 2020), and local search methods (Joshi, 2019) can be applied for better performances. After the agent has selected an action, the environment moves to a new state, and the agent receives a reward for the action it has made. The process then repeats from a new state within the allocated time budget. Once the model parameters have been trained, the agent is capable of searching the solutions for unseen instances of the problem. The organization of this chapter is listed as follows. The related works about DRL and its applications in related CO problems will be presented firstly, followed by the mathematical foundation of DRL and CO problem. Then DRL algorithms and the experimental results for TSP problems will be discussed in detail.

RELATED WORK

In recent years, the success of DRL has attracted increasing attention and motivates the proposal of versatile DRL algorithms. Silver et al. (Silver, 2014) proposes the deterministic policy gradient algorithm and prove its advantages in high-dimensional action space over the stochastic policy gradient algorithms. To tackle the headache of the convergence property of DRL, Kakade et al. (Kakade, 2001) introduces the natural policy gradient and restrict the updating steps of neural networks' parameters. Furthermore, to guarantee the effectiveness of each parameter's updating step, the trust region policy optimization (TRPO) algorithm and its simplification version of the proximal policy gradient (PPO) algorithm are proposed by (Schulman, 2015) and (Schulman, 2017). To adopt the advanced Kronecker-factored approximation function for computing parameters' gradients, Wu et al. (Wu, 2017) propose the Kronecker-Factored Trust Region (ACKTR) algorithm. For solving the data inefficiency issue, Mnih et al. (Mnih, 2016) adopt parallel policy models with shared parameters. Haarnoja et al. (Haarnoja, 2018) propose a soft actor-critic (SAC) algorithm to emphasize the significance of maximizing the entropy in the objective function. Wang et al. (Wang, 2021) propose a compatible critic network to boost the cooperation among the actor and the critic networks. Barth-Maron et al. (Barth-Maron, 2018) introduce confidence coefficient into Q value to provide more information for the policy improvement process.

The traveling salesman problem is a typical CO problem that has wide applications. In recent years, researchers have proven the success of solving complex TSP problems with deep reinforcement learning. Bello et al. (Bello, 2016) first introduce the Pointer network into DRL for solving the TSP problem, which is a combination of RNN and Attention architecture. The A2C algorithm is taken for the training process. Nazari et al. (Nazari, 2018) replace RNN with CNN and prove noise introduced by RNN can decrease the performance. Khalil et al. (Khalil, 2017) first combine the graph neural network into DRL, which can extract edge information for further heuristic methods. Chaitanya et al. (Chaitanya, 2019) introduce GCN into DRL and boost the performance. Kool et al (Kool, 2018) propose to adopt multi-head self-attention architecture to extract features from data and improve accuracy.

Coverage path planning (CPP) can be viewed as a variant of TSP (Kyaw, 2020). Lakshmanan et al. (Lakshmanan, 2020) prove the performance through the comparison among zigzag, spiral, greedy search schemes and other heuristic methods, like ant colony optimization and particle swarm optimization. Theile et al. (Theile, 2020) utilize the double deep Q-network to balance the limited power budget and coverage goal. Xiao et al. (Xiao, 2020) input the γ point map representing the continuous coverage process into DRL to generate a no-hole coverage policy.

Compared with the TSP problem, vehicle routing (Wang, 2018) problem raises new challenges with complex constraints. Different variants of vehicle routing problems have been studied for decades while it is still challenging to generate fast solutions to large-size problems with high performance. In the simplest sub-problem, a vehicle starts and ends at the depot while satisfying certain constraints. James et al. (James, 2019) point that complex VRP is becoming more computationally complex than before, which raises a challenge for existing mathematical programming-based algorithms. DRL is a potential method providing near-optimal solutions with minimal computation time. Guo et al. (Guo, 2020) compare DRL with other methods, which are based on ad-hoc decision rules and optimization tools, in VRP. They find that rules-based methods require intensive manual tuning while tools-based methods need an accurate system model, both of which add uncertainties to the solution quality.

The combination of deep reinforcement learning algorithms and heuristic methods is a hot topic. The fact is that although using neural networks to generate a complete solution from scratch will avoid the pain of searching and tuning heuristic methods, the difficulties of prediction increase as the number of variables grows. The combination of heuristics will shrink the solution space vastly and thus increase the convergence speeds. Moreover, it is proved that researchers can improve the performance of DRL further with an extra local search part. Qin et al. (Qin, 2021) propose a deep reinforcement learning-based hyper-heuristic method to solve the VRP of a heterogeneous fixed fleet vehicle. Deep reinforcement learning serves as a strategies selector to combine different heuristic methods, like the time-delay neural network (Tyasnurita, 2017) and NeuRewriter (Chen, 2019). Wu et al. (Wu, 2021) extend NeuRewriter to capacitated vehicle routing problems. Zhao et al. (Zhao, 2021) propose an adaptive critic network that adapts its structure to speed up the convergence process. Lin et al. (Lin, 2021) introduces a graph structure into the pointer network to solve vehicle routing problems with a time window. Zhang et al. (Zhang, 2020) propose a multi-agent attention model to solve multi-vehicle routing problems with soft time windows (MVRPSTW). For the energy-aware vehicle routing problem, Qian et al. (Qian, 2019) point out that a vast number of uncertainties are behind VRP, such as the fluctuation of charging prices and waiting time at charging stations, while DRL can approach the optimal solution without any prior knowledge of these uncertainties. Zhang et al. (Zhang, 2018) employ a DRL algorithm to solve the VRP with a mobile charging station. However, the charging point is predetermined. Agents' velocity and mobile charging stations' velocity are assumed to be the same. Besides, the mobile charging station must stay at the predetermined charging point before the agent's arrival. The agent can only be charged once.

Unlike VRP, the bin packing problem is another typical CO problem practically applied in the logistic industries. The first attempt to solve the 3D bin packing problem with DRL is studied by Hu et al. (Hu, 2017). Zhao et al. (Zhao, 2020) assume that the information of items is limited. When one item arrives, it should be packed at once without buffering, like (Verma, 2020). Jiang et al. (Jiang, 2021) study the influence of sequence, orientation, and position with a multi-model DRL. Kundu et al. (Kundu, 2019) study 2D online bin packing problems through inputting images into DRL. Zhang et al. (Zhang, 2021) proved a DRL baseline with a self-attention trick and prioritized oversampling trick. Laterre et al. (Laterre, 2018) prove the performance of the proposed ranked reward DRL through the comparison among generic Monte Carlo tree search, heuristic, and integer programming methods.

MATHEMATICAL FOUNDATION OF DEEP REINFORCEMENT LEARNING

In DRL, return value, the discounted accumulative reward, is denoted as Eq. (1).

$$R_t^\gamma = \sum\nolimits_{i=t}^{\infty} \gamma^{i-t} r\left(s_i, a_i\right), 0 < \gamma < 1, \tag{1}$$

where γ is the discounted coefficient. Value function $V\pi^{(S)}$ is the expectation of the return starting from the state s *a*nd the policy π as Eq. (2).

$$V^\pi\left(s\right) = \mathbb{E}\left[\sum\nolimits_{t=0}^{\infty} \gamma^t r\left(s_t\right) \mid \pi, s_0 = s\right], \tag{2}$$

State-action value function $Q^\pi(s,a)$ is the expectation of the return starting with the state s and action a and the policy π as Eq. (3).

$$Q^\pi\left(s,a\right) = \mathbb{E}\left[\sum\nolimits_{t=0}^{\infty} \gamma^t r\left(s_t, a_t\right) \mid \pi, s_0 = s, a_0 = a\right], \tag{3}$$

Moreover, $V^\pi(S)$ and $Q\pi^{(s}, a)$ can be transited into each other with the following transition function as Eq. (4).

$$V\pi^{(s)} = \max a Q_\pi(^s,a), \tag{4}$$

R

Here, this chapter takes DQN and A2C as examples to illustrate the training process. DQN is a popular value-based method. As demonstrated in Eq (5), the agent iteratively updates the state-action value function based on samples from the environment using the update rule.

$$Q\left(s_t, a_t\right) \leftarrow Q\left(s_t, a_t\right) + \alpha\left[r_t + \gamma \max_{a'} Q\left(s_{t+1}, a'\right) - Q\left(s_t, a_t\right)\right], \tag{5}$$

where α is the step size. To parameterize the Q value with θ, the loss function can be written as Eq. (6).

$$L\left(\theta_i\right) = \mathbb{E}_{\left(s_t, a_t, r_t, s_{t+1}\right) \sim D}\left[\left(r_t + \gamma \max_{a'} Q_{\theta_i}\left(s_{t+1}, a'\right) - Q_{\theta_i}\left(s_t, a_t\right)\right)^2\right], \tag{6}$$

D denotes the experience replay buffer storing the trajectory $\left(s_t, a_t, r_t, s_{t+1}\right)$.

A2C is a popular policy-based method, which directly discover the optimal policy parameterized by θ as π_θ^*. Without experience replay buffer, the training data is collected with current policy. The objective function is denoted as Eq. (7).

$$\nabla_\theta J\left(\pi_\theta\right) = \mathbb{E}_{\pi_\theta}\left[\sum_{t=0}^H \nabla_\theta \log \pi_\theta(a_t \mid s_t) A\left(s_t, a_t\right)\right], \tag{7}$$

where H is the length of the time steps. The advantage is represented as Eq. (8). $V(s_t)$ serves as the baseline to stabilize the training process by reducing the bias.

$$A\left(s_t, a_t\right) = Q\left(s_t, a_t\right) - V\left(s_t\right) = \mathbb{E}\left[r_{t+1} + \gamma V\left(s_{t+1}\right) - V\left(s_t\right)\right], \tag{8}$$

PROBLEM DEFINITION OF TYPICAL COMBINATROTIAL OPTIMIZATION PROBLEM

For the traveling salesman problem, given a sequence of task points in a 2-dimensional space, the goal is to find a tour with the minimum Euclidean distance. An intelligent agent should start from a starting point, visit all task points once, and return to the starting point. TSP is a typical NP-hard problem. It is computationally intractable for the TSP with a large number of visiting points. As a CO problem, an optimal visiting sequence is required to be solved.

This chapter considers the vehicle routing problem with single-agent and multiple constraints for the vehicle routing problem. The object is to minimize the total traveling distance or the combination of traveling distance, traveling time or energy consumption. Starting from the starting point and returning to the endpoint, an intelligent agent should visit a series of task points and gas/charging stations if required. For the capacity constraints, the agent needs to pick up goods at each task point. However, the agent has a limited loading capacity. For time windows constraints, the agent should visit each task point within a specific time slot. For energy constraints, the agent should choose gas/charging stations to visit to increase its working time. VRP has been proved to be the NP-hard problem, which requires a sequential solution while satisfying versatile constraints.

For the bin packing problem, with a collection of items of different sizes, the goal is to assign these terms into a minimized number of bins. Each bin has a limited capacity. The 3D-bin packing problem increases the complexity by restricting three-dimensional constraints, including maximal length, width, and height. In addition, some bin packing problems in the logistic industries require not only the optimal items-selecting sequence but also the optimal geometric directions and locations. Bin packing problem is another NP-hard problem, the decision variables of which include sequences and other discrete variables.

PROCEDURE OF SOLVING COMBINATORIAL OPTIMIZATION PROBLEM

Given a CO problem, the objective function and constraints functions should be firstly figured out. The next step is to build a Markov Decision Process Model with properly defined states, actions, rewards, and stationary transition functions. In particular, the definition of states is of great importance, which serves as the inputs of neural networks and directly determines the choice of the neural network architectures and the selections of DRL algorithms. Actions are typically defined as decision variables that determines the selection of DRL algorithms. For instance, if a problem involves continuous decision variables, the action space is large enough that DQN cannot tackle the problem. Rewards denote the objective functions. Normally, the rewards are maximized through the training process. The equivalence problem of minimizing objective functions is maximizing the corresponding negative values. Besides, for some kinds of DRL algorithms, the handcraft reward engineering works are required to provide domain knowledge, serve as step-rewards or increase the exploration ability. For instance, (Burda, 2018) introduces curiosity into DRL to explore the less touched solution spaces. Another example is multi-step DDPG which requires step-rewards for the bootstrapping strategy.

To solve the TSP, researchers first represent the given problem as a Markov Decision Processing model. States, actions, rewards and transition function are four essential parts, the definitions of which directly influence the neural network frameworks and loss functions of the following DRL method. Here the author presents one of the possible definitions for these four parts. The state is the currently selected tour of nodes. The action is to choose one of the remaining available nodes. Reward refers to the negative total tour length. The stationary transition function is deterministic here, which returns the next node of the tour deterministically until satisfying the terminal conditions. Given the MDP model, the next step is to select the suitable DRL algorithms, including A2C, A3C, DQN, PPO, DDPG and, others. Table 2 summarizes recently proposed DRL algorithms in solving TSP-related problems. Encoder and Decoder are constituent parts of the neural network architecture, which will be discussed soon. In general, the encoder is for feature extraction from the inputting data, while decoder serves as the feature fusion work. Besides, this chapter illustrates the pseudocode of the A2C method in Algorithm 1.

Table 1. Algorithm 1

Algorithms	Encoder/Decoder	DRL Algorithm
(Bello, 2016)	Pointer Network	A2C
(Khalil, 2017)	S2V	DQN
(Nazari, 2018)	Pointer Network + CNN	A2C
(Chaitanya, 2019)	GCN	A2C
(Kool, 2018)	Pointer Network + Attention Encoder	A2C

R

Based on the selected MDP models and DRL algorithm, the next essential step is to design suitable neural networks for the encoder and the decoder. For specific requirements and functions, researchers design a problem-depend neural network framework. For example, 1-dimension CNN serving as an encoder can extract feature vectors with fewer parameters. LSTM/GRU, serving as decoder, can generate sequential outputs. GCN/GAT, serving as decoder, can aggregate the features among neighbors. This chapter takes the pointer network as an example for further illustration. In the Pointer Network framework, the encoder and decoder are composed of two Long Short-Term Memory modules. The encoder inputs the sequence of the location information of the task points and stores the extracted features into the memory states. The decoder maintains the generated memory states, inputs the last node's location in the current tour, and outputs a distribution over the remaining nodes. To further increase the performance, the attention mechanism is applied.

Table 3 compares the performances of various methods, including exact methods, heuristic method, and learning-based methods. It is clear that the computational time of the exact method increases exponentially as the size of the TSP increases. Thus, the exact method is intractable for complex CO problems with large sizes. The heuristic methods can solve TSP efficiently, but the accuracy is not guaranteed. If the heuristics are not designed well, the performance cannot be acceptable. Moreover, DRL methods can obtain near-optimal solutions within an extremely short time.

Table 2. Summary of recent DRL algorithms in solving TSP related problems

Algorithm 1 Pseudocode of the A2C algorithm	
Input: number of epochs E, steps per epoch T', batch size B	
1:	*Initialize actor parameters θ and critic parameters φ*
2:	**for** epoch i=1 to E **do**
3:	**for** step t=1 to T' **do**
4:	*Run the policy $\pi_i(S_i, p_\theta)$ in a batch of environments (i=1,...,B) until the terminating condition is satisfied*
5:	Run the critic to get the baseline $b_i(S_i, p_\phi)$
6:	Compute the reward R_i and the advantage A_i
7:	$$\nabla\theta \leftarrow \sum_{i=1}^{B} A_i \nabla_\theta \log_{p_\theta}(\pi_i)$$
8:	$$\nabla\phi \leftarrow (R_i - b_i(S_i, p_\phi))^2$$
9:	*Update θ and φ*
10:	**end for**
11:	**end for**

CONCLUSION

With the rapid development of deep reinforcement learning in vast application domains, deep reinforcement learning is an indispensable research field in machine learning and deep learning domains. Besides, combinatorial optimization is a core optimization research field related to artificial intelligence, machine learning, auction theory, and software engineering. Traditional approaches to CO problems have nonnegligible shortcomings, including complicated hand-craft heuristics, unguaranteed performance, and extensive computational time. Because of the vast essential applications of CO problems, there is an urgent need to solve CO problems fast with near-optimal solutions. This chapter illustrates the core concepts related to DRL and CO problems, presents the solving process of CO problems with DRL, and shows the recent works and advantages of DRL in four CO problems. In conclusion, this chapter proves that DRL is a promising approach to the CO problem.

Table 3. Comparison among different methods in TSP

	Algorithm	Distance	Time	Accuracy Gap
TSP20	Exact	3.84	18s	-
	Nearest Insertion	4.33	1s	12.76%
	Random Insertion	4.00	1s	4.17%
	Farthest Insertion	3.93	1s	2.34%
	Nearest Neighbor	4.50	1s	17.19%
	(Bello, 2016)	3.89	0.01s	1.30%
	(Khalil, 2017)	3.89	0.01s	1.30%
	(Nazari, 2018)	3.97	0.01s	3.39%
	(Chaitanya, 2019)	3.86	0.01s	0.52%
	(Kool, 2018)	3.85	0.01s	0.26%
TSP50	Exact	5.70	5m	-
	Nearest Insertion	6.78	2s	18.95%
	Random Insertion	6.13	1s	7.54%
	Farthest Insertion	6.01	2s	5.44%
	Nearest Neighbor	7.00	1s	22.81%
	(Bello, 2016)	5.95	0.01s	4.39%
	(Khalil, 2017)	5.99	0.01s	5.09%
	(Nazari, 2018)	6.08	0.01s	6.67%
	(Chaitanya, 2019)	5.87	0.01s	2.98%
	(Kool, 2018)	5.80	0.01s	1.75%
TSP100	Exact	7.76	20m	-
	Nearest Insertion	9.46	6s	21.91%
	Random Insertion	8.52	3s	9.79%
	Farthest Insertion	8.35	7s	7.60%
	Nearest Neighbor	9.68	1s	24.74%
	(Bello, 2016)	8.30	0.01s	6.96%
	(Khalil, 2017)	8.42	0.01s	8.51%
	(Nazari, 2018)	8.44	0.01s	8.76%
	(Chaitanya, 2019)	8.41	0.01s	8.38%
	(Kool, 2018)	8.12	0.01s	4.64%

REFERENCES

R

Al-Emran, M. (2015). Hierarchical reinforcement learning: a survey. *International Journal of Computing and Digital Systems, 4*(2).

Arulkumaran, K., Deisenroth, M. P., Brundage, M., & Bharath, A. A. (2017). Deep reinforcement learning: A brief survey. *IEEE Signal Processing Magazine, 34*(6), 26–38. doi:10.1109/MSP.2017.2743240

Asgari, M., & Khasteh, S. H. (2022). *Profitable Strategy Design by Using Deep Reinforcement Learning for Trades on Cryptocurrency Markets.* arXiv preprint arXiv:2201.05906.

Barth-Maron, G., Hoffman, M. W., Budden, D., Dabney, W., Horgan, D., Tb, D., . . . Lillicrap, T. (2018). *Distributed distributional deterministic policy gradients.* arXiv preprint arXiv:1804.08617.

Bello, I., Pham, H., Le, Q. V., Norouzi, M., & Bengio, S. (2016). *Neural combinatorial optimization with reinforcement learning.* arXiv preprint arXiv:1611.09940.

Bharati, P., & Pramanik, A. (2020). Deep learning techniques—R-CNN to mask R-CNN: a survey. In *Computational Intelligence in Pattern Recognition.* Springer.

Burda, Y., Edwards, H., Pathak, D., Storkey, A., Darrell, T., & Efros, A. A. (2018). *Large-scale study of curiosity-driven learning.* arXiv preprint arXiv:1808.04355.

Chen, X., & Tian, Y. (2019). Learning to perform local rewriting for combinatorial optimization. *Advances in Neural Information Processing Systems, 32.*

Dewey, D. (2014, March). Reinforcement learning and the reward engineering principle. *2014 AAAI Spring Symposium Series.*

Du, Z., Yang, N., Yu, Z., & Yu, P. (2022). Learning from Atypical Behavior: Temporary Interest Aware Recommendation Based on Reinforcement Learning. *IEEE Transactions on Knowledge and Data Engineering.*

Guo, M., & Bürger, M. (2020, May). Predictive Safety Network for Resource-constrained Multi-agent Systems. In *Conference on Robot Learning.* PMLR.

Guo, S. (2020, July). A Survey on GAT-like Graph Neural Networks. In *2020 International Conference on Communications, Information System and Computer Engineering (CISCE).* IEEE.

Haarnoja, T., Zhou, A., Abbeel, P., & Levine, S. (2018, July). Soft actor-critic: Off-policy maximum entropy deep reinforcement learning with a stochastic actor. In *International conference on machine learning.* PMLR.

Henderson, P., Islam, R., Bachman, P., Pineau, J., Precup, D., & Meger, D. (2018, April). Deep reinforcement learning that matters. *Proceedings of the AAAI Conference on Artificial Intelligence, 32*(1).

Hu, H., Zhang, X., Yan, X., Wang, L., & Xu, Y. (2017). *Solving a new 3d bin packing problem with deep reinforcement learning method.* arXiv preprint arXiv:1708.05930.

Huang, Z., Heng, W., & Zhou, S. (2019). Learning to paint with model-based deep reinforcement learning. *Proceedings of the IEEE/CVF International Conference on Computer Vision.*

James, J. Q., Yu, W., & Gu, J. (2019). Online vehicle routing with neural combinatorial optimization and deep reinforcement learning. *IEEE Transactions on Intelligent Transportation Systems*, *20*(10), 3806–3817.

Jiang, Y., Cao, Z., & Zhang, J. (2021, May). Solving 3D Bin Packing Problem via Multimodal Deep Reinforcement Learning. *Proceedings of the 20th International Conference on Autonomous Agents and MultiAgent Systems*.

Joshi, C. K., Laurent, T., & Bresson, X. (2019). *An efficient graph convolutional network technique for the travelling salesman problem.* arXiv preprint arXiv:1906.01227.

Kakade, S. M. (2001). A natural policy gradient. *Advances in Neural Information Processing Systems*, 14.

Khalil, E., Dai, H., Zhang, Y., Dilkina, B., & Song, L. (2017). Learning combinatorial optimization algorithms over graphs. *Advances in Neural Information Processing Systems*, 30.

Konda, V., & Tsitsiklis, J. (1999). Actor-critic algorithms. *Advances in Neural Information Processing Systems*, 12.

Kool, W., Van Hoof, H., & Welling, M. (2018). *Attention, learn to solve routing problems!* arXiv preprint arXiv:1803.08475.

Kundu, O., Dutta, S., & Kumar, S. (2019, October). Deep-pack: A vision-based 2d online bin packing algorithm with deep reinforcement learning. In *2019 28th IEEE International Conference on Robot and Human Interactive Communication (RO-MAN)*. IEEE.

Kyaw, P. T., Paing, A., Thu, T. T., Mohan, R. E., Le, A. V., & Veerajagadheswar, P. (2020). Coverage path planning for decomposition reconfigurable grid-maps using deep reinforcement learning based travelling salesman problem. *IEEE Access: Practical Innovations, Open Solutions*, *8*, 225945–225956.

Lakshmanan, A. K., Mohan, R. E., Ramalingam, B., Le, A. V., Veerajagadeshwar, P., Tiwari, K., & Ilyas, M. (2020). Complete coverage path planning using reinforcement learning for tetromino based cleaning and maintenance robot. *Automation in Construction*, *112*, 103078.

Laterre, A., Fu, Y., Jabri, M. K., Cohen, A. S., Kas, D., Hajjar, K., ... Beguir, K. (2019). *Ranked reward: enabling self-play reinforcement learning for bin packing.* Academic Press.

Lin, B., Ghaddar, B., & Nathwani, J. (2021). Deep reinforcement learning for the electric vehicle routing problem with time windows. *IEEE Transactions on Intelligent Transportation Systems*.

Mazyavkina, N., Sviridov, S., Ivanov, S., & Burnaev, E. (2021). Reinforcement learning for combinatorial optimization: A survey. *Computers & Operations Research*, *134*, 105400.

Nazari, M., Oroojlooy, A., Snyder, L., & Takác, M. (2018). Reinforcement learning for solving the vehicle routing problem. *Advances in Neural Information Processing Systems*, 31.

Oh, S. H., Lee, S. J., & Park, J. (2022). Precision Medicine for Hypertension Patients with Type 2 Diabetes via Reinforcement Learning. *Journal of Personalized Medicine*, *12*(1), 87. doi:10.3390/jpm12010087 PMID:35055402

Osband, I., Blundell, C., Pritzel, A., & Van Roy, B. (2016). Deep exploration via bootstrapped DQN. *Advances in Neural Information Processing Systems*, 29.

Peng, B., Xie, Y., Seco-Granados, G., Wymeersch, H., & Jorswieck, E. A. (2022). Communication Scheduling by Deep Reinforcement Learning for Remote Traffic State Estimation with Bayesian Inference. *IEEE Transactions on Vehicular Technology*.

Qian, T., Shao, C., Wang, X., & Shahidehpour, M. (2019). Deep reinforcement learning for EV charging navigation by coordinating smart grid and intelligent transportation system. *IEEE Transactions on Smart Grid*, *11*(2), 1714–1723.

Qin, W., Zhuang, Z., Huang, Z., & Huang, H. (2021). A novel reinforcement learning-based hyper-heuristic for heterogeneous vehicle routing problem. *Computers & Industrial Engineering*, *156*, 107252.

Schulman, J., Levine, S., Abbeel, P., Jordan, M., & Moritz, P. (2015, June). Trust region policy optimization. In *International conference on machine learning*. PMLR.

Schulman, J., Wolski, F., Dhariwal, P., Radford, A., & Klimov, O. (2017). *Proximal policy optimization algorithms*. arXiv preprint arXiv:1707.06347.

Silver, D., Lever, G., Heess, N., Degris, T., Wierstra, D., & Riedmiller, M. (2014, January). Deterministic policy gradient algorithms. In *International conference on machine learning*. PMLR.

Sutton, R. S., & Barto, A. G. (2018). *Reinforcement learning: An introduction*. MIT Press.

Theile, M., Bayerlein, H., Nai, R., Gesbert, D., & Caccamo, M. (2020, March). UAV coverage path planning under varying power constraints using deep reinforcement learning. In *2020 IEEE/RSJ International Conference on Intelligent Robots and Systems (IROS)*. IEEE.

Tyasnurita, R., Özcan, E., & John, R. (2017, June). Learning heuristic selection using a time delay neural network for open vehicle routing. In *2017 IEEE Congress on Evolutionary Computation (CEC)*. IEEE.

Verma, R., Singhal, A., Khadilkar, H., Basumatary, A., Nayak, S., Singh, H. V., ... Sinha, R. (2020). *A generalized reinforcement learning algorithm for online 3d bin-packing*. arXiv preprint arXiv:2007.00463.

Wang, D., & Hu, M. (2021). Deep Deterministic Policy Gradient With Compatible Critic Network. *IEEE Transactions on Neural Networks and Learning Systems*.

Wang, D., Hu, M., & Gao, Y. (2018, August). Multi-criteria mission planning for a solar-powered multi-robot system. In *International Design Engineering Technical Conferences and Computers and Information in Engineering Conference*. American Society of Mechanical Engineers.

Wang, F., & Tax, D. M. (2016). *Survey on the attention based RNN model and its applications in computer vision*. arXiv preprint arXiv:1601.06823.

Wu, Y., Mansimov, E., Grosse, R. B., Liao, S., & Ba, J. (2017). Scalable trust-region method for deep reinforcement learning using kronecker-factored approximation. *Advances in Neural Information Processing Systems*, *30*.

Wu, Y., Song, W., Cao, Z., Zhang, J., & Lim, A. (2021). Learning Improvement Heuristics for Solving Routing Problems. *IEEE Transactions on Neural Networks and Learning Systems*.

Wu, Z., Pan, S., Chen, F., Long, G., Zhang, C., & Philip, S. Y. (2020). A comprehensive survey on graph neural networks. *IEEE Transactions on Neural Networks and Learning Systems*, *32*(1), 4–24.

Xiao, J., Wang, G., Zhang, Y., & Cheng, L. (2020). A distributed multi-agent dynamic area coverage algorithm based on reinforcement learning. *IEEE Access: Practical Innovations, Open Solutions*, 8, 33511–33521.

Yuan, X., Wang, Y., Liu, J., & Sun, C. (2022). Action Mapping: A Reinforcement Learning Method for Constrained-Input Systems. *IEEE Transactions on Neural Networks and Learning Systems*, 1–13. doi:10.1109/TNNLS.2021.3138924 PMID:35025751

Zhang, B., Liu, C. H., Tang, J., Xu, Z., Ma, J., & Wang, W. (2017). Learning-based energy-efficient data collection by unmanned vehicles in smart cities. *IEEE Transactions on Industrial Informatics*, *14*(4), 1666–1676.

Zhang, J., Zi, B., & Ge, X. (2021). *Attend2Pack: Bin Packing through Deep Reinforcement Learning with Attention.* arXiv preprint arXiv:2107.04333.

Zhang, K., He, F., Zhang, Z., Lin, X., & Li, M. (2020). Multi-vehicle routing problems with soft time windows: A multi-agent reinforcement learning approach. *Transportation Research Part C, Emerging Technologies*, *121*, 102861.

Zhao, H., She, Q., Zhu, C., Yang, Y., & Xu, K. (2020). *Online 3D bin packing with constrained deep reinforcement learning.* arXiv preprint arXiv:2006.14978.

Zhao, J., Mao, M., Zhao, X., & Zou, J. (2020). A hybrid of deep reinforcement learning and local search for the vehicle routing problems. *IEEE Transactions on Intelligent Transportation Systems*, *22*(11), 7208–7218.

Zhao, J., Mao, M., Zhao, X., & Zou, J. (2020). A hybrid of deep reinforcement learning and local search for the vehicle routing problems. *IEEE Transactions on Intelligent Transportation Systems*, *22*(11), 7208–7218.

ADDITIONAL READING

Barrett, T., Clements, W., Foerster, J., & Lvovsky, A. (2020, April). Exploratory combinatorial optimization with reinforcement learning. *Proceedings of the AAAI Conference on Artificial Intelligence*, *34*(04), 3243–3250. doi:10.1609/aaai.v34i04.5723

Haj-Ali, A., Ahmed, N. K., Willke, T., Gonzalez, J., Asanovic, K., & Stoica, I. (2019). *A view on deep reinforcement learning in system optimization.* arXiv preprint arXiv:1908.01275.

James, J. Q., Yu, W., & Gu, J. (2019). Online vehicle routing with neural combinatorial optimization and deep reinforcement learning. *IEEE Transactions on Intelligent Transportation Systems*, *20*(10), 3806–3817. doi:10.1109/TITS.2019.2909109

Khalil, E., Dai, H., Zhang, Y., Dilkina, B., & Song, L. (2017). Learning combinatorial optimization algorithms over graphs. *Advances in Neural Information Processing Systems*, 30.

Wang, Q., & Tang, C. (2021). Deep reinforcement learning for transportation network combinatorial optimization: A survey. *Knowledge-Based Systems*, *233*, 107526. doi:10.1016/j.knosys.2021.107526

KEY TERMS AND DEFINITIONS

R

Combinatorial Optimization: A subfield of optimization aims to find an optimal object from a finite set of objects where the set of feasible solutions is discrete or can be reduced to a discrete set.

Deep Learning: A kind of machine learning technique teaches computers to do what comes naturally to humans.

Deep Reinforcement Learning: A learning algorithm allows the agent to make decisions by trial and error.

Gradient: The steepness of the slope at that point is given by the magnitude of the gradient vector.

Loss Function: A function maps values of variables into a real number.

Markov Decision Process: A discrete-time stochastic control process models the decision-making process in environments with randomness.

Neural Network: A series of algorithms can extract relationships from data through mimicking the operation way of human brain.

Section 48
Simulation and Modeling

A Simulation Model for Application Development in Enterprise Data Platforms

Nayem Rahman

Portland State University, USA

INTRODUCTION

In spite of continuous refinement over the last four-five decades, the software development industry is still not free from many genuine criticisms in terms of providing the best or perfect possible products & services up to the level of high expectations of the increasingly growing software/application users around the world. On the basis of the experiences of working on or being involved in different important software application development projects as an industry professional, and an academician respectively, the authors have been searching for suitable answers to these criticisms.

In the process, from the similar research, or related studies done by the authors in the recent past, they identified the major critical areas which need to be addressed relentlessly, and more & more thoroughly always. Those are i. Controlling Cost, ii. Maintaining Schedule, iii. Ensuring Quality (Khanam and Rahman, 2019). There are many tits and bits to deal with to address these major issues. The authors attempted to develop a simulation model showing the possible solutions to the root problems in each of these major areas by investigating the resolved and unresolved challenges faced by the software development projects undertaken by the renowned supplier of software application programs in the world. The prepared simulation model for application development in Enterprise Data Platforms (EDPs) aims to analyze all the related & root causes of criticism to ensure an efficient life cycle of software development, optimized cost throughout the process, and improved performance of the launched & marketed applications.

It is important that code defects at each stage of software development need to be scrutinized very strictly. This paper illustrates it by adding two extra phases viz. code inspection and code score carding to the usual phases of software application development life cycle in the Enterprise Data Platforms (EDPs). With the proven experiences gained from other similar studies done by the authors in the past, it can be claimed that defect removal rate is much higher in the process having these two extra phases compared to the usual process not quite caring about code inspection and code score carding in every major stage of software development. It is highly expected that the simulation model presented in this paper would certainly enable the developers to improve their existing practices in giving quality and timely output of application software in EDPs (Dabab et al., 2018).

The authors have revised, enhanced, and updated their related research papers for the purpose of preparing this paper to present the said model. The due effort was given to bring appropriate answers to the following questions in the simulation process:

1. How much improvement may be made in process performance by introducing source code inspections?
2. Does the error detection capability of source code inspection leave any impact on the software development process in EDPs?

DOI: 10.4018/978-1-7998-9220-5.ch171

3. What are the risks of not going beyond the lowest rate of error detection even after adding the phase of code inspections?
4. How to choose only one between source code inspection and unit test?
5. How to justify the benefit of source code inspections if the starting source code shows more errors?
6. How to compare the existing cost of any incorrect unit test done in a software development process in EDPs?

BACKGROUND

From the results of the similar studies done by the authors, the authors got more or less conclusive answers to these questions as apprehended, to justify the inclusion of code inspection in the planned simulation model for application development in EDPs (Dabab et al., 2018). Software development is laborious, expensive, and unreliable. Hence, software development projects quite often encounter schedule slippage, cost overruns, and poor quality software in both commercial and government sectors (Fatin and Rahman, 2020; Raffo and Wernick, 2001). To address this potential issue, thoughts of bringing changes to the software development process got momentum. Smith and Rahman (2017) observe that "without efficient processes through which Information Technology (IT) builds and supports the technology, the full business-value potential will remain unrealized." Bringing the software project lifecycle under the radar of simulation models could be a good effort (Kellner et al., 2001). For the last four decades, systems dynamics modeling and simulation techniques were applied in diverse disciplines of science, engineering, and manufacturing processes (Richardson, 2013; Rashidi, 2016). According to the Merriam-Webster Online Dictionary, "simulation is the imitative representation of the functioning of one system or process by means of the functioning of another." Simulations run in simulation time, an abstraction of real-time (Rahman, 2018b; Imagine That Inc., 2014).

Simulation models are used to solve problems that arise in manufacturing (Barra Montevechi, 2016), business process design (Liu and Iijima, 2015), inventory management system (Cobb, 2017) and health care decision-making (Chick, 2006; Chen and Zhao, 2014). Martinez-Moyano and Richardson (2013) and others (Morrison, 2012; Mould and Bowers, 2013) listed 41 best practices of systems dynamics modeling and categorized them in terms of problem identification and definition, system conceptualization, and model formulation. Hughes and Perera (2009) argue that simulation could be integrated as a daily tool to solve problems. They present an easy-to-follow framework – consisting of five key stages, such as foundation, introduction, infrastructure, deployment and embedding - for enabling companies to embed simulation technologies into their business processes (Hughes and Perera, 2009). The work of Eatock et al. (2001) indicates that describing the dynamic behavior of IT could be very helpful for business process modelers in predicting the impact on organizational processes (Dabab et al., 2018; Eatock et al. 2001). Software process simulation is suggested to be helpful to achieve higher Capability Maturity Model (CMM) levels in software development (Rahman, 2018b; Raffo et al., 1999).

In software engineering, simulation modeling has attracted considerable interest during the last decade (Rahman, 2018b; Ahmed et al. 2008). Software process simulation is used mainly to address the challenges of strategic management of software development and to support process improvements (Raffo and Kellner, 2000). In this work, we are making an attempt to leverage simulation modeling in a data warehouse application development (Rahman, 2018a). We developed a simulation model based on defined processes for the application development of a data warehouse reporting environment called Next Generation Capital Reporting (NGCR). In our recent project, we developed and implemented a

Financial Reporting System (FRS) in the Enterprise Data Platform (EDP) environment. A data platform is used as a central repository of data of medium and large business organizations. A data platform is considered one of the key infrastructures of IT. And the capability of IT has a strong correlation between the agility and performance of an organization (Rahman et al., 2021; Rahman, 2016a).

Industry and academic research suggest that when an EDP becomes successful at an initial stage more and more application development and reporting projects start to land each year. Research suggests that there is a correlation between the increase of the size of the data warehouse and the increase of the value it brings to an organization (Rahman, 2016b). Engineering projects are complex (Rahman et al., 2016). From the standpoint of EDP projects complexity arise from multiple factors including different stakeholders' buy-in, software development effort, frequent changes of relevant tools and technologies, query performance issue, data validation, data quality, and production release timeliness. Therefore, it is quite challenging to maintain a stable data warehouse environment given it is an enterprise platform as well as a shared environment (Rahman, 2018a). Hence, some degree of discipline is needed in code development, code changes, testing, code performance optimization, system resource usage, and configuration of integration specification (Rahman, 2016b). An EDP-specific simulation model can help bring discipline in data platform applications development and improve the overall quality of application development and reporting environment.

The new EDP application development and reporting project undertaken by the authors was as big as the previous project (FRS). An attempt was made to simulate the software development process for the new project based on available data from a recently completed project. Using this data, different if-then scenarios were developed, and a process of software development was simulated for the new project to better manage, control, and measure its success of it. Through this model, requirement analysis, design process, construction & unit testing, code score-carding, integration, function testing, system testing, and deployment into the production environment, etc., were simulated. The goal was to reduce defects in each stage of the application development.

The recent project (FRS) life cycle had issues in the development and testing phases which impacted system availability and performance in the production system and took a while to stabilize. There were job failures in production after go-live. In the past project, it was noticed that requirements, designing decisions, and coding have changed repeatedly in each wave of development. This made the life-cycle unpredictable and often resulted in extensive overtime to meet the project deadlines. In a past project, prior to the unit test code inspections were not done. In this earlier project, codes were tested and moved to production without meeting performance measurement criteria and based on whatever code developers had written. Code rework had to be done after production release as part of stabilization. The cost of fixing defective code in production is 100 to 200 times more than fixing them in the early stage of software development (Fatin and Rahman, 2020; Boehm and Turner, 2003; Khramov, 2006).

In implementing technically challenging projects it is important to make sure technological product breakthroughs are achieved and emerging tools and technologies are adopted (Rahman et al., 2021; Rahman et al., 2016). This helps in delivering a project successfully and on time. The new project envisioned a new way of thinking to develop a state-of-the-art reporting system. At the very beginning finding, answers to various questions were practiced. How to track the actual effort to understand the inefficiencies? Is it possible to drive down the rework by doing a better job upfront during explore and requirements analysis phase? How to reduce the construction work by doing code inspection? How easy it would be to drive down the testing effort, reduce failure rates while in the testing phase by properly managing design and construction and also give adequate time to the tasks? What is the probability of reducing the defect rate, maintaining a good coding standard, and improving the performance of objects by doing code inspection? Is it feasible to drive down the change request for the product in the production environment, where change requests originate due to defects in production?

So, in their current project, the authors have added one new phase called "Inspect Code" to the application development life-cycle. In this phase developers' code in terms of database management systems (DBMS) objects (business views, stored procedures, and macros) will be peer-reviewed by all developers in a code review meeting. Once it is verified and confirmed by the developer team chaired by the Developer Lead the subsequent steps of the life cycle will be done. Based on past project experience the authors added one more phase called "Score-card Code" to the application development life cycle. Once coding and unit testing is done, a senior developer from the EDP will score-card the code using some SQL's suggested by the data platform DBMS (database management system) vendor to identify the performance issue. If the score-carding indicates that it would cause performance issues the code would be re-worked in order to make sure that the code does not cause performance issues in terms of virtual spool space usage, longer run time, use of huge CPU and IO on the production data platform server. This phase will be done after coding and unit testing and before the integration process phase. These new steps were added to make sure that the authors do not have to re-work code much once landed on the production server. They modeled both previous project data and current project process improvements via two simulation models – ASIS (previous project's life cycle stages) versus new model (with code inspection and code score-card steps introduced to the development lifecycle).

RESEARCH FOCUS AND METHODOLOGY

Research suggests that data availability and data quality are the most challenging issues in many simulation projects (Khanam and Rahman, 2019; Onggo and Hill, 2014). For this paper data were collected from the authors' previous project implementations. Here is a brief description of the data collection method and sources of data. The authors collected data regarding development and database objects from EDP source control repositories and Online Change Management (OCM) tools. The data consists of Extract-Transform-Load (ETL) code, defects in code, code-rework, and code-score-card. The authors looked at the history of code changes and rework in each of the code units (stored procedures, macros, and business views) under the previous project (FRS) and current project (NGCR system) and collected the statistics in terms of mean (average) values.

Based on the source control repository the authors collected documentation relating to different phases of a past project. The repository was used to identify change requests and reworks in different phases. Gantt charts were used in the past project were utilized to get the data on resources used, amount of work, and rework done in different releases of a past project. The OCM tool was used to track the list of items, implemented objects, failed objects, and error logs of different releases of the past project. The configuration management reports in terms of EDP source control and OCM tools have been used as the data source for each of the project phases. The EDP source control and OCM information against each code module and phases of the project life cycle were translated into effort/time used for each phase of project life. For simulation model purposes they are compiled in a spreadsheet.

Simulation experimentation and analysis provided several opportunities (Smith et al., 2019; Taylor and Robinson, 2009): better integration of optimization, better visualization for experimentation, guidance on scenario selection, various options for exploring solution space, quick model development, easy to understand analysis, real-time experimentation to assess likely effect of making different decisions, recommendations for the number of replications, and wider experimentation support. Lorenzo and

Diaz (2005) suggest a framework for process gap analysis and modeling of enterprise systems. They propose a four-step method which includes current situation analysis; business process improvements and requirements; gap analysis; and to-be processes based on which simulation is developed (Lorenzo and Diaz, 2005). Yang et al. (2015) propose adopting a simulation-based optimization algorithm in achieving performance and efficiency.

Figure 1 provides different stages of the system to be tested in the model presented in this paper. First, the authors get business requirements from the business analysts (BA). They review the requirements with different stakeholders including customers, data analysts, developers, and business intelligence (BI) analysts (Rahman, 2018a). Project BA's are contacted if more information is needed. After requirements are finalized, data analysts (DA) are contracted to design the tables to create underlying tables for reporting environments. Data analysts will also provide design documents. The design documents are reviewed with ETL developers and handed over to the developers. The ETL developers will write code to perform ETL work. Their code will be reviewed by ETL architects. If changes are needed, code rework will be done and a later unit test will be conducted.

Before moving code from the development environment to the testing environment, ETL code will be score-carded using some pre-defined guidelines (Rahman, 2016c). This score-card involves selecting units of complex code and putting them in a SQL score-card tool and then running the code to identify if the program units were written with poor coding including longer runtime and database spool space, heavy utilization of computing resources such as IO and CPU. After identifying these issues, a senior developer will re-work the code. This sometimes requires a significant amount of code change as well as table structure change. After the score-card is completed the unit test of the code will be conducted again. If the unit test does not pass, re-work of the code will be needed. The next step is to perform functional testing of the system. If the objects do not pass the testing, then send for code rework. Once testing cycles go through successfully and user acceptance testing is completed the code will be deployed into production.

Lee et al. (2009) observe that the development of enterprise software systems requires the collaboration of many stakeholders to allow them to perform what-if analyses before making their decisions (Lee et al. 2009). For data warehousing projects, the authors show stakeholders in the behavioral diagram consisting of requirements gathering, analysis, design, development testing, score-carding, unit and functional testing, and then implementing in the production environment (Figure 1). "The utility and benefits of a well-defined requirements engineering process are cited in many articles describing software engineering research and similar industry studies" (Arthur and Nance, 2007). Ryan and Heavey (2006) present a process modeling technique and Simulation Activity Diagrams (SADs) which could be used to support the initial requirements gathering phases of a simulation project.

Figure 2 depicts the model process flow diagram used to build the simulation model. The purpose of building the simulation model is to (1) determine actual effort; (2) see how to reduce the re-work; (3) see how to reduce construction work by code inspection; (4) identify how to reduce testing effort and failure rates; (5) identify how to reduce defect rate; and (6) drive down job failure rate by code inspection.

Figure 1. Behavioral Diagram of ETL Development

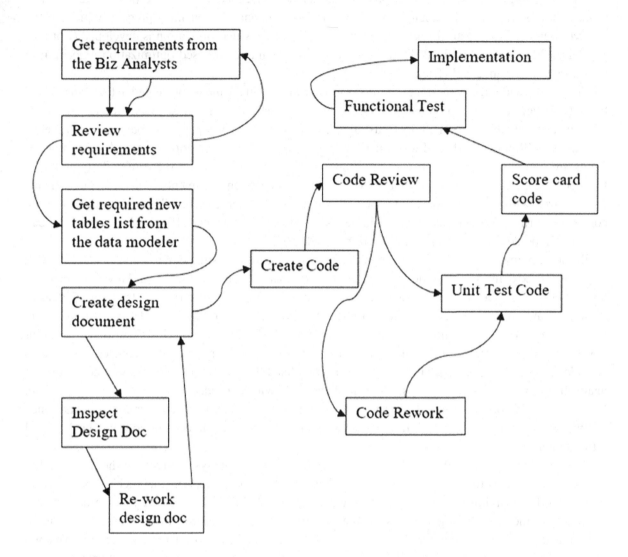

THE SIMULATION PROCESS MODEL: ANALYSES AND FINDINGS

The simulation model was built based on a certain timeframe, spatial boundaries, entities, attributes, and key assumptions. "A model is an abstracted and simplified representation of a system at one point in time" (Imagine That Inc., 2014). In this work, the simulation model was divided along with the major lifecycle phases. As a result, there is a separate model for requirement process, design process, code and unit test process, integration process, function testing process, and system testing process. These steps are incorporated into simulation and tested under different scenarios. Possible what-if analysis fills this gap by enabling users to "simulate and inspect the behavior of a complex system under some given hypotheses" (Golfarelli and Rizzi, 2009).

Figure 2. Process Flow Diagram

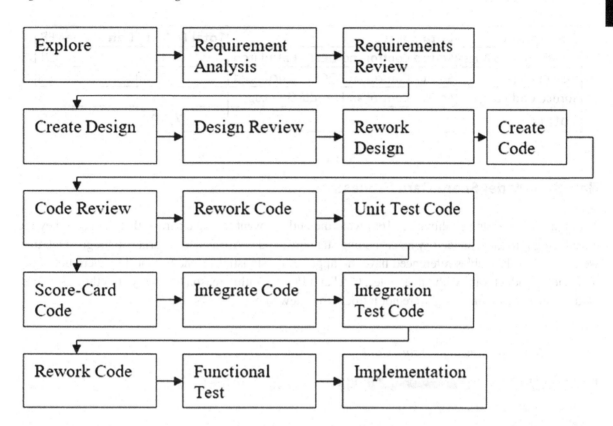

For this project, the authors used the ExtendSim® simulation software (Imagine That Inc., 2014) to build the model. In ExtendSim® blocks are used to model activities, resources, and the routing of jobs throughout the process. Additional blocks are used to collect data, calculate statistics, and display output graphically with frequency charts, histograms, and line plots (Imagine That Inc., 2014). The model predicts the number of person-months of efforts, calendar months of schedule, and remaining defects shipped to the customer for about 1500 function point systems. These 1500 function points flow through the model as a set of about 20 entities. Here the authors are using the same number of FP as used by Jones' baseline model (Jones, 2008). In his seminal book titled, Applied Software Measurement: Global Analysis of Productivity and Quality' Jones (2008) states that "a function point is an abstract but workable surrogate for the goods that are produced by software projects. Function points are the weighted sums of five different factors that are of interest to users (inputs, outputs, logical files, inquiries, and interfaces)."

The organizations where the authors are attached, do not have any pre-defined function point (FP) system for software projects. So, they decided to use an FP of about 1500. They are virtually calculating a total defect of 7500 to flow through the model. The defect per function point comes from requirements bugs, design bugs, and source code bugs (Table 1). And defect per FP is calculated based on recent project data pulled from the EDW source code control, Visual Source Safe (VSS), OCM tool, and log files.

Table 1. Defects per origin, per Function Point

Description	Data Source	Total Defects	Defects per FP
Requirements Bugs	Source Control and OCM - Calculated	1125	0.75
Design Bugs	Source Control and OCM - Calculated	2700	1.8
Soruce Code Bugs	Source Control and Production Logs	3675	2.45
Total		7,500	5

New Sub-Model Score Card Process

Through score-carding (Rahman, 2016a) what the authors want to make sure is that the code they are introducing into the data factory meets coding standards and performance criteria. At a high level, they were ensuring that tables referenced have the appropriate statistics on them, that they were not doing inefficient product joins with large tables, CPU and I/O are within reason for the system they are score-carding against, and that they were not introducing skewed processes on the system.

Figure 3. New Component for Score Card

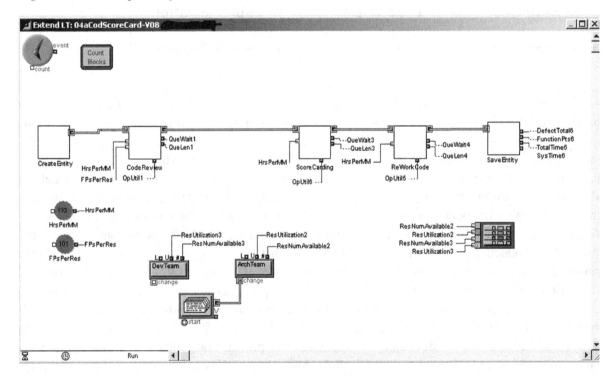

Figure 3 has the following underlying equations and calculations:

1.   **Creates Entity:** has inFile; Decision5: if(EntityNum >= 1) Path = Path1; else Path = Path2;

2.   **CodeProcess:** Eqn to Calculate different values; defect rate=0.0
3.   **ScoreCarding:** Eqn to Calculate different values; defect removal
rate= triangular
4.   **ReworkCode:** Eqn to Calculate different values;
5.   **SaveEntity:** Has two out files
File-1:
EntityNum=Generated19
TotalTime=64105
FunctionPts= Generated -1565
DefectTotal=6265
DefectRem=563
File-2:
TotOpr=37231
EntityNum=Generated19

Table 2 shows the triangular operation values per function point.

Table 2. Score Carding, Code Re-Work Process

Activity	Data Source	Average Effort per FP/SM	Distribution/Comments
Import	Overall Model	0	None
Code Process		0.009 (Min = 0.0072; Max = 0.0108)	Triangle Operation - +/- 20%
Score Card Code		0.009 (Min = 0.0144; Max = 0.0216)	Triangle Operation - +/- 20%
Re-Work Code		0.002 (0.0016/0/0024) & 0.019 (0.0152/0.0228)	Operation - Number of Defects X Re/Def; Triangle Operation - +/- 20%
Export	Overall Model	0	None

Triangular provides a good first approximation of the true values consisting of three pieces of information (the minimum, the maximum, and the most likely values) which are known. (Imagine That Inc. 2014). A triangular distribution is flexible and it prevents extremes compared to uniform and normal distributions (Doane, 2004). The authors came up with parameter values based on previous data as well as the current project's preliminary data. Parametric uncertainties in system dynamics models can cause undesirable behavior (Ng et al. 2012). They used Average Effort per FP/ SM and defects removal percent. And they used Triangular distribution with different values to handle uncertainty. The simulation software ExtendSim uses three parameters to sample from the triangular distribution.

Interpretation of the Results

Code inspection gives tremendous improvement. Table 3 shows that defect has reduced from 43% (AS-IS) to 86% (full model). Score-carding process has reduced defect rates and spool space, CPU/IO.

Table 4 shows that after introducing code inspection and score-carding the defect export to the next phases of the life-cycle has reduced significantly - AS-IS vs. Full model. The score-carding process had made it possible to send fewer defects in terms of spool space issues, CPU consumption, and IO generations.

Table 3. Defect Removal Summary

Activity	Total Defects; Defect Remaining	New Model	AS-IS Model
Requirements	Defect Total = 1179; Defect Remaining = 353	70% Removed	70% Removed
Design	Defect Total = 3995; Defect Remaining = 1433	64% Removed	60% Removed
Code Unite Test	Defect Total = 6265; Defect Remaining = 879	86% Removed	43% Removed
Code Score Card	Defect Total = 6265; Defect Remaining = 563	91% Removed	Not used
Integration	Defect Total = 6265; Defect Remaining = 396	93% Removed	50% Removed
Functional Test	Defect Total = 6265; Defect Remaining = 274	95% Removed	65% Removed
System Test	Defect Total = 6265; Defect Remaining = 144	97% Removed	82% Removed

Table 4. Decreased defect export to the next phase

Activity	Total Defects; Defect Remaining	New Model	AS-IS Model
Requirements	Defect Total = 1179; Defect Remaining = 353	30% defect sent	30% defect sent
Design	Defect Total = 3995; Defect Remaining = 1433	36% defect sent	40% defect sent
Code Unite Test	Defect Total = 6265; Defect Remaining = 879	14% defect sent	57% defect sent
Code Score Card	Defect Total = 6265; Defect Remaining = 563	9% defect sent	Not used
Integration	Defect Total = 6265; Defect Remaining = 396	7% defect sent	50% defect sent
Functional Test	Defect Total = 6265; Defect Remaining = 274	5% defect sent	35% defect sent
System Test	Defect Total = 6265; Defect Remaining = 144	3% defect sent	18% defect sent to Prod

Questions Investigated and Results Obtained

The authors pondered several questions in the simulation process:

1. Do source code inspections offer an improvement in process performance?
2. What would be the impact of reducing the error detection capability of source code inspection?
3. Would source code inspections still be worthwhile if the lowest reported error detection capability in the literature was achieved?
4. If there was only time to conduct either a source code inspection or a unit test, which method would be more effective?
5. Would source code inspections still be beneficial if the starting source code had more errors?
6. What is the cost currently being paid for conducting unit the test incorrectly?

They reached the following conclusions:

1. Source code inspections significantly increase the quality of the resulting code.
2. The source code inspection process is an efficient error detection method if implemented correctly.
3. The process with source code inspections and unit tests offers an overall improvement even if the inspection performance is poor.
4. If pressed for time, it is better to reduce unit testing rather than reduce inspections.
5. Inspections have a greater impact when the starting quality of the code is poor.

A

6.   The process change offered significant reductions in remaining defects.
     a.   Code inspection causes significant increases in error detection and does re-work
     b.   Score-carding makes sure code would perform efficiently in production
     c.   Doing code review would be a more effective process improvement than the creating unit test plans process change

The authors decided not to relate the model with Return on Investment (ROI) and Net Present Value (NPV) due to the lack of specific data related to the ETL development part of the project. They spoke with the business analysts to see if they could determine the ROI specifically for the ETL part. They said the ETL portion is not useful without the Front-End portion of the program/ system. The whole project has a total ROI of several million dollars. Therefore, there was no need to value the simulation model's value in terms of ROI or NPV.

SIMULATION PROCESS RECOMMENDED

"Discrete event simulation is a powerful tool that can address many problems that arise in manufacturing, business process design, health care decision-making, and a host of other areas" (Chick, 2006). This project was designed to simulate the ETL development process for the new project. In this model, the authors simulated requirement analysis, design process, construction and unit testing, code score-carding, integration, function testing, and system testing before the deployment of application development into the production environment.

To see the difference between past and present project performance they made two versions of existing of the model. One contains only those life cycle phases that they had in the previous projects (FRS). In this simulation model, the authors have not used the 'code inspection' phase. This model is called AS-IS by the authors. The other model, meant for a new project, contains all phases of the simulation model provided by Jones (2008). In addition, they added one more sub-model/phase called "Score-card Code". This was introduced between sub-models Code-Unit-Test and Integration.

Figure 4. Overall Simulation Process Model

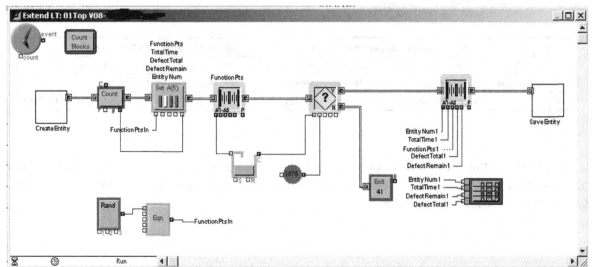

Figure 4 has the following underlying equations and calculations:

```
1.        Creates Entity
2.        Random Input Number generates function points - triangular: min-25,
max-150, mostlikely-75
3.        Constant value (limit function point): 1575
4.        Decision block:
if (TotalFpts < LimitFpts)
   Path = YesPath;
else
   Path = NoPath;
5.        SaveEntity: Has outfile
EntityNum=Generated19
TotalTime
FunctionPts= Generated -1565
DefectTotal=0
DefectRem=0
```

Based on the new model and simulation the authors are able to improve the ETL development, testing, and production deployment significantly. We added one new phase, "Inspect Code", to the life-cycle. In this phase developers' code (business views, stored procedures, and macros) are reviewed by all developers in a code review meeting. Based on past project experience the authors added another phase named "Score-card Code" to the life cycle. Once coding and unit testing is done, a senior developer from the EDP does score-card the code using some SQL's suggested by the DBMS vendor to identify the performance issue (Rahman, 2016c).

If the score-carding indicates that it might cause a performance issue, the code would be re-worked in order to make sure that the code does not cause a lot of spool space, longer run time, use of lot CPU/ IO on the production server. These new steps are added to make sure that the concerned people do not have to re-work code much once deployed into production.

Table 5. New Model Defects Reduction

Activity	Total Defects; Defect Remaining	New Model	AS-IS Model
Code Unit Test	Defect Total = 6265; Defect Remaining = 879	14% defect sent	57% defect sent
Code Score Card	Defect Total = 6265; Defect Remaining = 563	9% defect sent	Not used
System	Defect Total = 6265; Defect Remaining = 144	3% defect sent	18% defect sent to Prod

Table 5 shows that code inspection gives tremendous improvement – system defect has reduced from 82% (AS-IS) to 97% (full model). Score-carding has reduced defect rates, huge spool space generation, CPU consumption and IO generation.

MODEL VERIFICATION AND VALIDATION DONE FOR FUTURE USE OF IT

Verification and validation are the critical aspects of a simulation model (Sargent, 2013). Any model is expected to operate as intended and hence needs to be verified and validated. Model verification is the process of determining that a model operates as intended. Model verification is also meant for the "process of debugging a model to ensure that every portion operates as expected" (Imagine That Inc., 2014). With the help of the verification process, the authors try to find and remove unintentional errors in the logic of the model. Using this process, they determine if they have to build the model right (i.e., if it matches our mental model). Verification compares implemented model to the conceptual model. Model validation is the process of reaching an acceptable level of confidence that the inferences drawn from the model are correct and applicable to the real-world system being represented (Laguna and Markland, 2005).

The authors compared data with simulation results in terms of Average Effort per FP/ SM, add/ remove Defects Percent. They verified that measures are calculated in the same manner throughout the model in both as-is and to-be. They verified that simulation results accurately represented the data that was gathered. The model represents the assumptions (e.g., defects per FP, defect removal rate) that were made regarding how the system operates.

Different phases of the software life cycle correspond to the underlying structure of the model. The authors looked at the data of the system and it confirms that the simulation model works as intended. The results of the simulation made sense to us. Simulation tests reveal that the flow of function points, defect accumulation, and defect removal worked properly through the model. Comparison of simulation results with historical data from the past projects and with some data from new projects validated the results.

In the testing phase the authors did sensitivity analysis which allowed to vary a parameter incrementally, randomly, or in an ad hoc manner to determine how sensitivity model results look when a change is made to one variable. They used sensitivity set-up dialog and conducted a sensitivity analysis on Average Effort per FP/ SM (Triangle Operation), Defects per FP, Defects Percent removal (Triangle Operation), and resource usage to see the total defects and defects remaining, etc.

CONCLUSION

The authors have developed two simulation models, one (AS-IS model) based on software life-cycle phases/ steps of the previous project (FRS), and the other (NGCR Model) is based on the current project (NGCR). The AS-IS model contains no Code Inspection and Score-carding steps as we did the previous project without these steps. The NGCR model contains Code Inspection and Score-card phase/ step as we introduced these processes in a new project.

After doing several runs of both AS-IS and new models we found that Code inspection gives a tremendous improvement in driving down defects at the initial phase of PLC rather compared to the as-is model in which defects were exported to the last phases and even in production. The results show that the new model is able to remove 86% of defects compared to 43% in the as-is model. This indicates that the 'code inspection' process worked well to achieve this defect removal rate.

The results also showed that the new model was able to remove 91% of defects at Score-card and rework phase. The results also showed that under the new model, 97% of defects are removed before it went to Production compared to 82% under the as-is model. The overall simulation result showed a pretty impressive overall defect removal rate at early stages compared to the as-is model.

The newly introduced Score-carding phase in the NGCR model also worked well to reduce defect rates and generate less spool space, CPU/IO. This phase has helped reduce by 5% defects after code unit testing and re-work phase and before the integration phase. The source-code inspections and score-carding have significantly increased the quality of the resulting code. It has proved to be an efficient error detection method if implemented correctly.

Even with poor inspection methodologies, the process with source code inspections and the unit tests still seemed to offer an overall improvement. Inspections made an even greater impact when the starting quality of the code is poor. Installing defective code in production causes job failure issues which in turn causes failure to meet service level agreement (SLA). The authors found it challenging to overcome this issue. The new steps under the NGCR simulation model show that they performed well in production with regard to meeting the SLA.

The presented/prepared simulation model is expected to bring visible changes in an application/ software developing company with notable positive impact in the application development process in EDPs. The model will have an impact on ETL projects, business case analyses, risk assessment for introducing process changes, etc. e.g.: (1) it supports strategic process improvement goals of higher CMM levels (Sen et al. 2006); (2) the upcoming EDP ETL development projects will be benefited from the results of this simulation model; (3) it supports business case analysis of process changes; (4) it provides quantitative risk assessment prior to the introduction of process changes; and (5) it helps to obtain management buy-in for process change and collection of further metrics.

REFERENCES

Ahmed, R., Hall, T., Wernick, P., Robinson, S., & Shah, M. (2008). Software process simulation modelling: A survey of practice. *Journal of Simulation*, *2*(2), 91–102. doi:10.1057/jos.2008.1

Arthur, J. D., & Nance, R. E. (2007). Investigating the use of software requirements engineering techniques in simulation modelling. *Journal of Simulation*, *1*(3), 159–174. doi:10.1057/palgrave.jos.4250021

Barra Montevechi, J., da Silva Costa, R., de Pinho, A., & de Carvalho Miranda, R. (2016, February). A simulation-based approach to perform economic evaluation scenarios. *Journal of Simulation*. Advance online publication. doi:10.1057/jos.2016.2

Boehm, B., & Turner, R. (2003). Observations on balancing discipline and agility. *Proceedings of the IEEE Agile Development Conference (AGILE'03)*, 32-39.

Chen, C., & Zhao, S. X. (2014). Modeling and simulation analyses of healthcare delivery operations for inter-hospital patient transfers. *International Journal of Operations Research and Information Systems*, *5*(1), 76–94. doi:10.4018/ijoris.2014010106

Chick, S. E. (2006). Six ways to improve a simulation analysis. *Journal of Simulation*, *1*(1), 21–28. doi:10.1057/palgrave.jos.4250006

Cobb, B. R. (2017). Optimization models for the continuous review inventory system. *International Journal of Operations Research and Information Systems*, *8*(1), 1–21. doi:10.4018/IJORIS.2017010101

Dabab, M., Freiling, M., Rahman, N., & Sagalowicz, D. (2018). A Decision Model for Data Mining Techniques. *Proceedings of the IEEE Portland International Center for Management of Engineering and Technology (PICMET 2018) Conference*. 10.23919/PICMET.2018.8481953

Doane, D. P. (2004). Using simulation to teach distributions. *Journal of Statistics Education: An International Journal on the Teaching and Learning of Statistics, 12*(1).

Eatock, J., Paul, R. J., & Serranto, A. (2001). A study of the impact of information technology on business processes using discrete event simulation: A reprise. *International Journal of Simulation Systems, Science & Technology, 2*(2), 30–40.

Fatin, T., & Rahman, N. (2020). Measuring Digital Marketing Performance: A Balanced Scorecard Approach. *International Journal of Applied Management Theory and Research, 2*(1), 1–15. doi:10.4018/IJAMTR.2020010101

Golfarelli, M., & Rizzi, S. (2009). What-if simulation modeling in business intelligence. *International Journal of Data Warehousing and Mining, 5*(4), 1–20. doi:10.4018/jdwm.2009010101

Hughes, R. W. C., & Perera, T. (2009). Embedding simulation technologies into business processes: Challenges and solutions. *International Journal of Simulation and Process Modelling, 5*(3), 184–191. doi:10.1504/IJSPM.2009.031093

Imagine That Inc. (2014). *ExtendSim user guide, ExtendSim®*. Available online at: http://www.extendsim.com/

Jones, C. (2008). *Applied software measurement: Global analysis of productivity and quality*. McGraw-Hill Osborne Media.

Kellner, M. I., Madachy, R. J., & Raffo, D. M. (1999). Software process simulation modeling: Why? What? How? *Journal of Systems and Software, 46*(2-3), 91–105. doi:10.1016/S0164-1212(99)00003-5

Khanam, F., & Rahman, N. (2019). Measuring the Quality of Healthcare Services in Bangladesh: A Comparative Study of two Hospitals. *International Journal of Big Data and Analytics in Healthcare, 4*(1), 15–31. doi:10.4018/IJBDAH.2019010102

Khramov, Y. (2006). The cost of code quality. *Proceedings of the IEEE Agile 2006 Conference (AGILE'06)*, 119-125. 10.1109/AGILE.2006.52

Laguna, M., & Markland, J. (2005). *Business process modeling, simulation, and design*. Pearson Education, Inc.

Lee, S., Celik, N., & Son, Y.-J. (2009). An integrated simulation modelling framework for decision aids in enterprise software development process. *International Journal of Simulation and Process Modelling, 5*(1), 62–76. doi:10.1504/IJSPM.2009.025828

Liu, Y., & Iijima, J. (2015). Business process simulation in the context of enterprise engineering. *Journal of Simulation, 9*(3), 206–222. doi:10.1057/jos.2014.35

Lorenzo, O., & Diaz, A. (2005). Process gap analysis and modelling in enterprise systems. *International Journal of Simulation and Process Modelling, 3/4*(3/4), 114–124. doi:10.1504/IJSPM.2005.007642

Martinez-Moyano, I. J., & Richardson, G. P. (2013). Best practices in system dynamics modeling. *System Dynamics Review, 29*(2), 102–123. doi:10.1002dr.1495

Morrison, J. B. (2012). Process improvement dynamics under constrained resources: Managing the work harder versus work smarter balance. *System Dynamics Review, 28*(4), 329–350. doi:10.1002dr.1485

Mould, G., & Bowers, J. (2013). A comparison of process modelling methods for healthcare redesign. *International Journal of Simulation and Process Modelling, 8*(2/3), 168–176. doi:10.1504/IJSPM.2013.057539

Ng, T. S., Sy, C. L., & Lee, L. H. (2012). Robust parameter design for system dynamics models: A formal approach based on goal-seeking behavior. *System Dynamics Review, 28*(3), 230–254. doi:10.1002dr.1475

Onggo, B. S. S., & Hill, J. (2014). Data identification and data collection methods in simulation: A case study at ORH Ltd. *Journal of Simulation, 8*(3), 195–205. doi:10.1057/jos.2013.28

Raffo, D. M., & Kellner, M. I. (2000). Empirical analysis in software process simulation modeling. *Journal of Systems and Software, 53*(1), 31–41. doi:10.1016/S0164-1212(00)00006-6

Raffo, D. M., Vandeville, J. V., & Martin, R. H. (1999). Software process simulation to achieve higher CMM levels. *Journal of Systems and Software, 46*(2-3), 163–172. doi:10.1016/S0164-1212(99)00009-6

Raffo, D. M., & Wernick, P. (2001). Guest Editorial: Software Process Simulation Modelling. *Journal of Systems and Software, 59*(3), 223–225. doi:10.1016/S0164-1212(01)00063-2

Rahman, N. (2014). A system dynamics model for a sustainable fish population. *International Journal of Technology Diffusion, 5*(2), 39–53. doi:10.4018/ijtd.2014040104

Rahman, N. (2016a). *An empirical study of data warehouse implementation effectiveness. International Journal of Management Science and Engineering Management.* doi:10.1080/17509653.2015.1113394

Rahman, N. (2016b). Enterprise data warehouse governance best practices. *International Journal of Knowledge-Based Organizations, 6*(2), 21–37. doi:10.4018/IJKBO.2016040102

Rahman, N. (2016c). SQL scorecard for improved stability and performance of data warehouses. *International Journal of Software Innovation, 4*(3), 22–37. doi:10.4018/IJSI.2016070102

Rahman, N. (2018a). Data Warehousing and Business Intelligence with Big Data. *Proceedings of the 2018 International Annual Conference of the American Society for Engineering Management.*

Rahman, N. (2018b). A Simulation Model for Application Development in Data Warehouses. *International Journal of Operations Research and Information Systems, 9*(1), 66–80. doi:10.4018/IJORIS.2018010104

Rahman, N., Daim, T., & Basoglu, N. (2021). Exploring the Factors Influencing Big Data Technology Acceptance. *IEEE Transactions on Engineering Management*, 1–16. doi:10.1109/TEM.2021.3066153

Rahman, N., Wittman, A., & Thabet, S. (2016). Managing an engineering project. *International Journal of Information Technology Project Management, 7*(1), 1–17. doi:10.4018/IJITPM.2016010101

Rashidi, H. (2016, May). Discrete simulation software: A survey on taxonomies. *Journal of Simulation.* Advance online publication. doi:10.1057/jos.2016.4

Richardson, J. (2013). The past is prologue: Reflections on forty-plus years of system dynamics modeling practice. *System Dynamics Review, 29*(3), 172–187. doi:10.1002dr.1503

Ryan, J., & Heavey, C. (2006). Requirements gathering for simulation, United Kingdom Operational Research Society, Simulation Study Group. *Proceedings of the 3rd Simulation Workshop*, 1-13.

Sargent, R. G. (2013). Verification and validation of simulation models. *Journal of Simulation, 7*(1), 12–24. doi:10.1057/jos.2012.20

Sen, A., Sinha, A. P., & Ramamurthy, K. (2006). Data warehousing process maturity: An exploratory study of factors influencing user perceptions. *IEEE Transactions on Engineering Management, 53*(3), 440–455. doi:10.1109/TEM.2006.877460

Smith, A. W., & Rahman, N. (2017). Can agile, lean and ITIL coexist? *International Journal of Knowledge-Based Organizations, 7*(1), 78–88. doi:10.4018/IJKBO.2017010105

Smith, A. W., Rahman, N., Saleh, M. A., & Akhter, S. (2019). A Holistic Approach to Innovation and Fostering Intrepreneurship. *International Journal of Knowledge-Based Organizations, 9*(2), 62–79. doi:10.4018/IJKBO.2019040104

Sterman, J. D. (2000). *Business dynamics: Systems thinking and modeling for a complex world.* McGraw-Hill Higher Education.

Taylor, S. J. E., & Robinson, S. (2009). Simulation software: Evolution or revolution? *Journal of Simulation, 3*(1), 1–2. doi:10.1057/jos.2008.25

Yang, N., Wang, S., & Schonfeld, P. (2015). Simulation-based scheduling of waterway projects using a parallel genetic algorithm. *International Journal of Operations Research and Information Systems, 6*(1), 49–63. doi:10.4018/ijoris.2015010104

Ontological Metamodel of Sustainable Development

Boryana Deliyska

(iD) https://orcid.org/0000-0002-7791-4623

University of Forestry, Bulgaria

Adelina Ivanova

University of Forestry, Bulgaria

INTRODUCTION

In recent years, one of the most important research areas is that of Sustainable Development (SD). In its various aspects, SD is a multifaceted, complex and contradictory concept, interpreted in numerous studies. According to the most known and commonly accepted definition, "SD is a development that meets the needs of the present without compromising the ability of future generations to meet their own needs" (Brundtland, 1987, p.37). SD studies are inseparable from their modeling implemented by interdisciplinary researchers in a wide range of natural, engineering, mathematical, social, and economic sciences. Recently, a new scientific direction has emerged, called *sustainability science*. As in any science, in the core of the sustainability science is its conceptualization, i.e. clarifying and establishing a set of concepts that characterize it. One of the most effective approaches for this purpose is the ontology building. The notion *ontology* has two aspects. On the one hand, the ontology, as a branch of philosophy, studies, classifies and explains the entities and the nature of human beings. On the other hand, in informatics and computer science, an ontology is a computational data model representing concepts of given knowledge domain and their relationships. The main advantage of the computational ontology (referred briefly ontology from here below) compared to other domain conceptualization frameworks is that it represents widely available, shareable and reusable by human and computers domain knowledge and enable automated reasoning about data. Currently, the ontological modeling often precedes concrete researches and projects in different areas seeing the need for the non-ambiguous interpretation of the area's inherent terminology. Moreover, an ontology is a means for formal knowledge representation and machine-understandable knowledge generation based mainly on artificial intelligence (AI) theory, web technologies, data science and informatics methods and algorithms. For example, the background knowledge available in ontologies can be used to expand or enrich features in machine learning and to constrain the search for solutions to an optimization problem (Kulmanov, Smaili, Xin, & Hoehndorf, 2021). In other words, the ontology engineering is an AI technology for knowledge structuring, interchange and presentation. For these reasons, in the last 30 years ontologies have been actively developed.

Due to the interdisciplinarity of the SD field, in this work a conceptual model of SD in the form of set of interrelated ontologies (ontological metamodel) is developed. In view of the rapid SD evolution, a continuous generalization, clarification and refinement of its knowledge is necessary and the need of full SD ontological modeling arises. The generally shared view is that SD has three interdependent dimensions (pillars or constituents): ecological, social and economic. A coevolutionary approach is ap-

DOI: 10.4018/978-1-7998-9220-5.ch172

plied as a framework for analyzing the mutual causal influences between the natural (environmental) and human (social and economic) dimensions.

The current work is intended for a wide range of specialists involved in the data science theory and practice including ontological data modeling and extracting knowledge in the various fields related to the SD. The goal of the work is to present a SD ontological metamodel which systematizes and brings together SD terminology, activities and documents as well as to provide the possibility for knowledge extraction. The metamodel includes two layers – conceptual and physical. At the conceptual layer, a hierarchical structure of three levels is built including: Common Ontology of SD (COSD) as a top ontology; related to it domain ontologies of SD in economy, society and nature; and application ontologies concerning specific SD object and processes. As example, an application ontology of firm sustainability is developed. The physical layer consists of instance databases (databases containing instances of the ontology concepts). As whole, for each ontology of the metamodel links to other external ontologies are established.

The remainder of this article contains the following. The next background is a review of SD ontological modeling. Then, a methodology of SD ontological metamodel development is exposed followed by description of reasoning and verification of the created ontologies. The metamodel publication and the problems of ontology knowledge extraction are presented. On the base of the results, solutions and recommendations are discussed. In the end, future research directions and conclusion are proposed.

BACKGROUND

A review of the achievements in ontological SD modeling discovers several ontologies that can be considered as parts of a common SD ontology:

- The Sustainable Development Goals Interface Ontology (SDGIO), elaborated by United Nations (UN) Inter-Agency Expert Group on Sustainable Development Goals (IAEG-SDG) in 2016-2017 (Jensen, 2016). SDGIO is the most developed ontology in the SD area and its last version from 08.10.2018 includes 906 terms (OLS, n.d.).
- The Ontology of Sustainable Development Indicators called SDI-Economics (Brilhante, Ferreira, Marinho, & Pereira, 2006). This ontology does not support all Sustainable Development Goal (SDG) indicators.
- The Ontology of Sustainability Assessment (SA) (Konys, 2018) and the Ontology for Sustainability Indicator Sets (OSIS) (Ghahremanloo, Thom, & Magee, 2012) containing mainly methodological issues about sustainability measurement and assessment.

These ontologies have some overlapping concepts but they are not related each other.

Claiming that a lack of knowledge systematization in the SD field exists, Deliyska, Todorov, & Ivanova (2020) have presented an elementary schema of SD ontological metamodel including a top SD common ontology and planned development of corresponding domain ontologies. In other works (Ivanova, Deliyska, & Todorov, 2018; Ivanova, Deliyska, & Todorov, 2021; Ivanova, & Deliyska, 2020), domain ontologies of SD in economy (called OSDE), in society (OSSD) and in environment (OESD) were presented. Besides OSDE, OESD and OSSD, other domain SD ontologies were not found, excluding Ontology for Bioeconomy (BiOnto) (Bicchielli, Biancone, Ferri, & Grifoni, 2021), which is associated with the economic and the environmental SD pillars.

On the other hand, several SD application ontologies exist, for example: SD-based social ontology within a university system (Bankole, Fidelis, & Alfred, 2016), Strongly Sustainable Business Models Ontology (Upward, & Jones, 2016), Social ontology of sustainability of construction projects (Edum-Fotwe, & Price, 2009), Ontology of sustainable building technology (Abanda, & Tah, 2008), and others.

It can be said that there is a research gap in respect of consolidating all types of ontologies in the SD area. Moreover, some principal concepts are missing in them. In view of the dynamics of measures and actions in SD, a continuous generalization, clarification and refinement of the SD knowledge is necessary. Exploring the latest achievements in SD knowledge, described mainly in UN initiatives and documents as well as its links to other scientific areas, the existing elementary ontological SD metamodel is improved and enriched as a conceptual framework for explaining, classifying and justifying SD in its entirety.

METHODOLOGY OF THE SD ONTOLOGICAL METAMODEL CREATION

Generally, the ontology building includes AI methods and technologies, and Semantic Web resources. The main components of an ontology are concepts (called also classes), relations, properties and instances (individuals). The other ontology components (functions, axioms, etc.) are not covered in this work. The concepts are core components, generalized and hierarchically connected categories of the knowledge domain that build the skeleton of the ontology. Instances represent concrete examples of the concepts while properties (called also attributes or slots) characterize the concepts. The relations are links between the ontology components (concepts, instances). For example, *Sustainable development indicator* is a concept with instances *Human Development Indicator* and *Millennium Development Goals Indicator* and is linked to the concept *Sustainable development* with relation *is-subclass-of*. To this example concept can be added properties as definition, abbreviation, synonyms, etc. as well as more links to other ontology components.

The methodology of the SD ontological metamodel building compiles with the coevolution principles, meaning that SD is considered as natural result of the harmonious interaction between the processes of social, economic and natural development (Todorov, & Marinova, 2009). Specifically, the effective building of the proposed metamodel is associated with its clear modularization (partitioning or segmentation) into several ontologies and interconnectedness establishment between them. In this case, the leading rule of the ontology modularization is to differentiate the natural (environmental) and human (social and economic) dimensions of SD and to define requirements of their applications. The interconnectedness is implemented by common concepts participating in the particular metamodel ontologies. Thus, greater reusability, flexibility, scalability and maintainability of the separate modules is achieved.

The current methodology includes following stages: (1) creating a schema of the SD ontological metamodel; (2) a contemporary SD text corpus compilation; (3) research and selection of an annotation software tool for SD text corpus mining and SD concept extraction; (4) creating a common controlled vocabulary and a thesaurus; (5) generating the common and the domain ontologies; (6) creating an example firm sustainability application ontology; (7) reasoning, consistency verification and querying the particular ontologies.

SD Ontological Metamodel Schema

There are different definitions of metamodel. Commonly, metamodel is model of models (model generalization) or a set of elements (models), their mutual relationships and development rules. As far as an ontology is a data model, a set of mutually connected ontologies can refer to ontological metamodel. Then, SD ontological metamodel is a set of ontologies organized in a hierarchical system covering: common SD entities, specific SD dimension entities and specific applications in different SD areas. Moreover, this metamodel includes links to external ontologies and instance databases. More precisely, the SD ontological metamodel contains two main layers – conceptual and physical (Figure 1).

Figure 1. Schema of sustainable development ontological metamodel

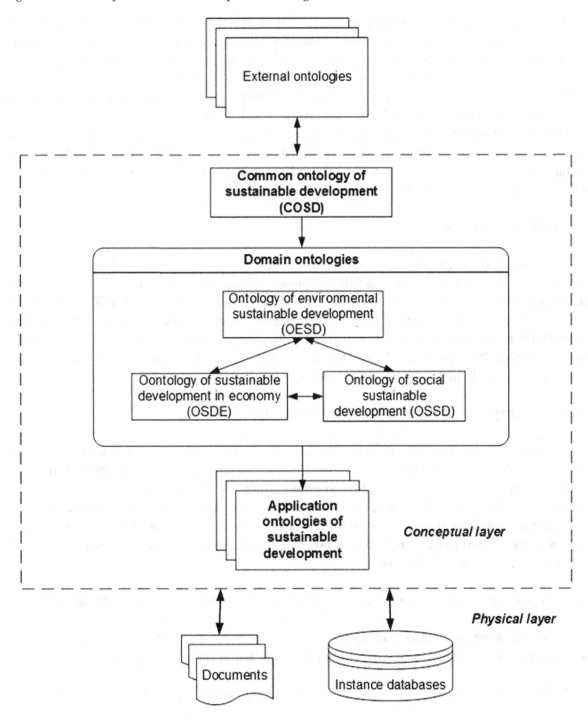

The conceptual layer consists of ontologies:

- COSD (as a top ontology);
- domain ontologies OSDE, OESD and OSSD, subordinate to COSD and having reciprocal links between them;
- an unlimited set of application ontologies structuring SD knowledge for concrete SD processes and objects.

The external ontologies have concepts related to those of the metamodel. Each of the metamodel ontologies is connected to its relevant external ontologies by equal concepts. For example, in Environment Ontology (ENVO) (Buttigieg et al., 2016) and in OESD have the same concept *Safe environment*. By analogy, Common Ontology of System and Process (COS) (Borydel/COS, 2019) is connected to COSD, Population and Community Ontology (PCO) (Buttigieg, Osumi-Sutherland, Walls, & Zheng, 2021) – to OSSD, Protein Ontology (PRO) (Natale et al., 2016) – to OESD, etc.

On the other hand, the instances (including reports, standards, statistics, regulations, images, software code, etc.) are organized in databases and as individual documents representing the physical layer of the metamodel. The most used of them are the SDG indicators database (UN DESA, n.d.), the documents of UN Sustainable Development Knowledge Platform (n.d.), etc.

SD Text Corpus Compilation

The text corpus consisting of a set of text files in the research area serves for analysis and extraction of the essential terms (concepts, instances), their relations and structure. A contemporary SD text corpus has been compiled including five important documents in the SD area: the last 2021 SD report (Sachs, Kroll, Lafortune, Fuller, & Woelm, 2021), a practical guide about stakeholder engagement in the 2030 Agenda (UN DESA & UNITAR, 2020), global SDG indicator framework (UN DESA, n.d.), SD literature review (Mensah, 2019) and issues about SD education (Hoffman, & Siege, 2018). Applying text mining methods and tools, from the corpus updated and new concepts and instances are derived.

SD Text Corpus Mining and Concept Extraction

In this work, a mixed approach combining automatic software tools and manual methods for text corpus mining is used. The text mining is a process including: text cleaning, preprocessing, entity designation and co-reference resolution. Firstly, the SD text corpus is manually cleaned which means deleting of unnecessary objects (images, diagrams, pictures, shapes, and etc.) and removing of any text and characters that aren't relevant. After that, the corpus is processed by text analytics software tool. By Harvey (2021), the contemporary text analytics tools use AI-powered natural language processing (NLP). In that, the following steps are sequentially performed:

- preprocessing – tokenization (splitting sentences into individual words/terms) and part-of-speech (POS) tagging;
- entity designation including gazetteer lookup, named entity tagging, etc.;
- co-reference resolution identifying mentions that refer to the same entities across the entire corpus.

In the end, the extracted concepts and instances are manually reviewed, selected and specified.

In (Sheets for Marketers, 2021) and (Harvey, 2021) the top text analytic software tools are discussed. Overall, there are a few dozen commercial and free such tools. The aim of this research is not their detailed analysis, but a choice of suitable and friendly tool helping the subsequent manual concept selection. Due to its user friendliness, possibility of free access and clear results, TextRazor (Sheets for Marketers, 2021) was selected. Using TextRazor, from the SD text corpus were extracted terms about:

- the SD index with instances: global SDG index and its 231 unique indicators;
- the instances of SD organizations, documents and events;
- sustainability science, SD education; and etc.

Common Controlled Vocabulary and Thesaurus Creating

The most specific terms extracted from the text corpus are arranged in a common controlled vocabulary. Each term of this controlled dictionary is specified by term identifier (TID), syntactic category (part of speech), relations with other terms and definition. According to the standard for controlled vocabularies (ANSI/NISO Z39.19-2005, 2010), TID has values: top term (TT), preferred term (PT), related term (RT), narrower term (NT), non-preferred term (NPT), etc. Adding hierarchical relations (of type *is-a/has-a* and *is-part-of/has-part*) between the TT and the PTs, this vocabulary is transformed into thesaurus. Obviously, TT is unique and in this case is *Sustainable development*. The TT and the PTs compose taxonomy. Each taxonomy has two main parts – classification (subsumption) and mereology. The classification scheme begins with a *type-of node* label and contains PTs of concepts linked with relations *is-a/has-a* (*is-subclass-of/has-subclass*). In turn, relations of the type *is-part-of/has-part* link the PTs concepts belonging to the mereology. An example of SD upper level taxonomy on Figure 2 is shown.

Figure 2. Upper level of COSD taxonomy

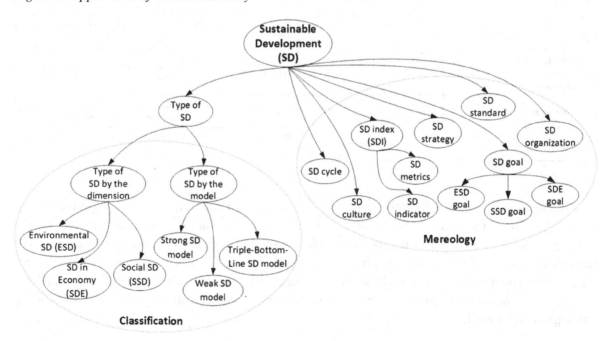

The terms of type RT, NT, NPT explain PTs by various relations. RTs are connected to PTs by associative relations (*is-kind-of*, *is-located-in*, *is-version-of* and many others) depending on the specifics of the subject area. The NTs are the subordinate terms in a hierarchical relation while NPTs are terms connected by equivalence relations (for example, *is-synonym-of/has-synonym*). For denoting the affiliation of each term to the concrete ontology within the metamodel, a new identifier "ontology range" (OR) with values SD, SSD, ESD or SDE to each term in thesaurus is added.

For example, in Table 1 a partial description of some terms of the common thesaurus is represented.

Table 1. An Excerpt of Common SD Thesaurus Content

Term	TID	OR	Relation	Related to	Definition
Ecological footprint	PT	ESD	is-subclass-of	ESD index	A measure of the demands made by a person or group of people on global natural resources.
Economic and Social Council	RT	SD	is-instance-of	SD organization	UN organ, responsible for coordinating the economic and social fields of the organization.
Education for SD	PT	SD	is-subclass-of	SD culture	UN program for education concerning knowledge, skills, values and attitudes to enable a more sustainable and just society for all.
High-Level Political Forum on SD	PT	SD	is-instance-of	SD event	The main UN platform on SD having a central role in the follow-up and review of the 2030 Agenda.
SCI	RT	SSD	is-abbreviation-of	service coverage index	A dimensionless index (of 0 to 100), geometric mean of 14 tracer indicators of health service coverage.
SD event	PT	SD	is-subclass-of	SD organization	SD conference, workshop, exhibition, meeting, and etc.
SD strategy document	PT	SD	is-subclass-of	SD strategy	Report, review, plan, schedule, paper, and etc. on SD.
Sustainable development in microeconomics	PT	SDE	is-subclass-of	Type of SDE	A set of SD activities at microeconomic level (SMEs).
Service coverage index	PT	SSD	is-subclass-of	SSD index	Average coverage of essential health services based on tracer interventions.
UN Agenda 30	RT	SD	is-instance-of	SD strategy document	UN plan for humanity SD adopted in 2015 to 2030

Although a thesaurus has all components as an ontology, due to its inability for logic-based reasoning it is not reusable in the Semantic Web (called also Linked Data Web and Web of Data). In other words, "an important reason for converting thesaurus into a formal ontology is the necessity of its machine readability and reuse." (Deliyska, 2007, p. 644). Then, the SD thesaurus is implemented in MS Access database because at the next stage by the software application presented in (Deliyska, 2007) the database is converted to ontology. Each of its term becomes concept, instance or property of an ontology of the ontological metamodel.

Generating the Common and the Domain Ontologies

Using the software application, the SD thesaurus database is converted into OWL ontologies – the top COSD and the domain OESD, OSSD, OSDE. The Web Ontology Language (OWL) is recommended by World Wide Web Consortium (W3C) for formal ontology description (DeBellis, 2021). For generating each of these ontologies, OR identifier is taken into account. It should be noted that the predominant part of the main concepts of these ontologies have the same meaning: goal, standard, justice, indicator, metrics, organization, etc. Their interconnections are organized in similar internal hierarchy. Then, the main concepts of the domain ontologies, are related to the respective COSD concepts. For example, the concept *SD goal* has subconcepts *SDE goal*, *SSD goal* and *ESD goal* (Figure 2) which at the same time are concepts of OSDE, OSSD and OESD, respectively. Latter, in these ontologies, according to IAEG-SDG (2018):

- *SDE goal* has subconcepts *Affordable and clean energy, Decent work and economic growth, Industry, innovation and infrastructure, Responsible consumption and production*;
- *ESD goal* subconcepts are: *Climate action, Life below water, Life on land*;
- *SSD goal* has subconcepts: *No poverty, Zero hunger, Good health and well-being, Quality education, Gender equality, Clean water and sanitation, Reduced inequalities, Sustainable cities and communities, Peace, justice and strong institutions*.

The OWL codes of the metamodel ontologies are introduced and edited in Protégé 5.5 ontology editor which is freely available and currently is the most used (DeBellis, 2021). The links of each ontology to external ontologies as well the links to the instance databases/documents are manually established in the Protégé 5.5 environment.

Currently, COSD contains 64 concepts, OESD – 44, OSSD – 28, and OSDE – 77, accompanied by their instances and properties.

Creating Firm Sustainability Application Ontology

The application ontologies are at the lowest level of the SD metamodel conceptual layer. It should be noted that a major problem for building any SD application ontology is the difficulty and even sometimes the impossibility to collect and to specify information about a variety of SD activities and indicators. As an example of microeconomic SD knowledge and using previous works on firm competitiveness and sustainability (Ivanova et al., 2020), an application ontology of firm sustainability (OFS) has been developed. For the purpose, following the above methodology steps, firstly a particular text corpus has been compiled. The text corpus includes journal articles (Adams, Thornton, & Sepehri, 2011; Gonga, Gaob, Koha, Sutcliffeb, & Cullena, 2019; Stocchetti, 2012; Toha, Johl, & Khan, 2020; Radzi, Jenatabadi, & Hasbullah, 2015) and a survey (Finansinspectionen, 2018). The most specific concepts extracted from the text corpus are collected in a firm sustainability (FS) controlled vocabulary and the main ones are: *FS goal, FS index, FS metrics, FS strategy, FS standard*, etc. On the base of this vocabulary, the FS thesaurus and the respective OWL ontology are created. The upper level of the FS taxonomy is shown on Figure 3.

Figure 3. Upper level of FS taxonomy

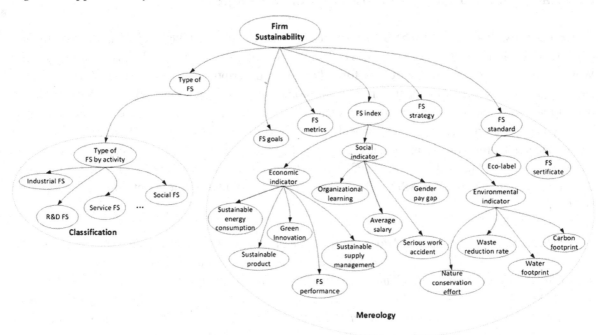

FSO as a part of the SD ontological metamodel is connected to the other ontologies by some of its concepts. For example:

- the top concept *Firm sustainability* is subconcept of *Sustainable development in microeconomics* of OSDE;
- *Gender pay gap* is connected to OSSD's *Social equity*;
- *FS economic indicator* – to OSDE's *SDE indicator*, etc.

On the other hand, FSO has connections to various instance databases. For example, one of the instances of the concept *FS index* is *Industrial FS Index* (*IFSI*) (Ivanova, Deliyska, & Popova-Terziyska, 2021) which is connected to an Excel sample of firm database containing calculated IFSI's together with data for their indicators. The Excel sample is published as repository of the same name in the OMSD project (Borydel/OMSD, 2021).

Reasoning, Consistency Verification and Querying Particular Ontologies

Ontology reasoning and verification means checking semantic structure and mutual consistency of the ontological units. For the purpose, appropriate semantic reasoner is used. In Protégé environment, these operations are executed through the embedded Pelet, FaCT++ or HermiT reasoners (DeBellis, 2021). The reasoner can also examine the hierarchy correctness. The reasoning, verification and querying of each metamodel ontology is implemented separately. Then, the ontologies can be used for knowledge extraction by some query language. For the purpose, a set of sample queries over them are implemented. The native formal languages in Protégé, generally intended for knowledge representation and querying, are Description Logics (DL), SPARQL, and SQWRL

Other knowledge extraction queries about hierarchy, class instances, annotations, data/object properties, etc. can be composed and eventually saved in the ontology repository for future reuse. A key problem in the Semantic Web is that these languages are not suitable for non-expert users, unfamiliar with the semantic technologies.

SOLUTIONS AND RECOMMENDATIONS

The focus of current SD activities is mainly on the practice and there is a lack of theoretical researches in the SD area. In the beginning of the 21st century, sustainability science emerged as theoretical foundation and a practical SD guidance. It explores the sustainability of the interactions between economic, social, and natural systems. Various methods and models are proposed for achievement of sustainability in each human activity. As each interdisciplinary science, the own terminology of the sustainability science is limited. Moreover, a gap in the terminology range and clarification exists. As a result of this work, an ontological metamodel of SD is proposed and developed on the base of a methodology covering: defining metamodel schema; SD text corpus composition, mining and concept extraction; controlled vocabulary and thesaurus creating; ontology formalization; reasoning, verification and querying. This metamodel systematizes and brings together knowledge about SD terminology, activities and documents. Moreover, it provides a possibility for knowledge extraction.

At present, the SD ontological metamodel description and its OWL codes are published and freely available in their GitHub repositories under the OMSD project (Borydel/OMSD, 2021).

FUTURE RESEARCH DIRECTIONS

The presented ontological SD metamodel has future development in three main research directions. The first is further enrichment and extension of the metamodel ontologies since SD is constantly evolving process and without alternative. Due to the rapid evolution of SD theory and practice, their continuous updating is necessary. Moreover, the links to the external ontologies need to be revised due to ongoing updating the latter.

The second direction concerns improvement of the knowledge extraction. Currently, a direct knowledge extraction from the metamodel ontologies is possible by Protégé editor query languages. The other more user-friendly ontology query methods and languages are not sufficiently developed. Another approach for knowledge acquisition and extraction consists of ontology-to-database transformation and following ontology database querying (Deliyska, & Manoilov, 2015). The advantage of this approach is in well-developed and convenient database querying user interfaces. On the other hands, the development of direct ontology query methods and tools for knowledge extraction is much more promising and effective. Creating convenient and unified cross-ontology query interface should provide introduction of a query in natural (or near to natural) language, visual language, SQL or in some other user-friendly language. In any case, a software application for conversion of the input query language to some ontology query language should be developed, bearing in mind the specifics of the SD ontological metamodel.

The third direction is related to the use of the SD ontological metamodel for structuring machine learning models of SD processes. Using the metamodel as a background knowledge for enriching end expanding the machine learning predictive models of these processes is promising investigation.

CONCLUSION

In this work, the necessity of a continuous generalization, clarification and refinement of the SD knowledge is underlined keeping in mind the rapid development of the sustainability science and practice. The review and the analysis of the state-of-the-art of SD data modeling confirm the hypothesis for lack of a common conceptual framework in this area. The advantage of ontologies as computational data models for provision of widely shareable and reusable by human and computers domain knowledge is justified. Applying the coevolutionary approach and the ontology modularization principle, an SD ontological metamodel is proposed. The metamodel is hierarchically structured and includes a conceptual layer of interconnected top ontology; related to it domain ontologies of SD in economy, society and nature; and application ontologies concerning specific SD object and processes; and a physical layer of instance databases. Using Semantic Web technologies, the particular OWL ontologies of the metamodel are developed and connected to the respective external ontologies. The proposed SD ontological metamodel would be useful for a wide range of specialists in the data science and in the sustainability science for SD knowledge extraction as well as knowledge base for future structuring of machine learning models of the SD processes.

REFERENCES

Abanda, F. H., & Tah, J. H. M. (2008). Towards developing a sustainable building technology ontology. In A. Dainty (Ed.), *Proceedings of 24th Annual ARCOM Conference*. Association of Researchers in Construction Management.

Adams, M., Thornton, B., & Sepehri, M. (2011). The impact of the pursuit of sustainability on the financial performance of the firm. *Journal of Sustainability and Green Business*, *1*, 1–14.

ANSI/NISO Z39. 19-2005. (2010). *Guidelines for the Construction, Format, and Management of Monolingual Controlled Vocabularies*. https://groups.niso.org/apps/group_public/download.php/12591/z39-19-2005r2010.pdf

Bankole, A., Fidelis, E., & Alfred, N. (2016). Towards a social ontology on sustainable development in CUT: Understanding stakeholder perceptions. In Handbook of theory and practice of sustainable development in higher education. Springer. doi:10.1007/978-3-319-47889-0_30

Bicchielli, Ch., Biancone, N., Ferri, F., & Grifoni, P. (2021). BiOnto: An ontology for sustainable bioeconomy and bioproducts. *Sustainability*, *13*(8), 4265. doi:10.3390u13084265

Borydel/COS. (2019). *Common ontology of system*. https://github.com/Borydel/COS/blob/master/OntologySystem.owl

Borydel/OMSD. (2021). *OMSD project*. https://github.com/Borydel?tab=projects

Brilhante, V., Ferreira, A., Marinho, J., & Pereira, J. S. (2006). Information integration through ontology and metadata for sustainability analysis. *Proceedings of International Congress on Environmental Modelling and Software*. https://scholarsarchive.byu.edu/iemssconference/2006/all/191

Brundtland, G. H. (1987). Our common future, chairman's foreword. *Report of the World Commission on Environment and Development (WCED)*. http://www.un-documents.net/ocf-cf.htm

Buttigieg, P. L., Osumi-Sutherland, D., Walls, R., & Zheng, J. (2021). *Population and community ontology*. https://www.ebi.ac.uk/ols/ontologies/pco

Buttigieg, P. L., Pafilis, E., Lewis, S. E., Schildhauer, M. P., Walls, R. L., & Mungall, C. J. (2016). The environment ontology in 2016: Bridging domains with increased scope, semantic density, and interoperation. *Journal of Biomedical Semantics*, *7*(1), 57. doi:10.118613326-016-0097-6 PMID:27664130

DeBellis, M. (2021). *A practical guide to building OWL ontologies using Protégé 5.5 and plugins*. https://tinyurl.com/NewPizzaTutorialV1

Deliyska, B. (2007). Thesaurus and domain ontology of geoinformatics. *Journal Transactions in GIS*, *11*(4), 637–651. doi:10.1111/j.1467-9671.2007.01064.x

Deliyska, B., & Manoilov, P. (2015). *Ontology-based system and process modeling*. Lambert Academic Publishing.

Deliyska, B., Todorov, V., & Ivanova, A. (2020). Common ontology of sustainable development. *International Journal of Information Systems and Social Change*, *11*(4), 55–69. doi:10.4018/IJISSC.2020100104

Edum-Fotwe, F. T., & Price, A. D. F. (2009). A social ontology for appraising sustainability of construction projects and developments. *International Journal of Project Management*, *27*(4), 313–322. doi:10.1016/j.ijproman.2008.04.003

Finansinspectionen. (2018). *Integration of Sustainability into Corporate Governance*. https://www.fi.se/contentassets/b631b84ddc5f4f03bd3085966328ff29/integrering-hallbarhet-foretagsstyrningen-eng.pdf

Ghahremanloo, L., Thom, J., & Magee, L. (2012). An ontology derived from heterogeneous sustainability indicator set documents. *Proceedings of ADCS*, *12*, 72–79. doi:10.1145/2407085.2407095

Gonga, M., Gaob, Y., Koha, L., Sutcliffeb, Ch., & Cullena, J. (2019). The role of customer awareness in promoting firm sustainability and sustainable supply chain management. *International Journal of Production Economics*, *217*, 88–96. doi:10.1016/j.ijpe.2019.01.033

Harvey, S. (2021). *Top 10 text analysis solutions*. https://www.datamation.com/big-data/text-analysis-tools/

Hoffman, T., & Siege, H. (2018). What is education for sustainable development (ESD)? *ESD Expert Net*. https://esd-expert.net/files/ESD-Expert/pdf/Was_wir_tun/201012_EduForSustDevelopment.pdf

Ivanova, A., & Deliyska, B. (2021). Ontological modeling of environmental sustainable development. *AMEE'2021 Conference*. http://amee.tu-sofia.bg/section-40-page.html

Ivanova, A., Deliyska, B., & Popova-Terziyska, R. (2021). Information modeling of firm competitiveness. *AIP Conference Proceedings*, *2333*, 110005. doi:10.1063/5.0042961

Ivanova, A., Deliyska, B., & Todorov, V. (2018). Domain ontology of sustainable development in economy. *AIP Conference Proceedings*, *2048*, 020004. doi:10.1063/1.5082022

Ivanova, A., Deliyska, B., & Todorov, Vl. (2020). Model of GIS-based application for firm competitiveness analysis. *Knowledge – International Journal*, *42*(3), 549-553.

Ivanova, A., Deliyska, B., & Todorov, V. (2021). Domain ontology of social sustainable development. *AIP Conference Proceedings*, *2333*, 110005. doi:10.1063/5.0042961

Ivanova, A., Todorov, Vl., Popova-Terziyska, R., Stefanova, E., & Marinova, M. (2021). *Modeling and assessment of the firm sustainability and competitiveness of Bulgarian furniture and forestry industry by geoinformational portal building*. Report of Project B-1087/16.03.2020, University of Forestry.

Jensen, M. (2016). Sustainable development goals interface ontology. *Proceedings of International Conference on Biomedical Ontology and BioCreative, 1747*.

Konys, A. (2018). An ontology-based knowledge modelling for a sustainability assessment domain. *Journal of Sustainability*, *10*(2), 1–27. doi:10.3390u10020300

Kulmanov, M., Smaili, F. Z., Xin, G., & Hoehndorf, R. (2021). Semantic similarity and machine learning with ontologies. *Briefings in Bioinformatics*, *22*(4), bbaa199. Advance online publication. doi:10.1093/bib/bbaa199 PMID:33049044

Mensah, J. (2019). Sustainable development: Meaning, history, principles, pillars, and implications for human action: Literature review. *Cogent Social Sciences*, *5*(1), 1653531. doi:10.1080/23311886.2019.1653531

Natale, D. A., Arighi, C. N., Blake, J. A., Bona, J., Chen, Ch., Chen, S. C., Christie, K. R., Cowart, J., D'Eustachio, P., Diehl, A. D., Drabkin, H. J., Duncan, W. D., Huang, H., Ren, J., Ross, K., Ruttenberg, A., Shamovsky, V., Smith, B., Wang, Q., ... Wu, C. H. (2016). Protein ontology (PRO): Enhancing and scaling up the representation of protein entities. *Nucleic Acids Research*, *45*(D1), D339–D346. doi:10.1093/nar/gkw1075 PMID:27899649

OLS (Ontology Lookup Service). (n.d.). *Sustainable Development Goals Interface Ontology*. https://www.ebi.ac.uk/ols/ontologies/sdgio

Radzi, W. M., Jenatabadi, H. S., & Hasbullah, M. B. (2015). Firm sustainability performance index modeling. *Journal of Sustainability*, *12*(7), 16196–16212. doi:10.3390u71215810

Sachs, J. D., Kroll, Ch., Lafortune, G., Fuller, G., & Woelm, F. (2021). *Sustainable development report 2021*. Cambridge University Press. doi:10.1017/9781009106559

Sheets for Marketers. (2021). *Text Analytics API*. https://sheetsformarketers.com/marketing-apis/text-analysis-apis/

Stocchetti, A. (2012). The sustainable firm: From principles to practice. *International Journal of Business and Management*, *7*(21). Advance online publication. doi:10.5539/ijbm.v7n21p34

Todorov, V., & Marinova, D. (2009). Models of sustainability. *Proceedings of 18th World IMACS/MODSIM Congress*, 1216-1222. https://mssanz.org.au/modsim09

Toha, A., Johl, S. K., & Khan, P. A. (2020). Firm's sustainability and societal development from the lens of fishbone eco-innovation: A moderating role of ISO 14001-2015 environmental management system. *Processes (Basel, Switzerland)*, *8*(9), 1152. doi:10.3390/pr8091152

UN DESA. (n.d.). *SDG indicators*. https://unstats.un.org/sdgs/indicators/database/

UN DESA & UNITAR. (2020). *Stakeholder engagement & the 2030 agenda. A practical guide*. https://sdgs.un.org/sites/default/files/2020-07/2703For_distribution_Stakeholder_Engagement_Practical_Guide_spreads_2.pdf

UN Sustainable Development Knowledge Platform. (n.d.). *Document Library*. https://sustainabledevelopment.un.org/index.html

Upward, A., & Jones, P. (2016). An ontology for strongly sustainable business models. *Journal of Organization & Environment, 29*(1), 97-123. . doi:10.1177/1086026615592933

ADDITIONAL READING

Codescu, M., Kuksa, E., Kutz, O., Mossakowski, T., & Neuhaus, F. (2017). Ontohub: A semantic repository engine for heterogeneous ontologies. *Journal Applied Ontology, 12*(3-4), 275–298. doi:10.3233/AO-170190

Crisóstomo, V. L., & Oliveira, M. R. (2014). Corporate social and sustainability performance and ownership concentration – an analysis of Brazilian firms. *Proceedings of EnANPAD.*

D'Aquin, M., Schlicht, A., Stuckenschmidt, H., & Sabou, M. (2007). Ontology modularization for knowledge selection: Experiments and evaluations. In R. Wagner, N. Revell, & G. Pernul (Eds.), *Database and Expert Systems Applications (DEXA)*. Springer Verlag. doi:10.1007/978-3-540-74469-6_85

Eurostat. (n.d.). *Database*. https://ec.europa.eu/eurostat/data/database

Ezoji, A., & Matta, N. (2019). Assist the sustainable development within industries through the territorial knowledge ontology. *KMIS*, 102-112. . doi:10.5220/0008165201020112

Malek, S. M., & Ukre, E. (2013). Agriculture ontology for sustainable development in Nigeria. *Advances in Computers, 3*(3), 57–59. doi:10.5923/j.ac.20130303.04

Neves, M., & Ševa, S. (2021). An extensive review of tools for manual annotation of documents. *Briefings in Bioinformatics, 22*(1), 146–163. doi:10.1093/bib/bbz130 PMID:31838514

Nielsen, L., & Faber, M.H. (2021). Toward an information theoretic ontology of risk, resilience and sustainability and a blueprint for education – Part I. *Journal of Sustainable and Resilient Infrastructure*, 1-46. . doi:10.1080/23789689.2021.1937775

Sullivan, S. (2017). What's ontology got to do with it? On nature and knowledge in a political ecology of the 'green economy'. *Journal of Political Ecology, 24*(1), 217–242. doi:10.2458/v24i1.20802

KEY TERMS AND DEFINITIONS

Coevolutionary Approach: A research approach for investigation and analyzing the reciprocal evolutionary change in group of species in the nature or the mutual causal influences between the natural (environmental) and human (social and economic) dimensions.

Controlled Vocabulary: A dictionary containing approved (preferred) terminology along with the definitions.

Ontological Metamodel: A set of ontologies on a common topic organized in a hierarchical system or in a network.

Ontology Instance (Individual): An ontology element denoting an example of a concept (i.e., United Nations is an instance of concept organization).

Semantic Reasoner (or Simply Reasoner): A software application verifying semantic structure and mutual consistency of the ontological units as well as deriving new facts from ontologies.

Taxonomy: A scheme (a tree structure) of a categorization and hierarchical classification of things or concepts in given area.

Text Analytics (With Synonyms Text Analysis, Text Mining, Text Annotation): Automated Natural Language Processing (NLP) technology in AI for unstructured text data treatment to extract topics, entities and keywords.

Text Corpus: A set of texts of specific topic used for research and analysis of the content in order to extract main components (parts of speech, concepts, relations, etc.).

Thesaurus: In informatics, a controlled vocabulary supplemented with hierarchical and nonhierarchical (associative) relationships between terms.

Web Ontology Language (OWL): A standard formal language recommended by World Wide Web Consortium (W3C) for formal ontology description.

Section 49
Smart City

Death Analytics and the Potential Role in Smart Cities

James Braman

iD https://orcid.org/0000-0001-6080-3903

Community College of Baltimore County, USA

Alexis D. Brown

Community College of Baltimore County, USA

INTRODUCTION

The massive amounts of data available today have opened an unprecedented opportunity for data analysis and understanding trends for improving many aspects of our lives. Through the advancements of the Internet of Things (IoT) and as more and increasingly sophisticated devices are brought online, the ability to collect rich data points as well as the variation in the data collected, will continue to grow. Society as a whole can certainly benefit from knowing more about how people interact and use resources to further make improvements to these tools. As an example, consider the growing number of devices and internet-connected services incorporated into our homes; many can now be considered "smart" homes due to this added technology. Through IoT, more items in our personal spaces contain sensors and the ability to perform tasks, enhancing automation and our productivity. In addition, the proliferation of artificial intelligence and digital assistants in our homes coupled with IoT is likely to grow at a rapid pace. As these devices are scaled from homes to cars and offices, a clear progression can be seen at the macro level.

IoT technology embedded in everyday devices on a macro scale allows us to consider impacts at the city level. Smart cities, therefore, have the potential to record and analyze massive amounts of information at a societal level. When considering the concept of a smart city, there is the potential for widespread continued automation and technology integration. Many people will end up living in these areas as populations increase and as technology evolves. Some estimates suggest that over sixty percent of the world population will live in metropolitan areas by 2030 (United Nations, 2015). As more significant percentages of people live in burgeoning and densely packed smart cities, there are opportunities to utilize this data to help residents make their lives easier and improve their quality of life. However, what is meant by the term smart city? This concept can be interpreted in many ways including measuring the levels of technological use, innovation metrics, goals, and project implementations within a city. Many cities have different approaches to technology, including changing needs, varying budgets, and technology infrastructures.

There still is a need for a clear definition of what exactly constitutes or defines a smart city (Dameri, 2013). It can be said that a smart city is a city whose very infrastructure aims to use technology and its interconnectedness, along with the intentions of its residents, businesses, and governments to use data to automate, monitor, and utilize information sharing to improve the lives and wellbeing of its communities. At the same time, a smart city should be designed in such a way as to minimize the negative impacts of technology use and, given the potential for large population size, strive to be "green" through its use of resources. As both technology and people are the main components of a smart city, these spaces should

DOI: 10.4018/978-1-7998-9220-5.ch173

enhance each other for the greater good. Smart cities should be able to address concerns associated with increasing urbanization to address the scarcity of resources, inadequate and deteriorating infrastructure, energy shortages and price instability, environmental changes, and various economic and social needs (Washburn & Sindhu, 2010). It can be said that the overall idea that describes a smart city is one that uses technology to solve urban problems (Dameri, 2013).

A few examples of smart cities include Songdo IBD and Hwaseong Dongtan in South Korea, Masdar City in Abu Dhabi, PlanIT Valley in Portugal, and SmartCity in Malta (Washburn & Sindhu, 2010). Although some smart cities were designed with a technological infrastructure in mind from its original inception, other cities have the potential to grow into a technological mindset as infrastructure is added, changed, and improved over time. Indeed, many cities in the future will experience changes as a society, and needs will evolve that will lend themselves to technological solutions. For this chapter, we can use a definition of a smart city by Dameri (2013) that states, "A smart city is a well-defined geographical area, in which high technologies such as ICT, logistics, energy production, and so on, cooperate to create benefits for residents in terms of wellbeing, inclusion and participation, environmental quality, intelligent development; it is government by a well-defined pool of subjects, able to state the rules and policy for the city government" (2013, p 2549). Indeed, there is a need for a highly coupled system between technology, resources, data, and the city's residents.

BACKGROUND

Data in various forms collected from multitudes of sensors and applications in a smart city is particularly useful. Significant information can be collected and analyzed based on how residents interact with city resources, travel, use energy, live, work, and interact with each other. While there are many security risks with having such enormous amounts of information related to people (Wang, Ali & Kelly, 2015), this chapter highlights the positive aspects. Consider one such positive aspect of digitizing the infrastructure - the improvement of public safety and a decrease in response times for medical and fire services. This can be achieved through better tracking, surveillance, and traffic routing during emergency situations. A plethora of data points can be collected through sensors in highways, buildings, power grids, school systems, hospitals, airports, and much more. Hashem *et al.* present how such IoT-connected sensor systems can be linked through various communication technologies contributing to big data systems that can be analyzed to support smart cities (2016). Real-time data analysis opens the door for ongoing research and improvements. Numerous components of a city infrastructure can be designed with data collection, management, and analysis and are possible to improve traffic, wastewater, power use, and more (Bawany & Shamsi, 2015).

Consider the case where power needs are significant on a scorching day to keep indoor environments comfortable. Reducing strain on city power generation and distribution during peak heavy demand times could be very beneficial. Otherwise, power demand could outpace supply which would be detrimental to critical systems. Instead of having potential shutdowns or brownouts which could impact key infrastructure such as public safety, transportation, traffic or schools, a smart city could automatically determine areas where power can be limited based on population density or current use and thus rerouted as needed. Buildings not in use, streetlights, and other non-essential city components could have their power consumption temporarily suspended or reduced. Another example would be the use of current weather data that can be analyzed to make informed decisions for tasks and scheduling of the day based on a customizable interface that learns the needs of a user (Richard, Braman & Colclough, 2020). Although this is a small example, many problems can be tackled using real-time data collection and automated processes based on analytics. Through this vast amount of collected data, smart cities can apply analytic tools, machine learning, and modeling to predict, interpret trends and make informed decisions.

Interactions of residents could also be analyzed for a better understanding of behavior patterns, preferences, and resource use. While it is a daunting task to capture such a vast amount of data on people, in addition to capturing data from embedded city sensors and applications, a wealth of useful predictive information can be made. With IoT devices embedded in smart cities, it is possible to monitor trends in behaviors and data related to residents' overall health. A recent example is an IoT real-time monitoring system and cloud-based analytics project for the detection of COVID-19 outbreaks based on analysis of wastewater (Steward, 2020). There is a great potential for other similar projects that could be deployed and connected to monitor other health-related elements such as water and air pollution, contaminants, environmental status of buildings, and much more. There have been recent initiatives using sensor networks to monitor air quality around the globe, with data available in real-time through a project such as PlanetWatch (PlanetWatch, 2022). As an incentive for individuals to buy sensor equipment and keep systems running in and around their homes, PlanetWatch uses its own utility token based on the Algorand blockchain (PlanetWatch, 2021). In this project, there are several sensor types available, each with varying capabilities and required licenses. As more technology becomes available that encourages residents to make use of data collection to improve their lives through monitoring aspects of health, the environment, and more; there will most likely be growing interest and more innovation around these areas. In this project, there are several sensor types available, each with varying capabilities and required licenses.

There has been significant progress made in the areas of using IoT devices to monitor older adults and to assist those with various disabilities or cognitive decline (Srivastava, 2022; Shahrestani, 2018; Mainetti, Patrono, Secco, & Sergi, 2016). For instance, with some monitoring systems, a family member can be notified if someone has not moved from their current position in some time, or has fallen (Bhoi et al., 2018) or where they may be located in their home. As IoT devices and their accuracy improve, the collection of movement and other activity data points can be used for more precise location tracking (Huh & Seo, 2017). IoT devices can be used to assist with reminding individuals to take medications at the correct time of day (Ahmad, Hasan, Shahabuddin, Tabassum, & Allvi, 2020). From a smart city viewpoint, there is research underway to make these types of systems scalable and potentially integrated into other systems to improve quality of life in an unobtrusive way for older adults and people with disabilities (Mulero, Almeida, Azkune, Abril-Jiménez, Waldmeyer, Castrillo, Patrono, Rametta & Sergi, 2018). As a larger sector of the current population ages and people continue to live longer lives, these types of assistive technologies designed around IoT will be advantageous. Despite the benefits of these IoT devices, there is some concern between maintaining an individual's safety and the potential privacy or computer security tradeoffs.

DATA, ANALYTICS AND DEATH

One overlooked aspect of data-driven decisions and analysis is the human element, specifically death and loss. With large populations living in these smart cities, a corresponding increase in the number of deaths will certainly follow. Western culture tends to purposefully overlook or avoid topics related to death despite it being a natural and unavoidable physical process. How then does this fit into data analytics and smart cities? Consider all the possible data points that can be collected about a user, and then extend this over the period of an individual's entire life span. This information can be used and analyzed in many ways, even after a person's death. We can specifically say that *Death Analytics* can be thought of as the analysis of data related to or about a specific person's death, death and dying (generally), or concerning the needs of terminally ill people. This is a broad definition that could be extended into other domains and for other use cases. While there can be more facets than just keeping track of the mortality rates of a population and performing calculations, we see it as a more detailed representation of key metrics of an individual or group. Within the scope of a smart city, seeing potential anomalies, trends, or other behaviors that are impacting death rates would be incredibly beneficial both from a health and safety aspect and city planning, and many others. In addition, there are benefits to maintaining digital artifacts left by the deceased to benefit the living.

Managing and maintaining all this data could be used to assist families of those who have died. We need to investigate ways we can best leverage technology to help those in need and those that have experienced the death of a loved one. Automated tools have the potential to collect changes in behavior, health, illness, and more as it relates to death and loss. Systems could track the utilization of resources and could be used to assist those in need. Just as smart city frameworks could adjust resources for traffic and energy, so too could automation be used to assist resource allocation for hospitals, palliative care and for other medical needs. In addition, this can be beneficial to ensure that those who experienced a loss can access grief counseling or other support services to aid the community (Breen, Kawashima, Joy, Cadell, Roth, Chow and Macdonald, 2020). If a city experiences a major event such as a natural disaster, tracking the needs of residents following a traumatic loss would also help support them (Walsh, 2007). Consider recent tracking of death rates, hospitalizations, and infections related to COVID-19 and how this was used to make important health decisions for cities, counties, and states. One can examine numerous data visualizations related to COVID-19 online. For example, consider Johns Hopkins Coronavirus Resource Center, where there are numerous data dashboards available with current data (Johns Hopkins Coronavirus Resource Center, 2022). However, there are other types of relevant data related to mortality rates that are also valuable.

The term thanatology can be defined as "the description or study of the phenomena of death and of psychological mechanisms for coping with them" (Merriam-Webster, n.d.). Whereas the related term thanatechnology is any technology that "include[s] all types of communication technology that can be used in the provision of death education, grief counseling, and thanatology research" (Solfka, 2012, p. 33). The related technology considered here is the data collected as part of a smart city framework using IoT devices in the context of death and dying to perform data analysis or in the context of examining or representing one's life after they have died. This data may be examined in order to perform some analysis on their life, trends leading to their death or to simply preserve their digital content. As more data is collected within this framework, information can be used in new and innovative ways. Technology has influenced how we deal with and interact with death in many new and profound ways. Some of this impacts how we grieve and how we interact with digital content that a loved one leaves behind (Bassett, 2022). Using the large amounts of data from smart cities, we can enhance residents' ability to deal with death, provide grief counseling, and provide additional options for memorialization. Digital memorialization allows explicitly for many opportunities for analyzing the impacts of death. In addition, residents can codify their final wishes, wills, and other documentation in a format that can be preserved and made available through technological means. Because blockchain technology can be used in conjunction with smart cities and IoT (Theodorou & Sklavos, 2019), consider the possibility of one's final wishes being preserved and secured through blockchain technology as this information would be open and immutable. Blockchain technology can be used in conjunction with smart cities and IoT (Theodorou & Sklavos, 2019).

CONSIDERING SOCIAL MEDIA

Imagine the case where residents in a smart city use technology, social media, cell phones, and more, along with interacting with a smart city's IoT sensor network and related applications over one's lifetime. As they would interact with this technology over their lifespan, this data would therefore contribute to the data left behind when they were to die. This would involve considerable information, mainly if most activities and life events could be recorded and stored. This could include keeping track of educational records, purchase history, medical information, communications, food consumption, transportation usage, resources, and much more. There would be massive amounts of data collected on each person. In other words, the data collected by the smart city infrastructure would become part of our digital footprint or digital legacy. In addition, posts on social media inevitably construct a narrative of our life events (Mitra, 2010), particularly if such use is over prolonged periods of our life, complete with timestamps and often even with geolocation information, images and/or video. Posts across social networking sites, blogs, and other social media become (intentionally or unintentionally) part of the online legacy one leaves behind. This information is often unintentional, considering that the metadata might be saved as part of a post. Posts on social media can have negative effects as well and cause feelings of regret after certain content has been posted, particularly if the content is very personal. This could be particularly troublesome if the content becomes part of someone's digital legacy and content is taken out of context. Also, one should consider posts that may be viewed by unintended audiences (Wang, Norcie, Komanduri, Acquisti, Leon, Cranor, 2011). All of this data has the potential to be analyzed and used in various ways. As mentioned earlier, if substantial amounts of data are retained (such as educational records, purchasing habits or more) then these digital artifacts would certainly be something one would not want publically available after their death. This also raises the question as to who would then be responsible for curating or managing that content, making sure that the data is shared, protected or deleted as the originator desired or would have desired.

In previous research, several key questions have been proposed that one can use to assess content as they are posting or storing information online or on a social networking site, or even in the context of virtual worlds, which include (Braman, Thomas, Vincenti, Dudley, Rodgers, 2013):

1.   Is this content something I'm alright with if it becomes part of my digital legacy?
2.   Is this content something that should be protected if something were to happen to me?
3.   If this content should be protected, how can it be protected?

These guiding questions can be used to assess if posted content could be potentially negative or contain content that one would not want to be saved as part of their legacy. Although this was originally aimed at social networking sites or thinking about virtual worlds, this can also be scaled to a larger context when thinking about the future potential of data collection in a smart city. It may be beneficial to add to these questions as other considerations are needed. This would include discovering what data has been collected on an individual. Has it been anonymized, or can this information lead to identifying the person? Who owns and manages the data? How is it being used? After the person is deceased, there is no way to monitor or assess how the data is being used (at least easily or directly). In some cases, if some of the collected data cannot be erased entirely (based on a person's final wishes), there should be a way to at least anonymize the data if it is still vital or beneficial. For example, consider the educational records of a student that dies suddenly. The school system may need some records to be maintained, but should that student's test scores or attendance records still be utilized? It can be argued that we have the right to be forgotten and deleted or, in other words, "exorcised" from various systems if that is one's final wishes (Braman & Dudley, 2022).

Considering Question number one can be difficult if one considers all content posted, saved, or recorded digitally in the context of a smart city. Many data points could be collected, often without a user's knowledge. The concern here would be data that may be private or data that could be aggregated to identify an individual can be used to discern more information about the individual. Question one is aimed at specific content that is posted that could potentially become part of a person's digital legacy. Consider when someone goes out to dinner and posts a photo of their food along with images of the friends they are with and the location. Compare this with a smart city view where that transaction for purchasing that dinner is saved and logged into a server or saved to the blockchain. The first situation is something that can be better controlled. Question two is difficult to assess as it is very subjective. Pictures, writings, videos, or even receipts may be meaningless to the creator but may have significant value to another person, particularly after death. Even insignificant data may have meaning to a loved one as it serves as a reminder and the fact that this data can never be created again by that person now that they are deceased. If a person knows, however that some information will be very helpful to others and should be protected in the event they were to die, then this would be relevant to what Question two is asking, for instance, a digitized family photo album, electronic documents, deeds, financial records, etc.

Question 3 is helpful in determining if content has value and needs to be protected, saved, or maintained in some way but with a focus on how it should be protected. Thinking about those sentimental photos or important financial records, how should they be protected, and how can they be passed on so that others can view them? Preserving important content in a digital format has also become a changing practice related to expressing grief through the digitization of pictures and other content (Gray & Coulton, 2013). Popular digital content often includes photographs, video, and text. Reminiscing through photographs is a way to interact with memories about the deceased that evokes emotions and can be seen as a ritual activity to help cope with the loss (Winokuer & Harris, 2016). A major concern would be how this concept is integrated into a smart city framework as thanatosensitive design would need to be considered in handling and maintaining data points from deceased users (Massimi & Charise, 2009).

In a related project that would be helpful in the case of a smart city system would be a program under development named SADD - A Social Media Agent for the Detection of the Deceased (Braman, Dudley & Vincenti, 2018). The SADD project aims to systematically identify accounts of users that are deceased on social networking sites. Although the automatic detection of accounts of deceased users is inherently problematic, there are many aspects that can lead to detection through various analyses of posted content, interactions and connections of accounts. Through the implementation of SADD we intend to research social media related to deceased user-profiles and explore how other users interact with the content. There are several benefits of the implementation of SADD, such as:

1. Potentially assisting families and friends in discovering unknown accounts of loved ones that have died.
2. Assisting social networking providers with an automated process to detect deceased users' accounts.
3. Identifying these accounts can help memorialize and save content.
4. Identifying accounts of deceased users can be beneficial for security reasons.

The detection of these profiles can allow family members to preserve content such as images, posts, and videos posted or stored within the deceased's account. In other studies, users have expressed the desire to have content preserved, either their own content when they are deceased or to protect a loved one's content (Braman, Dudley, Vincenti, 2017). There are complex issues related to the final wishes of the deceased if they are not known or ambiguous. Some questions to consider include:

- Who should maintain the profiles of the deceased?
- Is it known and verified that the original owner is indeed deceased?
- What were the final wishes of the deceased?
- What are the Terms of Service related to the accounts being considered?
- What content remains in the account?
- Is the content public or private information?

As technologies improve in the future, it will become easier to manage the social media content of the deceased as well as other information. Social media data combined with other collected information can provide meaningful insights on both individuals and on society. Data analysis of the data of the deceased within the context of smart cities can provide additional insights on how resources can be prioritized, data secured, and the health and wellbeing of its residents improved.

FUTURE RESEARCH DIRECTIONS

As part of our future work on this initiative, we are planning to examine and evaluate several IoT mesh networks and to evaluate and compare several smart city frameworks and the potential for integration. This will be insightful as we employ a close examination of the details of what specific types of data can be collected over time and how this information could impact users after their death. Expanding previous work, we will continue to gain feedback from users and their evaluation of the importance of the data they generate and the value they place on their social media content, as well as other data points that are collected during their lifetime in the context of their death. Additionally, as a next step based on feedback, we will examine ways to expand the above-mentioned questions (Braman et al., 2013) better to fit a smart city context for death-related analytics.

CONCLUSION

There is significant potential for research into the data analysis of the data generated by residents living in smart cities both from IoT sensors as well as the broader aggregate of their lifespan digital footprint, especially those that are deceased and how useful data can be collected through IoT. As an increasing amount of data is collected by these means, the ability to collect rich data points will continue to grow. Using this data to help those that are bereaved, terminally ill or to carry out the final wishes of the deceased (and to protect their data) will be advantageous. As the proliferation and popularity of smart cities invite more people to move to and work in them, considering death analytics and the data it can provide will be more important to consider.

REFERENCES

Ahmad, S., Hasan, M., Shahabuddin, M., Tabassum, T., & Allvi, M. W. (2020). IoT based pill reminder and monitoring system. *International Journal of Computer Science and Network Security*, *20*(7), 152–158.

Bassett, D. J. (2022). *The Creation and Inheritance of Digital Afterlives: You Only Live Twice. Palgrave Studies in the Future of Humanity and its Successors.* Palgrave Macmillan. doi:10.1007/978-3-030-91684-8

Bawany, N. Z., & Shamsi, J. A. (2015). Smart city architecture: Vision and challenges. *International Journal of Advanced Computer Science and Applications*, *6*(11).

Bhoi, S. K., Panda, S. K., Patra, B., Pradhan, B., Priyadarshinee, P., Tripathy, S., Singh, M., & Khilar, P. M. (2018). FallDS-IoT: a fall detection system for elderly healthcare based on IoT data analytics. In *2018 International Conference on Information Technology (ICIT)* (pp. 155-160). IEEE. 10.1109/ICIT.2018.00041

Braman, J., & Dudley, A. (2022). Do we need a digital data exorcism? End of life considerations of data mining educational content. In G. Trajkovski, M. Demeter, & H. Hayes (Eds.), *Applying Data Science and Learning Analytics Throughout a Learner's Lifespan.* IGI Global. doi:10.4018/978-1-7998-9644-9.ch013

Braman, J., Dudley, A., & Vincenti, G. (2017). Memorializing the deceased using virtual worlds: A preliminary study. *Proceedings of the 19th HCI International Conference on Online Communities and Social Computing.* 10.1007/978-3-319-58562-8_5

Braman, J., Dudley, A., & Vincenti, G. (2018). Designing SADD: A Social Media Agent for the Detection of the Deceased. *Proceedings of the 20th HCI International Conference on Online Communities and Social Computing.* 10.1007/978-3-319-91485-5_26

Braman, J., Thomas, U., Vincenti, G., Dudley, A., & Rodgers, K. (2013). Preparing your Digital Legacy: Assessing Awareness of Digital Natives. In G. Mallia (Ed.), The Social Classroom: Integrating Social Network Use in Education. Academic Press.

Breen, L. J., Kawashima, D., Joy, K., Cadell, S., Roth, D., Chow, A., & Macdonald, M. E. (2020). Grief literacy: A call to action for compassionate communities. *Death Studies*, 1–9. PMID:32189580

Dameri, R. (2013). Searching for smart city definition: A comprehensive proposal. *International Journal of Computers and Technology*, *11*(5), 2544–2551. doi:10.24297/ijct.v11i5.1142

Gray, S. E., & Coulton, P. (2013). Living with the dead: Emergent post-mortem digital curation and creation practices. In *Digital Legacy and Interaction* (pp. 31–47). Springer. doi:10.1007/978-3-319-01631-3_2

Hashem, I. A. T., Chang, V., Anuar, N. B., Adewole, K., Yaqoob, I., Gani, A., Ahmed, E., & Chiroma, H. (2016). The role of big data in smart city. *International Journal of Information Management*, *36*(5), 748–758. doi:10.1016/j.ijinfomgt.2016.05.002

Huh, J. H., & Seo, K. (2017). An indoor location-based control system using bluetooth beacons for IoT systems. *Sensors (Basel)*, *17*(12), 2917. doi:10.339017122917 PMID:29257044

Johns Hopkins Coronavirus Resource Center. (2022). *Follow global cases and trends. Updated daily.* https://coronavirus.jhu.edu/data

Mainetti, L., Patrono, L., Secco, A., & Sergi, I. (2016). An IoT-aware AAL system for elderly people. In *2016 International Multidisciplinary Conference on Computer and Energy Science (SpliTech)* (pp. 1-6). IEEE. 10.1109/SpliTech.2016.7555929

Massimi, M., & Charise, A. (2009). Dying, death, and mortality: towards thanatosensitivity in HCI. In CHI'09 Extended Abstracts on Human Factors in Computing Systems (pp. 2459-2468). doi:10.1145/1520340.1520349

Merriam-Webster. (n.d.). Thanatology. In *Merriam-Webster.com dictionary*. Retrieved February 1, 2022, from https://www.merriam-webster.com/dictionary/thanatology

Mulero, R., Almeida, A., Azkune, G., Abril-Jiménez, P., Waldmeyer, M. T. A., Castrillo, M. P., Patrono, L., Rametta, R., & Sergi, I. (2018). An IoT-aware approach for elderly-friendly cities. *IEEE Access: Practical Innovations, Open Solutions, 6*, 7941–7957. doi:10.1109/ACCESS.2018.2800161

PlanetWatch. (2021). *PlanetWatch White paper. Version 1.1*. https://www.planetwatch.us/white-paper/index-h5.html?page=1#page=1

PlanetWatch. (2022). https://www.planetwatch.us/

Richard, J., Braman, J., Colclough, M., & Bishwakarma, S. (2020). A Neural Affective Approach to an Intelligent Weather Sensor System. In C. Stephanidis, M. Antona, & S. Ntoa (Eds.), *HCI International 2020. "Late-Breaking Posters. HCII 2020. Communications in Computer and Information Science* (Vol. 1293). Springer. doi:10.1007/978-3-030-60700-5_46

Shahrestani, S. (2018). *Internet of things and smart environments*. Springer International Publishing.

Sofka, C., Cupit, I., & Gilbert, K. (2012). *Dying, death, and grief in an online universe: For counselors and educators*. Springer Publishing Company.

Srivastava, V. (2022). Cognitive Internet of Things: Exploring New Horizons for Elderly Care by Training Intelligent Devices. In *Information and Communication Technology for Competitive Strategies (ICTCS 2020)* (pp. 1085–1095). Springer. doi:10.1007/978-981-16-0739-4_100

Steward, K. (2020). *Real-time wastewater monitoring enables rapid COVID-19 outbreak detection*. Technology Networks. Retrieved from https://www.technologynetworks.com/applied-sciences/blog/real-time-wastewater-monitoring-enables-rapid-covid-19-outbreak-detection-337391

Style, A. P. A., & Mitra, A. (2010). Creating a Presence on Social Networks via Narbs. *Global Media Journal*, (9), 16.

Theodorou, S., & Sklavos, N. (2019). Blockchain-based security and privacy in smart cities. In *Smart Cities Cybersecurity and Privacy* (pp. 21–37). Elsevier. doi:10.1016/B978-0-12-815032-0.00003-2

United Nations. (2015). *The World Population Prospects: 2015 Revision*. https://www.un.org/en/development/desa/publications/world-population-prospects-2015-revision.html

Walsh, F. (2007). Traumatic loss and major disasters: Strengthening family and community resilience. *Family Process, 46*(2), 207–227. doi:10.1111/j.1545-5300.2007.00205.x PMID:17593886

Wang, P., Ali, A., & Kelly, W. (2015). Data security and threat modeling for smart city infrastructure. In 2015 international conference on cyber security of smart cities, industrial control system and communications (SSIC) (pp. 1-6). IEEE. doi:10.1109/SSIC.2015.7245322

Wang, Y., Norcie, G., Komanduri, S., Acquisti, A., Leon, P. G., & Cranor, L. F. (2011) I regretted the minute I pressed share: A qualitative study of regrets on Facebook. In *Proceedings of the Seventh Symposium on Usable Privacy and Security* (p. 10). ACM. 10.1145/2078827.2078841

Washburn, D., Sindhu, U., Balaouras, S., Dines, R. A., Hayes, N., & Nelson, L. E. (2009). Helping CIOs understand "smart city" initiatives. *Growth*, *17*(2), 1–17.

Winokuer, H., & Harris, D. (2016). *Principles and practice of grief counseling* (2nd ed.). Springer Publishing Company.

ADDITIONAL READING

Atitallah, S. B., Driss, M., Boulila, W., & Ghézala, H. B. (2020). Leveraging Deep Learning and IoT big data analytics to support the smart cities development: Review and future directions. *Computer Science Review*, *38*, 100303. doi:10.1016/j.cosrev.2020.100303

Beaunoyer, E., & Guitton, M. J. (2021). Cyberthanathology: Death and beyond in the digital age. *Computers in Human Behavior*, *122*, 106849. doi:10.1016/j.chb.2021.106849

Boyd, D., & Ellison, N. (2008). Social Network Sites: Definition, History, and Scholarship. *Journal of Computer-Mediated Communication*, *13*(1), 210–230. doi:10.1111/j.1083-6101.2007.00393.x

Carroll, E., & Romano, J. (2011). *Your Digital After Life*. New Riders.

Hughes, M. (1995). *Bereavement and Support: Healing in a Group Environment*. Taylor & Francis Publishing.

Littlewood, J. (1992). *Aspects of Grief: Bereavement in Adult Life*. Routledge.

Murthy, D. (2008). Digital Ethnography An Examination of the Use of New Technologies for Social Research. *Sociology*, *42*(5), 837–855. doi:10.1177/0038038508094565

Ren, Y., Harper, F. M., Drenner, S., Terveen, L., Kiesler, S., Riedl, J., & Kraut, R. E. (2012). Building member Attachment in Online Communities: Applying theories of group identity and interpersonal bonds. *Management Information Systems Quarterly*, *36*(3), 841–864. doi:10.2307/41703483

Sofka, C. J., Cupit, I. N., & Gilbert, K. R. (2012). *Dying, Death, and Grief in an online universe*. Springer Publishing Company.

Toh, C. K., Sanguesa, J. A., Cano, J. C., & Martinez, F. J. (2020). Advances in smart roads for future smart cities. *Proceedings of the Royal Society of London. Series A*, *476*(2233), 20190439. doi:10.1098/rspa.2019.0439 PMID:32082053

KEY TERMS AND DEFINITIONS

Bereavement: The condition of sorrow one experiences when they lose someone close to them especially through death.

Death Analytics: The analysis of data related to or about a specific person's death, death and dying (generally), or concerning the needs of terminally ill people. This is a broad definition that could be extended into other domains and for other use cases.

Digital Legacy: The remembrance or reflection of an individual through various digital mediums. This can be constructed through various ways included intended or unintended digital artifacts.

Memorialization: Process of preserving memories, information, a profile or other content of people or events. This can be done in memory of someone that has passed away.

Smart City: In general terms, a city that effectively leverages various technologies such as IoT to manage assets and monitor resources to better the lives of citizens.

Social Networking Site: An online service, platform or site that focuses on building and maintaining relationships which often includes various forms of interaction and the construction of a public representation for the user.

Thanatechnology: Technological mechanisms that are used to access information or aid in topics concerning thanatology. This can include technologies related to bereavement, memorialization and information preservation related to death.

Thanatology: Scientific study of death.

Section 50
Social Media Analytics

Usage of the Basic Facebook Features as Befitting Marketing Tools

Fahima Khanam

Business Administration, BSMR Aviation and Aerospace University, Bangladesh

Muhammad Omar Al-Zadid

Carson College of Business, Washington State University, USA

Mahmud Ullah

 https://orcid.org/0000-0001-7472-2477

Department of Marketing, University of Dhaka, Bangladesh

INTRODUCTION

The vital role of social media in modern business arena can hardly be overemphasized for both businesses and customers. During the last one decade or so, online shopping has become very popular among customers, especially buying from Facebook pages is pretty common. Facebook is the most preferred platform to the entrepreneurs for starting their business, out of all kinds of existing social media sites. They prefer to conduct many traditional marketing activities through online sites, preferably Facebook, to supplement the usual marketing activities of their offline businesses. Active existence of the businesses on both online & offline platforms is spurred mainly by the astonishing behavior of modern-day customers to use online channels to shop around and then actually buy from the offline stores ultimately.

In this technological world, customers are no longer in dark, rather they can get any kind of information, product reviews, recommendations etc. from social media sites at any time. This trend has created a scenario which empowers the customers with lots of options for taking their purchase decisions. On the other hand, businesses can grab this trend as an opportunity for expanding current customer base and flourishing profit line.

Today, most of the marketers in Bangladesh too, extensively use social media to remain well connected with the customers, and competitive in their respective business field. Strategically, businesses are using Facebook for branding their products and services as it will help increase the awareness level of customers resulting into reaching and creating more and more customer bases. However, the growing popularity of social media, particularly Facebook, is also bringing up the issues of trustworthiness and effectiveness of these sites.

Customers verify the quality of products or services based on various factors as they do not always feel safe to purchase online randomly because of some negative incidents take place every now and then. Businesses use certain tools and policies for promoting and branding products and services which have significant effects on customers' purchase decisions.

This chapter intends & aims to focus on identifying and analyzing the effective and befitting Facebook marketing tools and features used by marketers. It also examines how these Facebook marketing strategies influence or affect customers' purchase decisions. The very technological, visual, and universally

DOI: 10.4018/978-1-7998-9220-5.ch174

accepted content design of Facebook provides many befitting marketing tools which have beneficial scopes for conducting business operations.

BACKGROUND

Facebook has become the most effective platform for promoting different brands of almost all kinds of products and services because of its enviable popularity as the most widely reached medium for selling and buying activities in Bangladesh during the recent few years. Facebook applications and features are designed in such a way which can be used to attract consumers' attention and address the issues of customization as per their specific individual needs.

Another beneficial thing about using Facebook to promote and sell products and services is the opportunity to remain connected 24/7 with all the relevant parties in a cost-effective way. Most importantly, this 24/7 connectivity at a low cost is a highly favorable feature for the small businesses who are basically doing business only on Facebook. Facebook, one of the most profitable medium, is way more superior to, and influential over the traditional marketing strategies.

People can get reviews and feedbacks from other users about products and services by joining in a group or just from a page. They can observe the friends' activities as well as the advertisements pop up on the screen while scrolling their home pages on Facebook. User experiences and promotional materials affect the perception level of customers regarding a brand. Strategically, customers check their familiar persons' Facebook profile or the profile of the celebrities for getting the idea of the products and brands they are using or planning to use sometime in future.

Undoubtedly, pages with more likes and shares are considered to be the more authentic ones by the customers in general. More updated information and posts with wide engagement with various sources can increase the level of acceptance of a business to customers. Companies and service providers have begun to research and investigate the usage and efficiency of Facebook advertising, the applications, and the various ways customers are using to judge a brand in order to improve their brand position.

It is necessary for the companies and brands to find out the factors, definitely the most influential ones, for building up their strategies to boost their business performance. Customers' shared posts and check-ins are the most influential tools for a business. While consumers steadily choose brand groups on Facebook as trusted sources of information, new opportunities arise to build unique brand awareness and viral advertising platforms. This study is attempting to have a better understanding the influence and impact of the Facebook features, or Facebook marketing in a word, on the ultimate buying / purchase intention or behavior of the consumers.

The authors basically attempt to measure the utilities and effects of the Facebook features to be used as befitting marketing tools to influence consumers to make their purchases or demonstrate their responses on Facebook. The survey was designed to collect data to find whether Facebook marketing had ever affected them and generated their intention to purchase a particular product on or from Facebook shops, and if it had, to what extent. Though Facebook marketing is a rapidly growing concept in Bangladesh, not much of notable research has yet been done in this area so far.

In this context, this study / paper would definitely enrich the understanding level of the people engaged in Facebook marketing or just in any business as such, regarding the customers' perception of the Facebook features as the effectively used marketing tools. These results can be used in global context as well.

FOCUS OF THE STUDY

Facebook Features

Just like almost all the countries around the world, Bangladesh also has enormous number of Facebook users. It is widely used by the Bangladeshi people for various purposes - from mere social contact to establishing or running an online business. As a result, online businesses are growing and expanding by opening Facebook pages, which is a very easy, simple and convenient process to operate and handle. There are many other ways to start and boost businesses via Facebook (Al-Hadban, AL-Ghamdi, Al-Hassoun and Hamdi, 2014).

Facebook Page

A Facebook page is the most effective way for an organization to get engaged with the customers and create a favorable network for the customer base. People, generally share the page link to their friends and familiar members if they want to recommend a brand to them. This process increases the opportunities for the brand to grow, leads to increased sharing of information, and results into gradual increase in sales at the end.

News Feed

The main part of the Facebook where people can find all the information of the pages of brands, other people's profile or related/suggested pages/links and updates of friends' activities within the site is known as homepage. Facebook users can customize their options. The users have the option to filter of what they would like to see to be displayed at a given time.

Wall Posts

People who are the holders of Facebook ids can post messages, thoughts, contents, stories, or pictures from their profile which will be shown in the homepage/wall. A person can comment on others' wall posts. A wall is often the overview of a user's profile or page.

Groups

According to Facebook, groups are "for members of groups to connect, share and even collaborate on a given topic or idea". Generally, a group can be formed based on common thing or interest and is created by individual or an organization. This is a very effective Facebook application tool for sharing common thoughts and building up a community for a purpose.

Events

The most recent popular aspect of Facebook is creating events for inviting people for inauguration of shops, seminars, fairs, selling products, announcing food fair, or special celebration, for example, celebrating 50 years or birthdays etc. A user can create an event invitation and sent to as many registered users as the creator desires. These events can be location based or online platform based or both.

Discussion Boards

This feature can be enabled on many types of websites, allowing users to post questions, ideas, or comments in order to get responses and prompting a discussion. This is a useful application to create an interactive environment and to get feedback on a topic.

Pictures

Facebook has earned the high-ticket image for its suitability for sharing pictures of memories, and moments or happiness. Users can add a visual element to Facebook profiles, pages, groups, and event invitations, or they simply may share images to their friends. For a business organization, this feature is mostly perfect for promoting a brand, or showing the details of an offering. In case of online businesses, it can be detrimental as well. Pictures of products of a business page is very often taken and used by other pages without any permission.

Literature Review

The rapid growth of social media platforms has permanently altered the way that numerous consumers interact with each other, and organizations. Hence, this has changed the way that organizations attract and retain prospective consumers (Leung et al., 2015). Previously, marketers would create captivating advertising messages and purchase space in the mass media in the hope that consumers would become aware of, develop a preference to, and eventually purchase the brand. Social media has irrevocably altered marketing communications by shifting ways in which consumers select, share, and appraise information.

Social Media as Marketing Platforms

In today's technology driven world, social networking sites have become an avenue where retailers can extend their marketing campaigns to a wider range of consumers. Chi (2011) defines social media marketing as a "connection between brands and consumers, [while] offering a personal channel and currency for user centered networking and social interaction." The tools and approaches for communicating with customers have changed greatly with the emergence of social media; therefore, businesses must learn how to use social media in a way that is consistent with their business plan (Mangold and Faulds, 2009).

Consequently, marketers are increasing their social media budgets with digital interactive advertising forecasted to reach $138 billion in 2014, a growth rate of nearly 15 per cent in comparison to 2013 (eMarketer, 2014a). Furthermore, the Middle East and Africa are predicted to have the highest social media advertising spend growth (64 per cent) in 2014 (eMarketer, 2014c). Business-to-consumer (B2C) ecommerce revenue is expected to reach $1.5 trillion in 2014 (an increase of 20 per cent), with growth primarily coming from emerging markets (eMarketer, 2014b). Current figures reveal that the largest online social medium in the world is Facebook, with 1.32 billion active members, and it is also the largest social commerce site that accounts for 85 per cent of all orders from social media (Facebook, 2014a; Shopify, 2014).

The aforementioned evidence necessitates research into behavioral attitudes towards Facebook in an emerging country like Bangladesh which will be of interest to managers and their organizations.

Communication Efficacies in Facebook Marketing

The worldwide adoption of mobile phones has driven Facebook's mobile impetus, as the number of consumers that access the internet via mobile is closing the gap on computer-based online users. World Wide Worx indicated that there are 9.4 million active Facebook users in SA (making it the largest social medium in the country), with 87 per cent accessing Facebook via mobile devices such as cell phones and smart phones (Wronski and Goldstruck, 2013). Few studies have determined whether social media advertising is effective when accessed via mobile devices, which is examined in this paper. A review of Facebook's global advertising performance indicated that click-through rates had improved by 20 per cent from 2011 to 2012 (AYTM, 2012).

Furthermore, the cost per click had risen by over a quarter and the cost per thousand increased by more than half. However, Greenlight (2012) found that 44 per cent of consumers did not ever click on Facebook advertisements, 31 per cent rarely did, 10 per cent often did and 3 per cent clicked regularly. While Associated Press and CNBC (2012) reported that over eight out of ten Facebook users never or seldom viewed Facebook advertisements or their sponsored content. However, Reuters and Ipsos (2012) revealed that one in five Facebook users had purchased products as a result of advertisements and/or comments that they viewed on Facebook.

Chandra *et al.* (2012) conducted research into attitudes towards SNA among undergraduate and postgraduate students. The study found that social media advertising aided the purchase decision and resulted in more competitive prices but held unfavorable attitudes in terms of various cognitive (information) and affective (enjoyment, entertainment value and authenticity) components (lower level pyramid activities). Powers *et al.* (2012) agreed with the aforementioned sentiments and disclosed that over 20 per cent of consumers believed that social media was important for their final purchase decision; while another 20 per cent stated that it helped them to decide what to purchase.

Consumer Attitudes/Motives

It is vital for retailers and marketers to be aware of the factors that affect consumer attitudes and motives because consumers are increasingly creating content about brands, something previously controlled solely by companies (Heinonen, 2011). As a result, current research has examined what aspects of social media sites affect consumer attitudes and motives.

Chu (2011) examined the link between Facebook brand related group participation, advertising responses, and the psychological factors of self-disclosure and attitudes among members and nonmembers of Facebook groups. The study determined that users who are members of groups on Facebook are more likely to disclose their personal data than nonmembers are. Chu (2011) explains group participation and engagement with online ads requires a higher level of personal information because users openly reveal their connections with Facebook groups and promote brands or products when they pass on ads to their friends. "Facebook groups provide channels that consumers deem useful when seeking self-status in a product category, as does passing on viral content about brands to their social contacts" (Chu 2011).

Chu (2011) also found that users who are Facebook group members maintain a more favorable attitude toward social media and advertising. Users who have more positive attitudes toward advertising are more likely to join a brand or a retailer's Facebook group to receive promotional messages. Based on this result, Chu (2011) suggests that a link exists between consumers' use of and engagement in group applications on a social media site.

The relationship between consumers' use of and engagement with group applications influences the rate and effectiveness of advertising on social media, particularly Facebook. Generally, as Chu (2011) notes, Facebook's college-aged users have the most favorable attitudes toward social media advertising and are the largest growing demographic, which suggests that social media sites are a potentially rich platform for online advertising campaigns, especially for companies with a younger target market.

Cox (2010) also investigated the correlation between age and attitude and found that social network user attitude toward online advertising formats (i.e. blogs, video, and brand channel or page) differed to some extent across age groups. She explains that users who fall in the 18- 28 age brackets had strong positive attitudes towards blogs, video, and brand channel ad formats. This was because users found these ad formats to be eye catching, informative, and amusing. The 35-54 age groups preferred ad formats on video and brand channels.

User Generated Content

The fact that social media, despite being technology-driven, will be stranded without human users from society renders a different view of social media. As Gonzalez (2010) describes it, the individuals play the main role as influencers instead of technology and thus endless ways of communication emerge across social media. These individual users are the fuel of the social media concept. In order to distinguish a brand, a value is required which is well represented by the content generated by all these users. According to Kaplan and Haenlein (2010), user generated content takes into account all the ways used by people to utilize social media and also encompasses all the content created and made available by the users.

One type of user generated content is Consumer Generated Advertising (CGA) which requires consumers to generate the idea of a brand and devise specific messages in order to disseminate the message to other users (Campbell et al. 2011). Campbell et al. (2011) claim that traditional marketing might be either positively or negatively supported by CGA. Therefore, social media marketers must be vigilant about any negative effect of CGA on traditional marketing campaign. This trend is also reflected in Cheong and Morrison's (2010) study which recommended marketers to obtain a greater understanding of UGC in order to trace any negative impact of it on the conventional marketing campaigns. It is evident that consumers are actively participating in product reviewing, publicly consuming products and services, establishing various platforms within social media (Heinonen, 2011).

Another type of UGC is Firm Generated Advertising (FGA) which is yet more different from CGA (Pehlivan, Sarican, and Berthon, 2011). FGA generates a completely different type of discussion regarding the advertisement of a product. Though FGA is more likely to affect the consumers positively, consumers find CGA more engaging and interesting as well. (Pehlivan, Sarican, and Berthon, 2011).

According to Taylor, Strutton, and Thompson (2012), the tendency of social media users to express different messages about an offering is triggered by people's desire for self-enhancement. Consumers are more likely to share their feelings and messages about a product as they find it synchronizing with their personality and preferences. This way they can express their identity in the form if us\age of a product. Taylor, Strutton, and Thompson (2012, 13) also support this view by suggesting advertisers to look for different symbols and signs related to targeted consumer's identity and personality and express them in their ads in order to align them with consumers' self-perceptions. In these studies, the importance of CGA is reflected in a very convincing manner.

Richard and Guppy (2014) examined the effect of Facebook marketing on consumer purchase intention in which five distinct 5 variables were used such as Likes, Friends' Likes, Location-based Check-ins, Comment posting and Sharing. Friends' likes were found to have the strongest effect on consumers' purchase intention.

Whereas Location-based check-in and Sharing moderately influenced consumers' purchase intention, comment postings were found to have little or no effect at all.

Like

One of the most popular and iconic features of Facebook is a blue thumb up button which is called Like. How many people are liking a particular content is reflected by this sign. Apart from evaluating the quality of a content, the "Like" feature also provides valuable information about an individual's personality and preferences (Kosinski, et al., 2013). "Like" function is used in both content and pages in Facebook. This function allows users to get engaged with a page on regular basis. Whenever a user "likes" a certain page, he/she becomes a regular viewer of its content. Nowadays, businesses open their own Facebook page and attract users through various means to "like" their pages. Such a "like" turns a normal user a subscriber/fan of this page and send regular updates to the users' newsfeed. Even users are also exposed to the activities of other fans of this page as well. (Nelson-Field et al., 2012). This is how businesses can also make their advertisements, reviews, recommendations more visible to a certain number of users.

Friends' Likes

Harris and Denis (2011) explain that friends' reviews on social media sites, due to their credibility, cast a great impact on consumers' purchase decisions. Therefore, Friends' Likes are often taken into account with greater importance for its substantial effect on consumers' decision-making process during forming a purchase intention. Harris and Dennis (Harris and Dennis, 2011) claimed that people tend to shop through both online and social media as well. Though both trends were rising, consumers are more likely to use social media for purchases by observing friends' recommendations through Facebook. Even though Google is the most-acclaimed search that caters to the varying needs of people, they trust what their friends recommend purchasing.

Comment

Businesses commonly participate in interactive conversations with their customers online through the "Comment" feature of Social media. (Kietzmann et al., 2011; Kwok & Yu, 2012; Linke, & Zerfass, 2012; Lipsman et al., 2012; Lovejoy et al., 2012; Mangold and Faulds, 2009; Rao, 2012; Yan, 2011; Zauner et al., 2012). Social media have facilitated the interaction between parties to such a larger degree that consumers can communicate with other unknown customers beside businesses only by the means of "Comment" feature (Porter et al., 2011).

Debatin et al. (2009) also identifies that the short comments a user leaves are exposed to the other users of his/her network instantaneously on their newsfeed. Hennig-Thurau et al., (2004) describes the act of posting a comment and writing a review of an offering similar to the electronic word of mouth disseminated among a wide range of users. Comments have a powerful impact on consumers' perception.

On the other hand, positive comments act as non-paid advertisements for businesses involved. Today many consumers log into Facebook in order to search different products and services. In such cases, the comment section of an offering of a business can play a tremendously effective role in shaping the consumers' purchase intention. However, the effect of comments posted by friends and other users on purchase intention has been studied on a very limited scale.

Location Based Check-In Service

The location tracking is widely used today in all mobile applications. Using this facility, a user can express her/his position on a certain place, such as restaurants, tourist spots, coffee shops, fashion houses, shopping malls, convention centers, etc. by selecting the place name on Facebook. This act is distinctively called "Check-In, more specifically "Location Based Check- In".

This feature is perfectly used by retailers by offering discounts and other benefits to the customers who make a "Check-in" in their business outlet. Such a practice has the potential to be used as an alternative of Coupon card and loyalty user facilities (Slutsky, 2010). Bilogrevic et al. (2015) views "Location Based Check-in" in a subtler manner by claiming that such a feature often reveals the geographical coordinates and other semantic information of a particular place such as a restaurant, or a place of event or gathering more available to other users, while consumers are also accepting such a practice very positively.

Share

Another popular feature of Facebook is the option to "Share" a certain page, content, or post. Simply by clicking on the "Share" button, a user shares a post, or page with all his/her friends on Facebook, even with all public. Every 20 minutes one million links are shared on Facebook (Branckaute, 2010). Generally, consumers share a content or a business page when they find it worthy or important. Even this feature is so interactive that if a page or business page is shared several times on Facebook it makes a post/business page widely exposed throughout the newsfeed of many other users by showing how many times it has been shared by other users or friends. The more a post/business page is visible on others' newsfeed, the more likely is it that other users will also share the same content/business page which will lead to a manifold spread of a certain content/business page.

Conceptual Framework and Hypothesis Development

This study will try to measure the significance of the Facebook features as marketing tools in online marketing. From the study of Richard and Guppy (2014) mentioned in the literature review section, 5 distinct variables have been used in this study to measure their influence on consumers' perception of Facebook as an online shopping platform and their intention to make a purchase on or from it in the context of Bangladesh. They are: likes, friends' likes, location based check-ins, comment posting, and sharing. Using this model, the hypotheses can be developed as below:

H_0: Facebook features are not befitting and effective marketing tools and do not significantly influence consumers' intention to purchase online on Facebook platform.

H_1: Facebook features are befitting and effective marketing tools and significantly influence consumers' intention to purchase online on Facebook platform.

Figure 1. Conceptual Framework
(developed by the authors)

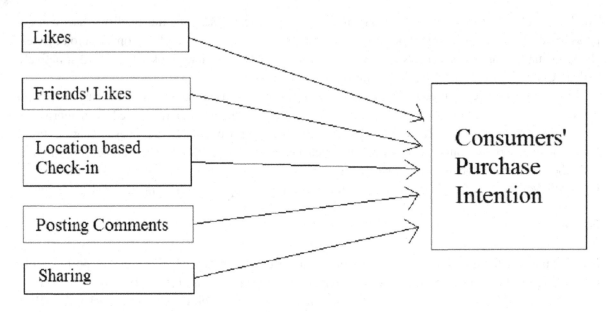

RESEARCH DESIGN, ANALYSES, AND FINDINGS

Both primary and secondary data have been collected for analyses. A Questionnaire having structured questions with multiple answers on five-point Likert scale was administered on respondents chosen by convenience sampling to collect primary data. All possible sources were explored to collect secondary data.

Since this is quantitative research, it involved some quantitative analyses with the use of statistical tools (descriptive and inferential). Multiple Linear Regression Model has been used to measure the association between five Facebook variables and consumers' purchase intention on the basis of acceptance and non-acceptance of the formulated hypothesis. SPSS version 16 package was used for the analyses of data. Descriptive statistics was used that mainly contained in the model summary, ANOVA table, coefficient chart, and correlation matrix.

Model Summary

See Table 1.

Table 1. Model Summary

Model	R	R Square	Adjusted R Square	Std. Error of the Estimate
1	.587	.344	.315	.873

a. Predictors: (Constant), Share, Comment, Like, Friends' Likes, Location based Check-in

Explanation

Here, by stating the model summary of the research, the researchers have tried to identify the association between Facebook marketing and purchase intention created in consumers. R is called the correlation coefficient that represents the strength of association between dependent variable and independent variables. Its value ranges between -1 and +1. When the value of **R** is positive, it suggests a positive association between dependent variable and independent variables (Malhotra and Dash, 2012-2013). From the above table, the value of **R is .587** which indicates that there is a positive association between Facebook marketing and consumers' purchase intention in Bangladesh.

From the aforementioned figure, it can be observed that the value of **R square is .344** which means that dependent variable is weakly associated with independent variables, i.e. **34.4%** of variance in dependent variable is explained by independent variables. "The strength of association is measured by the coefficient of determination, R^2. It varies between 0 and 1 and signifies the proportion of the total variation in Y that is accounted for by the variation in X." (Malhotra and Dash, 2012-2013).

Here, the value of adjusted R square is **.315**. As little difference between R square and adjusted R square can be noticed, there is no opportunities to add more variables. "R^2 is adjusted for the number of independent variables and the sample size to account for diminishing returns. After the first few variables, the additional independent variables do not make much contribution." (Malhotra and Dash, 2012-2013).

ANOVA Table

See Table 2.

Table 2. ANOVA

	Model	Sum of Squares	df	Mean Square	F	Sig.
	Regression	45.557	5	9.111	11.965	.000[a]
1	**Residual**	86.810	114	.761		
	Total	132.367	119			

a. Predictors: (Constant), Share, Comment, Like, Friends' Likes, Check-in
b. Dependent Variable: I would like to try a product recommended in Facebook.

Explanation

According to Malhotra and Dash (2012-2013), "the F test is used to test the null hypothesis that the coefficient of multiple determination in the population R^2 is zero. This is equivalent to testing the null hypothesis." The significance level in the model was 0.00 which is less the 5% level of significance used in the model. It therefore follows that the model is statistically significant in predicting how the independent variables affect consumers' online purchase intention. On the other hand, F critical at 5% significance level is 3.17 while the F - calculated is 11.965. It therefore follows that the overall model is significant since the F - calculated is greater than the F-critical.

Coefficient Analysis

Using the values shown in table 3, the regression model developed is as follows:

Consumers' purchase intention = .981 (Constant) + .026 (Likes) - 0.146 (Friends' Likes) + 0.067 (Location Based Check-In) + 0.200 (Comment) + 0.500 (Share) + e_i (error term).

Table 3. Coefficient Chart

Model		Unstandardized Coefficients		Standardized Coefficients	t	Sig.
		B	Std. Error	Beta		
1	(Constant)	.981	.429		2.288	.024
	Like	.028	.092	.026	.300	.765
	Friends' Likes	-.145	.093	-.146	-1.564	.121
	Check in	.063	.088	.067	.713	.477
	Comment	.201	.082	.200	2.436	.016
	Share	.624	.117	.500	5.322	.000

a. Dependent Variable: I would like to try a product recommended in Facebook.

The beta coefficients are the partial regression coefficients obtained. It "denotes the change in the predicted value Y, per unit change in X when the other independent variables are held constant." (Malhotra and Dash, 2012-2013)

Standardized coefficients calculated for each predictor variables, showing the percentage of variation in the dependent variable caused by the individual independent variables. It can be revealed that only the variable **'Share'** is significant at **5%** level. The Standardized beta coefficient of using **share** function is **0.500** (the highest) which means it is also the most important variable that influences purchase intention. The second important variable is **'Comment'**. Its standardized coefficient is **0.200.** The third most important variable is **'Check-in'** having a standardized coefficient of **0.067.** The next important variable is **'Like'** having a standardized coefficient of **0.026.** The only variable that has a negative standardized beta coefficient is **'Friend's Like'.** However, except the **'Share'** variable, no other variables are significant at 5% level.

Correlation Matrix Analysis

From the correlation matrix shown below in table 4, it is evident that maximum correlation values are less than 0.5. If the maximum values of correlation matrix exceed 0.5, then the research result is suffering from multi-collinearity problem. "Multi-collinearity arises when the inter-correlations among the predictors are very high." (Malhotra and Dash, 2012- 2013). So it can be concluded that the research result is not suffering from the multi-collinearity problem.

Table 4. Correlation Matrix

	Try a Product Recommended in Facebook (DV)	Like	Friends' Likes	Check-in	Comment	Share
Try a product recommended in Facebook. (DV)	1.000	.235	.168	.287	.356	**.544**
Like	.235	1.000	.345	.298	.155	.417
Friends' Likes	.168	.345	1.000	**.516**	.251	.440
Check-in	.287	.298	.516	1.000	.320	.448
Comment	.356	.155	.251	.320	1.000	.334
Share	.544	.417	.440	.448	.334	1.000

Hypothesis Testing

H_0: Facebook features are not befitting and effective marketing tools and do not significantly influence consumers' intention to purchase online on Facebook platform.

H_1: Facebook features are befitting and effective marketing tools and significantly influence consumers' intention to purchase online on Facebook platform.

From the coefficient table, there are no values of significance level which are below 0.05. The significance values for the five independent variables are 0.765, 0.121, 0.477, 0.016, 0.000.

So, the null hypothesis - Facebook features are not befitting and effective marketing tools and do not significantly influence consumers' intention to purchase online on Facebook platform - can be rejected. And hence, it can be concluded that the basic Facebook features are befitting and effective marketing tools and significantly influence consumers' intention to purchase online on Facebook platform.

MANAGERIAL IMPLICATIONS AND RECOMMENDATIONS

The study digs out several implications for the managers who are intending to promote their products or brands on Facebook. The following implications may be considered, and the recommendations made thereof may be followed.

- **Making the consumers more aware of the Facebook functions:** It is clearly seen from the study that the Bangladeshi consumers are using the Facebook functions subconsciously. Their participation is confined to only liking products' pages or posts and sharing them. So, marketing managers might think of making them understand the significance of likes, comments, and shares. They can be informed that these functions matter for the brand, and the product.
- **Importance of sharing:** According to the result, since sharing is the most important variable to influence the purchase intention, the marketers can leverage out of this function by engaging the consumers with more and more sharing.
- **Boosting check-in:** It is interesting that check-in is positioned in the middle of the coefficients in terms of importance. It might imply that the managers might generate more check-ins to their stores or events to capture the potentials.

FUTURE RESEARCH DIRECTIONS

The basic Facebook features have been proven to be perfectly befitting, effective, and efficient marketing tools, and have been happily used by the established and new businesses and entrepreneurs. Due to its unstoppable ever-increasing growth in an exponential rate for more than almost two decades now, new issues of concerns regarding its overall management as a giant are evolving and are very likely to amplify in the coming years. This could be a field of future research to develop and implement timely strategies to manage Facebook, so that it continues to provide improved services to the world.

Most alarming concern is the negative use of these Facebook features as fruitful marketing tools at all levels, viz. individual, group, social, national, and global. People take the advantages of the Facebook facilities to do fraudulent practices with others. At individual level, anyone with a bad motive may plot an apparently decent financial or relationship scheme full of fraudulent intentions to cheat anyone anytime anywhere in the world. At upper levels, i.e., group, social, national, or global levels, much more harmful, dangerous, and perilous uses of these basic Facebook features as befitting marketing tools are already evident in many incidences in different countries around the world during the last couple of decades or so. Conduct mass campaign on some social, political, national, or international issues with bad intention to create unrest and chaos in the society, country, or world has become a common practice during the last few years, especially during the Corona pandemic in the last couple of years. This is a one of the most important aspects to deal with to protect people and the whole world from the harmful uses of the Facebook, and hence lot of research opportunities are and will be there to serve the mankind by preventing the fraudsters from using these Facebook features negatively to implement their evil intentions for personal purposes at the cost of others' comfort.

The authors suggest that these fields of research relating to the Facebook features used negatively as effective marketing tools may be generously funded by the Facebook itself, and the other corporate funding agencies as a part of their corporate social responsibilities (CSR) to explore all these issues to find sustainable solutions to the seriously dreadful problems evolved out of the negative uses of these Facebook features as marketing tools for evil purposes.

CONCLUSION

Today social media is considered to have superseded all other media and platforms and conquered the people's internal lives and even privacy to such an extent that most of the people cannot even think of their lives without having presence in the social media sites. The advantages and comforts of social media turned us severely & helplessly dependent on them. Keeping this reality in mind, it has become obligatory for marketers to make a wise use of social media for widespread marketing of their offerings. Facebook based marketing has already become a new discipline for students to study, and for researchers to unfold more of it. The more such ways will come forward, the stronger the social media-based marketing will become to attract customers.

In such a scenario, the businesses that will ignore the new trend and practice, and neglect consumers' new mindset, will lose the game in the long run. However, marketers will also continue to innovate new sorts of campaigns that might be run on social media as it has apparently no limit at all. Besides, social media-based marketing must be concurrent with the conventional marketing strategies with a similar pace and focus. Lastly, the fact that the number of customers of various businesses in Facebook is ever-growing in Bangladesh, marketers must ensure that they will grab the attention of this portion of customers to make the best use of this marketing platform.

REFERENCES

Al-Hadban, N., AL-Ghamdi, H., Al-Hassoun, T., & Hamdi, P. R. (2014). The effectiveness of Facebook marketing tool: Saudi Arabia case study. *International Journal of Management & Information Technology*, *10*(2), 1815–1827. doi:10.24297/ijmit.v10i2.637

Associated Press & CNBC. (2012). *Is there a problem with Facebook advertising?* www.emarketer.com/Article.aspx?R=1009065. 2017/07/27.

AYTM. (2012). *Facebook marketers find better payoff with sponsored stories.* www.emarketer.com/Article/Facebook-Marketers-Find-Better-Payoff-with-Sponsored-Stories/1009109. 2017/07/27.

Bilogrevic, I. (2015). Predicting users' motivations behind location check-ins and utility implications of privacy protection mechanisms. *NDSS Symposium 2015, Internet Society.* 10.14722/ndss.2015.23032

Branckaute, F. (2010). *Facebook statistics: The numbers game continues.* Web blog post. https://www.blogherald.com/

Campbell, Pitt, L. F., Parent, M., & Berthon, P. R. (2011). Understanding consumer conversations around ads in a web 2.0 world. *Journal of Advertising*, *40*(1), 87–102. doi:10.2753/JOA0091-3367400106

Cheong, H. J., & Margaret, A. M. (2008). Consumers' reliance on product information and recommendations found in UGC. *Journal of Interactive Advertising*, *8*(2), 38–49. doi:10.1080/15252019.2008.10722141

Chi, H-H. (2011). Interactive digital advertising vs virtual brand community: Exploratory study of user motivation and social media marketing responses in Taiwan. *Journal of Interactive Advertising, 12*(1), 44-61.

Chu, S-C. (2011). Viral advertising in social media: Participation in Facebook groups and responses among college-aged users. *Journal of Interactive Advertising, 12*(1), 30-43.

Cox, S. A. (2010). *Online social network member attitude toward online advertising formats* [MA thesis]. The Rochester Institute of Technology.

e-Marketer. (2014a). *Digital ad spending worldwide to hit $137.53 billion in 2014.* www.emarketer.com/Article/Digital-Ad-Spending-Worldwide-Hit-3613753-Billion-2014/1010736/8

e-Marketer. (2014b). *Global B2C ecommerce sales to hit $1.5 trillion this year driven by growth in emerging markets.* www.emarketer.com/Article/Global-B2C-Ecommerce-Sales-Hit-15-Trillion-This-Year-Driven-by-Growth-Emerging-Markets/1010575

Facebook. (2014a). *Company info.* https://newsroom.fb.com/company- info/

Gonzalez, C. (2010). *Social media best practices for communication professionals through the lens of the fashion industry* [MA thesis]. The University of Southern California.

Greenlight (2012). *Facebook sponsored advertisements – 44% of people say they would never click on them.* www.bizcommunity.com/Article/196/12/75429.html

Hague, P., & Jackson, P. (1996). *Marketing research: A guide to planning methodology and evaluation* (1st ed.). Kogan Page.

Harris, L., & Dennis, C. (2011). Engaging customers on Facebook: Challenges for e-retailers. *Journal of Consumer Behaviour, 10*(6), 338–346.

Heinonen, K. (2011). Consumer activity in social media: Managerial approaches to consumers' social media behavior. *Journal of Consumer Behaviour, 10*(6), 356–364.

Kaplan, A. M., & Haenlein, M. (2010). Users of the world, unite: The challenges and opportunities of social media. *Business Horizons, 53*(1), 59–68.

Kietzmann, J. H., Hermkens, K., Mccarthy, I. P., & Silvestre, B. S. (2011). Social media? Get serious! Understanding the functional building blocks of social media. *Business Horizons, 54*(3), 241–251.

Kosinski, M., Stillwell, D., & Graepel, T. (2013). Private traits and attributes are predictable from digital records of human behavior. *Proceedings of the National Academy of Sciences of the United States of America.* doi: 10.1073/pnas.1218772110

Leung, X. Y., Bai, B., & Stahura, K. A. (2015). The marketing effectiveness of social media in the hotel industry: A comparison of Facebook and Twitter. *Journal of Hospitality & Tourism Research (Washington, D.C.), 39*(2), 147–169.

Malhotra, N. K., & Dash, S. (2012-2013). Correlation and regression. *Marketing research: An applied orientation,* 529-530.

Mangold, G. W., & Faulds, D. J. (2009). Social media: The new hybrid element of the promotion mix. *Business Horizons, 52*(4), 357–365.

Pehlivan, E., Funda, S., & Berthon, P. (2011). Mining messages: Exploring consumer response to consumer vs. Firm generated ads. *Journal of Consumer Behaviour, 10*(6), 313–321.

Porter, C., Donthu, N., MacElroy, W., & Wydra, D. (2011). How to foster and sustain engagement in virtual communities. *California Management Review, 53*(4), 80–110.

Powers, T., Advincula, D., Austin, M. S., Graiko, S., & Snyder, J. (2012). Digital and social media in the purchase decision process. *Journal of Advertising Research, 52*(4), 479–489.

Reuters & Ipsos. (2012). *Can Facebook go beyond earned media success?* www.emarketer.com/Article/Facebook-Go-Beyond-Earned-Media-Success/1009127

Richard, J. E., & Guppy, S. (2014). Facebook: Investigating the influence on consumer purchase intention. *Asian Journal of Business Research, 4*(2), 11.

Shopify. (2014). *Facebook is no. 1 for social commerce.* www.emarketer.com/Article/Facebook-No-1-Social-Commerce/1010721

Taylor, D. G., Strutton, D., & Thompson, K. (2012). Self enhancement as a motivation for sharing online advertising. *Journal of Interactive Advertising, 12*(2), 13–28.

Wronski, M., & Goldstruck, A. (2013). *South African social media landscape 2014*. www.worldwide-worx.com, www.fuseware.net

Younus, S., Rasheed, F., & Zia, A. (2015). Identifying the factors affecting customer purchase intention. *Global Journal of Management and Business Research: Administration and Management*, *15*(2), 9.

Zikmund, W. G. (2000). *Business research methods* (6th ed.). The Dryden Press, Harcout Brace College Publishers.

ADDITIONAL READING

Akar, E., & Dalgic, T. (2018). Understanding online consumers' purchase intentions: A contribution from social network theory. *Behaviour & Information Technology*, *37*(5), 473–487. doi:10.1080/0144 929X.2018.1456563

Chepkemoi, C., Zakayo, C., & Koima, J. (2018). Facebook as a competitive social media marketing tool on sales performance for small and medium enterprises in Nakuru CBD, Kenya. *World Journal of Innovative Research*, *5*(4), 5–11.

Chetioui, Y., Butt, I., & Lebdaoui, H. (2021). Facebook advertising, eWOM and consumer purchase intention - Evidence from a collectivistic emerging market. *Journal of Global Marketing*, *34*(3), 220–237. doi:10.1080/08911762.2021.1891359

Gunawan, D. D., & Huarng, K. H. (2015). Viral effects of social network and media on consumers' purchase intention. *Journal of Business Research*, *68*(11), 2237–2241. doi:10.1016/j.jbusres.2015.06.004

Hooda, A., & Hooda, A. (2018). Acceptance of social media as a marketing tool: A quantitative study. *The East Asian Journal of Business Management*, *8*(3), 5–12. doi:10.13106/eajbm.2018.vol8.no3.5

Imtiaz, R., Alsoud, M. A. S., Ramish, M. S., Aziz, A., & Anwar, A. (2021). Impact of Facebook on advertising: Analysis of effectiveness of Facebook on enhancing customer purchase intention. *Ilkogretim Online*, *20*(5), 7130–7149.

Jermsittiparsert, K. (2019, November). Impact of Facebook advertising on purchase intention. In *Proceedings of the 2019 3rd International Conference on E-Business and Internet* (pp.1-7). 10.1145/3383902.3383903

Joshi, A., & Kalia, A. (2017). Conceptual analysis of effectiveness of Facebook advertisements in India and abroad. *Journal of Content. Community & Communication*, *6*(3), 71–77.

Lutfie, H., & Marcelino, D. (2020, October). Investigating Facebook advertising feature through performance expectancy on customer purchase intention. In *2020 8th International Conference on Cyber and IT Service Management (CITSM)* (pp. 1-7). IEEE. 10.1109/CITSM50537.2020.9268905

Manzoor, U., Baig, S. A., Hashim, M., & Sami, A. (2020). Impact of social media marketing on consumer's purchase intentions: The mediating role of customer trust. *International Journal of Entrepreneurial Research*, *3*(2), 41–48. doi:10.31580/ijer.v3i2.1386

Saima & Khan, M. A. (2020). Effect of social media influencer marketing on consumers' purchase intention and the mediating role of credibility. *Journal of Promotion Management*, *27*(4), 503-523.

Vaidya, R. (2020). Effectiveness of Facebook as a marketing tool: A study among the users in Kathmandu valley. *World Academics Journal of Management*, 8(4), 14–20.

KEY TERMS AND DEFINITIONS

Brand Awareness: Knowledge of a person up to any extent from minimum to the most about the details of any offering, for example, features, utility, source, cost, availability, etc. which creates an overall image about the offering that pops up in that person's mind or memory, whenever the person may think of that kind of offering in general.

Comment: A verbal or written short statement, most of the times made instantly but sometimes pretty thoughtfully too, in response to an instigating or inspiring incidence, talk, dialogue, conversation, object etc., which may be live in person, and in a virtual world as well.

Communication Efficacy: Degree of abilities to convey one's thoughts and ideas to others, or comprehend the same conveyed by others, as closely as intended by either of the parties to convey or comprehend.

Discussion Board: A platform operated and used mainly virtually to invite and connect people to put and share their opinions on a commercial, political, social, technical, or any usual issue to help the community joining the specific platform on a specific issue.

Location-Based Check-In: A technical feature used by the social media, specially by Facebook to allow its clients to inform their connected people about their important activities and movements while using some service providing facilities to help everyone use the same, if and when any of them might be interested.

Perception: Process of organizing and interpreting any information or stimulus received by a living being, with the required intelligence to do so, in the perspectives of all the background knowledge already stored in the specific being's cognitive system.

Purchase Intention: Active or dormant desire to bring an offering under one's own possession, which ensures the title of ownership of that particular offering to the inclining person, with or without having the actual capability to exchange something of value, money in most of the cases, to actualize the desire driven by many complex factors.

Section 51
Supply Chain Analytics and Management

A Bio-Inspired Approach to Solve the Problem of Regular Carpooling

Khadidja Yachba

(iD) https://orcid.org/0000-0002-7754-2823

LIO Laboratory, University of Relizane, Algeria

Zakaria Bendaoud

(iD) https://orcid.org/0000-0003-3091-5044

GeCoDe Laboratory, University of Saida Dr. Moulay Tahar, Algeria

Karim Bouamrane

LIO Laboratory, Oran 1 University, Algeria

Rachid Kaleche

LIO Laboratory, Oran 1 University, Algeria

INTRODUCTION

The idea of carpooling is to share a car with several people making the same trip. Unlike hitchhiking, transportation costs are shared by everyone in the vehicle (Teal, 1987). It can be casual (travel, music festivals, etc.), or regular, such as carpooling with colleagues. Due to its economic and ecological benefits, carpooling is becoming more and more popular (Vanoutrive et al, 2012).

In most cases, carpooling reduces the cost of car trips. In fact, all the passengers of the vehicle share the expenses related to the displacement, such as the fuel cost and toll fees. The cost of this solution is significantly lower than that of taking public transportation or traveling alone by car.

Keeping in mind the time constraints of the operation, this work aims to minimize the number of vehicles used and the total distance travelled by all users.

Carpooling can be seen as a combination of a clustering and routing problem.

Using the Firefly algorithm, this work seeks to solve the problem of regular large carpools and extensions in a more effective way.

Numerous government agencies and employers have used carpooling as an effective strategy to address a wide range of climate, environmental, and congestion mitigation goals, while simultaneously increasing roadway and parking capacity for decades. (Shaheen et al, 2018).

The authors of this study are interested in regular carpooling. Finding the best groups under different constraints is the challenge.

The main objective of this study is to provide companies with efficient use of transport increase their returns. As a result, several questions are required:

- How the best group be properly determined?
- How the distances be minimized?
- How should we proceed to reduce transport costs?

DOI: 10.4018/978-1-7998-9220-5.ch175

The rest of the chapters are organized as follows: section 2 provides an overview of the subject area. Sections 3, 4, and 5 describe the method used to develop the contribution. In section 6, the authors present the results obtained using the proposed approach. These results are discussed in section 7. The authors finish with a conclusion, including future possibilities.

Figure 1. Regular carpooling

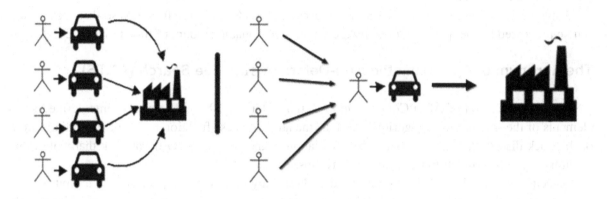

BACKGROUND

This section presents an overview of the methods used to solve carpooling problems.

In 2021, Kaleche (Kaleche et al, 2021) presented An Improved Biogeography Based Optimization for the Long Term Carpooling Problem.

Unlike the popularity of its related problems, little literature exists on carpooling. In the literature, different approaches have been proposed to solve the problem of regular carpooling, including an algorithm based on recording functions (Ferrari, 2003), The ANTS algorithm (Akka, 2018), a simulation-based approach (Viegas, 2010), a multi-matching system (Yan, 2011), and the Bird swarm algorithm for solving the long-term carpooling problem (Bendaoud, 2018). In this section, the authors classify resolution methods into two main categories: heuristics and metaheuristics.

Saving Functions Based Algorithm (SFBA)

In the SFBA Algorithm, a heuristic information processing routine is used to support efficient matching in carpool systems.

In addition, they are based on saving functions and belong to two distinct classes of algorithms to provide two deferential models of this problem. The focus is primarily on modeling the problem, rather than resolving it.

By associating different users to the support of the body model, resolution methods are relatively simple. In real-world applications, the approach has shown to be able to reduce travel distance by a significant amount.

Despite this, the approach relies heavily on the distribution of users; only benchmarks with clustered distributed users have achieved satisfactory results (Ferrari, 2003).

The Simulation-Based Method

Simulation-based methods use a division-and-conquest approach. In the division step, the K-means clustering algorithm (Macqueen, 1967) is used to classify objects into groups based on their attributes.

In grouping, the sum of the squares of the distances between the users and the corresponding center of concentration is minimized. In order to ensure good correspondence between users, the authors also considered users' departure and arrival times as part of the distance between users and the corresponding concentration center.

Using the K-means clustering algorithm, all users are divided into small groups so that each group can be processed by the optimization software within a reasonable amount of time (Viegas, 2010).

The Acronym of Approximated Non-Deterministic Tree Search (ANTS)

ANTS is an extension of ACO Column Optimization (Dorigo, 1992). There are some defined sub-elements of the original ACO algorithm, such as the attractiveness function to use or the initialization of the track distribution. It turns out to be a variation of the general ACO framework that makes the resulting algorithm similar to tree search algorithms.

In each step, a partial solution is generated by branching on any possible offspring; a limit is then calculated for each offspring, perhaps on the basis of dominance, and the partial solution associated with the surviving offspring is selected based on lower constraints.

The algorithm also includes a local search procedure, implemented as a variable neighborhood search. Each neighbor is taken into account in a main loop. After each neighbor has been used to obtain its local optimum, the next neighbor is considered. Optimisation ends when no neighbor can improve the current solution. When it comes to large instances scales, however, tree search structures and variable neighborhood search are less efficient (Maniezzo, 2004).

Trajectory-Based Methaheuristics (TBM)

In general, the trajectory-based algorithm works on one solution at a time, which will trace a path in the search space as iterations continue.

Paths are created by moving from one solution to another in the solution space iteratively. The walks start with a solution generated at random or obtained from another optimization algorithm, called the initial solution.

During each iteration, the current solution is replaced by another selected from among its neighbors. A better displacement or a solution is always accepted, whereas a not so good movement can be accepted with a certain probability. The steps or the movements trace a trajectory in the space of search, with a non-zero probability that this trajectory can to reach the global optimum.

The search process is stopped when a given condition is satisfied, such as a maximum number of generations, finding a solution with a target quality or no improvement for a given time, and so on this type of meta heuristic performs the movements in the vicinity of the solution.

Bird Swarm Algorithm for Solving the Long-Term Car-Pooling Problem

The purpose of this work is to benefit from web 2.0 tools in order to adopt the ideal strategy for carpooling. The article focused on the family of regular carpool families; the problem is to find the optimal groups of people who make the same trips every day and in a predictable manner. (BirdSwam Algorithm) (Bendaoud, 2018) was adapted to reach the goal.

FOCUS OF THE CHAPTER

In this chapter, the authors tackle the problem of regular carpooling using an organic method inspired by Fire Flight while taking into account new constraints.

SOLUTIONS AND RECOMMENDATIONS

As part of the research on decision support systems, transport, Maritime transportation (Bendaoud and Yachba, 2017), logistic (Yachba et al., 2021), optimization (Belayachi et al., 2017;Amrani et al., 2018;Yachba et al., 2018) and multicretaria methods (Yachba and Bouamrane, 2015;Yachba et al., 2018;Tahiri et al (a).2022;Tahiri et al (b).,2022).

In this section, the authors present their solution to the problem of regular carpooling using the Firefly algorithm.

Firefly Algorithm

To develop heuristics inspired by nature, ideas from nature were exploited in order to solve complex problems. Meta-heuristics were inspired by various fields, such as biology or ethology (study of animal behavior). 'FireFlies' are small winged beetles that produce a cold flashing light for mutual attraction.

In order to attract males, females mimic the light signals of other species, which they capture and devour. Fireflies possess a capacitor-type mechanism that slowly discharges until a certain threshold is reached at which point they release energy as light. This cycle occurs repeatedly. Yang's Firefly Algorithm is inspired by the attenuation of light with distance and mutual attraction, but he considers all fireflies to be unisex.

(Fister et al., 2017) developed the algorithm to solve optimization problems, but later it was used to solve problems such as roaming vendors and in digital image processing, compression, and clustering.

The algorithm takes into consideration the following three points (Yang, 2010):

1. Fireflies are all unisex, so the attraction between these is not based on their gender.
2. The attraction is proportional to their luminosity, so for two fireflies, the less luminous will move towards the brightest. If no firefly is bright than a particular firefly, the firefly will move randomly.
3. The brightness of fireflies is determined according to an objective function (to be optimized).

Based on these three rules, the Firefly algorithm is as follows:

1. Random generation of the initial population each firefly parent a solution,
2. Each firefly is rated according to brightness, distance function,
3. Comparison: If ($I_i < I_j$) The less luminous firefly will be attracted by the brightest,
4. Move the firefly i to the firefly j,
5. Evaluation of new solutions and update light intensity,

6.   Classify fireflies and find the best solution.

The Firefly algorithm can be further illustrated in the flowchart shown in Figure 3.

Figure 2. FireFly Algorithm
(Yang et al, 2018), (Farahani et al, 2011).

Generate a population of fireflies x_i ($i = 1, 2, ..., n$)
Set the intensity of light I to a point x_i by the objective function $f(x_i)$
t = n ;
While (t < Max Generation)
For i = 1 to n
For j = 1 to n
If ($f(x_i) < f(x_j)$)
            Move firefly x_i to firefly x_j
Else Move x_i randomly
End if
            Evaluate new solutions and update light intensity
    End for j end for i
      Classify fireflies and find the best solution
    t++ ;
End While
View the results

Artificial View versus Real View

Researchers have adapted the regular carpool problem using the FireFly algorithm in Table 1.

Setting Firefly Algorithms

Developing the firefly algorithm poses no major difficulties. An algorithm's parameterization, rather than its selection of values, is important. In most cases, the values of these parameters are determined by the experimental results. They depend closely on the type of problem to be solved.

The Firefly Algorithm (Johari et al.,2013) takes into account the following parameters:

Number of Firefly

Firefly population size affects directly the Firefly algorithm, so it is important to choose this parameter carefully to ensure the best compromise between the quality of the result and the speed of the algorithm.

In various tests, it has been found that the larger the population, the greater its diversity, and therefore the better the quality of the solution.

Consequently, if the execution time of an algorithm increases, it affects its efficiency.

Alternatively, if the number of fireflies is small, then a local optimum is more likely to result, so having many fireflies ensures diversity and prevents the phenomenon of local minima.

Figure 3. FireFly Algorithm Flowchart
(Gandomi et al, 2012)

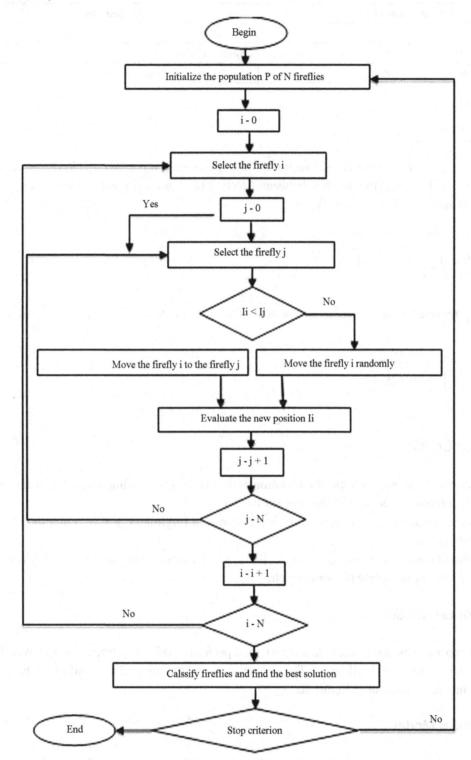

Table 1. Artificial View VS Real View

Artificial View	Real View
Fireflies	Individual
Brightness	Objective function
Number of fireflies	Size of the population, number of individuals

The Distance

The distance between two fireflies is a very important parameter, it is evaluated in different ways.

For the used algorithm, the distance between two fireflies i and j at positions x_i and x_j is defined by the following Cartesian distance (Yang, 2010):

$$r_{ij} = ||x_i - x_j|| = \sqrt{\sum_{k=1}^{d} \left(x_{i,k} - x_{j,k} \right)^2} \tag{1}$$

When $x_{i,k}$ represents the $k^{ème}$ spatial component of the coordinate x_i firefly i. In a den 2-D, the formula r_{ij} becomes:

$$r_{ij} = \sqrt{\left(x_i - x_j \right)^2 + \left(y_i - y_j \right)^2} \tag{2}$$

Absorption Coefficient

The absorption coefficient γ controls the variation of the brightness as a function of the distance between two fireflies communicated. It is in the interval $[0, \infty]$.

$\gamma = 0$ corresponds to no change, no variation or constant brightness, $\gamma = \infty$, corresponds to a complete random search.

The authors prefer to keep the value of $\gamma \in [0,1]$, $\gamma = 1$ leads to a brightness close to zero which is still equivalent to the complete random search.

Number of Generation

Even if the experiments demonstrate that the method performs well, convergence to the overall optimal solution is not guaranteed in all cases. The output scope of the algorithm should thus be defined by defining a maximum number of iterations.

Mathematical Model

The problem of regular carpool can be modeled by means of a directed graph **G = (U, A)**, when U is the set of users, and **A = {arc(i, j) / U, j ∈U}** is the set of arcs. Each user u ∈ U is associated with a house.

A is a set of directed weighted arcs where each arc(i, j) ∈A is associated with a positive displacement cost that is equivalent to the distance r in our model.

Each registered carpool user specifies: an original position (x_i, y_i), and another position to which he will move.

Objective Function

In order to achieve optimum carpooling, the total travel costs of all users must be minimized while minimizing the number of cars. In order to achieve these two objectives, the authors developed four objective functions.

Before Moving

The intensity of light at a particular distance from the source of light obeys the law of inverse squares. That is, the intensity of the light I decreases as the distance r increases as a function of $I \propto 1/r^2$. or this purpose each firefly calculates the brightness of the other fireflies in relation to it with the following formula (Yang, 2009):

$$I(r) = \frac{1}{r^2} \tag{3}$$

r: the distance between the Firefly i and the Firefly j.

Otherwise, for a firefly to calculate its luminosity, it divides the sum of the luminosities of the other fireflies compared to it on the number of the other members of the subgroup minus one:

$$I(r) = \frac{\sum \frac{1}{r^2}}{k-1} \tag{4}$$

k represents the number of members of the subgroup.

After Moving

As mentioned above the intensity of the light decreases with the growth of the distance from the source. This makes the attraction vary depending on the degree of absorption. For simplicity, the intensity of light $I(r)$ varies according to the law $I(r) = I_s / r^2$ when I_s is the intensity at the source. For a constant value of γ, the intensity varies according to the distance r, Which give: $I = I_0 e^{-\gamma r}$, when I_0 is the intensity of light from the source. The combination of the two effects of the inverse square law and the absorption can be approximated with the following Gaussian formula (Yang, 2009):

$$I(r) = I_0 e^{-\gamma r^2} \tag{5}$$

Formula (5) is used for a firefly to calculate its brightness after moving to another brighter firefly.

On the other hand, after moving a firefly its brightness varies with respect to other fireflies, so these will calculate their brightness in relation to it as follows:

$$I(r) = I_j e^{-\gamma r^2} \tag{6}$$

When: I_j represents the brightness of the other fireflies in relation to the firefly to which the firefly i moved.

Runtime Scenario

In the following example, the Firefly algorithm is applied to the carpool problem:

Assuming we have five individuals who want to make the same journey on a regular basis using the same vehicle, the proposed solution is to find the most suitable individual to transport them.

The link adaptation procedure is performed by applying the Firefly algorithm on this example as follows:

```
1)          Initialize the parameters of the algorithm:
2)          Grouping of people into subgroups of 5, 4 or 3 individuals minimum.
3)          Evaluate the light intensity of all fireflies using the objective
function.
4)          Update the position of fireflies by the following loop:
•           For i = 1 at the population size
•           For j = 1 at the population size
•           If the objective function (i) <the objective function (j) then
•           Move the firefly i to the firefly j
•           Otherwise move the firefly i randomly
•           End if
•           End for j
•           End for i
•           Classify fireflies according to their objective functions.
•           Update the generation index (incremented index t).
•           If t <generation number then
Return to step 3.
Else
Finish the algorithm by:
Choose the subgroup firefly that has the best function.
```

γ presented in equation (5) and (6), the index t, and the maximum number of generations.

Table 2 shows the X and Y coordinates of each individual from [0 to 4].

Table 3 represents the luminosities calculated by the fireflies before displacement, the brightness in red is calculated by the formula (4) and the black one calculated by the formula (3).

When launching FireFly Algorithm, the authors compare the brightness of each person in the subgroup with the brightness of all other people in the subgroup until the algorithm arrives at the best person with the highest brightness. The authors initialized the parameter γ to 0.001.

Figure 4. The graph of 5 individuals

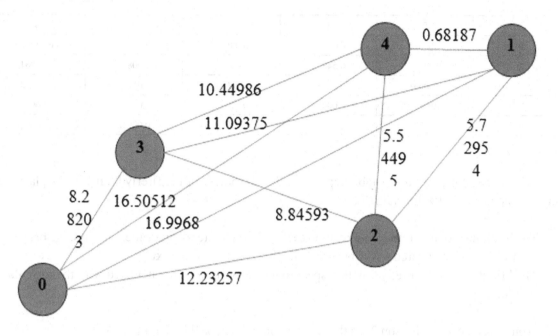

Table 2. Coordinates of members of the subgroup

The People	Coordinated x_i	Coordinated y_i
0	35.288882	-1.004364
1	35.398903	-0.874809
2	35.34568	-0.896024
3	35.368482	-0.981494
4	35.399226	-0.88162

Table 3. The luminosities calculated by the fireflies before displacement

	0	1	2	3	4
0	0.0071	0.00346	0.00668	0.01458	0.00367
1	0.00346	0.54822	0.03046	0.00813	2.15081
2	0.00668	0.03046	0.02061	0.01278	0.03252
3	0.01458	0.00813	0.01278	0.01116	0.00916
4	0.00367	2.15081	0.03252	0.00916	0.54904

Comparison of Person 0 With Person 1

The researchers will compare the brightness (00) with (01) means that the brightness of the person 0 with the brightness of the person 1 relative to 0, the authors find that (0.0071> 0.00346), so the person 0 will move randomly to the person 2. After the displacement one obtains Table 4.

Table 4. Comparison of person 0 with person 1

	0	1	2	3	4
0	0.00611	0.03046	0.00668	0.01278	0.03252
1	0.02623	0.54822	0.03046	0.00813	2.15081
2	0.00668	0.03046	0.02061	0.01278	0.03252
3	0.011	0.00813	0.01278	0.01116	0.00916
4	0.028	2.15081	0.03252	0.00916	0.54904

The brightness in green in the table represents the brightness of the firefly 0 after its displacement and it is calculated by the formula (5).

- The brightness of other people in relation to the person 0 after displacement is the same brightness of other people compared to the person 2 (in pink) because it is next to it.
- The brightness of the firefly 0 with respect to the other fireflies is calculated with the formula (6) (in blue).

Person 0 has moved to Person 2, so the second comparison will be with Person 3.

Figure 5. The movement of Person 0 to Person 2

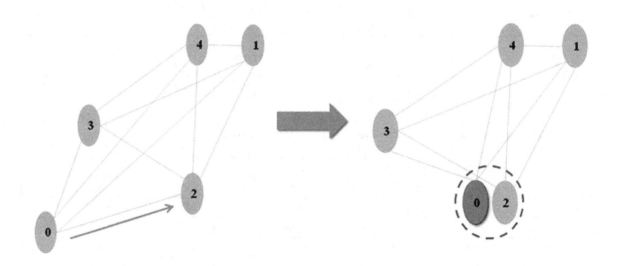

Comparison of Person 0 With Person 3

The authors compare the brightness (00) (22) with (03) which means that the sum of the brightness of the person 0 and 2 because they are adjacent to the brightness of the person 3 with respect to 0, the authors find that (0.00611 0.2061> 0.01278), so the person 0 will move randomly to the person 4. After moving we get the Table 5.

Table 5. Comparison of person 0 with person 3

	0	1	2	3	4
0	0.00592	2.15081	0.03252	0.00916	0.03252
1	1.56801	0.54822	0.03046	0.00813	2.15081
2	0.02371	0.03046	0.02061	0.01278	0.03252
3	0.00668	0.00813	0.01278	0.01116	0.00916
4	0.028	2.15081	0.03252	0.00916	0.54904

The brightness in green in the table represents the brightness of the firefly 0 after its displacement and it is calculated by the formula (5).

- The brightness of other people in relation to the person 0 after displacement is the same brightness of other people compared to the person 4 (in pink) because it is next to it.
- The brightness of the firefly 0 with respect to the other fireflies is calculated with the formula (6) (in blue).

As long as the person 0 is next to the person 4, we go to the comparison of the firefly 1 with all the other people (Figure 6).

Figure 6. The movement of Person 0 to Person 4

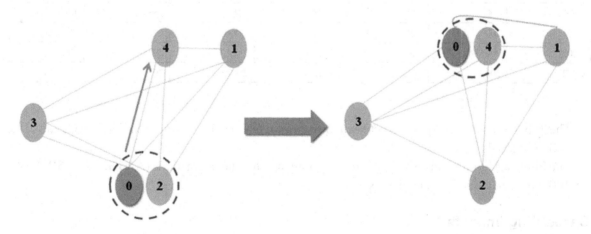

And the authors continue to make comparisons and displacements until get the final graph of displacement (Figure 7).

Simulation and Result

The researchers performed 30 simulation operations for each instance of problem. The machine used has a Windows 10 operating system with Intel Core i5 6200 CPU @ 2.30 GHz and 4 GB of RAM.

The following table show the results obtained from the proposed approach for 100 and 200 individuals.

Figure 7. The final Graph of Movement

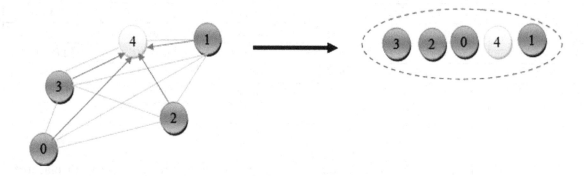

In order to situate the proposed approach with other approaches of the literature, the experimental results were compared to three other approaches to solving the carpooling problem, namely: ANTS and the simulation-based approach (SB), as well as as the Guided Genetic Algorithm (GGA). The results are given in Table 6.

Table 6. Comparison between Firefly Algorithm and other algorithms

Instances	Size	FF(FireFly)	GGA	ANTS	SBS	BSA
C101	100	744	1585.5	1585.5	1647.4	1481.35
C102	100	908	1701.9	1706.8	1717.5	1411.01
C103	100	923	1513.7	1512.6	1532.2	1433.06
C201	200	1599	2749.4	2784.4	2761.7	4676.23
C202	200	1688	2836.7	2879.2	2975.1	4000.69
C203	200	1945	2716.8	2769.3	2975.1	3759.36

The Table 6 shows a comparison between the experimental results of instances C101, c102 and c103 for 100 individuals.

The FireFly Algorithm gives us better results compared to other algorithms (ANTS, GGA, SB, BSA) for 100 individuals and 200 individuals.

Carpooling Impacts

Because carpooling reduces the number of automobiles needed by travelers, it is often associated with numerous societal benefits including (Li et al, 2018), (Shaheen et al, 2018).:

1. reductions in energy consumption and emissions,
2. congestion mitigation, and
3. reduced parking infrastructure demand.

Figure 8. Comparison between FireFly

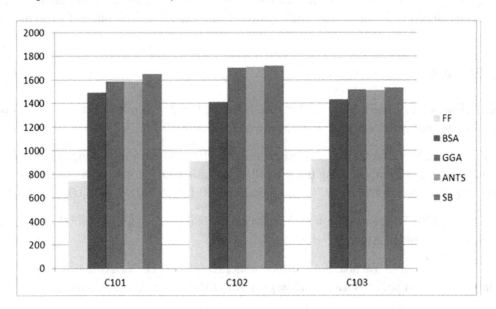

Advantages of the Proposed Approach

With the Firefly Algorithm, one can quickly arrive at solutions which are close to the optimal solution because of the movements of the fireflies based on the attractiveness and intensity that is defined by the objective function. Each iteration changes the locations, so the solutions change as well

In addition, to determine what is the best compromise between quality of the solution and the algorithm's speed of the algorithm.

FUTURE RESEARCH DIRECTIONS

To complete the research conducted, the authors wish to continue in this line of research. The authors hope to incorporate other bio inspired methods and enhance the comparative study as perspectives to this work.

CONCLUSION

In this work, the authors proposed an approach based on FireFly Algorithm to solve the problem of long-term carpooling. By adopting this approach, the number of groups and the distance traveled overall are minimized.

In order to explain the proposed approach, the authors first explained how it works, then demonstrated the results for different situations.

Using the FireFly Algorithm allows for quick solutions that are close to the optimal solution due to the movement of fireflies according to attraction and intensity, which are defined by the objective function and are the basis of all calculations. In order to determine the best compromise between the quality of the solution and the speed of the algorithm, the locations change at each iteration, and so do the solutions.

REFERENCES

Akka, K., & Khaber, F. (2018). Mobile robot path planning using an improved ant colony optimization. *International Journal of Advanced Robotic Systems*, *15*(3). doi:10.1177/1729881418774673

Amrani, F., Yachba, K., Belayachi, N., & Hamdadou, D. (2018). A decision-making system for container storage management in a seaport using the ant-colony optimisation algorithm. *International Journal of Management and Decision Making*, *17*(3), 348–367. doi:10.1504/IJMDM.2018.093501

Beghoura, M. A. (2012). *Segmentation multi sources des Images Satellitaires par l'algorithme Firefly* [PhD Thesis]. USTO6MB, Algeria.

Belayachi, N., Gelareh, S., Yachba, K., & Bouamrane, K. (2017). The Logistic of Empty Containers¢ Return in the Liner-Shipping Network. *Transport and Telecommunication Journal*, *18*(3), 207–219. doi:10.1515/ttj-2017-0018

Bendaoud, Z., & Yachba, K. (2017). Towards A Decision Support System for Optimization of Container Placement in a Container Terminal. *International Journal of Strategic Information Technology and Applications*, *8*(3), 59–72. doi:10.4018/IJSITA.2017070104

Bendaoud, Z., Yachba, K., & Bouamrane, K. (2018). Bird swarm algorithm for solving the long-term car pooling problem. 7th Edition de la Conférence internationale sur l'Innovation et Nouvelles Tendances dans les Systèmes d'Information, Marrakech, Morocco.

Dorigo, M. (1992). *Optimization, learning and natural algorithms* [Ph.D. Thesis]. Politecnico di Milano.

Farahani, S. M., Abshouri, A. A., Nasiri, B., & Meybodi, M. R. (2011). A Gaussian firefly algorithm. *International Journal of Machine Learning and Computing*, *1*(5), 448–453. doi:10.7763/IJMLC.2011.V1.67

Ferrari, E., Manzini, R., Pareschi, A., Persona, A., & Regattieri, A. (2003). The car pooling problem: Heuristic algorithms based on savings functions. *Journal of Advanced Transportation*, *37*(3), 243–272. doi:10.1002/atr.5670370302

Fister, I., Fister, I. Jr, Yang, X. S., & Brest, J. (2013). A comprehensive review of firefly algorithms. *Swarm and Evolutionary Computation*, *13*, 34–46. doi:10.1016/j.swevo.2013.06.001

Gandomi, A. H., Yang, X. S., Talatahari, S., & Alavi, A. H. (2013). Firefly algorithm with chaos. *Communications in Nonlinear Science and Numerical Simulation*, *18*(1), 89–98. doi:10.1016/j.cnsns.2012.06.009

Johari, N. F., Zain, A. M., Noorfa, M. H., & Udin, A. (2013). Firefly algorithm for optimization problem. *Applied Mechanics and Materials*, *421*, 512–517. doi:10.4028/www.scientific.net/AMM.421.512

Kaleche, R., Bendaoud, Z., & Bouamrane, K. (2021). An Improved Biogeography-Based Optimization for the Long-Term Carpooling Problem. *Applied Artificial Intelligence*, *35*(10), 745–764. doi:10.1080/08839514.2021.1935586

Li, R., Liu, Z., & Zhang, R. (2018). Studying the benefits of carpooling in an urban area using automatic vehicle identification data. *Transportation Research Part C, Emerging Technologies*, *93*, 367–380. doi:10.1016/j.trc.2018.06.012

MacQueen, J. (1967, June). Some methods for classification and analysis of multivariate observations. *Proceedings of the Fifth Berkeley Symposium on Mathematical Statistics and Probability*, *1*(14), 281-297.

Shaheen, S., Cohen, A., & Bayen, A. (2018). *The benefits of carpooling*. Academic Press.

Tahiri, H., Bouamrane, K., & Yachba, K. (2022). An Approach to Optimize Container Locations in a Containership With Electre III. *International Journal of Decision Support System Technology*, *14*(1), 1–18. doi:10.4018/IJDSST.286681

Tahiri, H., Khadidja, Y., & Bouamrane, K. (2022). Towards a Multi-Criteria Decision Approach to Solving the Container Storage Problem: Container Ship Loading Component. *International Journal of Organizational and Collective Intelligence*, *12*(1), 1–21. doi:10.4018/IJOCI.2022010105

Tahiri, H., Yachba, K., & Bouamrane, K. (2020, December). A container placement approach in a containership based on the electre 2 method. In *2020 4th International Symposium on Informatics and its Applications (ISIA)*. IEEE.

Teal, R. F. (1987). Carpooling: Who, how and why. *Transportation Research Part A, General*, *21*(3), 203–214. doi:10.1016/0191-2607(87)90014-8

Vanoutrive, T., Van De Vijver, E., Van Malderen, L., Jourquin, B., Thomas, I., Verhetsel, A., & Witlox, F. (2012). What determines carpooling to workplaces in Belgium: Location, organisation, or promotion? *Journal of Transport Geography*, *22*, 77–86. doi:10.1016/j.jtrangeo.2011.11.006

Viegas, J., Correia, G., Martinez, L., & Antunes, A. (2010). *A simulation procedure for measuring the market potential of shared taxis: An application to the Lisbon metropolitan area*. Academic Press.

Yachba, K., Bendaoud, Z., & Bouamrane, K. (2018). A Technique for Resolution of the Assignment Problem Containers in a Container Terminal. In *Handbook of Research on Biomimicry in Information Retrieval and Knowledge Management*. IGI Global. doi:10.4018/978-1-5225-3004-6.ch008

Yachba, K., Bendaoud, Z., & Bouamrane, K. (2018). Toward a Decision Support System for Regulation in an Urban Transport Network. *International Journal of Strategic Information Technology and Applications*, *9*(2), 1–17. doi:10.4018/IJSITA.2018040101

Yachba, K., Bouamrane, K., & Gelareh, S. (2015). Containers storage optimization in a container terminal using a multimethod multi-level approach. *The International Conference on Computers & Industrial Engineering (CIE45)*. 28-30.

Yachba, K., Chaabane, A., & Benadda, M. A. (2021). Un système d'aide à la décision pour l'optimisation de processus de distribution des produits finaux [A decision support system for optimizing the distribution process for end products]. Séminaire international sur les mathématiques et l'informatique.

Yan, M., Li, J., & Sha, B. (2011). Structural analysis of the Sil1–Bip complex reveals the mechanism for Sil1 to function as a nucleotide-exchange factor. *The Biochemical Journal*, *438*(3), 447–455. doi:10.1042/BJ20110500 PMID:21675960

Yang, X. S. (2010). *Nature-inspired metaheuristic algorithms*. Luniver press.

Yang, X. S., & He, X. S. (2018). Why the firefly algorithm works? In *Nature-Inspired Algorithms and Applied Optimization* (pp. 245–259). Springer. doi:10.1007/978-3-319-67669-2_11

ADDITIONAL READING

Amrani, F., Yachba, K., Belayachi, N., & Hamdadou, D. (2018). A decision-making system for container storage management in a seaport using the ant-colony optimisation algorithm. *International Journal of Management and Decision Making*, *17*(3), 348–367. doi:10.1504/IJMDM.2018.093501

Belayachi, N., Gelareh, S., Yachba, K., & Bouamrane, K. (2017). The logistic of empty containers¢ return in the liner-shipping network. *Transport and Telecommunication*, *18*(3), 207–219. doi:10.1515/ttj-2017-0018

Bendaoud, Z., & Yachba, K. (2017). Towards A Decision Support System for Optimization of Container Placement in a Container Terminal. *International Journal of Strategic Information Technology and Applications*, *8*(3), 59–72. doi:10.4018/IJSITA.2017070104

Bouamrane, K., Hamdadou, D., Yachba, K., & Guenachi, K. (2012). Towards a decision support system, application: itinerary road modification for road transport of hazardous materials. *International Journal of Decision Sciences, Risk and Management, 4*(3-4), 175-196.

Tahiri, H., Bouamrane, K., & Yachba, K. (2022). An Approach to Optimize Container Locations in a Containership With Electre III. *International Journal of Decision Support System Technology*, *14*(1), 1–18. doi:10.4018/IJDSST.286681

Tahiri, H., Yachba, K., & Bouamrane, K. (2020, December). A container placement approach in a containership based on the electre 2 method. In *2020 4th International Symposium on Informatics and its Applications (ISIA)*. IEEE. 10.1109/ISIA51297.2020.9416536

Yachba, K. (2011). *Identification des itinéraires et des flux relatifs aux risques liés aux transports routiers de matières dangereuses: analyse et redéploiement des infrastructures* [Identification of routes and flows relating to the risks associated with road transport of hazardous materials: analysis and redeployment of infrastructures] [Doctoral dissertation]. Université d'Oran1-Ahmed Ben Bella.

Yachba, K., Bendaoud, Z., & Bouamrane, K. (2018). Toward a Decision Support System for Regulation in an Urban Transport Network. *International Journal of Strategic Information Technology and Applications*, *9*(2), 1–17. doi:10.4018/IJSITA.2018040101

Yachba, K., Gelareh, S., & Bouamrane, K. (2016). Storage management of hazardous containers using the genetic algorithm. *Transport and Telecommunication*, *17*(4), 371–383. doi:10.1515/ttj-2016-0033

KEY TERMS AND DEFINITIONS

Best Solution: Research and develop better alternatives to any and all entry level accounting programs Bio inspired: Bio-inspiration is a paradigm shift that leads designers to draw inspiration from nature to develop new systems.

Carpooling: The activity of a group of people travelling together in a car, especially to work or school.

Firefly: The Lampyridae are a family of insects in the beetle order Coleoptera, with more than 2,000 described species, many of which are light emitting.

Firefly Algorithm: Is a population-based optimization algorithm and mimics a firefly's attraction to flashing light.

Group: A group of people who share the same journey.

Individual: A person.

Optimization: Action to obtain the best, to improve functioning, performance, use.

A

A Review on the Use of Artificial Intelligence in Reverse Logistics

Abhishek Kumar Sinha
National Institute of Technology, Calicut, India

Sajan T. John
Viswajyothi College of Engineering and Technology, India

R. Sridharan
 https://orcid.org/0000-0002-0186-6442
National Institute of Technology, Calicut, India

INTRODUCTION

Logistics has a long and illustrious history. The phrase "logistics management" was initially used by the United States to control the transit and supply of munitions during WWII (Zhang et al., 2020). Following WWII, the term "logistics" expanded and gained a foothold in fields such as business, procurement, distribution, reverse supply chain, green logistics, domestic logistics, humanitarian logistics, and so on. The physical distribution of commodities is the emphasis, which includes order fulfilment, product distribution, storage, production planning, and customer support. Logistics, as described by the Council of Logistics Management, is the process of planning, implementing, and regulating the efficient, effective movement and storage of products, services, and associated information from point of origin to point of consumption in order to meet customer expectations (Swamidass, 2000).

The closed-loop supply chain (CLSC) is an emerging topic of research in terms of sustainability in different dimensions of environmental, economic, and social, in connection with the circular economy (Islam & Huda, 2018). "A circular economy is a regenerative system in which resource input and waste, emission, and energy leakage are minimized by slowing, closing, and narrowing the material and energy loops," (Geissdoerfer et al., 2017). This can be accomplished by long-term planning, maintenance, repair, reuse, remanufacturing, refurbishment, and recycling (Geissdoerfer et al., 2017). CLSC management, according to Guide and Van Wassenhove (2009), is the design, control, and operation of a system to optimize value creation across a product's complete life cycle with the dynamic recovery of value from various types and volumes of returns over time (Guide et al., 2009). CLSC's research includes a wide range of topics, including the return of products, product maintenance, product refurbishing, component reuse, prefabrication, and waste (Jaehn., 2016).

Stock (1992) defines RL as the term typically used for the function of logistics in recycling, waste disposal, and hazardous material management; a broader view covers all concerns pertaining to logistical actions carried out in source reduction, recycling, substitution, reuse, and disposal (Stock., 1992).

"Reverse logistics is the process of planning, implementing, and controlling the efficient, cost-effective flow of raw materials, in-process inventory, finished goods, and related information from the point of consumption to the point of origin for the purpose of recapturing or creating value or proper disposal," according to Rogers and Tibben-Lembke (1999).

DOI: 10.4018/978-1-7998-9220-5.ch176

Due to a growth in e-commerce firms that allow quick and free product returns and businesses that manage end-of-life/reusable products, RL has lately gained increased interest and relevance among scholars and practitioners. Firms are using it as a strategic strategy for gaining economic advantages and improving their company's social image (Kannan et al., 2012). Wang et al. (2017) describe the content of reverse logistics, which includes transportation, storage, product recovery, recycling, remanufacture, redistribution, and discarding. The concept of RL or CLSC as a component of the Circular Economy has long piqued the interest of supply chain researchers. However, the present decade's technological development has made it difficult to integrate its tools with supply chain operations.

BACKGROUND

Artificial Intelligence (AI)

Artificial Intelligence is a multidisciplinary field that includes mathematical methodologies, computer science, and associated engineering disciplines. Intelligence simply refers to the ability to learn and solve problems, whereas AI is concerned with the development of algorithms and systems that are intelligent in the same way that humans are. Artificial intelligence is the result of the theory and idea underlying the invention of the artificial brain in the 1940s and 1950s. Companies and the government have invested money into research and development since then. As a result, the Checkers chess programme (skilled enough to challenge a respectable amateur), geometric and algebraic problem solvers, intelligent humanoid robots, IBM's Deep Blue computer (which defeated the world chess champion) were born. Storage and processing limits have hindered AI growth. The recent technological boom, on the other hand, has accelerated the development and deployment of AI-based applications. Image, audio, or video processing, business decision making, forecasting or predictions, creation, solving a complex problem, systematic search, natural language processing, decision making, pattern recognition, and other applications can be found in a wide range of industries, including healthcare and pharmaceuticals, supply chain and logistics, agriculture, education, security, defence, and humanitarian work.

Computational search and optimization methods, deep learning (neural network-based approaches), and methods based on statistics and probability are some of the instruments utilized in AI. In the supply chain area, optimization methods are commonly utilized for planning, inventory management, scheduling, routing, packing, and loading. These approaches provide the best optimum approach or answers that are close to ideal. For optimization, Heuristics, and Meta-Heuristics search strategies are used, giving AI systems cognitive capacity. Heuristics programming is a method for finding optimum or near-optimal solutions at a low cost of computation. These are intended to discover good, approximate solutions to challenging combinatorial problems that the present optimization technique cannot handle. The greedy search rule, which finishes the search at the local optimum when no more improvements are conceivable, is used by classical heuristics. Meta-heuristics are a type of non-traditional, high-level algorithmic process for locating a suitable answer. They are inspired by nature and assist in escaping local minima. Genetic algorithms, Simulated Annealing, Tabu search, Ant Colony Optimization, and, Particle Swarm Optimization are few examples of meta-heuristic models (Zhang et al., 2001; Pradhan & Kumar, 2019; Taha., 2017; Sokolov, 2019).

Machine Learning (ML)

Machine Learning is the practice of using algorithms to parse data, learn from it, and takes decisions. There are several ML algorithms which are commonly categorized as:

Supervised Learning Algorithms

This is applicable for a set of data that includes both independent and dependent variables. The algorithm is trained until it achieves the necessary degree of accuracy. Supervised learning problems are further divided into Regression and Classification models based on the outcome variable. If the data type of the result variable is continuous, regression-based supervised learning techniques are utilized, whereas classification models are used for discrete data types. Regression-based supervised learning algorithms include Linear Regression, Regression (Decision) trees, Random Forest regressor, Support Vector Machine (SVM) regressor, Bagging and Boosting regressor, and Logistic regression. Classification (Decision) trees, SVM classifier, Random Forest classifier, Bagging and Boosting classifier are examples of classification-based supervised learning algorithms.

Unsupervised Learning Algorithms

It is used for the data set, which does not have a target, outcome, or dependent variable. The model is widely used for clustering populations in different groups. K-means Clustering, K-Nearest Neighbour (KNN), Principal component analysis (PCA) are examples of unsupervised learning.

Reinforcement Learning Algorithms

This technique has a feedback type of algorithm or in another term, it has a reward and penalty type system. Based on the outcome, the user will decide what to offer. The model has to take sequential actions to maximize reward. Markov chain and Markov decision process are examples of reinforcement learning. (Pradhan & Kumar, 2019; Taha., 2017 ; Sokolov, 2019)

E-Commerce

In this chapter, we'll look at reverse logistics in the context of e-commerce product returns and e-waste management. "E-commerce" is defined as "the sale of goods and services via the internet through the use of a website" (Kotler & Keller, 2016). Amazon (Americas, Europe, and India), Walmart (Americas), eBay (Americas, Europe, China, and India), Flipkart (India), and Taobao (China) are some of the most well-known and widely utilized e-commerce websites (UPS Report). Business-to-Business (B2B), Business-to-Consumer (B2C), and Consumer-to-Consumer (C2C) are the three categories of e-commerce (C2C). The transaction takes place between two businesses on the B2B platform, but on the B2C platform, businesses offer their products directly to customers, enabling them to order at their convenience. A customer sells their old goods to another consumer in a C2C transaction. The user, consumer, or buyer orders the product (product selection, addition to cart, address selection, payment, and final confirmation), the retailer ships the goods (bill preparation, shipment to warehouse, packaging, and dispatch), and the consumer uses or consumes the product. Due to the participation of a large number of participants in the mechanism, the procedure is not straightforward.

According to an Invespcro analysis, at least 30% of all things bought online are returned, totalling $642.6 billion globally (Khalid, 2016; UPS, 2019). According to a UPS survey, 30% of returns are due to a broken or damaged product, 27% are due to poor quality, 20% are due to numerous purchases of the same product, 17% are no longer interested, and 27% are due to the incorrect item, item did not match description, and delivery delay (UPS pules of the online shopper, 2019). One or even more reasons might be responsible. According to a study by Magnetoitsolutions, 56 percent of total Cloths/shoe items ordered are returned: 30 percent of accessories/jewellery orders are returned; 42 percent of electronic items are returned; 22 percent of Health and Beauty products are returned, and 21 percent of entertainment products are returned (Magnetoitsolutions, 2021).

E-Waste

In 2003, the European Union (EU) established the "Waste Electrical and Electronic Equipment Directive," or the "WEEE directive" framework. The goal of this directive was to regulate and encourage electronic trash recycling and reuse. Over time, the council made changes to the decree. "Electrical and electronic equipment," or "EEE," is defined as "equipment that requires electric currents or electromagnetic fields to function properly, as well as equipment for the generation, transfer, and measurement of such currents and fields, and designed for use with a voltage rating not exceeding 1000 volts for alternating current and 1500 volts for direct current" (WEEE Directive, 2012).

The same directive also defined 'waste electrical and electronic equipment,' or 'WEEE' as any substance or object that the holder discards, intends to discard, or is required to discard, including all components, sub-assemblies, and consumables that are part of the product at the time of discarding (WEEE Directive, 2012). Now that we have some knowledge of e-waste, let us look at what precisely e-wastes. EEE is divided into 54 separate product-centric groups according to the E-waste Statistics Guidelines on Classification Reporting and Indicators (Forti et al., 2018). They then divided the items into six categories, which are as follows:

1. Temperature exchange equipment: Refrigerators, freezers, air conditioners, and heat pumps.
2. Screens and Monitors: Televisions, Monitors, laptops, notebooks, and tablets.
3. Lamps: Fluorescent lamps, high-intensity discharge lamps, and LED lamps
4. Large equipment: Washing Machine, clothes dryers, dishwashing Machine, electric stoves, large printing machines, and photovoltaic panels
5. Small equipment: Vacuum cleaners, microwaves, ventilation equipment, toasters, electric kettles, electric shaves, scales, calculators, radio sets, video cameras, electronic toys, electronic tools, etc.
6. Small IT and Telecommunication equipment: Mobile phones, Global Positioning System devices, pocket calculators, routers, personal computers, printers, and telephones

The question now is why e-waste management is so important. What impact does its existence have on the environment, social life, and human life? How might artificial intelligence (AI), machine learning (ML) technologies help to increase e-waste collection through formal processes?

Let's see if we can answer some of these questions. When an e-product has been used for a long time and is approaching its end-of-life phase, it generates e-waste. Some e-waste can be immediately repurposed or repaired and resold to consumers, while others can be collected by the official or informal sectors (Yang, et al., 2008).

From the report of "The Global E-waste Monitor 2020: Quantities, flows, and the circular economy potential" (Forti et al., 2020), "Children and digital dumpsites: e-waste exposure and child health" (WHO, 2021):

1. In 2019, global e-waste production reached 53.6 million tonnes (Mt) (excluding PV panels). Furthermore, it is predicted that by 2030, the volume would surpass 74Mt.
2. Only 9.3 million tonnes of e-waste were collected formally, accounting for 17.4% of total e-waste created.
3. Formal collections refer to e-waste gathered by recognized organizations, companies, and government agencies. Retailers, municipal corporations, and pick-up services are used to collect the trash. The garbage is then delivered to a special treatment plant where precious materials, critical raw materials can be recovered. The informal collections are all the waste collected against formal means. This includes garbage cans, second-hand markets, door-to-door collections from individuals, companies, and governmental organizations, as well as landfills. The issues with the informal collection are improper disassembly (manually breaking the equipment with no safety precautions taken), and backyard recycling (equipment left unhandled, causing serious environmental and human health harm).
4. People participating in the informal collecting and management of e-waste face the following health issues:
   a. Injuries and Short-term effects: Wounds, burns, cuts, sprains, puncture wounds, fractures. Some self-reported cases involve insomnia, weakness, muscle atrophy, headaches, cough chest pain, dizziness
   b. Adverse neonatal outcomes: Stillbirth, premature birth, shortened gestational age, lower birth weight and length, reduced body mass index, leanness, and smaller head.
   c. Growth: it shows mixed results, in some cases reduced growth, while in some cases increased height and weight in children is noted.
   d. Affects neurodevelopment, learning, and behavioural outcomes
   e. Suppresses immune system function
   f. Damages thyroid function, lung function, respiratory symptoms, and asthma.
   g. Changes in cardiovascular regulation can be a cause of heart attack and stroke.
   h. Hearing loss, olfactory memory, and rapid onset blood coagulation in children.

The list and details are wide and large. Refer to the WHO, 2021 report for a detailed explanation and study.

5. E-waste is also disposed of in large numbers at landfills. E-waste contains both ecologically toxic compounds (mercury, cadmium, lead, chromium, ozone-depleting chemicals like CFC, etc.) and valuable critical raw materials (CRM) (Kumar et al., 2017; Işildar et al., 2017). There are 30 CRMs, according to the European Commission. (Table 1). Non-critical metals (Aluminium and Iron), as well as precious metals, are found in e-waste (gold, silver, copper, platinum, palladium, ruthenium, rhodium, iridium, and osmium).

Table 1. List of Critical raw material (CRM) [29]

Antimony	Germanium	Phosphate Rock
Baryte	Hafnium	Phosphorus
Bauxite	Heavy Rare Earth Elements	Platinum Group Metals
Beryllium	Indium	Scandium
Bismuth	Light Rare Earth Elements	Silicon metal
Borate	Lithium	Strontium
Cobalt	Magnesium	Tantalum
Coking Coal	Natural Graphite	Titanium
Fluorspar	Natural Rubber	Tungsten

6. E-product life cycle analysis based on closed-loop supply networks, as depicted in Figure 1 (Hammond & Beullens., 2007; Georgiadis & Besiou, 2008). E-product can be manufactured and produced with extracted raw materials and semi-finished materials. The e-product can then be purchased by customers or users through distribution. The procedure is referred to as e-product forward logistics. Now that the product is in use, it will eventually reach its end. The product is then either sold to the next user or discarded (waste). Then, the formal and informal sectors collaborate to collect e-waste.

For questions that have been left unaddressed. The following portion of this chapter will review some of the previous work. This study attempts to present a brief review of the published literature on reverse logistics issues within the scope of product returns in e-commerce businesses and e-waste management. The remaining part of this chapter is organized as follows: A quick literature review with future areas of study and conclusion.

REVIEW OF THE LITERATURE

The works of literature are investigated in this section. The purpose is to identify the conceptual content of the research area. With few adjustments, the study processes followed the protocols used by Islam et al. (2018) and Cui (2020). Three phases are used to examine the literature: material gathering, descriptive analysis, and material assessment.

Material Collecting: The material collection is done using the Web of Science (WOS) database. For the search operation, two keywords ("Reverse Logistics" and "Closed-loop supply chain") were initially employed in all fields categories (Topic, Title, Author, Publication Titles, Publisher, Abstract, Language, and WOS categories, among others). Between 2001 and September 2021, the search yielded 2808 collections of articles, reviews, papers, chapters, and editorials. Biotechnology, applied microbiology, development studies, geology/pharmacy, neuroscience, chemistry, metallurgy, toxicology, tropical medicine, medical informatics, marine freshwater biology, and other similar papers were all excluded from the search results due to a lack of papers and out of the topic discussion. Book reviews, reprints, and revisions were also not allowed. The WOS core collection yielded 2622 results that had been filtered (2449 articles, 162 review articles, 55 proceedings papers, and 82 early access). The analysis of the WOS analysis feature result was recorded and given the designation "Group A." In the all-fields category, the

Figure 1. The entire life cycle of e-product including forward logistics and reverse logistics
(Hammond & Beullens., 2007)

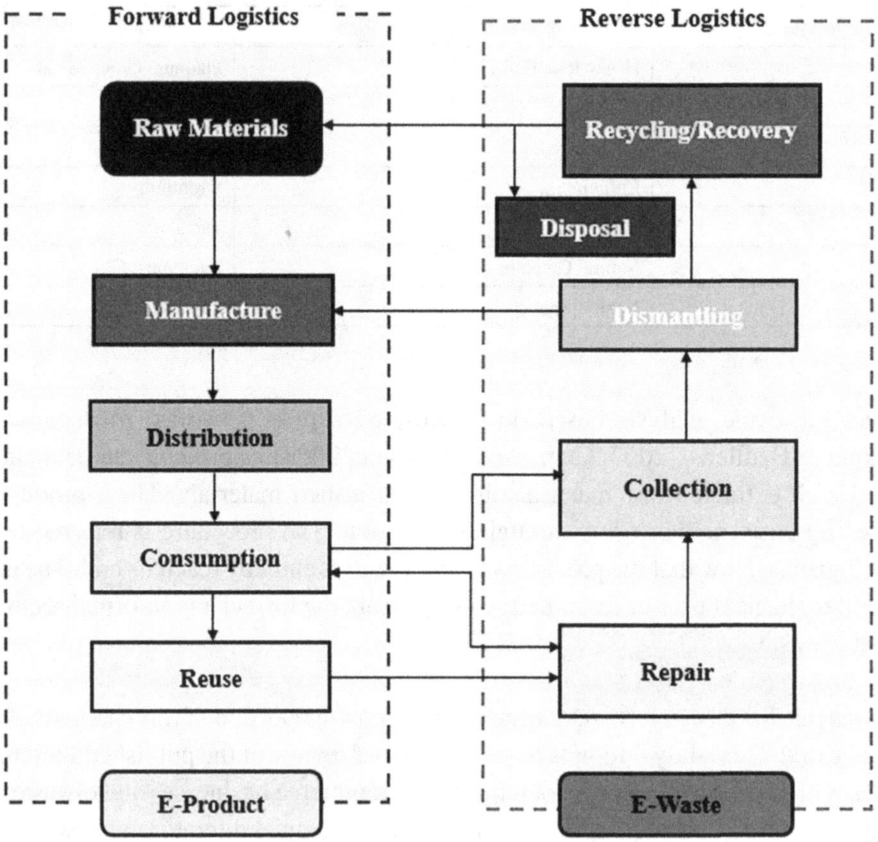

search result was further changed using the terms "Product return*" OR "Returns Management*" OR "WEEE" OR "e-waste" OR "e-commerce" (Topic, Title, Author, Publication Titles, Publisher, Abstract, Language, and WOS categories, etc.). There were 415 papers found in the search results (392 articles, 23 reviews articles, 8 proceedings papers, and 9 early access). The search result was subjected to a similar analytical procedure. "Group B" was the designation given to the observation. One additional search result is logged and designated "Group C" to note the relevance and existence of the following keywords: artificial intelligence, machine learning, optimization, and algorithm. Despite the fact that there have been a fair number of publications and reviews in the past addressing fundamental challenges and methods in RL. To the best of my knowledge, there has never been a review that discusses the use of machine learning and artificial intelligence in RL applications. Even the amount of work completed is insignificant. There are only 64 search results in Group C. After further investigation, it was discovered that all of the publications were published after 2006. Researchers from 25 different nations contributed, with China, the United States, and India topping with 22, 12, and 7 publications, respectively.

Descriptive Analysis: Figure 2-4 shows the comparison (between Group A and Group B). Due to frequent modifications, the search result numbers are dynamic. Operations research, management science, environmental science, industrial engineering, manufacturing, multidisciplinary sciences, telecommunication, instrumentation, medical and pharma industry, agriculture, social science, and biodiversity conservation are the topics covered in these papers. The figure for a count of publications based on

WOS categories is shown in Figure 2. In Group A and Group B, there were 40 and 31 WOS categories, respectively. Transportation, energy fuels, multidisciplinary material science, textiles, telecommunications, and corporate finance were the least common categories, as seen in the graph. The number of publications in a given year is represented in Figure 3.

The graphic shows a huge increase. The booming of e-commerce, as well as the challenges that come with it, has piqued the interest of experts in this field. Figure 4 depicts the countries that are investing in this field. By number, China, the United States, Iran, India, England, and Canada are at the top, while by percentage, the Netherlands, Norway, the United States, Brazil, Australia, and Canada are at the top.

Figure 2. Plot for the count of papers according to WOS categories

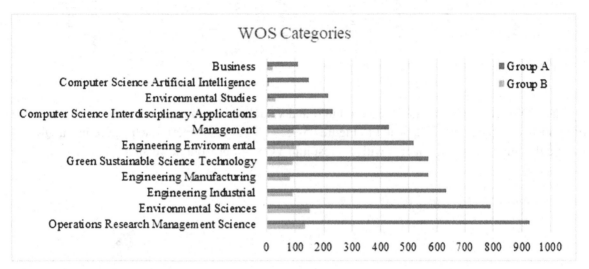

Figure 3. Plot for the count of publication in different year

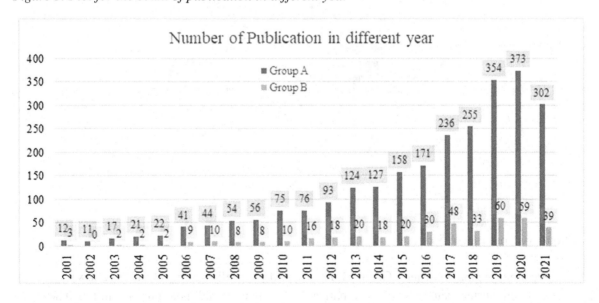

Figure 4. Number of publications by different countries

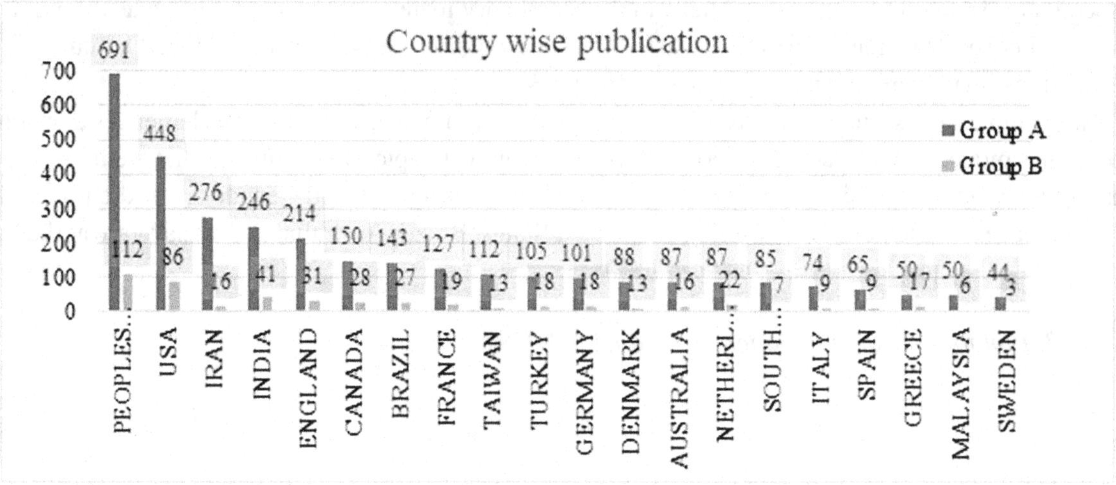

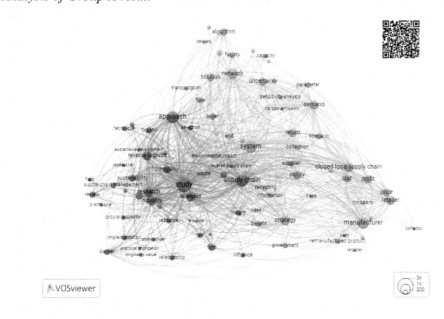

The VOSviewer programme is used to build and visualize bibliometric networks. The assessment of published publications is depicted in Figures 5-7. (Titles and abstract). Each figure has a QR code picture that may be used to interact with the result in VOSviewer's online version.

Figure 5. Analysis of Group A result

Summary from Figure 5 are:

1. There are three main clusters (Green, Blue, and Red), as well as a tiny cluster (Yellow).
2. The Green cluster focuses on a mathematical and computational model for a solution. The green cluster, in general, comprises the majority of words (capacity, network, demand, order, transpor-

tation, delivery, GA, return, uncertainty, location, total cost, parameter, and so on), leading to optimization or prescriptive analysis.

3. The blue cluster contains qualitative or subjective terms such as strategy, trade, closed-loop supply chain, policy, retailer, third party, collector, information, and so on.

4. The red cluster is a subjective blend that provides in-depth information on actors, opportunity, sustainability, relationship, methodology, and barriers, among other things.

5. The yellow cluster showed the long-term viability (waste, environmental impact, recovery, reuse, recycling, environment, weee, etc.).

6. The thickness of the link determines the strength and relationship between terms.

The data for figure 6 is derived from Group A. The dominance of terms like weee, e-waste, recycling, collection, network, recovery, product return, demand, uncertainty, retailer, manufacturer, closed-loop supply chain, environment, reverse logistic, barrier, etc. assures the collection of appropriate papers.

Figure 6. Analysis of Group B result

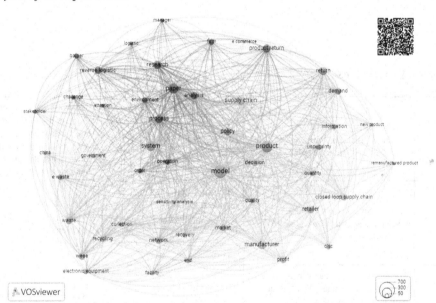

Group C is derived from Group B to find the relevance of ML, AI in RL (though review paper is screened from group B). Figure 7 presents the 6 different clusters- Green, Red, Blue, Cyan, Yellow, and Purple representing product collection and order, collaboration and coordination, return rate, logistics analytics, and logistics management respectively.

Material Evaluation: Group B results (415 papers) were screened manually. Articles and review papers were examined, based on the relevance with the topic; Table 2 presents the summary.

Figure 7. Analysis of Group C

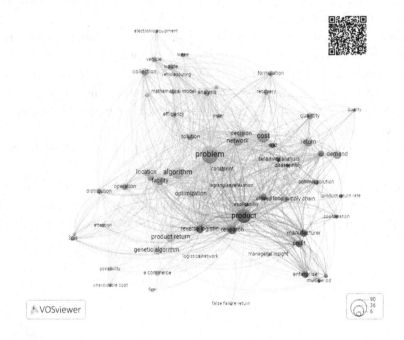

Table 2. Summary of Articles

Future scope	Development of alternative metaheuristic algorithms such as Tabu Search (TS), Scatter Search	_____	Network optimization with the uncertainty of return, to design a sustainable network for product returns, which aims equally at sustainability in economic, environmental, and social dimensions.
Research gap	Insufficient study on VRP for reverse logistics and its real-world applications	Optimization of the numbers and location of collecting points, recycling centers, and remanufacturing centers for E-commerce based on genetic algorithm	MPGSA algorithm was not used earlier to address the mentioned problem. Earlier used model (GA, SA, AIS)
Findings	The algorithm satisfactorily handles a real-life problem as well as other random instances generated. The algorithm is convenient to solve problems in which the date windows and collection capacity are tightly constrained.	The authors conducted the calculation 10 times with different initial values. And found, model of the paper is effective with an ideal fitness	The average total cost of the product returns network using MPGSA reaches the lowest level, reduced by 9.26% compared to Artificial immune system (AIS), 8.32% compared to SA, and 5.85 when compared to PGSA.
Methods	ANOVA test, Mixed-integer linear programming, GRASP based meta-heuristic model	Genetic Algorithm (GA)	MPGSA based optimization model.
Objective	To design a Greedy Randomized Adaptive Searching Procedure (GRASP) algorithm to solve a real-world problem where a fixed and heterogeneous fleet of capacitated vehicles with special features is used in the collection of WEEE from a set of customers.	A GA-based model is proposed for the design of reverse logistics network site handling product returns.	A mixed-integer non-linear programming model to mi a high-efficiency method, the Modified Plant Growth Simulation Algorithm (MPGSA), to optimize the problem.
Author, Year	Mar-Ortiz et al., 2013	Liu., 2014	Wang et al., 2017

continues on following page

Table 2.Continued

Future scope	Adding more EE equipment, Increasing the size of the dataset	To evaluate information system and novel body design of the vehicle to compare loading and handling times for various categories of e-waste.	To study the potential cost and benefits of retailer return policies.
Research gap	The gap in communication between residents and waste collection companies.	Previous work used SA, Bee Colony Algorithm, TS, Greedy Algorithm	Previous work studies were returned from the retailer's perspective. Lack of study from manufacturer's perspective.
Findings	The recognition and classification accuracy of the selected e-waste categories ranged from 90 to 97%.	The number of collection points calculated by the HS algorithm could be higher from 1.2% to 6.6%; Potential profit from the secondary raw materials from the waste collection could be higher 5.1% to 13.2% and the total mass of collected waste appliance up to 7%.	LASSO model achieved the highest accuracy in predicting future return volume.
Methods	Deep Learning Model, Convolution neural network (CNN)	Harmony Search (HS) Algorithm used for solving the vehicle routing problem with time windows.	Least Absolute Shrinkage and Selection Operator (LASSO), based predictive model, ML, Random Forest, Gradient Boosting
Objective	To develop an image recognition system for the identification and classification of weee from photos in purpose to facilitate the information exchange between waste collection point and waste collector.	An integrated approach with an improved information system designed to support the mobile collection of e-waste on demand.	To build a good data-driven model to predict return volume in the future.
Author, Year	Nowakowski & Pamula, 2020	Nowakowski et al., 2020	Cui et al., 2020
Future scope	The approach can be applied to dynamic and static network analysis such as risk interaction and project governance networks.	To consider traffic density on the road and congestion parameters for route planning.	Further studies can be extended to VRP with refurbished products and the uncertainties related to loading/unloading of products and Stochastic nature of distribution centre and uncertainties in resource allocation.
Research gap	———	Test four algorithms to solve VRP for weee collection.	Insufficient study on the application of forward and reverse logistics in VRP. Some studies failed to properly integrate realistic factors in e-commerce logistics.
Findings	Improved SA performs better than standard SA for all three problems (5, 10, 15 nodes).	SA is best and TS is worst for the support of mobile collection at request.	CPLEX gives optimal solution when compared to the proposed metaheuristic approach; For a large data set, CPLEX computation time is too high to obtain the solution, Par-DE performs better than the DE, GA, and BBGA algorithms
Methods	Matrix-based simulation model for uncertainty, SA, and improved SA	SA, TS, Greedy Search, Bee colony optimization	Exact optimization (CPLEX tools), Metaheuristic algorithm (Differential evolutionary algorithm (DE), Parallel DE algorithm (Par-DE), GA, Block-based GA (BBGA)

continues on following page

Table 2.Continued

Objective	To design a reverse logistics network for increasing the storage capacity.	To build artificial intelligence algorithms for solving VRP with time windows for a heterogeneous fleet of waste.	To develop a Mixed-integer non-linear programming model to address a VRP with simultaneous pickup and delivery with time windows from multiple depots over a time horizon in the B2C e-commerce logistics system to minimize the total transportation cost and penalty due to delay by logistics service providers.
Author, Year	Wang et al., 2018	Nowakowski et al., 2018	Zhang et al., 2020
Future scope	Tracking previous local optima or intelligent clustering techniques, Improvement of existing metaheuristic model. Development of Adaptive operators, stagnations prevention mechanisms, integration with data mining techniques to increase exploration ability.	Improvement of MLAFF with various cubing strategies like extreme point, Options for selecting solutions for varying cartoon set size, Unsupervised learning method for cartoon grouping phase, Minimizing the total void in cartoons or no. of cartoons prices by dimensional weight considering multi-objective strategies.	
Research gap	——	Insufficient and limited papers that directly address the carton set optimization problem. In addition, there is a gap between theory and practice of supply chain operational issues in terms of the problem investigated and methodologies utilized.	
Findings	In-depth study of 14 algorithms, a brief explanation of another 70 algorithms, discussion on the hybrid model.	Carton utilization rate is negatively related and positively related to the shipping cost and annualized saving respectively, Due to various sizes of cartons (shipping cost will be different), it is inaccurate to utilize per-item shipping cost, Order cubing based on MLAFF is a heuristic algorithm, which can lead to suboptimal solutions. The three-stage model can also lead to a suboptimal solution.	
Methods	Review	Three Stages: 1. Order Cubing- Modified largest area fit first (MLAFF) method. 2. Carton Grouping: Sort by descending volume, remove or add 3. Selecting optimal cartoon set- GA	
Objective	Review of new generation metaheuristics algorithms	To construct an optimal carton set, given the original carton set and the order shipping data of the warehouse.	
Author, Year	Dokeroglu., 2019	Singh & Ardimand., 2020	

FUTURE RESEARCH DIRECTIONS AND CONCLUSION

The conveyance of items from a point of origin to a point of consumption relies heavily on logistics. Reverse logistics is a term that refers to the movement of goods from point of consumption to point of origin with the aim of resale, repair, remanufacture, reuse, or recapturing. The information technology systems used in conjunction with AI and ML can help to improve reverse logistics. This chapter focuses on e-commerce and e-waste. According to the literature, 30 percent of products bought online are returned, costing over $640 billion. Furthermore, damaged or poor quality and malfunctioning items account for more than half of all returns. Necessary steps are important to reduce the return rate. The paper summarised past research on creating unsupervised learning approaches to sort or categorize the products, as well as forecasting the number of product returns for early decision-making. From a sustainability standpoint, an E-waste management system is urgently required. Studies in the literature presented the development of an information technology system to connect users to the collection center. CNN-based image recognition techniques are suggested to sort and manipulate the product. The inclusion of a heterogeneous set of EEE with large data is suggested for the further scope of the study. In the domain of RL, there are a substantial number of research on vehicle routing challenges for minimizing distance and cost. Study on VRP with new generation meta-heuristic and hybrid meta-heuristic model needed to be tested.

REFERENCES

Cui, H., Rajagopalan, S., & Ward, A. R. (2020). Predicting product return volume using machine learning methods. *European Journal of Operational Research*, *281*(3), 612–627. doi:10.1016/j.ejor.2019.05.046

DIRECTIVE. 2002/96/EC OF THE EUROPEAN PARLIAMENT AND OF THE COUNCIL of 27 January 2003 on waste electrical and electronic equipment (WEEE) (2003 EU WEEE directive), https://eur-lex.europa.eu/resource.html?uri=cellar:ac89e64f-a4a5-4c13-8d96-1fd1d6bcaa49.0004.02/DOC_1&format=PDF DIRECTIVE 2012/19/EU

Dokeroglu, T., Sevinc, E., Kucukyilmaz, T. & Cosar, A. (2019). A survey on new generation metaheuristic algorithms. *Computers & Industrial Engineering*.

E-commerce product return rate statistics and trends 2020. (2021). Accessed September 12, 2021, https://magnetoitsolutions.com/infographic/e-commerce-product-return-rate

Forti, V., Baldé, C. P., & Kuehr, R. (2018). E-waste Statistics: Guidelines on Classifications, Reporting and Indicators (2nd ed.). United Nations University, ViE – SCYCLE.

Forti, V., Baldé, C. P., Kuehr, R., & Bel, G. (n.d.). *The Global E-waste Monitor 2020: Quantities, flows and the circular economy potential*. United Nations University (UNU)/United Nations Institute for Training and Research (UNITAR) – co-hosted SCYCLE Programme, International Telecommunication Union (ITU) & International Solid Waste Association (ISWA). https://globalewaste.org/

Geissdoerfer, M., Savaget, P., Bocken, N. M., & Hultink, E. J. (2017). The Circular Economy–A new sustainability paradigm? *Journal of Cleaner Production*, *143*, 757–768. doi:10.1016/j.jclepro.2016.12.048

Georgiadis, P., & Besiou, M. (2008). Sustainability in electrical and electronic equipment closed-loop supply chains: A System Dynamics approach. *Journal of Cleaner Production*, *16*(15), 1665–1678. doi:10.1016/j.jclepro.2008.04.019

Guide, V. D. R. Jr, & Van Wassenhove, L. N. (2009). OR FORUM—The evolution of closed-loop supply chain research. *Operations Research*, *57*(1), 10–18. doi:10.1287/opre.1080.0628

Hammond, D., & Beullens, P. (2007). Closed-loop supply chain network equilibrium under legislation. *European Journal of Operational Research*, *183*(2), 895–908. doi:10.1016/j.ejor.2006.10.033

Işıldar, A., Rene, E. R., van Hullebusch, E. D., & Lens, P. N. L. (2017). Electronic waste as a secondary source of critical metals: Management and recovery technologies. *Resources, Conservation and Recycling*.

Islam, M. T., & Huda, N. (2018). Reverse logistics and closed-loop supply chain of Waste Electrical and Electronic Equipment (WEEE)/E-waste: A comprehensive literature review. *Resources, Conservation and Recycling, 137*(48-75).

Jaehn, F. (2016). Sustainable operations. *European Journal of Operational Research, 253*(2), 243–264. doi:10.1016/j.ejor.2016.02.046

Kannan, G., Palaniappan, M., Zhu, Q., & Kannan, D. (2012). Analysis of third-party reverse logistics provider using interpretive structural modeling. *International Journal of Production Research, 140*(1), 204–211. doi:10.1016/j.ijpe.2012.01.043

Khalid Saleh. (2016). *E-commerce Product Return Rate – Statistics and Trends.* Accessed September 12, 2021, https://www.invespcro.com/blog/ecommerce-product-return-rate-statistics/

Kotler, P., & Keller, K. L. (2016). *Marketing Management.* Pearson Education Limited.

Kumar, A., Holuszko, M., & Espinosa, D. C. R. (2017). E-waste: An overview on generation, collection, legislation and recycling practices. *Resources, Conservation and Recycling, 122,* 32–42. doi:10.1016/j.resconrec.2017.01.018

Liu, D. (2014). Network site optimization of reverse logistics for E-commerce based on genetic algorithm. *Neural Computing & Applications, 25*(1), 67–71. doi:10.100700521-013-1448-1

Mar-Ortiz, J., González-Velarde, J. L., & Adenso-Díaz, B. (2013). Designing routes for WEEE collection: The vehicle routing problem with split loads and date windows. *Journal of Heuristics, 19*(2), 103–127. doi:10.100710732-011-9159-1

Nowakowski, P., & Pamuła, T. (2020). Application of deep learning object classifier to improve e-waste collection planning. *Waste Management (New York, N.Y.), 109,* 1–9. doi:10.1016/j.wasman.2020.04.041 PMID:32361385

Nowakowski, P., Szwarc, K., & Boryczka, U. (2018). Vehicle route planning in e-waste mobile collection on demand supported by artificial intelligence algorithms. *Transportation Research Part D, Transport and Environment, 63,* 1–22. doi:10.1016/j.trd.2018.04.007

Nowakowski, P., Szwarc, K., & Boryczka, U. (2020). Combining an artificial intelligence algorithm and a novel vehicle for sustainable e-waste collection. *The Science of the Total Environment, 730,* 138726. doi:10.1016/j.scitotenv.2020.138726 PMID:32388362

Pradhan, M., & Kumar, U. D. (2019). *Machine Learning using Python.* Wiley India Pvt. Ltd.

Rogers, D. S., & Tibben-Lembke, R. S. (1999). *Going Backwards Reverse Logistics Trends and Practices.* Reverse Logistics Executive Council.

Sharma, M., Ammons, J. C., & Hartman, J. C. (2007). Asset management with reverse product flows and environmental considerations. *Computers & Operations Research, 34*(2), 464–486. doi:10.1016/j.cor.2005.03.009

Singh, M., & Ardjmand, E. (2020). Carton Set Optimization in E-commerce Warehouses: A Case Study. *Journal of Business Logistics, 41*(3), 222–235. doi:10.1111/jbl.12255

Sokolov, I. A. (2019). Theory and Practice of Application of Artificial Intelligence Methods. *Herald of the Russian Academy of Sciences, 89*(2), 115–119. doi:10.1134/S1019331619020205

Stock, J. R. (1992). *Reverse logistics: White paper.* Council of Logistics Management.

Swamidass, P. M. (2000). *Encyclopedia of Production and Manufacturing Management*. Springer. doi:10.1007/1-4020-0612-8

Taha, H. A. (2017). *Operations Research an Introduction*. Pearson Education.

The Economist. (2014). *The business of reselling returned shop items: What happens to all the goods shoppers don't want*. Accessed September 12, 2021, https://www.economist.com/news/business/21710855-what-happens-all-goods-shoppers-dont-want-business-reselling-returned-shop-items

Wang, L., Goh, M., Ding, R., & Mishra, V. (2018). Improved Simulated Annealing Based Network Model for E-Recycling Reverse Logistics Decisions under Uncertainty. *Mathematical Problems in Engineering*, 1–17.

Wang, X., Qiu, J., Li, T., & Ruan, J. (2017). A Network optimization research for product returns using modified plant growth simulation algorithm,. *Scientific Programming*.

Yang, J., Lu, B., Xu, C., (2008). WEEE flow and mitigating measures in China. *Waste Management, 28*, 1589-1597.

Zeng, X., Li, J., Stevels, A. L. N., & Liu, L. (2013). Perspective of electronic waste management in China based on a legislation comparison between China and the EU. *Journal of Cleaner Production, 51*, 80–87.

Zhang, M., Pratap, S., Zhao, Z., Prajapati, D., & Huang, G. Q. (2020). Forward and reverse logistics vehicle routing problems with time horizons in B2C e-commerce logistics. *International Journal of Production Research*.

Zhang, W., Dechter, R., & Korf, R. E. (2001). Heuristic Search in Artificial Intelligence. *Artificial Intelligence, 129*(1-2), 1–4.

Zhang, X., Li, Z., & Wang, Y. (2020). A Review of the Criteria and Methods of Reverse Logistics Supplier Selection. *Processes (Basel, Switzerland)*.

ADDITIONAL READING

Critical Raw Materials Resilience. (2020). *Charting a Path towards greater Security and Sustainability*. European Commission.

KEY TERMS AND DEFINITIONS

Closed-Loop Supply Chain: A system consisting of both logistics and reverse logistics.

E-Commerce: An internet-based platform to buy or sell a product.

E-Waste: Any electrical or electronic item which is of no use or discarded.

Meta-Heuristic Algorithm: Heuristic algorithms that are inspired by nature and help to get out of local minima.

Reverse Logistics: Performing logistic activities from customer to producer.

Artificial Intelligence for Sustainable Humanitarian Logistics

Ibrahim Opeyemi Oguntola
Dalhousie University, Canada

M. Ali Ülkü
🆔 https://orcid.org/0000-0002-8495-3364
Dalhousie University, Canada

INTRODUCTION

Artificial Intelligence (AI) involves the ability of machines to make decisions and do activities smartly with little or no human intervention. It is also famously described as an "agent" that can perceive its environment and perform actions to maximize its chances of achieving its goal. (Nilsson 1996). Since its boom in the 1980s, AI has been judiciously applied to a wide range of sectors, including social media (e.g., user behaviour analysis, language translation), banking (e.g., fraud detection), e-commerce (e.g., recommendation systems, AI-powered assistants), automotive (e.g., auto-pilot, auto-parking, road traffic analysis), healthcare (e.g., early disease detection, the discovery of new drugs, evidence-based telehealth) and even in governmental and justice decisions. This chapter seeks to discuss its application to sustainable humanitarian logistics.

Some of the factors powering the advances in AI include the increasing availability of supercomputing power and cloud resources, the efficient generation and documentation of data through various sources such as blockchain, Internet of Things (IoT), social media, mobile technologies, and the continuous emergence of innovative algorithms. Some of the standard algorithms or techniques used in AI modelling include single or hybrids of Artificial Neural Networks (ANN), Fuzzy Logic (FL) models, Genetic Algorithms (GA), Swarm Intelligence (SI), Random Forest (RF), Support Vector Machines (SVM), Naïve Bayes (NB), Optical Character Recognition (OCR), Natural Language Processing (NLP), among others. These algorithms support AI-based programs in performing specific tasks and can be incorporated into software or tools. In general, AI methods fall under supervised models, unsupervised models, deep learning (DL), reinforcement learning, deep reinforcement learning and optimization (Sun et al., 2020). Other applications of AI include computer vision, robotics, expert systems and speech recognition.

As an Industry 4.0 technology, AI is already a buzzword in logistics management, capable of revolutionizing supply chains (SCs) and unleashing new levels of efficiency. It has become even more accessible and affordable in recent times, making it more available. At large, AI can better coordinate the flow of information, goods and personnel between the elements of any SC network while enhancing its sustainability.

Humanitarian Logistics (HL), a specific field of logistics management, aids efforts in the response system to natural or manmade disasters. It involves the planning and activities to resolve the complicated logistical challenges that might be present. Disaster response management approaches utilizing the latest technologies such as AI are necessary to ensure smoother implementations as poor response to disasters could directly lead to loss of lives. Stages such as Risk assessment, Preparation, Response, and Recov-

DOI: 10.4018/978-1-7998-9220-5.ch177

ery/Relief have to be fine-tuned for each type of disaster to ensure more efficient and effective rescue and de-escalation missions. By nature, disasters generally have high levels of uncertainty. In assessing the situation, having accurate and timely information is crucial. Precise prediction of how the situation could escalate is critical to ensure robust preparations. There is also a need for coherent coordination of all the elements (such as personnel, equipment, food, organizations) involved to ensure the smooth transition of all planned activities. AI can tackle each of the highlighted demands while helping to save lives, reduce environmental impact and preserve cultural heritage at the lowest cost possible. The authors of this chapter define *Sustainable Humanitarian Logistics* (SHL) as

the design and implementation of all the humanitarian logistics systems and operations directed to save as many lives as possible (societal) at the least cost possible (economical) while reducing the impact of disasters on the environment (e.g. reducing hazardous debris) and ensuring the conservation of the cultures disasters might impact (cultural).

These four sustainability factors (economical, social, environmental, and cultural) are jointly referred to as the Quadruple Bottom-Line (QBL) pillars from whose lens any activity has to be analyzed before being considered sustainable or not (see, Ülkü & Engau (2020) and Figure 1).

Figure 1. Summary of the QBL pillars

In what follows, a brief introduction to SHL is given, followed by a review of published studies showing the state of research on the application of AI methods to sectors of HL. Most of these studies offer the generation of new algorithms and tools that could be used to enhance specific logistics operations. This is followed by a table showing AI-based decision support tools already available in practice. Future research directions and a Conclusion are then provided.

BACKGROUND

Humanitarian Logistics (HL) is a sector of logistics management that aids efforts in the response system to manmade (e.g., nuclear explosion, tanker oil spills, climate refuge) or natural (e.g., earthquakes, floods, pandemics) disasters that negatively impact a community leading to human life, economic, cultural or environmental losses. It includes all the processes involved in planning and mobilizing resources and support to aid communities afflicted with disaster to relieve human suffering and reduce the loss of lives and properties. When HL processes abide by the four pillars of QBL, it can be termed Sustainable Humanitarian Logistics (SHL).

HL is different from Business Logistics in that: 1- The objective is not to maximize profit but to save as many lives as possible; 2- There is uncertainty in most of the parameters involved; 3- There is a high stake associated with timely relief to reduce the chances of losing more lives; 4- There might be complex operational conditions such as transportation routes being cut off, lack of required resources etc.; finally, 5- There is a need for proper coordination between the multiple relief organizations that might be present. Also, during widespread pandemics such as COVID-19, little information might be known about the cause of the catastrophe or how to deal with it, thereby sending a large portion of the logistical system into disarray and necessitating the design of entirely new systems.

With the climate crisis, natural disasters are on the rise and AI may prove useful in mitigation efforts (e.g., Heteren et al., 2020). Kaveh et al. (2020) point out that considering the various uncertainties under catastrophic conditions, complex human behaviour (especially when agitated as in a disaster situation), among other factors, there is a need to develop better decision-making models or systems and to establish a worldwide standard database management system (DBMS) to make data gathering and sharing available for use in current and future disaster situation assessment. This indeed points to an area where AI can be judiciously utilized. With an open database, AI can provide insight into disaster situations, make accurate visual models, run simulations on possible disaster escalations and evacuation routes, and more while considering many uncertain and specific parameters. It can also be used to develop more sophisticated decision-making models on where to locate relief facilities, how and when to transport human and material resources safely and efficiently, and how to allocate these resources more efficiently to meet the uncertain needs of the different groups of people impacted. Some of the AI tools and algorithms generated in research and their application to different phases of HL will be highlighted.

There is a sustainability requirement in attempts to find appropriate mitigation, response or curbing solutions to the increasingly complex systems of relief operations. SHL can be divided into risk assessment, preparedness, immediate response and ongoing recovery/relief, as displayed in Figure 2.

Risk Assessment and Disaster Preparedness

Any disaster response activity aims to ensure that as many lives as possible are saved, and the situation is mitigated. Therefore, it is crucial to perform a risk assessment before taking action carefully. This would ensure that nothing is missed and the best course of action is taken after viewing the situation and possible escalations. After risk assessment, critical logistical decisions such as what response options are available, delivery method and network design, whether and where to pre-position relief supplies, how to orchestrate relief organizations, staffing, and resource sharing requirements are to be made in preparation for response operations.

Figure 2. Depiction of Sustainable Humanitarian Logistics stream

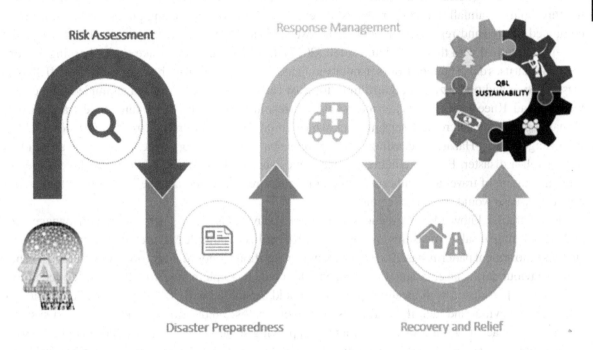

Considering human computational capacity and urgent situations, the final decisions might not be the most timely and efficient. There is an increasing necessity to incorporate AI into the risk assessment and response planning procedure. Utilizing the possible application of AI to predict uncertainties, we can aim to make decisions so robust they are relatively unaffected by complications unless highly unexpected. Using data obtained from simulations and past occurrences, AI with innovative algorithms could take advantage of advanced computational capabilities to hasten the decision-making process while considering many more factors, even if some are uncertain. More comprehensive planning would reduce the impact of the disaster smoothen evacuation if necessary while saving as much cost as possible hence enabling the sustainability of the recovery process. AI could also predict where and when disasters will strike, allowing escalation through widespread warnings, early evacuation and strategic pre-positioning of supplies. Some of the past applications and research carried out in this area are discussed in the following paragraphs.

The utilization of AI to predict the possible impact of an impending disaster would enable disaster managers to make appropriate mitigatory plans. Reed (2008) trained a regression model using historical data to predict potential infrastructural service disruptions due to hazards. This is necessary to identify the most vulnerable areas and populations as they might be disproportionately affected by natural hazards. Jeong and Yoon (2018) employed regression analysis to analyze ten vulnerability indicator factors on disaster damage in 230 local communities in South Korea. The model enabled recognizing the relationship between vulnerability factors and the accompanying disaster damage, identifying the most vulnerable communities. Wu et al. (2013) used a fuzzy clustering iterative model to study the agricultural drought vulnerability of 65 cities in the Yellow River basin. Identifying vulnerable areas is vital for disaster management to enable plans that mitigate disaster consequences, such as activities related to risk reduction, education to improve disaster awareness, better preparedness and proper allocation of resources. This would protect the minorities and vulnerable people, thereby enhancing cultural sustainability.

In terms of early detection or hazard forecasting to enable proactivity, Naidu et al. (2018) determined the threshold of rainfall that triggers landslide events in a sample city using an algorithm based on a combined cluster and regression model. The next landslide event could be predicted and necessary measures actioned with this. Rafiei and Adeli (2017) developed an Earthquake Early Warning System (EEWS) that uses data obtained from seismicity indicators in conjunction with a combination of ML-based classification and optimization algorithm to forecast earthquakes' occurrence magnitude and location weeks ahead. Rhee and Im (2017) formulated a high-resolution drought forecasting model trained using climatological data and remote sensing data, which could be used for drought-related decision-making in ungauged areas. Hazard forecasting could thereby spark the building of preventative infrastructures to forestall a disaster. Early prediction of pandemics such as COVID-19 could necessitate the early implementation of travel and gathering limitations measures. AI could also be further used to map out how the disease would spread over time.

In preparation, knowledge of evacuees' movement behaviour is beneficial to evacuation management and the building of safety measures. Wang et al. (2019) utilized multiple ML methods to study evacuees' stepwise movement patterns based on experimental evacuation videos, thereby obtaining findings on human behaviour during an emergency evacuation. This could be implemented for other real-life scenarios. Videos from past disasters in locations prone to it could be studied with ML algorithms. Preemption of evacuees' behaviour and identifying the best evacuation paths can develop evacuation support systems to smoothen evacuations and save lives, thereby improving societal sustainability (Peng et al., 2019).

In strategy development, proper situation assessment is needed. Zhang (2016) demonstrates how computer-vision methods can be used for assessing the state of affairs, such as target recognition and scene understanding, with data obtained from remote-sensing-enabled apparatuses using DL.

In summary, AI could forecast hazards, build disaster sensing and early warning systems, estimate impact, assess vulnerability, develop strategies, plan evacuations and determine how to pre-position resources most efficiently in preparedness. Altogether, AI could assist in the development of a disaster management strategy that aims to consider as many of the present factors as possible to obtain a plan of action to prevent or mitigate the impact of disasters, thereby enhancing SHL.

Response Management

This phase begins immediately after a disaster has occurred to restore access to essential services, provide supplies to the highest number of beneficiaries possible in the shortest time (Cozzolino et al., 2012), avoid or reduce damages and rescue as many people as possible if the location is deemed inhabitable. There is usually limited information about the exact requirements, making response operations a 'reactionary logistics' (Apte 2009). However, suppose supplies have been strategically pre-positioned (maybe due to predictions) and response networks pre-planned. In that case, these 'silent networks' could be activated to provide quick channels for the flow of resources, information and humans (Cozzolino et al., 2012).

Collaboration and coordination among all the actors involved in the response operation are critical. There might be a need to revise the initial plans or troubleshoot as the situation unfolds. Last-mile transportation networks might have to be determined on the field while considering all the parameters and obstacles present (e.g. unmotorable roads). Optimal distribution of available resources, facility location, and medical assistance deployment would also generally be determined on the field. In widespread epidemic (pandemic) situations, a response step would also be to find the root cause of the epidemic and efficiently tackle it. This might not be easy as the present COVID-19 outbreak has shown that it

A

could take time to devise a solid solution. Therefore, there is a need for mitigation steps to manage the pandemic's effects while searching for a definitive resolution.

AI could be quite impactful to disaster response as it can evaluate the situation in real-time while generating timely suggestions. Drones endowed with AI capabilities can be used to take a bird-eye view of the area and run quick vehicle routing problems (VRP) to figure out how best to navigate transport. Automated robots could go into dangerous areas to protect victims and perform surveillance operations. AI could also improve disaster response outcomes through real-time feedback and improvement recommendations on how effective the response procedures are while also gathering data to train itself in preparation for future disasters. In a review of academic research and practices that have been done on the application of AI to disaster response, a few of such studies are referenced below.

Imran et al. (2020) postulated how textual messages, images, and videos posted on social media such as Twitter during and post disasters could be incorporated as data sources for humanitarian organizations. The paper then discusses that some of the challenges to this, such as information overload, noisy data, real-time information processing, information extraction, summarization and verification of content, could be tackled using AI. For example, big data analytics techniques could handle vast volumes of data, NLP and DL algorithms for summarization and extraction of helpful content, ML algorithms such as naïve Bayes classifiers for verification of textual content etc. More research is being done to develop more sophisticated techniques that can handle each of the challenges faced more efficiently, thereby making this more viable as time goes on.

Demertzis et al. (2021) introduced a Geo-AI disaster response system based on computer vision capable of mapping out a large area. During disaster response, this could be used to obtain an updated map of the site, thereby enabling proper planning of vehicle routes, last-mile distribution, rescue and evacuation paths. Hayakawa et al. (2012) proposed a disaster recognition algorithm based on SVM, which uses a particular Emergency Rescue Evacuation Support System (ERESS) and obtains data from various sensors to detect disaster outbreaks, determine their position immediately and the appropriate evacuation routes to reduce the number of victims in panic-type disasters. Rahman and Hasan (2018) presented a DL model for predicting traffic speeds in freeways during periods of high demand such as disaster-induced evacuation thereby enabling emergency managers to respond to changing traffic conditions and smoothen evacuation operations actively.

There is a need to keep predicting how the situation would unfold or change to adjust plans appropriately during a disaster. Jhong et al. (2017) proposed an SVM-based two-stage forecasting system that could be used during a typhoon to forecast inundation depth as soon as hours earlier using past data from observed inundation maps. Khouj et al. (2011) modelled a reinforcement learning-based agent trained on simulated disaster scenarios to enable the agent to gather experience, capture knowledge and take actions that could help mitigate damage and casualties to assist human emergency responders. As an extension to Khouj et al. (2011), a three-dimensional (3D) real-time view of the affected area obtained from a drone circumnavigating the airspace above a disaster-struck area would enable the continuous inflow of recent data to such an agent, thereby enabling it to make timely and applicable suggestions.

Other applications of AI in assisting disaster management experts in mapping the event (Yu et al., 2005; Kovordányi and Roy, 2009; Yang and Cervone, 2019), assess the damage (Bandara et al., 2014, Cooner et al., 2016, Rudner et al., 2019), optimize resource allocation (Bayerlein et al., (2018), Chaudhuri and Bose (2020)) and enhance collaboration between relief organizations (Morito et al., (2016), Neppalli et al., (2018)) have also been explored. In terms of sustainability, the implementation of AI solutions to disaster response would improve the sustainability of HL by ensuring the objective of saving lives is more achievable (societal) at the least cost possible (economical). At the same time, incurred damage is mitigated by protecting infrastructures of sentimental values (cultural) and limiting the amount of waste generated (environmental).

Recovery and Relief

As the consequences of a disaster can be felt for a long time, even after its occurrence, the recovery phase looks into the effects of a disaster from a long-term perspective. This includes plans to handle future disaster risks, reducing the possibility of re-occurrence and its impacts. Preventive and mitigative measures have to be set as long-term recovery plans in areas with repeated catastrophic potentials and areas of forecasted occurrence. An example is building flood shelters in coastal regions prone to flooding. This is in line with making the community more prepared for potential future disasters (Yadav & Barve 2016). This phase also involves post-disaster reconstruction, including steps such as the adequate assessment of damage and needs, building houses and infrastructures, resuscitation of communication facilities, management of disaster waste, provision of medicine to prevent common diseases, and rehabilitation of the people impacted and revitalization of the economy. Governmental and Non Governmental Organizations (NGOs) are usually very involved in providing relief to disaster-hit communities. AI could be employed to estimate loss and repair costs, thereby providing a basis for seeking contributions from these parties.

Considering the complexity of the situation, AI could be utilized to support disaster recovery in various ways, including the accurate and quick assessment of the impact of the disaster in detail, development and tracking of recovery plans, evaluation of repair cost, coordination, among all organizations involved, re-evaluation of disaster response and determination of what could be done better in the future. These could be done faster as AI can take advantage of high computational speed and data obtained from aerial images, social media imagery data, remote sensing devices and other sources. Another benefit of AI may emerge in coordinating relief donations; see, Ülkü et al. (2015) for modelling donor behaviours and their possible ramifications in humanitarian operations.

AI can be used to assess infrastructural damage, social and psychological impact on humans and the economic impacts. For instance, to quickly assess the full impact, Xu et al. (2019) used ML techniques to automate the detection of damaged buildings in disaster-hit areas with satellite imagery data obtained from remote sensing. Khaloo et al. (2018) utilized a combination of UAVs, computer vision, data capture and data analysis to produce optimized 3D models of target infrastructure for defect monitoring purposes. These and similar works provide a quicker and less labour-intensive alternative to visual inspection. AI methods can also be used to track human activity patterns on social media or through survey data to conduct sentiment analyses on the disaster-induced impact on humans (Gong et al., 2014, Sun et al., 2020). Estimates on the economic effects of a disaster, in-depth insights and possible ways forward could also be obtained using AI (Cheng & Zhang, 2020; Qiang et al., 2020).

It is then necessary to develop a recovery plan and formulate metrics to measure how well recovery activities progress and effectiveness, considering the communities' recovery. The optimal distribution of resources, recovery of communication, and repair of roads after a disaster are significant steps to recovery. AI can be used to ensure equity in rationing and allocation. Li & Teo (2019) developed a genetic algorithm-based model to schedule and optimally route repair crews during post-disaster road network repair to enable its quick return to accessibility. Orabi et al. (2010) built a multi-objective genetic algorithm-based model to allocate limited reconstruction resources to competing recovery projects while optimizing the reconstruction duration and cost. To restore communication, Zhong et al. (2018) suggest using a fleet of UAVs as data mules to provide communication means to survivors and then propose a model to generate suitable flight paths for the UAVs. Hackl et al. (2018) used simulated annealing to build a restoration model to determine the most effective restoration program while minimizing the cost, resources, and time needed to fully recover after a disruptive event. Such a model can assist infrastructure restoration managers by estimating the likely time to complete restoration, simulating multiple restoration strategies, thereby helping to revise operational plans. AI methods can also map disaster waste (debris), efficiently analyze disposal options, optimally decide where to locate temporary and permanent storage sites(landfills) and do route optimization to transport the waste.

In tracking post-disaster recovery, social media data can again be analyzed by AI to obtain insight into how well the community is recovering. Malawani et al. (2020) examined posts on Twitter about Typhoon Washi, especially posts from regions impacted by the disaster, to obtain general insights on public clamour about issues being faced by disaster victims. The paper by Mabon (2016) shows that Google Street View video and imagery data can also be a viable source of data for the rudimentary tracking of recovery and rehabilitation progress (decontamination, resettlement, infrastructural restoration, etc.). AI could also be used to detect and prevent disaster-related rumours and frauds. For example, an insurance company could compare the before and after satellite images to claim a flooded house (Gilmour, 2019; Sun et al., 2020).

The recovery phase ensures that societal normalcy is swiftly reinstated for societal sustainability. Also, the focus on providing necessary assistance to the vulnerable and minority will further ensure cultural sustainability. At the same time, the seeking of optimal methods of recovery using optimization models and ML techniques will enable that the cost incurred in recovery is as low as possible, hence economic sustainability. The removal of disaster waste and the recovery of road networks will reduce pollution, enabling environmental sustainability.

Research institutes and companies have developed numerous AI-based decision support tools to facilitate SHL practice. Some of these tools gathered from Google scholar [Accessed 26 April 2022] and Sun et al. (2020) are presented in Table 1.

Table 1. A few examples of HL tools

Tool	Owner	Applicable Phase	Hazard	Website
One Concern	One Concern, Inc.	Preparedness, response	Seismic, flood	https://oneconcern.com
TweetTracker	Arizona State University	Preparedness, response	General	http://blogtrackers.fulton.asu.edu
CrisisMappers	Crisis Mappers Net	Preparedness, response	General	https://crisismapping.ning.com
INFORM	Multi-government-industry collaborations	Situation assessment	General	https://drmkc.jrc.ec.europa.eu/inform-index
Adashi FirstResponse MDT	Adashi	Response	Fire	https://www.adashi.com
Tractable	Tractable	Recovery	Flood, fire, hurricane	https://tractable.ai

FUTURE RESEARCH DIRECTIONS

AI can increase humanitarian logistics efficiencies while embracing the QBL sustainability pillars. AI could prove immensely useful in collecting data and turning it into informed real-time decision alternatives for better collaboration of humanitarian assistance and concrete actions. As the climate crisis exacerbates, more and more disasters are surfacing worldwide. Any technology that could prevent, predict, and respond to disasters is invaluable. Implementing that technology itself is not damaging the environment, societal and cultural viability and is economically feasible. To that end, future research includes what humanitarian SC locations and to what level AI needs to be gauged in logistics operations, the optimal design of AI-enabled disaster management systems, and the determination of the carbon and water footprint of AI in such uses. For instance, devising AI tools in estimating the impact of climate change on remote and dense communities (e.g., Tiller et al., 2022) and aiding climate and war refugees (e.g., Salman et al., 2021) would be excellent research extensions. Nevertheless, as AI transitions from a paradigm to reality, more data sources must be explored, and better algorithms for extracting valuable and timely insights must be developed for current and emerging humanitarian problems.

CONCLUSION

Integrating AI into SHL provides avenues for enhancing all four pillars of sustainability (economic, environmental, societal and cultural). A few such applications have been highlighted above, but there are even more both in ongoing research works and in software being developed for usage in the industry. Despite the initial implementation cost of AI sometimes being relatively expensive, there are significant advantages in supporting humanitarian logistics. Smoothening the collaboration of humans and AI seamlessly, especially during disaster response operations, is very important. In SHL, AI-based systems learn from historical data and might not be capable of dealing with drastic changes and revolutions such as the impacts the COVID-19 pandemic had on supply chain networks. Therefore, there might be a need to incorporate worst-case scenarios into the design and implementation of AI-based systems to make them more resistant. Overall, the trend in research promises to increase the viability of AI in all spheres.

REFERENCES

Apte, A. (2009). Humanitarian logistics: A new field of research and action. Foundations and Trends® in Technology. *Information and Operations Management*, *3*(1), 1–87. doi:10.1561/0200000014

Bandara, R., Chan, T., & Thambiratnam, D. (2014). Structural damage detection method using frequency response functions. *Structural Health Monitoring*, *13*(4), 418–429. doi:10.1177/1475921714522847

Bayerlein, H., De Kerret, P., & Gesbert, D. (2018). Trajectory Optimization for Autonomous Flying Base Station via Reinforcement Learning. *2018 IEEE 19th International Workshop on Signal Processing Advances in Wireless Communications (SPAWC)*, 1-5. 10.1109/SPAWC.2018.8445768

Chaudhuri, N., & Bose, I. (2020). Exploring the role of deep neural networks for post-disaster decision support. *Decision Support Systems*, *130*, 113234. doi:10.1016/j.dss.2019.113234

Cheng, L., & Zhang, J. (2020). Is tourism development a catalyst of economic recovery following natural disaster? An analysis of economic resilience and spatial variability. *Current Issues in Tourism, 23*(20), 2602–2623. doi:10.1080/13683500.2019.1711029

Cooner, A., Shao, Y., & Campbell, J. (2016). Detection of Urban Damage Using Remote Sensing and Machine Learning Algorithms: Revisiting the 2010 Haiti Earthquake. *Remote Sensing (Basel, Switzerland), 8*(10), 868. doi:10.3390/rs8100868

Cozzolino, A., Rossi, S., & Conforti, A. (2012). Agile and lean principles in the humanitarian supply chain. *Journal of Humanitarian Logistics and Supply Chain Management, 2*(1), 16–33. doi:10.1108/20426741211225984

Demertzis, K., Iliadis, L., & Pimenidis, E. (2021). Geo-AI to aid disaster response by memory-augmented deep reservoir computing. *Integrated Computer-Aided Engineering, 28*(4), 383–398. doi:10.3233/ICA-210657

Gilmour, P. (2019). The application of photography in investigating fraud. *Imaging Science Journal, 67*(4), 215–223. doi:10.1080/13682199.2019.1600254

Gong, Q., Li, L., Tognin, S., Wu, Q., Pettersson-Yeo, W., Lui, S., & Mechelli, A. (2014). Using structural neuroanatomy to identify trauma survivors with and without post-traumatic stress disorder at the individual level. *Psychological Medicine, 44*(1), 195–203. doi:10.1017/S0033291713000561 PMID:23551879

Hackl, J., Adey, B., & Lethanh, N. (2018). Determination of Near-Optimal Restoration Programs for Transportation Networks Following Natural Hazard Events Using Simulated Annealing. *Computer-Aided Civil and Infrastructure Engineering, 33*(8), 618–637. doi:10.1111/mice.12346

Hayakawa, Y., Mori, K., Ishida, Y., Tsudaka, K., Wada, T., Okada, H., & Ohtsuki, K. (2012). Development of emergency rescue evacuation support system in panic-type disasters. *2012 IEEE Consumer Communications and Networking Conference (CCNC)*, 52-53. 10.1109/CCNC.2012.6181047

Heteren, A. V., Hirt, M., & Veken, L. V. (2020, January 14). *Natural disasters are increasing in frequency and ferocity. Here's how AI can come to the rescue.* Retrieved April 27, 2022, from https://www.weforum.org/agenda/2020/01/natural-disasters-resilience-relief-artificial-intelligence-ai-mckinsey/

Imran, M., Ofli, F., Caragea, D., & Torralba, A. (2020). Using AI and Social Media Multimodal Content for Disaster Response and Management: Opportunities, Challenges, and Future Directions. *Information Processing & Management, 57*(5), 102261. doi:10.1016/j.ipm.2020.102261

Jeong, S., & Yoon, D. (2018). Examining Vulnerability Factors to Natural Disasters with a Spatial Autoregressive Model: The Case of South Korea. *Sustainability (Basel, Switzerland), 10*(5), 1651. doi:10.3390u10051651

Jhong, B., Wang, J., & Lin, G. (2017). An integrated two-stage support vector machine approach to forecast inundation maps during typhoons. *Journal of Hydrology (Amsterdam), 547*, 236–252. doi:10.1016/j.jhydrol.2017.01.057

Kaveh, A., Javadi, S., & Moghanni, R. (2020). Emergency management systems after disastrous earthquakes using optimization methods: A comprehensive review. *Advances in Engineering Software, 149*, 102885. doi:10.1016/j.advengsoft.2020.102885

Khaloo, A., Lattanzi, D., Cunningham, K., Dell'Andrea, R., & Riley, M. (2018). Unmanned aerial vehicle inspection of the Placer River Trail Bridge through image-based 3D modelling. *Structure and Infrastructure Engineering, 14*(1), 124–136. doi:10.1080/15732479.2017.1330891

Khouj, M., Lopez, C., Sarkaria, S., & Marti, J. (2011). Disaster management in real time simulation using machine learning. *2011 24th Canadian Conference on Electrical and Computer Engineering(CCECE),* 1507-1510. 10.1109/CCECE.2011.6030716

Kovordányi, R., & Roy, C. (2009). Cyclone track forecasting based on satellite images using artificial neural networks. *ISPRS Journal of Photogrammetry and Remote Sensing, 64*(6), 513–521. doi:10.1016/j.isprsjprs.2009.03.002

Li, S., & Teo, K. (2019). Post-disaster multi-period road network repair: Work scheduling and relief logistics optimization. *Annals of Operations Research, 283*(1-2), 1345–1385. doi:10.100710479-018-3037-2

Mabon, L. (2016). Charting Disaster Recovery via Google Street View: A Social Science Perspective on Challenges Raised by the Fukushima Nuclear Disaster. *International Journal of Disaster Risk Science, 7*(2), 175–185. doi:10.100713753-016-0087-4

Malawani, A., Nurmandi, A., Purnomo, E., & Rahman, T. (2020). Social media in aid of post disaster management. *Transforming Government: People. Process and Policy, 14*(2), 237–260. doi:10.1108/TG-09-2019-0088

Morito, T., Sugiyama, O., Kojima, R., & Nakadai, K. (2016). Partially Shared Deep Neural Network in sound source separation and identification using a UAV-embedded microphone array. *2016 IEEE/RSJ International Conference on Intelligent Robots and Systems (IROS),* 1299-1304. 10.1109/IROS.2016.7759215

Naidu, S., Sajinkumar, K., Oommen, T., Anuja, V., Samuel, R., & Muraleedharan, C. (2018). Early warning system for shallow landslides using rainfall threshold and slope stability analysis. *Geoscience Frontiers, 9*(6), 1871–1882. doi:10.1016/j.gsf.2017.10.008

Neppalli, V., Caragea, C., & Caragea, D. (2018). Deep neural networks versus Naïve Bayes classifiers for identifying informative tweets during disasters. *Proceedings of the 15th Annual conference for Information Systems for Crisis Response and Management (ISCRAM 2018).*

Nilsson, N. (1996). Artificial intelligence: A modern approach. *Artificial Intelligence, 82*(1-2), 369–380. doi:10.1016/0004-3702(96)00007-0

Orabi, W., Senouci, A., El-Rayes, K., & Al-Derham, H. (2010). Optimizing Resource Utilization during the Recovery of Civil Infrastructure Systems. *Journal of Management Engineering, 26*(4), 237–246. doi:10.1061/(ASCE)ME.1943-5479.0000024

Peng, Y., Li, S., & Hu, Z. (2019). A self-learning dynamic path planning method for evacuation in large public buildings based on neural networks. *Neurocomputing (Amsterdam), 365,* 71–85. doi:10.1016/j.neucom.2019.06.099

Qiang, Y., Huang, Q., & Xu, J. (2020). Observing community resilience from space: Using nighttime lights to model economic disturbance and recovery pattern in natural disaster. *Sustainable Cities and Society, 57,* 102115. doi:10.1016/j.scs.2020.102115

Rafiei, M., & Adeli, H. (2017). NEEWS: A novel earthquake early warning model using neural dynamic classification and neural dynamic optimization. *Soil Dynamics and Earthquake Engineering*, *100*, 417–427. doi:10.1016/j.soildyn.2017.05.013

Rahman, R., & Hasan, S. (2018). Short-Term Traffic Speed Prediction for Freeways During Hurricane Evacuation: A Deep Learning Approach. *2018 21st International Conference on Intelligent Transportation Systems (ITSC)*, 1291-1296. 10.1109/ITSC.2018.8569443

Reed, D. (2008). Electric utility distribution analysis for extreme winds. *Journal of Wind Engineering and Industrial Aerodynamics*, *96*(1), 123–140. doi:10.1016/j.jweia.2007.04.002

Rhee, J., & Im, J. (2017). Meteorological drought forecasting for ungauged areas based on machine learning: Using long-range climate forecast and remote sensing data. *Agricultural and Forest Meteorology*, *237-238*, 105–122. doi:10.1016/j.agrformet.2017.02.011

Rudner, T., Rußwurm, M., Fil, J., Pelich, R., Bischke, B., Kopackova, V., & Bilinski, P. (2019). Multi3Net: segmenting flooded buildings via fusion of multiresolution, multisensor, and multitemporal satellite imagery. *Proceedings of the AAAI Conference on Artificial Intelligence*, *33*, 702–709. 10.1609/aaai.v33i01.3301702

Salman, F. S., Yücel, E., Kayı, İ., Turper-Alışık, S., & Coşkun, A. (2021). Modeling mobile health service delivery to Syrian migrant farm workers using call record data. *Socio-Economic Planning Sciences*, *77*, 101005. doi:10.1016/j.seps.2020.101005

Sun, W., Bocchini, P., & Davison, B. (2020). Applications of artificial intelligence for disaster management. *Natural Hazards (Dordrecht)*, *103*(3), 2631–2689. doi:10.100711069-020-04124-3

Tiller, S. J., Rhindress, A. P., Oguntola, I. O., Ülkü, M. A., Williams, K. A., & Sunadararajan, B. (2022). Exploring the impact of climate change on Arctic shipping through the lenses of Quadruple Bottom Line and Sustainable Development Goals. *Sustainability (Basel, Switzerland)*, *14*(4), 2193. doi:10.3390u14042193

Ülkü, M. A., Bell, K. M., & Wilson, S. G. (2015). Modeling the impact of donor behavior on humanitarian aid operations. *Annals of Operations Research*, *230*(1), 153–168. doi:10.100710479-014-1623-5

Ülkü, M. A., & Engau, A. (2021). Sustainable Supply Chain Analytics. Industry, Innovation and Infrastructure, Encyclopedia of the UN Sustainable Development Goals, 1123-1134. doi:10.1007/978-3-319-95873-6

Wang, K., Shi, X., Goh, A., & Qian, S. (2019). A machine learning based study on pedestrian movement dynamics under emergency evacuation. *Fire Safety Journal*, *106*, 163–176. doi:10.1016/j.firesaf.2019.04.008

Wu, D., Yan, D., Yang, G., Wang, X., Xiao, W., & Zhang, H. (2013). Assessment on agricultural drought vulnerability in the Yellow River basin based on a fuzzy clustering iterative model. *Natural Hazards (Dordrecht)*, *67*(2), 919–936. doi:10.100711069-013-0617-y

Xu, J., Lu, W., Li, Z., Khaitan, P., & Zaytseva, V. (2019). Building Damage Detection in Satellite Imagery Using Convolutional Neural Networks. *33rd conference on neural information processing systems (NeurIPS 2019)*. 10.48550/arXiv.1910.06444

Yadav, D., & Barve, A. (2016). Modeling Post-disaster Challenges of Humanitarian Supply Chains: A TISM Approach. *Global Journal of Flexible Systems Managment, 17*(3), 321–340. doi:10.100740171-016-0134-4

Yang, L., & Cervone, G. (2019). Analysis of remote sensing imagery for disaster assessment using deep learning: A case study of flooding event. *Soft Computing, 23*(24), 13393–13408. doi:10.100700500-019-03878-8

Yu, L., Wang, N., & Meng, X. (2005). Real-time forest fire detection with wireless sensor networks. *Proceedings. 2005 International Conference on Wireless Communications, Networking and Mobile Computing, 2,* 1214-1217. 10.1109/WCNM.2005.1544272

Zhang, L., Zhang, L., & Du, B. (2016). Deep Learning for Remote Sensing Data: A Technical Tutorial on the State of the Art. *IEEE Geoscience and Remote Sensing Magazine, 4*(2), 22–40. doi:10.1109/MGRS.2016.2540798

Zhong, L., Garlichs, K., Yamada, S., Takano, K., & Ji, Y. (2018). Mission planning for UAV-based opportunistic disaster recovery networks. *2018 15th IEEE Annual Consumer Communications & Networking Conference (CCNC),* 1-6. doi:10.1109/CCNC.2018.8319233

ADDITIONAL READING

Özdamar, L., & Ertem, M. A. (2015). Models, solutions and enabling technologies in humanitarian logistics. *European Journal of Operational Research, 244*(1), 55–65. doi:10.1016/j.ejor.2014.11.030

Rahimi, I., Gandomi, A. H., Fong, S. J., & Ülkü, M. A. (Eds.). (2020). *Big Data Analytics in Supply Chain Management: Theory and Applications.* CRC Press. doi:10.1201/9780367816384

Rodríguez-Espíndola, O., Chowdhury, S., Beltagui, A., & Albores, P. (2020). The potential of emergent disruptive technologies for humanitarian supply chains: The integration of blockchain, Artificial Intelligence and 3D printing. *International Journal of Production Research, 58*(15), 4610–4630. doi:10.1080/00207543.2020.1761565

Talavera, A., & Luna, A. (2020). Machine learning: A contribution to operational research. *IEEE Revista Iberoamericana de Tecnologias del Aprendizaje, 15*(2), 70–75. doi:10.1109/RITA.2020.2987700

Tomasini, R., & Van Wassenhove, L. (2009). From preparedness to partnerships: Case study research on humanitarian logistics. *International Transactions in Operational Research, 16*(5), 549–559. doi:10.1111/j.1475-3995.2009.00697.x

Woschank, M., Rauch, E., & Zsifkovits, H. (2020). A Review of Further Directions for Artificial Intelligence, Machine Learning, and Deep Learning in Smart Logistics. *Sustainability (Basel, Switzerland), 12*(9), 3760. doi:10.3390u12093760

KEY TERMS AND DEFINITIONS

Algorithm: A set of well-defined steps in problem-solving.

Artificial Intelligence (AI): Intelligence by machines.

Intelligent Technology: Application of scientific knowledge to perform decision-making functions that formerly have required human intervention, e.g., AI.

Machine Learning (ML): A branch of AI that automates data-driven analytical modelling.

Optimization: Determining the best solution(s) among feasible alternatives.

Quadruple Bottom Line (QBL): Economy, environment, society, and culture (four pillars) should collectively constrain decision-making, not just the profit.

Supply Chain (SC): All the parties and activities involved in fulfilling a customer order.

Sustainability: Meeting the needs of today without sacrificing those of the future.

Sustainable Humanitarian Logistics (SHL): All logistical operations based on QBL pillars and involved in preparing for, responding to, and mitigating disasters.

Blockchain Technology, Vanilla Production, and Fighting Global Warming

Robert Leslie Fisher

Independent Researcher, USA

INTRODUCTION

"Climate change is the defining issue of our time." The United Nations has predicted that "From shifting weather patterns that threaten food production, to rising sea levels that increase the risk of catastrophic flooding, the impacts of climate change are global in scope and unprecedented in scale." Nor is the U.N. alone in calling for urgent action. World leaders have spoken out about it including Presidents Xi Jin-Ping (China), Vladimir Putin (Russian Federation) and Joseph Biden (USA).

Although everyone agrees we must keep global warming from rising more than one-and-a-half degrees Celsius, this unanimity does not extend to how it will be accomplished. Developing nations have been arguing that they should be excused from giving this priority while they focus on growing their economies. As Shyam Saran points out, "There is a difference between the emissions of developing nations which are 'survival' emissions and those of developed countries which are in the nature of 'lifestyle' emissions. They do not belong to the same category and should not be treated equivalently" (Saran, 2015).

Saran warned that if we "blur this distinction [between the two kinds of emissions]," we have "to accept the argument that because 'we got here first, so we get to keep what we have, while those who come later must stay where they are for the sake of saving the planet from the threat of climate change'...."

Are developing nations saying they do not intend to help in the fight against global warming? No, they are not. They understand that would make it all but impossible to achieve the goal of preventing a rise in average temperature of one-and-a-half degrees Celsius within the next decade. Even as he was upbraiding the developed nations for "their historic emissions" Saran appealed to them to contribute the funds and transfer the technologies to developing countries needed to help them avoid dangerous climate change" (Saran 2015).

Is there a way to help developing nations grow their economies over the next ten years while taking serious steps to control air and water pollution? The author is convinced there is. It was proposed in 2015 by Saran. He rhetorically asked, "Why not create a global technology platform which can then be disseminated as global public goods?" In this author's opinion, if we are to achieve the goal of preventing catastrophic global warming, we must rally behind Saran's suggestion for a global technology platform to share the best ideas for fighting global warming.

Implicit in Saran's call for assistance to developing nations in growing their economies is the idea that a **benefit-cost analysis** done correctly would lead to donor nations offering to assist by selecting those technologies that would most advance the goal of growing the recipient nation's economy.

From this standpoint, an especially valuable form of assistance for implementing the global technology platform is offering to share **blockchain** technology with the developing nations of the world. The decision to do this must be made soon, however, as China is ready to offer this technology based on technology standards it is endorsing. Allowing China's authoritarian regime to impose its technical

DOI: 10.4018/978-1-7998-9220-5.ch178

standard and to exercise control over who has access to the technology opens the door to their "weaponizing" it, an undesirable outcome as far as freedom loving peoples of the world are concerned.

MAIN FOCUS

This paper inquires whether it is cost effective to apply **blockchain** technology to vanilla production in the island nation of Malagasy (more familiarly known as Madagascar), one of the most impoverished countries of the world. (In 2012, according to the C.I.A. World Factbook, Madagascar ranked 178 out of 188 entities [nation states for the most part] on the G.D.P. per capita, a standard measure used in macroeconomics.

Although more will be said about **blockchain** below, here it is useful to note a **blockchain** is essentially a digital ledger of transactions that is duplicated and distributed across the network of computer systems of stakeholders. Before diving into the case study of **blockchain** technology applied to vanilla production in Madagascar, however, it is useful to address the question of what is the strategy we need to use to partner with developing nations in the fight against global warming?

A Strategy for Economic Development of Developing Nations

The author maintains that partnering with developing nations to fight global warming begins with accepting that their primary objective is economic growth and development. People of these countries want to live in housing that is warm in the cold weather and cool in the hot weather. They want modern ovens and microwaves to cook because these are time and work saving devices. They want vacuum cleaners and other labor-saving equipment to clean and keep their homes looking nice. And they want fast transportation to get to their jobs but also to go out and enjoy themselves.

An acceptable plan for controlling air and water pollution leading to global warming must provide a feasible means for the country to acquire the money its inhabitants need to achieve their lifestyle goals. Clearly this plan for each country must have certain common features.

First, although tailored to meet their distinct circumstances, each country's plan will be composed insofar as possible of standardized elements. Next, we must tackle the question of what the appropriate elements are. An element such as planet friendly ways of manufacturing concrete and asphalt would be part of every country's plan (Watts, 2019). The same might be said of **computer assisted diagnosis (CAD)** in health care. However, perhaps in the Republic of the Congo in Africa, the computerized system might be heavily oriented to treatment of parasitic diseases endemic to tropic countries whereas in Argentina it might be heavily weighted to heart disease and cancer (J. L. Fisher, 2018).

Second, every country's development plan must have an appraisal of what areas of the economy might be suitable for investment that would help the nation earn foreign exchange it needs to buy what it cannot produce. For instance, suppose the country sees tourism as an area where it can invest to earn foreign exchange. In the case of Madagascar, it might decide that there is a demand from foreigners to visit the country to see its scenic wonders including its unique fauna and flora. However, before the tourists from developed nations will come in large numbers, Madagascar will need to invest in hotels and other amenities and infrastructure that meet European standards of comfort and technological advancement.

Transfer of technology to developing nations that allows them to achieve economic growth in planet friendly ways can be encouraged in various spheres. Transportation is a good example. In populous countries such as Nigeria, Indonesia, and India, **aerotropolises** could be built to speed the flow of goods and people into and out of the country. Elsewhere modernization of ground links to airports creating **"quasi-aerotropolises"** could accomplish most of the main benefits of **an aerotropolis** (R. L. Fisher, 2014; Kasarda and Lindsay, 2011).

Transportation systems in developing countries based on planet friendly technologies could be encouraged. For instance, these countries might be encouraged to buy and/or assemble hydrogen power trains. Alternatively, they could be offered the technology to assemble electric battery-operated vehicles including motorized bicycles for commuters (K. Chu, 2010; Toplensky, 2021). Fuel stingy Zeppelins currently under development could be used to ferry people across large bodies of water or mountain ranges instead of slow ferries and heaver-than-air aircraft that are fuel guzzlers with a big carbon footprint (Topham, 2016). Ultra light flying machines etc. would address the problem of newly prosperous consumers buying vehicles that worsen environmental pollution. An example of this problem is the many consumers in Kosovo buying environmentally polluting used diesel powered cars that Germans no longer want.

A potentially even more powerful way to solve the global warming problem would be the creation of a new industry in countries such as Mauretania that uses peridotite, a mineral of which the mantle of the earth is largely composed, to absorb carbon dioxide out of the atmosphere. The peridotite would be laid down across barren stretches of the Sahara if the technology is perfected and would react with atmospheric carbon dioxide pulling it out of the atmosphere and locking it away (Fox, 2021).

Wherever feasible and cost effective, solar, wind, and nuclear power generation to heat homes, power electric trains, or for other uses could be encouraged while coal and other fossil fuel use could be discouraged. Geothermal energy could be harnessed near tectonic plates that are grinding against each other; wind would be harnessed in areas with high winds, and solar power would be ideal near the Equator where there is ample sunlight all year long. Counties near the equator that receive a lot of sun could be encouraged to use solar power. Those bordering the ocean with arid areas such as Namibia, Libya, Saudi Arabia or Chile might be encouraged to do desalination to get fresh water for drinking, irrigation or industry using solar and wind power. New technologies for manufacturing concrete and asphalt that consume less fuel than the standard methods are now being introduced and this technology should be transferred to developing countries, especially those planning large scale construction projects such as international hub airports (Watts, 2019).

While the author is enthusiastic about the many new technologies that are coming online, it is important to keep in mind that they may not be suitable everywhere for various reasons. Solar and wind power projects have well known adverse impacts on wildlife and flora in locations that might otherwise seem ideal. Sometimes it is the sheer size of the planned project that arouses deep concern. Large solar plants such as the Battle Born Solar Project of "California-based Arevia Power [that] would carpet 14 square miles … with more than a million solar panels 10 to 20 feet tall…. "(Carlton, 2021).

This is a useful point to reiterate that although this paper favors technology transfer to developing countries of a variety of planet friendly technologies, its main interest is in advocating sharing **blockchain** technology with developing nations. **Blockchain** might be suitable to the production of items where a country enjoys a **comparative advantage** and where the high technology can be utilized in a **cost-effective** way. Many developing nations have goods to sell that are potentially a lucrative source of foreign exchange that they can use to modernize their economies in a planet friendly way. For instance, the African nation of Sierra Leone sells diamonds. One of the earliest commercial applications of **blockchain** technology was to help in the fight to keep diamonds off the market that come from areas controlled by criminal gangs that sell the diamonds to fund their terrorism. (Marr, 2018)

Is Madagascar a Suitable Candidate for Blockchain Technology?

B

Two reasons account for the author's enthusiasm for applying **blockchain** technology to vanilla production in Madagascar. One is that buyers are willing to pay a sufficiently high price that it will be profitable enough to justify farmers raising it in commercial quantities. (Steavenson [2019] thinks that a price of $(US) 150-$180 a kilo might be satisfactory to both buyers and sellers).

A second reason is that Madagascar has a commanding position in its production of vanilla for sale to foreign buyers since it supplies currently 80 percent of the market for natural vanilla.

As regards the high price vanilla commands, it is pertinent to point out that natural vanilla has numerous uses as a flavoring agent (e.g. cold drinks, ice cream, chocolate candy, cakes and even some perfumes). Artificial vanilla, sometimes referred to as vanillan—the main ingredient in vanilla-- is used as a flavoring also but has not dented demand for the natural product except when the supply drops and the price soars.

The lofty price of vanilla, which makes it an attractive candidate for **blockchain** technology, is actually a recent phenomenon. Steavenson, writing in mid-2019, credits two main reasons. One is the success of Haagen-Dazs in convincing people their vanilla ice cream was a luxurious treat worth a hefty premium over ordinary ice cream. And the other was the fact that "over the past 15 years, food companies have faced increasing pressure from consumers to use natural, ethically sourced ingredients. Flavour companies began to trace beans back to their original villages and farms in order to earn certifications of fair trade and sustainability that commanded top prices."

Were it not for the lofty price it commands, it might not make sense to grow vanilla at all. According to "Vanilla: Its History, Cultivation, and Processing" (accessed on the internet on January 16, 2022), "The plant requires time consuming labor" and "much of the work is done by hand" including pollination which must be completed in "a few days."

The vanilla plant is the only edible member of the large orchid family. "It takes months for seedlings to develop" and the flower will not develop "until three years after they are planted." And then, "the pods, which resemble big green beans, must remain on the vine for nine months in order to completely develop their flavor potential." At least in Madagascar, it seems that all the while during this waiting period, the plants must be guarded because "Vanilla thievery is common." As if this were not enough to discourage people from bothering, "processing vanilla is time consuming and laborious. It takes months to cure the seeds and weeks more to extract the concentrated flavoring from the pods. The pods are then thrown into 'boiling water" for a specified amount of time that seems to be a jealously guarded secret after which "they are dried on bamboo tables for around ten weeks until they have shrunk … to about 20 percent of their original size." The last step is to "store away [the pods] for a month or two more" to allow them to "reach peak flavor and fragrance" but not before "they are sorted again for size and quality."

The Madagascar vanilla industry "is highly secretive." Companies such as Haagen-Dazs "send their representatives travelling private aircraft under false names to remote locations to get an edge over their competitors. They carry suitcases full of cash to buy the vanilla from "warehouses surrounded by razor wire and watched over by armed guards. Extortion, fraud, and even murder are all elements of the trade."

This short discussion of the organization of the vanilla industry in Madagascar yields a couple of important observations. One is that as currently organized the big winners are the rich companies from abroad while the farmers get just a small fraction of the retail price and endure the threat of robbery, the vagaries of the weather, and endless toil. And second, the survival of the natural vanilla industry depends on stability of demand and high prices for the product.

The history of vanilla production over the centuries is not reassuring on that count. Though today Madagascar is the main producer the plant is not native to that country. Like cacao, much of which nowadays comes from Ghana, vanilla originated in Mexico. The Aztecs reportedly so esteemed vanilla that they made a drink of cacao, vanilla and sugar that they sipped out of gold cups, tossing the cups away after just one drink. When the Spaniards came in the sixteenth century, they took it back to Spain where it became popular with wealthy people who flavored their desserts with it. Eventually, it also was adopted as a flavoring elsewhere in Europe and the United States. Wendell Steavenson reports that it was featured in a "recipe for 'vanilla ice' in a cookery book published in Naples in the 1690s." Thomas Jefferson apparently also enjoyed it.

Over the intervening centuries it has gone from luxury flavoring agent to a product used in "thousands of the food products we find in our supermarkets." And "plain vanilla" has come to mean "anything that is bland, unchallenging and ordinary." But as noted above, lately vanilla's reputation has vastly improved, and with it, the price it commands.

The price of vanilla paid by the foreign buyers, like the price of oil since 2015, has swung wildly since the early 1990s. In the early 1990s after a period of relative price stability enforced by the central government of the island nation it went from eighty dollars down to forty dollars a kilo, partly because the World Bank insisted that the price be allowed to float. By 2018, however, it had risen as high as $600 before falling back to $400 according to Steavenson.

Turbulence in the vanilla market has not been good for Madagascar and cannot be allowed to continue if we hope to put the country on the path to planet friendly growth. True, a few people have done handsomely by local standards but as already pointed out the majority of vanilla farmers have not and no money has flowed to the government for projects that would grow the economy in a planet friendly way.

According to Steavenson, in Belambo, a village in the heart of the vanilla producing region of Madagascar, "people complain that there is no drinking water, that the school building is dilapidated, the teachers barely literate and that there is no clinic or doctor."

Up to this point, the discussion has focused on the vanilla industry's organization and structure, emphasizing that it needs to be modernized to stabilize prices and properly compensate the farmers. But agreeing on the need to modernize the vanilla industry is one thing. Deciding how to do this is another.

A technology such as **blockchain** may or may not be suitable for this purpose in Madagascar. Here we present the case that the island nation of Madagascar could be a suitable candidate for **blockchain** technology. The purpose of this technology transfer is rationalizing the market for vanilla, an agricultural product that it grows in commercial quantities. A search engine inquiry into the definition of **blockchain** technology yielded the following definition. "**Blockchain** is a system of recording information in a way that makes it difficult or even impossible to change back or cheat the system. A **blockchain** is essentially a digital ledger of transactions that is duplicated and distributed across the network of computer systems on the **blockchain**."

Blockchain technology, hailed by its champions as an innovation that like double entry bookkeeping when it was invented hundreds of years ago, may transform the way business is done in society. According to R. A. Farrokhnia, "blockchain is a true paradigm shift…[potentially] helping us to design alternative models that could redress some of the shortcomings and structural challenges of our finance and banking industries" (Lee, 2021-2022). However, it currently suffers from two major problems hobbling its broad application. In a *Wall Street Journal* article of May 12, 2021, James T. Areddy sees it as "hobbled by a lack of uniform technical standards," a point echoed by Martin Walker (2022), while in a personal message, an expert in the area of **blockchain** technology pointed out that "I think over time blocked will become an essential part of all supply chain management programs." However, he pointed out that "the big problem we have … is that most food processing systems don't do a very good job of accurately capturing all the data." And, he added, somewhat apologetically, that "unfortunately I don't see a strong interest on the part of large companies [in investing in applying this technology to food and food waste] because the cost of food is so low and the penalty for wasting is consequently very small…. * (Anon. April 21, 2021 personal message).

These observations are certainly an incubus to rushing out and ordering a **blockchain** program to be written. But if in general **blockchain** technology is not feasible for the application under consideration, exceptional situations might exist where its application is appropriate. And the author maintains that vanilla production just might be such a promising application. Farrokhnia points out that "blockchain is being used to support fair-trade cooperatives and microfinance initiatives"—exactly the sort of initiative that might be the solution to the current dysfunctional structure of the Madagascar vanilla industry.

This author maintains **blockchain** technology is a logical choice for addressing the turbulence in the vanilla market and putting Madagascar on the road to planet friendly economic development. In a *Wall Street Journal* article of May 12, 2021, James T. Areddy shows why they are so ecstatic: Its big "selling point," he observes, "is to eventually allow numerous parties in a transaction to interact simultaneously and securely transfer assets over the net." He gives the example of a house sale. "To replace email chains and paperwork in a house sale, for example, the buyer, seller and brokers would tap into the same system as lawyers, mortgage bankers and title examiners." The potential for a great improvement in speed over the current system would result, as Areddy notes, since right now "After three decades, most internet applications are links between just two points at a time, even at high connections speeds" and this constitutes "a choke point on potential uses."

How much improvement in speed are we talking about? We can get some idea of the improvement from the following example of an application to the food industry. In 2017, for instance, Walmart teamed with IBM to develop a system for tracking foodstuffs from their point of origin through their arrival at Walmart superstores. Parallel testing using mangoes showed with the then standard technology it took six days plus to trace mangoes back to the harvesting plantation. And with the new **blockchain** technology system, it took two seconds (Areddy, 2021; Hackett, 2017).

These results are not simply impressive. They are policy relevant. **Blockchain** could make it possible to detect food borne pathogens quickly and give us a chance to nip the problem in the bud before it affects large numbers of victims (human or animal).

True, **blockchain** technology has been hampered by a lack of uniform technical standards and high costs of development. Experts on the technology with whom the author consulted were skeptical that big companies that are the main players in **blockchain** are interested in most agricultural uses because food waste (which could be reduced with **blockchain**) is not a sufficiently expensive cost for them to worry about (Anonymous, May 2021).

Blockchain being more hype and promise than reality may be about to change. "With an offer of ultra cheap server space, Beijing is beckoning **blockchain's** global community of developers to adopt its vision for the technology. Success could put China in a powerful position to influence future development of the internet itself and promote international use of Chinese innovations, like a homegrown Global Positioning System and a digitized national currency" (Areddy, 2021).

Will the world heed the siren song of the Chinese? It is more than likely that it will respond as it has to China's bid for dominance in 5G networks. Quite simply, western nations will mount a challenge to Beijing sooner rather than later. Signs of stirring by the developed nations of the west already are visible. Yaya J. Fanusie, formerly with the Central. Intelligence Agency, told a U.S. congressional research panel, "The Chinese government aims for the BSN [the Chinese proposal for a **blockchain** service network] to give China strategic global leverage." Without a doubt China's attempt to use its dominant position in rare earth metals to strong arm other nations' foreign policy was on everyone's mind in that room.

Areddy suggests that the U.S. might use "muscle to compel the **blockchain** community, including leading cloud companies like Amazon.com Inc., Microsoft Corp, and Alphabet Inc.'s Google "to suspend competition and agree on a single **blockchain** solution. Frankly, this author thinks China's push for preeminence in key technologies is not only of concern to American government experts on national security. **Blockchain's** potential is simply too huge while the development costs might be too forbiddingly lofty for the major high tech companies in the west to go it alone. The chances are very good that they will not require any push from Uncle Sam to see that their future prosperity, if not their survival depends on cooperating with one another and perhaps other firms as well. They might very well have started quietly discussing this already although nothing has appeared in the press to suggest that.

These arrangements among high tech companies while perhaps not common are certainly not unheard of. Similar alliances such as the Nanotech Center in Albany, New York already exist for other technologies, a natural result given research on new drugs and IT is a hugely expensive activity. The median drug development cost of was estimated by Prasad and Mailankody [2021] to be $648 million.

But some drug research can run into the billions of dollars, such as the so far elusive search for a drug to cure Alzheimer's Syndrome. A search on the internet for the estimated cost of an Alzheimer's treatment drug came up with the following, "An Alzheimer's disease drug development program's total cost is estimated at $5.7 billion with an expected study time of 13 years from preclinical studies to market approval." The statement was put on the internet on April 22, 2021. When the costs reach that level (with no certainty of success) even very rich companies will prefer to spread the costs across many players and content themselves with just a share of the market rather than trying to get a dominant position.

This is a good point to reiterate that although a uniform standard for **blockchain** development would be welcome, the author does not see its absence as necessarily inhibiting **blockchain's** application to vanilla production. Quite possibly, if the **blockchain** were developed for the vanilla production, it might be adapted to fit the uniform standard that came into existence subsequently or replaced by it. In the meantime, it could still be valuable and its development can proceed.

Nor is the American government the only one unlikely to sit idly by as the Chinese try to gain an overwhelming advantage in the competition to perfect this highly promising technology. The most likely scenario is that the U.S. will respond, as it has with 5G technology, with a competitive rival technology not controlled by Chinese companies beholden to Beijing.

Areddy suggests that the U.S. might use "muscle to compel the **blockchain** community, including leading cloud companies like Amazon.com Inc., Microsoft Corp, and Alphabet Inc.'s Google "to suspend competition and agree on a single **blockchain** solution." Alternatively, this writer believes that the companies will spot the common threat coming.

FUTURE RESEARCH DIRECTIONS

The logical future direction is papers on other applications of **blockchain** in developing nations on one hand and other technologies that would be suitable to transfer perhaps under license etc. For instance, Israel has advanced technology for seawater desalination. The United States is working on making fresh water by combining oxygen and hydrogen using a catalytic technology. This is still at the laboratory stage.

CONCLUSION

B

John Wang has written that, "Big Data and Machine Learning (BD and ML) are driving the Fourth Industrial Revolution, also referred to as Industry 4.0. Big Data has now become a critical part of the business world and daily life, as the synthesis and synergy of Machine Learning and Big Data has enormous potential" including to "maximize the citizens' wealth" and "promote all society's health" (Wang, 2021).

Can the new technology overcome the hurdles that have kept the nations of the world from cooperating in the fight against global warming? Until now there has been an impasse over developed nations' insistence that more be done in this fight by the less developed countries, while they in turn demand that developed nations provide the technology to allow the other nations to catch up to the technologically advanced nations in their development before they join the fight against global warming.

The author maintains that there might be a way out of this dilemma: perhaps the answer is individual nation development plans tailored to the needs of each sovereign nation, albeit composed primarily of certain standardized elements ((e.g. applying high technology to the production of items where a country enjoys a comparative advantage and where the high technology can be utilized in a cost effective way).

In this case study the author illustrates for the island nation of Madagascar a possible solution to the dilemma of development consistent with the goal of reducing the threat to the planet from global warming. The major element in the solution is **blockchain** technology.

If **blockchain** could make a major difference for Madagascar, it would be tempting for other countries dependent on a single crop or other export to follow suit. Examples might be Congo (cobalt), Bolivia (tin), Ghana (cacao) etc. **Blockchain** is currently an expensive technology but the price could be coming down fast thanks to China's bid to set the standards for this program. The author proposes that through the global technology platform modality Madagascar get access to **blockchain** technology to apply to vanilla production. The aim would be to stabilize the prices for this important commodity and provide reliable decent income for the vanilla farmers. The government of the nation would also get a cut of the price to help it with infrastructure investment.

REFERENCES

Areddy, J. (2021, May 12). China seeks leading role in blockchain. *The Wall Street Journal*.

Chu, K. (2010, February 12). Electric bikes face long road in U.S. *USA Today*.

Davenport, T. H. (2014). *Big data at work*. Harvard Business Review Press. doi:10.15358/9783800648153

Fisher, J. L. (2018). Sociological perspectives on improving medical diagnosis emphasizing CAD. In M. Khosrow-Pour (Ed.), *Encyclopedia of Information Science and Technology* (4th ed., pp. 1017–1026). doi:10.4018/978-1-5225-2255-3.ch088

Fisher, R. L. (2015). Research universities of the future: An 'aerotropolitan' perspective. *International Journal of Society Systems Science*, 7(2), 135–150. doi:10.1504/IJSSS.2015.069735

Fisher, R. L., & Fisher, J. L. (2014) Improving medical diagnosis: A sociological perspective. In Encyclopedia of Business Analytics and Optimization. doi:10.4018/978-1-4666-5202-6.ch107

Goodman, J. D. (2010, January 31), An electric boost for bicyclists. *The New York Times*.

Hackett. R. (2017, September 1), Block-chain mania! *Fortune*, 44-51.

Kasarda, J. D., & Lindsay, G. (2011). *Aerotropolis: The way we'll live next*. Farrar, Straus, and Giroux.

Lee, S., (2021, Winter). The future of your money. *Columbia*, 40.

Lostumbo, A., Suzuki, K., & Dachman, A. H. (2010). LFlat lesions in CT colonography. *Abdominal Imaging*, *35*(5), 578–583. doi:10.100700261-009-9562-3 PMID:19633882

Marr, B. (2018, March 14). *How blockchain could end the trade In blood diamonds*. Forbes.com.

Prasad, V., & Mailankody, S. (2017, November). Research and development spending to bring a single cancer drug to market and revenues after approval. *JAMA Internal Medicine*, *177*(11), 1569–1575. doi:10.1001/jamainternmed.2017.3601 PMID:28892524

Steavenson, W. (2019, June/July), Vanilla fever. *1843*, 54-63.

Toplensky, R. (2021, May 27). Hydrogen powered trains arrive. *The Wall Street Journal*.

United Nations Website. (n.d.). *Climate Change*. Available at https://www.un.org/en/global-issues/climate-change#:~:text=Climate

Walker, M. (2022, January 29). The pitfalls of blockchains. *The Economist*, 14.

Watts, J. (2019). *Concrete: The most destructive material on earth*. Available at https://www.theguardian.com/cities/2019/feb/25/-the-most-destructive-material-on-earth

ADDITIONAL READING

Hassol, S. J. (2004). *Impacts of a warming Arctic, Arctic Climate Impact Assessment (ACIA)*. Cambridge University Press.

PwC (PricewaterhouseCoopers). (2018). *Building block (chain)s for a better planet*. Fourth Industrial Revolution for the Earth Series. September.

Zheng, Z., Dai, H. N., & Xie, S. (2017). An overview of blockchain technology: architecture, consensus, and future trends. *Proceedings of the IEEE International Congress on Big Data*, 557-564. 10.1109/BigDataCongress.2017.85

KEY TERMS AND DEFINITIONS

Aerotropolis: A planned city incorporating an international hub airport and linked by rapid ground transportation to nearby urban areas. It is distinguished from a quasi-aerotropolis which is an international hub airport linked to one or more large densely populated urban agglomerations by rapid ground transport in that the urban agglomerations preceded the airport and have been retrofitted to link to the airport. Schiphol in the Netherlands is an aerotropolis whereas New York City, which is linked to JFK International Airport and Newark International Airport by rapid ground transportation is a quasi-aerotropolis.

Blockchain: The term for a system of recording information in a way that makes it difficult or even impossible to change back or cheat the system. A block chain is essentially a digital ledger of transactions that is duplicated and distributed across the network of computer systems on the block chain. Because all parties involved in the production and distribution of the goods or services see every transaction simultaneously, not only is system integrity enhanced, so is speed of movement, facilitating planning based on estimates of costs of inputs and profit targets, etc.

Computer-Aided Diagnosis (CAD): Any of several computer assisted technologies used in medicine to achieve more rapid diagnosis of an illness such as cancer. Some of these systems work by producing tentative diagnoses after specific diagnostic information inputted to the system. They then offer all the diagnoses that fit that information and invite the physician to offer additional pivotal information to winnow the list. This process is iterative until just one or a few possible diagnoses remain. Other systems built around imaging may be used to "detect earliest signs of abnormality" that would be impossible for a human professional is unable to spot without this assistance. Examples are symptoms of diabetic retinopathy, and non-polypoid lesions in CT colonography.

Cost Effective: In healthcare management science it refers to a form of management ensuring the maximization of the benefits that can be obtained from the resources allocated to health and the reduction of costs. Generally, it refers to the achievement of desirable outcomes of a process (e.g., the process achieves intended and/or unintended results that can be quantified in monetary terms and this occurs at a cost that is minimized compared to alternative process for achieving comparable results).

Global Technology Platform: A list of high technologies maintained by an international organization and accessible to any country that is a member of the United Nations and approved by the list maintenance organization to access this technology. Once a country is approved to use the technology, it can retain a suitable service provider to implement the technology and parallel test it if appropriate. Furthermore, the country may qualify for financial aid in whole or in part from the United States or for low-cost financing. Technologies available on the platform must be planet friendly and for use only to grow the economy or other legitimate use such improving health, life expectancy, increasing literacy, or advancing the rights or wellbeing of people in a country who are currently deprived of rights others enjoy or have a lower qualify of life than others, etc. Transfer of technology that can be used both for military and non-military purposes must include safeguards to prevent its application for military purposes.

Parallel Testing: The process of running multiple test cases on multiple combinations of operating systems and browsers at the same time. The process may be automated and often runs on virtual machines. In general, this is a process of experimentally validating a new procedure (nowadays usually computerized) against a current standard procedure (which may be an earlier computerized or partially computerized process to determine if the new procedure is better on some policy relevant variable. For example, it may be evaluated as to speed, cost, error rate or some combination of these if relevant.

Data Analytics in the Global Product Development Supply Chain

Kamalendu Pal

(iD) https://orcid.org/0000-0001-7158-6481

City, University of London, UK

INTRODUCTION

As more and more manufacturing business operational activity is digitized, a new source of data and ever-cheaper equipment combine (known as software system technology) to usher manufacturers into a new business world in which vast amounts of digitized data exist on virtually any topic of interest to regular operation. Web-based ordering, online shopping, digital communication, and instrumented machinery generate torrents of data as a by-product of their day in day out operations. Each of these is now a dynamic data creator. The data available are often unstructured, not organized in a database, and unwieldy, but there is a massive amount of unwanted information in it, simply waiting to be released. Besides, analytics brought rigorous decision-making techniques, and big data is more straightforward and robust. In this way, SST, particularly *data analytics*, significantly impacts the manufacturing industry. However, manufacturing professionals have been slow to exploit the full potential of SST. Instead of using SST to maximize productivity and revenue-generation ability, SSTs have been used mainly for *enterprise resource planning* (e.g., accounting, inventory management, human resource management) purposes within the manufacturing industry. As a result, the manufacturing industry has not yet exploited data analytics-based SST as an effective tool.

In addition, the advantage of globalization has simulated different initiatives in global product manufacturing and marketing business activities. For example, in the 1980s, the *"quick response"* strategy was developed to maintain a competitive advantage (Porter, 1985) for the domestic manufacturing of products. Technological innovations have made fast electronic communication a global phenomenon (Pal, 2022), and the rapid acquisition of technical skills in various countries has meant that many professional tasks could be outsourced (quality control, raw materials purchasing, sample making). Researchers (Gereffi, 1999) (Pal & Yasar, 2020) identified some of the trends for the manufacturing business. Also, the globalization trends have continued, and the radical social reform idea of making more from fewer resources (known as *Gandhian Engineering*) (Prahalad & Mashelkar, 2010) has become the business rule in today's global market. Also, operational planning – and appropriate information system (IS) – drives the whole business, where customers play a pivotal role.

With the technological advances, manufacturing companies regularly employ data mining techniques to explore the contents of data warehouses looking for trends, relationships, and outcomes to enhance their overall operations and discover new patterns that allow companies to serve their customers better. This way, manufacturing organizations rely on business processes related data to formulate strategy and succeed under value-based reimbursement models. The new paradigm requires data-driven insights that can help operational managers reduce unnecessary variation in business and make more informed service-line decisions across the enterprise. In this way, intelligent data processing plays a key role.

DOI: 10.4018/978-1-7998-9220-5.ch179

D

This chapter presents some of these issues identifying in particular: (i) the concept of big data, (ii) data gathering, (iii) data processing, and (iv) the broader research dilemmas. Hence, the central theme of this chapter is to expose the reader to some of the more interesting insights into how data and information systems (IS) to help run manufacturing supply chain management.

Evolution in computer processing power and storage capacity has enabled organizations to develop data-rich IS for daily operations, and therefore, there has been tremendous growth for data stored. In addition, business data collection itself has progressed from the transcription of paper-based records via manual data-entry processes to the use of smart cards, mobile phones (Location Data, GPS), Internet of Things (IoT) (e.g., radio frequency identification (RFID) tags, sensors), webcasting and Internet users' mouse clicks. In turn, this data generation has generated a need for new techniques and technologies that can transform these data into appealing and valuable information and knowledge.

Today, big data is generated by web applications, social media, intelligent machines, sensors, mobile phones, and other intelligent hand-held devices, bacterized by velocity, volume, and variety it produces along the supply chain. Such decision-support software applications employ pure mathematical and artificial intelligence techniques and sometimes use both methods to perform analytical operations that uncover relationships and patterns within the manufacturing supply chain generated Big Data.

Business processes along the supply chain must balance to provide customer service at no additional cost or workload. It also requires trade-offs throughout the supply chain. Therefore, it is necessary to consider a single interconnected chain rather than narrow functional business processes when considering practical mechanisms, which help find acceptable solutions at the time of need.

Real-time supply chain decision-making and coordination are essential in the international marketplace, shortening product life cycles and fast-changing trends. Technological evolution and the latest information-sharing techniques make real-time decision-making and coordination easier than in the recent past. In addition, the importance of integrating and coordinating supply chain business partners have been appreciated in many manufacturing industries (Pal, 2016).

Manufacturing supply chain managers are seeking ways to manage Big Data sources effectively. There are many examples of manufacturing business operations using Big Data solutions that highlight the wealth of business process enhancement scopes available through the clever use of data:

- Big Data-based applications, which help integrate strategic business planning, are recently assisting manufacturing businesses to coordinate more susceptible supply chains as they better apprehend operating market tendencies and customer desires. It forms the triangulation of a range of marketing and operating business environment data (e.g., social media discussion forums, demographic information, other static and dynamic data from diverse sources), giving the ability to forecast and proactively formulate strategies for manufacturing supply chain businesses.

- Software-defined machines, data-driven predictive analyses, Internet of Things (IoT), and soft-computing based machine learning mechanisms are ushering in a new industrial revolution. These new breeds of computing power are being used in predictive asset maintenance to avoid unplanned downtimes in the manufacturing shop floor.

- IoT can provide real-time telemetry data to reveal the details of production processes. In addition, machine learning algorithms are used to analyze the data to reveal the details of production processes that can correctly forecast near future machine failures and appropriate actions.

- Big Data-based solutions are helping avoid delivery delays and create pollution-reduced environments by analyzing Global Positioning Systems (GPS) data with the help of traffic and meteorological data, which actively plan and find cost-effective delivery routes.

- Extensive Data-based software systems are helping manufacturing supply chains for self-critiquing (rather than a reactive) response to supply chain risks (e.g., supply chain failures due to natural or synthetic problems).

These examples give just a few insights into the numerous advantages derived from the analysis of Big Data sources to enhance supply chain proactiveness. In this way, appropriate data manipulation techniques within special-purpose software, generally known as business analytics, are used for timely decision making.

Supply chain managers are now increasingly seeking to '*win with data*'. They rely on data to gain visibility into expenditure, look for trends in corporate operational cost and related performance, and support process control, inventory monitoring, production optimization, and process improvement efforts. In addition, many businesses are collecting vast amounts of data, with many using it to capitalize on data analytics to gain a competitive advantage (Davenport, 2006). In this way, appropriate-data capture, data cleaning, different data analysis techniques, and Big Data are all thought to be part of an emerging competitive area that will transform how manufacturing supply chains are managed and designed.

The rest of the chapter is structured as follows: Section 2 describes the extended supply chain network concept and includes the overview of the value chain network of participating partners in a manufacturing business. Additionally, this section explains the Supply Chain Council's SCOR (Supply Chain Operations Reference) model and its relevance for supply chain performance measurement. Section 3 discusses the era of Big Data analytics, sources of Big Data, and various kinds of analytics and their techniques applicable to corporate decision-making. Section 4 identifies data-based supply chain decision making related research. Finally, section 5 illustrates a Big Data-based framework for SCM; and it also provides a few examples of diverse types of manufacturing supply chain analytics. Section 6 describes the future research plan. Finally, Section 6 presents some concluding remarks.

EXTENDED SUPPLY CHAIN NETWORK

Business opportunities with better incentives that drive manufacturing workload to geographically distributed locations are enabled by a few factors - the growing modernization of international business, advancements in manufacturing product manufacturing technology with related information systems capabilities, and improvement in multimodal transportation and services. In this way, global supply chains are formed where cost reduction strategies result in ultimate products and services being produced with intermediate input originating from several countries, and this practice is now widespread in many business sectors. In addition, it extends overall business activities to more globally participating alliance partners. Moreover, a manufacturing business can create a business environment in many collaborative supply chains, ultimately creating a new complex makeup of related business activities.

These new intricate arrangements are based on three main motivating influences: (1) the geographical location and nature of connections between tasks in the chain; (2) the allocation of power among dominating business alliances and other associates in the chain; and (3) the role of government agencies and policies informing business alliances and business location. The geographical location is defined by splitting production activities and their delocalization.

Management teams are puzzling to substantiate their investment in traditional legacy systems for SCM purposes. The essential purpose is that systems mainly cater to transaction-based corporate activity. However, they lack the intellectual, analytical ability needed for an integrated view of the global supply chain management system. This way, it is where Business Intelligence (BI) tools like data warehousing, ETL (Extraction, Transformation, and Loading), data mining, and OLAP (On-Line Analytical Processing) can cater capability to analyze operational effectiveness and performance management across the global supply chain.

Supply Chain Performance Measurement

Supply Chain performance measurement is crucial for a manufacturing enterprise to survive in the competitive world of business. Some well-known manufacturing enterprises currently use supply chain performance measurement, consisting of *Business Intelligence* (BI) software applications and in-house business practices. It also measures the performance of the enterprise's internal business processes in consideration, but it also takes consideration of extended enterprise activities.

In order to tackle some of these drawbacks in traditional financial accounting-based practices for measuring supply chain performance, a variety of measurement mechanisms have been introduced. They include Balance Scorecard, Supply Chain Council's SCOR (Supply Chain Operations Reference) model, Logistics Scoreboard, Activity-Based Costing (ABC), and Economic Value Analysis (EVA). In this chapter, the SCOR model has been used for manufacturing supply chain decision making. A brief introduction of the SCOR model is described below.

SCOR Model

The Supply Chain Operations Reference (SCOR) model prescribes a general business process management approach to the supply chain community. This reference model was initially introduced by the Supply Chain Council (SCC) in 1996. The SCOR model deals with the supply chain management activities from an operational purpose. It includes corporate customer engagement information, day-to-day business transactions, and relevant market reactions. This model encapsulates business process activity management, benchmarking with market-leading enterprises, and best practices into a single framework. Many well-known companies have used the SCOR model (e.g., Intel, General Electronic, Airbus, DuPont, and IBM) (Supply Chain Council, 2010). Intel Corporation used its first SCOR for its resellers' product department in 1999. Then it used the SCOR model for its system manufacturing department. The benefits of implementing the SCOR model to handle business process management includes improvement in operational cycle time, fewer inventories in storage, enhanced visibility of the supply chain, and timely access to customer engagement information. General Electric (GE) has also used the SCOR model for its transportation management department, and it has reported operational improvement of its transportation service after using the SCOR model (Poluha, 2007).

The SCOR is a standardized multi-level framework with Key Performance Indicators (KPIs) attached to its Level. According to SCOR, five business entities are involved in the supply chain performance management: the enterprise itself, supplier of the enterprise, suppliers to suppliers, the customer of the enterprise, and customers of the customers. These five categories of business entities have their own SCOR. Individual SCOR is composed of the five-integrated corporate operational behaviours: Plan (P), Source (S), Make (M), Deliver (D), and Return (R) – from the suppliers' supplier to customers' customer, and all aligned with leading enterprise's operational strategy, material, work, and information flow.

Figure 1. An organizational overview of the SCOR model

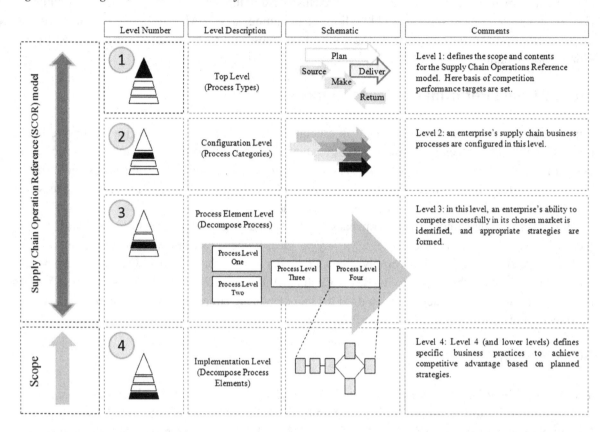

There are four levels in the SCOR framework: Top Level, Configuration Level, Process Element Level, and Implementation Level, as shown in Figure 1. It is considered a best practice framework for evaluating performance in supply chain management. The framework uses many performance measurement metrics and their relevant attributes. In this way, the SCOR framework creates business process improvement by using benchmarking techniques. The top three levels of the SCOR model are as follows:

1. Level-1(Process Types): This Level defines the scope and contents for the Supply Chain Operations Reference (SCOR) model. Here the basis of competition performance targets is set. To express the detailed requirements, it uses the following criteria:

    a. **P**lan (P): a process that balances requests of demand-side and supply-side and has a smooth sub-process for sourcing, making, and delivery activities under the best business plan.

    b. **S**ource (S): a process that procures raw materials and relevant services to fulfil strategic or practical needs.

    c. **M**ake (M): a process that transforms raw materials to finish or semi-finished goods to fulfil strategic requirements.

    d. **D**eliver (D): a process that transports finished goods or services to fulfil plans or strategic requirements.

    e. **R**eturn (R): a collection of return products for several reasons.

2. Level-2 (Process Categories): The second SCOR level defines the configuration of planning and execution processes in material flow, using standard process categories such as make-to-order, engineer-to-order, or make-to-stock categories. This Level derives from Level 1, which settles on more concrete strategies.

3. Level-3 (Process Element Level): The third Level contains the main process elements and their process flows. This lower Level of the SCOR model is most significant to business data analytics. It includes process element definitions, inputs and outputs, relationships, performance metrics, and best practices.

This way, all process metrics use aspects of a performance characteristic. For example, the performance characteristics for any given process are characterized as either customer-facing (reliability, responsiveness, and flexibility) or internal-facing (cost and assets) metrics. Level 1 metrics are primary, high-level measures that may cross multiple SCOR processes.

Performance metrics help measure the business intelligence (BI) for key performance indicators (KPIs). Each Level 1 metric can be disintegrated to the lower Level 2 and Level 3 metrics, thus providing standardized operational, tactical, and strategic performance measurements across the supply chain.

Business Intelligence

Gartner, an information technology research company, introduced the term *"Business Intelligence"* (BI) during the 1990s. BI is a process by which corporate operational information can be gathered, cleansed, stored, and made available to decision-makers who need it in its most helpful form. This can range from simple business reports, through trend analysis to complicated dashboards and even predicting the future. However, data in raw form is of limited use, and manufacturing enterprises are increasingly opting to use dedicated BI software to appreciate their data's full capability. BI commercial vendors specialize in an automated Big Data analytic platform that allows an enterprise to easily collect all corporate data, manipulate them, and display them as actionable information or information that can be acted upon in making informed decisions.

Moreover, enterprises of all sizes can connect to and analyze data (even Big Data) to produce better quality business decision-making environments in recent years. Interactive visualizations and dashboards enhance analyzing and interpreting data to make prudent business decisions nearly in real-time. In addition, BI enables manufacturers to enhance the way they do day-to-day business. Manufacturing enterprises are empowered to offer products and services at the lowest possible cost and with the highest degree of productivity and efficiency possible – while returning the highest revenues and profits.

BI platform can collect valuable data from many sources and assemble it into a central Data Warehouse (DW). It can be validated, cleaned, summarised, standardized, and even enhanced by copying the data. Moreover, BI capabilities are spreading to virtually all parts of the manufacturing enterprise as businesses strive to put critical data into the hand of business operational decision-makers who need it to do their jobs. The Big Data user community wants the following from the real-world BI systems:

- The capability to execute ad hoc queries
- Access and use multiple databases
- Scalability, affordability and reliability of data and the related operations
- Ease of integration with heterogenous internal and external data sources

In this way, BI refers to a set of methods and techniques that manufacturing enterprises use for tactical and strategic decision making. For example, it leverages technologies that focus on counts, statistics, and business objectives to improve business performance.

The goal of a DW is to hold the data needed by business managers to make decisions. The next step is to document the data warehouse. *Metadata* describes the source data, identifies the transformation and integration steps, and defines how the data warehouse is organized. This step is crucial to help decision-makers understand what data elements are available. Once the data requirements and data sources have been identified, the data must be transformed and integrated so that it can be searched and analyzed efficiently by the decision-makers. The main activities of this process flow are to extract, clean, transform, and load this data into the data warehouse. This process flow is also known as Extract, Transform, and Load (ETL).

Thus, the data warehouse process contains the following steps: (i) data extraction from multiple sources, databases, and files; (ii) data transformed and cleaned before loaded; and finally (iii) data is loaded into the data warehouse. So, the first step in the data warehouse is to extract data from different business data sources; and then transform it using built-in transformation processes. In addition, the data flow loading the warehouse dimensions are first passed to a short editor that removes any duplicated rows of data before being passed on to other processing units.

By itself, stored data does not create any business value, which is true of traditional databases, data warehouses, and the new Big Data technologies (e.g., Hadoop) for storage. However, once the data is appropriately stored, it can be analyzed, creating tremendous value. In addition, various analysis technologies and approaches have emerged that are especially applicable to Big Data sources within SCM.

THE ERA OF BIG DATA ANALYTICS

The main objective of processing Big Data is to generate differentiated value, which can be trusted. This is done by applying *advanced analytics* against the complete data collection regardless of scale. To understand the critical issues of Big Data, one needs to understand the *data sources* of business processes within manufacturing enterprises.

New breeds of manufacturing business organizational process automation software, such as Enterprise Resource Planning (ERP), Supply Chain Management (SCM), Supplier Relationship Management (SRM), Global Positioning Systems (GPS), Social Media (SM) analysis systems, adoption of digital sensors and radio frequency identification (RFID) tags leading to the 'Internet of Things (IoT), and digitization of voice and multimedia are capable of collecting substantial data sets and unlock valuable information from it.

Before Big Data can be used for business purposes, it must be stored, managed, and analyzed appropriately for decision-making purposes. Distributed file systems, flexible storage systems, and massively parallel processing databases enable much larger volumes at low-cost infrastructure (e.g., Data Center, Private Cloud, Public Cloud, and Hybrid Cloud). In addition, processing a high volume of complex data in a distributed manner needs different techniques (e.g., time series analysis, knowledge-based classification, scenario-based analysis, and other statistical analysis methods). A diagrammatic representation of Big Data Infrastructure and its processing capabilities is shown in Figure 2.

Figure 2. Typical types of Big Data application systems

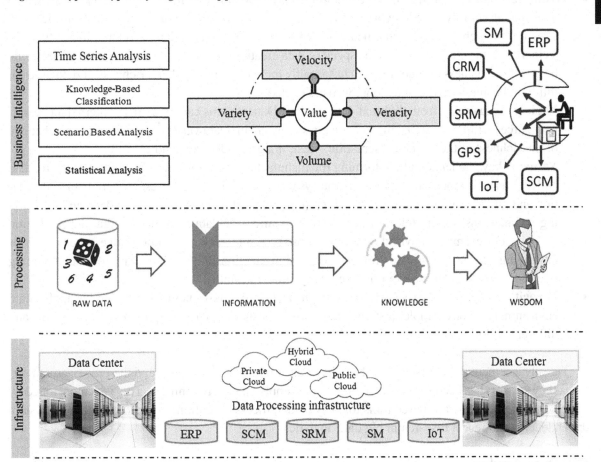

Data streams can come from internal and external sources within the global manufacturing chain. In addition, data can come in various formats such as transaction and log data from multiple applications, structured data as database tables, semi-structured data such as XML, unstructured data such as text, images, video streams, and audio statements. In order to process these data, other information systems are now making a revolution in sensing technology, computing and communication power that brings together a variety of resources. These resources range from networked embedded computers and mobile devices to multimodal data sources.

New breeds of manufacturing business automation software, such as Enterprise Resource Planning (ERP), Supply Chain Management (SCM), Supplier Relationship Management (SRM), can collect substantial data sets and create valuable information for the company. Additionally, the extended enterprise is enabled by web technologies, e-business for customers, supplier portals, and information technology innovations targeted at supply chains and customer relationships.

As Big Data is one of the most 'excited' terms in today's business computing, there is no consensus on defining it. Instead, the term is often used synonymously with related concepts such as Business Intelligence (BI) and data mining. This also forms the basis for the most used definition of Big Data, the five Vs: Volume, Velocity, Variety, Value, and Veracity, as shown in Figure 2.

- **Volume:** Data volume signifies the amount of data available to a manufacturing business, which does not necessarily have to own all of it if it can access it. Data is in text and videos, music, click stream from web queries, social media (e.g., Facebook, Twitter) update, and large image files.
- **Velocity**: Data velocity assesses the speed of data creation, streaming, and aggregation. Electronic business (e-business or e-commerce) has rapidly increased the speed and richness of data used for different business transactions (e.g., website clicks).
- **Variety**: Data comes from different data sources. Data streams can come from internal and external sources within the global manufacturing supply chain. Data variety is a measuring mechanism of the richness of the data representation – text, images, video, and audio.
- **Value:** A key challenge in transforming the manufacturing supply chain from infrastructure, data collection and remote sensing information system to a provision that presents actionable information and guides humans in decision making (e.g., relevant data, knowledge on data, and inferencing mechanisms) of the relevant information required for data analytics design and prediction purpose. For example, a hybrid of statistical methods and declarative knowledge is beneficial for leveraging sensor data streams for personalized production line machine care to reduce redoing rates among scheduled jobs to improve plant efficiency quality.
- **Veracity**: Veracity's key issues relate to the messiness of data generated in dynamic supply chain environments. For example, just consider Twitter posts with hashtags, abbreviations, typos, and different colloquial speech.

The advancement of understanding the behaviour of information systems and the processes and services they support has become a critical issue in the supply chain environment. This is demonstrated by the proliferation of software-based tools to analyze the process executions, system interactions, system dependencies and recent research in big data analytics.

Big Data Analytics

It is worth recognizing that the term '*analytics*' is not used consistently. It is used in at least three yet related ways (Watson, 2013a). An initiation point for understanding and appreciating data analytics is to examine its origins. The Decision support systems (DSS) in the 1970s were the first computerized systems to support decision making (Power, 2007). DSS appeared to be used to characterize special type software system applications and an academic research area. Over time, various decision support applications such as executive information systems (EISs), online analytical processing (OLAP), and dashboards/scorecards became very popular. Then in the 1990s, Howard Dresner, a business analyst at Gartner, customized the term *business intelligence* (BI). A simple definition is that "BI is a wider group of software applications, technologies, infrastructure, and processes for gathering, storing, accessing, and analyzing data to help business users make operational decisions" (Watson, 2009).

Various Kinds of Analytics

Big Data-based analytics is a rapidly developing field which already attracted attention from academics and practitioners. It is important to differentiate three diverse types of analytics because the differences have significance for the software system technologies and technical platform architectures used for Big Data analytics.

- **Descriptive Analytics**: Descriptive analytics is backwards-looking and expose what has happened. Descriptive data analytics, such as business reporting, dashboards, and data visualization, have been comprehensively used for some time and are the main applications of typical BI.
- **Predictive Analytics:** Predictive analytics suggest what will occur in future. The techniques and algorithms for predictive analytics such as statistical regression analysis, machine learning, and other soft-computing methods have been used for some time. However, commercial software systems like SAS Enterprise Miner have made them easier to use and apprehend.

Prescriptive analytics can find optimal solutions, often for scarce corporate resources. For example, mathematical techniques for revenue management are increasingly general for manufacturing enterprises that have "*perishable*" inventories (e.g., rental cars, hotel rooms, airline seats). In this way, modern data analytic techniques help enterprises to discover deeper insights from collected data.

Techniques for Analytics

Most of the techniques used to analyze Big Data analytics are based on applied mathematical computation and machine learning paradigms. However, Big Data analytics techniques are widespread and context specific. These techniques can be classified and discussed according to the data under investigation. Depending on the type of data, four central Big Data analytics can be defined:

- **Text Analytics:** This technique is used to find-out relevant information from textual data. Text analysis uses statistical computation, natural language processing techniques, and machine learning methods. Some of the essential techniques for text analytics are information extraction, text summarization, question answering, and sentimental analysis.
- **Audio Analytics**: Techniques deployed to extract information from unstructured audio data. Customer service telephone conversations with customers are the primary source of audio analytics. Some of the main techniques used for audio analytics include large vocabulary, continuous speech recognition and phonetics-based systems.
- **Video Analytics:** Techniques used to monitor and analyze video streams. Video analytics has been mainly used as a replacement for labour-intensive observation. In addition, many business applications of video analytics are being used in manufacturing to collect data on customer demographics and preferences.
- **Social Media Analytics:** Techniques used to analyze structured and non-structured data from social media channels (e.g., Twitter, Facebook). Some exciting techniques used to analyze social media data are community detection, social influence analysis and link prediction.

Many successful manufacturing enterprises have invested large sums of money in business intelligence and data warehousing tools and technologies. These manufacturers believe that up-to-date, accurate and integrated information about their supply chain, products and customers is critical for their survival.

RESEARCH IN BIG DATA-BASED SUPPLY CHAIN MANAGEMENT

In SCM, there is a growing interest in *business analytics* (BA), also known as supply chain analytics (SCA), in academic literature. These analytics use data and quantitative techniques to analyze business performance in different functional areas of supply chain management (Handfield, 2006) (Davis-Sramek, Germain, & Iyer, 2010) (Davenport & O'dwyer, 2011) (O'dwyer & Renner, 2011). This section presents a brief review of Big Data-Based SCM.

In recent research, J R Stock (Stock, 2013) proposes a Big Data-driven SCM. He suggests that Big Data-Based analytics for SCM will allow decision-makers to make decisions faster with the help of circumstance specific actions. An industry survey conducted by Mitsubishi Heavy Industries and consulting company Deloitte (Deloitte & MHI, 2014); and questioned supply chain executives about innovations that drive supply chains. The main objective was to get the views of business executives on emerging technology trends that could dramatically impact the supply chains of the future. A critical issue that emerged from the survey was *supply chain analytics*. The survey also identified areas for analytics-based SCM. The Council for Supply Chain Management Consultants published a report (Richey et al., 2014) on Big Data in SCM, based on interviews with supply chain managers.

Many commercial Big Data applications related to SCM are attracting the attention of academics and practitioners (Watson et al., 2014) (Davenport, 2006) (Davenport & Harris, 2007) (McAfee & Brynjolfsson, 2012) (Deloitte & MHI, 2016). For example, a few Big Data applications in corporate marketing management show tremendous opportunity in Big Data-based business analytics (Szilard et al., 2013). The number of publications on supply chain network design using Big Data and business analytics is also growing steady (Baesens, 2014) (Dietrich et al., 2014) (Sathi, 2012) (Siegel, 2013) (Watson et al., 2012).

There are many successful cases of SCA implementation by well-known manufacturing enterprises. For example, Proctor & Gamble and Walmart are reported to have enhanced operational performance using data and analytical decision-support software for their day-to-day functions (Davenport & Harris, 2007) (Davenport & O'dwyer, 2011) (O'Dwyer & Renner, 2011) (SAS, 2012). One of the well-known high-street manufacturers in the United Kingdom (UK), TESCO has experienced substantial cost savings by using Big Data analytics (Clark, 2013).

Big Data analytics in SCM is not necessarily a new idea (Davenport & O'dwyer, 2011) since different quantitative techniques and modelling mechanisms have long been used in manufacturing companies (Turban & Sephora, 1986) (Shapiro, 2000) (Kuaka, 2006) (Turkmen et al., 2010). However, there has been considerable interest in Big Data analytics in recent years, and it has also ushered new technical challenges for research communities. These challenges include technical issues regarding data volume and its storage facilities, data Provence (e.g., syntax, semantics, pragmatic), data quality and availability; and importantly, data uncertainties (Hanfield & Nichols, 2004) (Liberatore & Luo, 2010) (Hunter et al., 2011) (Lavallel et al., 2011) (Manyika et al., 2011).

The first significant challenge for manufacturing businesses, innovative information technology and related electronic devices used in SCM is generating and capturing massive amounts of data. This data has been used to change companies' performance (Kohli & Grover, 2008). For example, a well-known consumer goods company, Li & Fung, reported the flow of over 100 gigabytes of data through the company's supply chain network on a given day in 2009 (Economist, 2010). The opportunity to gain a competitive advantage may thus arise from how companies manage data (Vosburg & Kumar, 2011) (Forslund & Jonsson, 2007) (Oliva & Watson, 2011). The second challenge for business is the increasing uncertainty in both the demand (e.g., consumer market) and the supply side of manufacturing supply chains. One solution proposed by academics (Oliva & Watson, 2011) (Demirkan & Delen, 2012) is proper supply chain planning to tackle demand and supply uncertainty.

It is evident from the research literature that SCM's critically important organizational function will need to evolve and adapt to Big Data analytics. For example, in a recent industry report (Deloitte & MHI, 2016), Mitsubishi Heavy Industries highlighted the potential of supply chains to deliver mas-

D

sive economic and environmental rewards for society. However, the report suggests that technological innovation will play a vital role in fulfilling this potential. For example, big data analytics can provide step-change improvements in supply chain visibility, cost savings, and customer service. The key is to generate insightful data analysis and share it between business partners within manufacturing supply chains to act on it.

In response to these challenges, Big Data Analytics has been proposed as a promising approach to managing data better, utilizing IT resources and preparing for effective supply chain planning (Handfield, 2006) (Davenport, Harris & Morison, 2010) (Davis-Sramek, Germain & Iyer, 2010) (Viswanathan & Sadlovska, 2010). This new generation of analytics tools can develop a manufacturing enterprise's IT infrastructure and data management capabilities to improve strategic planning and enhance operational performance (Kohl & Grover, 2008) (Shapiro, 2010) (Mithras, Ramasubba & Sambamurthy, 2011). Additionally, it has been proposed that manufacturing enterprises can use SCA from acquired data using electromechanical devices (e.g., RFID tags, Sensors) and storing repositories of packaged software (e.g., CRM, ERP, SCM) to enhance manufacturing chain planning through IT-enabled planning and scheduling systems (Davenport & O'Dea, 2011) (Dwyer & Renner, 2011).

In order to solve a problem, the Big Data-based application used intelligent reasoning in automated software that helps users apply analytical and scientific methods to business decision making. The software applications that focus on the manufacturing chain domain are referred to as manufacturing decision support systems, providing Big Data-based tools to support a user global supply chains related reasoning process to develop a solution to the problem. This type of reasoning can be considered an intellectual process by which manufacturing operation managers use distinct artificial intelligence-based inference mechanisms to solve global operations problems.

PROPOSED BIG DATA FRAMEWORK FOR SCM

As the global supply chain's information system's architecture expands over the Internet to envelop the entire supply chain, so does BI. The Internet broadens the information sources of data storage. It expands beyond what is contained within the organization's internal systems across the Internet to include business partners, suppliers, and customer relations.

In order to collaborate efficiently, business organizations must coordinate their regular activities. The essential elements of a collaborative environment are operational data store, data warehouse (e.g., data and metadata information), data mart (data warehouse, which concentrates on a particular subject area within the business operations), ETL tools, OLAP engine, analytical tools (reporting, data mining, and so on) and web portals. Combinations of these elements make different scenarios that depend on an organization's organizational administration, informational architecture, and supply chain. A data warehouse system must:

- Make an organization's information easily accessible.
- Present the organization's information consistently
- Be adaptive and resilient to change
- Serve as the basis of improved decision making.

Figure 3 shows how the SCOR reference model can be utilized in Big Data for the supply chain management. The SCOR model allows identifying the origins of Big Data in supply chain activities. This can initially be applied at elevated levels and drilled down as required; secondly, it will identify potential users of such Big Data and their information requirements. Finally, the originating and communicating activities will need access to and analysis of Big Data sets. Finally, the approach allows specifying the type of IT infrastructure required to process such data, i.e., whether a batch or real-time streaming capability will be required or a combination of these two.

Additionally, the framework can accommodate the enterprise potential of augmented reality (AR) and virtual reality (VR). These efforts increasingly intersect with opportunities made possible by the Internet of Things (IoT) technology (e.g., sensors and connected devices) that help build a more integrated and extended digital and physical environment. Finally, the framework can help define a typical Big Data strategy for the whole supply chain.

Figure 3. Big Data potential for SCM according to the SCOR model

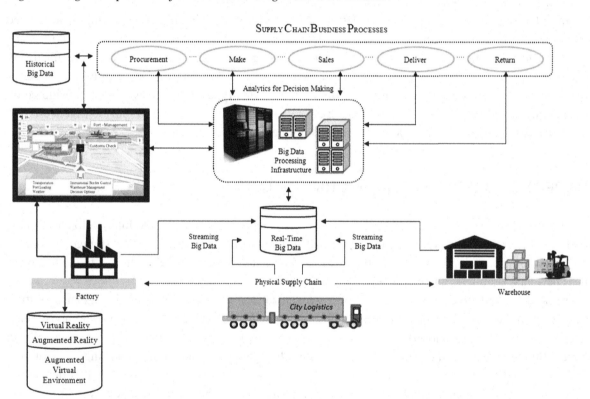

This framework allows the problem of utilizing Big Data for supply chain management to be viewed from the perspective of vital managerial components of business logistics and distinct categories of stakeholders. It can encompass all essential supply chain business foundations such as forecasting, inventory management, transportation, and human recourses management. Different stakeholders such as manufacturers, carriers, and manufacturers can then identify ways to benefit from the supply chain Big Data.

FUTURE RESEARCH DIRECTIONS

D

Business analytics (BA) design and development face numerous future success challenges, such as implementation cost and complexity. BA software systems often consist of multiple elements that do not integrate well, including best-of-breed components from different commercial vendors. In addition, the biggest challenge is the users' ability to determine how to act based on the results of BA analysis in a manufacturing business. Tradition BA applications have been slow at gathering and analyzing data. This makes the short-term and day-to-day decision making unsuitable.

Consequently, real-time data gathering, storing, and processing are fundamental challenges. Therefore, the best manufacturing supply chains will be those that can quickly analyze enormous amounts of distributed data and disseminate business insights to decision-makers as close to real-time as possible. In future, the current research will focus on the above issues and the useability of the BA software systems.

CONCLUSION

This chapter provides a systematic approach for using frameworks such as SCOR for supply chains, identifying the potential of Big Data within them, and identifying practical analytics applications for manufacturing supply chain management. The current business environment pushes manufacturing enterprises to optimize business processes and holding costs. At the same time, the extensive availability of data makes customers increasingly knowledgeable about products, prices, and other essential information. At first, manufacturing supply chain networks appear to easily manage abstract operational frameworks such as SCOR's Plan, Source, Make, Deliver and Return. However, upon deeper examination, manufacturing chains need real-time business process integration, coordination, and collaboration to deliver a higher level of corporate performance.

The emergence of Big Data Analytics opens excellent opportunities in manufacturing business communities. Also, current Information and Communication Technology (ICT) architectures enabled by Big Data can help optimize manufacturing supply chains with shared real-time data, coordination and altering capabilities. Additionally, this architecture needs to accommodate the enterprise potential of augmented reality (AR) and virtual reality (VR) that help build a more integrated and extended digital and physical environment.

REFERENCES

Baesens, A. (2014). *Analytics in a big data world: The essential guide to data science and its applications*. John Wiley & Sons.

Clark, L. (2013). *Tesco Uses Supply Chain Analytics to Save £100 m a Year*. https://www.computerweekly. com/news/2240182951/Tesco-uses-supply-chain-analytics-to-save-10-m-a-year

Cooke, J. A. (2013). Three trends to watch in 2013. *Perspective. Supply Chain Quarterly, 1*, 11.

Davenport, T., & O'dwyer, J. (2011). Tap into the Power of Analytics. *Supply Chain Quarterly*, 28-31.

Davenport, T. H. (2006). *Competing on analytics. Harvard Business Review*.

Davenport, T. H., Barth, P., & Bean, R. (2012). How Big Data is different. *MIT Sloan Management Review*, (Fall), 22–24.

Davenport, T. H., & Harris, J. G. (2007). *Competing on analytics – The new science of wining*. Harvard Business School Publishing Corporation.

Davenport, T. H., Harris, J. G., & Morison, R. (2010). *Analytics at work – Smart decisions, better results*. Harvard Business Press.

Davenport, T. H., Harris, J. G., & Morison, R. (2010). *Analytics at work – Smart decisions, better results*. Harvard Business Press.

Davenport, T. H., & O'dwyer, J (2011). Tap into the Power of Analytics. *Supply Chain Quarterly*, 28-31.

Davenport, T. H., & Prusak, L. (2000). *Working knowledge: How organizations manage what they know*. Harvard Business Press.

Davis-Sramek, B., Germain, R., & Iyer, K. (2010). Supply Chain Technology: The Role of Environment in Predicting Performance. *Journal of the Academy of Marketing Science, 38*(1), 42–55. doi:10.100711747-009-0137-1

Deloitte & MHI. (2014). *The 2014 MHI Annual Industry Report – Innovation the driven supply chain*. MHI.

Deloitte & MHI. (2016). *The 2016 MHI Annual Industry Report – Accelerating change: How innovation is driving digital, always-on Supply Chains*. MHI.

Demirkan, H., & Delen, D. (2012). Levering the Capabilities of Service-oriented Decision Support Systems: Putting Analytics and Big Data in Cloud. *Decision Support Systems, 55*(1), 412–421. doi:10.1016/j.dss.2012.05.048

Dietrich, B., Plachy, E. C., & Norton, M. F. (2014). *Analytics across the enterprise: How IBM realize business value from big data and analytics*. IBM Press Books.

Forslund, H., & Jonsson, P. (2007). The Impact of Forecast Information Quality on Supply Chain Performance. *International Journal of Operations & Production Management, 27*(1), 90–107. doi:10.1108/01443570710714556

Gereffi, G. (1999). International trade and industrial upgrading in the apparel commodity chain. *Journal of International Economics, 48*(1), 37–70. doi:10.1016/S0022-1996(98)00075-0

Handfield, R. (2006). *Supply Market Intelligence: A Managerial Handbook for Building Sourcing Strategies*. Taylor & Francis. doi:10.4324/9780203339527

Handfield, R., & Nichols, E. Jr. (2004). Key Issues in Global Supply Base Management. *Industrial Marketing Management, 33*(1), 29–35. doi:10.1016/j.indmarman.2003.08.007

Kohli, R., & Grover, V. (2008). Business Value of IT: An Essay on Expanding Research Directions to Keep up with the times. *Journal of the Association for Information Systems, 9*(1), 23–39. doi:10.17705/1jais.00147

Lavalle, S., Lesser, E., Shockey, R. H., & Crosthwait, N. M. (2011). Big Data, Analytics and the Path from Insight to Value. *MIT Sloan Management Review, 52*(2), 21–32.

Liberatore, M., & Luo, W. (2010). The Analytics Movement. *Interface: a Journal for and About Social Movements*, *40*(4), 313–324. doi:10.1287/inte.1100.0502

Mayika, J. M., Chui, B., Brown, J., Bughin, R., Roxburgh, C., & Byers, A. (2011). *Big Data: The Next Frontier for Innovation, Competition, and Productivity*. McKinsey Report.

McAfee, A., & Brynjolfsson, E. (2012). Big data: The management revolution. *Harvard Business Review*, *90*(10), 61–68. PMID:23074865

McAfee, A., & Brynjolfsson, E. (2012). Big data: The management revolution. *Harvard Business Review*, *90*(10), 61–68. PMID:23074865

Mithas, S., Ramasubbu, N., & Sambamurthy, V. (2011). How Information Management Capability Influences Firm Performance. *Management Information Systems Quarterly*, *35*(1), 237–256. doi:10.2307/23043496

O'dwyer, J., & Renner, R. (2011). The Promise of Advanced Supply Chain Analytics, Supply Chain. *Management Review*, *15*, 32–37.

Oliva, R., & Watson, N. (2011). Cross-Functional Alignment in Supply Chain Planning: A Case Study of Sales & Operations Planning. *Journal of Operations Management*, *29*(5), 434–448. doi:10.1016/j.jom.2010.11.012

Pal, K. (2016). *Supply Chain Coordination Based on Web Service, Supply Chain Management in the Big Data Era*. IGI Publication.

Pal, K. (2020). Information sharing for manufacturing supply chain management based on blockchain technology. In Cross-Industry Use of Blockchain Technology and Opportunities for the Future. IGI Global.

Pal, K. (2021). Applications of Secured Blockchain Technology in Manufacturing Industry. In Blockchain and AI Technology in the Industrial Internet of Things. IGI Global.

Pal, K. (2022). A Decentralized Privacy-Preserving Healthcare Blockchain for IoT, Challenges, and Solutions. In Prospects of Blockchain Technology for Accelerating Scientific Advancement in Healthcare. IGI Global.

Pal, K., & Yasar, A. (2020). Internet of Things and blockchain technology in apparel manufacturing supply chain data management. *Procedia Computer Science*, *170*, 450–457. doi:10.1016/j.procs.2020.03.088

Poluha, R. G. (2007). *Application of the SCOR Model in Supply Chain Management*. Youngstown.

Porter, M. E. (1985). *Competitive Advantage: Creating and Sustaining Superior Performance*. The Free Press.

Power, D. J. (2007). *A Brief History of Decision Support Systems*. http://DSSResource.COM/history/dsshistory.html

Prahalad, C. K., & Mashelkar, R. A. (2010, July). Innovation's Holy Grail. *Harvard Business Review*.

SAS. (2012). *Supply Chain Analytics: Beyond ERP and SCM*. SAS.

Sathi, A. (2012). Big data analytics: Disruptive technologies for changing the game. MC Press.

Shapiro, J. (2010). Advanced Analytics for Sales & Operations Planning. *Analytics Magazine*, (May-June), 20–26.

Siegel, E. (2013). *Predictive analytics: The power to predict who will click, buy, lie or die*. John Wiley & Sons Inc.

Stock, J. R. (2013). Supply chain management: A look back, a look ahead. *Supply Chain Quarterly*, 2, 22–26.

Supply Chain Council. (2010). http://supply-chain.org/f/down-load/726710733/SCOR10.pdf

Svilvar, M., Charkraborty, A. & Kanioura, A. (2013, Oct. 22). Big data analytics in marketing. *OR/MS Today*.

The Economist. (2010). *Data, Data Everywhere*. https://www.economist.com/node/15557443

Trkman, P., McCormack, K., de Oliveira, M. P. V., & Ladeira, M. B. (2010). The Impact of Business Analytics on Supply Chain Performance. *Decision Support Systems*, *49*(3), 318–327. doi:10.1016/j. dss.2010.03.007

Turban, E., & Sepehri, M. (1986). Applications of Decision Support and Expert Systems in Flexible Manufacturing Systems. *Journal of Operations Management*, *6*(34), 433–448. doi:10.1016/0272-6963(86)90015-X

Turban, E., Sharda, R., Delen, D., & King, D. (2011). *Business Intelligence: A Managerial Approach* (2nd ed.). Prentice-Hall.

Viswanathan, N., & Sadlovska, V. (2010). *Supply Chain Intelligence: Adopt Role-based Operational Business Intelligence and Improve Visibility*. Aberdeen Group.

Vosburg, J., & Kumar, A. (2011). Managing Dirty Data in Organizations Using ERP: Lessons from a Case Study. *Industrial Management & Data Systems*, *101*(1), 21–31. doi:10.1108/02635570110365970

Watson, H. J. (2009). Tutorial: Business Intelligence – Past, Present, and Future. *Communications of the Association for Information Systems*, *39*(25). Advance online publication. doi:10.17705/1CAIS.02539

Watson, M., Lewis, S., Cacioppi, P., & Jayaraman, J. (2013). *Supply chain network design – applying optimization and analytics to the global supply chain*. FT Press.

KEY TERMS AND DEFINITIONS

Augmented Reality: It is a modern technology that involves the overlay of computer graphics on real-world applications.

Big Data Analytics: Analytics is the discovery, interpretation, and visualization of meaningful patterns in Big Data. In order to do this, analytics use data classification and clustering mechanisms.

Decision-Making Systems: A decision support system (DSS) is a computer-based information system that supports business or organizational decision-making activities, typically ranking, sorting, or choosing from among alternatives. Decision support systems can be either fully computerized, human-powered or a combination of both.

Internet of Things: The Internet of things (IoT) is the inter-networking of physical devices, vehicles (also referred to as "connected devices" and "smart devices"), buildings, and other items; embedded with electronics, software, sensors, actuators, and network connectivity that enable these objects to collect and exchange data.

Neural Network: Neural network is an information processing paradigm inspired by how biological nervous systems, such as the brain, process information. It uses a classification mechanism that is modelled after the brain and operates by modifying the input through weights to determine what it should output.

Radio Frequency Identification (RFID): This wireless technology is used to identify tagged objects in certain vicinities. Generally, it has three main components: a tag, a reader, and a back-end. A tag uses the open air to transmit data via a radio frequency (RF) signal. However, it is also weak in computational capability. Finally, RFID automates information collection regarding an individual object's location and actions.

Supply Chain Management: A supply chain consists of a network of key business processes and facilities involving end-users and suppliers that provide products, services, and information.

Virtual Reality: It is a term used for computer-generated three-dimension (3D) environments that allow the user to enter and interact with synthetic environments. The users can immerse themselves to varying degrees in the artificial computer world, which may either be a simulation of some form of reality or a complex phenomenon.

Digital Twins, Stress Tests, and the Need for Resilient Supply Chains

Ronak R. Tiwari
National Institute of Techcnology, Calicut, India

Vishnu C. R.
Xavier Institute of Management and Entrepreneurship, Kochi, India

R. Sridharan
 https://orcid.org/0000-0002-0186-6442
National Institute of Techcnology, Calicut, India

P. N. Ram Kumar
Indian Institute of Management, Kozhikode, India

INTRODUCTION

The human civilization has evolved from the invention of the wheel to self-driving cars. While technology has made our lives easier, it has also made the world around us more complex to maintain. For instance, the scope of developing a new automobile now, is not only to make it functional, but also to make it safer, appealing, and cost effective at the same time. **D**ata, **I**nternet-of-Things (IoT), **S**ensors, **Co**mputers (DISCO) form a set of essential tools which can help us maintain and better manage this complexity. Industry 4.0 is a term given to indicate the direction in which the future of the industry lies. It essentially stresses on use of DISCO to build a world that is more sustainable, resilient and agile.

The focus of this article is on Supply Chains (SCs). SCs undoubtedly form an integral part of the modern economies. Last two decades have particularly tested the SCs in every aspect. Issues like Climate change have become more evident with frequent natural disasters persistently occurring in different parts of the world. With SCs getting more global, diverse, and interdependent they have become prone to disruption risks from all over the globe. The challenge for modern SCs is therefore to be able to recover from a disruption, back to its original state, with least impact possible. This ability is defined as resilience in SCs (Christopher & Peck, 2004). The word resilience is borrowed from ecology, which refers to a system's capacity to resist damage and recover after a perturbation or disruption (Peck, 2005). The audience from material science/engineering background may find acquaintance with the term too, where it is described as a material's property to absorb some amount of energy and return back to its original form. It could be argued that incorporating resilience aspects in new supply network is probably easier compared to altering the existing network which is already complex, and a result of years of relationship and trust built with suppliers. Hence, the bigger question that organizations are looking an answer for is, how to build resilience in existing SC networks? Or for that matter how to asses an organization's current state of resilience?

DOI: 10.4018/978-1-7998-9220-5.ch180

One of the key ideas promulgated in risk management, after the 2008 financial crisis, was the notion of 'Stress Tests' (Bank Stress Test, 2021). Stress tests in banking imply that the banks are exposed to a standard set of extreme scenarios, and the banks are assessed on their ability to withstand these events. The banks which fail the stress test are accordingly guided to shape their strategy. The practice of stress tests which originated with banks has been adapted and used in many different fields. After the Covid outbreak especially, many governments are considering stress testing their critical SCs (Tausche, 2021). The motivation for stress testing a SC is not to build an invincible SC, but to point out the weak links in the existing network. Identification of such vulnerabilities using stress tests and strengthening those weak links could be an important step towards SC resilience. For example, the disruptions like natural disasters, or pandemics are extremely difficult to predict, but these events can severely impair the recoverability of a SC. Fortifying each node with additional inventory, or multiple backup sources can kill the efficiency of the business, and therefore, an imperative is to use data to continually monitor potential threats in the network using stress-testing. Hence, Stress-testing can push the momentum towards data-driven and proactive risk management.

An easy way to conduct a stress test for SCs is to simulate the behavior of the SC under a set of extreme disruption scenarios. But, to be even capable of doing that, an organization would probably first need to collect a lot of data about the existing supply network configuration. For instance, the data needed to build a simulation model could be: the inventory levels at each echelon, the ordering frequencies and quantities, the location of supplier facilities, the lead times between echelons, etc. The obvious limitation which surfaces here, is that an SC is dynamic in nature. The lead times, inventory levels, demand, capacity, and other aspects that build SC, keep changing with time. It is very much possible that the stress test conducted for one instance of data could be absolutely non-value adding for other instances. The imperative therefore, is to think of a digital model of a SC which can be updated in real time using data collected from sensors, servers, IoT devices, etc. This digital model is referred to as a 'Digital Twin' of a SC. A digital twin of a SC, coupled with computing infrastructure can provide invaluable insights about the SC network and its state of resilience. It can serve as a great tool to make better and timely decisions in the times of disruptions.

The objective of this article is to introduce the terms, problems, and solutions keeping students and learners in mind, which very few studies consider. This article will act as a good start for students, early-stage researchers and professionals who are interested in understanding the need for digitalization in SCs. Funding on the wide literature, this chapter attempts to answer five important questions:

1. Why SCs need to be resilient?
2. How digital transformation can enable SCs to become resilient?
3. What are digital twins in SC context and how do they look like?
4. How to use digital twins of SCs for resilience building?
5. How to measure SC resilience?

This article is divided into 5 sections. The following section provides a broad background on current state of industry resilience, and the rush for digitalization. With supply chain resilience at the center of discussion, the next section describes in detail, the concept of a 'Digital Twin' and 'Stress Test'. Building on the ideas developed in the previous section, the third section attempts to demonstrate through three simple and short examples (a) an Arena based application of performance analysis in SC digital twin, and (b) ways to stress test a supply chain (c) recent metrics for measuring supply chain resilience. The last two sections summarize the article, present some new research directions, and finally provide some concluding remarks.

BACKGROUND

Digitalization and Visibility are the first few steps towards a viable SC. Digitalization augments visibility in SCs, and visibility aids agility in decision making. A study conducted among approximately 500 SC professionals on SC visibility, suggests lack of visibility across SCs as one of the top 3 obstacles in achieving their organizational objectives (Gartner, 2021). A 2020 survey on SC resilience revealed, only about 21% companies believe that they are resilient, and have good visibility of their SC (Gartner, 2020). A similar survey from Fortune reported that, around 94% of the Fortune 1000 companies experienced supply disruptions in some form or the other in 2020 (Sherman, 2020). Another report from PwC, on SC disruptions, indicates that the firms who actively invested in digitalization saw significantly higher numbers in terms of revenue and service levels compared to the ones who did not (PwC, 2021). The studies, surveys, and research on the status quo of the industry resilience, support the rush for digitalization. Covid has only reinforced the trust on digitalization and its promising benefits to organizations. Furthermore, the accelerated investments in digital technology after Covid-19 outbreak, indeed corroborate the fact that digitalization is no longer a competitive advantage, but a necessity to sustain.

An early study done by Wall Street Journal in the year 2000 published, that businesses were ready to take the risk of occasional supply disruptions attributed to single sourcing, due to benefits in quality, cost, and reduced inventory. But, with more global and leaner SCs, decrease in time to market, and more frequent disruptions hitting every part of the world, the same logic is no longer sustainable. Designing a resilient SC network transcends the traditional cost-centric network design approaches in many ways (Ivanov & Dolgui, 2019). Creating strategic redundancies, risk mitigation inventory, internal product flexibility, agility, multi-sourcing, visibility, and rate of digital adoption, to name a few, are some of the most important factors governing the resilience of a network. Christopher and Peck (2004), and Peck (2005) suggest two important points on building resilience in existing SC network (a) Understanding of the existing Supply network and (b) awareness of the vulnerabilities and what drives those vulnerabilities in the network. From a digital SC perspective, the first point (a) corresponds to the digital mapping of the existing network or building a digital twin, while (b) encourages use of the digital twin to identify bottlenecks or weak links. It is in identification of the vulnerable nodes in the network, that SC stress tests can add value to the decision makers and SC leaders.

An SC digital twin of an existing SC network, can fantastically complement the decision-making capabilities of a firm both pre-disruption, post-disruption, and during disruptions. The digital twin enables simulation of what-if scenarios, and optimal decision-making, in real time. SC Stress tests are in fact, simulations of extreme disruptions performed on digital models of SCs. The results of a SC stress test, can reveal the nodes, which if fail, the SC will see a maximum impact. SC managers can use this knowledge for informed risk planning, and disruption risk management. This digital advantage, consequently reduces the impact of disruptions on SCs, and ultimately increases the resilience of a SC.

THE DIGITAL SUPPLY CHAIN

Digital Twin

Although the terminology and the concept of 'Digital Twin' seems to be pretty recent, it is actually not. NASA used the simulators for its Apollo missions in late 60s, which fulfilled the same need as digital twins do. However, it is the maturity with digital technology, development in IT (Information Technol-

D

ogy), ubiquitous access to better computing infrastructure, development in sensor technology, etc. that has complemented the network effects. The notion of a digital twin was first formally conceptualized by Dr. Michael Grieves, in the year 2002, in a presentation at University of Michigan, PLM Centre (Grieves & Vickers, 2016). The phrase 'Digital Twin' although was a suggestion from John Vickers, a colleague of Professor Grieves, at NASA. The same concept has been referred to with many names including 'Mirrored Spaces Model' and 'Information Mirroring Model', but it is the phrase Digital Twin which has been simple and descriptive enough to be adopted by the industry as well. Product Lifecycle Management (PLM) was the area where the term found initial of its few applications, but with the pervasive goals of Industry 4.0 of creating a digital and connected ecosystem, it has found applications everywhere. The focus of this section is to present the concept of a digital twin in SC context.

An existing SC network can very well be mapped on a sheet of paper (albeit a big sheet). But it is the real-time data collection, advanced computing, and simulation capability that motivates the digitalization and hence digital mapping of SCs. This is also where the sensors, IoT devices, data warehouses play a key role. These devices and infrastructures, facilitate the real time data collection from several points all across the SC network. This could be equipment utilization data, inventory levels, location data, production schedules, demand data, to name a few. Ready availability and accuracy of such necessary information to SC managers and leaders adds immense value to an organization's ability to respond to changes. The mapping of the existing supply chain network can be done in many different ways. There are several commercial as well as opensource tools like anyLogistix from AnyLogic, Arena from Rockwell Automation, Simpy in Python, to name a few, that can technically support in preparing a digital model of the entire SC. The present article uses the DES (Discrete Event Simulation) software Arena which is a general-purpose simulation software, to demonstrate an example of how a digital model of a SC can appear like.

Stress Tests

In early 90s internal stress tests used to be conducted by some big players in the banking industry. The motivation to conduct such an exercise was to remain aware of the worst-case economic downturns where the banks could plunge into a crisis. It was in 2009 however, after the Great Recession, that Federal Reserve in United States, and several other government-run institutions worldwide, made it compulsory for banks (of specific size) to undergo stress tests. The term 'Stress Test', is actually borrowed from medicine. It is also a well-known term in risk management. In fact, in material science, stress-testing (Tensile test) describes the process of assessing a material's yield strength, through a destructive test on its specimen. Similarly, an SC stress test can be conveniently understood as a test to find out the strength of the SC. Here, the strength of SC can be defined as its ability to meet demand with supply in the face of disruptions. The last few sentences, not only explore the ties of the concept with material science stress tests, but also establish a direct conceptual link between stress tests and SC resilience. Furthermore, with Covid exposing a lot of pre-existing vulnerabilities in the SC, stress test is one of the few ideas which can immensely contribute towards a resilient future.

In the last decade, the increase in global SC risk and frequency of disruptions has encouraged huge research on disruption risk management, SC risk management, and resilience. There were several studies, done in the aftermath of 2011 Tsunami and Thailand floods. An important study conducted by Simchi-Levi *et al.* (2015)onFord's SC network, describes the Risk-exposure Model for stress testing SCs under supply disruptions. The model presented in the paper uses metrics like Time-To-Recover (TTR), Time-To-Survive (TTS), and Risk Exposure Index (REI) to pin point vulnerable and risky nodes in the network.

Another recent example of such stress tests being conceptualized is from Kearney (Kearney, 2021). Kearney's resilience stress test widens the scope of resilience for an organization. Kearney's stress test considers several dimensions of geography, working capital, suppliers, planning, to name a few to assess the resilience of an existing network. A similar stress test proposed by Accenture, is an adapted version of the Risk-exposure Model (Accenture, 2020). But what all ideas have in common here is: the need to understand end-to-end SC network. This inevitably aligns with the suggestions made by Christopher and Peck (2004). And it is in filling this gap, where digital mapping, and ultimately digitalization can help.

USING DATA TO MANAGE SUPPLY CHAINS

Modelling and Performance Analysis of a SC Digital Twin Using Arena

Arena provides an internal, ready-to-use logic, to model real world interactions between entities. The entities in a SC network can be imagined to be echelons, Automated Guided Vehicles (AGVs) being used at an echelon, suppliers, transportation vehicles, etc. depending on the abstraction and scope. Figure 1 shows a multi-echelon serial SC model built in Arena. It is evident that a digital representation of SC need not look any similar to its real-world counterpart (although, there are great visualization options available too). It is the information and data that matters. There are 4 echelons presented in the Arena simulation model below. All four stages interact with each other using simple set of rules. These rules form the basis for simulating transactions between entities in the model.

Figure 1. Arena based digital model of a multi-echelon serial SC

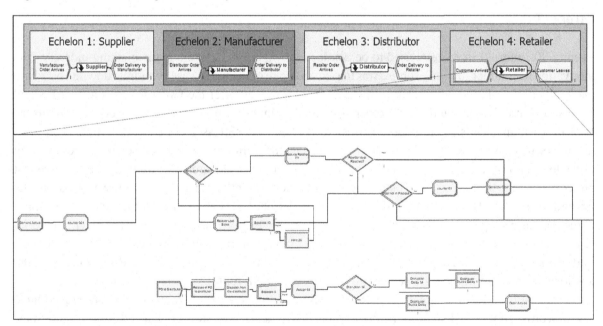

Arena provides built in modules to model standard processes. For illustration purposes, the flowchart or the logic at retailer's stage is magnified in Figure 1. It is important to recognize that, it is the scale of the model, number of entities involved, and number of possible transactions which the entities can do, that makes the SC complex and unpredictable. Preparing a digital twin equips us with the tools to tackle this complexity and uncertainty. *For the SC model to be referred to as digital twin, there has to be a continuous synchronization of data between the model and the real world. In other words, the digital model should mirror the real-world process in real time.* A digital model of the existing SC network can nevertheless be useful for scenario-analysis and evaluating different strategies. After appreciating the simulation and process modelling challenges with the existing tools, it is evident that there is at least some level of abstraction from real world, in the digital world. There for a digital twin is not an accurate but a needful and apt representation of the real world.

Arena uses a set of building blocks called modules. These modules form the basis in defining and modelling the sequential processes, events, and activities in the SC. Once the model is built, Arena enables the system to function/evolve on the basis of defined rules, and aids in calculating the metrics, and required performance measures for the system. Building upon the Arena model described in Figure 1, Arena generates the customer entities according to a known arrival pattern at the last echelon, Retailer. Those entities in turn, demand a certain quantity of product, based on the underlying demand distribution. Arrival of a customer stimulates the inventory management system of the retailer to check for product availability. If the specified quantity is less than or equal to the existing inventory at retailer, the demand is met and the inventory is adjusted accordingly. The inventory management system again checks for the number of units present in inventory. If the number of units turn out to be less than the pre-decided Re-order Level at retailer, the inventory management logic generates a Purchase Order (PO) to the Distributor which is the third echelon. The same process of verifying the inventory levels, meeting the demand, adjusting the inventory is iterated at Distributor stage. Next step, as soon as the capacity is realized, the delivery is initiated. The delivered quantity is replenished at retailer stage after the specified transportation lead time. This forms a set of simple rules through which the distributor and retailer stages interact. The same logic is used between all the stages to simulate the echelon interactions. This is a fairly simplified case of how interactions take place in SCs. The point to note here however, is that all the capabilities and interactions are modelled using variables and logic developed in the simulation environment, in Arena.

To illustrate with an example, the simulation model used in Figure 1 was made to run in Arena for 5 replications with a replication length of 2 years. Fill rate was used to measure the performance of the SC. Table 1 furnishes different lead time scenarios used for measuring the Fill rates. It can be observed that, with reduction in lead times, the retailer fill rate witnesses a significant rise, which is expected. The analysis presented here, although trivial can become a challenge if the data about inventory levels, lead times, inventory policies, capacity constraints, demand, etc. is not readily available. The ready availability of data across the network coupled with simulation capabilities, makes digital twins extremely valuable for SC planning and management.

Table 1. Performance Analysis of a SC using Arena

Sr. No.	Lead Time(Days)	Retailer Fill Rate
1	TRIA (0.75, 1, 2)	88.07%
2	TRIA (0.5, 0.75, 1.5)	96.61%
3	TRIA (0.25, 0.5, 1)	99.91%

REM for Stress Testing Supply Chains

This part of the article aims to delineate the major features of the Risk-exposure Model (REM) described in Simchi-Levi *et al.* (2015). REM attempts to answer two important questions:

1. What is the value of the risk, that a particular supplier node exposes the SC network to?
2. Which nodes in the SC network are the weakest links of the network?

To answer the first question, REM suggests two metrics, namely Time-To-Recover (TTR), and Performance Impact (PI) to measure the risk-exposure of each node in the network.

"TTR for a node is defined as the time that the supplier node would need, to resume the supply back after a disruption has occurred."

"PI for a node is defined as the change in chosen performance measure that the SC network will witness, if that node is disrupted for the duration equals to its TTR."

TTR should be obtained from the suppliers. PI could represent change in any of the performance measures viz. service level, lost sales, lost profit, lost revenue, etc. depending upon the business goals. Figure 2 shows an illustrative SC network with multiple-tiers. Each circle in the figure represents a node in the supply network, and each arc represents an existing material and information flow between the nodes. Each node behaves as a supplier stage for the lower tiers. After checking the TTR with the suppliers, PI for a node is calculated by simulating a disruption of a duration equal to its TTR, and measuring the change in performance measure. For example, the node 'A' has a TTR of 1 week and can cause a performance impact of $1M in lost profits (assuming zero lost profit without a disruption). *The PI of each node is also the value of risk that the node exposes the network to. It is also referred to as the 'Risk-exposure' of that particular node.*

Figure 2. TTR, PI and TTS for all nodes in SC network

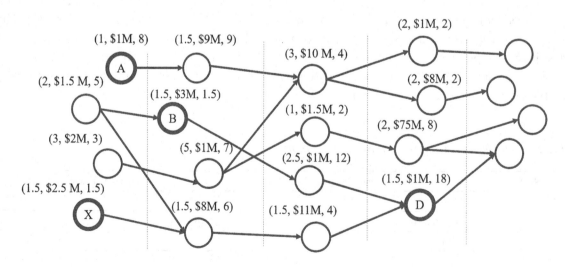

(TTR, PI, TTS)

A SC is a complex network of interconnected nodes. When a disruption is induced at one particular node in an interconnected and complex network, several other interconnected nodes get affected too. This is because of the propagation of disruptions across the network. This propagation of disruption across the SC is defined as ripple effect (Ivanov *et al.*, 2013). And, for PI to be able to qualify as the risk exposure for a particular node, the rest of the network should be least affected by ripple effects. To make an adjustment for this issue Simchi-Levi *et al.* (2015) describe a Linear Programming approach to calculate the risk exposure of each node. The linear programming model suggested in the paper ensures that once a disruption hits, the rest of the network behaves optimally. PI thus calculated, is the guaranteed best estimate of the Risk Exposure of that node.

The optimization model used in the study can be described as follows:

$$Minimize : \sum_{j \in P} p_j l_j^{(k)}$$

Subject to...

$$\sum_{i \in F^{(k)}} d_j t^{(k)} - q_{ji}^{(k)} - f_{ji} \leq l_j^{(k)}, \forall j \in \overline{P} \tag{1}$$

$$\sum_{j \in F^{(k)}} q_{ji}^{(k)} \leq c_i t^{(k)}, \forall i \in S \setminus k \tag{2}$$

$$q_{ji}^{(k)}, l_j^{(k)} \geq 0, \forall i \in S, j \in \overline{P} \tag{3}$$

The notation used in the model is summarized in Table 2. The objective is to minimize the lost profit over all disruption scenarios, for a set of products being produced, at a set of nodes. Constraint 1 balances the lost production with finished goods inventory and production quantity. The second inequality takes care of the production capacity constraints. Finally, the third constraint is for non-negativity of decision variables. The present linear optimization model directs to optimal allocation of resources, such that the disruption impact on the network is minimized. For one instance of the problem, the objective function value obtained is called the risk-exposure value of the node. At this point, it is important to note that the scope of this section is only to share the possibility of the use of linear programming formulations in stress testing. Therefore, the optimization model furnished here, is a simpler version of the model described in the paper.

A similar optimization approach is followed for calculating the TTS values for each node in the paper. It can be noted, that TTS is an alternate way to look at the same problem. TTS can also be described as the maximum value for TTR for which the SC network sees a zero change in PI.

"TTS for a node is defined as the duration for which the business can survive without being impacted by the disruption at that node"

Table 2. Summary of notations used in the Optimization Model

Sr. No.	Notation	Description of the Variable
1	p_j	Lost profit margin of product j
2	(k)	Denotes a particular disruption scenario out of k total scenarios for k nodes in the network
3	l_j	Lost production volume for product j
4	d_j	Demand per unit time for product j
5	$t^{(k)}$	TTR value for a particular node
6	$q_{ji}^{(k)}$	Quantity of product j produced at plant i under disruption scenario (k)
7	f_{ji}	Finished goods inventory of product j at plant i
8	c_j	Production capacity per unit time of plant i
9	$\overline{P}$	Set of products being produced in the network
10	S	Set of production sites
11	$F^{(k)}$	Set of production nodes under the impact of disruption scenario (k)

TTS has three benefits: (a) It keeps the business from falling into trap of a supplier's tendency to be optimistic about the TTR values. (b) TTS along with TTR values for each node in the network can give great insights on risky suppliers (essentially, where there is no slack). (c) Nodes with very high TTS values can be taken as potential opportunities for reducing inventory in the network. Figure 2 also shows an illustrative example of TTS values of each node in the network. It can be observed that supplier node 'A' has a TTS of 8 weeks. This means that there will be no performance impact observed because of disruption at this node, unless the disruption duration is more than 8 weeks. Similarly, for node 'C' there will be a negative impact on performance, if the disruption duration at this node exceeds a week. Collectively for a complex network with thousands of suppliers and distribution nodes, this approach can point out the hidden vulnerabilities. For example, if there are a few suppliers with a zero TTS span, then these few are the risky suppliers. The network will be at greater risk to disruptions from these suppliers because, the network quickly starts to starve. *These nodes can be identified as the weakest links of the network. Efforts should be taken to understand these suppliers, and investments in building resilience can be directed to such suppliers.* Whereas, if the majority of supplier nodes map to higher TTS values, this will serve as an opportunity to reduce inventory levels at nodes dependent on those suppliers (See node 'D'). Ideally, TTR and TTS complement each other for decision making. To be resilient or for that matter robust against disruptions, every node in the network should ideally have TTS > TTR. The problem is with the suppliers where TTS £ TTR. These are also the suppliers where most of the risk is concentrated. An organization's limited risk management resources can be concentrated on these nodes.

Risk Exposure Index

In a network of thousands of suppliers, it becomes a little tricky to pin point to a set of risky suppliers. But, even from those set of suppliers, TTR and TTS fail to give a complete picture. This is because a node can still have same values for both TTR and TTS (See node 'B' and 'X' in Figure 2). To solve this, and for cross scenario comparisons Simchi-Levi *et al.* (2015) define the Risk Exposure Index (REI). REI is a number that lies between 0 and 1. REI is maximum (1) for the node with the maximum PI in the network, and minimum (0) for the node with minimum PI. REI for any node (Ω) in the network can be calculated using Equation 4. given below.

$$REI_\Omega = 1 - \frac{PI_{(max)} - PI_\Omega}{PI_{(max)} - PI_{(min)}} \tag{4}$$

Notice that using the REI, it becomes evident that node B is riskier compared to node X, because REI_B (0.03) > REI_X (0.02).

REM uses simple metrics to identify vulnerable links in the network and uses a linear programming approach to stress test the SC for extreme scenarios. Ultimately it is the ability of the organization to use the insights and act accordingly to increase the resilience of the network with respect to supplier disruptions.

Stress Testing Using Simulation

Stress testing in SCs has a lot in common with simulations and what-if scenario analysis. Ivanov (2017) proposed a simulation modelling exercise for ripple effect analysis. The ideas shared in the paper can be taken as one of the ways for stress-testing the SC network. The first step however is always, the digital representation of the SC network using modelling and simulation tools like any Logistix, Arena, etc. The next step is to test the model for extreme disruption scenarios. It is important to note that, the selection scenarios are purely based on the knowledge of the manager about the SC network, and the disruptions. This approach can still identify the vulnerable links, given the performance impact a disruption in that particular node has on the network. This kind of analysis has been referred to as ripple effect analysis in the literature. To put the topic of the article in context, and with reference to the scope of interest of the present chapter, the disruption scenarios presented in Table 3 are considered for stress testing the Arena model described in Figure 1. The inventory, and other SC policy parameters have been presumed for simplicity.

Table 3. Retailer Fill Rate for sub-tier supplier disruptions

Sr. No.	Disruption Delay at a Sub-tier Supplier (Days)	Retailer Fill Rate
1	0	86.70%
2	20	87.0%
3	30	87.3%
4	40	87.13%
5	50	87.10%
6	60	86.9%
7	70	85.3%
8	80	82.70%
9	90	80.60%
10	120	64.70%

The simulation study conducted here successfully captures that for the given model parameters, the network easily withstands a 60 days sub-tier disruption (referring back to REM, 60 days is TTS of the sub-tier supplier node). An additional inference from the results is that there is too much inventory in between the intermediate stages/tiers, because the Fill rate measures don't drop significantly until a disruption of 70 days is induced in the model. The ability to do such simulation experiments in real time can tremendously increase the decision-making capability of an organization in the wake of disruptions.

Quantifying Supply Chain Resilience

Digital twins and stress tests are supplements for resilient SCs. However, to be able to compare SC networks or strategies based on their resilience, an organization would still need a numerical measure for resilience. Chritopher and Peck (2004) defined and proposed the idea of SC resilience in their seminal work, after observing resemblance of the term with ecological systems. Sheffi *et al.* (2005) extended the concept through the disruption profile, and vulnerability framework. Evidently, there was a shift of the SC research community towards resilience in early 2000s, but there's no widely accepted metric to measure SC resilience yet (Behzadi *et al.*, 2020). This is partly because resilience is a multi-faceted concept and includes elements of time, cost, adaptability, risk diversification and demand volatility, just to name a few. Quantifying resilience for a network is important for several reasons, but the main motivator is that it allows an objective comparison between strategies. To answer this question, over the recent few years there have been several research efforts on developing a metric to measure resilience. The research on SC resilience has evolved from qualitative to quantitative, with more quantitative approaches incorporating interdisciplinary concepts recently (Foroozesh et al., 2022; Ozdemir et al., 2022; Suryawanshi & Dutta, 2022; Hoseini et al., 2021; Moosavi & Hosseini, 2021; Hosseini et al., 2020; Li *et al.*, 2020; Ojha *et al.*, 2018; Torabi *et al.*, 2015; Cardoso *et al.*, 2015; Simchi-Levi, 2013). This section explains two of such easy-to-use metrics to measure a SC's resilience using the disruption profile described by Sheffi *et al.* (2005). Figure 3 shows an illustrative profile of a firm's performance in the event of a disruption and how recovery might look like, post-disruption.

Figure 3. Disruption Profile
(adapted from Sheffi and Rice (2005))

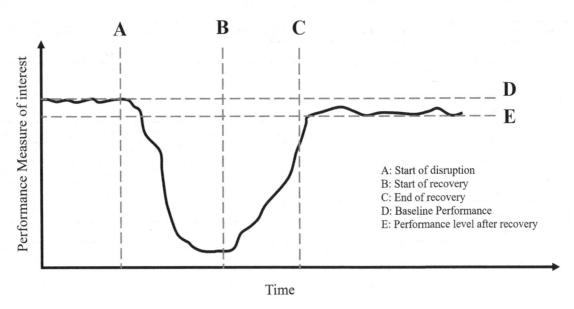

A: Start of disruption
B: Start of recovery
C: End of recovery
D: Baseline Performance
E: Performance level after recovery

Recovery Level (RL)

Recovery level (RL) is defined as the fraction of baseline performance (D) that the SC is able to attain and maintain after the recovery (E).

For example: If the Service level before the disruption was 90% and after the recovery is 85%, then the RL is calculated as:

$$RL = \frac{85}{90} \times 100 = 94.4\%$$

Lost Profits During Recovery (LPR)

LPR is defined as the total loss in profits witnessed by the business between the start of disruption (A) and the end of recovery (C).

For example: If the business expects that it could have produced and sold 1 million products more with a profit margin of $0.5 then the LPR is calculated as:

$$LPR = 1Mn \times \$0.5 = \$0.5Mn$$

These metrics although intuitive and simple, might not necessarily give the complete picture of a SC network's state of resilience. They tend to limit the scope of resilience to a single performance measure, and only to supply disruptions, while resilience is a much wider concept. Spiegler *et al.* (2012) also suggest a control-engineering based perspective to define a better measure-ITAE (Integral of Time Absolute Error) which considers a combination of these metrics along with the time element.

FUTURE RESEARCH DIRECTIONS

The present article explores recent research trends and capabilities needed to build resilience in SCs. It also puts digitalization as the first transformative step for a resilient and sustainable future. But even with this first step there are many challenges for the research fraternity to move the society towards viability. Some of the challenges and research directions which can help realize the full potential of digitalization are as follows:

1. With governments and businesses investing more on digital initiatives, designing new, and exhaustive SC stress tests could be a promising research arena for future.
2. Majority of the current research on SC resilience is qualitative. The dearth of quantitative studies on network resilience indicate that it is still in its infancy (Behzadi *et al.*, 2020). New avenues on measuring SC resilience considering its multi-faceted scope can be reckoned as a future trend.
3. Network design approaches to balance resilience and cost can be seen as an emerging trend.
4. 'Ripple effects' proposed by Ivanov *et al.* (2013) point towards a different perspective on resilience. The quantification and visualization of ripple effects in a network bears parallel paths of research with SC resilience and can likely converge and support the research on resilience.

The value that Data Science and Machine Learning techniques generate for the businesses, hugely depend on the accuracy and quality of the data. Pandemic induced rush towards adoption of digital technology by businesses and governments should fill in the missing gaps and accelerate the use of these techniques industry wide. This trend will also ultimately fuel a rapid development in sensor technologies, IoT devices and digital ecosystems on the whole. However, the first step still remains, end-to-end digitalization.

CONCLUSION

Covid is not the reason for failure of SCs. The pandemic has only revealed the pre-existing vulnerabilities in design, as well as planning of SC networks. The primary objective of this article is to shed some light on what could be done to deal with these vulnerabilities. The first section provides a brief background on the current state of industry resilience and motivates the need for SC resilience. It also puts in context; the urge for digitalization and how it can benefit at large. The next section lays down the history, emergence and meaning of the terms 'Digital Twin' and 'Stress Test' in the context of SCs. The third section tries to motivate some of the basic problems in SCs and how an Arena based digital modelling (similar to a digital twin) can be used to analyze a SC's performance. The next sub-part of this section focuses on stress tests and the REM as one of the techniques to conduct the same, followed by simulation. In the end some recent metrics to measure SC resilience are described. Ultimately, some future research directions at the intersection of resilience and ripple effects are also appreciated as future trends.

It is very important to mention that data-driven modelling and decision making in SCs is not as easy as it seems. The biggest challenge lies in the data availability, and visibility across a network that a company has. For example, at present, the companies are really struggling with the sub-tier visibility of their supply network. And, this is where organizations can run into a problem, if some event of disruption strikes in a country where a major sub-tier supplier is affected, about whom the company didn't even knew. Even if sub-tier visibility was not a problem, the benefits of operating such a sophisticated real time digital twin system should really outweigh operating costs, which is something that only big corporations can afford, as of now. Secondly, many of these sub-tier supply networks operate in emerging economies, where even small disruptions can unfold into devastating impacts (Tukamuhabwa et al., 2017).

Not only is it difficult to collect data and use it for risk assessment in SCs, but also a challenge for the SC directors, is to justify this cost of barricading. This is also the reason why most organizations see stress-testing as audits to comply with, and prefer fire-fighting in the event of disruptions instead of bearing the cost of redundancies beforehand. In fact, enterprise-wide SC risk management programs are rarely appreciated (encouraged) in an organization, and what organizations rely on, are usual risk registers, and standard risk assessment Key Performance Indicators (KPIs), or Key Risk Indicators (KRIs) like Supplier Credit Rating, On-time delivery performance of the suppliers, to name a few. However, using digitalization, and stress-testing models like REM, can enable SCs to continuously monitor the risks at different levels through data, and provide an updated report on the ever-changing map of vulnerabilities in the network. This will enable a firm, in developing a culture of risk management as suggested in the empirical studies done by Tukamuhabwa et al. (2017), instead of occasional epiphanies.

Research and knowledge on digitalization, and how it can fill the gaps is extremely important for the coming generation of SC managers and early-stage researchers or professionals. This article fills the exact same void through simple and appropriate examples, along with recent concepts without getting into more details. This article can contribute greatly towards their understanding of resilient SCs, why they require to be resilient, and how digital technology can help in building them resilient.

REFERENCES

Accenture. (2020). *Measuring and managing supply chain resilience.* https://www.accenture.com/us-en/services/supply-chain-operations/resilient-supply-chain

Behzadi, G., O'Sullivan, M. J., & Olsen, T. L. (2020). On metrics for supply chain resilience. *European Journal of Operational Research, 287*(1), 145–158. doi:10.1016/j.ejor.2020.04.040

Cardoso, S. R., Paula Barbosa-Póvoa, A., Relvas, S., & Novais, A. Q. (2015). Resilience metrics in the assessment of complex supply-chains performance operating under demand uncertainty. *Omega, 56,* 53–73. doi:10.1016/j.omega.2015.03.008

Christopher, M., & Peck, H. (2004). Building the Resilient Supply Chain. *International Journal of Logistics Management, 15*(2), 1–14. doi:10.1108/09574090410700275

Foroozesh, N., Karimi, B., & Mousavi, S. M. (2022). Green-resilient supply chain network design for perishable products considering route risk and horizontal collaboration under robust interval-valued type-2 fuzzy uncertainty: A case study in food industry. *Journal of Environmental Management, 307,* 114470. doi:10.1016/j.jenvman.2022.114470 PMID:35085967

Gartner. (2021). *The Increased Role of Visibility in Supply Chain: Surviving in the Era of Supply Chain Disruption.* Author.

Grieves, H. & Vickers, J., (2016). *Origins of the digital twin concept.* doi:10.13140/rg.2.2.26367.61609

Hoseini, S. A., Hashemkhani Zolfani, S., Skačkauskas, P., Fallahpour, A., & Saberi, S. (2021). A Combined Interval Type-2 Fuzzy MCDM Framework for the Resilient Supplier Selection Problem. *Mathematics, 10*(1), 44. doi:10.3390/math10010044

Hosseini, S., Ivanov, D., & Blackhurst, J. (2020). Conceptualization and Measurement of Supply Chain Resilience in an Open-System Context. *IEEE Transactions on Engineering Management,* 1–16.

Ivanov, D. (2017). Simulation-based ripple effect modelling in the supply chain. *International Journal of Production Research, 55*(7), 2083–2101. doi:10.1080/00207543.2016.1275873

Ivanov, D., & Dolgui, A. (2019). New disruption risk management perspectives in supply chains: Digital twins, the ripple effect, and resileanness. *IFAC-PapersOnLine, 52*(13), 337–342. doi:10.1016/j.ifacol.2019.11.138

Ivanov, D., Sokolov, B., & Dolgui, A. (2013). The Ripple effect in supply chains: Trade-off "efficiency-flexibility-resilience" in disruption management. *International Journal of Production Research, 52*(7), 2154–2172. doi:10.1080/00207543.2013.858836

Kearney. (2021). *Strategic options to build resilience.* Retrieved September 29, 2021, from https://www.kearney.com/operations-performance-transformation/article/?/a/strategic-options-to-build-resilience

Moosavi, J., & Hosseini, S. (2021). Simulation-based assessment of supply chain resilience with consideration of recovery strategies in the COVID-19 pandemic context. *Computers & Industrial Engineering*, *160*, 107593. doi:10.1016/j.cie.2021.107593 PMID:34511708

Ojha, R., Ghadge, A., Tiwari, M., & Bititci, U. (2018, April 10). *Bayesian Network Modelling for Supply Chain Risk Propagation*. Academic Press.

Ozdemir, D., Sharma, M., Dhir, A., & Daim, T. (2022). Supply chain resilience during the COVID-19 pandemic. *Technology in Society*, *68*, 101847. doi:10.1016/j.techsoc.2021.101847 PMID:35075312

Peck, H. (2005). Drivers of supply chain vulnerability: An integrated framework. *International Journal of Physical Distribution & Logistics Management*, *35*(4), 210–232. doi:10.1108/09600030510599904

PwC. (2021). *PwC's perspective on digital supply chain*. PwC.

Sherman, E. (2020, February 21). *94% of the Fortune 1000 are seeing coronavirus supply chain disruptions*. Fortune. https://fortune.com/2020/02/21/fortune-1000-coronavirus-china-supply-chain-impact/

Simchi-Levi, D., Schmidt, W., Wei, Y., Zhang, P. Y., Combs, K., Ge, Y., Gusikhin, O., Sanders, M., & Zhang, D. (2015). Identifying Risks and Mitigating Disruptions in the Automotive Supply Chain. *Interfaces*, *45*(5), 375–390. doi:10.1287/inte.2015.0804

Spiegler, V. L. M., Potter, A. T., Naim, M. M., & Towill, D. R. (2015). The value of nonlinear control theory in investigating the underlying dynamics and resilience of a grocery supply chain. *International Journal of Production Research*, *54*(1), 265–286. doi:10.1080/00207543.2015.1076945

Suryawanshi, P., & Dutta, P. (2022). Optimization models for supply chains under risk, uncertainty, and resilience: A state-of-the-art review and future research directions. *Transportation Research Part E, Logistics and Transportation Review*, *157*, 102553. doi:10.1016/j.tre.2021.102553

Tausche, K. (2021, April 1). *White House studying supply chain "stress tests" after semiconductor shortages, sources say*. CNBC. https://www.cnbc.com/2021/04/01/white-house-studying-supply-chain-stress-tests-after-semiconductor-shortages-sources-say-.html

Tukamuhabwa, B., Stevenson, M., & Busby, J. (2017). Supply chain resilience in a developing country context: A case study on the interconnectedness of threats, strategies and outcomes. *Supply Chain Management*, *22*(6), 486–505. doi:10.1108/SCM-02-2017-0059

ADDITIONAL READING

Bank Stress Test. (2019). *Investopedia*. https://www.investopedia.com/terms/b/bank-stress-test.asp

de Arquer, M., Ponte, B., & Pino, R. (2021). Examining the balance between efficiency and resilience in closed-loop supply chains. *Central European Journal of Operations Research*. Advance online publication. doi:10.100710100-021-00766-1 PMID:34413704

Gartner. (2020). *Weathering the storm: supply chain resilience in an age of disruption*. https://www.gartner.com/en/supply-chain/trends/weathering-the-storm-supply-chain-resilience-in-an-age-of-disruption

Ponis, S. T., & Koronis, E. (2012). Supply Chain Resilience: Definition Of Concept And Its Formative Elements. *Journal of Applied Business Research*, 28(5), 921. doi:10.19030/jabr.v28i5.7234

Rajesh, R. (2018). Measuring the barriers to resilience in manufacturing supply chains using Grey Clustering and VIKOR approaches. *Measurement*, *126*, 259–273. doi:10.1016/j.measurement.2018.05.043

Schlegel, G. L., & Trent, R. J. (2015). *Supply chain risk management: An emerging discipline*. CRC Press.

Simchi-Levi, D. (2010). *Operations rules:Delivering customer value through flexible operations*. MIT Press.

Torabi, S. A., Baghersad, M., & Mansouri, S. A. (2015). Resilient supplier selection and order allocation under operational and disruption risks. *Transportation Research Part E, Logistics and Transportation Review*, *79*, 22–48. doi:10.1016/j.tre.2015.03.005

KEY TERMS AND DEFINITIONS

Digital Twins: Digital twins refer to a connected digital model or a digital replica of a real-world system.

Digitalization: Digitalization refers to the shift from paper-based transactions to computer based digital transactions.

Disruption: Disruption is defined as a complete facility stoppage.

Fill Rate: Percentage of demand met out of total demand observed is called fill rate.

Ripple Effects in Supply Chains: Ripple effects in supply chains are defined as the propagation of disruptions to other dependent nodes across the network.

Supply Chain: Supply chain or a supply chain network refers to all the entities who collaborate to meet the demand with supply. Right from the raw material suppliers to the last mile delivery vans forms a part of the supply chain network.

Supply Chain Resilience: Supply chain resilience is an attribute of supply chains to be able to recover back from disruptions to a more desirable state or the same state.

Supply Chain Stress Test: Supply chain stress tests are defined as techniques to assess the ability of the supply chain to meet demand with supply, in the face of disruptions.

Section 52
Symbolic Learning

Knowledge–Based Artificial Intelligence:
Methods and Applications

Sotiris Batsakis
Technical University of Crete, Greece

Nikolaos Matsatsinis
 https://orcid.org/0000-0003-0150-7615
Technical University of Crete, Greece

INTRODUCTION

Artificial Intelligence (AI) and Data Science are among the most (if not the most) transformative scientific and engineering disciplines of our era, impacting many aspects of everyday lives and science itself. Availability of data and computing power makes data-based machine learning approaches particularly efficient but also raises questions about the trustworthiness of deployed systems especially in critical applications (Wing, 2021). This important issue causes the re-examination of pure machine learning based approaches and the employment of formal knowledge-based approaches that have been used extensively in AI. Knowledge-Based approaches are often contrasting Data-Based approaches such as Neural Networks, although this distinction is actually not as sharp as past debates imply and they are both needed in order to achieve deployment of efficient AI systems (Goel, A., 2022).

Based on the above observations and the misconception that AI and Data Science are only about Machine Learning, often ignoring alternative and complementary approaches the current chapter is focused on Knowledge Based methods in order to provide to the reader an overview of this vast and fruitful area of research. Being able to deploy and combine both Machine Learning Based and Knowledge Based approaches in practice will be crucial in overcoming limitations of pure Machine Learning systems and building explainable and trustworthy systems, thus an overview of Knowledge Based methods will be useful to an AI practitioner and will help avoiding a narrow focus on a specific set of methods often ignoring useful existing methods following a different approach. The chapter contains a background section followed by presentation of various logic-based approaches in AI including classic logic, logic programming and non-monotonic logics, modal and temporal logics and the more recent Semantic Web and Answer Set Programming methods. This is followed be presenting recent work on large scale semantic reasoning which brings symbolic knowledge-based methods to the Big Data era and finally concussions and discussion about future work.

BACKGROUND

Since the emergence of Artificial Intelligence in 50s, approaches based on logic based reasoning combined with formal encoding of human knowledge have been of the forefront of artificial intelligence research, due to their similarly to the human way of thinking and their suitability for automation (Van Harmelen et al., 2008). Having lost their preeminence since the so called "AI winter" of late 80s and early 90s and

DOI: 10.4018/978-1-7998-9220-5.ch181

currently overshadowed by data intensive Machine Learning (ML) approaches, especially deep learning approaches, the Knowledge Based (KB) approaches are currently not in the focus of attention of the majority of AI community and the public in general to the same degree as in the early days of AI. On the other hand they still remain a crucial building block of AI applications and an important approach for overcoming current problems caused when deploying AI systems.

As machine learning approaches are applied in an ever-increasing number of application domains several issues are raised related to biases of Machine learning generated models, resulting from biases in training datasets, and the explainability of produced models which contradicts the requirement of accountability of deployed Artificial Intelligence Applications. Since AI is getting more important and ML is applied to critical tasks, such as medical diagnosis and self-driving cars, accountability becomes a major issue as exemplified by EU's regulations (Goodman & Flaxman, 2017) and DARPA's explainable AI initiative (Gunning & Aha, 2019).

Neural Networks in particular, although achieving human level, or higher, performance on various applications such as image recognition and automatic translation and being the leading paradigm in current AI research, suffer from their lack of explainability. Specifically the structure of Neural Networks is complex and the interpretation of internal nodes and weights of edges is typically missing making them a "black box" approach, non-compatible with accountability requirements. Deploying such non interpretable systems for a critical task contradicts with the accountability requirements typical for critical applications such as autonomous vehicles and medical diagnosis (Tjoa & Guan, 2020).

Knowledge Based approaches, whose development is based on constant involvement of domain experts, on the other hand, are based on formal encoding of human knowledge and logic rules, thus offering transparent models and leading to an explainable decision making process. In addition, recent research activity on knowledge based systems has led to novel formalisms having increased expressivity and performance. Various approaches have been developed, optimized for specific types of applications and theoretical work has led to a clear understanding to the tradeoff between expressivity and performance of employed approaches allowing of optimal decisions with respect to the selected formalism for each application type. Table 1 summarizes the main characteristics of symbolic and ML based approaches.

Large scale semantic reasoning is an active area of research, bringing knowledge based approaches to the big data era and making such approaches suitable to data intensive applications. The abovementioned advances in Knowledge Based AI offer alternative or complementary solutions to machine learning based approaches, especially deep learning, bringing with them the deep understanding which is needed for efficient and accountable deployment of Artificial Intelligence. An overview of the current landscape and the state of the art of Knowledge Based AI approaches is presented in the following, containing related work and methods.

CLASSIC LOGIC

Logic has been studied extensively since ancient times beginning with Aristotle and continuing throughout the Middle Ages. Modern Logic has been introduced by Boole and Frege and advanced rapidly in the 20th century combined with the advent of computers (Robinson, 2000). Propositional Logic used to reason about sentences and propositions is the basic widely studied logic and several approaches for reasoning have been proposed, leading to decidable (i.e., there is an effective method for determining whether an arbitrary propositional formula is logically valid) and efficient methods for automatic reasoning, especially in knowledge bases in restricted forms. In particular Satisfiability Solvers (SAT Solvers)

Table 1. Comparison of Knowledge Based and Machine Learning Based approaches

	Knowledge Based Methods	**Machine Learning Methods**
Data requirements	• Low volume of Data required. • Typically, quality of Data is not critical for performance	• High Volume of Data required • Performance Highly Dependent on Quality of Data
Hume expertise Requirements	• Hume expertise and involvement is required on all phases of the process • Performance is highly dependent on quality of human knowledge encoded in the system	• Process is automated to a large degree • Human expertise is still required in complex domains e.g. for data preprocessing and cleaning, feature selection and construction • Performance is highly dependent on human expertise in complex applications
Computational Complexity	• Depending on formalism, ranges from undecidable to linear time complexity. • Complexity is typically formally analyzed and well understood • Tradeoff between expressivity and performance, expressive formalisms typically non scalable	• Depended on algorithm and on Data characteristics • Typically, scalable (depending on the method) to large volume of Data • Difficult to analyze formal properties and convergence criteria
Explainability	• Models created are interpretable	• Typically, non-interpretable models are created • Interpretability can be achieved on simple domains and for specific algorithms (e.g. decision trees, linear regression • Important methods (SVM, Neural Networks) don't produce interpretable models
Applications	• Suitable for high level applications involving symbolic data (e.g. medical, legal) and for qualitative reasoning	• Suitable for applications involving large volume of quantitative data (e.g. image and speech recognition)

are widely used for reasoning over propositional formulars. First Order Logic offers greater expressivity in comparison with propositional logic by means of quantifiers (existential and universal) predicates and variables and it can be used to represent not only facts and propositions but also classes of objects, their properties and relations, functions and information about specific individuals. Also reasoning over First Order Logic is semi decidable since there are methods such as natural deduction and tableaux that correctly identify all the valid first-order logic statement that belong to a First Order theory, but they may not terminate when presented with certain statements not belonging to the theory.

An advantage of First Order Logic is that efficient algorithms for specific knowledge bases (consisting of definite and Horn clauses) such as forward chaining and backward chaining exist. Horn clauses (i.e. disjunctive formulas with at most on positive literal) can encode rules of form "if conditions are true then implication is true" which are typically used for representing human reasoning, thus they are a very important category of formulas, used extensively in practice. Definite clauses i.e., formulas with exactly one positive literal is a more restrictive form also very important in practice, especially in logic programming. Conditions of the rules also called bodies of rules and the result of applying the rule when conditions are met is also called head of a rule. Notice that Horn formulas allow for expressing restrictions (i.e., rules with empty head) which is not the case for definite clauses.

In addition to the above the resolution method (Robinson, 1965) is an efficient, and suitable for automation, general purpose algorithm for decidability of First Order Logic Formulas. Based on efficient reasoning methods First Order Logic theorem provers have been introduced and used extensively since the early steps of Artificial Intelligence and related work was initially the focus for AI related research effort. The result of this effort is the availability of a large collection of benchmark datasets and reasoning tools (Sutcliffe, 2017).

EXTENSIONS TO LOGIC AND LOGIC PROGRAMMING

Classic Logic although offering an efficient method for symbolic reasoning, doesn't support directly representation and reasoning of uncertainty which is the focus of probabilities and related formalisms such as Bayes Networks and specialized logics such as fuzzy logics that form an independent and vast area of research (Li et al., 2012). Another issue identified during the early research on logics is the mismatch between databases which adopt the closed world assumption (i.e., if a fact in not proven true then it is false) and open world assumption adopted by First Order Logic (if a fact is not proven to be either true or false then it's truth value is unknown). The closed world assumption is suitable for commonsense reasoning in settings that we don't want to explicitly assert facts that do not hold. For example, when checking departures at an airport it is assumed that available flights are only those presented on the departure board. Another example is a customer database where it is assumed that all customers are included and persons that are not included are not customers, without having to explicitly assert that fact. Although the closed world assumption can be represented using First Order Logic axioms for a specific domain, alternative approaches adopting directly in their semantics the Closed World Assumption (and often the Unique Name assumption i.e., that two objects with distinct names are distinct unless explicitly asserted that they are equal) have been introduced leading to the emergence of logic programming.

Prolog developed in the 70s is a programming language adopting a form of the Closed World Assumption and representing logic programs in the form of Horn clauses, i.e. implications (Colmerauer & Roussel, 1996). Efficient backward chaining reasoning (i.e., given the statement to prove, the reasoning implementation detects rules having this statement as a conclusion and checks if preconditions for the rule hold, if not it tries to prove iteratively these preconditions) was the basis of Prolog inference mechanism combined with several heuristics. This reasoning mechanism is actually a variant of the resolution method called SLD resolution. Although reasoning is typically efficient and Prolog is a Turing complete language (i.e., can compute every function on natural numbers that a Turing machine can compute) Prolog programs aren't guaranteed to terminate, actually even a terminating program can become non terminating by changing the order of rules in the program.

The rationale behind adoption of backward chaining in Prolog was to focus the search for a solution by deriving facts relevant to the fact to prove and thus speed up the reasoning process, especially in question answering tasks. Based on Prolog the logic programming paradigm became the main symbolic reasoning mechanism adopted in practice. Datalog, being a less expressive variant of Prolog (having similar syntax but without functions and with syntactic restrictions) has been developed in order to achieve large scale deductive reasoning in Databases (Maier et al., 2018). Such advances both in Logic programming, and deductive databases in particular, adopting forward chaining reasoning (which triggers rules when their preconditions are met, then adding implications to the known facts and repeating until no rule can be triggered), which is more suitable for updating databases, led to the development of expert systems that are still an important category of AI systems applied in numerous application areas (Liebowitz, 2019).

NON-MONOTONIC LOGICS

An important problem that AI practitioners faced when working on logic based approaches was the non-monotonicity problem (i.e. new facts contradicting with existing inferences and causing removal of already inferred facts). Soon research over non-monotonic logics led to the development and formal specification or related logics such as Default Logic, Auto- epistemic Logic, Circumscription, Argumentation, and Defeasible Rules, offering direct support over defeasible rules (Antoniou & Williams, 1997). Using the above mentioned logics users can express facts that hold by default (e.g., birds typically fly so if a knowledge base contains information about a bird it can be inferred that it flies), but when specific information is asserted that contradicts the default information (e.g., a bird belongs to a species that doesn't fly such as penguins) then the default inferences must be retracted. This is achieved for example in the case of defeasible reasoning (Maher et al., 2001) using facts as in classic logic and different types of rules. Specifically defeasible reasoning supports three types of rules namely strict rules that are similar as rules in classic logic (i.e., inferences cannot be retracted), defeasible rules that their conclusions can be defeated by contrary evidence and defeaters that are rules that are used only to prevent some conclusions from other rules rather than draw conclusions. Finally a superiority relation between conflicting rules can be defined.

Notice that logic programming approaches such as Prolog can also express such cases indirectly by proper use of negation as failure, which is combined with the closed world assumption adopted in Prolog. When using negation as failure a precondition of a rule can be in the form "not A" meaning that the condition holds when A is not proven to be true (which is different than proven to be not true as in strong negation of classic logic), so if new information is asserted proving that A is true then the precondition no longer holds true and corresponding inferred facts by the rule must be retracted. Using logic programming and negation as failure, exceptions to rules and priority of conflicting rules can be defined as in the case of the British Nationality Act represented using a logic program (Sergot et al., 1986). Typical applications include the medical and legal domain where rules leading to contradicting results often exist and a priority between them in case of contradiction must be expressed (Batsakis et al., 2018).

SEMANTIC WEB

The advent of Web in 90s brought in the spotlight another direction of research, the Semantic Web, in order to deal with large scale interconnected data. According to the Semantic Web vision as expressed by Tim Berners Lee, information of the Web should be semantically annotated so as to allow for automated reasoning and thus execution of various tasks by intelligent agents instead of end users (Berners-Lee et al., 2001). Semantic Web is based in the Description Logics (although compatibility of standards with other formalisms such as conceptual graph exists) which are typically, with proper selection of allowed constructs, a decidable subset of first order logic as illustrated in Figure 1 (Baader et al., 2003).

Extensive research identifying the trade of between expressivity and efficiency led to the adoption by W3C of the OWL language standard based on decidable and expressive description logics (Hitzler et al., 2009). OWL complements RDF for representing data in the form of subject-predicate-object triples, typically using XML syntax, RDFS for definition of simple data schemas and taxonomies and SPARQL query language forming the set of Semantic Web standards (Antoniou et al., 2012). The current version of OWL is OWL 2, offering rich expressivity for complex concepts definitions and the characteristics of their properties while retaining decidability, while OWL profiles such as OWL ER, OWL QL and OWL RL offer optimized performance by restricting allowable constructs. Semantic Web standards and recommendations also include the SWRL rule language and SHACL for data validation against a set of conditions (See Figure 2). The emergence of the Semantic Web and development of related tools for representing, editing, querying and reasoning over ontologies and knowledge bases, tools such as the Protégé ontology editor (Musen, 2015), led to wide scale practical applications to a level not seen before for Knowledge Based AI.

Figure 1. Relation between Logic Based Formalisms

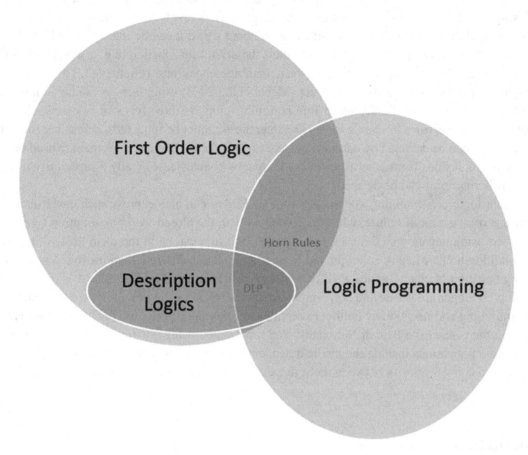

Figure 2. Semantic Web technologies and standards

Querying: SPARQL	Ontologies: OWL	Rules: SWRL	Validation: SHACL
	Taxonomies: RDFS		
Data: RDF			
Syntax: XML			

Notice that application on the Web scale led to a different approach for the Semantic Web than logic programming. The openness and diversity of the Web linking different sources of information on grand scale led to the adoption of the Open World Assumption, while Unique Name Assumption is not adopted, thus semantics of OWL are close to these of First Order Logics, actually in terms of expressivity OWL is a proper subset of first order logic, and not those of Logic Programming Paradigms (see Figure 1). Nevertheless, the subset of Horn formulas of Logic Programming is also a subset of First Order Logic and a restricted form of Horn Formulas called Description Logic Programs (DLP) can be also expressed using Description Logics, thus represented using Semantic Web standards. Today a large part of Web information, forming the linked Open Data cloud (McCrae et al., 2019) is represented using Semantic

Web standards, while Semantic interoperability and representation of complex domains with formal conceptualizations called ontologies such as the medical domain also led to the widespread use of Semantic Web standards. The medical domain in particular, where complex definitions and automated reasoning is important for assisting decision making process, has greatly benefited from Semantic Web technologies as illustrated by the development of a large number of medical ontologies (Ivanović & Budimac, 2014). Furthermore in recent years information represented in the form of Knowledge Graphs has widespread use in the industry offering increased expressivity and reasoning capabilities, beyond those of traditional database systems (Hogan et al., 2021).

MODAL AND TEMPORAL LOGICS

Research on Knowledge Based Artificial Intelligence is also active towards other directions related to representing beliefs, obligations and dynamic information evolving in time. Extending classical Logics to represent beliefs and knowledge led to the development of Modal Logics that include operators for necessity and possibility (Goldblatt, 2003) and the closely related Deontic Logics (representing modalities such as obligation, prohibition and allowance). Deontic logic is particularly suitable for normative and legal reasoning, an application area in which it has been extensively applied (Navarro & Rodríguez, 2014). Another related area is that of Temporal Logics, with theoretical properties closely related to these of modal logics and direct support of expressions such as "eventually", "always in the future/past" (Demri et al., 2016). Many temporal logics have been proposed including LTL, CTL and CTL* and their classification is depended on whether they are point or interval based, representing linear or branching time and the allowable constructs and combinations of temporal expressions in each language.

Temporal Logics have been adopted widely in applications such as system modeling and verification in the software and hardware industry using techniques known as model checking (Clarke et al., 2018) for formally verifying the properties of complex systems. In various application domains logic based approaches are used when quantitative (i.e. numeric) information is missing and facts are expressed using qualitative expressions (such as "before" for temporal information and "borders with" for spatial information). Qualitative temporal and spatial reasoning and qualitative physics are applications for such approaches (Ligozat, 2013), while planning is also a domain where symbolic approaches are widely used (Kress-Gazit et al., 2009). In addition, qualitative spatiotemporal formalisms (Cohn & Renz, 2008) can be combined with other knowledge based formalisms such a Description logics leading to more expressive formalisms such as Temporal Description Logics (Lutz et al., 2008).

ANSWER SET PROGRAMMING

While application of knowledge based approaches to the Web led to the development of the Semantic Web and the need for specialized modal and temporal operators led to theoretical and practical advances in modal and temporal logics, important new theoretical and practical contributions appear in the area of logic programming. Specifically, an important recent development in the area logic programming in general, also related with Datalog and Prolog in particular (although in fact covering many areas of logic programming) is Answer Set Programming (ASP). Having similar rationale as Datalog but with support for additional constructs (such as disjunction on rule heads) related research led in late 90s to the Answer Set Programming paradigm (Lifschitz, 2019). Adding disjunction on rule heads allows for expressing non determinism and choices using Answer Set Programming, which was not typically the case with traditional logic programming. In addition, ASP programs are guaranteed to terminate which is not the case of Prolog.

Based on the stable model semantics of Prolog for negation as failure and extending them in presence of rules having disjunctive heads Answer Set Programming has clearly defined semantics that specify the so-called answer sets which are sets of solutions that satisfy the set of rules contained in an ASP program. ASP systems typically consist of an "instantiator" or "grounder" that replaces variables with all corresponding constants and then the grounded (i.e., propositional) form of the ASP program is the input of the ASP solver. Since the input to the solver is in propositional form, SAT solvers are used extensively in ASP solvers. The solver in turn consists of two subsystems the ground reasoner that generates possible answer sets and the model checker that filters out answer sets not compatible with constrains expressed using the rules of the ASP program. The resulting sets are the final output of the ASP system. Recent additions to ASP systems include aggregates (e.g., summation, min, max) and optimization statements that in addition to generating answer sets also rank these sets according to optimization criteria. Being suitable for representing and solving hard problems such as NP problems, because of the increased expressivity offered and combined with solid theoretical foundations and the availability of stable implementations and tools Answer Set Programming is the typical choice for solving hard problems including problems with non-monotonic information (Gebser et al., 2018), thus complementing approaches based on classic logic (such as the Semantic Web). Related application domains of ASP include planning, business intelligence and medical reasoning among others (Leone & Ricca, 2015).

LARGE SCALE SEMANTIC REASONING

The availability of large amounts of Data is a crucial factor for the success of data driven artificial intelligence in recent years but also poses new challenges to all AI approaches both data driven and knowledge based, thus the large scale of data calls for efficient big data implementations of symbolic AI approaches too. Besides theoretical properties and expressivity, performance and scalability are major areas of knowledge based AI research and optimized implementations are of crucial importance for their adoption in practice. SAT solvers in particular being the core part of many reasoning systems is an active area of research related to performance optimization (Nawaz et al., 2019).

In addition to optimizations of reasoning engines large scale reasoning has been achieved by combining symbolic reasoning with big data frameworks such as the Map-Reduce paradigm bringing symbolic reasoning to the big data era. This is necessary in order to deal with the large volume of data available on the Web. The main approach is to efficiently split data and or rules and apply reasoning in a distributed way. Following this distributed processing approach, efficient parallel reasoning implementations have been deployed for formalisms such as RDF, RDFS, fragments of OWL having desirable computational properties such as the OWL RL profile but also for more complex formalisms such as defeasible rules, being able to deal with billions of triples in the case of the simpler formalisms (Antoniou et al., 2018). Being a generic method for dealing with big data, parallelization has been recently applied in more specialized formalisms such as qualitative spatiotemporal reasoning (Mantle et al., 2019).

Besides using parallelization for large scale semantic reasoning, the availability of big data and advances in machine learning can improve the process of generating symbolic representations and rules as the output of a machine learning process over raw data. This approach, called Inductive Logic Programming, has demonstrated the advantages of combining data driven and knowledge based approaches but also the limitations of data driven approaches for generating symbolic representations were human expertise still plays a major role (Cropper et al., 2020). Similarly, data driven approaches have been applied in conjunction with Semantic Web technologies (Martinez-Rodriguez et al., 2020).

FUTURE RESEARCH DIRECTIONS

Using knowledge based methods also leads to AI systems that are interpretable and their functionality can be understood by human users, typically in hybrid settings were machine learning is used for extracting low level features (such as object recognition from images) and then symbolic approaches combining human expertise are applied for high level reasoning and decision making. This combination brings together learning capabilities of data driven approaches and understanding capabilities of knowledge based approaches which are needed for efficient deployment of AI in critical applications. Another direction of research is towards integrating knowledge and machine learning approaches, for example neural networks and logic rules (Towell & Shavlik, 1994). Finally, knowledge based systems can be used for ensuring trustworthiness and security of AI systems by analyzing their formal properties in the way model checking techniques are used for software and hardware verification (Wing, 2021).

CONCLUSION

Knowledge based AI has been a mature technology offering solutions to a wide range of problems where representation of data is inherently symbolic, thus making quantitative techniques non applicable. Table 2 summarizes main symbolic formalisms in terms of their expressivity and complexity.

Table 2. Overview of Main Symbolic Formalisms

Formalism	Expressivity	Complexity
Propositional Logic	Sentences	Decidable, exponential in worst case, linear to specific subsets (e.g. Horn clauses)
First Order Logic	Objects, Relations, Categories, Quantifiers	Semi-decidable linear to specific subsets (e.g. Horn clauses)
Logic Programming-Prolog	Horn Clauses, Turing Complete	Depending on order of rules a program may not terminate, typically efficient in practice.
Non-Monotonic Logics	Extends classic logic with ability to express non monotonic information (i.e. new facts make previous inferences invalid)	Most expressive non-monotonic Logics are not decidable but formalisms with efficient reasoning systems exist, e.g. the propositional Defeasible Logic has linear time complexity
Modal Logics	Expressiveness depending the logic: necessity, possibility, belief and knowledge	Main Modal logics are decidable
Temporal Logics	Expressing temporal statements such as aways or possible in the future	Typically decidable, specific logics have very efficient reasoning mechanisms in practice
Semantic Web/ OWL	Subset of First Order Logic	Decidable, tractable subsets of OWL have been defined
Answer Set Programming	Horn clauses extended with support of disjunctive rules	Decidable

Interpretability and explainability are major requirements of current AI systems because of legal and ethical reasons, gradually bringing back knowledge based approaches, that are the topic of the this chapter, to the forefront of AI research and practice. In particular, in case of critical domains such as medical and legal applications were accountability is a major requirement, knowledge based systems are very important and the availability and extended range of knowledge based formalisms and tools covering diverse needs regarding expressiveness and efficiency make such approaches of paramount importance in practice.

REFERENCES

Antoniou, G., Batsakis, S., Mutharaju, R., Pan, J. Z., Qi, G., Tachmazidis, I., Urbani, J., & Zhou, Z. (2018). A survey of large-scale reasoning on the web of data. *The Knowledge Engineering Review, 33*, 33. doi:10.1017/S0269888918000255

Antoniou, G., Groth, P., Van Harmelen, F., & Hoekstra, R. (2012). *A Semantic Web Primer*. MIT Press.

Antoniou, G., & Williams, M. A. (1997). *Nonmonotonic reasoning*. MIT Press. doi:10.7551/mitpress/5040.001.0001

Baader, F., Calvanese, D., McGuinness, D., Patel-Schneider, P., & Nardi, D. (Eds.). (2003). *The description logic handbook: Theory, implementation and applications*. Cambridge University Press.

Batsakis, S., Baryannis, G., Governatori, G., Tachmazidis, I., & Antoniou, G. (2018). Legal Representation and Reasoning in Practice: A Critical Comparison. JURIX, 31(4).

Berners-Lee, T., Hendler, J., & Lassila, O. (2001). The semantic web. *Scientific American, 284*(5), 34–43. doi:10.1038cientificamerican0501-34 PMID:11681174

Clarke, E. M. Jr, Grumberg, O., Kroening, D., Peled, D., & Veith, H. (2018). *Model checking*. MIT Press.

Cohn, A. G., & Renz, J. (2008). Qualitative spatial representation and reasoning. *Foundations of Artificial Intelligence, 3*(3), 551–596. doi:10.1016/S1574-6526(07)03013-1

Colmerauer, A., & Roussel, P. (1996). The birth of Prolog. In History of programming languages-II (pp. 331-367). doi:10.1145/234286.1057820

Cropper, A., Dumančić, S., & Muggleton, S. H. (2020). *Turning 30: New ideas in inductive logic programming*. doi:10.24963/ijcai.2020/673

Demri, S., Goranko, V., & Lange, M. (2016). *Temporal logics in computer science: Finite-state systems (58)*. Cambridge University Press. doi:10.1017/CBO9781139236119

Gebser, M., Leone, N., Maratea, M., Perri, S., Ricca, F., & Schaub, T. (2018). Evaluation Techniques and Systems for Answer Set Programming: A Survey. IJCAI, (18), 5450-5456. doi:10.24963/ijcai.2018/769

Goel, A. (2022). Looking back, looking ahead: Symbolic versus connectionist AI. *AI Magazine, 42*(4), 83–85. doi:10.1609/aimag.v42i4.15111

Goldblatt, R. (2003). Mathematical modal logic: A view of its evolution. *Journal of Applied Logic, 1*(5-6), 309–392. doi:10.1016/S1570-8683(03)00008-9

Goodman, B., & Flaxman, S. (2017). European Union regulations on algorithmic decision-making and a "right to explanation". *AI Magazine, 38*(3), 50–57. doi:10.1609/aimag.v38i3.2741

Gunning, D., & Aha, D. (2019). DARPA's explainable artificial intelligence (XAI) program. *AI Magazine, 40*(2), 44–58. doi:10.1609/aimag.v40i2.2850

Hitzler, P., Krötzsch, M., Parsia, B., Patel-Schneider, P. F., & Rudolph, S. (2009). OWL 2 web ontology language primer. *W3C Recommendation, 27*(1), 123.

Hogan, A., Blomqvist, E., Cochez, M., d'Amato, C., Melo, G. D., Gutierrez, C., Kirrane, S., Gayo, J. E., Navigli, R., Neumaier, S., Ngomo, A. C., Polleres, A., Rashid, S. M., Rula, A., & Zimmermann, A. (2021). Knowledge graphs. *ACM Computing Surveys, 54*(4), 1–37. doi:10.1145/3447772

Ivanović, M., & Budimac, Z. (2014). An overview of ontologies and data resources in medical domains. *Expert Systems with Applications, 41*(11), 5158–5166. doi:10.1016/j.eswa.2014.02.045

Kress-Gazit, H., Fainekos, G. E., & Pappas, G. J. (2009). Temporal-logic-based reactive mission and motion planning. *IEEE Transactions on Robotics, 25*(6), 1370–1381. doi:10.1109/TRO.2009.2030225

Leone, N., & Ricca, F. (2015). Answer set programming: A tour from the basics to advanced development tools and industrial applications. In *Reasoning web international summer school* (pp. 308–326). Springer. doi:10.1007/978-3-319-21768-0_10

Li, Y., Chen, J., & Feng, L. (2012). Dealing with uncertainty: A survey of theories and practices. *IEEE Transactions on Knowledge and Data Engineering, 25*(11), 2463–2482. doi:10.1109/TKDE.2012.179

Liebowitz, J. (Ed.). (2019). The handbook of applied expert systems. CRC Press.

Lifschitz, V. (2019). *Answer set programming.* Springer. doi:10.1007/978-3-030-24658-7

Ligozat, G. (2013). *Qualitative spatial and temporal reasoning.* John Wiley & Sons. doi:10.1002/9781118601457

Lutz, C., Wolter, F., & Zakharyaschev, M. (2008). Temporal description logics: A survey. In *2008 15th International Symposium on Temporal Representation and Reasoning* (pp. 3-14). IEEE. 10.1109/TIME.2008.14

Maher, M. J., Rock, A., Antoniou, G., Billington, D., & Miller, T. (2001). Efficient defeasible reasoning systems. *International Journal of Artificial Intelligence Tools, 10*(04), 483–501. doi:10.1142/S0218213001000623

Maier, D., Tekle, K. T., Kifer, M., & Warren, D. S. (2018). Datalog: concepts, history, and outlook. In Declarative Logic Programming: Theory, Systems, and Applications (pp. 3-100). doi:10.1145/3191315.3191317

Mantle, M., Batsakis, S., & Antoniou, G. (2019). Large scale distributed spatio-temporal reasoning using real-world knowledge graphs. *Knowledge-Based Systems, 163*, 214–226. doi:10.1016/j.knosys.2018.08.035

Martinez-Rodriguez, J. L., Hogan, A., & Lopez-Arevalo, I. (2020). Information extraction meets the semantic web: A survey. *Semantic Web, 11*(2), 255–335. doi:10.3233/SW-180333

McCrae, J. P., Abele, A., Buitelaar, P., Cyganiak, R., Jentzsch, A., Andryushechkin, V., & Debattista, J. (2019). *The linked open data cloud.* Lod-cloud.net.

Musen, M. A. (2015). The protégé project: A look back and a look forward. *AI Matters, 1*(4), 4–12. doi:10.1145/2757001.2757003 PMID:27239556

Navarro, P. E., & Rodríguez, J. L. (2014). *Deontic logic and legal systems.* Cambridge University Press. doi:10.1017/CBO9781139032711

Nawaz, M. S., Malik, M., Li, Y., Sun, M., & Lali, M. (2019). *A survey on theorem provers in formal methods.* arXiv preprint arXiv:1912.03028.

Robinson, J. A. (1965). A machine-oriented logic based on the resolution principle. *Journal of the Association for Computing Machinery, 12*(1), 23–41. doi:10.1145/321250.321253

Robinson, J. A. (2000). Computational logic: Memories of the past and challenges for the future. In *International Conference on Computational Logic* (pp. 1-24). Springer. 10.1007/3-540-44957-4_1

Sergot, M. J., Sadri, F., Kowalski, R. A., Kriwaczek, F., Hammond, P., & Cory, H. T. (1986). The British Nationality Act as a logic program. *Communications of the ACM, 29*(5), 370–386. doi:10.1145/5689.5920

Sutcliffe, G. (2017). The TPTP problem library and associated infrastructure. *Journal of Automated Reasoning, 59*(4), 483–502. doi:10.100710817-017-9407-7

Tjoa, E., & Guan, C. (2020). A survey on explainable artificial intelligence (xai): Toward medical xai. *IEEE Transactions on Neural Networks and Learning Systems.* PMID:33079674

Towell, G. G., & Shavlik, J. W. (1994). Knowledge-based artificial neural networks. *Artificial Intelligence, 70*(1-2), 119–165. doi:10.1016/0004-3702(94)90105-8

Van Harmelen, F., Lifschitz, V., & Porter, B. (Eds.). (2008). *Handbook of knowledge representation.* Elsevier.

Wing, J. M. (2021). Trustworthy AI. *Communications of the ACM, 64*(10), 64–71. doi:10.1145/3448248

ADDITIONAL READING

Akerkar, R., & Sajja, P. (2009). *Knowledge-based systems.* Jones & Bartlett Publishers.

Baader, F., Calvanese, D., McGuinness, D., Patel-Schneider, P., & Nardi, D. (Eds.). (2003). *The description logic handbook: Theory, implementation and applications.* Cambridge University Press.

Genesereth, M. R., & Nilsson, N. J. (2012). *Logical foundations of artificial intelligence.* Morgan Kaufmann.

Hagras, H. (2018). Toward human-understandable, explainable AI. *Computer, 51*(9), 28–36. doi:10.1109/MC.2018.3620965

Minker, J. (Ed.). (2012). *Logic-based artificial intelligence.* Springer Science & Business Media.

Norvig, S., & Russel, P. (2016). *Artificial Intelligence: A modern approach* (3rd ed.). Pearson Education.

Poole, D. L., & Mackworth, A. K. (2010). *Artificial Intelligence: foundations of computational agents.* Cambridge University Press. doi:10.1017/CBO9780511794797

Siau, K., & Wang, W. (2020). Artificial intelligence (AI) ethics: Ethics of AI and ethical AI. *Journal of Database Management*, *31*(2), 74–87. doi:10.4018/JDM.2020040105

KEY TERMS AND DEFINITIONS

Artificial Intelligence: A branch of computer science focusing on building systems that perform tasks that are typically performed by humans.

Knowledge Representation: A field of Artificial Intelligence focusing on representing knowledge in such a way that a software system can use directly for completing tasks and solving problems.

Logic Programming: A programming paradigm based on formal logic where a program consists of a set of logic rules and facts about an application domain.

Logic Reasoner: A software system that infers logical consequences from a set of asserted facts and axioms.

Machine Learning: Branch of Artificial Intelligence based on building models by learning directly from data while minimizing human effort.

Modal Logics: Logics that formally represent the notions of necessity and possibility.

Non-Monotonic Logics: Logics that allow of making previous axioms invalid and retracting some inferred facts in addition to adding new inferences.

Ontology: A formal conceptualization of a domain.

Semantic Web: A set of standards and tools for making Web information machine readable.

Section 53

Time Series Analysis

Statistical Model Selection for Seasonal Big Time Series Data

S

Brian Guangshi Wu
Southwestern University, USA

Dorin Drignei
Oakland University, USA

INTRODUCTION

Seasonal time series abound in areas such as environmental sciences and economics. For example, seasonal temperatures (e.g., Chen et al., 2016; Murthy & Kumar, 2021), seasonal precipitation (e.g., Sayemuzzaman & Jha, 2014; Martin et al., 2020) or seasonal wind speed (e.g., Shih, 2021) are common in environmental sciences, while seasonal business cycles (e.g., Gregory & Smith, 1996) or seasonal labor data (e.g. Liebensteiner, 2014) can be found in economics. Analyzing such data sets provides useful insight into seasonal patterns that have an impact on human activities and economic development. Due to recent capabilities to collect large amounts of data, however, classical statistical analysis methods have limitations, the big time series data sets posing new computational and modeling challenges.

In time series analysis, order identification refers to the selection of a time series model characterized by non-negative integer orders, which is followed by parameter estimation, diagnostic checking and forecasting. Despite being a critically important early step in time series analysis, order identification is perhaps the least developed among these steps. In autoregressive $AR(p)$ processes the partial autocorrelation function is zero after lag p, thus identifying the AR order p. The autocorrelation function of moving average $MA(q)$ processes is zero after lag q, providing a convenient method to identify the MA order q. The least-squares type method ESACF using the extended sample autocorrelation function has been proposed in Tsay and Tiao (1984) for the order identification of mixed autoregressive moving average $ARMA(p,q)$ models. This method uses a sequence of linear regression models to identify the orders (p,q). A related method called SCAN has been proposed by the same authors in Tsay and Tiao (1985), using a canonical correlation approach. The applicability of these methods is facilitated by tables from which the orders p, q are identified. These methods can also be used for integrated ARMA (i.e. ARIMA) models. However, these methods are not directly applicable to other time series models, such as seasonal autoregressive integrated moving average (SARIMA) models, or certain types of nonlinear models. Cross-validation for time series model selection is a potential alternative, but it may be nontrivial to apply due to the inherent serial correlation (Bergmeir et al., 2018).

The most commonly used method for time series model selection is based on evaluating an information criterion for a few plausible time series models and choosing the model that minimizes such a criterion (e.g. Brockwell & Davis, 2016; Shumway & Stoffer, 2017). When a small set of plausible models is not available, one performs an exhaustive computation and minimization of the information criterion over a large enough grid of orders (Brockwell & Davis, 2016). However, choosing the best model using this exhaustive method is computationally challenging for big time series data, which could be a univariate large-sample time series (e.g. appliances energy consumption time series of length 19,735 in Candanedo

DOI: 10.4018/978-1-7998-9220-5.ch182

et al., 2017), a collection of large-sample time series (e.g. 438 stocks over 1,495 days in Lunde et al., 2016), or it can occur in a less common format (e.g. a temporal sequence of 606 facial expressions in Xu et al., 2020; Wang et al., 2020).

A method for the order identification of big time series data was developed in Wu and Drignei (2021), which was applied to ARMA models and ARMA-GARCH models, where the latter part stands for generalized autoregressive conditionally heteroscedastic. The goal of the current paper is to help time series practitioners better understand how to apply the method outlined in Wu and Drignei (2021) to SARIMA models of seasonal big time series. Here we focus on univariate large-sample seasonal time series, and the method can be summarized as follows. We compute the information criterion for a random sample of orders for the SARIMA model and use kriging-based methods to emulate (i.e. approximate) the information criterion for any new SARIMA orders. Then we use an efficient global optimization (EGO) algorithm to minimize the emulated information criterion, thus identifying efficiently the orders of SARIMA models for seasonal big time series. Both simulations and real temperature time series will be used to illustrate the method.

BACKGROUND

This paper focuses mainly on the challenges of statistical model selection for seasonal big time series, and potential solutions to address such challenges. However, such data sets have also generated much interest recently in other areas, such as machine learning. It is useful to review some recent works in such areas, while acknowledging that they discuss aspects of seasonal big time series data other than statistical model selection. Bachechi et al. (2022) incorporated information visualization methods into a system that can detect trends, seasonality, or anomalies in traffic flow over space and time. Castan-Lascorz et al. (2022) proposed a new prediction algorithm for time series, both univariate and multivariate, that uses clustering, classification and forecasting techniques. First, windows of time series values with similar patterns are grouped using clustering. Subsequently, for each pattern a prediction model is constructed only from the time windows associated with the pattern. The method can handle a large variety of time series behaviors, including seasonality. Guo et al. (2021) developed a hybrid model that combines the traditional time series model with an artificial neural network to predict the monthly mean atmospheric temperature profile. Carlini et al. (2021) proposed a method using graphs over time to study seasonal and trending patterns in world-wide maritime applications. Yi et al. (2021) used a penalized regression with inferred seasonality module (PRISM) and online internet search data to forecast unemployment initial claims. Poussin et al. (2021) used satellite-derived annual and seasonal time series of normalized difference water index to study implications of changing climatic conditions. Kumari and Toshniwal (2021) investigated a new hybrid deep learning model for global horizontal irradiance forecasting, which takes into account the spatio-temporal features of the data set. Wang et al. (2021) used a classification model that integrates the terrain, time series characteristics, priority, and seasonality with satellite images. Hewamalage et al. (2021) performed an empirical study to investigate the seasonal forecasting properties of recurrent neural networks. Da Silva et al. (2020) developed time series classification methods to monitor an agricultural area, based on active learning (AL) that selects limited seasonal time series information to generate the training set. Chen et al. (2019) proposed a Periodicity-based Parallel Time Series Prediction (PPTSP) algorithm for large-scale time series data showing periodicity characteristics. Jurman (2019) used a database including a large number of seasonal time series to predict the results of sport matches and competitions. Yeh and Yeh (2019) used queries on mortality related terms from Google

Trends, along with time series and wavelet scalogram of search terms, to classify the patterns of search queries into various levels of periodicity. Such studies are valuable in developing early surveillance tools for causes of death and can help with prevention against diseases. Kim et al. (2018) used cyclostationary empirical orthogonal function analysis for big space-time data exhibiting temporal periodicity to determine important modes of variability. The method was applied to hourly passenger subway traffic data. Saez et al. (2018) proposed to use functional data analysis techniques to characterize temporal variability in data recorded over long periods of time. They illustrated the proposed method with a data set including a large number of hospital discharges over a decade and were able to detect seasonal patterns in the estimated data trajectories. Giordano et al. (2017) proposed a clustering technique for large time-dependent databases characterized by strong seasonality components. The method is presented in the frequency domain and involves an efficient algorithm that needs less computational and memory resources. Both simulations and an electricity big time series database were used to illustrate the method. Chou et al. (2016) proposed a method that combines seasonal time series models with metaheuristic firefly algorithm-based least squares support vector regression to predict building energy consumption data collected by a smart grid.

FOCUS OF THE ARTICLE

Differencing at lag s a seasonal time series $\{X_t\}$ with period s is a common approach to eliminating seasonality. More generally (e.g. Brockwell & Davis, 2016; Shumway & Stoffer, 2017), if f and F are nonnegative integers, then $\{X_t\}$ is a multiplicative *SARIMA* $(p, f, q) \times (P, F, Q)_s$ process if the differenced

series $Y_t = (1 - B)^f (1 - B^s)^F X_t$

satisfies

$$\varphi(B)\Phi(B^s)Y_t = \theta(B)\Theta(B^s)Z_t, \tag{1}$$

where $\{Z_t\} \sim WN(0, \sigma^2)$ and

$$\varphi(z) = 1-\varphi_1 z - \cdots -\varphi_p z^p,$$

$$\Phi(z) = 1-\Phi_1 z - \cdots -\Phi_P z^P,$$

$$\theta(z) = 1 + \theta_1 z + \cdots + \theta_q z^q,$$

$$\Theta(z) = 1 + \Theta_1 z + \cdots + \Theta_Q z^Q$$

are polynomials having roots outside the unit circle. Note that both f and F can be set to zero without losing generality because one can perform f successive differencing at lag 1 and F successive differencing at lag s on the original series. The resulting differenced series will have $f = 0$ and $F = 0$.

For the SARIMA$(p, 0, q) \times (P, 0, Q)_s$ seasonal model with period s defined in (1) we consider an information criterion $S(p, q, P, Q)$, such as the Bayesian information criterion (BIC)

$$S(p, q, P, Q) = -2 \log L + (p + q + P + Q) \log T,$$

where L is the time series likelihood function computed at the maximum likelihood estimates of model parameters and T is the time series length (e.g. Psaradakis et al., 2009; Pena et al., 2001). Here we assume that $S = S(p, q, P, Q)$ is conditioned on the observed time series. While in this paper we work with BIC due to its consistency property (e.g. Brockwell & Davis, 2016), other information criteria can be used, such as the Akaike's information criterion (AIC).

The definition of the multiplicative SARIMA model requires considering all four orders (p, q, P, Q) simultaneously; it is not possible to analyze the (p, q) part separately from the (P, Q) part of the model. Therefore, we consider that the orders (p, q, P, Q) belong to

$$\{0, \ldots, M_a\} \times \{0, \ldots, M_a\} \times \{0, \ldots, M_s\} \times \{0, \ldots, M_s\},$$

a practically large-enough four-dimensional grid input space. Computing the S values for a SARIMA$(p, 0, q) \times (P, 0, Q)_s$ model is computationally intensive for big time series because the model fitting relies on the repeated computation of the likelihood function to estimate the parameters. Therefore, computing all $(M_a + 1)^2 (M_s + 1)^2$ information criterion values S on the grid becomes computationally challenging for big time series data.

SOLUTIONS AND RECOMMENDATIONS

We propose to compute S for a subset of (p, q, P, Q) orders, sampled according to a space filling design in the input space. We then use kriging-type methods to emulate S in the entire input space and identify the orders (p, q, P, Q) that minimize the criterion S using the efficient global optimization (EGO) method.

Kriging Emulator of the Information Criterion

Using terminology from the general area of computer experiments (e.g. Sacks et al., 1989), let (p, q, P, Q) be the input in the computer model $S(p, q, P, Q)$. A sample of D inputs

$$\{(p_1, q_1, P_1, Q_1), \ldots, (p_D, q_D, P_D, Q_D)\}$$

is chosen in $[0, 1]^4$ using a maximin Latin hypercube design, multiplying the first two components by M_a, the last two components by M_s, and then rounding them to the nearest non-negative integer. We retain a sample that includes only distinct inputs. As a rule of thumb in the design and analysis of computer experiments, at least 10 sampled inputs per input dimension are needed to construct an accurate kriging emulator, thus D should be at least 40. The corresponding outputs are

$$\mathbf{S} = [S(p_1, q_1, P_1, Q_1), \ldots, S(p_D, q_D, P_D, Q_D)]',$$

and we assume that they follow a multivariate normal distribution of constant mean vector $\gamma \mathbf{1}_D$ and covariance matrix $\tau^2 \mathbf{R}_D$ of dimension D. Examples of correlations $\mathbf{R}_D$ often used in the analysis of computer experiments are the power exponential and Matern (e.g. Sacks et al., 1989; Roustant et al., 2012). The parameters of $\mathbf{R}_D$, as well as τ^2, γ are estimated by maximizing the likelihood of $\mathbf{S}$. Note that the likelihood function of $\mathbf{S}$ is different from the likelihood function of the observed time series $\{X_t\}$.

Let (p, q, P, Q) be an arbitrary input in the input space

$\{0, \ldots, M_a\} \times \{0, \ldots, M_a\} \times \{0, \ldots, M_s\} \times \{0, \ldots, M_s\}.$

The kriging emulator of $S(p, q, P, Q)$ is then given by

$$\hat{S}(p, q, P, Q) = \hat{\gamma} + \boldsymbol{R}_0' \boldsymbol{R}_D^{-1} (\boldsymbol{S} - \hat{\gamma} \boldsymbol{1}_D).$$

The emulator variance is

$$V(p, q, P, Q) = \hat{\tau}^2 \left[1 - \boldsymbol{R}_0' \boldsymbol{R}_D^{-1} \boldsymbol{R}_0 + \frac{\left(1 - \boldsymbol{R}_0' \boldsymbol{R}_D^{-1} \boldsymbol{1}_D \right)^2}{\boldsymbol{1}_D' \boldsymbol{R}_D^{-1} \boldsymbol{1}_D} \right]$$

where $\hat{\gamma}$, $\hat{\tau}^2$ are the maximum likelihood estimators of γ, τ^2, respectively, and $\boldsymbol{R}_0$ represents the vector of model correlations between $S(p, q, P, Q)$ at the new input and

$$\{S(p_1, q_1, P_1, Q_1), \ldots, S(p_D, q_D, P_D, Q_D)\}.$$

Both $\hat{S}(p, q, P, Q)$ and the emulator variance involve very simple algebra and usually the value of D is small because only a small number of information criterion evaluations is computationally affordable. Therefore, the kriging emulator $\hat{S}(p, q, P, Q)$ is a fast approximation of the computationally intensive information criterion $S(p, q, P, Q)$ for seasonal big time series data.

Order Identification Using the EGO Algorithm

The goal is to choose the optimal orders (p, q, P, Q) in the input space given by

$$\{0, \ldots, M_a\} \times \{0, \ldots, M_a\} \times \{0, \ldots, M_s\} \times \{0, \ldots, M_s\},$$

minimizing $S(p, q, P, Q)$.

Since minimizing $\hat{S}(p, q, P, Q)$ by itself does not take into account the emulator variance, possibly leading to erroneous solutions, we maximize instead the "expected improvement" (EI) function (e.g. Jones et al., 1998; Roustant et al., 2012)

$\mathrm{EI}(p, q, P, Q) =$

$$\left(S_{min} - \hat{S}(p, q, P, Q) \right) G \left(\frac{S_{min} - \hat{S}(p, q, P, Q)}{\sqrt{V(p, q, P, Q)}} \right) + \sqrt{V(p, q, P, Q)} \, g \left(\frac{S_{min} - \hat{S}(p, q, P, Q)}{\sqrt{V(p, q, P, Q)}} \right)$$

where

$$S_{min} = \min \{ S(p_1, q_1, P_1, Q_1), \ldots, S(p_D, q_D, P_D, Q_D) \},$$

G is the cumulative distribution function of $N(0, 1)$, g is the probability distribution function of $N(0, 1)$. Intuitively, this method samples a new point (p, q, P, Q) where $\hat{S}(p, q, P, Q)$ improves over S_{min} or where $V(p, q, P, Q)$ is large (i.e. in previously unexplored parts of the in- put space). It leads to the following "efficient global optimization" (EGO) algorithm:

1.   Sample D inputs $\{(p_1, q_1, P_1, Q_1), \ldots, (p_D, q_D, P_D, Q_D)\}$ and compute the out- put information criterion values $\{S(p_1, q_1, P_1, Q_1), \ldots, S(p_D, q_D, P_D, Q_D)\}$.
2.   Construct the kriging emulator $\hat{S}(p, q, P, Q)$ and its variance $V(p, q, P, Q)$, for any (p, q, P, Q) in the input space.
3.   Choose $(p_{D+1}, q_{D+1}, P_{D+1}, Q_{D+1})$ that maximizes the expected improvement $EI(p, q, P, Q)$.
4.   Augment the set of sampled inputs as

$$\{(p_1, q_1, P_1, Q_1), \ldots, (p_D, q_D, P_D, Q_D), (p_{D+1}, q_{D+1}, P_{D+1}, Q_{D+1})\}$$

and the corresponding set of outputs as

$$\{S(p_1, q_1, P_1, Q_1), \ldots, S(p_D, q_D, P_D, Q_D), S(p_{D+1}, q_{D+1}, P_{D+1}, QD+1)\}.$$

5.   Iterate the steps above until $S(p_{D+1}, q_{D+1}, P_{D+1}, Q_{D+1}) < S_{min}$ and the relative error is smaller than a positive number (e.g. $\varepsilon = 0.0001$):

$$\frac{\left| S\left(p_{D+1}, q_{D+1}, P_{D+1}, Q_{D+1}\right) - S_{min} \right|}{\left| S_{min} \right|} < \varepsilon.$$

Note that

$$\{0, \ldots, M_a\} \times \{0, \ldots, M_a\} \times \{0, \ldots, M_s\} \times \{0, \ldots, M_s\},$$

the four- dimensional grid input space, will include a larger number of points, but it is still finite. Therefore the EGO algorithm will eventually converge and find the true orders in a finite number of steps if it is allowed to run long enough. However, as the examples will show, the guided search provided by the EGO can find the true orders (or orders close enough) in a smaller number of steps without going through the entire finite set of inputs on the grid. Note also that the EGO algorithm could select the next point (p, q, P, Q) to have non-integer components. While the formulas for the emulator $\hat{S}(p, q, P, Q)$ and its variance $V(p, q, P, Q)$ can be applied to any real numbers p, q, P, Q, if such values are chosen by the EGO algorithm we round them to the nearest non-negative integer.

Design and analysis of computer experiments for time-dependent output data has been addressed in the literature (e.g. Fang et al., 2007; Drignei, 2010). The problem addressed in this paper, however, has a different focus. It develops kriging-based emulators for the information criterion $S(p, q, P, Q)$ as scalar output, which is conditioned on the observed big time series.

Figure 1. Identified orders from 500 simulated series SARIMA (2, 0, 2) × (2, 0, 1)$_4$ of length 1000; Left: p, q orders; Right: P, Q orders.

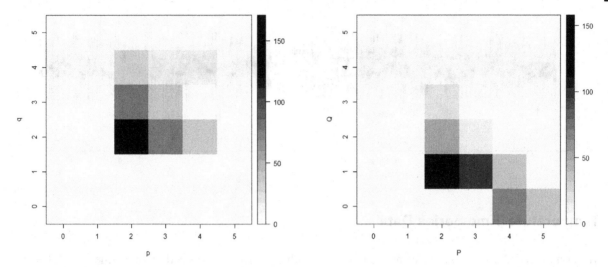

Simulations

We simulated 500 time series of length 1,000 from a SARIMA $(p, 0, q) \times (P, 0, Q)_s$ model using the *sarima* R package (Boshnakov & Halliday, 2019). The goal was to verify the accuracy of the proposed method by identifying the prespecified orders p, q, P, Q. Specifically, we considered the SARIMA(2, 0, 2) × (2, 0, 1)$_4$ model of zero mean and unit variance, AR coefficients $\varphi_1 = 0.35$, $\varphi_2 = -0.60$, MA coefficients $\theta_1 = 0.20$, $\theta_2 = 0.80$, SAR coefficients $\Phi_1 = 0.70$, $\Phi_2 = -0.40$ and SMA coefficient $\Theta_1 = 0.50$. We choose the period $s = 4$ because we used the same value in the real application to be discussed later. We considered the practical maximal orders $M_a = M_s = 5$, leading to a grid input space of $6^4 = 1,296$ points. For each simulated time series we used the method described above starting with D = 41 sampled inputs (p, q, P, Q), fitting the corresponding SARIMA$(p, 0, q) \times (P, 0, Q)_4$ models and computing the D output BIC values. Next, the R package DiceKriging was used with the default Matern(5/2) covariance to fit the kriging emulator for the BIC output values. Finally, the R package DiceOptim was used to run the EGO algorithm until convergence. Details about both R packages DiceKriging and DiceOptim can be found in Roustant et al. (2012).

Figure 1 shows image plots of the identified orders. While the mode of the distribution identifies the true orders $(p, q) = (2, 2)$ and $(P, Q) = (2, 1)$, some of the model orders are over-identified. However, the over-identification is rather mild since most of such models have at most two additional orders than the true model. The average number of iterations that the EGO algorithm took to converge was 61. All of the computations were performed in R, on a Windows 10 laptop with 16GB RAM and 2.30GHz i7 processor. The image plots were obtained using the *plot3D* R package (Soetaert, 2017).

Figure 2. Differenced temperature series.

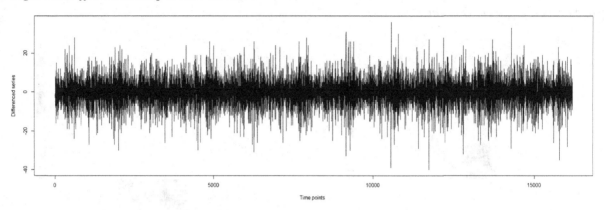

Temperature Time Series Data

We considered daily temperatures at the Chicago Midway airport, recorded at four time points (3am, 9am, 3pm and 9pm), between January 1, 2010 and February 1, 2021. This temperature data set has 16,200 time points and it was downloaded in a straightforward format from "Reliable Prognosis" (2021). According to their website, information on the actual weather was obtained from NOAA (US). A very small number of days didn't have complete temperature records at the hours mentioned above, in which case we completed the data set with temperatures from "Weather Underground" (2021). There are two cycles of yearly and daily temperatures in the data set, which were removed by differencing at lag 4. The autocorrelation function of the seasonally differenced series decayed slowly, therefore we performed an additional differencing at lag 1 resulting in the differenced time series plotted in Figure 2. We inspected the autocorrelation and partial autocorrelation functions of this series. There are significant autocorrelations at lags 4 and 8, as well as significant partial autocorrelations at lags multiple of 4, showing that this series may be modeled by a multiplicative SARIMA$(p, 0, q) \times (P, 0, Q)_4$ process.

To demonstrate the efficiency and accuracy of the proposed method, we computed first the BIC values on the entire four-dimensional grid and obtained the actual orders $(p, q, P, Q) = (3, 4, 2, 1)$ where BIC is minimized. The estimated parameters of this SARIMA model along with their standard errors are given in Table 1. It took about 75 minutes of computing time to fit all 1,296 SARIMA models of orders given by the coordinates of the points on this grid.

Table 1. Differenced temperature series. Parameter estimates (upper row) and standard errors (lower row) for the SARIMA(3, 0, 4) × (2, 0, 1)₄ model.

φ_1	φ_2	φ_3	θ_1	θ_2	θ_3	θ_4	Φ_1	Φ_2	Θ_1
-0.2038	0.4022	0.3512	0.1789	-0.6028	-0.4799	-0.0626	0.1248	-0.0160	-0.9441
0.1077	0.0312	0.0808	0.1088	0.0310	0.1026	0.0186	0.0158	0.0086	0.0033

We then implemented the proposed kriging-based optimization method with $D = 41$ initial kriging points followed by the EGO algorithm until convergence. The method identified the correct orders $(p, q, P, Q) = (3, 4, 2, 1)$ after 55 EGO iterations. Thus, the proposed method needed only 96 fitted SARIMA models overall. The two-dimensional projection plots including the initial kriging points (blue triangles), the points visited during first and last two EGO iterations (red circles and green star) are shown in Figure 3. The proposed method took only about 6 minutes, more than 12 times reduction in the computing time. The BIC values at each iteration of the EGO algorithm display a zigzagging pattern indicative of inputs where BIC is small or inputs selected in a previously unexplored part of the input space. The log kriging standard error at the next input chosen by the EGO algorithm shows a decreasing trend, indicating a reduction of the uncertainty in the rest of the input space as the EGO algorithm progresses.

Figure 3. Temperature series example. Sample inputs for the initial kriging model (blue triangles), along with the first and last two iterations of the EGO algorithm (number-marked points). Left: projection on the (p, q) subspace; Right: projection on the (P, Q) subspace.

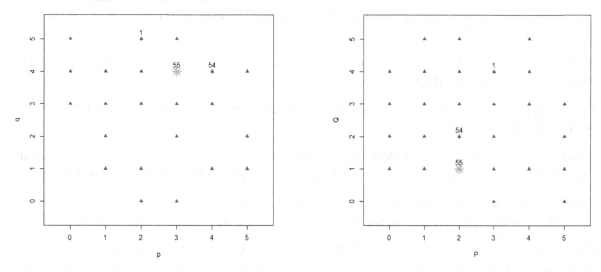

FUTURE RESEARCH DIRECTIONS

A potential future research direction on this topic would be to investigate simultaneously multiple seasonal big time series instead of just one. For example, it may be necessary to model simultaneously seasonal temperature time series at multiple locations, or seasonal labor time series data from multiple countries. The computational challenges will be even greater in the multiple time series case, the number of computationally affordable fitted time series models being much smaller. One must investigate potential adjustments in the methodology outlined in this paper to address such challenges.

CONCLUSION

Big time series data sets pose new computational and modeling challenges. In this paper we discussed a computationally efficient method for order identification in SARIMA models of seasonal big time series data sets. It starts with sampling a small set of non-negative integer orders on a practically large enough grid, where the SARIMA models are fitted and information criteria such as BIC are computed. A kriging-based emulator that predicts the information criterion at any set of orders on the grid is used in conjunction with an EGO algorithm to identify the optimal orders of the SARIMA model. The simulations indicate that the method identifies accurately and efficiently prespecified orders or their close neighbors. We also demonstrated the method using a very long time series of temperatures recorded at the Chicago Midway airport. The method correctly identifies the SARIMA model, while decreasing the computing time by more than twelve times.

REFERENCES

Bachechi, C., Po, L., & Rollo, F. (2022). Big data analytics and visualization in traffic monitoring. *Big Data Research*, *27*, 100292. doi:10.1016/j.bdr.2021.100292

Bergmeir, C., Hyndman, R. J., & Koo, B. (2018). A note on the validity of cross- validation for evaluating autoregressive time series prediction. *Computational Statistics & Data Analysis*, *120*, 70–83. doi:10.1016/j.csda.2017.11.003

Boshnakov, G. N., & Halliday, J. (2019). *Sarima: Simulation and prediction with seasonal ARIMA models*. R package version 0.8.1.

Brockwell, P. J., & Davis, R. A. (2016). *Introduction to time series and forecasting* (3rd ed.). Springer. doi:10.1007/978-3-319-29854-2

Candanedo, L. M., Feldheim, V., & Deramaix, D. (2017). Data driven prediction models of energy use of appliances in a low-energy house. *Energy and Building*, *140*, 81–97. doi:10.1016/j.enbuild.2017.01.083

Carlini, E., de Lira, V. M., Soares, A., Etemad, M., Brandoli, B., & Matwin, S. (2021). Understanding evolution of maritime networks from automatic identification system data. *GeoInformatica*.

Castan-Lascorz, M. A., Jimenez-Herrera, P., Troncoso, A., & Asencio-Cortés, G. (2022). A new hybrid method for predicting univariate and multivariate time series based on pattern forecasting. *Information Sciences*, *586*, 611–627. doi:10.1016/j.ins.2021.12.001

Chen, J. G., Li, K. L., Rong, H. G., Bilal, K., Li, K. Q., & Yu, P. S. (2019). A periodicity-based parallel time series prediction algorithm in cloud computing environments. *Information Sciences*, *496*, 506–537. doi:10.1016/j.ins.2018.06.045

Chen, Y., Morton, D. C., Andela, N., Giglio, L., & Randerson, J. T. (2016). How much global burned area can be forecast on seasonal time scales using sea surface temperatures? *Environmental Research Letters*, *11*(4), 045001. doi:10.1088/1748-9326/11/4/045001

Chou, J. S., & Ngo, N. T. (2016). Time series analytics using sliding window metaheuristic optimization-based machine learning system for identifying building energy consumption patterns. *Applied Energy*, *177*, 751–770. doi:10.1016/j.apenergy.2016.05.074

Da Silva, J. P., Zullo, J., & Romani, L. A. S. (2020). A time series mining approach for agricultural area detection. *IEEE Transactions on Big Data*, *6*(3), 537–546. doi:10.1109/TBDATA.2019.2913402

Drignei, D. (2010). Functional ANOVA in computer models with time series output. *Technometrics*, *52*(4), 430–437. doi:10.1198/TECH.2010.10029

Fang, K. T., Li, R., & Sudjianto, A. (2007). *Design and modeling for computer experiments.* Chapman and Hall.

Giordano, F., La Rocca, M., & Parrella, M. L. (2017). Clustering complex time-series databases by using periodic components. *Statistical Analysis and Data Mining: The ASA Data Science Journal, 10*(2), 89–106. doi:10.1002am.11341

Gregory, A. W., & Smith, G. W. (1996). Measuring business cycles with business- cycle models. *Journal of Economic Dynamics & Control, 20*(6-7), 1007–1025. doi:10.1016/0165-1889(95)00887-X

Guo, X., Zhu, S. L., & Wu, J. J. (2021). A hybrid seasonal autoregressive integrated moving average and denoising autoencoder model for atmospheric temperature profile prediction. *Big Data*, big.2021.0242. doi:10.1089/big.2021.0242 PMID:34918943

Hewamalage, H., Bergmeir, C., & Bandara, K. (2021). Recurrent neural networks for time series forecasting: Current status and future directions. *International Journal of Forecasting, 37*(1), 388–427. doi:10.1016/j.ijforecast.2020.06.008

Jones, D. R., Schonlau, M., & Welch, W. J. (1998). Efficient global optimization of expensive black- box functions. *Journal of Global Optimization, 13*(4), 455–492. doi:10.1023/A:1008306431147

Jurman, G. (2019). Seasonal linear predictivity in national football championships. *Big Data, 7*(1), 21–34. doi:10.1089/big.2018.0076 PMID:30888213

Kim, K. Y., Lim, C. Y., & Kim, E. J. (2018). A new approach to the space-time analysis of big data: Application to subway traffic data in Seoul. *Journal of Big Data, 5*(1), 5. doi:10.118640537-018-0116-9

Kumari, P., & Toshniwal, D. (2021). Long short term memory-convolutional neural network based deep hybrid approach for solar irradiance forecasting. *Applied Energy, 295*, 117061. doi:10.1016/j.apenergy.2021.117061

Liebensteiner, M. (2014). Estimating the income gain of seasonal labor migration. *Review of Development Economics, 18*(4), 667–680. doi:10.1111/rode.12110

Lunde, A., Shephard, N., & Sheppard, K. (2016). Econometric analysis of vast covariance matrices using composite realized kernels and their application to portfolio choice. *Journal of Business & Economic Statistics, 34*(4), 504–518. doi:10.1080/07350015.2015.1064432

Martin, G. M., Brooks, M. E., Johnson, B., Milton, S. F., Webster, S., Jayakumar, A., Mitra, A. K., Rajan, D., & Hunt, K. M. R. (2020). Forecasting the monsoon on daily to seasonal time-scales in support of a field campaign. *Quarterly Journal of the Royal Meteorological Society, 146*(731), 2906–2927. doi:10.1002/qj.3620

Murthy, K. V. N., & Kumar, G. K. (2021). Structural time-series modelling for seasonal surface air temperature patterns in India 1951–2016. *Meteorology and Atmospheric Physics, 133*(1), 27–39. doi:10.100700703-020-00732-7

Pena, D., Tiao, G. C., & Tsay, R. S. (2001). *A course in time series analysis.* Wiley.

Poussin, C., Massot, A., Ginzler, C., Weber, D., Chatenoux, B., Lacroix, P., Piller, T., Nguyen, L., & Giuliani, G. (2021). Drying conditions in Switzerland - indication from a 35-year Landsat time-series analysis of vegetation water content estimates to support SDGs. *Big Earth Data*, *5*(4), 445–475. doi:10.1080/20964471.2021.1974681

Psaradakis, Z., Sola, M., Spagnolo, F., & Spagnolo, N. (2009). Selecting nonlinear time series models using information criteria. *Journal of Time Series Analysis*, *30*(4), 369–394. doi:10.1111/j.1467-9892.2009.00614.x

Reliable Prognosis. (2021). https://rp5.ru/

Roustant, O., Ginsbourger, D., & Deville, Y. (2012). DiceKriging, DiceOptim: Two R packages for the analysis of computer experiments by kriging-based meta-modeling and optimization. *Journal of Statistical Software*, *51*(1), 1–55. doi:10.18637/jss.v051.i01

Sacks, J., Welch, W. J., Mitchell, T. J., & Wynn, H. P. (1989). Design and analysis of computer experiments. *Statistical Science*, *4*, 409–423.

Saez, C., & Garcia-Gomez, J. M. (2018). Kinematics of big biomedical data to characterize temporal variability and seasonality of data repositories: Functional data analysis of data temporal evolution over non-parametric statistical manifolds. *International Journal of Medical Informatics*, *119*, 109–124. doi:10.1016/j.ijmedinf.2018.09.015 PMID:30342679

Santner, T. J., Williams, B. J., & Notz, W. I. (2003). *The design and analysis of computer experiments*. Springer. doi:10.1007/978-1-4757-3799-8

Sayemuzzaman, M., & Jha, M. K. (2014). Seasonal and annual precipitation time series trend analysis in North Carolina, United States. *Atmospheric Research*, *137*, 183–194. doi:10.1016/j.atmosres.2013.10.012

Shih, D. C.-F. (2021). Rotary spectral analysis for directional time series: Seasonal variation of wind speed on a subtropical island near the western Pacific ocean. *Pure and Applied Geophysics*, *178*(4), 1369–1385. doi:10.100700024-021-02708-z

Shumway, R. H., & Stoffer, D. S. (2017). *Time series analysis and its applications* (4th ed.). Springer. doi:10.1007/978-3-319-52452-8

Soetaert, K. (2017). *plot3D: Plotting multi-dimensional data*. R package version 1.1.1.

Tsay, R. S., & Tiao, G. C. (1984). Consistent estimates of autoregressive parameters and extended sample autocorrelation function for stationary and nonstationary ARMA models. *Journal of the American Statistical Association*, *79*(385), 84–96. doi:10.1080/01621459.1984.10477068

Tsay, R. S., & Tiao, G. C. (1985). Use of canonical analysis in time series model identification. *Biometrika*, *72*(2), 299–315. doi:10.1093/biomet/72.2.299

Wang, L., Chen, D., Zomaya, A., Yang, L. T., & Georgakopoulos, D. (2020). Editorial for the special issue on big time series data. *Computing*, *102*(3), 741–743. doi:10.100700607-020-00793-x

Wang, L. J., Wang, J. Y., & Qin, F. (2021). Feature fusion approach for temporal land use mapping in complex agricultural areas. *Remote Sensing*, *13*(13), 2517. doi:10.3390/rs13132517

Weather Underground. (2021). https://www.wunderground.com/

Wu, B., & Drignei, D. (2021). Emulated order identification for models of big time series data. *Statistical Analysis and Data Mining: The ASA Data Science Journal*, *14*(2), 201–212. doi:10.1002am.11504

Xu, R., Chen, J., Han, J., Tan, L., & Xu, L. (2020). Towards emotion-sensitive learning cognitive state analysis of big data in education: Deep learning-based facial expression analysis using ordinal information. *Computing*, *102*(3), 765–780. doi:10.100700607-019-00722-7

Yeh, F. C., & Yeh, C. H. (2019). Developing mortality surveillance systems using Google trend: A pilot study. *Physica A*, *527*, 121125. doi:10.1016/j.physa.2019.121125

Yi, D. D., Ning, S. Y., Chang, C. J., & Kou, S. C. (2021). Forecasting unemployment using internet search data via PRISM. *Journal of the American Statistical Association*, *116*(536), 1662–1673. doi:10.1080/01621459.2021.1883436

ADDITIONAL READING

Askari, S. (2021). A critical note on inverse fuzzy time series algorithms. *Fuzzy Sets and Systems*, *421*, 193–199. doi:10.1016/j.fss.2020.11.007

Davis, R. A., Sousa, T. D., & Kluppelberg, C. (2021). Indirect inference for time series using the empirical characteristic function and control variates. *Journal of Time Series Analysis*, *42*(5-6), 653–668. doi:10.1111/jtsa.12582

Diop, M. L., & Kengne, W. (2021). Piecewise autoregression for general integer-valued time series. *Journal of Statistical Planning and Inference*, *211*, 271–286. doi:10.1016/j.jspi.2020.07.003

Drees, H., Janssen, A., & Neblung, S. (2021). Cluster based inference for extremes of time series. *Stochastic Processes and Their Applications*, *142*, 1–33. doi:10.1016/j.spa.2021.07.012

Hu, H. C., Hu, W. F., & Yu, X. X. (2021). Pseudo-maximum likelihood estimators in linear regression models with fractional time series. *Statistische Hefte*, *62*, 639–659.

Liu, X. L., & Zhang, T. (2022). Estimating change-point latent factor models for high-dimensional time series. *Journal of Statistical Planning and Inference*, *217*, 69–91. doi:10.1016/j.jspi.2021.07.006

Philips, A. Q. (2020). An easy way to create duration variables in binary cross-sectional time-series data. *The Stata Journal*, *20*(4), 916–930. doi:10.1177/1536867X20976322

Truquet, L. (2020). Coupling and perturbation techniques for categorical time series. *Bernoulli*, *26*(4), 3249–3279. doi:10.3150/20-BEJ1225

KEY TERMS AND DEFINITIONS

Computer Experiment: An experiment intended to study how the changes in the inputs of a computer model affect the outputs.

Emulator: A simplified model that mimics the behavior of a more complex model.

Kriging: An interpolation method initially developed in geostatistics.

Model Selection: A procedure that chooses the best model among a set of competing models.

Optimization Algorithm: An iterative process leading to an optimal solution.

Seasonality: The cyclic behavior of a process or phenomenon.

Time Series: A sequence of observations recorded over time.

Section 54
Transfer Learning

Integration of Knowledge Sharing Into Project Management

Zinga Novais
ISEG, Universidade de Lisboa, Portugal

Jorge Gomes
 https://orcid.org/0000-0003-0656-9284
Universidade Lusófona das Humanidades e Tecnologias, Lisboa, Portugal

Mário Romão
 https://orcid.org/0000-0003-4564-1883
ISEG, Universidade de Lisboa, Portugal

INTRODUCTION

An increasing number of organizations have implemented their business operations through projects (Todorović, et., 2015). Projects that can be defined as a temporary effort to create a specific product or service (PMI, 2017). Temporary, in the sense that a project has a defined beginning and end, and unique, in the sense that the product/service is different in some way, distinct from other products/services (Owen & Burstein, 2005; PMI, 2017). Projects are collective endeavors with goals based on the development of common understandings, which generate personal and group knowledge that contributes to their own success (Sankarasubramanian, 2009).

For many organizations, knowledge is the most important asset and its survival depends on the organization's ability to effectively use existing knowledge and to effectively create, develop and use new knowledge (Pascoe & More, 2005). Proper knowledge is a basic prerequisite for effective project management (Gasik, 2011) and the knowledge management is vital factor to successfully undertake projects (Sokhanvar, 2014). According to Koskinen and Pihlanto (2008), projects are often dependent on knowledge that is not in their possession. Within this context, the integration of knowledge management in project management is necessary to share information and knowledge to solve problems effectively and efficiently (Yeong & Lim, 2010). Knowledge, defined by Gao et al (2018) as the practical and theoretical understanding of a subject, is considered as an essential organizational resource (Buvik & Tvedt, 2017; Hanisch et al., 2009) and its management is considered as a fundamental tool for the success of the projects (Romani, 2017).

Generically knowledge management represents the set of processes and practices carried out in organizations with the objective of increasing intellectual potential, improving the effectiveness and efficiency of the management of organizational knowledge resources (Heisig, 2009; Andreeva and Kianto, 2012). The basic purpose of knowledge management is to create and share knowledge within organizations (Chen et al., 2018). Knowledge sharing is especially important in a project environment and contributes significantly to the performance of organizations (Buvik & Tvedt, 2017) and to understand the best way to share knowledge between teams and between members of a project (Fernie et., 2003). Further, Al Ahbabi et al. (2019) conclude that the dimensions of knowledge management had a positive impact on

DOI: 10.4018/978-1-7998-9220-5.ch183

innovation, quality and operational performance of employees. Gürlek & Çemberci (2020) shows that firms under the leadership of knowledge-oriented leaders have high knowledge management capacity, innovation performance and firm performance. Also, due to the temporary nature of projects, knowledge management in project-based organizations is not like functional companies (Kasvi, Vartiainen, & Hailikari, 2003). Project team members split up or leave after project completion and this poses several challenges to projects and project-based organizations (Ajmal, Helo, & Kekale, 2010)

Through a case study approach, it is proved that team members use different knowledge sharing practices, in addition to recognizing its importance for the most successful management of their projects.

BACKGROUND

Knowledge

"Knowledge is seen as an intangible asset, which is valuable, distinctive, path-dependent, causally ambiguous and hard to substitute or replicate" (Fang et al., 2013, p. 945). Knowledge is considered an essential strategic resource that allows organizations to maintain competitive advantage in a dynamic market environment (Rashed, 2016).

There is no single definition of knowledge, it has different understandings depending on the context in which it is being defined (Ekambaram et al., 2018). It can be defined as the practical and theoretical understanding of a subject (Gao et al., 2018), the ability to make judgments (Fernie et al., 2003), based on reflection and human experience (De Long & Fahey, 2000), a system of connections between facts and ideas (Romani, 2017) or information combined with experience, context, interpretation and reflection (Davenport, De Long & Beers, 1998).

De Long and Fahey (2000) believe that there are three types of knowledge: human knowledge, social knowledge and structured knowledge. In addition, they believe that there are two dimensions to understanding knowledge in an organizational context: first, that knowledge can exist at the individual, group or organizational level; and second, that knowledge can be tacit or explicit (De Long & Fahey, 2000). This latter dimension, between tacit knowledge and explicit knowledge, is frequently mentioned in the literature (Buvik & Tvedt, 2017; Chen et al., 2018; De Long & Fahey, 2000; Fernie et al., 2003; Hoorn & Whitty, 2019; Nonaka, 1994).

Explicit knowledge consists of words and numbers that are easily accessible (Uğurlu & Kizildağ, 2013), information defined in a tangible way (Gao et al., 2018; Owen & Burstein, 2005), formal and well structured, through documentation, databases and reports (Terzieva, 2014; Mazur et al., 2014). Explicit knowledge refers to knowledge that is transmissible in a formal and systemic language (Nonaka, 1994; Nonaka & Takeuchi, 1995).

Tacit knowledge is defined as what we know, but we cannot explain (De Long & Fahey, 2000), the experience rooted in the individual's mind (Koskinen et al., 2003; Chen et al., 2018). Tacit knowledge is not in a structured or documented form. It is internalized by the experience, intuition and insight of individuals who are experts within their organizations (Terzieva, 2014; Mazur et al., 2014; Davenport et al., 1998). Tacit knowledge has a personal quality, which makes it difficult to formalize and communicate (Nonaka, 1994; Nonaka & Takeuchi, 1995). According to the same author, tacit knowledge has two types of elements or dimensions. A cognitive dimension based on paradigms, beliefs and points of view that provide individuals with unique perspectives, and a technical dimension supported by informal skills and know-how applied to a specific context (Nonaka, 1994; Nonaka & Konno, 1998). Tacit knowledge is expressed by human action (Koskinen et al., 2003), know-how (Bryde et al., 2018), characterized by being complex and dynamic (Chen et al., 2018), personal and context dependent (Fernie et al., 2003), and subjective (Hoorn & Whitty, 2019). However, according to Owen & Burstein (2005), there is a third type of knowledge, implicit knowledge, which, like tacit knowledge, is present in the individual's mind. The same authors explain that the main difference between implicit and tacit knowledge is the fact that the latter can be captured and transferred within the organization through social networks, while the implicit knowledge can potentially be captured, encoded and stored in databases or documents (Owen & Burstein, 2005).

Knowledge Management

Knowledge management has a fundamental role in the success of organizations' activities and strategies, namely in the effective support to environmental changes, in increasing productivity, in the relationships between employees, and in opening the way for development and innovation (Castrogiovanni et al., 2016; Ekambaram et al., 2018; Mueller, 2012). It is considered a key element for organizations looking to obtain a competitive advantage (Wang & Ko, 2012). In a simplified way, the concept is based on the vision of the strategic value of organizational knowledge, using information technologies (e.g., databases and others) to facilitate the acquisition, sharing, storage, retrieval and use of knowledge (Easterby- Smith & Lyles, 2011).

Inkinen (2016) defines knowledge management practices as the conscious organizational and managerial practices intended to achieve organizational goals through efficient and effective management of the firm's knowledge resources.

Several studies define knowledge management processes in different ways, according to Costa & Monteiro (2016) and Inkinen (2016), knowledge management is an aggregated process composed of the acquisition, creation, transfer, storage and application of knowledge. However, in operational terms, the definition of knowledge management processes is related to the creation, sharing and use of knowledge (Ahmad et al., 2017; Shujahat et al., 2017).

Knowledge creation is a process in which new knowledge is created through the four sub-processes of organizational knowledge creation (Andreeva & Kianto, 2011; Collins & Smith, 2006), namely through socialization, combination, externalization and internationalization (Collins & Smith, 2006; Lai et al., 2014)

Knowledge sharing is the donation and collection of knowledge between different knowledge units in a company (Becerra-Fernandez, Gonzalez, & Sabherwal, 2004). It is the act of transferring the respective insights between workers (Hooff & De Ridder, 2004). It can be categorized as formal versus informal elements or donation versus collection of knowledge (Hooff & De Ridder, 2004; Taminiau, Smit, & Lange, 2009). Singh et al (2021) claims that organizations with strong knowledge sharing practices are more competent in chasing open innovation. Abbas et al (2019) shows a substantial positive linkage between knowledge sharing and organizational innovation in Pakistani Islamic banks. Therefore, to have an effective knowledge exchange among employee and employers, there must be effective knowledge sharing and helping (Singh et al., 2021). A complete process of knowledge sharing includes sharing intention, sharing behaviours, and sharing results (Akhavan &Mahdi Hosseini, 2016).

The use of knowledge is the application of knowledge that has been shared (Song, Bij, & Weggeman, 2005). It is a newly created knowledge that becomes part of organizational behavior and processes for problem solving through assimilation (Chen et al., 2012).

Seiner (2001), defined knowledge management as the way the company collects, organizes, shares and analyzes the knowledge of individuals and groups, and the ways that directly affect organizational performance (Mazur et al., 2014). Mahdi et al. (2019) see knowledge as a dynamic and recurring process, in which employees must constantly connect with information and obtain new knowledge and apply that knowledge to improve their decision making, while developing knowledge and information new in the process. Knowledge management describes all methods, instruments and tools in a holistic approach to generate, store, distribute and apply knowledge supported by the identification of knowledge and the definition of knowledge goals in all areas and levels of the organization (Mahdi et al., 2019; Rashed, 2016). It is also considered as a cyclical system that allows the organization to efficiently achieve its objectives by the ability to transform tacit and explicit learning into habits, to better plan and execute (Mazur et al., 2014).

Knowledge Management Strategies

Knowledge management ensures the correct flow of knowledge through two main strategies: coding and personalization (Shujahat et al., 2017). The coding strategy is related to extracting and storing knowledge explicitly through the ICT framework, while the personalization strategy focuses on direct human interactions for the purposes of knowledge sharing (Curado & Bontis, 2006; Merat & Bo, 2013; Shujahat et al., 2017).

In the coding strategy, knowledge is encrypted and stored in databases, which allows for easy access and reuse of knowledge (Hans & Skiver, 2007; Hansen et al., 1999; Kasvi et al., 2003; Ruuska & Vartiainen, 2005). Organizations that adopt the coding strategy depend on the "economics of reuse", and once acquired or developed, knowledge assets can be used multiple times. The reuse of knowledge reduces the volume of work, reduces costs and allows the organization to take on more projects (Hansen et al., 1999). This strategy is considered a good mechanism for storing large amounts of knowledge and creating an organizational memory for all employees (Polyaninova, 2011).

Opposite to the coding strategy, there is the personalization strategy (Bolisani et al., 2017) in which knowledge is linked to the person who developed it (Hansen et al., 1999; Mannan et al., 2013; Polyaninova, 2011). This strategy focuses on the contribution of tacit knowledge (Bolisani et al., 2017). Personalization as a knowledge sharing mechanism has the flexibility to transmit tacit knowledge and allows discussions and the sharing of interpretations that may lead to the development of new knowledge (Polyaninova, 2011).

Knowledge is transmitted and shared through personal interaction, which focuses on dialogue between individuals, in brainstorming sessions, in building networks of people, a "person-to-person" approach (Hansen et al., 1999; Mannan, et al., 2013; Polyaninova, 2011). Information technologies, when it comes to personalization, have the main purpose of facilitating communication and sharing tacit knowledge (Hansen et al., 1999).

The organizations that successfully generate knowledge are those that identify the knowledge management strategy that best fits their competitive strategy, using this as their main strategy and the other as support (Greiner et al., 2007; Hansen et al., 1999).

Bolisani et al. (2017), present a third strategy, the sharing strategy, which refers to an approach where individuals are assumed to work better collectively, arguing that there is a need to share and socialize the elements of their private knowledge. This strategy exists under the premise that no individual has all the knowledge necessary to perform a complex task, that individuals should be encouraged to put their experiences and knowledge in common, leading to the creation of specialized islands of knowledge, where they can create and sharing knowledge and implementing collective learning processes (Bolisani et al., 2017).

Sharing Knowledge in Project Management

Knowledge sharing refers to the dissemination of organizational knowledge to all the organization's stakeholders (Kishore, et al., 2009), playing a critical role in the growth of companies' businesses, through the generation of new ideas, products or services (Fields, 2017) and by the transfer of thoughts, information, perceptions and experiences and, consequently, becoming a source of creativity and innovation in organizations (Ciulli & Kolk, 2019). Love, Fong and Irani (2005) have made a valuable contribution to understanding knowledge management in project environments. Considering the role and processes of knowledge management in project environments, they focus on knowledge management in the context of cross-functional project teams, as well as the role of organizational learning in projects.

Knowledge is considered an essential asset for a project (Holzman, 2013), and is linked to the methodology and communication practices used in projects (Hanisch et al., 2009; Frey et al., 2009). Consequently, knowledge management is an essential tool, available to the project manager for the successful completion of a project (Romani, 2017). Some researchers have linked knowledge and learning from project performance (Reich et al., 2008). Several empirical studies show a strong correlation between project management and knowledge management practices (McElroy, 2000) and between good knowledge management practices and project performance (Leseure & Brookes, 2004).

Project knowledge management is defined as the application of concepts, tools and techniques to complete a project within the defined time and budget, responding to the client's needs (Romani, 2017). Project knowledge management, especially in complex projects, is one of the main success factors in project management and it lack is one of the main reasons for failure (Desouza & Evaristo, 2004). Frey et al. (2009), states that project knowledge management comprises not only knowledge within projects, but also between different projects and about projects. Soderlund (2010) stated that in large transformation projects, it is necessary to integrate several knowledge bases in these projects. For these projects, knowledge integration depends on the ability of the people involved to relate to each other, share and absorb findings and knowledge assets that have been developed in the project, and adjust them to the speed of other parts of the project. Polyaninova (2011) states that knowledge management in the project environment occurs in the transfer of experience between projects or between project teams and in the dissemination and development of new competences from central departments to project teams.

For Bassi (2014), within an organization there are two levels of knowledge to be managed: individual knowledge and organizational knowledge. The first refers to what individuals learn during project execution, while the second refers to what the organization has developed and learned from managing its projects. Hanish et al. (2009) states that knowledge in projects is linked to the project management methodology and communication practices in projects, making project knowledge contribute to the organizational knowledge base.

According to Pretorius & Steyn (2005), the challenge of knowledge management in project environments is in the documentation and management, as well as the distribution and sharing of newly created knowledge. Failure in this knowledge transfer within the organization leads to waste and impacts project performance (Leseure & Brookes, 2004).

Knowledge about project management, explicit or tacit, plays a decisive role in understanding this discipline (Morris, 2002). Knowledge increases in value, when it is shared (Cabrera & Cabrera, 2002), knowledge sharing is potentially considered the most important activity in knowledge management (Chen et al., 2018). Sharing is recognized as strategically important for organizations, as it allows individuals to acquire the necessary knowledge to improve their performance (Wang & Ko, 2012). It is a key process in translating individual knowledge into organizational knowledge (Nesheim & Hunskaar, 2015), and vital to innovation, increasing productivity and maintaining competitive advantage (Mueller, 2015).

Knowledge sharing can be defined as the action of disseminating knowledge among individuals, groups and organizations (Chen et al., 2018), the organizational processes associated with making knowledge available to others (Chen et al., 2018). However, some authors (Alavi & Denford, 2011), differentiate the concepts of knowledge sharing and transfer.

Knowledge transfer is considered as the communication of knowledge from a source to a recipient. Knowledge transfer involves the transmission of knowledge from its original location, to where it needs to be applied (Alavi & Denford, 2011). Some authors argue that knowledge sharing is a voluntary act, suggesting that the individual presents the knowledge so that it can be used by others, and that it involves conscious action and active participation by the individual who possesses the knowledge (Wickramasinghe & Widyaratne, 2012). Others, in turn, suggest that knowledge sharing may not only be voluntary, but also requested, referring to the sending and receiving of requests for knowledge and the consequent fulfillment of those same requests (Wickramasinghe & Widyaratne, 2012). Knowledge sharing is especially important within the context of the project, where individuals work together and interact to perform their tasks and is positively associated with project performance (Buvik & Tvedt, 2017).

However, it is necessary to be aware of any barriers that may develop within the organization. There are numerous barriers that we can group into three homogeneous dimensions (Crupi et al., 2020):

- Cultural dimension - The culture of an organization can be a barrier to interorganizational knowledge sharing (Lotti Oliva, 2014). The culture can impact the knowledge sharing by not implementing knowledge management tools, not providing an adequate reward system, changing the organizational climate and relationships (Zawawi et al., 2011).
- Structural dimension - Organizational relationships seems to be an important barrier to the transfer of information from the organization to the team (Connelly & Kelloway, 2003). For this reason, organizations must promote the culture of teamwork as a knowledge sharing generating factor, facilitating the work conditions and the adequate infrastructure (Mariotti, 2007).
- Strategic dimension - Strategy development and collaborative encouragement require leadership. Knowledge is an individual resource that needs to be coordinated and integrated at the organizational level (Tiwari, 2015).

At individual level, we highlighted some dimension, namely, Culture (Chmielecki, 2013), emotions (Riege, 2005), trust (Park & Kim, 2018), communication skills and social networks' breadth (Riege, 2005) and time constraints (Razmerita et al., 2016). Technology issues, cross-organizational information transfer, the idea of taking tangible advantage from the information exchange, situations where one of the organizations involved in the KS imposes the sharing of information with other organizations, configure a set of barriers at the interorganizational level (Boonstra & de Vries, 2005).

CASE STUDY

Company Z

Company Z is a multinational company within the financial sector. Its subsidiary in Portugal has project teams made up of project managers and local and central project management professionals, who represent the parent company.

The organization has several project teams within its departments. The target department of this study is made up mostly of project teams whose scope applies to different areas and, in turn, have different project management methodologies. This means that, depending on the type of project carried out by the team, we can find teams that adopt different project management methodologies (Cascade, Agile, Lean Six Sigma, among others).

The project team under study is a team that carries out projects for internal clients, that is, for other business areas within the organization. It consists of a sub-team of project managers and a sub-team of PMO which, in turn, is subdivided into two teams: the coordination team, responsible for supporting the project managers and a PMO team that is part of the team at the company's headquarters.

Figure 1. Structure of the project team

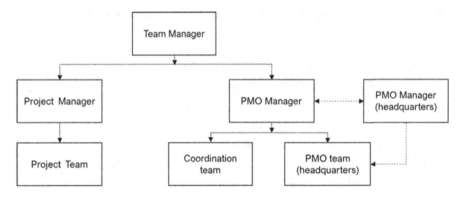

Data Collection Instrument

To understand the perception of individuals in relation to the topic of knowledge sharing, an interview guide was created based on a literature review and applied within a project team in a financial sector organization.

The questions created can be categorized using the knowledge sharing inventory, developed by Liebowitz and Megbolugbe (2003) to assess how well an organization implements the knowledge management and sharing structure. This approach is divided into 4 categories (Liebowitz & Megbolugbe, 2003):

- Communication flow - how knowledge and communication exchanges are captured and disseminated by the organization.
- Knowledge management environment - which looks at the internal cultural factors related to knowledge management within the organization.

- Organizational availability - which assesses the sophistication of the knowledge management infrastructure and the ability to share knowledge within the organization.
- Measurement - which measures the likelihood of knowledge sharing and knowledge management being successful within an organization.

The categorization and references are detailed in the table 1.

Table 1. Categorization of the interview guide (pre-validation)

The Categorization	Question	References
Communication flow	Q.3 Q.4 Q.6	(Liebowitz & Megbolugbe, 2003) (Schindler & Eppler, 2003) (Terzieva, 2014)
Knowledge Management Environment	Q.2 Q.5 Q.6a Q.9	(Bryde et al., 2018) (Chen et al., 2018) (Todorović et al.,2015) (Liebowitz & Megbolugbe, 2003)
Organizational availability	Q.1 Q.2 Q.6b Q.6c	(Bryde et al., 2018) (Hanisch et al., 2009) (Liebowitz & Megbolugbe, 2003) (Liebowitz & Megbolugbe, 2003)
Measurement	Q.7 Q.8	(Liebowitz & Megbolugbe, 2003) (Liebowitz & Megbolugbe, 2003)

The script's structure asked about: The perception of the relevance of the knowledge sharing theme within the project management; the existence of a project management methodology, knowledge sharing and existing knowledge sources; the incentive for top management to share and the currently used methodologies.

The responses obtained were categorized to observe the frequency of the topics mentioned by the respondents.

ANALYSIS AND DISCUSSION

The unit of analysis for this study was the members of the project and PMO teams. Answers were obtained from 10 respondents (Table 2).

According to the results obtained, most (7 in 10) apply Cascade Project Management methodology and most affirm that the applied methodologies incorporate knowledge management practices (6 in 10). All respondents believe it is relevant to share knowledge within a project environment. The most common sources of knowledge are guides/procedures (23%), SharePoint/Share Drive (16%), experts (13%), reports (10%) and repositories (10%).

Regarding incentives by top management, there is no consensus among respondents, and the answers indicated, both, the existence of incentives and the absence of them.

Notwithstanding the divergence of opinion in relation to the previous question, there is a consensus that the sharing of knowledge between project managers is a common practice among respondent teams. During their projects, most of them claim to use knowledge acquired by other project managers, information which is found in the form of project reports, digital databases and direct contact with project managers.

Table 2. Respondent's profile

Member	Job	Age	Sex
GP01	Project Manager	30 - 40	Male
GP02	Project Manager	> 40	Male
GP03	Project Manager	> 40	Male
GP04	Project Manager	20 -30	Male
GP05	Project Manager	20 - 30	Female
PMO01	Project Manager Officer	20 - 30	Male
PMO02	Project Manager Officer	20 - 30	Female
PMO03	Project Manager Officer	20 - 30	Female
PMO04	Project Manager Officer	20 - 30	Male
L01	Coordination Team Manager	30 - 40	Male

When asked about the adequacy of the currently used methodology, the general opinion is that it is in fact adequate, but subject to improvement.

The main problems pointed out are cantered on the lack of compliance in the preparation of project documentation and on the lack of harmonization and practicality in the information storage processes.

Respondents also identified several aspects whose improvement would benefit the development of their projects, namely:

- Reducing bureaucracy in general.
- Increase of knowledge sharing sessions between teams.
- Creating new tools that are easier to use.
- Increased level of contact between the various project managers.
- Greater promotion of collaborative work.
- Awareness of filling in the data associated with each project.
- Simplification and harmonization of information sources.
- Simplification of project documentation to avoid duplication of work.
- Simplification of reports for better understanding.

CONCLUSION

This study was aimed to investigate the way knowledge was shared in a project environment and how it is observed from the perspective of individuals belonging to project teams. The results obtained reveal that knowledge sharing is considered important, both by project management managers and professionals, and at the organizational level, identified in the existence of knowledge management practices and tools, and incorporated into the methodologies adopted by the team's project management.

The study concludes that, despite the lack of incentives on the part of top management, project managers and other members belonging to project teams, considered knowledge sharing as a relevant contribution to a more successful execution of projects.

It was also concluded that, given the disparity of projects, in type and dimension, knowledge sharing practices are not yet standardized in the organization's project management methodologies. Aspects related to the simplification and harmonization of documentation and information sources should be improved to enhance the dissemination of knowledge and benefit the end results of the projects.

Also, most respondents seemed to be aware that it would be important to define more explicit methods and practices for obtaining, storing and sharing knowledge.

LIMITATIONS AND FUTURE WORK

The small sample size makes the study reflect only the specific reality of the studied project team, within the specific organizational context.

For future research, it would be of interest to analyze how geographically distant project teams deal with knowledge sharing. Additionally, how organizational cultures and subcultures impact the sharing of knowledge in different project teams within an organization, since the culture under which projects operate has a significant impact on knowledge sharing between projects. Finally, having carried out the study on knowledge sharing, it would be of interest to study the use of knowledge in the project environment, and to analyze the benefits observed by the project managers.

REFERENCES

Abbas, J., Hussain, I., Hussain, S., Akram, S., Shaheen, I., & Niu, B. (2019). The Impact of Knowledge Sharing and Innovation on Sustainable Performance in Islamic Banks: A Mediation Analysis through a SEM Approach. *Sustainability*, *11*(4049), 4049. Advance online publication. doi:10.3390u11154049

Ahmad, N., Lodhi, M. S., Zaman, K., & Naseem, I. (2017). Knowledge management: A gateway for organizational performance. *Journal of the Knowledge Economy*, *8*(3), 859–876. doi:10.100713132-015-0282-3

Ajmal, M. M., Helo, P., & Kekale, T. (2010). Critical factors for knowledge management in project business. *Journal of Knowledge Management*, *14*(1), 156–168. doi:10.1108/13673271011015633

Akhavan, P., & Mahdi Hosseini, S. (2016). Social capital, knowledge sharing, and innovation capability, an empirical study of R&D teams in Iran. *Technology Analysis and Strategic Management*, *28*(1), 96–113. doi:10.1080/09537325.2015.1072622

Al Ahbabi, S. A., Singh, S. K., Balasubramanian, S., & Gaur, S. S. (2019). Employee perception of impact of knowledge management processes on public sector performance. *Journal of Knowledge Management*, *23*(2), 351–373. doi:10.1108/JKM-08-2017-0348

Alavi, M., & Denford, J. S. (2011). Knowledge Management: Process, Practice and Web 2.0. In M. Easterby-Smith & M. A. Lyles (Eds.), Handbook of Organizational Learning & Knowledge Management (2nd ed., pp. 105–124). Academic Press.

Andreeva, T., & Kianto, A. (2011). Knowledge processes, knowledge-intensity and innovation: A moderated mediation analysis. *Journal of Knowledge Management*, *15*(6), 1016–1034. doi:10.1108/13673271111179343

Bassi, A. (2014). Human and Organizational Knowledge in a Project Management Context. *Modern Management Review*, *19*(21), 7–19. doi:10.7862/rz.2014.mmr.29

Becerra-Fernandez, I., Gonzalez, A., & Sabherwal, R. (2004). *Knowledge management challenges, solutions, and technologies*. Pearson Prentice Hall.

Bolisani, E., Debei, S., & Savino, N. (2017). Renovating Project Management: Knowledge Personalization and Sharing. In M. Handzic & A. Bassi (Eds.), *Knowledge and Project Management: A Shared Approach to Improve Performance* (Vol. 5, pp. 131–153). doi:10.1007/978-3-319-51067-5_6

Bryde, D. J., Unterhitzenberger, C., Renzl, B., & Rost, M. (2018). KM and Project Management. In J. Syed, P. A. Murray, D. Hislop, & Y. Mouzughi (Eds.), *The Palgrave Handbook of Knowledge Management* (pp. 539–561). Palgrave Handbooks. doi:10.1007/978-3-319-71434-9_22

Buvik, M. P., & Tvedt, S. D. (2017). The Influence of Project Commitment and Team Commitment on the Relationship Between Trust and Knowledge Sharing in Project Teams. *Project Management Journal*, *48*(2), 5–21. doi:10.1177/875697281704800202

Cabrera, Á., & Cabrera, E. F. (2002). Knowledge-sharing Dilemmas. *Organization Studies*, *23*(5), 687–710. doi:10.1177/0170840602235001

Castrogiovanni, G., Ribeiro-Soriano, D., Mas-Tur, A., & Roig-Tierno, N. (2016). Where to acquire knowledge: Adapting knowledge management to financial institutions. *Journal of Business Research*, *69*(5), 1812–1816. doi:10.1016/j.jbusres.2015.10.061

Chen, H., Nunes, M. B., Ragsdell, G., & An, X. (2018). Extrinsic and intrinsic motivation for experience grounded tacit knowledge sharing in Chinese software organizations. *Journal of Knowledge Management*, *22*(4), 478–498. doi:10.1108/JKM-03-2017-0101

Chen, S. H., Tao, C. Q., & He, W. (2012). Empirical research on relationship of knowledge integration and innovation ability of IT enterprise. *International Journal of Networking and Virtual Organisations*, *11*(3), 315–328. doi:10.1504/IJNVO.2012.048913

Ciulli, F., & Kolk, A. (2019). Incumbents and business model innovation for the sharing economy: Implications for sustainability. *Journal of Cleaner Production*, *214*, 995–1010. doi:10.1016/j.jclepro.2018.12.295

Collins, C. J., & Smith, K. G. (2006). Knowledge exchange and combination: The role of human resource practices in the performance of high-technology firms. *Academy of Management Journal*, *49*(3), 544–560. doi:10.5465/amj.2006.21794671

Costa, V., & Monteiro, S. (2016). Key knowledge management processes for innovation: A systematic literature review. *VINE Journal of Information and Knowledge Management Systems*, *46*(3), 386–410. doi:10.1108/VJIKMS-02-2015-0017

Curado, C., & Bontis, N. (2006). The knowledge-based view of the firm and its theoretical precursor. *International Journal of Learning and Intellectual Capital*, *3*(4), 367–381. doi:10.1504/IJLIC.2006.011747

Davenport, T. H., De Long, D. W., & Beers, M. C. (1998). Successful Knowledge Management Projects. *Sloan Management Review*, 43–57.

De Long, D. W., & Fahey, L. (2000). Diagnosing cultural barriers to knowledge management. *Academy of Knowledge Executive*, *14*(4), 113–127.

Desouza, K. C., & Evaristo, J. R. (2004). Managing knowledge in distributed projects. *Communications of the ACM*, *47*(4), 87–91. doi:10.1145/975817.975823

Ekambaram, A., Sørensen, A. Ø., Bull-Berg, H., & Olsson, N. O. (2018). The role of big data and knowledge management in improving project-based organizations. *Procedia Computer Science, 138,* 851–858. doi:10.1016/j.procs.2018.10.111

Fang, S. C., Yang, C. W., & Hsu, W. Y. (2013). Inter-organizational knowledge transfer: The perspective of knowledge governance. *Journal of Knowledge Management, 17*(6), 943–957. doi:10.1108/JKM-04-2013-0138

Fernie, S., Green, S. D., Weller, S. J., & Newcombe, R. (2003). Knowledge sharing: Context, confusion and controversy. *International Journal of Project Management, 21*(3), 177–187. doi:10.1016/S0263-7863(02)00092-3

Fields, Z. (Ed.). (2017). *Collective Creativity for Responsible and Sustainable Business Practice.* IGI Global. doi:10.4018/978-1-5225-1823-5

Frey, P., Lindner, F., Muller, A., & Wald, A. (2009). Project Knowledge Management Organizational Design and Success Factors - An Empirical Study in Germany. *Proceedings of 42nd Hawaii International Conference on System Sciences,* 1-14.

Gao, T., Chai, Y., & Liu, Y. (2018). A review of knowledge management about theoretical conception and designing approaches. *International Journal of Crowd Sciences, 2*(1), 42–51. doi:10.1108/IJCS-08-2017-0023

Gasik, S. (2011). A Model of Project Knowledge Management. *Project Management Journal, 42*(3), 23–44. doi:10.1002/pmj.20239

Greiner, M., Böhmann, T., & Krcmar, H. (2007). A strategy for knowledge management. *Journal of Knowledge Management, 11*(6), 3–15. doi:10.1108/13673270710832127

Gürlek, M., & Çemberci, M. (2020). Understanding the relationships among knowledge-oriented leadership, knowledge management capacity, innovation performance and organizational performance: A serial mediation analysis. *Kybernetes, 49*(11), 2819–2846. doi:10.1108/K-09-2019-0632

Hanisch, B., Lindner, F., Mueller, A., & Wald, A. (2009). Knowledge management in project environments. *Journal of Knowledge Management, 13*(4), 148–160. doi:10.1108/13673270910971897

Hans, P. E., & Skiver, J. (2007). Organizational Culture Restraining In-House Knowledge Transfer Between Project Managers - A Case Study. *Project Management Journal, 38*(1), 110–122. doi:10.1177/875697280703800111

Hansen, M. T., Nohria, N., & Tierney, T. (1999). What's Your Strategy for Managing Knowledge? *Harvard Business Review,* 1–11. PMID:10387767

Heisig, P. (2009). Harmonisation of knowledge management – comparing 160 KM frameworks around the globe. *Journal of Knowledge Management, 13*(4), 4–31. doi:10.1108/13673270910971798

Holzman, V. (2013). A meta-analysis of brokering knowledge in project management. *International Journal of Project Management, 31*(1), 2–13. doi:10.1016/j.ijproman.2012.05.002

Hooff, B. V. D., & De Ridder, J. A. (2004). Knowledge sharing in context: The influence of organizational commitment, communication climate and CMC use on knowledge sharing. *Journal of Knowledge Management, 8*(6), 117–130. doi:10.1108/13673270410567675

Hoorn, B., & Whitty, S. J. (2019). The five modes of comportment for project managing: Disclosing the tacit in project work. *International Journal of Project Management, 37*(3), 363–377. doi:10.1016/j.ijproman.2019.01.009

Inkinen, H. (2016). Review of empirical research on knowledge management practices and firm performance. *Journal of Knowledge Management, 20*(2), 230–257. doi:10.1108/JKM-09-2015-0336

Kasvi, J. J., Vartiainen, M., & Hailikari, M. (2003). Managing knowledge and knowledge competences in projects and project organisations. *International Journal of Project Management, 21*(8), 571–582. doi:10.1016/S0263-7863(02)00057-1

Kishore, J. K., Sandhu, M. S., & Wai Ling, C. (2009). Knowledge sharing in an American multinational company based in Malaysia. *Journal of Workplace Learning, 21*(2), 125–142. doi:10.1108/13665620910934825

Koskinen, K. U. (2004). Knowledge Management to Improve Project Communication and Implementation. *Project Management Journal, 35*(1), 13–19. doi:10.1177/875697280403500203

Koskinen, K. U., & Pihlanto, P. (2008). Knowledge Sharing and Methods of Knowledge Sharing. In K. U. Koskinen & P. Pihlanto (Eds.), *Knowledge Management in Project-Based Companies: An Organic Perspective* (pp. 80–157). Palgrave Macmillan. doi:10.1057/9780230595071_6

Koskinen, K. U., Pihlanto, P., & Vanharanta, H. (2003). Tacit knowledge acquisition and sharing in a project work context. *International Journal of Project Management, 21*(4), 281–290. doi:10.1016/S0263-7863(02)00030-3

Lai, Y. L., Hsu, M. S., Lin, F. J., Chen, Y. M., & Lin, Y. H. (2014). The effects of industry cluster knowledge management on innovation performance. *Journal of Business Research, 67*(5), 734–739. doi:10.1016/j.jbusres.2013.11.036

Leseure, M. J., & Brookes, N. J. (2004). Knowledge management benchmarks for project management. *Journal of Knowledge Management, 8*(1), 103–116. doi:10.1108/13673270410523943

Liebowitz, J., & Megbolugbe, I. (2003). A set of frameworks to aid the project manager in conceptualizing and implementing knowledge management initiatives. *International Journal of Project Management, 21*(3), 189–198. doi:10.1016/S0263-7863(02)00093-5

Love, P., Fong, P., & Irani, Z. (2005). *Management of knowledge in project environments*. Elsevier.

Mahdi, O. R., Nassa, I. A., & Almsafir, M. K. (2019). Knowledge management processes and sustainable competitive advantage: An empirical examination in private universities. *Journal of Business Research, 94*, 320–334. doi:10.1016/j.jbusres.2018.02.013

Mannan, B., Jameel, S. S., & Haleem, A. (2013). *Knowledge Management in Project Management: An ISM Approach*. Lambert Academic Publishing.

Mazur, M., Spahić, A., Grabar, D., Grd, P., Sedlbauer, G., Sikorska, K., & Beamonte, E. P. (2014). Knowledge Management 2.0 - Handbook for companies. Lifelong Learning Programme, European Commission.

McElroy, M. W. (2000). Integrating complexity theory, knowledge management and organisational learning. *Journal of Knowledge Management, 4*(3), 195–203. doi:10.1108/13673270010377652

Merat, A., & Bo, D. (2013). Strategic analysis of knowledge firms: The links between knowledge management and leadership. *Journal of Knowledge Management, 17*(1), 3–15. doi:10.1108/13673271311300697

Morris, P. (2002). Science, objective knowledge and the theory of project management. *Proceedings of the Institution of Civil Engineers. Civil Engineering, 150*(2), 82–90. doi:10.1680/cien.2002.150.2.82

Mueller, J. (2012). Knowledge sharing between project teams and its cultural antecedents. *Journal of Knowledge Management, 16*(3), 435–447. doi:10.1108/13673271211238751

Mueller, J. (2015). Formal and Informal Practices of Knowledge Sharing Between Project Teams and Enacted Cultural Characteristics. *Project Management Journal, 46*(1), 53–68. doi:10.1002/pmj.21471

Nesheim, T., & Hunskaar, H. M. (2015). When employees and external consultants work together on projects: Challenges of knowledge sharing. *International Journal of Project Management, 33*(7), 1417–1424. doi:10.1016/j.ijproman.2015.06.010

Nonaka, I. (1994). A Dynamic Theory of Organizational Knowledge Creation. *Organization Science, 5*(1), 14–37. doi:10.1287/orsc.5.1.14

Nonaka, I., & Konno, N. (1998). The Concept of "Ba": Building a Foundation for Knowledge Creation. *California Management Review, 40*(3), 40–54. doi:10.2307/41165942

Nonaka, I., & Takeuchi, H. (1995). *The Knowledge-creating Company – How Japanese Companies Create the Dynamics of Innovation*. Oxford University Press.

Owen, J., & Burstein, F. (2005). Where Knowledge Management Resides within Project Management. In *Case Studies in Knowledge Management*. doi:10.4018/978-1-59140-351-7.ch009

Pascoe, C., & More, E. (2005). Communication Climate and Organizational Knowledge Sharing. *Journal of Information and Knowledge Management, 4*(04), 247–255. doi:10.1142/S0219649205001225

PMI. (2017). A Guide to the Project Management Body of Knowledge (PMBOK) (6th ed.). Project Management Institute, Inc.

Polyaninova, T. (2011). Knowledge Management in a Project Environment: Organisational CT and Project Influences. *VINE Journal of Information and Knowledge Management Systems, 41*(3).

Pretorius, C. J., & Steyn, H. (2005). Knowledge management in project environments. *South African Journal of Business Management, 36*(3), 41–50. doi:10.4102ajbm.v36i3.634

Rashed, M. (2016). The Readiness of Banks in Knowledge Management: A Study of Three Private Commercial Banks in Bangladesh. *Journal of Business and Financial Affairs, 5*(2), 1–5.

Reich, B. H., Gemino, A., & Sauer, C. (2008). Modeling the knowledge perspective in IT projects. *Project Management Journal, 39*(1_suppl), S4–S14. doi:10.1002/pmj.20056

Romani, M. (2017). Lessons Learnt Support System. In M. Handzic & A. Bassi (Eds.), *Knowledge and Project Management: A Shared Approach to Improve Performance* (Vol. 5, pp. 95–129). doi:10.1007/978-3-319-51067-5_5

Ruuska, I., & Vartiainen, M. (2005). Characteristics of knowledge sharing communities in project organizations. *International Journal of Project Management, 23*(5), 374–379. doi:10.1016/j.ijproman.2005.01.003

Sankarasubramanian, S. (2009). *Knowledge management meets project management.* Paper presented at PMI® Global Congress 2009—Asia Pacific, Kuala Lumpur, Malaysia.

Schindler, M., & Eppler, M. J. (2003). Harversting project knowledge: A review of project learning methods and success factors. *International Journal of Project Management, 21*(3), 219–228. doi:10.1016/S0263-7863(02)00096-0

Shujahat, M., Hussain, S., Javed, S., Thurasamy, R., & Ali, J. (2017). Strategic management model with lens of knowledge management and competitive intelligence: A review approach. *VINE Journal of Information and Knowledge Management Systems, 47*(1), 55–93. doi:10.1108/VJIKMS-06-2016-0035

Singh, S. K., Gupta, S., Busso, D., & Kamboj, S. (2021). Top management knowledge value, knowledge sharing practices, open innovation and organizational performance. *Journal of Business Research, 128*, 788–798. doi:10.1016/j.jbusres.2019.04.040

Soderlund, J. (2010). Knowledge entrainment and project management: The case of large-scale transformation projects. *International Journal of Project Management, 28*(2), 130–141. doi:10.1016/j.ijproman.2009.11.010

Sokhanvar, S., Matthews, J., & Yarlagadda, P. (2014). Importance of Knowledge Management Processes in a Project-based organization: A Case Study of Research Enterprise. *Procedia Engineering, 97*, 1825–1830. doi:10.1016/j.proeng.2014.12.336

Song, M., Bij, H. V. D., & Weggeman, M. (2005). Determinants of the level of knowledge application: A knowledge-based and information-processing perspective. *Journal of Product Innovation Management, 22*(5), 430–444. doi:10.1111/j.1540-5885.2005.00139.x

Taminiau, Y., Smit, W., & Lange, A. D. (2009). Innovation in management consulting firms through informal knowledge sharing. *Journal of Knowledge Management, 13*(1), 42–55. doi:10.1108/13673270910931152

Terzieva, M. (2014). Project Knowledge Management: How organizations learn from experience. *Procedia Technology, 16*, 1086–1095. doi:10.1016/j.protcy.2014.10.123

Todorović, M. L., Petrović, D. Č., Mihić, M. M., Obradović, V. L., & Bushuyev, S. D. (2015). Project success analysis framework: A knowledge-based approach in project management. *International Journal of Project Management, 33*(4), 772–783. doi:10.1016/j.ijproman.2014.10.009

Uğurlu, Ö. Y., & Kizildağ, D. (2013). A Comparative Analysis of Knowledge Management in Banking Sector: An Empirical Research. *European Journal of Business and Management, 5*(16), 12–19.

Wang, W.-T., & Ko, N.-Y. (2012). Knowledge sharing practices of project teams when encountering changes in project scope: A contingency approach. *Journal of Information Science, 38*(5), 423–441. doi:10.1177/0165551512445240

Wickramasinghe, V., & Widyaratne, R. (2012). Effects of interpersonal trust, team leader support, rewards, and knowledge sharing mechanisms on knowledge sharing in project teams. *VINE Journal of Information and Knowledge Management Systems, 42*(2), 214–236.

Yeong, A., & Lim, T. T. (2010). Integrating knowledge management with project management for project success. *Journal of Project, Program & Portfolio Management, 1*(2), 8–19. doi:10.5130/pppm.v1i2.1735

ADDITIONAL READING

Alavi, M., & Leidner, D. (1999). Knowledge management systems: issues, challenges, and benefits. *Communications of the AIS*, *1*(2).

Alavi, M., & Leidner, D. (2001). Review: Knowledge Management and Knowledge Management Systems: Conceptual Foundations and Research Issues. *Management Information Systems Quarterly*, *25*(1), 107. doi:10.2307/3250961

Bontis, N., & Choo, C. W. (2002). *The Strategic Management of Intellectual Capital and Organizational Knowledge*. Oxford University Press.

Davenport, T. H., & Prusak, L. (1998). *Working Knowledge: How Organizations Manage What They Know*. Harvard Business School Press.

Easterby-Smith, M., & Lyles, M. A. (2011). The Evolving Field of Organizational Learning and Knowledge Management. In M. Easterby-Smith & M. A. Lyles (Eds.), Handbook of Organizational Learning & Knowledge Management (2nd ed., pp. 1–20). Academic Press.

Fong, P. S. (2005). Co-creation of knowledge by multidisciplinary project teams. In P. E. Love, P. S. Fong, & Z. Irani (Eds.), *Management of Knowledge in Project Environments* (pp. 41–36). Elsevier Butterworth-Heinemann. doi:10.1016/B978-0-7506-6251-2.50007-9

Gupta, J., & Sharma, S. (2004). *Creating Knowledge Based Organizations*. Idea Group Publishing. doi:10.4018/978-1-59140-162-9

Kogut, B., & Zander, U. (1992). Knowledge of the firm, combinative capabilities, and the replication of technology. *Organization Science*, *3*(3), 383–397. doi:10.1287/orsc.3.3.383

Koskinen, K. U. (2000). Tacit knowledge as a promoter of project success. *European Journal of Purchasing & Supply Management*, *6*(1), 41–47. doi:10.1016/S0969-7012(99)00033-7

Maier, R. (2007). *Knowledge Management Systems: Information and Communication Technologies for Knowledge Management* (3rd ed.). Springer.

Nonaka, I. (1991). The knowledge creating company. *Harvard Business Review*, *69*(6), 96–104.

Nonaka, I., & von Krogh, G. (2009). Tacit Knowledge and Knowledge Conversion: Controversy and Advancement in Organizational Knowledge Creation Theory. *Organization Science*, *20*(3), 635–652. doi:10.1287/orsc.1080.0412

Nonaka, I., von Krogh, G., & Voelpel, S. (2006). Organizational knowledge creation theory: Evolutionary paths and future advances. *Organization Studies*, *27*(8), 1179–1208. doi:10.1177/0170840606066312

Polanyi, M. (1966). *The Tacit Dimension*. Routledge & Kegan Paul.

KEY TERMS AND DEFINITIONS

Explicit Knowledge: Refers to knowledge that is transmissible in a formal and systemic language (Nonaka, 1994; Nonaka & Takeuchi, 1995).

Knowledge: Seen as an intangible asset, which is valuable, distinctive, path-dependent, causally ambiguous and hard to substitute or replicate (Fang et al., 2013, p. 945).

Knowledge Creation: The process in which new knowledge is created through the four sub-processes of organizational knowledge creation (Andreeva & Kianto, 2011).

Knowledge Management: The set of processes related to the creation, sharing and use of knowledge (Ahmad et al., 2017; Shujahat et al., 2017).

Knowledge Sharing: The action of disseminating knowledge among individuals, groups and organizations (Chen et al., 2018).

Knowledge Transfer: The communication of knowledge from a source to a recipient (Alavi & Denford, 2011).

Project Knowledge Management: The application of concepts, tools and techniques to complete a project within the defined time and budget, responding to the client's needs (Romani, 2017).

Section 55
Transport Analytics

Improving Transportation Planning Using Machine Learning

Satish Vadlamani

Kenco Management Services, LLC, USA

Mayank Modashiya

Kenco Management Services, LLC, USA

INTRODUCTION

Companies can no longer rely on lack of dependencies and integrations with suppliers or customers. Companies that are successful are the ones that have a focus on supply chain (Anderson, Britt, & Favre, 2007). Will (2021) published an article in which supply chain is described as follows: "A supply chain is a network between a company and its suppliers to produce and distribute a specific product to the final buyer. This network includes different activities, people, entities, information, and resources. The supply chain also represents the steps it takes to get the product or service from its original state to the customer". Lummus and Vokurka (2001) provide definitions from different article and finally provide a summarized definition of supply chain as; "all the activities involved in delivering a product from raw material through to the customer including sourcing raw materials and parts, manufacturing and assembly, warehousing and inventory tracking, order entry and order management, distribution across all channels, delivery to the customer, and the information systems necessary to monitor all of these activities". Another term supply chain management (SCM) is key in understanding supply chains and their management. The Council of Supply Chain Management Professionals defines SCM as "encompasses the planning and management of all activities involved in sourcing and procurement, conversion, and all logistics management activities. Importantly, it also includes coordination and collaboration with channel partners, which can be suppliers, intermediaries, third party service providers, and customers. In essence, supply chain management integrates supply and demand management within and across".

As per the definition of supply chain, product moving from raw material stage to final customer, is physical movement, but there is information/ data being transferred from systems at every stage of the supply chain. A study by Forrester Research suggests that U.S. manufacturers are benefiting from using information technology (IT) to improve supply chain agility, reduce cycle time, achieve higher efficiency, and deliver products to customers in a timely manner (Radjou, 2003). Wu, Yeniyurt, Kim, & Cavusgil (2006) discuss the importance and competitive advantage IT can create for supply chains. The authors also discuss IT related resources, IT advancement, IT alignment and the role of these in a supply chain or a company. With the use of IT systems to improve efficiencies in the supply chain, comes a very compelling biproduct, i.e., data.

Transportation is a very important part of the supply chain. Because of the globalization of supply chains, the transportation networks must connect more effectively across different regions to meet increase in customers' demands, such as ensuring on-time delivery. The global nature of transportation networks and competition among companies to serve customers better leads to increase in demands of

DOI: 10.4018/978-1-7998-9220-5.ch184

service and faster delivery times with cost efficiency. This adds greater complexity in transportation networks which results in vulnerability.

With massive amounts data being generated in supply chains (Schoenherr & Speier-Pero, 2015) it is very crucial that supply chain management professionals are using predictive analytics to improve supply chain performance and competitive advantage (Waller & Fawcett, 2013a). McAfee and Brynjolfsson (2012) note that use of predictive analytics has a potential for significant above-average returns. Predictive analytics is a quantitative and qualitative approach of using historical data to answer questions of the future. Predictive analytics is a positioned within the domain of data science (Schoenherr & Speier-Pero, 2015). Data Science (DS) is an art of using science to tell a story about the data that allows for better decision making (Van Der Aalst, 2016) and (Provost & Fawcett,).

The importance of supply chain management has encouraged modern researchers to explore predictive analytics techniques to solve complex problems (Dubey et al, 2018), (Seyedan & Mafakheri, 2020) and (Govindan, Cheng, Mishra, & Shukla, 2018). Some of the areas of recent focus are demand forecasting using machine learning (Feizabadi, 2022), predicting supply chain risks using machine learning (Baryannis, Dani, & Antoniou, 2019). There is a need for more researchers to solve traditional supply chain problems like forecasting, planning and risk mitigation with more modern predictive analytics techniques.

The major contributions of this paper are 1) bring forward the complexity of supply chains 2) discuss challenges of transportation planning 3) provide insights into data science techniques 4) solve a real-world transportation planning problem using data science techniques.

BACKGROUND

Because of the complexity and global nature of supply chains, providing visibility of where the product is in the supply chain is necessary for better planning. To increase this visibility, most companies use transportation management systems (TMS) and other tracking software. TMS in general use order information, cost of shipping, etc. to help plan shipments. TMS' also provide visibility into where the shipment is currently. The limitation of TMS and the tracking software is that they can only provide information of what has happened so far and where the shipment is currently, but not what can happen further to the shipment.

There are different techniques employed to help understand how a shipment would potentially move further down the supply chain. One such technique is building simulation models, here are some simulation software OpenTrack (Nash & Huerlimann, 2004) and Railsys (Radtke and Hauptmann, 2004). These simulation software work for intermodal shipments. Researchers have used event graphs (Goverde, 2010), activity graphs (Büker, & Seybold, 2012), and Petri nets (Zegordi & Davarzani, 2012) to predict delays in shipments. Markov chains designs have been used to solve delay predictions as queuing theory models. Some of the challenges of traditional methods are that they cannot account for all the complex relationships in real-world and only a simplified version of the problem can be solved (Balster, Hansen, Hanno, & Ludwig, 2020). Predicting delays in advance helps plan better as there is more visibility into the future. There are not many papers in literature for predicting delays within the transportation area using predictive analytics, but there are a few general delay prediction problems (Yaghini, Khoshraftar, & Seyedabadi, 2013) and (van Riessen, Negenborn, & Dekker, 2016)

Data science techniques have been used in literature for wider variety of transportation problems like smart transportation planning (Karami, & Kashef, 2020), choosing the correct travel mode (Hagenauer, & Helbich, 2017) and a comprehensive survey on the using predictive analytics for international freight transportation management (Barua, Zou, & Zhou, 2020). This article focuses on domestic transportation in the USA and specifically around using data science techniques to help transportation planning more reliable. As far as the authors are aware, there are not many papers in the literature that address this issue. In the following sections, the authors will illustrate the complexity of domestic transportation and the need for using data science vs traditional planning techniques.

FOCUS OF THE ARTICLE

Brief Introduction to Domestic Transportation

Supply chain networks are very critical to ensure essential items like medicines, food etc. are delivered to the everyone across the globe. The vulnerability of supply chain networks was exposed during the COVID-19 pandemic, which was further fueled by the network nature of supply chains, i.e., a disruption in one node in the supply chain can impact other nodes in the network making it a very challenging problem to solve. A node in the supply chain network can be the manufacturing plant, the port, the warehouse/service c enters, or the end consumer. These nodes are connected via multiple paths, called lanes. The products are shipped on these lanes via multiple modes, such as ship, train, truck, air. With many nodes, lanes, and modes makes planning very complex.

With the ever-expanding global nature of supply chain networks and considering the vulnerabilities at the pandemic scale, but also at the local scale like weather, traffic, port, or service center congestions is essential. With the pandemic there was a rise in e-commerce which meant consumers are looking for better service. Speed to ship adds another dimension of complexity to planning a shipment.

With the boom in e-commerce in the USA domestic shipment needs to ensure timely deliveries. Transportation cost contributes the most to the over supply chain cost and in the USA, trucking is the most widely used, because of it reach. There are three major types of trucking Full-Truckload (FTL), Less-Than-Truckload (LTL), and Parcel that are used to ship domestically in the USA. Products are shipped FTL when there is enough volume to fill the truck either by weight or by volume and usually ships cross country. Example of FTL provides in the USA are U.S. Express, J.B. Hunt etc. In the case of LTL there is not enough volume to fill the truck, so the LTL providers pick up smaller volumes or weights from multiple shippers and take them to a service center or a consolidation center where they combine all the LTL volume to create cost effective routes. Here a shipper is a person or entity that is shipping the products to either the receiver or the end customer (a store, or a residential address). In the case of Parcel shipments, these are packages that are not big enough to be shipped LTL. Examples of LTL providers are Old Dominion Freight Line Inc., XPO Logistics etc. Parcel providers usually deliver to end customer at a residential address. Some examples Parcel providers are FedEx, UPS etc.

Another key player in the supply chain networks is the Third-Party Logistics Provider (3PL). The 3PLs help run parts or the entire supply chains for their customers. They are responsible for ensuring that the product is shipped in the most efficient way possible. 3PLs have access to a lot of customers information in the supply chain and they take that into consideration for planning the supply chain for their customers.

As it can be seen with so many players involved in ensuring a shipment is delivered to the customer when needed with most cost-effective way, planning is very important. And with so many parties involved and with external factor like nature, capacity etc. planning becomes more challenging. With lots of data and too many variables to consider, traditional planning by TMS' and manual techniques is not optimal and effective.

With so many nodes, lanes, carriers, and other key players planning coordinating to make sure a shipment arrives to the destination as planned is a challenge. External factors can add additional challenges to the planning of the shipment. For example, to ensure an on-time delivery of shipments, planners need to choose the right carrier, the day to ship, be aware of the weather, holidays, labor shortages, market conditions (supply and demand of trucks) etc. And manually planning for this can be very complex and traditional TMS' or manual planning does not scale.

Brief Introduction to Data Science

DS includes analyzing large amounts of data, statistical analysis, visualizing data to help decision makers. Data scientists use different computer science and linear algebra concepts to help solve complex problems. Machine Learning (ML) or Artificial Intelligence (AI) are few techniques a data scientist uses to predict/prescribe what would be the outcome of the future based on what happened in the past. ML is a programmatic technique where the computers can learn past behaviors to predict the future. ML is a subset of AI, which is a technique where the computer is in the process of using artificial neural networks or statistical models to learn patterns like the human brain. In 2015 AI gained tremendous popularity because of AlphaGo (Silver et al, 2016) an AI program developed by Google. AlphaGo was able to beat the world champion the board game Go. Although AI has gained popularity recently, example self-driving cars, image recognition etc., in 1950, Turing (1950) published an article about intelligent machines and how can they be tested. In 1956 Marvin Minsky and John McCarthy hosted Dartmouth Summer Research Project on Artificial Intelligence (DSRPAI) at Dartmouth College in New Hampshire (McCarthy, Minsky, Rochester, & Shannon, 2006). This workshop is the birth of AI, and the scientist were later considered the founding fathers of AI. It must be noted that DS practitioners usually hold titles such as data scientist, data analyst etc. In this paper, we will use title data scientist to refer to the practitioner of DS.

There are four major categories of problems that can be solved using ML, 1) Supervised Learning; 2) Unsupervised Learning; 3) Semi-Supervised Learning; 4) Reinforcement Learning.

Supervised Learning

Supervised learning a type of machine learning where the algorithm learning from being supervised, i.e., the algorithm is provided with input data and corresponding output data. When solving a supervised learning problem, the algorithm needs to be trained, i.e., feed both input and output to the algorithm to learn the patterns. Then test or validate the performance of the algorithm with a new data which is exactly like the training data but without the desired output. The key is that algorithm should not be exposed to the test or validation data set before or during the training. The process where the algorithm is provided with both input and output to learn is referred to as training. Once the algorithm has been trained, a new data set (test or validation data) is pass through the algorithm to make predictions, this process is called inferencing. The process of training is usually an optimization function that aims minimize the error of prediction vs actual in an iterative process. Once the predefined threshold or iteration limit or algorithm converges to the optima, the algorithm stops and is trained.

There are two categories in supervised learning 1) Regression and 2) Classification:

In regression, the goal of the algorithm is to find a relationship between input and the output using a continuous function. The algorithm tries to understand how the output changes when the input changes. An example of regression is predicting house prices in a city based on factors like size and year of construction (new vs old). Here inputs to the algorithm are two variables size and year of construction and the output is price of the house is dollars. Here the output is a continuous value and hence this problem is categorized as regression.

A classification problem is a type of ML problem where given a set of inputs the algorithm predicts a class or the probability of falling into a category. For classification problem, the training data includes input and output that are categorized into classes. An example could be given the feature set; color, size, shape, taste, the algorithm can classify if it is an orange or an apple.

Unsupervised Learning

Unsupervised learning is a type of machine learning where the algorithms find hidden patterns in the data and do not rely on input and output data set being provided. In the case of unsupervised learning, the training of the algorithm involves only reading the input without any output and predict an output based on relationships in the input. There are two popular unsupervised technique: clustering and association.

Clustering

Clustering algorithms aim at grouping data into two or more groups based on relationship between data points. Generally, clustering methods are mathematical models that identify similarities between data points without any prior information about the expected output. Various algorithms are distance based they use methods such as Euclidean distance to identify similarities in the data points

Association

In association the focus is on identifying a particular or trends in the data that can be used to represent major data patterns or has a significant association rule to connect data patterns. We recommend the readers read about semi-supervised (Zhou, & Belkin, 2014) and reinforcement learning (Buşoniu, Babuška, & De Schutter, 2010) to get a better understanding of the full breadth of ML.

With supply chains generating data large amounts of data (Talwar, Kaur, Fosso., & Dhir, 2021) companies are trying harness the power of data to make decisions. One such problem, that the authors worked on was predicting service failures in the transportation industry using ML. As mentioned earlier high level of service especially due to the boom in e-commerce is very important. And the cost of the transportation is a big contributor to the overall cost of the supply chain which would increase the cost of the product for the end customer. The authors worked with a 3PL and focused on the LTL shipments, to predict service failure (resulted from complexity of planning) and recommend the correct course of action (best days to ship to improve service) using ML. The 3PL the authors worked with used a TMS MercuryGate (https://mercurygate.com/tms-solutions/transportation-management-system/), which did not have any predictive capability like most of the traditional TMS'.

SOLUTIONS AND RECOMMENDATIONS

Any data science project usually follows the following process;

1. Understand the problem
2. Data collection
3. Data and business understanding
4. Feature engineering
5. Feature selection
6. Model training
7. Modeling testing
8. Re-train model until agreed upon satisfactory results based on a predetermined metric is achieved
9. Model deployment, and
10. Getting feedback and starting from step 1, if needed.

Understanding the Problem

It is very important for the data scientist to understand the problem needed to be worked on and quantify the benefit of solving the problem. It is at this step that the metric to optimize is determined and what would be the threshold to accept the results of the algorithm. In this paper, the authors worked with a 3PL's transportation team to understand the problem and determined the metric for evaluating the performance of the algorithm. The problem was defined as: "Predict service failures or predict LTL shipment not making it to the destination at the promised time based on current plan; and recommend the best day to ship to improve service and ensure LTL shipment reaches destination as promised. So that the transportation team can change plans and implement the best plan that improves service." *Accuracy score* was metric to optimize and a threshold to beat was 80%. This threshold is defined based on input from the business users and the data scientist after understanding the complexity of the problem. More details on *accuracy score* is covered later in the paper.

As it can be imagined the LTL providers are trying to always improve their service levels, so the probability of failures is not very high and not a common event. Based on the data the authors analyzed the carriers are 90% reliable to deliver the product on-time and remaining 10% the carriers do not deliver on-time for various reasons, such as picked up late, day of the week (congestion in service centers varies by day of week), origin/destination, weather etc. In a classification problem it is very important that both the binary classes have similar number of the rows to avoid bias towards the majority class. If the one of the classes has more than the other, this is called class imbalance (Amin et al, 2016).

It is important to understand that for classification problems with class imbalance, just looking at *accuracy score* is not enough, and the results of the *confusion matrix* are very important. More details on this in will be provided in the later steps.

Data Collection

In this step, it is important to collect all the data that may seem relevant to the business directly and indirectly. In this paper, the authors worked with the transportation team at the 3PL to collect LTL shipping data from 2016 till 2021 and developed a ML model that could learn from past patterns and current trends to make predictions of failures in service and recommend best course of action. The data consists of variables or features such as, origin, destination, carrier, customer name, distance, current location of the product, date of shipment, weather, seasons etc.

Data and Business Understanding

The key to be a good data scientist is to have good understanding of the data and business understanding or more commonly known as domain knowledge. It is widely accepted that 80% of data scientist's time is spent cleaning the data plugging gaps in the data. Below is an example of plugging gaps in the data; the transit times (time it takes to go from origin to destination) between city A and city Z historically for three shipments were 10 days, 12 days, and 15 days. There is a fourth shipment in the data, but the transit time is missing, one way of plugging the data would be to take an average of previous three shipments, i.e., 12.333 days. Another way could be to use the most recent transit time 15 days in this case. The choice of plugging in the data could come from business understanding. In this example, maybe using 15 days would more accurate, because of the recent changes made to that lane that now needs more time to ship. In this paper, the authors who are experts in the transportation and supply chain domain discussed the data with the transportation team before data cleaning or model development.

Feature Engineering and Feature Selection

As a data scientist it is important to extract information from the data, that would not be easily visible to everyone. The data scientist must try to mine for more information and create new variables based on the data. The process of creating new variables or features that is relevant to the problem from the data is called feature engineering. An example of feature engineering could be extracting information from the date of shipping. From that one column date of shipping, we can extract the month, day of the week (Monday – Sunday), day of year (1-365), week number (1-52) etc. In this paper the authors used Pandas' *DatetimeIndex* Python package (https://pandas.pydata.org/docs/reference/api/pandas.DatetimeIndex.html) to extract the columns. For example, to get the day of the week from a date column we could use *shipdate.dt.dayofweek,* where *shipdate* is the date when a an order was shipped. Once we have engineered the data features, we must select the features that will help improve the results. Here are some techniques; correlation, statistics methods, an example could be chi-squared test, feature importance scores (https://scikit-learn.org/stable/auto_examples/ensemble/plot_forest_importances.html), and dimensionality reduction, an example of dimensionality reduction could be principal component analysis (PCA). The authors encourage the readers to read more on these topics. Another technique to ensure good model performance as a part of feature engineering would is using standardization transformation (Eq. 1) and/ or normalization transformation (Eq. 2).

$$X' = \frac{X_{actual} - \mu}{\sigma}, \tag{1}$$

$$X' = \frac{X_{actual} - X_{min}}{X_{max} - X_{min}}, \tag{2}$$

Where X' is output after transformation. X_{actual} is actual data, μ is the mean of the column, σ is the standard deviation of the column. Xmi_{n_i}s the minimum value in the column and Xma_{x_i}s the maximum value in the column. The authors finally created a data set of 110 features and about one million rows of data after cleaning, feature engineering and feature selection.

Model Training

As noted in the previous section, in supervised learning the model needs to be fed with historical input and corresponding output. It is important for data scientist to formulate the problem correctly (is it a regression, classification etc.) to solve for the problem statement. The authors in this paper treated this as a binary (0 or 1) classification problem. In this paper, the authors used the features available to predict the target; if a shipment will be on-time (1) or not (0) and provide the probability of being on-time. The authors also recommend the best day to ship to increase the probability of being on-time (1).

The problem with class imbalance is that if the algorithm is trained, the algorithm will learn to predict the majority class as there were mostly rows from that class. The algorithm would do poor job in predicting the minority class. To solve the problem of class imbalance there are few techniques (Longadge & Dongre, 2013) such as over-sampling (duplicate few rows from the minority class at random) the minority class, under-sampling (remove rows from the majority class at random) and Synthetic Minority Oversampling Technique (SMOTE). The authors used SMOTE to remove class imbalance and then trained the model with the new data.

Model training step and the model testing and re-training happen simultaneously although it is shown here as two different steps. Typically, the models are trained, tested, evaluated and re-trained (if needed) together. The authors used Python 3.6, Scikit-learn (Pedregosa et. Al, 2011), and used Amazon Sage-Maker for development of the model. To train a model in Python and Scikit-learn a simple way would be to first instantiate the algorithm to use and then using the *fit()* method or function. For example:

clf = SVC()

clf.fit(X, y)

Where *SVC()* is an algorithm called *support vector classifier*, *clf* is the object that is assigned the *SVC()* object. *X* is the input and *y* is the target variable or the value we want to predict. By fitting the algorithm to the data both input *X* and target *y* we create a model that can "learn" patterns or relations between the input and the output.

Model Testing and Re-training

After we have trained the models, we use the *predict ()* method to predict what the future values will be for a given new data set that is statistically similar to the training data, but not the exact same data. For example, *clf.predict(X_test)*, where *X_test* is the data, we want to make predictions on. Notice, there is no *y* term in the *predict()* because the aim is to predict *y* given an *X*. During the model testing step, usually multiple algorithms are trained and tested to meet the desired output. The metric and threshold that are predetermined are used to evaluate the performance of testing. When working on a classification problem, domain expertise would be very important to evaluate the model, just using a metric is not completely useful for the business user. Here is where the *confusion matrix* will help; a *confusion matrix* contains four quadrants *True Positive (TP): predicting on-time, when the shipment is on-time; True Negative (TN): predicting late, when the shipment is late; False Negative (FN): predicting shipment will be late, when it is on-time, and False Positive (FP: predicting the shipment will be on-time, when it is late.* As it can be seen the first three values (TP, TN, and FN) are proactive measures and do not impact the business even if the prediction was wrong. But, having a high FP can have a huge financial impact on the business, because if the model predicts on-time and the plan is executed, if the shipment is delayed, will lead to failure in service and a penalty must be paid. *Accuracy score* is calculated as shown in Eq. 3.

$$accuracy\ score = \frac{T_P + T_N}{T_P + T_N + F_P + F_N},$$

(3)

Accuracy score is the number of correct predictions by the total number of predictions. In this paper, the authors experimented with various algorithms, with aim to meet the threshold *accuracy score* of greater than 80%, but also improve the *precision. Precision* is defined as the number of shipments predicted to be on-time by the total number of on-time predictions $\frac{T_P}{T_P + F_P}$. Re-training is when data scientist is not satisfied with the results and goes back to experiment again with the feature engineering or feature selection or changing the algorithm or changing the parameters of the algorithm, until satisfactory results are achieved. In this paper, the authors used XGBoost (Chen & Guestrin, 2016) to predict if a given shipment will be on-time or not and then recommend the best day to ship to improve the reliability of being on-time. XGBoost is a tree-based algorithm. The simplest of the tree-based algorithms is a decision tree with parent and child nodes leading to a final decision. The authors were able to predict service failures with an 85% *accuracy score*.

Model Deployment and Feedback Loop

Model deployment is to take the model developed in the previous steps and move it to environment/ system/ server where the predictions can run at a desired time. The model once deployed should not typically be changed until there is a drop in the accuracy or drop in the metric below the predefined threshold. Model can be generally deployed to perform two things: batch prediction or real-time prediction. In batch prediction, the model runs and makes predictions to a batch of rows at once. In real-time predictions, the model runs on demand or whenever it is called or triggered to run via an Application Programming Interface (API). Model deployment is typically a function of the IT team or MLOPS (Machine Learning OPS) teams. MLOPS like the traditional DevOPS teams that maintained software once in production, maintains the ML models in production.

Once the model is deployed it is very important to get feedback from the end user and put checks and balances in place to ensure that the model is performing as desired and if the metric drops below the predefined threshold there are alerts sent to the data scientist. There are many reasons the model's performance can change after the model has been moved to production, such as, the business has changed, COVID-19 pandemic etc. which then reflects in the data, which in turn leads to models training not being totally effective. Generally, retraining the model with the changes in the data can improve the performance. If that does not work the data scientist would have to start from step one to ensure a good model.

In this paper, the authors deployed the model on Amazon Web Services (AWS) EC2 instance. An EC2 instance can be thought of as a computer or server on the cloud. The authors are using batch predictions based on the business needs and have alert mechanisms in place to catch any errors or dip in model performance. The authors worked with the business intelligence team to develop dashboards that visualize the results of the predictions.

FUTURE RESEARCH DIRECTIONS

This paper focuses on using ML to help transportation planning and prevent service failures. That means even before a shipment is ready to be shipped and planners are trying to ensure that the product reaches its destination on-time, this ML model would provide decision support. For future research there is a need to use ML to predict shipment delays while the shipment is in transit. That means while the shipment is travelling from origin to destination, use ML to dynamically predict if the shipment will make it on-time. Some of the factors to consider would be real-time traffic, weather, and real-time congestion at the service center. Each party in the supply chain is focusing on optimizing their network, a model that can optimize globally across all parties would be an area of further research.

Another thing to consider for future research would be to be able to dynamically re-route shipments to find the best route. There is a need for further research on how ML or data science techniques can replace or compliment operations research methods, specifically for route-optimization using real-time data.

CONCLUSION

This paper discusses the use of data science in the supply chain industry with a focus on domestic LTL transportation planning and predict service failures to allow for corrective actions. Because supply chains are so critical to our day-to-day life and with any disruption to it can cause severe shortages of essential items, improving planning under uncertainty is very important. With many variables such as weather, origin, destination, carrier etc. having an impact on whether a shipment will make it on-time, it is not easy for humans to plan accurately. Hence the use of advanced techniques like ML can help improve the planning thereby ensuring consumers have the essential products when needed.

The paper also goes into the details of various steps from start to finish of using data science from the domestic LTL transportation planning perspective. Provides interested researchers to dig deeper into using ML to solve some of the classical transportation problems. Because this paper is a real-world example of using data science, young professionals and researchers alike can benefit from understanding how the supply chain industry can leverage advanced techniques to improve efficiency and better service.

The paper also highlights the need for having domain expertise and involving the business users through the process of development of the data science projects. Success of data science at any organization will depend on the collaboration from multiple teams within the company.

REFERENCES

Amin, A., Anwar, S., Adnan, A., Nawaz, M., Howard, N., Qadir, J., Hawalah, A., & Hussain, A. (2016). Comparing oversampling techniques to handle the class imbalance problem: A customer churn prediction case study. *IEEE Access: Practical Innovations, Open Solutions, 4*, 7940–7957. doi:10.1109/ACCESS.2016.2619719

Anderson, D. L., Britt, F. F., & Favre, D. J. (2007). The 7 principles of supply chain management. *Supply Chain Management Review, 11*(3), 41–46.

Anonymous. (2021, September 20). *CSCMP Supply Chain Management Definitions and Glossary.* https://cscmp.org/CSCMP/Educate/SCM_Definitions_and_Glossary_of_Terms.aspx

Balster, A., Hansen, O., Hanno, F., & Ludwig, A. (2020). An eta prediction model for intermodal transport networks based on machine learning. *Business & Information Systems Engineering*, *62*(5), 403–416. doi:10.100712599-020-00653-0

Barua, L., Zou, B., & Zhou, Y. (2020). Machine learning for international freight transportation management: A comprehensive review. *Research in Transportation Business & Management*, *34*, 100453. doi:10.1016/j.rtbm.2020.100453

Baryannis, G., Dani, S., & Antoniou, G. (2019). Predicting supply chain risks using machine learning: The trade-off between performance and interpretability. *Future Generation Computer Systems*, *101*, 993–1004. doi:10.1016/j.future.2019.07.059

Beth, S., Burt, D. N., Copacino, W., Gopal, C., Lee, H. L., Lynch, R. P., & Morris, S. (2003). Supply chain challenges. building relationships. *Harvard Business Review*, *81*(7), 64–73. PMID:12858712

Büker, T., & Seybold, B. (2012). Stochastic modelling of delay propagation in large networks. *Journal of Rail Transport Planning & Management*, *2*(1-2), 34–50. doi:10.1016/j.jrtpm.2012.10.001

Buşoniu, L., Babuška, R., & De Schutter, B. (2010). Multi-agent reinforcement learning: An overview. *Innovations in Multi-Agent Systems and Applications, 1*, 183-221.

Chen, I. J., & Paulraj, A. (2004). Understanding supply chain management: Critical research and a theoretical framework. *International Journal of Production Research*, *42*(1), 131–163. doi:10.1080/00 207540310001602865

Chen, T., & Guestrin, C. (2016, August). Xgboost: A scalable tree boosting system. In *Proceedings of the 22nd acm sigkdd international conference on knowledge discovery and data mining* (pp. 785-794). 10.1145/2939672.2939785

Dubey, R., Luo, Z., Gunasekaran, A., Akter, S., Hazen, B. T., & Douglas, M. A. (2018). Big data and predictive analytics in humanitarian supply chains: Enabling visibility and coordination in the presence of swift trust. *International Journal of Logistics Management*, *29*(2), 485–512. doi:10.1108/IJLM-02-2017-0039

Feizabadi, J. (2022). Machine learning demand forecasting and supply chain performance. *International Journal of Logistics Research and Applications*, *25*(2), 119–142. doi:10.1080/13675567.2020.1803246

Goverde, R. M. (2010). A delay propagation algorithm for large-scale railway traffic networks. *Transportation Research Part C, Emerging Technologies*, *18*(3), 269–287. doi:10.1016/j.trc.2010.01.002

Govindan, K., Cheng, T. E., Mishra, N., & Shukla, N. (2018). Big data analytics and application for logistics and supply chain management. *Transportation Research Part E, Logistics and Transportation Review*, *114*, 343–349. doi:10.1016/j.tre.2018.03.011

Haenlein, M., & Kaplan, A. (2019). A brief history of artificial intelligence: On the past, present, and future of artificial intelligence. *California Management Review*, *61*(4), 5–14. doi:10.1177/0008125619864925

Hagenauer, J., & Helbich, M. (2017). A comparative study of machine learning classifiers for modeling travel mode choice. *Expert Systems with Applications*, *78*, 273–282. doi:10.1016/j.eswa.2017.01.057

Karami, Z., & Kashef, R. (2020). Smart transportation planning: Data, models, and algorithms. *Transportation Engineering*, *2*, 100013. doi:10.1016/j.treng.2020.100013

Longadge, R., & Dongre, S. (2013). *Class imbalance problem in data mining review.* arXiv preprint arXiv:1305.1707.

Lummus, R. R., Krumwiede, D. W., & Vokurka, R. J. (2001). The relationship of logistics to supply chain management: Developing a common industry definition. *Industrial Management & Data Systems*, *101*(8), 426–432. doi:10.1108/02635570110406730

McAfee, A., & Brynjolfsson, E. (2012). Big Data. The management revolution. *Harvard Business Review*, *90*(10), 61–68. PMID:23074865

McCarthy, J., Minsky, M. L., Rochester, N., & Shannon, C. E. (2006). A proposal for the dartmouth summer research project on artificial intelligence, august 31, 1955. *AI Magazine*, *27*(4), 12–12.

Nash, A., & Huerlimann, D. (2004). Railroad simulation using OpenTrack. *WIT Transactions on the Built Environment*, 74.

Pedregosa, F., Varoquaux, G., Gramfort, A., Michel, V., Thirion, B., Grisel, O., ... Duchesnay, E. (2011). Scikit-learn: Machine learning in Python. *Journal of Machine Learning Research, 12*, 2825-2830.

Provost, F., & Fawcett, T. (2013). Data science and its relationship to big data and data-driven decision making. *Big Data, 1*(1), 51–59. doi:10.1089/big.2013.1508 PMID:27447038

Radjou, N. (2003). US manufacturers' supply chain mandate. *World Trade, 16*(12), 42–46.

Radtke, A., & Hauptmann, D. (2004). Automated planning of timetables in large railway networks using a microscopic data basis and railway simulation techniques. *WIT Transactions on the Built Environment*, 74.

Schoenherr, T., & Speier-Pero, C. (2015). Data science, predictive analytics, and big data in supply chain management: Current state and future potential. *Journal of Business Logistics, 36*(1), 120–132. doi:10.1111/jbl.12082

Seyedan, M., & Mafakheri, F. (2020). Predictive big data analytics for supply chain demand forecasting: Methods, applications, and research opportunities. *Journal of Big Data, 7*(1), 1–22. doi:10.118640537-020-00329-2

Silver, D., Huang, A., Maddison, C. J., Guez, A., Sifre, L., Van Den Driessche, G., ... Hassabis, D. (2016). Mastering the game of Go with deep neural networks and tree search. *Nature, 529*(7587), 484-489.

Talwar, S., Kaur, P., Fosso Wamba, S., & Dhir, A. (2021). Big Data in operations and supply chain management: A systematic literature review and future research agenda. *International Journal of Production Research, 59*(11), 3509–3534. doi:10.1080/00207543.2020.1868599

Turing, A. M. (1950). Computing machinery and intelligence. *Mind, LIX*(236), 433–460. doi:10.1093/mind/LIX.236.433

Van Der Aalst, W. (2016). Data science in action. In *Process mining* (pp. 3–23). Springer. doi:10.1007/978-3-662-49851-4_1

van Riessen, B., Negenborn, R. R., & Dekker, R. (2016). Real-time container transport planning with decision trees based on offline obtained optimal solutions. *Decision Support Systems, 89*, 1–16. doi:10.1016/j.dss.2016.06.004

Waller, M. A., & Fawcett, S. E. (2013). Data Science, Predictive Analytics, and Big Data: A Revolution That Will Transform Supply Chain Design and Management. *Journal of Business Logistics, 34*(2), 77–84. doi:10.1111/jbl.12010

WillK. (2021, August 29). *Supply Chain*. https://www.investopedia.com/terms/s/supplychain.asp

Wu, F., Yeniyurt, S., Kim, D., & Cavusgil, S. T. (2006). The impact of information technology on supply chain capabilities and firm performance: A resource-based view. *Industrial Marketing Management, 35*(4), 493–504. doi:10.1016/j.indmarman.2005.05.003

Yaghini, M., Khoshraftar, M. M., & Seyedabadi, M. (2013). Railway passenger train delay prediction via neural network model. *Journal of Advanced Transportation, 47*(3), 355–368. doi:10.1002/atr.193

Zegordi, S. H., & Davarzani, H. (2012). Developing a supply chain disruption analysis model: Application of colored Petri-nets. *Expert Systems with Applications, 39*(2), 2102–2111. doi:10.1016/j.eswa.2011.07.137

Zhou, X., & Belkin, M. (2014). Semi-supervised learning. In *Academic Press Library in Signal Processing* (Vol. 1, pp. 1239–1269). Elsevier.

ADDITIONAL READING

Friedman, J. H. (2017). *The elements of statistical learning: Data mining, inference, and prediction.* Springer Open.

KEY TERMS AND DEFINITIONS

Data Science: Is the art of using to tell a story from the data, involves advanced mathematical and statistical techniques that solve complex problems.

Machine Learning: A computer programming technique that enables computers to learn from historical data and make predictions into the future.

Predictive Analytics: A subset of data science, where the main goal is to predict the future outcomes.

Supply Chain: Link between the manufacturer and the consumer that involves various people, modes, and systems.

Section 56

Unsupervised and Supervised Learning

AUTOMATON:
A Gamification Machine Learning Project

Adam Palmquist

iD https://orcid.org/0000-0003-0943-6022

University of Gothenburg, Sweden

Isak Barbopoulos

iD https://orcid.org/0000-0003-2485-0184

Insert Coin, Sweden

Miralem Helmefalk

School of Business and Economics, Sweden

INTRODUCTION

This chapter aims to highlight opportunities, challenges and future research on an ongoing development project - the AUtonomous TailOred gaMificATiON (AUTOMATON) - at a gamification start-up for gamified machine learning acting in Scandinavia. Gamification refers to using game elements in non-game situations (Deterding et al., 2011) and has been discussed in various domains, such as crowd-sourcing, tourism, computer science, sustainability, software development, health and wellness as well as in business (Helmefalk, 2019). A considerable amount of literature emphasizes these elements being defined as game mechanics (e.g., badge, level, leaderboard, points), supporting various processes while being engaging and motivating (Looyestyn et al., 2017; Reiners & Wood, 2015; Sailer et al., 2017; Wee & Choong, 2019).

During its relatively brief existence, the multifaceted concept of gamification has gained much attention in the last decade in both business and academia (Nacke & Deterding, 2017). Regarding search trends (Figure.1), it has also surpassed its older sibling Serious games, a game designed for purposes other than entertainment such as learning. Ironically, the last decade of gamification hype might be to gamification's detriment. This is because even though several established advisory firms and research institutes (see Burke, 2012; IEEE, 2014) have predicted a promising future for the use of game elements in the non-game context, several of these predictions have failed to actualize.

DOI: 10.4018/978-1-7998-9220-5.ch185

Figure 1. "Gamification" surpassed "Serious Games" in search trends in 2012 (Google Trends, 2021)
(The "Obs!" annotation marks the date of an update in the way search trend data was collected via Google Trends: "An improvement of our (Google) data collection has been applied from 2016-01-01.")

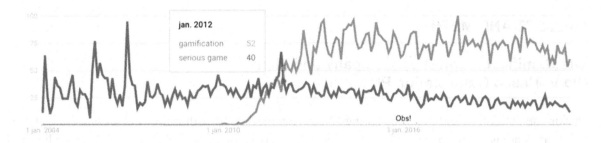

BACKGROUND AND PROBLEM

Gamification researchers have suggested that gamification, probably due to its rapid rise to fame, has largely failed to evolve with the fields that elevated it (Raftopoulos, 2020). Also, even though research on gamification shows promise in several fields (Koivisto & Hamari, 2019), the gamification industry has not yet refined any rigorous and verified standards (Nacke & Deterding, 2017), resulting in an uncertain market in the hands of various gamification consultants – with slim possibilities of developing and validating industry standards due to the many different design approaches (Koivisto & Hamari, 2019). To illustrate, while one industry may apply best practices, standards or solutions that generate promising results, other industries have their own. Consequently, inputs, outputs and data become too eclectic to (dis)confirm the wider efficiency of gamification. Last but not least, gamification scholars and practitioners alike have argued that gamification designs are context-dependent (Palmquist et al., 2021). Transferring a successful design from one context to another can have serious consequences in the gamified situation, affecting the users negatively. A gamified solution that have showed promise in increasing engagement among students in education, may not only be different from other contexts such as health and fitness services, but may also differ from other courses. Needless to say, context is important. This predicament has made gamification demanding in terms of resources such as capital and time; likewise, it makes gamification hard to generalize and scale up effectively. Solving these problems is not a simple matter, but requires long-term methods, designs, systems and technical solutions that aid our understanding how people think, feel and use gamified services.

In a systematic literature review, Khakpour and Colomo-Palacios (2021) investigated the convergence of gamification and machine learning. One of the research questions raised was which aspects of gamification were impacted by developments in the field of machine learning. They highlight various potential implementations, such as user personalisation, as well as adaptation of gamification mechanics during use. Instead of letting users set their preferences at the start of using the system, based on factors which may change as time goes and the users progress, these adaptive processes can offer dynamic and engaging tasks during the whole use. While A.I. and machine learning has gained considerable momentum in Information Technology (IT) and learning, it has as of yet received less attention in the context of gamification. A significant amount of conceptual research has been conducted, showcasing how gamification could *potentially* benefit from utilising A.I.; however, validated and consistent smart gamification products developed for, and deployed in, real-life situations are scarce. To address these issues, this chapter aims *to approach these problems by highlighting opportunities, challenges, and the need for future research in machine learning in gamification, as well as describe an ongoing case study where machine learning techniques are used in a gamified service.*

PROJECT AND METHOD

The Gamification Start-up Company and Their Cloud-Based Gamification Platform

During the autumn of 2020 and the spring of 2021, author 1 and author 2 of the present chapter participated as advisors in a machine learning research and development (RnD) project at a Scandinavian gamification start-up. Due to the apparent lack of published investigations and insights on real-world A.I. projects in the field of gamification, author 1 and 2 decided early in the project that they should ask the studio for consent for monitoring the project and later publicize articles covering the project, which the studio approved. Henceforth author 1 and 2 outlined an explorative information systems design ethnography study (Baskerville & Myers, 2015) and began studying the start-up's existing scale-able gamification platform GWEN, and their novel machine learning project AUTOMATON.

The gamification start-up company running AUTOMATON uses an in-house developed cloud-based interoperable business process-agnostic gamification application programming interface (API)-platform providing gamification as a service (GaaS) by applying a software licensing model in which the gamification API services is licensed on a subscription basis and is centrally cloud-hosted. The platform launched late in 2018 and is continuously developed. The start-ups' goal with the gamification platform is to lower the resource-cost for companies interested in implementing gamification in their information system, quicken the design and development process, accelerate time to market, and lower the decision thresholds from clients and at the same time making gamification more scalable across multiple clients.

The GWEN API may be integrated with various cloud-based software- services or products such as Websites, Smartphone applications or Cloud-platforms, e.g., Learning Management systems or Human Resources. The GWEN API is implemented and connected with or without a user interface depending on the client's need[1].

The event structure of the GWEN API links the present clients' software product with a gamification library through a unique API key. The API-key isolates the clients' individual gamification design logic from the GWEN APIs internal logic. The procedure allows for a non-invasive introduction of game elements and game logic into the clients' software products. Each GWEN API implementation involves one or more setups within the platform's framework through an API key, allowing for the definition of standardised interfaces and design artefacts while at the same time giving each client the ability to adapt and modify their gamification design without affecting other clients' designs (Figure 2).

The platform was designed for scalability providing the gamification designer with a modular-based design interface. At the time of writing the start-ups' gamification platform GWEN serves 4.84 million accounts[2] in several businesses. The core business area of the gamification start-up is the digitalization of the production and manufacturing industry (Industry 4.0), thus gamifying various software services used by Human Resources departments such as Employee Training-, Digital Fitness- and Corporate Sustainability systems.

Figure 2. Gamification platform system architecture

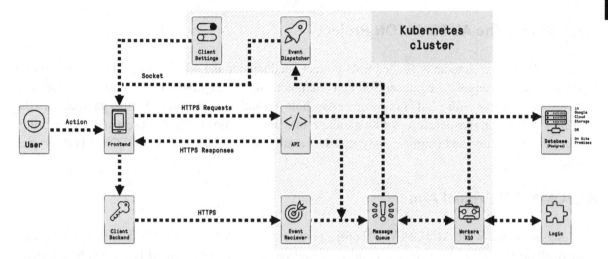

Design Ethnography in Information System

The chosen academic approach in the AUTOMATON project is Design ethnography in information systems (Baskerville & Myers, 2015). The method stands on the shoulders of Design science and Action research (Järvinen, 2007) and makes the researcher a temporary yet formal design team member. Also, like Design science and Action research, Design ethnography is an applied research praxis operating in real-world settings (Dresch et al., 2015). The method blends different stages of design science, action research and ethnography, engaging the researcher in the actual context providing him/her a design functional role in the team. Rather than beginning with a problem formulation (Whyte et al., 1991) or one of the six steps of the design science research methodology (DSRM) (Peffers et al., 2007), the process of Design ethnography starts with the socialisation of the researcher(s) into the development project, learning the practices of the team, grasping the project scope and its stakes (Baskerville & Myers, 2015). The method stresses that the researchers do not initially have to be part of the project; it may be a long-enduring endeavour.

Design ethnography in the information system emphasises the importance of constructing well-defined rules for the dilemmas that might arise from engaging a researcher in practical action. This could be divergences in the roles and goals of researcher and designer or conflicts regarding the ethics of research and the ethics of practice (Baskerville & Myers, 2015). The method advocates data gathering and analysis corresponding to the day-to-day actions designing and developing the intended artefacts. This can include objective observations, artefact analysis, stakeholder analysis, instrumented measurements of artefact performance, benchmarking. By participating, collecting and analysing information needed for the artefact design, the researcher gains insight into the cultural and societal aspects that determine what information designers define as essential for designing a digital artefact.

OPPORTUNITIES AND CHALLENGES WITH AUTOMATION

Case Study: The AUTOMATON Project

AUTOMATON is an internally funded RnD project conducted at the start-up Insert Coin. The project is staffed with one senior AI-engineer/Solution Architect with a background in the automation industry and one data scientist with a PhD in consumer psychology (author 2). The project runs parallel with the start-up's tech-team, five developers with a background in interaction design and software engineering. Also, one gamification and learning analytics advisor are partly included in the AUTOMATON project (author 1).

AUTOMATON Project Aim

The long-term aim of the AUTOMATON project is to create an A.I.-driven procedure that can autonomously identify user segments (stage 1) in any gamification implementation it is applied to, and then evaluate, suggest, apply or adjust gamification modules for each segment in that implementation (stage 2).

The procedure is intended to be used for a wide variety of clients in different industries. Therefore, the autonomous aspect of the project is of critical importance, ensuring that the procedure is scalable as well as time- and cost-effective to implement on new clients and datasets. To this end, it is also important to avoid any steps that may be specific for any client or industry, as it must work the same regardless of the specifics of the dataset.

Automated User Segmentation: Proof of Concept

For the sake of developing a proof of concept for the automation of user segmentation, a dataset was chosen consisting of approximately 1 year's worth of user events from a gamified fitness-app. In this app, users could record different types of physical activities (e.g., cycling, running, weightlifting), enter or check their weight or get a count of burned calories, connect and interact with friends and get achievements as they complete different exercise goals (e.g., based on distance or time). In total, the dataset contained 1,116,126 such events, recorded by 19,576 unique users.

Since the physical activities could either be selected among a list of predefined activities, or entered as free text by the users themselves (e.g., "went for a run"), it was decided that every activity should be treated as text data, in other words, users can besides select pre-set activities also insert and define own and unique physical activities. Therefore, it was necessary to find patterns among all the entries of text. This was done though vectorizing the text entries and using the *term frequency–inverse document frequency* (TF-IDF) statistic, following clustering practices commonly used in natural language processing (e.g., Gowtham et al., 2014). K-means clustering was then used to identify segments of users based on the vectorized events.

A problem that arises when trying to find a standardized and automated procedure for conducting cluster analysis across many datasets is that the analysis itself does not offer a definitive answer on *how many* clusters there actually are in a given dataset (Yu et al., 2014). Answering this question typically involves evaluating and comparing multiple models across a variety of metrics and validation criteria, while sometimes simultaneously varying hyperparameters to see whether the models can be improved further. Furthermore, in order to ensure that the selected cluster model is *useful*, the external validity of the clusters often has to be tested on new data. The fact that this would then have to be repeated every time the segmentation procedure is applied to a new client's service, or whenever a significant change has been made to an existing gamification implementation, means that the project would suffer in terms of scalability and autonomy. Thus, a slightly different approach was developed:

1. Rather than evaluating and making adjustments/refinements iteratively, the procedure was set so that all potentially interesting combinations of data extraction/cleaning methods and hyperparameters (e.g., number of clusters) could be defined as separate models from the start. For the sake of this proof of concept, the only hyperparameter that was varied was the number of clusters, which was set to a minimum of 1 and a maximum of 12, resulting in a total of 12 unique cluster models.
2. Each predefined cluster model was then trained on data from the designated training sample (60% of the total sample).
3. In order to automatically select a single cluster model out of the 12 predefined models, a validation task was constructed:
    a. Sequential Long Short-Term Memory (LSTM) neural networks were trained to analyze a fixed-length sequence of events and predict the event following that sequence. After each prediction, the input sequence was shifted forward one event, so that the previous "target" event was now incorporated into the fixed-length input sequence, and it then predicted the next event following that sequence, until every event associated with the given cluster had been processed. One such model was trained for each unique cluster in each of the 12 cluster models, for a total of 78 sequential models.
    b. After the cluster models and the sequential models had been trained and stored, the training sample was set aside, and the trained cluster models were then used to predict the cluster labels of the users in the test sample (comprising 40% of the total sample). Note that the most recent days worth of events for every user had been excluded from the input data, to be used as a target for the sequential models.
    c. Each sequential model was given the events from the 2nd, 3rd and 4th most recent dates for each user associated with its cluster, and was then tasked with predicting the most likely event to occur on the most recent date (i.e., the target day). A given sequential model would score a hit if it predicted an event that occurred on the target day; otherwise the prediction would count as a miss.
    d. For each cluster model, the total number of hits and the total number of predictions were summed for all the sequential models associated with its clusters, and the models **total** percent of correct predictions was calculated. For instance, a cluster model with three clusters would be associated with three corresponding sequential models. If the sequential models scored 200/300, 300/400 and 400/500 hits respectively, then the total number of hits/predictions for that cluster model would be 900/1200, which would equal a score of 75%.
    e. The cluster model that attained the highest total score compared to all other cluster models was the one selected as the final model.

Automated User Segmentation: Results

The sequential models had to pick one out of a total of 1,446 unique events that could occur, with an average of ~3 events occurring on the same day (although events could be performed multiple times per day, so there might not be ~3 *unique* events per day on average). The most common event happened in ~54% of the marked days. In order to be worthwhile, the sequential models therefore had to attain a score better than 54%, since a "dumb model" can predict the most common event over and over and be correct 54% of the time. Notably, the baseline model - the model in which all users belong to the same cluster (i.e., the same as there being no clusters) - attained a score of 55%, only slightly better than the "dumb model".

As shown in Figure 3, with just two clusters, the prediction score improved by 13.5 percentage points, to 68.5%. As more clusters were added, the score continued to increase until it hit a peak at 76% for the 7-cluster model. Importantly, every model with more than one cluster performed substantially better than the lowest acceptable score of 54%, showing that clustering consistently improves the ability of the sequential models to predict the next event. In other words, seven clusters were optimal for predicting correct events, as more clusters did not show any improvements in efficiency (see Figure 3).

Figure 3. The total percent of correct predictions for each cluster model (with the best performing model identified by the dotted vertical line)

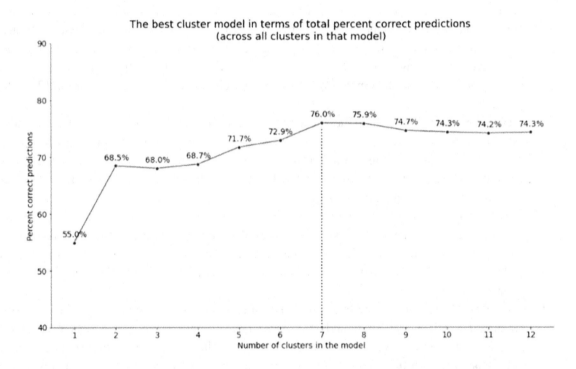

Automated User Segmentation: Conclusion

Overall, the results show that it is feasible to use prediction models to automate the selection of cluster models, thereby ensuring that the project can produce useful user segments in a way that is highly autonomous, and therefore more scalable and less time-consuming to implement across different services/ datasets. There are several additional benefits with this approach compared to traditional clustering procedures:

1.   While inertia is a good way to find a model with distinct and well-defined clusters, well-defined clusters are not necessarily useful in and of themselves. By instead selecting the model associated

with the highest number of correct predictions, it is ensured that the extracted clusters are informative and useful. The selection procedure may therefore also double as a validation procedure.

2. Since models may vary not only in number of extracted clusters, but also in a variety of other hyperparameters, data extraction/cleaning techniques, and may even be based on different clustering techniques altogether, trying to select models based on abstract and contextual metrics such as inertia and silhouette quickly becomes a daunting task that is hard to automate and scale effectively. The predictive success rates of the competing models instead offer a more intuitive and clear-cut metric that is comparable across any number of model variations.

3. Finally, while cluster models take the frequencies of events into account (regardless of in which order they were recorded), sequential models instead look at the order in which the events were recorded. Both kinds of models offer interesting and unique perspectives on the data, and are therefore useful in their own right. Thus the "validation tasks" may find plenty of potential uses outside of simply selecting the optimal cluster model.

AUTOMATON Opportunities

Automated gamification systems such as AUTOMATON might fuse well with domains such as smart-learning and training systems as well as automated transportation and sustainability systems (Uskov & Sekar, 2015). The field of learning analytics is particularly interesting, especially where efforts have been made to tailor the learning experience with the use of recommender-systems, providing learners with feedback based on their persona/player types (Hallifax et al., 2021), or automated adaptation of teaching material difficulty depending on the learner skill (Lopez & Tucker, 2021). Automated gamification systems may also find applications in e-health, which is the second-largest field for gamification research and business applications, e.g., as applied to data from wearables for exercise and fitness (Zhao et al., 2015), health informatics (Croon et al., 2018) and Virtual Reality Therapy (Lindner et al., 2020).

AUTOMATON Challenges

While the proof of concept was largely satisfactory, the chosen approach also shed light on some of the challenges in building automated gamification systems:

1. The single-cluster baseline model in this trial only performed marginally better than the "dumb model", suggesting that the sequential models set up in this project likely were not that effective in predicting future events. The fact that the performance improved substantially following clustering can likely be attributed to the fact that dividing users into more and more distinct clusters also reduces the range of possible events that can occur, thereby making predictions easier. However, given that the goal was to select the cluster model that most facilitates prediction models, selecting the number of clusters that makes for the "easiest" predictions, is in fact in-line with the intended purpose.

2. Neural networks require careful hyperparameter fine-tuning to perform optimally, which can in itself be a time-consuming process that may require some level of automation of its own in order to be sufficiently scalable. The fine-tuning and optimizing neural networks was unfortunately outside of the scope of this proof of concept. Going forward, it may be more worthwhile to either use simpler and less hyperparameter-sensitive models, alternatively, purposefully develop predic-

tive models for the sake of making predictions (which can then also be used for selecting cluster models, thereby spreading the development cost across multiple uses).

3. These points transcend into the temporal and resource-based discussion often present in real-world gamification applications, namely that constructing and implementing gamified solutions is a time-consuming process (Morschheuser et al., 2018). Theories within gamification are still eclectic and choosing a context-fitting model requires adopting and gathering valid qualitative as well as quantitative validation theories and data (Palmquist et. al., 2021; Helmefalk, 2019).

FUTURE RESEARCH DIRECTIONS

In light of the discussed automation opportunities and challenges, there are several research avenues to be explored within gamification. First, as stated by Khakpour and Colomo-Palacios (2021), "there is the possibility of predicting future user behaviour and using this prediction to provide suggestions to users as a type of motivating element." (p. 622). As these systems are constantly improving and evolving, it is important to examine how automated adaptations and decisions based on prediction models impact the attitudes and goals of users, and how it affects their long term-engagement with a platform.

Future research should also examine how segments and clusters can be utilized to understand user paths leading to different outcomes. For instance, qualitative analyses could be conducted to find patterns of meaning within specific clusters that can aid in understanding why certain behaviours persist or diminish. Similar to Helmefalk (2019), future research may focus on further exploring how gamification mechanics influence different psychological constructs and how they in turn mediate certain outcomes.

Clustering would likely prove useful in understanding and suggesting mechanics that improve the user experience for different types of users. Automating such procedures may aid designers in selecting suitable mechanics and eliminating unnecessary mechanics, as the sheer amount of combinations of user types and gamification mechanics across different industries and domains are staggering.

Research should also attempt to find procedures for validating the effectiveness of recommender-systems as applied to gamification, e.g., in terms of their ability to improve user engagement, sense of flow and performance compared to non-adaptive systems or compared to other personalization methods, as suggested by Rodrigues et al. (2021).

CONCLUSION

This chapter has touched on multiple concepts, issues, challenges, innovations, and opportunities in the field of adaptive gamification, reflecting the multidisciplinary nature of gamification itself, taking cues from the fields of machine learning, cloud-based system infrastructures, as well as motivational and consumer psychology. The chapter has discussed gamification from the perspective of the AUTOMATON project, a case study based on the prospects of using machine learning as a way to create an autonomous, scalable and adaptive gamification system. The mix of machine learning and gamification paints a picture of a possible future of gamification that diverges from the field's earlier days, where self-proclaimed gamification gurus and costly consultants created gamification systems that were hard to evaluate and benchmark, due to imprecise and obscure practices. Furthermore, the chapter raises opportunities, issues, and potential research directions for scholars investigating industry 4.0 in general and machine learning for gamification applications in particular.

REFERENCES

Baskerville, R. L., & Myers, M. D. (2015). Design ethnography in information systems. *Information Systems Journal*, 25(1), 23–46. doi:10.1111/isj.12055

Burke, B. (2012, November). *Gartner Says by 2014, 80 Percent of Current Gamified Applications Will Fail to Meet Business Objectives Primarily Due to Poor Design.* Gartner.Com.

Croon, R. D., Wildemeersch, D., Wille, J., Verbert, K., & Aheele, V. V. (2018). Gamification and Serious Games in a Healthcare Informatics Context. *2018 IEEE International Conference on Healthcare Informatics (ICHI)*, 53–63. 10.1109/ICHI.2018.00014

Deterding, S., Dixon, D., Khaled, R., & Nacke, L. E. (2011). Gamification: Toward a Definition Sebastian. *CHI*, *1–4*. Advance online publication. doi:10.1007/978-3-642-13959-8_1

Dresch, A., Lacerda, P., Antônio, J., & Antunes, V. (2015). *Design Science Research A Method for Science and Technology Advancement.* Springer London.

Google Trends. (2021). https://trends.google.com/trends/explore?date=all&q=Gamification,Serious%20 Games

Gowtham, S., Goswami, M., Balachandran, K., & Purkayastha, B. S. (2014). An Approach for Document Pre-processing and K Means Algorithm Implementation. *Fourth International Conference on Advances in Computing and Communications*, 162-166. https://doi:10.1109/ICACC.2014.46

Hallifax, S., Serna, A., Marty, J., Lavoué, E., Hallifax, S., Serna, A., Marty, J., Lavoué, E., Cnrs, I. D. L., Umr, L., & France, L. (2021). Dynamic gamification adaptation framework based on engagement detection through learning analytics. *Companion Proceedings 11th International Conference on Learning Analytics & Knowledge (LAK21).*

Helmefalk, M. (2019). An interdisciplinary perspective on gamification: Mechanics, psychological mediators and outcomes: Mechanics, mental mediators and outcomes. *International Journal of Serious Games*, 6(1), 3–26. doi:10.17083/ijsg.v6i1.262

IEEE. (2014). *Everyone's a gamer: IEEE experts predict gaming will be integrated into more than 85 percent of daily tasks by 2020.* http://www.ieee.org/about/news/2014/ 25_feb_2014.html,

Järvinen, P. (2007). Action research is similar to design science. *Quality & Quantity*, 41(1), 37–54. doi:10.100711135-005-5427-1

Khakpour, A., & Colomo-Palacios, R. (2021). Convergence of gamification and machine learning: A systematic literature review. Technology. *Knowledge and Learning*, 26(3), 597–636. doi:10.100710758-020-09456-4

Koivisto, J., & Hamari, J. (2019). The rise of motivational information systems: A review of gamification research. *International Journal of Information Management*, 45, 191–210. doi:10.1016/j.ijinfomgt.2018.10.013

Lindner, P., Rozental, A., Jurell, A., Reuterskiöld, L., Andersson, G., Hamilton, W., Miloff, A., & Carlbring, P. (2020). Experiences of Gamified and Automated Virtual Reality Exposure Therapy for Spider Phobia: Qualitative Study. *JMIR Serious Games*, 8(2), e17807. doi:10.2196/17807 PMID:32347803

Looyestyn, J., Kernot, J., Boshoff, K., Ryan, J., Edney, S., & Maher, C. (2017). Does gamification increase engagement with online programs? *Systematic Reviews*, *12*(3), e0173403. Advance online publication. doi:10.1371/journal.pone.0173403 PMID:28362821

Lopez, C. E., & Tucker, C. S. (2021). HCI in Games: Experience Design and Game Mechanics. *Third International Conference, HCI-Games 2021, Held as Part of the 23rd HCI International Conference, HCII 2021, Virtual Event, July 24–29, 2021, Proceedings, Part I. Lecture Notes in Computer Science*, 327–341. 10.1007/978-3-030-77277-2_25

Morschheuser, B., Hassan, L., Werder, K., & Hamari, J. (2018). How to design gamification? A method for engineering gamified software. *Information and Software Technology*, *95*, 219–237. doi:10.1016/j.infsof.2017.10.015

Nacke, L. E., & Deterding, S. (2017). The maturing of gamification research. *Computers in Human Behavior*, *71*, 450–454. doi:10.1016/j.chb.2016.11.062

Palmquist, A., Munkvold, R., & Goethe, O. (2021). *Gamification Design Predicaments for E-learning*. In X. Fang (Ed.), Lecture Notes in Computer Science: Vol. 12790. *HCI in Games: Serious and Immersive Games. HCII 2021*. Springer. doi:10.1007/978-3-030-77414-1_18

Peffers, K., Tuunanen, T., Rothenberger, M. A., & Chatterjee, S. (2007). A design science research methodology for information systems research. *Journal of Management Information Systems*, *24*(3), 45–77. doi:10.2753/MIS0742-1222240302

Raftopoulos, M. (2020). Has gamification failed, or failed to evolve? Lessons from the frontline in information systems applications. *CEUR Workshop Proceedings*, *2637*, 21–30.

Reiners, T., & Wood, L. C. (2015). *Gamification in education and business*. doi:10.1007/978-3-319-10208-5

Rodrigues, L., Toda, A. M., Oliveira, W., Palomino, P. T., Vassileva, J., & Isotani, S. (2021). *Automating Gamification Personalization: To the User and Beyond*. arXiv preprint arXiv:2101.05718.

Sailer, M., Hense, J. U., Mayr, S. K., & Mandl, H. (2017). How gamification motivates: An experimental study of the effects of specific game design elements on psychological need satisfaction. *Computers in Human Behavior*, *69*(January), 371–380. doi:10.1016/j.chb.2016.12.033

Uskov, A., & Sekar, B. (2015). Smart gamification and smart serious games. In *Fusion of smart, multimedia and computer gaming technologies* (pp. 7–36). Springer. doi:10.1007/978-3-319-14645-4

Wee, S. C., & Choong, W. W. (2019). Gamification: Predicting the effectiveness of variety game design elements to intrinsically motivate users' energy conservation behaviour. *Journal of Environmental Management*, *233*, 97–106. doi:10.1016/j.jenvman.2018.11.127 PMID:30572268

Whyte, W. F., Greenwood, D. J., & Lazes, P. (1991). Participatory action research: Through practice to science in social research. *Participatory Action Research*, 19–55.

Yu, H., Liu, Z., & Wang, G. (2014). An automatic method to determine the number of clusters using decision-theoretic rough set. *International Journal of Approximate Reasoning*, *55*(1), 101–115. doi:10.1016/j.ijar.2013.03.018

Zhao, Z., Etemad, S. A., & Arya, A. (2015). Gamification of Exercise and Fitness using Wearable Activity Trackers. *Advances in Intelligent Systems and Computing*, 233–240. doi:10.1007/978-3-319-24560-7_30

ADDITIONAL READING

Arnedo, J., Nacke, L. E., Abeele, V. V., Toups, Z. O., Hallifax, S., Serna, A., Marty, J.-C., Lavoué, G., & Lavoué, E. (2019). Factors to Consider for Tailored Gamification. *Proceedings of the Annual Symposium on Computer-Human Interaction in Play*, 559–572. 10.1145/3311350.3347167

Khakpour, A., & Colomo-Palacios, R. (2021). Convergence of gamification and machine learning: A systematic literature review. Technology. *Knowledge and Learning*, 26(3), 597–636. doi:10.100710758-020-09456-4

López, C., & Tucker, C. (2018). Toward personalized adaptive gamification: a machine learning model for predicting performance. *IEEE Transactions on Games, 12*(2), 155-168. doi:10.1109/TG.2018.2883661

Tondello, G. F., Orji, R., & Nacke, L. E. (2017). Recommender Systems for Personalized Gamification. *UMAP 2017 - Adjunct Publication of the 25th Conference on User Modeling, Adaptation and Personalization*, 425–430. 10.1145/3099023.3099114

ENDNOTES

[1] See further GWEN API documentation.
[2] See Grafana snapshot (number of users, 1 sept, 2021): https://grafana.gwen.insertcoin.se/dashboard/snapshot/4yFlaSxl4Q14QDLalXYyVRlUuk0vfOxY.

Employee Classification in Reward Allocation Using ML Algorithms

Parakramaweera Sunil Dharmapala

(iD) https://orcid.org/0000-0003-4050-6754

Lone Star College, Cypress, USA

INTRODUCTION

Authors were primarily motivated by a research study reported by Olsen (2015), where he presented a theoretical model based on arguments of prior research. Prior research suggested that cultural values affect individuals' preferences in work rewards (i.e., pay and benefits) and are allocated according to rules based on 'equity', 'equality', or 'need'. Drawing on equity and social exchange theories, Olsen (2015) presented a theoretical model with nine propositions that incorporated both individual and societal values as determinants of the reward allocation preferences. He proposed that societal values and individual values had main and interactive effects on reward allocation preferences and that the effects of societal values are partially mediated by individual values. He opined that prior research on reward allocation preferences focused mostly on the effects of societal or individual values and claimed that his theoretical model attempted to clarify and distinguish values at these two levels and to better understand their main and interactive effects on individual reward allocation rule preferences. Prior research included the publications listed under Literature Review. Olsen's model considered only three categories; 'equity', 'equality', and 'need', whereas in this study the authors expand it to four and include 'seniority' as well, and they analyze reward allocation preferences from a different perspective using machine learning algorithms (MLAs).

An advantage of using MLAs in our study is that the string variable 'employee category' is multinomial with values 'performer', 'starter', 'needy' and 'senior', and it does not have to be coded with numerical values as it is done in statistical methods and then use 'dummy' variables to run in Regression Analysis. Same advantage applies to other string variables that are categorical input features.

LITERATURE REVIEW

This work reports the research studies conducted in the past relevant to 'reward allocation' in various groups and organizations with a wide spectrum of backgrounds.

Datta (2012) addressed the issue of, "How can managers optimally distribute rewards among individuals in a job group? His research introduced an innovative portfolio management scheme for employee rewards distribution and created a process that exemplifies rewards distribution using four different rewards allocation scenarios based on varying managerial prerogatives. Markovsky and Eriksson (2012) offered a comparison between direct and indirect methods for measuring perceptions of 'distributive justice' in reward allocations. The direct method simply asks respondents what they would consider to be a fair salary for a particular person in a given set of circumstances. In contrast, the indirect method infers fair salaries from respondents' judgments about the relative unfairness of hypothetical salaries.

DOI: 10.4018/978-1-7998-9220-5.ch186

They concluded that the two methods yielded incompatible results and that neither was immune to bias, and they suggested new directions for research to gain a better understanding of these problems and to circumvent them. Fischer (2007) presented a six-nation study where they showed associations between (i) organizational performance and equity, (ii) unemployment and need, and (iii) income inequality and need. While focusing on 'Rewarding Seniority', Fischer (2008) explored cultural and organizational predictors of seniority allocations. And earlier, Fischer (2004) highlighted cross-cultural differences in reward allocation while presenting two studies that investigated the use of reward allocation principles based on equity, equality, need and seniority by work organizations in Germany and the UK. He also suggested that more research focusing on real-life allocations was needed to develop a better understanding of cross-cultural differences. He et al. (2004) studied the reward allocation preferences of Chinese employees where they reported the effects of ownership reform, collectivism and goal priority. In order to test their hypotheses, they conducted hierarchical multiple regression analyses on differential and equalitarian allocation preferences. Tajima (1997) investigated people's expectation of others' ingroup favoritism, and the effect of expecting others to take part in reward allocation decision on ingroup favoritism in reward allocation. His findings suggested that ingroup favoritism was not a result of quasi-strategy of self-interest in an attempt to maximize own gains, but of psychological group formation. Younies et al. (2008) studied how medical sector employees in the private and public health sector view the Reward and Recognition (RR) systems in the UAE, where outstanding employees expect their effort to be acknowledged by the organization. However, they claimed that the variety of rewards and recognitions systems used by organizations may be perceived differently by different employees. Hu et al. (2004) investigated the relationships between employee categorization criteria and Chinese managers' allocation behaviors. They examined, using a vignette approach and a four-factor within-subjects design, the effects of relationship (guanxi), loyalty, and competence, as well as their interactions with allocation context (private vs public). Their results showed that subordinates who had a close relationship with the allocator, high loyalty, or high competence were rewarded more. Ng (2011) conducted an experiment that examined the effect of personal status on bias, and how such an effect might vary with group status. When asked to allocate money rewards directly to ingroup and outgroup members who had done equal works, subjects allocated equally regardless of status manipulations, indicating that personal status could lead to bias either by itself or jointly with group status. Islam and Ismail (2003) presented a research study that intended to find out the specific reward and recognition ways preferred by the employees working in various Malaysian organizations. They opine those employees who perform exceptionally well expected their contributions to be recognized or to be appreciated by the top management. Bamberger and Levi (2009) examined the effects of two key team-based pay characteristics – (i) reward allocation procedures (i.e., reward based on norms of equity, equality or some combination of the two) and (ii) incentive intensity – on both the amount and type of help given to one another among members of outcome-interdependent teams. They used a (2 x 3) experimental design with ANOVA and hierarchical regression analyses to test their hypotheses. Tower et al. (2011) conducted a study to examine the extent to which individualist–collectivist values were endorsed by Russian and British participants and the relationship between these values and allocation of rewards to self and co-worker in a hypothetical scenario. In addition, qualitative data from group discussions were used to explain reward allocation decisions and to explore the specific ways in which Russian collectivism differed from British individualism. Krishnan (2000) re-examined the consistently reported strong 'need' and weak 'merit' preference in reward allocation under collectivism, including allocator-recipient relationship, the nature of the resource, and resource scarcity as independent variables. Responses by 76 female college students in India to allocation scenarios indicated both significant merit and need preference depending largely on the nature of the resource and partly on the allocator-recipient relationship. Krishnan and Carment (2006) examined, among Indian and Canadian university students, senior/junior recipient status as a possible determinant of perceived fairness of given allocations and allocation preference. They reported that Canadians perceived more fairness and less unfairness than Indians, and they favored 'seniority' to a greater extent than Indians, possibly because they treated seniority as a component of merit. Indians manifested an 'equality' orientation and gave variable responses to seniority depending on the nature of allocation, allocator/recipient role, rule combination and their interactive effects.

In earlier studies, Murphy-Berman et al. (1984) presented the factors affecting the allocation of reward to needy and meritorious recipients, in a cross-cultural comparison of India versus U.S. male and female groups. Their findings supported the idea that perceptions of fairness are culturally relative and bound to specific socialization practices and societal norms. In comparing Chinese and U.S. business organizations, Chen (1995) explored and identified trends in allocation preferences for both material and emotional rewards, where the Chinese employees were economically oriented and preferred to invoke differential rules, whereas their American counterparts preferred a performance rule for material rewards and equality rules for socioemotional rewards. Chen and Church (1993) presented an article focusing on the factors that affected the selection and implementation of three principles of 'distributive justice', namely, equity, equality, and need, to reward systems in group and organizational settings.

BACKGROUND AND DATA ACQUSITION

The description of the data used in this paper and stated below is taken from the data set presented in the article of Dharmapala et al. (2015).

Suppose you are a supervisor of a work unit of 4 employees that assemble computer keyboards, on average 25 keyboards per day. And you must decide how to allocate a bonus of $50,000 among the 4 employees for working exceptionally well last year. All 4 employees have worked for the company all their working life. The description of the employees is as follows.

'Performer'; is a single 30-years old woman with no children and lives with her parents. She has been with the company for about 10 years and assembles about 32 keyboards per day – an exceptional performer.

'Starter'; is a single 20-years old man with no children and lives with his parents. This is his first year with the company. He is an average worker who also assembles about 25 keyboards per day.

'Needy'; is a single 35-years old woman with 3 little children. She is the sole provider of her family and has been working with the company for 15 years. She is an average performer who has been assembling about 25 keyboards per day.

'Senior'; is a 60-years old widowed man. He has 2 children who have jobs and are married with families of their own. He has worked for this company all his life since the age of 19. He is an average performer who assembles about 26 keyboards per day.

Present study conducted a survey with a questionnaire of 8 questions and distributed it among 350 respondents and collected about the same number of responses. See Appendix-1 for the questionnaire distributed. Addressing their main question, "What factors influence your decision in allocating a reward among the four employees?", the researchers started the survey with the first question to the respondents. The target variable 'Category' was our second question, …, and the remaining questions follow. Out of the 338 complete responses we collected, 320 were included in our sample of observations, and the remining 18 responses formed the out-of-sample for future prediction and verification of the best MLA selected using the methodology described below.

Appendix-2 shows a partial set of data with 11 columns; first 10 columns are input features and the last column is 'Category' of 4 employees that the researchers intend to classify using MLAs. The first 4 columns show the allocation of the bonus among the 4 employee categories (total adds up to 50 in $1000 units), and the remaining 6 columns capture the responses to the survey questions.

METHODOLGY

According to Wikipedia (2021), "Machine learning is the study of computer algorithms that improve automatically through experience. Machine learning algorithms build a mathematical model based on sample data, known as 'training data', in order to make predictions or decisions without being explicitly programmed to do so." Nilsson (2005) opines, "It is possible that hidden among large piles of data are important relationships and correlations. Machine learning methods can often be used to extract these relationships (data mining)." He further states that a machine learns whenever it changes its structure, program, or data (based on its inputs or in response to external information) in such a manner that its expected future performance improves.

Machine learning task of assigning input features to an output target is called 'Supervised Learning'. We explain that relationship in the form of a function (unknown), $h: X \circledR Y$, where vector $x_i = (x_{i1}, x_{i2}, ..., x_{ik})$ of k input features in X, of observation i, is mapped on to output target y_i in Y. Thus, we have a set of n observations (examples) $\{(x_1, y_1), (x_2, y_2), ..., (x_n, y_n)\}$ in the product space $(X \times Y)$, part of which will be selected as 'training data' and the remaining part as 'validation data'. The model, $y = h(x) +$ *error*, is fitted on the training data, and the fitted model is used to predict responses on the validation data. The function h itself is treated as a hypothesis that links input features $x = (x_1, x_2, ..., x_n)^T$ to output target $y = (y_1, y_2, ..., y_n)^T$. The goal is to estimate the function h with $\hat{h}$, such that $y \gg \hat{h}(x)$. What is really wanted to see is, $y \gg \hat{h}(x)$, where x is from validation & testing data after determining the pattern of $\hat{h}$ from training data. If too many $\hat{h}$ are consistent with the training data, then there may exist the *overfitting* problem in training data that impacts on out-of-sample prediction.

This study addresses the *overfitting* problem through *cross-validation* by partitioning the full data set of 320 observations in 10 folds in the following fashion: every time data are shuffled (random sampling with replacement), 10 models will be trained and validated in such a way that the training set will have 288 observations and the validation & testing set will have the remaining 32 observations.

Under supervised learning, we perform 'classification learning' (see Hastie et al., 2009). It is widely believed that there is no single MLA that works best for all supervised learning problems, and each method has its own strengths and weaknesses. In this study, the target variable is the Categories of 4 employees, n=320 total observations (examples), k=10 input features for the full model, and k=7 input features for the reduced model. Both models include qualitative and quantitative predictors.

This study asserts that there is a nonlinear statistical relationship between the four categories and the allotted amounts of the bonus and other input features that describe the respondents. This work uses four primary classification methods of machine learning available in MATLAB® to analyze this relationship that are listed in Table 1.

Table 1. MLA classification learners

(1) Classification Trees	(i) Fine tree	(ii) Medium tree
	(iii) Coarse tree	(iv) Optimizable tree
(2) Naïve Bayes	(i) Gaussian	(ii) Kernel
	(iii) Optimizable	
(3) Support Vector Machines	(i) Linear	(ii) Quadratic
	(iii) Cubic	(iv) Fine Gaussian
	(v) Medium Gaussian	(vi) Coarse Gaussian
	(vii) Optimizable	
(4) Ensemble Methods	(i) Boosted trees	(ii) Bagged trees
	(iii) Subspace discriminant	(iv) Subspace KNN
	(v) RUS Boosted	(vi) Optimizable

RESULTS AND DISCUSSION

Graphical Summary of Responses

Here this study presents the graphical summary of respondents' allocations for each employee, starting with 'Performer'. Figure 1 shows the allocations for 'Performer'. See Appendix-3 for the histograms of 'Starter', 'Needy', and 'Senior'. We summarize the allocations depicted in all four histograms in Table 2. Considering the modal class, 'Needy' has secured the largest allocation of $20,000.

Figure 1. Histogram for 'Performer'

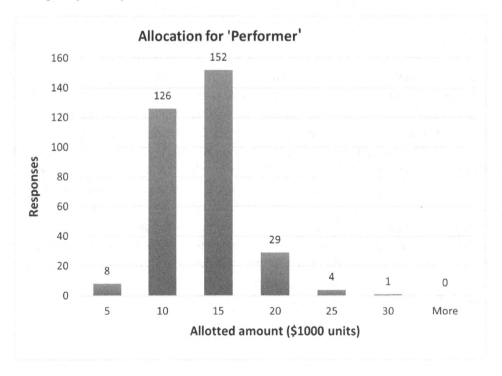

Table 2. Allocations depicted in Histograms for all 4 categories

	Performer	Starter	Needy	Senior
Highest allocation	$15,000	$10,000	$20,000	$15000
Number of respondents	152	183	130	177

Classification by MLAs

This research trained the survey sample data on classifiers that are listed in Table 1, and from them we selected 4 classifiers with high Accuracy rates and AUC (area under ROC curve) scores shown in Tables 3 and 4. From them, the authors selected the best classifier(s) that predicted the employee categories for out-of-sample observations.

Table 3. Accuracy and AUC scores of 10 predictor classification

Classifier	Accuracy Rate (%)	AUC (%)
(1) Optimized tree	86.9%	90%
(2) Naïve Bayes Gaussian	83.1%	95%
(3) SVM Optimizable	88.8%	98%
(4) Ensemble Optimizable	89.4%	97%

Table 4. Accuracy and AUC scores of 7 predictor classification

Classifier	Accuracy Rate (%)	AUC (%)
(1) Optimized tree	89.4%	93%
(2) Naïve Bayes Gaussian	86.9%	96%
(3) SVM Optimizable	90.6%	98%
(4) Ensemble Optimizable	90.9%	97%

Tables 3 and 4 clearly show that the 7-predictor classification has higher Accuracy rates and AUC scores. The reduced model with 7 predictors has 'education', 'industry' and 'job position' dropped from the 10-predictor model. That means these 3 qualitative predictors have no relevance to the allocation of the bonus among the 4 categories of employees. Authors take (3) and (4) classifiers of this reduced model for out-of-sample prediction and select the better classifier. The out-of-sample data and prediction results for both classifiers are shown in Appendix-5. Detailed publications about Ensemble methods and SVM classifiers are listed under Additional Reading.

Figure 2 shows the 'Confusion Matrix' for 7-predictor Optimizable Ensemble classifier, and below it is shown how to calculate the accuracy rate. Here, on-diagonal observations (Blue) are correctly classified, while off-diagonal observations (Red) are misclassified. The matrix displays that 10 'Needy', 10 'Performer', 7 'Senior', and 2 'Starter' categories are misclassified.

Accuracy Rate = number of on-diagonal observations / Total observations = 291/320 = 90.9%

Figure 3 shows the Confusion Matrix for 7-predictor Optimizable SVM classifier, and the Appendix-4 shows the AUC plots for both classifiers.

Figure 2. Confusion matrix for 7-predictor Ensemble classifier

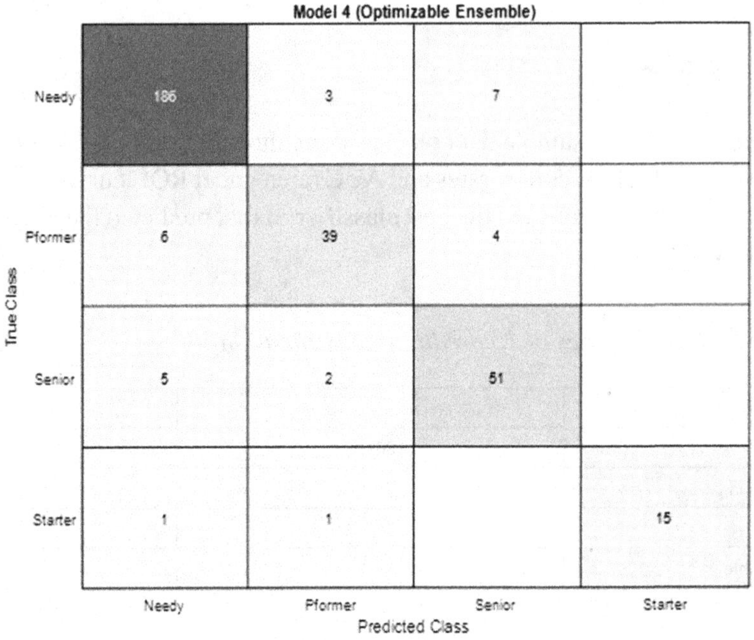

Figure 3. Confusion matrix for 7-predictor SVM classifier

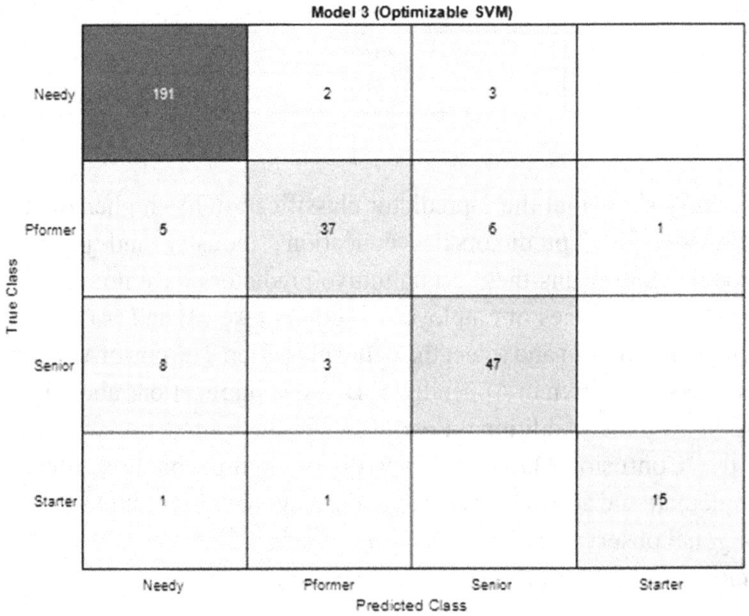

Figures 2 and 3 display that both classifiers heavily favored 'Needy' in the allocation of bonus, followed by 'Senior', 'Performer', and 'Starter'.

FUTURE RESEARCH DIRECTIONS

1. This study opened a new direction using four primary MLAs. Future research can be extended to using other classification learners not listed here, including the hybrid versions.
2. The input features included in this research were limited to 10, but more input features can be added and tested their viability in future research studies.

CONCLUSION

As the study wraps up its findings, the following conclusions are in order:

1. Respondents' input features 'education', 'job industry' and 'job position' bear no relevance to determine the employee category in allocating the bonus, but 'age', 'gender' and 'experience' appear relevant, in addition to the allocations for four employees.
2. Graphical summary of histograms of responses (320) reveals that 'Needy' has secured the largest allocation of $20,000, considering the modal class of allotted amounts.
3. The 7-predictor model trained on sample responses selected both Optimizable Ensemble and Optimizable SVM as best classifiers, based on higher Accuracy Rates and equal AUC scores over their counterparts in the 10-predictor model.
4. With the selection of the 7-predictor model for out-of-sample prediction, the three qualitative predictors 'education', 'industry' and 'job position' seem to have no relevance to the allocation of the bonus among the four categories of employees.
5. Ensemble and SVM classifiers heavily favored 'Needy' employee in the allocation of bonus followed by 'Senior', 'Performer' and 'Starter'.
6. Ensemble and SVM classifiers were used to predict employee categories for out-of-sample observations, and both classifiers predicted the categories with perfect accuracy.
7. As for managerial implication, both graphical summary result in 2. and MLA-classifier selection in 4. of 'Needy' employee highlight that majority of respondents was inclined to believe that 'need' overwhelms 'equity' 'equality' and 'seniority'.

REFERENCES

Bamberger, P. A., & Levi, R. (2009). Team-based reward allocation structures and the helping behaviors of outcome-interdependent team members. *Journal of Managerial Psychology*, 24(4), 300–327. doi:10.1108/02683940910952705

Chen, C. C. (1995). New trends in reward allocation preferences: A Sino-U.S. comparison. *Academy of Management Journal*, 38(2), 408–428. doi:10.5465/256686

Chen, Y.-R., & Church, A. H. (1993). Reward allocation preferences in groups and organizations. *International Journal of Conflict Management, 4*(1), 25–59. doi:10.1108/eb022720

Datta, P. (2012). An applied organizational rewards distribution system. *Management Decision, 50*(3), 479–501. doi:10.1108/00251741211216241

Dharmapala, P. S., Bachkirov, A. A., & Shamsudin, F. M. (2015). Employee reward allocation based on 'Equity', 'Need', 'Equality' and 'Seniority': A probabilistic analysis. *Proceedings of the International Conference on Organization and Management (ICOM)*. https://www.researchgate.net/publication/290045891_Employee_reward_allocation_based_on_performance_need_seniority_and_equality_A_probabilistic_analysis

Fisher, R. (2004). Organizational reward allocation: A comparison of British and German organizations. *International Journal of Intercultural Relations, 28*(2), 151–164. doi:10.1016/j.ijintrel.2004.03.002

Fisher, R. (2007). How Do Organizations Allocate Rewards? The Predictive Validity of National Values, Economic and Organizational Factors Across Six Nations. *Journal of Cross-Cultural Psychology, 38*(1), 3–18. doi:10.1177/0022022106295437

Fisher, R. (2008). Rewarding Seniority: Exploring Cultural and Organizational Predictors of Seniority Allocations. *The Journal of Social Psychology, 148*(2), 167–186. doi:10.3200/SOCP.148.2.167-186 PMID:18512417

Hastie, T., Tibshirani, R., & Friedman, J. (Eds.). (2009). *The Elements of Statistical Learning: Data Mining, Inference, and Prediction* (2nd ed.). Springer-Verlag. doi:10.1007/978-0-387-84858-7

He, W., Chao, C. C., & Zhang, C. C. (2004). Reward allocation preferences of Chinese employees in the new millennium: The effects of ownership reform, collectivism, and goal priority. *Organization Science, 15*(2), 221–231. doi:10.1287/orsc.1030.0049

Hsu, C.-W., & Lin, C.-J. (2002). A Comparison of Methods for Multiclass Support Vector Machines. *IEEE Transactions on Neural Networks, 13*(2), 415–425. doi:10.1109/72.991427 PMID:18244442

Hu, H.-H., Hsu, W.-L., & Cheng, B.-S. (2004). Reward allocation decisions of Chinese managers: Influence of employee categorization and allocation context. *Asian Journal of Social Psychology, 7*(2), 221–232. doi:10.1111/j.1467-839x.2004.00146.x

Islam, R., & Ismail, A. Z. H. (2003). Ranking of employees' reward and recognition approaches: A Malaysian Perspective. *Journal for International Business and Entrepreneurship Development, 2*(10809), 113. Advance online publication. doi:10.1504/JIBED.2004.007860

Krishnan, L. (2000). Resource, relationship and scarcity in reward allocation in India. *Psychologia, 43*(4), 275–285.

Krishnan, L., & Carment, D. W. (2006). Senior/Junior Recipient Status and Reward Allocation. *Psychology and Developing Societies, 18*(1), 15–35. doi:10.1177/097133360501800102

Markovsky, B., & Eriksson, K. (2012). Comparing Direct and Indirect Measures of Just Rewards. *Sociological Methods & Research, 40*(1), 199–216. doi:10.1177/0049124112437712

Murphy-Berman, V., Berman, J. J., Singh, P., Pachauri, A., & Kumar, P. (1984). Factors affecting allocation to needy and meritorious recipients: A cross-cultural comparison. *Journal of Personality and Social Psychology*, *46*(6), 1267–1272. doi:10.1037/0022-3514.46.6.1267

Ng, S. H. (2011). Biases in reward allocation resulting from personal status, group status, and allocation procedure. *Australian Journal of Psychology*, *37*(3), 297–307. doi:10.1080/00049538508256407

Nilsson, N. J. (Ed.). (2005). *Introduction to Machine Learning*. Stanford University Computer Science Department. https://ai.stanford.edu/people/nilsson/MLBOOK.pdf

Olsen, J. E. (2015). Societal values and individual values in reward allocation preferences. *Cross Cultural Management*, *22*(2), 187–200. doi:10.1108/CCM-09-2013-0130

Organ, D. W. (1988). A Restatement of the Satisfaction-Performance Hypothesis. *Journal of Management*, *14*(4), 547–557. doi:10.1177/014920638801400405

Tajima, T. (1997). Expectation of others' reward allocation, and ingroup favoritism in reward allocation. *The Japanese Journal of Psychology, 68*(2), 135-139. doi:10.4992/jjpsy.68.135

Tower, R. K., Kelly, C., & Richards, A. (2011). Individualism, collectivism and reward allocation: A cross-cultural study in Russia and Britain. *British Journal of Social Psychology*, *36*(3), 331–345. doi:10.1111/j.2044-8309.1997.tb01135.x

Wikipedia. (2021). https://en.wikipedia.org/wiki/Machine_learning

Younies, H., Barhem, B., & Younis, M. (2008). Ranking of priorities in employees' reward and recognition schemes: From the perspective of UAE health care employees. *The International Journal of Health Planning and Management*, *23*(4), 357–371. doi:10.1002/hpm.912 PMID:18000918

ADDITIONAL READING

Bzdok, D., Altman, N., & Krzywinski, M. (2018). Statistics versus Machine Learning. *Nature Methods*, *15*(4), 233–234. doi:10.1038/nmeth.4642 PMID:30100822

Christian, B., & Griffith, T. (2017). Overfitting, Algorithms to Live By. In W. Collins (Ed.), The computer science of human decisions (pp. 149–168). Academic Press.

Cortes, C., & Vapnik, V. N. (1995). Support-vector networks. *Machine Learning*, *20*(3), 273–297. doi:10.1007/BF00994018

Deery, S., Rayton, B., Walsh, J., & Kinnie, N. (2016). The Costs of Exhibiting Organizational Citizenship Behavior. *Human Resource Management*. Advance online publication. doi:10.1002/hrm.21815

Hinton, G., & Sejnowski, T. (Eds.). (1999). *Unsupervised Learning: Foundations of Neural Computation*. MIT Press. doi:10.7551/mitpress/7011.001.0001

James, G., Witten, D., Hastie, T., & Tibshirani, R. (Eds.). (2021). *An Introduction to Statistical Learning with Applications in R*. Springer Texts in Statistics. doi:10.1007/978-1-0716-1418-1

Opitz, D., & Maclin, R. (1999). Popular Ensemble Methods: An Empirical Study. *Journal of Artificial Intelligence Research*, *11*, 169–198. doi:10.1613/jair.614

Organ, D. W., Podsakoff, P. M., & MacKenzie, S. P. (Eds.). (2006). *Organizational citizenship behavior: Its nature, antecedents, and consequences.* Sage Publications. doi:10.4135/9781452231082

Rokach, L. (2010). Ensemble-based classifiers. *Artificial Intelligence Review*, *33*(1–2), 1–39. doi:10.100710462-009-9124-7

KEY TERMS AND DEFINITIONS

Accuracy Rate: In classification learning, a measure to determine the accuracy of prediction using $\hat{h}$ of a machine learning method, by plotting a 'confusion matrix' with predicted classes as columns and true classes as rows. On-diagonal elements show the correctly predicted classes and off-diagonal elements show the falsely predicted classes. The percentage of correctly predicted classes to the total predicted classes forms the accuracy rate.

Area Under ROC Curve (AUC): ROC curve, or receiver operating characteristic curve, is a graphical plot that illustrates the diagnostic ability of a binary classifier system. ROC space is defined by FPR (false positive rate) and TPR (true positive rate) as x and y axes, respectively, which depicts a relative trade-off between truly predicted and falsely predicted classes. The total area is bounded by the unit square [0 to 1] on x-axis, and [0 to 1] on y-axis. AUC area extends from the 45°-line (that connects (0,0) and (1,1)) towards the top left (0,1) covering 100% total area. A higher AUC area closer to (0,1) depicts a stronger classification method.

Classification Learning: Under Supervised Learning, the output target is a categorical variable representing categories/classes/attributes that the inputs map into after determining the pattern of the function from training data.

Cross-Validation: A statistical technique used in machine learning to overcome the *Overfitting* problem. The full data set is partitioned into 'training data' and 'validation and testing data' by creating multiple manyfold samples using random sampling with replacement. The number of folds determines the number of times the full data set is shuffled and partitioned, and that many models are built to determine the pattern of $\hat{h}$.

Histogram: A frequency bar graph that plots the allotted amounts on the horizontal axis and the number of responses on the vertical axis depicting the allocation favored by respondents.

Overfitting: In machine learning, the fitting of $\hat{h}$ corresponds too closely to the training data set and may therefore fail to fit validation and testing data. An overfitted model is a statistical model that contains more parameters than can be justified by the sample data and therefore fails to predict out-of-sample data reliably.

Reward Allocation: In industrial and organizational psychology, 'organizational citizenship behavior' (OCB) is a person's voluntary commitment within an organization that is not part of his or her contractual tasks. Organ (1988) defines OCB as "individual behavior that is discretionary, not directly or explicitly recognized by the formal reward system, and that in the aggregate promotes the effective functioning of the organization". Reward allocation is designed to promote OCB in an organization.

Supervised Learning (SL): Machine learning task of learning a function that maps an input (mostly a vector) to an output, based on input-output pairs of observations in the training data set.

Unsupervised Learning (UL): There is no target output variable in UL, nor the data are tagged as in SL. UL methods exhibit self-organization that captures patterns as probability densities.

APPENDIX 1

Survey Questionnaire

Write down the amount of your allocation for each employee (Total = $ 50,000)
- ◦ 'Performer': _____
- ◦ 'Starter': _____
- ◦ 'Needy': _____
- ◦ 'Senior': _____

1. Which one of the following influenced your decision? Mark each one with the appropriate number
   a. Performance: number of keyboards assembled by each employee
   b. Need: the extent to which each employee needed the money
   c. Seniority; length of service on the job
   d. Equality: treat all 4 employees equally regardless of their need, seniority or performance
2. Which employee deserves the bonus the most?
   a. 'Performer'
   b. 'Starter'
   c. 'Needy'
   d. 'Senior'
3. Your age (to the nearest year) _____
4. Your gender: 1 – Male 2 – Female
5. Your highest level of education
   a. Secondary school
   b. College
   c. BA/BS degree
   d. MA/MS degree
   e. PhD/DBA degree
6. Industry you work for
   a. Oil & Gas
   b. Tourism
   c. Education
   d. Aviation
   e. Other
7. Position in your job
   a. Supervisor
   b. Middle manager
   c. Top manager
   d. Novice
8. Years of work experience _____

APPENDIX 2

Table 5. Partial Set of Observations in the 10-Predictor Model

Performer	Starter	Needy	Senior	Age	Gender	Educatn	Industry	JobPost	Experence	Category
15	10	15	10	30	Female	Bachelor	Eductn	MidMngt	8	Pformer
10	5	20	15	37	Female	College	Other	Supvisor	15	Pformer
10	12	14	13	25	Male	Bachelor	Oil&Gas	TopMngt	2	Needy
10	10	17.5	12.5	34	Male	Masters	Oil&Gas	MidMngt	10	Needy
15	10	10	15	27	Female	College	Oil&Gas	Novice	4	Pformer
11	11	15	13	30	Male	Bachelor	Other	MidMngt	10	Needy
2.5	2.5	30	15	36	Male	PhD	Tourism	MidMngt	14	Needy
15	5	15	15	29	Male	Masters	Other	Supvisor	5	Pformer
12	8	16	14	27	Male	College	Other	Supvisor	5	Needy
8.5	8.5	20	13	36	Female	Bachelor	Other	MidMngt	0	Needy
12	12	14	12	56	Male	PhD	Eductn	Novice	26	Needy
11.5	11.5	15	12	47	Male	College	Aviation	TopMngt	23	Needy
8	10	18	14	45	Male	Masters	Eductn	TopMngt	22	Needy
8	10	20	12	40	Female	Masters	Other	TopMngt	18	Needy
9	5	18	18	47	Male	HS	Other	TopMngt	27	Needy
10	9	20	11	36	Female	PhD	Other	TopMngt	9	Needy
20	11	11	8	35	Male	HS	Other	TopMngt	31	Pformer
12	12	13.5	12.5	31	Male	Bachelor	Other	Supvisor	8	Needy
10	8	20	12	43	Female	HS	Other	TopMngt	0	Needy
10	20	10	10	46	Male	PhD	Other	TopMngt	21	Starter
8	7	17	18	34	Female	College	Eductn	Supvisor	10	Needy
11	10	17	12	26	Male	Bachelor	Tourism	Supvisor	2	Needy
12	10	13	14	28	Female	College	Aviation	MidMngt	5	Senior
13	2	15	20	28	Female	Bachelor	Other	Supvisor	1	Senior
7.5	7.5	20	15	28	Female	College	Other	Supvisor	2	Needy
11.5	10.5	15	13	30	Female	Bachelor	Other	Supvisor	4	Needy
15	7	8	20	29	Female	College	Other	Supvisor	1	Senior
14	7	16	13	40	Female	College	Other	Supvisor	7	Needy
10	10	15	15	37	Male	Masters	Eductn	Supvisor	15	Senior
11.5	11.5	15	12	45	Male	Bachelor	Other	MidMngt	17	Needy
10	10	18	12	40	Male	Masters	Other	Supvisor	5	Needy
12.5	10	15	12.5	38	Male	Bachelor	Other	MidMngt	18	Needy
11	11	16	12	24	Male	College	Other	MidMngt	30	Needy
10	10	18	12	40	Male	Bachelor	Other	TopMngt	25	Needy
10	9	13	18	58	Female	Bachelor	Tourism	MidMngt	12	Senior
10	9	13	18	56	Male	College	Other	MidMngt	2	Senior
15	5	13	17	42	Male	Bachelor	Tourism	MidMngt	10	Senior
14	7	16	13	30	Male	College	Other	Supvisor	6	Needy
20	15	10	5	38	Male	College	Other	MidMngt	22	Pformer

APPENDIX 3

Histograms of Responses for Other 3 Employees

Figure 4. Histogram for 'Starter'

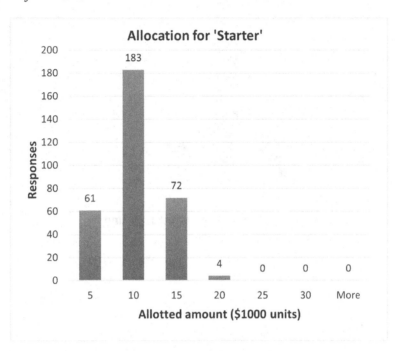

Figure 5. Histogram for 'Needy'

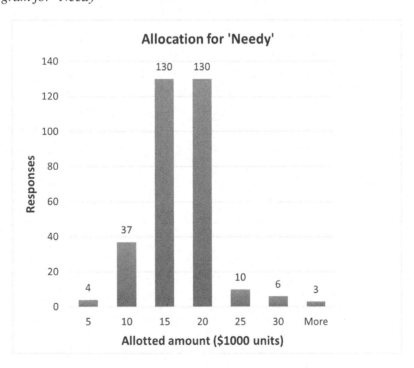

Figure 6. Histogram for "Senior'

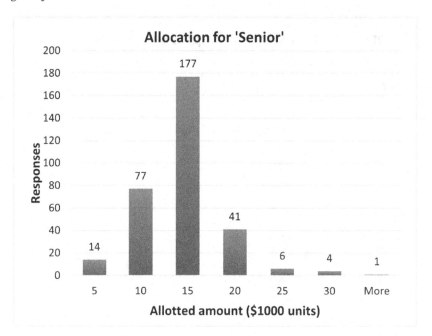

APPENDIX 4

AUC Plots for 7-Predictor Classifiers

Figure 7. AUC plot for Ensemble classifier

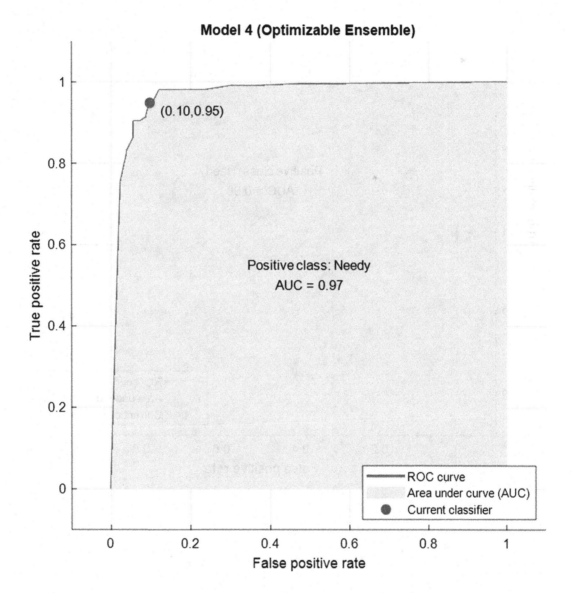

Figure 8. AUC plot for SVM classifier

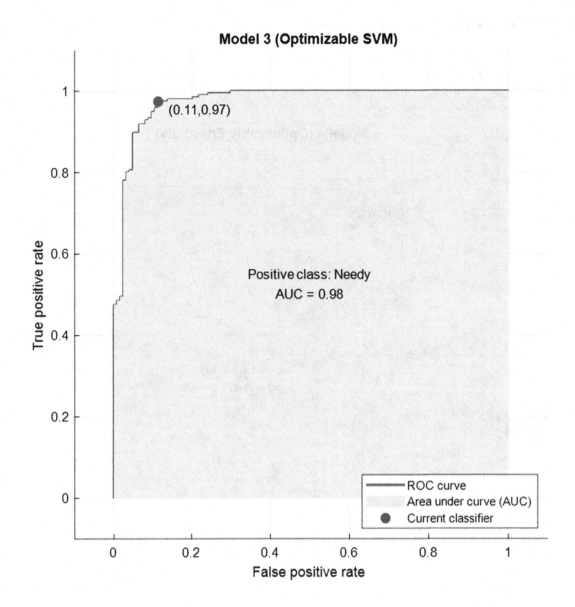

APPENDIX 5

E

Table 6. Out-of-sample data for prediction using Optimizable SVM classifier

Performer	Starter	Needy	Senior	Age	Gender	Experience	True Category	Predicted Category
20	5	15	10	62	Male	16	Pformer	Pformer
5	5	30	10	25	Female	14	Needy	Needy
15	5	20	10	45	Male	17	Needy	Needy
19	7	12	12	27	Male	20	Pformer	Pformer
10	10	20	10	26	Female	12	Needy	Needy
10	10	12	18	24	Male	13	Senior	Senior
10	10	20	10	40	Male	33	Needy	Needy
12	14	13.5	10.5	45	Female	0	Starter	Starter
10	5	15	20	28	Male	10	Senior	Senior
20	5	15	10	36	Male	25	Pformer	Pformer
12.5	13	14	10.5	55	Male	13	Needy	Needy
20	5	10	15	28	Female	8	Pformer	Pformer
11	4	15	20	26	Female	9	Senior	Senior
15	15	20	12	31	Female	7	Needy	Needy
11	9	17	13	46	Male	7	Needy	Needy
12.5	12.5	12.5	12.5	34	Male	23	Starter	Starter
15	5	20	10	37	Male	18	Needy	Needy
12.5	12.5	12.5	12.5	38	Female	5	Starter	Starter

Table 7. Out-of-sample data for prediction using Optimizable Ensemble classifier

Performer	Starter	Needy	Senior	Age	Gender	Experience	True Category	Predicted Category
20	5	15	10	62	Male	16	Pformer	Pformer
5	5	30	10	25	Female	14	Needy	Needy
15	5	20	10	45	Male	17	Needy	Needy
19	7	12	12	27	Male	20	Pformer	Pformer
10	10	20	10	26	Female	12	Needy	Needy
10	10	12	18	24	Male	13	Senior	Senior
10	10	20	10	40	Male	33	Needy	Needy
12	14	13.5	10.5	45	Female	0	Starter	Starter
10	5	15	20	28	Male	10	Senior	Senior
20	5	15	10	36	Male	25	Pformer	Pformer
12.5	13	14	10.5	55	Male	13	Needy	Needy
20	5	10	15	28	Female	8	Pformer	Pformer
11	4	15	20	26	Female	9	Senior	Senior
15	15	20	12	31	Female	7	Needy	Needy
11	9	17	13	46	Male	7	Needy	Needy
12.5	12.5	12.5	12.5	34	Male	23	Starter	Starter
15	5	20	10	37	Male	18	Needy	Needy
12.5	12.5	12.5	12.5	38	Female	5	Starter	Starter

Identifying Disease and Diagnosis in Females Using Machine Learning

Sabyasachi Pramanik

https://orcid.org/0000-0002-9431-8751

Haldia Institute of Technology, India

Samir Kumar Bandyopadhyay

Bhawanipore Educational Society, India

INTRODUCTION

When a human body doesn't produce insulin or doesn't produce sufficient insulin or doesn't use it efficiently it can lead to dangerous complications called Diabetes (Lee et. al. 2021). This disorder occurs when the glucose of our blood gets high, also known as blood sugar. In the human body the main source of energy is blood glucose and they are getting energy from whatever we eat. For having energy, this glucose gets into the body cells to be used with the help of insulin. Possessing extra visceral fat is significantly connected to having the highest risk of developing diabetes, such as type 2 diabetes. Obese women are also more likely than males to have a healthy metabolism. The present epidemic of diabetes in India is mostly due to changes in lifestyle. Increasing prevalence may be attributed to a variety of factors, including fast changes in food habits, lack of physical activity, and increase in body weight, particularly the build-up of belly fat.

Types of Diabetes

1. Type 1 Diabetes (De Bois, M., et al. 2022): This is also known as autoimmune disorder. Here the diabetes pancreatic cells are damaged and for that the pancreas fails to produce enough body insulin.
2. Type 2 Diabetes (Yang, L., et al. 2021): It is also known as Adult-Onset Diabetes. Here the pancreas either produces excessive insulin or it resists insulin and it affects the way body processes blood sugar.
3. Pre-Diabetes (Harimoorthy, K., et al. 2021): Pre-Diabetes is nearly same as Type 2 Diabetes. Here, in the Pre-Diabetes stage the amount of blood sugar is not greater than Type 2 Diabetes.
4. Gestational Diabetes Mellitus (GDM) (Barik, S., et al. 2021): This type of diabetes consists of carbohydrate of varying intensity during pregnancy. GDM has no specific clinical features, it is diagnosed after screening.

Symptoms of Diabetes

1. Excessive thirst
2. Slow healing sores and recurrent infection
3. Feeling lazy
4. Blurred vision

DOI: 10.4018/978-1-7998-9220-5.ch187

5.   Tingling in hand and feet
6.   Swollen gums
7.   Excessive urination
8.   Weight lost

Causes of Diabetes

1.   Diabetes due to obesity
2.   Hereditary
3.   High sugar levels during pregnancy
4.   Blood vessel diseases
5.   High blood pressure & high cholesterol
6.   Pre-diabetes or impaired fasting glucose

BACKGROUND

The research of (Karatsiolis and Schizas, 2012) implemented a modified Support Vector Machine technique is used to solve the challenge of diagnosing Pima Indian Diabetes using data from UCI Repository of Machine Learning Databases (Akter, L., et al. 2021). The suggested algorithm's performance is compared to that of other categorization algorithms in order to show that it outperforms them. The purpose of this study is to provide readers an understanding of a technique that may be utilised to improve classification success rates attained by using traditional methodologies like Neural Networks, RBF networks (Meng, X., et al. 2021) and K-nearest neighbours. The proposed technique separates the training set into subgroups: one resulting from the combining of coherent data areas, and the other containing data that is difficult to cluster. As a result, the first subset is being used to train an RBF kernel Support Vector Machine, whereas the second subset is utilised to train a polynomial kernel Support Vector Machine. The method can determine whichever of the two Support Vector Machine algorithms to utilise during classification. The proposed approach is based on the assumption that the RBF Support Vector Machine architecture is more suited to use on data sets with varying features than the polynomial kernel (Mahindru, A., et al., 2021). The recommended technique improved the average classification success rate to 82.2 percent in this investigation, whereas the greatest performance attained in earlier experiments was 81 percent using a fine-tuned very complicated ARTMAP-IC model (Bascil, M. S., et al. 2012).

The outcome of the study by (Kaur et al., 2018) used the diabetes in a serious metabolic illness that may have a negative impact on the overall body system. Diabetic nephropathy, myocardial stroke, and other complications may all be exacerbated by undiagnosed diabetes. This illness affects millions of individuals all over the globe. Diabetes must be detected early in order to live a healthy life. Diabetes is a worldwide problem, since the number of patients is continually increasing. Machine learning (ML) (Pramanik, S. et al., 2021) is a computer technology that enhances performance by automatically learning from experience and making more accurate predictions. In this study, the authors used the R data (Li, W. et al., 2021) manipulation programme to generate trends and uncover patterns in the Pima Indian diabetes dataset using machine learning techniques. Using the R data manipulation tool, we constructed and assessed five alternative prediction models to categorise patients as diabetic or non-diabetic. We employed supervised machine learning methods such as the linear kernel support vector machine (SVM-linear), the radial basis function (RBF) kernel support vector machine, the k-nearest neighbour (K-NN), the artificial neural network (ANN), and multifactor dimensionality reduction for this (MDR) (Coffey, C. S. et. al., 2004).

The results of the research conducted by (Nilashi, M., et al., 2017) shows that the utilization of medical datasets has piqued the interest of scholars all around the globe. The application of data mining methods in the development of decision support systems for illness prediction using a collection of medical datasets (Ahmed, S. T., et al. 2021) is common. In this study, we use clustering, noise (Jeba Kumar R.J.S., et al., 2022) reduction, and prediction algorithms to offer a novel knowledge based (Samanta, D., et al., 2021) approach for illness prediction. The fuzzy rules (Amuthadevi, C., et al. 2021) for the knowledge-based system are generated using Classification and Regression Trees (CART). We put our suggested strategy to the test on a number of publicly available medical datasets. The suggested strategy significantly increases illness prediction accuracy in the Pima Indian Diabetes, Mesothelioma, WDBC, StatLog, Cleveland, and Parkinson's telemonitoring datasets. The findings revealed that using a mix of fuzzy rule-based, CART with noise reduction, and clustering algorithms to predict illnesses from real-world medical datasets may be beneficial. As a clinical analytical approach, the knowledge-based system may support medical practitioners in their healthcare practise.

The outcomes based on the research by (Naz, H. et al., 2019) conducted by Purpose International Diabetes Federation (IDF) shows that 382 million people worldwide have diabetes. Diabetes' influence has risen dramatically in recent years, making it a worldwide problem. Diabetes has risen to the top of the list of leading causes of mortality in recent years. By 2045, the number of individuals impacted would have risen to 629 million, a 48 percent increase. Diabetes, on the other hand, is mainly avoidable and may be prevented by changing one's lifestyle. These adjustments may also help to reduce the risk of cancer and heart disease. As a result, there is an urgent need for a prognostic tool that may assist clinicians in early illness diagnosis and, as a result, propose the lifestyle adjustments necessary to halt the fatal disease's development. Method Diabetes, if left untreated, may be deadly and can lead to a variety of other ailments, including cardiac arrest, heart failure, brain stroke, and many more. As a result, early identification of diabetes is critical in order to take prompt treatment and prevent the condition from progressing and causing additional difficulties. Healthcare companies amass massive amounts of data (Pramanik, S. et al., 2019), such as electronic health records, pictures (Pramanik, S. et al., 2020; Pramanik, S. et al., 2014), omics data, and text (Pramanik, S. et al., 2014), but extracting (Pramanik, S. et al., 2014) insight and knowledge into that data remains a major difficulty. The newest breakthroughs in machine learning technology may be used to uncover hidden patterns, which might lead to an early diagnosis of diabetes. Utilizing the PIMA dataset, this research study proposes an approach for diabetes diagnosis using a variety of machine learning algorithms. Results of Artificial Neural Network (ANN), Naive Bayes (NB), Decision Tree (DT), and Deep Learning (DL) are functional classifiers that attain accuracy in the 90–98% range. On the PIMA dataset, DL had the best outcomes for diabetes onset among the four, with an accuracy rate of 98.07 percent. As a result, the suggested approach offers healthcare administrators with an effective predictive tool. The findings might be utilised to create a new automated prognostic tool that could aid in illness diagnosis early on. The study's findings show that DL produces the greatest outcomes with more promising extracted characteristics. DL obtains a 98.07 percent accuracy rate, which may be utilised to improve the automated prognosis tool. The accuracy of the DL technique may be further improved by including omics data for illness start prediction.

FOCUS OF THE ARTICLE

Dataset

The dataset we plan to use is Pima Indians Diabetes Database. In CCO Public Domain Pima Indians Diabetes database is available and maintained by UCI Machine Learning.

Pima Indian Dataset is basically from the National Institute of Diabetes and Digestive and Kidney Diseases organization. It can be found on the website named Kaggle (Patwa, P. et al., 2021). Based on the certain measurement of the diagnostic behaviour, the dataset is to diagnostically predict whether or not a woman patient has diabetes, based on certain diagnostic measurements included in the dataset. It is the main objective of this dataset. It is a larger dataset. In this dataset, all the patients are 21 years old females having Pregnancy Induced Hypertension (PIH) (Ebadi, A., et al. 2021).

This dataset has many medical independent attributes and a dependent attribute. Independent attributes consist of the pregnancies number, level of the insulin, age of the patient, BMI etc.

In this dataset there are 768 records of the patients. In the dataset there are some missing values which are filled with zero.

In Pima Indian dataset, out of the 768 records, only 268 records are true who are diabetic and the rest are false which are Non-Diabetic (Math, L. et al., 2021).

Dataset Information

- Total number of records: 768
- Number of the attributes: 9
- Name of the attributes: Pregnancies, Glucose, Blood Pressure, Skin thickness, Insulin, BMI, Diabetes Pedigree, Age and Outcome
- Missing values: 0 (0.0%)
- Duplicate rows: 0 (0.0%)

Class Distribution

- 0: 500
- 1: 268

Warnings

- Blood Pressure has 35 (4.6%) zeros
- Glucose has 5 (0.8%) zeros
- BMI has 11 (1.4%) zeros
- Insulin has 374 (48.7%) zeros
- Pregnancies has 110 (14.5%) zeros
- Skin Thickness has 227 (29.6%) zeros

Details About the Dataset

- Pregnancies: Number of times the person has been pregnant.
- Glucose: Patient's blood glucose level on testing.
- Blood Pressure: Patient body's Diastolic blood pressure.
- Skin Thickness: Skin fold thickness of triceps.
- Insulin: In two hour's serum test of the amount of insulin.
- BMI: Body Mass Index of the patients (kg/m^2)
- Diabetes Pedigree: The total family medical history of the patient.
- Age: Age (years) of the patient.
- Outcome: Diabetic – 1 /Non-Diabetic – 0.

The following table shows the data for age vs. no of female patients, age vs. no of pregnancies, age vs. Glucose Level for females, age vs. Blood Pressure for females, age vs. skin thickness, age vs. insulin taken by a female, age vs. BMI of a woman and age vs. Diabetic pedigree function

Table 1. Data for age vs. no of female patients, age vs. no of pregnancies, age vs. Glucose Level for females, age vs. Blood Pressure for females, age vs. skin thickness, age vs. insulin taken by a female, age vs. BMI of a woman and age vs. Diabetic pedigree function

	Age			
	80 – 60	**59 – 40**	**39 – 20**	**19 – 1**
No. of Female Patients	53	37	61	24
No. of pregnancies (Mean)	4	3	2	1
Glucose Level for females (mm/dL) (Mean)	130.85	116.21	106.84	105.72
Blood Pressure for females (mmHg) (Mean)	74.57	68.64	67.34	60.22
Skin Thickness	20.22	18.66	16.78	13.27
Insulin taken by a woman (Mean)	76.54	82.31	68.97	54.81
BMI of a woman (Mean)	28.83	26.87	30.25	23.54
Diabetic Pedigree Function (Mean)	0.48	0.34	0.37	0.45

The maximum number of pregnancies that a woman had was 17 while the minimum was 0 and the Mean is 3.845 and Median is 3 Pregnancy per woman.

The maximum glucose a Pima Indian woman had was 199 mg/dL and mean glucose level is 120.9 mg/dL with median of 117 mg/dL.

The maximum Blood Pressure of a Pima Indian woman had was 122 mmHg and mean Blood pressure is 69.11 mmHg with median of 72 mmHg

The maximum skin thickness a Pima Indian woman had was 99 and mean skin thickness is 20.54 with a median value of 23

The maximum insulin a Pima Indian woman had was 846 and mean insulin is 79.8 with median of 30.5

The maximum BMI a Pima Indian woman had was 67.1 and mean BMI is 31.99 with median of 32

The maximum diabetes pedigree function a Pima Indian woman had was 2.42 and mean diabetes pedigree function is 0.4719 with median of 0.3725

The maximum age of a Pima Indian woman had was 81 years and mean age is 33.24 years with median of 29 years.

Comparison of Mean of Independent variables of Pima Indian Women with and without Diabetes: From the data it can be visualized that BP level, BMI, Glucose Insulin and Age are higher for diabetic women as compared to women without diabetes. The findings are on expected lines.

Table 2. Details of Dataset

	Pregnancies	Glucose	BP	Skin Thickness	Insulin	BMI	DPF	Age	Outcome
0	6	148	72	35	0	33.6	0.627	50	1
1	1	85	66	29	0	26.6	0.351	31	0
2	8	183	64	0	0	23.3	0.672	32	1
3	1	89	66	23	94	28.1	0.167	21	0
4	0	137	40	35	168	43.1	2.288	33	1

Limitations of the Dataset

1. In the dataset all the records are of female patients.
2. The race of patients in the dataset is Pima Indians.

Before we processed for the regression, we have divided the data into three parts.

Training data set contains 70% of the total observations, Validation data set contains 20% of the total observations, and Test data set contains 10% of the total observations.

COMMON MACHINE LEARNING ALGORITHMS

Here, the Decision Tree Classifier and Random Forest Classifier. Let's go on a basic idea on these algorithms.

Decision Tree Algorithm

Decision Tree (Hancock et al., 2021) is a classifier which is tree structured. It can be used as a classifier and also it can be used for regression. Based on a training dataset as an input, this algorithm generates a model or a classifier. When we give couple of unlabelled examples as an input to the model or classifier, the classifier assigns or finds the class for the examples based on the input mechanism. There are 2 types of nodes in Decision Tree, one is decision node and another is leaf node. Decision nodes are nothing but test and the result of the test is either Yes or No, are indicated by the branches. The test is performed on the feature or the attribute value of the input dataset. And the leaf node represents the final results.

Example

Here we represent an example as picture. We take a dataset of salary and a facility tree. At first, the decision node checks whether the salary is between $50000-$80000 or not. According to the result decision tree splits the dataset. One of them is another decision node and another is the leaf node. It again checks the decision node and according to the result, decision tree splits the dataset again. By this process finally the decision tree gives the results in the leaf node.

Figure 1. Pictorial representation of Random Forest

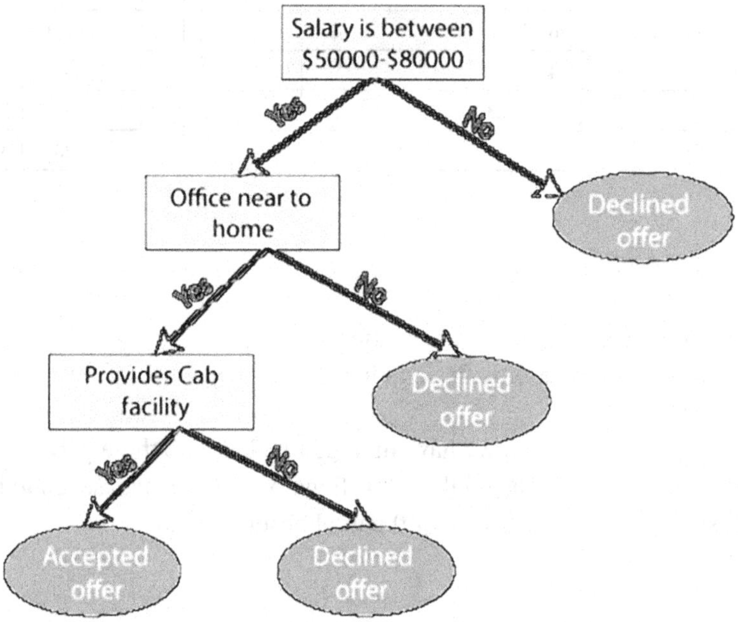

Algorithm:

- STEP 1: Starts from the root node which contains complete dataset.
- STEP 2: Split the dataset into subsets which contains the data with the same value for an attribute.
- STEP 3: Generate Decision node which contains the best attribute.
- STEP 4: Repeat above steps on each subset until it finds leaf nodes in all the branches of the tree.

Random Forest Algorithm

It is the most popular and powerful supervised machine learning algorithm. It creates the forest with the help of decision trees. If we take most of the number of decision trees in the forest, it gives high accuracy. This algorithm collects the results from decision trees and find out the optimal result by majority. Random forest can be used as a classifier and regression also, handle the missing values in an optimal way and maintain the accuracy for the missing data.

The main hypermeters of using Random Forest (Simseklar, et al. 2021) over any model is

1. Increasing the predictive power of the model.
2. Increasing the model's speed.

Example

We can take 9 Decision trees to create forest, 6 of those predict a value of 1 and 3 of those predicts a value of 0. Random forest algorithm checks the majority of the values and predicts the result; here random forest predicts a value of 1 because a major part of the decision trees (6 decision trees) predicts a value of 1. This is the way by which a Random Forest Algorithm works.

Algorithm:

- STEP 1: Selects random data points from the training set.
- STEP2: Create Decisions trees associated with the selected data points (subsets).
- STEP 3: Choose the number N for decision trees.
- STEP 4: Repeat step 1 and step 2
- STEP 5: When it finds new data points then it looks for the predictions of each decision tree and by considering the majority of the result it assigns the category to the new data point.

K-Nearest Neighbor

K-nearest neighbor algorithm (El-Magd et al., 2021) is a supervised machine learning (Muhammad, 2021) algorithm used for both classification (Cvitic, et al. 2021) and regression (Shah et al., 2021) also. K nearest algorithm assigns or predicts a class/category for a new datapoint by considering the K-nearest neighbor of that datapoint. It is known as lazy learner algorithm because it doesn't learn using training data prior. It stores the data and when it gets new datapoint then the algorithm classifies that datapoint into a category which is similar to its k-Nearest neighbors. The algorithm finds k nearest neighbors by using Euclidean Distance (Liang, J., 2020) formula. The Euclidean Distance between two points $p(x1, y1)$ and $p(x2, y2)$ is $ED= sqrt((x2-x1)^2 + (y2-y1)^2)$

Example

As we see if there are total 7 data points, out of which 3 red belongs to class R, 3 belongs to class B and yellow one is a new datapoint. K nearest neighbor algorithm will classify that the new data point belongs to class R because its k nearest neighbors are red and belongs to class R.

Algorithm:

- Step 1: Load training data.
- Step 2: Prepare the data by data scaling, missing value treatment and dimensionally reduction as required.
- Step 3: Find the value for k.
- Step 4: Class prediction for a new data point.
  - Calculate the distance between new data point and training data.
  - Add the distance and the index of train data to an ordered collection.
  - Sort the distances in ascending order with corresponding train data.
  - Select top k entries from the sorted list.

       ◦   Find the most frequent category of chosen k entries. And assign that category or class to the new data point.

The code for importing libraries is shown here

```
In [ 1 7]: import pandas as pd
import numpy as np import OS
import itertools
import matplotlib.pyplot as plt import seaborn as sns
```

The libraries have been imported. The file diabetes.csv is shown in Table 3.

```
In (60): df=pd.read_csv("C:\\Users\\SUCHISMITA\\Desktop\\final year\\diabetes.
csv") df .head (10)
Out (60):
```

Table 3.

	Pregnancies	Glucose	Blood Pressure	Skin Thickness	Insulin	BMI	Diabetes Pedigree Function	Age	Outcome
0	6	148	72	35	0	33.6	0.627	50	1
1	1	85	68	29	0	26.6	0.351	31	0
2	8	183	64	0	0	23.3	0.672	32	1 1
3	1	89	68	23	94	28.1	0.167	21	0
4	0	137	40	35	168	43.1	2.288	33	1
6	5	116	74	0	0	25.6	0.201	30	0
6	3	78	50	32	88	31.0	0.248	26	1
7	10	115	0	0	0	35.3	0.134	29	0
8	2	197	70	45	543	30.5	0.158	53	1 1
9	8	125	96	0	0	0.0	0.232	54	1

Then the dataset has been recorded. In total there are 768 pregnant women records in the dataset. The first ten pregnant women records have been visualized for better understanding. Information of the dataset is shown in Table 4.

```
In [ 22]: data.info()
<class 'pandas.core.frame.DataFrame'>
Rangeindex: 768 entries, 0 to 767 Data (total 9 columns) columns):
```

Here we have plotted the graphical representation of the dataset variables. This graphical visualization can help us to understand the dataset in better way.

Then the information of dataset has been checked.

Table 4.

#	Column	Non-null	Count	Dtype
0	Pregnancies	768	non-null	int64
1	Glucose	768	non-null	int64
2	BloodPressure	768	non-null	int64
3	SkinThickness	768	non-null	int64
4	Insulin	768	non-null	int64
5	BMI	768	non-null	float64
6	DiabetesPedigreeFunction	768	non-null	float64
7	Age	768	non-null	int64
8	Outcome	768	non-null	int64

Figure 2. Graphical representation of dataset

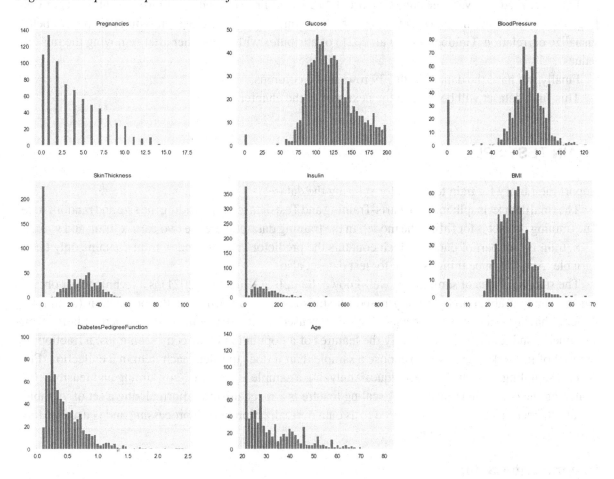

For cleaning (Rawat et al., 2021) the data (Pramanik, S. et al., 2021) the number of missing values in the dataset is found out for each predictor variable. To count the missing values, summation of the columns is performed and then the sum is subtracted from 768. This is done for every predictor variable and then finally the no of zeros for every predictor variable is calculated. It is shown in Table 5.

Table 5. Number of zeros for every predictor variable

Number of values zero in pregnancies: 111
Number of values zero in pregnancies: 5
Number of values zero in pregnancies: 35
Number of values zero in pregnancies: 227
Number of values zero in pregnancies: 374
Number of values zero in pregnancies: 11
Number of values zero in pregnancies: 0
Number of values zero in pregnancies: 0

Here, the total no of zeroes for each predictor variable has been shown. It is seen that the Skin Thickness and Insulin have maximum no of missing values (Gupta, H. et al., 2021). As it is known that Machine Learning algorithms don't work well when data is missing, so it is required to clean the dataset. For cleaning the dataset, the SkinThikness and Insulin columns has been removed from the dataset as these two columns have maximum no of missing values.

For other predictor variables like Glucose, BMI, Blood Pressure the no of missing values is not very large so only the rows have been removed which contain zeroes. Here, we present a pair-plot to better visualize correlation (Goldberg, P., et al. 2021) of attributes with each other after removing the missing values.

Finally, we have the dataset with 729 rows and 7 columns.

This final dataset will be used in the next part of the chapter.

TRAIN TEST SPLIT

Import the library for train test split for splitting the dataset.

The final dataset is split into two parts-Training and Test dataset by providing the size and random state. The training dataset is for fitting the model. In the training dataset there are two parts x_train and y_train.

x_train is that part of dataset which contains the predictor variable and y_train contains only target variable. And the same thing is done for test dataset also.

The statistical idea of sampling is well-known. Sampling (Liu et al., 2021) is a technique for obtaining information about a community based on statistics from a portion of the population (a sample), rather of having to analyze each person. Sampling is used to derive conclusions about a population from specimens, and it allows us to identify the features of a population by directly seeing just a fraction (or sample) of it. It takes less time to choose a sample than it does to select each item in a collection. Purposeful sampling is a low-cost technique. Analyzing a sample is less time-consuming and feasible than analyzing the complete population. A scaling feature is a mechanism for normalizing a set of variables or data characteristics. It is also referred to as data normalization in data processing and is usually done during the data preparation stage.

Experimental Setup

In the experiment, PYTHON v3.8.5 (Mandal et al., 2021) has been used on PC with 2.00GHz in i5-10210U processor to run the desired model classifier and bring out the efficiency (Hamdia et al., 2021) of our proposed model. In the experiment, we have used the Pima Indians Dataset. The whole of the experiment has been done in Jupyter-Notebook, as python 3.8.5.

Figure 3. Final outcome

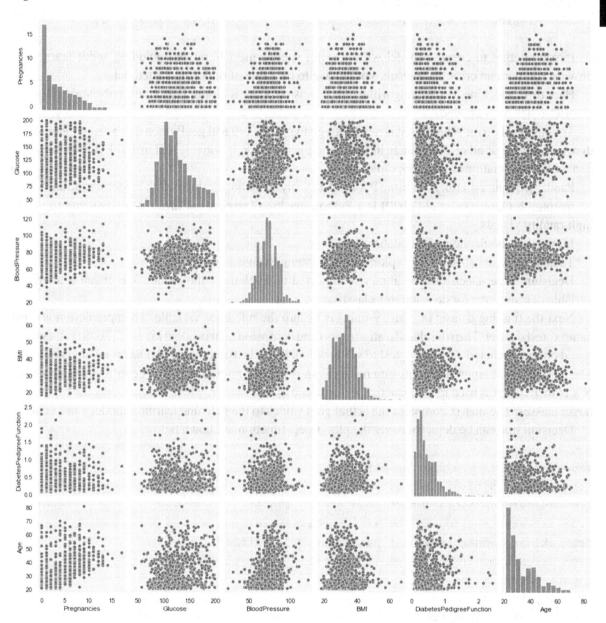

Data Processing

The dataset is saved in CSV file (Cagirici et al., 2021) named diabetes.csv. First, we have to read the dataset. To read the dataset we have to import the following modules.

After adding a constant value to each variable value, do a log transformation. With the mean, one may infer a value of zero. For transformation, use square root rather than log.

Missing numbers are represented in Python libraries as nan, which stands for "not a number." You may use the command to find out which cells contain missing values and then calculate how many are out there in each column:

```
missing val count by column = (data.isnull().sum())
print (missing val count by column [missing val count by column > 0])
```

If you attempt to create a model with missing values, most libraries (including scikit-learn) will provide you with an error. As a result, you'll have to pick one of the tactics listed below.

Here three machine learning algorithm i.e., Decision Tree, Random Forest and K-Nearest neighbor algorithm has been applied.

To setup Python on Windows, it is needed to go to python.org and get Python 2.7. x from there. After that, acceptance of all of the settings in the Python installation is done. It will install Python and set up certain file associations in the root directory.

Pandas (Mohamed, et al. 2021) are a Python data analysis toolkit that helps with modeling and analytics.

matplotlib (Mohanty, et al., 2020) is a Python machine learning package that allows you to create high-quality visuals.

Jupyter notebook allows for collaborative work.

Tableau provides strong data exploration and interactive visualization tools.

Decision Tree: Decision tree library is imported to implement the model. We create a reference variable decision tree for decision tree classifier.

Next the training dataset (x_train, y-train) is fit into the reference variable. Then prediction is done using x_test dataset. Then the classification report and confusion matrix (Dourjoy et al., 2020) is found out based on the predicted data and y_test to see how much the decision tree model has predicted correctly. The classification report and confusion matrix is shown in the above diagram. A confusion matrix is an N x N matrix that is used to evaluate the performance of a classifier, where N represents the number of target classes. The matrix compares the actual goal values to the machine learning model's predictions.

Decision tree can be depicted using the plot_tree() function as shown below.

```
import matplotlib.pyplot as plt
from sklearn.datasets import load_iris
from sklearn.datasets import load_breast_cancer
from sklearn.tree import DecisionTreeClassifier
from sklearn.ensemble import RandomForestClassifier
from sklearn.model_selection import train_test_split
import pandas as pd
import numpy as np
from sklearn import tree
```

Then the accuracy of the decision tree model is found out. The accuracy of this model is 73.39449%.

Random Forest

First the RandomForestClassifier library is imported to implement the model. A reference variable rfc is created for RandomForestClassifier providing the no of decision tree. Next the training dataset (x_train, y-train) is fit into the reference variable.

Then the prediction has been done by using x_test dataset

Then we have printed the classification report and confusion matrix on the basis of predicted data and y_test to see how much the random forest model has predicted correctly. The classification report and confusion matrix is shown in the above diagram.

The accuracy for Random forest is 78.440367%.

K-Nearest Neighbor

First K-NeighborClassifier library is imported to implement the model. A reference variable KNN is created for KNeighborClassifier providing the no of nearest points. Next the training dataset (x_train,y-train) is fit into the reference variable.

Then, prediction has been done using the x_test dataset.

Then we have print the classification report and confusion matrix on the basis of predicted data and y_test to see how much our model has predicted correctly. The classification report and confusion matrix is shown in the above diagram.

Then the accuracy for this algorithm is found out. And the accuracy is 74.770642%.

SOLUTIONS AND RECOMMENDATIONS

Data pre-processing is the procedure for preparing raw data (Janiesch, et al. 2021) for use in a machine learning algorithm. It's the first and most important stage in building a machine learning approach. It is not always the case that we come across clean and prepared data while working on a machine learning project. And, before doing any data-related activity, it is necessary to clean the data and format it. As a result, we utilise a data pre-treatment activity for this. Real-world data sometimes includes noise, missing values, and is in an unsuitable format that cannot be utilised directly in machine learning models. Data pre-processing is a necessary step for cleaning data and making it acceptable for a machine learning model, which improves the model's accuracy and efficiency.

Confusion matrix is associated with the following terms:

1. True Positives (TP): True positives occur when the data point's actual class is 1 (True) and the anticipated class is likewise 1. (True)

True positive refers to a situation in which a person has diabetes and the algorithm classifies his case as cancer (1).

2. True Negatives (TN): True negatives occur when the data point's actual class is 0(False) and the projected class is likewise 0(False).

True Negatives are used in situations when a person does not have cancer yet the model classifies his condition as such.

3. False Positive (FP): False positives occur when the data point's real class is 0 (False) but the anticipated value is 1 (True). It is false because the model anticipated the wrong thing, and true since this class predicted the right thing (1). False Positives are when a person does not have cancer yet the model classifies his situation as cancer.

4.   False Negatives (FN): False negatives occur when the data point's real class is 1 (True) but the anticipated value is 0 (False). It is false because the model anticipated the wrong thing, and negative since the class predicted the wrong thing (0). False Negatives are when a person has cancer and the algorithm classifies his condition as non-cancer.

It is needed for the model to produce 0 False Positives and 0 False Negatives in the ideal case. However, this is not the situation in real life since no model is 100 percent correct majority of the time.

What Should Be Minimised and When?

We know that any model we employ to forecast the real class of the target attribute will have some inaccuracy. False Positives and False Negatives will happen as a consequence of this (i.e., Algorithm classifying things incorrectly as model compared to the actual class). There is no hard and fast rule that states what should be reduced in every circumstance. It all relies on your company's requirements and the circumstances of the issue one is attempting to address. As a result, we may desire to reduce the number of False Positives or False Negatives.

Reduce False Negatives

Let's imagine that, in our diabetes detection scenario, only 5 persons out of 100 have cancer. We want to accurately categorise all malignant patients in this situation since even a very BAD model (trying to predict everyone as NON-diabetes) would give us a 95 percent accuracy (will come to what accuracy is). However, in trying to catch all cancer instances, one may wind up creating a categorization in which a person who is not suffering from cancer is labelled as cancerous. This may be acceptable since it is less risky than failing to identify/capture a malignant patient, as we will be sending the cases of cancer for additional investigation and reporting anyhow. Missing a cancer patient, on the other hand, would be a tremendous error since they would not be examined further.

Reduce False Positives

Let's look at another scenario where the model identifies how an email is spam or not to better understand False Positives. Assume that one is anticipating a crucial email, such as a response from an employer or an acceptance letter from an institution. Assign the target variable a label, such as 1: "Email is a spam" and 0: "Email is not a spam". Let's say the Model categorises the critical email you've been waiting for as Spam (case of False positive). Now, this is a lot worse than labelling a spam email as essential or not important, since in that instance, we can still manually remove it, and it's not a big deal if it occurs once in a while. As a result, when it comes to spam email categorization, reducing false positives seems to be more essential than reducing false negatives.

Accuracy

In classification problems, accuracy refers to the number of accurate predictions produced by the model across all types of predictions. Our accurate predictions (True positives and True negatives) (shown in red in the diagram above) are in the numerator, while the type of all predictions generated by the algorithm is in the denominator (Right as well as wrong ones).

When Should One Utilise Accuracy?

When the target variable classes in the data are approximately balanced, accuracy is a good metric. For example, apples account for 60% of the classes in our fruit picture collection, whereas oranges account for 40%. In this case, a model that correctly predicts whether such a new picture is an Apple or an Orange 97 percent of the time is a very excellent metric.

When to Avoid Using Accuracy?

When the target variable classes in the data are a majority of one class, accuracy should never be utilised as a metric. In our diabetes detection scenario, only 5 persons out of 100 have cancer. Let's pretend our model is terrible and every instance is predicted to be cancer-free. As a result, it properly categorised 95 non-cancer patients as non-cancerous and 5 malignant patients as non-cancerous. Despite the fact that the model is lousy at predicting cancer, it has a 95 percent accuracy rate.

Precision

Let's utilise the same confusion matrix we used for our cancer diagnosis example before. Precision is a metric that informs us what percentage of cancer patients we diagnosed truly had cancer. People who are expected to be malignant (TP and FP) and those who actually have cancer are both TP. In the related cancer scenario, only 5 persons out of 100 have cancer. Let's pretend our model is terrible and incorrectly diagnoses every instance as cancer. Our denominator (True positives and False Positives) is 100, while the numerator (individual with cancer and model estimating his case as cancer) is 5. So, in this case, we may claim that the precision of this model is 5%.

Recall

Recall is a metric that shows us what percentage of patients with cancer were mistakenly identified as having cancer by the algorithm. Actual positives (people with cancer are TP and FN) and persons diagnosed with cancer by the model are both TP. (Note: FN can be included since the Person was diagnosed with cancer against the model's prediction.)

Ex: Of the 100 persons in our cancer example, only 5 have cancer. Let's imagine the model predicts cancer in every instance. As a result, our denominator (True Positives and False Negatives) is 5, and our numerator (individual with cancer and model predicting his case as cancer) is likewise 5. (Since we predicted 5 diabetes cases correctly). As a result, in this case, we may state that the model's recall is 100 percent. And, as previously stated, the precision of such a design is 5%.

When Should You Use Precision and When Should You Use Recall?

It is self-evident that recall informs us about a classifier's performance in terms of false negatives (how often did we miss), whereas precision informs us about its performance in terms of false positives (how often did we miss) (how many did we caught). Being exact is what precision is all about. So, even if we just managed to catch one cancer case and accurately recorded it, we are 100 percent exact.

Recall isn't so much about accurately recording cases as it is about capturing all instances when the response is "cancer." So, if we just refer to every instance as "cancer", we will have 100% recall. So, if we want to concentrate on reducing False Negatives, we need our Recall to be as near to 100 percent as feasible without sacrificing accuracy, and if we want to emphasis on reducing False Positives, we want Precision to be as close to 100 percent as possible.

Specificity

Specificity is a metric that indicates how many patients who did not have diabetes were projected as non-cancerous by the algorithm. The genuine negatives (those who do not have cancer) and the persons who are diagnosed as not having cancer by us are FP and TN. (Note: FP is also included because, despite what the model predicted, the Participant did not develop cancer.)

Ex: Of the 100 persons in the related cancer example, only 5 have cancer. Let's imagine the model predicts cancer in every instance.

As a result, our denominator (False Positives and True Negatives) is 95, while the numerator (individual without diabetes and model projecting his case as diabetes-free) is 0 (Since we predicted every case as diabetic). So, in this case, we can see that the model's specificity is 0%.

FUTURE RESEARCH DIRECTIONS

Researchers showed that Diabetes mellitus, often referred to as diabetes, is a collection of metabolic illnesses that affects millions of individuals worldwide. Diabetes identification is critical due to the serious problems it may cause. Many research studies on diabetes detection have been conducted, some of which are dependent on the Pima Indian diabetes data collection. It's a data collection that dates back to 1965 and looks at women in the Pima Indian group, where the diabetes onset rate is rather high. Most previous research studies largely concentrated on one or two sophisticated approaches to evaluate the data, however a complete study covering a wide range of techniques is lacking. In the future, we will examine the most widely used strategies for detecting diabetes and data preparation methods (e.g., RNN (Recurrent Neural Network), CNN (Convolutional Neural Network) and Generative Adversarial Networks (GANs)), and so on. We will test these strategies on the Pima Indian data set to see how accurate cross-validation is. We will test each classifier's performance across a variety of data pre-processors and tweak the parameters to increase accuracy. We will also look at the relationship between each characteristic and the categorization outcome.

CONCLUSION

The main aim of this chapter was to design and implement Diabetes Prediction using Machine Learning Methods and Performance Analysis of that methods and it has been achieved successfully. The proposed approach uses various classification and ensemble learning method in which Random Forest, Decision Tree and K-NN classifiers are used. Here it is seen that the random forest classifier achieves better compared to others and give 78% accuracy. The diagram represents the comparison of the used Machine Learning methods. The experimental results can assist health care professionals to take early prediction and make early decision to cure diabetes and save humans life.

REFERENCES

Ahmed, S. T., Sankar, S., & Sandhya, M. (2021). Multi-objective optimal medical data informatics standardization and processing technique for telemedicine via machine learning approach. *Journal of Ambient Intelligence and Humanized Computing, 12*(5), 5349–5358. doi:10.100712652-020-02016-9

Akter, L., Al-Islam, F., & Islam, M.M. (2021). Prediction of Cervical Cancer from Behavior Risk Using Machine Learning Techniques. *SN Comput. Sc, 2,* 177-188. doi:10.1007/s42979-021-00551-6

Amuthadevi, C., Vijayan, D. S., & Ramachandran, V. (2021). Development of air quality monitoring (AQM) models using different machine learning approaches. *Journal of Ambient Intelligence and Humanized Computing, 22*(3), 1–13. doi:10.100712652-020-02724-2

Bandyopadhyay, S., Goyal, V., Dutta, S., Pramanik, S., & Sherazi, H. H. R. (2021). Unseen to Seen by Digital Steganography. In S. Pramanik, M. M. Ghonge, R. Ravi, & K. Cengiz (Eds.), *Multidisciplinary Approach to Modern Digital Steganography*. IGI Global. doi:10.4018/978-1-7998-7160-6.ch001

Barik, S., Mohanty, S., Mohanty, S., & Singh, D. (2021). Analysis of Prediction Accuracy of Diabetes Using Classifier and Hybrid Machine Learning Techniques. In D. Mishra, R. Buyya, P. Mohapatra, & S. Patnaik (Eds.), *Intelligent and Cloud Computing. Smart Innovation, Systems and Technologies* (Vol. 153). Springer. doi:10.1007/978-981-15-6202-0_41

Bascil, M. S., & Oztekin, H. (2012). A Study on Hepatitis Disease Diagnosis Using Probabilistic Neural Network. *Journal of Medical Systems, 36*(3), 1603–1606. doi:10.100710916-010-9621-x PMID:21057884

Cagirici, H. B., Galvez, S., Sen, T. Z., & Budak, H. (2021). LncMachine: A machine learning algorithm for long noncoding RNA annotation in plants. *Functional & Integrative Genomics, 21*(2), 195–204. doi:10.100710142-021-00769-w PMID:33635499

Coffey, C. S., Hebert, P. R., Ritchie, M. D., Krumholz, H. M., Gaziano, J. M., Ridker, P. M., Brown, N. J., Vaughan, D. E., & Moore, J. H. (2004). An application of conditional logistic regression and multifactor dimensionality reduction for detecting gene-gene Interactions on risk of myocardial infarction: The importance of model validation. *BMC Bioinformatics, 49*(1), 22–37. doi:10.1186/1471-2105-5-49 PMID:15119966

Cvitić, I., Peraković, D., Periša, M., & Gupta, B. (2021). Ensemble machine learning approach for classification of IoT devices in smart home. *International Journal of Machine Learning and Cybernetics, 12*(11), 3179–3202. doi:10.100713042-020-01241-0

De Bois, M., Yacoubi, M. A. E., & Ammi, M. (2022). GLYFE: Review and benchmark of personalized glucose predictive models in type 1 diabetes. *Medical & Biological Engineering & Computing, 60*(1), 1–17. doi:10.100711517-021-02437-4 PMID:34751904

Dourjoy, S. M. K., Rafi, A. M. G. R., Tumpa, Z. N., & Saifuzzaman, M. (2021). A Comparative Study on Prediction of Dengue Fever Using Machine Learning Algorithm. In A. Tripathy, M. Sarkar, J. Sahoo, K. C. Li, & S. Chinara (Eds.), *Advances in Distributed Computing and Machine Learning. Lecture Notes in Networks and Systems* (Vol. 127). Springer. doi:10.1007/978-981-15-4218-3_49

Dutta, S., Pramanik, S., & Bandyopadhyay, S. K. (2021). Prediction of Weight Gain during COVID-19 for Avoiding Complication in Health. *International Journal of Medical Science and Current Research, 4*(3), 1042–1052. doi:10.20944/preprints202105.0177.v1

Ebadi, A., Xi, P., Tremblay, S., Spencer, B., Pall, R., & Wong, A. (2021). Understanding the temporal evolution of COVID-19 research through machine learning and natural language processing. *Scientometrics*, *126*(1), 725–739. doi:10.100711192-020-03744-7 PMID:33230352

El-Magd, S. A. A., Pradhan, B., & Alamri, A. (2021). Machine learning algorithm for flash flood prediction mapping in Wadi El-Laqeita and surroundings, Central Eastern Desert, Egypt. *Arabian Journal of Geosciences*, *14*(4), 323. doi:10.100712517-021-06466-z

Goldberg, P., Sümer, Ö., Stürmer, K., Wagner, W., Göllner, R., Gerjets, P., Kasneci, E., & Trautwein, U. (2021). Attentive or Not? Toward a Machine Learning Approach to Assessing Students' Visible Engagement in Classroom Instruction. *Educational Psychology Review*, *33*(1), 27–49. doi:10.100710648-019-09514-z

Gupta, A., Pramanik, S., Bui, H. T. & Ibenu, N. M. (2021). Machine Learning and Deep Learning in Steganography and Steganalysis. *Multimedia Approach to Modern Digital Steganography*, 75-98. . doi:10.4018/978-1-7998-7160-6

Gupta, H., Varshney, H., & Sharma, T. K. (2021). Comparative performance analysis of quantum machine learning with deep learning for diabetes prediction. *Complex Intell. Syst*, *12*, 41–53. doi:10.100740747-021-00398-7

Hamdia, K. M., Zhuang, X., & Rabczuk, T. (2021). An efficient optimization approach for designing machine learning models based on genetic algorithm. *Neural Computing & Applications*, *33*(6), 1923–1933. doi:10.100700521-020-05035-x

Hancock, J. T., & Khoshgoftaar, T. M. (2021). Gradient Boosted Decision Tree Algorithms for Medicare Fraud Detection. *SN. Computer Science*, *2*(4), 268–279. doi:10.100742979-021-00655-z

Harimoorthy, K., & Thangavelu, M. (2021). Multi-disease prediction model using improved SVM-radial bias technique in healthcare monitoring system. *Journal of Ambient Intelligence and Humanized Computing*, *12*(3), 3715–3723. doi:10.100712652-019-01652-0

Janiesch, C., Zschech, P., & Heinrich, K. (2021). Machine learning and deep learning. *Electronic Markets*, *31*(3), 685–695. doi:10.100712525-021-00475-2

Jayasingh, R., Kumar, R. J. S., Telagathoti, D. B., Sagayam, K. M., & Pramanik, S. (2022). Speckle noise removal by SORAMA segmentation in Digital Image Processing to facilitate precise robotic surgery. *International Journal of Reliable and Quality E-Healthcare*, *11*(1), 1–19. Advance online publication. doi:10.4018/IJRQEH.295083

Karatsiolis, S., & Schizas, C. N. (2012). Region based Support Vector Machine algorithm for medical diagnosis on Pima Indian Diabetes dataset. *IEEE 12th International Conference on Bioinformatics & Bioengineering (BIBE)*, 139-144, 10.1109/BIBE.2012.6399663

Kaur, H. & Kumari, V. (2022). Predictive modelling and analytics for diabetes using a machine learning approach. *Applied Computing and Informatics, 18*, 99-100. . doi:10.1016/j.aci.2018.12.004

Lee, S., Zhou, J., Wong, W. T., Liu, T., Wu, W. K. K., Wong, I. C. K., Zhang, Q., & Tse, G. (2021). Glycemic and lipid variability for predicting complications and mortality in diabetes mellitus using machine learning. *BMC Endocrine Disorders*, *21*(1), 94. doi:10.118612902-021-00751-4 PMID:33947391

Li, W., Chai, Y., Khan, F., Jan, S. R. U., Verma, S., Menon, V. G., Kavita, & Li, X. (2021). A Comprehensive Survey on Machine Learning-Based Big Data Analytics for IoT-Enabled Smart Healthcare System. *Mobile Networks and Applications*, 26(1), 234–252. doi:10.100711036-020-01700-6

Liang, J., Wei, Y., Qu, B., Yue, C., & Song, H. (2021). Ensemble learning based on fitness Euclidean-distance ratio differential evolution for classification. *Natural Computing*, 20(1), 77–87. doi:10.100711047-020-09791-6

Liu, Y., Bai, F., Tang, Z., Liu, N., & Liu, Q. (2021). Integrative transcriptomic, proteomic, and machine learning approach to identifying feature genes of atrial fibrillation using atrial samples from patients with valvular heart disease. *BMC Cardiovascular Disorders*, 21(1), 52–68. doi:10.118612872-020-01819-0 PMID:33509101

Lu, G., Li, S., Guo, Z., Farha, O. K., Hauser, B. G., Qi, X., Wang, Y., Wang, X., Han, S., Liu, X., DuChene, J. S., Zhang, H., Zhang, Q., Chen, X., Ma, J., Loo, S. C. J., Wei, W. D., Yang, Y., Hupp, J. T., & Huo, F. (2012). Imparting functionality to a metal–organic framework material by controlled nanoparticle encapsulation. *Nature Chemistry*, 4(4), 310–316. doi:10.1038/nchem.1272 PMID:22437717

Mahindru, A., Sangal, A., & Droid, F. S. (2021). A feature selection technique to detect malware from Android using Machine Learning Techniques. *Multimedia Tools and Applications*, 80(9), 13271–13323. doi:10.100711042-020-10367-w PMID:33462535

Mandal, A., Dutta, S. & Pramanik, S. (2021). Machine Intelligence of Pi from Geometrical Figures with Variable Parameters using SciLab. *Methodologies and Applications of Computational Statistics for Machine Intelligence*, 38-63. doi:10.4018/978-1-7998-7701-1

Math, L., & Fatima, R. (2021). Adaptive machine learning classification for diabetic retinopathy. *Multimedia Tools and Applications*, 80(4), 5173–5186. doi:10.100711042-020-09793-7

Meng, X., Zhang, Y., & Qiao, J. (2021). An adaptive task-oriented RBF network for key water quality parameters prediction in wastewater treatment process. *Neural Computing & Applications*, 33(17), 11401–11414. doi:10.100700521-020-05659-z

Meslie, Y., Enbeyle, W., Pandey, B. K., Pramanik, S., Pandey, D., Dadeech, P., Belay, A., & Saini, A. (2021). Machine Intelligence-based trend analysis of COVID-19 for total daily confirmed case in Asia and Africa. *Methodologies and Applications of Computational Statistics for Machine Intelligence*, 164-185. . doi:10.4018/978-1-7998-7701-1

Mohamed, A., Abuoda, G., & Ghanem, A. (2021). RDFFrames: Knowledge graph access for machine learning tools. *The VLDB Journal*, 18, 88–99. doi:10.100700778-021-00690-5

Mohanty, S., Mishra, A., & Saxena, A. (2021). Medical Data Analysis Using Machine Learning with KNN. In *International Conference on Innovative Computing and Communications. Advances in Intelligent Systems and Computing* (vol. 1166). Springer. 10.1007/978-981-15-5148-2_42

Muhammad, L. J., Algehyne, E. A., Usman, S. S., Ahmad, A., Chakraborty, C., & Mohammed, I. A. (2021). Supervised Machine Learning Models for Prediction of COVID-19 Infection using Epidemiology Dataset. *SN Comput Sci*, 2(1), 11–19. doi:10.100742979-020-00394-7 PMID:33263111

Naz, H., & Ahuja, S. (2020). Deep learning approach for diabetes prediction using PIMA Indian dataset. *Journal of Diabetes and Metabolic Disorders*, *19*(1), 391–403. doi:10.100740200-020-00520-5 PMID:32550190

Nilashi, M., Ibrahim, O., Dalvi, M., Ahmadi, H., & Shahmoradi, L. (2017). Accuracy Improvement for Diabetes Disease Classification: A Case on a Public Medical Dataset. *Fuzzy Information and Engineering*, *9*(3), 345–357. doi:10.1016/j.fiae.2017.09.006

Pandey, B. K., Mane, D., Kumar, V., Nassa, K., Pandey, D., Dutta, S., Ventayen, R. J. M., Agarwal, G. & Rastogi, R., (2021). Secure text Extraction form Complex Degraded Images by Applying Steganography and Deep Learning. *Multimedia Approach to Modern Digital Steganography*, 146-163. doi:10.4018/978-1-7998-7160-6

Patwa, P. (2021). Fighting an Infodemic: COVID-19 Fake News Dataset. In T. Chakraborty, K. Shu, H. R. Bernard, H. Liu, & M. S. Akhtar (Eds.), *Combating Online Hostile Posts in Regional Languages during Emergency Situation. CONSTRAINT 2021. Communications in Computer and Information Science* (Vol. 1402). Springer. doi:10.1007/978-3-030-73696-5_3

Pramanik, S., & Bandyopadhyay, S. K. (2013). Application of Steganography in Symmetric Key Cryptography with Genetic Algorithm. *International Journals of Engineering and Technology*, *10*, 1791–1799.

Pramanik, S., & Bandyopadhyay, S. K. (2014). An Innovative Approach in Steganography. *Scholars Journal of Engineering and Technology*, *2*, 276–280.

Pramanik, S., & Bandyopadhyay, S. K. (2014). Image Steganography Using Wavelet Transform and Genetic Algorithm. *International Journal of Innovative Research in Advanced Engineering*, *1*, 1–4.

Pramanik, S., Galety, M. G., Samanta, D., & Joseph, N. P. (2022). *Data mining approaches for Healthcare decision support systems*. In 3rd International Conference on Emerging Technologies in Data Mining and Information Security (IEMIS 2022) at Institute of Engineering & Management, Kolkata, West Bengal. India.

Pramanik, S., & Raja, S. S. (2019). Analytical Study on Security Issues in Steganography. *Think-India*, *22*(35), 106-114.

Pramanik, S., Sagayam, K. M. & Jena, O. P. (2021). Machine Learning Frameworks in Cancer Detection. *ICCSRE 2021*. . doi:10.1051/e3sconf/202129701073

Rawat, R., Mahor, V., Chirgaiya, S., Shaw, R. N., & Ghosh, A. (2021). Sentiment Analysis at Online Social Network for Cyber-Malicious Post Reviews Using Machine Learning Techniques. In J. C. Bansal, M. Paprzycki, M. Bianchini, & S. Das (Eds.), *Computationally Intelligent Systems and their Applications. Studies in Computational Intelligence* (Vol. 950). Springer. doi:10.1007/978-981-16-0407-2_9

Samanta, D., Dutta, S., Galety, M. G. & Pramanik, S. (2021). A Novel Approach for Web Mining Taxonomy for High-Performance Computing. *CIIR 2021*.

Shah, M. I., Javed, M. F., & Abunama, T. (2021). Proposed formulation of surface water quality and modelling using gene expression, machine learning, and regression techniques. *Environmental Science and Pollution Research International*, *28*(11), 13202–13220. doi:10.100711356-020-11490-9 PMID:33179185

Simsekler, M. C. E., Alhashmi, N. H., Azar, E., King, N., Luqman, R. A. M. A., & Al Mulla, A. (2021). Exploring drivers of patient satisfaction using a random forest algorithm. *BMC Medical Informatics and Decision Making*, *21*(1), 157–168. doi:10.118612911-021-01519-5 PMID:33985481

Yang, L., Xue, Y., Wei, J., Dai, Q., & Li, P. (2021). Integrating metabolomic data with machine learning approach for discovery of Q-markers from Jinqi Jiangtang preparation against type 2 diabetes. *Chinese Medicine*, *16*(1), 30–48. doi:10.118613020-021-00438-x PMID:33741031

ADDITIONAL READING

Albahri, A. S., Hamid, R. A., Alwan, J. K., Al-qays, Z. T., Zaidan, A. A., Zaidan, B. B., Albahri, A. O. S., AlAmoodi, A. H., Khlaf, J. M., Almahdi, E. M., Thabet, E., Hadi, S. M., Mohammed, K. I., Alsalem, M. A., Al-Obaidi, J. R., & Madhloom, H. T. (2020). Role of biological Data Mining and Machine Learning Techniques in Detecting and Diagnosing the Novel Coronavirus (COVID-19): A Systematic Review. *Journal of Medical Systems*, *44*(7), 122. doi:10.100710916-020-01582-x PMID:32451808

Arpaci, I., Huang, S., Al-Emran, M., Al-Kabi, M. N., & Peng, M. (2021). Predicting the COVID-19 infection with fourteen clinical features using machine learning classification algorithms. *Multimedia Tools and Applications*, *80*(8), 11943–11957. doi:10.100711042-020-10340-7 PMID:33437173

Chugh, G., Kumar, S., & Singh, N. (2021). Survey on Machine Learning and Deep Learning Applications in Breast Cancer Diagnosis. *Cognitive Computation*, *13*(6), 1451–1470. doi:10.100712559-020-09813-6

Donohue, C., Mao, S., Sejdić, E., & Coyle, J. L. (2021). Tracking Hyoid Bone Displacement During Swallowing Without Videofluoroscopy Using Machine Learning of Vibratory Signals. *Dysphagia*, *36*(2), 259–269. doi:10.100700455-020-10124-z PMID:32419103

Jefferies, J. L., Spencer, A. K., Lau, H. A., Nelson, M. W., Giuliano, J. D., Zabinski, J. W., Boussios, C., Curhan, G., Gliklich, R. E., & Warnock, D. G. (2021). A new approach to identifying patients with elevated risk for Fabry disease using a machine learning algorithm. *Orphanet Journal of Rare Diseases*, *16*(1), 518. doi:10.118613023-021-02150-3 PMID:34930374

Kadhim, A. I. (2019). Survey on supervised machine learning techniques for automatic text classification. *Artificial Intelligence Review*, *52*(1), 273–292. doi:10.100710462-018-09677-1

Kenny, L. C., Dunn, W. B., Ellis, D. I., Myers, J., Baker, P. N., & Kell, D. B. (2005). Novel biomarkers for pre-eclampsia detected using metabolomics and machine learning. *Metabolomics*, *1*(3), 227. doi:10.100711306-005-0003-1

Kinreich, S., Meyers, J. L., Maron-Katz, A., Kamarajan, C., Pandey, A. K., Chorlian, D. B., Zhang, J., Pandey, G., Subbie-Saenz de Viteri, S., Pitti, D., Anokhin, A. P., Bauer, L., Hesselbrock, V., Schuckit, M. A., Edenberg, H. J., & Porjesz, B. (2021). Predicting risk for Alcohol Use Disorder using longitudinal data with multimodal biomarkers and family history: A machine learning study. *Molecular Psychiatry*, *26*(4), 1133–1141. doi:10.103841380-019-0534-x PMID:31595034

Mejdoub, M., & Ben Amar, C. (2013). Classification improvement of local feature vectors over the KNN algorithm. *Multimedia Tools and Applications*, *64*(1), 197–218. doi:10.100711042-011-0900-4

Muhammad, L. J., Algehyne, E. A., Usman, S. S., Ahmad, A., Chakraborty, C., & Mohammed, I. A. (2021). Supervised Machine Learning Models for Prediction of COVID-19 Infection using Epidemiology Dataset. *SN. Computer Science*, *2*(1), 11. doi:10.100742979-020-00394-7 PMID:33263111

Okagbue, H. I., Adamu, P. I., Oguntunde, P. E., Obasi, E. C. M., & Odetunmibi, O. A. (2021). Machine learning prediction of breast cancer survival using age, sex, length of stay, mode of diagnosis and location of cancer. *Health Technology (Hong Kong)*, *11*(4), 887–893. doi:10.100712553-021-00572-4

Peng, G. C. Y., Alber, M., & Tepole, A. (2021). Multiscale Modelling Meets Machine Learning: What Can We Learn? *Archives of Computational Methods in Engineering*, *28*(3), 1017–1037. doi:10.100711831-020-09405-5 PMID:34093005

Sha'abani, M. N. A. H., Fuad, N., Jamal, N., & Ismail, M. F. (2020). kNN and SVM Classification for EEG: A Review. In ECCE2019. Lecture Notes in Electrical Engineering, 632. doi:10.1007/978-981-15-2317-5_47

Shah, K., Patel, H., Sanghvi, D., & Shah, M. (2020). A Comparative Analysis of Logistic Regression, Random Forest and KNN Models for the Text Classification. *Augment Hum Res*, *5*(1), 12. doi:10.100741133-020-00032-0

Shan, G., Bernick, C., Caldwell, J. Z. K., & Ritter, A. (2021). Machine learning methods to predict amyloid positivity using domain scores from cognitive tests. *Scientific Reports*, *11*(1), 4822–4838. doi:10.103841598-021-83911-9 PMID:33649452

Silva, I. S., Ferreira, C. N., & Costa, L. B. X. (2022). Polycystic ovary syndrome: Clinical and laboratory variables related to new phenotypes using machine-learning models. *Journal of Endocrinological Investigation*, *45*, 497–505. doi:10.100740618-021-01672-8 PMID:34524677

Song, D. Y., Topriceanu, C. C., Ilie-Ablachim, D. C., Kinali, M., & Bisdas, S. (2021). Machine learning with neuroimaging data to identify autism spectrum disorder: A systematic review and meta-analysis. *Neuroradiology*, *63*(12), 2057–2072. doi:10.100700234-021-02774-z PMID:34420058

Yusof, A. R., Udzir, N. I., & Selamat, A. (2016). An Evaluation on KNN-SVM Algorithm for Detection and Prediction of DDoS Attack. In H. Fujita, M. Ali, A. Selamat, J. Sasaki, & M. Kurematsu (Eds.), Lecture Notes in Computer Science: Vol. 9799. *Trends in Applied Knowledge-Based Systems and Data Science. IEA/AIE 2016.* Springer. doi:10.1007/978-3-319-42007-3_9

KEY TERMS AND DEFINITIONS

Decision Tree: A decision tree is a decision-making aid that employs a tree-like model of choices and their potential results, such as chance event outcomes, cost objects, and usefulness. It's one approach to show an algorithm made up entirely of conditional control statements.

Diabetes Mellitus: A condition in which the body's capacity to create or react to the hormone insulin is hampered, resulting in improper carbohydrate metabolism and high blood glucose levels.

K-Nearest Neighbour Algorithm: The k-nearest neighbours' technique is a non-parametric supervised learning approach invented by Evelyn Fix and Joseph Hodges in 1951 and subsequently extended by Thomas Cover in statistics. It is used in the categorization and regression of data. In both circumstances, the input is a data set with the k closest training samples.

Pima Indian Diabetes: The National Institute of Diabetes and Digestive and Kidney Diseases provided this data. The dataset's goal is to diagnose if a person has diabetes using diagnostic metrics provided in the collection.

Random Forests: It known as random decision forests is an ensemble learning approach for classification, regression, and other tasks that works by building a large number of decision trees during training. For classification tasks, the random forest's output is the class chosen by the majority of trees.

Support-Vector Machines: They are supervised learning models using learning algorithms that evaluate data for classification and regression analysis in machine learning.

About the Contributors

John Wang is a professor in the Department of Information Management and Business Analytics at Montclair State University, USA. Having received a scholarship award, he came to the USA and completed his Ph.D. in operations research at Temple University. Due to his extraordinary contributions beyond a tenured full professor, Dr. Wang has been honored with two special range adjustments in 2006 and 2009, respectively. He has published over 100 refereed papers and seventeen books. He has also developed several computer software programs based on his research findings.

* * *

Nassir Abba-Aji, PhD, is a Senior Lecturer at the Department of Mass Communication, University of Maiduguri, Borno State, Nigeria, and the Sub-Dean, Faculty of Social Sciences of the university. He is a one-time Chairman, Jere Local Government Area, Borno State, as well as Commissioner for Religious Affairs during the Senator Ali Modu Sheriff Administration in Borno State. Dr Nassir has published several articles and book chapters, and has presented papers at several conferences.

Peter Abraldes completed his BA in political science at the University of Pittsburgh. He completed graduate work in statistics and earned his masters in data analytics at the Pennsylvania State University. Peter also spent time studying development economics in Argentina and Brazil, especially how international trade impacts developing countries. His studies include labor economics, trade export policies, and national industrial development policies. He is a maritime trade analyst for the Philadelphia Regional Port Authority, focused on optimizing the organization's cargo development strategy. The strategy includes understanding how the port can differentiate itself and make it more resilient to supply chain disruptions and international policy changes. He has been the scholarship chair for the World Trade Association of Philadelphia since 2018.

Anal Acharya is currently Assistant Professor in Computer Science department in St. Xavier's College, Kolkata. His current research interest is Educational Data Mining.

Prageet Aeron is presently an Assistant Professor at the department of Information Management at MDI Gurgaon. He is a Fellow (FPM) of Computers and Information Systems Group from the Indian Institute of Management Ahmedabad, and a B.Tech from the Indian Institute of Technology-BHU, Varanasi. He has over 10 years of teaching experience across various B-schools in NCR and is actively engaged in teaching and research in the areas of Entrepreneurship, Strategic Information Systems, e-Commerce and Big Data Applications in Management. His research work has been regularly accepted in reputed International Journals and Conferences.

Javier M. Aguiar Pérez is Associate Professor at University of Valladolid, and Head of the Data Engineering Research Unit. His research is focused on Big Data, Artificial Intelligence, and Internet of Things. He has managed international research projects and he has contributed in the standardisation field as expert at the European Telecommunications Standards Institute. He serves as editor, guest editor and reviewer, and author in several international journals, books and conferences. Furthermore, he has been involved as reviewer and rapporteur in several international research initiatives.

Gilbert Ahamer is inclined to analyse fundamentals of philosophy for the target of designing new paradigms driven by foresight when it comes to develop policies for mastering globalisation. As a physicist, environmentalist, economist, technologist, and geographer, he suggests that radically new concepts might beneficially contribute to solving the pressing problems of global change. He co-founded the 'Global Studies' curriculum at Graz University, Austria, studied and established global long-term scenarios when affiliated to the International Institute for Applied Systems Analysis IIASA, and is active in institutionalised dialogue-building for the Environment Agency Austria in Central Asia, Ukraine, and Georgia since his earlier affiliation to the Austrian Academy of Sciences.

Md. Omar Al-Zadid is currently working as a Senior Officer in Bank Asia Limited, Dhaka, Bangladesh. He began his career as a corporate professional in The Daily 'Prothom Alo', one of the top ranking newspapers in Bangladesh. His primary responsibilities in Prothom Alo included key account management and customer relationship management in advertisement department. He achieved 2nd Category Ptak Prize Award in recognition of global supply chain understanding and leadership in the young supply chain community organized by International Supply Chain Education Alliance (ISCEA) in 2013. He obtained Certificate of Achievement for completion of ITES Foundation Skills Training on Digital Marketing under NASSCOM IT-ITES sector Skill Council Certification in 2015. He holds an MBA in Marketing from the University of Dhaka, Bangladesh. His principal research interests include marketing analytics, innovation adoption, digital marketing, online banking, consumer behavior and psychology, Blue Ocean marketing strategy etc.

İnci Albayrak is an Professor in the Department of Mathematical Engineering at Yildiz Technical University (YTU),Turkey, where she has been a faculty member since 1992. She received her BS in 1990, MS in 1993 and PhD in 1997 in Mathematical Engineering from Yildiz Technical University. She had studied spectral theory and operator theory. She has lots of papers in these areas. In recent years, she has collaborated actively with researchers and focused on fuzzy mathematics. She has ongoing research projects about fuzzy linear equation systems and fuzzy linear programming problem.

Dima Alberg is a Researcher in SCE – Shamoon College of Engineering. His areas of specialty are financial data mining, scientific programming, and simulation methods. His current and future research plans focus on developing new models and tools that allow researchers and practitioners to analyze and solve practical problems in data science research areas.

Miguel Alonso Felipe received his M.S. degrees in telecommunication engineering from the University of Valladolid, Spain. In addition, he is PhD Candidate at University of Valladolid and Researcher of the Data Engineering Research Unit. His research is mainly focused on Big Data, Artificial Intelligence, and Internet of Things. Besides, he is co-author of some publications in journals, dealing with topics related to his lines of research.

Yas Alsultanny is the scientist of machine learning, data mining, and quantitative analysis, he is a computer engineering and data analysis PhD holder. He was spent his past 30 years of his life dedicated to the advancement of technological convergence and knowledge transfer to students. He was developed a high standard of research methods for graduate students and MBA through his supervising 100 MSc and PhD theses, and consulting 140 MBA projects, moreover he supervised 40 higher diploma projects and 100 BSc projects. Professor Alsultanny served for a reputed university in Bahrain: Arabian Gulf University (AGU), French Arabian Business School, and University of Bahrain. In Jordan: Applied Science University (ASU), Amman Arab University, Al-Balqa Applied University, and the Arab Academy for Banking and Financial Sciences. In Iraq: University of Baghdad, University of Technology, Al-Mustansiriya University, and Institute of Technology. In Germany: Arab German Academy for Science and Technology (online). Besides these, he was held position director of the AGU University Consultations, Community Services, Training, and Continuous Teaching Centre in Bahrain. And the position of head of the Computer Information Systems department and vice dean College of Information Technology in ASU University in Jordan. Alsultanny was worked a chair of statistical and KPIs committees in AGU University, chair of quality assurance and accreditation committee in Amman Arab University, member of quality assurance and accreditation committee in ASU and AGU Universities, member of establishing PhD Innovation Management programme in AGU University, member of establishing the college of Information Technology, ASU University, member of establishing Graduate College of Computing Studies, Amman Arab University, member of developing MSc Technology Management programme, member council of College of Graduate Studies, AGU University, and member council of College of Information Technology, ASU University. He is a trainer and a consultant for several public and private organizations, he led more than 100 workshops, and main speaker in many symposiums and conferences. He is a main writer of the UN Environment report, as well as member of writing AGU university strategic plans. In addition, he is reviewer and editor for various international journals.

Gerardo Amador Soto is a PhD student in Energy Systems from the National University of Colombia, Researcher in Energy Efficiency for Complex Systems.

Billie Anderson is an Assistant Professor of Applied Statistics at UMKC's Henry W. Bloch School of Management. Billie earned her Ph.D. in Applied Statistics from the University of Alabama, Masters of Mathematics and Statistics from the University of South Alabama, and her Bachelor of Mathematics from Spring Hill College. Before entering academia, Billie was a Research Statistician for SAS. SAS is a statistical software company headquartered in North Carolina. Billie wrote data mining algorithms for the banking and insurance industries. Billie maintained a consultancy relationship with SAS as an analytical trainer from 2012-2020. In this role, she taught analytical-based classes to professionals in organizations to help promote best statistical practices. And, she has consulted with different companies like Ann Taylor, Dunn & Bradstreet, Blue Cross Blue Shield of Michigan, Lowes Home Improvement Store, and Starbucks. She assisted these organizations in applying analytics to solve their business problems. Billie's research focus is in the statistical modeling of credit scoring with a particular interest in reject inference.

Issa Annamoradnejad is a Ph.D. candidate at the Sharif University of Technology, Tehran, Iran.

Rahimberdi Annamoradnejad wrote a chapter on the current and potential application of machine learning for predicting housing prices. He is an Iranian urban planner and an associate professor of geography and urban planning at the University of Mazandaran.

Joel Antúnez-García was born in Ensenada B. C., México, in 1975. He received the B. Sc. degree in Physics from Universidad Autónoma de Baja California (UABC), México, in 1999. The M. Sc. from Centro de Investigación Científica y de Educación Superior de Ensenada (CICESE), México, in 2004. The Ph. D. in Physical-Industrial Engineering from Universidad Autónoma de Nuevo Léon (UANL), Méxio, in 2010. From 2012 to 2013, he did a postdoctoral stay at Centro de Nanociencias y Nanotecnología at UNAM, working on DFT calculations to obtain different zeolites' electronic properties. From 2013-2015 he worked as a professor at Centro de Enseñanza Técnica y Superior (CETYS university). From 2016 to date, he has been involved in the theoretical study of bi-and tri-metallic catalysts based on MoS2 compounds and zeolites.

Dounia Arezki (), after obtaining an MSc in Artificial Intelligence, pursued her Ph.D. program in information technology at the Computer Science faculty of Science and Technology university of Oran (USTO) from 2017 to 2021. January 2022, she started an MSc program in international business. Presently her research interests are focused on spatial data processing, clustering algorithms, data analysis, risk, and project management.

Heba Atteya is the Senior Director of Business Intelligence and Data Analytics unit at The American University in Cairo (AUC). She led the founding team who built AUC's enterprise data-warehouse and business intelligence (BI) platform. In her current role, she manages the full-spectrum of the BI process including: setting AUC's BI roadmap, leading the data architecture and modeling functions, as well as the automated data extraction from the different source systems. Heba completed her MSc in Computer Science at AUC in Spring 2017 in the topic of visualizing large datasets. She earned her bachelor of science in Information Systems with honors in 2010 and joined AUC as a full-time staff member since 2011. She had a successful track record of achievements which qualified her for the position of BI and Data Analytics Director in 2017. Ever since then, she has successfully expanded the BI platform to extract data from the main ERP of the University, the main student information system, and the university CRM, as well as several other source systems providing a 360-degree view of student, faculty, staff and alumni of the University. Recently, she has led the efforts of the AUC's first big data project, analyzing Wi-Fi big data streams to support COVID-19 contact tracing process, as well as AUC's first AI-powered Chat-bot supporting the IT Help Desk function. She has always found inspiration in working with data and finding its underlying hidden patterns. She believes that informed decision-making is what every institution needs to compete in this highly competitive market.

Antonio Badia is an Associate Professor in the Computer Science and Engineering department at the Speed School of Engineering, University of Louisville. His research focuses on database systems and data science; his previous projects have been funded by the National Science Foundation and US Navy. He's the author of over 50 publications and 2 books.

Youakim Badr is an Associate Professor of Data Analytics in the Great Valley campus of the Pennsylvania State University, USA. He earned his Ph.D. in computer science from the National Institute of Applied Sciences (INSA-Lyon), where he worked as an associate professor in the computer science and engineering department. Over the course of his research, Dr. Badr has worked extensively in the area of service computing (distributed systems) and information security. His current research strategy aims at developing a new software engineering approach for designing and deploying "smart connected devices" and building "smart service systems" for the Internet of Things.

Surajit Bag is an Associate Professor at the Institute of Management and Technology, Ghaziabad, India (AACSB accredited). He is also working as a Visiting Associate Professor in the Department of Transport and Supply Chain Management, University of Johannesburg, South Africa. He has 11 years of industry experience. He has teaching experince from India, Morocco, South Africa and U.K. Educationally, Dr. Surajit earned his second Ph.D. in Information Management from the Postgraduate School of Engineering Management, University of Johannesburg, South Africa, and holds his first Ph.D. in Supply Chain Management from the School of Business, University of Petroleum and Energy Studies, India. Prior to getting a Ph.D., he obtained an MBA in Marketing Management (major) from MAKAUT (formerly the West Bengal University of Technology), India. His substantive areas of interest include Industry 4.0, big data, artificial intelligence applications in marketing and supply chain, sustainability. His expertise lies in the areas of Multivariate Data Analysis Techniques, Mediation Analysis, Moderation Analysis, and Structural Equation Modeling. He is familiar with data analysis software such as WarpPLS, PLS-SEM, SPSS, and Python. Surajit has published some of the most cited papers in the Industrial Marketing Management, International Journal of Production Economics, International Journal of Production Research, Technological Forecasting & Social Change, Production, Planning & Control, IEEE Transactions on Engineering Management, Journal of Cleaner Production, Annals of Operations Research, Information Systems Frontiers, Journal of Business Research, and Supply Chain Management: An International Journal. He is the proud recipient of the "AIMS-IRMA Young Management Researcher Award 2016" for his significant contribution to management research. He is the proud recipient of best "Doctoral Research Award 2020" from the Postgraduate School of Engineering Management, University of Johannesburg in recognition of the outstanding academic excellence. Dr. Surajit was listed in World's Top 2% Scientists which was released by Stanford University. He is a professional member of the Association of International Business, (AIB), Chartered Institute of Procurement and Supply (CIPS); Association for Supply Chain Management (ASCM); Institute of Electrical and Electronics Engineers (IEEE); Indian Rubber Institute; Association of Indian Management Scholars (AIMS International); and Operational Research Society of India (ORSI).

Sikha Bagui is Professor and Askew Fellow in the Department of Computer Science, at The University West Florida, Pensacola, Florida. Dr. Bagui is active in publishing peer reviewed journal articles in the areas of database design, data mining, Big Data analytics, machine learning and AI. Dr. Bagui has worked on funded as well unfunded research projects and has 85+ peer reviewed publications, some in highly selected journals and conferences. She has also co-authored several books on database and SQL. Bagui also serves as Associate Editor and is on the editorial board of several journals.

Samir Bandyopadhyay is presently a distinguished professor of The Bhawanipur Education Society College.

Soumya Banerjee is the Chief Technical Advisor & Board member of Must with specialised on ML & Security.

Sarang Bang is currently Studying at Vellore Institute of Technology, Vellore (India) pursuing Btech in Computer Science with Specialization in Data Science. He completed his schooling from Bhavan's Bhagwandas Purohit Vidya Mandir, Nagpur wherein he secured 10 cgpa in 10th grade and few other merit awards . He has been District Level Volleyball player during his schooling year. After choosing PCM and completing his 12th grade with 86.7 percentage he developed a lot of interest in coding and hence chose Computer Science as his career. In VIT, he is core committee member at VIT Mathematical Association Student chapter and also member at Lions Club International Leo Club Victory, Nagpur. He is passionate about Web Development and has worked on many projects as well as contributed to Hackathons as a front end developer. He also has interest in flutter development, machine learning. He wants to focus on a career in research and is currently exploring Machine learning and Artificial Intelligence.

Bazila Banu is a Professor and Head in the Department of Artificial Intelligence and Machine Learning at Bannari Amman Institute of Technology, India. She received her PhD degree in Information and Communication Engineering at Anna University, India in 2015 and guiding PhD Scholars. She holds 16 years of professional experience including academic and software Industry. She published 15 articles in National and International journals . She is an active reviewer and Guest Editor for International journals and technical committee member for International conferences. Her research interest includes Big Data and Data Analytics. She has filed three National level Patents and received grants from AICTE for Margdarshan scheme (19 Lakhs) and National Commission for women.

Isak Barbopoulos, PhD, has worked as a research psychologist studying the situational activation of consumer motives. He is currently working as a data scientist at Insert Coin, where he is developing and implementing a system for adaptive gamification.

Mikel Barrio Conde is a PhD candidate at University of Valladolid, who received his M.S. degrees in telecommunication engineering from the University of Valladolid, Spain. He is researcher of the Data Engineering Research Unit and his research is focused on Artificial Intelligence, and Internet of Things. Also, he is co-author of some publications in journals, dealing with topics related to his lines of his research.

Sotiris Batsakis is a Laboratory Teaching member of the Technical University of Crete, Greece and he has worked as Affiliated Senior Researcher and Senior Lecturer at the University of Huddersfield, UK. He received a diploma in Computer Engineering and Informatics from the University of Patras, Greece with highest distinction, and a Master's degree and a Ph.D. in Electronic and Computer Engineering from the Technical University of Crete Greece. He is an experienced researcher having participated on various research projects and with over 50 research publications in the areas of Knowledge Representation, Artificial Intelligence and Information Retrieval.

Andrew Behrens is an Instructor of business analytics courses at Dakota State University and is pursuing a Ph.D. in Information Systems at Dakota State University. He has worked with Cherie Noteboom for three years and has published in IS Conferences (MWAIS, IACIS, and AMCIS).

Santiago Belda https://orcid.org/0000-0003-3739-6056 (ORCID ID) From 2011 to 2015, he engaged in a PhD in Mathematical Methods and Modeling in Science and Engineering at Universidad de Alicante. He worked in various projects and is currently affiliated to Universidad de Alicante as a Distinguished postdoc researcher Presently his research interests are Astronomy, VLBI, Earth Orientation Parameters, Terrestrial and Celestial Reference Frames. Santiago Belda was partially supported by Generalitat Valenciana SEJIGENT program (SEJIGENT/2021/001), European Union – NextGenerationEU (ZAMBRANO 21-04) and European Research Council (ERC) under the ERC-2017-STG SENTIFLEX project grant number 755617.

Zakaria Bendaoud is an associate professor at the University of Saida. His research focuses on information retrieval, supply chain and transportation.

Mustapha Benramdane is a Ph.D. student in Computer Science at CNAM. His main research domains are matchmaking and Intent-based Contextual Orchestration inside Digital Business Ecosystems and Platforms.

Níssia Bergiante is a Doctor in Transportation Engineering (COPPE UFRJ– Federal University of Rio de Janeiro - Brazil). Production Engineer with a Master in Production Engineering (UFF-Brazil). Background in Production Engineering, focusing on Operational Management and Operational Research, acting on the following subjects: Decision Analysis and Soft Operation Research (Problem Structuring Methods); Operation Management and Process improvement.

Aditi A. Bhoir is a final year undergraduate student, currently pursuing Bachelor of Technology (B. Tech.) in Mechanical Engineering, at Sardar Patel College of Engineering, Mumbai, India. She will be doing Master of Science (MS) in abroad from fall 2022. Her focus research interest is design and robotics.

Trevor J. Bihl is a Senior Research Engineer with the Air Force Research Laboratory, Sensors Directorate where he leads a diverse portfolio in artificial intelligence (AI) and autonomy. Dr. Bihl earned his doctorate in Electrical Engineering from the Air Force Institute of Technology, Wright Patterson AFB, OH, and he also received a bachelor's and master's degree in Electrical Engineering at Ohio University, Athens, OH. Dr. Bihl is a Senior Member of IEEE and he has served as a board member as Vice President of Chapters/Fora for INFORMS (The Institute of Operations Research and the Management Sciences). His research interests include artificial intelligence, autonomous systems, machine learning, and operations research.

Sanjay Krishno Biswas is a faculty of Anthropology at Shahjalal University of Science and Technology, Bangladesh. He is currently pursuing his Ph.D. His academic interest includes Anthropological Theory, Mobility, and Migration, Diaspora and Transnationality, Ethnicity and Marginality, and Ecology and Climate Change. Mr. Biswas has a number of articles in reputed journals and book chapters from reputed publishers including Routledge.

Karim Bouamrane received the PhD Degree in computer science from the Oran University in 2006. He is full Professor of computer Science at the same university. He is member of computer science laboratory (LIO). He is the head of the team decision and piloting system. His current research interests deal with decision support system, transportation system, risk management, Health system, bio-inspired approach. He participates in several scientific committees' international/national conferences in Algeria and others countries in the same domain and collaborate in Algerian-French scientific projects. He is co-author of more than 60 scientific publications and communications.

Samia Bouzefrane is Professor at the Conservatoire National des Arts et Métiers (Cnam) of Paris. She received her PhD in Computer Science from the University of Poitiers (France) in 1998. After four years at the University of Le Havre (France), she joined in 2002 the CEDRIC Lab of Cnam. She is the co-author of many books (Operating Systems, Smart Cards, and Identity Management Systems). She is a lead expert in the French ministry. She is involved in many scientific workshops and conferences. Her current research areas cover Security and AI Internet of Thing.

Paul Bracewell is Co-Founder of New Zealand-based data science firm, DOT loves data and Adjunct Research Fellow at Victoria University of Wellington. He received his PhD in Statistics from Massey University and has contributed to more than 50 peer reviewed publications.

James Braman is an Associate Professor in the Computer Science/Information Technology Department at the Community College of Baltimore County for the School of Business, Technology and Law. He earned a B.S. and M.S. in Computer Science and D.Sc. in Information Technology from Towson University. He is currently pursuing a M.S. in Thanatology from Marian University. From 2009 to 2017 he was a joint editor-in-chief for the European Alliance for Innovation (EAI) endorsed Transactions on E-Learning with Dr. Giovanni Vincenti. Dr. Braman's research interests include thanatechnology, virtual and augmented reality, e-Learning, affective computing, agent-based technologies, and information retrieval.

Alexis D. Brown is an Assistant Professor in the Computer Science & Information Technology Department at the Community College of Baltimore County. They hold a master's degree in Management Information Systems from the University of Maryland Baltimore County. Their main research interests focus on education and instructional technology but includes varied technology-related topics.

Joseph Budu is an award-winning research scholar within the information systems discipline. He received the University of Ghana Vice Chancellor award for the outstanding doctoral dissertation for the humanities for the 2019/2020 academic year. Prior to this feat, he has undertaken several academic research and consultancies. Dr. Budu has written one mini-book, and one research workbook to guide students in conducting academic research. See https://bit.ly/BuduContentfolio for various contents Joseph has produced (e.g. manuals, blog posts, lead magnets, and presentations).

Rachel Cardarelli graduated from Bryant University with a degree in Actuarial Mathematics and concentration in Applied Statistics. Since graduating, she has been working as an Actuarial Analyst.

Ferhan Çebi is a Professor in Istanbul Technical University Faculty of Management, Management Engineering Department. She holds a B.S. in Chemical Engineering from ITU, a M.S. and a Ph.D. in Management Engineering from ITU. She gives the lectures on Operations Research and Operations Management at the undergraduate level and graduate level. Her main research areas are application of Operations Research techniques to the manufacturing and service problems, production planning and control, fuzziness and mathematical modelling, decision analysis, decision support systems, information technology for competitiveness. She is acting scientific committee member and organization committee member for a number of national & international conferences. Ferhan Cebi is member of editorial boards of International Journal of Information Systems in the Service Sector, International Journal of Information & Decision Sciences, and International Journal of Data Sciences. Her works have been published in several international and national conference proceedings and journals such as Computers and Industrial Engineering, Information Sciences, Information Systems Frontiers, Journal of Enterprise Information Management, Logistics Information Management, International Journal of Information and Decision Sciences.

Shuvro Chakrobartty has made significant contributions to identifying, conceptualizing, and formulating the research objective and methodology, the proposed framework, and the analysis of the findings. With a prior educational background in Computer Science and Business, currently, he is a Ph.D. student of Information Systems at Dakota State University. His research interests lie in responsible AI and data analytics. He has work experience in multiple industries within the software, cloud, and data engineering domain. He is a member of the Association for Information Systems (AIS) professional organizations and serves as a peer-reviewer for multiple conferences, books, and journal publications.

Hannah H. Chang is Associate Professor of Marketing at Lee Kong Chian School of Business, Singapore Management University. She received a PhD in Marketing from Graduate School of Business, Columbia University.

Hsin-Lu Chang is a professor in the Department of Management Information Systems, National Chengchi University. She received a Ph.D. in information systems at the School of Commerce, the University of Illinois at Urbana-Champaign. Her research areas are in E-Commerce, IT value, and technology adoption. She has published in Decision Support Systems, Information Systems Journal, International Journal of Electronic Commerce, Journal of Organizational Computing and Electronic Commerce, and Information Systems and e-Business Management.

D. K. Chaturvedi is Professor in Electrical Engineering at DEI, Agra, India.

Akhilesh Chauhan is a fourth-year Ph.D. (IS) student in the College of Business and Information Systems at the Dakota State University (Madison, S.D., USA). He is received a master's degree in Analytics from Dakota State University. He is currently working as a graduate research assistant at DSU. His current research interest includes association rule mining, machine learning, healthcare informatics, transfer learning, text mining, and data mining.

Tanvi Chawla completed her B.Tech in Information Technology (IT) from MDU, Rohtak in 2012 and received her M.Tech in Software Engineering (SE) from ITM University, Gurgaon in 2014. She has completed her Ph.D. in Computer Science and Engineering (CSE) from Malaviya National Institute of Technology (MNIT), Jaipur in 2022. During her Ph.D. she published articles in premier journals and conferences. Her research interests are Semantic Web, Big Data, Distributed Data Storage, and Processing.

Xi Chen is a lecturer in the College of Humanities at Beijing University of Civil Engineering and Architecture. She is also a research assistant in the Beijing Research Base for Architectural Culture. Her current research interests include English academic writing, settlement evolution, and urbanization in China and the U.S., etc.

Xiaoyan Cheng is a professor at University of Nebraska at Omaha. Dr. Cheng's research has been published in Auditing: A Journal of Practice & Theory, Advances in Accounting, Review of Quantitative Finance and Accounting, Research in Accounting Regulation, Global Finance Journal, Asian Review of Accounting, and Review of Pacific Basin Financial Markets and Policies.

Xusen Cheng is a Professor of Information Systems in the School of Information at Renmin University of China in Beijing. He obtained his PhD degree from the University of Manchester, UK. His research is in the areas of information systems and management particularly focusing on online collaboration, global teams, the sharing economy, e-commerce, and e-learning.

Paula Chimenti is an Associate Professor of Strategy and Innovation at COPPEAD graduate school of business, Federal University of Rio de Janeiro, Brazil. She holds a PhD in Administration from Coppead. She is the coordinator of the Center of Studies in Strategy and Innovation, where she develops research about the impact of disruptive innovations on business ecosystems. She has several works published in journals in Brazil and abroad, such as JGIM and JCR. Her article on Business Ecosystems received the first prize in one of the most important academic conferences in Brazil. She teaches Management Networked Businesses, Digital Marketing and Research Methodology in the Executive MBA, Master's and Doctorate programs at COPPEAD / UFRJ. She coordinated the Master program and Executive MBA programs at COPPEAD. Paula is the cases for teaching Editor for RAC - Revista de Administração Contemporânea, one of the top journals in Brasil.

Jahid Siraz Chowdhuy is a Fellow Ph.D. the program, Department of Social Administration and Justice, Faculty of Arts and Social Sciences, University of Malaya, 50603, Kuala Lumpur, Malaysia and Ex-faculty of Anthropology, Shahjalal University of Science and Technology, Bangladesh.

Parvathi Chundi is a professor of computer science at University of Nebraska at Omaha. Her primary research interests are in the fields of data mining, big data, and computer vision. She is currently focused on developing algorithms for automatic labeling of data for semantic and instance segmentation of biofilm images.

William Chung is an associate professor of Management Sciences at the City University of Hong Kong. He earned his Ph.D. in Management Sciences at the University of Waterloo, Canada. His personal research interests mainly focus on developing mathematical methodologies for energy-environmental policy problems, like large-scale equilibrium models, benchmarking methods for the energy consumption performance of buildings, and decomposition analysis of energy intensity. His papers can be found in the following journals: Operations Research, European Journal of Operational Research (EJOR), Computational Economics, Energy Economics, Energy Policy, Energy, Applied Energy, and Energy and Buildings. In addition, he is the director and founder of the Energy and Environmental Policy Research

Unit at the City University of Hong Kong. He was a visiting professor of the Center for International Energy and Environment Strategy Studies, Renmin University of China.

Mateus Coimbra holds a PhD in Administration from COPPEAD school of business in Federal University of Rio de Janeiro, Brazil.

Mirko Čubrilo is BSc in Mathematics, MSc in Mathematics, PhD in Computer Science (all from Zagreb University, Croatia). Full professor with tenure (Zagreb University, Croatia). Currently engaged at the University of the North (Varaždin, Croatia). Scientific interest includes mathematical logic, theory of algorithms, logic programming, artificial intelligence in a broad context, including neural nets and deep learning. Author of two books on the topics of mathematical logic and programming and more than fifty papers, published in journals and conference proceedings around the world (Germany, Japan, UK, USA, Egypt, Slovakia, Greece, Italy).

Marcin Czajkowski received his Master's degree (2007) and his PhD with honours (2015) in Computer Science from the Bialystok University of Technology, Poland. His research activity mainly concerns bioinformatics, machine learning and data mining, in particular, decision trees, evolutionary algorithms and relative expression analysis.

Jeya Mala D. has a Ph.D. in Software Engineering with Specialization on Software Testing and is currently working as 'Associate Professor Senior' in Vellore Institute of Technology, Chennai, India. She had been in the industry for about 4 years. She has a profound teaching and research experience of more than 24 years. She has published a book on "Object Oriented Analysis and Design using UML" for Tata McGraw Hill Publishers, also she has published 2 edited books for IGI Global, USA. She has published more than 70 papers about her research works at leading international journals and conferences such as IET, ACM, Springer, World Scientific, Computing and Informatics etc. As a researcher, Dr. Jeya Mala had investigated practical aspects of software engineering and object oriented paradigms for effective software development. Her work on Software Testing has fetched grants from UGC under Major Research Project scheme. Her dissertation has been listed as one of the best Ph.D. thesis in the CSIR – Indian Science Abstracts. She has successfully guided numerous Software Development based projects for the IBM- The Great Mind Challenge (TGMC) contest. The project she has mentored during 2007, has received national level Best Top 10 Project Award – 2007, from IBM. Currently she is guiding Ph.D. and M.Phil research scholars under the areas of Software Engineering and optimization techniques. She is a life member of Computer Society of India and an invited member of ACEEE. She forms the reviewer board in Journals like IEEE Transactions on Software Engineering, Elsevier – Information Sciences, Springer, World Scientific, International Journal of Metaheuristics etc. She has organized several sponsored national level conferences and workshops, notably she is one of the organizers of "Research Ideas in Software Engineering and Security (RISES'13) – A run-up event of ICSE 2014 sponsored by Computer Society of India". She has been listed in Marquis Who's Who list in 2011. She has completed certification on Software Testing Fundamentals, Brain bench certification on Java 1.1 programming, IBM certification as Associate Developer Websphere Application Studio. She is a proud recipient of several laurels from industries like Honeywell, IBM and Microsoft for her remarkable contributions in the field of Software Development and Object Orientation.

Karim Dabbabi is currently working as an assistant professor at the Faculty of Sciences of Tunis (FST). He held the postdoctoral position for a year and a half at the same faculty. He obtained his doctorate degree in electronics in July 2019 from the FST in addition to that of a research master's degree in automatic and signal processing from the National School of Engineers of Tunis in 2014. He has worked on various research projects in Automatic Speech Recognition (ASR), speaker diarization, automatic indexing of audio documents, audio segmentation and natural language processing (NLP) in general. In addition, he has worked on the identification of different neurological diseases, including Parkinson's and Alzheimer's using different voice features.

Indraneel Dabhade completed his M.S. in Engineering at Clemson University. He is a CISSP and has studied Cybersecurity from the Massachusetts Institute of Technology Center for Professional Education. He is currently pursuing an advanced certification in information security at the Stanford Center for Professional Development. Indraneel is a published author in Data Science, Human Factors, and Intellectual Property Rights. He has over 7 years of industry experience. Currently, Indraneel heads an automation firm (O Automation) in India.

Debabrata Datta is currently an Assistant Professor In Computer Science at St. Xavier's College (Autonomous), Kolkata. His research interest is Data Analytics and Natural Language Processing.

Magdalene Delighta Angeline D. is currently in the Department of Computer Science and Engineering as Assistant Professor, Joginpally B.R Engineering College, Hyderabad, India. Her research area includes data mining, computer networks. She has a good number of research publications.

Boryana Deliyska is professor retired in Department of Computer Systems and Informatics of University of Forestry, Sofia, Bulgaria. She obtained a PHD Degree in Computer Science from Technical University of Sofia, BG. She has long-standing research and practical experience in Semantic Web technologies, e-learning, computer lexicography, ontology engineering, web design and programming, geographical information systems (GIS), databases and information systems. She teaches information technologies, programming, CAD, computer graphics and computer networks. She is an author of 4 monographies, 7 Elsevier's dictionaries, 18 textbooks, more of 130 journal articles and conference papers.

Javier Del-Pozo-Velázquez received his M.S. degrees in telecommunication engineering from the University of Valladolid, Spain. In addition, he is PhD Candidate at University of Valladolid and Researcher of the Data Engineering Research Unit. His research is mainly focused on Big Data, Artificial Intelligence and Internet of Things. Besides, he is co-author of some publications in journals, dealing with topics related to his lines of research.

Chitra A. Dhawale (Ph.D in Computer Science) is currently working as a Professor Department of Computer Engineering P.R. Pote College of Engineering and Management, Amravati (MS), India. Earlier She worked as a Professor at Symbiosis International University, Pune (MS). To her credit, 06 research scholars have been awarded PhD. so far under her guidance, by S.G.B. Amravati and R.T.M. Nagpur University. Her research interests include Image and Video Processing, Machine Learning, Deep Learning, Multi-Biometric, Big Data Analytics. She has developed many projects for Machine Learning, Deep Learning, Natural Language Processing Algorithms using python. She also has hands on experience in

R-Programming, Hadoop-MapReduce, Apache Spark, Tableau. She has published 02 books, 08 Book Chapters, 26 Research papers in Journals (02- SCI-Indexed,15-Scopus Indexed, 06-UGC Journals and 03 in other research journals) and presented 35 papers in International Conferences (Abroad Conference-08, IEEE-18, ACM-02, Elsevier-01,Springer-04, Others-02) and 19 papers in National Conferences. She has reviewed 09 books for various publishers.

Kritika Dhawale is working as Deep Learning Engineer at SkyLark Drones, Bangalore. She has published 2 book chapters on Deep Learning. Her Research interest is Deep Learning and Cloud Computing.

Harini Dissanayake is a research student at Victoria University of Wellington, New Zealand working on her project 'Data informed decision bias.' The project focuses on identifying discriminatory bias in operational algorithms and remedying sample selection bias in datasets used for informing both commercial and government decisions.

Emmanuel Djaba is an early-stage academic with an avid interest in data science and machine learning. With extensive experience in industry, he is interested in doing innovative research that can be readily applied to interesting problems. He is currently a PhD student at the University of Ghana where he is pursuing a PhD in information systems.

Matt Drake has been a researcher in supply chain management for twenty years, focusing mainly on the areas of supply chain education and ethics. He has published over 30 articles and book chapters during this time. His chapter discusses the use of IoT technology to improve supply chain management. As firms look to improve their supply chain resilience in response to the COVID-19 pandemic and other disruptions, IoT data increases visibility, traceability, and can help firms to mitigate risks through added agility and responsiveness. The improved decision making made possible from IoT data creates a competitive advantage in the market.

Dorin Drignei received his PhD in Statistics from Iowa State University in 2004. Following his graduation, he was a postdoctoral researcher at the National Center for Atmospheric Research for two years. In 2006 he joined Oakland University where he is currently a Professor of Statistics. His current research interests include statistical modeling of big time series data.

Yuehua Duan is a PhD student in Computer Science Department at the University of North Carolina, Charlotte. Her research interests include recommender systems, business analytics, data mining, natural language processing, and machine learning.

Dishit Duggar is currently Studying at Vellore Institute of Technology, Vellore (India) pursuing Btech in Computer Science with Specialization in Information Security. He completed his schooling from Delhi Public School, Jaipur wherein he secured 10 cgpa in 10th grade and was a gold medal recipient for being a scholar for 6 consecutive years. After choosing PCM and completing his 12th grade with 93.8 percentage, He developed a lot of interest in coding and hence chose Computer Science as his career. In VIT, he is the App Lead of VinnovateIT which is a lab setup by Cognizant and also a member at Student Technical Community which is backed by Microsoft. He is passionate about Apps, Blockchain and Machine Learning and has worked on many projects as well as contributed and lead teams in multiple Hackathons. He wants to focus on a career in research and is currently exploring Cyber Security and Artificial Intelligence.

Ankur Dumka is working as Associate Professor and head of department in Women Institute of Technology, Dehradun. He is having more than 10 years of academic and industrial experience. He is having more than 60 research papers in reputed journals and conferences of repute. He contributed 4 books and 12 book chapters with reputed publisher. He is also associated with many reputed journals in the capacity of editorial board members and editor.

Abhishek Dutta has completed BS in Computer Science from Calcutta University and MS in Data Science and Analytics from Maulana Abul Kalam Azad University of Technology, Kolkata, India in 2020. He has authored seven conference papers which are published in IEEE Xplore and Springer Link. His research areas include Machine Learning, Deep Learning and AI applications in Finance.

Santosha Kumar Dwivedy received the Ph.D. in Mechanical Engineering from Indian Institute of Technology Kharagpur (IIT Kharagpur), India in 2000. He is currently Professor in Department of Mechanical Engineering at Indian Institute of Technology Guwahati (IIT Guwahati). He was also a Visiting Professor at Institute of Engineering and Computational Mechanics, University of Stuttgart, Germany under DAAD-IIT faculty exchange scheme. He has over 180 journal and conference publications with a focus on integrating robotics and dynamics in various fields. His research interests include both industrial and medical robotics, biomechanics, nonlinear vibration, and control along with the applications.

Brent M. Egan, MD, is Vice-President, Cardiovascular Disease Prevention in the Improving Health Outcomes group of the American Medical Association. He also serves as Professor of Medicine at the University of South Carolina School of Medicine, Greenville and as Past-President of the South Carolina Upstate affiliate of the American Heart Association. He received his medical degree and training in medicine and hypertension at the University of Michigan. He also served on the Board of Directors and President of the International Society of Hypertension in Blacks for many years. His professional interests center on hypertension, metabolic syndrome and vascular disease, which led to some 350 original papers and reviews. Dr. Egan remains committed to working with colleagues to translate the evidence-base into better cardiovascular health, especially for medically underserved populations.

Amal El Arid has earned a Masters' degree in Electrical and Computer Engineering from the American University of Beirut. She has been an instructor in the Department of Computer Science and Information Technology at the Lebanese International University since 2012. In addition, she specializes in programming and networking fields, earning a trainer certificate from the CISCO organization as a CCNA instructor since 2016. She is now working in the artificial intelligence and machine learning research field.

Houda El Bouhissi graduated with an engineering degree in computer science from Sidi-Bel-Abbes University - Algeria, in 1995. She received her M. Sc. and Ph. D. in computer science from the University of Sidi-Bel-Abbes, Algeria, in 2008 and 2015, respectively. Also, she received an M. Sc. in eLearning from the University of sciences and technologies, Lille1, France. Currently, she is an Assistant Professor at the University of Bejaia, Algeria. Her research interests include recommender systems, sentiments analysis, information systems interoperability, ontology engineering, and machine learning.

Mohamed El Touhamy is a Senior Data Engineer at The American University in Cairo (AUC). He completed his undergraduate studies at the Faculty of Computers and Information, Cairo University, earning a bachelor's degree in Computer Science. Mohamed started his journey in data science in 2017, participating in and leading many mega projects. He has excellent experience in big data engineering, data extraction using different technologies, data quality checks automation, and data warehouse enterprise solution management. He is also a graduate student at The American University in Cairo, seeking his master's degree in Computer Science.

Caner Erden, currently working as Assistant Professor in the Faculty of Applied Sciences, Sakarya University of Applied Sciences, Sakarya, Turkey. He worked as resarch assistant of Industrial Engineering at Sakarya University and researcher at Sakarya University Artificial Intelligence Systems Application and Research between 2012-2020. He holds a PhD degree in Industrial Engineering from Natural Science Institue Industrial Engineering Department, Sakarya University, Turkey with thesis titled "Dynamic Integrated Process Planning, Scheduling and Due Date Assignment". His research interests include scheduling, discrete event simulation, meta-heuristic algorithms, modelling and optimization, decision-making under uncertainty, machine learning and deep learning.

Omar El-Gayar has made a significant contribution to the conceptualization and formulation of the research objective and methodology, the proposed framework, and the interpretation of the findings. He is a Professor of Information Systems at Dakota State University. His research interests include analytics, business intelligence, and decision support. His numerous publications appear in various information technology-related venues. Dr. El-Gayar serves as a peer and program evaluator for accrediting agencies such as the Higher Learning Commission and ABET and as a peer reviewer for numerous journals and conferences. He is a member of the association for Information Systems (AIS).

Gozde Erturk Zararsiz is a faculty member in Biostatistics Department of Erciyes University. Her research mostly focuses on statistical modeling, method comparison, survival analysis and machine learning. Zararsiz completed her M.Sc. from Cukurova University, Institute of Health Sciences, Department of Biostatistics with the thesis entitled as "Evolution of Competing Risks Based on Both Dependent-Independent Real and Simulated Data by Using Self-Developed R Program". In 2015, Zararsiz has started her Ph.D. in Department of Biostatistics of Eskisehir Osmangazi University. During her Ph.D. in 2016, Zararsiz worked as a visiting researcher under the supervision of Prof. Dr. Christoph Klein at the laboratory of the Dr von Hauner Children's Hospital, LMU in Munich. During her research period, Zararsiz has published international papers and received awards. Zararsiz completed her PhD with the thesis entitled as "Bootstrap-Based Regression Approaches in Comparing Laboratory Methods".

Tasnia Fatin is a PhD Candidate in Management at Putra Business School, UPM, Malaysia. She has been a Lecturer of Marketing at Northern University Bangladesh (BBA, MBA) where she has taught Brand Management, Strategic Marketing, Principles of Marketing and Marketing Management. She had also been a Lecturer at Independent University Bangladesh. She takes keen interest in Entrepreneurship and has been running her own Business Solutions Agency and a Skill Training Institute. She holds an

MBA in Marketing from the University of Dhaka. She has also worked as a Strategic Marketing Manager for Prasaad Group of Companies to develop real estate projects home and abroad. She has also separately worked on projects in Urban Waste Management and Sustainable Agriculture that has been presented at George Washington University (USA), MIT (USA), Queens University (Canada) and at KLCC (Malaysia). Her research interests include digital marketing, disruptive innovations and the way they shape the world, IoT (Internet of Things), and sustainable business practices. She participated in several national level, Government level, and International level Youth Conferences and Forums home and abroad mentored by Industry leaders, experts, and professors from Harvard, Oxford, and many other prestigious institutions.

Arafat Febriandirza is a junior researcher at the Research Center for Informatics, The Indonesia Institute of Sciences (LIPI), Indonesia since 2020. He obtained his bachelor degree in Electrical Engineering from University of General Achmad Yani, Indonesia in 2008. He earned a Master's degree in Information Technology from the University of Indonesia in 2011 and a Doctorate in Communication and Transportation Engineering from Wuhan university of Technology in 2018. Arafat Febriandirza's research interests include issues in the field of Machine Learning, Modeling, Simulation, and Social Informatics.

Egi Arvian Firmansyah is a permanent lecturer at the Faculty of Economics and Business Universitas Padjadjaran, Indonesia. He has been published numerous journal articles and conferences proceedings. He is also a finance and managing editor at Jurnal Bisnis dan Manajemen, which is an accredited and reputable journal in Indonesia. Currently, he is a Ph.D student in finance at Universiti Brunei Darussalam.

Robert Leslie Fisher was educated in New York City. He attended Stuyvesant High School, a special science high school, has a bachelors degree (cum laude) in sociology from City College of New York, and a graduate degree in sociology from Columbia University. He is the author of several books including "Invisible Student Scientists (2013)" and the forthcoming Educating Public Interest Professionals and the Student Loan Debt Crisis." He has previously contributed chapters to encyclopedias and handbooks published by IGI Global including John Wang International Handbook of Business Analytics and Optimization as well as the International Encyclopedia of Information Sciences and Technology, and the International Encyclopedia of Modern Educational Technologies, Applications, and Management (both edited by Mehdi Khosrow-Pour). Mr. Fisher resides in the USA. He is an independent contractor.

Wendy Flores-Fuentes received the bachelor's degree in electronic engineering from the Autonomous University of Baja California in 2001, the master's degree in engineering from Technological Institute of Mexicali in 2006, and the Ph.D. degree in science, applied physics, with emphasis on Optoelectronic Scanning Systems for SHM, from Autonomous University of Baja California in June 2014. By now she is the author of 36 journal articles in Elsevier, IEEE, Emerald and Springer, 18 book chapters and 8 books in Springer, Intech, IGI global Lambert Academic and Springer, 46 proceedings articles in IEEE ISIE 2014-2021, IECON 2014, 2018, 2019, the World Congress on Engineering and Computer Science (IAENG 2013), IEEE Section Mexico IEEE ROCC2011, and the VII International Conference on Industrial Engineering ARGOS 2014. Recently, she has organized and participated as Chair of Special Session on ''Machine Vision, Control and Navigation'' at IEEE ISIE 2015-2021 and IECON 2018, 2019. She has participated has Guest Editor at Journal of Sensors with Hindawi, The International Journal of Advanced

Robotic Systems with SAGE, IEEE Sensors, and Elsevier Measurement. She holds 1 patent of Mexico and 1 patent of Ukraine. She has been a reviewer of several articles in Taylor and Francis, IEEE, Elsevier, and EEMJ. Currently, she is a full-time professor at Universidad Autónoma de Baja California, at the Faculty of Engineering. She has been incorporated into CONACYT National Research System in 2015. She did receive the award of "Best session presentation" in WSECS2013 in San-Francisco, USA. She did receive as coauthor the award of "Outstanding Paper in the 2017 Emerald Literati Network Awards for Excellence". Her's interests include optoelectronics, robotics, artificial intelligence, measurement systems, and machine vision systems.

Jeffrey Yi-Lin Forrest is a professor of mathematics and the research coach for the School of Business at Slippery Rock University of Pennsylvania. His research interest covers a wide range of topics, including, but not limited to, economics, finance, mathematics, management, marketing and systems science. As of the end of 2020, he has published over 600 research works, 24 monographs and 27 special topic edited volumes.

Raksh Gangwar is working as Professor and Director in Women Institute of Technology, Dehradun. He is having more than 35 years of experience. He has guided many Ph.D and M.Tech scholars. He is also member of many committee of national/international repute. He has contributed many research papers. He has also contributed many patents under his name.

Ge Gao is a Professor at Zhuhai College of Science and Technology and Management School at Jilin University. Her research focuses on Blockchain application, Supply Chain Management, Big Data application, user interface management in mobile commerce, and Social electronic commerce.

Araceli Gárate-García is a full-time professor at the Universidad Politécnica de Baja California (UPBC) since 2017. She received her PhD in electronics and telecommunications in conjoint between the CICESE research center, Mexico and the IRCCyN research center of the ECN university, France in 2011, the M.Sc. degree in electronics and telecommunications from CICESE research center in 2006 and her bachelor degree in Electronic Engineering in 2003 from the ITM university. Her main research interests are the analysis and control of nonlinear systems with and without time delays and the symbolic computation.

María J. García G. is Bachelor in Chemistry and has a master in Operations Research (OR). Together others authors had increase their investigations, already two hundred and forty, mainly in the areas of Evaluation and Management of Projects, Knowledge Management, Managerial and Social Decision making and OR, especially in multi-criteria decision. They have been presented or published in different countries, having publications and offering their reports, chats or conferences in: Azerbaijan, Finland, Poland, Croatia, Switzerland, Greece, Germany, Italy, Czech Republic, Iceland, Lithuania, Spain, France, Portugal, United States, Panama, Uruguay, Brazil, Mexico, Argentina and Chile besides attending as guest speaker, in lectures to relevant events in Colombia, Peru, Spain and Venezuela. Among other works she is coauthor of: "Inventories control, the Inventory manager and Matrixes Of Weighing with multiplicative factors (MOWwMf)"; "A Methodology of the Decision Support Systems Applied to Other Projects of Investigation"; "Matrixes Of Weighing and catastrophes"; "Multiattribute Model with Multiplicative Factors and Matrixes Of Weighing and the Problem of the Potable Water"

Nuno Geada has a Master's degree in Systems Information Management by Polytechnic Institute of Setúbal - School of Business Sciences and Management -Setúbal, Degree in Industrial Management and Technology by Polytechnic Institute of Setúbal - School of Technology of Setubal. He has written chapters, and papers to journals about topics regarding information technology management and strategic change management. He is from the Editorial Board - Associate Editor from International Journal of Business Strategy and Automation (IJBSA). He is the Editor of the book Reviving Businesses with New Organizational Change Management Strategies. His main research interests in information systems management, strategy, knowledge management, change management, and information technology management adoption in business contexts throw models and frameworks. He works as a Professor and a Researcher.

Natheer K. Gharaibeh is currently Associate Professor at College of Computer Science & Engineering at Yanbu - Taibah University from June 2016. He has more than 17 years of experience: He worked as Assistant Professor at College of Computer Science & Engineering at Yanbu – Taibah University from September. 2013 till June 2016. Before that he worked as an Assistant Professor at Balqa Applied University. He also worked as part-time Lecturer at Jordan University of Science and Technology (JUST) and other Jordanian universities. He published many papers in International Journals and participated in several International Conferences. His current research interests are: Business Intelligence, NLP, IR, Software Engineering, and Knowledge Societies. He got a grant for a joint project from the DFG with Rostock Technical University - Germany. He is editorial board Member, reviewer, and Keynote speaker in many International Journals and Conferences, he also has membership in many International and Technical Societies.

Abichal Ghosh is a final year B.E. student pursuing his degree in Computer Science from BITS Pilani K.K. Birla Goa campus. His field of interest lies in the research areas of Artificial Intelligence, Machine Learning, Deep Learning, Image Processing, Computer Vision and their application in various fields such as Desalination by Membrane technology, Ozonation, and more. Recently, he has been working for the prediction of the optimal conditions of Thin Film Nanocomposite Membranes for efficient desalination. For the topics related to Computer Vision, he has previously worked in the topic of Segmentation and is also currently working on the topic of Learned Image Compression.

Christoph Glauser was born in Berne in 1964. After studying History, Political Science and Media Science in Berne and Law in Geneva, he obtained a doctorate at the University of Berne in 1994. Christoph Glauser then participated in the national research programme, NFP27 at the University of Geneva. As a lecturer in Journalism and Online Research, he worked at various universities. He lectured in the subject, „Organisational Learning" in Social Psychology at the University of Zurich and for six years, he was the leading researcher and lecturer at ETH Zurich. In 1997-1998 he was a Visiting Lecturer at the University of Washington in Seattle, for which he continued to lecture their graduate students in Rome until 2006. During that time, he was Visiting Lecturer for online research at various universities both in Switzerland and abroad. Since 1998, Christoph Glauser has developed a successful career as online expert, CEO and delegate of governing boards, in particular (delete 'of') MMS – Media Monitoring Switzerland AG - and in diverse IT companies. Since 1994, he has been running the Institute for Fundamental Studies in Computer-assisted Content Analyses IFAA in Berne. In 2001, Glauser founded the URL study factory for competition analyses, ArgYou (Arguments for You), in order to study content of websites on the internet and compare these via search engines with the searched-for content (online effect research). In 2006, this company evolved into ArgYou AG in Baar (Switzerland), where he has remained as Chair of the governing board up to the present. For some years, Glauser has been serving on several European committees as an expert in e-governance. Subsequently, in 2007, he was one of the sixteen members of the jury for the European Union e-Government award, which honours the best European e-government projects on behalf of the European Commission. Since 2014 he has been operating the IFAAR find-engine set up directly for purposes of digital evaluation.

Rajesh Godasu is pursuing a Ph.D. in information systems at Dakota State University, his research interest is Deep learning in medical images. He has worked with Dr. Zeng for the past three years on different Machine Learning, Data Science, and Predictive Analytics topics. Conducted research on the Topic "Transfer Learning in Medical Image Classification" and published two papers in Information systems conferences, MWAIS and AMCIS.

Jorge Gomes is a researcher at ADVANCE, ISEG, School of Economics & Management of the Universidade de Lisboa. He holds a PhD in Management from ISEG and a Masters in Management Sciences from ISCTE-IUL, He also have a post-graduation in Project Management from INDEG/ISCTE, and a degree in Geographic Engineering from the Faculty of Sciences of the Universidade de Lisboa. During the past 30 years, he has worked as an engineer, project manager, quality auditor and consultant. Teaches Management at ULHT, Lisboa. His research interests include Benefits Management, Project Management, Project Success, Maturity Models, IS/IT Investments, IS/IT in Healthcare, and IS/IT Management.

Hale Gonce Kocken is an Associate Professor in the Department of Mathematical Engineering at the Yildiz Technical University (YTU), Istanbul, Turkey. She has been a faculty member of YTU since 2004. She completed her Ph.D. entitled "Fuzzy approaches to network analysis" in Applied Mathematics (2011) from the same department. Her current area of research is mathematical programming, supply chain management, and some related Operational Research subjects in multi-criteria and fuzzy environments.

Rick Gorvett is Professor and Chair of the Mathematics Department at Bryant University. He is a Fellow of the Casualty Actuarial Society.

M. Govindarajan is currently an Associate Professor in the Department of Computer Science and Engineering, Annamalai University, Tamil Nadu, India. He received the B.E, M.E and Ph.D Degree in Computer Science and Engineering from Annamalai University, Tamil Nadu, India in 2001, 2005 and 2010 respectively. He did his post-doctoral research in the Department of Computing, Faculty of Engineering and Physical Sciences, University of Surrey, Guildford, Surrey, United Kingdom in 2011 and at CSIR Centre for Mathematical Modelling and Computer Simulation, Bangalore in 2013. He has visited countries like Czech Republic, Austria, Thailand, United Kingdom (twice), Malaysia, U.S.A (twice), and Singapore. He has presented and published more than 140 papers at Conferences and Journals and also received best paper awards. He has delivered invited talks at various national and international conferences. His current research interests include Data Mining and its applications, Web Mining, Text Mining, and Sentiment Mining. He has completed two major projects as principal investigator and has produced four Ph.Ds. He was the recipient of the Achievement Award for the field in the Conference in Bio-Engineering, Computer Science, Knowledge Mining (2006), Prague, Czech Republic. He received

Career Award for Young Teachers (2006), All India Council for Technical Education, New Delhi, India and Young Scientist International Travel Award (2012), Department of Science and Technology, Government of India, New Delhi. He is a Young Scientists awardee under Fast Track Scheme (2013), Department of Science and Technology, Government of India, New Delhi and also granted Young Scientist Fellowship (2013), Tamil Nadu State Council for Science and Technology, Government of Tamil Nadu, Chennai. He also received the Senior Scientist International Travel Award (2016), Department of Science and Technology, Government of India. He has published ten book chapters and also applied patent in the area of data mining. He is an active Member of various professional bodies and Editorial Board Member of various conferences and journals.

Ashwin Gupta has currently completed his BSc with Major in Computer Science from St. Xavier's College, Kolkata. His current research interest is Data Analytics and Machine Learning.

Neha Gupta is currently working as an Professor, Faculty of Computer Applications at Manav Rachna International Institute of Research and Studies, Faridabad campus. She has completed her PhD from Manav Rachna International University and has done R&D Project in CDAC-Noida. She has total of 12+ year of experience in teaching and research. She is a Life Member of ACM CSTA, Tech Republic and Professional Member of IEEE. She has authored and coauthored 30 research papers in SCI/SCOPUS/Peer Reviewed Journals (Scopus indexed) and IEEE/IET Conference proceedings in areas of Web Content Mining, Mobile Computing, and Web Content Adaptation. She is a technical programme committee (TPC) member in various conferences across globe. She is an active reviewer for International Journal of Computer and Information Technology and in various IEEE Conferences around the world. She is one of the Editorial and review board members in International Journal of Research in Engineering and Technology.

Jafar Habibi is an associate professor at the Computer Engineering Department, Sharif University of Technology, Iran. He has been the head of the Computer Society of Iran and the Department of Computer Engineering. His main research interests are Internet of Things, Simulation, System Analysis and Design, and Social Network Analysis.

Christian Haertel studied business informatics at Otto von Guericke University Magdeburg. He joined the VLBA research team in 2021 and accompanies research projects with external partners (e.g., Google Cloud, Accenture Digital). The modelling and development of concepts in the areas of data science and cloud computing are his main areas of research.

J. Michael Hardin is the Provost and Vice President and Professor of Quantitative Analysis at Samford University. Dr. Hardin came to Samford University in July 2015 from the University of Alabama at Tuscaloosa, where he served as the Culverhouse College of Commerce and Business Administration dean. Dr. Hardin had previously served as Culverhouse's senior associate dean, associate dean for research, director of the University of Alabama's NIH Alabama EPSCoR Agency and director of Culverhouse's Institute of Business Intelligence. Dr. Hardin's service as a Culverhouse professor of quantitative analysis, business and statistics was widely credited for establishing the University of Alabama as an internationally-known resource in the field of data analytics. His Culverhouse career followed his numerous administrative and faculty appointments at the University of Alabama in Birmingham in biostatistics, biomathematics, health informatics and computer science. Dr. Hardin holds a Ph.D. in Applied Statistics from the University of Alabama, M.A. in Mathematics from the University of Alabama, M.S. in Research Design and Statistics from Florida State University's College of Education, B.A. in Mathematics from the University of West Florida, B.A. in Philosophy from the University of West Florida and M.Div. from New Orleans Baptist Theological Seminary. He is an ordained Southern Baptist minister. Dr. Hardin has authored or co-authored more than 150 papers in various journals, edited numerous professional journals, authored multiple book chapters, presented more than 250 abstracts at national meetings and given more than 150 invited lectures or talks. For 25 years he served as a National Institutes of Health (NIH) grant reviewer and participated as Investigator or co-Investigator on more than 100 U.S. Department of Health and Human Services/NIH-funded projects. He has served as a consultant for other national healthcare and financial organizations and was among the inventors receiving a U.S. patent licensed to MedMined, a Birmingham-based firm dedicated to controlling hospital infection rates and improving patient care.

Shanmugasundaram Hariharan received his B.E degree specialized in Computer Science and Engineering from Madurai Kammaraj University, Madurai, India in 2002, M.E degree specialized in the field of Computer Science and Engineering from Anna University, Chennai, India in 2004. He holds his Ph.D degree in the area of Information Retrieval from Anna University, Chennai, India. He is a member of IAENG, IACSIT, ISTE, CSTA and has 17 years of experience in teaching. Currently he is working as Professor in Department of Computer Science and Engineering, Vardhaman College of Engineering, India. His research interests include Information Retrieval, Data mining, Opinion Mining, Web mining. He has to his credit several papers in referred journals and conferences. He also serves as editorial board member and as program committee member for several international journals and conferences.

Budi Harsanto is a lecturer at Universitas Padjadjaran, Bandung, Indonesia. His research interests are in sustainability innovation, and operations and supply chain management.

Md Salleh Salleh Hassan, Prof., PhD, is a retired Professor at the Department of Communication, Faculty of Modern Languages and Communication, Universiti Putra Malaysia. He has graduated many PhD, master's and undergraduate students. He was once the Deputy Dean of the Faculty, and has published many research papers, attended many conferences both local and international.

Miralem Helmefalk, PhD, is an assistant senior lecturer at the Department of Marketing in School of Business and Economics at Linnaeus University in Sweden. Miralem's research interests lie in concepts within consumer psychology, digitalization, gamification as well as sensory marketing. He believes that machine learning represents the perfect storm for his research interests.

Gilberto J. Hernández is a Bachelor in Chemistry and have a master in Technology of foods. Together others authors had increase their investigations, mainly in the areas of Food technologies, Playful, in particular in the fantastic sports leagues, Knowledge Management, Managerial and Social Decision making, Logistics, Risk Management and Operations research, especially in multi-criteria decision and making decision under uncertainty and risk. They have been presented or published in different countries, having publications and offering their reports, chats or conferences in: Finland, Poland, Croatia, Switzerland, Greece, Czech Republic, Spain, Portugal and United States besides attending as guest speaker, in lectures to relevant events in Costa Rica and Venezuela. Among other works he is coauthor of: "Enterprise Logistics, Indicators and Physical Distribution Manager"; "Multiattribute Models with Multiplicative factors in the Fantasy Sports"; "The Industrial design manager of LoMoBaP and Knowledge Management"; "Dynamic knowledge: Diagnosis and Customer Service".

José Hernández Ramírez is a Chemical Engineer and have a master in Operations Research. Together others authors had increase their investigations, already above two hundred and forty, mainly in the areas of Knowledge Management, Managerial and Social Decision making, Logistics, Risk Management and Operations research, especially in multi-criteria decision. They have been presented or published in different countries, having publications and offering their reports, chats or conferences in: Azerbaijan, Finland, Croatia, Switzerland, Greece, Germany, Italy, Czech Republic, Iceland, Lithuania, Spain, France, Portugal, United States, Panama, Paraguay, Uruguay, Brazil, Cuba, Mexico, Argentina and Chile besides attending as guest speaker, in reiterated occasions, in lectures to relevant events in Colombia, Peru, Costa Rica, Brazil, Spain and Venezuela. Among other works he is coauthor of: "Teaching Enterprise Logistics through Indicators: Dispatch Manager"; "Enterprise diagnosis and the Environmental manager of LoMoBaP"; "Logistics, Marketing and Knowledge Management in the Community of Consumer".

Thanh Ho received M.S. degree in Computer Science from University of Information Technology, VNU-HCM, Vietnam in 2009 and PhD degree in Computer Science from University of Information Technology, VNU-HCM, Vietnam. He is currently lecturer in Faculty of Information Systems, University of Economics and Law, VNU-HCM, Vietnam in 2018. His research interests are Data mining, Data Analytics, Business Intelligence, Social Network Analysis, and Big Data.

Victoria Hodge is a Research Fellow and Software Developer in the Department of Computer Science at University of York. Her research interests include AI, outlier detection, and data mining. She is currently researching the safety assurance of machine learning for autonomous systems. A focus of this research is assuring robot navigation including localisation. She is on the editorial board of two journals and has authored over 60 refereed publications. She has worked in industry as a software architect for a medical diagnostics company; and as a software developer on condition monitoring in industrial environments, and deep learning for robot navigation.

Essam H. Houssein received his PhD degree in Computer Science in 2012. He is an associate professor at the Faculty of Computers and Information, Minia University, Egypt. He is the founder and chair of the Computing & Artificial Intelligence Research Group (CAIRG) in Egypt. He has more than 100 scientific research papers published in prestigious international journals in the topics for instance meta-heuristics optimization, artificial intelligence, image processing, IoT and its applications. Essam H. Houssein serves as a reviewer of more than 40 journals (Elsevier, Springer, IEEE, etc.). His research interests include WSNs, IoT, AI, Bioinformatics and Biomedical, Image processing, Data mining, and Meta-heuristics Optimization techniques.

Adamkolo Mohammed Ibrahim is a Lecturer at the Department of Mass Communication, University of Maiduguri, Nigeria and a PhD Research Scholar at Bayero University, Kano (BUK), Nigeria. He received his master's degree in Development Communication at Universiti Putra Malaysia (UPM) in 2017. In 2007, he had his first degree (BA Mass Communication) at the Department of Mass Communication, University of Maiduguri, Nigeria. Currently, he teaches mass communication at the University of Maiduguri. He conducts research and writes in ICT adoption for development, social media, cyberbullying, cyber terrorism/conflict, gender and ICT, gender and conflict and online shopping. He has published several journal articles, book chapters and a few books. His most recent work explores the impacts of fake news and hate speech in Nigerian democracy and proposes a theoretical model as a fact-checking tool. More details on his most recent works and all his other publications can be accessed on his website: https://unimaid.academia.edu/AdamkoloMohammedIbrahim. Malam Adamkolo is currently serving as an Editorial Board Member of Jurnal Komunikasi Ikatan Sarjana Komunikasi Indonesia (the Communication Journal of the Indonesian Association of Communication Scholars) and a co-researcher in a research project by The Kukah Centre, Abuja, Nigeria. The proposed title of the research is: "Engaging Local Communities for Peacebuilding, Social Cohesion, Preventing and Countering Violent Extremism in Nigeria's northeast". Adamkolo has received Publons Top Reviewer Award in 2018 (for being among the top 1% global peer reviewers in Psychiatry/Psychology). In 2017, Elsevier had awarded him a certificate of outstanding peer review with one of Elsevier's prestigious journals, Computers in Human Behaviour (CHB) which he reviews for; he also reviews for Emerald's Journal of Systems and Information Technology (JSIT) and several other journals. Much earlier, from 2000 to 2010, he worked as a broadcast journalist in Yobe Broadcasting Corporation (YBC) Damaturu, and from 2008 to 2010 was deployed to Sahel FM (formerly Pride FM, a subsidiary of YBC Damaturu as DJ-cum-producer/presenter/journalist). From 2008 to 2010, he worked as YBC's focal person on UNICEF and Partnership for the Revival of Routine Immunisation in Northern Nigeria-Maternal, newborn and Child Health (PRRINN-MNCH). From September to October 2018, he served as a consultant to ManienDanniels (West Africa Ltd.) and MNCH2 programme.

Funda Ipekten's research focused on a statistical analysis of high-throughput metabolomics data, multi-omics data integration, feature selection for multi-omics.

Adelina Ivanova is Assisted Professor Dr. in Department of Computer Systems and Informatics of University of Forestry, Sofia, Bulgaria. Her research interests are in the areas of ontology engineering, sustainable development, databases, and office information systems.

Sajan T. John is an Associate Professor of Industrial Engineering in the Department of Mechanical Engineering at Viswajyothi College of Engineering and Technology, Vazhakulam, Kerala. He received PhD from the National Institute of Technology Calicut in 2015. His research interests are in the areas of operations research, mathematical modelling, supply chain management and reverse logistics. He has published papers in international journals and proceedings of international and national conferences.

Rachid Kaleche is a PhD student of computer science since 2018. He is member of computer science laboratory (LIO) of Oran 1 university in Algeria. His current research interests deal with artificial intelligence, transportation system, logistic systems, machine learning, and bio-inspired approach. He is co-author of many publications and communications.

Reddi Kamesh received B.Tech in Chemical engineering from Acharya Nagarjuna University, Guntur, India, in 2011, and M.Tech and Ph.D. from Academy of and Innovative Research (AcSIR), CSIR-Indian Institute of Chemical Technology (IICT), Campus, Hyderabad, India, in 2014 and 2019 respectively. Dr. Kamesh has extensive experience in the field of Process Systems Engineering (PSE), Artificial Intelligence (AI) and Machine Learning methods, Integrated Multi-Scale Modelling methods, and Process Intensification. He is working as a scientist in CSIR-IICT since 2016. He has actively engaged in basic research as well as applied research. He has developed process model-based as well as AI-based methodologies to simulate, design, control, and optimize processes, for accelerated product and process design, and to achieve performance improvements to existing processes in terms of improving productivity and selectivity while maintaining their safety and environmental constraints. Dr. Kamesh was a recipient of the Ambuja Young Researchers Award in 2014 from Indian Institute of Chemical Engineers (IIChE).

Shri Kant has received his Ph. D. in applied mathematics from applied mathematics departments of institute of technology, Banaras Hindu University (BHU), Varanasi in 1981. He is working as a Professor and head of "Center of Cyber Security and cryptology", Department of Computer Science and Engineering of Sharda University, India and involved actively in teaching and research mainly in the area of cyber security and Machine learning. His areas of interest are Special Functions, Cryptology, Pattern Recognition, Cluster Analysis, Soft Computing Model, Machine Learning and Data Mining.

Nurdan Kara is an Assistant Prof. in the Department of Mathematics at National Defence University (MSU), Istanbul, Turkey. She has been a faculty member of Ankara University since 1998. She completed her Ph.D. entitled "Fuzzy approaches to multiobjective fractional transportation problem" in Applied Mathematics (2008) from Yildiz Technical University. Her current area of research is mathematical Programming, fractional programming, supply chain management and some related Operational Research subjects in multi criteria and fuzzy environments.

Prasanna Karhade is Associate Professor of IT Management, Shidler College Faculty Fellow and a Faculty Fellow at the Pacific Asian Center for Entrepreneurship [PACE] at the University of Hawai'i at Mānoa. His research interests include digital innovation and digital platforms in growing, rural, eastern, aspirational and transitional [GREAT] economies.

Bouamrane Karim received the PhD Degree in computer science from the Oran University in 2006. He is Professor of computer Science at Oran1 University. He is the head of "Decision and piloting system" team. His current research interests deal with decision support system and logistics in maritime transportation, urban transportation system, production system, health systems and application of bio-inspired based optimization metaheuristic. He participates in several scientific committees' international/national conferences in Algeria and others countries in the same domain and collaborated in Algerian-French scientific projects. He is co-author of more than 40 scientific publications.

Joseph Kasten is an Assistant Professor of Information Science and Technology at the Pennsylvania State University in York, PA. He earned a PhD in Information Science at Long Island University in Brookville, NY, an MBA at Dowling College in Oakdale, NY, and a BS in engineering at Florida Institute of Technology in Melbourne, FL. Before joining academia, Joe was a senior engineer with the Northrop-Grumman Corp. where he worked on various military and commercial projects such as the X-29 and the Boeing 777. His research interests center on the implementation of data analytics within the organization as well as the application of blockchain technology to emerging organizational requirements. Professor Kasten's recent research appears in the International Journal of Business Intelligence Research and International Journal of Healthcare Information Systems and Informatics.

Tolga Kaya is a full-time researcher and lecturer at the department of Management Engineering in Istanbul Technical University. His research areas are consumer modeling, statistical decision making, input-output modeling, multicriteria decision making, machine learning and fuzzy applications in business and management. He has published several papers and presented his research at a number of international conferences in these areas.

Wei Ke, Ph.D., is the Adjunct Associate Professor of Quantitative Revenue and Pricing Analytics at Columbia Business School. Previously, he was Managing Partner and the head of financial services practice in North America at Simon-Kucher & Partners. Wei received a Ph.D. in Decision, Risk, and Operations from Columbia Business School, and a BSc in Electrical Engineering & Applied Mathematics, summa cum laude, from Columbia University.

Vanessa Keppeler is a Senior Associate with PwC Germany's Financial Services Consulting practice. She specializes on the design and implementation of Data and AI Governance. Her research and studies focus on the practical enablement of Explainable AI in Financial Institutions. Vanessa holds a master's degree in Management (Finance).

Mehrnaz Khalaj Hedayati is an Assistant Professor of Management at Georgia College & State University, J. Whitney Bunting College of Business. Mehrnaz received her Ph.D. from the University of Rhode Island in 2020. Mehrnaz has published several academic journal articles. She is a Lean Six Sigma Certified from the URI College of Business. She has taught undergraduate and master's level courses in Business Quantitative Analysis, Business Statistics, and Operations Management. She has also served as ad-hoc reviewer for several academic journals.

Fahima Khanam is a Lecturer in the department of Aviation Operation Management at Bangabandhu Sheikh Mujibur Rahman Aviation and Aerospace University. Prior to joining the BSMRAAU, she served as Lecturer in the Department of Business Administration at Sheikh Burhanuddin Post Graduate College, European University, Victoria University and German University, Bangladesh where she taught Principles of Marketing, Marketing Management, Operations Management, International Business, and Business Communication. She also worked as a corporate professional in The Daily 'Prothom Alo', one of the top daily newspapers in Bangladesh. She holds an MBA in Marketing from University of Dhaka, Bangladesh. Her most recent publication appeared in the International Journal of Big Data and Analytics in Healthcare (IJBDAH). Her principal research interests include e-commerce, online shopping, social media marketing and branding strategy, marketing strategy and technology adoption.

Shardul Khandekar has his BE completed in E&TC and his research area includes machine learning and deep learning.

Mubina Khondkar serves as a Professor in the Department of Marketing at the University of Dhaka. She has interdisciplinary knowledge in the areas of marketing and development economics. She has both industry and research experiences with organizations including ANZ Grindlays Bank, Care Bangladesh, USAID, DFID, Concern, IFPRI, World Bank, SEDF, IFC, JICA, CIDA, UNICEF, BIDS, the University of Manchester, and the University of Cambridge. Her research interests include value chain analysis, marketing, poverty, microfinance, development economics, gender, and women's empowerment. Further details can be found here: https://www.researchgate.net/profile/Mubina-Khondkar.

Soumya Khurana has his BE completed in E&TC and his research area includes machine learning and deep learning.

Necla Koçhan is currently working as a postdoctoral researcher at Izmir Biomedicine and Genome Center, IBG. Her research interests are computational biology, statistical data analysis, fuzzy theory, classification, and biostatistics.

Koharudin is a master student in IPB University, Indonesia. In 2014 he joined the Bureau of Organization and Human Resource, Indonesian Institute of Sciences (LIPI), as IT Engineering. In 2020 He moved to Center for Scientific Data and Documentation, Indonesian Institute of Sciences (LIPI). His current roles include building and maintaining web applications, designing database architecture, integrating data and providing data through service point. He obtained his bachelor degree in Computer Science from the Sepuluh Nopember Institute of Technology in 2011. He has developed some applications such as Human Resources Information System, Mobile applications and API Gateway. His research interests include Bioinformatics, High Performance Computing and Machine Learning.

Tibor Koltay is Professor retired from the Institute of Learning Technologies at Eszterházy Károly Catholic University, in Hungary. He graduated from Eötvös Loránd University (Budapest, Hungary) in 1984 with an MA in Russian. He obtained there his PhD in 2002. In 1992 he was awarded the Certificate of Advanced Studies in Library and Information Science at Kent State University, Kent. OH.

Xiangfen Kong is an Associate Professor from the Civil Aviation University of China. Her research interests include smart airports, system reliability, operational research, and big data.

Elena Kornyshova is an Associate Professor at CNAM, Ph.D. in Economics and Management Sciences and Ph.D. in Computer Science. Her main research domains are method and process engineering, decision-making, enterprise architecture, and digitalization. She is/was involved in organization of multiple international conferences and workshops. She has significant experience in industry and consultancy sector mainly in the fields of IS engineering and enterprise architecture.

Maximiliano E. Korstanje is editor in chief of International Journal of Safety and Security in Tourism (UP Argentina) and Editor in Chief Emeritus of International Journal of Cyber Warfare and Terrorism (IGI-Global US). Korstanje is Senior Researchers in the Department of Economics at University of Palermo, Argentina. In 2015 he was awarded as Visiting Research Fellow at School of Sociology and Social Policy, University of Leeds, UK and the University of La Habana Cuba. In 2017 is elected as Foreign Faculty Member of AMIT, Mexican Academy in the study of Tourism, which is the most prominent institutions dedicated to tourism research in Mexico. He had a vast experience in editorial projects working as advisory member of Elsevier, Routledge, Springer, IGI global and Cambridge Scholar publishing. Korstanje had visited and given seminars in many important universities worldwide. He has also recently been selected to take part of the 2018 Albert Nelson Marquis Lifetime Achievement Award. a great distinction given by Marquis Who´s Who in the world.

Mika Kosonen is a graduate student in University of Lapland. He has bachelor's degree in social sciences and is currently finishing his master's degree. His bachelor's thesis was concerning artificial intelligence and ethics, and master's thesis contributes to morality in human-technology interaction, both with excellent grades. With strong interest in technology and human experience he is always wondering the world where technology mediates the reality, whether in suburbans or the wilderness found in northernmost parts of Europe.

Anjani Kumar is a Ph.D. student of computer science at the University of Nebraska at Omaha. He is working as a Data Scientist at Data Axle Inc. His primary research interests are in the fields of Big Data, Deep Learning, and Machine Learning.

Sameer Kumar is an Associate Professor at Universiti Malaya, Malaysia.

Madhusree Kundu is presently Professor, Department of Chemical Engineering, National Institute of Technology Rourkela, Orissa, India. Currently, HOD, Central Instrument Facility (CIF), NIT Rourkela. Experience: Worked as Process Engineer in Simon Carves India Limited (A Design Consultancy). First Academic Appointment: Assistant Professor, Birla Institute of Technology and Science (BITS) Pilani, Rajasthan, India. PhD: Indian Institute of Technology Kharagpur Research Interest: Fluid Phase equilibrium and its application, Modeling, & Simulation and Control, Chemommetrics/Machine Learning applications, Process Identification monitoring and Control, Biomimetic device development and Digitized Sustainable Agriculture.

Mascha Kurpicz-Briki obtained her PhD in the area of energy-efficient cloud computing at the University of Neuchâtel. After her PhD, she worked a few years in industry, in the area of open-source engineering, cloud computing and analytics. She is now professor for data engineering at the Bern University of Applied Sciences, investigating how to apply digital methods and in particular natural language processing to social and community challenges.

Kevin Kwak is an Information Systems and Accounting student at the University of Nebraska at Omaha. He received a Master's in Accounting and as of this writing is pursuing a Master's in Information Systems. His current interests of study are accounting, data security, and data mining. Currently, he has had five articles published in various journals.

Wikil Kwak is a Professor of Accounting at the University of Nebraska at Omaha. He received Ph.D. in Accounting from the University of Nebraska in Lincoln. Dr. Kwak's research interests include the areas of mathematical programming approaches in bankruptcy prediction, capital budgeting, transfer pricing, performance evaluation and Japanese capital market studies. He has published more than 57 articles in the Engineering Economist, Abacus, Contemporary Accounting Research, Review of Quantitative Finance and Accounting, Management Accountant, Journal of Petroleum Accounting and Financial Management, Business Intelligence and Data Mining, Review of Pacific Basin Financial Markets and Policies, and Multinational Business Review.

Georgios Lampropoulos received his BSc degree with the title of Information Technology Engineer specialized as a Software Engineer from the Department of Information Technology at Alexander

Technological Educational Institute of Thessaloniki (currently named International Hellenic University) in 2017 and he received his MSc in Web Intelligence from the same department in 2019. Currently, he is a PhD candidate and Visiting Lecturer in the Department of Information and Electronic Engineering at International Hellenic University and a MEd student in Education Sciences at Hellenic Open University. He has published his work in several peer reviewed journals and conferences, he has taken part in international research programs and he has also served as a reviewer and a member of the organizing and scientific committees of international conferences and international journals.

Torben Larsen is an MSc Econ from University of Aarhus and an international Degree in Strategic Management from University of Maryland-Tietgenskolen Dk. He has broad experience in regional planning of healthcare with Academic Awards from 1) Association of Hospital Managers in Norway, Lundbeck Fonden Dk and MIE96. He is a former Chief Research Consultant at University of Southern Denmark which included leadership of an EU-sponsored research project in Integrated Homecare. He has been involved with various courses and conferences and has written research papers in Health Economics, Neuroeconomics, Meditation and Biofeedback. 2017 he published "Homo Neuroeconomicus" (IJUDH(1)). 2020 he published "Neuroeconomic Pcyshology. 3 Modules for End-users . . . .", IJPCH Actually, he is giving guest lectures in cybernetic economics.

Matthias Lederer is Full Professor of Information Systems at the Technical University of Applied Sciences Amberg-Weiden. Prior to this, he was a professor at the ISM International School of Management Munich and at the same time Chief Process Officer at the IT Service Center of the Bavarian justice system. His previous positions include research assistant at the University of Erlangen-Nuremberg and strategy consultant at the German industrial company REHAU. His research and studies focus on business process management and IT management. Prof. Lederer holds a doctorate as well as a master's degree in international information systems and is the author of over 70 scientific publications in this field.

Eva Lee applies combinatorial optimization, math programming, game theory, and parallel computation to biological, medical, health systems, and logistics analyses. Her clinical decision-support systems (DSS) assist in disease diagnosis/prediction, treatment design, drug delivery, treatment and healthcare outcome analysis/prediction, and healthcare operations logistics. In logistics, she tackles operations planning and resource allocation, and her DSS addresses inventory control, vehicle dispatching, scheduling, transportation, telecom, portfolio investment, public health emergency treatment response, and facility location/planning. Dr. Lee is Director of the Center for Operations Research in Medicine and HealthCare, a center established through funds from the National Science Foundation and the Whitaker Foundation. The center focuses on biomedicine, public health and defense, translational medical research, medical delivery and preparedness, and the protection of critical infrastructures. She is a subject matter expert in medical systems and public health informatics, logistics and networks, and large-scale connected systems. She previously served as the Senior Health Systems Engineer and Professor for the U.S. Department of Veterans Affairs and was Co-Director for the Center for Health Organization Transformation. Dr. Lee has received numerous practice excellence awards, including the INFORMS Edelman Award on novel cancer therapeutics, the Wagner prize on vaccine immunity prediction, and the Pierskalla award on bioterrorism, emergency response, and mass casualty mitigation She is a fellow at INFORMS and AIMBE. Lee has served on NAE/NAS/IOM, NRC, NBSB, DTRA panel committees related to CBRN and WMD incidents, public health and medical preparedness, and healthcare systems innovation. She holds ten patents on medical systems and devices. Her work has been featured in the New York Times, London Times, disaster documentaries, and in other venues.

Jinha Lee is an Assistant Professor in the Department of Public and Allied Health at Bowling Green State University. His research interests include healthcare operations, data analytics, economic decision analysis, and system modeling in healthcare service. His work has examined practice variance and systems analysis for quality and process improvement and new clinical guidelines establishment. Also, his research has focused on economic analysis on industry networks, resource allocations, and the R&D process in healthcare services. His research primarily utilizes large datasets and clinical observations derived from various healthcare databases and field studies in clinical facilities. He has collaborated actively with hospitals, healthcare research institutes, and healthcare delivery organizations both in the U.S. and in foreign countries.

Ulli Leucht is a Manager in PwC Germany's Financial Services Technology Consulting team. He is an expert in AI and its use in Financial Institutions - which includes how AI use cases are identified, perceived, implemented, operated and surrounding governance, compliance, and legal requirements. Prior to joining PwC Germany, he worked with some of the most innovative FinTechs in the United Kingdom and the United States in the context of AI. Ulli's research and studies focus is the usage of AI in Financial Institutions. He holds a master's degree in Sensors and Cognitive Psychology.

Carson Leung is currently a Professor at the University of Manitoba, Canada. He has contributed more than 300 refereed publications on the topics of big data, computational intelligence, cognitive computing, data analytics, data mining, data science, fuzzy systems, machine learning, social network analysis, and visual analytics. These include eight chapters in IGI Global's books/encyclopedia (e.g., Encyclopedia of Organizational Knowledge, Administration, and Technology (2021)). He has also served on the Organizing Committee of the ACM CIKM, ACM SIGMOD, IEEE DSAA, IEEE ICDM, and other conferences.

Siyao Li is a student at the City University of Macau. She studies in the International Business program.

Gilson B. A. Lima is a Professor in the Industrial Engineering Department at Federal Fluminense University (UFF), Brazil. He received his PhD in the Rio de Janeiro Federal University, Brazil. His current research interests include industrial safety, risk management, industrial maintenance and industrial environmental management.

Yu-Wei Lin is an assistant professor in the Leavey School of Business, Santa Clara University. He received a Ph.D. in information systems at Gies College of Business, the University of Illinois at Urbana-Champaign. His research interests are in User-Generated Content, Healthcare Analytics, Online Review Analysis, Machine Learning, Decision Making, and Decision Support Systems.

Fangyao Liu is an assistant professor in the College of Electronic and Information at the Southwest Minzu University, China. He received Ph.D. in Information Technology from the University of Nebraska at Omaha, USA. Dr. Liu's research interests include the areas of data mining, artificial intelligence, and statistics. He has published more than 20 articles in the International journal of Computers Communications & Control, Journal of Urban Planning and Development, Journal of software, Journal of Asian Development, Journal of Contemporary Management, Procedia Computer Science, and several IEEE conferences.

Haoyu Liu is an assistant professor at the Faculty of Business, City University of Macau. He received an MPhil and a PhD in Operations Management from HKUST Business School in 2017 and 2020, respectively. He serves as a reviewer for Manufacturing & Service Operations Management (MSOM), Naval Research Logistics (NRL), International Journal of Applied Management Science (IJAMS), International Journal of Retail & Distribution Management (IJRDM), International Journal of E-Business Research (IJEBR), International Conference on Information Systems (ICIS), and INFORMS Conference on Service Science (ICSS). He has broad interests in issues related to healthcare, emerging technologies, charitable organizations, and marketing. In solving problems, he employs various techniques, ranging from game-theoretical and stochastic models to typical tools in empirical and experimental studies.

Ran Liu is an Assistant Professor in the Marketing department at Central Connecticut State University. His research focuses on online relationships, user-generated content (UGC), data modeling, and International businesses. He serves as Associate Editor (Asia) for Journal of Eastern European and Central Asian Research (JEECAR) and Faculty Advisor for American Marketing Association Collegiate Chapter.

Cèlia Llurba is currently a PhD student in Educational Technology in the Department of Pedagogy at the URV. Graduate in East Asian Studies from the UOC and a graduate in Mining Engineering from the UPC. She is currently a teacher of Technology in a high school in Cambrils (state employee) and also teaches in the subjects of Vocational Guidance and Citizenship, and Educational Processes and Contexts, within the Master's Degree in Teacher Training at the URV. Her main lines of research are: intellectual learning environments, data analytics and artificial intelligence in intellectual areas.

Manuel Lozano Rodriguez is American University of Sovereign Nations (AUSN) Visiting Prof. in his own discipline that takes bioethics off the medical hegemony to land it on social sciences, futurism, politics and pop culture through metaphysics of displacement. Born in Barcelona in 1978, Ph.D. in Bioethics, Sustainability and Global Public Health, AUSN; Master of Science in Sustainability, Peace and Development, AUSN; Graduate in Fundamentals of Sustainability Organizational, Harvard.

Lorenzo Magnani, philosopher, epistemologist, and cognitive scientist, is a professor of Philosophy of Science at the University of Pavia, Italy, and the director of its Computational Philosophy Laboratory. His previous positions have included: visiting researcher (Carnegie Mellon University, 1992; McGill University, 1992–93; University of Waterloo, 1993; and Georgia Institute of Technology, 1998–99) and visiting professor (visiting professor of Philosophy of Science and Theories of Ethics at Georgia Institute of Technology, 1999–2003; Weissman Distinguished Visiting Professor of Special Studies in Philosophy: Philosophy of Science at Baruch College, City University of New York, 2003). Visiting professor at the Sun Yat-sen University, Canton (Guangzhou), China from 2006 to 2012, in the event of the 50th anniversary of the re-building of the Philosophy Department of Sun Yat-sen University in 2010, an award was given to him to acknowledge his contributions to the areas of philosophy, philosophy of science, logic, and cognitive science. A Doctor Honoris Causa degree was awarded to Lorenzo Magnani by the Senate of the Ştefan cel Mare University, Suceava, Romania. In 2015 Lorenzo Magnani has been appointed member of the International Academy for the Philosophy of the Sciences (AIPS). He currently directs international research programs in the EU, USA, and China. His book Abduction, Reason, and Science (New York, 2001) has become a well-respected work in the field of human cognition. The book Morality in a Technological World (Cambridge, 2007) develops a philosophical and cognitive theory of the relationships between ethics and technology in a naturalistic perspective. The book Abductive Cognition. The Epistemological and Eco-Cognitive Dimensions of Hypothetical Reasoning and the last monograph Understanding Violence. The Intertwining of Morality, Religion, and Violence: A Philosophical Stance have been more recently published by Springer, in 2009 and 2011. A new monograph has been published by Springer in 2017, The Abductive Structure of Scientific Creativity. An Essay on the Ecology of Cognition, together with the Springer Handbook of Model-Based Science (edited with Tommaso Bertolotti). The last book Eco-Cognitive Computationalism. Cognitive Domestication of Ignorant Entities, published by Springer, offers an entirely new dynamic perspective on the nature of computation. He edited books in Chinese, 16 special issues of international academic journals, and 17 collective books, some of them deriving from international conferences. Since 1998, initially in collaboration with Nancy J. Nersessian and Paul Thagard, he created and promoted the MBR Conferences on Model-Based Reasoning. Since 2011 he is the editor of the Book Series Studies in Applied Philosophy, Epistemology and Rational Ethics (SAPERE), Springer, Heidelberg/Berlin.

Mazlina Abdul Majid is an Associate Professor in the Faculty of Computing at University Malaysia Pahang (UMP), Malaysia. She received her PHD in Computer Science from the University of Nottingham, UK. She held various managerial responsibilities as a Deputy Dean of Research and Graduate Studies and currently acts as the head of the Software Engineering Research Group in her Faculty. She also taught courses on the undergraduate and master's levels. She has published 130 research in local and international books, journals and conference proceedings. She is also a member of various committees of international conferences. Her research interests include simulation, software agent, software usability and testing.

Jasna D. Marković-Petrović received her B.Sc. (1992) and M.Sc. (2011) degrees in electrical engineering and her Ph.D. degree (2018) in technical sciences, all from the University of Belgrade, Serbia. She is with the Public Enterprise "Electric Power Industry of Serbia" for more than 25 years. Her activities involve implementation of the technical information system, participation in projects concerning upgrading the remote control system of the hydropower plant, and implementation of the SCADA security system. She is a member of the Serbian National CIGRÉ Study Committee D2. As author or coauthor, she published a number of book chapters, journal articles and conference papers in her field. Her main research interests involve smart grids, SCADA and industrial control systems security, and cyber risk management.

Roberto Marmo received the Laurea (cum laude) in Computer Science from Salerno University (Italy) and Ph.D. in Electronic and Computer Engineering obtained from the University of Pavia (Italy). He is presently contract teacher of computer science at Faculty of Engineering of Pavia University, Italy. His most recent work is concerned with mathematical models and software for social network analysis. He is author of "Social Media Mining", a textbook in Italian language on extraction of information from social media, website http://www.socialmediamining.it.

Nikolaos Matsatsinis is a full Professor of Information and Decision Support Systems in the School of Production Engineering and Management of the Technical University of Crete, Greece. He is President of the Hellenic Operational Research Society (HELORS). He is Director of DSS Lab and Postgraduate Programs. He has contributed as scientific or project coordinator on over of fifty national and international projects. He is chief editor of the Operational Research: An International Journal (Impact Factor 2020: 2.410) and International Journal of Decision Support Systems. He is the author or co-author/editor of 25 books and over of 120 articles in international scientific journals and books. He has organized and participated in the organization of over of ninety scientific conferences, including EURO 2021, and he has over of one hundred and ninety presentations in international and national scientific conferences. His research interests fall into the areas of Intelligent DSS, Multi-Agent Systems, Recommendation Systems, Multicriteria Decision Analysis, Group Decision Making, Operational Research, e-Marketing, Consumer Behaviour Analysis, Data Analysis, Business Intelligence & Business Analytics.

Hubert Maupas is graduated from Ecole Centrale de Lyon (France) and holds a PhD in Integrated Electronics, obtained with several patents and publications. He has spent most of his career in medical device industry and is currently working as COO of MUST, a all-in-one B2B Metaverse platform to manage DBE (Digital Business Ecosystem) embedding advanced matchmaking algorithms.

Iman Megahed is the AVP for Digital Transformation, Chief Strategy and Knowledge Officer at the American University in Cairo (AUC). She is currently responsible for all Information Technology, Information Security, Business Intelligence and institutional effectiveness functions. She co-founded the business intelligence and data governance functions to support informed based decision making. She also founded the office of Online Student Services which applied web services and portal technology to enhance student services. With a successful track record in technology and effectiveness administrative positions in Higher Education since 1992, Iman has accumulated extensive technical expertise, unique project management skills coupled with results-oriented leadership style and passion for informed based decision making. Iman earned her PhD in Organizational Behavior from Cairo University, MBA and BS in Computer Science from The American University in Cairo.

Natarajan Meghanathan is a tenured Full Professor of Computer Science at Jackson State University, Jackson, MS. He graduated with a Ph.D. in Computer Science from The University of Texas at Dallas in May 2005. Dr. Meghanathan has published more than 175 peer-reviewed articles (more than half of them being journal publications). He has also received federal education and research grants from the U. S. National Science Foundation, Army Research Lab and Air Force Research Lab. Dr. Meghanathan has been serving in the editorial board of several international journals and in the Technical Program Committees and Organization Committees of several international conferences. His research interests are Wireless Ad hoc Networks and Sensor Networks, Graph Theory and Network Science, Cyber Security, Machine Learning, Bioinformatics and Computational Biology. For more information, visit https://www.jsums.edu/nmeghanathan.

Abelardo Mercado Herrera has a PhD from the National Institute of Astrophysics, Optics and Electronics (INAOE), specializing in Astrophysics, Postdoctorate in Astrophysics from the Institute of Astronomy from the National Autonomous University of Mexico (UNAM), Electronics Engineer from the Autonomous University of Baja California (UABC). He is a specialist in the mathematical-statistical description of stochastic processes and/or deterministic systems, nonlinear systems, complex systems, chaos theory, among others, as well as its application to physical phenomena such as astronomy, medicine, economics, finance, telecommunications, social sciences etc., in order to determine the dynamics underlying in such processes, and given the case, its connection with real physical variables and possible prediction. He has worked on the development of interfaces and programs to carry out electrical tests in industry, as well as in scientific instrumentation, applied to telemetry, infrared polarimetry, optics and spectroscopy. He has also specialized in image analysis, measurement techniques and noise reduction.

Shivlal Mewada is presently working as an Assistant Professor (contact) in the Dept. of CS, Govt. Holkar (Autonomous, Model) Science College, Indore, India. He shared the responsibility of research activities and coordinator of M.Phil.(CS) at Govt. Holkar Sci. Collage, Indore. He has also received JRF in 2010-11 for M.Phil. Programme under UGC Fellow scheme, New Delhi. He is a member of IEEE since 2013 and editorial member of the ISROSET since 2013. He is a technical committee and editorial member of various reputed journals including Taylor & Francis, Inderscience. He chaired 5 national and international conferences and seminars. He organized 2 special for international conferences. He also contributed to the organization of 2 national and 4 virtual international conferences. Mr. Mewada has published 3 book chapters and over 18 research articles in reputed journals like SCI, Scopus including IEEE conferences. His areas of interest include; cryptography, information security and computational intelligence.

Tanish Ambrishkumar Mishra is an undergraduate student at Sardar Patel College of Engineering, Mumbai, India. Currently pursuing his Bachelor of Technology (B.Tech) in Department of Mechanical Engineering. His research areas of interest are mobile robotics, biomimetic robot design, robotic prosthetic limb design, control systems and AI/ML.

Mayank Modashiya is a Data Scientist 1 at Kenco Group, Chattanooga, TN, USA. He earned is Bachelor's in Engineering in Mechanical Engineering, India. He earned his Masters in Industrial Engineering from the University of Texas at Arlington. Mayank has passion for applying machine learning (ML) and artificial Intelligence (AI) to solve complex supply chain problems. Mayank has more than 2 years' experience in developing and implementing AI/ML for problem solving. His research interest includes supply chain networks, logistics and manufacturing. He is member of INFORMS and IISE.

Jordi Mogas holds a PhD in Educational Technology and a Bachelor's in Information and Documentation with mention in information systems management. Currently, he is a postdoc researcher at GEPS research center (Globalisation, Education and Social Policies), at the Universitat Autònoma de Barcelona, and belongs to ARGET (Applied Research Group in Education and Technology). Dr. Mogas teaches at both the Department of Pedagogy at the Universitat Rovira i Virgili (professor associate) and at the Department of Education at the Universitat Oberta de Catalunya (professor collaborador). His main research lines are: Smart Learning Environments, Virtual Learning Environments and Self-Regulated Learning.

Siddhartha Moulik is working as a Scientist in CSIR-IICT. His field of specialization deals with wastewater treatment, cavitation based advanced oxidation processes, sonochemistry as well as in membrane separation technology along with experiences in practical field applications.

Adam Moyer is an Assistant Professor in the Department of Analytics and Information Systems at Ohio University's College of Business. Moyer received a BBA from Ohio University and has had experience managing information systems for non-profit organizations, has worked as a systems engineer, and has consulted for various companies. While earning an MS in Industrial & Systems Engineering at Ohio University, Adam developed and taught courses related to information systems, programming, system design and deployment, business intelligence, analytics, and cybersecurity at Ohio University. After gaining additional professional experience in the counterintelligence community, Moyer returned to Ohio University and earned a Ph.D. in Mechanical and Systems Engineering.

Anirban Mukherjee is faculty in marketing. He received a PhD in Marketing from The Samuel Curtis Johnson Graduate School of Management, Cornell University.

Anweshan Mukherjee has completed his BSc with Major in Computer Science from St. Xavier's College, Kolkata and is currently pursuing MSc in Computer Science from the same college. His current research interest is Data Analytics and Machine Learning.

Partha Mukherjee, assistant professor of data analytics, received his bachelor's degree in mechanical engineering in 1995 from Jadavpur University in India. He received his Master of Technology in Computer Science from Indian Statistical Institute in 2001. He earned his second graduate degree in computer Science from the University of Tulsa in 2008. He completed his Ph.D. from Penn State in information and technology with a minor in applied statistics in 2016.

Fabian N. Murrieta-Rico received B.Eng. and M.Eng. degrees from Instituto Tecnológico de Mexicali (ITM) in 2004 and 2013 respectively. In 2017, he received his PhD in Materials Physics at Centro de Investigación Científica y Educación Superior de Ensenada (CICESE). He has worked as an automation engineer, systems designer, as a university professor, and as postdoctoral researcher at Facultad de Ingeniería, Arquitectura y Diseño from Universidad Autónoma de Baja California (UABC) and at the Centro de Nanociencias y Nanotecnología from Universidad Nacional Autónoma de México (CNyN-UNAM), currently he works as professor at the Universidad Politécnica de Baja California. His research has been published in different journals and presented at international conferences since 2009. He has served as reviewer for different journals, some of them include IEEE Transactions on Industrial Electronics, IEEE Transactions on Instrumentation, Measurement and Sensor Review. His research interests are focused on the field of time and frequency metrology, the design of wireless sensor networks, automated systems, and highly sensitive chemical detectors.

Balsam A. J. Mustafa holds an MS.c in Information Systems from the UK and earned her Ph.D. in Computer Science (Software Engineering) from Malaysia. Her research interests are in the areas of empirical software engineering, intelligent health care systems, and data mining & analytics. Dr. Balsam has served on more than 25 international conference program committees and journal editorial boards, and has been a keynote and invited speaker at several international conferences. She is a member of IEEE and a professional member of the Association of Computing Machinery (ACM). Dr. Balsam has published 30 technical papers in various refereed journals and conference proceedings.

Ambika N. is an MCA, MPhil, Ph.D. in computer science. She completed her Ph.D. from Bharathiar university in the year 2015. She has 16 years of teaching experience and presently working for St.Francis College, Bangalore. She has guided BCA, MCA and M.Tech students in their projects. Her expertise includes wireless sensor network, Internet of things, cybersecurity. She gives guest lectures in her expertise. She is a reviewer of books, conferences (national/international), encyclopaedia and journals. She is advisory committee member of some conferences. She has many publications in National & international conferences, international books, national and international journals and encyclopaedias. She has some patent publications (National) in computer science division.

Jyotindra Narayan is a regular doctoral fellow at the Department of Mechanical Engineering, Indian Institute of Technology Guwahati, currently practicing and working on "Design, Development and Control Architecture of a Low-cost Lower-Limb Exoskeleton for Mobility Assistance and Gait Rehabilitation". Moreover, he employs the intelligent and soft computing algorithms in his research. He has a substantial experience in kinematics, dynamics and control of robotic devices for medical applications. He has published several journals, book chapters and conference papers on the broad topic of medical and rehabilitation devices.

Ghalia Nasserddine is a Ph.D in information technology and systems. She has been an assistant professor at Lebanese International University since 2010. In addition, she is active research in machine learning, belief function theory, renewable energy and High voltage transmission.

Son Nguyen earned his master's degree in applied mathematics and doctoral degree in mathematics, statistics emphasis, both at Ohio University. He is currently an assistant professor at the department of mathematics at Bryant University. His primary research interests lie in dimensionality reduction, imbalanced learning, and machine learning classification. In addition to the theoretical aspects, he is also interested in applying statistics to other areas such as finance and healthcare.

Van-Ho Nguyen received B.A. degree in Management Information System from Faculty of Information Systems, University of Economics and Law (VNU–HCM), Vietnam in 2015, and Master degree in MIS from School of Business Information Technology from University of Economics Ho Chi Minh City, Vietnam in 2020, respectively. His current research interests include Business Intelligence, Data Analytics, and Machine Learning.

Shivinder Nijjer, currently serving as Assistant Professor in Chitkara University, Punjab, has a doctorate in Business Analytics and Human Resource Management. She has authored books and book chapters in the field of Business Analytics, Information Systems and Strategy for eminent publication groups like Taylor and Francis, Emerald, Pearson and IGI Global. She is currently guiding two PhD candidates and is on reviewer panel of three Scopus indexed journals.

Roberto Nogueira is Grupo Globo Full Professor of Strategy at COPPEAD Graduate School of Business, The Federal University of Rio de Janeiro, where he is also executive director of the Strategy and Innovation Research Center. He joined COPPEAD in 1984 and since that teaches at the MSc, PhD and Executive Education courses. He was visiting professor at the University of San Diego (USA), San Jose State University (USA), Alma Business School (Italy), Audencia (France) and Stellenbosch (South

Africa). He is co-founder and board member of the Executive MBA Consortium for Global Business Innovation, encompassing Business Schools from five continents - Alma Business School (Italy), Cranfield (UK), Coppead (Brazil), ESAN (Peru), FIU (USA), Keio Business School (Japan), Kozminski (Poland), MIR (Russia), Munich Business School (Germany), San Jose State (Silicon Valley - USA) and Stellenbosch (South Africa) promoting the exchange of Executive MBA students. Nogueira wrote two books and has published dozens of scholarly articles on such topics as Corporate Strategy, Business Ecosystems, Innovation and Emerging Technologies and Business Reconfiguration, analyzing sectors such as Health, Energy, Education, Media and Entertainment and Space.

Cherie Noteboom is a Professor of Information Systems in the College of Business and Information Systems, Coordinator of the PhD in Information Systems and Co-Director of the Center of Excellence in Information Systems at Dakota State University. She holds a Ph.D. in Information Technology from the University of Nebraska-Omaha. In addition, she has earned an Education Doctorate in Adult & Higher Education & Administration & MBA from the University of South Dakota. She has a BS degree in computer science from South Dakota State University. She researches in the areas of Information Systems, Healthcare, and Project Management. Her industry experience runs the continuum from technical computer science endeavors to project management and formal management & leadership positions. She has significant experience working with Management Information Systems, Staff Development, Project Management, Application Development, Education, Healthcare, Mentoring, and Leadership.

Zinga Novais is a project manager. She holds a Master's in Project Management from ISEG, School of Economics & Management of the University of Lisbon. She also holds a post-graduation in Project Management and a postgraduation in Management & Business Consulting, both from ISEG - University of Lisbon; and a degree in Public Administration from ISCSP, School of Social and Political Sciences of the University of Lisbon.

Poonam Oberoi is an Associate Professor of Marketing at Excelia Business School. She joined Excelia Group in 2014 after successfully defending her thesis at Grenoble Ecole de Management the same year. On the research front, Dr. Oberoi's primary focus is in the area of innovation and technology management. Her work examines the technology and innovation sourcing decisions that firms make, and the consequences of these decisions. Since her appointment at Excelia Business School, she has published research papers on these topics in well-regarded, peer reviewed, international journals such as M@n@gement and Journal of Business Research. Furthermore, she has published many book chapters and case studies on related topics. For more information, please visit: https://www.excelia-group.com/faculty-research/faculty/oberoi.

Ibrahim Oguntola is a Research Assistant, Industrial Engineering, Dalhousie University, Canada.

Kamalendu Pal is with the Department of Computer Science, School of Science and Technology, City, University of London. Kamalendu received his BSc (Hons) degree in Physics from Calcutta University, India, Postgraduate Diploma in Computer Science from Pune, India, MSc degree in Software Systems Technology from the University of Sheffield, Postgraduate Diploma in Artificial Intelligence from the Kingston University, MPhil degree in Computer Science from the University College London, and MBA degree from the University of Hull, United Kingdom. He has published over seventy-five international research articles (including book chapters) widely in the scientific community with research papers in the ACM SIGMIS Database, Expert Systems with Applications, Decision Support Systems, and conferences. His research interests include knowledge-based systems, decision support systems, blockchain technology, software engineering, service-oriented computing, and ubiquitous computing. He is on the editorial board of an international computer science journal and is a member of the British Computer Society, the Institution of Engineering and Technology, and the IEEE Computer Society.

Ramon Palau is a researcher and lecturer in the Pedagogy Department of the Rovira and Virgili University. As a researcher he did internships in UNESCO París and Leipzig University. His current work as a researcher is in ARGET (Applied Research Group of Education Technology) focused in e-learning, digital technologies, digital competences and educational application of digital technologies. In this group he has participated in several research projects. Currently his research is centered in smart learning environments publishing the first fundings. He has worked as a content developer for several institutions as Universitat Oberta de Catalunya, Fundació URV, Fundació Paco Puerto, Editorial Barcanova and Universitat de Lleida. Previously of the works in academia, he has worked as a primary and secondary teacher as a civil servant. From 2003 until 2007 he had been a principal in a public school. Concerning teaching, in higher education level, he has taught in Master of Educational Technology in Universitat Rovira i Virgili and Universitat Oberta de Catalunya and the Master of Teaching in Secondary School where is the director of the program.

Adam Palmquist is an industrial PhDc at the department of Applied IT at Gothenburg University and works as Chief Scientific Officer (CSO) at the Swedish Gamification company Insert Coin. Palmquist has a background in learning and game design. He is the author of several books addressing the intersection of design, technology, and learning. Adam has worked as a gamification and learning advisor for several international companies in the technology and production industries. His PhD-project is a collaboration between Gothenburg University and Insert Coin concerning Gamified the World Engine (GWEN), a unique system-agnostic API constructed to make gamification designs scalable. The interdisciplinary project transpires at the intersection of Human-Computer Interaction, Design Science in Information Systems and Learning Analytics.

Chung-Yeung Pang received his Ph.D. from Cambridge University, England. He has over 30 years of software development experience in a variety of areas from device drivers, web, and mobile apps to large enterprise IT systems. He has experience in many programming languages, including low-level languages like Assembler and C, high-level languages like COBOL, Java and Ada, AI languages like LISP and Prolog, and mobile app languages like Javascript and Dart. For the past 20 years he has worked as a consultant in various corporate software projects. He worked in the fields of architecture design, development, coaching and management of IT projects. At one time he was a lead architect on a project with a budget of over $ 1 billion. In recent years, despite limited resources and high pressure in some projects, he has led many projects to complete on time and on budget.

Severin Pang completed a combined degree in mathematics, statistics, and economics at the University of Bern. He also received the Swiss federal state diploma for computer engineers. He has more than 10 years of experience in computing engineering in companies such as Swiss Re, Zurich Insurance and IBM. At IBM he implemented AI functionalities for a hovering robot to support ISS astronauts. Severin Pang is currently working as a data scientist at Cognitive Solutions & Innovation AG in Switzerland, where he formulates mathematical models for predictive maintenance of machines, develops an intelligent sensor to detect anomalies in the frequency spectrum, and verifies the effectiveness of fuel-saving measures for Airbus aircraft and optimizes the energy consumption of more than 6000 hotels around the world. He has contributed to a number of publications in the fields of data science, AI, and software engineering.

Renan Payer holds a PhD and a Master's degree in Production Engineering from Fluminense Federal University (Brazil). Graduated in Chemical Engineering (University of the State of Rio de Janeiro UERJ) in Industrial Chemistry (Fluminense Federal University - UFF). He has an MBA in Production and Quality Management. It carries out academic research in the area of sustainability, circular economy and digital transformation.

Jean-Eric Pelet holds a PhD in Marketing, an MBA in Information Systems and a BA (Hns) in Advertising. As an assistant professor in management, he works on problems concerning consumer behaviour when using a website or other information system (e-learning, knowledge management, e-commerce platforms), and how the interface can change that behavior. His main interest lies in the variables that enhance navigation in order to help people to be more efficient with these systems. He works as a visiting professor both in France and abroad (England, Switzerland) teaching e-marketing, ergonomics, usability, and consumer behaviour at Design Schools (Nantes), Business Schools (Paris, Reims), and Universities (Paris Dauphine – Nantes). Dr. Pelet has also actively participated in a number of European Community and National research projects. His current research interests focus on, social networks, interface design, and usability.

María A. Pérez received her M.S. and Ph.D. degrees in telecommunication engineering from the University of Valladolid, Spain, in 1996 and 1999, respectively. She is presently Associate Professor at University of Valladolid, and member of the Data Engineering Research Unit. Her research is focused on Big Data, Artificial Intelligence, Internet of Things, and the application of technology to the learning process. She has managed or participated in numerous international research projects. She is author or co-author of many publications in journals, books, and conferences. In addition, she has been involved as reviewer in several international research initiatives.

Vitalii Petranovskii received the Ph.D. degree in physical chemistry from the Moscow Institute of Crystallography in 1988. From 1993 to 1994, he worked as a Visiting Fellow at the National Institute of Materials Science and Chemical Research, Japan. Since 1995, he has been working with the Center for Nanotechnology and Nanotechnology, National University of Mexico, as the Head of the Department of Nanocatalysis, from 2006 to 2014. He is a member of the Mexican Academy of Sciences, the International Association of Zeolites, and the Russian Chemical Society. He has published over 160 articles in peer-reviewed journals and five invited book chapters. He is also a coauthor of the monograph Clusters and Matrix Isolated Clustered Superstructures (St. Petersburg, 1995). His research interests include the synthesis and properties of nanoparticles deposited on zeolite matrices, and the modification of the zeolite matrices themselves for their high-tech use.

Frederick E. Petry received BS and MS degrees in physics and a PhD in computer and information science from The Ohio State University. He is currently a computer scientist in the Naval Research Laboratory at the Stennis Space Center Mississippi. He has been on the faculty of the University of Alabama in Huntsville, the Ohio State University and Tulane University where he is an Emeritus Professor. His recent research interests include representation of imprecision via soft computing in databases, spatial and environmental and information systems and machine learning. Dr. Petry has over 350 scientific publications including 150 journal articles/book chapters and 9 books written or edited. For his research on the use of fuzzy sets for modeling imprecision in databases and information systems he was elected an IEEE Life Fellow, AAAS Fellow, IFSA Fellow and an ACM Distinguished Scientist. In 2016 he received the IEEE Computational Intelligence Society Pioneer Award.

Birgit Pilch studied Biology and then Technical Protection of Environment at Graz University and Graz University of Technology.

Matthias Pohl is a research associate in the Very Large Business Application Lab at the Otto von Guericke University Magdeburg since 2016. His main research and work interests are data science, statistical modeling and the efficient design of innovative IT solutions. Matthias Pohl studied Mathematics and Informatics and holds a Diplom degree in Mathematics from Otto von Guericke University Magdeburg.

Peter Poschmann, M.Sc., works as a research associate at the Chair of Logistics, Institute of Technology and Management, at the Technical University of Berlin. Within the scope of several research projects, he focuses on the technical application of Machine Learning to logistic problems, in particular the prediction of transport processes. Previously, he worked as a research associate at a Fraunhofer Institute with a focus on Data Science. He graduated in industrial engineering with a specialization in mechanical engineering at the Technical University of Darmstadt.

Brajkishore Prajapati is an associate Data Scientist at Azilen Technologies Pvt. Ltd. He is living in Gwalior, Madhya Pradesh. He is very passionate and loyal to his work and finishes his work on time. His dream is to become one of the great researchers in the field of Artificial Intelligence. He is a very big fan of cricket and reading.

Sabyasachi Pramanik is a Professional IEEE member. He obtained a PhD in Computer Science and Engineering from the Sri Satya Sai University of Technology and Medical Sciences, Bhopal, India. Presently, he is an Assistant Professor, Department of Computer Science and Engineering, Haldia Institute of Technology, India. He has many publications in various reputed international conferences, journals, and online book chapter contributions (Indexed by SCIE, Scopus, ESCI, etc.). He is doing research in the field of Artificial Intelligence, Data Privacy, Cybersecurity, Network Security, and Machine Learning. He is also serving as the editorial board member of many international journals. He is a reviewer of journal articles from IEEE, Springer, Elsevier, Inderscience, IET, and IGI Global. He has reviewed many conference papers, has been a keynote speaker, session chair and has been a technical program committee member in many international conferences. He has authored a book on Wireless Sensor Network. Currently, he is editing 6 books from IGI Global, CRC Press EAI/Springer and Scrivener-Wiley Publications.

Abdurrakhman Prasetyadi is a junior researcher at the Research Center for Data and Information Science, The Indonesia Institute of Sciences (LIPI), Indonesia since 2019. He was a researcher at the Center for Information Technology (UPT BIT LIPI) for 6 years. He obtained his bachelor's degree in

Library and Information Sciences from the University of Padjadjaran, Indonesia in 2008. He earned a Master's degree in Information Technology for Libraries from the IPB University in 2017. Abdurrakhman Prasetyadi's research interests include issues in the field of Library and Information Science, Social Informatics, and Informetrics.

Bitan Pratihar obtained his Bachelor of Technology degree in Chemical Engineering from National Institute of Technology Durgapur, India, in 2017. He completed his Master of Technology degree in Chemical Engineering department of National Institute of Technology Rourkela, India, in 2019. His research interests were the application of Fuzzy Logic in data mining, controller design, and soft sensor design for several chemical engineering applications and others. Currently, he is a doctoral student in Membrane Separation Laboratory of Chemical Engineering Department, Indian Institute of Technology Kharagpur, India.

Alessandro Puzzanghera is a PhD student at the University for foreigners "Dante Alighieri" in Reggio Calabria. He worked many years as legal assistant at the FIDLAW LLP a law firm in London. He successfully completed her studies in the Master of Studies (MSt) postgraduate level degree program of the European Law and Governance School at the European Public Law Organization in Athens. His fields of research include: Artificial Intelligence, Administrative law, Personal Data in particular about GDPR. He published papers for Hart publishing (Oxford), EPLO publication (Athens) and various italian scientific journals.

John Quinn is a Professor of Mathematics at Bryant University and has been teaching there since 1991. Prior to teaching, he was an engineer at the Naval Underwater Systems Center (now the Naval Undersea Warfare Center). He received his Sc.B. degree from Brown University in 1978, and his M.S. and Ph.D. degrees from Harvard University in 1987 and 1991, respectively. Professor Quinn has published in multiple areas. He has done previous research in mathematical programming methods and computable general equilibrium models. He currently does research in probability models and in data mining applications, including the prediction of rare events. He is also doing research in pension modeling, including the effects of health status on retirement payouts.

Parvathi R. is a Professor of School of Computing Science and Engineering at VIT University, Chennai since 2011. She received the Doctoral degree in the field of spatial data mining in the same year. Her teaching experience in the area of computer science includes more than two decades and her research interests include data mining, big data and computational biology.

Sreemathy R. is working as Associate Professor in Pune Institute of Computer Technology, Savitribai Phule Pune University, India. She has her Master's degree in Electronics Engineering from college of Engineering, Pune. Savitribai Phule Pune University and Doctoral degree in Electronics Engineering from Shivaji University, India. Her research areas include signal processing, image processing, Artificial Intelligence, Machine Learning and Deep Learning.

Kornelije Rabuzin is currently a Full Professor at the Faculty of organization and informatics, University of Zagreb, Croatia. He holds Bachelor, Master, and PhD degrees - all in Information Science. He performs research in the area of databases, particularly graph databases, as well as in the field of data warehousing and business intelligence. He has published four books and more than eighty scientific and professional papers.

Kaleche Rachid is a PhD student of computer science since 2018. He is member of computer science laboratory (LIO) of Oran1 university in Algeria. His current research interests deal with artificial intelligence, transportation system, logistic systems, machine learning, bio-inspired approach. He is co-author of many publications and communications.

Rulina Rachmawati earned a bachelor degree in Chemistry from the Sepuluh Nopember Institute of Technology, Indonesia, in 2009. She started her career as a technical librarian at the Library and Archive Agency of the Regional Government of Surabaya city, Indonesia. Her passion for librarianship brought her to pursue a Master of Information Management from RMIT University, Australia, in 2019. Presently, she is a librarian at the Center for Scientific Data and Documentation, the Indonesian Institute of Sciences. Her current roles include providing library services, providing content for the Indonesian Scientific Journal Database (ISJD), and researching data, documentation and information. Her research interests include bibliometrics, library services, information retrieval, and research data management.

Nayem Rahman is an Information Technology (IT) Professional. He has implemented several large projects using data warehousing and big data technologies. He holds a Ph.D. from the Department of Engineering and Technology Management at Portland State University, USA, an M.S. in Systems Science (Modeling & Simulation) from Portland State University, Oregon, USA, and an MBA in Management Information Systems (MIS), Project Management, and Marketing from Wright State University, Ohio, USA. He has authored 40 articles published in various conference proceedings and scholarly journals. He serves on the Editorial Review Board of the International Journal of End-User Computing and Development (IJEUCD). His principal research interests include Big Data Analytics, Big Data Technology Acceptance, Data Mining for Business Intelligence, and Simulation-based Decision Support System (DSS).

Vishnu Rajan is an Assistant Professor in the Production & Operations Management Division at XIME Kochi, Kerala, India. His current research interests include supply chain risk management, operations research, reliability engineering, manufacturing systems management, quantitative techniques and statistics. He has published research articles in reputed peer-reviewed international journals of Taylor & Francis, Emerald, Inderscience, Elsevier, IEEE and IIIE publications. He also has a scientific book chapter to his credit. Besides this, Vishnu serves as an editorial board member of the International Journal of Risk and Contingency Management (IJRCM) of IGI Global.

T. Rajeshwari is freelancer and Yagyopathy researcher. She usually writes up article in science forums related to Hindu Mythology and their scientific proofs. She belongs to Kolkata and travels across globe for social work and spreading the science of Hindu rituals.

P. N. Ram Kumar is Professor in the QM & OM area at the Indian Institute of Management Kozhikode. Prior to this appointment, he had worked as a Post-Doctoral Research Fellow in the School of Mechanical and Aerospace Engineering at the Nanyang Technological University, Singapore. He obtained his Bachelor in Mechanical Engineering from the JNTU Hyderabad in 2003, Master in Industrial Engineering from the PSG College of Technology, Coimbatore in 2005 and PhD from the IIT Madras in 2009.

His primary areas of research include, but not limited to, transportation network optimisation, military logistics, reliability engineering and supply chain management. He has authored several international journal papers and his work has been published in reputed journals such as Journal of the Operational Research Society, Defense and Security Analysis, Strategic Analysis, and Journal of Defense Modeling & Simulation, to name a few.

Perumal Ramasubramanian holds BE, ME from Computer Science and Engineering from Madurai Kamaraj University and PH.D Computer Science from Madurai Kamaraj University in the year 1989, 1996 and 2012. He has 31 years teaching experience in academia. He was published 55 papers in various international journal and conferences. He has authored 14 books and has 135 citations with h-index 5 and i10 index 4. He is also actively involved in various professional societies like Institution of Engineers(I), Computer Science Teachers Association, ISTE, ISRD, etc.

Célia M. Q. Ramos graduated in Computer Engineering from the University of Coimbra, obtained her Master in Electrical and Computers Engineering from the Higher Technical Institute, Lisbon University, and the PhD in Econometrics in the University of the Algarve (UALG), Faculty of Economics, Portugal. She is Associate Professor at School for Management, Hospitality and Tourism, also in the UALG, where she lectures computer science. Areas of research and special interest include the conception and development of business intelligence, information systems, tourism information systems, big data, tourism, machine learning, social media marketing, econometric modelling and panel-data models. Célia Ramos has published in the fields of information systems and tourism, namely, she has authored a book, several book chapters, conference papers and journal articles. At the level of applied research, she has participated in several funded projects.

Anshu Rani has more than 12 years of experience in teaching and learning at various reputed institutes. She is a researcher associated with the online consumer behaviour area.

Bindu Rani is a Ph.D. scholar from Department of Computer Science and Engineering, Sharda University, Greater Noida, India and works as assistant professor in Information Technology Department, Inderprastha Engineering College, Ghaziabad, Dr. A.P.J Abdul Kalam Technical University, India. She received Master in Computer Science and Application degree from Aligarh Muslim University (AMU), India. Her research interests are Data Mining, Big Data and Machine learning techniques.

N. Raghavendra Rao is an Advisor to FINAIT Consultancy Services India. He has a doctorate in the area of Finance. He has a rare distinction of having experience in the combined areas of Information Technology and Finance.

Zbigniew W. Ras is a Professor of Computer Science Department and the Director of the KDD Laboratory at the University of North Carolina, Charlotte. He also holds professorship position in the Institute of Computer Science at the Polish-Japanese Academy of Information Technology in Warsaw, Poland. His areas of specialization include knowledge discovery and data mining, recommender systems, health informatics, business analytics, flexible query answering, music information retrieval, and art.

Rohit Rastogi received his B.E. degree in Computer Science and Engineering from C.C.S.Univ. Meerut in 2003, the M.E. degree in Computer Science from NITTTR-Chandigarh (National Institute of Technical Teachers Training and Research-affiliated to MHRD, Govt. of India), Punjab Univ. Chandigarh in 2010. Currently he is pursuing his Ph.D. In computer science from Dayalbagh Educational Institute, Agra under renowned professor of Electrical Engineering Dr. D.K. Chaturvedi in area of spiritual consciousness. Dr. Santosh Satya of IIT-Delhi and dr. Navneet Arora of IIT-Roorkee have happily consented him to co supervise. He is also working presently with Dr. Piyush Trivedi of DSVV Hardwar, India in center of Scientific spirituality. He is a Associate Professor of CSE Dept. in ABES Engineering. College, Ghaziabad (U.P.-India), affiliated to Dr. A.P. J. Abdul Kalam Technical Univ. Lucknow (earlier Uttar Pradesh Tech. University). Also, he is preparing some interesting algorithms on Swarm Intelligence approaches like PSO, ACO and BCO etc.Rohit Rastogi is involved actively with Vichaar Krnati Abhiyaan and strongly believe that transformation starts within self.

Mark Rauch is a database administrator and a graduate student in the program for Database Management at the University of West Florida. Mark Rauch is actively working in the healthcare industry and has experience working with several Oracle database platforms as well as SQL Server. His experience extends across Oracle 11g, 12c, and 19c. He has also supported several aspects of Oracle Middleware including Oracle Data Integrator, Oracle Enterprise Manager, Web Logic, and Business Publisher.

Yuan Ren is an instructor in Shanghai Dianji University. He was born in 1984. He got his bachelor's degree in mathematics from Jilin University in 2007, and doctor's degree in computer software from Fudan University in 2013. His multidisciplinary research interests include image understanding, artificial intelligence, and data science.

M. Yudhi Rezaldi is a researcher at the Research Center for Informatics, National Research and Innovation Agency (BRIN). His academic qualifications were obtained from Pasundan Universiti Bandung for his bachelor degree, and Mater degree in Magister of Design from Institut Teknologi Bandung (ITB). He completed his PhD in 2020 at Computer Science from Universiti Kebangsaan Malaysia (UKM). And he is also an active member of Himpunan Peneliti Indonesia (Himpenindo). His research interests include visualization, modeling, computer graphics animation, multimedia design, Information Science, particularly disaster. He received an award The best researcher in the 2011 researcher and engineer incentive program in Indonesian Institute of Science (LIPI). and once received the Karya Satya award 10 years in 2018 from the Indonesian government for his services to the country.

Moisés Rivas López was born in June 1, 1960. He received the B.S. and M.S. degrees in Autonomous University of Baja California, México, in 1985, 1991, respectively. He received PhD degree in the same University, on specialty "Optical Scanning for Structural Health Monitoring", in 2010. He has written 5 book chapters and 148 Journal and Proceedings Conference papers. Since 1992 till the present time he has presented different works in several International Congresses of IEEE, ICROS, SICE, AMMAC in USA, England, Japan, turkey and Mexico. Dr. Rivas was Dean of Engineering Institute of Autonomous University Baja California, Since1997 to 2005; also was Rector of Polytechnic University of Baja California, Since2006 to 2010. Since 2012 to 208 was the head of physic engineering department, of Engineering Institute, Autonomous University of Baja California, Mexico. Since 2013 till the present time member of National Researcher System and now is Professor in the Polytechnic University of Baja California.

Julio C. Rodríguez-Quiñonez received the B.S. degree in CETYS, Mexico in 2007. He received the Ph.D. degree from Baja California Autonomous University, México, in 2013. He is currently Full Time Researcher-Professor in the Engineering Faculty of the Autonomous University of Baja California, and member of the National Research System Level 1. Since 2016 is Senior Member of IEEE. He is involved in the development of optical scanning prototype in the Applied Physics Department and research leader in the development of a new stereo vision system prototype. He has been thesis director of 3 Doctor's Degree students and 4 Master's degree students. He holds two patents referred to dynamic triangulation method, has been editor of 4 books, Guest Editor of Measurement, IEEE Sensors Journal, International Journal of Advanced Robotic Systems and Journal of Sensors, written over 70 papers, 8 book chapters and has been a reviewer for IEEE Sensors Journal, Optics and Lasers in Engineering, IEEE Transaction on Mechatronics and Neural Computing and Applications of Springer; he participated as a reviewer and Session Chair of IEEE ISIE conferences in 2014 (Turkey), 2015 (Brazil), 2016 (USA), 2017 (UK), 2019 (Canada), IECON 2018 (USA), IECON 2019 (Portugal), ISIE 2020 (Netherlands), ISIE 2021 (Japan). His current research interests include automated metrology, stereo vision systems, control systems, robot navigation and 3D laser scanners.

Mário José Batista Romão is an Associate Professor of Information Systems, with Aggregation, at ISEG – University of Lisbon. He is Director of the Masters program in Computer Science and Management. He holds a PhD in Management Sciences by ISCTE-IUL and by Computer Integrated Manufacturing at Cranfiel University (UK). He also holds a MsC in Telecommunications and Computer Science, at IST - Instituto Superior Técnico, University of Lisbon. He is Pos-Graduated in Project Management and holds the international certification Project Management Professional (PMP), by PMI – Project Management International. He has a degree in Electrotecnic Engineer by IST.

James Rotella did his BS in physics at Pennsylvania State University and MS in physics at the University of Pittsburgh. While at the University of Pittsburgh he focused on doing epigenetic research in the biophysics department. He went on to work for 4 years as a failure analysis engineer at a Dynamics Inc. working on improving their lines of flexible microelectronics. He focused on improving yield internally in the factory, and designing and carrying out accelerated life and field tests to improve field performance. After working at Dynamics, he moved on to begin work programming at K&L Gates where he maintains analytics pipelines, models, and databases. While at K&L Gates, he completed an Masters in Data Analytics at Pennsylvania State University.

Anirban Roy is the founder of Water-Energy Nexus Laboratory in BITS Pilani Goa Campus Founder and Promoter and CEO of Epione Swajal Solutions India LLP, focussing on Membrane Manufacturing. Experience in membrane synthesis, manufacturing, handling, devices, and prototypes.

Parimal Roy studied in Anthropology. Later he obtained papers on MBA, Project management, and Criminology (paper is better than a certificate) to enhance his knowledge. He is currently working in a state own institution in the field of Training & Development. Decolonizing, Marginal community, subaltern voice, Project management - all are interest arena in academic world. His written book is

Extra-marital love in folk songs. Co-author of Captive minded intellectual; Quantitative Ethnography in Indigenous Research Methodology; and so many book chapters and journals.

Saúl Rozada Raneros is a PhD candidate at University of Valladolid, who received his M.S. degrees in telecommunication engineering from the University of Valladolid, Spain. He is researcher of the Data Engineering Research Unit and his research is focused on Internet of Things, and Virtual Reality. Also, he is co-author of some publications in journals, dealing with topics related to his lines of his research.

Rauno Rusko is University lecturer at the University of Lapland. His research activities focus on cooperation, coopetition, strategic management, supply chain management and entrepreneurship mainly in the branches of information communication technology, forest industry and tourism. His articles appeared in the European Management Journal, Forest Policy and Economics, International Journal of Business Environment, Industrial Marketing Management, International Journal of Innovation in the Digital Economy and International Journal of Tourism Research among others.

Rashid bin Mohd Saad is an educationist and serving as an Assistant professor at the Department of Education at Universiti Malaya. At present, he is working in the Drug Discoveries of Indigenous communities in Bangladesh.

Sheelu Sagar is a research scholar pursuing her PhD in Management from Amity University (AUUP). She graduated with a Bachelor Degree of Science from Delhi University. She received her Post Graduate Degree in Master of Business Administration with distinction from Amity University Uttar Pradesh India in 2019. She is working at a post of Asst. Controller of Examinations, Amity University, Uttar Pradesh. She is associated with various NGOs - in India. She is an Active Member of Gayatri Teerth, ShantiKunj, Haridwar, Trustee - ChaturdhamVed Bhawan Nyas (having various centers all over India), Member Executive Body -Shree JeeGauSadan, Noida. She is a social worker and has been performing Yagya since last 35 years and working for revival of Indian Cultural Heritage through yagna (Hawan), meditation through Gayatri Mantra and pranayama. She is doing her research on Gayatri Mantra.

Rajarshi Saha has currently completed his BSc with Major in Computer Science from St. Xavier's College, Kolkata. His current research interest is Data Analytics and Machine Learning.

Sudipta Sahana is an Associate Professor at a renowned University in West Bengal. For more than 11 years he has worked in this region. He has passed his M.tech degree in Software Engineering and B.Tech Degree in Information Technology from West Bengal University of Technology with a great CGPA/DGPA in 2010 and 2012 respectively. He completed his Ph.D. from the University of Kalyani in 2020. He has published more than 60 papers in referred journals and conferences indexed by Scopus, DBLP, and Google Scholar and working as an editorial team member of many reputed journals. He is a life member of the Computer Society of India (CSI), Computer Science Teachers Association (CSTA), and also a member of the International Association of Computer Science and Information Technology (IACSIT).

Pavithra Salanke has more than a decade of experience in Teaching and she is an active member in the research area of HR using social media.

Hajara U. Sanda, PhD, is an Associate Professor at the Department of Mass Communication, Bayero University, Kano, Kano State, Nigeria. She is also a former Dean, Student Affairs of the university, and has published many research articles, presented many conference papers, and published a couple of books.

Enes Şanlıtürk holds B.S. in Industrial Engineering in Istanbul Technical University and M.S. in Management Engineering in Istanbul Technical University. Also, his Ph.D. education continues in Industrial Engineering in Istanbul Technical University. He has study in Machine Learning. His main contributions is enhancing defect prediction performance in machine learning on production systems. In addition, he works in private sector as an Analyst.

Loris Schmid was born in 1992 in Visp, Switzerland. Studying at the University of Berne he attained a Master of Science in Economics. During the UMUSE2 (User Monitoring of the US Election) project, Loris Schmid was employed by the University of Neuchâtel from August 2020 until February 2021 performing data analysis and processing. He works as an Analyst and Research Assistant at IFAAR since 2019.

Dara Schniederjans is an Associate Professor of Supply Chain Management at the University of Rhode Island, College of Business Administration. Dara received her Ph.D. from Texas Tech University in 2012. Dara has co-authored five books and published over thirty academic journal articles as well as numerous book chapters. Dara has served as a guest co-editor for a special issue on "Business ethics in Social Sciences" in the International Journal of Society Systems Science. She has also served as a website coordinator and new faculty development consortium co-coordinator for Decisions Sciences Institute.

Jaydip Sen obtained his Bachelor of Engineering (B.E) in Electrical Engineering with honors from Jadavpur University, Kolkata, India in 1988, and Master of Technology (M.Tech) in Computer Science with honors from Indian Statistical Institute, Kolkata in 2001. Currently, he is pursuing his PhD on "Security and Privacy in Internet of Things" in Jadavpur University, which is expected to be completed by December 2018. His research areas include security in wired and wireless networks, intrusion detection systems, secure routing protocols in wireless ad hoc and sensor networks, secure multicast and broadcast communication in next generation broadband wireless networks, trust and reputation based systems, sensor networks, and privacy issues in ubiquitous and pervasive communication. He has more than 100 publications in reputed international journals and referred conference proceedings (IEEE Xplore, ACM Digital Library, Springer LNCS etc.), and 6 book chapters in books published by internationally renowned publishing houses e.g. Springer, CRC press, IGI-Global etc. He is a Senior Member of ACM, USA a Member IEEE, USA.

Kishore Kumar Senapati's experiences at BIT, Mesra complement both teaching and research, which brought innovation culture at academia and Industry. He has significant Industry driven research and teaching experience in the leading organizations of the country working nearly two decades, including ≈ 16 years at current place as an Assistant Professor in the Department of Computer Science and Engineering at Birla Institute of Technology, MESRA, Ranchi, INDIA. He has obtained PhD in Engineering from Birla Institute of Technology, MESRA. He has Master of Technology in Computer Science from UTKAL University, ODISHA. He has more than 18 years of teaching and research experience. He has guided more than 41 students of ME & M. Tech and four PhD scholars are currently working under his supervision in Computer Science field. He has capabilities in the area of algorithm design, Image processing, Cyber Security and Machine learning. He has published more than 40 peer reviewed papers on various national and international journals of repute including conference presentations. He has delivered invited talks at various national and international seminars including conferences, symposium, and workshop. He is also professional member of national and international societies. He was also active members in various program committees of international conference and chaired the sessions. He serves as editor of International and National Journal of high repute. He has successfully conducted several workshops in his organization on various topics. He is an honorary computer science expert and serves the nation in multiple areas.

Oleg Yu. Sergiyenko was born in February, 9, 1969. He received the B.S., and M.S., degrees in Kharkiv National University of Automobiles and Highways, Kharkiv, Ukraine, in 1991, 1993, respectively. He received the Ph.D. degree in Kharkiv National Polytechnic University on specialty "Tools and methods of non-destructive control" in 1997. He received the DSc degree in Kharkiv National University of Radio electronics in 2018. He has been an editor of 7 books, written 24 book chapters, 160 papers indexed in Scopus and holds 2 patents of Ukraine and 1 in Mexico. Since 1994 till the present time he was represented by his research works in several International Congresses of IEEE, ICROS, SICE, IMEKO in USA, England, Japan, Canada, Italy, Brazil, Austria, Ukraine, and Mexico. Dr.Sergiyenko in December 2004 was invited by Engineering Institute of Baja California Autonomous University for researcher position. He is currently Head of Applied Physics Department of Engineering Institute of Baja California Autonomous University, Mexico, director of several Masters and Doctorate thesis. He was a member of Program Committees of various international and local conferences. He is member of Academy (Academician) of Applied Radio electronics of Bielorussia, Ukraine and Russia.

Martina Šestak received her Master's degree in Information and Software Engineering from the Faculty of Organization and Informatics, University of Zagreb in 2016. She is currently a Ph.D. student in Computer Science at Faculty of Electrical Engineering and Computer Science in Maribor. She is currently a Teaching Assistant and a member of Laboratory for Information Systems at the Faculty of Electrical Engineering and Computer Science, University of Maribor. Her main research interests include graph databases, data analytics and knowledge graphs.

Rohan Shah is a Director in the Financial Services practice at Simon-Kucher & Partners. Rohan holds a Master's degree in Operations Research, specializing in Financial and Managerial Applications from Columbia University in the City of New York.

Aakanksha Sharaff has completed her graduation in Computer Science and Engineering in 2010 from Government Engineering College, Bilaspur (C.G.). She has completed her post graduation Master of Technology in 2012 in Computer Science & Engineering (Specialization- Software Engineering) from National Institute of Technology, Rourkela and completed Ph.D. degree in Computer Science & Engineering in 2017 from National Institute of Technology Raipur, India. Her area of interest is Software Engineering, Data Mining, Text Mining, and Information Retrieval. She is currently working as an Assistant Professor at NIT Raipur India.

Michael J. Shaw joined the faculty of University of Illinois at Urbana-Champaign in 1984. He has been affiliated with the Gies College of Business, National Center for Supercomputing Applications, and the Information Trust Institute. His research interests include machine learning, digital transformation, and healthcare applications.

Yong Shi is a Professor of University of Nebraska at Omaha. He also serves as the Director, Chinese Academy of Sciences Research Center on Fictitious Economy & Data Science and the Director of the Key Lab of Big Data Mining and Knowledge Management, Chinese Academy of Sciences. He is the counselor of the State Council of PRC (2016), the elected member of the International Eurasian Academy of Science (2017), and elected fellow of the World Academy of Sciences for Advancement of Science in Developing Countries (2015). His research interests include business intelligence, data mining, and multiple criteria decision making. He has published more than 32 books, over 350 papers in various journals and numerous conferences/proceedings papers. He is the Editor-in-Chief of International Journal of Information Technology and Decision Making (SCI), Editor-in-Chief of Annals of Data Science (Springer) and a member of Editorial Board for several academic journals.

Dharmpal Singh received his Bachelor of Computer Science and Engineering and Master of Computer Science and Engineering from West Bengal University of Technology. He has about eight years of experience in teaching and research. At present, he is with JIS College of Engineering, Kalyani, and West Bengal, India as an Associate Professor. Currently, he had done his Ph. D from University of Kalyani. He has about 26 publications in national and international journals and conference proceedings. He is also the editorial board members of many reputed/ referred journal.

Aarushi Siri Agarwal is pursuing an undergraduate degree in Computer Science Engineering at Vellore Institute of Technology Chennai. Her interest is in using Machine Learning algorithms for data analysis, mainly in areas such as Cyber Security and Social Network Analysis.

R. Sridharan is a Professor of Industrial Engineering in the Department of Mechanical Engineering at National Institute of Technology Calicut, India. He received his PhD in 1995 from the Department of Mechanical Engineering at Indian Institute of Technology, Bombay, India. His research interests include modelling and analysis of decision problems in supply chain management, job shop production systems and flexible manufacturing systems. He has published papers in reputed journals such as IJPE, IJPR, JMTM, IJLM, IJAMT, etc. For the outstanding contribution to the field of industrial engineering and the institution, he has been conferred with the Fellowship award by the National Council of the Indian Institution of Industrial Engineering in 2017.

Karthik Srinivasan is an assistant professor of business analytics in the School of Business at University of Kansas (KU). He completed his PhD in Management Information Systems from University of Arizona and his master's in management from Indian Institute of Science. He has also worked as a software developer and a data scientist prior to joining academia. His research focuses on addressing novel and important analytics challenges using statistical machine learning, network science, and natural language processing. His research has been presented in top tier business and healthcare analytics conferences and journals. Karthik teaches database management, data warehousing, big data courses for undergraduates and masters students at KU.

Gautam Srivastava is working as an Assistant Professor with GL Bajaj Institute of Management and Research. He has 15+ years of academic experience. He has completed his Ph.D. from the University of Petroleum and Energy Studies, India. His area of specialization is Marketing. He has published and presented many research papers in national and international journals.

Daniel Staegemann studied computer science at Technical University Berlin (TUB). He received the master's degree in 2017. He is currently pursuing the Ph.D. degree with the Otto von Guericke University Magdeburg. Since 2018, he has been employed as a research associate with OVGU where he has authored numerous papers that have been published in prestigious journals and conferences, for which he is also an active reviewer. His research interest is primarily focused on big data, especially the testing.

Mirjana D. Stojanović received her B.Sc. (1985) and M.Sc. (1993) degrees in electrical engineering and her Ph.D. degree (2005) in technical sciences, all from the University of Belgrade, Serbia. She is currently full professor in Information and Communication Technologies at the Faculty of Transport and Traffic Engineering, University of Belgrade. Previously, she held research position at the Mihailo Pupin Institute, University of Belgrade, and was involved in developing telecommunication equipment and systems for regional power utilities and major Serbian corporate systems. Prof. Stojanović participated in a number of national and international R&D projects, including technical projects of the International Council on Large Electric Systems, CIGRÉ. As author or co-author she published more than 170 book chapters, journal articles, and conference papers in her field. She was lead editor of the book on ICS cyber security in the Future Internet environment. Mirjana Stojanović also published a monograph on teletraffic engineering and two university textbooks (in Serbian). Her research interests include communication protocols, cyber security, service and network management, and Future Internet technologies.

Frank Straube studied Industrial Engineering, received his doctorate in 1987 from the Department of Logistics at the Technical University of Berlin under Prof. Dr.-Ing. H. Baumgarten and subsequently worked in a scientifically oriented practice, including more than 10 years as head of a company with more than 100 employees planning logistics systems. After his habilitation (2004) at the University of St. Gallen, Prof. Straube followed the call to the TU Berlin and since then has been head of the logistics department at the Institute for Technology and Management. He is a member of the editorial boards of international logistics journals. Prof. Straube founded the "International Transfer Center for Logistics (ITCL)" in 2005 to realize innovative planning and training activities for companies. He is a member of different boards at companies and associations to bridge between science and practice.

Hamed Taherdoost is an award-winning leader and R&D professional. He is the founder of Hamta Group and sessional faculty member of University Canada West. He has over 20 years of experience in both industry and academia sectors. Dr. Hamed was lecturer at IAU and PNU universities, a scientific researcher and R&D and Academic Manager at IAU, Research Club, MDTH, NAAS, Pinmo, Tablokar, Requiti, and Hamta Academy. Hamed has authored over 120 scientific articles in peer-reviewed international journals and conference proceedings (h-index = 24; i10-index = 50; February 2021), as well as eight book chapters and seven books in the field of technology and research methodology. He is the author of the Research Skills book and his current papers have been published in Behaviour & Information Technology, Information and Computer Security, Electronics, Annual Data Science, Cogent Business & Management, Procedia Manufacturing, and International Journal of Intelligent Engineering Informatics. He is a Senior Member of the IEEE, IAEEEE, IASED & IEDRC, Working group member of IFIP TC and Member of CSIAC, ACT-IAC, and many other professional bodies. Currently, he is involved in several multidisciplinary research projects among which includes studying innovation in information technology & web development, people's behavior, and technology acceptance.

Toshifumi Takada, Professor of National Chung Cheng University, Taiwan, 2018 to present, and Professor Emeritus of Tohoku University Accounting School, served as a CPA examination commissioner from 2001 to 2003. He has held many important posts, including the special commissioner of the Business Accounting Council of the Financial Service Agency, councilor of the Japan Accounting Association, President of the Japan Audit Association, and Director of the Japan Internal Control Association. Professional Career: 1979-1997 Lecturer, Associate Professor, Professor of Fukushima University, Japan 1997-2018 Professor of Tohoku University, Japan 2018-present Professor of National Chung Cheng University, Taiwan.

Neeti Tandon is Yagypathy researcher, scholar of fundamental physics in Vikram University Ujjain. She is active Volunteer of Gayatri Parivaar and highly involved in philanthropic activities.

Ahmet Tezcan Tekin holds B.S. in Computer Science in Istanbul Technical University and Binghamton University, a M.S. and Ph.D. in Management Engineering in Istanbul Technical University. He has studies in Machine Learning, Fuzzy Clustering etc. He gives lectures on Database Management and Big Data Management in different programs. His main contributions in this research area is improving prediction performance in machine learning with the merging Ensemble Learning approach and fuzzy clustering approach.

Gizem Temelcan obtained her Ph.D. entitled "Optimization of the System Optimum Fuzzy Traffic Assignment Problem" in Mathematical Engineering from Yildiz Technical University in 2020. She is an Assistant Professor in the Department of Computer Engineering at Beykoz University, Istanbul, Turkey. Her research interests are operational research, optimization of linear and nonlinear programming problems in the fuzzy environment.

Ronak Tiwari is a graduate student of Industrial Engineering and Management in the Department of Mechanical Engineering at National Institute of Technology Calicut, India. He worked in the industry for two years after receiving his bachelor's degree. He received his bachelor's degree in Industrial Engineering, in 2018, from Pandit Deendayal Petroleum University, Gujarat, India. He also received a silver medal for his academic performance during his undergraduate studies. He received a Government of India Scholarship under INSPIRE scheme to pursue basic sciences. He is an active researcher, and his research interests are mainly in supply chain risk, supply chain resilience, location theory problems, and humanitarian logistics. He has also acted as a reviewer of some internationally reputed journals.

Carlos Torres is CEO of Power-MI, a cloud platform to manage Predictive Maintenance. Born in San Salvador, 1975. Mechanical Engineer, Universidad Centroamericana "José Simeon Cañas", El Salvador. Master in Science Mechatronics, Universität Siegen, Germany. INSEAD Certificate in Global Management, France. Harvard Business School graduated in Global Management Program, USA.

Cahyo Trianggoro is Junior Researcher at Research Center for Informatics, Indonesia Institute of Science (LIPI). Cahyo is completed study from University of Padjadjaran, where he received a Bachelor degree in Information and Library Science and currently pursue for master degree in graduate school University of Padjadjaran. Cahyo having research interest study in data governance, digital preservation, and social informatics.

B. K. Tripathy is now working as a Professor in SITE, school, VIT, Vellore, India. He has received research/academic fellowships from UGC, DST, SERC and DOE of Govt. of India. Dr. Tripathy has published more than 700 technical papers in international journals, proceedings of international conferences and edited research volumes. He has produced 30 PhDs, 13 MPhils and 5 M.S (By research) under his supervision. Dr. Tripathy has 10 edited volumes, published two text books on Soft Computing and Computer Graphics. He has served as the member of Advisory board or Technical Programme Committee member of more than 125 international conferences inside India and abroad. Also, he has edited 6 research volumes for different publications including IGI and CRC. He is a Fellow of IETE and life/senior member of IEEE, ACM, IRSS, CSI, ACEEE, OMS and IMS. Dr. Tripathy is an editorial board member/reviewer of more than 100 international journals of repute.

Gyananjaya Tripathy has completed his graduation in Information Technology in 2012 from Biju Patnaik University of Technology, Odisha. He has completed his post graduation Master of Technology in 2016 in Computer Science & Engineering (Specialization- Wireless Sensor Network) from Veer Surendra Sai University of Technology, Burla (Odisha) and pursuing his Ph.D. degree in Computer Science & Engineering from National Institute of Technology Raipur, India. His area of interest is Wireless Sensor Network and Sentiment Analysis.

Klaus Turowski (born 1966) studied Business and Engineering at the University of Karlsruhe, achieved his doctorate at the Institute for Business Informatics at the University of Münster and habilitated in Business Informatics at the Faculty of Computer Science at the Otto von Guericke University Magdeburg. In 2000, he deputized the Chair of Business Informatics at the University of the Federal Armed Forces München and, from 2001, he headed the Chair of Business Informatics and Systems Engineering at the University of Augsburg. Since 2011, he is heading the Chair of Business Informatics (AG WI) at the Otto von Guericke University Magdeburg, the Very Large Business Applications Lab (VLBA Lab) and the world's largest SAP University Competence Center (SAP UCC Magdeburg). Additionally, Klaus Turowski worked as a guest lecturer at several universities around the world and was a lecturer at the Universities of Darmstadt and Konstanz. He was a (co-) organizer of a multiplicity of national and international scientific congresses and workshops and acted as a member of several programme comitees, and expert Groups. In the context of his university activities as well as an independent consultant he gained practical experience in industry.

Mousami Turuk is working as Assistant Professor in Pune Institute of Computer Technology, Savitribai Phule Pune University, India. She has her Master's degree in Electronics Engineering from Walchand College of Engineering, Sangli, Shivaji University Kolhapur. She has Doctoral degree in Electronics Engineering from Sant Gadge Baba, Amaravati University India. Her research areas include computer vision, Machine Learning and Deep Learning.

M. Ali Ülkü, Ph.D., M.Sc., is a Full Professor and the Director of the Centre for Research in Sustainable Supply Chain Analytics (CRSSCA), in the Rowe School of Business at Dalhousie University, Canada. Dr. Ülkü's research is on sustainable and circular supply chain and logistics management, and analytical decision models.

Mahmud Ullah is an Associate Professor of Marketing at the Faculty of Business Studies, University of Dhaka, Bangladesh. He teaches Behavioral and Quantitative courses in Business, e.g., Psychology, Organizational Behavior, Consumer Behavior, Business Mathematics, Business Statistics, Quantitative Analyses in Business etc., in addition to the Basic and Specialized Marketing courses like Marketing Management, Non-Profit Marketing, E-Marketing etc. He also taught Basic & Advanced English, and IELTS in a couple of English language Schools in New Zealand during his stay over there between 2002 and 2006. He has conducted a number of research projects sponsored by different international and national organizations like the World Bank (RMB), UNICEF, UNFPA, USAID, JAICA, AUSAID, IPPF, PPD, Die Licht Brucke, Andheri Hilfe, BNSB, FPAB etc. He did most of his research in the field of Health, Education, and Environment. His research interests include ethical aspects of human behavior in all these relevant fields, specifically in the continuously evolving and changing field of Digital Business and Marketing.

Nivedita V. S. is an Assistant Professor in the Department of Computer Science and Technology at Bannari Amman Institute of Technology, India. She is pursuing her doctoral degree in Information and Communication Engineering at Anna University, India. She holds 6 years of professional experience in academic institutions affiliated under Anna University. Her research interests include information filtering and retrieval, explainable intelligence, big data, etc.

Satish Vadlamani is a Director of Data Science and BI at Kenco Group, Chattanooga, TN, USA. He earned B.Tech. in Electronics and Communications Engineering, India. A Masters and Ph.D. in Industrial and Systems Engineering from Mississippi State University, USA. Before joining Kenco, Dr. Vadlamani worked at other global supply chain companies like APLL and XPO. Dr. Vadlamani has passion for applying operations research, machine learning (ML) and artificial (AI) intelligence to solve complex supply chain problems. Dr. Vadlamani has seven years of experience applying ML and AI for problem solving. Dr. Vadlamani has published at multiple journals and conferences and teaches data science and analytics to people around the globe. His research interests include networks, wireless sensor networks, wireless ad-hoc networks, supply chain networks, network interdiction, location problems, transportation, and meta-heuristics. Dr. Vadlamani has been an invited speaker at various colleges, universities, and other professional organizations across the globe. He is a member of IEOM, INFORMS and IISE.

Phuong Vi was born in Thai Nguyen, Vietnam. She is a lecturer at the Faculty of Journalism - Communications, Thai Nguyen University of Science, Vietnam. Her current research focuses on the following: Media culture; Social Media; Journalism History; Online newspaper; Journalism and public opinion; Public Relations. Her research is articles about journalism - modern media; books and book chapters have been published in prestigious international journals. "I am a journalist, researcher, author, writer, and university lecturer that never tires of learning and learning and teaches others for posterity, and for social development."

Takis Vidalis completed his basic legal studies at the University of Athens. In 1995, he received his Ph.D. in law. In 2001 he was elected a senior researcher and legal advisor of the Hellenic National Bioethics Commission (now, Commission for Bioethics and Technoethics). He is the author (or co-author) of 7 books and more than 50 academic papers in topics related to ethics and law of advanced technologies, constitutional law, philosophy of law, and sociology of law. Currently, he teaches "Artificial Intelligence: Ethics and Law", at the Law School of the Univ. of Athens, and "Biolaw and Bioethics," at the International Hellenic University. He is the president of the Research Ethics Committee of the National Centre for Scientific Research "Democritos" (the largest multidisciplinary research centre of Greece), and a member of the European Group on Ethics in Science and New Technologies (European Commission).

Fabio Vitor is an Assistant Professor of operations research in the Department of Mathematical and Statistical Sciences at the University of Nebraska at Omaha. He received a Ph.D. in Industrial Engineering and M.S. in Operations Research from Kansas State University, and a B.S. in Industrial Engineering from Maua Institute of Technology, Brazil. Dr. Vitor has nearly 10 years of industry experience, working for companies such as Monsanto, Kalmar, and Volkswagen. Dr. Vitor's research includes both theoretical and applied topics in operations research. His theoretical research creates algorithms to more quickly solve continuous and discrete optimization problems while some of his applied research has involved the application of optimization models and other operations research tools to reduce inventory costs, improve delivery routings, optimize nursery planting allocation, improve airport operations, and create strategies to overcome human trafficking.

Rogan Vleming is the Head of Data Science & Engineering at Simon-Kucher & Partners. Rogan received an M.B.A. in Finance specializing in financial engineering from McMaster University's De-Groote School of Business, and a B.Sc. in Mechanical Engineering from McMaster University.

Haris Abd Wahab, PhD, is an Associate Professor in the Department of Social Administration and Justice, Faculty of Arts and Social Sciences, University of Malaya, Malaysia. He graduated in the field of human development and community development. He has conducted studies on community work, community development, volunteerism, and disability. He has extensive experience working as a medical social worker at the Ministry of Health, Malaysia.

Chaojie Wang works for The MITRE Corporation, an international thinktank and operator of Federally Funded Research and Development Centers (FFRDC). In his capacity as a principal systems engineer, Dr. Wang advises the federal government on IT Acquisition & Modernization, Data Analytics & Knowledge Management, Health IT and Informatics, and Emerging Technology Evaluation & Adoption. Dr. Wang currently serves as the Editor-in-Chief for the International Journal of Patient-Centered Healthcare (IJPCH) by IGI Global and is on the Editorial Review Board of the Issues in Information System (IIS) by the International Association for Computer Information Systems (IACIS). Dr. Wang teaches Data Science graduate courses at University of Maryland Baltimore County (UMBC) and Healthcare Informatics graduate courses at Harrisburg University of Science and Technology. Dr. Wang holds a Bachelor of Engineering in MIS from Tsinghua University, a Master of Art in Economics and a Master of Science in Statistics both from the University of Toledo, an MBA in Finance from Loyola University Maryland, and a Doctor of Science in Information Systems and Communications from Robert Morris University.

Di Wang received his B.S. and M.S. degree in electrical engineering from Fuzhou University, China and Tianjin University, China. He is currently pursuing his Ph.D. degree in the Industrial Engineering Department, University of Illinois at Chicago, USA. His current research interests include multi-agent systems, distributed control, and energy schedule in the smart city.

Yue Wang is a doctoral candidate at the Computer Network Information Center, Chinese Academy of Sciences. Her research interests cover data mining, machine learning, user behavior analysis, etc. She has been working at the intersection of machine learning and information management for several years. Recently, she is working on NEW ARP technical research. In this paper, she handles the research on the technologies of the NEW ARP.

Manuel Weinke works as a research associate at the Chair of Logistics, Institute of Technology and Management, at the Technical University of Berlin. Within the scope of several research projects, he focuses on the utilization of Machine Learning in logistics management. Previously, he worked as a senior consultant in a management consultancy. He graduated in industrial engineering with a major in logistics, project, and quality management at the Technical University of Berlin.

Thomas A. Woolman is a doctoral student at Indiana State University's Technology Management program, with a concentration in digital communication systems. Mr. Woolman also holds an MBA with a concentration in data analytics from Saint Joseph's University, a Master's degree in Data Analytics from Saint Joseph's University and a Master's degree in Physical Science from Emporia State University. He is the president of On Target Technologies, Inc., a data science and research analytics consulting firm based in Virginia, USA.

Brian G. Wu received his Bachelor of Arts in Mathematics & Piano Music from Albion College in 2014. He pursued his graduate education at Oakland University, where he received his MS in Applied Statistics in 2016 and his PhD in Applied Mathematical Sciences, Applied Statistics Specialization, in 2020. His PhD thesis addressed computational and modeling aspects of big time series data. He will continue his career as a Visiting Assistant Professor at Southwestern University in the 2021-22 academic year.

Tao Wu is an assistant professor of Computer Science at SUNY Oneonta. He has extensive research experience in the fields of data science, information science, wireless communications, wireless networks, and statistical signal processing. He is also an expert in computer hardware and programming.

Mengying Xia's research interests focus on molecular epidemiology and women's health. Her current research involves molecular predictors of ovarian cancer severity, recurrence, and prognosis.

Hang Xiao is a project manager in SSGM at State Street Corporation. He earned a M.S. in Information System from Northeastern University in 2012. His research interests include IoT, AI, Big Data, and Operational Research.

Khadidja Yachba (born in Oran, Algeria) is a Teacher (Assistant Professor) in Computer sciences department of University Centre Relizane and a research assistant at LIO Laboratory, Oran, Algeria. She received her Ph. D. in transport maritime and optimization at University of Oran 1, Ahmed Benbella in 2017. Her research interests are in Decision Support Systems (urban, road, maritime transportation, and health), Optimization, Simulation, Cooperative and Distributed System, Knowledge bases and Multi Criteria Decision Making. Khadidja Yachba has published in journals such as transport and telecommunication, International Journal of Decision Sciences, Risk and Management.

Ronald R. Yager has worked in the area of machine intelligence for over twenty-five years. He has published over 500 papers and more then thirty books in areas related to artificial intelligence, fuzzy sets, decision-making under uncertainty and the fusion of information. He is among the world's top 1% most highly cited researchers with over 85,000 citations. He was the recipient of the IEEE Computational Intelligence Society's highly prestigious Frank Rosenblatt Award in 2016. He was the recipient of the IEEE Systems, Man and Cybernetics Society 2018 Lotfi Zadeh Pioneer Award. He was also the recipient of the IEEE Computational Intelligence Society Pioneer award in Fuzzy Systems. He received honorary doctorates from the Azerbaijan Technical University, the State University of Information Technologies, Sofia Bulgaria and the Rostov on the Don University, Russia. Dr. Yager is a fellow of the IEEE and the Fuzzy Systems Association. He was given a lifetime achievement award by the Polish Academy of Sciences for his contributions. He served at the National Science Foundation as program director in the Information Sciences program. He was a NASA/Stanford visiting fellow and a research associate at the University of California, Berkeley. He has been a lecturer at NATO Advanced Study Institutes. He is a Distinguished Adjunct Professor at King Abdulaziz University, Jeddah, Saudi Arabia. He was a distinguished honorary professor at the Aalborg University Denmark. He was distinguished visiting scientist at King Saud University, Riyadh, Saudi Arabia. He received his undergraduate degree from the City College of New York and his Ph. D. from the Polytechnic University of New York. He was editor and chief of the International Journal of Intelligent Systems. He serves on the editorial board of numerous technology journals. Currently he is an Emeritus Professor at Iona College and is director of the Machine Intelligence.

Jing Yang is an associate professor of management information systems at the State University of New York at Oneonta. She has authored multiple research papers on consumer reviews that have been published in a variety of high-quality peer-reviewed journals, including Decision Support Systems, Nakai Business Review International, Wireless Personal Communications, and the International Journal of Operations Research and Information Systems.

Lanting Yang is a student at the City University of Macau. She studies in the International Business program.

Pi-Ying Yen is an assistant professor at the School of Business, Macau University of Science and Technology. She received her PhD in Industrial Engineering and Decision Analytics from HKUST in 2020. She serves as a reviewer for Manufacturing & Service Operations Management (MSOM) and Naval Research Logistics (NRL). Her research interests include socially responsible operations, supply chain management, and consumer behavior.

Iris Yeung received her B.Soc.Sc. Degree from the University of Hong Kong, M.Sc. degree from Imperial College, University of London, and a Ph.D. degree from University of Kent at Canterbury, UK. Her major research and teaching areas are time series analysis and multivariate data analysis. She has published articles in the Journal of Statistical Computation and Simulations, Statistica Sinica, Journal of Royal Statistical Society: Series C, Journal of Applied Statistical Science, Environmental Monitoring and Assessment, Environmental Science and Pollution Research, Waste Management, Marine Pollution Bulletin, Energy Policy, Applied Energy, Energy and Buildings, and Energy for Sustainable Development. She has participated in a number of consulting projects, including the British Council, Mass Transit Railway Corporation, Hong Kong Ferry (Holdings) Co. Ltd., Greenpeace East Asia, and Environmental Protection Department, The Government of the Hong Kong Special Administrative Region.

Selen Yılmaz Işıkhan carried out an integrated master and doctorate education in biostatistics department of Hacettepe University Faculty of Medicine. She has been working as a lecturer at the same university since 2010. Some examples of her research interests are machine learning, data mining, multivariate statistical analyses, regression analysis, meta analysis, and gut microbiota analysis.

Ambar Yoganingrum is a senior researcher at the Research Center for Informatics, National Research and Innovation Agency (BRIN), Indonesia, since 2019. She was a researcher in Center for Scientific Documentation and Information, Indonesian Institute of Sciences (PDII LIPI) for 18 years. She obtained her bachelor degree in Pharmaceutical Sciences from University of Padjadjaran, Indonesia in 1990. She earned a Master's degree in Health Informatics from the University of Indonesia in 2003 and a Doctorate in Information Systems from the same university in 2015. Ambar Yoganingrum's research interests include issues in the field of Library and Information Sciences, Information processing, Applied Informatics for Social Sciences purposes, and Multimedia.

M. Yossi is an Associate Professor and the Head of the Department of Industrial Engineering and Management at SCE – Shamoon College of Engineering. His areas of specialty are work-study, DEA, and ranking methods. He has published several papers and six books in these areas. He received his BSc, MSc, and Ph.D. (Summa Cum Laude) in Industrial Engineering from the Ben-Gurion University of the Negev, Israel.

William A. Young II is the Director of the Online Masters of Business Administration (OMBA) program, the Director of the Online Masters of Business Analytics (OMBAn), and a Charles G. O'Bleness Associate Professor of Business Analytics in the Department of Analytics and Information Systems. As an Associate Professor, Young received Ohio University's University Professor Award in 2020. Young earned his doctorate in Mechanical and Systems Engineering from Ohio University's Russ College of Engineering and Technology in 2010. William also received a bachelor's and master's degree in Electrical Engineering at Ohio University in 2002 and 2005, respectively. William has collaborated with multidisciplinary teams of faculty, students, and professionals on projects and programs that have been funded by General Electric Aviation, the National Science Foundation, Sogeti Netherlands, and Ohio's Department of Labor. Young's primary research and teaching interests relate to business analytics and operations management.

Jianjun Yu is currently the researcher, doctoral supervisor at the Computer Network Information Center, Chinese Academy of Sciences. His research interests cover big data analysis, collaborative filtering recommendations, and cloud computing. Recently, he is working on New ARP technical research.

Gokmen Zararsiz is a PhD researcher working in Dept. of Biostatistics, Faculty of Medicine, Erciyes University, Turkey.

Alex Zarifis is passionate about researching, teaching and practicing management in its many facets. He has taught in higher education for over ten years at universities including the University of Cambridge, University of Manchester and the University of Mannheim. His research is in the areas of information systems and management. Dr Alex first degree is a BSc in Management with Information Systems from the University of Leeds. His second an MSc in Business Information Technology and a PhD in Business Administration are both from the University of Manchester. The University of Manchester PhD in Business Administration is ranked 1st in the world according to the Financial Times.

David Zeng is a faculty member in College of Business and Information Systems at Dakota State University. David received his PhD at University of California, Irvine specializing in Information Systems. David's Teaching Interests include Predictive Analytics for Decision-making, Programming for Data Analytics (Python), Business Intelligence & Visualization, Deep Learning, AI Applications, Applied AI & applications, and Strategy & Application of AI in Organizations. David's research has been published at top-tier, peer-reviewed journals including MIS Quarterly, and has been funded by both internal and external grants. David received the Merrill D. Hunter Award of Excellence in Research in 2020. David is the Director of Center for Business Analytics Research (CBAR) at DSU.

Jin Zhang is a full professor at the School of Information Studies, University of Wisconsin-Milwaukee, U.S.A. He has published papers in journals such as Journal of the American Society for Information Science and Technology, Information Processing & Management, Journal of Documentation, Journal of Intelligent Information Systems, Online Information Review, etc. His book "Visualization for Information Retrieval" was published in the Information Retrieval Series by Springer in 2008. His research interests include visualization for information retrieval, information retrieval algorithm, metadata, search engine evaluation, consumer health informatics, social media, transaction log analysis, digital libraries, data mining, knowledge system evaluation, and human computer interface design.

Peng Zhao is a data science professional with experience in industry, teaching, and research. He has a broad range of practical data science experience in different industries, including finance, mobile device, consumer intelligence, big data technology, insurance, and biomedical industries. He is a leading machine learning expertise in a Big Data & AI company in New Jersey. He also manages a data scientist team providing a variety of data consulting services to individuals, businesses, and non-profit organizations.

Yuehua Zhao is a research assistant professor at the School of Information Management, Nanjing University, China. Her research interests include consumer health informatics, social network analysis, and social media research.

Index

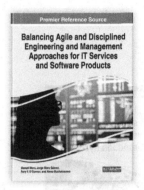

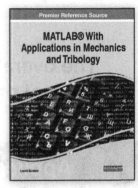

Ensure Quality Research is Introduced to the Academic Community

Become an Evaluator for IGI Global Authored Book Projects

Premier Reference Source

Stabilizing Currency and Preserving Economic Sovereignty Using the Grondona System

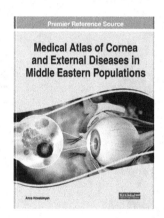

Premier Reference Source

Medical Atlas of Cornea and External Diseases in Middle Eastern Populations

Premier Reference Source

Examining Biophilia and Societal Indifference to Environmental Protection

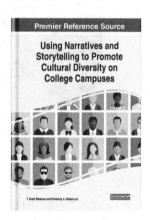

Premier Reference Source

Using Narratives and Storytelling to Promote Cultural Diversity on College Campuses

The overall success of an authored book project is dependent on quality and timely manuscript evaluations.

Applications and Inquiries may be sent to:
development@igi-global.com

Applicants must have a doctorate (or equivalent degree) as well as publishing, research, and reviewing experience. Authored Book Evaluators are appointed for one-year terms and are expected to complete at least three evaluations per term. Upon successful completion of this term, evaluators can be considered for an additional term.

If you have a colleague that may be interested in this opportunity, we encourage you to share this information with them.

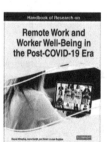

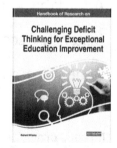

Printed in the United States
by Baker & Taylor Publisher Services